CW01334504

1 MONTH OF FREE READING

at
www.ForgottenBooks.com

By purchasing this book you are eligible for one month membership to ForgottenBooks.com, giving you unlimited access to our entire collection of over 700,000 titles via our web site and mobile apps.

To claim your free month visit:
www.forgottenbooks.com/free876179

* Offer is valid for 45 days from date of purchase. Terms and conditions apply.

ISBN 978-0-265-65168-1
PIBN 10876179

This book is a reproduction of an important historical work. Forgotten Books uses state-of-the-art technology to digitally reconstruct the work, preserving the original format whilst repairing imperfections present in the aged copy. In rare cases, an imperfection in the original, such as a blemish or missing page, may be replicated in our edition. We do, however, repair the vast majority of imperfections successfully; any imperfections that remain are intentionally left to preserve the state of such historical works.

Forgotten Books is a registered trademark of FB &c Ltd.
Copyright © 2017 FB &c Ltd.
FB &c Ltd, Dalton House, 60 Windsor Avenue, London, SW19 2RR.
Company number 08720141. Registered in England and Wales.

For support please visit www.forgottenbooks.com

HISTORY

OF

THE CITY OF DUBLIN,

FROM THE

EARLIEST ACCOUNTS TO THE PRESENT TIME;

CONTAINING

ITS ANNALS, ANTIQUITIES, ECCLESIASTICAL HISTORY, AND CHARTERS;

ITS PRESENT EXTENT, PUBLIC BUILDINGS, SCHOOLS, INSTITUTIONS, &c.

TO WHICH ARE ADDED,

BIOGRAPHICAL NOTICES OF EMINENT MEN,

AND

COPIOUS APPENDICES OF ITS POPULATION, REVENUE, COMMERCE, AND LITERATURE.

BY

The late J. WARBURTON, Deputy-keeper of the Records in Birmingham Tower;
The late Rev. J. WHITELAW, M. R. I. A. Vicar of St. Catherine's;
And the Rev. ROBERT WALSH, M. R. I. A.

At hæc omnia tractari præcipimus, ut non criticorum more in laude et censura tempus teratur, sed plané, historicè res ipsæ narrentur, judicium parcius interponatur.
Bacon de Augmen. Scientiæ, Lib. 2, cap. 4.

IN TWO VOLUMES,
ILLUSTRATED WITH NUMEROUS PLATES, PLANS, AND MAPS.

VOL. II.

LONDON:

PRINTED FOR T. CADELL AND W. DAVIES, IN THE STRAND,
BY W. BULMER AND CO. CLEVELAND-ROW, ST. JAMES'S.

1818.

DA995
.D75W37
1818x
FOLIO
v.2

TO HIS EXCELLENCY

CHARLES, EARL TALBOT,

LORD-LIEUTENANT OF IRELAND,

&c. &c. &c.

My Lord,

The Institutions of every people are intimately connected with their most important social relations; they, therefore, cannot fail to be objects of interest to him who is appointed to govern them. Those of the Irish Metropolis engaged the particular attention of your predecessors; and many of our most noble and useful Establishments bear the name and attest the care of former Viceroys.

Recently arrived in Dublin, your Excellency has not yet had that local knowledge and experience which a longer residence would bestow; I have therefore presumed to offer to your notice a detailed account of our Institutions, civil, religious, charitable, and literary, in the hope you would not decline any information which proposes to enlighten such important subjects; and in condescending to accept the Dedication of This Volume, you encourage a pleasing hope, that you will not withhold patronage to encourage, where you are pleased to evince a wish to be informed.

I have the honour to be,

Your Excellency's

faithful Servant,

ROBERT WALSH.

Dublin,
March 3, 1818.

CONTENTS.

		Page			Page
Medical Hospitals.	{ Lying-in-Hospital	669		George's	784
	Stevens' Hospital	682		Knight's	785
	St. Patrick's, or Swift's Hospital	690		Parochial	785
	Westmoreland, or Lock Hospital	696		Clergymen's	786
	Sir Patrick Dun's Hospital	700		Methodists	787
	Meath Hospital	705		Presbyterian	789
	House of Recovery, or Fever Hospital,			Independants	789
	Cork-street	707		Moravian	789
	———— George's	716		Catholic	789
	Royal Military Infirmary	720	Female Servants.	{ Aged and Infirm	790
	Infirmary, Jervis-street	723		House of Refuge	792
	St. Mark and St. Anne's Hospital	727		Stanhope-street	793
	Hospital for Incurables	728	Old Men.	Russel-place	795
Dispensaries.	Dispensaries in General	730		Dorset Institution	797
	St. Thomas and St. Mary	735		Drumcondra Retreat	798
	Dublin General	736	Schools and Congregations.	{ Protestant Parochial	799
	Liberties	737		Roman Catholic	806
	St. George's	740		Presbyterians	813
	North-West	741		Seceders	817
	Eye Infirmary	744		Independents	819
	Vaccine	744		Methodists	820
	Vaccine Institution	745		Kilhamites	827
	Apothecaries' Hall	746		Moravians	827
Royal College	of Surgeons	750		Baptists	829
	of Physicians	753		Quakers	830
Asylums for the Blind.	{ Simpson's	761		Walker's Sect	836
	Harp Society	765		Kelly's	839
	Richmond Institution	767	Foreign Congregations.	{ French Refugees	840
	Molyneux	768		German Lutherans	842
Magdalen Asylums.	{ Leeson-street	770		Jews	845
	Lock Penitentiary	773	Table of Sects.		847
	Circular-road	775	FemaleOrphan. Circular-road		849
	Bow-street	775		Masonic	851
	Townsend-street	776	Mixed.	Free School	852
Widows.	St. James's-street	778		North Strand	855
	Great Britain-street	782		General Daily	856
	Denmark-street	783		Linen-Hall	857
	Retreat	784		St. James	858

CONTENTS.

		Page			Page
	Kellet's - - -	858		Corn Trade and Exchange	994
	South-east District -	859		Provision Trade -	998
	Erasmus Smith - -	860		Breweries and Distilleries -	999
	Marble-street -	860	Public Offices.	Post Office - -	1001
	Young Sweeps - -	861		Stamp Office - -	1009
	Deaf and Dumb	862		Record Office - -	1011
noptical	Table of Schools -. -	866	Courts of Law.	Inns of Court -	1015
arity Sermons	- - -	868	Ecclesiastical.	Convocation - -	1027
cieties of ⎱	Poor of Ireland - -	872		Delegates - -	1028
lucation. ⎰	Cheap Book - -	874		Prerogative - -	1028
	Baptist Corresponding -	875		Consistorial - -	1029
	Board of Education -	880		Admiralty - -	1029
	Literary Teachers - -	882		First Fruits -	1030
ligious.	Association for Discountenancing Vice	885		Sessions House -	1033
	Hibernian Bible -	894		Police - -	1037
	Religious Tracts - -	898	Manors.	Glasnevin - -	1040
	Church Missionary -	898		Donore - -	1042
	Methodist Missionary -	899		St. Sepulchre's -	1044
	Indigent Room-keepers -	900		Deanry of St. Patrick -	1046
	Stranger's Friend -	901	Prisons.	Newgate - -	1047
	Charitable Association -	901		Sheriffs - -	1052
	Industrious Poor -	901		Marshalsea - -	1055
	Debtors' Friend - -	902		City Marshalsea - .	1058
	Confined Debtors -	902	,	Kilmainham Gaol -	1059
	Comforts of the Poor -	902		Dublin Penitentiary -	1061
	Decayed Musicians -	903		House of Correction -	1062
	Charitable Loan -	913	Public Bodies.	Corporation - -	1063
	Meath Loan - -	913		Aldermen of Skinners'-alley	1068
	Goldsmith Jubilee -	913		Pipe Water Committee -	1069
	Ouzel Galley - -	914		Commissioners of Paving and Lighting	1075
	Charitable Donations -	914		———————Wide Streets	1078
terary.	Royal Irish Academy -	916		Ballast Office - -	1083
	Kirwanian - -	922	Public Works.	Quays - -	1093
	Gaelic, or Hiberno-Celtic	926		Bridges - -	1094
braries.	Trinity College - -	937	Monuments.	Equestrian Statue of William III.	1098
	Marsh's Library -	940		———————————— George I.	1099
	Dublin Library - - -	942		———————————— George II.	1099
	——— Institution	943		Pedestrian Statue of George III.	1099
·ts and ⎱	Dublin Society -	944		Nelson's Pillar -	1100
·iculture. ⎰	Farming - -	960		Wellington Trophy , -	1103
anufactures.	Linen and Linen-Hall -	965	Public ⎱	Barracks - -	1106
	Cotton - -	971	Buildings. ⎰	Theatres - -	1108
	Silk - - -	976		Markets - -	1123
	Woollen - -	980	New Buildings ⎱	Richmond Lunatic Asylum	1146
	Tenter-House - -	984	and Improve- ⎰	St. Stephen's-Green -	1147
mmerce.	Commercial Buildings -	987	ments.	New North Wing of Trinity College	1149

CONTENTS.

	Page		Page
Castle Chapel	1150	Situation, Climate, Soil, and Diseases	1328
Metropolitan Roman Catholic Chapel	1153		
County Infirmary	1154	Appendices.	
New Fever Hospital	1154	No. 1. Population of Dublin	iii
Carlisle Buildings	1155	2. ———— Tables	xi
Charitable Institution	1155	3. Synopsis of Down Survey	xxvi
Free Masons' Hall	1155	4. Reports of Boards of Education	xxxviii
te of Literature and the Fine Arts	1155	5. Salaries of Custom-house Officers	xliii
of Society and Manners	1167	6. Exports of Corn	xlv
denda. Artists who practised in Dublin	1179	7. Ancient Ecclesiastical Revenue	xlvi
Biographical Sketches of Eminent Natives	1189	8. Rental of Corporation Tolls and Customs	xlvii
VIRONS. Grand and Royal Canals	1221	9. List of City Magistrates	lxiii
Howth, New Harbour	1249	10. State of Accounts of Canal Companies	lxvii
New Pier, Dunleary	1273		
Botanic Garden, Glasnevin	1279	11. Comparative Population Returns from 1798 to 1813	lxxiv
———————- College	1304		
Phœnix Park	1306	12. Irish Manuscripts	lxxvi
Observatory	1312	13. Botany of Environs	lxxxvi
Roman Catholic College, Maynooth	1317	14. Conchology of Dublin Bay	cxvi

Lying in Hospital.

HISTORY OF DUBLIN.

LYING-IN HOSPITAL.

Dr. Bartholomew Mosse, deeply affected by those scenes of misery, which in the course of his practice he was called on to witness among the poor, conceived the truly humane idea of opening an asylum for poor lying-in women. For this purpose, on the 25th of March 1745, this amiable philanthropist opened a large house in George's-lane, which at his own expence, he had previously furnished with beds and other necessaries. He continued also for some time to support it at his sole expence, till its evident and striking utility obtained for it other supporters.

This was the first hospital of the kind attempted in any part of his Majesty's dominions; and the great advantage of it being soon observed, application was made to Dr. Mosse in the year 1747, by several persons in London, (particularly Dr. Layard) for his plan, scheme, and regulations, which he transmitted to them; and the year following, an hospital was established in Brownlow-street, London, on the same plan.

In the year 1750, Dr. Mosse, finding the house in George's-lane too small (and upon many accounts inconvenient) for the reception of the great number of women applying for admittance, took a lease of a piece of ground in Great Britain-street, whereon to build a large hospital: and in order to secure a probability of maintaining such hospital, he first, at the risk of his whole fortune, laid out and finished the present garden, which is justly admired for its many beauties: this he intended as a place of public resort, applying the profits arising, to the purpose of his intended plan.

On the 24th of May, 1751, (old style) being the birth-day of his present Majesty King George the Third (then Prince of Wales) the foundation stone was laid by the Right Honourable Thomas Taylor, then lord mayor of the city of Dublin, who, with the aldermen, recorder, sheriffs, common-council, the masters and wardens of the several companies of the city, attended on that occasion, and were all entertained in a genteel and hospitable manner by the Doctor.

He continued to carry on the building, and raised money for that purpose by lottery schemes, and on his own credit, until he had expended thereon above £8,000. But in the year 1754, failing in a scheme, which he expected would have enabled him to complete the building, and being on that account involved in many difficulties, he petitioned the House of Commons in 1755; a grant was in consequence made of six thousand pounds, which enabled him to proceed in his undertaking until the session following, when a further sum of six thousand pounds was granted for finishing the Hospital, and two thousand for the Doctor's own use, as a reward for his services.

Thus we see a public building, useful in its design, and beautiful in the execution, begun and carried on by the address and resolution of a single person, without either the security of fortune, or patronage of the great; and yet no application to parliament, till facts had silenced malice, and extorted a general approbation.

In the year 1756, he obtained a charter from his late Majesty King George the Second, incorporating a number of noblemen and gentlemen as governors and guardians of the Hospital, with proper powers for the regulation and management thereof; and appointing himself master of the Hospital during life.

The structure being nearly finished, and the upper floor furnished with fifty beds, and other necessaries, it was opened for the reception of patients, on the 8th day of December, 1757, by his Grace the Duke of Bedford, then lord-lieutenant of Ireland, and fifty-two poor women, great with child, who then attended for admittance, with proper certificates and recommendations, were received; and being all decently clothed in an uniform, at the expense of the corporation, appeared in the hall before his Grace and the rest of the governors and guardians of the Hospital, together with many of the nobility and gentry.

Before the opening of the new, Dr. Mosse published a full account of the old Hospital in George's-lane; whereby it appeared, that in the space of twelve years, 3975 women were delivered therein of 2101 boys, and 1948 girls, in all 4049 children, 74 women having had twins; and that the expense of supporting the Hospital, in that time, amounted to no more than £3913..13: which was about 19s. 8¼d. for each woman and her child. By the said printed account, the following curious and satisfactory calculations (among others) appear to have been made by Dr. Mosse.

Proportion of males to females born, about twelve males to eleven females.
Women having twins as 1 to 53¼.
Women dying in child-bed as 1 to 90⅓.
Children dying in the month as 1 to 17.
Children still-born, as 1 to 34.

Women delivered from the age of 15 to 21	-	-	409
from 21 to 31	-	-	2542
from 31 to 41	-	-	935
from 41 to 53	-	-	89

The whole number delivered in that Hospital - 3,975

Dr. Mosse having impaired his health, by superintending the building, as well as several fatiguing journies to London, to forward his scheme, and by his close attention to the business of the Hospital, did not long enjoy the pleasure which must have arisen from his indefatigable labours; for on the 16th day of February 1759, he departed this life, in the 47th year of his age, and left the new Hospital as a monument to posterity of his surprising perseverance, diligence, and ingenuity, and indeed one of the most beautiful architectural ornaments of the city of Dublin. By his last Will he made over the same to the Right Honourable James Earl of Kildare, and the Right Honourable Lord Viscount Sudley, ancestors of the present Duke of Leinster and Earl of Arran, and their heirs, to the only use of the said corporation and their successors for ever.

It has often been regretted that this fine edifice did not face Sackville-street, to which it would have formed a noble termination, and such we are told was the founder's wish; but a refusal on the part of the proprietor of that street to accede to the proposed exchange of some ground necessary for this purpose, obliged him to relinquish a plan, which none but a man devoid of taste and judgment could reject. It is, however, an elegant structure, and does great credit to Mr. Cassels, architect, by whom it was built, from his own designs. The centre building, 125 feet by 82 in depth, has two fronts of excellent mountain granite, that to the garden plain but elegant, that to Britain-street more ornamental; in the centre of this four semi-columns of the Doric order, on a basement story, support the entablature and pediment, which are beautifully proportioned: at either end curved colonnades, intended not for use but ornament, serve, however, to gain a court yard in front, which is secured by a handsome iron balustrade; these colonnades in the original plan had no proper terminations; they, however, have been in part supplied by the taste of Mr. Trench; that to the east, already finished and ornamented with Doric columns and vases, serves as a handsome entrance to the Rotunda and new rooms: the intended site of the other is at present occupied by an old house which disfigures this part of Rutland-square, and which it is hoped the Governors of the Hospital may be enabled to purchase and remove.

The interior of this Hospital possesses that kind of merit which is suitable to such an edifice, solidity, convenience, and neatness, without that display of ornament which, however graceful, is at the expense of charity. A spacious hall, nearly 35 feet by 33, communicates with a gallery, off which the apartments open, and opposite to it is the grand stair-case of Portland stone with a neat iron balustrade of open work: this stair-case is lighted by a large Venetian window decorated with Ionic columns, and between these stands a marble bust of the founder, on the pedestal of which is the following concise but expressive inscription:

Bart. Mosse, M. D.
Miseris Solamen
Instituit
MDCCLVII.

The chapel directly over the hall and of the same dimensions, is very neat and elegant; the seats, which are of mahogany, are rented annually on very easy terms to the neighbouring gentry and nobility, whose contributions go to the general fund of the Hospital; the gallery is ornamented with iron open works, and the ceiling exhibits some fine figures and ornaments in alto-relievo boldly executed in stucco by an Italian artist.

In 1764 a marble font of curious workmanship, raised on an elevated base with ascending steps, was erected in the anti-chapel, the bequest of the late Dr. Robert Downes, bishop Raphoe.

The wards, which in the upper stories open off galleries running the entire length of the building, are airy and spacious, varying from 31 to 36

THE CITY OF DUBLIN. 673

feet in length by 23 in breadth. Of these, three have been munificently endowed by individuals whose names should never be forgotten. Over the entrance of that entitled the Primate's ward is a tablet with the following inscription :

His Grace the most Rev. and Rt. Hon.
Richard Robinson
Lord Archbishop of Armagh,
Primate and Metropolitan of all Ireland,
Baron Rokeby of Armagh, and Baronet,
Bequeathed by Will the Sum of
One Thousand Pounds ster.
To establish this Ward.
The Governors of this Hospital,
anxious to perpetuate the Memory
of this exemplary Prelate,
whose Virtues
added Dignity to his exalted Station,
have caused this Tablet to be erected,
MDCCXCVI.

This ward, 34 feet by 23, contains seven beds, and off it are two smaller rooms with two beds each, which being in a more retired situation, are assigned to women of a more decent description.

Over the entrance of a ward of similar dimensions, and entitled Mr. Preston's ward, is a tablet with the following inscription:

This ward, containing eight beds, was formed at the express desire of Thomas Preston, Esq. late of Merion-street, Dublin, and by his liberal donation of One Thousand Pounds ster.—Of his extensive benevolence many foundations in this city bear ample testimony.

MDCC,XCIX.

Over the entrance of a ward 31 feet by 23, is a tablet with the following inscription:

" This ward, containing twelve beds, received perpetual endowment on the 22nd of March, 1789, by the humane and liberal application of £3000. directed by the will of the late William Raphson, Esq. deceased, to such charitable disposition as might be appointed by his Trustees, the Earl of Bective and James Somerville, Esq. who have associated with them his

4 R

Grace Charles Agar Lord Archbishop of Cashell—to their joint benevolence the publick are indebted for this extensive support."

Of the beds in his ward four are in small adjoining apartments, and appropriated to women of a better description.

"The Hospital gardens (says Mr. Malton) for the capability so small a spot could afford, are beautiful in a very eminent degree, and contain a variety that is astonishing; in a hollow below a terrace on the north side, is an excellent bowling-green, and all around is thickly planted with well-grown elm, disposed in a variety of walks that are really romantic, and afford delightful recreation to the inhabitants of its neighbourhood. The Rotunda gardens were originally inclosed by a high wall, which was taken down in 1784, and a handsome iron railing, on a dwarf wall, with lamps thickly placed, put in its stead; this was done in the administration of his Grace Charles Duke of Rutland, when it was called after him Rutland-square.

"The Rotunda, and new rooms adjoining, now form a very distinguishing feature in the city: this noble circular room was built in the year 1757, for a place of public entertainment. In 1785 an elegant suite of rooms were begun to be added to the Rotunda, and the Rotunda itself to be much beautified in its external appearance, by Mr. Richard Johnston, architect, assisted by Frederick Trench, Esq. to whose exertions and taste in architecture these buildings are much indebted. The foundation stone of the new rooms was laid by the Duke of Rutland on the 17th of July 1785: the tympan of the pediment in the centre is adorned with his arms encircled by the collar of the garter, and other ornaments: the new rooms form a pleasing range of building 101 feet in extent, parallel with Cavendish-row, the east side of the square.

"The inside of the Rotunda has a very pleasing appearance; it is 80 feet in diameter, and is 40 feet in height, and without any middle support: it is decorated around with pilasters of the Corinthian order, eighteen in number, and 25 feet high, standing on pedestals; above which, between the pilasters, are enriched windows, which appear on the outside: the ceiling is flat, with large and bold compartments: the ornaments of the whole are now somewhat antiquated, but it has nevertheless a grand effect on public nights, when illumined and filled with the native beauty and fashion of the country: the orchestra projects into the room, and is generally filled with the best musical abilities the city can afford; the effect of sound is good.

"The new rooms are superb; they consist of two principal apartments, one over the other, 86 feet long by 40 broad; the lower is the ball, the upper the supper and tea room. There is a smaller ball room on the ground floor 60 feet by 24, which also serves as a room for refreshments when the larger is occupied. The upper room is very elegantly enriched; between pilasters against the walls are trophies, where shields of cut glass and other glittering ornaments have a very brilliant appearance. There are several lesser rooms for cards and refreshments. Besides weekly concerts in the winter season, there are here held subscription balls, supported by the first nobility and gentry; card assemblies; and every season, a masquerade or two. The entertainments of the Rotunda during the winter form the most elegant amusements of Dublin; it is opened every Sunday evening in summer, for the purpose of a promenade, when tea and coffee are given in the superb upper room.* The receipts of the whole, after defraying the incidental expenses, go to the support of the Hospital."

In this asylum for the reception of indigent females, during the perils and pains of parturition, and for a reasonable time after it (usually nine days), the formality of a recommendation is not required, and certain relief, with comfortable accommodation, is afforded to the destitute and unfortunate at all hours of the day and night. The governors of this Hospital have exerted themselves to their utmost in order to obtain sufficient accommodation for the increasing numbers who apply for admission, so as at the same time not only to supply well aired beds, but to increase the other means of contributing to the health of the patients and their helpless offspring. Supplies of flannels and linens are given occasionally to the poorest and most needy of the patients, together with other little comforts which their destitute and wretched circumstances may render necessary. When the necessity of overseeing their families at home requires them to leave the house before the expiration of the ninth day, such of the patients as require it are supplied with a carriage under the directions and at the discretion of the master or his assistants. The strictest attention is paid to the cleanliness of the wards, as well as to the proper means of ventilation; all apartments of parade have been converted into wards, and the occupation of rooms by the officers of the house has been narrowed in some instances, and abolished

* The Rotunda is no longer open on Sunday evenings, the promenades having been discontinued from motives hereafter stated.

altogether in others. The apartments formerly occupied by the chaplain, according to the old establishment, have been fitted up for wards, and the holder of that office has become a non-resident, and the junior assistant to the master has no longer any rooms. A large room called the anti-chapel, has been turned into a ward, and the master and other officers of the house have willingly submitted to considerable inconvenience for the accommodation of the poor; and have thus promoted the general objects of the charity: thus the hospital contains at present eighty-seven beds for patients, which are usually occupied; and of these twenty-five have been added since the year 1804. By an Act passed in 1785, the grand juries of the respective counties in Ireland were enabled to present a sum of money not exceeding £30. for the purpose of educating a midwife, who should settle in the county in which the money was assessed: but the grand juries having failed, with a very few exceptions, to execute the intentions of the legislature, and frequent complaints having come to the knowlegde of some of the governors of the great want of qualified midwives in the country parts of Ireland, the attention of the Board was directed to this subject, and, with a view of extending the benefit of the instruction and experience, which the Lying-in Hospital affords, to every part of Ireland, it was determined that a certain number of female pupils should be taken in and supported in the Hospital, for such a period as might be sufficient to enable them to acquire, not only a competent knowledge of the common practice of a midwife, but of those accidents and extraordinary occurrences sometimes attendant on parturition, and such a steadiness in their business as might render them more eminently serviceable to the public: an idea also has been suggested of rendering these pupils useful in extending the practice of Vaccination, by obliging them to attend occasionally at the Vaccine institution, in order to acquire an adequate knowledge of the true vaccine pock, so as to enable them to introduce this practice advantageously amongst the lower orders of the people in the country. The principal support of this useful institution was derived from concerts of music given at the Rotunda, which proved lucrative for many years, but which gradually declined, and finally ceased to be productive enough to pay the expense of the performances. There was no inattention on the part of the governors and conductors of these musical entertainments, but a change in the taste of the public; for private individuals of great musical skill have several times since hired the rooms for concerts, and, although they have provided excellent performers, they have uniformly in the event lost money by the speculation. After the rooms in Fishamble-street fell into ruin, the scheme of building, by subscription, public rooms in the neighbourhood of the Hospital, under the direction of the governors, was adopted; but the subscription proving inadequate to the execution of the design, a grant was made, by Act of Parliament, of a tax on private sedan chairs in favour of the governors, to enable them to erect a suite of rooms calculated to answer the purpose of a place of public resort and entertainment. In order to carry this plan into effect, the sum of £11,000. was borrowed on debentures at 4 per cent. chargeable on the chair-tax; and, at the same time, government guaranteed payment to the holders of these debentures, in case at any time the funds of the Hospital should fail. This charge for interest makes an item in the yearly expenditure of the Hospital to this day of £440. although the chair-tax, which was intended to cover that demand, has now fallen to £90. per annum. From the countenance and protection afforded to the entertainments held in their assembly rooms, the governors derived a fund fully adequate to their expenses, and the patronage of the public increased in proportion as the demands on the charity were extended. The public agitation excited by the disturbances, in 1798, gave the first check to the numerous and fashionable resort, which hitherto had attended the assemblies; and subsequent events, by causing the absence and emigration of almost all those whose rank and distinction had so eminently contributed to advance the purposes of the entertainments, caused such a deficiency as to force the governors to look for other and less fluctuating means of supporting the institution. They found themselves, in the year 1803, under the necessity, for the first time, of laying their case before the government. The Earl of Hardwicke having maturely examined the circumstances of the Hospital, and having taken into consideration, that the governors, in compliance with a solemn remonstrance from the Society for discountenancing Vice, had relinquished the most lucrative fund which they had ever devised, namely, the Sunday evening promenades, was most graciously pleased to recommend to them, to petition the House of Commons for relief; and they have from that period to acknowledge the bounty of Parliament, which has yearly granted them a sum equivalent to the deficiency occasioned by their diminished resources, the increased demands against the charity, and the high price of all articles of consumption for the use of the establishment.

During the year 1798, and for three years subsequent thereunto, the Rotunda and public rooms were occupied as barracks; but on the times becoming more settled, they were again restored to the governors, who endeavoured to revive entertainments similar to those which had formerly been productive, but their efforts were attended with very inadequate success.

The average profits from the rooms for three years preceding 1798, amounted to £1450. but the average of the last three years does not produce £300. per annum. The governors have frequently advertised the rooms for hire, and have even offered to let them, under proper restrictions, for any term of years, but without being able to make any bargain advantageous to the public. Another source of emolument arose from the Sunday collections in the chapel; on an average of twelve years, ending 1786, the medium profit of the chapel amounted to the sum of £158. yearly, whereas the profit, on an average, of the last three years does not exceed £32. notwithstanding that the governors have, in the latter period, let out the seats in the chapel at a very high price, with a view to extend the means of the establishment. The collection at a charity sermon still forms an item in the calculation of the casual income of this Hospital, as a fund which may be had recourse to, although there has not been any sermon preached for it for some years past. The sum arising from this resource was very considerable when a late preacher undertook the cause of the charity; but, in ordinary cases, it latterly fell off so much, that, in stating the casual income, it is only taken at £150. When the frequency of appeals of this kind is considered, and that they are made for parish schools and minor charities depending solely on such casual means for support, and moreover that, in general, these collections arise from the charitable dispositions of the same set of individuals nearly, who go from Sunday to Sunday from one charity sermon to another, it is hoped that the governors and guardians of the Lying-in Hospital will not appear remiss to the general interests of the charity, in waving this form of appeal to the public for the support of an institution of such general utility.

The casual income of the Lying-in Hospital on an average of three years may be thus estimated.

THE CITY OF DUBLIN.

Occasional benefactions - - - -	£ 60	0 0
Profit of chapel - - - - -	32	0 0
Rent of a room hired to the Anacreontic Society for a private concert - - - - - -	34	2 6
Profit from the gardens - - - -	50	0 0
Profit from the Rotunda - - - -	300	0 0
Charity sermon - - - -	150	0 0
Chair tax -	90	0 0
	£716	2 6

Fixed or permanent Income of the Lying-in Hospital.

Rent of vaults under the Rotunda - - -	£200	0 0
Ground rents belonging to the charity -	202	12 9
Interest on debentures purchased by the governors by means of legacies left to the charity - - - -	72	10 0
Interest on Mr. Daniel's bequest - - -	30	0 0
Bed money collected from certain governors who pay £12..10..0. per annum each for supporting a bed in the hospital -	350	0 0
Wine license - - - - - -	10	6 3
Astley's annuity - - - - -	100	0 0
	£ 965	9 0
Casual income - - - - -	716	2 6
Total income - - - - - -	£1681	11 6

It has been computed that £1..10..0. for each patient delivered in the Hospital is sufficient to cover the entire expenditure of the institution, the interest of £11,000. borrowed and guaranteed by government at the building of the new rooms, and the expense of the eight female pupils already mentioned excepted; and, as the number of patients annually delivered may at present be stated at about 2500, the annual sum necessary to support the institution may be thus estimated.

2500 patients at £1..10..0. per head - - -	£3750	0 0
Debenture interest - - - - -	440	0 0
Carry forward -	£4190	0 0

Brought over,	£4190 0 0
Maintenance and education of eight female pupils to be instructed in midwifery	160 0 0
	£4350 0 0
Casual and permanent income	1681 11 6
Deficit	£2668 8 6

The following Parliamentary grants have been made to supply the deficit, viz. Session 1803, £2619—1804, £2245..11..6—1805, £2521..8..5—1806, £2218..1..5—1807, £2457..0..2½—1808, £2588—1809, £2668..8..6—1810, £2518..5..8. and 1811, £3195.—Total £23,048..15..8¼.; and it is but justice to observe that the bounty of Parliament seems, in few instances, to have been more judiciously bestowed, than in support of an institution, the funds of which have been diminished from events out of the power of the governors either to foresee or to remedy; an institution peculiarly calculated to relieve the rapidly increasing population of Ireland, and which from its foundation has been deservedly held in good repute by the middle and lower orders of the community.

The following abstract of the registry kept at the hospital from the 8th day of December 1757, (the day it was first opened) to the 31st day of December 1811, will supply much curious and satisfactory information. In this table every year is distinguished, and the first line contains the admissions, &c. from the 8th to the 31st of December 1757, only.

THE CITY OF DUBLIN.

Year ending the 31st of December	Number of Patients admitted.	Went out not delivered.	Delivered in the Hospital.	Boys Born.	Girls Born.	Total Number of Children.	Women having Twins and more.	Children Dead.	Children Still Born.	Women Dead.
1757	55	-	55	30	25	55		6	3	1
1758	455	1	454	255	207	462	8	54	21	8
1759	413	7	406	228	192	420	13 (1 had 3)	95	22	5
1760	571	15	556	300	260	560	4	116	35	4
1761	537	16	521	283	249	532	11	104	29	9
1762	550	17	533	279	266	545	12	106	33	6
1763	519	31	488	274	224	498	10	94	29	9
1764	610	22	588	287	308	595	7	83	26	12
1765	559	26	533	288	251	539	6	94	25	6
1766	611	30	581	324	261	585	4	111	18	3
1767	695	31	664	373	301	674	10	124	29	11
1768	689	34	655	362	302	664	9	154	47	16
1769	675	33	642	350	301	651	9	152	38	8
1770	705	35	670	372	305	677	7	107	37	8
1771	724	29	695	370	341	711	16	102	44	5
1772	725	21	704	368	344	712	8	116	32	4
1773	727	33	694	367	344	711	17	136	31	13
1774	709	28	681	357	334	691	10	134	29	21
1775	752	24	728	364	378	742	14	122	27	5
1776	833	31	802	418	407	825	22 (1 had 3)	132	39	7
1777	872	37	835	452	395	847	12	145	35	7
1778	961	34	927	476	460	936	9	127	39	10
1779	1064	53	1011	550	476	1026	15	146	59	8
1780	967	48	919	499	441	940	21	115	41	5
1781	1079	52	1027	598	447	1045	18	121	38	6
1782	1021	31	990	549	458	1007	17	127	57	6
1783	1230	63	1167	632	553	1185	17 (1 had 3)	91	72	15
1784	1317	56	1261	643	641	1284	23	76	68	11
1785	1349	57	1292	711	610	1321	28 (1 had 3)	87	75	8
1786	1396	45	1351	716	656	1372	21	51	101	8
1787	1418	71	1347	705	670	1375	28	59	95	10
1788	1533	64	1469	725	771	1496	25 (1 had 4)	55	72	23
1789	1497	62	1435	745	707	1452	17	38	84	25
1790	1610	64	1546	813	766	1579	32 (1 had 3)	61	88	12
1791	1671	69	1602	842	782	1624	22	75	87	25
1792	1701	70	1631	858	806	1664	31 (1 had 3)	65	83	10
1793	1811	64	1747	941	845	1786	38 (1 had 3)	68	71	19
1794	1595	52	1543	835	744	1579	34 (3 had 3)	70	60	20
1795	1585	82	1503	827	719	1546	42 (1 had 3)	72	57	7
1796	1684	63	1621	857	788	1645	23 (1 had 3)	67	83	10
1797	1768	56	1712	908	840	1748	35 (1 had 3)	41	97	13
1798	1674	70	1604	845	789	1634	29 (1 had 3)	47	103	8
1799	1620	83	1537	829	748	1577	38 (1 had 3)	53	84	10
1800	1907	70	1837	965	899	1864	27	51	116	18
1801	1804	79	1725	864	894	1758	31 (1 had 3)	37	111	30
1802	2018	33	1985	1055	957	2012	25 (1 had 3)	27	124	26
1803	2065	37	2028	1065	1000	2065	35 (2 had 3)	74	116	44
1804	1980	65	1915	1013	936	1949	34	54	119	16
1805	2277	57	2220	1239	1031	2270	50	51	138	12
1806	2519	113	2406	1247	1204	2451	45	43	151	23
1807	2603	92	2511	1306	1249	2555	44	50	145	12
1808	2763	98	2665	1375	1334	2707	42	49	149	13
1809	2966	77	2889	1493	1442	2935	45 (1 had 3)	45	165	21
1810	3016	162	2854	1546	1350	2896	42	54	179	29
1811	2720	159	2561	1363	1250	2613	52	50	169	24
Total	73,176	2852	70323	37336	34258	71592	1230	4605	3928	708

Proportion of Males and Females born, about *Twelve* Males to *Eleven* Females.
Children dying in the Hospital, about *One* to *Fifteen*.
Children still-born, about *One* to *Eighteen*.
Women havin T   d   about *One* to *Fifty seven*.

THE HISTORY OF

Salaries and Allowances to the Officers and Servants.

Master allowed for coals	£.10	0 0
Assistant ditto	5	0 - 0
Pupils ditto	5	0 0
Chaplains' salary	110	0 0
Superannuated ditto	55	0 0
Register and agent	90	0 0
Matron (with diet and coals)	60	0 0
Chapel clerk	12	0 0
Sextoness	10	0 0
Porter, £5. for coals, £5. for clothes, and £10. salary	20	0 0
One midwife with diet	18	4 0
Nine nurses, with diet wages £7.	63	0 0
Eight ward-maids ditto, £4.	32	0 0
One cook ditto	6	16 6
One kitchen maid ditto	4	0 0
One house and chapel maid ditto	5	0 0
One messenger	11	2 9
Total salaries, &c.	£497	3 3
Diet of matron, servants, and female pupils, about	570	0 0
Expense of establishment, about	£1067	3 3

DR. STEEVENS'S HOSPITAL.

Dr. Richard Steevens, a physician of Dublin in 1710, bequeathed his real estate, situate in the county of Westmeath and King's County, and set for lives, renewable for ever, at the yearly rent of £604..4..0. to his sister, Grisilda Steevens, during her life, and after her decease vested it in trustees,[*] for the purpose of erecting and endowing an hospital near

[*] The trustees were the Right Honourable Robert Rochfort, Chief Baron of the Court of Exchequer; the Rev. Doctor Stearne, Dean of St. Patrick's, afterwards Bishop of Clogher; Doctor William Griffith, with Thomas Proby, and Henry Aston, Esquires.

THE CITY OF DUBLIN.

Dublin, for the relief and maintenance of curable poor persons, and to be called Steevens's Hospital.

Mrs. Steevens becoming possessed of the estate, was extremely desirous to see her brother's intention executed, and with a disinterestedness truly Christian, soon after his death purchased ground for the purpose, situate near the southern bank of the Liffey, to the north-eastward of the Royal Hospital, on which she commenced the present spacious edifice in 1720.

The plan was obviously too extensive for the endowment, but she adopted it with the hope, that the contributions of others, who felt a benevolence like her own, would enable her to complete the original design; nor was she disappointed in this hope, for benefactions were so considerable, that about two-thirds of the building were finished in July 1733, and the wards being furnished with every necessary accommodation, the governors met on the 2d of that month to appoint officers and servants, and to admit patients, 40 of whom it was then capable of accommodating.

In 1729, Doctor Stearne, Bishop of Clogher, was the only survivor of the trustees named in Doctor Steevens's will, and it being apprehended that his death might render the intention of the testator ineffectual, as the estate might thus descend to minors incapable of executing the trust, an act of parliament was obtained, which took place on the 25th of April, 1730, appointing twenty-three governors,* (of whom the surviving trustee was one) and their successors, to be a body politic and corporate for ever, by the name of the governors and guardians of Doctor Steevens's Hospital, vested with all the powers of the trustees, and all estates and legacies that were, or might thereafter be left for the use of the Hospital, with power to purchase lands of inheritance to the annual amount of £2000. to have a common seal, to sue and be sued, and also to make leases of 61 years in cities and towns corporate, and for 31 years in any other place.

* These governors were the Lord Primate, the Lord Chancellor, the Lord Archbishop of Dublin, the Chancellor of the Exchequer, the Chief Justice of the King's Bench, the Chief Justice of the Common Pleas, and the Chief Baron of the Exchequer; the Deans of Christ Church and St. Patrick, the Provost of Trinity College, and the Surgeon General, all for the time being; together with the Right Reverend Doctor John Stearne, Bishop of Clogher, Frederick Hamilton, Esq., Doctor Marmaduke Coghill, Richard Tighe, Esq., Sir William Fownes, Bart., George Rochfort, Esq., John Rochfort, Esq., Thomas Molyneux, M. D. Edward Worth, M. D. Richard Helsham, M. D. Bryan Robinson, M. D. Thomas Burgh, Esq., and John Nicholls, Esq.

Mrs. Steevens appropriating only about £120. per annum of her brother's estate to her own use, with apartments in the hospital, with the remainder, and a subscription of about £1400. the governors soon completed the present spacious building.

Steevens's hospital consists of two stories, with a third contained in a very elevated roof, forming a square of 233 by 204 feet, and enclosing an area of 114 by 94 feet: this is surrounded by piazzas 8 feet 6 inches wide, off which, and the galleries over it, the wards and other apartments open. The architecture of the four fronts is plain and unornamented, and over the entrance, which is by a large gate in the east front, is the following inscription:

Ricardus Steevens, M. D. Dotavit.
Grissell Steevens soror ejus Ædificavit,
Anno Dom.
1720.

Over the pediment is a cupola, containing a clock and well-toned bell; and in this front are convenient apartments for the resident-surgeon, chaplain, steward, and matron. In the south-eastern angle is a neat chapel, 54 by 35 feet, in which divine service is performed on Sundays, Wednesdays, and Fridays, and the sacrament administered on festivals, and once in every three months; it has seats for the officers of the house, with a gallery for the nurses and convalescent patients: the chaplain's salary from the establishment is only £20. per ann. with coals, candles, apartments, and a garden, but he receives also £121..2..0. per ann. from lands situate in the county of Meath—purchased by a legacy of £1000. bequeathed for that purpose by Mrs. Esther Johnston, the celebrated Stella, and also from Doctor Stearne, Bishop of Clogher's legacy of £40. per annum, making in all a yearly income of £181..2..0.

The library, which is also in the eastern front, is a handsome room, 31 feet by 25, and 16 feet high, furnished with glazed cases, filled with a curious and valuable collection of medical, classical, and other books, of the finest editions, and elegantly bound; these were bequeathed by Doctor Edward Worth for the use of the physicians, surgeons, and chaplains of the Hospital: many of the persons to whom exclusively this library is accessible, are men of acknowledged literature, but from the want of leisure in some, and the want of taste in others, the books lie unmolested on their shelves;

so that this truly valuable collection is totally useless. Doctor Worth, with a laudable desire of promoting education, bequeathed part of his property to found exhibitions in our University, and thither should his books have been sent; but fearing, as it is said, that they would be unnoticed and lost in the vastness of the library of Trinity College, he preferred consigning them to this hospital, where they are, it must be acknowledged, in a state of excellent preservation. It is to be lamented, that this library cannot be disposed of for the uses of the hospital, having obviously failed in supplying medicine to the mind, as all libraries should, it would thus supply it to the body.

On a tablet over the entrance, is the following inscription:

Ægris sauciisque sanandis,
Ric[dus] Steevens, M. D. Reditus,
Gris[da] Steevens superstes Ædes basce
Dono dedere.
Edwardus Worth Archiater
Bibliothecam quam vides
Eruditam, nitidam, perpolitam.

In a compartment over the fire-place, decorated by two fluted Corinthian columns, hangs the portrait of Dr. Worth, and over the entrance to the Committee room, that of Mrs. Steevens.

The governors assemble in the library: adjoining to it is a committee-room, where the physicians and surgeons meet to examine the patients for admission. The entrance to this room is through the surgery, where the patients for admission wait to be called for examination.

The north, south, and west sides, are divided into different wards for the accommodation of patients, the ground floor for the men and the upper for the women.

In the west front is a theatre where surgical operations are performed, and warm and cold baths, an apothecary's shop and elaboratory. The under ground vaults serve for kitchen, laundries, store-rooms, and such other conveniencies as are necessary appendages to so great a building.

The whole is enclosed by a court to the front with an iron gate, by yards and gardens on the other sides, for the convenience of the officers and servants.

THE HISTORY OF

The present officers are,

1 Treasurer without salary.
2 Visiting surgeons, non-resident; £10. each for coach hire yearly.
1 Physician, non-resident; £30. yearly for coach hire.
1 Assistant physician, non-resident; no allowance.
2 Assistant surgeons, non-resident; £10. each for coach hire yearly.
1 Resident surgeon, salary £60. per annum, with coals, candles, apartments, and a garden.
1 Steward, resident; salary £40. per annum, with coals, candles, apartments, and a garden.
1 Apothecary, resident; salary £33. per annum, with coals, candles, and apartments.
1 Matron, resident; salary £30. per annum, with coals, candles, apartments, and a garden.
1 Register and receiver, non-resident; salary £40. per annum.
1 Chaplain, resident; salary £20. per annum, with coals, candles, apartments, and a garden.

The present servants are,

1 Porter, coals and candles;   £16. per annum.
1 Messenger, coals, and candles; £18. per annum.
1 Cook,   -   -   -   £16. ditto.
1 Laundress,   -   -   £20. ditto.
2 Nurses, -   -   -   £20. each.
4 Ditto,   -   -   -   £16. each.

Those servants all reside in the hospital, but diet themselves.

The hospital receives medical and surgical cases, with all sudden accidents, and since the opening of the house to the 30th of September, 1808, 49,336 patients have been admitted into it.

The yearly nett income of the hospital, exclusive of the parliamentary grant of £500. amounts to £2425..17..10. as appears from the following rental.

THE CITY OF DUBLIN.

ANNUAL INCOME OF DR. STEEVENS'S HOSPITAL, DUBLIN.

By whom bequeathed.	Lands, where situated.	Yearly Rents.	General Observations.
Doctor Steevens,	County of Westmeath and King's County, - No. 1	604 4 0	For lives renewable for ever.
	County of Carlow, - 2	76 10 1	Determinable, one excepted, at $L.2..6..8.$ per ann. for lives renewable for ever.
Edward Cusack,	—— of Meath, - 3	910 6 0½	Determinable, one excepted, at $L.3..7..6.$ per ann. for lives renewable for ever.
	—— of Kildare, - 4	110 8 9	Determinable; an order has been made to set part of those lands at an increase of $L.93..11..3.$ per ann.
	& City of Dublin, - 5	85 0 0	Determinable.
Col. Alex. Montgomery,	County of Dublin, - 6	6 0 0	Determinable.
Doctor Stearne, Bishop of Clogher,	County of Dublin, - 7	298 9 7	Determinable; a considerable rise may be expected on this lease, which expired in 1810, but the governor's interest is determinable.
Philip Ramsay,	City of Dublin, - 8	43 0 0	
Lewis Moore,	Ditto, - 9	28 0 0	
William Golding,	Ditto, - 10	40 0 0	Determinable.
A purchase made by the Governors,	Ditto, - 11	232 0 0	
	Part of the hospital ground set to the governors of Swift's Hospital,	10 0 0	On all these lands considerable rises of rent may be expected, except on No. 1, and parts of Nos 2 and 3. Besides the lands here enumerated, there are lands appropriated to the sole use of the chaplain, not included in the foregoing rental.—Mrs. Esther Johnson left L1000. to be laid out in the purchase of lands for the use of the chaplain: these lands are now set at $L.121..2..0.$ per annum.
		L. 2442 18 5½	
	Deduct quit and ground-rent,	370 10 7¼	
	Nett annual profit, - L.	2073 7 10	
	Yearly interest of Turnpike Debentures,	5 10 10	
	Ditto, of 42 Government Debentures, at 3¾ per cent.	152 10 0	
	Rent of Military Hospital hired to Government,	200 0 0	
		2425 17 10	

The gentlemen appointed by the Lord Lieutenant in 1808, to inspect the state of certain charitable establishments in the city of Dublin, which receive aid from parliament, have made the following important observations on this Hospital.

From the first erection of the Hospital to the present day, the funds have at all times been inadequate to the maintenance of the number of patients for which the buildings would have afforded accommodation. Hence, in the year 1803, the governors felt it their duty to accede to a proposal from government, to allot, during the war, the upper story of the building, for the reception of military patients, in consideration of an annual payment of £200. in aid of the funds of the institution.

The wards thus appropriated to the use of the army, are completely shut out from all communication with the rest of the hospital, and under the direction of an establishment, totally distinct from its ordinary government; and as they must, in consequence of the limited amount of the funds, have remained unoccupied and unproductive, and as there is no reason to apprehend, that the accommodation thus afforded to the military establishment of the country, has in any degree impeded or interfered with the original objects of the institution, the measure appears to us to have been, on the part of the governors, not only unexceptionable under the actual circumstances, but judicious.

As after a period of 70 years, and upwards, this hospital, (originally erected by contract,) had fallen greatly into decay, especially in the roof, the timber of which had in many places become so rotten, as not even to admit of temporary slating with safety, the governors were induced, in 1805, to make these facts known to parliament by memorial, for the purpose of procuring aid to enable them to put the buildings in thorough repair.

In consequence of said application, the following grants have been successively made, namely:

In 1805	-	-	£4942	0 0
1806	-	-	4243	3 0½
1808			1295	3 10
Making for repairs a total of	-	£10480	6 10½*

In addition to these grants, a yearly sum of £500. commencing in 1806, has been voted by parliament in aid of the permanent funds of the charity and one or more wards are now fitting up to hold from 20 to 30 additional beds, to be maintained from said fund.

When we visited the hospital, (December 1808,) we found that the repairs had been completed, and the new furniture and bedding provided, and all

* A small part of this sum has been appropriated to the purchase of new bedding and furniture.

the wards seemed to be in good order, the whole house having been lately white-washed.

We could, however, plainly discern, that in the essential point of cleanliness, the surgical wards in particular were behind those in some of our best hospitals, although, from the recent expenditure, every thing was necessarily viewed by us under favourable circumstances in this respect. This great charity ought, for obvious reasons, to yield to no other in any country in every matter conducive to the appearance and comfort, as well as to the relief of the sick poor.

By a reference to the list of governors, it will be seen that many of the persons so appointed are high in official situation in Ireland, and for the above reason so occupied with other important duties, as to have little, if any time, to appropriate to the minute details of an hospital: On this account, a standing committee of five has been chosen out of the body at large, whose duty it is to examine into all accompts and expenditure of every sort, and to inspect into the conduct of the officers and servants, and make their report quarterly to the board, which is regularly convened by a summons from the register, in consequence of a requisition to him signed by five governors.

Under a constitution so framed, we admit it to be indispensibly necessary, that a delegated trust of this kind should be conferred on a few persons.

The point however for consideration in the present case is, whether it has generally been easy to find five members of the board who were ready and willing, and had sufficient leisure to enable them to execute, in a complete and satisfactory manner, the task of managing so extensive an establishment.

If the question cannot be answered in the affirmative, which we have reason to think is the fact, the consequences attendant on a lax administration are obvious, and follow from inevitable necessity, although the zeal and exertions of two or three governors may have protected the charity from glaring abuses.

We consider it to be important to call the attention of the highly respectable persons who compose the present board of governors of this valuable institution to the above defect; the remedy appearing to us to be within their reach, as it consists in nothing more than in endeavouring to fill up future vacancies, by selecting men of good character, usually resident in or near to Dublin, who could, with convenience to their private engagements, allot a certain portion of their time to the discharge of their duty as governors; and if such men are sought for, as they ought to be, when vacancies occur, and every species of solicitation resisted by the board which shall not accord with the foregoing rule, we are warranted, from experience, to state that the object, though difficult, is not unattainable.

The only observation we have to add for the consideration of the board, relates to the physician, who, by the rules of the establishment, is required to visit the hospital twice only in every week, (namely on Mondays and Fridays, at 11 o'clock in the forenoon,) except in cases of particular emergency, and whose sole remuneration consists in an allowance of £30. a year for coach hire.

We have no hesitation in pronouncing the above allowance to be too small, even for the attendance required; but thinking, as we do, that a daily visitation of the physician is indispensible for the safety and speedy cure of the medical patients, we cannot too strongly press an alteration in the existing system, which ought to be met on the part of the governors by a proportionate liberality to this officer.

In truth, there is no position in hospital administration better established than this, that all large institutions of the kind require one or more physicians and surgeons, and an apothecary, as distinct officers, either resident or attending daily on the sick at stated hours; and when those persons have been selected with care and judgment, they should be rewarded suitably to the rank they hold in their respective professions, and to the nature and importance of the duties which they severally discharge.

ST. PATRICK'S HOSPITAL.

This charitable institution for lunatics and ideots, owes its existence to the celebrated Doctor Jonathan Swift, Dean of St. Patrick's, who dying in 1745, bequeathed the entire of his property, subject to a few inconsiderable legacies, for this purpose.* The patent of incorporation bears date the 8th of

* It is well known that the Dean lent money in sums of 5l. to poor industrious manufacturers, interest free, to be repaid at the rate of 2s. 2d. per week; and we find that at the period of his death,

THE CITY OF DUBLIN. 691

August, 1746, and in 1749, Mr. Semple, the builder employed by the governors, was ordered to commence the intended hospital on a piece of ground on the north side of Bow-lane, which they had taken for that purpose from the governors of Stevenson's Hospital, at an annual rent of £10. The bequest has been stated at about £11000., but the governors met with such difficulties in calling it in, that the last gale was not paid by the executors until 1752; and in the preceding year £7720. only appears to have carried interest. The hospital, built partly from the issues of the Deans' bequest, and partly from voluntary donations,* with a parliamentary grant of £1000. in 1755, was, with the aid of a second grant of a similar sum in 1757, supplied with the necessary furniture, and on the 19th of September, in that year, opened for the reception of 50 patients. The original plan was so judiciously arranged, that additions might be made at any time that the resources

208*l*. 2*s*. 4½*d*. of this money was in the hands of the borrowers, exclusive of a balance of 27*l*. 8*s*. 3*d*. paid to the governors by Mrs. Whiteway, the Dean's housekeeper, who appears to have managed this charity for him, and who, as her books were confused and unintelligible, ascertained this balance by oath, which, in consequence of her established reputation for honesty, the governors accepted. The monument in memory of the Dean, in St. Patrick's Cathedral, was erected by the governors in 1747, at an expense of 25*l*.

* Subscription rolls were sent through the kingdom for the purpose of procuring donations, but with a success very inadequate to the proposed end, as of sixty rolls sent out, one only at the termination of the first year appears to have been returned. The following donors to this truly humane institution deserve to be had in remembrance: Doctor Stearne, Bishop of Clogher, 500*l*. Lord Chief Justice Singleton, 100*l*. Mr. Henry Land and Mrs. Land, 145*l*. Sir Richard Levenge, 500*l*. Mr. Thomas Hollingworth, 20*l*. Alderman Bowen, 250*l*. Doctor Christopher Donnellan, 200*l*. Doctor Joshua Pulleine, 500*l*. Rev. John Worral, 500*l*. Rev. John Worral also a leasehold interest, then producing 9*l*. 14*s*. for 97 years, from 1750, conditional for an annuity of 30*l*. for Winifred Conolly. Mr. Bolton, 1000*l*. conditional for receiving from the institution an annuity of 50*l*. during his life. All these donations were prior to opening the hospital in 1757. In 1764, Mrs. Jane Bury gave a donation of 200*l*. A person unknown, 50*l*. Doctor Thomas Smith, 100*l*. In 1771, Sir Richard Wolsely, 24*l*. Mrs. Echersell, 20*l*. Mr. Kane, 20*l*. In 1778, Mr. Patrick Tool, of Trim, 500*l*. In 1783, ten canal debentures of 100*l*. each, by Mr. Timothy Dyton, late master of the hospital. In 1785, Mr. Arthur Gore, 500*l*. In 1793, Miss Keon, 1000*l*. In 1798, the trustees of the late Bishop Stearne's estate, 100*l*. per annum, to commence from June 24, 1799. In 1799, Mrs. Walcot, 500*l*. In 1803, Doctor Stewart, Lord Primate, 50*l*. In 1805, Susannah Barton, 50*l*. In 1807, Mr. Tench, 100*l*. In 1808, Doctor Hastings, Archdeacon of Dublin, the reversion of his house in Dublin on the demise of his widow, for which the governors accepted a composition of 600*l*.

The parliamentary grants to this hospital were, in 1755, 1000*l*. 1757, 1000*l*. 1764, 1000*l*. 1767, 1000*l*. 1778, 2940*l*. 1781, 3000*l*. 1783, 1500. 1791, 2568*l*. 1811, 4000*l*. and 1812, 4180. Total, 23188.

of the institution might enable the governors so to do, without any interruption, and with very little inconvenience to the business of the hospital: it has accordingly, in consequence of parliamentary grants for that purpose, received two successive additions, so as to be at present capable of conveniently accommodating 177 patients.

The hospital presents a front to the south of 147 feet, consisting of a rusticated centre of about 100 feet, of hewn mountain granite, rising two stories above the basement, with lower wings of plain masonry, the whole neat, simple, and substantial. The area before it, which is separated from Bow-lane by a substantial wall, strengthened by plain pilasters of hewn stone, consists of a grass plat, surrounded by a gravel walk, in which the patients of a better description are permitted to exercise. The basement story contains the kitchen, scullery, stores, bread-room, cellerage, &c. with convenient baths, all which open off a gallery that runs the entire length of the building; and off similar galleries, in the second and third stories, open the apartments of the master and matron, with seven others, which are assigned to the class of patients called chamber-boarders. The stair-case, which occupies a semicircular projection of the building, communicates with the galleries, and is ingeniously planned.

The wards, six in number, are situated in the rear, and occupy two long parallel buildings of 327 feet by 33 each, three stories high, and separated from each other by an area open to the north, and 32 feet wide: the three wards in the eastern building are exclusively appropriated to the male, and the three in the western to the female patients, between whom there is no communication whatever. Each ward consists of a spacious, lofty, well-ventilated gallery, 325 feet long, by 14 wide, with the cells and other apartments that open off it, communicates with its corresponding gallery in the front building, and is furnished with fire-places to render it comfortable to the patients in cold weather. The cells, which are universally 12 feet by 8, and vaulted, are 158 in number, the two upper wards having each 27, and the four other 26 each, and exclusive of these cells, each of the six wards has a water closet, two apartments for chamber-boarders, 16 feet by 12 each, with a parlour and dormitory for the ward-keeper. The windows in the cells and galleries are well secured, placed at an elevation above the reach of the lunatics, and with a large open casement at the northern end of each gallery: hey admit an abundant supply of air. All parts of the house are plentifully supplied with water, that prime necessary of life, which from the great elevation of the bason, naturally ascends, by a well known law of hydrostatics, to its highest apartments; and through the entire establishment there obviously prevails, not only a strict attention to neatness and cleanliness, but an anxious desire to contribute, as far as their circumstances will admit, to the comfort of the unhappy objects of the charity.

There are 19 apartments for chamber-boarders, viz. 7 in the front buildings, and 12 in the wards: of these 17 are at present occupied by 13 males and 4 females, who pay the institution 100 guineas per annum each, and have an apartment and servant for their own use exclusively. There are also at present 44 ward-boarders, of whom 26 are males and 17 females, who pay 60 guineas per annum each, and occupy cells in the wards, where they receive reasonable attendance. The pauper patients, at present 107, of whom 50 are males, and 57 females, occupy cells, and are clothed, dieted, and supplied with medicine, medical advice, and attendance.*

The officers and servants of the house are,

A physician, non-resident, but who pays an unremitting attention to the charity. Instead of a salary, he receives four guineas per annum for every boarder, with two guineas entrance for each when admitted.†

A surgeon, non-resident, whose salary, formerly £56..17..6. is discontinued; he receiving in lieu of it two guineas per annum for each boarder.

A master, at £80. per annum salary, with apartments, coals, soap, and candles.

A matron, at £60. per annum salary, with ditto.

Six ward-keepers, at £28..8..9. each.

Two laundry-maids, at £22..15. each.

A cook, at £20..9..6.

A porter, at £18..4.

Thirteen chamber-keepers, at £22..15. each.

A barber, at £13..13..0.

The dietary of the male chamber and ward-boarders is as follows: Break-

* Doctor Halliday, of Manchester, has, no doubt from erroneous information, fallen into a very great mistake in his pamphlet on the expediency of the establishing lunatic asylums in Ireland, in which he says, " that the only public asylum in Dublin, and in Ireland, for the reception of lunatics, is that which was established and endowed by Swift, *and that even this Asylum is shut to the pauper.*"

† When the late Doctor Emmet, to whom the governors appear to have been wonderfully liberal, held this employment, his emoluments were double the above.

fast, 8 oz. of bread, with tea, milk, and butter. Dinner, 1¼ lb. of roast meat, 8 oz. of bread, and one quart of beer. Supper, 6 oz. of bread, and a pint of new milk. The dietary of the females is the same, except that the allowance of bread at breakfast and dinner is only 6 oz.

The dietary of the pauper patients: Breakfast always stir-about, and one pint of beer. Dinner on Monday, Wednesday, and Friday, callcannon and one pint of beer. Supper, 6 oz. of bread and one pint of beer. Dinner on Sunday, Tuesday, and Thursday, 1 lb. of boiled meat without bone, 8 oz. of bread, and one pint of beer. Supper, 6 oz. of bread, with broth from the meat at dinner. On Saturday, dinner, 8 oz. of bread and three half-pints of new milk; supper, stir-about, and one pint of beer. It is but just to observe, that every article of food used in this hospital is excellent in its kind.

The limited income of the institution not enabling the governors to support as many pauper patients as the hospital could accommodate, they were induced to adopt the system of chamber and ward boarders: thus an asylum is afforded to persons in moderate circumstances at an expense within their means, by admitting them to the second class, and the fund for support of the paupers is encreased, by relieving the charity from the burden of paying salaries to the physician and surgeon, whose meritorious services are recompensed by the savings arising from the maintenance of these classes of patients.

The deficiency of accommodation for pauper lunatics and ideots in Ireland has been often noticed with regret. This hospital, until very lately, has been the sole asylum in this kingdom for persons of this unhappy description; and the pressure for admission has been at all periods, since it was first opened, so importunate and unremitting, that the governors, yielding to the suggestions of humanity, rather than those of prudence, have, by applying nearly their entire income to the support of pauper patients, so far neglected the buildings of the hospital, that a thorough repair became absolutely necessary: to this, however, their funds appearing totally inadequate, an application to the bounty of the Imperial Parliament was made with success in 1811, when the sum of £4000. was granted, and in the session of 1812, a further aid of £4180. As this very liberal grant is at the disposal of a committee, consisting of gentlemen whose intelligence, energy, and integrity are unquestioned, it will, no doubt, be judiciously and faithfully expended. The entire of the extensive roof of this hospital has been already repaired and covered with ton slates of the best quality, the ruinous stacks of chimneys have been rebuilt, the windows renewed, and improved by the addition of window-stools: the flags of the ground-floor, universally rough, uneven, and of a quality producing damp, have been entirely removed, and replaced with others from Yorkshire of the finest grain, and perfectly smooth and dry; and the entire building is to be pebble-dashed in the best and most durable manner. Other improvements are in contemplation, calculated to render the situation of the quiet and peaceable patients more comfortable, by securing them more effectually from the noise and turbulence of the outrageous maniacs; and an hope is also entertained that removing some old buildings that at present greatly annoy the hospital, may be found compatible with that system of œconomy which the governors are so judiciously determined to pursue.

There are enclosures perfectly distinct for the male and female patients to enjoy air and exercise, with gardens for the master and matron; the entire forming a rectangular area of 490 feet by 180.

Of the various donations to the hospital, a considerable part had been vested in government securities; but, in consequence of the continually increasing demands of the institution, and a judicious purchase of chief rent, to which the Saggard estate was subject, and to effect which the debentures were disposed of, at present nothing remains for its future support, exclusive of the money received from chamber and ward-boarders, but the annual income of its estates. The present income of the hospital may be stated as follows:

The Saggard estate, in the county of Dublin, purchased in 1760 for £7010.
part of the property bequeathed by Dean Swift near £1600   0
The Ferns estate in the county of Wexford, above   600   0
Doctor Taylor's estate in the city of Dublin, near   600   0
To the above we may add
Income arising from 17 chamber-boarders at
  100 guineas per annum   -   -   -   1933 15
Do. from 44 ward-boarders, at 80 guineas
  per annum   -   -   -   -   -   -   3003   0
From the Trustees of Bishop Stearne's charity   100   0
                                                        ─────────
                                                        £7856 15

The expenditure of the hospital, for one year, ending 25th December, 1811, (buildings and repairs not included) amounted to £5282..5..6¼

The expense of a pauper patient, which in 1787 was estimated at £14..7..6., amounts at present, in consequence of the rise which has of late years taken place in the necessaries of life, to £15..10.* and the savings made in former years, from the sums received for the maintenance of chamber and ward-boarders, have, from the same circumstance, been so reduced, that it is in contemplation to encrease the latter, in such a moderate degree however, as may serve the interest of the institution, without materially discouraging the application of persons of these descriptions for admission.

WESTMORLAND LOCK HOSPITAL.

THE Buckingham Hospital, on Donnybrook road, originally intended for a small-pox hospital, was, for some time prior to 1792, used as a Lock hospital; but being insufficient for that purpose, and inconveniently situated for the necessary medical attendance, it was in that year transferred to the governors of the charitable foundation for incurables, who gave in exchange their hospital in Townsend-street, which has since that period been denominated the Westmorland Lock Hospital, from the nobleman who was then Viceroy, and at whose instance the exchange was effected.

It was opened on the 20th of November, 1792, for the indiscriminate admission, without recommendation, of indigent persons affected with the venereal disease, and was placed under a Board of Directors consisting of five physicians and nine surgeons, all resident in Dublin: two physicians were appointed to it annually, and ten surgeons, who served without fee or reward, but this arrangement was soon found defective, the attendance on the part of the surgeons became irregular, and of course productive not only of injurious effects to the patients, but of a variety of contingent expenses to the institution, and the members of the Board of Directors were, after an experience of four years, convinced, of what is indeed a truism, that where a daily and laborious duty is required from professional men, they have a fair claim to be paid for their time and trouble: they accordingly, in 1796, recommended to government to appoint two senior surgeons to be selected exclusively from the body of members, or licentiates of the college

* This is exclusive of the expense of clothes, bedding, fire, candle-light, washing, &c. which being fluctuating, cannot be accurately ascertained.

of surgeons, with an annual salary of £182..10..0. each; and three assistant or junior surgeons to be elected biennially by the directors from the same body, with a salary of £50. per annum each; two of the latter are capable of being re-elected; but by a regulation adopted in 1808, the former can hold their offices for seven years only, and cannot be re-appointed at any subsequent period.

For several years prior to 1792, the number of indigent persons affected with the venereal disease, and earnestly requesting to be received into the house of industry and the other hospitals in Dublin, was so great, as to prove a heavy burden on establishments with limited funds; for, when admitted, they too often occupied the beds which were wanted for other descriptions of sick poor, better entitled to relief. A wish to meet this evil by an adequate remedy, induced government to open this hospital, which was directed to contain 300 beds; and the original building not appearing sufficient for this purpose, additional wings have been erected, the whole containing seventeen wards for patients, exclusive of apartments for the resident officers, with a surgery and shop, and the other accommodations necessary for such an institution: it consists of a centre three stories high, with wings of inferior elevation; the whole forming a front of 120 feet, and built of mountain granite, of the Doric order, and in a style plain, solid, and durable: it is almost completely furnished; but notwithstanding its original destination for 300 beds, it will not, in the opinion of the best judges, be capable of accommodating more than 260 without overcrowding, it being very desirable that one or two wards should be always kept empty, and in a state of cleansing and purification, to admit the removal of patients in succession from a close and heated atmosphere, to breathe a pure air: and this provision seems to be the more necessary, as some of the apartments in the old part of the house, which contain 17 or 18 beds, have no ventilators, and are so filled with a mercurial atmosphere, as to produce a premature spitting, which by no means contributes to the cure of the venereal disease.

In the sixteen years that have elapsed since the opening of this charity, to the 4th of June 1808, 22,811 patients have been admitted, and a much greater number of externs have received advice and medicines; but though for a few years it seemed to answer the expectations of the founders by relieving the immediate pressure on the Dublin hospitals, the applications for admission have latterly, from various concurring causes, become so numerous, that the vacant beds, occasioned by the dismissal of those who have been cured, are not sufficient to accommodate more than one-sixth part of the applicants. This is no doubt a melancholy indication of the profligacy of the lower orders, not only of this capital, but of the country parts of this kingdom, from whence numbers infected with this dreadful malady crowd to this institution for relief, in consequence of the total neglect of establishing venereal wards in the country hospitals; and in the opinion of those who have bestowed much serious attention on the subject, it is one of the many evils naturally attendant on the present unparalelled state of Europe: large standing armies have unhappily become necessary for our protection; in every large town, nay, in every small village, troops are now quartered permanently; and that to this circumstance, the more extensive propagation of the venereal disease in the capital, and throughout every part of Ireland is to be attributed, the sick reports of the army afford irrefragable proofs; nor can it be concealed or denied, that an increased profligacy of manners amongst the lower order of females is distinctly to be traced to the same origin.*

In consequence of an arrangement adopted at the desire of Marquis Cornwallis in April 1799, an establishment for providing trusses and bandages for the ruptured poor was annexed to this hospital. As the predisposing cause of rupture is weakness and relaxation of the muscular fibre, this disease is frequent among the manufacturing classes of this kingdom, from their sedentary habits of life; and the relief afforded by a well made elastic bandage, properly fitted to the part, is so considerable, and so generally enables poor people labouring under this complaint to earn a livelihood by trade, or as menial servants, who would otherwise, with their family, be thrown upon charity for support, that the expenditure incurred to attain so useful and benevolent a purpose, must meet with general approbation. The expence of this department has varied from £296..14..6. to £492..14..9½ per annum. With respect to the crowd of miserable objects, both male and

---

* The chastity of the Irish female character in every class of life, has long been a subject of merited eulogy. Ireland, happily not far advanced in that progress of refinement which depraves the morals, while it gives a false polish to the manners, retained her primitive simplicity—the upper classes undisgraced by public scandal, and the lower undebauched by private profligacy. Dublin was, and perhaps still is, in that respect, the least vicious metropolis in Europe. It is therefore deeply to be regretted that any cause should tend to debase this excellent character. E.

female, at present and for some time past soliciting to be admitted into this charity, priority is generally given to the latter, not only from the obvious tendency of this arrangement to check the further propagation of the disease, but from a consideration that females are certainly more helpless than males, and have therefore a stronger claim to compassionate attention.

This institution, supported entirely by parliamentary grants, has cost the public since its first opening, to January 4th, 1808, £76..302..4..7. of which £2876..1..4. has been expended for trusses. In that period 22,811 were admitted, of whom 21,181 were discharged cured, 523 died in the hospital, and 833 either eloped or were dismissed for irregular conduct: the annual expense of each bed for provisions only, calculated on an average of thirteen years, was £8..15..4.; and the annual expense of each bed, the charge for trusses and also for repairs and buildings not included, and calculated on the same average, was £19..19..1. Since that period, however, the expenditure of the hospital has increased considerably, as appears from the following comparative statement for the years ending Jan. 5th, 1808, and Jan. 5th, 1811.

1808.	£.	s.	d.	1811. £.	s.	d.
Officers' salaries and wages,	1234	7	9	1602	8	1½
Provisions, - -	3150	6	11	4512	16	8
Medicines, &c. - -	436	10	6	1010	11	10½
Firing, soap, oil, and candles,	494	1	1	491	15	3½
Furniture, - - -	406	15	5	188	16	0½
Repairs, - - -	714	0	10	528	18	4½
Bedding, &c. - -	722	18	9¼	965	7	3½
Stationary, - - -	46	4	4	64	13	3½
Trusses and bandages,	315	10	1½	442	11	8½
Incidents, - - -	274	13	10½	222	0	5½
Rent and taxes, - -	32	3	0	20	0	0
Auditor-general's fees -	4	7	9	4	13	10
	£7812	0	4¼	£10,050	12	11¼

SIR PATRICK DUN'S HOSPITAL.

Sir Patrick Dun having bequeathed estates for the establishment of a professorship or professorships in the College of Physicians, and his executors having failed in the execution of his will, the trust of the estates were, by a decree of the Court of Chancery, vested in the College of Physicians. The income of the estate having considerably risen, by an act of parliament in 1781, the professorships, stiled King's professorships, were appointed, providing for instructions in departments of medicine which were not filled by the lecturers then appointed in Trinity College. The estates having still risen in value, and the income of the three professors having been so large, as to render the instruction of pupils an object of no consequence, and which was of course neglected, an act was passed in 1785, which limited the salaries of the King's professorships to one hundred pounds per annum; and to complete the system of medical education, directed that clinical lectures should be given, and that they should be supported out of the surplus fund, the professors' salaries first being paid: it also anticipates the foundation of an hospital, directing, " that until an hospital can be provided for giving clinical lectures, they shall be given in some hospital of the city, appointed by the president and fellows of the College of Physicians;" the experience of six years having evinced that no hospital in the city was adapted to the purpose of medical instruction, and that houses taken for the temporary reception of the sick, were both inconvenient and expensive, an act passed in 1791, empowered the College of Physicians to raise £1000. on the estates of Sir Patrick Dun, in order to defray the expense of a building, which might make a portion of an extensive hospital, to be supported partly out of the surplus fund of Sir Patrick Dun's estates, and partly by public subscription.

The construction of the act of 1785 having been contested at law, the foundation of the hospital was postponed; at length, in the year 1800, an act was passed, which finally removed all existing difficulties, and appointed eight commissioners, with full power to contract for a lot of ground for the site of the intended hospital, at a rent not exceeding £150. per annum, and to carry the building of it into effect and execution. The difficulty, however, of procuring ground sufficiently spacious and open for such an edifice, at a convenient distance from the college, prevented the commis-

St. Patrick's Inns. Hospital.

sioners from beginning this work until the year 1803, when, owing to the peculiar situation of the ground, much expense was necessarily incurred in levelling, fitting, draining, and enclosing it.

It consists of a centre, and wings which project about 11 feet, and terminate in angular pediments; the whole two stories high, exclusive of the under-ground offices, and forming a handsome front of 194 feet, substantial, plain, and neat, its only ornaments consisting of a niche for a statue in the front of each wing, with a flat pediment in the centre, supported by four composite columns resting on the basement story: the centre, exclusive of a spacious hall and stair-case, will contain on the first floor, convenient apartments for the house-keeper and apothecary, pupils in waiting, &c. with a lecture-room in the rear nearly semicircular, 42 feet by 31; and on the upper floor a board-room, apartments for the professors, with a spacious library to contain the books bequeathed by Sir Patrick Dun to the institution. The wings contain the wards for patients; and in these the sexes will be completely separated, as the eastern wing is to be exclusively appropriated to males, and the western to females. In these wings the convalescent wards and other apartments of the first floor are vaulted: this construction, besides preventing disturbance, obviating accidents by fire, and affording an opportunity of lime-whitening the floors, in case of violent infection, has enabled the architect to collect all the flues of the under apartments into the thickness of the walls of the great upper ward, destined for the reception of fever patients.

This ward, which is 66 feet by 38, and 20 feet high, is subdivided by partitions of the height of 7 feet 6 inches, into six apartments, four of which are capable of containing four beds, and two of which may contain ten. The ward is ventilated on both sides by windows, and at top by a louvre. Besides the flues in the wall, it is heated by three open fire-places. The great body of air which it contains, it is hoped, will afford security against contagion. The plan was adopted in consequence of what is recommended by Howard in his work on lazarettos, and of observations which evinced that, in the best regulated hospitals, the wards of which were of the ordinary height, (from eleven to thirteen feet,) infectious diseases were propagated, notwithstanding every attention paid to ventilation and cleanliness. The building is furnished with water-closets, and hot and cold baths supplied by a forcing pump.

Sir Patrick Dun's Hospital, as a public institution, is to be regarded in two different points of view : first, as an asylum calculated to afford relief to the poor oppressed with sickness and disease; and next, as being connected with the school of physic, and likely to afford in time an ample field for medical experience, where the young student in medicine will see the most interesting and critical cases of diseases, whether chronic or acute, treated by learned and ingenious professors. It must be admitted, that much has been done in the space of a few years to alleviate the sufferings of the distressed poor of the City of Dublin, and to prevent disease from making the unresisted ravages among them, which it was wont to do even recently. The active benevolence and generosity of private individuals, have been powerfully and successfully supported by the wisdom of government, and the good policy of the legislature ;—still, however, much remains to be done: and even as a public hospital for the relief of the sick labouring under disease, whether contagious or otherwise, this institution, calculated to contain, when it shall be finished, 100 patients, may be truly considered as deserving public support and approbation. As the building is not merely calculated for an hospital, but is likewise intended to accommodate the professors of medicine in the school of physic, with a theatre, where their lectures on the cases of their patients may be held, together with a room to contain the very valuable collection of books, constituting Sir Patrick Dun's library, and other apartments necessary for the accommodation of the professors and their pupils, it is therefore obvious, that to answer those different purposes, it must be finished on a great scale. The hospital is built on such a principle as to ensure stability, and every accommodation which has been approved of by the most inquisitive into the subject of buildings of this kind. It is true it has been an expensive building, but not more so than might be expected from its durable structure, and the increased expense of all those materials necessary in erecting such an hospital.

As this volume may fall into the hands of persons not acquainted with the nature of the instruction afforded to students in medicine, by attendance on the professors, who are to give what are termed clinical lectures in this hospital, it may not be amiss to add a few words in explanation, pointing out the advantages of such lectures, and the way in which the business is conducted. The act of parliament directs, that two of the six medical professors shall annually, in such rotation as they shall agree upon among themselves, attend the patients, who are to be the subjects of the clinical lectures in Sir Patrick Dun's Hospital, for the six months during which medical lectures are given in the school of physic, and that each of them shall attend three months, and lecture at least twice a week. A professor attends daily, and when a patient is brought to the hospital, his case is accurately noted in a book kept by the professor's clerk, (generally a student advanced somewhat in a knowledge of his profession,) and is read aloud by him in presence of the professor and the different students, who are in attendance at the bed-side of the patients: and hence it is that this kind of instruction has been called clinical. Any circumstance omitted by the clerk, or any new occurrence in the case since he had stated it in the report, is now reported aloud by the physician, and is copied into the report book by the clerk.

Thus from day to day the various patients who are to be the subjects of the clinical lectures are visited, and every variety in their situation is carefully remarked and noted down in these reports before all the students, and the prescriptions of the professor are reported in the same manner. It is obvious that it would be attended with great inconvenience, and even danger, were the professor to deliver his opinion on the nature of their diseases, and the probable events likely to occur in the course of treating them, in the presence of the patients; hence the necessity of a proper theatre where these lectures may be given. At stated times, twice in the week, the students are convened to hear the professor comment at large on the cases of the patients, and at the same time explain the nature of his practice. It is obvious that the delay occasioned in remarking the symptoms of the diseases, and prescribing the necessary remedies, and also for the clerk and students to take them down in their report books, and notes, does not admit of the professor attending many patients within one hour, which is the time allotted for these reports in each day. As the house is calculated to contain 100 patients, the professors will have it in their power always to select the most critical and instructive cases to be the subjects of their lectures. It may be observed, that the number of students who are witnesses of the practice of the professor, and the necessity he is under of giving a rational account of his practice to them at his lectures, are well calculated to stimulate him to exert all the powers of his mind in attending to the various changes in his patients, and in prescribing those medicines the best calculated to alleviate or to remove the disorder.

On this hospital, the centre of which is built and roofed, and the western wing completely finished, £15,460..18..0. have been already expended, exclusive of £1500. ground rent for ten years, and £1062..19..8. the expense of the temporary establishment for patients admitted into the western wing : making a total of £18,023..17..8. of which £10,242. were supplied by parliamentary grants, and the remainder has arisen from the surplus funds of Sir Patrick Dun's estate : these, however, are no longer applicable to this purpose, as by the act regulating these funds, the hospital being now capable of containing thirty patients, they are applicable to their maintenance only, and are barely sufficient for that purpose and other appropriations contained in the act : an additional parliamentary grant has been accordingly obtained, and the commissioners, who have hitherto paid an unremitting attention to the trust reposed in them, will no doubt expedite the completion of this edifice.

Sir Patrick Dun's estates in the county of Wexford contain 2181 acres, 3 roods, 12 perches, producing at present an annual rent of £1574..0..0. but subject to £121..5..10. head rents, payable to Lord Ormond and Joseph Henry, with a quit rent under the denomination of King's silver of £51..8..0. leaving a clear profit rent of £1401..6..2. : it is set under determinable leases which will expire in 1814, 1817, and 1820, when it is highly probable the rental will not fall short of £4000. per annum, which will be more than sufficient to maintain the number of patients which the hospital is calculated to hold. When the estate can afford it, the surplus fund, which will remain after maintaining the hospital, will be applied, agreeably to the act of parliament, in maintaining new professorships, and to increase the library.

The following is the present establishment.

Three professors, at £100. per annum,	£300 0 0
Librarian,	70 0 0
Treasurer,	50 0 0
Apothecary,	68 5 0
House-keeper,	56 17 6
Cook,	23 8 0
Laundry-maid,	23 8 0
House-maid,	23 8 0
Three nurses, at £23..8..0. each,	70 4 0
Gate-porter,	31 4 0
	£716 14 6

THE CITY OF DUBLIN. 705

When the above sum of £716..14..6. with £150. the ground rent of the hospital, is deducted from the clear profit rent of the estates of Sir Patrick Dun, £534..11..8. only will remain for the maintenance of the patients, and for incidents: and it is but justice to observe, that in consequence of the insufficiency of this fund, the hospital could not be kept open during the current year, were it not for the humane donation of the Provost of Trinity College, and Doctor Percival, of £100. each.

Of 214 patients admitted from its opening, to the 27th June, 1809, 108 were dismissed cured, 39 were relieved, and 19 only died.

MEATH HOSPITAL.

THE Meath Hospital, originally instituted for the relief of poor manufacturers in the Earl of Meath's liberty, was entirely supported by private subscription; and subscribers paying one guinea, or upwards, together with the physicians and surgeons, were the governors. Its first site was in Meath-street, from whence it was removed to a larger and more commodious house in Earl-street: this also proving insufficient for the numbers that applied for relief, several humane persons, by private subscription, erected, on the Coomb, at an expense of above two thousand pounds, the present Meath Hospital.

In the act of the 5th year of the reign of his present Majesty, for establishing infirmaries in the different counties of Ireland, the county of Dublin was, by some unaccountable mistake, omitted; and the proprietors of this hospital generously and humanely offering to give it up, with all its furniture, utensils, and appurtenances, to the use of the county for ever, it was, on the 24th day of June, 1774, constituted by act of parliament, the County of Dublin Infirmary, with the usual allowance of £100. per annum, to be appropriated, however, to the general fund for necessaries, and not to the use of the attending physicians and surgeons, who, as in former years, continued to act without any reward, save the satisfaction arising from the consciousness of disinterested humanity. This appropriation of the hospital, it may be necessary to observe, has not interfered with its original destination, any

4 X

further than by extending it, the Earl of Meath's liberty being in the county. In July, 1805, the annual presentment was raised to £600.

The governors, who are a body corporate, are his Grace the Archbishop of Armagh, his Grace the Archbishop of Dublin, the Lord High Chancellor, and the Vicar of St. Catherine's, all for the time being, with donors of £10. or upwards, and annual subscribers of one guinea. The two physicians and six surgeons of the hospital, in consideration of their gratuitous attendance and disinterested exertions in its support during a period of seventeen years, and in consideration of their relinquishing, for themselves and successors, all claim to an annual salary in future, were continued in office, with a power to fill up by election all vacancies made in their number by death or removal.

The hospital, which is substantially built, has a handsome front of mountain granite: the wards, four in number, are spacious and airy, two of them being 45 by 20 feet, and the others 30 by 20: they at present contain 40 beds, admitting only one patient each, but are capable of holding more without inconvenience; the wards for males and females being on separate floors, the sexes are completely separated, and through every department of the institution the greatest attention to neatness and cleanliness prevails.

Two medical gentlemen, a physician and surgeon, attend every day at half past ten o'clock, and remain for an hour: during which time they prescribe not only for the intern patients, but for a very considerable number of externs, who apply for relief; at the same time two medical and surgical pupils are present for their improvement in the medical science, who occasionally assist in dressing wounds, &c.

The establishment consists at present of two physicians and five surgeons, who receive no salary.

An apothecary at an annual salary of	£50 0 0
A register and collector,	40 0 0
A house-keeper,	38 0 0
Two nurses, wages and allowances for tea and beer £11. each,	22 0 0
One house-maid, wages and allowances for tea and beer,	8 14 6
One porter ditto,	8 14 6
	£167 9 0

Its income, permanent and casual, may be thus estimated:

Permanent Income.

Annual treasury grant,	- - -	£96 10 3
County presentment	- - -	600 0 0
Interest on government debentures, and on a mortgage of £200. - - - -		47 10 0
		£743 10 3

Casual Income.

Collection at an annual charity sermon, averaged about	£250	0 0
Annual subscription very fluctuating, at present about	150	0 0
	400	0 0

Total - £1143 10 3

This hospital is much indebted to a late excellent citizen, Arthur Guinness, Esq. who for several successive years discharged the duties of treasurer: as useful in public, as he was amiable in private life, he devoted much of his time and attention to this favorite institution, whose interests he promoted with an unwearied solicitude, that seems hereditary in his son, Arthur Guinness, Esq. who happily for this most humane establishment, has succeeded to the same trust, at the unanimous solicitation of the governors.

There were in this hospital, 25th December 1809	-	31
Admitted in the year ending 25th December 1810	-	395
		—— 426
Discharged	- -	369
Died	- - -	19
Remained in the hospital		38
		—— 426

DESCRIPTION AND HISTORY OF THE HOUSE OF RECOVERY, OR FEVER HOSPITAL, IN CORK-STREET.[*]

THE miseries occasionally suffered by the labouring poor in all parts of Ireland, in consequence of the prevalence of the low contagious fever, are well

[*] This article is taken principally from an account of this Hospital, by William Disney, Esq.

known to those who are acquainted with the circumstances of the lower classes in that part of the united kingdom. It is by no means uncommon to see whole families, down in the fever (to use the vulgar phrase) at once; and this even in country villages and detached cabins ; and relapses after temporary recovery are also extremely frequent. But the calamity becomes much more grievous and formidable in its appearance, when it breaks out in the close parts of a populous city, inhabited thickly by sedentary manufacturers and artisans; and in the midst of an accumulation of causes, tending to generate, propagate, and (so long as they are suffered to exist) perpetuate contagion. These causes are no where perhaps found to prevail in greater force and number, than in those parts of the city of Dublin which constitute the liberties of St. Sepulchre, Thomas-court, and Donore ; close and ruinous habitations, unfurnished with any means of cleanliness, and crowded with inhabitants; narrow lanes and alleys, in the rear of which the filth of years is often suffered to accumulate ; a total relaxation of police as to almost every species of nuisance that can offend the senses, disgust the mind, or impair the health of the citizens; all operate with combined and continued force; nor can any person who has not visited this quarter of the metropolis, form a just or full conception of the circumstances and situation of the inhabitants.

When the Dispensary in Meath-street (commonly known by the name of the Sick Poor Institution) was first opened, the promoters of this salutary and highly useful establishment were fully aware of these circumstances; and the adoption of measures calculated to check the progress of contagion, and promote cleanliness among the people, formed a part of their original plan, and such means have (particularly of late years) been resorted to by them. But the managers found all their operations imperfect with respect to fever patients, so long as the infected person was suffered to remain to spread the disorder over the whole house in which he lodged. Their funds, however, never enabled them to erect or procure a distinct, separate house, for the reception of such patients, and consequently this part of their plan though the want of it was severely felt) was never fully carried into execution.

The accounts of the fever hospital at Manchester, and of a similar establishment at Waterford, had furnished new proofs of the efficacy and utility of such establishments; and the conviction of the benefit to be

THE CITY OF DUBLIN.

derived from them had been daily gaining strength. It was felt, that the health of the poor (in this respect at least) was the security of the rich, and motives of self-preservation and public policy operated to enforce the suggestions of benevolence. The subject attracted the attention of the Imperial Legislature; and in the session of 1802, on the recommendation of his Excellency the Lord Lieutenant, £1000. was voted by parliament towards erecting a building, and £500. towards the annual support of an establishment for the reception of fever patients residing in that part of the City of Dublin, which comprises the liberties on the south side of the river Liffey.

The vote of parliament was founded on the expectation, that the public liberality would be seconded by large private subscriptions, which had commenced previous to the parliamentary grant in the month of October, 1801; and in this expectation the legislature were not disappointed. Before the 7th of March, 1803, the sum of £6,330..18..1½ was subscribed, and the above sum has been since augmented by fresh subscriptions to the amount of £8,935..7..1¼, (exclusive of a sum of £200. bequeathed by the will of a respectable merchant lately resident in Dublin) ; and an hospital, consisting of two parallel buildings, the one for fever, and the other for convalescent patients, has been erected, and was opened for the reception of patients on the 14th May, 1804.

On the 23d day of October, 1801, fifteen persons were elected by the subscribers, in whom the management of the funds destined for the building of the hospital, and the furnishing thereof, was vested. On these fifteen persons, and six others, annually elected by the subscribers, the whole conduct of the institution now rests.

The first object that occupied the attention of the trustees, was the choice of a proper situation for the house; three points were necessary for this purpose : 1st, Proximity to the patients; 2dly, Abundance of pure and fresh air ;. 3dly, A copious supply of water. These advantages were all combined in the ground which, after much diligent search, was selected for the site of the hospital : it is a field of nearly 3 acres, on the south side of Cork-street, and in the immediate vicinity of the district intended to be relieved. It is nearly the highest ground in the neighbourhood of Dublin; the surface of the soil is perfectly dry, and an abundant and never-failing supply of water runs through it. It is situate on the south-western side of the City, consequently, from the prevalence of winds from this quarter, it is but seldom involved in the smoke or effluvia which would otherwise reach it, and it is exposed to the continued influx of fresh air from the mountains south of Dublin, on which side it is perfectly open.

In forming the plan of the building, they were aided by the experience of Dr. Currie of Liverpool, Doctors Percival and Bardsley of Manchester, and other eminent physicians, whose sentiments on the subject were obligingly communicated by Thomas Bernard, Esq. of the Foundling Hospital, London. To procure a complete separation of the sick from those who are recovering, two parallel buildings, 89 by 35 are constructed, at the distance of 116 feet from each other, and connected only by a covered colonnade, which serves the purpose of conveying the patients from the sick to the convalescent side of the house, and as a walk for the convalescents, for which it is well fitted, as it is open on one side to the south. The eastern building contains the sick, the western the convalescents, by which arrangement the probability of the transmission of noxious effluvia from the sick to the convalescent wards is diminished, in consequence of the prevalence of westerly winds. The direction of the building is from north to south; thus the inconvenience of much light, and a meridian sun on the wards, is obviated as far as possible; and as the windows of all the wards have an eastern or western aspect, ventilation is at the same time promoted by the prevailing wind from the west.

Each of the buildings is three stories high, exclusive of the basement stories, and that appropriated to the sick contains thirty-five wards, two of which are assigned to the apothecary, four to nurses, two to baths, two are used as reception rooms, for washing patients when admitted; and these last are the only part of the basement story, which as yet it has been found necessary to occupy.

It was at first a question, whether large or small wards were to be preferred: the larger wards were recommended by their more complete ventilation, by the smaller surface of walls for contagion to attach itself to, and by the lesser expense; the smaller, by their affording the means of separating the patients, and by the inconvenience being avoided of the patients disturbing each other, as well as of the shock which the appearance of death must at times occasion: the smaller wards would also admit of more frequent cleansing and fumigation. The opinion and reasons of Dr. Percival, in favour of small wards, were adopted, and experience seems to justify the preference. These wards are ranged along each side of a long gallery, that extends the whole length of the building, and the dimensions of each ward are 16 feet by 11 feet 3 inches, and 10 feet and a half high: the floors are tiled, and the walls are perfectly plain, without any cornice or projection that might impede the operation of sweeping or white-washing, or increase the surface to which dust or contagious matter might attach itself: similar principles have been observed in the construction of the window frames. The fever wards were originally intended to contain two beds, but in consequence of the extension of the district to be relieved, three beds have been introduced. The bedsteads are of cast iron, with boards laid across, on which ticks filled with straw are placed; the blankets are rather of the better kind, and the sheets are of bleached linen. Ventilation in the galleries is effected by three open grates in each floor, vertically opposite to each other, and two louvres in the roof; and there is a window at each extremity of the gallery that opens from above. Each of the wards is ventilated by the door, window, fire-place, and a tube inserted in the extremitity of the ceiling most remote from the fire-place, and continued to the upper part of the house. The ventilation is so complete, that no disagreeable smell is ever perceptible. Different galleries are appropriated to the different sexes; and to insure cleanliness, there are water-closets on each gallery. Each of the nurse's apartments, of which there is one on each gallery, is provided with a water-cock and bason, supplied by a forcing pump, which tends to the protection of the nurses, by affording them the means of washing themselves, after they have been in contact with the patients: all the painted parts of the house are white; the articles of dress and furniture are of the same colour, (with exception of the quilts, which are of materials that can be washed,) which affords the advantage of the immediately detecting dirt, and allowing fumigation with the usual materials when deemed necessary; and to prevent unnecessary intercourse between the sick and convalescent parts of the establishment, the servants, furniture, dresses, and various accommodations of each, are perfectly different and distinct.

The system of the House of Recovery has in view,—1st, To select the particular disease which it is the object of the charity to prevent; 2dly, To free the patient from contagion, and expedite his recovery; and, 3dly, To apply the means for destroying contagion within his habitation.

In conducting the hospital, every thing is carried on according to a general system of rules, previously arranged, and well matured and considered: strict regularity is observed as to hours of meals, bed-time, &c. with respect to the convalescents: the utmost attention is paid to cleanliness throughout; the wards are washed every day, all dirty clothes are immediately immersed in cold water, and removed to the under-ground apartments: after the removal or death of a patient, the ward is fumigated, and occasionally white-washed before the admission of another; the straw of the beds is frequently changed; and it may with truth be affirmed, that no sick room, under any circumstances, can present an appearance less offensive than the fever wards of this hospital.

In the basement story of the western or convalescent building, are the kitchen, scullery, store-rooms for bread, &c., with two large apartments for coffins, and the reception of the dead, which, opening outwards, have no communication with the other parts of the building. The first story contains, exclusive of the hall and stair-case, the board-room, convenient apartments for the master and house-keeper, with spacious store-rooms for the latter; and over these in the second and third stories, are four spacious convalescent wards, 33 feet 6 inches, by 31 feet 6 inches, two for males, and two for females, with intermediate apartments for the attending nurses; these wards having fire-places at each end, and windows on their sides, commanding a view of verdant fields and distant mountains, are well ventilated, lightsome, cheerful, and comfortable.

There are two different entrances with porters' lodges, one appropriated exclusively to the admission of patients, the other at the extreme end of the premises, which are enclosed by a substantial wall; and in convenient situations, detached from the hospital, there are stables, a laundry, and house for fumigation. In this edifice, nothing has been sacrificed to ornament; it is built with the best brick and mountain granite; it is throughout solid, plain, neat, and convenient, and may, we think, be proposed as a model for future fever hospitals.

The relief of the labouring and manufacturing poor, and the checking the progress of contagion, being the primary object of the instiution, a system has been adopted that seemed most likely to promote a plan so truly beneficent. Three physicians visit the hospital each day between 10 and 11 o'clock; to facilitate the patients' admission no recommendation is re-

THE CITY OF DUBLIN.

quired, but any application is attended to if made before ten o'clock in the morning; a physician from the hospital immediately visits at their dwelling the sick thus applying, selects from them those who labour under fever, and gives a ticket of admission: when this is received at the hospital, a covered carriage placed on springs, applied to this use only, so constructed as that the patient can lie at ease in an horizontal position, and furnished with a bed, is sent, in which the patient is slowly and cautiously conveyed to the house.* He is stripped in a reception-room appropriated to this use, and his wearing apparel put into cold water, preparatory to its undergoing a complete cleansing. The patient's face, hands, and feet, are washed with warm water, he is provided with clean linen, and conveyed to bed. The most striking effects have been produced by the mere cleansing the persons of the patient, and his removal to a clean bed in the airy, sweet, and well ventilated ward: profound sleep has very frequently followed, and been attended with an immediate favourable change in the symptoms of the disorder. To any person acquainted with the places from which the majority of patients are removed, the effects of such a transition will not appear surprising.

He is visited every day by a physician, who keeps the journal of the case, marks in a table the diet to be used, and gives directions as to his medical treatment, which are speedily carried into effect; when the patient is able to sit up, he is provided with a white wrapper, stockings, and slippers, which he wears until he is fit for removal; when this is the case, he is furnished with the dress appropriated to convalescents, and passes to the convalescent building.

When fit to be dismissed, the wearing apparel brought by him into the house is returned, after having undergone purification and exposure to the air. Such are the means by which contagion is suppressed in the person of the sick; to the beneficial consequences of which may be added, the effect produced on the mind of the patient, by having a system of cleanliness pursued in his person for a considerable time, and by shewing the possibility of the practice of cleanliness, as well as the comfort it produces.

Such is the outline of this establishment as to its internal management. With respect to the external measures to be pursued by the managing

---

* The bed, as soon as the patient is lodged at the hospital, is taken out and well aired; and there is no permanent lining in the carriage to retain infection.

committee, "for checking the progress of contagion, and introducing habits of cleanliness among the poor within the district," a wide field of exertion is open, in which they have been hitherto able to make little progress. On the dismissal of a patient, a printed ticket of advice is given to his friends, in which various particulars conducive to the destruction of contagion are recommended; but with this exception, little has been hitherto attempted, save the white-washing the apartments, from whence the sick have been removed; which department has been hitherto conducted by the managers of the sick poor institution. The efficacy of this process in such cases, has been long established: lime is known to occasion the decomposition of animal matters; and this perhaps operates in destroying the matter of contagion, which is probably of an animal nature. In the directions issued from the Manchester House of Recovery, it is said, the lime should be slacked when it is to be used, and that the white-washing should be practised while the mixture is bubbling and hot. These circumstances are important, as lime is more active when fresh, or before it has been exposed to the air, and as the vapours that rise from fresh slacked lime hold the latter substance in a state of minute division, therefore are likely to come in contact with and destroy any contagious effluvia that may float in the atmosphere. The removal of the infected patient from the midst of his family, and the cleansing his dwelling, are indeed justly ranked among the means which tend to cut off the very source of the evil, yet they are of themselves insufficient for the attainment of this great object, without attention to the removal of those causes, which either generate contagion, or dispose the body to receive it, such as the accumulated filth of back yards, and other intolerable nuisances, already mentioned, as the result of a total relaxation of police. Those objects have not escaped the vigilant attention of the committee, and will no doubt be met with the zeal and activity which their importance merits: it is obvious, however, that to render their endeavours completely effectual, co-operation must be sought for and obtained from other quarters, and a vigilant and active police established in the district of the hospital It must be a pleasing reflection to those engaged in this work of mercy, that even the remote effects of their exertions will tend to the attainment of the objects of this charity: the prevention of poverty, by obviating sickness, the improvement of the constitutions of the poor, by removing nuisances, the introduction of cleanliness, by facilitating the means

THE CITY OF DUBLIN. 715

for obtaining it, will all be the consequence of such benevolent endeavours, will all tend to eradicate contagion.

To the two buildings which originally constituted this hospital, a third has been added, which occupies the centre between them, opens off the connecting gallery or colonnade, and is built in the same plain substantial manner : to this, in consequence of the convenience of its central situation, the apothecary and house-keeper have been judiciously removed: in its two upper stories there are eight additional wards; and it terminates in a cupola containing a clock and bell. In consequence of this extension, and occupying the basement story, which is airy and lightsome, there are at present 132 beds for fever patients, which it is presumed will be sufficient, as the number of that description in the house has not at any time exceeded 118, although the hospital, originally intended for fever patients from the Liberties of Dublin only, at present receives them indiscriminately from all parts of the city, within the Circular Road.

The establishment consists at present of

Four physicians,	A collector,
A surgeon,	A house-keeper,
A register and purveyor,	Eight nurses,
An apothecary,	Seven servant maids.

This hospital has no estate, real or personal, save the premises on which it stands, which are held by a lease of lives renewable for ever, subject to a rent of £70..12. per annum; and £1693..15..2½, 3½ per cent. government stock.

In the year ending the 25th December, 1810, the subscriptions to this charity amounted to £1156..16..3.; the donations to £93..18..3.; and on an especial appeal to the public on the necessity of extending its beneficial influence; further donations were obtained to the amount of £2057..1..8., to which we may add, the parliamentary grant, which amounted to £999..12..11. In the same year, the expenditure was as follows:

Provisions	-	-	-	-	£919	18	6¼
Coal, soap, and candles	-	-	-	386	18	4
Medicines, & c.	-	-	-	-	333	15	11
Clothing	-	-	-	-	-	21	9	4½
Building and repairs	-	-	-	247	6	5
Rent and taxes	-	-	-	-	78	18	0
		Carried forward	-	£1988	6	6¼

Brought forward	-	£1988	6	6¼
Salaries and wages,	- - -	1036	10	3
Printing, stationary, and advertising,	-	58	2	3
Whitewashing the habitations of the poor,	-	89	8	4
Incidents,	- - - -	140	10	9½
Total expenditure,	- - -	£3465	17	3¾

Patients in the house, 5th January 1810, -	32
Admitted from that period to 5th January 1811,	1774
	1806
Discharged cured, - - -	1610
Died, - - - -	158
Remained in the Hospital, 5th January 1811,	38
	1806

GEORGE'S FEVER HOSPITAL.

This Hospital is annexed to the dispensary institution of St. George's parish. The great distance of this part of the city from Cork-street having rendered the conveyance of patients inconvenient and distressing, a house was taken on the Circular Road, Dorset-street, and fitted up for the purposes of a Fever Hospital. Its situation is healthy, being ventilated by the sea breezes from the Bay of Dublin, to which it lies in some measure open, but sufficiently remote from the marsh miasma which is sometimes exhaled from the low grounds at the entrance of the Liffey. The house contains 4 wards; 2 for male and 2 for female patients. In these are 17 beds, which are not always full. The number of patients admitted for the year 1814, was 129, and since its commencement in 1804, 1834, giving an average of 183 annually.

The medical attendants and expenditure are in common with the dispensary for St. George's parish.

OF MERCER'S HOSPITAL IN STEPHEN-STREET.

SEVERAL attempts were made by some of the surgeons of the City of Dublin to prepare an hospital for the relief of the sick poor, which, for want of a fund to commence with, proved abortive; till Mrs. Mary Mercer, in the year 1734, gave the large stone house, at the end of Stephen's-street, for an hospital for the reception of sick poor; and, by her deed of conveyance, appointed governors and directors of the hospital: the ground on which the house stands, being glebe, was given by Dr. Whittingham, the then archdeacon of Dublin: at the same time, upon the application of the late Rev. Dr. William Jackson, the City of Dublin gave the sum of fifty pounds towards fitting up the house; and soon after several charitable persons contributed in such manner, that by the 17th of August, 1734, ten beds were fitted up for the reception of sick poor, and immediately filled; the physicians and surgeons, who were appointed governors, undertook to attend the patients gratis, and several eminent apothecaries and druggists subscribed annually towards supplying the hospital with medicines. As more contributions came in, the number of beds was increased to forty; and in the year 1738, by means of a legacy left by Captain Hayes, the governors built a considerable addition to the house on ground given for that purpose by the then archdeacon of Dublin.

Until the governors were incorporated, they could not legally recover legacies; they therefore thought it expedient to apply for an Act of Parliament; and obtained one in the year 1750; by which they were enabled to receive donations, purchase lands, and recover legacies, &c. By this act, the dean and chapter of Christ-church, and the minister, churchwardens, and parishioners of the parish of St. Peter, are empowered to grant in fee-farm to the governors of this hospital, such part of their ground contiguous to the house, as may hereafter be found necessary towards the enlargement of the hospital. There is also a clause in this act formed to perpetuate the gratuitous attendance of the physicians and surgeons.

A committee has been lately appointed by the governors, consisting of fifteen persons selected from their own body, to be kept up as vacancies occur, who meet at the hospital on the first and third Tuesday in every month, and under whose inspection every thing relative to the management and expenditure must come, subject however to the revision of the board of governors: the committee appoint two of their number to visit the house occasionally, and *unexpectedly*, in order to the better carrying into effect every arrangement. A dietary hangs in each ward, which enables the patients to judge whether their food is administered according to the directions of the medical gentlemen, and all complaints are to be laid before the managing committee. Rules for the conduct of the officers and servants employed in the establishment have been framed, and are hung up in the wards and other apartments. The attention of strangers, and all persons who desire to inspect the hospital, is requested, and a book is kept, in which any 'observation may be entered by them, when it will be certain to meet the eyes of the managing committee.

The late surgeon Hume, who for 60 years gave the most constant and gratuitous attendance to this establishment, bequeathed to it a legacy of £300., which has induced the governors to prepare an additional ward, denominated from this circumstance *Hume's Ward*, and for the future support of which they depend on the humanity of a liberal public. There has been also an engraved portrait of this worthy benefactor published at the expence of the establishment, which, while it is only a merited tribute of respect to Mr. Hume, will, they trust, from the esteem that gentleman was held in, add something to the fund by the profits arising from the sale of it. And in consequence also of a liberal donation of £500. by two benevolent females, Mrs. Pleasants, and Miss Daunt, another ward has been opened; but this, like the former, must depend upon the benevolence of the public.

Of the six wards, two are at present appropriated to females, and four to males; and one of the former and two of the latter are for the reception of patients labouring under accidental injuries, such as wounds, fractures, &c. In these wards, the number of beds have been lately encreased from 38 to 48; and although on occasions of great pressure there have been 52 patients at the same time in the house, yet a circumstance which requires that two persons should occupy the same bed, and which of course should be avoided, has but seldom occurred, and the average number of patients constantly in the house may be estimated at 40.*

---

* Before the building of Sir Patrick Dunn's, four wards of this hospital had been appropriated to his Professors, who gave Clinical Lectures on the cases that occurred. As the causes assigned for discon-

The principal support of this Hospital was (besides casual benefactions and annual subscriptions) the benefit arising yearly from the performance of sacred musick in St. Andrew's church; but this becoming at length unproductive has been relinquished, and its present income, 1812, may be stated as follows:

Profit rents of lands in the Counties of Armagh and Longford,	£140	6	0¼
Ditto of houses in the City of Dublin,	111	1	6
Interest on £8198..10..6. securities,	464	8	2
Parliamentary grant of £50. net.	48	5	1
Grand Jury presentment,	50	0	0
Additional ditto,	50	0	0
Certain annual income,	904	0	9¼
Annual Subscriptions about	134	0	0
	1038	0	9¼

tinuing these Lectures forms an extraordinary fact in the medical practice of Dublin, we shall subjoin it. The frequent victims to Hydrophobia, had drawn the attention of the faculty to this dreadful malady, and the inefficacy of every tried remedy had induced some of them to determine on adopting some practice hitherto unattempted. A Sweep in passing through the College Courts was bitten by a mad dog. The usual precautions were taken immediately after: the parts were cauterised; and no apprehensions were entertained by himself of any ill consequences; nevertheless he was seized with rabid symptoms, and he died in four days, notwithstanding every effort to save him. It was found, however, that in this and similar cases, the application of a tight ligature above the wound, produced a temporary suspension of the symptoms, by interrupting, it was supposed, the communication between the sensorium and the wounded part; and hence it was concluded, that amputation of the part altogether might, on the same principle, produce a permanent and effectual relief. It was determined, therefore, to try. In a short time afterwards, a poor girl was brought to the Hospital who had been bitten in the leg, and at the time was labouring under symptoms of the incipient complaint. The Professor consulted with some medical friends, and it was determined to take off the limb. As it was a new and untried experiment, it became in the Hospital a subject of much debate and controversy. The Surgeon who had originally undertaken to perform the operation, was deterred from attempting it, and another, much less skilful, was prevailed on to try. The time was lost, the limb was mutilated, the woman died, the clamour was loud, the wards were resumed by the Governors of the Hospital, and the medical students were deprived of the benefit of Clinical Lectures. In justification of the experiment, it has been fairly stated, that there never has yet been recorded an instance of recovery from Hydrophobia, after the symptoms had unequivocally appeared; therefore no chance of recovery was hazarded where mortality was so certain; and further, that in a disease of such rapid progress, every fair chance of success was destroyed by the unwarrantable delays and impediments that obstructed it. Be this as is may, it is deeply to be regretted that any possible chance of relieving the most dreadful malady that can afflict the human frame,

Expenditure.

Provisions	- - - -	£584 11 5¼
Coals, soap, and candles	- - · ·	117 6 2¼
Medicines, &c.	- - - -	69 4 6¼
Repairs	-	21 13 10½
Stationary	- - - -	2 9 7
Salaries and wages	- - -	131 13 10
Contingencies	-	28 1 4
		£955 0 10

ROYAL MILITARY INFIRMARY.

The Royal Military Infirmary is a well built fabric of Portland stone. Its front consists of a centre surmounted by an handsome cupola and clock, and two returning wings 90 feet in depth. The whole extends 170 feet, exhibiting a façade by no means inelegant in itself, and adding a striking feature to the surrounding beautiful scenery.

It is delightfully situated on a high ground in the south-east angle of the Phœnix Park, commanding extensive and uninterrupted prospects over the Park, and a fine country; which lavishly displays a great variety of land richly embellished with wood and water, assisted with various works of art: thus deriving all the advantage that can be desired from a free and salubrious air. Over against this building to the south, on an equally elevated situation, stands the Old Soldier's Asylum at Kilmainham. Between the two buildings, at the bottom of a valley, runs the river Liffey, whose pleasing windings for a considerable extent enriches the beauty of the scene; to which Sarah's Bridge, consisting of one elegant and light arch, some short distance up the river, contributes not a little.

should be prevented by unfair obstruction on the one hand, or precipitate trial on the other; and that the consequences should be, that medical men were deterred from a similar attempt, and medical students deprived of the important benefits of Clinical Lectures, and from these circumstances that the progress of medical science should be long retarded in the city of Dublin.

THE CITY OF DUBLIN.

The building formerly used for the purposes of this Infirmary, is situated in St. James's street, within the city; but being much decayed, and, besides too small for the number of patients, this pleasing structure was raised in its present eligible situation, during the administration of the Duke of Rutland, who was present at the ceremony of laying its foundation stone, on the 17th of August, 1786. The plan, which seems to be excellent, was drawn by Mr. William Gibson, architect, and the work was executed by a Mr. Handy, for the sum of £9000., who completed it in 1788, in which year it was visited on the 21st of March, by the celebrated Mr. Howard, who then expressed his entire approbation of it, which he has confirmed in his work since published.

The interior consists of thirteen lofty and well ventilated wards, of which seven are medical, and six surgical; of these, six are 48 feet by 23 wide, six 24 feet by 23, and one, called the cupola ward, 34 feet by 26. The seven larger wards contain nineteen double beds each, and the six smaller nine double beds each, making a total of one hundred and eighty-seven beds. The bedding is excellent, the bedsteads of cast metal, and placed at proper distances from each other; the floors are tiled, and the pernicious practice of washing them, and covering them with sand or saw-dust, strictly forbidden, as in all other military hospitals. To the wards are attached convenient rooms for nurses, &c.; there are water-closets when necessary, and an ample supply of good water from a cistern on the top of the building. The wards are in the wings on each side of the hall, which occupies the centre of the building, separating the medical patients from the surgical: this latter, which is plain and neat, is fifty-two feet by twenty-three, accommodated with a gallery on one side, and at present serves as a chapel, though it has occasionally, in times of great pressure, been converted into a medical ward. In the parts between the centre and wings most of the officers of the house are accommodated. By the judicious construction of the areas, which are very wide, the under-ground story is well lighted, and rendered sufficiently agreeable for a residence. Here some of the officers are accommodated with airy and convenient apartments, by which means the upper and more ventilated parts of the building are occupied almost exclusively by patients' wards.

At the rear of the Infirmary, in an airy situation, and perfectly detached, is a new fever hospital. This on the upper floor has four wards, containing four single beds each, very well ventilated, but obviously much too small, a circumstance which however can be easily remedied, by removing some partitions, taking in the dividing galleries, and thus throwing the four wards into two. On the ground-floor are wards with cells most absurdly intended for lunatics, but which will answer for convenient apartments, as they are perfectly ventilated.

A few acres of the Phœnix Park have been walled off, and attached to this Infirmary; these consist of the platform on which it stands, and a bank descending rapidly to a valley, through which runs a lively stream, with a neat gravel walk along its margin, where the convalescents are permitted to enjoy air and exercise; the whole forming a scene cheerful and comfortable. In a distant angle of this ground, some of the officers of the house have small gardens: and here is a range of buildings which contains the laundry, the prison wards for sick deserters, &c. lunatic cells, medical board stores, with the charnel or dead house.

This hospital not having been found sufficient for the sick soldiers of the garrison of Dublin, government has for some years rented the upper story of Stevens's hospital at £500. per annum: this is considered as part of this establishment, the entire expense of which last year amounted to £8554. nearly £4600. of which was supplied by parliamentary grant, and £3954. by a stoppage of 10d. per day from each patient's pay, while in the Infirmary. The average expense of supporting one patient in the Infirmary, (salaries of officers, and all other expences included) is nearly £33. per annum, of which government pays nearly £17.

Exclusive of the occasional attendance of the state physician and surgeon-general, a non-resident surgeon attends daily, and an apothecary constantly resides, each having a salary of ten shillings per day, which is also the allowance of the resident steward or purveyor. The deputy purveyor and store-keeper, who are also resident, have each five shillings per day. It is scarce necessary to add, that the most perfect order, decency, neatness, and cleanliness are visible in every part of this institution.

The instructions from the army medical board enjoin, that all soldiers that belong to regiments on duty in Dublin, who shall be afflicted with fevers, and other acute disorders, shall be sent to this Infirmary within twenty-four hours at the utmost after sickening; and all soldiers labouring under diseases arising from accidents, or other cases which require immediate medical assistance, shall be sent to the Infirmary within twelve hours. All cases which are not of the above description are received into the regimental hospitals,* and attended by the respective medical officers of each corps, who in addition to their ordinary duty, are enjoined to attend at the military infirmary on two days in the week. .

The number of patients received is very fluctuating. Notwithstanding the extensive accommodation of the establishment, occasions have occurred on which they have been found insufficient. When an exchange took place between the two militias of England and Ireland, the influx of the military into Dublin was attended with much sickness: the fatigue of marching and other causes created so many cases, which were appropriate subjects for this hospital, that it was found necessary to erect tents in the lawn before the building to accommodate them. The number of patients at present is remarkably small: to account for this, a cause perhaps not altogether adequate, is assigned. The regiments composing the garrison of Dublin are constantly exercised in military manœuvres in the Phœnix Park : it was some time ago the practice not to commence this duty till after mid-day, and the soldiers were exposed in summer to all the morbid effects produced by the heat of a burning sun, which in a body of five or six thousand men were very numerous. This practice has now been changed ; the hours of exercise are from seven in the forenoon till ten ; and correspondent good effects are said to have followed the alteration. Perhaps the improved state of medical practice in the army may be the principal cause.

CHARITABLE INFIRMARY, JERVIS-STREET.

This venerable establishment is particularly entitled to public notice, as the first charitable institution of the kind established in Dublin, and is therefore the parent from which all the others have proceeded. So early as the beginning of the last century, some benevolent gentlemen of the faculty resolved

* There are seven fabrics erected for this purpose at the rear of the royal barracks, to which the sick of the different regiments, composing the garrison of Dublin, are conveyed, except such cases as are subjects for the royal infirmary. These are attended by the respective surgeons and assistants.

on founding some asylum, to which the afflicted might apply for medical aid, and where they might be removed and taken care of during the continuance of their malady. For this purpose, in the year 1728, six surgeons* associated together, and took a small house in Cook-street, capable of accommodating four intern patients, which they supported by subscription of individuals who approved of the project. In a short time the subscriptions increased so rapidly, as to enable them to increase their establishment beyond their then limited accommodation. They therefore removed it from their small house to one considerably larger on the King's Inn quay, where they accommodated fifty patients. This continued to flourish till the site of the four courts was determined on, which comprehending the ground on which the infirmary stood, it was necessary again to remove it. An eligible situation offering in Jervis-street, an advantageous bargain was made with Lord Charlemont, and the institution transferred thither. In the year 1792, the governors feeling the inconvenience of acting without the confidence of sufficient sanction, made application to government for a charter. Their petition stated, "that for many years past the institution had been of great and manifest advantage to the sick and wounded poor of the north parts of Dublin, by supplying them with medical and surgical assistants, medicine, and all manner of necessaries, without fee or reward. That it was supported entirely by the charitable contributions of the public, and that several persons who are disposed to contribute liberally to its support, are deterred from so doing because the present governors are incompetent to receive and manage the same from the want of a charter of incorporation to insure the funds, and enforce the necessary regulations." The charter was forthwith granted, and the governors were incorporated by the name of "*the Guardians and Governors of the Charitable Infirmary, Dublin.*" The good effects of this measure were soon apparent, and enabled the governors to

* The memory of these benevolent men are preserved by the following inscription on one of the walls.
SOLI DEO GLORIA.
The Charitable Infirmary was first founded and opened August 1728, at the sole expence of the following surgeons:

George Duany,   John Dowdall,
Patrick Kelly,   Fr. Duany,
Nath. Handson,   Peter Brenan,

who served the poor without fee or reward.

make considerable improvements. Their house was old, and it was determined to rebuild it. In the year 1803 it was taken down, and the present spacious building erected in its place. As it stands in a situation little exposed to public view, no attention has been paid to exterior decoration.. It has a plain brick front, differing only from the adjoining houses in size, and a certain air of gloominess. Its interior consists of a large reception room, which is also the apothecary's shop, a board room, a lecture room, and six wards, which are capable of containing seventy-five beds; but at present they are not all occupied. An excellent arrangement has been lately adopted, which distinguishes this useful institution. There is a class of society above the description of those poor who are usually candidates for admission into hospitals, and yet so limited in their circumstances, as to feel great distress under the pressure of sickness, from the expense of medicine and medical attendants: to accommodate such individuals, it was resolved to fit up two of the large and commodious wards for their reception, upon the terms of supporting themselves with food, and looking to the house only for advice, medicine, and beds. This humane and considerate arrangement has been of infinite comfort to many of the more decent classes of the labouring poor. They are not exposed in the public room, or associated with the usual paupers of an hospital, while they have all the comforts of fire, candle-light, warm room, and regular attendance, in addition to medicine, which a dispensary would not supply. The number of poor, who avail themselves of this privilege, is considerable. A recommendation is seldom necessary to obtain relief from this institution, all persons applying are indiscriminately received, either as intern or extern patients. Though originally intended for a surgical hospital only, all cases are admitted, except such as are contagious. This general practice induced the medical officers to establish lectures in the infirmary. In the year 1808, therefore, it was erected into a school for medical and surgical education, and a course of lectures commenced on the theory and practice of physic and clinical surgery; and a small library was also established for the use of the students. This school has added another important advantage to the medical education of this metropolis, the facility and excellence of which are now so acknowledged, as to rival the reputation of the most celebrated in other countries. The average number of pupils who attend, are forty annually; but last year they were increased to seventy, a proof of the growing reputation of this infant school.

The average number of extern patients daily prescribed for, amonut to one hundred and twenty.

The average number of intern patients, annually received, one hundred and ninety.*

Officers of the Institution.

Two physicians, Housekeeper resident,
Nine surgeons, Two nurses,
Register,   Porter.

Annual Income of the Establishment.

	£.	£	s.	d.
Interest on £7000. { 4000 Public security	-	277	10	0
{ 3000 on private ditto	-	180	0	0
From Treasury, deducting fees	- - -	48	5	1½
City Grand Jury cess '	- - -	216	13	4
Rents	- - - -	76	17	6
Annual subscriptions	- - - -	120	0	0
		919	5	11½

Annual Expenditure.

Provisions	- - - -	350	0	0
Medicines	- - - -	165	0	0
Coals, Candles, &c.	- - - -	76	0	0
Repairs	- - - - -	46	0	0
Furniture and utensils	- - -	24	0	0
Rent	- - - -	48	8	9
Salaries and wages	- - - -	233	15	0
Contingencies	- - - -	50	0	0
		993	3	9

The expenditure of this excellent institution for some years considerably exceeded its receipts, but a recent appeal to the public has been very successful, and commensurate to its extensive relief. The number of interns admitted from January 1812 to January 1816, amounted to 762.

* The number admitted from April 1808, to April 1812, amounted to six-hundred and seventy-seven.

UNITED HOSPITAL OF ST. MARK'S AND ST. ANNE'S.

This Hospital was originally opened in the year 1753, in Francis-street, and intended for the then destitute poor of the parishes of St. Nicholas and St. Catherine. It was supported by subscriptions, and the interest of a fund raised by lottery. On the expiration of the lease of the house in 1804, the governors, considering the west end of the town now liberally supplied with means of relief to the sick poor, turned their attention to the parish of St. Mark, as the only part of the metropolis which stood in need of an hospital. Accordingly, in the year 1808, it was transferred to Mark-street, and intended for the relief of the poor of St. Anne's and St. Mark's parishes. Part of the district to which it extends is very poor and sickly, and sent more cases to the Dublin General Dispensary than all the rest of the metropolis. It includes the low, dank, and unwholesome lanes and alleys, which run to George's quay and the Liffey, comprising the Wapping of Dublin. The inhabitants are the poor who are connected with a seafaring life, and are more liable to the usual excitements of disease, privation, exposure, hardship and intemperance, than any other class of the community. Notwithstanding this, the hospital remains untenanted : the funds are not able to support any internal patient, and its 10 beds remain unoccupied. This is much to be regretted, as the extensive relief it gives to externs as a dispensary, affords a melancholy proof of its necessity. The number of patients relieved in 1815, were—

Medical - - 3276
Surgical - - 3101
Total 6377

Attached to the institution are two physicians and six surgeons.

HOSPITAL FOR INCURABLES.

THE establishment of hospitals for the relief of the poor, is perhaps one of the most benevolent and judicious efforts of the human mind. It is to alleviate at once the two most afflicting incidents of human life, and disarm of their severity, the associated evils of poverty and distemper. But there is yet a stage of wretchedness beyond the scope of ordinary hospitals, which seems to point at a defect of no inconsiderable magnitude, in the principles of their establishment. The unhappy object may be afflicted with a distemper which no medical aid can eradicate, and he then finds no longer an asylum. He is thus rejected when his affliction becomes most extreme, and removed from all charitable aid, when his hopeless misery has the strongest claims on the compassion of the humane heart. In this state, he encounters all the evils of penury and distemper in their truest form: he is turned into our streets to become a loathsome object to every eye, reprobating at once the deficiency of human precaution, and shocking the feelings of human sensibility. For a long time this evil was obtruded on the public eye of Dublin. The numerous hospitals of the city rejected their incurable patients, who wandered about the streets, expelled from one asylum, and refused admittance to every other. It was not till a late period that this melancholy evil excited due attention. Lord Mornington, father to the Duke of Wellington, was the first who interested himself with effect for this most afflicted class of fellow creatures. This nobleman's love of music is well known, and the specimens he has left behind of his proficiency in this art are very celebrated. He conceived the happy idea of converting this talent into a source of charity, and appealing to the public benevolence, through the medium of his favourite science. A musical society was formed, under his patronage, for the object of holding public concerts, the profits of which were applied to the purpose of making provision for such poor patients as laboured under incurable diseases, which by being exposed in the streets, exhibited objects not only offensive to humanity, but dangerous to delicate and pregnant females. The first efforts of this benevolent society were not very extensive; in the year 1744, they rented, and fitted up with suitable accommodations, a small house in Fleet-street, into which were removed the diseased objects, whose exposure in the public streets was most offensive. The success of this society and the interest excited by the project, soon enabled them to erect a larger and more complete asylum; and the extensive hospital in Townshend-street was completed. This building was very spacious, and well calculated for the purposes of its erection. It consisted of six wards, and was capable of containing above 100 patients; but the zeal and ability evinced in its erection, were not continued for its support: for several years this excellent charity languished in an obscure and negligent manner, part of their funds had been lent out on securities, and there seems to have been considerable difficulty in again recalling them. In the year 1790, but two of its wards were occupied by a few patients of both sexes, who were seldom supplied with clothes, and exhibited an appearance equally squalid and offensive. About this time, the governors finding themselves unable to occupy the wards of this extensive building, and unwilling that four spacious wards should remain useless to the public, and unengaged in any purpose of charity, made application to the governors of the house of industry, and permitted them to send from one hundred to one hundred and twenty of such of their patients as was deemed incurable, to occupy those wards. This plan, which was dictated by a benevolent spirit and a sense of public utility, was very unfortunate in its consequence. The class of patients sent from the house of industry were necessarily of the lowest description; they brought with them all the vicious and immoral practices of early habits, and soon introduced among the established patients of the house, who were selected from decent classes of society, their own habits and propensities. In a short time the hopeless irregularities and profligacy of the house induced the governors to render up the whole establishment to the governors of the house of industry, from a despair of managing it as they intended. This proposal was strenuously opposed by the late Lord Kilwarden and Arthur French, Esq. the treasurer: happily their opposition was successful, and the measure was abandoned. In the year 1790, a legacy of £4000. was bequeathed to the charity by Theobald Wolf, Esq., and from this period its affairs began to revive. Lord Kilwarden, his executor, in conjunction with the treasurer, thought it his duty to inquire strictly into the internal management of this charity, and to correct all its imperfections and abuses. This superintendance they continued till a thorough reformation was effected; a system of perfect order and regularity was restored, the comfort and convenience of the

* See article Lock Hospital, p. 696.

patient more attended to in the article of food, and a suit of clothes with an additional shirt and shift was annually provided. In this thriving state the institution continued till the year 1792, when a material alteration took place in its establishment. It was found that the house in Donnybrook, as a Lock hospital, was entirely unfit for the purpose. Government therefore proposed to the managers of this charity to exchange the house and lands of Donnybrook for their concerns in Townshend-street. This judicious proposal readily met with their approbation.

The Lock hospital was removed to the city, where the constant attendance of medical men is given without professional inconvenience, and the asylum for incurables was transferred to the country, where the unhappy patients have the advantages of pure air and rural retirement, supplying to their hopeless misery the only solace their state is susceptible of. Since that period the Institution has been much indebted to the exertions of Dr. Percival; he visited the house with a constant assiduity, and drew up a form of acts for its internal regulation highly beneficial. In the reception of a patient three things are scrupulously attended to: 1st, misery of the complaint; 2d, age of the patient; 3d, former good conduct. A consideration of these qualifications is so strict as to supersede every other recommendation, however extensive the influence or high the authority.

A system also has been adopted highly conducive to the interests of the charity. A certain number of patients are received who are supported by particular subscription of individuals. These not only set an example of good conduct, by the greater decorum of their demeanor, but also the funds have been thus so increased as to admit 50 patients, which is the present establishment.

GENERAL OBSERVATIONS ON DISPENSARIES.

A Dispensary is an institution where medicine and advice are given gratis to the poor without any other accommodation. It usually consists of a small house, which can be procured on moderate terms, the house is divided into two apartments, the medical and surgical, to which is attached an apothecary's shop, from whence such medicines as are prescribed are *dispensed* to the poor. The institution is either general or parochial, supported by subscriptions annual or occasional, and sometimes charity sermons. When sickness renders medical assistance necessary, application is made for a recommendation, which is readily procured in every parish; on the emergency of accident none is necessary. This is brought at stated hours to the dispensary, where, in appropriate apartments, physicians and surgeons sit to examine and prescribe for such as are able to attend in person. If their maladies are so severe as to confine them to their own houses, they are immediately and regularly visited in any part within the precincts of the respective districts to which the dispensary is appropriated.

It is singular that dispensaries, which of all institutions for the relief of the sick poor, seem best calculated sometimes for effectual relief, and always for extensive utility, should be so recent in their first establishment, and so tardy in their general adoption. Hospitals, where the patient becomes an inmate in the institution, and are supplied with other accommodations, which the poor themselves can seldom provide, are certainly very well arranged to meet those poignant afflictions, which poverty and distemper united, seldom fail to create; but then there are many reasons which militate against their general utility.

From the very liberality of their object they must be extremely limited in the extent of their utility. The expense of their establishment necessarily restricts their number to a few, and the patients admitted bear no kind of proportion to the numerous poor who require medical assistance. Thus a recommendation to an hospital is not easily procured, and a vast majority of the sick poor would be left to perish, if they depended only on such partial accommodation. But in dispensaries this is entirely obviated. There is no limited space exclusively occupied; there is no assistance besides medicine and advice called for, to exhaust a limited fund. The expense of the institution is comparatively small, the subscriptions are moderate, the subscribers many, and there are no patients, however friendless or numerous, to whom its relief is inaccessible, where there are so many in every parish to whose recommendation it is open. The moderate expenditure, and extensive relief of such institutions may be estimated by the following fact: In the year 1807, the number of patients admitted into the Meath-street Dispensary, was 7437, and the expense for medicine and stationary £199.; by which it appears that a large portion of the poorest population has received advice from the most eminent practitioners, and medicines of the best quality, and in every quantity, at the moderate sum of 6½d. for each individual.

Children are not subjects for hospitals. The numbers afflicted with distempers, and the minute attention which their helpless age individully requires, necessarily preclude them from institutions whose arrangements, however extensive, are yet so comparatively limited in the means of accommodation, and the number of their attendants. It is from dispensaries alone that this interesting class of society can be relieved; and while the mother's watchful anxiety can alone distinguish, for the physician's guidance, symptoms impervious to any other but a mother's eye, the progress of the disease is watched, and the salutary medicine is aided by that maternal care at home, which the promiscuous accommodation of an hospital could never bestow on so many helpless individuals.

Even of adults the most numerous cases are those where the stage of the distemper, or its kind, does not render confinement or restraint from ordinary avocation necessary, while medical advice is absolutely called for, to arrest the progress, or remove altogether, a complaint whose neglect might be fatal. To such, dispensaries afford salutary relief. The poor artizan is not impeded in the exercise of his profession, on the returns of which himself and his family depend for support; while the best advice and medicine the nature of his case demands, are gratuitously supplied him.

Even of those adults whose cases are subjects for admission into an hospital, there are many, and those of the valuable and interesting class of the poor, who would not submit to it. The rooted prejudice of unconquerable aversion, the strong attachment to his own house, frequently render removal exquisitely painful to the irritable mind of a sick man, and is found to exasperate in no small degree the symptoms of the disorder; not to say that the nature and stage of the distemper, may sometimes render removal on another account highly dangerous. But in dispensaries, there is nothing in the manner in which the relief is applied that can, in the smallest degree, wound the sensibilities, or exasperate the disease. The poor artizan is not torn from his family; the little arrangements of his domestic life are not disturbed; and while those decent proprieties so natural to the heart of man are not violated in the promiscuous publicity of an hospital, and the best advice humanely attends at his bed side, the soothing consolations of his own home, and the assiduity of his own family, are powerful auxiliaries in aid of medicine to restore him. There is strongly marked in the Irish character a social propensity, which pines at separation; there is a prejudice, a pride, that clings to home, however wretched, and shrinks from public exposure, however modified. If then a mind calm and undisturbed be one great essential in the cure of disease, how judicious is that institution which thus adapts itself to the disposition of the patient, combats not the feelings of his heart, and while it even condemns the prejudice, kindly concedes to the propensity.

On the whole of this subject, should certain regulations, which are partially adopted, become essential in the establishment of them all, dispensaries might not only relieve, as they do, every possible case, but meet every possible emergency to which the sick poor are liable; particularly since the establishment of fever hospitals. The certain consequence of sickness among the poor is to increase their poverty still more, by preventing their exertions for their own support, and the debility which follows is rendered still more tedious and distressing by the want of that cordial and nutritious diet, which the poor cannot themselves provide, and which humane societies in general withdraw when the the patient is no longer sick. Small sums of money should therefore be given, by appointed visitors, to purchase such nourishment as might materially contribute to restore more speedily his strength to the convalescent. To the remedies already provided should be added wine, whose medicinal qualities to those whose constitutions are not familiarised to its effects, are found to be so powerful in counteracting disease, and whose cordial qualities are such noble restoratives; and finally, to prevent the attack of distemper in the first instance, to destroy its malignity, arrest its progress, and prevent its return, the poor should be supplied with the means of, and to a certain degree compelled to cleanliness; their apartments should be purified by ablutions, and the foulness of the air corrected by lime and white-washing.

The establishment of dispensaries originated in London, in the year 1687. The College of Physicians issued, in that year, an edict, enjoining all Fellows, Candidates, and Licentiates, to give medical advice gratuitously to the neighbouring poor. This edict was sent to the board of aldermen; and a question arising as to what description of the community the term *poor* should apply, it was answered by the College, that it would be sufficient to bring a certificate from the clergymen of the parish in which the applicant resided: to this it was afterwards added by the aldermen, that the certificates of the churchwardens and overseers should be also received; and further, that all hired servants and apprentices to handicraftsmen should be deemed poor, and objects of the intended charity; and a committee was appointed to consider the best mode of administering it.

Still the high price of medicine was an object which rendered the benevolent intentions of the physicians almost nugatory, as the poor had seldom the means of paying for the prescription after it was written. To obviate this, and render to the poor a facility of availing themselves of this gratuitous advice, the laboratory of the college was fitted up for the preparation of medicine, to be distributed to them at reduced prices; and another room was provided for the reception of those who applied for advice. Such was the origin of dispensaries.

It is an extraordinary fact in the history of the human character, that a design of this kind could meet with any opposition; that there could be found any members of the community so meanly interested as to cling to the profits of poverty under its most afflicting circumstances, or so absurdly avaricious, as to fear such an arrangement would be disadvantageous to their trade, when it was notorious that few of the description for whom the relief was intended, attempted to procure advice or medicine at all, except gratuitously and at reduced; prices yet so it was, that an opposition so violent commenced against the plan, and a persecution so vexatious against all the faculty who favoured it, that after nine years laudable exertion to establish it, the fellows, and other members of the college, were themselves obliged to enter into voluntary subscriptions of £500. and thus not only gave gratuitously the valuable exercise of their professional skill, but provided their patients with the medicines they themselves prescribed.*

* Each of them subscribed 10*l.* to purchase medicines to be distributed to the poor in the form of recipes, *at their intrinsic value:* it is stated in the instrument to which their names are annexed, "that prescribing for the poor gratis was hitherto rendered ineffectual, for no method was taken to furnish them with medicines for their aid, at low and reasonable rates." Among the names is to be seen the celebrated Sam. Garth, whose admirable satire, written on the occasion of this inhuman opposition, has the following lines put into the mouth of one of the opponents, at a supposed meeting of the apothecaries:

" The faculty of Warwick-lane, design,
If not to storm, at least to undermine;
Their gates each day ten thousand night-caps crowd,
And mortars utter their attempts aloud;
Our manufactures now they meanly sell,
And spitefully the intrinsic value tell." *Disp. Canto* 2.

ST. THOMAS'S AND ST. MARY'S DISPENSARY.

ALMOST a century elapsed before the establishment of a similar institution in Dublin; at length, in the year 1782, by the exertions of Doctors Law and Paul, ministers of St. Mary's and St. Thomas's parishes, aided by Dr. Purcel, and Surgeon Kuig, the first dispensary was established in Dublin for those parishes. This primitive institution was, and still continues to be, very simple: there is no local aparatus or medical establishment; there is no printed rules of its regulations; the poor recommended assembled at an apothecary's shop appointed for that purpose, produced the recipes prescribed for them, received the medicines, and the account was periodically sent in to the subscribers and settled. At present the house of assembly is in Coles-lane, where, on two days in the week, the surgeon and one physician of the institution attend; their prescriptions are brought to an apothecary's shop in Great Britain-street, not far from the house where the medicines are compounded and delivered. This institution, though simple in its establishment, and limited in its means, has nevertheless been of most essential service in promoting the purposes intended. As the first institution of the kind in Ireland, and setting an example since so laudably followed, it merits our gratitude; while its arrangements perhaps have this advantage over others, that the convenience of the poor is more consulted, the times of giving out the medicine not being limited to any particular hour as in other dispensaries.*

Five physicians and one surgeon attend, who receive no salary. The expenditure may be thus stated:

	£.	s.	d.
Medicines	100	0	0
Rent	14	0	0
Attendants	4	11	0
Contingencies	20	0	0
	138	11	0

The number of patients at present annually relieved - 3,400
Entire number since the commencement, being thirty-four years, 76,000
Annual average - - - - - - 2,200

* The written rules of the institution are as follows:
No person to be elected a governor but by ballot, and one black bean excludes. Three boards to be

THE DUBLIN GENERAL DISPENARY.

This was established in April 1785, under the patronage of his Grace the Duke of Leinster president, and Lord Donoughmore, vice president. Its attention is not confined to the precincts of a single parish or district, but, as its name imports, extends its inspection to the remotest parts, calls to it with equal affection the friend and stranger, and pours wine and oil into the wounds of every afflicted traveller. The house is situated on Temple Bar, nearly in the centre of the city. Besides the usual surgery, apothecary's shop, &c. there are a few apartments where those patients may be occasionally accommodated with beds, whom sudden accident, or any important operation, might render it dangerous to remove. There is also an apparatus to restore suspended animation, to which, from its vicinity to the river, those may be immediately brought who meet with such accidents, and the expiring spark of life speedily revived, which the delay of a few minutes might for ever extinguish. This apparatus consists of a sand bath, constructed of stone, having under it a furnace, by means of which a moderate degree of warmth is diffused through the sand, in which the patient's body is immersed. Though this contrivance may be well devised for restoring a uniform animal heat to the body, were it always ready, yet the process of preparing it is so prolix, in cases of pressing emergency, where a minute's delay might be fatal, that it has hitherto been attended with little efficacy, and from frequent failure, has been latterly altogether disused. However, so necessary a part of the institution was too important to forego. The place has been recently improved; and under the patronage of his Grace the Duke of Bedford, a Humane Society has been formed, on a more extended plan, connected with this institution. Its object is, exclusively, to recover persons drowned, or in a state of suspended animation, from any other cause. The Dublin General Dispensary, and Stevens' Hospital, both

held in the year, and three governors constitute a board. The treasurer's accounts to be audited every stated board. A list of medical and surgical patients to be laid annually before the board, and published with a list of the subscribers. An annual charity sermon to be preached alternately in the parish churches of St. Thomas and St. Mary. Patients to attend on Tuesdays and Saturdays; but home patients to be visited at any time at their own houses. It is supported by subscriptions and an annual charity sermon.

THE CITY OF DUBLIN.

in the vicinity of the Liffey, are appointed receiving houses; these are provided with complete apparatus for inflating the lungs, and performing every other necessary operation. Boats, provided with drags, poles, and other implements, are placed convenient to both places, and are to hold themselves always in readiness. The expences of this establishment are defrayed in the same manner as those of the vaccine institutions, by annual memorials to his Excellency the Lord Lieutenant.

The number of patients annually relieved, are on an average, about 4000, and the average annual expence about £225. computing from its commencement to the present day. The particulars are as follow:

	£.	s.	d.
Salary of Apothecary	60	0	0
Ditto Porters	18	8	3
Rent of House	30	0	0
Drugs and incidental expences	116	11	9
	£225	0	0

DISPENSARY FOR THE LIBERTIES.

The decided benefits derived to the poor from the Dublin General Dispensary, were so obvious and striking, as to call for the establishment of similar institutions. In a metropolis of more than ten English miles in circumference, and containing a population of 172,000 individuals, it is scarcely possible that two institutions, however general one was in its plan, and however assiduous both were in their execution, could immediately attend to every call in so great an extent, and effectually relieve every individual in so great a number; even if the people tried to avail themselves of the benebenefits, which many would not, or could not do, from the inconvenient distance of the extremities of a large city from the centre.

Accordingly, several parishes where the inconvenience was most felt, formed themselves into a separate district, and established a dispensary appropriated to the poor within their limits. Those are the parishes of St. James, St. Luke, St. Nicholas without, St. Catharine, and St. Audoen, comprising a considerable part of the liberties of the city. The poor of every large town must be ever more subject to disease than the rich, from the circumstances connected with their situations; food, scanty in its quantity, and unwholesome in its quality, exposure to heat and cold, without the protection of sufficient covering, want of timely medical aid to meet the commencement and remove the consequences of disease, habits of intoxication from the immoderate use of ardent spirits, confined unwholesome streets, and crowded dirty apartments, together with those moral causes, which through the medium of the mind, affect the physical frame, the depression of despondency and the irritations of violent passions. These are additional causes of distemper, ever to be found among the poor of populous cities, from which the opulent are in a great measure exempt; no wonder then if, where these causes are found in the greatest extreme, the quantity of sickness should be correspondent, and extreme also. The district for which this dispensary is established, contains a population of 50,000 individuals, by far the greater part of whom are in the lowest stage of human wretchedness: they for the most part inhabit narrow lanes, where the insalubrity of the air usual in such places, is increased to a pernicious degree by the effluvia of putrid offals, constantly accumulating both in front and rear; the houses are very high, and the numerous apartments swarm with inhabitants. It is not unfrequent for one family or individual to rent a room, and set a portion of it by the week, or night, to any accidental occupant, each person paying for that portion of the floor which his extended body occupies. In this way it will not appear incredible, that 108 individuals have been reckoned in one building, and that seven persons were found lying in a fever on the floor at one time, out of twelve that occupied the small apartment.*

Among this population so lodged, every thing that privation and nakedness from extreme poverty can effect; every thing that despondency can produce, from decay of trade and want of employment; every thing that ebriety can cause, from facility of procuring ardent spirits, and unrestrained indulgence of them; every thing, in fine, that can be supposed to engender disease, and extend its baneful consequence, here exerts its influence, and produces morbid effects, the most melancholy and deplorable. To counteract those effects, many benevolent plans were proposed and adopted

* The first occurred to the Rev. Mr. Whitelaw, the other to the Rev. R. Walsh.

by the more opulent inhabitants, but none more efficacious to meet the evil than the dispensary opened in Meath-street, in the year 1794.

This institution is indebted for its support not only to the actual residents, but to many others, who had been inhabitants of the Liberties in their more flourishing state ; and who having retired with ample fortunes to more eligible residences, with no less propriety than retributive humanity, returned part of that wealth to relieve the distresses of those manufacturers, from whose labours, in better times, they had derived it: nor do the subscribers limit their liberality to mere medical assistance ; but where the mass of human misery calls for every aid that a fellow creature can bestow, it is humanely provided for, and no ordinary distress is met by no ordinary exertions of benevolence. Many of the subscribers themselves inspect personally into the wants of the sick poor, to supply them and their families with pecuniary and other aids, whenever the case requires it; and thus men of different avocations, and far other pursuits in life, unite in searching for objects of distress, and bound by no tie, and called by no professional duty, wreckless of danger, and intrepid in humanity, are daily seen penetrating into the most dangerous contagion and revolting wretchedness, for the noble and disinterested motive alone of seeing best how they may relieve it Another feature which distinguishes this noble institution is, that it is supported exclusively by subscriptions, without charity sermons, or any other appeal to the public.

The total number of patients relieved since the establishment of the institution in 1794, to the end of the year 1807, was 58,780, giving an average of 4521 annually. But this average, in fact, gives no accuracy as to the numbers annually relieved, they never continuing stationary, but increasing in a most extraordinary progression. In 1804, the numbers were 4132; in 1805, 5125; in 1806, 6369 ; and in 1807, 7487 ; the fever hospital had been opened in the interval, substracting from the dispensary 600 annual patients : if those therefore be added, it will give an increase of sickness in this district of from 4000 to 8000 in four years. It is surely an object for the philantropic enquirer, to endeavour to account for this rapid and alarming increase. It is not sufficient to say, that the prejudices of the people to such institutions are wearing away ; if that were all, the increase would be regular, since its commencement, which it is not, the number being less in some of the subsequent years than in the preceding ; besides, there is no cause of prejudice to dispensary institutions; the very nature of them yields to every objection a poor man could make, even though near thirty years experience of them in this city had not long removed it; while the population of the Liberty has remained the same; while the usual causes of disease, arising from poverty, nakedness, and vicissitude of weather, remained nearly the same in this period; it would be very difficult to account for this increase, did not one acknowledged pregnant cause of distemper, *the consumption of spirits*, encrease at the same time in nearly a correspondent progression. Among the returns for the diseases of one of the last years are found 30 cases of paralysis, 15 of palpitations, 287 of dropsy, and 264 of dyspepsia, distempers amongst the poor notoriously the consequence of the immoderate use of spirits; within that time the number of licences had increased in the same proportion; and the number of shops vending spirits in one street alone in the district to FIFTY-THREE!!

Annual Expenditure as follows:

	£.	s.	d.
Medicines	179	0	0
Stationary	27	0	0
Rent	40	0	0
Whitewashing, and distributing to poor, &c.	51	0	0
Salaries	227	0	0
	£524	0	0

ST. GEORGE'S DISPENSARY.

FROM the increasing size and population of St. George's parish, a dispensary was there also found to be essential to the relief of the poor: accordingly, in January, 1801, some gentlemen of the parish, among whom were three of the present medical attendants, entered into a subscription, and opened a dispensary in Dorset-street, together with a fever hospital annexed to the establishment, on the Circular Road. The house in which the dispensary is established is a recent erection: it had some years ago, in the times of scarcity, contained boilers, and apparatus for supplying the poor with soup; but when that practice was discontinued, a part of the building was appropriated to a school, and the other to the dispensary, which is remarkably neat and well kept. The regulations and expenditure of this institution are in common with those of the fever hospital. Those which relate to the dispensary exclusively, have nothing to distinguish them from the other institutions. Of five physicians and two surgeons attached to the whole establishment, one or more of each, if necessary, attend every day the dispensary. The apothecary, who is to reside at the fever hospital, is to attend the medical gentlemen in the morning at the dispensary, and also at five in the evening, to make up such recipes as are sent from patients visited at their own houses. The medical officers receive no salaries ; and the annual expenditure of both establishments, £450. is defrayed by donations, subscriptions, charity sermons, and other appeals to the public.

The number of patients relieved at the dispensary since its commencement - - - - - - - 35,000
Annual average - - - - - 5000

This number of patients seems to bear a much greater proportion to the population of St. George's parish, than the circumstances of it would warrant us to expect, as the greater part of it is exempt from those causes which generate disease among the people, being recently built, the inhabitants opulent, and the number of poor comparatively few. But as its regulations extend its attentions beyond the precincts of the parish, much of the poor of other parishes are included, particularly those of the country and suburbs, at that side of the city which are contiguous to St. George's dispensary, and have no institution of their own to apply to.

NORTH-WEST DISPENSARY.

THE liberties are not the only part of Dublin, where poverty and disease call for humane inspection ; another considerable portion of the town, including many old streets, was too remote and too extensive, for the superintendance of any dispensary beyond its precincts, and imperiously called for some institution of its own to meet, in any degree, the incessant and numerous demands for medical assistance. The parishes of St. Michan's and St. Paul's, therefore, in the year 1804, impressed with the melancholy necessity of such an establishment, resolved to erect a dispensary for their own poor, including the north-west portion of the city. It is a singular fact, that where experience had already pointed out the great utility of such institutions at an age so liberal and enlightened as the present, and in a city so eminent for its humane establishments, there could be found any opposition to the plan, yet it met with an opposition almost as violent, though not from the same cause, as that which retarded the original establishment of dispensaries; till at length, by the persevering benevolence of some individuals, particularly a medical gentleman, all parties were reconciled, the plan adopted, and a house of reception opened in Beresford-street, in October, 1804. As much of this portion of the town resembled the Liberties, in confined streets and crowded population, similar regulations were called for, to meet, with any success, the necessities of the poor. The distribution, therefore, of pecuniary aid, and an attention to cleanliness, form prominent features in the regulations.

And as arresting the progress of contagious diseases is of the last importance, and one of the prime objects of the institution, the most particular attention is to be always paid to this subject.

It is supported by subscription, and an annual charity sermon. The expences annually are as follow:

	£.	s.	d.
Rent	25	0	0
Apothecary's salary	50	0	0
Porter	25	0	0
Medicine and distributing to poor	150	0	0
	250	0	0

Number of patients admitted since its establishment - 12,100
Annual average - - - 3000

N.B. The 9 parishes, comprising the south-eastern division of the city, have no appropriate dispensary. To these the Dublin General Dispensary has been very much confined; yet it is not considered as an appropriate dispensary, nor supported as such; but two subscribe a small sum for its support, five pay near 150l. per annum to individuals for medicines, for their poor, and the other two have no medical aid provided. There appears then an obvious necessity for some particular institution, which would be an object of œconomy to some, and meet the wishes of all. A plan was therefore submitted some time ago to the governors, and the several parishes concerned, to erect the general dispensary, into a local one for these parishes. The whole city of Dublin would then be regularly and equally divided into four medical districts, having a dispensary peculiarly attached to each, which if regulated by a central committee, elected from the respective governors, would afford effectual medical relief to all the poor. This proposal was approved of, and a committee appointed to carry it into effect; but it yet remains to be done. As we know no relief which charity can dispense more cheap and effectual than those excellent institutions, we wish much to see them placed under some general and permanent regulations, and the more so, as we are sorry to find that the north-west dispensary is not in a flourishing situation, and St. George's is for the present suspended.

The following Table exhibits in one point of view, the state of the Dispensary Institutions, calculated in round numbers, from the date of their respective establishments to the end of the year 1808; since which year no material alteration has occurred.

Dispensaries.	When established.	Annual Expence.	Whole Expence.	Annual Patients.	Total Number.
St. Thomas and St. Mary.	1782	£ 140 0 0	£ 3640 0 0	2000	52000
Dublin General Dispensary.	1785	225 0 0	5175 0 0	4000	92000
Dispensary for the Liberties.	1794	524 0 0	7336 0 0	5500	63000
St. George's Dispensary.	1801	100 0 0	700 0 0	5000	35000
North-West Dispensary	1804	250 0 0	1000 0 0	3000	12000
Total.		1239 0 0	17857 0 0	19500	254000

Thus it appears, then, that Dublin is so poor, that 19,500 individuals, or about one-eighth part of its whole population, are not able to procure medicine or advice themselves, but are annually indebted to dispensaries for relief; and that that number is annually afflicted with distempers, which are not venereal, or contagious, or in general confining the patients to their beds, and to the relief of which hospitals would be inapplicable.

It further appears that five medical institutions, attended by thirty-six medical gentlemen of the first respectability, provided with apothecaries' shops, and other necessary apparatus, and established in parts of the town convenient for every purpose of aid to the poor, from whence they derive not only medical assistance, but in many instances proper nourishment for themselves, and support for their families, are kept up for the annual sum of £1239; little more than the expence of a single hospital.

And lastly, it appears, that notwithstanding the general adoption of these institutions is but yet in its infancy in the metropolis, yet even already 254,000 fellow creatures have been assisted with the best advice and medicine, at the moderate sum of 1s. 4¼d. for each individual.

NATIONAL EYE INFIRMARY.

This institution, devoted exclusively to the diseases of the eye, was opened in Mary's Abbey, in October, 1814. It has made reports of its progress, which are highly satisfactory. In nine months 800 persons have derived benefit from it; 58 were restored to complete vision, among whom were five cases of cataract, two of closed pupil, and four of gutta serena. Some of the patients were blind from their birth, and some for years totally deprived of sight. From this auspicious commencement, sanguine hopes are deservedly entertained of the great benefit of this infant institution. It is supported by private subscriptions.

VACCINE INSTITUTION, AND DISPENSARY FOR INFANT POOR.

The baneful effects that were known to result from inattention to the diseases of children, and the salutary consequences which immediately followed a regular inspection and careful treatment of this helpless and interesting class of the poor community, induced the governors of the Foundling Hospital to extend to others those benefits which the infants of their institution had so effectually experienced. They therefore readily complied with the suggestions of their surgeon, and established in the year 1800 in Clarendon-street, a Dispensary for infant poor, to which children from any part of the city or country might apply for relief. To this was annexed a VACCINE INSTITUTION, being the first of either kind ever established in Ireland. From this establishment infection is distributed gratis, to every one who applies; and it is asserted, that no instance has yet occurred, to the knowledge of any person, where small-pox has succeeded to cow-pock in a practice of fourteen years at this dispensary. A third department is attached with this, as in some measure connected with its peculiar objects, the diseases to which mothers and adult females are subject. The following are the numbers relieved in each department,—from March 1800 to September 1814:

Infants and children - - 69,007
Vaccinated - - - 19,911
Adult females - - - 1872

The expence is supported by a charity sermon every third year, producing on an average £200.

VACCINE INSTITUTION.

This was opened in Sackville-street, under the direction of six of the most eminent physicians and surgeons in the city, on the 14th of January, 1804. It is supported partly by the sale of infection, and partly by an annual grant from government; the first produces about £250. and the latter £150. per annum. The only officer attached to the institution is a secretary, who attends on two days in the week to vaccinate, and report the progress of the disease in a registry kept for that purpose. Through him a regular correspondence is kept up on the subject of the progress of vaccination, through different parts of Ireland, and packets of infection are forwarded through the post office, free of postage. In this way, the several dispensaries, &c. in Ireland, are furnished with a constant and regular supply of vaccine matter for one guinea per annum, or 2s. 6d. for each packet. To ascertain the certainty and progress of the disease, is of much consequence in extending its beneficial effects through the country, while at the same time the careless habits of the people frequently disappoint the practitioner, as they sometimes do not return to the institution after the infection has been communicated. To obviate this, it is always required that the parents shall deposit a small sum of money, which is to be refunded on their regular attendance. This simple precaution has been found so effectual, that in no instance have the people neglected to return to claim their deposit. The growing confidence of the public in this institution, is remarkably exemplified by the following fact. It was rumoured, that a very malignant small pock had appeared in a particular part of the town. Immediately the children of the neighbourhood crowded to the institution, so that in four successive days, no less than 700 were vaccinated, and effectually protected from the variolous contagion. The progress of the institution, since its commencement, will be seen by the following table:

	Patients Inoculated.	Packets issued to Practitioners in general.	Packets to Army Surgeons.
1804	578	776	236
1805	1,032	1,124	178
1806	1,356	1,340	220
1807	2,156	1,790	320
1808	3,002	2,285	333
1809	3,941	2,540	244
1810	4,084	3,249	281
1811	4,157	3,838	368
1812	5,162	3,901	402
1813	4,968	4,465	314
1814	4,585	4,899	301
Totals.	35,021	30,207	3200

APOTHECARIES HALL.

Previous to the year 1746, the corporation of Apothecaries was blended with that of Barbers : and continued quietly in that universal but disreputable connection. The liberal and intelligent of the profession, began now however to feel the consequence and dignity of their avocation. They knew that on them ultimately depended the health and lives of the community; that the skill of the physician was unavailing, if the medicines he prescribed were compounded bad in their quality or inaccurate in their quantity: still more so, if those substances which not only injure but extinguish human life, were left to the disposal of the ignorant or the unprincipled. Accordingly in the year 1742, the Apothecaries of Dublin presented a petition to the Lords' Justices, setting forth that divers frauds and abuses were imposed on many of his majesty's subjects, by the ignorance and unskilfulness of divers persons pretending to the art and mystery of an apothecary: and that no sufficient rules or regulations had been yet established to prevent or correct them. And further prayed for a charter of incorporation, with such powers, jurisdictions, and authorities, as might be necessary for the purpose of correction. This petition and prayer were referred to the college of physicians, who reported that it would be expedient to incorporate the Society of Apothecaries with such powers, providing however that they should make no bye-laws concerning the composition of medicines, unless first approved of by the College of Physicians. Accordingly, in the year 1745, letters passed the great seal, constituting the guild or fraternity of Apothecaries to be a body politic or corporate, within the city or liberties of Dublin. Though this charter was of considerable use in giving a more reputable character, a distinctive name, and a separate jurisdiction, still their powers and means were very limited; they could only regulate the concerns of their trade within the city of Dublin; and they compounded medicines which they were supplied with by the druggist, the quality of which was frequently very indifferent. To remedy these inconveniences also, another petition was presented to the Irish Parliament in the year 1790, praying to be allowed to raise a fund for erecting an Apothecary's Hall, to be supplied with medicines of the purest quality, and prepared under the inspection of persons skilled in the art and mystery of such preparations, the want of which, as the act states, as well as the unskilfulness and ignorance of divers persons who pretend to the art, caused injury to the fair trader, disappointment to the physician, and infinite hazard to the lives of his Majesty's subjects, as well in the city of Dublin as in divers parts of Ireland. In the year following, the prayer of the petition was complied with, and an act passed to carry its object into effect. Subscriptions were immediately opened for creating a fund for erecting the hall, and 60 debentures issued for £100. each; with the produce of this, amounting to £6000. the building was erected in Mary's-street, without any aid from government. The exterior consists of a plain front of Portland stone, and the interior of a large shop for vending drugs, and an elaboratory for compounding chemicals, with other apartments. To supply the shop with stock, the sum of £2000. was borrowed, and an assortment of the best medicines provided; and to superintend the elaboratory, an eminent chemist[*] was engaged at

[*] Mr. Higgans, the present Professor of Chemistry to the Dublin Society. In this elaboratory are made all preparations of antimony and mercury, all volatile spirits and æthers, all syrups, confections, and distilled waters; in effect, every medicament and chemical combination except those prepared in extensive manufactories, only such as the mineral acids, neutral salts, &c. &c. &c. Essential oils were tried, but at length discontinued, it having been found that they could be imported cheaper and better from England, where it is supposed the recent herb yields a more abundant oil, and of a stronger odour. It had been objected, that the medicines vended here are of a very high price, and not of cor-

£300. per annum; under whose direction it was arranged and conducted. The next important object was to regulate the sale and composition of medicines in other places, and prevent the unskilfulness and ignorance so universally complained of.

Heretofore there had been no examination as to the capability of the persons conducting apothecarys' shops, and the most illiterate were to be found in the practice of an art, the very terms, direction, and language of which required a competent share of classical knowledge to comprehend. Why the directions of the art of healing, which should of all others be the most clear and simple, should be wrapt up in the mysteries of an occult language, is not easy to say, but as long as it is so, it is of the last consequence that it should be so perfectly understood as not to be liable to mistake.

By the regulations of the act, every candidate, apprentice,* assistant, or

responding excellence. A simple fact will illustrate the justice of this objection. A few years ago, there was a considerable importation of Peruvian bark made at the same time by the Hall, and a druggist of this city: as a very extraordinary difference of duty was paid for the same quantity of the same article at the same time by two different importers, it excited enquiry, and it was found that the goods paid then a duty *ad valorem*, and the quality of that imported by the druggist was very inferior to the other, and the smaller price paid for it, was the cause of the smaller duty. Intermittent fevers were about that time prevalent, and there was a general complaint of the inefficacy of the bark then prescribed. Apothecaries bills are complained of like those of attorneys: in certain cases the Hall has a jurisdiction in taxing bills; and reducing them to a reasonable amount. Schedules also of the fees to which an apothecary is entitled for attendance, is made out, which not only prevents arbitrary charges, but enables him to demand a fair compensation for his personal exertions. This circumstance confers additional respectability on the profession, by sanctioning their practising physic, in some cases where it would not be convenient to fee a physician—a sanction which their improved education fully justifies. There are few apothecaries who have attended any time in a Dublin shop, who have not also availed themselves of the opportunity of attending a course of medical and surgical lectures;—a stipulation to this effect is usually made with their master. It is the intention also to establish a course of pharmaceutical lectures in the elaboratory, in which the combinations of antimony, mercury, salts, and all officinal preparations, will be displayed and elucidated; a department of chemistry highly useful, though but little attended to in a general course.

* Apprentices are expected to have read Cæsar, Sallust, Justin, Ovid's Metamorph., Virgil and Horace; and in Greek, the four Gospels. Assistants, besides these books, must be able to read with facility any modern abbreviated prescription into good grammar, and demonstrate a perfect acquaintance with the materia medica, pharmacy, and pharmaceutic chemistry. Masters must shew themselves perfectly well acquainted with whatever is required of assistants; and the Court strictly investigates the result of those studies to which every one who proposed to become a master ought to have devoted his time, and distinguish in terms of approbation, in their certificate, any person who shall have made an eminent progress.

master, must undergo a strict examination before the governors and court of examiners, who shall be on oath to examine impartially their respective qualifications, and refuse a certificate to any who shall be found incompetent.* By this regulation, the profession has become highly respectable. Young persons of reputable situations in life alone are educated for it, and their qualifications are such as those required for any other learned profession. In order to ensure the vending of such medicines as are salutary, it is prohibited to any apothecary to keep oils and colours, or arsenic, in the shop where he compounds his medicine, or sell less than one pound of the last to any persons unknown, or to any who will not sign an entry in a book, that it has been sold to them.† To insure these and similar regulations, four physicians and two apothecaries are appointed as inspectors of shops, who examine four times a year the state of the medicines, and take care that the salutary are prepared, and the deleterious prohibited. Local inspectors are appointed in country towns for the same purpose. It is, however, a subject of complaint that these salutary regulations are sometimes defeated by the insufficiency of the act. The penalties can only be levied by a regular legal process, and a record to recover £20. has cost the prosecutors £100. The act therefore defeats itself; for who would enforce any regulation attended with such difficulty and expence? To render it effectual, a power should be given of summary conviction before a magistrate, as in the case of other penalties. A clause for that purpose has been introduced into the London act: we trust it will be extended to Dublin.

* We know however these excellent regulations to have been evaded in a very unworthy manner. Candidate apprentices in the country have been represented in Dublin by persons of their own age, and having passed the examination of the Hall in this way by their representatives, were bound on the surreptitious certificates thus obtained by others assuming their name. The notice of this fact is not intended as any imputation upon the examiners; any institution would be liable to such a deception; but we mention it in the hope that its notoriety will prevent any similar attempt, and exclude the ignorant and unprincipled from a profession where they would be so dangerous.

† The act appointing inspectors of shops, was brought into Parliament by the celebrated Dr. Lucas, and from him called Lucas's act. At the time of its passing, he was member of parliament for the city of Dublin, and kept an apothecary's shop in Charles-street. Having had some quarrel with the College of Physicians, he revenged himself in a singular manner: he obliterated all the labels of his shop, and disguised sundry substances, so as to make them resemble different kinds of medicines. When the inspecting physicians came to examine, they were exceedingly embarrassed to ascertain the different kinds; and he boasted that they actually acknowledged a substance to be good rhubarb, which he afterwards proved to be toast and turmeric.

The corporation is directed by a governor, a deputy governor, and thirteen directors, who are annually chosen. The affairs of the corporation are so prosperous, that the original shares for £100. now sell for £600., no mean proof of good conduct, supported by public approbation.

ROYAL COLLEGE OF SURGEONS.

IF it be admitted that Ireland had, at all times, produced her proportion of skilful and accomplished surgeons, yet this was to be attributed rather to their own genius or application, or to an education in foreign seminaries, than to any advantages or resources derived from well regulated establishments at home. At length, the rapidly increasing population, together with the numerous hospitals and charitable institutions of the metropolis, induced the necessity and importance of an immediate improvement in the state of surgery in Ireland. The surgeons of Dublin having, in consequence, formed themselves into a society, and having first taken a comprehensive view of the various schools and institutions of surgery in the different states and kingdoms of Europe; adopting the most useful, and rejecting the inefficient and faulty systems, so as to profit by the experience of all,—resolved to petition the legislature for the establishment and incorporation of a Royal College of Surgeons; and in this resolution they were assisted by all the respectable practitioners in every part of the country.

This charter of incorporation was accordingly granted early in the year 1784, and on the second day of March of the same year, the surgeons of Dublin held their first meeting as a College. From that period the progress of surgical science in Ireland, made rapid and important improvements. These advantages are chiefly to be attributed to the wisdom and liberality of the framers of its original regulations. Their prospects for the public good, and for the advancement of the profession, were not circumscribed by narrow tenets, nor actuated by those selfish monopolizing motives which so frequently influence the acts and proceedings of incorporated societies. Men of all persuasions were admitted members, and the most lucrative and honourable situations were as open to the licentiates of every other sect, as to those of the established church.

With a view of giving the utmost efficacy and estimation to the surgical profession, the college extended its care and circumspection to the examination of the professional qualifications of practitioners. It next provided, that none but those who had received a liberal education should enter into the profession. For this intention the pupils were examined respecting their proficiency in the classics, as a preliminary step to their being registered. And further, to complete a finished surgical education, the college extended its superintendence to make the different hospitals of Dublin subservient to that intention. The hours of attendance are so arranged as not to interfere with the lectures of the school, and the clinical lectures take place in the same orderly succession.

Finally, to fulfil every purpose and object of an extensive surgical seminary, a school of surgery was established, and the following professorships were instituted, under the direction of the court of examiners of the college, each of whom gives a full course of lectures on the professional science allotted to him. 1 Anatomy and Physiology. 2. Theory and Practice of Surgery. 3. The Practice of Physic 4. Surgical Pharmacy. 5. Midwifery, and the Diseases of Women and Children. 6. Botany.*

The theatre in which the lectures are delivered is capable of accommodating between three and four hundred students, besides what the gallery may contain, which is opened for the public during the dissection of malefactors. Adjoining the theatre are the professors' dissecting room, and two museums.

The lectures on anatomy and surgery commence annually in October, and continue for six months, to illustrate which, besides the recent dissections, there is a fine collection of preparations. The course of practical anatomy is conducted on a scale far exceeding that of any other school in the united kingdom. The dissecting rooms are very commodious, and were added but lately to the building. They consist of a public and private dissecting room, with suitable apartments and lofts for making and drying preparations. The public dissecting room is furnished with twenty tables, at each of which two students are placed. There is moreover, adjoining, a

---

* The present professors are, 1. Richard Dease, M. D. and Ab. Colles, M. D.; 2. The same; 3. John Cheyne, M. D.; 4. Andrew Johnston; 5. John Creighton; 6. Walter Wade, M. D.

theatre for demonstration, which may contain upwards of one hundred spectators.

The lectures on the practice of physic are delivered three days in the week during the term, for the first three months alternately with those on surgical pharmacy, and for the remainder with those on midwifery. These lectures are particularly calculated to illustrate the diseases incidental to the army and navy. The course on surgical pharmacy comprehends pharmaceutical chemistry and the materia medica; and the lectures on midwifery include the diseases of pregnant women and infants. The botanic course commences in the month of April and continues during the summer.

The court of examiners are impowered to grant licences for the practice of surgery to those only who have served a five years apprenticeship to regular surgeons, on judging them to be properly qualified. But in case of rejection, the candidate has it in his power to appeal from the judgment of this court and demand a re-examination by the court of assistants, who are on taking the oath prescribed by the charter, authorised to examine, and grant letters testimonial to the candidate on approval. The court of examiners are further empowered to examine candidates for medical appointments in the army and navy. Formerly the examination was confined to those who were to obtain such appointments in Ireland only, but by a late order of his Royal Highness the Commander in Chief, the certificates of the college of surgeons in Dublin, are now admitted as qualifications for appointments on the English establishment also.

The various small buildings which the college in its infancy had been able to procure, being found inadequate to its subsequent accommodation, government, at the solicitation of the late surgeon-general, and of the present inspector-general, agreed to supply funds to build a hall with suitable apartments annexed. These, though extensive, were, after a few years, found insufficient for the purposes of the still increasing establishment, so that new grants have been lately obtained, by means of which the present handsome structure has been finished, and the establishment completed.

To effect all these purposes, a sum of money, not less than thirty-five thousand pounds, was voted in successive sessions of parliament; and the views of the college were thus ably aided and supported by the enlightened policy and liberality of government, though amidst the most pressing exigencies of the state.

THE CITY OF DUBLIN. 753

The Royal College of Surgeons is well situated at the corner of York-street, the front facing St. Stephen's Green. It is extremely well-built, the basement story being of mountain granite, and the superstructure of Portland-stone ; the façade is simply elegant, and ornamented with six columns of the Doric order. The interior consists of the apartments already noticed, together with a spacious hall and handsome stair-case, surrounded by suitable lodging rooms and offices adapted to every purpose of the institution.

The whole structure, including the purchase of the ground, has cost about forty thousand pounds. The establishment is wholly supported by its own resources, derived chiefly from sums paid by the pupils and students, but no officer is allowed a salary.

The number of students has continually increased during the last ten years from sixty to two-hundred and twenty. And thus has the college, progressively and rapidly advancing, matured in a few years a system of surgical education which, for extent of views and utility of application, may vie with any other in Europe.

COLLEGE OF PHYSICIANS.

THE first charter of incorporation granted to the physicians in Ireland, was in the reign of Charles the Second. This was not effectual for the purpose intended, for it appears that the number of unskilful and illiterate practitioners had increased, and the frauds and deceits of empirical apothecaries and druggists abounded, to the dishonour of the government, and the prejudice and destruction of the subject.* Accordingly, in the year 1692, it was surrendered, and a new one was obtained from William and Mary, by which the college was incorporated by the name of the King and Queen's College of Physicians. It consisted of one president, to be chosen annually, on the 18th day of October, and 14 fellows. Their duty was to supervise all practitioners in physic, to summon them before them in order that they might be examined, as to their qualifications, to prohibit the unqualified from practising, and even to inflict the punishment of fine and imprison-

* Preamble to Charter of William and Mary.

ment upon the ignorant and contumacious, on those who presumed to practise without due qualifications, or on those who refuse to appear to verify them. They were further allowed to summon before them druggists and apothecaries, to enter their warehouses and shops, to examine their medicines, investigate their qualities and compositions, and what they might deem unfit or improper for use, to burn or destroy according to their discretion.

These powers, it should appear, were abundantly competent to prevent any abuses in the practice of so important a profession, and to give ample security that the health and lives of the community should be entrusted only to the learned and the skilful not only in Dublin but all over Ireland, for the operation of the charter and the powers it conferred were equally extensive. But this, like the former, seems to have been defeated by the want of sufficient sanction. The charter was never confirmed by the legislature of Ireland, and thus a constitutional authority, which alone could give confidence to their proceedings, and validity to their powers, was withheld. No control was exercised, no restraint was imposed on the practice of physic, or penalties inflicted on the venders of deleterious drugs.[*] To remedy the defects of this charter also, an act[†] was introduced into the Irish House of Commons in the year 1761, by Dr. Lucas, which modified the charter in some respects. It enacts that no limitation shall be made to the number of fellows, but extends it at the discretion of the college, and it confirms to them a most important privilege, which is not possessed even by that of London. It provides that no quack medicine or nostrum can be exposed to sale but under the sanction of the college: it enjoins in the first instance that its composition be made known, and it empowers them to prohibit the sale of it altogether if it be disapproved of. This clause forms a striking feature in the Irish act, and accounts in some measure for the comparatively small quantity of quack medicines used in this country. Did they possess a similar power in England it is highly probable it would be exerted to

---

[*] The powers conferred by the charter extend to fine and imprisonment, at the discretion of the president and fellows. Such arbitrary authority, unconfirmed by legislative enactment, is deemed unconstitutional and therefore is never exercised.

[†] It is this which enacts that the physician shall set down in words at length, and not in chemical or numerical characters, the quantity of every ingredient prescribed, under a penalty of forty shillings. 1 George III. Sect. 19.

restrain the extraordinary multitude of nostrums, with which that country abounds.

A still further alteration was made in the constitution of the college in the year 1800, by the act for establishing a complete school of physic. By this act the choice of fellows is restricted to those physicians only who have taken a degree in arts or medicine in one of the universities of Oxford, Cambridge, or Dublin; and thus though the number be indefinite, the objects of selection are very limited, the great majority of practitioners in Dublin having graduated in proscribed universities. This act further enjoins, that all who shall accept professorships shall cease to be fellows, though they continue to be members of the college. Thus then it appears that the present state of the college differs materially from its chartered constitution. It consists of three bodies, the fellows elected under the charter, the licentiates, or those who receive a license from the college to practise physic,* and an intermediate class, called honorary fellows, who consist chiefly of those ex-fellows who having accepted professorships have vacated their fellowships. Of the first there are 16, of the second 43, and of the third 12.

The college seem to possess no real power except as to their licentiates, and even of these they take but little account, as they do not belong to the corporation. They never interfere with any other practitioner. They direct the forms under which Apothecaries make up their shop medicines, throughout Ireland. They have sometimes seized on the medicines they disapproved of, but very rarely burned them before the shops, which the act empowers them to do. Four physicians are appointed to examine and make a report of the state of apothecaries shops, four times in each year. The examination is seldom made, and the report is never published, though it is a circumstance which it imports the public to know.

The college of physicians have no local habitation; their meetings are held at the house of the president for the time being, to which they are convened. They have a small library at Sir P. Dunn's Hospital, for which a

* There are two days appointed for examining a candidate for a license. On the first he is examined by the two junior censors; in anatomy and physiology by the one, and in chemistry, botany, and the materia medica by the other. On the second day he is examined by the president and four censors; by the president in the Greek physicians, by the junior censor in botany, chemistry, and anatomy, by the next in an acute disease, by the next in a chronic disease, and by the last censor in the non-naturals. The fee paid by a licentiate is 50l. which is disposed of at the discretion of the college.

librarian is appointed with a salary, but no fund is appropriated for the purchase of new books; nor does it appear that they have any manuscript archives or records in this library, notwithstanding their early incorporation. The only publication under their sanction or authority is a small pharmacopœia, which was published in Latin in the year 1806, and has never been revised or republished since.

The school of physic as established by act of parliament in 1785, consists of six professors. Those of anatomy and surgery, of chemistry, and of botany, are on the establishment of the university: those of the practice of medicine, of the institutes of medicine, and of the materia medica, and pharmacy, are on the foundation of Sir Patrick Dunn.* The lectures of the university professors, are delivered in Trinity college; those of Sir Patrick Dunn at the hospital, in a new and beautiful theatre lately finished. The several courses commence on the first Monday in November, except that on botany, which begins on the first Monday in May, and continues to the end of July. Each of the professors attends in turn at the hospital, and delivers a course of clinical lectures on the cases which occur.† No candidate is qualified for a degree in medicine, until he has attended those six courses, together with six months at the clinical hospital. The number of pupils is annually increasing; those now in attendance on the several professors exceed 100.

The present professors are,—

    Practice of Medicine - Dr. Tuomy
    Institutes of Medicine - Dr. Boyton.
    Materia Medica and Pharmacy, Dr. Crampton.
    Anatomy and Surgery - Dr. Macartney.
    Chemistry - - - Dr. Barker.
    Botany - - - - Dr. Alman.

* The three first are elected by the provost and senior fellows, and are paid by the under graduate classes, and their emoluments fluctuate between 200*l.* and 400*l.* per annum. The three last receive a salary from the funds of Sir P. Dunn's estate, which is now limited to 10*l.* per annum; and their mode of election is as follows: when a vacancy occurs, the president convenes the College of Physicians, who select by ballot three of their body, to those are added the provost and professor of physic in Trinity College, who together fill up the vacancy. No elector can himself be eligible. 25 Geo. III. Sect. 4, *et seq.*

† See Sir P. Dunn's Hospital, page 702.

Formerly, a degree from Edinburgh was deemed essential to the reputation of the medical practitioner in Dublin. The high and deserved celebrity of the university of that city conferring a comparative consequence on all those who graduated in it. Since some time, however, no small revolution has taken place in the public opinion of this city. Many practitioners of high reputation have graduated at home, and the consequence of our school of physic is progressively increasing. Before the act which established it was passed, it was the custom for the professors to dictate their lectures in Latin: besides this they enjoyed the whole emolument of Sir P. Dunn's estate. The consequence was, that their professorships were sinecures, the language they used was little calculated to instruct those to whom in general it was not perfectly known, and their great salaries rendered them careless of pupils, of whom they were intirely independent. It followed, therefore, that few attended, and those few were uninstructed. Since the establishment of the school of physic, the professorships have become really efficient. The professors were all men well qualified for their important duty. Their education was regular, and their acquisitions extensive. In the university course, they displayed talents and industry. They acquired reputation in other departments of science before they applied themselves to the study of physic, and a regular degree in arts, was preparatory to one in medicine. Their lectures were not given as heretofore in the college terms, but they continued for six months in one consecutive course. In their lectures, the absurd practice of conveying oral instruction in a dead language, was laid aside, and knowledge was communicated in sounds that every one understood.* It was besides the object of the professors to increase their moderate salaries by a reputation which their own industry and exertions should create. And as their professorships became vacant every seven years, they were anxious to insure a re-election. The result was that their lectures were valuable, the reputation of the school was established, and their pupils increased. The facilities of practice also, and the variety

* The practice of lecturing in Latin had fallen into disuse before the year 1785, though in the act passed in that year it was abolished by the following clause: "And be it enacted by the Authority aforesaid, that the said several Lectures shall be given in the English language, unless specially ordered, &c." 25 George III. Sect. 30.—It appears to have been in use in the year 1749, as about that time a liberal offer was made to a celebrated German professor to hold lectures, who could not speak the language of this country, and must have used Latin as his medium of communication.

of cases which occur in Dublin, present another important means of improvement to the young practitioner. As soon as he graduates, his first care is to be elected physician to some dispensary, which is not very difficult. Here abundant objects present themselves to improve both his practice and his humanity. It is but justice to the medical profession of Dublin to say, that this disinterested pursuit is followed with zeal, kindness, and assiduity. Nor is it alone confined to men commencing their profession, and to whom the improvement of their practice would be as valuable as its emoluments; many of high established reputation devote much of their valuable time to this humane pursuit. They not only prescribe for those who attend at the dispensaries, but visit those who are confined at home; and thus deserting the mansions of opulence, and the emoluments of practice, voluntarily penetrate into those numerous mansions of misery, with which some districts of the metropolis abound, and seek out the most revolting objects of distemper and distress for the sole and disinterested purpose of relieving them.

The profession of surgery, for the same reasons, the establishment of a complete school of surgery, and the selection of able professors, has attained to considerable reputation. Another circumstance may also contribute to this end, the facility of procuring human subjects for dissection. A reason assigned for the imperfect knowledge of the ancients in the anatomy of the human frame, was that all their observations were taken from the dissection of inferior animals, and hence that confusion of anatomical terms where the name conveys such incorrect ideas of the same parts in the human frame. The dissection of human bodies has been a most important improvement in modern practice, and the accuracy of the surgeon must depend very much on his having been able to avail himself of it. In several countries this however is a matter of extreme difficulty. Strong prejudices against disturbing the repose of the dead, and feelings of unavailing affection in the living so guard the tomb, that attempts to procure a body, have been often attended with great personal danger. But in Ireland it is not so. Though there is no country where the sick are attended with more disinterested zeal and affection by their friends, the memory of the deceased cherished with more tender regard, or the souls of the dead prayed for with more fervent devotion, yet there is none where the inanimate body is looked upon with more philosophic indifference. After it is consigned to the earth with the ceremonies of pious respect, it is in general a subject of no further concern.* Precautions are seldom taken, or a watch seldom placed to preserve it, and hence dissecting pupils have abundant opportunities of improving themselves in the most important part of their education, with little interruption to the progress of their enquiries. Nor is it uncommon for this dissection to take place at the especial request of the sick. A poor woman in early life, was attended in her room from the Dublin General Dispensary: she was affected by a pulmonary complaint, and as there was something unusual in the progress of it, she was impressed with an opinion that if the internal cause could be investigated, the effects might be removed. As she had no hopes for herself, she made it an earnest request to the attending physician, that her body might be opened after her death, in order that her family, whom she apprehended had an hereditary tendency to the complaint, might derive benefit from any discovery made in the dissection. This is one of many similar instances which occur in medical practice among the poor, examples of such philosophic and rational fortitude being very common among the lower orders in Ireland.

It is perhaps a matter to be regretted that the different departments of medicine are not more distinctly marked, and confined to their appropriate practitioners. Accoucheurs, surgeons, physicians, and apothecaries, prescribe indiscriminately for all diseases, and the three first are frequently met on the same consultation, in purely medical cases. The accoucheur and the surgeon receive a suitable education to practise very valuable departments of the healing art, and which are sufficiently extensive to occupy their entire and undivided attention; but their professions are in some measure mechanical, and their excellence manual dexterity; and surely a degree in medicine cannot confer a qualification which their course of study and habits of practice cannot bestow. Apothecaries also frequently visit and prescribe for their patients, but they are never consulted with by regular practitioners. Their practice is confined to the less dangerous diseases

* Though this be generally true, it is not universally so. Instances have occurred where strict precautions were taken, and those who have attempted to remove the bodies have been assaulted and severely wounded, by the watching friends of the deceased. The great cemetery of the poor is a large space of ground called the Hospital Fields, in the vicinity of Kilmainham. Within it is a monument said to have been erected over Brian Boromhe, the celebrated Irish king, who was slain by the Danes at the battle of Clontarf.

760   THE CITY OF DUBLIN.

of children, or to those of people in limited circumstances, whose means do not enable them to fee a physician. In general, in all cases of incipient disease the apothecary of the family is first called in, and by his advice the physician is sent for.

The following is a statement of the actual number of medical practitioners in Dublin :—

Physicians	-	96
Surgeons	-	57
Accoucheurs	-	42
Dentists	-	8
Occulist	-	1
		204
Apothecaries	-	76
		280

The following is the detail —Members of the College of physicians, 58 ; Graduates of different universities, who are not members of the College : Dublin, 16; Edinburgh, 22 ; Glasgow, 1 ; St. Andrews, 2 ; Cambridge, 1 ; Oxford, 1 ; Rheims, 3 ; Leyden, 1 ; Universities not known, 14; Surgeons who have graduated in medicine, 7 ; Dentists ditto, 3 ;—making the number of practising graduates 129 ; of whom 30 practise midwifery. Members of the College of Surgeons, 53 ; not of the College, 23(deducting those who have graduated in medicine) ; of these 12 practise midwifery.

Among the irregular practitioners of Dublin are two advertising doctors, and one female, who cures the king's evil ; but besides, there is another so remarkable as to deserve notice. In passing through Mitre-alley, an obscure part of the old city, near St. Patrick's cathedral, the eye is attracted by an angular sign board projecting from the wall, on which is the following inscription,—" Domestic Medicine prescribed from Irish Manuscripts,"— and a couplet of Irish poetry follows,—

*A Chpṁoṛc leiṡeaṡ aṅ laṡ
Sviōim oṗc aṡ-caibaiṗ*

which is literally, " Oh ! Christ the sick relieve,—to their aid I thee implore." Attracted by this notice we visited the doctor, in the hope of meeting those Irish MSS. from which he derived his prescriptions. Nor were we disappointed. We found an old man of a genuine Milesian aspect, possessed of 73 very old and valuable volumes of vellum, bound in modern covers. They contained several thousand recipes in Latin and Irish, written in a very beautiful but very old Irish character. The title pages were wanting, but they were supposed to be a collection of native and other recipes, made in the 13th century, and from that period traditionally descending from family to family. From this sacred repertory the venerable doctor collected all his knowledge of the healing art, and practised with some success among the poor in his vicinity.

BLIND ASYLUMS.

SIMPSON'S HOSPITAL.

In no instance is the selfish and odious maxim of Rochfocault[*] so completely refuted as in the public charities erected for the cure of human malady, or the alleviation of human calamity; and that we are not pleased with the misfortunes of our fellow creatures, every new asylum is a new example. Swift himself, though he defended the maxim,[†] acted in direct opposition to its principles, by erecting an asylum for the reception of those who were afflicted with a calamity with which he himself was threatened: and the benevolent founder of the present establishment adopted his practice, though not his opinion. Geo. Simpson was a respectable merchant; he was subject to severe and protracted fits of the gout, and laboured under the infirmity of weak eyes. It does not appear that he ever exulted in the similar afflictions of his neighbours, on the contrary, it is certain he felt the greatest sympathy and compassion. He founded an asylum exclusively for the reception of blind and gouty patients, and by his will, bearing date

---

[*] " Dans l'adversité de nos meilleurs amis nous trouvons toujours quelque chose qui ne nous deplait " pas."

[†] " As Rochfocault his maxim drew
" From Nature, I believe it true."

the 11th Sept. 1778, he bequeathed a large estate to its support; and in the 39th of the present king, the establishment was incorporated, by act of parliament. The excellence of this interesting charity has induced others to make similar bequests, but they do not exceed £4000. in the aggregate; so that the institution is still almost exclusively supported by the generosity of its original founder.

The first establishment, like most recent charities, was an inconvenient receptacle in a private house in Great Britain-street; from hence the patients were removed to Jervis-street, where the present char. infirmary stands, while the old house was thrown down, and a new edifice erected on the same site. It was finished at the expence of £6458. and the patients returned to it. The edifice stands on the west side of Great Britain-street, the perspective of the façade occupying the whole-breadth of Jervis street, which it fronts, and seems to terminate. It presents a handsome and extended front of mountain granite, simply chaste in its design and construction; though plain and massive it is by no means gloomy or unornamental, as a public edifice. In the rear are extensive offices, and a garden containing about a rood of ground, laid out in grass plats and gravel walks, with wooden benches at intervals, shaded with trees, on which the venerable patients are fond to repose.

The wards of the hospital, 24 in number, are spacious and airy, they are approached by two flights of stairs at opposite ends of the building. Some contain four and others three beds; the total number 72, each person being allowed a bed to himself. For the more perfect accommodation of the patients a new spacious dining hall was lately erected by the trustees, at the expense of £2000. and over the hall a dormitory, capable of containing as many beds as would make the whole establishment accommodate 100 patients. It is much to be regretted that this benevolent purpose, not only has not succeeded, but the number of patients is reduced to fifty, from the inadequacy of the present funds.

It is impossible to contemplate this establishment without an earnest wish that its benefits were more extended. The patients for whom its relief is intended, are not taken indiscriminately from those classes of society where familiarity with distress reconciles them to suffering, and blunts that sympathy in others, which they are supposed not to feel acutely for themselves. The first recommendation for admission, is the former respectability and irreproachable character of the applicants. The next is their advanced age, the severity of their distemper, and their inability of support. In the election of a candidate for a vacancy, these considerations are most scrupulously attended to. The visitor to this charity, therefore, sees himself surrounded by men who moved in a sphere of life perhaps equal to, and with a character as fair as his own, and while they are snatched from poverty, and its worst consequence, mendicity, every little comfort is afforded to them compatible with their former situations and habitual feelings. A plain but decent suit of clothes is provided; their food is of the very best kind, prime joints of beef and mutton, &c.; their rooms are neat, and if more than one individual occupies the same apartment, it only promotes that social gratification which the blind and the lame must feel in mutual society and assistance. It is a singular and interesting spectacle to see this interchange of offices, each making use of that organ of his neighbour of which he is himself deprived. In this way, the patients who are deprived of the use of their limbs by the severity of the gout are supported about by their blind friends, whose motions they direct and guide; while in return, a lame patient is frequently seen surrounded by a group of the blind, to whom he reads a newspaper which is supplied for that purpose, or some book of entertainment or instruction. In the spring and summer, the gay sound of the flute and violin is often heard from the benches of their little garden, and the whole institution has an air of cheerful content. The patients are freely allowed to walk abroad, and wherever they are met in the streets, and recognized by their dress, they never fail to excite in no small degree, the interest and good-will of the passengers, who are glad to accord to their infirmity any assistance in their power, a feeling, which at once evinces a general respect for the character and circumstances of the men, and for the excellent institution which supports and protects them.*

* The indignation of the public was considerably excited some years ago, by a horrid atrocity practised on one of the harmless members of this community. Early one morning a person demanded admission from the porter to visit a blind patient, whom he named. When brought to him, he pretended to impart some communications from his friends in the country, and at parting, presented him with a cake, as a little token of their regard. Immediately after, the blind man and others with whom he shared the cake, were seized with excruciating pains. It appeared that the cake was poisoned: he for whom it was intended died, and the others were recovered with great difficulty. The miscreant who perpetrated the murder, was traced to a remote part of the country, by the laudable exertions of the

THE HISTORY OF

The Income and Expenditure of the House is as follows:

Income permanent.

		£. s. d.
Rents of G. Simpson - annual		1990 12 10
Interest on private securities - -		192 0 0
Ditto on ten shares in the Hibernian Insurance Company - - - -		65 0 0
Government securities - -		715 0 0
Total annual income - -		2962 12 10
Deduct for head rent - - -		268 15 10
Net income - -		2693 17 0
Income casual		None.

Expenditure.

Officers, Medical.

Two Physicians, each per ann.   11l. 7s. 6d. Apothecary is paid for the medicine used.
One Surgeon - -   22 15 0

Officers of the House.

Registrar - -   30l. 0s. 0d.   Housekeeper - -   20l. 0s. 0d.
Agent paid by centage on money collected.   Steward - -   20 0 0

Servants.

Three Nurses, each	-	5l. 13s. 9d	One Kitchen-maid	-	5l. 13s. 9d.
Four House-maids	-	5 13 9	One head Porter	-	8 0 0
One Cook	-	6 16 6	Under Ditto	-	6 0 0

There are on the establishment at present,

Blind patients   -   25
Gouty ditto   -   25

The annual expense for each, including all incidents, is estimated at £50.

---

trustees of the charity, but he unfortunately escaped into the mountains. No certain cause could ever be assigned for this diabolical act, but it is thought that considerable property depended on the man, who was once in opulent circumstances.

IRISH HARP SOCIETY.

BLINDNESS is an infirmity which peculiarly excites the compassion of the human heart, and we feel that it is not sufficient to relieve it by the ordinary employment which might occupy others, but it requires a means of solace and consolation, great in proportion to the greatness of the privation. The highest gratification which a blind man seems to derive from external causes, arises from musical sounds, and he flies himself to the practice of some musical instrument, as his prime source of consolation. To afford him therefore the means of proficiency, and make the source of his subsistance the solace of his misfortune, cannot be the project of a fanciful imagination, but the dictates of a pure and liberal charity. It is to Ireland that these observations apply with peculiar force : a propensity for music celebrated from the earliest times ;[*] a perfection in musical instruments which was the admiration of a remote age ;[†] and a beauty of musical composition which is the delight of the present age; all attest the universal gratification received from this science, and held out a prospect that the poor professor would be as liberally rewarded as he was personally delighted, by the practice of his art in a country where that art was so highly prized and so early cultivated.

[*] See Geraldus Cambrensis on this subject. When he speaks of the proficiency of the Irish in music he says, " Præ omni natione quam vidimus admirabiliter est instructa." And he describes their mode of performance and the effect it produced in terms as creditable to his own taste and judgment as to their skill and execution. " Mirum quod in tanta tam præcipiti digitorum rapacitate musica servatur " proportio, et arte per omnia indemni inter crispatos modulos organaque multipliciter intricata, tam " suavi velocitate, tam impari paritate, tam discordia consona redditur et completur melodia, tam " subtiliter modulos intrant et exeunt, sicque sub obtuso grossioris chordæ sonitu gracilium tinnitus " licentius ludunt. Hinc accidit ut ea subtilius intuentibus et artis arcana acutè discernentibus internas " et ineffabiles comparant animi delicias." *Topog.* cap. 11, p. 739.

This " extorted praise," as Ledwich calls it, from a man so hostile in other respects, is very conclusive. Gerald Barry was an accomplished scholar, and well acquainted with the state of music in other countries through which he had travelled. He was among the first who landed from England, in the 12th century, and was astonished to find in this sequestered island, that this delightful art had arrived to such a scientific and unknown perfection.

[†] Irish melodies and other native musical compositions, lately revived and published by Bunting, Moore, Stevenson, and Fitzsimmons.

In the year 1792 some patriotic and benevolent individuals conceived the idea of collecting together all that remained of the once celebrated Irish harpers, and having gathered from them the remnants of Irish music which existed only in their memories, to educate a number of blind boys to practise it; thus catching the transient melodies, and perpetuating the race of ancient bards at the moment they were both about to expire for ever. Emissaries were sent for this purpose to different parts of Ireland, and a few very old and venerable men were assembled at Belfast, where an ingenious professor of music* noted down, and secured in permanent characters, those exquisite compositions, which till then existed only in the memory of those who played them; and immediately after an asylum was opened for a certain number of poor blind pupils, who were instructed to play on the Irish harp, and to learn these melodies. This benevolent and patriotic example was followed in Dublin, and in the year 1809, a society was formed similar to that in Belfast, called the Irish Harp Society, the preamble of whose resolutions states its objects in the following terms:

"The Society was formed to revive the native music and poetry of Ireland, to make further improvements in the Irish harp, and to excite a correspondent feeling in the country by instructing a number of blind and destitute children on the Irish harp, thus combining a patriotic object with a most interesting charity."

Its affairs are conducted by three committees—of finance, music, and literature. The first regulates its receipts and expenditure; the second arranges its concerts and musical concerns, and the third is appointed to search out and preserve such songs as may yet be found treasured in the manuscripts or traditions of the country. This interesting society was patronised by many persons eminent for rank or talents, not only in Dublin but in other parts of Ireland. The venerable General Valancy became its first president. He was succeeded by the Bishop of Kildare, who liberally accommodated the society with the use of a large mansion at Glassnevin, for the reception of pupils. In aid of the funds an annual concert was performed, and "The Commemoration of Carolan" revived the memory of an old and

---

* Mr. Bunting, who some time after published a most interesting volume of genuine Irish airs, collected on this occasion. This seems to have been the first collection ever made; and the parent of all that followed.

almost forgotten Irish bard. Those who witnessed the effects of these exhibitions testify the enthusiastic feelings they excited; they seemed to be a pledge of universal support to the charity. After some time, however, it was found that the support was not adequate to the expectations raised, and for want of sufficient funds the objects of this national society are not yet carried into effect. As yet no bard from this seminary has illumined Ireland " with the light of his song;" but several blind minstrels educated in the seminary at Belfast are found wandering through different parts of the country, affording a pleasing and harmless amusement to the people who hear them, providing a comfortable support for their necessities, and a sweet source of consolation to their infirmities.

RICHMOND NATIONAL INSTITUTION.

THE benevolence of Simpson had long established in Dublin an asylum to support the aged blind. But to prevent the necessity of such an establishment, and to teach the blind to support themselves, had long been a desideratum in the annals of charity. The example set however in Liverpool and Bristol, was soon followed in Dublin, and the Richmond Institution was opened in Great Britain-street, in the year 1809, upon the same principles. The pupils are taught netting, weaving, and basket-making, mending and sewing sacks, and a few have acquired expertness in them all. There are now in the house 26, admitted from different parts of Ireland, and of different ages from 10 to 30. They shew in general great inclination and aptitude to learn, though instances have occurred to the contrary. It is pleasing however to remark, that even already the institution has evinced its utility not merely as an asylum for distress, but as a school for correcting it. One pupil has already acquired sufficient skill to set up for himself. He has learned the mystery of an ingenious trade in less time than an apprentice bound in the ordinary way, and with the approbation of the governors, is settled in Dublin making baskets on his own account. It had been a question whether music should not make a part of the instruction given here; and such pupils as shewed a decided taste, be selected and taught some instrument. This however was thought inexpedient, and music is proscribed in a seminary where of all others it would be most grateful. The blind employed in any useful art must be a sight highly gratifying to a benevolent mind, but it would be more so perhaps if they could enjoy that sense of which they are not deprived, and pleasing sounds enlivened the monotony of their dark and silent industry.

The affairs of the institution are prosperous. The house in Great Britain-street not being deemed sufficiently convenient for the growing establishment, it has been disposed of to the governors of the Lying-in Hospital, to encrease their accommodation; and another more spacious taken in Sackville-street, to which the pupils are now removed. They already possess a property of £3395..12s..11d. including £1600. vested in government debentures. It is supported by subscriptions, charity sermons, and profit of the sale of work, as follows :—

Account of Income and Expenditure of the RICHMOND NATIONAL INSTITUTION, *for the year ending 31st of March*, 1814.

Dr.	L.	s.	d.	Cr.	L.	s.	d.
To Provisions	407	15	10½	By Donations	86	19	10
Clothing	94	10	6	Subscrips. to 31st Dec. 1813, £391 18 2			
Fuel	32	2	4½	Less, Poundage to Collector 14 18 5½			
Soap and Candles	20	2	4		376	19	8½
Rent, Taxes, and Insurance £135 ·12 11				Cash found in Poor-boxes	24	19	7
Less, Rent............ 40 0 0				One year's interest on 160ul. 3½ per cent.			
	95	12	11	funded stock	56	0	0
Repairs and Alterations	15	17	3½	Amount collected at a Charity Sermon	282	6	9
Furniture, 10 per cent. allowed for wear				Profit on Basket manufacture	80	8	4½
and tear	25	14	7	N. B. 83l. paid teacher, charged to the			
Salary to Superintendant and Matron	75	0	0	manufacture			
Gratuity	20	0	0	Profit on Net manufacture	12	11	8
Servants' Wages	24	12	5½	Profit on Weaving account	60	19	1½
Printing, Stationary, and Advertising	65	4	8	N. B. 66l. 12s. 6d. paid teacher, charged			
Medicines	18	1	10	to the manufacture.			
Incidents	8	14	10½				
Proportion of earnings paid pupils........... £4 16 9							
Ditto to be paid on leaving the Institution......... 26 9 8							
	31	6	5				
Excess of Income, above Expenditure	29	8	11				
	£963	5	0½		£963	5	0½

MOLYNEUX ASYLUM.

WHILE a revolution of religious impressions has converted on the continent houses consecrated to pious purposes to scenes of pleasure, the feelings of the metropolis of Ireland seem to have taken an opposite direction, and within a few years some of the gayest resorts of fashion and dissipation have been transformed into edifices of devotion and charity; Ranelagh has become a convent, Smock-alley play-house a parochial chapel, and Astley's Amphitheatre, a house of worship and an asylum for blind females. Among the very few objects of charity overlooked in Dublin, blind females had been undeservedly one. The late Duke of Dorset used to declare an establishment for them was the only one which seemed to be wanting, and he expressed a strong desire to patronise it : but the premature death of that amiable young nobleman anticipated his intentions, and deprived the Institution of the benefit it might derive from his rank and consequence. But the necessity of such an establishment had long impressed a number of benevolent individuals. Accordingly with very limited means, they undertook to establish this interesting charity on an extensive scale. The amphitheatre in Peter-street, had long afforded amusement to the gay. The house had been originally the family mansion of Sir Thomas Molyneaux. It was erected in 1711, and was at that time a grand residence surrounded by a fashionable vicinity. When that part of the town was deserted by its gay inhabitants, the family mansion was let by the late Sir C. Molyneaux to a professional gentleman, whose representatives disposed of it to the well-known Mr. Astley, who built on the ground and offices in the rear of the dwelling-house, his Amphitheatre, where he continued to amuse the public many years with feats of horsemanship. From him it was taken by a candidate* for public favour, who proposed to make it the rival of Crow-street. The attempt failed, and the whole concern reverted by process of ejectment to the family of the original proprietor. This seeming a fit opportunity for effecting their purpose, the subscribers to the blind asylum in 1815 took the whole concern at the annual rent of £100. and applied it to the several purposes of the charity. The dwelling-house, which is roomy and spacious, they fitted up for the reception of fifty blind females, and the amphitheatre, with some alteration, has passed into a chapel connected with the Institution. Where the scenes formerly stood, now stands the altar of God, on the stage is erected the pulpit, the pit and galleries retain their former destination, and are crowded with the usual concourse of people; but how different is the motive which attracts them, and the language in which they are addressed from the same place ! The pursuers of gaiety and pleasure here frequent their haunts of former dissipation, to hear that pleasure censured and that dissipation proscribed—

And those who came to scoff remain to pray.

* Mr. H. Johnstone.

The charity is intended not merely as an asylum for the old, but as a school of instruction for the young. It is therefore open to all ages as well as all religious persuasions. The pupils are taught to plait straw, to twist cords for window-curtains, &c. In addition to this, a taste for music is assiduously cultivated. Such as display any talent are instructed on the piano-forte, and in this way qualified to become organists to different houses of worship. There are already admitted 14, of whom three have shewn decided musical abilities.

The institution is under the direction of a guardian, five trustees, a chaplain, and 15 visiting ladies. It is supported by the receipts of the chapel, an annual charity sermon, and private subscriptions. Among these last is £100. the rent of the house, which has been liberally returned by the proprietor.

Summary of Blind Asylums.

Simpson's	72
Harp Society	0
Richmond	26
Molyneaux	14
	112

MAGDALENE ASYLUMS.

ASYLUM, LEESON-STREET.

This most interesting institution, owes its origin, as many others in the city of Dublin, to the benevolent sympathies of the female heart. Lady Arabella Denny, long known and prized in this country for her pure piety and active charities was the founder of this establishment. Hitherto, the unhappy class of females who had deviated from virtue, were not only excluded from every communication and intercourse with their own sex, but they were looked upon with a horror that deemed any approach contamination, and a prejudice that supposed any attempt to reform a visionary project. Without weakening the first, this amiable woman undertook to remove the latter impression. In obedience to the dictates of that religion of which she was so sincere a professor, she founded an institution which opened its bosom to the repentant sinner, removed the prejudices which obstructed her return to the pale of society, and by the strongest motives, the bitter experience of the past, and the joyful hope of the future, called upon her to " go and sin no more." This asylum, the first of the kind established in this country, was opened in Leeson street, on the 11th of June 1766, for unfortunate females abandoned by their seducers, and rejected by their friends, who were willing to prefer a life of penitence and virtue to one of guilt, infamy, and prostitution. To the other charities of whch lady Arabella was a promoter, she gave a due attention, but to promote the objects of this her own and favourite institution, she was constant and ardent in her exertions. She obtained for it the patronage of her Majesty, in right of which the Lady Lieutenant of Ireland, as her representative, is claimed its patroness, a claim which is generally answered by donations, visits, and exertions in its behalf. She drew up a code of laws for its internal regulations, which with little variation is still in force, and by the liberal donations and subscriptions which her example and influence obtained, she had the happiness to see this novel and interesting charity completely established, and in high prosperity, when it pleased God to call her from its superintendance, and receive the reward of her profitable stewardship.

The excellent example of this lady continued to operate after her decease, and a number of governesses, equally distinguished for their rank in life and zealous charity, have since continued to promote its objects with the same laudable assiduity, and the institution has gone on with an uniform progression. The house has been nearly rebuilt, and considerable additions made to its accommodations; and the congregation which attends the interesting service in its chapel is so increased, that it has been found necessary to enlarge it at two different times, till it was capable of containing nearly 700 people, whose weekly contributions are the principal support of the institution. In this chapel divine service is performed every Sunday and holiday, the Magdalenes answering the responses, and giving to the service, by the pensive sweetness of their voices, a peculiarly interesting solemnity. Here also the chaplain lectures the penitents every week, expounds the scriptures preparatory to the sacrament, exhorts and reproves them when required, and reads, whenever it has been unfortunately necessary, the form of expulsion of the irreclaimable. To give greater efficacy to such exhortations, none are received into the house after the age when they would be supposed incapable of instruction. Candidates past the age of twenty are inadmissible. The greater number have been taken into the asylum under the age of 17, when the effects of bad education are with less difficulty counteracted by the contrary habits of discipline and regularity. Not a few of these poor creatures are so very young as to be fit inmates for a school, and being unhappily but necessarily excluded from the society of those of their own age, find here a safe retirement from infamy and insult. In the bosom of this retreat they sometimes receive the whole of their education, and are frequently restored to their friends reformed, and instructed for their future duties in society, having passed through the extremes of vice, and returned again to virtue before the age when they would have been qualified for any station in life by the ordinary period of education. The general period of probation is from two to three years; but not even then is the well conducted penitent sent home till a means of honest livelihood is provided, or a reconciliation with her friends effected, if they be themselves in reputable circumstances. There are innumerable instances of their having proved exemplary and trusty servants, particularly in attendance on children, whom they are qualified to instruct in the first rudiments of learning; they have likewise given much satisfaction to elderly ladies who require good readers.

The rules of the establishment are in general founded on those of the Magdalene House in London, erected a few years prior to it. The interior concerns are conducted by a committee of 15 ladies, who visit the house, and are elected from the subscribers. These are the only persons allowed to see the penitents, unless by special order.

The institution is supported by subscriptions, the receipts of the chapel, and an annual charity sermon. The first are very limited for so popular and excellent an institution, amounting only to £100. per annum. The second are very considerable, from the opulent and respectable congregation which crowd to the interesting service. The third has been remarkably productive. It has called forth the talents of the most celebrated preachers in the country, and the contributions have been proportionably liberal.

The penitents are employed in the usual works of female industry, but the produce of their labour forms no part of the funds of the institution. One quarter of it is given to themselves immediately, as an incentive and reward to exertion, and the remainder is distributed in gratuities and clothes, to them on leaving the asylum. In order to extend further the benefits of the institution as far as possible, by increasing its means, it is expected that the friends of those who are received will contribute something to their support: this amounts usually to the small sum of ten guineas per annum, and is not exacted, when they are not in circumstances to pay it.

The house in its present improved state, is calculated to receive 60 penitents, and 48 have been at one time accommodated. But the admirable example of this asylum having been followed up in other instances, other establishments of the same kind divide the public attention, and its means of support are proportionably lessened. At the conclusion of the year 1814 42 were in the house. Since the commencement, 726 have been received, and as far as it was possible to trace their future progress through society, those who have been dismissed have evinced with few exceptions a thorough reformation. To the excellent family of Latouche this asylum is much indebted, particularly to its vice patroness, the Hon. Mrs. D. Latouche, who is indefatigable in her attention to its interests.

LOCK PENITENTIARY.

In the year 1783, Wm. Smyth[*] of the city of Dublin, erected at his own private expense a chapel, called Bethesda, and appointed two clergymen of the established church as chaplains, who were to officiate according to the liturgy and forms of the establishment. The building occupies a considerable portion of the east side of Dorset-street. Though spacious, it is insufficient to accommodate the congregations that crowd it, and it is less remarkable for architectural ornament than for the excellent uses to which it has been applied. To the chapel, its founder shortly after annexed a female orphan asylum, and appropriated to its accommodation a suit of apartments situated over the chapel. In the year 1794, he extended it to a further use, no less benevolent than judicious. Among the unhappy class of females who deviate from virtue, there is sometimes an obduracy so confirmed by habit, that even the powerful admonitions of contumely, poverty, and dis-

---

[*] This benevolent gentleman was nephew to Dr. Arth. Smyth, late archbishop of Dublin, whose worth is recorded on an inscription on his monument in St. Patrick's cathedral, by the classic pen of Dr. Lowth. (See p. 478.)

tress cannot reclaim: but there is one monitory warning that few are proof against, and the progress of a painful and loathsome distemper seldom fails to effect that change of mind which less severe afflictions could not accomplish. To open an asylum for these unhappy females, at a moment when their hearts are softened by pain of body and anguish of mind; to give them the alternative of comfort, health, and tranquillity, when they are about to encounter again distress, disease, and affliction, never fails to influence the mind with the most salutary impressions.* He therefore vested the Bethesda chapel with some adjoining houses, in the hands of five trustees, who undertook to open a Lock Penitentiary, for the reception and employment of women leaving the Lock hospital, and wishing to return again to the pursuits of industry and virtue. Since the commencement of this excellent charity 520 females have been received into it, who have in general evinced a sincere and perfect reformation. Some have been restored to their families, and some placed out at services or other employments recommended by the governors of the house and their own good conduct Fifty-four remain in the asylum. They are kept constantly employed; all branches of washing, mangling, and plain work, are carried on, and are so productive as to evince the severe and incessant industry to which these poor penitents cheerfully accommodate themselves. The institution is principally supported by their labour, which produces £500. per annum. This is aided by subscriptions, and an annual charity sermon.

Since the formation of the orphan asylum, about 250 young females have been supported, clothed, and educated, and at present 35 remain in the house. This charity, like the penitentiary, is supported by the industry of it's objects, subscriptions, and a charity sermon.

The chapel of the Bethesda is unusually crowded during divine service, either because it is supposed the service is performed with more solemnity, the preaching more impressive, or the doctrine more pure. Perhaps the excellent uses to which the establishment is applied may attract many to

* The medical gentlemen who attend at the Lock Hospital give an afflicting picture of the distress of some of these poor women. They sometimes try to remain in the house after their cure has been pronounced complete, earnestly intreating to be placed in any receptacle which would protect them from the horrors which they had experienced: and it has been even necessary to remove them from the hall and galleries of the house, where for weeks they continued to linger, still clinging to the hope of shelter in some asylum.

THE CITY OF DUBLIN.

this house of worship. They hear on the one side the voice of the female penitent, and on the other, of the female orphan, joining in divine service ; the first having passed through the extremes of misery and vice, returning chastened and reformed to the house of God; the second, as yet pure and unacquainted with sin and wretchedness, contrasted with their unhappy sisters and taking a solemn warning by their example. The impression of this is very affecting, and the voice of one penitent in particular has been long celebrated for its pensive sweetness.

DUBLIN FEMALE PENITENTIARY.

In the year 1813 this asylum was opened, and in the year following was removed to a new and extensive building erected for the purpose on the North Circular-road. It is directed by a committee of ladies, who daily attend. They do not confine their superintendance to the mere regulations of industry, but their exertions are directed to the moral and religious improvement of the unhappy women, with whom they do not hesitate to converse; and by kind condescension to their fallen sister, and by gentle and friendly exhortation gradually inculcate principles in a persuasive way that distant reserve or repulsive severity would often defeat. Besides this, habits of industry and order are strictly attended to. In addition to the ordinary avocations of washing and plain work, a repository is opened at the house for the sale of fancy and ornamental works. This is a well judged addition to such an institution, as these unfortunates frequently possess a peculiar talent for fancy needle-work, and display much ingenuity.

The building contains accommodations for 70 females. There are at present 40 on the establishment.

It is supported by subscription, the profits of the repository, and an annual charity sermon.

BOW-STREET ASYLUM.

This Institution is connected with circumstances somewhat curious and romantic. Some years ago a young child was sent to the house of a poor tradesman residing in Church-street, with a request that he would bring it up, and a promise of a certain annual sum for its support. This sum was regularly paid, and the child grew up under the care of his adopted parents, without the smallest knowledge of his own. When of a competent age, he learned the trade of a bricklayer from his adopted father, and worked at it for his support. In this state of indigent obscurity, he was returning home one night from his daily occupation, when he was accosted in Dame-street, by an unfortunate female as desolate as himself. Being a young man of moral principles, he was shocked at the address, and being of a serious turn of mind he exhorted her on her mode of life. The unfortunate female told a story of desertion and distress somewhat similar to his own, and excited his sympathy to such a degree that he invited her to his poor dwelling, till he could provide her temporary accommodation elsewhere. Having related the circumstance to some companions as well disposed as himself, a small sum was raised from their daily labour, and an humble asylum was established, of which this poor sincere penitent became the first inmate. In some time after, a letter was received from abroad by a mercantile house of great eminence, enquiring anxiously for the boy. His name was now ascertained to be Dillon, and his family of much opulence and respectability. He subsequently became a merchant of high repute, and in prosperity supported that estimable moral character which he so strikingly evinced in adversity. He at present resides in Monte Video, in South America: meanwhile his asylum continues to prosper. It soon attracted the notice of the Roman Catholic clergy, to which persuasion he belongs, and the public patronage sanctions the undertaking. It is now established in Bow-street, and receives into its bosom 50 repentant sinners.

GENERAL ASYLUM, TOWNSEND-STREET.

This, like the former, owes its origin to the exertions of virtue in obscurity. A poor and pious weaver in the Liberties, of the name of Quaterman, was struck with the guilt and misery in which unfortunate females of this class are involved, and he determined from his scanty ability to alleviate them. He began with an individual whom he endeavoured by persuasion to reclaim, and having succeeded, he applied to his serious and equally indigent acquaintance to assist him. From their united exertions, they were enabled to raise a small fund for this purpose, and a few poor females were reclaimed by the exhortations and supported by the patient industry of these benevolent moralists, whose utmost efforts, in the most prosperous times, scarcely sufficed for their own support. From this commencement, it gradually increased, and in process of time attracted the notice of the public, who now liberally support it. The asylum is in Townshend-street, where the penitents are employed in the more laborious occupations of female industry. They have erected a steam engine for the purpose, and all the operations of washing are carried on by it. This asylum, like the former, has a clergyman of the Roman Catholic church attached to it, and is considered as a charity supported exclusively by that persuasion. There are at present 45 penitents on the establishment.

These instances of considerate benevolence which have been displayed in the establishment of asylums for these unfortunates, are highly creditable to those excellent individuals, whose names we have had great pleasure in recording; but they are so in different degrees. The first moved in a sphere of society, where such principles and feelings would naturally operate in such a way; where the horror at the vice and the wish to reclaim it, would be no less the result of a good heart than of a good education; and where feelings implanted by nature, would be further promoted by the example of the society in which they lived, and the morality they constantly heard inculcated. The second were humble moralists who had no such incentives. They were persons of the lowest rank, associates of the meanest companions; they lived among a class where principle is said to be extinct, depravity universal, and morals absorbed in vice and profligacy. And we record those instances of excellent principle in the lower class with the more pleasure, as we know they are not solitary exceptions. We can assert from our experience of the poor of this city, that there is yet an admirable feeling that poverty and ignorance cannot entirely extinguish; a virtue which, independent of sect or party or persuasion, displays itself as the natural endowment of the mind, not to be obliterated by adventitious circumstances. It is to this cause we are to attribute the number of asylums for penitents of this class, which so much exceed the comparative size of our metropolis. It arises not from any greater profligacy, for we trust it will be admitted, that there are fewer deviations among the upper classes, and less systematic depravity among the lower, than are to be found in most of the cities of

Europe of equal population: but it is to be attributed, on the one hand, to an horror of the crime, and an anxiety to restrain it so great as to out-run absolute necessity, that so many houses of this kind are established: and on the other, to that disposition which it is more difficult to confirm in vice than to persuade to virtue, that such houses become immediately crowded with inmates, wherever they open their bosoms to repentant sinners.

Summary of Magdalene Asylums.

Leeson-street	42
Lock Penitentiary	54
Dublin Female	40
Townshend-street	52
Bow-street	45
	233

ASYLUMS FOR WIDOWS.

WIDOWS' ALMS-HOUSE OF ST. JAMES'S PARISH.

THE very singular origin of this institution entitles it to particular notice, and we feel pleasure in rescuing from oblivion, a few anecdotes of its founder, John Loggins.

This extraordinary man was a native of Bow-bridge, in this parish, where he filled for many years the humble occupation of a hackney-coachman; at length by persevering industry, becoming the proprietor of two coaches, he drove only occasionally, and particularly when the judges of assize, with whom he appears to have been a favourite, went on circuit. His circumstances continuing gradually to improve, he became possessed of a small property in houses in Bow-bridge and its vicinity, to the value of about £40. per annum; but fell at length into the most abandoned state of drunkenness and profligacy. As his little property does not appear to have been dissipated, it is probable he did not continue long in a state which may be considered as truly wretched, as few are known to recover from its deplorable infatuation. A gracious Providence, however, that often produces good through the instrumentality of the mean and humble, seems to have destined this obscure individual to be the father of an institution which should supply comfort and consolation to many of his fellow creatures through succeeding generations. The life of a drunkard is necessarily exposed to various instances of distress, disgrace, and infamy; and of these John Loggins experienced a full proportion. He was arrested and imprisoned for drunken debts, and often by those whom he deemed his sincerest friends; and it is recorded of him, that having reduced himself at a public tavern to a state of beastly intoxication, he was in that situation placed in a basket on a porter's back, and thus carried in open day through the public streets, to his house in Bow-bridge. To a mind whose sensibilities were strong, the recollection of such scenes of disgrace was extremely painful: he frequently deplored them to his acquaintance, and made repeated efforts at amendment. But the first instance of an actual reformation in John Loggins was produced by the following incident. One of his coach-horses was so extremly vicious as to be approached with danger, and had often hurt those employed in cleaning his stall; yet this man passed an entire night in a state of senseless intoxication under this animal's feet, who during that time did not attempt to lie down, or injure him. This he immediately conceived, and indeed ever after maintained, to be an obvious interposition of Divine Providence in his favour, and produced immediately a visible and steady change in his conduct, impressed with an ardent impulse of gratitude to that Being who so visibly protected a wretch so unprepared to enter into his presence; and feeling also a sense of obligation to the animal that spared him, he instantly not only determined on a total reformation of life, but formed a resolution that the Sabbath should be thenceforward a day of rest to his horses, and he never afterwards was known to allow his coaches to ply on Sunday.

While on circuit with the judges he fared sumptuously, and had his bottle of wine regularly charged and allowed in the bill. On his return from the last circuit he ever went, the wheels of his carriage had scarcely cleared Kilcullen-bridge, when the arch over which he had just passed, instantly gave way, and tumbled in ruins into the Liffey. This second interference of a protecting Providence determined his resolves for ever. He instantly relinquished a profession which exposed him to peculiar temptations, sold his carriages and horses, and consecrated to fervent piety and active virtue the remnant of a life so long disgraced by irreligion and impurity. To indulgence of appetite succeeded the most rigid temperance; animal food he scarce ever tasted; bread and milk became his constant diet; milk and water his only drink; and to the close of life, two days in each week were assigned to mortifying the flesh by a total abstinence from food, with a perseverance from which no solicitations could tempt him to recede. The ridicule of his former associates had no effect in suspending his devotions public or private, which, without being ostentatious were frequent, regular, and ardent. Twice every day he attended prayers at the chapel of the Royal Hospital; frequently in the evening he went to hear the methodist preachers, though never, I believe, in their society; and at the cathedral of St. Patrick, where the eucharist is every Sunday administered, he was a constant guest.

He now conceived the idea of converting his unoccupied stables into an alms-house for poor widows; but in the ardour of his zeal he seemed to forget the total incompetence of his means. His wife indeed appears to have patiently submitted to his frugal fare and rigid œconomy; yet an income not exceeding £40. per annum, could afford but little for charitable exertion: but a mind ardent in a generous cause is not easily discouraged. In the execution of his favourite plan he became mason and carpenter, and with his own hands by incessant labour fitted up in a short time his stable and hay-loft for the accommodation of poor widows. Some truly amiable females, who were induced by the history of this singular man to patronise his plan, supplied beds and bedding, and six indigent and aged females were, to his great satisfaction, admitted into this asylum, but at what precise period we are not informed; to these he supplied every comfort within the reach of his humble means, and where these failed, he was so indefatigable in his solicitations to the humane and wealthy in their behalf, that even on his fast days he has been known to undertake for this purpose long journeys on foot into the country, without relaxing the severity of abstinence, or taking any refreshment except a drink of his usual beverage, milk and water. Of this adopted family of helpless females, he became at once virtually the parent and pastor; and while he relieved their necessities he forgot not their better interests, but taught them to seek comfort under the pains and infirmities of old age, in the bosom of that religion whose consolations he could, from experience, so well attest. One of these poor widows still survives, and expressed a grateful recollection of the warm affection with which this good man entered into all their little interests, and the fervour with which he offered up his prayers and intercessions for their welfare.

The success of his solicitations encouraged him to extend his views. His dwelling-house was contiguous to his little asylum, and room after room was added to it as his means increased; and at length purchasing the interest of an under tenant, to whom he had set the lowest apartment, this too was converted to the same humane purpose, and he had the happiness to live to see twenty widows comfortably settled in his alms-house.

He died on the 23d of July 1774, exhibiting in his life and death, a fine example of what ardent zeal, even with the humblest means, may perform, in the sacred cause of charity and humanity.

By his will dated October 13, 1771, he appointed the vicar and church wardens of the parish of St. James, and their successors, trustees and guardians of the charity; and for that purpose devised to them the alms-house, at a pepper-corn rent, with forty shillings per annum towards its support. The trust has been hitherto faithfully executed.—An annual charity sermon, producing generally about £130., with the interest of about £800. saved from former collections, when the necessaries of life were more moderate, form the sole support of this institution. The house is old, and mean in its external appearance, and from its former destination destitute of that symmetry and solidity so pleasing to the eye in buildings of this description; the apartments, however, are sufficiently spacious, and are kept neat, clean, and comfortable; the bedding is good, firing and candles abundant, but though the quantity of clothing and sustenance may be sufficient for those who by their industry can make some addition to their comforts, it is to be lamented that the fund will not allow any extension in favour of the infirm and sickly. We found them in general disposed to acknowledge with gratitude the comforts they enjoyed; an air of religion seemed to pervade the place; and one who was labouring under a heavy visitation of Providence, appeared to be deeply pious. We mention these circumstances, as they are so very different from what is usually seen in a Dublin alms-house.

Such was the state of this charity in 1806. We are happy however in being able to add, that on re-visiting it in 1812, we found the comforts of the poor widows much improved. In lieu of their former scanty allowance of provisions, they now receive 3s. 3d. with a half-quartern loaf each per week; they are fully clothed every second year, and in the intermediate year receive each a shift and petticoat, with a pair of stockings and shoes.

WIDOWS' ALMS-HOUSE, IN GREAT BRITAIN-STREET.

THIS edifice, 60 feet by 36 in the clear, is substantially built of stone, the quoins, jambs of windows, &c. being of hewn mountain-granite. It consists of three stories exclusive of the basement, which is below the level of the street, and has a spacious area both in front and rear. The apartments, eight on each floor, open off a gallery six feet wide, and running the entire length of the building; and this is crossed in the centre by another, about eight feet wide, one end of which is occupied by the staircase; the other forms the hall, with closets over it in the upper stories. The apartments, thirty-two in number, are fourteen feet by twelve each, furnished with a fire-place, and lighted by a single window; but those on the upper floor alone are ceiled; in the rest the naked joists are exposed to view, which form receptacles for cobwebs, and have an unpleasing effect.

In the front area is a pipe and cock affording a plentiful supply of water, and at the rear is a spacious yard, above 60 feet square.

The number of widows at present in the house are 32, each occupying a room, and receiving from the endowment two guineas per annum, which is paid at Christmas; and one of their number, who acts as housekeeper, has an additional gratuity of four guineas per annum, with a guinea for coals.

The intentions of the founder of this charity were certainly laudable, in a city where the most wretched room, in the most wretched situation, rents from one to two shillings per week. A comfortable apartment, with even the small pittance of two guineas per annum, must, to a poor widow, be an object of some importance. The building is in an airy situation, seems to have been well-planned, and is executed in that stile of plainness and solidity most suitable to its destination: but the benevolent views of the founder are in a great measure frustrated by a degree of neglect distressing to humanity; instead of that cheerful neatness and cleanliness so grateful to the eye of the spectator in the habitations of the poor, it is here disgusted with walls embroidered with dirt and smoke, windows from filth scarce pervious to the light, and by a ruinous ceiling, threatening destruction to

THE CITY OF DUBLIN. 783

the inhabitants, of which some fragments have already fallen. The roof has lately been repaired, but the other timber work not having been painted, as we were informed, since 1797, is rapidly hastening to decay; and we must add, that the window which originally lighted the lower gallery having been accidentally damaged, it has been injudiciously built up, so that the wretched inhabitants of this floor, are necessitated to grope their way to their apartments through darkness visible.

As the widows on this foundation receive nothing but the bare room with two guineas (as before stated) at Christmas, their bedding and furniture is of course their own, and the interior appearance of their apartments might be supposed to be proportioned to their respective means, but here a general character of gloom and dirt pervades every room, from which even the apartment of the housekeeper is not wholly exempt, though used occasionally as a board room by the governors.

FORTICK'S WIDOWS' ALMS-HOUSE, IN DENMARK-STREET.

THIS resembles that in Great Britain-street already described, both in the nature of the institution, and in the arrangement of the plan of the building; it is however on a smaller scale, the galleries being only five feet wide, and the apartments about 13 by 11 feet 6 inches, and not so lofty. The front is of brick, the rear of rough stone, and the latter has bulged and separated a few inches from the cross partitions, but as this fissure has not increased for many years it is not thought dangerous. The spacious area in front has a cock and pipe that supplies abundance of good water, and in the rear is a yard and grass plat of about 60 by 100 feet, well-secured. The apartments were originally 32 in number, but those on the ground-floor, the funds we suppose not being adequate to their support, have been judiciously divided into small coal holes, of which each widow has one appropriated to her sole use. There are twenty-four apartments, and as the housekeeper, who is also one of the widows, occupies two, the widows are 23 in number, who receive about £3. 10s. each per annum, with a bag of coals at Christmas.

Whether the inmates of this alms-house are more judiciously selected, or that the superintendance of the institution is more attended to, we do not presume to determine, but the appearance of the widows, and their apartments, is very different from what we see in the alms-house already alluded to. Here many of the rooms are uncommonly clean, with an air of neatness and comfort, to which the possession of a receptacle for their fuel separate from the apartment, must contribute much; some indeed were occupied by widows in extreme indigence, but even these, though destitute of furniture, were not rendered disgusting by dirt.

The superintendance of this Institution is under the direction of the Rector of St. Mary's, who with the Lord Chancellor for the time being, alternately fills up the vacancies which occur.

WIDOWS' RETREAT.

THIS excellent institution was erected in 1815, at the sole expence of the Latouche family. It is a new and neat brick building, situated at the extremity of Dorset-street, in the open and healthy outlet of Drumcondra. It consists of 12 rooms, each containing 2 beds, and accommodating two poor widows. The room is besides furnished with two arm-chairs, and a convenient press. It is in orders that no food shall be dressed in these apartments, and that they shall be regularly cleaned after breakfast at ten o'clock, each day. These and other regulations are strictly complied with, and the rooms are perfectly neat and comfortable. Beneath is a large kitchen, where the widows dine in common. In the rear is a flagged yard, and an extensive garden for their use. Besides the accommodations of the house they are allowed 2s. 6d. per week; and are received without distinction of religion, though the great majority are protestants. The whole has an aspect of great comfort and tranquillity.

GEORGE'S.

THIS Asylum supports 13 widows from the weekly receipts of the parochial church, which on an average amount annually to £380. It was erected in 1814, and is situated in George's-place. It is intended exclusively for poor protestant parishioners. They seem not uncomfortable; but there is an evident want of attention to neatness and regularity.

KNIGHT'S.

THE large and opulent parish of ST. PETER's has but one alms-house for widows, which is not a parochial establishment, but founded in the year 1713, by Mr. Knight. It accommodates four widows, and is under the superintendance of the Archdeacon of Dublin.

PAROCHIAL ALMS-HOUSES.

ST. THOMAS's.—This is situated in Cumberland-lane, and contains six rooms, which accommodate twelve widows. The only furniture given is a metal bedstead.

ST. MICHAN's.—This is a small house, situated in the Church-yard, where eight widows are lodged.

ST. PAUL's.—This is a large house on Arbour-hill, in which twenty-nine widows are at present lodged, of whom twelve receive a weekly stipend.

ST. CATHERINE's.—There are two asylums for widows in this parish, in which are lodged thirty-six widows; the excellent management of the parochial estate having allowed the parishioners to apply £100. a year to their support, beside the annual subscriptions.

ST. JOHN's.—This is situated in Rosemary-lane, and accommodates twelve widows.

ST. WERBURGH's.—This is in Derby-square, and receives twelve widows.

ST. ANDREW's—Receives two widows. The house is in Pie-corner-lane.

ST. MARK's.—This asylum had formerly been a soup-shop, but was fitted up for the reception of fourteen widows.

ST. ANNE's—Is situated in Kildare-lane. It is a large house, containing eight rooms, sufficiently spacious to accommodate four widows in each. Some of these poor creatures are extremely old and blind, and require the attendance of some friend to take care of them. There are thirty-six inmates at present in the house.

ST. BRIDE's—Is in Great Ship-street, and receives twenty widows.

The widows in all these houses receive a small stipend weekly, with coals generally in winter. The expence is defrayed from the collections of the Parish Church, aided by occasional donations and subscriptions. On the books of the remaining parishes are a certain number of widows, who receive a weekly proportion of bread and money from the church collections, but they have no asylum in which they are lodged.

ASYLUM FOR CLERGYMENS' WIDOWS.

This is situated in Mercer-street, and was founded by Lady Anne Hume, for six Clergymens' Widows, who, in addition to their lodging, receive a stipend of £10. per annum. When we consider the very slender provision made for the unbeneficed clergy of the established church during their life, we deeply regret that this mean mansion, however creditable to the individual who founded it, should be the only provision made for their families at their death. To remedy this deficiency, a subscription was some time ago entered into by the clergy themselves, to supply an annual income for the families of the deceased; but the poverty of the subscribers, and the number of applications, rendered this mode of relief hopeless. The number of unbeneficed clergymen in the diocese of Dublin, amounts to about seventy, and the only provision for their widows, is a small house, more mean and comfortless than a parish alms-house, into which six families are crowded, with an income of £60. a year to support them all!. Yet even for this poor provision, the claimants are so numerous and meritorious, as to render the selection extremely embarrassing. If integrity of life, extent of learning, and sincerity and zeal in the discharge of a sacred duty, should entitle any body of men to the consideration of the government under which they live, and the establishment which they serve, we trust it will be admitted, that the curates of this country have strong claims. Yet while the royal bounty has been liberally granted to aid the stipend of the clergy of one persuasion, and pressed upon the acceptance of those of another, the unbeneficed clergy of the established church remain with a salary not only inadequate to the present support and future provision of a family, but even inadequate to maintain the individual in that station of society which an expensive and liberal education has fitted him, which habit has used him to, and the decorum of his sacred profession calls on him to support. The many efforts made in Parliament, evince how much the subject is felt, and the necessity for some change acknowledged,—but these efforts have done no more than

> Keep the word of promise to our ear,
> And break it to our hopes.

Still are our clergy without an adequate provision for themselves, and their widows, in this diocese, without the common benefit of an adequate pauper asylum!

METHODIST ALMS-HOUSE, WHITEFRIAR-STREET.

In the year 1764 the Arminian Methodists of Dublin first conceived the idea of founding an alms-house for the poor widows belonging to their connection in this city, and who, from their exemplary piety, age, and infirmities, had a powerful claim on their humanity: the society, however, generally consisting of persons in the middle and lower classes of life, and of course equal to little more than the weekly supply of the numerous wants of their sick poor, were sensible that the proposed plan would require a fund, far beyond what their own unaided exertions could supply. Thus circumstanced, they communicated their intentions to the public, and religious persons of all denominations of Protestants, encouraged a plan obviously founded in piety and humanity: the contributions were liberal, and among the numerous promoters of this excellent charity, we record with pleasure the name of Mr. Joseph Terry, who, though unconnected with the society, gave a donation of one hundred pounds subject to interest during his life only. With the humane view of affording the comforts of public worship to its intended aged and infirm inhabitants, a site was selected immediately adjoining the society's meeting-house in Whitefriar-street, on which the house was erected in the year 1766, at an expense of about seven hundred pounds, and in the following year twenty widows were admitted, who were furnished with beds, bedding, coals and candles, and also with money in such proportions, from sixpence to four shillings English each per week, as their various necessities required, and the limited funds of the society could supply, while a very few, were, in consequence of other resources, independant of this pecuniary aid.

The institution fully answers the benevolent end proposed by its founders, and the spirit that gave it birth, continues to cherish and support it; its existence in a great measure depends on the annual collections made at charity sermons, in the meeting-houses of the society in Whitefriar-street, Gravel-walk, and in Westley Chapel, near Mountjoy-square, which are on this occasion attended by the pious of all denominations of Protestants, whose liberal contributions have enabled the trustees not only to enlarge the number of widows to twenty-four, but to encrease their comforts.

This alms-house contains twelve apartments, each about sixteen by fourteen feet, and occupied by two widows, who have separate beds, with warm comfortable bedding. The rooms have each a fire-place, are lighted by two windows, are kept neat and clean, and are well ventilated; such as had health and strength sufficient, we found endeavouring by some little exertion of industry, to add to their comforts, and we did not find any room without a bible.

It is perhaps to be lamented that persons are generally admitted into almshouses without any reference in the selection to their former habits of life, moral or religious; and hence it happens, that in these asylums of age and infirmity, we seldom meet with that pious resignation and cheerful acquiescence in their lot, which might be expected from persons looking forward to a better world; fretful bickerings but too often interrupt their little comforts; and it is a melancholy, but we fear a just observation, that a poor almshouse widow, with scanty means of subsistence, and destitute of religion, is of all human beings the most discontented and querulous.

In the alms-house of Whitefriar-street, a far different scene presents itself: we have frequently visited and conversed with its truly venerable inhabitants, and though not exempt from the usual maladies of infirm old age, we never heard one murmur of discontent; they appeared to live in the most perfect harmony, and seemed anxious by every little exertion of tender sympathy, to sooth each others sufferings: effusions of gratitude to Heaven and to their benefactors on earth, seemed to be the favourite theme of every tongue, and through the whole institution there reigned an air of pious humility, and patient but cheerful hope.

Since the opening of the house in 1767, to the commencement of the year 1809, ninety-eight widows have here found a refuge from the complicated sufferings of infirmity and poverty, and at a period of life when least able to sustain them; twenty-four remain in the house: seventy-four have died in peace, and of these Isabella Frazier, who attained the age of 77, is, after a lapse of thirteen years, remembered with veneration: this poor woman, who previous to her admission, had been long confined to her bed, continued in that situation seven and twenty years, evincing by her uniform cheerfulness and edifying conversation, during that long and painful visitation, the wonderful power of religion when it reaches and influences the heart.

This charity is greatly indebted to the active zeal of a worthy individual of the methodist connection, Arthur Keen, Esq. who for many years past has been indefatigable not only in soliciting aid for its support, but in his unwearied attention to its internal management and economy.

PRESBYTERIAN ALMS-HOUSE, CORK-STREET.

The congregation of Eustace-street meeting-house, appropriate the weekly contributions of the society to support a widows' house; these contributions are aided by a collection made on the last Sunday in each year, among the members themselves. The alms-house is situated in Cork-street, and comfortably maintains 12 poor widows.

INDEPENDANTS' ALMS-HOUSE, PLUNKET-STREET.

The congregation of Plunket-street meeting-house support an alms-house connected with their society. It accommodates 12 poor widows.

MORAVIAN ALMS-HOUSE, WHITEFRIAR-STREET.

This house is a bequest of the late Andrew Moller, Esq. a respected brother of the Moravian Society. He also left a sum of money, the interest of which provides the inmates with coals and candles; besides which they receive a weekly allowance from the receipts of the meeting-house. It accommodates 13 widows and aged females.

CATHOLIC ALMS-HOUSE, CLARK'S-COURT.

This charity is connected with a Sunday-school, and is supported by members of the Catholic persuasion, to which it exclusively belongs. The house is situated in a court off Great Ship-street, and supports 25 widows.

SUMMARY OF WIDOWS' ALMS-HOUSES.

James's supports	20
Great Britain-street	32
Forticks	23
Retreat	24
George's	13
Knight's	4
Parochial	181
Clergymens' Widows	6
Methodists	24
Presbyterian	12
Independants	12
Moravian	13
Catholic	25
	389

ASYLUMS FOR FEMALE SERVANTS.

ASYLUM FOR AGED AND INFIRM FEMALE SERVANTS.

This Institution was founded in 1809, by a few friends to the cause of humanity, who had long seen and lamented the deplorable situation of that useful class of their fellow creatures, female servants, who reduced by age and decrepitude, to undergo the extremes of human misery, were left to famish in unnoticed obscurity, or to supplicate in the streets for a precarious subsistence: and being convinced that the house of industry was not an adequate asylum for those who had been accustomed to the comforts of life; they were led to think of an institution solely for the reception of aged and infirm female servants, a home for the truly deserving of this class, where their weary limbs might rest, and where their minds, undisturbed by pecuniary cares, might repose in quietude and peace. Solid advantages, it was expected, might arise to society from such an establishment, and that the prospect of such an asylum might powerfully stimulate to integrity and sobriety, especially as certificates of good conduct from their masters or mistresses must necessarily be produced previous to admission.

In this humane and populous city, so abounding in the extremes of opulence and poverty, the helpless infant, the sick and the wounded, are provided with suitable receptacles, and almost every species of human misery has its appropriate asylum: that in such a city, those hands whose daily drudgery reserves to us the enjoyment of domestic ease, those limbs whose useful toil has left to ours the privelege of rest, should alone be forgotten, appeared to these amiable and excellent individuals, a neglect so unaccountable, that they were induced to conclude that it must have arisen from the subject not having sufficiently engaged the attention of the public: to the public therefore they made an earnest appeal, and with a success that realised their most sanguine hopes. The institution was opened on the 10th of June 1809, when 14 of the most deserving and necessitous old female servants (being the utmost number that the limited state of the funds could then support), were selected from a considerable number of candidates, and admitted into the house taken for the purpose on Summer-hill, in the vicinity of the circular road, in a situation healthy, cheerful and airy;

and in its internal arangements convenient and comfortable. This number has been already increased to 24, and as the guardians have a further extension of the charity in contemplation, they are looking out for a larger house.

The apartments of this institution are kept perfectly neat and clean, and the conduct of every individual hitherto admitted has been quite decent and exemplary. Religious distinctions are avoided; and to afford them the plain comforts of life, is the intention of the guardians: for this purpose, exclusive of a sufficient supply of coals, they receive a weekly stipend of 3s. 3d. each for their support; and in time of sickness, medical aid and such other comforts as appear to be necessary are provided.

It was at first doubted by some, whether deserving objects of the class intended to be relieved, could be found in this city, sufficiently numerous to warrant a call on the public bounty, in order to establish an institution exclusively for their reception and support; experience however has proved, that in this class numbers of highly deserving persons are to be met with, and when the two last vacancies were filled, 65 candidates appeared, whose characters, when particularly enquired into by members of the committee, corresponded with the written testimonials of good conduct which they produced from their respective masters or mistresses;[*] a circumstance which must fully convince the friends of this truly humane institution of the propriety of persevering in their exertions to relieve this deserving but long neglected class of their fellow creatures. Among the general rules for the government of the institution are the following.

Ten guineas in any one year shall constitute a governor for life: and an annual subscription of one guinea shall entitle the subscriber to the privilege of a governor for one year.—Persons applying for admission must bring a letter of recommendation from a subscriber, and produce satisfactory discharges from those with whom they have lived, certifying their sobriety, honesty, and peaceable demeanour.—Two of the committee to be appointed to investigate the character of each applicant, and report the result of their inquiries at the next meeting of the committee, for consideration and

[*] The number of claims for admission since the commencement till the expiration of the year 1812, were 125, who from every circumstance of character and conduct, was duly qualified. From these 32 were admitted, 8 died in the asylum, and there are now 24 in the house.

decision; and when there are more applications than one to fill a vacancy, the most meritorious and necessitous always to have the preference—due regard being had to length of service in one place.

Statement of the Income and Expenditure of the Asylum for Aged and Infirm Female Servants, for 1812.

Expenditure.

	£.	s.	d.
Paid Purchase of £300. at 3¼ per Cent. Stock,	218	2	10
Collection fees	10	15	3
Printing	12	2	3
Coals	22	18	0
Repairs and Taxes	7	18	0
Contingencies	4	8	1¼
Weekly Allowance to 24 Women	194	17	6
Balance in Treasurer's Hands	140	4	8
	611	6	7½

Receipts.

	£.	s.	d.
By Balance in Treasurer's hands, per Report last year	142	4	1
Net amount of Charity Sermon	131	17	2
Interest received on Stock	25	5	0
Subscriptions received this year	210	17	7¼
Donations	101	2	9
	611	6	7½

HOUSE FO REFUGE FOR SERVANTS OUT OF PLACE.

At this period of considerate charity, scarcely any object is passed over which really deserves the notice of the humane, and the temptations and errors to which unprotected females of the lower classes are exposed, have justly engaged no inconsiderable degree of attention. Female servants when disengaged from a family are peculiarly in this situation. Suddenly deprived of their usual means of support, and incapable of pursuing any other, they are temporary outcasts from the society in which they have lived, and liable to all the temptations of want and desertion. To obviate this, a House of Refuge was opened in Baggot-street, in the year 1802, for the reception of young women out of employment who could bring unquestionable testimonies of their modesty, honesty, and sobriety. Here they reside till they are accommodated with eligible services, and in the mean time are employed in washing and plain-work, &c. receiving a small daily allowance, to assist any deficiency in their earnings. The house is confided to the care of a matron; and the governesses meet every month, to examine candidates for admission, and recommend those in the house to such situations as they are qualified to undertake. The establishment is supported by subscription. Since its commencement, 584 have been admitted, and the number of candidates whose good conduct entitles them to a reception here is so great, that a house is now preparing to accommodate 60 young women.

HOUSE OF REFUGE, STANHOPE-STREET.

A pious widow in humble circumstances originated this establishment. She kept a fruit-shop at the corner of Bow-street, Mary's-lane, and having had frequent opportunities of witnessing the distress and danger to which servants of her own sex are exposed, when removed from the protection of the family in which they lived, she gratuitously assigned a part of her house for their reception, and invited to this asylum as many as it would accommodate until they should be again employed. The important service rendered in this way by this kind and considerate woman, induced the clergy of her own persuasion to interest themselves to enlarge her little establishment. They engaged the concurrence of many opulent Catholics, and a spacious house was purchased in Stanhope-street, (Grange Gorman-lane), and fitted up for the reception of females of this description. Forty females whose character and conduct entitle them to this protection, are here supported, and finally recommended to reputable services.

The advantages of these establishments cannot be too highly appreciated. The charity is not confined to those who receive, but extends also to those bestow it, and comes home to the domestic comforts of every individual in the community. When a servant left her situation before the establishment of those houses, her only resource was an application to a registry-office. Here she deposited a sum of money, her name was entered in a book, and she waited without home or protection an indefinite length of time till chance procured her another situation. Meanwhile, without employment, or the means of industry to support her, she every day attended at the office to learn her fate, and here she met with a crowd of men, who assemble at the same office, for the same purpose, and are as idle and unemployed as herself. To accommodate those loungers, a public-house is usually opened next door to the office, to which it seems to be a necessary appendage, and here they generally retire together to pass the time. The seductions of such a place are sufficient at any time, and under the best circumstances, to sap the principles, corrupt the morals, and destroy the reputation of any female who frequents it; but if she be without home to invite, a mistress to protect, or an employment to support her, can she possibly avoid any temptation, when thus invited by intemperance, seduced by example, and impelled by poverty? It was in vain, then, that such early precautions were taken to form the young mind in the numerous schools which instruct females in the qualifications necessary to form good servants, if, in more advanced years, they are constantly and periodically liable to a temptation, which, like the eternal enemy, sows the tares of vice and depravity amid the very best education. The notorious consequence has been, a general complaint of the intemperance, dishonesty, and profligacy of the servants of the metropolis, and the inefficacy of early education to restrain them. To remove the great evil, these judicious houses of refuge seem well calculated. The female is never out of the protection of guardians, never compelled to improper associations, never seduced to improper places, never idle, never in want; reputation is her best support, past character entitles her always to protection, and present conduct ensures her a future recommendation. If to these considerations be added, the asylum which holds out a support and shelter for her old age, we should hope that every reasonable precaution is taken to provide good servants, forming good principles in early life, and applying every incentive to ensure their practice.

The number of servants constantly out of place, and waiting to be employed in these houses of refuge, amount to 100, a number equal to that

THE CITY OF DUBLIN.

which is usually found in the registry offices. It is expected, therefore, that the public will always find a sufficient selection there, and the necessity of registry offices for females, be altogether superseded.

Summary of Asylums for Servants.

Aged - - -	24
Young, Baggot-street	60
——— Stanhope-Street	40
	124

ASYLUM FOR OLD MEN, RUSSEL-PLACE.

THE number of alms and widows' houses, in this metropolis shews that the claims of these superanuated members of the community, have not been urged in vain; but until lately, it had provided no establishment exclusively for the reception of old men. The well-tried attention of our citizens to every demand upon their liberality does not deserve to have it doubted, that the utility of such an institution had not before presented itself, though circumstances might have delayed the undertaking. In 1807, however, through the exertions of a foreigner, whose long residence in Dublin was marked by unceasing benevolence, a subscription was set on foot for this purpose, and small labelled boxes, to be opened at stated intervals by the collectors, were distributed to the subscribers and other persons, who placed them in conspicuous situations in their houses to receive further contributions. Thus, and with the additional aid of a charity sermon, a considerable fund was soon raised, which was vested in the hands of twelve trustees, and applied to the building and furnishing of the Asylum for Old Men; a small sum being reserved for the weekly stipends of six out-pensioners, who were supported during the progress of the work.

The asylum was completed in 1812, at an expence of £1296. besides £300. for furniture, and opened for the reception of 24 deserving objects. It stands on the south side of the Circular-road, near Mountjoy-square, in a pleasant and healthful situation, combining at the same time all the advantages of contiguity and retirement. The building is of brick, with rustic wings of mountain granite, and contains a kitchen, hall, housekeeper's room, which serves also the occasional purposes of a chapel and a committee-room, and six bed-chambers. It is in contemplation to enlarge the establishment by erecting a dining hall, and some additional apartments, one of which is intended to be fitted up as a work-shop, for the use of such of the old men as are able to employ themselves for their own amusement, in the occupation they have been accustomed to; and a considerable sum has been actually subscribed for the purpose. In the mean time, the old men have their meals comfortably provided for them in the house-keeper's room.

The applicants for admission are required to produce proofs that they are at least sixty years of age, incabable of earning a subsistence, and destitute of friends who can support them; that their moral character has been unexceptionable, and that they have not been servants, or retail venders of spirituous liquous. They are also required to be protestants; a stipulation which on first view may appear tainted with a spirit of party and intolerance, altogether inconsistent with the principles of charitable institutions: but it must be urged, in excuse for a rule apparently so illiberal, that perfect good will and harmony amongst the inmates, are essential to the ends proposed, in an establishment of this kind; and when it is recollected that the irritability and long confirmed sentiments and prejudices of old age are peculiarly excited by religious differences, which it is to be feared the severest prohibition could not prevent, it would be uncandid to question too closely the policy which decided, that it was better at once to avoid the consequences by excluding the cause.

The asylum is constantly open to the visits of strangers as well as subscribers, and all visitors are requested to write their remarks freely upon the institution. The book kept for this purpose already exhibits many most respectable and gratifying testimonials of the admirable cleanliness of the house, and of the comforts extended to its venerable inhabitants. Of these, some are now near 90 years of age, but the Asylum has not yet afforded any very striking instance of longevity.

The expense of the establishment is defrayed by private subscriptions and donations, and by the produce of an annual charity sermon.

The expenditure for the year 1815, amounted to £423. 3s. 8d.

THE CITY OF DUBLIN. 797

Subscriptions amount to £60. receipts of the boxes to about £30.; the remainder is defrayed by a charity sermon, the receipts of which has fluctuated between £353. 8s. 8d. and £185. 1s. 9d.

DORSET INSTITUTION.

Her Excellency the Duchess of Dorset was much occupied during the autumn of 1815, in devising some scheme of relief for the industrious females of the Metropolis, and under her patronage, this charity, embracing sundry useful objects, was opened in 1816, in Lower Abbey-street. The establishment of the straw-plait manufacture* in this city had long been an object of much interest to those who supposed it connected with many advantages to the poor. It requires neither capital or machinery; the raw materials cost nearly nothing, and the manufactured article bears a high price, and has a ready sale. Moreover, it tended to correct those faulty propensities to which the children of the poor are prone. It required a more than usual attention to cleanliness; called forth ingenuity and dexterity; could employ children at an early age, and give them support when other sources of industry failed. Attempts were therefore made to introduce it into several schools, and with considerable success. A manufactory of this kind forms a principal part of this establishment. Thirty children are

* In several counties in Ireland the peasantry are employed in making straw hats for their own use, particularly in the county of Wexford, where every female wears a bonnet of her own manufacture. The straw of this country was supposed inferior to that of England for this purpose, but our lime-stone soil has been found to produce straw of a quality equal to that of a chalky soil, which in fact it so exactly resembles in its chemical properties, any colouring matter being readily discharged by sulphureous acid gas in the process of stoving, which renders the straw perfectly white. To excite the public interest, the produce of these little factories were frequently patronised by the Lady Lieutenant; on which occasion, harps, shamrocks, and other devices, very ingeniously made of straw materials by the children were presented to her Excellency with some appropriate verses.

The manufacture of straw is introduced into "Leadbeater's Cottage Dialogues," a little work so admirably calculated to improve all the domestic habits and comforts of the Irish peasant.

Young children in this country soon acquire a surprising dexterity in this elegant manufacture, and some specimens have been produced excelling in texture that of any other. We know it has been the practice to vend such at an advanced price, as English, and we equally reprobate the deception and the perverse prejudice that renders it necessary.

ployed under the superintendance of a matron, in platting straw. The produce of their industry is disposed of in a warehouse attached to the factory; the children get their dinner and the produce of their labour as an incentive to their exertion. But the charity extends to other objects. In the ware-room is stored a quantity of wearing apparel, made up for the poor, and disposed of at reduced prices, to such as come recommended by a subscriber.—Another department receives and gives out work to poor room-keepers, unknown to the persons who send it. This procures employment for many people who could not otherwise obtain it, as the public institution is pledged for the safety, neatness, and punctual return of the work. Thus also many respectable females are enabled to maintain themselves, whose reduced circumstances require such means of support, but whose pride would prevent their publicly seeking it. In six months, 9641 yards of straw-plait, and 184 bonnets have been manufactured by the children, and 121 plain workers are now employed. The receipts of the institution for that period, were £982. 5s. 1d.; and the expenditure £524. 9s. 11d.; leaving a balance in the Treasurer's hands of £457. 15s. 2d.

THE RETREAT.

This establishment was formed in Drumcondra, in the year 1814. It affords lodging to a number of poor people of good character for a certain time. Here the poor artizans, when their usual means of support are suspended, retire for shelter. They are furnished with some means of employment for the present, and continue till better times enable them to resume their own. Here too the infirm and the aged, the orphan and the widow find shelter and relief. In effect, it is a general but temporary asylum for every species of distress. Nor is its value the less, because it is silent and unobtrusive. It is not enumerated among the public charities, and it is entirely supported by the contributions of a few private individuals; yet its benefits are very extensive. Within the last year 247 were admitted into the house, of whom 62 remain, the rest having been successively provided for in different ways. By a minute attention to cleanliness and order, this fluctuating mass of temporary residents are regular in their conduct while they remain, and do not discredit the recommendation they receive, when they leave it. The building cost £1500. and the annual expense of supporting the infirm and orphans from £150. to £200.

SCHOOLS, PLACES OF WORSHIP, AND CONGREGATIONS.

Protestant Parochial Schools.

The parochial distribution of Dublin with the respective places of worship is as follows:

On the North side of the Liffey, 5 : viz.

St. George's Parish Church, in Hardwick-place.
St. Mary's - - in Mary-street.
St. Thomas's - - in Marlborough-street.
St. Michan's - - in Church-street.
St. Paul's - - in King-street.

On the South side of the Liffey, 14: viz.

St. Andrew's - - in Andrew's-street.
St. Anne's - - in Dawson-street.
St. Audoen's - - in Audoen's arch.
St. Bridget's - - in Bride-street.
St. Catherine's - in Thomas-street.
St. James's - - in James-street.
St. John's - - in Fishamble-street.
St. Luke's - - on the Coombe.
St. Mark's - - in Mark-street.
St. Michael's - - in High-street (newly built).
St. Nicholas Within - in Nicholas-street.
St. Nicholas Without in ruins. The service is performed in the French Lutheran Chapel, St. Patrick.
St. Peter's - in Aungier-street.
St. Werburgh's - in Werburgh-street.

Besides these, are the two cathedrals and the following chapels where the Liturgy is read and the service of the established church performed.

St. Kevin's - - in Kevin's-street, (united to St. Peter's.)
St. George's. in Temple-street, (a chapel of ease).

Castle Chapel	in Castle-yard.
College Chapel	Trinity College.
Magdalene Asylum	in Leeson-street.
Bethesda	in Dorset-street.
Lying-in Hospital	in Britain-street.
Blue-coat Hospital	in Blackhall-street.
Foundling Hospital	Mt. Brown.
Sunday School	North Strand.
Marine School	Rogerson's Quay.
Molyneaux Asylum	Peter-street.
R. Hibernian School	Phœnix Park.

In each of the parishes[*] connected with the parochial church is a school for the education of a certain number of the children of poor Protestant parishioners, and they are supported, clothed, or only educated, as the circumstances of the parish admit.

We have already adverted to some of the inconveniences arising from the great disproportion that exists between the parishes of this metropolis;[†] but it may be affirmed with truth, that they do not vary more in extent than in their degrees of opulence; and, as the parishes where the poor are numerous are precisely those which possess the most scanty means of relief, while others can scarce find objects to employ their beneficence, it is obvious that the system, at present universally adopted, of each parish providing for its own poor only, is founded in absurdity itself. In no instance are the fatal effects of this unchristian principle more severely felt, than in our parochial establishments, for educating the children of poor Protestants. We have in this city parishes the most opulent, which, from their total neglect, or languid efforts, seem unconscious that poverty and ignorance have an existence. In five poor parishes, their utmost exertions are scarcely more than sufficient to supply a scanty salary to the master of a day-school, with clothing for a very limited number of children. These, unprovided with food or lodging, must of course, after school hours, mingle with the idle, the profligate, and the profane; among whom, unfortunately, we may often number their own parents. The utter inability of these neglected portions of our capital, is visible in the wretched state of their school-houses. These

[*] For an account of the extent and population of these parishes see Appendix No. II; and for a description of the most remarkable churches, see page 498, *et seq.*   [†] See page 447.

are situate in the midst of an extremely compressed population, in narrow streets, or filthy lanes, without any back-yards, and the ground-floor of course, occupied by the dirt-hole and necessary. In some of our parochial schools, that essential article the complete separation of sexes, is neglected, and in others, they have no play-ground except a church-yard, generally not exceeding a few yards in extent, and environed with lofty buildings, that interrupt a free circulation of the air, which alone could render such a situation tolerable.

The following table, which is the result of actual observation and minute inquiry, will not be uninteresting to the public. Such a simple statement of facts, will place in the strongest point of view the necessity of removing evils of such serious magnitude; and, at the same time, supply much of that preliminary knowledge, essential in forming any plan of amelioration.

THE HISTORY OF

Parish		Description
aul's	0 0 0	In King-street North. Play ground spacious. No separation of sexes, who have one common necessary, one common school-room, and sleep in adjoining dormitories, which are clean and airy.
Michan's	0 0 0	In Bow-street. Play-ground the Church-yard. No separation of sexes, who sleep in adjoining dormitories, which are clean and airy, have one common school-room, and necessaries in the same yard, 25 feet by 12.
Mary's	0 0 0	In Denmark-street. No separation of sexes, as their schools open off the same passage, and their necessaries are in the same common yard and play-ground, 39 feet by 37. Dormitories distinct, clean and airy.
Thomas's	0 0 0	In Mecklenburgh-street. No play-ground. The yard 38 feet by 14, including dirt hole and necessary. Dormitories clean and airy. The smallest establishment in the most opulent parish!
George's	0 0 0	Saint George's, though erected into a distinct parish in 1793, and very opulent, had no parochial school till 1811. The apartments for the children are in the east porch of the church over the vestry.
James's	0 0 0	The contributions of the parish were exclusively appropriated to the support o an alms-house for twenty poor widows, till 1805, when the school was opened in James-street.
atherine's	0 0 0	In Brown-street, near the Fever Hospital. Yard and play-ground spacious. Dormitories clean, large, and airy.
Luke's	0 0 30 0	In consequence of its poverty had no parochial establishment, though it contains above seven thousand souls, till 1810, when a school was openeued in New Market Liberties.
Nicholas Without	20 0 0	In New-stueet. Yard and play-ground spacious. Dormitories airy and clean, but the school room small, dark, and inconvenient. The population of this parish exceeds 12,000 souls.
Nicholas Within	0 0 15 0	In Nicholas-street. No yard : the dirt-hole and necessary on the ground-floor. Play-ground the church-yard, 50 feet by 20, and bounded by the lofty walls of the Church and Tholsel.
Audeon's	0 0 †26 t5	In Saint Audeon's arch. No yard. Dirt-hole and necessary on the ground-floor. Play ground the church-yard No separation of sexes, who have one common school-room.

THE CITY OF DUBLIN.

L SCHOOLS.	Boys.	Girls.	Day Boys.	OBSERVATIONS.
Michael's - - -	0	0	*35	In Michael's-lane, here 15 feet wide. No yard. Play-ground the church-yard and ruins of the church.
John's - - -	10	10	0	In John's-lane, here 17 feet wide. Play-ground the church-yard. No separation of sexes. Their dormitories which are clean, though small, having one common staircase, and their necessaries in the same yard, 18 feet by 12. School-room dark and gloomy; from the great elevation of the wall of the cathedral of Christ-church, only 17 feet distant.
erburgh's - -	0	16	20	Communicates with Castle-street by a narrow entry. Separate school-rooms. One common passage to the necessaries, which are in very confined situations. Dormitories very neat and clean. Play-ground the church-yard. The governors have anxiously endeavoured to procure a more airy situation for this school, in the vicinity, but without success.
Bridget's - -	20	0	10	In Michael-a-pole, a court off Great Ship-Street. Yard spacious; which with a burial-ground, forms the play-ground. Dormitories airy and clean.
Peter's - - -	25	25	0	The boys school in Charlemont-street; the girls school in Kevin's port. The establishments are of course perfectly detached, and are both excellent. No servant in the female school.
Anne's - - -				In School-house lane, off Kildare-street. The school-room and dormitories remarkably clean, airy, and spacious. No separation of sexes, there being only one common yard and play-ground, 37 feet by 18, and this incommoded by the dirt hole and boys' necessary. The present incumbent, who is possessed of zeal and energy, will no doubt remove, when possible, an evil which he feels and laments.
Andrews's - -				In Exchequer-street. The male and female schools in adjoining, but distinct houses, so that the sexes are separated. Girls yard and play-ground 46 feet by 25; boys yard flagged, 28 feet by 14; their play-ground the church-yard. The dormitories clean and airy.
Mark's - - -				In Mark-street. No play-ground. Yard only 18 feet by 16, including dirt-hole and necessary; reduced to these dimensions by building a soup-house on it. Dormitories and school-room clean and airy.
y of Saint Patrick's				School in ruins, and the salary paid to the former schoolmaster, who was superannuated and is now dead.

Expence of Ser

From the foregoing table it appears, that in the Protestant parochial schools of Dublin, 141 boys, and 218 girls, are educated, maintained, clothed, and lodged: and 144 day boys receive instruction and clothes; and 19 boys and 5 girls instruction only. It also appears that for these 359 boarders, and 163 day-children, there are no less than 20 different establishments: and that the salaries of masters, mistresses, and assistants, the wages and maintainance of servants, with the expenditure in coals, amount to the sum of £1173. 16s. 2d.

We may safely affirm, that by a different arrangement, nearly one half of the above expence might be saved, the number of children of course enlarged, the business of education at least as well executed, the objects of public humanity better selected, and, what is of still greater importance, the intercourse between the sexes totally removed: an intercourse so unfriendly to female purity and moral decency, that we are astonished how it has been so long permitted to exist.

We would propose that in the place of twenty parochial, four general schools should be established; two exclusively for males, and two for females, each to contain 120 children. That these should be built in the suburbs, in healthy airy situations, with large play-grounds; that to each should be annexed a small infirmary, with a cold-bath: that these schools should be supported in the usual manner by charity sermons, and subscriptions in the different parishes; and that each parish should be entitled to send to these schools a number in proportion to its poor Protestant population, and not to the extent of its contribution. Thus, as we conceive, all the above stated inconveniences would be at once removed; the schools would be capable of completely accommodating 480, instead of 359 children, and a considerable sum saved towards the maintainance of this increased number.

The expence of these establishments we state thus:

BOYS SCHOOL.

Master and Mistress's Salary	-	£50 0 0
Assistant - -	-	25 0 0
Two Servant maids -	-	20 0 0
Coals. 35 tons, at 33s. per.	-	5 5 0
		£152 5 0

THE CITY OF DUBLIN.

Girls School.

Master and Mistress	£50	0 0
Female Assistant	25	0 0
Servant maid	10	0 0
Coals, 35 tons at 33s. per.	57	5 0
	142	5 0

Thus the expence, as above, of the four establishments, will be   599   0   0

Expence as above of the present 20 parochial schools.   1173   16   2

Difference in favour of the former   £574   16   2

It may be thought by some, that one assistant in each school is not sufficient for 120 children; but we can assure the reader that the master of the free protestant school founded on the Coombe, by the governors of Erasmus Smith's schools, at present manages, with great ease, 160 boys, with the assistance of monitors only. One of these, who are selected from the best instructed and most orderly boys, is allowed for every ten or twelve children, and receives the small gratuity of 40s. from the foundation, which, however, in a parochial school, will be unnecessary. We can assert with great satisfaction, that this method, which may be considered as forming a kind of seminary for future school-masters, produces in these boys, without materially retarding their own advancement, an emulation and decency of manners truly pleasing. We have, however, in the above estimate, included an assistant, as the master himself must be frequently absent as providore to the school.

It is a circumstance lamented by many, that no system of industry has been introduced at any of our parochial schools; and that children are of course apprenticed from them, not only ignorant of any species of useful exertion, but averse to it from habit. The sedentary occupations of knitting, spinning, and plain work, are practised at most schools; but these, however useful, are very inadequate as the means of future subsistence. A better system is scarcely compatible with the contracted scale and resources of a parochial school, but might easily become an essential part of the larger establishments we recommend.

The principal superintendance of these establishments would of course devolve upon the parochial clergy, and other governors in rotation, who would thus find the business easy, and the returns of duty distant: at the same time, the attention would be unremitting, an essential point in the superintendance of a school: emulation would be excited among the governors; and individual zeal and energy, in some degree, pervade and invigorate the whole institution. Whereas, in the present system, should the incumbent be deficient in energy, his visits will be careless and unfrequent; too much will be entrusted to the master or mistress, and his school must infallibly suffer.

As to the first expence, the great objection to such a plan, we can only say, that a liberal government may do much; that at least two of the existing schools might, at a moderate sum, be so enlarged, as to answer the purpose; and that the rents at which the other schools would let, would greatly lighten the remaining expence.

ROMAN CATHOLIC SCHOOLS.

As these establishments form a striking feature in the toleration of the present day, we shall premise a brief sketch of the divisions of the city for which these schools were established, and give a general view of the parochial distribution of the Roman Catholic population. While the penal laws were in force, the clergy of that persuasion were obliged to administer spiritual consolation to their flock rather according to their temporary convenience than any systematic plan. No places of public worship were permitted, and the clergyman moved his altar, books, and every thing necessary for the celebration of his religious rites from house to house, among such of his flock as were enabled in this way to support an itinerant domestic chaplain; while for the poorer part some waste house or stable, in a remote and retired situation, was selected, and here the service was silently and secretly performed, unobserved by the public eye. But the spirit of toleration had already gone abroad, and an incident furnished a pretext for allowing places of public worship, while yet the statutes proscribed them. The crowds of poor people who flocked to receive the consolations of their religion were too great for the crazy edifices to contain or support them, and serious accidents, attended with the loss of sundry lives, occasioned by the falling down of these places of resort, called for the interference of a humane government.* In the year 1745, Lord Chesterfield, then viceroy of Ireland, permitted these congregations to assemble in more safe and public places. The old edifices

* Though the rigorous execution of the penal statutes subsided immediately after the reign of Queen Anne, yet they were occasionally revived, either partially or generally, as the state of politics abroad excited suspicions or apprehensions at home. One of these periods occurred in 1744, and is minutely described by Burke, in his Hibernia Dominicana, who was himself an eye-witness. The occasion of re-opening the chapels was well remembered by sundry old men in Dublin, not long since dead; and it is recorded by Burke in the following curious passage. The house alluded to was in Cook-street.

" Hac exardescente persecutione, sacro privati fuere dominicis eciam et festivis diebus Xtifideles demptis paucis qui missas audiebant in speluncis et cavernis terræ; Dublinii autem in equorum stabulis aliisve abditis locis; donec presbytero quodam Midensi cui nomen Johannes Geraldinus, sacrum in summitate domûs faciente jam minantis ruinam coram pleniore congregatione, dum data sub finem missæ benedictione surgeret populus, *illico cecidit domus* novemque laici utriusque sexus interiere, pluresque lethaliter vulnerati sunt. Exinde siquidem Prorex aliique Aulici atque Magistratus commiseratione tacti tacite innuerunt se velle potius, ut apperirentur sacella quam ut cives sic inopinate exterminarentur. Itaque sacella omnia Dubliniensia uperte fuere die 17mo Martii, S. Patricio sacrâ, atque ex eo tempore aperta manent usque ad hodiernum diem sæviente etsi domestico bello in Magna Britannia, sub exitum anni 1745, et ingressum anni 1746, idque tunc maturiori prudentia excellentissimi tunc Proregio celebris scilicet Comitis de Cestro Campo, vernacule Chesterfield, ea tempestate Dublinii residentis."

Hibernia Dominicana, p. 175, 176.

Doctor Thomas Burke was born in Dublin, in the year 1710. At the age of 13, he was sent to Rome, to prepare himself for orders, and at the early age of 15, he was invested with the habit of a Dominican; having first obtained a dispensation from the congregation of Cardinals In the year after he made his profession and became a monk at the age of 16. During his noviciate he studied Philosophy, and for five years after applied himself closely to Theology, in which he made such a progress as to attract the particular notice of Pope Benedict XIII. He was employed at this time to exert his learning and interest on a singular occasion. It appeared that ten Irish Saints of strong pretensions had been only invoked in the parishes of which they were the patrons. In 1741, Dr. Burke was engaged by the Irish Clergy to solicit the Holy See that they should be recognised through the whole island, and have particular offices for that purpose. These offices he himself composed, and by his exertions the saints were approved of by the Pope, and received all over Ireland, and in the Irish colleges abroad. About this time, he was sent on a mission to Portugal to restore the communication between that Court and the See of Rome, which had been for ten years suspended. It was the practice of the Court, that every person should retire from the presence with their face turned towards the throne. In this way he was retiring from an audience when he trod on the train of his own stole, and was immediately thrown prostrate on his back. From that time an edict issued, that all clergymen in their robes should be exempt from this ceremony. At Rome, he gradually rose to the highest theological honours, and returned to his native city in the year 1743. He continued in Ireland from that period, and was promoted by the

consecrated to public worship were re-opened, and new ones gradually built in the city. And a further toleration allowed their clergy unmolested to distribute their flocks into such parochial districts as might be convenient for their attendance. This distribution is as follows, designated from the street in which the chapel is situated.

ARRAN-QUAY, comprehends St. Paul's parish, and extends in that direction as far as the parish of Blanchard-town, including a portion of the Phœnix-Park as far as the Vice-regal lodge. On the east, it is bounded by a line along one side of Church-street, northward. Besides the parish chapel, there are in this district a friary in Church-street, and a nunnery in King-street.*

MARY's-LANE, comprehends part of St. Michan's and of St. George's parishes: it extends from the Liffey to the Tolka rivers, and is included between lines drawn from Old Church street to Glasnevin bridge, from thence down the right bank of the Tolka to Drumcondra bridge, and from thence through Arran-street to the Liffey. A new chapel is erected for this district in Arran-street. There is besides a nunnery on George's-hill.

LIFFEY-STREET, comprehends St. Mary's, St. Thomas's, and part of St.

Pope to the titular see of Ossory in the year 1759. This reward of his talents and virtues he only enjoyed seven years. He died at Kilkenny, on the 25th Sept. 1776, in the 66th year of his age, leaving behind him a high character for piety and erudition.

His works are "Promptuarium Morale," translated while at Rome from Spanish into Latin, with considerable additions, for the use of those who took orders or heard confessions.

A History of the Dominican Order in Ireland, to which he was appointed Historiographer. It was a work of seven years incessant application.

But his great work is his "Hibernia Dominicana," from which we have made the above extract. It is declared in the title page to be printed at Cologne; " Coloniæ Agrippinæ ex Typographia Metter-"nichia, sub signo Gryphi: anno 1762;" but it was actually executed by Edm. Fyn, of Kilkenny, under Dr. Burke's own inspection; and in 1772 he published a Supplement to it. This very curious and valuable work displays much learning and industry, but its principles have been disavowed by his own persuasion. In 1775, the titular Bishops met at Thurles, county of Tipperary, and published a declaration, to which seven signatures are annexed, entirely disapproving of the principles of the book, " because they weaken and subvert allegiance," "raise unnecessary scruples in the minds of people," and " give a handle to those who differ in religious opinions, to impute to us maxims that we entirely reject, as not founded in the doctrines of the Roman Catholic Church." In consequence of this disapprobation almost every person possessed of the work tore out the exceptionable passages. These castrated books, as they are called, are sufficiently common, but it is very rare indeed to meet with a perfect copy.

* This is intended for the reception of widows and unmarried ladies who wish to live retired from the world, and who pay a pension for their board and lodging.

THE CITY OF DUBLIN. 809

George's parishes. It is bounded on the west, by the east side of Arran-street, where it joins Ormond Quay, through Boot and Petticoat-lanes, Green street, Bolton-street, and Dorset-street, to Drumcondra bridge, thence down the river Tolka, by Ballybough bridge to the Liffey. It is for this extensive and populous district, the spacious metropolitical chapel is now erecting in Marlborough-street. There is also a friary in Denmark-street, a nunnery on Summer-hill, and a chapel in Hardwick-street, which belonged to a nunnery formerly in Dorset-street.

TOWNSEND STREET, comprehends St. Mark's, St. Anne's, St. Andrew's, and part of St. Peter's parish. There is a friary in Clarendon-street, and the friary of St. Patrick's in French-street.

ROSEMARY-LANE, comprehends the parishes of St. Michael, St. John, St. Bride, and St. Nicholas within, including the Castle Circuit, and Christ Church. For the congregation of this district, a spacious and handsome chapel has been erected in Lower Exchange-street, on the site of the old theatre in Smock-alley, and opened for divine service in 1815.

BRIDGE-STREET, comprehends only St. Audeon's parish. In this district is the friary of Adam and Eve, in Cook-street.

FRANCIS-STREET, includes St. Luke's, St. Nicholas without, the greater part of St. Peter's parish, Harold's Cross, and Rathmines, and extends as far as Miltown River. In this district are the nunneries of Ranelagh,* Harold's Cross, and Warren's Mount.

MEATH-STREET, comprehends St. Catherine's parish, with a rural district as far as the Canal. In this is the friary of St. John, for Augustinian friars, in Thomas-street.

JAMES-STREET, comprehends Kilmainham, Dolphin's Barn, and extends as far as the Canal. It has a nunnery in James-street.

For the Roman Catholic population of Dublin, then, there are—

Nine Chapels, viz.

Arran Quay.	Francis-street.
Mary's-lane.	Meath-street.
Townsend-street.	James-street.
Rosemary-lane.	Hardwick-street.
Bridge-street.	

* In this convent the daughters of the nobility and gentry are educated.

5 L

THE HISTORY OF

Six Friaries, viz.

Church-street (Capuchins). French-street (calced Carmelites).
Denmark-street (Dominicans). Cook-street (Franciscans).
Clarendon-street (discalced Carmelites). Mass-lane (Augustinians)

Seven Nunneries, viz.

Harold's Cross	16 Nuns.
James-street	8
Warren's Mount	14
George's Hill	11
Summer Hill	6
Ranelagh	18
King-street	6

In these officiate 70 secular clergymen belonging to the parochial establishments, and 40 regulars belonging to the different friaries.

These establishments support and paronise the following Schools.*

FEMALE SCHOOLS.

HAROLD's CROSS NUNNERY supports 100 female orphans. Attached to the nunnery is a long, spacious, and airy school-room, over which are two dormitories, each containing 50 beds. The benevolent sisterhood conduct the whole upon the most approved plan, and the children have all the symptoms of health and cheerfulness. They are instructed in all the usual branches of education, but writing was for a long time proscribed, as affording a vehicle for improper communication with the other sex. The prejudice is however removed, and this useful appendage to education is now permitted, with great benefit to the Institution. Several children who excel, are taken as clerks to people in business, and acquit themselves with great credit. A new and spacious edifice is now erecting for this school, to which is attached a chapel.

2. PARADISE-ROW, The Josephian Society patronise a school which is kept here, and conducted in a very neat and orderly manner. Twenty

---

* By the Act to restrain foreign education, passed in the 7th William III. and the Act to prevent the growth of popery, 8th Anne, Roman Catholics were prohibited from publicly teaching in schools, or even in private houses. These acts were repealed, 21st Geo. III. provided popish master took the oath of allegiance, and received no protestant child into his school; and further repealed by 33d Geo. III. by which a popish master is not obliged to take out a licence.

THE CITY OF DUBLIN. 811

female orphans are received at the age of three years, and supported and educated till they are apprenticed.

3. James-Street Convent has attached to it a school, where 18 girls are supported, clothed, and educated, and 160 educated.

4. George's Hill Convent supports 20 girls, and educates 300. This is one of the first schools permitted in Dublin, and is half a century established. The females who patronise it are called the Ladies of the Presentation.

5. Summer Hill Convent supports 14 girls, and educates 100.

6. Summer Hill Orphan House supports and educates 21 female orphans.

7. Clarke's Court is a sunday and day school for educating 90 girls.

8. Forbes-Street. Here 300 girls are educated on the Lancasterian plan, and provided with books and stationary.

9. Warren's Mount Convent supports 30 girls, and educates 200.

MALE SCHOOLS.

10. Clarendon-Street supports an evening school in which 200 boys are educated.

11. Meath-Street. One hundred and seventy boys are here daily instructed on Lancaster's plan, and provided with books and stationary. About 80 lads of a more advanced age are taught in the evening, whose avocations would not allow them to avail themselves of the instruction given in the day. The confined situation of the rooms, and the want of sufficient elevation in the cielings, are evils in these much frequented and useful schools, which ought to be remedied.

12. Skinner-Row School. This is an old establishment of the venerable Dr. Betagh. Here from 300 to 400 young men assemble after their daily labour, and are instructed on Lancaster's plan in reading, writing, and accounts. The situation of this useful school is even liable to more objection than the former; the rooms are low and narrow, and are both above and below the ground.

13. Lime-Street Presentation School educates 500 boys on Lancaster's plan, and supplies them with books and stationary.*

* The Presentation Orders for the education of the poor, commenced in Ireland in the year 1804, by an humble individual named Rice, under the auspices of Dr. Hussey, titular Bishop of Waterford. From that period, schools on the same plan, or rather branches from the original one, have extended their beneficial effects to Cork, Carrick-on-Suir, Dungarvan, Thurles, Limerick, Cappoquin, and Dublin. The

14. MARY's-LANE supports 18 boys, and educates 100.

15. DENMARK-STREET supports 24 boys, and educates 60.

16. JAMES-STREET CHAPEL clothes 20 boys, and educates 60, providing them with books and stationary.

MALE AND FEMALE SCHOOLS.

17. LIFFEY-STREET CHAPEL supports 30 girls, and educates 150; clothes 20 boys, and educates 100.

18. FRANCIS-STREET educates 150 girls and 150 boys. A certain number of both sexes are supported or clothed, as the fluctuating circumstances of the charity admit.

19. ST. JOHN's and ST. MICHAEL's SCHOOLS support 18 boys and 10 girls, and educates 40 boys.

20. TERESIAN SOCIETY supports 25 boys and 25 girls.

21. TOWNSEND-STREET supports 20 boys and 22 girls.

22. JOSEPHIAN SOCIETY supports 40 boys and 40 girls.

23. BRIDGE-STREET CHAPEL clothes, educates, and breakfasts 36 girls, and occasionally selects 10 of the most indigent, which are entirely supported. It also clothes and educates 36 boys.

24. ST. JOHN-STREET CHAPEL clothes and educates 23 boys and 20 girls.

25. MEATH-STREET CHAPEL educates 115 boys and 97 girls, of whom 70 boys and 30 girls receive clothes, and 20 of both sexes breakfast.

26. MEATH-STREET SUNDAY SCHOOL educates 80 boys and 100 girls.

27. FIRST TRINITARIAN DUBLIN SOCIETY supports 42 boys and 42 girls.

28. PATRICIAN SOCIETY supports 45 boys and 45 girls.

29. SECOND TRINITARIAN DUBLIN SOCIETY supports 48 boys and 48 girls. Their school is kept at Saggard.

30. ARRAN QUAY educates 45 boys and 40 girls, and clothes half that number.

gentlemen of the order after a probation of two years, make vows of poverty, chastity, and obedience. But their principal vow is the gratuitous instruction of youth, to which they devote their whole time and attention. In the school of Lime-street are six brothers, who live in seclusion and community. Some of them are very young, and all of them gentlemen in independent circumstances. They voluntarily left the world, without entering into holy orders, at a time when others begin to enjoy it, and feel more pleasure in the society of the poor children they instruct, than in any other source of social enjoyment. They wear a long close garment of black stuff, and are the only order in Dublin distinguished by a particular costume.

THE CITY OF DUBLIN. 813

31. CHURCH-STREET educates 45 boys and 45 girls, of whom 40 are clothed.

32. GENERAL ASYLUM. This was instituted in 1813, for the children of soldiers and sailors who had died fighting in the service of their country. As the great majority of those who enter the army and navy from this country are Roman Catholics, to provide a school exclusively for their children, which would not militate against their religious impressions, and to hold out a prospect of support and education for their orphans in the faith in which they had been brought up, was no less an act of justice in the community, than a strong incentive to themselves. This interesting school, therefore, seems to have met with such liberal support, that it maintains, clothes, and educates 150 boys and 150 girls.

These Schools are entirely supported by donations, subscriptions, and annual charity sermons. The children, who are maintained as well as educated, cost on an average from £7. to £8. each per annum: and the aggregate amount of the expenditure of all the schools is annually about £6000.

DISSENTING SCHOOLS AND CONGREGATIONS.

THE different denominations of Protestants who dissent from the established church[*] form a numerous and respectable body. They are distributed into twenty-four congregations as follow :

PRESBYTERIANS.[†]

It is not clearly known whether the Presbyterian congregations of Dublin existed as a body separated from the communion of the established church

[*] It is our intention to present a sketch of the origin and progress of these sects in Ireland, as forming a portion of the community of the metropolis, and as connected with their public schools ; but for the history of their original formation, and the tenets which distinguish them, we refer to Mosheim's Ecclesiastical History, Bogue and Bennet's History of Dissenters, &c. and for a more succinct account to Evan's Sketch and Buck's Dictionary, to which latter we have been ourselves referred by different sects, as containing the most concise and candid statement of their history and opinions.

[†] The Presbyterians, who are considered as the most numerous body of Protestants in Ireland, are chiefly settled in Ulster, and are but thinly scattered in the southern and western parts of this kingdom. They are descended, principally, from the Scotch Presbyterians, who were encouraged by King James I.

114   THE HISTORY OF

before the reign of Charles II. though many families of English Puritans and Scotch Presbyterians had settled in Dublin during the reigns of Eliza-

to settle in Ulster; partly from families of English Dissenters, who from time to time emigrated to this country; and partly from the French Protestants, who took refuge in Ireland after the revocation of the Edict of Nantz. To these have been added at various times, many families of Episcopalians, who left the communion of the established church, preferring the more simple form of Presbyterian worship.

The plantation of Ulster by Scotch Presbyterians was considered by King James I. as a work of great importance to the prosperity of the British empire. Before their settlement, the province of Ulster was the most uncultivated and unproductive district in Ireland, and its inhabitants the most turbulent and least industrious. It is now the most improved part of the kingdom in every respect.

In the prosecution of his scheme, King James gave the greatest encouragement to the settlement of Presbyterian churches in the northern counties; and granted for the support of their ministers, the tithes of the parishes in which their congregations were assembled. The Protestant bishops also, received them with the greatest cordiality, united with them in communion, and as Presbyters joined in their ordinations. The tithes which had been granted for their support, were some years afterwards resumed by the English government, and, in lieu of them, an endowment of 100*l.* per annum to each pastor was conferred on the Presbyterian ministers. This seems to have been the first origin of what is now callled " Regium Donum," which is the annual stipend provided for Presbyterian ministers in this kingdom, partly by an Act of the Irish Parliament, and partly by various grants from the Crown.

The Presbyterians of Ireland are divided into two Synods or General Assemblies, which have always been connected by a friendly intercourse, and community of interest. Their ecclesiastical discipline is modelled after the church of Scotland. They hold annual meetings, in which each congregation is represented by its pastor and a lay elder. The first is the Synod of Ulster, which consists of nearly 200 congregations. The second, called the Synod of Munster, or southern association, consisted formerly of 52 congregations, many of which have become extinct.

In the Presbyterian body, a considerable diversity of sentiment prevails with respect to theological opinions; without however disturbing the brotherly connection of the body at large. Many of their congregations are considered as Calvinists, and many as Unitarians, though not in the Socinian sense of that term. Of the latter description there may be some individuals, but no congregation in this kingdom.

The presend stipend allowed by government for the support of the Presbyterian ministers, arises from the following grants:

Some years after the restoration of King Charles II. a sum of 600*l.* per annum was, by the King's order, distributed among them, as an acknowledgement for their attachment to the royal cause, and as a partial compensation for the endowment of which they had been deprived during the civil wars. King William afterwards granted 1200*l.* a year for the same purpose; which grant was confirmed by Queen Anne. To this King George I. added 800*l.* per annum, in the year 1719. These grants have been further increased by his present Majesty, who added to them 1000*l.* per annum in the year 1783. In the year 1792, this sum was further augmented by an Act of the Irish Parliament; who voted the sum of 5000*l.* to be equally distributed among the Presbyterian ministers of Ireland. In the year 1803, this endowment was augmented; and an arrangement was formed, by which the ministers of each synod were divided into three classes, according to the population of their respective congregations.

beth, James I. and Charles I. The present churches of Presbyterians in Dublin were formed in the year 1662; when on the passing of the Act of Uniformity, a number of Protestant clergymen in this city, among whom were the Provost* and several of the Fellows of Trinity College, refusing, from conscientious motives, to subscribe to the 39 Articles, and to conform to the established church, resigned their benefices, and their situations in the university. As they were men of distinguished piety, learning, and eloquence, and were considered as suffering for conscience sake, the members of the parochial churches where they had officiated (among whom were many noble and opulent families), adhered to them after their resignation; and being united with the Presbyterians, formed several numerous congregations.

1. Wood-street, now Strand-street.
2. Cook-street.
3. New-row, now Eustace-street.
4. Plunket-street.
5. Capel-street.
6. Usher's Quay.
7. Mary's Abbey, formed at a later period.

Of these, Strand-street, Eustace-street, Cook-street, Plunket-street, and

> The Ministers of the First Class receive 100*l.* per annum, each.
> Second Class   75*l.*
> Third (in Ulster)   50*l.*
> Third (in Munster) 58*l.*

It has been erroneously reported, that the endowments of the Presbyterian ministers are a novel institution in this kingdom; whereas, on the contrary, they have existed upwards of two centuries, though exposed to considerable fluctuations, in the civil commotions that have intervened during that period. At the present day, the stipend allowed them by government, though liberal, falls far short of what their predecessors enjoyed 150 years ago: each of them receiving, at that time, a stipend from government of 100*l* per annum, which was equal to at least 300*l.* of our present currency. The regium donum, in whatever form it has existed, was originally intended as an encouragement to the settlement of a very valuable branch of the reformed church in this kingdom. To the sober, religious, and industrious habits of the congregations connected with this church, the civilization, cultivation, commerce, manufactures, and general prosperity of Ireland are mainly indebted. This endowment has been revived, continued, and augmented, by the British government, as an acknowledgement of these facts, and with a view to sustain the original purpose of the institution. It imposes no kind of shackle or restriction on the civil or religious liberty of the Presbyterians; nor has it ever produced, on the part of government, the least interference with their ecclesiastical discipline.

* Their names were,—Samuel Winter, Provost; Edward Veale, F. T. C. D.; Samuel Mather, F. T. C. D.; Robert Norbury, F. T. C. D. See Nonconformists' Memorial.

THE HISTORY OF

Mary's Abbey, have been in connexion with the Synod of Munster, and are considered Unitarians of the Arian persuasion; Capel-street and Usher's Quay belong to the Synod of Ulster, and are of the Westminster Confession.

Several of the pastors of these churches have attained to considerable eminence as theological writers. Charnock, Rule, Williams, Emlyn, Mather, Boyce, Duchal, and the late Dr. Moody, have been distinguished either by their controversial publications, or their sermons on miscellaneous subjects. Abernathy, by his Discourses on the Attributes; and Leland,[*] by his able Vindication of Christianity against Deism.

There are at present only four Presbyterian churches in Dublin:

1. Strand-street, (formerly Wood-street) into which the congregations of Cook-street and Mary's Abbey have merged. The present ministers are the Rev. James Armstrong, M. A. and the Rev. Wm. H. Drummond, D. D.[†] The number of its members is 560.

There is a charity school attached to it, consisting of 28 boys, who are lodged, dieted, clothed, educated, and when qualified apprenticed to useful trades. This school is principally supported by the collection at an annual charity sermon, which is preached on the last Sunday in February. The amount of the collection is at an average £420. annually. There is also a small permanent fund of £30. per annum, for the support of this school. On the poor list of Strand-street congregation there are 26 widows of different religious denominations, who receive each a weekly stipend from the Sunday's collection. To this church there is attached a congregational library; and a permanent fund for the pastors' widows, amounting to £100. per annum.

2. Eustace-street (formerly New Row). The present ministers are the Rev. Philip Taylor, and the Rev. Joseph Hutton. The number of its members is 200. Its charity school consists of 20 boys, for whose support there are considerable permanent funds. The annual charity sermon for this school is preached on the fourth Sunday in November. The amount of the collection is at an average, £160. Attached to this congregation is an alms-house, noticed under its proper head before. There is also a perma-

[*] This gentleman is not to be confounded with Dr. Leland, author of the History of Ireland, &c. He was a clergyman of the established church, and a fellow of Trinity College, Dublin.

[†] Dr. Drummond has distinguished himself in the walks of Literature by an admired poem on the Giant's Causeway, a spirited Translation of Lucretius, and other poetical productions.

ment fund for a female charity school, which is at present suffered to accumulate.'

3. Capel-street (now called Mary's Abbey). The present ministers are the Rev. Benjamin M'Dowel, the Rev. James Horner, and the Rev. James Carlisle. The number of its members is 2000. Its charity school consists of 20 boys, and 10 girls. The annual charity sermon is preached on the first Sunday in March. The average amount of the collection is £480. There is no permanent fund for the support of this school.

4. Usher's Quay, into which the Presbyterian congregation of Plunket-street merged. The present ministers are the Rev. Hugh Moore, and the Rev. Samuel Simpson. The number of its members is 200. Their charity school consists of 20 girls, and also of 20 boys. The latter are only clothed and educated. The permanent funds for the support of these schools amount to little. The annual charity sermon is preached on the third Sunday in January. The average amount of the collection is £150.

SECEDERS.

This sect established their first congregation in Skinner's-alley in Dublin, in the year 1765.* There are at present two congregations in Dublin, which comprise 140 individuals.

Burghers, who assemble at the meeting-house in Mass-lane,† and compose

* About the year 1746, the Rev. Messrs. Black, Clarke, Main, Hume, Arnot, and Reid, passed over from Scotland, and formed the first congregations in the North of Ireland, from which time they have gradually and, comparatively speaking, greatly multiplied. There are at present 98 congregations, including the two in Dublin, whose pastors enjoy the regium donum, and 12 whose pastors do not. They have no congregations in Munster. There were formerly two in Connaught, one near Castlebar, the other near Killala. The first was under the protection of the celebrated G. Rob. Fitzgerald, who by a strange inconsistency wished to encourage bodies of men of peaceable and industrious habits in a country which he continually disturbed by his lawless outrages. After his death, they were compelled to fly from the local jealousy of the peasantry, who set upon them in their retreat, and despoiled their property. They are all Calvinists in doctrine, and Presbyterians in discipline. The whole Presbyterian body in Ireland is divided, popularly speaking, into the old light and the new. The first are Trinitarians, the second Unitarians. The Seceders professs to be rigidly of the old light principles.

* This lane was so called from one of the chapels of the Dominican Friary, suppressed by Henry, and presented to the Society of the King's Inns, which stood there. This was converted into the chapel of the Society, till James II. restored it to its ancient use, and attended mass there himself. On the

the smaller congregation. Their meeting-house standing in the way of the projected new street leading from Richmond-bridge, is about to be taken down, and a new one erected, more convenient and on a more eligible site. Their present minister is the Rev. Mr. Hutchinson.

ANTI-BURGHERS, assembled originally in Back-lane, but have now removed to a new Meeting-house in Mary's-Abbey, erected at the expence of an individual of their body on the site of the old bank. Their present minister is the Rev. Mr. Stewart.

These congregations support no schools or other charitable institutions. They are under the direction of the Associate Synods of Ulster,* and their ministers receive the regium donum of the higher class. They adhere to the Westminster Confession, avow the doctrinal articles of the Church of England, and the larger and shorter chatechisms of the Church of Scotland. Their ministers were heretofore educated in Scotland, but the Synods have now agreed to receive the certificates of the Academy of Belfast, as equivalent to a degree in an University, on which young candidates are sent to the respective congregations, to be approved of, and then ordained by the Presbytery.

As there is no difference in doctrine, and little in discipline between these congregations, a junction has been resolved on between the Burghers† and Anti-Burghers, and delegates have been appointed on both sides to digest the articles of an union similar to that which has taken place in North America. It is supposed also when this is effected here, that a junction will be formed with the general Synod of Presbyterians. A principal point of difference with the Kirk of Scotland, and an occasion of secession, was

Revolution, William presented it to the French Hugonots, with the consent of the Society. It finally became the property of the Burgher Seceders, having passed through a variety of religious revolutions.

* The Associate Synod of Burghers in Ireland have no particular connection with that of Scotland. That of the Anti-Burghers have. This will cease when an union takes place between the sects.

† As the reason of these appellations is but little known, at least in this country, we give it here. At the meeting of the Ascociate Synod of Perth and Stirling, in 1745, their attention was called to the following clause in the Burgess oath: " I profess and allow in my heart the true religion professed in this realm, and authorised by the law thereof," which it was contended Seceders could not lawfully swear. The minority, who held it might be lawful, were called Burghers, and separated on this consideration from the majority, who denied it, and were called Anti-Burghers. The former were deemed the schismatics on the occasion, though it was the latter who removed a step farther from the established Kirk. Where no such oath is taken, no such cause of separation exists. (See Narative and Testimony.)

THE CITY OF DUBLIN. 819

the patronage* exercised by individuals in the appointment of ministers. As this has never been exerted in Ireland, where every Presbyterian congregation freely elects its own pastor, this primary cause of secession does not exist, and it is to be hoped that the whole Presbyterian body will be united in this country.

INDEPENDENTS.†

WHEN the Presbyterian congregation established itself at Usher's Quay, the vacant meeting-house in Plunket-street was occupied by a congregation of Independents in 1774, which seems to have been the first regular congregation formed in Dublin: their pastor was the Rev. Mr. Hawksworth. He

* This made the principal charge of Ebenezer Erskine, the founder of the Seceders, in his sermon, preached before the Synod of Perth and Stirling, in 1732; and in the Narrative and Testimony, agreed on and published by the general associate Synod in 1804, the violent exercise of this patronage, forms a prominent feature of their complaint, and "the right of Christian people to choose their own pastor, "a special cause of secession." , (See Narrative, Part III. p. 46.)

† The Independent structure of the churches of the sect in this country who call themselves Independents, seems to have prevented that union and connection necessary for any regular detail of their history. Little is known even to themselves of their origin and progress in Ireland, and that little is very imperfect and contradictory. Some with whom we have conversed, deduce their origin from the Puritans who followed Cromwell to this country. But Mr. Whitfield seems to have been the first to introduce the doctrines at present recognised by the sect, and by his connection their pastors were supplied, and their discipline regulated. His first visit to Ireland was compulsory. In the year 1738, he embarked at Charles-town, to return to England, but after a perilous voyage he was driven into the Shannon, from whence he proceeded through Limerick to Dublin, and was kindly received by Archbishop Bolton, Bishop Rundel, and Dr. Delany. In 1741, the schism took place between the Arminian and the Calvinist Methodists; those of the latter opinion followed Mr. Whitfield, who a few years after became one of Lady Huntingdon's preachers. In 1751 he again visited Ireland, and proceeded from Dublin to Athlone, Limerick and Cork, where his doctrines, he says, were well received, while those of the Methodists met with violent persecution. In 1757 he came to Dublin, for the last time, and preached in Oxmantown Green. Here he was violently attacked by the Ormond and Liberty boys, while he was praying for the success of the King of Prussia's arms. He endeavoured to retreat into the barracks, but was not permitted to enter: he was bathed in blood from the wounds he received, and narrowly escaped the death of St. Stephen, which at the time he wished for. (See Seymour's Life of Whitfield, p. 164.) He was succeeded by some preachers of Lady Huntingdon's connection, who supplied the different meetings established in Dublin and other towns. There are now in Ireland twenty-five congregations, comprising about six thousand individuals; the most numerous are those established in Dublin, Cork, Belfast, Armagh, Sligo, and Youghal.

was sent from Lady Huntingdon's connection in England, which for many years supplied preachers to this meeting-house. Their first permanent pastor was the Rev. Mr. Cooper. They are about to establish a college in Dublin for the education of ministers to supply their congregations in this country.* In discipline they are independents in the strictest sense of the word; they acknowledge no person by whose name they are distinguished; they hold that every congregation has in itself what is necessary for its own government, and that their clergy owe no subordination to or dependancy on any other assemblies. In doctrine, they are rigid Calvinists, and are generally denominated Calvinistic Methodists. There are three congregations in Dublin.

Plunket-street contains the largest; their present pastor is the Rev. Mr. Cooper. In practice they differ from Independents in general by celebrating the Lord's Supper every week. The number of the congregation is 1000, of whom they reckon 250 communicants. They support an almshouse for widows, mentioned before, and a Sunday-school. The school was originally in Malpas-street. A new school-house has been recently built in the yard of the meeting-house, and 130 children of both sexes and all religious denominations receive weekly instruction.

York-street contains 500, of whom 40 are communicants. Their meeting-house is a new and spacious edifice, erected in the year 1808, capable of containing a much greater number. Their present pastor is the Rev. Mr. Stratton.

Pool Baggot-street contains 200, of whom 25 are communicants. They use as a meeting-house, the temporary accommodation of the Dutch church, and are rather a secession than a regular congregation. Their present pastor is the Rev. John Davies.

METHODISTS.

Mr. WILLIAMS, a preacher of the Methodist Society, was the first person who introduced them into Dublin. About the year 1746 he passed over to Ireland, and began to preach in Dublin, where multitudes flocked to hear him, and much disturbance ensued. He soon however formed a small

---

*. The Irish Evangelical Society has established a seminary, which was supposed to appertain to this sect. It is situated in Manor-street, and receives eight students, who are educated for the ministry.

society, and wrote an account of his success to Mr. Wesley,* who determined to visit Ireland immediately himself. He accordingly landed in

* Shortly after the arrival of Mr. J. Wesley he was followed by his brother Charles, who proceeded from Dublin to Cork, Athlone, and Bandon. He was in general well received, except at Cork, where a riotous mob, headed by a ballad singer of the name of Butler, persecuted him and his friends in such a way that they were obliged, for their own personal safety, to lodge examinations against them. About twenty-eight depositions of this kind were laid before the Grand Jury at the August assizes in 1749, who, instead of finding bills of indictment against the rioters, presented Charles Wesley, and nine of his friends, as " persons of ill-fame, vagabonds, common disturbers of his Majesty's peace, and prayed that they might be transported." This extraordinary display of prejudice and injustice so inflamed the mob that they paraded the streets with impunity, offering 5l. for a swaddler's head, a name this sect was first known by in Ireland. The Judge who presided at the ensuing assizes, however, repaid the injustice of this memorable Grand Jury. When he inquired who were the persons presented, and Mr. Wesley and his friends, who attended in court, were pointed out to him, he was astonished at the proceeding. He immediately dismissed them, expressing an apology for the improper treatment they had received, and a hope that the police would be better attended to in future. Since that period, the progress of methodism has been uniform in Ireland, interrupted by occasional disturbances, which the novelty of field preaching excited no less in this country than in England. At the conference held previous to the death of Mr. J. Wesley, which happened on the 21st March, 1791, the connection in Ireland comprehended 29 circuits, 67 preachers, and 14,106 members. In 1802, the number of Meeting-houses erected in different counties in Ireland was as follows : (See Myles' Chronology.)

Antrim	6	Dublin	5	Limerick	1	Sligo	2
Armagh	11	Fermanagh	8	Londonderry	4	Tipperary	6
Cavan	7	Galway	3	Longford	5	Tyrone	7
Clare	1	Kerry	1	Louth	4	Waterford	2
Cork	13	Kildare	1	Mayo	2	Westmeath	5
Carlow	4	Kilkenny	5	Monaghan	5	Wexford	3
Donnegal	3	Kings Co.	5	Queen's Co.	7	Wicklow	2
Down	5	Leitrim	1	Roscommon	2		

122

At the conference held in 1805, a remarkable addition was made to the preachers' establishment. Eight missionaries who spoke the Irish language with fluency, were chosen and sent to traverse the entire of the country. These missionaries had each a large circuit assigned to them, in the wildest parts, where no chapel or preacher's dwelling was yet established, and they continued sometimes for two years in these places. Finding that the Roman Catholic peasantry did not attend their meetings, they followed them into fairs and markets, and wherever a number of them was collected together for any purpose of business or amusement. Here they addressed them on horseback ; and to avoid the impropriety of wearing a hat, and at the same time to protect their heads from cold or violence, they assumed black leather caps, a costume by which they are particularly marked and distinguished. The labours of these equestrian missionaries are said not to have been in vain ; it is asserted in a printed statement that 800 converts have been made in this way from the Roman Catholic persuasion. In the year 1814, the numbers in Ireland were 29,388. The return for the present year is not so much. Subjoined is the

Dublin on the 9th of August, 1747: It happened to be on a Sunday morning, at ten o'clock, when the bells of the several churches were ringing for actual state of the Methodist connection in this country, as returned at the last conference held in Dublin in July, 1816. Ireland is divided into 10 districts, 48 circuits, and 14 missions, eight in which congregations are established, and six where they are not; these are attended by 112 itinerant, and 21 missionary preachers, who hold an annual conference in Dublin, to regulate the concerns of this extended establishment.

District.	Circuit.	No. of Preachers.	No. in Society.	District.	Circuit.	No. of Preachers.	No. in Society.
Dublin	Dublin	7	1420	Clones	Clones	3	1000
	Longford	4	230		Killessandra	2	600
	Drogheda	2	295		Cavan	2	880
	Oldcastle	2	392		Monaghan	4	560
	Wicklow	4	372	Enniskillen	Enniskillen	4	1350
Waterford	Waterford	2	252		Manorhamilton	2	540
	Carlow	2	290		Ballyshannon	2	850
	Newtown Bany	2	500		Ballynamallard	3	1763
					Brookborough	3	1012
Cork	Cork City	3	538	Derry	Londonderry	2	340
	Bandon	2	472		Strabane	2	680
	Skibbereen	1	205		Newtown Steward	2	800
	Mallow	1	150		Stranorlan	1	580
Limerick	Limerick	2	502	Belfast	Belfast	3	703
	Milltown	1	180		Carrickfergus	2	440
	Rosscrea	2	305		Coleraine	2	617
	Cloughjordan	2	301		Lisburn	2	700
	Mountrath	3	450		Downpatrick	3	510
Athlone	Athlone	3	340	Newry	Newry	3	450
	Aughrim	1	160		Dungannon	1	708
	Castlebar	2	206		Cookstown	2	758
	Ballina	1	225		Charlemont	1	680
	Sligo	2	400		Armagh	2	452
	Boyle	2	430		Lurgan	3	1054
					Tanderagee	2	896

MISSIONS.

Wicklow		1	40	Letterkenny		1	—
Youghal		1	—	Derry and Antrim		5	300
Cove		1	55	Cookstown		1	—
Clare		1	106	Castleblany		3	273
Aughrim		1	—	Belfast		1	—
Boylagh		1	232	Newry		2	25
Killesandra		1	—				
Donnegal		1	40			133	28,542

prayers.' This circumstance he, as usual, hailed as an omen for good, and immediately proceeded to church. At three o'clock of the same day he

The members of these societies strictly adhere to the methodical rules laid down by their founder. The noviciate is put into a suitable class, consisting of a class-teacher, and about ten, fifteen, or twenty members, who meet once a week for prayer, praise, and confessing their faults to each other. He then may or may not meet in *band*, which consists of two, three, or more, who have no leader, but pray in turn, and search out and confess their mutual spiritual faults. Every member on admission receives a ticket containing a scripture text, which admits him into society meetings. This is renewed every quarter, when his attendance in class and the state of his mind is particularly noticed. These tickets are supposed to resemble the επιστολαι συστατικαι, or commendatory letters, mentioned by the Apostle. This ticket admits him to the Αγαπαι, or LOVE-FEASTS, so called from the resemblance they are supposed to bear to those of the early christians. A basket of thin sweet cake is handed about with vessels of water, which are occasionally declared to be *no* substitute for the Eucharist. The *watch-night* lasts from seven to eleven o'clock, and consists in prayers, hymns, and exhortations, by several local preachers in succession; besides these, there are select meetings, in which prayers are offered for particular purposes,— the revival of christianity, the success of missionaries, and sundry others. The effects of this systematic regularity are remarkable wherever methodism has extended in this country; an exterior of decorum and good order, and habits of sobriety and industry have been introduced where they did not before exist, an improvement in the social and domestic comforts of the poor, which we think more than compensates for the enthusiasm and extravagance with which, in Ireland, it is more rarely accompanied.

In compliance also with the injunctions of their founder, they adhered to the church to which they originally belonged, either Presbyterian or Episcopalian, in the administration of the sacraments of baptism and the Lord's supper. The question, however, has been recently agitated, and much controversy has ensued. The Methodists of Dublin, Cork, Waterford, and other places, contended for " the " good old way ;" and strong remonstrances were published on the subject. Application had been even made to his Majesty's Attorney-General in this country for his opinion, and the interference of the civil law sought for against any innovation. The opposite party however have prevailed. The last conference has decided that the administration of the sacraments by their own preachers, and in their own chapels, is permitted in certain circuits, with the consent of two-thirds of the stewards of such circuits. Thus the innovation is made. The slender bond that united them to the established church is broken in this country as well as in England, and, contrary to the strong representations of their founder, the society now stands alone a distinct and separate body. " Finding themselves" as Dr. Priestley remarks upon another occasion, " by degrees at the head of a large body of people and in considerable power and influence, they must *not have been men* if they had not felt the love of power gratified in such a situation, and they must have been *more than men* if their subsequent conduct had not been influenced by it." Though the discipline of their founder has thus changed, his doctrine remains unaltered; they universally profess pure Arminianism.

After the death of Wesley, and his successor Coke, the care of the societies devolved upon Doctor Adam Clarke, a native of Ireland, who is their present superintendant, and was president at the late Irish conference. The piety, industry, and learning of this gentleman are not inferior to those of his predecessors. He was born in 1761. His father was a schoolmaster, and cultivated a small farm on the banks of the Morgala near Lough Neagh. From him, his son acquired the rudiments

preached by permission of the curate in St. Mary's church, and found, as he says himself, "as gay and senseless a congregation as he ever witnessed." On the next day he waited on the Archbishop, and during a conference of three hours, answered abundance of objections urged against him. From this time he continued preaching morning and evening in the meeting-house in Marlborough-street, to crowded congregations of all descriptions, including ministers of all denominations, who filled not only the house but the yard. He now examined the state of the society, which consisted of 280 actual members, and having explained at large his rules, and impressed on them the necessity of observing them, he returned to England, leaving his flock in the care of Messrs. Williams and Trembath. Soon after his departure a mob attacked his meeting-house, assaulted and rudely treated the preacher, and having torn down the pulpit and benches, burned them in the street. Notwithstanding, the society continued to increase in Dublin, and the progress of methodism was more rapid than in London in the same period.* After several visits to Dublin, from whence he extended his

of Greek and Latin, which he himself improved with laborious assiduity, and added to it an extraordinary zeal in the acquisition of Eastern literature. His knowledge of the Oriental as well as the European languages is said to be very extensive, and procured for him an honorary degree of LL.D. from the University of Cambridge. He was the founder of the Strangers' Friend Society in Dublin, and the Philological Society of Manchester, and is the author of the following works :—Translation of Sturm's Reflections,— Memoirs of Mrs. Mary Cooper.—Succession of Sacred Literature,—On the Eucharist,—A Pamphlet on the abuse of Tobacco, Tea, Coffee, and Spirituous Liquors,—An Edition of Baxter's Christian Directory,—of Henry's History of the Ancient Israelites,—of Harmer's Eastern Customs,—of Butterworth's Concordance,—with Letters and Sermons on different subjects. But his great work is his erudite Commentary on the Bible, which contains proofs and illustrations from the originals, the versions, the various readings and commentators, and evince him a biblical labourer of no mean skill and perseverance. From the sale of the edition, consisting of 10,000 copies, he has been enabled to extend his valuable collection of Oriental literature, and support in independence a wife and twelve children.

* In the year 1762, Mr. Wesley bears the following testimony of its progress, that it was far greater than in London, in proportion to the time and number of people; and that it was more pure. "In all " this time" said he " there were none of them headstrong or unadvisable, none who dreamed of being " immortal, or infallibly incapable of temptation, no whimsical or enthusiastic person, all were calm " and sober-minded."—*Coke's Life of Wesley*, p. 390.

This eulogy is the more remarkable as it applied to a people much accused of superstition and fanaticism on religious subjects, and at a time when " dreams, visions, and revelations, were more honoured " than the written word," by some of the Methodists in London.—See Wesley's Controversy with Bell and Owen, and his singular charges against them.—*Ib*. p. 335, et seq.

mission to other parts of Ireland, he held a conference of the several preachers of the societies then established in this country: between forty and fifty attended, of whose character he speaks in high terms of seeming surprise that such could be found in Ireland! He then took a solemn farewell of these his sons in the Gospel, and left Ireland in July, 1790, never to return.

The methodists of Dublin amount to 1420 individuals, who form four congregations in the following places of worship:

WHITEFRIAR-STREET—built in the year 1756. This is the most frequented place of worship, the assembly generally consisting of 1000 persons.

WESLEY CHAPEL, Mountjoy-square.—This edifice was erected in the year 1800. It is fronted with mountain granite, and ornamented with an Ionic pediment; and when the nakedness of its exterior is relieved by some plantation in the area in which it is placed, and the mean wall and wooden gates, which at present deform its front, are removed, and their places supplied by iron gates and railing, it will form a very ornamental termination to Upper Rutland-street * The original plan includes dwelling houses on each side of the chapel within the yard. The interior is calculated to contain 1000 persons, and accommodated the whole congregation of St. George's parish while their church was building. It is fitted up with great elegance without pews, which, in conformity to Wesley's request, are not permitted in the preaching houses in Ireland. The congregation which use this chapel formerly assembled in Marlborough-street: they amount to about 200.

HENDRICK-STREET, formerly called Gravel-walk, was built in the year 1771. It is calculated to contain 250. It is situated near the Royal Barrack, with a view to accommodate such of the garrison as may belong to the methodist connection. The permanent congregation amounts to about 100.

CORK-STREET CHAPEL in the Liberties was built in 1815. It may con-

* The Commissioners of Wide Streets, wished that this chapel should be built to front the extremity of a new street just commenced, and which was to be called Wesley-street; but this the Guardians could not comply with from the situation of their ground, and the chapel was erected on one side of the range of the intended street. But it was deemed too ornamental to be lost; and since the chapel could not be brought to the street, the street was brought to the chapel: the direction of it was changed, after the corner houses were built, which accounts for the awkward deviation in the direction of Upper and Lower Rutland-street, across Summer-hill.

tain about 200 people. The congregation which use it amounts to 100, and assembled for several years in a private house.

To these may be added twelve places of worship in the vicinity of Dublin, which are attended by local preachers appointed by the Strangers' Friend Society, who are persons in trade, and devote their leisure hours to this purpose. The members of this society also are, from their qualifications, to administer spiritual as well as temporal comfort to the distressed. They are divided into three classes, either to preach, exhort, or pray extempore, according to their several abilities, and they are appointed for the sabbath morning to minister in the several hospitals, jails, convict ships, schools, or villages as opportunities may present. The methodist ministry of Dublin then consists of five regular preachers and two supernumeraries, attached to the chapels, besides thirteen local preachers of the Strangers' Friend Society, and twenty-two others, who preach, exhort, or pray, as they are capable, and occasionally appointed.

The Society in Dublin supports the following schools.

Walker's Orphan House.—This school was founded by Mr. Solomon Walker, a gentleman long known in the Liberties for his active benevolence. At his death he bequeathed the sum of £100. per annum, arising from £2000. vested in government stock, to support a school for destitute female children of the methodist society; and £150. in money to purchase beds and other furniture necessary to establish it. To this fund were added subscriptions, and the occasional aid of a charity sermon, and by these means the governors have increased their children to twelve, who are maintained, clothed, and educated. The school is in Whitefriar-street.

Whitefriar-street Day School for Boys, educates forty, and clothes and apprentices a certain number.

Whitefriar-street Day School for Girls, educates twenty-four, and clothes and apprentices a certain number.

Hendrick-street Sunday School, principally intended for soldiers' children connected with the meeting-house, one hundred boys, one hundred girls.

Cork-street Sunday School, one hundred boys, one hundred girls.

A new School House is now building in Baggot-street, which will accommodate five hundred children.

THE CITY OF DUBLIN.

KILHAMITES.*

OF this sect of methodist seceders there are twenty individuals in Dublin. They hold their meetings in Taylors' Hall in Back-lane, and have long separated from the Church of England by having the sacraments of Baptism and the Lord's Supper celebrated by their own preachers. They support no school or other separate charity.

MORAVIANS.

IN the year 1745, Mr. Benjamin Latrobe, a student of divinity, formed a religious society in Dublin, of persons of various sects and opinions. He was a young man of considerable talents as a public speaker, and was at that time in connection with the Baptist society. He afterwards adopted Moravian tenets, and having heard that the Rev. Mr Cennick, who had left the methodists, and joined the brethren, was preaching with great acceptance in England, he invited him to this country. Mr. Cennick in consequence came to Dublin in June 1746, and on the 15th of that month, preached his first sermon in the Baptist Meeting-house in Swift's-alley.* The hearers

* This sect originated in 1797. Even then objections had been made to the establishment of an hierarchy among the methodists, and certain of their body seceded to establish a church government on popular principles, and unite the ministers and people in every part of it. They assumed the appellation of *New Methodists*, but are generally known by the name of Kilhamites, from *Alexander Kilham*, a preacher who first protested against the abuses of original methodism, and was silenced by the conference assembled in 1796. They hold the same doctrine and nearly the same discipline as the old methodists, but they immediately separated from the established church, by celebrating the sacraments among themselves. There are in the different congregations in Ireland about 5000.

† From Dublin Mr. Cennick proceeded to the north of Ireland, and preached in many places in the counties of Antrim, Down, Derry, Cavan, &c. He acquired the name of swaddler, from preaching frequently on the text, " you shall find a babe wrapt in swaddling clothes," a name which was indiscriminately applied both to Moravians and methodists, on their first introduction into Ireland. Being assisted by several other ministers, congregations of Moravians were formed in different parts of the kingdom, where there are at present six, as follow: Dublin, consisting of 230 members; Grace-hill, county of Antrim, 850; Ballinderry, 40; Gracefield, county of Derry, 180; Coothill, 40; Kilkeel, county of Down, 30; the total of Moravians in Ireland is 1370. These congregations are under the direction of the general synod of their church, at which ministers and deputies from all their congregations both in

of Messrs. Cennick and Latrobe, who approved of the doctrine and discipline of the Brethren, were in the year 1750 formed into a congregation of their persuasion, which has ever since been regularly served by ordained ministers of the Moravian church. Their meeting-house, with an adjoining dwelling for their pastor, is in Bishop-street; their present minister, the Rev. Mr. Holmes, a Dane, and their congregation consists of about 230 members, including children.

Christian and pagan countries assemble. This synod appoints a minister, who is consecrated a Bishop of their church, and to whose care are intrusted the ecclesiastical affairs of this country. In him is lodged the power of ordaining Presbyters and Deacons for the congregations under his direction. The Irish Moravian Bishop resides at Grace-hill, county of Antrim. They have also a Bishop resident in England; for by an Act of Parliament passed in 1747, the Brethren were acknowledged an Episcopal Church, and all the rights and privileges for which they petitioned were by it legally secured to them in his Majesty's dominions.

Their theological college is in Germany, to which theological students from these countries used to be sent; but as this became difficult during the war, an academy, designed to obviate the difficulty, was in the year 1808, established at Fulneck, in Yorkshire. They have no establishment of a similar kind in Ireland, but they have two large boarding schools at Gracehill for boys and girls, and one in Ballinderry for girls; to which, however, children of every denomination are admitted.

It does not come within our limits to detail the doctrines of any sect, unless they should be distinguished by some peculiar tenet in this country; but as much obloquy has been cast upon this sect for its supposed monstrous opinions, adopted, not in the dark and unsettled period of the Reformation, but so lately as the middle of the last century; as the Bishop of Gloucester has declared that their practices are "unspeakably flagitious," (See Doctrine of Grace), and as Dr. Maclane, the editor of Mosheim, has asserted that their doctrines "open a door to the most licentious effects of fanaticism," (See Mosheim, Vol. vi p. 23, note) we have enquired particularly into those that are held and practised in this country. The doctrine we are informed is essentially the same as that professed by the national church of these kingdoms, agreeably to the 39 Articles. They receive and hold the unaltered Confession of Augsburg, especially the first 21 doctrinal articles, as presented to the Emperor Charles V. in 1530, because they think it conformable to the holy scripture, and the synods have agreed that no doctrine repugnant to it shall be taught in any of their congregations. To Count Zinzindorf they owe the greatest gratitude, for the asylum afforded to their distressed congregations on his estates in Lusatia, by which their persecuted church was renewed at Hernhut; but "they do not *assent* to, or *adopt* all the *peculiar sentiments* and expressions contained in his writings." (See Crantz's History of the Brethren, p. 342, 526, &c.) Zinzindorf's opinions were those by which they are now particularly stigmatized. Like the Quakers, the Moravians hold it unlawful to take an oath, and an Act of Parliament has been passed, confirming to them the same indulgence, by receiving their affirmation in certain matters of testimony. Their practice is as pure as their principles: they are remarkable for their integrity of life, and simplicity of manners. Their dress, particularly of their females, resembles the plainness and neatness of quakers. All their establishments in this country are marked by industry and sobriety, and they display here the same benevolence and patient endurance, that has led their missionaries from the Pole to the Equator, from the coast of Labrador to the Nicobar Islands.

In the same street is likewise a house called the Moravian House, which is inhabited by a number of unmarried females, who are members of their church. This however is not a charitable establishment, for every resident supports herself. It serves merely as an accommodation to such pious females of the society as find it inconvenient to reside with their friends. No means of persuasion are ever resorted to, to induce any to enter the house, and the inmates are at liberty at any time to leave it. For the sake of order, one of this associate family is appointed superintendent, who regulates its concerns, and inspects the moral and religious conduct of its members.

The united Brethren in Dublin support two charities,—a Widows' House, mentioned before, and a Sunday Female School. The school is held in their house in Bishop-street, and is superintended by the female members of their church, who give their gratuitous attendance. The expences are defrayed by subscription. The school is open to children of all persuasions; and no books are read but the Old and New Testament. About 30 children attend.

BAPTISTS.

The first Baptist congregation was established in Dublin* prior to the year

* Several Baptist congregations were formed in Ireland coeval with that of Dublin. They came over with the crowd of Dissenters who colonised Ireland after Cromwell's victories, and established churches in Kilkenny, Wexford, Waterford, Clonmel, Cork, Kerry, Limerick, Galway, and near Carrickfergus. (Bogue and Bennet's History of Dissenters, vol. ii. p. 414.) Several of these have become extinct. The congregations at present in Ireland are, one in Waterford, which consists of 100 members; Cloughjordan, 100; Killtribber, 50; Cork, 100. Besides these, three congregations have been formed within the last year: Thurles, consisting of 70 members; Furban, 50; Clonmel, 40. In the north of Ireland there are eleven small congregations, but they have no particular connection with the rest. The whole number in Ireland amounts to about 2000. The Rev. Joseph Ivemey, Secretary to the Baptist Missionary Society, visited Ireland in 1814. His report states that the Baptists have only five churches in Ireland, out of eleven which existed and were highly prosperous a hundred and fifty years ago. "Sandimanianism," says he "has divided the larger societies, both of Independents and Baptists." (See Appendix to First Annual Report of the Baptist Missionary Society.) The Baptist churches applied to government, by a Memorial laid before the Lord Lieutenant of Ireland, for a participation of the Regium Donum granted to other Dissenters in Ireland, but hitherto without success,

The inoffensive Baptists of the present day form a strong contrast with the Anabaptists of the Befor-

1653, at which period it existed in Swift's-alley. In 1738, the old meeting-house was pulled down, and rebuilt on its former site. It is the meeting-house which accommodates the congregation at the present day, which consists of one hundred and fifty members, who hold no tenets different from those in England. In point of ceremony, their baptisms by immersion are performed in a baptistry within their meeting house, and never in the open air, as is sometimes the case in England and Wales. They have as yet no college for educating pastors in this country: they are periodically supplied from England and Wales. Their present minister is the Rev. Mr. West.

This congregation supports two schools. A day-school consisting of fourteen girls, who are clothed, maintained, and educated. This is supported by an annual charity sermon, producing with donations about £210. They also support a Sunday-school, in which sixty boys and seventy girls are taught. This latter school is distinguished by a remarkable feature: a master is provided who teaches Irish,* and about twenty of the children avail themselves of his instruction. It is found that they learn to read the language they have been accustomed to speak with greater facility than a foreign one: they are therefore first taught to read Irish books, and learn to read English through this medium.

QUAKERS.†

In the year 1655, two females, Elizabeth Fletcher, and Elizabeth Smith, landed in Dublin, and went to St. Audeon's church. They addressed the

mation, particularly those ferocious and impious fanatics, who seized on the city of Munster in the year 1535. Indeed they seem to consider the name as a term of reproach, and deny that there exists in Ireland a single Anabaptist. They hold the doctrine of adult baptism by immersion as of apostolic authority, and derived from John the Baptist; but they reject the necessity of rebaptising, from whence the original sect derived its name, and all those wild opinions which they pretended justified their practices. The Baptists of Ireland are remarkable for their sobriety, practical good sense, and submission to the civil magistrates.

* This School is thus noticed in the first Report of the Irish Baptist Society, for 1815. "A Sunday "School is opened in Dublin, which is conducted by some zealous young men, in which both English "and Irish are taught. Several young men designed for priests and schoolmasters have attended to "learn Irish. They all read the Irish Testament." An excellent Irish scholar of the Catholic persuasion has assured us that he was called upon to examine these scholars, and he was highly pleased with their proficiency.

† The first introduction of this sect into Ireland was by William Edmunson. While a soldier in

THE CITY OF DUBLIN. 831

congregation then assembled, and having declared their testimony of the truth, proceeded to publish it at the Baptist meeting-house which had been

Cromwell's army he was visited with conscientious scruples in Scotland, and was finally converted by G. Fox, and James Nailor, whom he met on his return to England. Having left the army, he was persuaded to go into Ireland by his brother. He brought goods with him, and settled as a merchant in Antrim, in 1653. On entering his goods at the Custom-house his deportment excited much surprise. His refusal to take off his hat, declining the usual oaths, and his peculiar dress and phraseology, were new and strange, and excited much offence. Some time after, he was joined by John Tiffin, from England, with whom he travelled to Belfast, where they proposed to preach. After being expelled from every house in the town, they were at length invited by a man of the name of Laithes, to his house in the vicinity; but when they arrived, he also refused to admit them; they accordingly sat down near his house, where three lanes ends meet, and there held their first meeting in the open air, exciting the wonder of all the people who gathered round them. About this time, William Edmunson removed to Lurgan from Antrim, and established there the first settled Quaker's meeting in Ireland. They were now joined by sundry friends from England, who spread the opinions of the sect through every part of the country.

These missionaries appear to have been very indefatigable, penetrating to the remotest parts of Connaught, a circumstance at that time of no less danger than difficulty. They suffered much persecution for their peculiarities. Their refusing to pay tythes, not observing holydays, but particularly their entering churches and chapels, interrupting the service, and bearing testimony against priests and ministers, subjected them to constant penalties of fine and imprisonment. A singular instance of this latter kind is recorded by Sewel. Solomon Eccles entered the chapel of Galway naked above the waist, with a chafing dish of coals and burning brimstone upon his head, asserting that God had sent him to testify against Idolaters, and to shew what would be their portion unless they repented. He some time after proceeded to the Cathedral of Cork, and rebuked the clergyman, who had been a Presbyterian, for preaching in a surplice. For this latter offence, he was committed to prison and publicly whipped. About the same time, John Perrot, a native of Dublin, left Ireland and went to Rome, to convert the Pope. He was imprisoned, but soon after enlarged as insane. On his return he wrote a book called the " Battering Ram against Rome." Notwithstanding these extravagances, which were not confined to the Quakers of that day, the converts in Ireland were as respectable as they were numerous. Amongst these was the celebrated William Penn. He was sent by his father, Admiral Penn, in the year 1666, to manage a considerable estate which he possessed in Ireland. Hearing that Thomas Loe, was to preach at a meeting at Cork, he went to hear him. Here he was converted, and became a constant frequenter of their meetings. He was arrested, with sundry others, by the Mayor of Cork, and cast into prison, from whence he was liberated by an admirable letter addressed to the Lord President of Munster, which is preserved in his works (vol. i.)

It is a remarkable fact, that during the turbulent period which occurred in Ireland from 1688, they assembled together without much disturbance from either party, and attended both monthly, provincial, and national meetings, travelling unarmed through hostile countries from remote and distant parts. They suffered great losses and alarms both from soldiers and rapparees; but during all this bloody period they never left their ordinary abode, and but four Quakers suffered death; two of whom exposed themselves to unnecessary hazard. They were at this time a numerous people, for about fifty meetings established a few years before. The Baptists merely rejected their testimony, but they were both sent to Newgate prison by the Lord Mayor, for

(Rutty's Table of Settlement, p. 342.) were established in Munster, Leinster, and Ulster; and an opulent people, for their loss of property by the war in 1692, was computed at 100,000*l*. (Rutty, p. 158.)

In the year 1750, the Quakers had 101 established congregations in Ireland; viz. in Leinster 49; in Ulster, 31; Munster, 23; Connaught, 1; for the greater part of which meeting houses had been built. Since that time, the sect has much declined; there are at present but 42 meetings in the country, each containing on an average 100 individuals, viz.

In ULSTER.

Lurgan	Lower Grange	Ballinderry	Richhill
Moyallon	Ballinacree	Belfast	Coothill
Rathfriland	Lisburn	Newtown	
Antrim	Hillsborough	Grange, near Charlemont	

In LEINSTER.

Moate	Ballinakill	Kilconner	Ross
Mountmelick	Edenderry	Enniscorthy	Ballimore
Montrath	Rathangan	Forrest	Ballinclay
Birr	Carlow	Cooladine	Dublin
Knockballymaher	Ballitore	Randlesmill	Wicklow

In MUNSTER.

| Cork | Garryroan | Limerick | Youghall |
| Clonmell | Waterford | Roscrea | |

In CONNAUGHT.——Ballimurry.

Total number of Friends in Ireland—about 4500.

The rural village of Ballitore has been long celebrated for the excellent Quaker school of A. Shackleton, where Edmund Burke was educated; and no less so for the birth of Mary Ledbeater, the daughter of Shackleton, and author of the inimitable " Cottage Dialogues."

The Quakers of Cork are very wealthy, and engross the Woolen trade. Those of Waterford form the most opulent and respectable part of the commercial interest of that town. In Clonmel they constitute the greater part of the wealthy Protestant population. They support three provincial schools—for Ulster at Lisburn; for Leinster, at Mountmelick; and for Munster, at Waterford. Each child is charged 3*l*. which however is remitted to those who cannot pay. The attention paid to ventilation and cleanliness in these schools is so remarkable, that the Apothecary's bill for twenty boys, and twenty-five girls at Lisburn, in one year amounted only to seven shillings.—*Wakefield*, vol. ii. p. 595.

In point of discipline and practice, the Quakers of the present day preserve unchanged the ordinances of their ancestors, and differ in nothing from those of England; for these we refer to Gough, Clarkson, and others. We shall merely notice the institution of Family Visits, for its peculiarity and excellence. At the yearly national meeting a recommendation for the purpose issues, and two or three names are sent down to each monthly meeting, of persons qualified to be visitors. If such are not found at a par-the offence committed against the congregation of St. Audeon's. After some time they were released, and held a meeting at the house of Richard Fowkes, a tailor, near Polegate, which was the first meeting of Quakers ever held in Dublin. In 1668, George Fox visited Ireland, and came to Dublin, when he settled the men and women meeting to be held every two weeks, and a general meeting of friends from the different provinces to be asssembled half yearly. The first provincial meeting took place in Dublin in March 1670, at which the sufferings of friends for conscience sake in different parts of Ireland, were collected and recorded, and application made for the release of such as were committed to prison. The systematic arrangements of George Fox, by giving regularity and stability to the sect, rapidly increased their numbers. The congregation in Polegate was soon divided, and removed, part to Bride's-alley, and part to Wormwood-gate. But in 1686, the former house being considered too small for the still encreasing congregation, a large meeting-house was erected in Meath-street, by the friends of Leinster province, to which the congregation of Bride's-alley removed; and in 1692 a new meeting-house was erected in Sycamore-alley, to which that of Wormwood-gate was transferred. In these houses they meet at the present day.

In common with the friends of England, those of Dublin suffered sundry

ticular meeting, they are called from a neighbouring one, and sometimes friends feel themselves inwardly called on to perform the service. These proceed from house to house, inspect the conduct of the individuals of the family, as far as relates to morality, adhering to the institutions of the society, and attending their meetings, reading the scriptures, and conforming themselves to the best models; and as the discipline of monthly meetings takes cognizance of any irregularities which are reported to have been committed, those family visits must have a strong tendency to prevent them. These friendly monitors are in every family kindly received and implicitly obeyed. In point of doctrine, there was some time ago a diversity of opinion. It has always appeared to be the wisdom of this people in general by holding matters of faith undefined, to avoid occasion of schism, depending more on purity of practice than abstract creeds, and modes of belief. A small deviation from their usual practice occasioned a temporary appearance of schism. Some of the schismatics conceived that they adhered more strictly to the primitive sentiments of the society; others went further, and asserted that the opinions of the society were incorrect *ab origine*. Of these latter was John Handcock, of Lisburn, who published a pamphlet vindicating his opinions. The two most essential positions in this pamphlet were, a denial of the inspiration of their extemporaneous preachers, and a doubt of the inspiration of the scriptures in the historical parts of the Old Testament. These opinions were adopted by some individuals, but no separate society was ever formed by the seceders. The schism seems now nearly forgotten: but originating at the period of the French revolution, when infidel doctrines were prevalent, the society in general was inconsiderately charged with adopting the opinions of Paine, and this most excellent and respectable body stigmatised with the errors of an ephemeral heresy.

5 O

persecutions and annoyances; the first, from the magistrates, for refusing to comply with the laws and ordinances which their consciences condemned; the latter, from riotous mobs which their peculiarities attracted. From most of these, the act of toleration passed in the reign of King William exempted them, in common with other dissenters, but there were some from which they still suffered great inconvenience. They held the observance of holidays as superstitious, and always opened their shops as a testimony against it. On these occasions riotous mobs of apprentices and other persons were allowed to assemble, who proceeded to their houses, and under the pretext of shutting down their shops, committed great outrages. In the year 1702 the Lord Mayor of Dublin, and the Seneschal of Downand Thomas Court, issued proclamations previous to Christmas day, prohibiting meetings for such purposes, and from that time the annoyance ceased. Their refusal to take an oath was also a pregnant source of vexation to the friends in Dublin. The crafty and litigious availing themselves of the circumstance, on every occasion filed bills in Chancery, to which a friend could put in no answer. They were harassed therefore with suits which they could not defend, and by dishonest men against whom they had no remedy. To relieve them from a vexation so serious and unjust, a Bill was passed in 1719, by which the Chancellor and Barons of the Exchequer were empowered to receive their answers on affirmation. This considerate law terminated the grievance, and their properties were rendered secure without violence to their conscience.

The year 1727 was rendered memorable by a resolution of the yearly meeting assembled at Dublin. *The practice of importing Negroes from their native country* was censured in the minutes of their proceedings.* The first published record of a similar resolution in London, was at the yearly meeting in 1758 : and thus it should appear that the Quakers of Ireland were the first public body who protested against the slave trade; and the abolition of a traffic which has clothed England with glory, and Europe with shame, originated in Dublin.

About the year 1798, Hannah Barnard came from America; she had imbibed, it is said, the opinions of the French philosophers, then prevalent in her own country, and came to disseminate them here. She met in Belfast and the north of Ireland, a few whose opinions were congenial to her own; but in Dublin she had no success. Having called a public meeting, she at-

* Rutty, p. 442.

tempted to inculcate her opinions, but she was opposed by Joseph Williams, of Cole-alley, who declared that such were not the doctrines of the society. From hence she went to England, where she was examined before a large meeting, but she refused to have her doctrine tried by the test of scripture; she was therefore silenced, and remitted to America, where she was expelled the society altogether, and now lives in poverty and obscurity. This circumstance excited some alarm among the sect; and to strengthen themselves against the innovations which such dangerous opinions might cause, an union was proposed between the yearly meetings of London and Dublin; and thus the projected union of the Quaker Societies, preceded that of the Legislature of the two countries; but it did not take place.

Among the Quakers of Dublin, Dr. Rutty, and John Gough, distinguished themselves as literary men, the first by his History of the County of Dublin, and other works, and the latter by his History of the Quakers, and Treatise on Arithmetic.*

There are at present resident in Dublin one-hundred and thirty families, containing about six hundred individuals. They form a highly respectable part of the commercial portion of the metropolis. Their appearance and manners still mark them as a distinct class, though much of the peculiarity of both is worn away. It is however very conspicuous at the yearly meeting which takes place the latter end of April: during its continuance for a week, the streets are crowded with friends from different parts of Ireland, who seem to have lost little of the primitive simplicity of dress or manners.

Their habits of industry, frugality and moderation, which the admirable regulations of their society still keep up, prevent the necessity of those charities among their body which are expedient among other societies. They have but one exclusive charity in Dublin, a retreat at Donneybrook, in the vicinity of the metropolis, for such of their friends as labour under mental derangement; and this is a recent establishment. But while they are thus exempt from charitable demands from their own sect, they are most prompt to dispense it to others, and those who most want it. The several charities for the Liberties of Dublin are principally indebted to Quakers for their support. The Meath Hospital, the Fever Hospital, the Sick Poor Institution, in Meath-street, and the extensive School, in School-street, are much indebted to them, and the two last almost exclusively supported by their exertions.

* JOHN RUTTY was born in Wiltshire, about the year 1698. In his youth, he was tutor to the

WALKER'S.

THE diversity of religious denominations received a recent addition by the establishment of a sect which appears to be as new in its discipline as in children of William Penn, who died in 1718, upon which, Rutty, being then only twenty years of age, went to Leyden, to study medicine, where he took out his degree.

In 1730, he appears to have settled in Dublin, when he became a member of the Physico Historical Society. Smith, employed by the Society, mentions Dr. Rutty as affording him essential assistance in compiling his County Histories.

Doctor Rutty kept an accurate Journal of the weather in Dublin, for more than fifty years. He died unmarried in 1775, aged 77, and left a character in the highest degree esteemed by all his friends and cotemporaries.

He was the author of the following useful works:

1. The History of the Rise and Progress of the People called Quakers; small 4to. 1751.
2. Natural History of the Mineral Waters of Ireland. This work was warmly attacked by that extraordinary genius Doctor Lucas, in his "Analysis," and answered by Rutty in his "Reply to the Analysis."
3. Natural History of the County of Dublin, 1772.
4. Moral and Religious Tracts.
5. A Materia Medica, a posthumous work, not published.

SAMUEL FULLER, first a school master, and then a bookseller in Meath-street, died in 1737.

He was the author of the Mathematical Miscellany, a Treatise on Astronomy, and several religious Tracts relative to the Quakers, one of which was called, "An Answer to the Abusive Queries of Samuel Roys, of the Presbyterian Meeting-house, New-row."

JOHN GOUGH was born at Kendal, in Westmoreland, in 1721. He came to Ireland about 1740, and settled in Cork, where he married, after which he removed to Dublin, in 1750.

Gough kept a school of much repute in the metropolis for twenty-four years, in which many persons, who became respectable for their talents or stations in life, were educated. He was afterwards appointed superintendant of the Quaker's Provincial School, at Lisburn, which he conducted with great reputation. There, whilst in the act of writing at his desk, his History of the Quakers, he was suddenly struck with an apoplectic fit, and died, leaving the sentence unfinished, 25th November, 1791.

Gough published the following works:

1. An English Grammar, in conjunction with his brother James, which became a school-book in much request, 1754.
2. Arithmetic in Theory and Practice, 1758. A second edition in 1770, and a third, 1786. He abridged this work for the use of schools in 1767, which has since gone through more than twenty numerous editions.
3. Several Religious Tracts in defence of the Quakers, one of which was a Reply to Misrepresentations of his Sect, made in Guthrie's Geography, which had the proper effect of causing the charge to be discontinued in the subsequent editions of that work.
4. History of the Quakers, in 4 vols. 8vo.

This work was published by subscription: about 2000 sets were made up in Dublin alone, for the subscribers in Ireland and America. Those in England were still more numerous. It was brought down only to the year 1764, in composing which period of the history, the author was seised with the fatal fit above mentioned.

its denomination. The Rev. John Walker, was conspicuous in the University of Dublin for his talents, particularly for the logical precision of his reasoning powers.* He obtained a fellowship with much credit, and took orders; he also became minister of Bethesda chapel, chaplain to the Lock Penetentiary, and a member of several religious and useful institutions. But in the year 1801, he conceived that his former adherance to the established form of worship was unscriptural, inasmuch as the offices of devotion are performed by all persons together without discrimination. He therefore withdrew from his former religious connections, resigned his valuable fellowship in the University, laid aside the garb which distinguished him as a clergyman, and selecting a few associates like-minded with himself, he formed an exclusive religious assembly, whose tenets do not seem to be adopted from those of any. In addition to their peculiar mode of faith, they carefully observe the external form of worship used among the early Christians. On this their discipline is established, which excludes from their communion all believers, however unexceptionable in essential faith, if after hearing a precept that could be fairly and generally applied, he should refuse to obey it. And this exclusion is of the most rigid kind; it extends not only to the communion of the Lord's Supper, but it does not suffer prayer to be offered up, hymns to be sung, or any other religious act to be performed in the same room with the excluded party, without removing to a distance, and expressing their separation by some external action; even conversation, if it should be directed to any religious subject, is strictly prohibited with those who are not of their church; not, as they assert, because they esteem themselves better than others, but because they hold that

* When an under graduate in the University, this gentleman distinguished himself in the walks of polite literature. One of his Essays, a critique on the Tempest of Shakspeare, was read before the Royal Irish Academy, where it was much admired, and published in their Transactions. He has since published some Tracts, on religious and other subjects, of which latter are Compendiums of Logic and Algebra. He has also written a Treatise on the Metres of Horace,—and edited two of the Classics. He proposed to superintend the University press in the publication of others, for an adequate salary. We regret that this proposal was not complied with. It would be rendering an essential benefit to classical students if new editions would supply that want of books which is frequently felt and complained of even in the University, and supersede those few which issue from the Dublin press, which are as disgraceful, particularly the Greek, by the inelegance of the type and courseness of the paper, as by the gross inaccuracy of the text. We counted 47 typographical errors in a Dublin edition of Lucian, some of which rendered the text altogether unintelligible. The Classics formerly edited in Trinity College were remarkable for their beauty and correctness.

true worship and Christian communion of conversation, is impossible, for it is unscriptural where persons do not receive the same truths in common. Hence, whenever they assemble for public worship, those who happen to be present not recognized as members of their society, are considered as cyphers, and deemed incapable of any act of devotion with them. They ordain no ministers. Any person of the society possessing the gifts of prayer or preaching, exercise them indiscriminately; and certain of the former are appointed to break the bread, and pour out the wine at their sacrament of the eucharist ; that of baptism they hold superfluous, unless to those who never before professed Christianity, and were then first converted. These singularities of faith and discipline were naturally subject to much animadversion. On the first establishment of the sect another was added no less extraordinary. Their meetings were held in Stafford-street, and on one day in the week, every person was invited to attend their service, and to propound their objections publicly, which would be as publicly answered. This invitation drew crowds from different motives, some to hear the doctrine, and some to object, but the greater part from curiosity, to be witness of so singular a controversy. After the service of the evening was performed, a sermon was preached on some appropriate text. A pause ensued, and the preacher again stood up, and asked the assembly if any one present wished to oppugn the tenets then delivered. The invitation was generally accepted, and a controversy ensued, in which the decorum of the sacred subject was lost, and scenes of outrage and violence too often terminated the contest. These disputations are now happily discontinued. Already has this sect divided upon a point of discipline : some of them hold that the words of the Apostle, " Salute one another with an holy kiss,"* is a precept of positive observance, and cannot in the public meetings be dispensed with; others hold that it is one of suitable but indifferent nature, and may be neglected or observed by those who hold it so. Mr. Walker adheres to the first opinion, and continued with his congregation in Stafford-street. Mr. Tuthil has adopted the latter, and retired to Cutler's-hall in Capel-street, with the seceders. The two congregations consist of about 140 individuals. There are similar churches in several towns in Ireland : they are independent of each other, or any church government, and disavow the name of any leader, but from their excluding discipline, more nearly resemble the followers of

* Romans, chap. xvi. verse 16.

Robert Sandeman, than any others. They support no school or other charity.*

KELLY'S.

The Rev. Thomas Kelly, the only son of the late Judge Kelly, left the established church in some time after he was ordained, and instituted one more new sect, for the accommodation of which he built a chapel at Black Rock, near Dublin, and another at Athy. For these he composed a book of hymns, both the music and poetry of which were original, and peculiar to his followers, and his service was a simple form of extemporaneous prayer and preaching. Several young men from Scotland joined this society, and planted similar meetings in other places.

* In the year 1804, a pamphlet was published by the founder of this sect, in which he assigns his reason for leaving the established church, and for the new opinions he had adopted. In this pamphlet are the following passages: " I wish to speak out and distinctly, upon a most important, though most " unpopular trait of the religion of Christ. Let the children of the world argue the political right or ex- " pediency of the matter; but there is no rule of scripture more plain than that which calls upon the " disciples of Christ to maintain, in all cases, a course of *passive obedience, and non-resistance* towards " the constituted authorities of the state. But what I assert is, that it is contrary to the nature and " laws of Christ's kingdom, that his disciples should acknowledge the State Religion as theirs, or hold " any connection with the religious establishment of the country. Protestants have greatly erred in " conceiving that many passages of scripture are exclusively applicable to the Popish corruptions; " which really are pointed against the corruptions in whatever body they exist. And wherever the " kings of the earth have committed fornication with any church, by attempting to introduce their laws " into Christ's kingdom, there is at least one of the progeny of Babylon, the mother of harlots, concern- " ing which the voice from heaven speaks,—*come out of her my people, that ye be not partakers of her* " *sins, and that ye receive not of her plagues*."—p. 43, 51. This view, he says, was accompanied by an immediate conviction and a clear perception of the path of duty, and he wrote the following letter to the Provost of Dublin College, October 8, 1804.—"Rev. Sir, I long since thought it probable that many things " which I was led to do from a sense of Christian duty, would eventually occasion my removal from the " situation I have held in the Establishment of this country, and in the University. That probability " has of late appeared to me to increase into a moral certainty; from the nature of some steps to " which I have been led by opening views of the rule of scripture. But until these very few days I " conceived that I might, consistently with that rule, remain in my present situation till I should be re- " moved from it. On this point I have now to avow to you a change of sentiment, and to inform you, " that I cannot longer conscientiously exercise any religious functions as a minister of the Establish- " ment." The Provost expostulated, but he was decided. He proposed to *resign*, but the Provost thought it his duty to *expel* him.—p. 43, 51-52.

When Walker published his sentiments on christian form and discipline, the Presbyterian form of Kelly's churches were conformed nearly to his plan, but the congregations profess themselves a distinct people, and keep up a conection with each other by occasional visits of the members, carrying commendatory epistles, as to the primitive meetings at Philippi and Ephesus, which they profess to imitate. At their meetings any of the brethren may administer the eucharist or exhort the rest. In public, strangers are separated from the body by a rail or other division, but in private they do not object to join in worship with any one who makes a true profession of Christianity. At their weekly meetings, which are held for the purpose of church government, any member of either sex may propose a rule, and have its adoption discussed. They allow every one to think and act as they please with respect to baptism. Their place of worship in Dublin is a school-room in Stephen-street, and their congregation consists of about sixty individuals.

FOREIGNERS.

[Of these there are two small congregations in Dublin, in French Refugees and German Lutherans.]

FRENCH REFUGEES.

WHEN Louis XIV. revoked the edict of Nantz, which had been enacted by Henry IV. to secure to his Protestant subjects the free exercise of their religion, the violent persecution which followed obliged all those who were attached to it to leave their property and fly from their country. Some of them found an asylum in Ireland.

William III. had a regiment of French Refugees at the battle of the Boyne, and when peace was established they settled in Ireland.* Among

* Some of these French Refugees settled in Waterford, and some in Lisburn, where congregations are found at this day. They have a pastor paid by government, who performs the service in the French language. The most important colony was that established at Portarlington, in the Queen's County, which has long been celebrated for the seminaries established there. It was in high repute for the excellent opportunities it afforded, and resorted to by all who deemed an accurate knowledge of French, an essential part of education. It was the language in common use there.

THE CITY OF DUBLIN.

them were many of the higher classes, who left their own country from pure principle, and their conduct in a strange one did them credit, and raised them to its highest ranks. The majority, however, were of the industrious part of the nation, and they brought with them their habits of labour and their skill in manufactures. The manufacture of silks was first introduced by them into Spitalfields, London; and from thence established in the Liberties of Dublin. To the Hugonots we are also indebted for the cultivation of flowers. This elegant pursuit was but little attended to, and exotics were scarcely known in Dublin before the reign of George I. At that time the resident Refugees formed themselves into a "Florists' Club," for the purpose of promoting the cultivation of flowers in this country.* They held their meetings for many years at the Rose tavern, in Drumcondra-lane, (now Dorset-street) and adjudged premiums to the members who produced the most beautiful flowers on stated days. This club existed till the reign of George II. and is still remembered. The Rose tavern was standing, before the late improvements in that outlet, now become a part of the town, obliterated all trace of what it formerly was.

The literature of Dublin is also indebted to the Refugees for some valuable improvements. The first Literary Journal which ever appeared in Ireland, was established in 1744, by the Rev. Mr. Droz, who kept a book shop in College Green, and exercised his clerical functions on Sunday. It was continued after his death by the Rev. Mr. Desveaux, and contained a view of the state of learning in Europe. The History of Greece by Dr. Gast, has received the merited eulogy of the Provost and Fellows of the University, and its extensive use proves the estimation in which it is held. The bar is also indebted to the legal knowledge of these foreigners. The grandfather of the present Attorney-General was a favourite of William III. and provided for by him in Ireland. His grandfather's brother was the celebrated preacher Saurin.

But perhaps the most valuable acquisition to Dublin, was the moral qualities brought and exercised by some of these men and their descendents. Their names are to be found among the promoters of all our religious or charitable institutions; and one is so conspicuous, that notice would be superfluous, and eulogy impertinent. Who does not know, and knowing prize, the excellent family of La Touche?

* Essay on Rise and Progress of Gardening in Ireland, by Jos. Coop. Walker.

The French Refugees were so numerous on their first introduction as to form, in the year 1695, three congregations. A meeting-house in Lucas-lane, and another in Peter-street, were erected for those of the Calvinist persuasion, and a chapel under the roof of St. Patrick's Cathedral was assigned to those who were of the established Church; but as they were not supplied by any accession from abroad, the members gradually amalgamated with the population of the Metropolis. Many families became extinct in the male line, and those who retained their name, lost, with their vernacular language, the distinctive character of their sect. The two first places of worship are closed, and the congregation of the latter is nearly extinct. It consists of about twenty individuals, for whom the liturgy is still read, and the sermon preached in the French language. Government allows the minister a stipend of £150. per annum. Their present pastor is the Rev. Mr. Letablere.

In 1723, a school was established in Myler's-alley, Patrick's-close, for the maintainance and education of those whose parents were in distress. At first it included boys and girls. It now supports only eight girls, who are lodged, maintained, educated, and apprenticed at a proper age. They are all the children of Refugees. The income of the school arises from the interest of debentures, occasionally a charity sermon, and a few subscribers.

GERMAN LUTHERANS.

ESDRAS MARCUS LIGHTENSTONE, the founder of the German congregation in Ireland, was ordained chaplain to the Duke of Brandenburgh's regiment in 1689, by the Lutheran divines of London, to accompany that regiment to Ireland, where he continued with it during the wars of that period. On disbanding the regiment at the peace of Ryswick, in 1697, it was proposed that he should endeavour to form a congregation of such of his countrymen as were settled in Dublin after the wars, or who traded there. In this he was encouraged by the then Lords Justices, who granted him a protection under the act for encouraging foreign protestants to settle in this kingdom.

THE CITY OF DUBLIN. 843

Of these he found about twenty individuals resident, and formed a congregation, occasionally augmented by foreigners of the Lutheran persuasion. Their first place of worship was the Lutheran church in Marlborough-street. For the more orderly government of this community, four Lutheran inhabitants, and one master of a ship, were appointed trustees with the minister to manage its affairs, which were for some time prosperous, but one of the trustees having convoked the congregation to meet at a public house without their pastor, the original regulations drawn up in their church were cancelled, and the affairs were so mismanaged, that Mr. Lightenstone found it necessary to make a collection among their friends resident in other countries. He therefore proceeded with a recommendatory patent from the Lords Justices, one of whom was the Archbishop, to England, and thence to the Continent, where he travelled through various parts of Holland, Germany and Denmark, making charitable collections, with which he returned to Ireland.*

This congregation originally included foreigners of all countries who professed the Lutheran doctrines, and the minister was required to know their respective languages. In the morning he addressed the Germans, in the afternoon the Danes, Swedes, and Norwegians. About the year 1725, a new edifice was erected in Pool-beg-street, with a residence for the minister annexed, which is the meeting-house used at the present day. Their pastor† was allowed a stipend by government, and was licenced by the Archbishop, to whose jurisdiction he was subject, and to whose visitation he was summoned, but he used either the liturgy of the consistory of Holstein, or extemporaneous prayer. The primitive opinions of Luther were still adhered to. They held the doctrine of the real presence,‡ and used the

* On his return, he appears to have been very cruelly and unjustly treated by his own flock. He was cast into prison, and suffered a violent persecution which his conduct little merited. He was charged with not accounting for the money he had received, though it appeared, that independent of his great personal exertions, which his congregation could not remunerate, they were actually his pecuniary debtors. He has published a vindication, which is a curious document. In it, he asserts, as worthy of note, that a Mr. K——z, one of his persecutors, was laid upon his sick bed, on which he died on the very day he (Mr. Lightenstone) was taken prisoner. A certificate of his character is annexed to this vindication, signed by those who knew him, which asserts that he was a man pious and industrious in his calling, and just and honourable in his dealings.

† First granted in the reign of Queen Anne. The licence granted by the Archbishop was of a late date.

‡ Luther's own explication of this doctrine is singular. "As in the red hot iron two distinct substances

wafer in the celebration of the Eucharist; they tolerated the use of images, practised a form of auricular confession, used an exorcism at baptism, and, in fine, adopted that crude mixture of rites and doctrines which marked the early periods of the Reformation.*

Their present pastor is the Rev. Mr. Shultze. He was not called from Germany to officiate here, as his predecessors had been. He had left his native country with three others, on a mission to the coast of Africa. Passing the south of Ireland, the vessel was wrecked off the coast of Wexford. From thence he proceeded to Dublin, to find the means of continuing his voyage. It happened that the congregation of the German church had, at that time no pastor, and Mr. Shultze was called upon to fill the vacancy. His mission thus terminated in Ireland, and his three coadjutors proceeded to their original destination. As the practice of preaching in the Danish language has been discontinued, the present congregation consists of but twelve individuals, who are resident, with the occasional addition of such seafaring people as may be in the port, and speak the German language. They support no school or other charity, but some of their congregation, particularly the late Mr. Eichbaum, were remarkable for promoting schools and charities among other persuasions. The allowance of Government to the minister is £50. per annum.†

"Iron and fire, are united; so is the body of Christ joined to the bread in the Eucharist." Melancthon, in his defence of the Confession of Augsburgh, whether from timidity or hesitation of mind, acceded to the opinion, though he afterwards seems to have adopted the contrary.

* The mixture of rites seems to have arisen from the famous edict of the *Interim*, published by the Emperor Charles V. from which the *Adiaphorists*, who held that compliance was due to the Imperial edict in things indifferent, arose; and which continued many years in the German reformed churches. "But as time and experience are necessary to bring all things to perfection, so the doctrine of the Lu- "theran church changed imperceptibly its original form, and was improved and perfected in many res- "pects."—Moshiem, vol. iv. p. 303. This is the case with the little congregation of which we are writing. They still indeed hold the doctrine of the real presence, as the word of him who could not lie; but they do not pretend to comprehend, much less to explain it. The forms of confession and exorcism have been discontinued, and their present pastor, Mr. Shultze, has substituted bread for the wafer in the Eucharist.

† To aid his small stipend, the present respectable minister proposed, to teach the German language, but the little success he has had is a proof how little that language is cultivated in a metropolis which supports so many French and Italian teachers. He has had but twelve pupils in ten years.

JEWS.

It is not very certain when the first Jews established themselves in Dublin. There is reason to suppose, however, that they were among the Dissenters who came to Ireland after Cromwell's conquests.* He wished to encourage a people whose supposed wealth and industry would be likely to advance the commercial interests of the country, and form with the rest a barrier against the Catholic population. On his invitation some Portuguese Jews settled in Dublin, where they became opulent merchants, and established a synagogue in Crane-lane. In process of time, they became so numerous as to engage the attention of the Legislature. In the year 1746 a bill was brought into the House of Commons for naturalising persons professing the Jewish religion in Ireland, where it passed, and in the year following it was again introduced, agreed to without any amendment, and presented to his Grace the Lord Lieutenant, to be transmitted to England. However, it never received the Royal assent, but miscarried, as a similar bill had done in England, in consequence, it should appear, of the popular clamour raised in that country against such a measure. There were about this time forty families settled in Dublin, comprising about two hundred individuals. They had removed their synagogue to Marlborough-green, and had purchased a burying ground at Ballybough-bridge.

Since that period they gradually declined. About the year 1800 there were not ten battelnim, or males, which are necessary to constitute a synagogue in Dublin: and it was therefore discontinued. The temple was converted into a glass-house, and the congregation is now reduced to two

---

* This is the account the Jews of Dublin give of themselves, which, however, is rather a matter of oral tradition than of written record among them. There were none settled in any other part of Ireland. There are a few individuals in Cork, and other commercial towns at present, but they are rather itinerants than fixed residents.—The Jews petitioned Cromwell for liberty to exercise their religion and carry on their trade in London. Manassez Ben Israel, with some of the chief Rabbis, came to Whitchall from Amsterdam for this purpose, whom the Protector treated with respect, and summoned a meeting of divines, lawyers, and merchants, to deliberate upon the affair. The assembly could not agree, and the affair was dropped. The Protector himself was well disposed to it, and ordered 200*l.* to be paid to the Rabbi out of the Treasury. The Jews offered him 200,000*l.* provided they might have Westminster Hall for a settlement.—Neale's History of the Puritans, vol. iv. p. 140, 141.

It is supposed to have been on this occason that the Jews first settled in Dublin.

families,* consisting of nine individuals, who perform their religious rites in their own houses.

Their cemetery, however, is carefully preserved, and gives some evidence of their former respectability. It is situated between Ballybough-bridge, and Philipsburgh-avenue. It contains about a rood of ground, is planted on the inside with shrubs and trees, and well inclosed with a high wall, which forms one side of the road. It is much larger than the Jewish population would at any time seem to require, did they not adhere strictly to the precepts of their rabbins, who teach that it is not lawful to disturb the repose of the dead, by opening the same grave twice. Their bodies are therefore laid side by side, with some space between; and never one above the other; and hence they require more space in their cemeteries, than any other sect. All the Jewish rites of sepulture are still carefully observed by this scanty remnant; under the head of the corpse is placed a bag of earth, the face is cautiously turned towards the east, and the mourners retiring from the grave, pluck the grass and strew it behind them. Near the west wall are erected some tomb stones, all of which are inscribed with Hebrew characters, on one of them is the device of two raised hands. It belongs to a family of the name of Kohen,† now resident in Dublin, and is the emblematic device of the tribe of Levi to which he belongs. There was formerly a much greater number of tombs visible in this grave-yard, but some have been overgrown with grass and sods, which the superstition of the Jews will not suffer them to remove, and others have disappeared in a more extraordinary manner. They have been stolen at different times for the purpose of converting them into hearth-stones or other uses,‡ the people of that

---

* There are two other families resident in Dublin, but they have mixed with the Christian community, and are disowned by those orthodox Jews, one of whom is a grocer, and the other a pencil maker. Their features and persons bear the indelible marks of their nation. Several efforts have been made to convert them, without success. They are honest harmless people. The paucity of Jews in Dublin, has been erroneously adduced as a proof of its poverty. Poland, the poorest country in Europe, contains the most Jews. Amsterdam, however, has only a population of 231,747 souls of whom 40,000 are Jews, forming 103 congregations. Dublin contains nearly as many people, of whom nine only are of that persuasion, not sufficient to constitute one synagogue.

† It is one of the two above mentioned. They derive their descent and name from Kohath, the second son of Levi. The device of the hands is adopted from the 9th Chapter of Leviticus, " And Aaron lift " up his hands to bless the people."

‡ A Jew a short time ago paid a visit to a Christian friend in the neighbourhood of Ballybough-bridge.

neighbourhood not deeming it any sacrilege to plunder the burying ground of a Jew, though they are very scrupulous in violating that of a Christian.

TABLE OF SECTARIAN POPULATION.

It is much to be regretted that no accurate estimate has been hitherto made of the comparative numbers of the different sects in the metropolis, though many orders have been issued for that purpose. In the year 1731, a return was made to the House of Lords of the Protestants of Ireland, but it is not to be found in the Record Office. In 1740, the Lord Lieutenant issued an order to the Commissioners of the Revenue, in consequence of which the Supervisors of hearth money, returned the Protestant housekeepers of Dublin county, including the city, at 7065, which at six to a family would give 42,390. In 1766, the House of Peers ordered the ministers and curates to make a return of the Protestant and Roman Catholic families of the respective parishes in the different dioceses. This was so imperfect, that of 209 parishes in the diocese of Dublin, 90 only were returned. A similar order was issued by the present Archbishop of Dublin to the clergy of his diocese, a few years ago, and circular letters sent to each; but the result has been as little satisfactory: and though we have by Mr. Whitelaw's indefatigable exertion an accurate return of the whole, the proportion of each yet remains to be ascertained. In the following table, the returns of the different dissenting congregations have been communicated to us by the respective pastors, or other members who had opportunity to know, and their accuracy may be relied on. But for the proportion of Protestants to Roman Catholics we have no certain data. Mr. Whitelaw ascertained the number of Protestants of all denominations in his own parish of St. Catherine, to be 2000, giving a proportion of 9 to 1 to the Roman Catholics; but he does not suppose that this may be adopted for the entire Liberties, much less for the eastern parts of the town, where the majority of householders are Protestants. A shrewd and learned, but not a very accurate statistical writer, in 1812, conjectures that the

---

He found him in the act of repairing his house. Examining his improvements, he perceived near the fire-place, a stone with a Hebrew inscription, which intimated to the astonished Israelite, that the body of his father was buried in the chimney.

Protestants of Dublin, are to the Roman Catholics as 1 to 6.* In the House of Industry, during six years, ending 1789, there were admitted, Protestants 6313, Roman Catholics 17,816, being a proportion of about 1 to 3.† In a letter published in the year 1814 by the guardians of the Methodist societies, the Protestant population of the metropolis is stated at 60,200, giving a ratio to the Roman Catholics of about 1 to 2. Thus then it appears, that in four different calculations in the course of twenty-five years, the proportions varied in the ratios of 9 to 1, 6 to 1, 3 to 1, and 2 to 1! We have been diligent in searching for some certainty on this subject, but we confess we have not been able to acquire any satisfactory information. We cannot even form an opinion, where evidence is so inconclusive, and conjecture so various; and we had rather confess our ignorance than add to error, by adding another hypothesis.‡

Synoptical Table of the different Sects in Dublin, with their Places of Worship, and Number of each, in round numbers, in the year 1816.

Presbyterian	Strand-street	500	2960	Milbamites		Tailor's Hall - - 20	20
	Eustace-street -	200		Moravians -		Bishop-street ♦ 230	230
	Mary's Abbey -	2000		Baptists - -		Swift's-alley · - 150	150
	Usher's Quay ·	200		Quakers -		Meath-street - -	650
Seceders -	Burgher's Mass-lane - - -	50	140	Walker's -		Sycamore-alley - -	
						Stafford-street - - 90	140
	Anti-Burghers,					Capel-steeet - - 50	
	Mary's Abbey	90		Kelly's - -		Stephen-street - - 60	60
Independents	Plunket-street ·-	1000	1700	Foreigners -		French, St. Patrick's 20	41
	York-street - -	500				German, Poolbeg-st. 12	
	Poolbeg-street -	200				Jews - - - - - 9	
Methodists	Whitefriar-street	1000	1420			Total Dissenters	7,491
	Wesley Chapel -	200					
	Hendrick-street -	120					
	Cork-street - -	100					

* Wakefield, vol. ii. p. 607.   † Essay on Comparative Population, p. 11.

‡ Of the uncertainty of Statistical results in general, (See page ix. Life of Whitelaw) the last returns of 1814, made by order of Government, is a striking instance. In these, two whole parishes, St. George's and St. Luke's, are omitted, because, being situated in the county of Dublin, they were returned for the latter, and not for the city. For the same reason, parts of other parishes in various directions are also omitted. The omissions may account, why —after 16 years, during which the buildings were increasing in those very places—the number of houses of the table of 1814, appears nearly the same as that of Mr. Whitelaw, in 1798. The accuracy even of the return, which was instituted with such precaution, and effected with considerable expence to Government, has been much canvassed; and there is reason to believe it incorrect in several parishes. We quoted it, because we think its general result a confirmation of Mr. Whitelaw's.

THE CITY OF DUBLIN. 849

ORPHAN SCHOOLS.

FEMALE ORPHAN HOUSE.

This excellent Institution owes its origin to the sympathetic feelings of female benevolence. In the year 1790, two ladies, Mrs. Ed. Tighe, and Mrs. Ch. Este, at their own private expence, took a small old house in Prussia-street, and placed in it five female orphans. This humane commencement soon met with corresponding feelings in the public. It was remarkable, that for 35 years an asylum had been opened in Dublin for the reception of unhappy females who had deviated from virtue, and as yet no precautionary Institution had been founded for the early reception of that class, who, bereft of their natural guardians and protectors, were in a peculiar degree the objects of unmanly seduction. When this example therefore was given, it was speedily followed. A subscription was opened the following year, which increased so fast that the present extensive building was erected, on the north Circular-road, two years after the plan was first proposed; and these amiable women had the heart-felt satisfaction to see a noble institution immediately rise upon their humble and limited establishment. The situation of the house is airy and healthy, having in front an area planted with trees and shrubs, and in the rear a large garden. It is held in perpetuity on a lease from Lord Monck. To this the governors have added ten acres of ground for the use of the establishment, rented on a terminable lease. The interior of the house has accommodations for 150 children, which are its proposed limitation. It has however been extended to 160, which number is now in the house. The qualifications for admission, require that the child be a real orphan, deprived of both father and and mother; and further, that she be not under five nor over ten years old; which must be certified by the minister and church-wardens of her parish.[*] All persuasions are

---

[*] A singular difference exists between this and one of the qualifications for admission into the Female Orphan Asylum, St. George's-fields, London; which require that " the settlement of the female orphan cannot be found." It has been remarked on this, that there is no such person existing. By

5 Q

received, but they are educated in that of the established church. Besides the usual education, they are carefully taught needle work and such other things as would qualify them for servants in different capacities, for which they are in great request. Their early introduction into the house, their being generally separated from those ties, and consequently from that intercourse with relatives in the lower classes, which too frequently counteract the strictest education; and above all, the particular care that is bestowed in giving them correct habits, and steady principles, confer on the children brought up in this establishment, a degree of consideration somewhat above those of ordinary schools; though it must be confessed, that this is not unattended with complaints that the servants educated here sometimes forget the humility of their station, and become unpleasant by the assumption of a fanciful superiority.

Since the commencement, 107 children have been apprenticed from the school, and nine have been returned, to their surviving relatives.*

The governors are now an incorporated society, and an annual sum is granted by Parliament, for its support. Its funds are as follow:

PERMANENT. £. . d.
Interest on £5700. accumulated from Subscriptions, Legacies, and Donations, and vested in 5 per cents. - 285 0 0

FLUCTUATING.
Charity Sermon - - - 500 0 0
Produce of Work - - - - - 110 0 0
Subscriptions and Donations - - - 160 0 0
Parliamentary Grant (average) - - - 1633 13 4

£2688 13 4

the Laws of England, the settlement of an orphan is in the parish in which it is found, when it can be referred no where else.

* The want of a domestic place of worship for so large an establishment was much felt, and the sum of 2500l. was granted by Parliament for building one. With this fund a chapel is now erecting contiguous to the house, which will not only be an essential appendage to the institution, but be very convenient to the inhabitants of the vicinity, who are on the confines of St. Mark's parish, and remote from the church of that and every other.

ESTABLISHMENT.

	£	s.	d.
Two Physicians }			
One Surgeon }			
Chaplain	30	0	0
Register	70	0	0
Matron	34	2	6
Assistant	20	0	0
Writing-master,	40	0	0
Five Girls Teachers, £7. 14s. 6d. each,	38	11	8
Books	12	0	0
	244	14	2
Total Expence, including children's maintainance, &c.	£2693	2	9

MASONIC FEMALE ORPHAN SCHOOL.

In the year 1790, a few freemasons conceived the project of establishing a school for the children of deceased brethren, and a subscription, amounting to a few shillings each, was entered into, by which a small school of about half a dozen children was supported. In a short time it attracted the attention of the body at large, the subscriptions increased, and the school, augmented to twenty female orphans, was opened in Domville-lane, Prussia-street. It is conducted on the same principles as parochial schools, save only that there is no inquiry made into the religious persuasion of the child till she is admitted into the school; her profession is then ascertained, and she is carefully brought up in its tenets. There are many schools where the children of all persuasions meet together for a few hours in the day, but this is perhaps the only one where they reside under the same roof, are clothed in the same uniform, and dieted at the same table; evincing by the amity and harmony of their lives, the facility of universal education without reference to religious opinions. This liberal school has fluctuated very much in its resources. It is at present reduced to 12 children, but from the support it has recently received, its funds are again so flourishing that the governors propose to take a new house, and enlarge their school to 25.

It is supported by subscription and a charity sermon, besides the fees paid by Masons on their initiation, which are appropriated to this purpose.

MIXED SCHOOLS.

DUBLIN FREE-SCHOOL, SCHOOL-STREET.

The first Sunday-school established in this city, and in Ireland, was opened in 1786, by the Rev. Richard Powell, rector of Dundrum, in the parish of St. Catherine's, of which he was at that time curate. The female children assembled in the parochial school-house, which the governors lent for that purpose; and the boys were accommodated by the Earl of Meath, an anxious friend to the institution, with the use of the Court-house of the Liberties of Thomas Court and Donore. From 300 to 500 children of all denominations generally attended, and exclusive of the usual course of reading, writing, and arithmetic, the sacred scriptures were admitted and read, but without any selection, explanation, or comment whatever. In consequence of the gratuitous assistance of many respectable persons who were friendly to the infant institution, the expences were so moderate, that the collection made at an annual charity sermon preached in the Church of St. Catherines, was sufficient to answer every demand. The accommodation, however, being not only indifferent, but insufficient for the continually increasing numbers in that poor but populous part of the city, an idea was conceived of erecting a school for the purpose, on a large scale, and with every neçessary convenience. Among the promoters of the Institution, the Friends, or as they are usually denominated the Quakers, who in the parish of St. Catherine's are numerous, took an anxious and decided part, and in consequence, in a great measure, of the active and unremitting exertions of Mr. Ephraim Bewley, one of their body, so many respectable and opulent citizens were induced to contribute liberally, that in a short time a sum was subscribed nearly sufficient to defray the expence of the intended edifice, when the work was commenced, and in 1798 finished, with a rapidity that evinces the energy of that respectable body, and with a substantial plainness and neatness that does equal credit to their taste and good sense.

This seminary, open to the children of all denominations of Christians, and therefore called the Dublin Free School-house, is situated in School-street,

THE CITY OF DUBLIN.

in the parish of St. Catherine; it is of a rectangular form, 156 feet by 37, of brick, and three stories high; of these, the basement story consists principally of stores rented by merchants in the vicinity, and on the two upper floors are the school-rooms, four in number, viz. two for males, and two for females; each 56 feet by 33, spacious, lofty, and well ventilated. The male and female schools have entrances perfectly distinct; and are separated from each other by a spacious Committee-room, and an apartment appropriated to the superintendant, who by an ingenious contrivance of the architect, is enabled by a small change in his position, to command an uninterrupted view of the four schools, though on different floors.* While he sits, the entire of the male and female schools on the first floor are open to his inspection, as are those on the second floor when he stands: thus a constant sense of his superintending eye, contributes greatly to preserve order and silence; while his communication with his assistants is direct, and unembarrassed by the necessity of moving from one school to another to give his directions.

From the commencement of this Institution in January, 1786, it was open for the admission of children on Sundays only until March, 1811, when the governors, anxious to extend its benefits to the utmost, opened it as a daily school also. Attendance from nine in the morning till one in the afternoon, and from three to six in the afternoon.

The Income and Expenditure of these schools for the year 1812, were as follow :—

INCOME.	£.	s.	d.
Subscriptions	377	10	1
Donations	23	0	0
Legacies	222	15	0
From scholars of weekly school	100	11	6
From scholars of daily ditto	256	10	0
For stationary sold, including payment for books lost by scholars	104	7	7
For work done in daily female school	36	17	1
From female scholars, for articles of clothing	54	3	6¼
	£1155	14	9¼

---

* This plan is deemed so efficient for the purposes of superintendance, that it is adopted in some extensive manufactories in the Liberties.

EXPENDITURE.

	£.	s.	d.
Balance due last year	194	10	5¼
Rent and insurance, one year	138	18	8
Superintendant	100	0	0
Teachers of Weekly School	90	10	0
Teachers of Daily ditto	150	12	0
Stationary	71	19	4
Furniture and Repairs	36	8	0
Coals and Candles	47	8	0
Printing and Advertising	5	2	2
Cleaning Schools	14	9	5¼
Threads, Needles, &c. &c. for Female Daily Working School	12	17	9
Articles for Clothing for Female Scholars	106	3	9¼
Balance in Treasurer's hands	183	14	8
	£1155	14	9¼

This school has been for many years conducted on a plan which does not involve in its management any of those doctrines in which the different sects of Christians disagree; and Mr. Joseph Lancaster's system, admitting of the same latitude, has been latterly introduced, and we think judiciously: such a system, indeed, seems to be best adapted to the peculiar circumstances of the children of the poor, in a district where Roman Catholics are to all other sects conjunctively as 9 to 1; and it has been attended with success. A sufficient knowledge in reading, writing, and arithmetic, is rapidly, and at a very moderate expense, communicated to the objects of its care, and with it what is perhaps still more valuable, habits of order, cleanliness, and decency, to which we may add of industry also among the females, in whose schools a mistress of superior qualifications superintends the working department: the remuneration here held out to the girls has been attended with very beneficial effects; they receive the entire of their earnings in clothes made in the schools; their improvement in this branch, to which they dedicate two days in the week, is considerable, and has eventually produced a considerable increase of attendance.

Since the commencement of the Weekly School up to the year 1814,

THE CITY OF DUBLIN. 855

24,361 have been taught, and there are now on the books 578. Since the commencement of the Daily School, 8089 have been received, and there are no less than 796 in daily attendance. The proficiency and regularity of this mass of children are really surprising; they are taken from the poorest classes of society, and pass from the licentious and irregular habits of the streets in the morning, and again return to them in the evening; yet they suddenly conform, and implicitly submit to the discipline of one another, without apparent coercion or corporal punishment while they are in school, and the whole machinery moves with the utmost regularity under one superintendant.

Contiguous to the school-house, but perfectly detached from it, are excellent soup-shops, which are at present unemployed, but have been found of great utility in facilitating the subsisting the poor in seasons of scarcity: they are neat and convenient, and situated in a yard flagged with mountain granite.

SUNDAY AND DAILY SCHOOL, NORTH STRAND.

In the same year and on the same principles as the preceding, was opened at the other extremity of the city, the Sunday School on the North Strand, for the reception and instruction of the poor children of the parishes of St. Mary's, St. Thomas's, and afterwards of St. George's. It consists of a neat building, not so extensive or so arranged as the former, but having the advantage of a chapel, in which divine service is performed every Sunday to a numerous congregation, whose weekly contributions materially assist the establishment. The Governors finding, on inquiry, that the children were for the most part unemployed during the week days, in a short time opened it for the reception of day scholars also. On this was engrafted a School for Female Industry, which has been very prosperous. Some of the regulations of these schools are peculiar, and seem very well adapted to the circumstances of them.*

* As they are open to all religious persuasions, one of the masters is a Catholic, who instructs his persuasion in their own catechism, and conducts them every Sunday to chapel. To induce an early attendance, bread was distributed to those who came soonest; and after some time clothing, as a reward;

In consequence of their being strictly enforced, this Institution, which is held together by no fund but the annual voluntary contributions of individuals, has continued to flourish for twenty-nine years. During that period 7000 boys and girls have been admitted, and there are now 340 in attendance, being an equal number of each sex; of whom one hundred of the most deserving are annually clothed. The annual expence amounts to £450. which is defrayed by subscriptions, a charity sermon, and by the profits of the children's work.

GENERAL DAILY FREE-SCHOOL.

This was established in the year 1796, in Abbey-street, and from thence transferred to the rear of the Linen-Hall. It consists of a lower room for girls, and an upper for boys. There are at present on the books, and in daily attendance, 64 boys and 77 girls, of all persuasions. It is much to be regretted that this well conducted school has not better accommodations. The rooms are small and inconvenient; but the excellent order, silent regularity, and decent cleanliness of the children, render it a practical model for such establishments. Among the annual expenditure of the school is a small sum given in rewards of soap, which seems to have produced an excellent effect. The apparel of the poor children is as worn, and their persons as naked as those of the lower classes usually are, but there is no offensive negligence to disgust the visitor: their hands and faces are washed, their hair combed, and the scanty portion of linen whole and white; and the crowded rooms in which they are obliged to be confined breathe an air of pure and wholesome cleanliness, affording a convincing proof that dirt is not a natural propensity, but the acquired habit of extreme poverty

to prevent the child from withdrawing from the school when this was obtained, a note for the amount was passed by the parent, on which he was liable to be sued. Woolen cloaks are lent out to the most deserving girls during the winter months, which are returned in spring; those who keep them best, receive a premium: one set of cloaks has in this way served for five winters. Advancement in education is considered not a task but a reward; and industry is made preparatory to learning. No girl is allowed to write till she has made a shirt. The superintendance of the schools naturally devolves on the Chaplain, who does not receive his salary unless he attends at least four days in the week, to be certified by his signature in the visitors' book.

among the poor of this country, and is readily corrected by kindness and attention. The excellence of this institution has made it very deservedly popular among those for whose benefit it is intended; but as the narrow limits of the house will contain but few, the subscribers are reluctantly compelled to dismiss a number of applications to an institution which they wish to be unlimited. There have been admitted since the commencement, 1126 boys, 1379 girls; total 2505. The income and expenditure are as follows:—

Income - - £98 2 9 | Expenditure - - £109 2 9

There is a sum of £190. 6s. 2d. in the hands of the Treasurer, which it is proposed to increase by subscription, and build with the amount a new school.

LINEN-HALL SUNDAY AND DAILY SCHOOLS.

THIS was opened in 1812, on a large scale. It was intended to rival the establishment in School-street, and supply the same means of instruction to the poor children of the north side of the city as that did to the south. Accordingly, a large building was taken in Yarn-hall-street, and three very large rooms completely fitted up for the reception of 400 children. But the progress of the school did not correspond to this commencement. The subscribers having once established it, failed to support or superintend it: the children were neglected, the subscriptions unpaid, and this large establishment exhibits all the symptoms of want of care, and disorder, and seems rapidly hastening to its dissolution. There are 114 boys and 65 girls on the books, but their attendance is very irregular, and their appearance squalid and neglected. Here then are two schools in the immediate vicinity, exhibiting all the opposite effects of care and inattention. The one useful and prosperous, but without sufficient means of accommodation; the other possessing extensive accommodation, but worthless and in disorder—scholars without a school, and a school without scholars. It would be well if they were united, and the excellent system of the one adopted in the extensive rooms of the other. The expenditure of this school is—Rent £30. Salary to Master £70 : total £120. The school is supported by subscription, and one penny per week from scholars.

ST. JAMES'S SUNDAY-SCHOOL.

This School was opened in 1812, and is connected with the parochial school, the master of which attends to the care of the books, &c. for which he is remunerated. It is conducted by a committee of ladies and gentlemen residing in its vicinity. Since its commencement fifty-four boys, and forty-eight girls have received premiums in clothes or books, the latter gratuitously supplied by the Association for Discountenancing Vice. The books not given in premiums are supplied by the Sunday School Society at reduced prices. Writing is not taught on Sundays, but the three most deserving in each class are instructed in it on Wednesday evenings, as a reward for their industry. It is supported by subscription.

Since its commencement 454 children have received instruction. There are now in attendance —

  Boys - - - - - 70
  Girls - - - - - 50
          Total 120

KELLET'S SCHOOL.

This school was founded in 1811, on a liberal bequest of £5000. left by Miss A. Kellet, of Fordstown, county of Meath, for that purpose. It is situated in Drumcondra, at the northern extremity of the city, a site judiciously selected, not only as being airy and healthy, but as affording means of education to the poor of this remote part of the city, who are too distant to avail themselves of any other. The building is constructed in the most permanent manner. Through the walls run brick flues, which effectually convey the heat of a stove through this extensive building. The ventilation in summer is equally effectual. The seminary consists of two apartments, 70 feet long and 35 broad; the lower prepared to accommodate 350 boys, and the upper as many girls. Both floors are constructed and arranged on Lancaster's principles, inclined planes, where the scholars sit so as always to front the superintendents, and be under their eye; while a visitor commands both schools at one view. The course of education is the same as that for which the Society for Promoting the Education of the Poor, received a grant from Parliament. The girls are taught needle-work half the day, and receive the produce of their labour in articles of clothing, as an incentive to their industry. Pupils pay three halfpence per week during the summer months, which is remitted in the winter to those who have been regular in their attendance. Annexed to the school is a house and garden for the accommodation of four teachers, a master, head monitor, and two mistresses. The whole cost £1740., and is built on a lease from Lord Mountjoy, for 1999 years. The expenditure of the school is

Rent   -   -   -   -   £ 17 10 0
Salaries   -   -   -   130 0' 0

Since its commencement 590 boys and 457 girls have been admitted, and are now in the school.

SOUTH-EASTERN DISTRICT SCHOOL.

This large school was opened in Stephen's Green, in the year 1813, for boys instructed on Lancaster's system. It was immediately filled, as well from the avidity of the poor to learn, as from the want of all other means of instruction in that part of the city. The number of boys upon the rolls amounts to 286, of whom 200 are in daily attendance, and being assembled at the same time, crowd the school. This circumstance compelled the governing committee to refuse admittance to more. There are 119 on their lists anxiously expecting vacancies, and 1000 children at least would avail themselves of the institution, if they could be accommodated. In 1814, a school was opened for girls under the same building, and there are already on the list 254. The cleanliness of the children, and the silent regularity of this large society, is another proof of the facility of correcting the habits of the poor, and the growing improvement in the systems of general education. The schools are supported by subscription, one penny a week paid by the children, and by work in the female school sold at the repository.

The expense of the boys, for the last year was, deducting £78. for repairs, £246. 19s.; that of the girls £99. 8s. 1d.

SCHOOLS ON ERASMUS SMITH'S FOUNDATION.

COMBE SCHOOL.

In the year 1805, the governors of Erasmus Smith's schools erected on the Combe a large school for children of both sexes. In the centre are the master and mistress' apartments, and at each end are two spacious school rooms, one for either sex. Over each of these are apartments of corresponding size, intended originally for factories, in which the children might be employed on alternate days in some system of industry. Unfortunately this plan has not been pursued, and these fine apartments remain unoccupied and useless. The building is erected in an elevated and open situation at the upper extremity of the Combe, and having an area both in front and rere, is airy and wholesome. Though there was no distinction made in the reception of children originally, those who attend are now exclusively Protestant.

Boys - - - -	160
Girls - - - -	153
Total -	315

The master receives a salary of £100., and the most deserving children premiums of clothes and shoes. The annual expenditure, including £40. rent, amounts to £216.

MARBLE STREET.

This school was erected in 1811, and intended to provide instruction for the very poor and populous district of St. Mark's parish. No religious distinction is made in the admission of children, though the great majority are Protestants, and Dr. Bell's system is adopted in the schools. The number of children in attendance daily is

Boys - - - -	90
Girls - - - -	60
Total -	150

The annual expenditure is £100.

THE CITY OF DUBLIN.

SCHOOL FOR YOUNG SWEEPS.

AMONG the many projects which the exuberant charity of the metropolis has indulged in, this school perhaps is the most fanciful. There is certainly no class of the community which has so much and so deservedly excited public commiseration as that of young sweeps, and we think the existence of such a trade is a reproach to the police of any state where it is permitted; but we think the only effectual remedy would be to remove the cause.* The dismal effects can be but feebly remedied, and the condition of a young sweep is but little improved because he knows how to read and write. The incident which called the public attention to this object, and gave rise to the establishment of this school, was as follows. A master-sweep had been tried and convicted of cruelty to his apprentice. He was sentenced to be publicly whipped; and the general indignation was strongly excited by the circumstances which appeared in evidence.† It was proved that the child had been blistered by lashes and burned with coals; and when the sores festered, to add to the poignancy of fresh burnings, he was dipped in cold water, and lashed and burned alternately. He was brought into court, wrapped in a blanket, covered with ointment, and shortly after the trial died, it is said, of a general mortification.

At the next yearly meeting of the Sunday School Society, this event excited much sympathy, and produced a determination to relieve this most forlorn and degraded class of society. In 1816 a society was founded, in which the lord mayor, who was also member for the city, took a leading part. At their first meeting various enormities were reported from the

* A machine for sweeping chimneys was sometime since invented by an ingenious man of the name of Robinson, which was approved of, and recommended, by the Dublin Society, to whose examination it was submitted: it consists of brushes fixed to flexible joints, so as to adapt themselves to the size of the chimney. This machine has been used with much success in Dublin, but it fails where the flues of the chimney are intricate or circuitous. Would it not be possible for the legislature, which taxes hearths, and regulates the size of bricks, to oblige chimneys to be built so as to be accommodated to such a machine, and for the public to supersede the necessity of employing sweeps by encouraging it?

† This feeling occasioned a melancholy catastrophe; an immense croud assembled on the steps of the Royal Exchange, and the pressure was so great that the whole range of the ponderous balustrades in the front gave way, and the mass of people was precipitated on the flags below; eleven men, women, and children were crushed to death by the fall.

best evidence. Several instances of murder, the constant practice of employing them to rob or steal by night; procuring young females, and using them as boys: in effect, such a system of cruelty, indecency, and moral depravity was displayed, as degraded the present state of these wretched children far below the level of humanity, and precluded all hope, by rendering them utterly unfit for any future state of society. To apply some remedy to these melancholy evils, it was resolved, in the first instance, to ascertain those master-sweeps who retain children without indentures, in order that steps might be immediately taken to put such children under the protection of the law. It was next considered, that, as they cannot pursue their trade, even if it was desirable, beyond a certain time of life, when they attain too large a stature, and as few can become masters, the great majority, at an adult age, must be thrown upon society without knowledge, principle, or employment. To counteract the present influence, and to qualify them for something better hereafter, a school was established to instruct them in reading, writing, and arithmetic. The trustee of Kellet's bequest readily granted the large rooms of that school for the purpose. Here they assemble every Sunday; a breakfast is provided by the subscribers; and they are supplied with shirts, cloaks, caps, and shoes; premiums of soap, combs, and money are given to excite a sense of decency and a feeling of cleanliness, and on one day of the week, at least, these forlorn outcasts are admitted to the rights and raised to the level of humanity. About forty attend every Sunday, and some of them evince a great desire to learn.*

* One child had learned to read from the labels on the doors of the houses where he waited to be admitted, and another who was not able to walk, from an accident, was carried to school at his own request, on the back of his companion. We are concerned, however, to state, that the charity is for the present suspended by the interference of their own clergy of the Roman Catholic persuasion, who suspect an intention of proselyting the children. Now, besides the usual precaution of using the Bible and other books of instruction without note or commentary, care is taken here, that no Protestant visitor shall even hold the book out of which the child is instructed, lest he might be suspected of supplying an oral commentary to a book that had none, and instil any doctrine inimical to the Roman Catholic Church. None but monitors of their own persuasion teach them, or hold the book while they learn. We respect that care which the pastor of every persuasion ought to pay to the flock he is appointed to watch over, and if there was reason to fear that any system of proselytism was concealed under the garb of charity, we should applaud the precautionary jealousy which defeated it even in the case of a degraded sweep; but it is not so; and we trust these forlorn outcasts will not be deprived of the new-born sensations of comfort, cleanliness, and wholesome food, by an unfounded suspicion.

THE CITY OF DUBLIN.

DEAF AND DUMB SCHOOL.

In the spring of the year 1816, a course of public lectures were delivered at the Rotunda by Doct. C. Orpen, on the instruction of the deaf and dumb, with a view to interest the humanity, and call the attention of the public to a subject little known in this country.* In order to afford a practical illustration of the principles of the science, and an example of the efficacy of their application, a deaf and dumb boy, who had already been partially instructed, was introduced to their notice. The interest excited by the novelty of the exhibition was considerable, and the progress which the

* To the venerable and amiable Abbé L'Epée, the world is indebted for the apparently hopeless, but successful attempt of supplying those organs to the deaf and dumb of which nature had deprived them. He was followed by the Abbé Sicard, who superintended a school founded for the deaf and dumb at Bourdeaux, in 1786; on the death of L'Epée, he was elected to that of Paris. There appeared besides, Le Père Famin and Perreira in France, Heinicke in Leipsic, Amman at Amsterdam, Peter Ponce and Bonnet in Spain, and Dr. Wallis and Braidwood in England; who engaged nearly at the same time in the same benevolent pursuit: of these Sicard published a treatise on the mode of instruction, in 1803. Another appeared in 1809, by Dr. Watson, master of the London school. The first suggestion of this kind which was ever submitted to the public in Ireland, appeared in the Anthologia Hibernica more than twenty years ago. It is a scheme for an universal alphabet, formed on a suggestion of Sir W. Jones, and is pointed out as a method to facilitate the instruction of the deaf and dumb. The author assumes a principle, that original alphabets were formed from an outline of the several organs of speech in the act of articulation, and he gives an engraved sketch of the section of the mouth, lips, teeth, tongue, palate, and nose, being the parts used in modulating the voice as it issues from the *glottis* in articulating the vowel, labial, dental, lingual, palateal, and nasal sounds, which constitute the elements of every oral language. Thus, the simple vowel sounds are formed by the mouth more or less opened, a section of which would form the characters ⊇ ⊆ ⊂ , which nearly resemble the Greek letters, Λ Ε Ω. The consonants are no less accurately defined, the letter B, particularly, which has the same figure in most existing languages. Its character is formed of the profile of the lips gently compressed, as |3. But for the further elucidation of this interesting idea, we must refer to the article itself in the Anthologia. See Anth. Hib. for July, 1793. As a mode of instructing the deaf and dumb, its application is obvious. The author of this ingenious essay was Doct. Edw. Walsh, since Physician to his Majesty's Forces, and author of " The Narrative of the Expedition to Holland," &c. He left Dublin shortly after, and his suggestion was not acted on.

A few years ago, the celebrated Robinson, who had been instrumental in bringing Romana's army from Denmark, came to Dublin. He found out here a number of deaf and dumb children, and proposed to government to establish and direct a national school for their instruction on the Abbé Sicard's plan, but his proposal was not acceded to, and his project fell to the ground till Doct. Orpen, happily revived it.

child had made in a short period of three months, as well in the art of writing and calculation, as in the power of conveying his meaning by articulate sounds, removed at once all objection to the practicability of the project, and made it the earnest wish of all the audience, not only that the education of this child should be completed, but that similar benefits should be extended to all other children in Ireland in the same unfortunate situation. A meeting was immediately called, by public advertisement, on the 18th of May, 1816, who founded an institution for the education of the deaf and dumb poor of Ireland. This was opened on the 19th of June following, under the patronage of His Excellency Lord Viscount Whitworth, and was the first public provision ever made in this country for such a purpose.

In order to ascertain the necessity of such an establishment, circular letters were sent to different parts of Ireland, containing certain queries, tending to ascertain the number of children of this description, and their capability of instruction. More than one hundred authenticated cases have been already laid before the committee who conduct the institution, and there is reason to believe that the number who stand in need of, and could derive benefit from it in different parts of Ireland is very considerable. As the claimants are thus numerous, and the object national, it is proposed, when circumstances will permit, to found an extensive seminary for their accommodation. Meantime the governors of the House of Industry, to further the present design, have given up a part of the Penitentiary in Smithfield, where 16 children can be accommodated. The school opened with 8 pupils. The number is now increased to 13, and 3 more are about to be admitted. They are all boys, as they have but one dormitory; but girls will be also received, as soon as they can be accommodated. They are of all ages, from six to sixteen. The institution is supported by subscriptions and donations; of which last £150. have been vested in government stock as the commencement of a permanent fund. The mode of instruction is adopted from the Abbé Sicard, but differs in some respects from that pursued in Paris and London.* Doct. C. Orpen, who had already

---

* The Abbé L'Epée's method was merely cultivating the memory of his pupils, and Sicard places no confidence in their mental powers, but talks as if he had formed their intellects. Doct. Orpen supposes them already supplied with mental faculties, which he endeavours to develope by teaching them how to communcate their own ideas to others by articulate sounds, and to comprehend those of others when

directed his attention so successfully to the subject, kindly gives his gratuitous services as instructor of the pupils and superintendant of the institution.

The first thing that strikes a stranger on his entrance, is the profound silence which reigns in the room, so different from the buzzing noise which assails him in every other school; but there is nothing melancholy connected with this absence of sound; the countenances of all the children around are remarkably cheerful and intelligent. Their propensities are very social, and every day increases their means of social communication. They always feel great joy when they are taught to expect the arrival of a new scholar, and testify it by their countenances whenever a stranger enters, as if he were the companion they looked for. Many of them came to the institution without knowing themselves that they laboured under any defect. Happily, the consciousness of the fact and the power to remedy it occurred at the same time, and they seemed delighted at the new prospect unfolded to their view. One boy had been sent from the Foundling Hospital, where he had learned mechanically to write an excellent hand, but annexed no meaning to the letters he had copied; his avidity for writing seemed wonderfully increased as he discovered the figures he copied were symbols of other things, and that he could communicate his thoughts, and learn those of his companions by means of them.*

communicated to them in a written language. In the process of teaching, no attempt has yet been made to point out to the pupils the resemblance between the organs of speech and the shape of the letters, though in forming the vowels the symbol which marks them denotes the manner in which the mouth is to be shaped. Thus, a perpendicular oval ( ) is put over a vowel which sounds like the *a*, in wall, &c. A transverse oval ⌒ over a vowel which sounds like the *o* in do, &c. and a circular mark ( ) over a vowel which sounds like the *o* in no, &c. because these symbols nearly give the shape of the lips in forming those sounds. We regret that our limits will not permit us to enter fully into this curious and interesting subject; we refer to the institution itself, where its founder readily points out the process, and freely communicates the principles of this school, so novel in our metropolis.

* Though this is the first school founded exclusively for the education of deaf and dumb in Ireland, a competent mode of instruction had been discovered and practised long since. In the beginning of the last century, John Burns was born deaf and dumb, in the town of Monaghan. He discovered a strong natural capacity, was taught to read and write, and acquired a considerable knowledge of arithmetic, geography, history, and chronology. In the humblest circumstances, he commenced life as a pedlar with a few shillings, which he improved into a considerable sum, and became a shopkeeper. He was unfortunate, however, in his connections, became a bankrupt, and was cast into prison. From hence he was liberated, and paid the full amount of his debts, by his literary talents. His misfortunes and abilities had attracted the notice of the eccentric and worthy Philip Skelton, under whose patronage he composed at an advanced period of life, "An Historical and Chronological Remembrancer," which was published by subscription, in Dublin, by William Watson, in 1775. It contains 500 pages of curious matter, and appears a surprising intellectual effort of a man born with his infirmities.

5 S

THE HISTORY OF

Synoptical Table of the Education of the Lower Class in Dublin for the year 1816.

		Sunday	Evening	
		Girls	Boys	Girls	Total of each School.

Protestant	Blue Coat Hospital	150
	Foundling Hospital*	624
	Hibernian School	510
	Marine School	114
	Bedford Asylum	710
	Penitentiaries	124
	Charlemont Street†	120
	Clontarf ‡	0
	Parochial School	7
	Orphan House	0
	Bethesda ditto	5
Catholic	Harold's Cross	0
	Paradise Row	0
	James Street Convent	8
	George's Hill ditto	0
	Summer Hill ditto	4
	Ditto Orphans	1
	Clarke's Court	0
	Forbes Street	0
	Warren's Mount Convent	0
	Clarendon Street	00
	Meath Street	
	Skinner Row	
	Lime Street	
	Mary's Lane	
	Denmark Street	
	James Street Chapel	
	Liffey Street ditto	
	Francis Street	
	St. John's and St. Michael's	
	Teresian Society	
	Townsend Street	
	Josephian Society	
	Bridge Street Chapel	
	St. John's ditto	
	Meath Street ditto	
	Ditto ditto	
	Trinitarian Society	
	Patrician ditto	
	Second Trinitarian ditto	
	Arran Quay	
	Church Street	
	General Asylum	
Presbyterian	Strand Street	
	Eustace Street	
	Mary's Abbey	
	Usher's Quay	
Independents	Plunket Street	
Methodists	Whitefriar s Street	
	Hendrick Street	
	Cork Street	
	Walkers	
Moravian	Bishop Street	
Baptists	Swift's Alley	
French	Meyler's Alley	
Mixed	Masonic	
	School Street	
	North Strand	
	General Daily	
	Linen Hall	
	James's	
	Kellett's	
	South East District	
Erasmus Smith's	Combe	
	Marble Street	
Sweeps	Drumcondra	
Deaf and Dumb	Smithfield	

In the foregoing Table all the seminaries are included which afford education to the poor of the metropolis; where it was possible, we have distinguished the children sent from Dublin in schools which receive them from other parts. In the Marine and Hibernian Schools, there may be some whose parents were not resident in Dublin, but we have not distinguished them. In calculating the expence of each, we found some difficulty, from various causes, and we give the following, rather as a probable average, than a certain estimate; we believe, however, it will be found near the truth.

29 Protestant schools educate		3194 children,	at an annual expence of	£44,000.
32 Catholic ditto	ditto	5095	ditto	ditto	8,000.
12 Dissenter ditto	ditto	906	ditto	ditto	2,500.
12 Mixed ditto	ditto	4402	ditto	ditto	2,500.
85		13,597			£57,700.

To account for this extraordinary difference of expence, it will be considered that in all the Protestant establishments, with the exception of the parochial, the children are maintained in large seminaries with liberal endowments, in one of which the average expence of each child is £29. 16s. 6d.* In the Roman Catholic schools, one-fifth only are maintained, and at the small average expence of £7. or £3. each; and in the mixed schools the children are only educated.

It might be presumed, however, that where so many children are educated, and at so great an expence, that education was afforded to every child in the metropolis who stood in need of it, and that every child who stood in need of it, availed themselves of it; but the fact is otherwise. The population of the lower classes of Dublin amounts to 115,174.†—Suppose, then, that each family averages at 5,‡ it will give 23,014 families; of these, 2 are usually the parents, 1 is either adult or infant,§ too old or too

* Blue Coat Hospital. See p. 577. † See Appendix, No. I. p. vii.

‡ Mr. Whitelaw found the average at Bray to be exactly 5¼, and in his own parish of St. Catherine's to be 4½. This difference he accounts for by the sedentary habits, and other causes of insalubrity among the lower classes of the Liberties. We suppose, however, that 5 is a fair average for the whole city.

§ From the improvident habit of early marriages among the lower classes in Ireland, it frequently happens that parents who are yet not old, have children of all ages; it is common to see a young man just married with his infant brother in his arms. Where the adult is of an age to earn his bread, the care of the child devolves upon one of the younger, hence it is frequently a cause of being absent from school; and where there are more children in a family, they " mind the child," and go to school in rotation.

young for education, and 2 are of an age to learn: and this is generally found to be the case. In schools where the admission is indiscriminate, a single child, or 3 children of the same family, are sometimes found, but 2 is the more frequent number; that we may not appear, however, to overrate it, we will assume only that in every 2 families 3 children are at the age of instruction, and those who are acquainted with the metropolis will admit that this is an underrated proportion. This would give 34,516 children who need education, of whom 13,597 only, receive it. In the year 1797 there were but 54 schools in the metropolis containing 7416 children. It was supposed at that time that the education of the poor was carried to its greatest extent; but while the population has scarcely increased since that time the number of children educated is nearly doubled. Thus then it appears, that much has been done, yet much remains undone; £57,000. are expended every year, yet 2 children out of 3 still remain uneducated.

CHARITY SERMONS.

THE greater number of the schools and other charities in Dublin, is supported by charity sermons, a mode of collecting money for a public object, which from the extent to which it is carried, the interest that it excites, and the universality of the practice, is a peculiar and distinguishing feature of the metropolis of Ireland. Having no poor rates to pay, they consider themselves exempt from a burthen heavily laid upon their neighbours, and they voluntarily impose upon themselves an annual contribution greater than any compulsory tax. Every charity has its stated time of the year for an appeal to the public, and so anxious are the governors to prevent the interference of any other, that it is no unusual circumstance to see it advertised for several months before. As the selection of a preacher is of considerable consequence, the earliest application is made to one of those who are most popular, and his assistance very early secured, and notified accordingly. As the day approaches, the whole parish is in commotion. Bills are posted, advertisements put forth, and letters every where circulated. Deputations of the parishioners set out in coaches to wait on the lord lieutenant, lord mayor, and other public or opulent characters to request their attendance. Ladies, the most remarkable for their rank and beauty, are appointed collectors. Every body takes an interest in the charity as if it was a personal concern,

THE CITY OF DUBLIN.

and every means are taken to insure its success. It is sometimes usual even to close the churches in the vicinity that the congregation may be compelled to that in which the sermon is preached. On the important day, if the preacher or the charity be at all popular, the church is generally crowded. It is held disreputable for any parishioners or other person connected with the charity, to absent themselves, and the additional congregation of strangers causes an overflow. Instances have frequently occurred where a guard of soldiers has been obliged to keep order among the crowd who were kept out, and certain stewards with white wands to mark their authority, to regulate the tumultuary congregation that had got in. Under such circumstances it is much to be regretted that scenes of irregularity, little according with the solemnity of the place, have sometimes occurred, and the whole of the service which preceded the sermon been entirely unattended to. But when the preacher ascends the pulpit, the scene suddenly changes; the wave of the multitude subsides, and every auditor is fixed in wrapt attention. After the sermon, the ladies attended by white rods, proceed from pew to pew with a silver plate.* The collection of each pew is poured into a bason held by her attendant, and the plate is presented empty to the next, that every one's donation may be conspicuous. Thus every engine is moved to increase the collection; and the charity of the congregation is so far from being the simple dictate of religion, that it is a mixed emotion, in which eloquence, pity, beauty and vanity have a considerable share.

Among the many incidents which have occurred to mark the deep interest which the people of the metropolis take in charity sermons, we shall mention one which, though sufficiently known, is too remarkable to be omitted. On the 30th of March, 1794, a sermon was announced for the Female Orphan House to be preached by the Rev. Dean Kirwan,† in

---

* In England and in the Roman Catholic chapels in Ireland the collectors stand at the door, and the congregation give as they go out.

† This extraordinary man was born in Galway, in 1754. He went at the age of seventeen to the Danish Island of St. Croix, in the West Indies, where he remained for six years. On his return he studied at St. Omer's, took orders, and became Roman Catholic chaplain to the Neapolitan Embassador, in 1778. After two years solemn deliberation, he conformed to the established church in 1787, and preached for the first time in St. Peter's Church in June in that year. Here immense crowds thronged to hear him, and on the following year the governors of the parochial schools came to a resolution, " that from the effects which the sermons of the Rev. W. B. Kirwan had from the pulpit, his officiating in the metropolis ought to be considered a peculiar national advantage, and that vestries

St. Peter's Church. The popularity both of the preacher and the institution was great, and the church was crowded with even a more than usual con-should be called to consider the most effectual method of securing to the city an instrument under Providence of such public benefit." He was now presented to the prebend of Howth, and the parish of St. Nicholas without, and in 1800 to the deanery of Kilalla by Lord Cornwallis. Every testimony that could mark the admiration of the public was conferred upon him. Besides the immense contributions which his sermons called forth, his portraits were painted and engraved; he was presented with addresses, pieces of plate, and the freedom of the corporations; and in 1792, a man whose energetic oratory was congenial to his own, introduced him to the notice of the Irish parliament in these words. " This man preferred our country, and our religion, and brought to both genius superior to what he found in either. He called forth the latent virtues of the human heart, and taught men to discover a mine of charity in themselves, of which the owners were unconscious. He came to interrupt the repose of the pulpit, and shakes one world with the thunder of another. But in feeding the lamp of charity, he exhausted the lamp of life." The violence of his efforts had brought on a spitting of blood, and he fell a victim to his exertions on the 7th of October, 1805. His funeral was attended by a long train of charity children from the different schools in Dublin, which his eloquence had so eminently contributed to support and extend.

Kirwan was the founder of a new school of pulpit oratory in Dublin. His sermons were the result of much labour and attention. He committed them to memory with the most exact precision, but he delivered them in a manner so apparently unpremeditated that they had the effect of natural and unstudied elocution. On one occasion, some interruption to the service in a crowded church, when he returned home he composed a discourse on the propriety of behaviour in the house of God, which he determined should be his subject when next called on to preach. Supposing, however, that it would have more effect if it seemed unpremeditated, and to arise from some immediate cause, he gave out a different text, and commenced on another topic: what he had calculated on took place: the disturbance again occurred. He broke off the discourse he had begun, and abruptly thundered a reproof from the pulpit, the more solemn and impressive as it seemed sudden and unpremeditated. We had heard this mentioned as a proof that all his sermons were extemporaneous; but his great mind was above disguise, and he candidly communicated to us the real circumstance. His action has been taxed with extravagance; he literally " came to disturb the repose of the pulpit;" it was his custom to remove the cushion, that the sound elicited from the boards both by his hands and feet might add to the effect of his empassioned delivery; strange as this was, the occasions were so appropriate, and accompanied by such energy of thought and potency of language, that the whole seemed perfectly natural and congruous. He had many personal deficiencies,—a weak voice, an oblique eye, and an unprepossessing countenance; but they were never noticed in the pulpit: the profound attention of his hearers remedied the one, and ardent feelings of his mind irradiated the other. His style of eloquence died with him. He had many imitators, but genius was wanting to sanction their attempts. They were principally distinguished by an extravagance of action, which is now happily banished from our pulpit, till some other Kirwan arise to give it currency. He has been succeeded by many charity sermon preachers of another school, whose high attainments and admirable compositions adorn and promote the sacred cause in which they are exerted,—but " the mine of charity" is not wrought as it was wont to be. The voice " that shook one world with the thunders of the other," is heard no more; he that uttered it has been removed to that other world, and the mantle of Elijah has fallen upon no successor.

course: when the preacher entered the pulpit a profound silence prevailed; every one listened anxiously to catch those sounds which never failed to make upon them the deepest impression; but they heard nothing: a sudden illness had seized the preacher, who was in a very feeble state of health, and he could do now no more than lay his hand upon his breast, and pointing with the other to his little flock, silently recommend them to the mercy of the congregation. The appeal was irresistible; and the mute eloquence of the preacher on this interesting occasion produced even more than his most laboured and powerful oratory. A sum exceeding £1000. was in a few minutes collected in the church. It was on this occasion, we believe, that a watch was found on the plate; the case was clasped on a bit of paper on which was a pencil-mark for £10., and the owner redeemed it next day, alledging that the sum he brought with him, and intended for the charity, he deemed insufficient for such an appeal. These are characteristic traits of the Irish disposition. A silent gesture produced more from a disappointed assembly, than they were prepared to give to the most powerful appeal of reason or religion.

Among the different parishes, and particularly among the different sects, there is great emulation. A good collection is mentioned with exultation, and a bad one deplored as if it was a personal concern. The result is published in the newspapers, and if there be any deficiency the public are called on to supply it. We have searched the books of the several charities for the collections of the year 1815, and we give the general result. We regret to find a considerable deficiency compared with the contribution of former years. We are afraid that commercial distress, and inability among the citizens of Dublin, are some of the principal causes.

Amount of Collections for Schools and other charitable purposes in the different Places of Worship in Dublin, in the year 1815.

Protestant churches	- - -	£7278 10 7½
Roman Catholic chapels	- -	3300 9 4
Presbyterian meeting-houses	-	1259 18 1
Independent ditto	- - -	1100 0 0
Methodist ditto	- - -	388 6 1
Baptist ditto	- - -	190 0 0
		£13517 4 1

THE HISTORY OF

SOCIETY FOR PROMOTING THE EDUCATION OF THE POOR IN IRELAND.

THE objections made to the schools hitherto established for the instruction of the poor of this country were, that books containing, and men professing, sectarian doctrines, were appointed to instruct the children of those who held it a point of salvation to reject them, and that the mode of instruction was expensive, its progress tedious, and its result ineffectual. With a view to remove these objections, a number of laymen formed a society on the broad principle of imparting education to the poor by a system which would embrace all sects and parties, and give offence to none, and which would extend the benefits to a greater number at a smaller expense by an efficient process of instruction. They held their first meeting at the Rotunda, on the 2d of December 1811, and declared their purpose by the following resolutions: "That the object of the society was to diffuse throughout the "country a well ordered system of education for the poor, which shall "combine economy of time and money, and bestow a due attention on "cleanliness and discipline; and the leading principle by which it shall be "guided is to afford the same facilities to all classes of professing Christians, "without any attempt to interfere with the peculiar religious opinions of "any." In pursuance of this purpose, they determined that the appointment of governors, teachers, and scholars should be uninfluenced by religious opinions. That the scripture should be used without note or commentary; and that all catechisms and books of religious controversy should be entirely excluded. This principle they are determined rigidly to adhere to, convinced by experience, that sectarian distinctions have opposed insurmountable barriers to the amelioration of the peasantry, and rendered abortive every attempt hitherto made to instruct them. Having thus removed the obstacles to receive instruction, their next care was effectually to impart it. With this view they propose to erect a *model school*, where lads may be trained to act as schoolmasters, and from whence they might be sent to organise and superintend schools on their plan in different parts of Ireland, as occasion might require

In promoting these excellent objects the society have received high encouragement. The Duke of Kent has become their Patron, and the

Duchess of 'Dorset their Vice-patroness, in order to interest the ladies of Ireland to establish and superintend a female school on a similar plan. At the summer assizes in the year 1814, the grand jury of the county of Limerick, and in 1815 those of Waterford and Tipperary, passed resolutions approving the plan and recommending it to the resident nobility and gentry; while the absentees, equally interested in its success, have taken measures to form a similar society in London. Mean time, the committee in Ireland have addressed the different trading companies in England, who possess estates in the north of Ireland, and naturally hope to derive assistance from those bodies. Nor is the interest excited by such a purpose confined to those who have a personal concern in it. A society has been formed in Edinburgh on the same plan, whose sole object is to extend to Ireland the benefit of general education, and co-operate with the society here for that end.

In 1815, a petition was presented to parliament for aid to build a model school, and the sum of £6980. was granted, with which it is intended to erect a building in Kildare-street, on the plan recommended in the Hints and Directions for building School-houses.* Mean while, a room in the establishment in School-street has been assigned to them, which is capable of containing 250 boys, and a person strongly recommended has been engaged at a salary of £200. per annum to superintend them. In this school 38 school-masters have been already trained; of whom 15 are Roman Catholics and 23 Protestants. These have left the school, and proceeded to organize and disseminate the system through the country. Attached to this society is a depository from which books and stationary are sold at reduced prices to different schools. The number of local esta-

* The foundation has been laid, and the buildings are now in progress. They consist of three edifices; the first, fronting Kildare-place, is intended for a depository for the sale of books and stationary; the second is detached from it in the rere, and is intended for a printing-office, in which will be printed such books as the society shall recommend or compose for the use of their schools. A committee of intelligent and judicious members has been appointed for this purpose, and parliament has granted the sum of 6000l. to carry it into effect, and enable them to undersell those of an immoral or pernicious tendency, and thus supersede their use. To render this department more effectual, it is proposed to amalgamate the Cheap Book Society with it. The third building is the model-school. In this edifice is a spacious school-room, 86 feet by 56, intended to contain 1200 children. The children of the South East District School are to be accommodated here, and the governors of it to coalesce with this society.

blishments supplied from hence in the last year amounted to 140, and similar ones are establishing in Cork and other places. For the extensive and most important objects proposed by this society, we regret to state, that, exclusive of parliamentary aid, their funds are very limited. The receipts of the last year, 1816, by donations and subscriptions, amounted only to the sum of £437. 0s. 7d. but they have increased since the year before..

The society is managed by a committee of 21, who report to a general meeting at the Rotunda on the 2d of May in each year, on which occasion there is usually a considerable attendance of the public and a great display of oratory.

CHEAP BOOK SOCIETY.

TEACHING the poor how to read may be communicating to them either an evil or a good. If the books they receive be such as communicate good principles, their accession of knowledge by these means will improve their moral practices. If they communicate bad ones, their effects will be accordingly. Within these few years the only books accessible to the poor were small volumes printed on coarse paper, bound in uniform white calf, and from their unvarying price called " sixpenny books," and sometimes " Burton books." The most popular of these were " the Life of James Freney* the Robber," " the History of the Irish Rogues and Rapparees," and others on similar subjects. These were generally printed in Dublin and sold by wholesale to country dealers for the use of country schools, where they were universally admired. The effects said to be produced in Germany by the publication of Schiller's Robbers are well known ; that such have followed in this country from the early admiration and study of such characters is highly probable. To supersede their use by supplying others of an opposite description, should have been a prime consideration with all who insisted on the necessity of public education. It was not, however, till very recently that any society was expressly instituted for that particular purpose. On the 26th of May, 1814, a meeting was called at the Rotunda,

* In Mr. Edgeworth's Letter to the Primate (See Ap. 12, Report of Board of Education.) this noted book is called the " Life of Captain Frene." After five years depredations this ruffian betrayed his friend who had saved his life, was rewarded with a situation in the revenue in New Ross, and wrote his life and adventures as an edifying example.

where it was resolved, " that it was expedient to form a society not for circulating bibles and religious tracts, but one whose sole object should be to provide good books for the use of the poor not of a religious description, and for printing and publishing at a cheap rate such useful books as may supersede the immoral publications now used in schools among the lower classes of the people." * A society was accordingly formed for this purpose, and its proceedings must form an essential preliminary to every system of education among the poor in this country. Every person subscribing one guinea, becomes a member, and has the privilege of obtaining books from the society gratis to the amount of one-fourth part of their subscription. We understand this society is likely to merge into that for Promoting the Education of the Poor.

HIBERNIAN BAPTIST CORRESPONDING SOCIETY.

This is a corresponding committee of the parent society which was instituted in London, in April, 1814. The society has three objects—to distribute religious books, send forth itinerant preachers, and establish schools; the last is that which peculiarly distinguishes them. They state that in the

* It may be asserted with truth, that any defect in the moral state of the peasantry of Ireland does not arise either from their ignorance of letters, or of their want of books. We have heard many intelligent and impartial men state it as their conviction that more than a comparative proportion know how to read, and we are assured that the experiment was tried. A certain number was taken indiscriminately from among the privates of an English and Irish regiment of militia, and it was found that a greater proportion of the latter than the former could read out of the book presented to them. We have not been able to ascertain to what shire or county the regiments belonged. From the number of Irish catechisms annually sold, it is inferred by Dr. Stokes that 20,000 persons in Ireland are able to read their native tongue. (See Dewar, p. 88.) The number of " sixpenny " or " Burton books" annually sold, was formerly immense. Four booksellers in Dublin used to deal exclusively in them, and one had four presses constantly employed, and published on an average 50,000 annually; besides these there were presses in Cork and Limerick employed on no other work. It was supposed that in this way 300,000 were every year printed and circulated. They were a principal commodity of hawkers and pedlars : and in every country town they were exposed on tables in the streets for sale, and the markets resembled a Leipsic fair. On the recurrence of a fair it was a practice with children to cry " my fairing on you " to whomsoever they knew. The person addressed usually gave some cheap article or small sum of money. To obtain in this way a sixpenny book for a fairing was the great object of young ambition. We believe this race of books is now becoming scarce, and their place already happily supplied by Hannah More's tracts and other cheap books circulated for several years by the " Association."

provinces of Munster and Connaught there are one million five hundred thousand who are incapable of receiving instruction in any other language than Irish; they, therefore, have resolved to establish schools for teaching *exclusively the Irish language,* and are in fact the only society, as they justly assert, who have taken this precise and exclusive ground. In this project they had much to encounter from the prejudices against teaching the Irish language, which existed among the friends of education in Ireland, and the difficulty of finding proper persons to become school-masters.* Their first attempt was made in the neighbourhood of Sligo, where they established two schools in the year 1814. At the end of the year a pædopaptist minister was strongly recommended to them, and they engaged him at a salary of £40. as a reader of the Irish scriptures. This zealous and laborious man traversed indefatigably the counties of Sligo, Mayo, and Roscommon, establishing evening schools for teaching Irish, and employing those who were capable, to read the scriptures to their neighbours in their native tongue.† In this way 16 schools and 16 sabbath readers were instituted at

* We do not believe there is much difficulty in finding masters to instruct in Irish, to which every teacher of a hedge-school is competent. In an excursion we made, last summer, to Glandelach, we found the Irish inscription on O'Toole's monument (see p. 261), and heard on inquiry that the schoolmaster could read it. We found him in a wretched hovel, with several scholars too tall to stand upright in his school-room. He freely decyphered the obsolete inscription, transcribed it into modern Irish with great neatness, and added a translation in classical Latin. His scholars were sitting on stones round the wall of the hovel, and none of them had shoes or stockings. Some time ago we were applied to by another professor of Irish, who was also a good classical scholar. He had acquired a knowledge of Greek, he said, from a woman who read Homer with him in a retired spot near the Lake of Killarney. He afterwards became a teacher in a baptist school, but is now struggling with poverty and a numerous family. "I was astonished," says Dewar (page 139) "to find in the wildest parts of Donegal a man with neither shoes or stockings, who gave me a clear and correct account of the peculiarities of Irish grammar." Mr. Dewar is himself from the Highlands, and a good Gaelic scholar. "One of the masters of a baptist school was a *poor scholar,* whom the master teaches free, and the scholars bring home every night in turn to their houses. He had received an Irish testament, which he read to the father and sisters of the priest of the parish. The old man was so pleased that he promised the boy a school if his testament was introduced without catechism or comment. The terms were agreed to, as they are the fundamental principles of the society, and the boy was given a school-house large enough to contain 120 children. (Report for 1815, p. 15.)

† Among the strangers who have visited Ireland to promote the project of instructing the natives through the medium of their own language, were the Rev. Dan. Dewar and the Rev. Cha. Anderson. They were both Scotchmen, and published accounts of their researches, the first in 1812, the latter in 1815. We refer to those works for much curious information; particularly the latter; it is written

the moderate sum of 2s. per week for each school and reader. To these were added 10 day schools, the masters of which receive 20 guineas per annum: and it is computed that there are at present 1000 children receiving instruction in the schools connected with the society, in which several young men designed for Roman Catholic priests and schoolmasters attend to perfect themselves in the Irish language. To provide suitable elementary books the Corresponding Committee in Dublin have printed 2000 copies of a spelling book in the English and old Irish letter in parallel columns, a copy of which when bound will cost the society about $3\tfrac{1}{2}d$.[*] There is besides a primer, containing about 4000 Irish monosyllables with corresponding explanations, as also a selection of Esop's Fables in the Irish

with a knowledge of the subject, a temperance, and a philanthropy that does equal credit to the understanding, the judgment, and the heart of the excellent writer. In a Letter to the Secretary of the Baptist Society, he thus expresses himself: "As I had been in Ireland, six years ago, I went this journey with impressions widely different from those of a mere stranger. I had not that strange and very erroneous idea that some have entertained, that deceitfulness and ferocity formed a part of the basis of the Irish character. But much as I was interested then, I am now much more so. With all the faults laid to their charge, there are still many things which endear the peasantry of those parts, (south and west) and raise them in the esteem of all who examine their condition with impartiality,—witness their hospitality and generosity of heart: were a traveller to walk into a cottage and say, he has come to take share of what they had to bestow, he is welcomed by all, and there is something quite characteristic in the whole family, parents and children expressing their "welcome to you," "kindly welcome." The strong natural capacity, the acuteness and genius of the Irish peasantry are known to be leading features in their character; and even among the inferior orders of the country there is a delicacy and richness of imagination to be met with that is truly surprising. We have heard of the superstition that reigns over their minds, the strong prejudices, the changeableness and want of perseverance, the impatience, the impetuosity of the Irish peasant; but I love rather to hold out as encouragements to a benevolent mind, their generosity, their warmth of heart, their strong family attachments, their thirst after knowledge and capacity for receiving and retaining it." This is the language of a liberal, unprejudiced mind, whose object is instruction, and whose means are conciliation and kindness. We are sorry that some parts of the Report of this Society are in a different spirit. One man talks of the degraded state of the Popish population, and the mountain where St. Patrick conquered the Devil's mother (p. 32). The Roman Catholic clergy are treated with wretched ribaldry, and the intention of proselytism is every where avowed in the most unqualified manner. As sincere and anxious friends to the establishment of Irish schools and the circulation of the Scripture in the Irish tongue, we deprecate this worse than folly in those who have undertaken to do it. It is not our design to defend a respectable body of men from silly aspersion, but to notice the impolicy of neglecting to engage the co-operation of those who could most promote the project, and compelling them from a sense of duty as well as of resentment to endeavour to oppose it. We trust the spirit of Mr. Anderson will pervade the next report of this society.

[*] See Report of Baptists' Society, for 1815, p. 17.

character. In addition to those, are two Irish grammars recently published; one by Doctor O'Brian, of Maynooth College, in the original character, the other by the Rev. Mr. Neilson of Dundalk in the Roman letter.

The funds of the society by donations and subscription amounted last year to £886. 2s. 3½d. and the disbursements to £574. 16s. 2d. leaving a balance in the treasurer's hands of £311. 6s. 1d.

THE HIBERNIAN SUNDAY SCHOOL SOCIETY.

THE extensive beneficial effects of Sunday schools have been long experienced and universally acknowledged in England, where the institution first originated; but how much greater benefits ought we not to expect from their establishment in a country which stands so much more in need of them?

In furthering this important object, "The Hibernian Sunday School Society" has ulterior views beyond the mere diffusion of the elements of education. For by this plan a more intimate knowledge is obtained of the character and manners of the Irish peasantry. An opportunity is thereby afforded to the benevolent managers of personally visiting and becoming acquainted with the poor families on whose children they are to bestow the inestimable blessings of an education suited to their wants and capacities; and the poor parents themselves, on perceiving that their own welfare is alone the object of these generous exertions, will by degrees discard from their minds that prejudice and hatred which their hitherto neglected and forlorn condition had inspired, and with better hope and prospect will, it is hoped, be at length reconciled to their fate.

In these Sunday schools all religious catechisms and tenets are excluded, and the children are initiated in their respective modes of faith at home without the smallest interference of the school managers, who confine themselves chiefly to the Lancasterian plan of instruction.

The society was first formed in 1783, but its establishment on the present plan was in November 1809. It is connected and corresponds with all the Sunday schools in Ireland, whose entire number, which it assisted since its establishment according to the last annual report of 1815, is as follows:

1810,   2 schools.
1811,   42 schools which had not before applied.
1812-13, 73 schools   idem.
1813-14, 58 schools   idem.
1814-15, 77 schools   idem.
1815-16, 98 schools   idem.

Making a total of 350 schools containing 38,598 children, of which 15 containing 1008 children have failed since 1809, the year in which the society began its operations.

Within the same period, the following assistance has been afforded gratuitously: 1,927 bibles, 14,912 testaments, 20,680 spelling-books No. 1, 19,295 spelling-books No. 2, 12,759 "alphabets," 514 "Hints for conducting Sunday schools:" and the following at reduced prices; 55 bibles, 885 testaments, 8,812 spelling books No. 1, 8,220 spelling-books No. 2, 1,522 "alphabets," 28 "Hints for conducting Sunday schools," and £235. 19s. 6d. in money.

The funds of the society are derived from annual subscriptions and donations; among which may be honourably mentioned one of £80. from the Edinburgh Bible Society, £162. from various other Bible Societies in Scotland, and one of £220. from an auxiliary Sunday School Society instituted by a number of patriotic and benevolent ladies in Dublin, by whose persevering zeal the institution has received the most effectual aid.

The affairs of the society are conducted by a committee, which reports its proceedings every year at a public meeting held at the Rotunda, where the means for promoting its interests are freely and often eloquently discussed. According to the last Report it appears that Sunday schools in Ireland are on the increase; that the sum of £675. 7s. 11d. remained in the hands of the treasurer, in April 1816, and that their present state is as satisfactory as could be hoped for by their warmest friends and ablest supporters. The society publish annual Reports of their progress, in which are to be found extracts from correspondence singularly illustrative of the moral and religious state of different remote parts of Ireland where Sunday schools are established or wanted, to which we refer for much curious information.*

* The following extract of a letter may serve as a specimen of the kind of information to be derived from this correspondence. It was written from Magilligan, the wildest district of the county of Londonderry on the east side of Lough Foyle, opposite the notorious barony of Inishowen.

" The interior is one vast circular-like breast of mountain and mountainous land, a great deal of it in

BOARD OF EDUCATION.

THE state of the endowed schools in Ireland had long been a subject of animadversion and censure. On the 6th April, 1786; Mr. Orde, secretary to the Duke of Rutland, brought the subject before the Irish House of Commons. He stated, that the masters either did no duty at all, or in so careless a way that the youth of the kingdom derived very little benefit from them, and he wished that some method might be devised to support young persons in a course of education, not merely by paying masters, but assisting scholars in the pursuit of knowledge; " and he moved that the national foundation of one or more public schools would be of great public utility."* This was unanimously agreed to, and an address presented to His

cliffs, from 3 to 500 feet high, and 'Benyvenagh,' filling a great space of about 1500 feet high. There are but two entrances, one towards Newtownlimabody, and the other at times impassable, by Coleraiu. These bounds contain about 3000 souls; 40 families, or 200 persons are of the established church; about 150 families, or 750 individuals are dissenters, and all the rest Roman Catholics. Great is the intermixture by marriage. One consequence is, that the children do not wish to disoblige either parent, and in many instances seem to have no place of worship. It has been and is still the outlet by which illicit distillation was and is effected. From this you may guess the description of the greater part of our population, living part of the time in stupid indolence on the profits of their adventures, and the rest in illegal acts. Until the late Hervey Bishop of Bristol built a small new church, and gave them the old one, they had no place of worship, except private houses and fields. There are four day schools, wretched hovels, 4 feet high on the sides, built of turf, without windows, except the hole in the roof. In general, stones are employed for seats, and little boards on the knees for tables, &c." Vide Sixth Report.

* Mr. Orde's object was to establish a general system of education for Ireland founded on the enquiry. In 1787 he submitted his plan, as follows:

1st. That the children of the lower order should be educated in parochial schools, which should be rendered effectual for that purpose by 6d. in the pound paid by every incumbent and proprietor of impropriate tythes.

2. That four large provincial schools should be established similar to the Blue Coat Hospital in each of the provinces, to which the funds of the charter schools and those of Erasmus Smith should be applied. In these seminaries mathematics, navigation, modern languages, and every thing necessary for a mercantile education should be taught.

3. That diocesan schools should be put on a better foundation to promote classical learning.

4. That two great academies should be instituted preparatory to the universities; to support which and aid the diocesan schools, the revenues and lands of some of the endowed classical schools should be applied. To the academies were to be annexed exhibitions, as a further incitement to ability or genius to persevere.

Excellency that he would give orders to prepare plans of the necessary arrangements. Meantime, it was ordered that proper persons should make a return of the schools of royal and other foundation, with their present yearly value and the allowance to masters and assistants, and the number of scholars, and also that the registers of the several dioceses should return to the House, an account of English schools kept by the rectors and vicars, with the number of scholars. In consequence of these resolutions, a Board of Education was formed in 1788, but it does not appear they made much progress in the object of their appointment.

In the year 1806, an Act passed to revive and amend the former, for enabling the Lord Lieutenant to appoint commissioners for enquiring into the several funds and revenues granted for the purposes of education and into the state and condition of all the schools.* This Board consisted of men eminent for rank and talents, and among them the primate, the provost, Mr. Grattan and Mr. Edgeworth. In consequence of the powers vested in them, they commenced a minute and laborious enquiry from the year 1806 to the year 1812. In the progress of it they presented 14 copious reports, which were printed by order of the House of Commons.† Having investigated every thing connected with this interesting subject, and pointed out what required correction, their functions expired. They were constituted only a Board of Enquiry, and could do no more than report and recommend. On their recommendation, a second Board was formed under a new Act passed in 1813, for the *Regulation* of the several endowed schools

---

5. That a SECOND UNIVERSITY should be founded situated in the north-west of Ireland, as well to accommodate those who went from those parts to foreign universities, as those from other countries who would prefer our university, if it was out of Dublin. To support this the revenues of several of the great endowed schools in the north-west should be blended together.—Col. Polit. vol. ii. p. 147 *et seq.*

* See 46 Geo. III.

† For a full analysis of the Reports, see Appendix, No. IV. It apears by them, that sums exceeding 80,000*l.* per annum have been allowed by different persons at different times for the establishment of schools in Ireland; that some of the money was never applied, and some was misapplied. That in the endowed classical schools few or none availed themselves of their being *free*, and the endowed English schools afforded education to so small a number that 162,476 poor children paid in 2736 other schools from 10s. to 1l. 6s. per annum each for their education. That of the diocesan schools, only 13 had been kept out of 34, and of parish schools only 549 had been returned out of 1125 benefices. In fine, that a great deal had been done for education in Ireland by prudent laws and liberal benefactors, and a great deal undone by neglect, abuse, and mismanagement.

of public and private foundation in Ireland,* who are now proceeding to correct the abuses pointed out by the former, and have presented two Reports on the progress they have made in the work of reformation.

LITERARY TEACHERS' SOCIETY.

It was formerly much the practice to send young persons of both sexes to England and elsewhere to acquire those accomplishments necessary for children of a certain rank in life, which it was presumed they could not not procure in any seminary at home. The consequence of this practice, we apprehend, was, that young minds early imbibed unfavourable impressions of their own country; the first feeling was that it was unfit to afford them education, and the next was that it was unfit to live in: they naturally returned, therefore, to reside in that place which early association had endeared, and left a country from which early prejudices had alienated them. Whether the crowd of absentees, which has long been assigned as a prime cause of our adversities, or their rooted prejudices, which have been deplored as a prime obstacle to our prosperity, may not have originated partly in this cause, we leave to their consideration, but we may assert, that whatever deficiency was heretofore found in our system, there is no want in the metropolis at the present day of ample means for an accomplished and classical education.

There are now in Dublin and the vicinity 90 reputable schools,† viz. 34 on the north side and 56 on the south side of the Liffey; of these about 50 are for young ladies. They are kept by very respectable characters, the classical schools generally by clergymen of different persuasions, among whom are many who had acquired reputation in the university.‡ The

* See 53 Geo. III.

† These are exclusive of schools of inferior respectability, which are numerous.

‡ Among the schools we shall notice two, as possessing distinctive characters. A school for young ladies kept at Russell-place, Circular-road, by Mrs. Kirkchoffer, one of the family of Brook, a name rendered respectable by patriotic enterprise and literary eminence. In this school are 50 pupils, and 6 governesses for French and English, besides masters who attend for drawing, music, dancing, and Italian. In addition to the usual course of education, history and practical astronomy are particularly attended to; for which latter purpose an Orrery on an ingenious principle is constructed in one of the rooms: a large concave hemisphere is suspended from the ceiling on which are marked the constellations

number of children in each is very various, some restricting themselves to a few, and some receiving an unlimited number; in this way they vary from 8 to 100, but the average is about 28, giving 2520 children of both sexes. The usual price for day scholars varies from 3 guineas to 1 per quarter: and for boarders from 30 to 50 guineas per annum. Those who take only a limited number, require higher terms for each. Modern languages and accomplishments are extra charges. The education of females includes French, Italian, drawing, music, fancy works, geography, history, and the elements of astronomy. But besides this, a more than usual attention has been latterly paid to the moral and religious instruction. Clergymen of the respective persuasions frequently give their attendance for this purpose; and at periodical examinations, a knowledge of the scriptures is particularly enquired into. We have known some young ladies, and have heard of others, who have been instructed in Greek and Latin; but we believe these literary extravagancies are very rare in Dublin. The course of education, and the books read in our classical schools, are those usually adopted, and have nothing particular to distinguish them: the old rules of Lily are generally exploded,

in metallic stars. In this space, corresponding with the visible firmament, the orbits of the planets, and their different phœnomena are more easily and distinctly explained, than on common globes, whose convex surface invert the natural position. Fellows of the college and other clergymen attend at public examinations, at which the young ladies display great knowledge. The moral, religious, and intellectual character of this seminary particularly recommended it to Mr. Whitelaw, who was a constant examiner.

The other is a seminary for young gentlemen conducted by Professor Von Feinaigle. This gentleman, a native of Germany, arrived in Dublin a few years ago and proposed a new system of artificial memory, founded on symbols which would be applicable to every purpose of intellectual attainment. Having explained his principles of mnemonics and methodics in several public lectures delivered at the Rotunda and elsewhere, a number of gentlemen, who approved of them, founded an institution by subscription in 1813, for establishing and perpetuating a system of education invented by Von Feinaigle, by which he asserts that " the period of education is considerably abridged, and the objects of instruction " are acquired with a facility, and retained with a certainty hitherto unknown." For this purpose the house of the Earl of Aldborough, on the Circular-road, was fitted up for a seminary, and called Luxembourg, from the territory which appertained to his family in Germany. The affairs of the institution are conducted by a committee of the proprietors. There are 130 pupils instructed, whose progress is displayed by periodical examinations, for which tickets of admission are issued, and the public attend, and are invited to examine. Opinions are much divided on this novel seminary, nor has it yet been satisfactorily ascertained to what extent its high pretensions are justified. The period of education is four years, which has not yet been completed since the opening of the seminary. A work has just been published in Dublin by M. Sandford, mnemonic draughtsman to the institution: it is entitled a Grammar of the Methodic and Mnemonic Art, as taught at the Feinaiglian Institution.

and the period of grammar is reduced to six months. It had been objected, however, that sufficient attention was not paid to history and geography, so necessary for the illustration of ancient authors; and that Latin composition has been more neglected than in English schools. The first of these objections has been removed, and those subjects are now taught with care; but we believe, there is some reason for the latter, and the cause has been attributed to our university, where science has been so much more highly prized than classical literature.

It was not till a comparatively late period that there had been any association among the numerous and respectable individuals who superintend those seminaries, to provide for the future support of their families; though it is notorious, as the preamble of the Act of incorporation truly states, "that " they obtain so scanty and inadequate a retribution, that many, if not most " of those who devote themselves to the service of the public, are barely " able during a period of strength and labour to earn a moderate subsistence, " and find it impossible to lay up any provision against accident, sick- " ness, or old age." In the year 1789, however, a voluntary association was formed, called *The Abecedarian Society*, whose object was the relief of decayed and indigent teachers and their families. In the year 1797, it availed itself of the Act for promoting friendly societies, and became incorporated under the name of *The Society for the Relief of Distressed Literary Teachers and their Families;* and in 1804, a committee was appointed to revise and alter its imperfect rules, which were submitted to the review of the justices, at a quarter sessions, and filed by the clerk of the peace, pursuant to the Act.* By these rules, any person of either sex actually engaged in the business of teaching, may be eligible to become a member on paying one guinea per annum, if under the age of 60, after which no professional candidate can be admitted. When the funds shall amount to a sum yielding an interest of £120. relief will be afforded to any member, or his family, who shall appear to be in *actual distress*, while the distress continues, and no longer; the sum not to exceed in any case one guinea per week; and when a member dies, a sum not exceeding £10. may be drawn for his interrment. The fund, at present, amounts to £2780. vested in government stock, from which 3 pensioners receive 16s..3d. 10s. and 7s..6d. per week. To the fund there are

* See an Act passed for encouraging friendly societies, 36 Geo. III. where these preliminaries are prescribed.

but 30 subscribers, who are with few exceptions themselves teachers, and ill able to afford a subscription. They have never received any aid from government, or grant from parliament. Such, then, in this city of considerate charity is the provision made for the emergency of a profession " that is among the most necessary and useful in a well regulated state, " and consequently the most truly honourable to those who ably and faithfully exercise its many arduous and important duties;"* a profession whose members are distinguished by literary attainments and moral excellence, and whose pretensions are acknowledged by having 2500 young persons, the rising hopes of the metropolis, confided to their care, whose conduct they are to direct, whose characters they are to form, and whose present and future prospects ultimately depend on their care and instruction. The obligations due to such a body are acknowledged by "a scanty and inadequate retribution" for the present, and for the future the hopes of a few shillings a week to three of their families when in actual want, and the chance of £10. to provide themselves with a decent funeral!†

ASSOCIATION FOR DISCOUNTENANCING VICE, AND PROMOTING THE KNOWLEDGE AND PRACTICE OF THE CHRISTIAN RELIGION.

Mr. William Watson, Sen. of Capel-street, known from his benevolence and genuine piety, first conceived the idea of forming this institution: he thought that the efforts of a number of individuals associated for the purpose of promoting religion and morality, would be more efficacious, acting in concert, than the individual and divided exertions of any persons, however numerous. He communicated his views on the subject to the Rev. Doct. O'Connor, of Castle Knock, and the Rev. S. Harpur, curate of Saint Mary's Dublin, who entirely coincided in his opinion. These three persons accordingly met at his house in Capel-street on the 9th October, 1792, and there held the first meeting of the society. The following

* See preamble to the Act of incorporation.
† The Literary Teachers' Society, in London, was established several years subsequent to that in Dublin, yet its present income is six times greater, and enjoys high and extensive patronage.

resolutions explanatory of their views were entered into: "That the rapid progress which infidelity and immorality are making throughout the kingdom calls loudly on every individual of the clergy and the laity who has at heart the welfare of his country and the honour of his God, to exert all his powers to stem the baneful torrent. That it appears advisable to enter into an association for that purpose; but, in order to guard against the danger of enthusiasm, it be established as a fundamental principle that nothing be attempted contrary to the doctrine and discipline of the established church, or that shall lead in the smallest degree to a separation from the same. That the subjects to be discussed be the religious education of the rising generation by parents, schoolmasters, &c. &c.; the best means of promoting a regular and conscientious attendance upon public worship and the holy communion: how to restore the practice of family prayer; how most effectually to prevent intemperance in all ranks of men; how to discourage and discountenance luxury, dissipation, and extravagance in the upper and middle classes, both male and female; how to prevent profane cursing and swearing, particularly perjury; what may be the best means of enforcing the laws in being against immorality, and whether it be expedient to solicit any, and what further laws for that purpose; the best means of promoting honesty and industry, and of discouraging idleness and beggary; how the real and necessitous may be the most effectually relieved; and in effect whatever may conduce to the temporal and external welfare of the public." Such were the very important and extensive duties undertaken to be performed by three individuals, without any other authority than that which the intrinsic importance of the objects themselves conferred on them:[*] and at a time when opinions subversive of all the established principles of morals and religion were widely spread and assiduously propagated by numerous societies of men, and the public mind unfortunately prepossessed very generally by their influence; no sooner, however, were their objects made known by a prospectus of their views, printed and circulated, than numbers pressed forward to be enrolled members of the association. It was a rallying point to the friends of order and good morals.

[*] A political revolution was effected in America through the agency, it is said, of Benjamin Franklin, George Washington, and J. Arnold; a bookseller, a farmer, and a horse-dealer. In Ireland, a more difficult moral revolution was attempted, and in many instances effected, by a country clergyman, a Dublin curate, and a bookseller.

In less than three years, the viceroy of Ireland* voluntarily proposed himself, and was elected, their president, their numbers were increased to nearly 500 persons, and the following important objects were undertaken, and most of them carried into effect.

Catechetical examinations were established among the children of all charitable seminaries in Dublin, and its vicinity, and finally extended to all classes of the established church in Ireland. Now, for the first time, were seen the young persons of the different schools in Dublin moving in an interesting procession annually to St. Werburg's and St. Mary's churches, and the laity as well as the clergy crowding to hear the examination of their progress, and distributing premiums to the best answerers.

On their application to the bishops of the different dioceses in every part of Ireland, directions were transmitted to the several parochial clergy to preach sermons on the observance of the sabbath day, and the lord mayor issued a proclamation to enforce it; and to give greater efficacy to the exhortation of the clergy, and the interference of the civil power, an abstract of the existing laws on the subject was printed and widely circulated by the society. Among other violations of the sabbath, were the promenades at the Rotunda, which, without sufficient motive or necessity were always held on Sunday evenings. On the representation of the association to the governors of the Lying-in Hospital, this practice was discontinued, and week days fixed on for their public exhibitions.

An exhortation at the same time was addressed to the public on the regular observance of family prayer, and a solemn engagement was entered into by the members themselves to practise and enforce the duty daily in their own families.

There is no time, perhaps, when exhortation would make deeper impression than previous to the execution of public justice on public offenders. The prospect of eternal judgment may sometimes be too indistinct or too remote to impress the careless mind; but temporal punishment comes home to every heart, because every heart must be conscious of the presence of actual evil; the association, therefore, established the practice of preaching *assize sermons* while the judges were on circuit, and the clergy of the different persuasions were engaged to preach appropriate discourses on the Sunday previous to that awful time, when justice makes its periodical visitation among their respective congregations.

* Lord Fitzwilliam.

The distribution of bibles was also among the earliest objects of the society. At this period 5000 octavo bibles were purchased and circulated. Having commenced thus early to act on their resolution, " That effectual " provision would be made, that no house, no cabin in the whole kingdom, " in which there is a single person who can read shall be destitute of the " holy scriptures." Thus a bible society was formed in Dublin, ten years previous to the establishment of the British and Foreign Bible Societies in London.*

Among the moral objects were many of great importance. The first to which they directed their attention was the suppression of licentious books, which at this time was particularly necessary. They were prime agents in the hands of infidelity to demoralize the people, and itinerants vending them were found in all directions. The Association prosecuted to conviction a hawker, who was detected with obscene books and prints for sale, which was the only instance in which they employed coercive measures; and they induced another to render up his impure commodities, which were burned by their direction; they preferring rather to succeed in their object by persuasion than by the arm of the law, in which way they have frequently interfered with success; since that period we believe Dublin to be remarkably exempt from this contagion. Among the publications of a less gross, though equally immoral tendency, was a magazine published in Dublin, which contained an engraving of the heads of notorious characters in a *tête-à-tête*, with an account of them annexed. In this way the public morals were insulted by the monthly exhibition of some intrigue in fashionable

* The state of the public circulation of the sacred volume in these countries was at this time very deplorable. An edition of 5000 had been some time before printed, but was found carefully shut up for several years in the warehouse of the King's printer in London, from whence the Association first liberated them; the patent for this purpose having been deemed of such little comparative value, that it was scarcely attended to. The fate of a subsequent edition in Dublin was singular; when it appeared it was found illegible, and consequently useless. It was, therefore, offered to a paper manufacturer for a smaller quantity of blank paper, who readily accepted a bargain which he thought so advantageous. He found, however, that the books were absolutely unsaleable, and he was compelled to work up the whole edition again into pulp, and re-produced it as blank paper, after discharging the ink. Two editions of the bible, consisting of upwards of 30,000 copies, printed at the recommendation of the Association, and almost entirely purchased by them, were of a large size and legible print, and not liable to the same objection. If, therefore, they did nothing more than cause these editions of the sacred volume to be printed in a manner capable of being read, they conferred an essential benefit on the public.

life, and the description heightened by language which took from vice its deformity, and familiarised the mind to it by the seduction of fashionable example; on the representation of the Society those *tête-à-têtes* were omitted, and decorum was no longer outraged by such an exhibition.*

The excess of gambling, and the misery and profligacy which insurance in the lotteries at that time gave rise to in Dublin, were also serious evils in the moral world; the multitudes of unhappy beings who crowded the lottery offices in Capel-street, and other public streets, and the distraction which they displayed, are still remembered by many in the city: during that period all industry was suspended, every faculty was absorbed in the chance of a number, every expedient that pawning, or selling, or robbing could supply was used to purchase the means of insurance, and every excess that has been attributed to gambling in the few of the upper classes who indulge in it, was here displayed among the whole poor population in the public streets, in frenzy and despair; the roads and streets were filled with robbers, and the rivers and canals with suicides.† On this subject the Association were deeply interested; they memorialed the chief governor, and after sundry regulations to restrain the practice, it was at length totally suppressed.

The consumption of spirituous liquors was also a pregnant source of immorality and misery. It was found that the sale of these on Sunday, besides leading to the violation of the sabbath, was the origin of all the intemperance which ensued for the remainder of the week, as that was an idle day, and the day on which the artizan could command the wages of his work and the means of intoxication. To put a stop to this serious evil the Association interfered, an application was made to the legislature to

* There were at this time, and had been, two Magazines established for several years in Dublin,— Exshaw's Gentleman and London, and Walker's Hibernian. These *tête-à-têtes* were in Walker's, and copied from the Town and Country Magazine.

† The mania had seized even the very beggars: a poor creature who was blind, used to attract the notice of the passengers by her silent and unobtrusive manners, and cleanly appearance. She had a little basket containing articles for sale with a net over it, which she held before her, and she received more alms than a common beggar. She unfortunately dreamed of a number that would make her fortune, and the next day she was led to the lottery office, and insured it. Her little store was soon expended. She sold her clothes and pledged her basket: but her number still remained in the wheel: she could no longer try her fortune: and the number was drawn the day after she ceased to insure. She groped her way to the canal and threw herself in.

prohibit the sale of spirits on the whole of Sunday; which after some time was adopted, and several acts passed for that purpose.*

The reform of young criminals was another moral object which was of much importance : heretofore they had been confined, without selection or distinction, with offenders of all ages, in a common prison ; this association with hardened vice seldom failed to establish the bad propensities of the yielding mind, and the young sinner emerged from his confinement confirmed in all his bad habits. The case also of the children of convicts suffering the sentence of the law was very deplorable; beside the example of their unhappy parents, they had to encounter the taunts and prejudices of the world; and character, that spring of all good actions, was lost, before it could serve them as an incentive. To provide an asylum for these objects, a house was taken on George's Hill, in which several young criminals and the children of convicts, were placed, and taught different trades. After this experiment the Association applied to parliament, for aid to extend the

* This pernicious habit has long been a subject of complaint. Sir William Petty, in the year 1656, asserted that the number of ale-houses was one-third of the whole number of houses in Dublin. In 1749, Dr. Rutty made a calculation on the average of several years, and found the proportion nearly the same: viz. 2000 ale-houses, 300 taverns, and 1200 brandy-shops, making altogether 3500 houses selling intoxicating liquors in the city and liberties of Dublin, which at that time contained 12,857 houses. He laments the growing use of whiskey, then first introduced, but beginning to prevail so enormously among the lower orders, that in the year 1749 ten persons, and in the year 1753 twenty-six had died of excessive dram-drinking ; and he deprecates its use not only as corrupting their morals, destroying their constitutions and producing sudden death, but also as debasing and enfeebling their progeny.—(Rutty's Natural History of Dublin, vol. i. p. 12.) —Notwithstanding this, no effectual means had been taken to prevent the use of ardent spirits, The Act of William III. enjoins that no keeper of a tavern or ale-house shall permit to remain any person in his house, or furnish them with liquor of any sort during the time of divine service on Sunday. It was justly remarked that this temporary suspension, when enforced, produced greater intoxication in the evening, when there was no restraint ; but, in fact, it was seldom enforced till the Association interfered to prevent the enormous evil. By Acts passed in 1797, and the subsequent years, severe laws were made to regulate the sale and restrain the use of ardent spirits, and at length an Act passed to prohibit the sale of them *on Sunday* altogether.— (See 37, 38, 39 and 41 of George III.)—In a sermon preached at this time on " the effects of intoxication" before the lord mayor and corporation of Dublin, and printed at their request, it was proved, that the number of licensed houses selling ardent spirits in the county of Dublin was 2000 ; of which 1052 was in the city, to which might be added 350 which vended without any license; that in each of these 10 persons were intoxicated every Sunday, and continued so for the two succeeding days; that each of these had at least two persons dependant on them for support : so that the sale of spirits on Sunday involved 40,000 persons for half the week in the greatest distress and misery !

THE CITY OF DUBLIN. 891

plan; they modestly asked £300. and were voted £3000. This was appropriated to building a large house in Smithfield, and the direction of it placed under the governors of the House of Industry, in whose department the Association properly deemed it.*

The deplorable state of the chimney sweepers also was taken into consideration. About the year 1788 an Act of Parliament had passed in England, for their better regulation, but no such law had been enacted in this country. It was computed that they amounted in the city of Dublin to 200 children, who beside the degrading and odious employment to which they are condemned, were not indented apprentices, and had no redress against the brutality of their masters. The Association had the Act copied in the form of a Bill, with necessary alterations and additions, with a view to have it presented to the Irish parliament. The object however was not attained.

The books which had been published and circulated for the instruction or entertainment of the lower orders of the people, were of the most immoral kind, and inculcated principles the most pernicious. To correct the impression made by such publications, it was resolved to substitute cheap books of a different tendency, to be distributed among the poor. This was proposed so early as the year 1795, but as no tracts on the subject were yet composed in Ireland, an edition of the excellent tracts of Hannah Moore was re-published in Dublin by Mr. Watson, and were received with such avidity that 120,000 were distributed in the first year to the poor at reduced prices.

Servants were a class of society which had engaged the sympathy and consideration of the Association, and they proposed to afford those of good characters who were past their labour, effectual relief. A committee was appointed to manage a fund to be raised by subscription, which was intended to be so extensive as that all deserving servants who could shew sufficient claims, should be entitled as a matter of right to demand support in their old age. This plan did not succeed according to the excellent intention, but a society more recently established for the same purpose has superseded the necessity of it.†

Emanating principally from the Association was at this time established the Howard Society, for visiting prisons and alleviating the distresses of the

* See page 627.   † See page 788.

prisoners: from this originated the present excellent institution, the Debtor's Friend Society.

But the great object to which their attention has been directed, was the establishment of schools and the extension of education. For this purpose, in the year 1799, circular letters were sent to the different dioceses in Ireland, with the approbation of the bishops, to get a return of the state of education. It appeared that in two dioceses alone there were 58,000 children who were of an age to be instructed; of these, only 14,000 received education, and that of a bad kind, while 44,000 were left in total ignorance. The Association therefore purposed to grant aid for building new school houses, and salaries to deserving masters. They commenced in the year 1805, with 10 schools, and the plan has now so succeeded, that grants have been made for the erection of 30 school houses, and 100 schools have been taken under their patronage, and salaries allowed to the masters.

A general complaint had been made of the want of proper schoolmasters, and the incapability and ill conduct of those employed. They therefore established a seminary for the instruction of parish clerks and school masters, who could be qualified to fulfil the respective duties of each, and sometimes of both departments: upwards of 50 have been already educated and established in different schools, and the demand has so much increased that the grant for this purpose, which commenced with £50. has been gradually augmented to £900. per annum, by which they propose in future to send out twenty schoolmasters every year.*

* In the year 1798, a parish school-master had been concerned in the rebellion in the county of Wicklow. This circumstance induced the Rev. Mr. Jones, the resident clergyman of the parish, to instruct the children himself, rather than entrust them to improper teachers. For this purpose a school house was procured, and Mr. Jones, with the assistance of an half-educated young man, commenced his plan in the year 1800. In a short time the young man became an excellent schoolmaster; and from this circumstance originated his plan of forming a *seminary* for training school masters in Ireland. Nothing impeded the attempt but the want of means; these, however, were liberally supplied by donations exceeding 1000*l.* from some distinguished persons in England, among whom was Mr. Wilberforce, and an experimental school was opened by Mr. Jones for three years in 1806. In 1808 Mr. Jones was promoted to the perpetual cure of Kildumo in the diocese of Limerick, the seminary was removed to that place also, and a large school house with dormitories was built, the expence of which was partly defrayed by the Association for Discountenancing Vice. Young men not less than eighteen years of age, are received here as vacancies occur, and after a probation of two months, are continued on the establishment, if their conduct and capacity be approved of. They are instructed in reading, writing,

In the year 1800 the society was incorporated. The measure was proposed to the Association without any application on their part, and effected without any expence.

To extend the general benefit of the institution, diocesan committees were formed in many dioceses to forward the several plans proposed by the society.

The institution is supported by subscription and parliamentary grants.

Subscriptions amount to £500. per annum.

Parliamentary grants commenced at £300. and have been increased the last year to £8000.

The Association since its commencement, to the end of the year 1816, has distributed at very reduced prices, nearly 50,000 bibles, 200,000 testaments and prayer books, and one million of other religious and moral books and tracts, at an expense of almost £25,000. Premiums have been granted to upwards of 9000 children, who distinguished themselves at catechetical examinations, at an expence of £4500. £1400. have been granted in aid of the erecting and building 32 school-houses, and £1500. per annum in salaries and rewards to masters of 100 schools; £100. were also granted in aid of building a seminary for educating young men for parish clerks and schoolmasters, and £500. annually for its support.

Thus it has proceeded steadily but silently in its objects; it makes no public display of its progress,* and seeks no applause; its meetings are still continued in the private house where it originated, and its existence is only known by the excellent effects which are produced by its unobtrusive perseverance.

and arithmetic on Dr. Bell's improved method. Those who display ability are taught book-keeping, English grammar, geography, geometry, trigonometry, mensuration, navigation and algebra; and by this diversity of attainments different masters are prepared for different situations. A master is usually qualified in eighteen months. Those pupils who have a good voice are instructed in psalmody, and qualified for parish clerks. A select but very useful library is attached to the seminary. Fifty schools have been already supplied from hence, and among the rest the original school in the county of Wicklow.

* A sermon is occasionally preached before the meeting, at which the Viceroy is usually present. This sermon is always printed, and contains a detail of their proceedings.

894   THE HISTORY OF

HIBERNIAN BIBLE SOCIETY.

WHEN this society was first established in the year 1805, it stood a separate society independent of and unconnected with any other, and was instituted for the sole purpose of encouraging a wider circulation of the Scriptures in Ireland. Immediately after its formation the example was followed in Belfast, which became auxiliary to it, and since that time by the zealous exertions of some of its members who make periodical circuits for that purpose, branches have extended through Ireland, and societies for similar objects have been formed in different places. It has been a subject of regret that the books distributed by this society have been hitherto from the presses of England and Scotland. On their first formation the business of the committee was suspended for several months for want of Bibles, and on several occasions since, they have had to wait the delay and expense of importation. For the last thirty years but four editions of the Bible were published in Dublin;[*] the first was so bad as to be illegible and unsaleable; the two last were published at the instance of the Association in 1801 and in 1809, and consisted of 15,000 copies each, which were almost entirely distributed by that society. A new arrangement has, however, commenced, which forms an important æra in the constitution and proceedings of the Bible Society. In the year 1814, an union was proposed and effected with that in England, and it is now auxiliary to the British and Foreign Bible Society; but from the peculiar situation of Ireland, it is allowed to maintain a controul over its own funds till a more extensive circulation of the Scriptures at home, shall allow it to act with the parent society in foreign operations. To enable them effectually to do this they have, after most mature deliberation, recommended to the society in England to publish an edition of the New Testament in Irish in the *Irish character*, with an English version in parallel columns;[†] the utility of which will be better appreciated by the consideration, that branches of the Bible Society have ramified through every county in Ireland except five, and there are now 58 centres, round which these Bibles will circulate among the peasantry, in their native tongue.[‡]

[*] In this is not included two quarto and two folio editions of the Douay Bible, published by Cross, in the year 1793 and in subsequent years.

[†] See Ninth Report, p. 18.

[‡] The cultivation of letters among the Irish ecclesiastics at an early period is now an indisputable fact; and it is more than probable, that among the Irish MSS. which at present exist in various libraries,

Besides these larger branches, St. George's parish in Dublin, has set the example of forming smaller ones, and ten parochial associations have been formed in different places on a similar plan.

an old copy of the Scriptures in the Irish language and character may be found. But the policy of the English government since the accession of Henry II. to the present time, to obstruct and suppress the use of the vernacular tongue, with the view of its ultimate extinction, has, more than the former devastations of the Danes, or all the subsequent ravages of civil war, rendered the earlier written documents very scarce, and has been partly successful in preventing the study of the written language. But the most arbitrary measures were ineffectual to prevent its oral practice.

From time to time there were good and eminent characters who deemed that Christianity and civilization would be best promoted by the cultivation, and not the suppression of the Irish tongue. Among these was Richard Fitz-Ralph, some time Chancellor of Oxford, and promoted in 1347 to the primacy of Armagh. This worthy prelate had a translation of the New Testament in Irish, which some suppose was done by himself, but finding his efforts were not in unison with the spirit of the times relative to Ireland, he concealed the MS. in the wall of his church. Fitz-Ralph died in 1360, and about the year 1530, the church of Armagh was repairing, the book was found, but it is doubtful if it exist at present. (See Usher's Hist. Dogm. and Foxes Acts.)

At length the Reformation operated more favourably for the encouragement of Irish; for though Henry VIII. passed an Act for the cultivation and universal practice of English, to the exclusion of the Irish, which policy was pursued by his son and successor Edward, yet Elizabeth finding prohibitory laws ineffectual, had the better policy of teaching her Irish subjects the doctrines of Christianity through the medium of their own language. In 1571, the Queen, at her own expence, provided a printing press, with types of the Irish character, and sent it over to Nicholas Walsh, chancellor, and John Kearney, treasurer of St. Patrick's, Dublin. (See Annals, p. 199, also Ware.) The first book printed in this Irish press was a catechism, composed by Kearney; whilst Chancellor Walsh, afterwards Bishop of Ossory, made progress in translating the New Testament, which he was prevented from completing by being unfortunately assassinated in his own house. Kearney and Donellan Archbishop of Tuam, endeavoured to finish the work, but it was still incomplete at their death. At length, in 1602, it was finished and published by William Daniel, Archbishop of Tuam, who in 1608 also published a translation of the Book of Common Prayer.

It was not until 1627, that the Old Testament was translated into Irish by that excellent prelate, Bishop Bedell, who to qualify himself for the propagation of the Irish Scriptures, actually became so great a proficient in the Irish language, at the age of 57, though by birth an Englishman, that he was enabled to publish a grammar of the tongue. This virtuous man died in the 71st year of his age, in 1641, the year of the great rebellion. This and the subsequent calamities into which Ireland was plunged, retarded the publication of the Irish Bible until 1685, when, owing to the munificence and exertions of the Hon. Robert Boyle, it was at length published, in a beautiful Irish character. (See Bedell's Life, by Clojy, and Boyle's Life.)

In 1634, a convocation met in Dublin, and drew up the Hundred Canons, which are bound up in our quarto Prayer Books and appointed to be read out periodically in our churches. The XCIVth canon enjoins that the church-wardens shall provide two Books of Common Prayer and a Bible, " and when

Among the applications made for the word of God the Wexford militia affords an excellent example: they subscribed a sum of money among "all or most of the people are Irish, they shall provide also the said books *in the Irish tongue*," the charge to be born by the whole parish. (See XCIVth canon.)

Notwithstanding the enlightened policy of Elizabeth, and the individual efforts of these excellent men already mentioned, whose example continued to be followed by others, yet no great progress was made in giving universal circulation to the Irish Scriptures among the poorer classes of the natives. In fact, the spirit of the English government remained hostile to the measure, and about 1711, the attempt to suppress the use of the Irish, by introducing and teaching the English in the remote districts, became a favourite project, but, like the former attempt, it totally failed.

In 1712, John Richardson, chaplain to the Duke of Ormond, translated and published an exposition of the church catechism into Irish; "though he knew the work would meet with discouragement and opposition yet he was resolved to proceed," he said, "hoping that God would raise up friends to his undertaking." He also published a history of the attempts made to convert the Irish; from which much of the foregoing account is extracted. In the year 1786 occurred the memorable controversy between Father O'Leary and the Bishop of Cloyne. His Lordship had proposed that the Irish language should be suppressed, in order that the people might be instructed by the clergyman of the parish; O'Leary suggested if it would not be easier for one man to learn Irish than for a whole parish to learn English; and said his Lordship's proposal reminded him of the echo in Erasmus *quid est sacerdotium ?—otium.*

In the year 1799, W. Stokes, M. D. was instrumental in publishing by subscription an edition consisting of 2000 copies of St. Luke's Gospel and the Acts of the Apostles in Irish, in the Roman character, and spelled as it is pronounced. It was supposed by some that those who did not understand Irish, might in this way read to and instruct those who could not speak or read English. The project, however, was not found to succeed; and in 1806, the four Gospels and Acts were published in the Roman character, but with the true orthography. This approximation to the genuine language had better success, and in 1810 the Foreign and British Bible Society published a similar edition of the whole New Testament in stereotype, the greater part of which was remitted to Ireland. In 1815, the Proverbs of Solomon were published in the genuine orthography in the *Irish character;* and thus the tortured language was once more restored to its rights. It is in this way the Bible Society rationally propose that their edition shall be published in conformity with the manner in which the language has always been, and is still read and taught in every part of Ireland where it prevails. The following calculation has been made by Dean Graves on the subject. It exhibits the proportion of the Irish to the English language in different parts of the country at the present day.

LEINSTER PROVINCE.	Irish	English	ULSTER PROVINCE.	Irish	English
South Meath and West Meath	5 to	2	Tyrone	$3\frac{1}{2}$ to	3
Dublin, Kildare, Wicklow	1 to	6	Donegal	4 to	3
King's and Queen's Counties	2 to	5	Armagh and Down	3 to	4
Carlow, south-west	4 to	3	Antrim, east coast	2 to	5
Kilkenny	5 to	2	Derry Mountains, south-west	2 to	5
Wexford, south-east	2 to	5	Fermanagh	1 to	6
Ditto north-west	5 to	2	MUNSTER PROVINCE	$5\frac{1}{4}$ to	$1\frac{1}{4}$
ULSTER PROVINCE.			CONNAUGHT PROVINCE	$6\frac{1}{4}$ to	$\frac{1}{2}$
Cavan and Monaghan	4 to	3			

THE CITY OF DUBLIN.

themselves when they were disbanded, that every man might bring home a bible to his family as the best acquisition of his campaigns. The convicts also of a prison ship on the eve of leaving this country for New Holland, were presented with a donation of the precious books. An affecting letter, signed by 169 of these forlorn men has been received, acknowledging with gratitude this considerate gift. " You gave," say they " to our solitude " the book of books, and it assures, that we in ' no wise can be cast out.'*

The number of bibles and testaments distributed by the society in the year 1815, amounted to 30,775, and for the last seven years to 160,000.

The income and expenditure are as follow :—

Ladies' Auxiliary Society, at subscriptions of 1d. per week	£338	10	0
Congregational collections in different parts of Ireland	408	10	4
Bibles sold at reduced prices - - - -	1451	8	6
Subscriptions and donations, &c. - - -	2378	0	2¼
	£4576	9	7¼
Paid for bibles and binding - - - -	3416	1	6¼
Travelling expences of secretaries forming branches, &c.	107	17	9
Other expences, printing, &c. - - -	1052	10	4
	£4576	9	7¼

If this calculation be correct, it appears that in seven centuries the English language has made its way through little more than half the country, that two millions and a half of the people yet use their native tongue, and that in one whole province but one man out of every thirteen has learned to speak English exclusively, though many of the peasantry are found to speak both English and Irish. In the Isle of Man it is not only the universal language of all classes of the natives with whom we conversed, but it is that generally used in the Deemster's Court in the capital, and that in which the service of the established church is performed for three Sundays out of four in some parts of the island. In Ireland, out of the metropolis, the sermon is almost always delivered in Irish in Roman Catholic chapels, and in all the country towns and fairs of three provinces it is the general language of commercial intercourse. We would strongly recommend the liberal and enlightened little work of Mr. Anderson to the perusal of those who wish for fuller information on this highly interesting subject than we could possibly give in our restricted limits.

* Ninth Report, p. 23.

RELIGIOUS BOOK AND TRACT SOCIETIES.

BESIDES the Bible Society there are two others instituted with the same view; one for distributing religious books, and the other religious tracts. The books and tracts are printed in Dublin, and on local subjects. They are distributed by appointing a district to every two members, who on intermediate Sundays proceed to their destination, and distribute them among the people they meet at the hospitals, barracks, jails, and other places. They are frequently given to beggars instead of money, who sell them at a profit, and return to purchase more. 130,000 tracts were printed, and 90,000 distributed, or sold at reduced prices in one year in Dublin, and repositories are appointed in town and in the country for a similar purpose.

HIBERNIAN AUXILIARY CHURCH MISSIONARY SOCIETY.

THE clergy and members of the established church, have been deemed by many remiss and supine, compared with the Dissenters, in the general promotion of Christian and charitable objects. But in the noble and extensive project for propagating the Christian religion among savage nations, which in its beneficent effects promises to transcend all other charitable institutions, they have now taken the lead.

The very interesting publications of the Missionary Societies furnish various examples of the happy effects of conversion to Christianity, but none is more striking than the success of the Quaker Mission among the Shawnese, a tribe of Canadian savages heretofore remarkable for their ferocity, but now converted from the wild hunter state into sober and industrious husbandmen.

"The Hibernian Church Missionary Society auxiliary to the Church Missionary Society for Missions to Africa and the East," was formed in Dublin, and their first meeting held at the Rotunda, 22d June, 1814. It has already established missionaries and schools in Africa. About 300 Negro children receive instruction, and half that number both maintenance and education. An annual subscriber of £5. has the right of adopting an African child, and giving it a name. The society is also attempting a settlement at New Zealand. Here a novel, dangerous, but in the event, it is hoped, glorious enterprise is opened to its exertions. In physical and intellectual energies the New Zealander far surpasses all the savages of the Pacific Ocean. He is, however, ferocious, treacherous, and vindictive, a cannibal and devourer of human flesh from appetite and choice. Such a being must be treated in no ordinary way; like the Shawnese above mentioned, his faith must be made conducive to his temporal interests. Already have some considerate traders introduced the potatoe into New Zealand, and the culture of this nutritious root in some degree has weaned the native from his thirst for human blood.*

The funds of this society arise from donations and annual subscriptions: the first already amount to more than £1000. and the other to about £200. per annum. In aid of this society there is another established at Armagh, which with the Dublin Missionary Society are composed of some of the most respectable names in the kingdom.

METHODIST MISSIONARY SOCIETY

Was established in 1815 and denominated itself the Methodist Missionary Society for the Dublin district in aid of the Methodist Missions. This Society is in connection with a smaller one in London. In the course of the last year £200. 13s. have been collected, a considerable portion of which arose from the contributions of penny-a-week societies. It is stated in one of their Reports,[†] that 120 itinerant preachers are employed in Ireland, many of whom are acquainted with the vernacular language of the country, and submitting to every possible inconvenience in streets, fields and cabins, have exerted themselves with great success.[‡]

The society meet annually in Whitefriars-street Meeting House, and elect a committee for the ensuing year.

* Savage's Voyage to New Zealand.
† See Reports for the year 1814 and 1815, where it is further stated that in Great Britain are 586 itinerant perachers, and 50 on foreign missions, besides 3700 local preachers and 21,000 persons who sustain the characters of leaders and exhorters whose labours are wholly gratuitous.
‡ See Methodist congregation and schools.

SICK AND INDIGENT ROOM-KEEPERS.

A few individuals in the middle ranks of life, inhabiting a part of the town where the population was poor and crowded, had daily opportunities of knowing, that many poor creatures who were unable to dig and ashamed to beg expired of want, and were often found dead in the sequestered garrets and cellars, to which they had silently retired; they resolved therefore to form a society for the purpose of searching out those solitary objects. In the year 1790 they first met, and called themselves a Society for the Relief of Sick and Indigent Room-keepers of all Religious denominations. Their first exertions were on a very limited scale: their subscriptions were confined to two-pence a week or eight shillings a year; and their visits extended only to Charles-street, Mountrath-street, and the neighbourhood of Ormond-market; to the poor housekeepers of which, they distributed occasionally food and fuel. But the obvious utility of the charity soon attracted public notice and support: they never gave to any object that was known to beg abroad; and the evident tendency of the society to check mendicity was a strong recommendation. In four years after its establishment, it was enabled to extend its relief to the verge of the city, which, for greater convenience was divided into four districts, viz. Barrack, Workhouse, Stephen's Green, and Rotunda divisions, where, at an appointed house in each, from twenty to forty members attend on one evening in every week. To these are sent in the petitions of such poor room-keepers as are in distress; an inspector proceeds to examine the case, and on his report a certain maintenance for one month is allotted. A remarkable feature in this society is, the total exclusion of all religious distinction in, not only its objects, but its members. The funds are aided by charity sermons in churches, chapels, and meeting-houses: its visitors are Protestants, Catholics, and Dissenters; the holy bond of charity has, in this instance, at least, united the most incongruous opinions, and for twenty-six years kept together a discordant body of men, who now amount to 1200 persons, to act on one object with the most cordial and regular co-operation. Its receipts for the year 1790 were £20. 2s. 4d.; for the year 1815, £1927. 13s. 10d.; the whole sum expended is £39,343. 2s. 4d., and the whole number relieved 312,248 persons, nearly twice as many as the whole population of Dublin.

STRANGERS' FRIEND SOCIETY.

This society was instituted in the same year as the former, 1790. Dr. Adam Clark was principally instrumental in its formation. Though its relief is equally afforded to all religious denominations, its subscribers and members are wholly of the Methodist persuasion. It professes to combine two objects, "relieving the wants of the body, and administering to the necessities of "the soul." When a poor creature is dejected by sickness and pressed by poverty, they apply to his softened heart. Every visitor is capable of exhortation, and while they supply his necessities, they endeavour to correct his offences. Their expenditure for the year 1815, amounted to £486. 4s. 10d.

CHARITABLE ASSOCIATION.

This was formed in 1806, on the principles of the two former, to afford relief to all but common beggars. Their funds are derived from small subscriptions; any sum not less than one penny a week constituting a member. Annexed to the society is a committee of work ladies, who provide employment for poor females who have seen better days, and also a lending fund. They hold their meetings at the Bethesda chapel, and the visitors of this society, as well as of the Strangers' Friend, annex to their annual report cases of particular distress, some of which are very affecting: their disbursements usually amount to £400. per annum.

SOCIETY FOR THE RELIEF OF INDUSTRIOUS POOR

Was formed in the year 1813 out of an Association for the Relief of the Poor. It originated with some members of the Quakers' Society, by whom it is principally conducted. It is intended to ameliorate the condition of those who have been in better circumstances. A sub-committee of ladies are appointed, who inspect the claims of the necessitous, and are allowed about £10. per month to distribute among them. The committee meets every Sunday morning at the Institution for Female Servants, in Dorset-street. It is supported by subscription.

DEBTORS' FRIEND SOCIETY.

There had been a society for this purpose in Dublin in the year 1775, but it is now discontinued. This society was formed on the plan of the Howard Association formerly emanating from the Association for Discountenancing Vice. It was established in 1813, and has for its object to compromise and liquidate the debts of small amount, for which deserving individuals may be confined. By its rules no composition shall be made for any debt exceeding £5. except under peculiar circumstances, and no debt shall be discharged which is contracted for spirituous liquors, or no person relieved who has been found guilty of combination. The lord mayor of Dublin, with the city and county sheriffs, are always of the committee. The report for the year ending January, 1816, states that seventy persons were liberated from the Four Courts and city Marshalsea, and their receipts were £221. including a bequest of £190. 17s. 1d. of Mr. Sican.

CONFINED DEBTORS.

To alleviate the situation of those for whom debts are not compromised, Mr. Powel left a legacy of £800. vested in the hands of the lord mayor and aldermen; from the interest of which a twelvepenny loaf, a piece of beef, some fuel, and £1. 1s. in money are distributed by the sheriffs on Christmas eve to each confined debtor.

SOCIETY FOR PROMOTING THE COMFORTS OF THE POOR.

A knowledge of the actual state of the poor is the first step to improve their condition. This was therefore instituted in 1799, with a view to collect information on the subject, and to guide and assist the efforts of individuals in the judicious direction of their charitable efforts so as to effect the greatest possible good with the smallest means, and encourage industry, while it relieved distress. It is patronised by his Excellency the Lord Lieutenant, who is president, and by the first characters in the country, it has for its extensive object, the improvement of all Ireland. The following are the subjects on which the society are more immediately desirous of collecting and circulating information. 1. Friendly societies. 2. Benevolent loans. 3. Agricultural societies. 4. Village shops. 5. Village mills. 6. Fuel. 7. Habitations of the poor. 8. Gaols, means of reforming them. 9. County infirmaries and local dispensaries. 10. Public kitchens and soup shops. 11. Education of the poor. 12. Employment of the poor. 13. Beggars, means of preventing them. On these topics, they have published two volumes of reports on the communications they have received from different parts of Ireland, and republished six volumes of English reports on the same subjects.

MUSICAL FUND FOR DECAYED MUSICIANS.

The last of our native Irish Bards whose compositions gave celebrity to their author was Carolan;* he died in the year 1738, and with him may be said to have expired what remained in Dublin of that taste for simple and touching melody so peculiar in its character and so long cherished in this country. Italian music had before this time been cultivated in England, and both vocal and instrumental performers had been brought at an enormous expence from Italy to London, and a taste for the complex produc-

* We are indebted to an old gentleman for the following traditionary anecdotes of Carolan and Dean Swift, which are not, we believe, except perhaps the first, in any account hitherto, published; for copious particulars of his life we refer to Walker's Irish Bards, 4to. Appendix, No. 4.

One of Carolan's early friends was Hugh Mac Gauran, a gentleman of the County of Leitrim, who excelled in ludicrous poetry. It was he who composed the celebrated Pleraucha na Rourcha, and from his English translation Dean Swift made the admirable version beginning "O'Rourke's noble feast will ne'er be forgot." Yet it was to Carolan he was indebted for some of the most striking parts of the translation. The Dean admired Carolan's genius, had him frequently at the Deanery House in Dublin, and used to hear him play and sing the Pleraucha. He was particularly struck with the happy and singular *onomatapoeia* in several passages of the original, particularly that which represented the sound of the wet in the dancers shoes, glug glug ionna m-bhroiga.

This was thought to be inimitable by English words, till Carolan bade him send his servant to walk over shoes in a pool of water, and then dance before him. This coincided with the Dean's own whimsical fancy. The experiment was made, and the Dean caught the sound and expressed it by,

"Splash, splash in their pumps," &c.

His esteem for Carolan, however did not prevent him seeing his faults and reproving them. Abstemious himself, he never passed by intemperance in others; and one day that he met our Bard, overtaken by the inspiring cup, reproved him with great asperity. Carolan no whit dismayed, told the boy who led him, to place his hand on the Dean's coat: when the Bard gently laying hold of the skirts with

tions of this school had already made its way to Dublin. The music hall in Crow-street was erected for the practice of Italian music and opened on one hand and raising the other in an attitude to bespeak attention, repeated the following lines in his native tongue.

> Sibshe, a chleir, na meallan an t-ōl
> Is ar gach aon ce mōr bhur smacht
> Ce mōr bhur milleann air chach
> Ni gheibh sibh fein bas le tart.

> Ye clergy who never deceive your drink,
> But censure our errors from last to first,
> However severe your correction, I think
> That none of yourselves ever died of thirst.

This extemporaneous effusion being explained in English, so pleased the Dean, that he compensated his rebuke by a pecuniary acknowledgement.

In Carolan's time public schools in Ireland were not numerous, and domestic education was very much the fashion; hence in most gentlemen's houses there was a room appropriated to the tutor and his pupils. It was here that our Bard was always ushered in, on his occasional visits to the gentry, obtaining a middle rank in the family, neither seated among the proud descendants of Irish kings, nor yet degraded among the domestics. One day, at a house where the Dean frequented, he was introduced, where a tutor, who had been just engaged, was sitting with his pupils: having never before seen Carolan, he asked the Dean in Latin, *Quis est Homo?* The Dean replied *est homo qui potest bibere.* Carolan, though not understanding Latin, treasured the words in his very tenacious memory, and whilst at table, asked the gentleman of the house their import; when explained, he turned round to where the tutor sat, and immediately said,

> Do ghlōr fa chloca tuigim go maith—
> Ce dhiultōch deoch a shliuga ionna thart?

> Your censure cloak'd I rightly scan ——
> Would you, when dry, reject a can?

While the penal statutes were in force in Ireland, there were sometimes found people to avail themselves of their odious clauses. A gentleman of the County of Galway had read his recantation under their sanction, and had eagerly seized on all the privileges they conferred to the oppression of his family and the aggrandizement of himself. It entitled him, among other things, to carry pistols in his holsters, which he never failed to do with much parade and ostentation. One day he met Carolan, whom he knew, and disliked for his known attachment to the religion of his ancestors, on the high road, in conversation with the Dean. Disregarding his helpless state, he was near riding over the blind Bard, who when he had passed, repeated the following extempore.

> Sin chughain data Padruig na cleiré
> A chul re Gaodhail is aghadh re Gaill
> A pheiré bhachal ar a bheuladh
> S-e beannughadb Eriond bun-os-cionn.

> See St. Patrick the Second, his clergy's disgrace,
> With his back to the Gaels, to the Saxons his face;
> His pistols before him for crosiers I pray,
> And he blesses poor Ireland—all the wrong way.

In the translation of the last line, the point is lost, though the sense is preserved ; in the original it is, he blesses the Irish by turning them up side down : *bun-os-cionn* is a proverbial expression, which literally taken, alludes to his riding over the Bard.

the 30th. Nov. 1731, with a Ridotto. A musical society was also formed and held at the Bull's head. By the subscribers to its funds, the Music-hall in Fishamble-street was built, and the first concert held in it, on the 1st. of October, 1741*. But a circumstance now occurred which seemed to give a decided turn to the taste of the town. Handel, banished from England by the spirit of party, sought refuge here, and found protection. Soon after his arrival he performed his oratorio of the Messiah for the benefit of the city prison, in the new Music-hall, and assisted by the violin of his friend Mat. Dubourg.† He effected a total revolution in the music of the metropolis. The simple strains of our native airs were now contemned, and fell into such disuse that they were totally forgotten, till they were revived, after nearly a century's oblivion, as new and extraordinary compositions. Meantime Italian singers were invited to Dublin, and operas established with an eagerness equal to that displayed in England. In the education of the youth of both sexes, a knowledge of the practice of some musical instrument was deemed an indispensable accomplishment; concerts were every where established, and became the favourite amusement in the houses of the nobility and gentry; and musical societies were formed in all the great towns in the kingdom.‡

In Dublin the Philharmonic Society was formed, and by its exertions several charities were founded, which are now among the most extensive and useful in the metropolis.§

But the MUSICAL ACADEMY formed the most conspicuous object, and eclipsed all the rest, not only by the superior skill, but the superior rank of its members. This institution was originally founded by the influence and

* On the site of the music hall in Crow-street, was afterwards built the Theatre, in 1752. Part of that in Fishamble-street fell down, and the remainder was converted into a Theatre, for which it is occasionally used.

† An anecdote is told of this performer, which indicates at the same time his skill, and the quick discrimination of the common Irish, in musical excellence. Eager to see the humours of an Irish fair, of which he had heard much, he left Dublin, and in the disguise of an itinerant fidler, entered the fair of Dunboyne, at a few miles distant from the metropolis. He was soon engaged to play in a tent, and endeavoured to acquit himself in the discordant notes of the character he personated: but, like the lyre of Anacreon, his instrument would not utter the sounds he wished, and the dancers, arrested in their notions, suspended the jig, and crowded round him to catch the sweet tones which they felt with irresistible force. With some difficulty he escaped from their hospitality, and was not inclined to renew the experiment.

‡ Walker's Bard, 4to. p. 160.   § See Hospital for Incurables, p. 728.

example of Lord Mornington. It comprised persons moving in the highest sphere of society; all professors or mercenary teachers of the art were strictly excluded. Their meetings were held at the Music-hall in Fishamble-street, and their proceedings were regulated by a body of statutes: they were divided into three degrees—Academics, Probationers, and Associates. They met once in each week for private practice; once in each month they held a more public meeting, to which a select number of auditors were admitted by tickets, and once in each year they made a public display of their talents for the benefit of some charity, to which all persons who paid were admitted. On these occasions crowds were naturally attracted, as well by the talents as the consequence of the performers. They saw on the stage all rank obliterated, profession disregarded, and female timidity overcome in the cause of charity; while noblemen, statesmen, lawyers, divines, and ladies, exerted their best abilities, like mercenary performers, to amuse the public. The musical academy continued its meetings for many years, but by the death of several of its male, and marriage of its female Academics, its principal supports were gradually withdrawn, till at length this curious and interesting society was dissolved, and charity lost a powerful and profitable advocate.*

* As every thing connected with this curious institution is interesting, we give an account of its statutes and members, which, though often spoken of, are little known. It was obligingly furnished by a female academic of high respectability, one of the last survivors of this society:

Statutes of the Musical Academy of Dublin, 1758.

1. This academy shall be composed of ladies patronesses, and of ladies and gentlemen. Vocal and instrumental performers of music only to be elected by ballot.
2. The male academics only shall have a right of suffrage in the Academy.
3. All power of enacting, altering, or annulling any statute or statutes shall vest solely in the male academics.
4. No public mercenary performer, professor, or teacher of music, shall ever be admitted into any rank of the Academy on any account whatsoever.
5. Ladies and gentlemen vocal and instrumental performers shall be admitted by ballot under the title of probationers.
6. Gentlemen instrumental performers, shall be admitted by ballot under the title of associate.
7. The ladies patronesses, female academics, and probationers, male probationers, and associates shall be exempt from all expences of the Academy, but obliged to an exact conformity to their statutes.
8. Appoints a president, four vice-presidents, treasurer and secretary.
9. A standing committee of nine.

But, not only the talents of amateurs, but those of the profession, were engaged and directed to the object of charity, and many of the foreign

10. An indefinite number of auditors to be admitted to be present at all concerts in the Hall.
11. The Academy to meet every Wednesday at seven o'clock, from November to May.
12. In every month there shall be three Wednesdays of private practice, and one or more of public performance. On these last strangers shall be admitted by tickets.
13. On evenings of private practice members may admit friends, who are on no account to be admitted again during the season.
14. No man to be admitted, except by the foregoing statute, unless to be a performer (not a professor), and actually capable and willing to give a specimen of his talents in the musical piece of the evening.
15. The voluntary absence of any academic for four successive evenings, shall be understood as a resignation.
16. Married male academics shall have the privilege of introducing their wives at every musical performance.
17. Once in every year a *public musical* entertainment shall be exhibited by the Academy for the benefit of the *charitable loan*, or any other which shall be deemed more worthy.
18. All debates decided by ballot.
19. A copy of statutes to be handed to every member, that all may know and expect no other than the privileges annexed to their several ranks.

MEMBERS.

President.
 Earl of Mornington.
Vice-President.
 Kean O'Hara.
Leader of Band.
 Earl of Mornington.
Violin Players.
 John Neal.
 Ed. B. Swan.
 Rt. Hon. Sackville Hamilton.
 Count M'Carthy.
 Rev. Dean Bayley.
 —— Connor.
 Dr. Hutchinson.
Tenors.
 —— Candler, &c. &c.
Bassoons.
 W. Deane.
 Col. Lee Cary, &c. &c.
Violoncellos.
 Earl of Bellamont.
 Hon. and Rev. Arch. Hamilton.
 Hon. and Rev. Dean Burke, since Archbishop of Tuan.
 Sir John Dillon.

Flutes.
 Lord Lucan.
 Captain Reid.
 —— Watson.
 Rev. Jos. Johnson.
Harpsichord.
 Rt. Hon. W. Brownlow.
 Dr. Quin.
 Lady Freke.
 Miss Cavendish.
 Miss Nichols.
Lady Patronesses.
 Countess of Tyrone.
 ———— Charleville.
 ———— Mornington.
 Lady Freke.
Lady Vocal Performers.
 Rt. Hon. Lady Caroline Russell.
 Mrs. Monk.
 Miss Stewart.
 Miss O'Hara.
 Miss Plunket.
Gentlemen ditto.
 Hugh Montgomery Lyons.
 Thomas Cobb.

singers and musicians were invited over for that purpose. Dr. Moss, the benevolent founder of the Lying-in Hospital, brought over the celebrated Castrucci,* the last pupil of Correlli, for the purpose of exerting his talents in the Concert Rooms, then erected in Rutland-square, for the benefit of his new institution. Castrucci died in Dublin, and was followed by De Mellos, a Portuguese, who established an opera in Fishamble-street, aided by Sestini and Pineti. About this time also the family of De Amici came to reside in Dublin: and in the year 1780, St. Georgio opened an opera in Smock-alley Theatre with Carnovalli, and continued it by subscriptions for twelve months.

But the taste of Dublin does not seem to relish the composition or the performance of the Italian school, and no efforts could establish a permanent opera on its principles. Individuals and companies make occasional visits at long intervals, and from time to time excite the public interest by a display of their complex powers. The periodical novelty attracts while it is new, but, from want of taste or want of money, the Dublin public are seldom visited by Italian performers. In the administration of Lord Hardwicke, the last effort was made to establish regular concerts on a grand scale, to be patronised by His Excellency and the principal nobility in Ireland, and several of the first public singers were engaged for this purpose, but the

---

Among these academics were many whose names have descended to posterity with their compositions. LORD MORNINGTON's sacred music holds a distinguished place in our cathedrals, as his catches and glees do in private societies; of which latter the beautiful glee of " Lightly tread—'tis hallowed ground," is a fine example. KEAN O'HARA, the author of " Midas," is well known. (See Biography of Dublin Men.) DR. HUTCHINSON published a volume of glees under the assumed name of Francis Ireland; having taken a fictitious name, because he did not think it reputable for a professional man to be a composer of music, though he had no objection to be a performer. JOHN NEAL was state surgeon: he attained an extraordinary proficiency on the violin, and was a member of all the musical societies. His fame in this way made him an object of public notice in England, and George II. expressed a wish to hear a man so celebrated. He was accordingly introduced at St. James's as an Irish gentleman, and delighted His Majesty with his performance.

* This extraordinary man, though capable of commanding by his talents wealth to any amount, was reduced, by his pride and extravagance, to great want. He was found by some friends who prized his genius, in the suit of black velvet in which he appeared in public, gathering chips to make a fire. He died shortly after in 1752. He was buried in St. Mary's Church yard, attended by several of the first characters, and so vast a concourse of people that the beadle of the parish was crushed to death in the execution of his duty. (Walker's Bards.)

THE CITY OF DUBLIN

project did not take place, and there has not been for many years any thing approaching to a regular public concert established in Dublin.* Meantime the taste of the town has suffered a second revolution, and reverted to its first principles, and the revival of our own sweet airs has removed what little interest was generally felt for the music of the continent. In the year 1792 those exquisite melodies were rescued from oblivion; and the united efforts of Bunting, Stephenson, and Moore presented them to the public in a new and interesting form. Societies were founded, and concerts held to revive the memory of Carolan and our forgotten bards. Successive volumes were published, containing their compositions, aided by the charms of appropriate poetry, and more are eagerly expected from this unexhausted source. They are now introduced on the stage and at public concerts, and in private musical parties they are sometimes exclusively practised. To give them greater effect, the use of the harp is generally superseding that of the piano-forte, and these airs are heard on the instrument for which they were originally composed.

Though there are no established concerts or operas in Dublin, there are several clubs and musical societies, who meet periodically, and display excellent specimens of the delightful art. In no city, perhaps, are catches sung with more humour, melodies with more feeling, or glees with more harmony, than in those societies. The Irish having, in general, little relish for the more complex excellencies of the science of music, have ever been remarked for their sensibility to the beauties of its more simple combination. The metropolis therefore is far inferior to others in furnishing the materials of an opera or concert, but it excels in those who delight by simple songs. It is the remark of the most celebrated singer of the present day, that he never heard melodies or glees sung with such taste and feeling as in Dublin.

Among the improvements in the instrumental parts of the science, there are some which have originated in Dublin. The Irish harp, eight centuries ago the most perfect instrument of its kind in Europe, and of which there

* Among other performers engaged on this occasion, were the Miss Cheeses from Manchester. They came to Dublin, and remained here; they established private concerts on a limited scale, which are continued every winter since the year 1803, and are the only regular musical performance held in the metropolis, unless we except the oratorio of sacred music performed on every Passion week at the Rotunda.

is a beautiful and curious specimen preserved in the College Musæum,* was capable only of playing on one key. The addition of pedals, while it gave an extent of compass, was liable to objections from the complex machinery, the manner in which it was used, and the increased expense; it was therefore inapplicable to the Irish harp; but Mr. Egan,† an ingenious artist in Dublin, has lately made the improvement so long sought for. He has rendered the Irish harp capable of being played on in every key, and of introducing half tones in every tune without pedals;- while the original structure of the instrument, with its number of brass strings remains unaltered. He has also much improved and simplified the complicated machinery of the double action pedal harp, imported from London and Paris, which are now much sought after for their brilliancy of tone.

The extent and variety of the piano-forte have been also much increased by the additional keys invented by Mr. Southwell. This improvement has been so much admired, that it has been universally adopted; and, we believe, there are no instruments now made of this kind in England, or the continent, without it.

The patent Kent bugle horn was invented by Mr. J. Halliday, which is now used in Dublin with such striking effect by Mr. Wilman.

But the invention of musical glasses by Mr. Pockrige‡ gave a dis-

* This is the celebrated harp of Brian Boromhe, and was brought to Rome by one of his sons, and presented to the Pope with Brian's golden crown. This was considered as an act of submission of the kingdom of Ireland, and afterwards alleged by Adrian IV. as one of his titles to the kingdom of Ireland, in his bull to Henry II. These regalia were deposited in the Vatican till the reign of Henry VIII. when the Pope sent the harp to Henry VIII. as Defender of the Faith, but retained the crown, which was of massive gold. Henry had no music in his soul; he therefore set no value on this harp, but gave it to the first Earl of Clanrickarde, whence it was traced through a variety of hands till it came into the possession of the Right Hon. W. Cunningham, who deposited it in the Museum, in 1782. For a full description of this harp, and the minute history of its descent from the Irish monarch, we refer to the thirteenth Number of the Collect. de Reb. Hibernicis; nor do we think the credit of the interesting account at all weakened by Dr. Ledwich, who asserts that it cannot be the harp of Brian, because it is ornamented with armorial bearings! Antiq. p. 232. The arms are chased on a silver plate, and it is evident, might have been an ornament subsequently added when gentilitial arms came into use.

† This humble but excellent artist was originally a blacksmith; following the irresistible bent of his genius, he commenced making Irish harps for itinerant musicians, but has now attained much celebrity and extensive patronage even out of Ireland. He is made honourable mention of by Miss Owenson (Lady Morgan), in her " Patriotic Sketches."

‡ This gentleman was possessed of a considerable estate in the county of Monaghan, but by imprudence and convivial expences into which an enthusiastic attachment to music led him, he exhausted his

tinguished æra to the music of Dublin, by the novel and exquisite tones it introduced. This instrument has since been imposed into the harmonica, but with much injury to the sweet and expressive sounds of the original.*

patrimony and outlived his fortune. In this state he was beset by two bailiffs sent to arrest him, but he so charmed their rugged nature by the sweet sounds of his musical glasses, that they were incapable of executing the writ, and suffered him to escape. He afterwards was compelled to practice his own instrument for a subsistence. He terminated an unfortunate life by an accidental fire at Cornhill, London. He published a volume of poems in 1755. (Walker, p. 160.) The instrument was improved and played on by Cartwright some years ago, in Dublin. He had previously visited the continent, and played before the court and the royal family of France. The late queen Maria Antoinette, he used to say, was particularly affected with the plaintive air of " Queen Mary's Lamentation," and turned away with an emotion she could not conceal whenever it was played. On one occasion she exclaimed, with a feeling prediction of her own fate, " Pauvre Marie."

* Among the men whose professional talents conferred celebrity on Dublin, we may enumerate the following.

Mr. S. Lee was the first Irishman who combined the ancient and modern style of music, and excelled in both. As a leader he was correct and chaste, and was much respected in his private character.

Mr. T. Carter set the music of " The Rival Candidates," and " The Maid of the Oaks ;" but he is better known as the author of the sweet air of " O, Nanny, wilt thou fly with me," which, had he composed nothing else, would have immortalised him.

Mr. T. Geary gave early promise of extraordinary musical genius, and the specimens he has left behind him indicate extraordinary musical talents ; but he was cut off prematurely before his powers could develope themselves. Labouring under some depression of mind he rushed out of his house, and was found drowned in the canal.

Mr. M. Kelly composed the music of " Blue Beard" and many other pieces which had great success. He was first singer at Drury Lane for many years, and was appointed director of the music at the Opera. He was much esteemed by Mr. Sheridan, who frequently visited him. He had at one time opened a music shop, and commenced the business of a wine-merchant, and supposing that an advertisement from the pen of Sheridan would ensure him success, he applied to his friend for the purpose. He immediately supplied him with one, commencing with " M. Kelly, composer of wine and importer of music," &c.

Among the present residents in the metropolis may be mentioned Dr. Coogan, who is considered as the father of modern music in this country, and deeply skilled in the theory as well as the practice of it. He composed the music of the " Rape of Proserpine," and the " Ruling passion," which were much admired.

Sir J. A. Stephenson claims a distinguished place by the number of glees, operas, and church services which he has composed, and the high repute in which they are held. It is said, however, that he has not much improved the original beauty and simplicity of the Irish melodies by its symphonies and additions.

Mr.-T. Cooke displayed much versatility of talents, and at an early period of life was selected to conduct the orchestra in Crow-street. He has composed many songs, operas, and overtures, and his musical abilities were much esteemed by Madame Catalani.

THE HISTORY OF

The Irish Musical Fund Society was founded in January, 1787, among the band of the Smock-alley Theatre, by the exertions of Mr. B. Cooke. Its object is to afford relief to distressed musicians and their families. By its rules no member can be admitted after the age of fifty. All members pay from two to ten guineas on admission, according to their age, and subscribe a sum not less than twelve shillings per annum, out of which any member, who has been a subscriber three years, or his family, may receive a weekly allowance not exceeding one guinea. All members who refuse their professional aid to a concert in aid of the funds to be fined half-a-guinea if absent from a rehearsal, and one guinea if absent from the principal performance, without sufficient cause. All members who promote dissention, or use ungentlemanly language to be expelled, never to be restored.

To increase the funds, the Philharmonic Society appropriated the profits of a concert; and in 1788, the receipts of the commemoration held in that year, amounting to £400., were applied to the same purpose. In 1794, the Society was incorporated by Act of Parliament, by the interest and exertions of Giordani, and there was such a feeling excited in the House, that the Speaker and all the officers relinquished their fees upon the occasion. The Society is patronised by every chief governor, and a highly respectable list of the most eminent of the nobility and gentry, who attend its concerts and add to its funds. The proprietors of the theatre always gratuitously permits the performers of the orchestra to assist, and no performer has yet been found who has refused his professional aid on these occasions.

In the year 1814 the stock in Bank amounted to sixty-three debentures yielding an annual interest of £239. 15s.; out of which eleven persons received support. We are much concerned, however, to state that the two last commemorations have added little to the funds; while the failure of the grand canal, in which they had vested nearly half their property, amounting to twenty-five debentures, has so embarrassed them that they are under the painful necessity of reducing half their pensioners.

THE CITY OF DUBLIN.

CHARITABLE LOAN.

This is one of the charitable institutions which owe their origin to the talents and propensity for music in this city. It was founded by the governors of the Charitable Musical Society, and was incorporated by Act of Parliament in the year 1780. The governors lend out money, interest free, to indigent tradesmen, in sums not less than two, nor exceeding five pounds, to be repaid at six-pence per week for every pound lent. They originally met at St. Andrew's vestry-room. They now meet at St. Anne's, on the first and second Tuesday in each month, to receive recommendations and interest, and issue loans. It is computed that above 4000 persons have been assisted in this way by loans, whose amount exceed £13,000.

MEATH LOAN.

In addition to what we have stated of the origin and progress of this Institution,* we have to add another circumstance of its utility. It has raised above 400 distressed journeymen weavers in the Liberties, to the rank of masters, by the important and well timed aid it afforded them; so that the credit of the greater part of what remains of the wreck of cotton woollen manufacturers, may be said to be founded on the judicious encouragement of this excellent charity.†

GOLDSMITHS' JUBILEE

Was established in the year 1809, at the celebration of the fiftieth anniversary of his Majesty's accession; and hence the charity is called the *Jubilee*. It was founded by the Goldsmiths' corporation, for the support of aged and indigent persons connected with their trade. They are dieted and lodged by contract, in a convenient house at Rathfarnham, and supplied with occasional clothing. The charity is supported by subscription, and by grants from the corporation, who appropriate to it also the fines of the members.

* See page iii. of Mr. Whitelaw's Life prefixed.
† Besides these, there is a parochial loan established in St. Peter's parish.

OUZEL GALLEY.

Though this society was not founded with a view to promote any particular charity, yet as it devotes much property to that purpose, it may be more properly classed under that denomination than any other. We have made due enquiry into the origin of its singular name,* and we have received the following account. Early in the year 1700, the case of a ship in the port of Dublin, excited much controversy and legal perplexity, without being brought to any satisfactory decision: to put an end to this delay and expence, it was finally referred to an arbitration of merchants, whose luminous investigation was highly approved of, and satisfactory decision cheerfully acquiesced in by the parties. On the utility of this precedent, a society was founded for determining commercial differences by arbitration. The vessel was called the *Ouzel Galley*, and the society adopted the name as their appropriate designation. Its members consist of a captain, lieutenants, and crew, who always have been, as they are now, the most respectable merchants in Dublin. They hold two or three convivial meetings annually, at which the general business of the Society is transacted. They assemble when and where the captain pleases to order. The expense of these meetings is defrayed out of a subscription fund. The costs decreed against the parties who submit to their arbitration, are always appropriated to charitable purposes.

BOARD OF CHARITABLE DONATIONS.

If there be any property in the State which should be guarded with more precaution than another, it is the sacred fund of charity. It is usually the

---

* The proverbial expression "very like an ouzel," is supposed to be borrowed from Hamlet; but in the original it is " very like a *weazel*;" *(see Malone)* of which the other is a common corruption, even on the stage. The word ouzel, however, occurs in Shakspeare:—

" The ouzel cock so black o' hue."

See Bottom's Song, Midsummer-night's Dream.

The ouzel is the black-bird. Many names of birds are to be found in the list of the British navy: Goldfinch, Nightingale, &c.

THE CITY OF DUBLIN.

bequest of the dying, to alleviate some distress of the living : to embezzle or misapply it would be destroying the sweetest consolation of many a parting, soul, adding to the sufferings of many a miserable body. It has therefore always been held as something sacred, and any fraud detected in its management, stigmatized with more than usual turpitude. Yet this moral feeling has not been found a sufficient protection against embezzlements, and the too frequent commission of this sacrilege, compelled the Legislature to fortify it with an additional guard. The first act was passed by the Irish Parliament, for this purpose, in the year 1763.* By this, every executor is bound under a penalty of fifty pounds, to advertise in the Dublin Gazette, within three months after obtaining probate, every charitable bequest contained in the will, whether he be of the Protestant or Catholic religion. To carry this act into effect, committees of charity were appointed in the Houses of Parliament, who watched over, and superintended charitable bequests and donations. At the period of the Union, these committees were about to cease, but that the pious intentions of charitable persons might not be defeated by having no guardians to their bequests, it was deemed expedient to appoint some permanent public body to watch over such charities, and enforce the application of them to the purposes intended. Accordingly, one of the last Acts of the Irish Legislature was, appointing and organizing this Board.† The powers, objects, and principal members of the Board, continue unchanged; its constitution only, is altered. In order to afford more certain means of information, the Act enjoins, that the registers of the Prerogative, and other offices in Ireland, shall make annual returns of all legacies left for charitable purposes, to the secretary of the Board, and empowers them to sue for, and recover any embezzled charity, and apply it according to the intentions of the donor; or if that be impracticable or unlawful, then to apply it to such charitable purposes as shall seem to be nearest and most conformable to his directions and intentions. It consists of the arch-bishops, bishops, chancellor, judges, dean of St. Patrick's, vicar-general of the diocese, and beneficed clergymen of the parishes of the city of Dublin. It has a secretary and law-agent, to prepare its business, and pass its cases for legal direction, into the hands of the attorney and

* See 3 Geo. III.
† See 40 Geo. III. ch. 75; whose preamble recites the above reasons for the Act.

solicitor-generals, or for information or advice elsewhere. It enforces the penalties of the law, without distinction, against all fraudulent persons who conceal or embezzle testamentary gifts, exacts the publication of them in newspapers, and prints a collection of such notices annually, with the returns of probate of wills made by diocesan registrars. It thus keeps a complete record of property devised for humane purposes, and has, in a variety of cases, instituted suits for the recovery of the sacred funds of charity, and compelled executors and trustees to apply them according to the intentions of the donor. The funds enabling the commissioners to act, are annually renewed at the discretion of Parliament, and consequently, the conduct of the Board is periodically subject to animadversion.* The only person who receives any compensation, is the secretary, who is remunerated by a salary of £150.

* In making enquiries into the funds of some charities, we were concerned to find a reluctance to communicate them, and that the cause was an apprehension of this Board. The origin of this, we apprehend, is the statement contained in the celebrated pamphlet on the penal laws, which avers, that it is "eager in pursuit of its prey, and armed with every authority to seize the funds devised by dying Catholics, for the maintenance of the pious and poor of their religion." The assertions of this book are without proof, but they are refuted by the positive facts adduced in the pamphlet, written in reply, which stands unimpeached. This states, that out of fifteen cases in which the Board interfered, two only, were against Catholics. One was a complaint against an executor, for not endowing an hospital according to the testator's bequest; and on the interference of the Board, the object was attained, and a useful and well regulated charity established in a country town, where it was most wanted. The other was the well known case of Mrs. Power, of Waterford, in which the Board interfered, only because the bequest appointed an *ecclesiastical* corporation, not recognised by the law. Meantime, a school was built, a nunnery established, a chapel repaired, and four hundred pounds applied to a secret purpose, without enquiry or molestation, by the commissioners. No suit, we believe, against a Catholic, has since occurred, though sundry have been instituted against Protestants, particularly at the suggestion of the Board of Education. We refer those to the pamphlets in question, who wish to judge of the merits of this controversy, which we do not desire to engage in, though it would be our anxious wish to remove impressions of such manifest injurious tendency.

ROYAL IRISH ACADEMY.

IN a country like Ireland, abounding with antiquities—high in reputation for ancient literature, and producing men of acknowledged talents in every walk of genius, it was long a national reflection that at a most

THE CITY OF DUBLIN. 917

enlightened period there existed no society of men under whose sanction and auspices these antiquities might be investigated, and the fugitive productions of genius, in other departments of literature, cherished and preserved. So early as the year 1683 an attempt was made by Mr. Mollyneaux to establish a society in Ireland, similar to the Royal Society in London. The temper of the times seemed very unfavourable to such an institution. Though aided by the talents and local knowledge of the celebrated Sir W. Petty, who was elected its president, it languished for five years, and finally expired amid the distractions of the country. In 1744 a Physico-Historical Society* was established. This society appointed a committee to explore the antiquities of Ireland, and proposed to examine each separate

* On the 14th of May, 1744, a number of noblemen and gentlemen associated in Dublin for the express purpose of enquiring into the ancient and present state of the several counties in Ireland, but they assumed no particular name; the original members were::

Lord Southwell.	Lionel Jenkin, M. D.
Lord Bishop of Dromore.	William Acton, Esq.
———— of Cork.	Reilley Towers, Esq.
———— of Clonfert.	James Ware, Esq.
Rev. Dean Owen.	John Coghlan, Esq.
Rev. Archdeacon Congreve.	Samuel Waring, Esq.
Rev. Dr. Jones.	Thomas Prior, Esq.
Rev. Dr. Ledwich.	Walter Harris, Esq.
Rev. Dr. Wynne.	Mr. Joseph Butler.
Rev. Archdeacon Howse.	Mr. John Lodge.
Rev. James Knight, F. T. C. D.	Mr. Robert Culderwood.
Rev. Brab. Disney, F. T. C. D.	Mr. Edward Exshaw.
Edward Barry, M. D.	Mr. George Fawlkner.
John Ferral, M. D.	

After entering on some matters of regulation, the society requested Mr. Harris and Dr. Jenkins to collect materials for a description of the city of Dublin, and also for the county. Dr. Samuel Madden made a donation of £10. which he proposed to continue annually; and he moreover undertook, in conjunction with the Rev. Philip Skelton, the histories of the counties of Fermanagh and Monaghan, and Mr. Harris engaged for the city of Dublin. The society applied to the Duke of Chandos for permission to examine his Irish MSS. and to the University of Dublin to peruse those of Dr. Gilbert, particularly Mr. Downing's Short Description of all the Counties in Ireland. On the 7th of May Dr. Jenkin read a treatise on the extinct birds and beasts of Ireland, particularly in the county of Dublin. At the same meeting Mr. Lodge produced a MS. relating to the county of Fermanagh. On the 15th of May, 1744, the society assumed the title of the *Physico Historical-Society*.

The following works were undertaken or published at the instance of this society:

A Tour through Ireland, ascribed to the P. H. Society, 1746.

county by a statistical survey—a plan which has since been so laudably acted on, but which yet remains to be completed. Under their auspices the accurate and indefatigable Smyth published his Histories of Waterford, Cork, and Kerry, executed in so masterly a manner as to have left little to be done in these counties at the present day. In the short space however of *two* years, their regular sittings ceased also, displaying a most extraordinary degree of national apathy in a country abounding with such testimony of former arts, and such capabilities for investigating them; but *two* transitory efforts were made to explore them, comprising an interval of seven years, in so long a period.* In the memorable year 1782, however, a new and general impulse seems to have been imparted to the human faculties in this country, and the investigation of civil rights called forth an emulation in every liberal art. A number of gentlemen, principally members of the university, associated together this year, for the purpose of investigating and communicating useful and entertaining knowledge. They assembled once a week, and each person read his productions in turn. Into this society were admitted, from time to time, such persons as were eminent in the different walks of literature in Ireland,† till at length the

---

* Smith's History of the Counties of Cork, Waterford, and Kerry, published with the approbation of the P. H. Soc. 1746.

Louthiana, or the Antiquities of the County of Louth.

But the most remarkable work published under their auspices, was Simon's Essay on Irish Coins, for which the thanks of the society were voted at a general meeting in 1747.

A History of the County of Down, and Rutley's History of the County of Dublin, were undertaken at the suggestion of this society, but afterwards " accommodated to the noble designs of the Dublin Society," and published in 1772.

Two Volumes of the Minutes of the P. H. Society are still extant.

The preliminary Discourse prefixed to the First Volume of the Transactions of the Royal Irish Academy, states that this P. H. Society was founded in 1740. The above dates of its meetings were taken from a MS. obligingly communicated by Dr. Ledwich.

* The Dublin Society for improving husbandry and other useful arts cannot be said to be of this description.

† Among the original members of the Academy was Colonel Charles Valancey. It has been asserted that he was an Englishman, and that he first came to Ireland with Lord Townshend. The following account was partly communicated by himself, a short time before his death. The ancestors of General Charles Valancey were distinguished on the Continent for their military character. His grandfather had been military governor of Calais. His father's name was Le Brun de Valançai, called from his territorial patrimony in Berry. It was in the castle of his ancestors that Ferdinand of Spain was confined by

society encreased to such magnitude that it was deemed necessary to give it a corporate form, to ensure its future permanence and respectability.

Napoleon; it had been offered to Col. Valancey by the French Government, on condition that he would reside on it, but he declined the proposal.

Charles Valancey himself was born in Flanders, but came to England when a child, and was educated in Eton college. He early entered the army, and obtained a captain's commission in the 12th regiment, and soon after was appointed to a corps of engineers on his regiment coming to Ireland. Here he began his literary labours. He first published his "Field Engineer" in 1756, and commenced a military survey of Ireland, which was particularly pleasing to his Majesty'; but after twenty years' progress it yet remains to be compleated. It was on these excursions that he had such an interesting view of the most unfrequented recesses of Ireland, and he determined to acquire a knowledge of its language. His occasional residence in Dublin gave him every facility. He commenced the study under Morris O'Gorman, clerk of Marys-lane chapel, and the Irish MSS. collected by Sir John Seabright, were presented to Trinity College, with a condition that Col. Valancey should first have permission to make such extracts as he thought proper. This was the origin of the "Collectanea," which was intended rather to excite than to gratify public curiosity. In 1773 he published his Irish Grammar, as a preparatory work, and in 1774 he began his "Collectanea de rebus Hibernicis," which contains such singular and fanciful matter, and excited so much attention by the novel and ingenious collation of the Irish and Punic languages. This was continued by a society formed to investigate the antiquities of Ireland, of which the Right Hon. Mr. Conyngham was president, but from some difference of opinion on etymology and colonization, the society was dissolved, though the Collectanea was continued till 1790, when it was finally concluded.

General Valancey died in Lower Mount-street, Dublin, August 8, 1812, at the advanced age of eighty-two. He was four times married, and was not very select in his choice of some of his wives.

At the sale of his books, the *Green Book* was bought for 100 guineas, containing an historical account of all the MS. and printed documents relative to Ireland. In this curious book was the following curious memorandum in his own hand writing. "Mr. Burton Conyngham had free access to my library in my absence, leaving a receipt for such books as he took out. I was absent six years on duty in Cork harbour leaving the care of my house in Dublin to a servant maid; this book was taken by Mr. C., and a receipt on a slip of paper given, which the servant put into a book on the shelf. She was some time after discharged, and another hired. On my return at the expiration of six years, I missed this book. In about two years, taking down the octavo in which Mr. B.'s note had been carefully deposited, the receipt fell out. Mr. Conyngham was dead, and died as was supposed intestate, and his great estate devolved upon Lord Conyngham, his nephew. I produced the receipt, and demanded the book, or the payment of 200*l*. The book was not to be found; with others it had been packed in boxes, and sent to an auction; not sold, and brought back. At length Mr. A. Cooper of the Treasury, who had the care of Mr. C.'s affairs, by long search discovered the book, when on opening it Mr. C.'s will fell out, by which it appeared that the estate was divided between Lord C. and his mother."

The Rev. Edward Ledwich, LL.D. is well known to the public, from two editions of his *Antiquities of Ireland*, and his decided opposition to his former literary associate, Gen. Valancey. We understand

In the commencement of the year 1786, it was incorporated by act of parliament under the name of the Royal Irish Academy, for the study of polite literature, science, and antiquities. The preamble of the act states, " that Ireland was in ancient time conspicuous for her schools and seminaries " of learning, and produced many persons eminent in every branch of " science," and that " lately several persons in the city of Dublin had met

he is preparing memoirs of his family from existing records, and which will elucidate many obscurities in Irish history. He was born in Nicholas-street, in Dublin, on the 29th of March, 1739, and received his education under the Rev. Dr. Sheil, master of the diocesan school of Dublin. He entered Trinity College in November, 1755, under his half-uncle the Rev. Dr. William Martin, and at a proper age was ordained in the church of St. Michael, of which his uncle, the Rev. Edward Ledwich, was prebendary. He was appointed vicar general of Dromore by Dr. Oswald, bishop of that see, who being soon removed to another diocese, and he expecting nothing from his successor, and wishing to see the world, obtained the chaplaincy of the 55th foot, and was for some time with the regiment in America. On his return to Europe he settled with some friends in Salisbury, and there began his literary career. He had before, in Wilson's Dublin Magazine for May, 1763, shewed his early fondness for antiquities, by endeavouring to prove that the celebrated battle of Clontarf, A. D. 1014, extended from that place as far as Granby-row, from the multitude of bones and military weapons discovered there on excavating the ground for a new street then building.

Having been appointed, by Dr. Barber, curate of Coome and Harnham, he published a pamphlet against inoculation, under the name of Dr. Langton. Shortly after he compiled the Salisbury Guide. In 1769 he printed Literatura Græca, being an abridgement of Potter's Antiquities ; and an Essay on the Greek language, tenses, and particles, under the name of William Jackson. (See Critical Review, vol. xxviii. p. 388. Monthly Review, vol. xlii. p. 70). In 1769 he gave an improved edition of the House-Catalogue of the antiquities at Wilton-House, the seat of the Earl of Pembroke ; and before he left England, he composed Antiquitates Sarisburienses, or the History of Old and New Sarum. (See Monthly Review, vol. xliv. p. 52). Mr. Gough, in his Topography, calls the writer Mr. Lescure. Having in 1772 exchanged his chaplaincy for the living of Aghaboe, he published the first annual report of the corporation instituted for the relief of the poor in the Queen's County ; it contains some valuable notices of mendicity, and similar establishments among the Greeks and Romans, and displays great learning. In 1781 he assisted Gen. Valancey in his Collectanea, by contributions to it ; but in his Antiquities of Ireland he has declared himself his decided opponent. The controversy exhibited a singular circumstance. A foreigner well versed in the language of Ireland, supporting its antiquities, and a native unacquainted with his vernacular tongue, endeavouring to subvert them.

In 1784 he was elected member of the Antiquarian Societies of London, Edinburgh, and Dublin. The same year and that following, he became a contributor to the London Archæologia, and in 1789 he published the first edition of the Antiquities of Ireland, and the second edition in 1804, of which the reviews spoke in high terms of approbation. Besides the foregoing works, he assisted Gough in his edition of Camden, as he acknowledges in his preface ; and he finished Grose's Antiquities of Ireland, who lived to write but seven pages.

THE CITY OF DUBLIN.

"together for their mutual improvement in the above studies, to which every encouragement should be given every where, especially in Ireland." It consists of a patron, who is the King, a visitor, who is the chief governor of Ireland; a president and vice-presidents, a treasurer, two secretaries, and a council of twenty-one, which is subdivided into three committees, of science, polite literature, and antiquities. The committe of science meets on the first Monday of every month—of polite literature on the second—of antiquities on the third—and the Academy at large on the fourth, at eight o'clock in the evening. All members are invited to attend and assist at the meeting of the committees. The Academy-house is situated on the west side of Grafton-street, nearly opposite the provost's house. It is a large edifice not distinguished by any architectural ornament, but furnished with a library* and suitable apartments. That in which the Academy meet is a spacious room, ornamented with striking portraits of Lord Charlemont and Mr. Kirwan. To stimulate exertion by the incentive of reward and reputation, the society occasionally propose prizes for the best compositions on given subjects, and periodically publish their Transactions, in which the most approved essays in the different departments of literature are laid before the public. In this way twelve quarto volumes have appeared, in which are to be found many curious and valuable papers on subjects very interesting to the country, the greater part of which would never have existed, or enriched the literature of Ireland, if not called forth by the incentives, and preserved in the Transactions of this society. The mode of admission is by ballot, and the terms five guineas entrance, and two guineas per annum; there are at present 180 members. The rent and taxes of the house, amounting to £166. were defrayed by an annual grant from government. The present grant from parliament is £309. besides £400. for the perfect repair of the house.†

* In the library are three valuable Irish manuscripts, viz. the Book of Balleymote, the Book of Lecau, and the Leabhar Breac M'Eogain, or the Speckled Book of M'Egan; they are bound in folio, and in good preservation. They treat of the history and affairs of Ireland at very early periods. These are the only MSS. in the possession of the society. The printed books have been lately enriched by the scientific works of Mr. Kirwan, of which the Academy had not copies. The library is not used as a reading room, but it is open every Monday for members to take such books as they may wish to borrow.

† The first society of this kind established in the University about the year 1782, was called the *Palæosophers*. Their object was the investigation of ancient learning, particularly the fathers of the Church.

THE HISTORY OF

KIRWANIAN SOCIETY.

This institution was founded in 1812, and assumed for its appropriate appellation the name of the great chemist of Ireland. Its objects are the

Dr. Percival had just returned from the Continent, and introduced the new system of chemistry, then almost totally unknown, and little attended to in this country. The investigation of this had excited a kindred zeal in the pursuit of other sciences, and Dr. Percival proposed to Dr. Usher to establish a new society to promote it. In the year 1785, therefore, another association was formed. Their object was the investigation of science and modern literature, and they denominated themselves *Neosophers*: into this, the Palæosophers in a short time merged. They met at each other's houses, dined together once every fortnight, read essays, and debated: they kept regular journals of their proceedings, but published no transactions. From these emanated the Royal Irish Academy, combining and enlarging the objects of both the former, and having distinct committees for the investigation of science, antiquities, and polite literature. The original Neosophers were, Drs. Usher, Marsh, R. Stack, Hall, Young, Hamilton, Waller, Kearney, F. T. C. D,. Drs. Perceval and Purcel, M. D., Messrs. W. Ball and W. Preston, barristers. Of these gentlemen but two are now (1816) living, Mr. Ball and Dr. Perceval. The former of these is rendered famous by a literary labour of uncommon magnitude, a complete and copious index of all the Irish statutes, by which he has acquired the well merited cognomen of Index Ball. Dr. Perceval was well known as professor of chemistry to the University for many years, where, though the promoter of the new school, he long adhered to the system of Stahl. His lectures excited an interest never known before in this city. The perspicuity of his matter was exceeded by the felicity of his manner: his language was a new invention, created for the occasion; it was happily characterised as "something above conversation, but below debate," which carried with it an irresistible charm. We take pleasure in noticing a trait of this gentleman's character: He never refuses his valuable professional aid to those who call upon him on Sundays, but he devotes, it is said, all the fees he receives on the Sabbath, to the necessities of the poor.

Among the early members who have paid the debt of nature, were many no less estimable. Doct. M. Young was born in the year 1750, and was elected a Fellow of the University in 1775. He was an enthusiastic admirer of the Irish language, in which he made a considerable progress under one of his own pupils, T. O'Flanagan, and in 1784 he proceeded to the Highlands of Scotland to collect information on the subject of Ossian's Poems: the result of his research he has published in the first volume of the Transactions of the Academy, where it forms an highly interesting article. In 1799 he was promoted to the See of Clonfert, which he enjoyed but a short period. He died in November, the following year, at Rochdale in Lancashire, of a cancer in his tongue. Besides several papers in the Transactions of the Academy, he published "An Essay on Sounds," and "An Analysis of Natural Philosophy."

Dr. W. Hamilton was also elected Fellow of the University, but retired on a living to Phanet, in the county of Donegal. From hence he proceeded to the Coast of Antrim, and erecting a hut on the summit of the Giant's Causeway, the foundation of which remains to this day, on the edge of the cliff, opposite Cape Pleaskin, he studied for several months the phenomena of this extraordinary production. He

cultivation and advancement of chemistry, mineralogy, and other branches of natural history, and keeping alive the spirit of philosophical enquiry in the country. The original members did not attempt more at the commencement than the appropriate business of such an institution. They simply met at stated periods and read communications, and held conversations on subjects connected with chemistry and natural history. Their next object was to make a collection of the most valuable books of science, to provide a chemical apparatus, and finally, as their means encreased and their views enlarged, to publish periodically a volume of their transactions.

But as mineralogy was a prime object, they immediately procured the most improved instruments requisite for geognostic researches; and written directions, pointing out the proper mode of collecting samples; were distributed by the members to all who might wish to contribute to a museum forming by the society, and all persons were requested to transmit to the secretary such specimens of the rarer natural productions as they might be able to collect. Such correspondents as wish to have ores, or indications of metals analytically examined, or who may desire information on the subject of mining, or economical chemistry, are duly attended to. As much controversy has arisen on the priority of chemical discoveries, it is intended that all communications to the society, previous to their insertion in the Transactions, shall be noticed without delay in the monthly philosophical journals.

As this society is but in its infancy its progress hitherto has been little noticed; it is proceeding silently in its march; already it has acquired a philosophical apparatus, and commenced its library by some valuable books. Several ingenious essays have been read at its meetings, and several members of zeal and penetration have been added to its list; and it is to

published the result of his examination in "Letters from the Coast of Antrim," an elegant and ingenious work, in which it was supposed he had satisfactorily established the volcanic origin of basaltes, though his theory has since been questioned. This ingenious scholar and enlightened patriot fell a victim to popular frenzy in the year 1797, after having evinced his zeal for Ireland by a most eloquent defence of her early pretensions. It was remarkable, that though no person of the many concerned in this atrocious murder was ever convicted, not one of them escaped punishment. It is generally known in the country where it happened, that they all died premature or violent deaths:

<blockquote>
Raro antecedentem scelestum,
Deseruit pede pœna claudo.
</blockquote>

be presumed, that a country which has already produced a Boyle,* a Black, a Kirwan, and a Chenevix, has still sufficient talent to render this young

* *Robert Boyle* was born in the castle of Lismore, county of Waterford, on 25th of January, 1627, and was one of a family whose names have illustrated Ireland. He acquired an incurable impediment in his voice while a child by the habit of mimicking a stuttering boy. During the troubles in Ireland he resided in Oxford, where he invented the air-pump, from an experiment made at Magdeburg. He was pressed to enter into orders, and promised a bishoprick, but he declined it from natural diffidence and a conscientious scruple that his writings as a layman would be more effectual in support of christianity. As director of the East India Company he procured a renewal of their charter, and required only as a remuneration, that they would print 500 copies of the New Testament in the Malayan tongue; and this appears one of the first efforts for propagating christianity in foreign countries, since so extensively followed up. In 1689 he was obliged to publish an advertisement to prevent the intrusion of visitors while he was engaged in a course of chemical experiments; at this time he invented the barometer. He died in 1691. His Works are published in 5 vol. folio. His life was written by Burnet, Bishop of Sarum. See also Smith's History of Waterford.

Joseph Black is said by Dr. Robison to have been born at Bordeaux, but it is generally believed that Belfast was the place of his birth, where he certainly received his early education. He took his degree as Doctor of Physic in Glasgow in 1754, at the age of 26. In 1766 he succeeded Dr. Cullen in the chemical chair at Edinburgh, and continued for thirty years, to devote his time wholly to science and the improvement of his pupils. He is still remembered with enthusiasm by the Irish students who attended his lectures. The modesty of his pretensions, the simplicity and perspicuity of his manner, and the extent and depth of his knowledge rendered him an object of affectionate respect and admiration to all who heard him. He first invented the inflammable air balloon by proposing to enclose hydrogen gas in the alantois of a calf. He was also celebrated for his discovery of latent heat. He died in 1799. His lectures are published in 2 vols. 4to. in 1803, to which is prefixed his life.

Richard Chenevix is, we believe, immediately descended from the amiable bishop of Waterford, whom Lord Chesterfield recommended for the see as " the man in whom there was no guile." He is a native of Ireland, and member of the Royal Irish Academy. He is the author of numerous papers in Nicholson's Journal, and the Phil. Mag. His observations on mineralogical systems contains a vigorous attack on Werner, and a philosophical defence of the rival system of Hauy. He is still enumerated among living authors, and quoted as one of the highest chemical authorities of the present day.—Biographical Dictionary of living Authors Thomps. Chem. &c.

Richard Kirwan was born in the year 1730, in the county of Galway, and his family was one of the twelve tribes of the town of that name. He received his early education at Ballyragget school, kept at that time by Patsull, a Carlow man, well known as the translator of Quinctilian, and compiler of the last volume of the " Modern Universal History." Here Kirwan shewed little talent, and in due time was sent to the Jesuit's college in Poictiers in France. While at that seminary his elder brother was killed in a duel at Lucas's coffee-house in Dublin, and he in consequence returned to Ireland to take possession of the family estate. At a shooting party in his native mountains at this time, he was compelled to a long abstinence from food, and the aperture of his stomach became so closed, and liable to spasmodic contractions, that he never after could take solid food without danger of suffocation, he therefore lived

THE CITY OF DUBLIN.

society, an useful and ornamental addition to the literary establishments of the metropolis. The terms of admission are one guinea per annum; and its members amount to about forty.

the greater part of his life on a milk diet. So great was his difficulty of deglutition, that a small particle of bread accidentally conveyed by his milk gave him intolerable agony. After persisting for fourteen years in this diet, he happened to stop at an inn where no milk could be procured; his companion found the remnant of a Westphalian ham, which had been boiled to jelly, after the mode of Continental cookery, and left by a foreigner sporting in that country a few days before: he was persuaded to try this, and found it not to disagree with him; it therefore continued ever after to be a favourite dish with him, though attended sometimes with very violent effects, accompanied with a convulsive rattling in his throat and a distortion of countenance, which he would not suffer even his own family to witness. After some time he removed to Dublin, and occupied a large house in Cavendish-row, in the rear of which was a small garden. Here he erected his laboratory, and pursued those chemical enquiries which have rendered his name so celebrated in Europe, as one of the most accurate and laborious investigators. His pursuits being the analysis of bodies, rendered his exertions equally useful to all systems, many of which he saw originate and expire without affecting the unalterable nature of his experiments. He, however, long adhered to the phlogistic theory of Stahl, from the defence of which he slowly retired before the superior one of Lavoisier; but he was inclined again to rally, when Davy confuted his too general principle of oxygen. He was the first who published in Ireland the Analysis of Soils, for a System of Agricultural Chemistry. He was a member and correspondent of most of the scientific societies in Europe, and a particular promoter of those in Dublin. Though educated a Roman catholic, he was in his religious opinions an Unitarian; but in his writings he gave no countenance to them, or frequented any place of worship where they were held. He was remarkably fond of music, and passed much of his latter time in listening to those young ladies who excelled on the harp or piano-forte, and to one of whom he left a legacy solely for her musical excellence; he however preferred the more complex combinations of Italian compositions to simple melodies, for which latter he seemed to have so/little taste or feeling, that he complained that Irish music "gave him the gripes." His objection arose from the associations connected with it; it reminded him, he said, of the plaintive moans of a hopeless and degraded people. So inveterate was his dislike, that he took pains to extirpate it from the country, by encouraging a taste for Italian music, and substituting it for the Irish melodies in use among the peasantry on his own and the neighbouring estates. He died in Dublin at the advanced age of eighty-two. His old servant, who had lived with him for fifty years, and had assisted him in all his chemical operations, survived him only a few days, and was buried with him in the same grave. Besides his chemical works, Kirwan was the author of many others on Happiness, Metaphysics, and Cosmography; he was also one of the most liberal contributors to some of the volumes of the Royal Irish Academy. Except a bust of him in the Dublin Library, and a portrait in the Royal Irish Academy, the only tribute of respect yet paid to this great man, in his native country, is the assumption of his name by this society; one of his legatees, however, has relinquished his legacy to erect a suitable monument to his remains in George's Chapel, Dublin.

GAELIC SOCIETY.

Since the revival of literature in Christendom, through the agency of the press, all those philosophers who have made language the subject of their investigation, have admitted, that the etymology of the names by which most of the promontories, mountains, rivers, and the other more permanent features of nature, are still denominated in the south of Europe, must be deduced from some other languages than those of Greece and Rome; nay, the more penetrating philologers of the seventeenth and eighteenth centuries, have indefatigably proved, that the radices of most of those names, and of the primitive appellatives of those languages, cannot be satisfactorily accounted for without a knowledge of the ancient Celtic, once the vernacular tongue, with a few dialectic variations, of all nations and states, from the Thracian Bosphorus to the Ultima Thule of the British isles. The learned Llhyd, eminently distinguished for his intimate acquaintance with the Cambrian, his native dialect, and with the Irish, or Erse, and Cornish, of all which, he made comparative vocabularies and grammars,[*] has abundantly demonstrated this. Leibnitz, and other continental philosophers after him, have asserted, that " were there a more sequestered isle than Ireland, where the language was still vernacular, it is to that they would look for the most unadulterated dialect of the Galatic, Gaelic, Keltic, or Celtic, now in existence." From the various disquisitions of our late Irish, British, and Continental philologers, it is evident, that without a knowledge of the Irish, or Erse, little progress can be made in the *genealogy* of the other European languages. This is fully proved from the numerous absurd etymologies to be met with in the philological works of Vossius, Menage, Littleton, Bailey, and even Johnson himself.

Notwithstanding this, and though the Gaelic is still, after an active proscription of many centuries, the vernacular language of three millions of people in Ireland, and of about one hundred thousand Albanian Gaels; and though there still exist many thousand Irish manuscripts on various subjects, in the British, Continental, and Irish libraries, both public and private, and though many of these contain treatises both in prose and verse, on the geography, botany, and jurisprudence of Ireland, the translation of which would enable antiquaries to trace the earlier

---

[*] See his Archæologia Britannica, printed at the Oxford Theatre Press, in the folio size, 1707.

periods of Irish history, Irish customs, and civilization, previously to the landing of the Anglo-Normans, yet, to our national shame, the well founded complaint of the Caledonian Doctor Carsuel, made two hundred and fifty years ago, holds equally true with respect to Ireland, in the nineteenth century, as at the time of his writing, which was but a few years after the invention of printing. Carsuel, in the dedicatory preface to his Gaelic translation of the Confession of Faith, published in 1567, pathetically laments in pure Irish, " that there is still one great disadvantage and want under which we Gaoidhils (Gaeils) of Albion and Ireland, above the rest of the world labour, that our Gaoidhilic dialect has never yet been committed to the press, as their vernacular dialects and languages have been by all other nations.". With respect to his native country, the grounds of Doctor Carsuel's complaints are now nearly removed by the patriotic exertions of the nobility and gentry of Scotland. A Gaelic society has been long established through the activity and agency of that body; schools for the instruction of the natives of Inchigael, in their own vernacular tongue, have been established among the Highland Scotch people; the Bible has been recently translated into Gaelic, and printed; many tracts on devotion, and various other subjects, have been published in that dialect, and among thirty-two members of that body, a sum of above £1200. British, was about sixteen months ago, subscribed, for enabling Doctor M'Leod, of Kilmarnock, and his associates, to commence the compilation of a Gaelic dictionary.

In the little principality of Wales, whose population, in 1811, amounted only to 607,388, less by about 3000, according to the Irish census, than that of the county of Cork alone, we have the assertion of the learned Mr. W. Owens,* that in the Cambrian language, about 20,000 tracts and books, on various subjects, have been already printed and published, among which, are repeated editions of bibles, common prayers, and books of devotion, in various sizes, bindings, &c. since the reign of Queen Elizabeth.† In this principality, Welsh schools have been, from very early times, erected, in which the national language has been taught; while in their churches,

* Author of the Repository of Cambrian Literature, and a Dictionary of the Welsh language, in two royal thick octavo volumes;—see the preface to it.

† The preamble to her Act for printing the bible in the Welsh language, declares, among the reasons for her permitting the impression, " that it will facilitate the acquisition of the English tongue."

they are also instructed, and have always been accustomed to bear sermons and read the word of God, and receive catechetical instruction in their native dialect, in which, books of geography, jurisprudence, and other subjects, are disseminated among them, for the propagation of knowledge, and the promulgation of the laws.

In Ireland alone, Bishop Carsuel's complaints are as well founded at this day, as when he published them two centuries and an half ago. Through national supineness, the reliques of Irish literature still remain neglected, and what is worse, become a daily prey to time, and subject to dispersion or total destruction.

Through the exertions of a few patriotic individuals, attempts have been made to remedy this complaint. Edmund Burke caused the Seabright collection of vellum manuscripts to be deposited in our College library, for facilitating the publication of the most valuable parts of their contents, and by his letters to General Valancey, frequently urged him to that undertaking. On the establishment of the Royal Irish Academy, all Europe looked up to that institute for the execution of that desirable work. In some of the first volumes of their Transactions, some few attempts have been made by the late learned Doctor Young, Bishop of Clonfert; but his premature death prevented the further accomplishment of his patriotic designs.

Henry Flood, a man who must ever stand high in the esteem of his countrymen, entering into the views of Burke, respecting the promotion of Irish literature, made Trinity College a residuary legatee to a considerable part of his property after his lady's decease, amounting now, it is said, to between £9000. and £12,000. a year. In his will, he directed, that on coming into possession, " they do institute and maintain, as a perpetual establishment, a professorship of, and for the native Irish, or Erse language; and that they should grant annual premiums for the two best compositions in prose or verse, in the native Irish, or Erse language, upon some point of ancient history, government, religion, geography, or literature of Ireland; and also that they should purchase books or manuscripts in that language." Through some informality in the wording of the will, the College has not as yet obtained possession of the estate, for which it is at present at law with Mr. Flood's heirs. Sir Lawrence Parsons[*] states, in

[*] Now Lord Ross.

his vindication of our ancient history, " that Mr. Flood's only object was, to enable men of letters to study the Irish, there being many curious and valuable records in that language, which would throw a considerable light upon a very early era in the history of the human race, as well as relieve this country from the most unjust charges of ignorance and barbarism, at a time when it was by far more enlightened and civilized than any of the adjacent nations." But might we not attribute another no less laudable motive for that great man's bequest: might it not be also for founding a professorship in that seminary, in order to qualify those intended for the clerical profession, for the mission of Ireland, by enabling them to preach and teach in their own tongue, especially when he saw field and street preachers in the provincial towns, sedulously employed in addressing the people in their vernacular dialect, to the no small discredit of the established church, whose ministers are not so qualified.

The conduct of Mr. Flood was imitated in an humbler sphere of life with better effect. Since the establishment of the college of Maynooth, for the domestic education of secular clergy for the Roman Catholic church, the want of a professorship for the Irish language, was felt and regretted by the people of that communion, in Connaught, Munster, and other parts of the nation where the majority spoke Irish. Young candidates for orders, born and bred generally in towns, when sent to country parishes, were unable to perform the duties of their profession, for want of a practical knowledge of Irish. To remedy this, a pious scrivener, of the name of Keenan, sunk one thousand pounds of his hard earned property, the produce of a long, laborious, and economical life, for £60. per annum, to support an Irish Professor for " teaching and instructing the students of the college of Maynooth the Irish language in the Irish character." From this fund the present Dr. Paul O'Brien, who according to the donor's wishes, was appointed the first Irish professor, and still continues to fill the Irish chair, is paid his annual salary.

Mr. Flood's legacy also had another tendency, though in an indirect way, to promote the study of Irish. When, through the activity of the press, his bequest for an Irish Institute and for the purchase of Irish manuscripts was publicly known, a great number of these, both on vellum and paper, were sent from various parts of Ireland to be disposed of in the metropolis:

the market was soon glutted with them ; they therefore became cheap, and many private individuals who had then but a smattering knowledge, and many who neither spoke nor read the language, became so intimately acquainted with the old vellum manuscripts, as to surpass in that study those whose vernacular tongue it was, and who could write and read the modern dialect.

The exertions of the late General Valancey tended in an eminent degree to render the study of Irish also fashionable.* Private tutors were employed, many of the clergy of the establishment, some of the junior and senior fellows of Trinity College applied themselves to the study of Irish. The present Bishop of Kildare,† to whom General Valancey inscribed one of the volumes of his learned works on Irish antiquities, on account of his Lordship's attachment to the language of Ireland, has also applied himself to the study of it, though his Lordship is not a native, and the use of the language is almost extinct in his diocese.

Such was the real state of Irish literature, and of the Irish language, when accident brought together a number of variously gifted individuals in the middle state of life, some endued with talents superior to their pecuniary means, and intimately acquainted with Irish literature; some others possessed of a great number of Irish manuscripts, and others whose inclination and means were ready to co-operate in rescuing from oblivion the remains of Irish literature. These frequently meeting with each other in their evening hours of relaxation, and rationally suggesting the means of furthering each others views, resolved to associate themselves into an active little institute, which they designated by the title prefixed to the present article.

The Gaelic Society of Dublin associated December 11, 1806, and at the same time developed its views in an address advertised in the Dublin Evening Post, wherein it is stated, that they embrace for their objects " The history, civil and ecclesiastical, of this island, long celebrated for

* Gen. Valancey's precursor in this neglected path was Miss Charlotte Brooke, daughter of the celebrated Henry Brooke of Rantavan, county of Meath, Esq. Her " Reliques of Ancient Irish Poetry," of which a second edition is lately published, served to attract the attention of men of taste by her charming English versification which accompanied the originals.

† Right Hon. and Right Rev. Ch. Lindsay, brother to the Earl of Ballcarras, and brother-in-law to Lord Hardwick.

" the piety and learning of its inhabitants. The former will present a
" picture of the laws, manners, and customs of Celtic Europe, previously
" to the Roman Conquest; the latter will fill a chasm in the history of
" religion during a period of darkness in Europe, save the light that shone
" in this nursery of learning. The translation of the ancient laws, annals,
" and other important documents, preserved from the ravages of times,
" and the more destructive waste of desolating revolutions, the affinities
" and connections of the ancient and modern languages elucidated from
" the mother tongue."

The terms of a member's admission are 2s. 2d. per month, or 24s. per year. By proposing terms so low, the society intended to ensure the co-operation of talents and genius in the humble walks of life. In this rank, in Ireland particularly, many are found who are most conversant in their native language. They are thus enabled to have deliberative voices in all transactions of the institution, a measure which is generally overlooked, or not attended to as it ought in societies of the literary kind.

For furthering the institute's view, they, in January 1807, took a suite of rooms in Saul's-court, Fishamble-street, balloted for members, appointed a committee of literature, vice president, and other officers. An excellent Irish scholar, Theophilus O'Flanagan,* was elected their secretary, and at

* Theophilus O'Flanagan, who was baptized Thadeus, was born near Tulla, in the county of Clare. He was sent to the school of John Nunan, who was esteemed the best classical teacher in Munster. From hence he entered Trinity College, under Dr. Young, where he obtained a scholarship. The Irish language was, at that time, through the exertions of General Valancey, becoming an object of literary enquiry and interest; Theophilus had come from a county where it was taught by his own father, and universally spoken by all, and he understood and wrote it as his vernacular tongue. His amiable tutor was an enthusiast in the study of it, and through his pupil's assistance soon attained a considerable proficiency. By him he was recommended to the notice of Lord Charlemont, and all the members of the Royal Irish Academy, by whom his abilities were much respected and highly spoken of. But an unfortunate propensity for intemperance and irregular habits, revolted those friends his talents had acquired, and having lost their patronage, he was compelled to withdraw from Dublin. Through the friendship of Sir L. Parsons he established an academy at Birr, and finally obtained a place in the post office; but inveterate habits still involved him in difficulties, and he was compelled to take refuge from his creditors in Kerry, where he superintended a roman catholic seminary: from hence he removed to Limerick in 1812, and was placed at the head of an Irish Institute established there by subscription. Here he continued to deliver weekly lectures till his death, which happened on the 4th of January, 1814, in the 53d year of his age. He had married the sister of Colonel Harvey Morris, who was

the same time, they employed, at a liberal stated annual salary, with other accommodations, as transcribing clerk, a Mr. Woulfe, a man of masculine genius, and by his knowledge of Irish, eminently qualified for copying old Irish manuscripts. This clerk copied many volumes of the ancient Brehon laws, from mannscripts lent the society for that purpose by John M'Nemara, now of Sandy-mount, Esq. one of the vice-presidents, in whose library fair transcripts lie ready for publication.

They also engaged the abilities of the late Father Dennis Taafe,* a man

co-heiress to an estate, for the recovery of which he commenced a suit which terminated in his favour a few months before his death.

Besides the tracts mentioned above, O'Flanagan furnished the first article ever published in the department of antiquities in the Transactions of the Royal Irish Academy. It contains an Essay and Elucidation of an Ogam inscription on a flag on the south-east side of Slieu Collaun in the county of Clare, to which he was sent in 1785, with Mr. Burton, who made a drawing of the stone, which is published in the same volume of the Transactions. This inscription purports to be the monumental tomb of Conawn, one of the Fenian heroes. The engraver informed Mr. Whitelaw, that O'Flanagan had altered and transposed the lines, and made them totally different from the original drawing. This circumstance was communicated by Mr. Whitelaw to Dr. Ledwich, and it induced them to doubt the existence of the Ogam altogether.

† O'Flanagan began a translation of Lynch's Cambrensis eversus from Latin into English, but he had as little perseverence as prudence; he printed only 112 pages.

* This extraordinary man was born near Mellifont, in the county of Lowth. His father was a farmer, and gave him a classical education, with a view to his taking orders in the church of Rome. He was sent at a proper age to Lovain, and becoming a Franciscan, he proceeded to the Irish convent of the brotherhood at Prague. Here he acquired an intimate knowledge of Hebrew from a poor Rabbi whom he supported out of his convent allowance, and after completing his studies he was remanded to his native country, with an excellent character for assiduity and correctness. In London on his way home he met with a countryman, and was induced to go with him to a tavern, where he became intoxicated. The next morning he found himself in Bridewell, without being able to account for the circumstance, and stripped of all the property he possessed in the world. This incident seems to have totally altered his nature. It was his first moral transgression, and induced habits of inveterate profligacy which he never after tried to correct. He could hear nothing of the man who had betrayed him to vice, and he was enabled to return to Ireland through the charity of some Irish sailors. By the order of his provincial, he was sent to the convent in Drogheda, where he soon became irregular, and was reprimanded for his conduct; he immediately left his convent, came to Dublin, and read his recantation in St. Peter's church, Dublin, Nov. 2, 1788. Taafe's brother having attempted at this time to take the life of a priest at the altar, with a bill hook, the grand jury of the county of Cork refused to allow him the usual stipend of £40. and Taafe, again irritated, returned to the bosom of the church he had left. Discountenanced however by all persuasions, he commenced a writer of pamphlets, and published

THE CITY OF DUBLIN. 933

endued with an extraordinary gift of analysing languages, at a certain stipend, to draw up dissertations illustrative of those subjects more intimately connected with the language and antiquities of Ireland; but after exciting much expectation, that eccentric person failed in fulfilling his engagements with the institute, or in realizing the hopes of his friends on that occasion.

Many members volunteered and sent in dissertations and tracts on various subjects of Irish antiquities or language; among the foremost was Dr. Paul O'Brien, Irish professor of Maynooth College, who compiled and forwarded for the society's emolument, a valuable grammar of the Irish language, subsequently printed, in the octavo size, by Fitzpatrick.

But of all the members of this infant institute, the late William Halliday, Esq.* was the most active and zealous in promoting its views and best

no less than *twenty* against government. He was convicted for writing "the Administration of England," confined, enlarged, and immediately committed again for writing "the Shamrock." Newgate was much crowded at this time, and none were willing to admit Taafe to their bed. It was his custom, on these occasions, to take a candle and deliberately set fire to the bed, then quietly take possession of the burning straw from which he had bolted the owner. An offer was now made to him by government to employ his pen in their cause. This offer he next day published, became connected with the insurgents, was pursued by the cavalry, and wounded by a blunderbuss, by which he lost the use of his left hand. He escaped to the Wicklow mountains through Dundrum, and afterwards boasted that he was present at the engagement in which Colonel Walpole was killed, and advised the plan of laying cars across the road, by which his detachment was intercepted. After escaping all the perils of those times, he commenced in 1808 a Continuation of Keating's History of Ireland, from 1172 till the Union in 1800, which he published in 3 vols. 8vo. He had been the means of rendering some service to the Duke of Richmond, when on his travels on the Continent, which he was willing to remunerate when viceroy in this country, and expressed his wishes to do so; but nothing could serve this impracticable man, he would not avail himself of the offer, and after alternately engaging in scenes of the grossest sensuality, and the most abject poverty, his powers were exhausted, he became debilitated in mind and body, and after an illness of three weeks, died a great penitent, in August 1813, in the 56th year of his age, a melancholy mixture of energy and weakness, of genius and profligacy.

* W. Halliday was the son of a respectable druggist and apothecary, in Dublin. He was bound to an attorney, and when out of his apprenticeship was patronised by Lord Norbury, and was appointed deputy filazer to the Court of Common Pleas. To a fine taste for the arts, he added a critical knowledge of the classics and modern languages; but that which particularly distinguished him, was a profound knowledge of the Irish language, with which he had been, till the last years of his life, entirely unacquainted. By close application to the vellum MSS., with the aid of imperfect Irish glossaries, he acquired such a facility in understanding the most ancient writings of the country, as surprised those whose native tongue it was from their infancy; a circumstance which should operate as an incentive

interests. He began, and published, a literal English translation of the first volume of Doctor Keating's History of Ireland, with the Irish original inthe collateral page.*

Mr. Halliday also composed an Irish Grammar of the duodecimi size, containing many curious observations on the declensions and prosody of the Irish language, indicative of its author's genius and taste.

To the perseverance and learning of Mr. Edward O'Reilly,† another member, the lovers of Irish literature, and the investigators of language in general, are indebted, for compiling and editing the completest Irish English dictionary of the language hitherto attempted. Of this work, two parts are already published in quarto, and the remaining two parts are now at press, and will soon be published at Barlow's, the Society's printer. Mr. O'Reilly has also ready for press, an English translation of the Annals of Innisfallan, and of the four Masters, generally called the Annals of Donegal, works which throw great light on Irish history, even since the

to the study of a language not difficult to acquire, and to which recent elementary works afford great facilities. He commenced a translation of Keating's History of Ireland, of which one volume was published; but his premature death, at the age of twenty-four, deprived the lovers of Irish literature of the further exertions of this promising and accomplished young man. Three months before his death he had married an amiable young lady, who has erected a monument to his memory, in Tawny Church, Dundrum, near Dublin. He died on the 26th of October, 1812.

* To this are prefixed a complete life and defence of the author, and his history, including curious anecdotes respecting Irish bardic schools before their suppression, about 1640, and the subsequent mode of educating Roman Catholic priests, and other scholars, in Munster and Connaught, by Mr. P. Lynch, vice-president of the society, who is now completing the translation of the second volume of the same work; printed by Barlow.

† Edward O'Reilly was born at Harold's Cross, and educated in Dublin, where he had never heard Irish spoken. He applied himself to the study of the language by accident. In the year 1794, a young man of the name of Wright, who was about to emigrate from his native country, had a number of books to dispose of, which chiefly consisted of Irish MSS. They had been collected by the industry of a man of the name of O'Gorman, who was clerk to Mary's-lane Chapel, and the person from whom Dr. Young, Bishop of Clonfert, and General Valancey, had learned Irish. This man's library, which filled five large sacks, Mr. O'Reilly purchased from Wright, and on examination found himself possessed of a collection of the rarest MSS., for one of which he has since refused fifty guineas. Master of this valuable repository, he commenced the study of the language, and by persevering application has acquired a deep knowledge of the ancient language of the country. Besides his dictionary, he is the author of several poetical pieces, tracts, and translations in the Anthologia, and other periodical publications.

landing of the English: he only awaits his countrymen's patronage for enabling him to defray the expences of the publication.

In 1808, a volume of transactions was published in the Society's name, comprising 412 octavo pages. It contains observations on the Gaelic language, by Richard M'Elligot, Esq. of Limerick, an honorary member. The remaining part of the volume contains two tracts; the first is Mr. O'Flanagan's Latin translation of an inauguration poem, by Thady M'Brodin, hereditary bard to the Prince of Thomond, at the coronation of Donach O'Brien, with the original in the opposite page, in Irish character; to which is prefixed, a version of the same, by William Lahy, Esq., then under-graduate of Trinity College. The second is an affecting romance from Irish history, called *Deirdre*, the Darthula of Mr. M'Pherson, or the lamentable fate of the Sons of Uisneach, translated into English prose, by Mr. O'Flanagan also, and accompanied with the original on the collateral page, in Irish character,*

In 1808, another adjument, and that the completest of any hitherto attempted, issued from the Dublin press. It is an introduction to the Irish, in three parts; first, an original and comprehensive grammar; second, familiar phrases and dialogues, all in the English character: but the mutable letters in the Irish words, instead of having an h annexed, have a point or dot over them, like the dagessated letters of the Hebrews, for designating their variation from the primitive. In the third part are comprised, extracts from Irish tracts, for habituating the student to the perusal of the language in its original Irish character.† On the whole, there never was such an apparatus as this, edited in one volume, for facilitating the knowledge of any national language, and does great credit to the author, the

---

* But in these, and in Mr. Haliday's grammar, there is one peculiarity which renders them more difficult to be read—an attempt to reduce them to the orthography of the fifteenth century. By this, more obstructions are opposed to the acquisition of a language, the spelling of which, even in its most improved state, presents obstacles not easily overcome, either by natives or foreigners.

† However judicious the adoption of the diacritical dots, yet it must be acknowledged, that placing the dagesh or dot in the body of the English letter would have been more striking to the eye. The dialogues are well chosen, not between shopkeepers or citizens, among whom the language is wearing out, as in other compilations, but between smiths, farmers, and country people, who most use it; but they are not always grammatical, a fault from which a grammar surely should be exempt.

THE HISTORY OF

Rev. Dr. William Neilson,* of Dundalk, M. R. I. A. and Member of the Gaelic Society.

In 1815, Mr. P. Lynch,† the present secretary, published synoptic tables of the alphabetic sounds, and also of the declinable parts of Irish speech,

* This gentleman is also author of the best Introduction for making Greek Exercises ever before attempted in the British Isles.

† P. Lynch was born near Quin, in the county of Clare, on St. Patrick's day, 1757. It is the practice in Ireland to call the child by the name of the saint whose day is next at hand, and he was called Patrick. He was educated near Ennis, under Donough an Charrain, or Dennis of the Heap. His master knew no English, and young Lynch learned the classics through the medium of the Irish language. After acquiring, in this way, an excellent knowledge of Greek, Latin, and Hebrew, he was compelled by family misfortunes to turn farmer, and for five years he held a plough. From this drudgery he was happily relieved, and was subsequently more fortunate, because he was more prudent, than Burns. He first was invited to Butler of Galmory's, where he passed six years as tutor to his children. After sundry experiments of the same kind, in different parts of Ireland, he at length settled in Carrick on Suir, and undertook to conduct the school of a respectable man who had just died, and became the only support of his widow and family. In the execution of this pious duty he was interrupted by a fanatic, who persecuted him for teaching school as a Catholic, and cited him to the Ecclesiastical Court of Waterford, over which at that time presided the amiable Bishop Newcome. He appeared in Court, accompanied by the widow, in mourning for her husband, and the good bishop was affected by the scene: " God forbid," said he, " that I should obstruct education in a country where it is so much wanted, and on such an occasion;" and he dismissed the complaint with a reprimand to the complainant. In him happily terminated this odious persecution, of which he was the last object.

In Carrick on Suir he commenced his career as an author. He had written a *Chronoscope*, but had no means of publishing it. In concert with a barber of the town, he procured some types, and by means of a bellows press, he set and printed his first work with his own hands, and established the first printing press ever seen in that town. He next wrote and printed, at the same press, a *Pentaglot grammar*, in which he instituted a comparison between English, Greek, Latin, Hebrew, and Irish. He has proved a singular coincidence between the two latter languages, and convicted Johnson of several errors in his Saxon etymologies. From Carrick he removed to Dublin, with his family, as affording a wider field for his literary labours. Here his merit was soon recognised. He was one of the first persons employed under the record commission, and has been since engaged in investigating the records of Ireland. His literary labours are various: besides editing, and adding to several elementary works in the languages, and other parts of education, he has written " Proofs of the Existence of St. Patrick," and " Life of Columkille." He is now engaged in a continuation of Keating's History, translated from the original Irish, and a " Geographical and Statistical Histoy of Ireland." He has also commenced a translation of Colgan's " Acta Sanctorum Hiberniæ," to which will be annexed, the whole of the valuable topographical notes which Valancey proposed should be published by themselves, and from which Archdal and others extracted their most valuable information.

THE CITY OF DUBLIN.

exemplifying the pronunciation of the Irish words, as far as could be effected by the substitution of English characters. In this little manual, entitled, "For ordeas Gnaith-Ghaoilge na h'Eirand," or an Introduction to the Irish as now spoken, he has attempted to shew all the variation of the Irish verbs in each person, as now spoken, more particularly in Munster and Connaught, thereby shewing the difficulty of giving rules with dogmatical decision, especially for the words of a language not yet collected with glossaries. He has given no rules: it has one perfection—it is short, and comprised in two sheets, on large type, of the octavo size.

On the whole, from what is here advanced, it will be seen, that there is a possibility of still obtaining a critical knowledge of the Hiberno-Celtic dialect, and by its agency of the old Celtic original, through the cò-operative means of the Gaelic societies of Scotland, London, and Ireland.

PUBLIC LIBRARIES.

TRINITY COLLEGE.

The first step towards the general diffusion of knowledge in any country must be the establishment of a public library. In early ages, when the transcription of copies rendered books, so scarce and valuable, it was absolutely necessary, and the libraries of Rome and Constantinople, destroyed by the Goths and Saracens, were noble monuments of such establishments. That such existed in the literary age of Ireland is highly probable, though similar ravages have, in like manner, left no trace of them in modern times. But it is a singular fact, that the same cause should, in this instance, produce opposite effects, and the ravages of war, which destroyed them, should be again the means of their re-establishment. The library of Trinity College, the first public library in modern times in Ireland, owed its establishment to the following incident. In the year 1603, the Spaniards were defeated by the English at the battle of Kinsale; the soldiers were determined to commemorate their victory by some permanent monument, and they collected among themselves the sum of £1800. to purchase books for a public library, to be founded in the then infant establishment of Trinity College, Dublin. This sum was handed to the celebrated Usher, who proceeded to London, and purchased the works necessary for the purpose.* From this commencement the library was encreased by many valuable donations,† at different periods, till at length

* It is a curious coincidence, that Usher, while purchasing these books, met in London, Sir T. Bodley, engaged in the same business, to establish his famous library at Oxford. It thus appears, that these libraries were exactly cotemporary establishments.—Parr's Life of Usher, p. 9. Folio. T.C.D.

† The first donation to the library was Usher's own collection, consisting originally of 10,000 vols. After his death, Cardinal Mazarine, and the King of Denmark, wished to purchase it, but Cromwell would not suffer it to be brought out of the kingdom. The soldiers at that time in Ireland wishing to emulate those of Elizabeth, purchased it in the same manner; but Cromwell again interfered, and would not suffer them to present it to the college. It was therefore deposited in the Castle, whence many valuable books and MSS. were stolen. At length, on the Restoration, it was given to the College, but not before the collection was reduced, both in the number and value of its books. It is said to have been given ex dono Car. II. though he had no other merit in the donation than complying with the original intentions of the purchasers.—Ibid. p. 10. See also Borlase's Reduct. of Ireland.

The following presents the state of the library as to the number of books and manuscripts, and by whom they were presented.

MSS. ROOM.

Usher A. Biblia Sacra, partes Bibliorum cum Commentariis.

    B. Breviaria, Missalia, Ecclesiæ Romanæ Rituales, Patres sancti et scriptores orientales.

    C. P. Sancti.—Scriptores Systematici, Scholastici, Polemici.

    D. Catalogi, Philosophi, Medici, et Historici.

    E. Genealogiæ et Historiæ Hiberniæ Ecclesiasticæ et Civilis.

Stearne F. Codices ejusdem argumenti, et Theologi.

    G. Historici et Theologi cum MSS. quæ præcipue tractant de rebus forensibus.

Nomina Benefactorum in Catalogo MSS.

Carolus II. qui anno 1661, dedit Bibliothecam Ussinanam, Jerome Alexander, 1674. J. Stearne, Episcop. Clogh. 1741, dedit MSS. Maddeni. Robert Huntingdon, Oriental. MSS. Miles Sumner, 1652. Peter Carew, president of Munster, Irish MSS. in Queen Elizabeth's reign. W. Gore, H. Prescott, 1680 H. Jones, T. Halley, 1672. Alexander Jephson, Archbishop Parker, W. Barry, John Lyon, Thomas Hay, Gordian Trowbridge, Murtogh Dowling, 1693. Charles Willoughby, Cornelius Higden, James Usher Armagh, Edward Worth,—21.

The MSS. are preserved in a room at the east end of the library, whence they are not permitted to be taken. The room is never to be opened, nor the MSS. to be inspected, unless in the presence of the librarian. These precautions are required by the statutes, as well with a view to their preservation, as to render them as authentic documents as possible. They are all in good preservation.

Number of printed Books.

Usher's	6,401	
Hallison's	4,109	
Gilbert's	12,749	
Other books	309	
		23,568
Other side, not including Smith's	11,850	
Smith's	629	
		12,479
		36,047

its growing magnitude demanding a corresponding encrease of room, the present library was built, forming, with the Fagel library recently added, a structure as elegant, and a collection as valuable, though not perhaps as extensive, as any in Europe. But the exclusive principles of such university institutions must, in their very nature, limit the extension of their utility, and the comparative few who are admitted to read in this noble library, bear no proportion to those who might benefit by such an establishment. The statutes enjoin that none but those who have taken a degree* shall be allowed to read in the library, who when this object is obtained generally leave the university. Thus not only the public at large are excluded, but students of the college are not admitted till the period arrives when they have no longer an opportunity to avail themselves of the privilege. The hours of admission also from 8 to 10, and from 11 till 1, are so brief a portion

Of Manuscripts.

Usher's	- - -	693
Stearne's	- - -	135
Stearne's and Alexander's	-	77
Others	- - -	102
		1,007
Printed books and prints	- -	104
		1,111

' The above account was taken in the year 1787; since that time great additions have been made to the library, particularly the collection of M. Fagel, pensionary of Holland, amounting to upwards of 20,000 volumes; it cost £8,000. granted by the trustees of Erasmus Smith. When the French invaded Holland in 1794, the collection was removed to England, where it was purchased by the College, with the above grant. This library is included in the bookseller's act, and receives a copy of every new publication. The total number is now supposed to amount to near 100,000 vols.

* The statutes thus prescribe the qualifications to read in the library: " ex iis qui in Collegio degant non alii ad usum librorum in bibliotheca admittantur quam qui saltem gradum Baculaureatus in Artibus suscepere, et ex iis isti soli qui presito prius juramento infra prescripto dabant fidem: de libris, &c." No person under the degree of master, shall introduce a stranger to read. " Nemo nisi socius hujusce collegii fuerit aut saltem magister in artibus in collegio degens quique dictum juramentum præstitit extraneum aliquem aut injuratum studendi causa in bibliothecam introducat, qui socius aut artis magisterei adstabit vel assideat quamdiu libro quolibet utetur." The time of admission, and the longer time of exclusion, are thus directed : " quotidie ab hora octava antemeridiana ad decimam et a secunda pomeridiana ad quartam in bibliotheca interuit (scil. Bibliothecarius) diebus festis exceptis uti et septimanis tribus." Stat. de Biblioth. cap. i. iii. The hours may be changed : " Concedimus potestatem horas quibus Bibliotheca patebit mutandi et alias constituendi quatuor nempe in die prout illis cum cæteris collegii officium optime videbitur conveniens," cap. vi. The hours have in consequence been altered, but the period, *quatuor nempe in die,* cannot be enlarged without a new statute.

of the day, and so ill adapted to the present arrangements of time, as to render them generally inconvenient to the graduate resident in the metropolis, who would wish to avail himself of the advantage of reading here. Added to this, the number of holidays which are religiously kept at the library, detract so much from this little space, as to render this noble edifice nearly useless for the general purposes of a public library, and indeed it ought not perhaps be classed as such.

MARSH'S LIBRARY.

In the year 1707, Narcissus Marsh, then archbishop of Dublin, established a public library contiguous to St. Patrick's Cathedral, on part of the ground attached to the archbishop of Dublin's palace.* The books which compose this collection, originally formed the library of the celebrated bishop Stillingfleet, and was purchased by Marsh for this purpose. The books are arranged in two long galleries, which meet each other at a right angle; in the first are the books of Stillingfleet. The second gallery contains the donations of others; at the angle is the reading room, in which the librarian sits, and commands a view of the whole library. Originally all gentlemen and graduates had free access, but some abuses occasioned more limited restrictions.† None can be now admitted but such as can produce a well attested certificate, and no book can be removed from its place unless in

* The establishment of this library forms a part of the eulogium inscribed on his monument in St. Patrick's Cathedral.

" Hinc Dubliniensis publicam hanc extruxit Bibliothecam, Armachianus auxit, instruxitque libris in omni eruditionis genere selectissimis."

And the invitation to study in it seemed to be very general to every reader,

" Qualis et quanta sit adspice et inspice."

See page 476.

† The cause of these restrictions is thus stated in an inscription near the entrance, dated October 1750. " A considerable number of books having been, from time to time, stolen from the library, by persons under the denomination of Gentlemen, claiming a privilege to read in it, according to the statutes, To guard against the thefts of such *infamous villains* in future, no person will be admitted unless he produce a well attested certificate to the librarian, of his being a scholar and a gentleman. An honest porter is appointed to watch and search every person leaving the library." This practice, however, is not continued.

the presence of the librarian. Extraordinary precautions were also taken to preserve the books. Each was fastened by a chain, terminated by a ring, which ran upon a wooden rod. This rod was close and parallel to the shelf to which the book belonged, and the chain was sufficiently long to suffer the book to rest upon any part of the reading desk below. The chains have been removed, but the rods yet remain to indicate the structure of this precautionary contrivance. The library is open every day, except Sundays and holidays, from 11 till 3; and notwithstanding these apparent precautions and restrictions few persons will find any difficulty in obtaining free access to it.* It is governed by trustees appointed by act of parliament, who make annual visitations; yet the public derive but little benefit from it. The books are extremely old, and on such subjects as but little interest the general reader, and the sum of £10. a year, allowed to purchase new ones, is altogether inadequate for any such purpose.† To this may be added, the remote situation, so distant from the general haunt, and so uninviting, deters many from attempting to avail themselves of it. In effect, the solitary individual now and then found in it, is a melancholy proof of its inutility, though it appears to have been, fifty years ago, in high estimation.‡

* In the reign of Anne, an act passed for regulating this library. It enacts, among other provisions, that it be vested in trustees, with the primate and archbishop of Dublin, the chancellor and chief judges, the deans of Trinity and St. Patrick's, the provost and their successors for ever. The property to be unalienable, free from taxes and incumbrances, unless particularly charged in future acts. The librarian to be appointed by the archbishop, to be a priest and A. M. Books hereafter to be given, if duplicates, may be changed or sold, and others bought. Librarian to keep the building in repair, or be suspended, and his income applied by the archbishop. Governors to visit second Thursday in October, yearly. 6 An. cap. 9, sect. 2. 3. 5. &c. The sum of £250. per annum is allowed to the librarian, out of which he keeps the building in repair. The number of books amount to about 25,000 vols. Among them are some valuable works on oriental literature, with a large proportion of polemic divinity. The Bampton Lectures are among the few recent purchases.

† Unfortunately the copy right act, which would confer on this library a gratuitous supply of new publications, does not extend to it. Dr. Radcliffe allotted £100. per annum, to purchase books for his library at Oxford, and a fund exceeding £400. a year, was established in 1780, to purchase books for the Bodleian library.—Chalmers's Hist. of Oxford, vol ii p. 163.

‡ "I am under the necessity," says Harris, "of acknowledging, from long experience, that this "is the only useful library in the kingdom, being open to all strangers and at all seasonable hours. "But there is one thing wanting to render it more complete, which is a supply of books, from the time "of its establishment there being only £10. per annum allotted for this purpose, which is little more "than sufficient to keep the books in repair."—Har. Cont. of Ware's Bps. p. 359.

DUBLIN LIBRARY SOCIETY.

The want of a public library on general principles, containing publications of universal interest, admitting all without any discrimination, except those of conduct and character, open at all convenient hours, and placed in a central situation, was long felt and acknowledged in the metropolis; yet it was not till the year 1791, that the want was supplied when the Dublin Society was established. Their first meetings were held at the house of Mr. Archer, an eminent bookseller, then in Dame-street. Into this society was admitted, every respectable person who paid a small entrance and annual subscription, and the numbers increased so rapidly, that it was soon necessary to take a suit of apartments for their accommodation. These apartments were first in Eustace-street, but the library has since been transferred to Burgh Quay, near Carlisle Bridge, for the further accommodation of the increasing members. The situation is extremely convenient: it is

The following MSS. illustrative of the history of Ireland, are contained in twelve small folio volumes, of rough paper.

Manuscripts:—Repertorium viride; Archbishop Alan's Account of the Churches in the Diocese of Dublin; Ecclesiastical Affairs of Ireland; Annales Hiberniæ; State of Ireland from 1640; Court Book of Esker and Crumlin; Liber Niger, seu Registrum Io. Aluni Archiepiscopi Dublin; Royal Grants in Ireland; State and Revenue of Bishops of Meath and Clunmacnoishe, as delivered to the King's Commissioners by J. Usher, 1622; same as returned by Anthony Dopping, 1693; Precedents, &c. of the Diocese of Armagh; Liber Precedentium Dud. Loftus; An Answer to Tyrone's Seditious Declaration sent to the Popish Priests in the Pale, written probably by Thomas Jones, bishop of Meath, afterwards archbishop of Dublin; Jurisdiction of the Prerogative Court of Ireland; Practice of Admiralty Court of Dublin; James the Second's Proclamation for Toleration in Scotland, with Remarks on it; Remarks on two Papers on Religion, by Charles IL; Articles of Peace, July 21, 1667, between Charles IL, States General, Lewis XIV., and King of Denmark; Proposals of Archbishop of Canterbury, with other Bishops to King James II. &c.

There are besides some Irish books in manuscript, viz. An Irish and Latin Dictionary in folio; Rudiments of Irish Grammar; Irish Romances, written 1331, folio, with several others.

The inconvenient situation of this library, has been long a subject of regret, and proposals have been made to remove it. In 1814, a memoir was presented to the trustees by the Dublin Society, stating, " that 20,000 books being in the library in a *remote and inconvenient* situation, so as to defeat the laudable object of the founder, that the Dublin Society, in furtherance of its chief objects, the diffusion of useful knowlege, have it in contemplation, to erect a building sufficiently extensive for their library, and capable of affording more accommodation than is necessary for their purpose, and propose to grant the trustees such a portion of ground as will enable them to erect a suitable building."
See Minutes, September, 1814.

contiguous to the great avenues which connect the north and south sides of the city, and it is the most frequented thoroughfare in the metropolis by that class who would be likely to avail themselves of such an institution. The house is new, spacious, and conveniently fitted up with suitable accommodations. In one apartment devoted to news and conversation, is collected every daily and other periodical publication of merit that can inform or amuse; in another, dedicated to silence and study, is found an elegant and extensive collection of every modern work of merit, in the different departments of poetry, history, or science, including the transactions of all the learned societies. The sum of £4000. has been already expended on the purchase of books, and the collection has been further increased by the accession of several valuable donations. The terms of admission are two guineas for the first year, and one guinea for every succeeding, but to officers of the army or navy, who are supposed to be only temporary residents, the additional subscription for the first year is liberally remitted. The library is open every day from ten o'clock in the morning till five in the afternoon, and from seven till ten at night. Thus the arrangements of this society are such as those of an institution intended to promote a taste for literature in a country ought to be. The terms of admission adapted to every ones means, the books to every ones taste, and the hours to every ones convenience. A lending library has been recently added.

The affairs of the society are conducted by a president, four vice-presidents, and a committee of twenty-one, who are chosen annually by ballot. The subscribers amount to about 1200.

DUBLIN INSTITUTION.

In a society constituted like that of Dublin, where topics are constantly agitated which involve such deep interest, it is impossible that any promiscuous assemblage of men should converse without a variety of conflicting sentiments. In the news room of the library society, where the most unrestrained freedom of conversation was allowed, and the newspapers and other periodical publications, naturally suggested a diversity of opinion, conversation sometimes assumed the form of debate, and discussions were carried on with less moderation than some members of more studious habits, thought comported with the privacy and silence of a literary institution. This

944   THE HISTORY OF

circumstance, combined with others, induced them to found a second society, where the admission should be less indiscriminate, and the objects more immediately literary and scientific. For this purpose a plan was published and circulated. It was proposed to establish a fund by subscription, and to issue debentures for certain shares, the holders of which should be the original proprietors of the institution. The proposal was readily adopted. In a short time 300 transferable debentures were issued for £50. each, and the sum of £15000. was raised. With this fund, a public library was opened in Sackville-street, in 1811, called the " Dublin Institution" for the purpose of enlarging the means of Useful Knowledge. Two features distinguish this society. A circulating library is attached to it, from which such members as find it inconvenient from any cause to go to the institution, receive books at their own homes, which they are allowed to keep a reasonable time. This addition to the general library is very judicious and accommodating, as it induces many persons to become members who could not otherwise avail themselves of the advantages of the institution, and brings home to the families of members, the most valuable publications which they could not otherwise procure. Besides this, lectures are established on the most useful subjects of science, and to promote their interest and value, a philosophical apparatus has been procured, and a lecturer on natural history appointed. A spacious lecture room has been erected, capable of containing three or four hundred persons: with this, any lecturer who applies is readily accommodated, so that there is a constant succession of lectures on a variety of interesting subjects. The terms of admission are three guineas per annum. The members amount to about 600, one half proprietors, and the other subscribers.*

DUBLIN SOCIETY.

THE Dublin Society was formed in the year 1731, by the voluntary union of several individuals† who had the best interests of their country at heart,

* Besides these, there are libraries attached to Stephen's Hospital, Kings Inns, Dublin Society, and other public institutions, which are noticed under their proper heads.

† Among those individuals whose exertions the society is particularly indebted to, were Dr. Samuel Madden, and Mr. Thomas Prior. Of the first of these excellent men, little was hitherto known, and

and, as Haller observes, was the first society ever formed for the improvement of agriculture. Their only fund was the small amount of their own

that little incorrect. We are happy to be able to rectify several mistakes which have appeared in every biography hitherto published of him: much of the account we subjoin, has been obligingly furnished by Colonel John Madden, his great grandson; it may therefore be relied on.

Doctor SAMUEL MADDEN was born of English parents, at Maddington, in Wiltshire, in the year 1690, and having received a liberal education at Oxford, he was entrusted with the care of the present king's father, who died without coming to the throne, or having it in his power to reward Mr. Madden; but the preceptor of the prince still retained great influence with the Government, and was held in high estimation, till he undertook to publish a book, entitled the "Memoirs of the Twentieth Century received and revealed in the Year 1733," exposing the conduct of persons then in power. Of six intended volumes, one only was printed, which gave such offence that government purchased up and destroyed the work. Of 1000 copies of this odd volume, there are now known to exist but three, one of which was sold at Dr. Kearney's (the late Bishop of Ossory) sale, in June 1815, for 8l. 2s. 6d. In order the more effectually to dispose of a person of whom they entertained apprehensions, the administration appointed him to the living of Newtown Butler, county of Fermanagh, in Ireland, contiguous to a property which had lately fallen to him in this country. There he fixed his residence, and for near forty years devoted his attention, time, and property to promote every thing which could contribute to the improvement of the people among whom he came to dwell. He proposed and established premiums for the best answers at quarterly examinations in Trinity College, Dublin, which are found to be such incentives, and at this day distinguish the system of education in that seminary. He was an original member of the *Physico-historical Society*, to which he gave liberal donations, and was one of the founders of the Dublin Society, in which the example of his premiums continues at this day to be laudably followed. In 1740, he allocated the sum of £100. to be distributed annually by the Society, in premiums for the encouragement of manufactures, sculpture, and painting; and in 1751, he encreased it to £275. to be extended to a greater number of objects. He was an intimate friend of Bishop Boulter, and all the then eminent men in Ireland; and having lived an exemplary life of piety and charity, and devoted his attention and liberal fortune to the judicious improvement of the condition of his fellow creatures, he died at Manor-Water-House, in 1772, at the advanced age of eighty two, leaving four sons and six daughters, and a name which, as Dr. Johnson says, "Every Irishman ought to honour."

He bequeathed a large and valuable collection of books to Trinity College, and several pictures now in the Provost's house. The only memorial which presents the likeness of this excellent patriot, is a mezzotinto print, with this appropriate inscription, "Quique sui memores alios fecere merendo." Besides the book above alluded to, he was the author of "Themistocles, or the Lover of his Country;" "Boulter's Monument;" also an exceedingly scarce work entitled "Reflections and Resolutions for the Gentlemen of Ireland;" these are summed up in thirty-two resolutions containing what ought to be their determinations as landlords, masters of families, &c. This curious work was first printed in 1738, in 8vo. and deemed of such excellence as to be reprinted in 1816, and distributed at the sole expence of Mr. Pleasants.

THOMAS PRIOR was a native of Rathdowny in the Queen's county. He was educated in Trinity

subscriptions, until 1749, when they were incorporated by his late majesty George II., by the title of The DUBLIN SOCIETY for promoting Husbandry and other useful Arts in Ireland, who was graciously pleased to grant the £500. per annum, on his civil establishment, since which period parliament has uniformly added its bounty every session; and it is but justice to acknowledge, that they have constantly and uniformly endeavoured to promote the beneficial objects of their institution, by applying the funds thus obtained in premiums and other means for improving agriculture, arts, and manufactures; and with a degree of success that enables this truly respectable, because truly useful body, to look back on its past labours with that satisfaction that results from the reflection, that its endeavours have not been fruitless. Though arts and manufactures have participated in their fostering care, yet agriculture, that most interesting of human pursuits, whether studied as a science, or practised as an art, appears to have been the favourite object of their attention, and at their weekly meetings, to use the language of a judicious writer on a similar subject, have been obviously calculated " to excite emulation and promote enquiry; to encourage and diffuse improvements in the construction and use of instruments for abridging labour; in adapting a proper rotation of crops, and a judicious selection of manures, to different soils; and to endeavour, for all these purposes, to combine the results of science with the practical knowledge of agriculture; to discuss and consider new projects; to recommend such as are useful; and to discountenance such as are visionary and impracticable." By these laudable exertions much has been effected, in the course of many years; the bounties of the Society, with the introduction of im-

College, Dublin, and is generally considered as the founder of the Dublin Society, which is commemorated on his monument. " Societatis Dubliniensis auctor, institutor, curator." (See Monument, p. 496.) He was certainly the first, and long continued, Secretary of the Society. The absentees of Ireland long engaged his attention, as a principal impediment to the prosperity of Ireland. In 1729 he drew up a list of them, with some excellent observations on the trade and manufactures of the country, and the condition of the kingdom. It was published without a name, but there is in Dublin a gentleman in possession of a copy which has these words in Prior's hand writing, " To Mrs. Dorothy Rawdon, from Mr. Thomas Prior." This lady was one of the excellent family of Lord Moira. Linen scarves, first used at the funeral of Mr. Conolly, Speaker of the House of Commons, in October 1729, were said to be his invention, as a means of encouraging the linen manufacture of Ireland. He died 21st October, 1751, in the seventy-first year of his age. Besides his List of Absentees, he was the author of some tracts on Coins and the Linen Manufacture.

plements, have brought into use some part of the British practice; yet we must state, with concern, that much remains to be done; local prejudices are maintained with obstinancy, and slowly give way; agriculture is still very far short of what it might be brought to; the modes in use are very deficient in making the soil produce what it is equal to, and what the modes practised in Great Britain would do. The success, however, that has hitherto attended the exertions of the Society will, no doubt, encourage them to persevere, and induce the Imperial Parliament to give that liberal aid, without which its exertions must be in vain, recollecting that a sister thus kindly fostered, may be, in time, enabled to supply to Great Britain those necessaries which her great population requires, which her own soil has not been found sufficient to produce, and for a great portion of which she is dependant on nations jealous of her power, and envious of her prosperity.

At the period of their incorporation, Ireland, though blessed with a genial climate and fertile soil, yet presented, almost every where, to the eye of the spectator, its naked and unsheltered fields; to encourage planting* became of course a favourite object of attention to the Society, and to restore those woods and groves that once entitled it to the emphatical appellation of the *woody island,* and of which so many indications still exist, but unfortunately beneath its surface, seems to have been an object of their laudable ambition; in this their labours have not been in vain; " many millions of trees have been planted, many large and extensive nurseries have been formed in divers parts of the kingdom, under their premiums, and the emulation that has arisen among gentlemen, of ornamenting and improving the value of their estates, has been sufficiently encouraged by the cheapness of the price, and facility of acquiring young trees, which those nurseries have produced. In this system the Society will, no doubt, persevere: thus the opprobrium, that Ireland is peculiarly deficient in timber, will be removed, and hundreds of thousands of acres, now waste and unprofitable, which by

* The excellent qualities of the Irish oak have long been known and appreciated. It was sent to England at an early period, where it is yet admired in the roofs of several public structures. The great wood of Kilcash in the county of Tipperary, not very long since, used to furnish quantities of the choicest timber for the navy. It is now, however, totally destroyed, as is also the famous wood of Shellala, with the exception of a few venerable trees, which are suffered to remain as specimens of its former grandeur.

sufficient encouragement, might be covered with trees, to the future wealth and aggrandizement of the country, and the support of the British navy, will be planted; and we sincerely hope that government will recollect, that the larger the encouragement is that the Society may be empowered to give, the greater and more speedy will be the benefit.

They also, under the encouragement and sanction of the legislature, procured land at Glasnevin, a village about a mile and a half from Dublin, which they have furnished and are continuing to furnish with various arrangements of plants, for the purpose of promoting a practical knowledge of botany, so far as it is useful to the farmer, the grazier, the planter, and the artificer; a knowledge hitherto much neglected in this kingdom, but very essential for forming a complete and profitable acquaintance with land, and its products. They have appointed a professor of skill and eminence to lecture on those plants, and on the various uses of all which are natives of Ireland; how far each is nutritious or injurious to each species of cattle, or can afford means of dyeing colours, or be useful in manufactures.* They had in contemplation the extending of their ground there, so as to procure the power of water which runs through it, for the purpose of trying experiments, and giving practical proof of the utility and application of many modern inventions in mechanics, for shortening labour in agriculture, arts, and manufactures: and they likewise proposed to erect sheds for their ploughs and other implements of husbandry, and to appropriate a field there, where country gentlemen and farmers may have ocular demonstration of their effects. But these objects come now within the plan of the Farming Society.

For the further execution of their trust in promoting the agriculture of their country, the Society have sent persons throughout the kingdom, for the purpose of making agricultural surveys of each of its counties, in the same manner as has been done in Great Britain by the Board of Agriculture there; in order that by a knowledge of the defects, or of any profitable practice in any place, they may be able to remedy the one, or to diffuse and extend the other, and may have the means of a continued correspondence with all parts, so as to suit their exertions from time to time, where necessary, with efficacy, and a surer prospect of success. Of these surveys, twenty-three have been finished, and printed for distribution, at an average expence of £140. each; of which £80. may be considered as the remuneration of

* See Botanic Garden.

the surveyor, and £60. as necessary to defray the expence of printing. These surveys, as might be expected, have been executed with very different degrees of ability, and while some are superficial and unsatisfactory, others reflect great credit on their authors, who appear to have engaged in the business with superior talents, and who, prompted by an ardent desire to serve their country, have executed their work with a degree of care and attention, to which the quantum of remuneration bears no proportion. At the head of these we may place Mr. Tighe's statistical survey of the county of Kilkenny.

The Society also established a Veterinary Institution, similar to that supported by the bounty of the Imperial Parliament in London, for promoting a knowledge of the diseases, the cures, and the treatment, not only of horses, but of neat cattle, sheep, and swine: two gentlemen of eminence, recommended from the Veterinary College in London, give lectures in this useful science, to promote which the Society has purchased a veterinary museum from Dr. Percival of London.

In 1792 the Society purchased the Leskean Museum. This celebrated collection is divided into the mineral and animal kingdoms, of which the former is peculiarly fine. The institutor, from whom it derives its name, was Mr. Leske, professor of natural history at Marburg, one of the earliest and most distinguished pupils of the celebrated Mr. Werner, upon whose principles, and with whose assistance it was arranged, between the years 1782 and 1787. Upon the decease of Mr. Leske it was revised, enlarged, and described by Mr. Karsten, also a disciple of Mr. Werner, and who deservedly ranks next to him among the mineralogists of Germany. To him we owe the catalogue of this truly valuable museum, which was printed in 1789, since which period no mineralogical work of note, has appeared on the Continent in which it is not mentioned with approbation, and confidently referred to. The museum being offered to sale by the family of the deceased possessor, was some time afterwards happily secured to this country, by the meritorious exertions of some distinguished members of the Dublin Society, for the moderate sum of £1350.

The mineral part of this collection, possessing such advantages from its first formation, and subsequent revision, by the most eminent mineralogists of Germany, was destined still to undergo a more rigorous examination, and to receive new improvements from the late Mr. Kirwan, a gentleman whose talents and genius are too well known in the world of science to need any eulogium. The collection is divided into five separate parts in conformity to the rules laid down by Mr. Werner, in his masterly treatise on the different sorts of collections which a complete cabinet of minerals ought to consist of.

The first, or characteristic collection, destined to convey to the young student a knowledge of the language employed in mineralogy, by exhibiting to the senses the characters described, consists of 580 specimens.

The second, or systematic collection, in which the more simple minerals are arranged, after their mutual relations of genera and species, in a natural order, exhibits 3,268 specimens, and is the most important, the study of it being indispensible to all persons employed in the cultivation of mineralogy in general, or any of its branches in particular.

In the third or geological collection, the minerals are arranged according to their position and relative situation in the internal structure of the earth; in this collection, which consists of 1,100 specimens, will be found a series of petrifactions, supposed to be one of the most perfect which is extant.

In the fourth, or geographical collection, the minerals are placed in geographical order: from this we may become aquainted with the mountains that occur in different countries, the minerals which these mountains contain, and where and under what circumstances they are found. This, which contains 1,909 specimens, is, as we might naturally expect, peculiarly rich in Saxon minerals, but does not exhibit a single specimen from Ireland.

The fifth, or economical collection, consists of 474 specimens, arranged merely according to the different uses to which they are applied in common life, and as objects of commerce: this exhibits for what purpose, and by what artist, each mineral is employed; and the utility of this collection is much augmented by having the product of each fossil, and the preparation of each mineral in general, laid contiguous to the substances in their natural state.

We have stated above, that Ireland has not furnished a single specimen to the Leskean collection of minerals: it is, however, but just to remark, and we do it with pleasure, that the Dublin Society, with an honourable solicitude to remove this opprobrium, and from the still more praise-worthy motive of bringing to light the hidden treasures of their native country, have, for some years, constantly employed one or more able mineralogists in exploring its minerals and fossils, the result of whose labours is disposed according to the order of the thirty-two counties of Ireland: from this collection, though still in its infancy, it appears that nature, profuse in the external blessings of an healthful climate, and a fertile soil, has not, in her less visible and more recondite treasures, been an unkind step-mother to our island. It is called Museum Hibernicum, Regnum Minerale.

Of the other additions made to this museum, one of the most important seems to be a collection of lavas, scorias, &c. from Vesuvius and other volcanoes, collected on the spot, and presented to the society, of which he was an active member, by the late Rev. George Graydon, for some years the excellent and amiable minister of St. John's, in this city, and with whose approbation they were, in 1801, added to the Leskean Museum.

The Society, sensible of the advantages to be derived from the institution of a museum under proper custody and regulations, by which the curiosity of the unlearned may be excited, and the researches of the scientific enquirer into nature assisted, have committed, this collection to the care of Mr. William Higgins, their professor of chemistry and mineralogy: the apartment in which it is deposited is open at stated hours, for the inspection of the curious, and always for the reception of mineralogical students, and the Society, with their usual attention to the advancement of useful science, have appropriated liberal premiums for the encouragement of young students in the attainment of excellence in the science of mineralogy.

That part of the Leskean collection that constitutes the animal kingdom*

* The animal kingdom is arranged under six classes, viz.
Class 1. Mammalia, divided into 5 orders, of which there are 27 specimens.
    2. Aves, 6 orders, and 161 specimens.
    3. Amphibia, 3 orders, 120 specimens.
    4. Pisces, 4 orders, 72 specimens.
    5. Insectæ, 8 orders, 2,773 specimens, of which the order of Eleutherata, or beetles, alone has 1005 specimens, and that of the Glossatæ, or butterfly, 643 specimens.
    6. Vermes, 5 orders, 1,562 specimens, of which the order of Testacea, or shells, has 1,326 specimens.

Nathaniel Gottfried Leske was borne on the 22d of October, 1752, at the village of Mascavia in Upper Lusatia, of which his father, Gottfried Leske, was minister: this excellent parent, who appears to have paid an anxious attention to the early education of his son, encouraged his strong predilection for natural history, which he cultivated with indefatigable industry and uncommon success to the close of a short existence of thirty-four years; an existence rendered uncomfortable by the frequent

is peculiarly rich in shells, butterflies, and beetles, of which there are not only a great variety, but many of uncommon beauty: the serpent tribe is also numerous and in good preservation; and here is to be seen the stuffed skin of the Boa constrictor, which was thirty feet long, though now shrunk to twenty-one. In beasts and birds the collection is deficient; there are however a few of the most beautiful of the latter, many of which have been preserved by Mr. Robert Glennon, and who has evinced much ingenuity in preserving the lustre of their plumage untarnished, and much taste in giving to each bird that ease and elegance which results from placing it in its natural and appropriate attitude. There are in this museum some specimens of Irish pearls, among which are two, procured by General Valancey, about the magnitude of a middle-sized pea, of the finest water, and not inferior to the best oriental pearls: they were found in a muscle in the lake of Killarney, and are valued at £50.

The venerable old General, always alive in his attention to this Museum, and particularly in its arrangement, has shewn much taste and judgment in selecting inscriptions: they are at once sublime and appropriate, irresistibly awakening those emotions with which such objects should be contemplated.

> Ask now the beasts and they shall teach thee; and the fowls of the air and they shall tell thee; or speak to the earth and it shall inform thee; and the fishes of the sea shall declare unto thee: who knoweth not in all these, that the hand of the Lord hath wrought this?—Job. xii. 7, 8, 9.

> Each moss,
> Each shell, each crawling insect, holds a rank
> Important in the plan of HIM who form'd
> The scale of beings; holds a rank, which lost,
> Would break the chain, and leave a gap
> Which Nature's self would rue!

recurrence of disease and pain, the consequence of an injury received in his infancy, which occasioned the distortion of the dorsal vertebræ. At the age of seventeen he entered the university of Leipzig, where, under the care of the celebrated Ludwig, he studied physic and anatomy, not with any professional views, but as subsidiary to his favourite science, natural history, of which he was appointed an *extraordinary* professor, with a salary from the Elector of Saxony, in 1775, when he had scarce attained his twenty-third year. In 1778 he became an honorary member of the Economic Society at Leipzig, and in 1786, professor of natural history at Marburg, where he died a few days after his appointment. His life, with a list of his useful works, has been prefixed by Karsten to his Catalogue of the Leskean Museum.

There are also some beautiful specimens of stained glass, executed by native artists, Messrs. Hen and M'Allister, and two good models, one of Stonehenge, shewing its present ruinous, and supposed former perfect state; and the other of a very curious edifice, called the Steag, or Stairs by the country people, in a remote and little frequented part of the county of Kerry, about twenty miles from Kenmare village, and three from the northern shore of the river, or more properly the bay of Kenmare. This edifice, which escaped the notice of Dr. Smith, who published his history of Kerry in 1756, was first discovered and described by Mr. Byers, General Valancey's assistant in his military survey of Ireland in 1787, but remained unknown to the public till 1811, when it was revisited by Mr. L. Foster and Mr. Rochfort, two of the bog-commissioners, from whose accurate drawings and description the model has been constructed. It is of considerable dimensions, being a circle of ninety feet diameter; the walls fourteen feet thick at the base, and seven at the top, constructed of small stones, unhewn, carefully fitted together without cement, and twenty feet high : it is surrounded by a fosse twenty feet wide, and from the top of the wall there is a descent into the area by no less than twenty flights of stairs. The General thinks that it was an Irish amphitheatre built by the Milesians, whom he derives ultimately from Indostan; and as it fortunately stands in a wild and desolate region, where no gentleman, or wealthy farmer has thought proper to settle, it is in a good state of preservation; otherwise, as he observes, like all the ancient buildings of this country, there would not now have been one stone of it left upon another. The museum has been lately enriched by valuable Greenland curiosities presented by sir C. Gisecké.[*]
The museum is open for the public every Monday, Wednesday, and Friday from 12 to 3 o'clock, and to a member at all times, who may introduce a stranger. The officers of the Society are strictly prohibited from exacting any gratuity from those who visit the museum, or any other part of the institution.

The fine arts have also largely participated in the fostering care of the Society; masters are provided to teach, and pupils are stimulated to exertion

[*] This gentleman is a native of Germany, and studied at Gottingen. In the year 1794 he applied himself to mineralogy under Count Blumenbach. When he left the University he proceeded over all the countries in Europe, including the Faroe islands. In 1806 he went to Greenland, where he continued seven years, and returned with valuable specimens of mineralogy, from the till then unexplored mountains of that remote country. He was elected Professor of Mineralogy to the Society in 1813, when he could not lecture in English, which he has since acquired.

by premiums for superior excellence in modelling, painting, statuary, and engraving, and the best models are provided for them to copy. These models are casts of busts and statues taken from the best originals, for the improvement of the young students, among which are the Laocoon and Apollo of Belvidere, the valuable gift of David La Touche, jun. Esq. to the Society; a Mercury, the gift of —— Weld, Esq.; a Venus de Medicis, a beautiful Bacchus, a Roman Gladiator, the Listening Slave, Roman Boxers, &c. with a beautiful groupe representing Sampson slaying the Philistines. In addition to these, casts of the Elgin Marbles were purchased by the Society in 1816 for the sum of £210. There are also a few figures in statuary marble, among which a dancing Faunus is highly esteemed, and the gratitude of the Society has added marble busts of the Earl of Chesterfield, Dr. Madden, Thomas Prior, and William Maple, Esqrs., to whose zeal and energy it, in some measure owes its existence.

The drawing school* is divided into four compartments—figure drawing, architecture, landscape, and sculpture. Over each compartment a master presides. They sit three times in the week, for three hours each time; and for the more perfect instruction of the pupils in the muscular anatomy of the human frame, a living figure is annually provided at the expence of the society. More than fifty pupils punctually attend each school; and some of the first artists in these kingdoms have been educated by the society. In them the education is entirely gratuitous, and

* This school was first founded in 1744, on a very limited plan. Mr. West, the grandfather of the present master, was employed by the Dublin Society to instruct twelve boys in drawing, at his own house in George's-lane, and soon after they built a room in Shaw's-court, Dame-street, for Mr. West, to which he removed. In 1753 Mr. Manning came to Ireland, and was engaged by the Society to instruct eight boys in ornamental and landscape drawing. An annual salary was now settled on Messrs. West and Manning; apartments were assigned them in the Society's house, Shaw's-court, and they engaged to receive as many pupils as the Society recommended, including a number of girls, to be instructed in ornamental drawing. On the removal of the house to Grafton-street, the girls were discontinued, and the masters were no longer accommodated with rooms in the house, but they still continued to superintend the school opened in the house adjoining. The Society appropriated £300. per annum for these schools, out of £5,000. at that time the parliamentary grant. The arrangements connected with the drawing school in Hawkins-street, would have been, when finished, very complete, particularly the Bust Gallery and Exhibition Rooms. The former is ninety-one feet in length, and thirty feet wide; and the latter sixty-seven by twenty-nine, and both are twenty-five feet in height, and lighted from the roof. The exhibition room has one continued upright lanthorn in the centre of the ceiling, which from thence is coved, and terminates in a stucco cornice. It was contrived by Mr. Baker, the superintendant of the school of architecture, and is, next the Louvre perhaps, the finest exhibition room in Europe. It is still used by the artists, at their annual exhibition, till the house in Hawkins-street shall be disposed of.

admission is open to all boys of a certain age. Independent of the improvement in the fine arts, these schools have rendered essential service to the different departments of manufacture; and the calico-printer, cabinet-maker, and glass-cutter, are indebted to them for many of their improvements. Many poor boys, educated as carpenters, who have evinced any abilities, have been sent to this school from the remote parts of the country. Here they acquire a knowledge of architecture and mechanics, and return to improve the place from which they came with their scientific acquisitions. In order to the further encouragement of unnoticed genius, and the developement of latent talents, they appropriate apartments to the Society of Artists, who hold their annual exhibition under their sanction Here the various productions of native talents are displayed—humble genius is drawn from the obscurity in which it lay concealed, real merit is discriminated, and diffident abilities are stimulated to exertion by the incentive of public approbation. Already have many paintings and specimens of sculpture been displayed highly creditable to the infant arts in Ireland, and to the society which first encouraged their cultivation; and it is much to be wished, that no misunderstanding among the artists themselves, may frustrate the excellent object of this department of the Society. As beautiful specimens of the graphic art, in Ireland, may be classed the bog-surveys. These are actual surveys made under the directions of the Bog Commissioners, for the purpose of furthering the very laudable plan of bringing into cultivation a vast tract of the surface of this kingdom, at present not only useless, but, in many instances, injurious; a plan which, when we consider the pressing wants of a rapidly increasing population, must appear to call for the most serious consideration. Of these surveys some may be admired, as specimens of beautiful drawing, and as all of them appear to have been executed with fidelity by able engineers; they may (exclusive of their primary destination) be justly considered as very valuable materials in the hands of some intelligent artist, who may undertake to give to the public that grand desideratum, an accurate map of Ireland.

The Society are possessed of a great number of valuable models of various implements of husbandry, and of several modern inventions in mechanics for abridging time and labour in agriculture and manufactures; among other curious specimens of mechanism, is to be seen a fine model of the celebrated wooden bridge over the Rhine at Schaffhausen in Switzerland, presented, in 1771, to the Society, by the late Lord Bristol, Bishop of Derry. This stupendous bridge, according to Mr. Cox, who saw it in 1786, when it was undergoing a thorough repair, is 365* feet long, and consists of two unequal arches, one of 172, the other of 193 feet, and which rest on a pier in the river, the remains of the former stone bridge, which the impetuosity of the stream had demolished: it was planned and executed by Ulric Grubenman, originally an illiterate carpenter, a native of Tuffen, a small village of the canton of Appenzel, but possessed of great natural talents, and a wonderful knowledge in the practical part of mechanics, and who raised himself to such eminence in his profession, that he has been justly considered as one of the most ingenious architects of the present century. On the Bishop's passing through Schaffhausen, an object whose vastness evinced the daring genius of the architect, naturally attracted the notice of a congenial mind, and anxious to have a bridge of a similar construction thrown over the Foyle at Londonderry, where that river is 900 feet wide,† he employed Ulric Grubenman the brother or nephew of the original architect, to make this model, which is executed with the most minute precision: it is 16 feet and 1 inch long, and 10 inches and six-tenths of an inch broad, and on a scale of nearly 2 feet to an inch. Mr. Andreæ, in his Letters on Switzerland, has given two engravings of the bridge of Schaffhausen, to which he has added a very accurate description of its mechanical construction, communicated by Mr. Jetzler; but as this bridge is no longer in existence, having been destroyed by the French in their retreat from Switzerland, before the victorious arms of the Archduke Charles, and this model of it (probably the only one in existence) conveying a much more accurate knowledge of its mechanism than any engravings can possibly do, it certainly merits more attention than it has hitherto experienced: the damages occasioned by carelessness and neglect have been lately repaired, and it is earnestly hoped that it may be placed in a situation, which

* These are probably Rhinland feet, and (as the London foot is to the Rhinland as 1352 to 1392 (nearly) are equal to 376 feet of our measure.

† The Bishop's ideas were magnificent but extravagant: his intended bridge over the Foyle was to consist of two arches, of 450 feet each: but though he subscribed liberally himself towards the execution of his plan, he failed in obtaining a sufficient sum for the purpose. On his application to a clergyman of his diocese (the Rev. Dr. Forster) the latter, it is said, expressed great admiration at the boldness of his plan, and the sublimity of the imagination that conceived so grand an idea; but when pressed for his subscription, shrewdly observed, that when his lordship had turned the arches, he would finish the superstructure at his own expense.

may at once shew to advantage, and protect from injury, a model which communicates to the intelligent spectator, who will take the trouble to examine it, a lively idea of what natural talents, in humble life, and unaided by science, may effect.

The following lectures are annually given by their respective professors:

NATURAL PHILOSOPHY. First course, first Tuesday in March; second course, first Tuesday in May. - - - Mr. Lynch.

BOTANY. First course, first Monday in May, at the Society-house; second course, second Tuesday in June, at the Botanic Garden. - - - - Dr. Wade.

CHEMISTRY. First course, first Tuesday in November; second course, first Tuesday in January. - - Mr. Higgins.

MINERALOGY. First Monday in March. - Sir C. Giseckè.

MINING. First Tuesday in February. - - Mr. Griffith.

VETERINARY ART. First Monday in May. - Mr. Peal.

To these lectures the public are liberally invited. Tickets of admission being readily and gratuitously procured, by application to the President of the Society.

The institution was originally supported by subscription, and parliamentary grants. The former have been discontinued, every person now paying at his admission fifty guineas, which constitute him a member for life. The latter amounted to £5,500. per annum, till the year 1800, when the Irish parliament made an additional grant of £10,000, since which period, the same sum has been annually continued by the Imperial Parliament. The Society consists of 490 members.

The house of the Society was originally in Grafton-street, but in the year 1800 they were enabled to take, or purchase ground between Poolbeg and Hawkins-street, from the Commissoners of Wide Streets, convenient for their necessary buildings; the rent was fixed at £842. 8s. 8d., that is £200. for ground rent, and £642. 8s. 8d. for the proprietor's profit rent. In the sessions of 1801 and 1802, the imperial parliament granted £9,000. for building; and on this site, and with these aids, they erected a very extensive edifice, which, for fourteen years, they continued to enlarge and improve. But when a sum exceeding £60,000. had been expended on the edifice, and its numerous and extensive compartments were nearly completed, an unexpected alteration took place, and the Society has again removed to another situation.*

* The necessity for this removal has been doubted, and its propriety much questioned. The

The noble mansion of the Duke of Leinster was purchased for the sum of £20,000.* by which the Society obtained the fee-simple of an area of an acre of ground, and a magnificent palace in the best part of the city; to this they removed in the year 1815, after considerable alterations had been made in it, for their reception. This building had long been celebrated as one of the most splendid private residences in Europe. It is approached from Kildare-street through a grand gateway of rustic masonry. This leads to a spacious court, forming an immense segment of a circle before the principal front. This front is ornamented with four beautiful Corinthian pillars, with their entablature, which rest on the rusticated part of the first story, and support a pediment, and between the pedestals of the columns are balustrades. The windows are all ornamented by architraves, and

building already erected was ornamental, and its parts built expressly for the purposes of the institution. It consisted of a front and sides, including a quadrangular area. The first is 97 feet in length, and presents an interesting façade to Hawkins-street. It is built of hewn granite, and forms a centre and two wings. The wings are of two stories, ornamented with Doric pilasters without bases, and the centre terminates in an attic story above the Doric entablature. The door is Doric, and in a niche over it, is a figure of Minerva with a cornucopiæ, the emblem of plenty, and on her shield the Irish harp, with the appropriate motto of the Society, NOSTRI PLENA LABORIS. The apartments within are, a broad room, lofty and well lighted by a beautiful and richly ornamented square lantborn in the centre, and two others of an oval form on each side, this room is 39 feet by 25. Two spacious apartments, erected for the purpose of displaying the Leskean Mineral Museum to the best advantage, and contiguous to it, a gallery for the Irish specimens. One 53 feet by 24, for displaying the animal collection; from hence was a noble and well proportioned gallery, 90 feet by 30, well lighted by three elegant lanthorns from above, round which were disposed to the best advantage, the busts and statues of the Society, the group of Laocoon terminating the vista. Off that was the drawing school, a fine apartment, 30 feet square, judiciously and well lighted from the roof. The library occupied three rooms. The exhibition room was lofty and spacious, built on the best model, with the light so disposed from the roof, as to display the paintings with the best effect. In the rear of the quadrangular court was an extensive chemical laboratory and lecture room, round which ran a gallery and seats for the accommodation of 800 people. It was suggested that a new front might be made on the south side of the building, to correspond with that of the college, as the origin of a fine square into which eight other streets would lead; in the centre of which the Wellington Trophy should be raised. The Society-house would be thus not only near the most central, but in the most ornamental part of the metropolis. This large edifice is now abandoned, its collections removed to an inconvenient distance, and crowded into ill adapted rooms, and the Society having expended vast sums to render one house unfit for any other purpose, have purchased another which no money will render suitable.—A splendid edifice well calculated for the mansion-house of the Lord Mayor, but ill adapted indeed for the residence of science and philosophy.

* The Society had their option, either to pay £20,000., or £10,000. and £600. per annum; they preferred the latter.

THE CITY OF DUBLIN.

those between the columns and at each side, by angular and circular pediments, placed alternately; connected with the front, at each side, are two correspondent colonnades of the Doric order. In the rere of the building is an extensive lawn extending to Merrion-square, separated from it only by a dwarf wall, which forms the greater part of the boundary of the western side of the square. This accidental contiguity adds considerably to the beauty of both, as they seem to form but one magnificent area. The building is entered by a very noble hall; round which several statues might be arranged with fine effect: at present, we observe but one, which though solitary, is very striking; a copy of the Belvidere Apollo. This hall leads to the board-room, news-room, secretary's office and house, and keeper's apartments, which entirely occupy the lower part of the building. On the second story are the library and the museum. The library occupies the western wing, extending the whole breadth of the building. It is a fine apartment, enlarged by a semicircular recess, and well calculated for the purpose to which it is appropriated: round the upper part of the room runs a light gallery: to clear the windows it was necessary to raise it almost to the cornice of the room; while it occupies much book space, it does not seem to give suitable convenience; its necessity is doubtful, and its deformity is certain.* The remaining part of this story is occupied by the museum. It is much to be regretted, that in this princely edifice there is not one apartment calculated for this purpose. *The rooms appointed are a suite of six apartments; of which four open into each other on one side of the corridor, and two on the other. These are small and deep, each lighted only by two narrow windows, which by no means afford a quantity of illumination sufficient for the purposes of display or exhibition. Those who have seen the museums of the Jardin des Plantes, in Paris, and that of Montague House, in London, will appreciate this defect. In the former, the works of nature are displayed round large and lofty rooms, where the

* In the library are about ten thousand volumes on the fine arts, architecture, Irish history, natural history, agriculture and botany: on this latter subject every rare and valuable work is to be found, and the botanical collection of books exceeds perhaps any in Europe. Besides these are copious collections of the transactions of other learned societies. The MSS. which may be consulted are contained in seventeen volumes folio, which are in good preservation. They were entirely collected by Walter Harris, and principally in his own hand writing; their authenticity therefore depends on the credit due to himself. The first volume of the second series, however, is a collection of Archbishop King's, and considered original; it is chiefly " de Hospitalibus cænobiis et Monasteriis Hibernicis." The whole were purchased by parliament from Harris's widow for £500. and presented to the Dublin Society.

effect of every thing is heightened by the abundance of light and extent of space in which they are judiciously arranged; in the latter they are crowded into small apartments, where light is excluded and space denied; and a collection which does not yield to any in the world, for extent, variety, and value, loses its effect by the manner in which it is displayed. It would be a subject of deep regret, if our museum should adopt the same defects. It has been said that the rooms which communicate with each other may be salooned into two grand apartments, and the windows splayed off so as to illumine them. If that be practicable, we earnestly hope it may be done; if not, that some other arrangement may be made which will do justice to this important department of the Society. The attic story of the house is spacious, but unfit for any purpose of the institution: dark rooms terminating long galleries,

"Windows that exclude the light,
And passages that lead to nothing." GRAY.

The chemical elaboratory and other necessary edifices are in progress in the rere of the main building. The kitchen is converted into a lecture room capable of accommodating 800 auditors.

THE FARMING SOCIETY OF IRELAND.

FROM the remotest times Ireland has been remarkable for the multitude and goodness of its flocks and herds. A mild and humid climate, with a fertile soil, produced luxuriant pastures, which remained verdant and fruitful the whole year round; but agricultural pursuits, though the natives had scarcely any others, were followed in a very imperfect and slovenly manner. The farmer supposed that he could not possibly thrive, if he did not religiously adhere to the system of his predecessors. It is not more than fifty years since ploughing by the traces fastened to the horse's tail, was practised in many parts of the country.

Whilst, with every natural advantage, this first of all occupations, continued so defective in Ireland, it had attained a high degree of perfection in Great Britain: there, every art and every science was made subservient to promote its improvements; and rural economy became itself a science of the greatest importance. This advantage was chiefly owing to the great encouragement and indefatigable exertions which many of the nobility,

THE CITY OF DUBLIN. 961

gentry, and the superior class of farmers bestowed on the theory and practice of agriculture, principally by means of farming societies formed for that purpose, at the head of which was that illustrious patriot the late Duke of Bedford.

At length the successful progress of the English societies excited in the land proprietors of Ireland a desire to form similar institutions; and in the month of March 1800, several noblemen, gentlemen, and practical farmers formed themselves into a Society to improve the agriculture and live-stock of Ireland. Of this most excellent institution the late Marquis of Sligo was the founder; and as a proof that the public good was his only motive, he proposed that the Right Hon. J. Foster should be president, whilst his lordship accepted, with pride, the subordinate situation of vice-president, which he filled till his death with the greatest zeal and activity.

The Farming Society is composed of a president, vice-president, secretary, register, and a committee, which has been increased at different times from thirteen to twenty-one members.

Candidates for admission are elected by ballot at two general meetings in the year; namely, the last week in March and the first in October. A deposit of ten guineas is required previous to the ballot. Members are chosen for life, and no further subscription is required. The Society has increased so rapidly, that it consists at present of about one thousand members, from among the most respectable and public spirited men in Ireland.

The Farming Society have two grand establishments and depôts; one in Dublin, and one in Ballinsloe. The former is situated on Summer Hill: it consists of an extensive concern, surrounding two large courts. Fronting the street is the house, in which are the board room, agricultural library, and suitable apartments for the clerk and servants, but the Society's officers provide residences for themselves. At the rere of the house is a small garden, for the conservation of the various grasses as specimens. Two sides of the yard are shedded for the reception of fat cattle at the spring show, and at the further end there is a large building, in which annual sales by auction of fine wool take place. Adjoining to this yard is the farming supplement factory, containing a foundery with extensive forges and workshops. Every kind of approved implement of husbandry and vehicle are there manufactured by numerous workmen and artizans, who,

6 G

until a late period, received constant employment. The Trustees, however, found it necessary to diminish the number, in consequence of the unparalleled circumstance of the times; but as the general depression under which the country at present labours, shall be gradually removed, the works will doubtless be carried on, and people employed as extensively as before.

The Society holds its spring show of fat cattle, sheep and swine, at its establishment in Dublin; and the show of breeding stock at its establishment in Ballinsloe, annually in October.

The business of the society has been most ably conducted by its committee, whose plans and exertions have been crowned with distinguished success, to the incalculable benefit of the agricultural interests of Ireland; as a proof of which, it is only necessary to enumerate its various labours.

The primary objects to which the society directs its attention, are the improvement of the agriculture and live-stock of the country, and the encouragement of planting; and subservient thereto, is the encouragement of industry, sobriety, and cleanliness among the lower orders connected with husbandry.

To remedy the very defective state of the implements of husbandry, and of wheel carriages, was one of the first objects of the committee. In 1803, an order was obtained from the commissioners of the revenue to admit farming implements free of duty, which before amounted nearly to a prohibition: upon which the importation of the best articles of this kind in Great Britain was encouraged, and the manufacture of them, as before mentioned, established in Dublin. Great numbers of these implements have been dispersed over the country, experienced persons have been employed to instruct the farmer in the management, and their use will by degrees become general; forasmuch as in every country which is so fortunate as to be the residence of public-spirited gentlemen, an improved system of agriculture has already taken place; but in no respect have the advantages of good machines been more general than in the improvement of land carriages. The miserable rickety little cars, which, until lately, were universal throughout the island, are now replaced by Scotch drays, which convey with greater ease double the load. In the north of Ireland, in particular, this advantageous change has been generally adopted.

The committee has been not less successful in removing impediments which interfered with the importation of live cattle and seed corn. In 1802 an agreement was made with the proprietors of the Liverpool and Parkgate packets, by which the freight of cattle and sheep was regulated, and considerably reduced; at the same period, an exemption from the duty to which seed-corn was then subject, was obtained.

The importation of live stock, and the annual exhibitions, have been attended with extraordinary success in the improvement of the native Irish animal. At these shows of cattle, sheep, and swine the greatest emulation is excited. There is a manifest improvement every year. The finest stock in the world has been introduced into Ireland, and nothing now remains but to disperse them, and keep them up.

The mode by which these improvements in rural economy are upheld and encouraged is by premiums, which are at once beneficial and honorary to those who obtain them. There is an annual ploughing-match near Dublin generally well attended. There are besides other ploughing-matches, promoted by the Society, in counties remote from the metropolis. The premiums for the improvement of live stock have had time to operate, and the annual shows at Dublin and Ballinsloe have tended to discover and make known the principles upon which that improvement ought to be attempted.

The Leicester, Hereford, North Devon, and Durham breeds of cattle are eagerly contending for superiority. The selection of each is conducted with so much skill, that, in no very distant period, Ireland will probably excel the whole world in beef and dairy stock.

By the introduction of the new Leicester rams the native sheep has been rapidly and highly improved in symmetry of form and early maturity. The importation of the Spanish Merino breed has not yet been made in sufficient numbers to effect an improvement in the staple of the wool, but the subject is most earnestly recommended to attention, as it is presumed that the mild climate and sweet herbage of the country would agree perfectly well with that celebrated breed. Meanwhile, to encourage as much as possible the improvement of Irish wool, premiums have been given by the Society for broad cloth manufactured in Ireland from wool entirely of Irish growth. This measure has caused a most spirited competition, and produced some pieces of a very excellent quality.

The improvement of swine* has been more rapid than that of any other animal; this has been effected by the introduction of the Leicester breed, and has become very general.

The old Irish hobby was once in great request; it was supposed to be derived from a Spanish race, in consequence of the intercourse that formerly subsisted between the two nations. The breed is perhaps extinct, if it be not to be found amongst the Connaught horses. All other species of Irish horses, being many of them half blooded, are in good repute, except only the draught cattle, to improve, therefore, this most useful kind, the Society has been no less sedulous than successful. Encouraged by its premiums, stallions and brood mares have been imported from England. The varieties brought over are the Suffolk Panch, and the black Leicester draught, but it remains yet to be decided which is the best adapted to the country.

The proceedings and operations of this Society have produced effects even beyond the objects for which it was founded. The half yearly exhibitions at Dublin and Ballinsloe are the means of bringing together numbers of the most intelligent farmers, from several parts of the United Kingdom, who associate and live together for some time, and who mutually communicate a fund of knowlege, grounded on experience, which could not possibly be derived from any other source. Intimacies have thus been formed between the most useful and best informed men in every county— the practical farmers and resident gentry. The income of the Society consists in parliamentary grants and casual subscriptions and donations. By the care of its committee a petition was presented to Parliament in the year 1801, which obtained a grant of £2000. per annum. In 1806 this sum was increased to £3000., and in 1807, to £5000, which has been continued ever since. The Dublin Society made a donation of £200., and each member on admisson subscribes ten guineas, as already noticed.

The Society possesses a well chosen, though not an extensive library. Regular minutes of its proceedings are kept. It has no branches, but

---

* The native Irish hog is an unsightly, bony, long-legged animal, notwithstanding which it fattens to an enormous weight, and makes the best pork in the world, being the only salted meat that remains equally good in all climates. The author of one of Cook's Voyages relates, that the Irish mess pork was found perfectly sweet and good at the end of a five years' voyage round the world. The old native cow of the country; though not so handsome, gives double the quantity of milk of the improved breed.

maintains an extensive correspondence, nor has it, as yet, published Transactions. The Society, as a body, does not set on foot any practical experiments relative to the objects of its institution, but it encourages everywhere the adoption of approved practices and experiments.

The salaries and wages of its officers and servants are as follow:

A Secretary - - - - £300. per annum.
Register - - - - - 150
Agriculture reporter - - - - 300
The same for travelling expenses - - 200
Clerk - - - - - 100
Overseer of buildings - - - - 20
Woolstapler - - - - - 20

When it is considered that the exports of Ireland, on which its prosperity depends, consist but of two branches, both derived from agriculture—linen and provisions; a just estimation may be made of the importance and beneficial pursuits of the Farming Society of Ireland.

THE LINEN MANUFACTURE AND HALL.

It is evident that linen made part of the dress of the ancient Irish, from the earliest account of their costume, as described in the Islandic Chronicle of A. D. 1129; and so great was their predilection for this fabric, that sumptuary laws were enacted by Henry VIII. to restrain its use. By these laws a shirt or smock was ordered to contain no more than seven yards of linen cloth. Prior thereto the shirt ordinarily contained thirty yards. It was dyed yellow, but not with saffron, as Moryson, Spencer, and Camden relate, for to obtain a sufficient quantity of the chives or filaments of the crocus would require plantations of that vegetable as extensive as those of the flax itself. The yellow dye for this purpose was really obtained from the *Buidhmor*, or great yellow wild woad, a plant that grew abundantly in all the moist soils of the country, and is used for dyeing yellow at this day.

Before linen became the staple commodity of Ireland, it was a domestic manufacture universally made for home consumption. The cloth was wove into narrow pieces, seven yards in length and eighteen inches in width, being sufficient to make a shirt for a labouring man; these pieces were called Bandel Linen, or Bandel Cloth, and they are still manufactured and sold at markets and fairs, chiefly in the south of Ireland.

It was the great, but unfortunate Earl of Strafford that must be considered as the real founder of the linen manufacture, which was commenced in his lieutenancy in 1642. He found the soil well adapted for the growth of flax, and the Irish women already expert spinners; and so confident was he of its ultimate success, that he embarked no less than £30,000 of his private fortune, a prodigious sum at that time, in the undertaking. After a few years it justified the sagacity of Lord Strafford; by becoming the staple manufacture of the country.

In the memorable year 1699, the liberty of exporting woollens from Ireland was taken away; but the Irish Parliament seemed so sensible of the injustice of the measure, and of the great loss sustained by the nation, that in lieu thereof, the people were invited, by every encouragement, to apply their industry to improve the linen manufacture, and to this end several laws were made to promote it. One law was of particular importance, and formed a remarkable era in its proceedings. In the 8th of Queen Anne's reign, an act was passed appointing a certain and equal number of persons in each province of Ireland, to be trustees for the disposal and management of the duties granted by the act. The Duke of Ormond, then Lord Lieutenant, appointed by name the several trustees, and having summoned them to meet him at the Castle of Dublin, on Wednesday the 7th of October, 1711, he read their deed of appointment, and having invested them with their powers, they elected a secretary, with whom was deposited their deed of trust, and other officers, and from that time they have held regular meetings in Dublin, and kept journals of their proceedings, giving to the linen and hempen manufacture a consistency and regularity which were not known before. Their first accommodation for so important a concern, was very inconvenient; they rented a room on Cork-hill, for £14 per annum; and Lord Galway, one of the Lord Justices, empowered them to use his name with the Lord Mayor, that their hemp and flax seed, lying in the custom house, might be deposited in the House of Industry. In 1716 they were accommodated with an apartment in the Castle, for dispatching their business, but in 1719, finding that the books, papers, and utensils belonging to the manufacture had very much encreased, and that the space was too scanty; the Trustees memorialed that larger rooms might be allotted them.

' In the following year, the Secretary was directed to enquire into the nature and constitution of 'Blackwell' Hall at 'Hamburgh, and a committee was appointed to consider how an office set up on such models might promote the trade and interests of the concern; and immediately after, the Trustees gave public notice to receive proposals for erecting a Linen Weaver's Hall in or near the City of Dublin, in the most convenient site. Among many situations proffered, one near Drumcondra first engaged the attention of the Board, as very convenient to the Ulster merchants; but another at the end of Capel-street was chosen, as affording accommodation to those from Leinster and Connaught, as well as from the North, being near the Inns in Church-street and Pill-lane, to which the carriers resort, and affording a considerable front to three intended new streets. This second plot of ground was therefore purchased of Mr. Everard, the proprietor, for £360., and the building was proceeded on, the sum of £3000. having been granted by Parliament for that purpose. In the year 1728, it was completed, and on Thursday the 14th November in the same year, it was opened by public advertisement. The original front of the Hall formed one side of Lisburn street, the façade, distinguished by a cupola over the gate of entrance, fronted Linen-Hall-street, which street was subsequently made the avenue of approach to it. The Hall consisted but of one quadrangle, the sides of which were formed by the chambers for the reception of linen goods; to this original square, subsequent additions have been made at different periods, as the necessities of the increasing trade required. It now consists of six large courts, surrounded by stores, which communicate below by piazzas and above by galleries. A Yarn Hall has been also added, and the whole is so extensive, as to occupy the space between Broad Stone and Bolton-street*. It is approached and entered by three avenues from three different streets. Among its other conveniences it contains a large and elegant coffee-room for the accommodation of factors and traders, who daily crowd its courts; and a Board Room, where the

* Besides the Linen and Yarn Hall, a warehouse was erected in Poolbeg-street for the reception of hemp and flax-seed imported, and all utensils provided by the Board. This has been long discontinued. It was assigned by the Board to the Dublin Society, and was the origin of their establishment in Hawkins-street.

Trustees meet as often as they deem convenient. Though at this Board the Trustees regulate the concerns of the linen trade in every part of Ireland, the Hall is only a local establishment, similar to that at Belfast, and has no jurisdiction or control beyond Dublin.

The regulations of the Hall appointed a chamberlain to keep the keys of the lockers and chambers, when the goods are deposited, to open and shut as occasion might require, and to keep a regular account of those to whom he assigns chambers, and to take care that no chambers shall be kept unoccupied by goods, or locked up during the hours of sale. Every person who brings goods to the Hall, must have them made up in packs, farldes, or boxes, and deposit them in some chamber, for which he pays no charge or storage duty. He may be allowed to sell his own linen, or employ a factor appointed by the Trustees for that purpose. These factors give security to the amount £1000., for the faithful discharge of the trust reposed in them, and are allowed to receive no fee or perquisite for selling flaxen or hempen goods over and above the sum of three-pence in the pound. No sale is allowed but with open doors, no retail is permitted, and the gates leading to the Hall are closed during the time of sale, except the one leading from Anne-street. The hours of sale are from eight in the morning to one in the afternoon every day, from April to October; and from nine to one from October to April, Sundays and holidays excepted. When the sale commences or terminates, it is notified by the ringing of a bell. No holiday, except Sundays, are admitted for one month before the cloth-fair of Chester and Bristol. The other officers of the Hall are a clerk, a gate-keeper, who wears a gown and staff during his attendance, porters, distinguished by a badge, and watchmen provided with fire-arms, who commence their watch every night at 8 o'clock*.

* Some of the original regulations have fallen into disuse, and some have been altered. The factors at present are merely approved of by the Board, and no security is required. The commission on the sale is regulated by the quality of the goods and the period of credit; $2\frac{1}{2}$ per cent. on all goods whose price does not exceed 2 shillings per yard, and 2 months credit, but $3\frac{1}{4}$ per cent. on all goods above 2 shillings, and whose credit runs to 4 months. The gates are all open during the sale. The hours are from 9 o'clock till half after 4 during the whole year. The bell is rung only when the gates are closed, to warn those to retire, who might be otherwise locked in, as no person has any access to the Hall after that time except the chamberlain, from whose house there is a passage. No light or fire of any kind is permitted; no holidays are recognised, except the King's birth-day, Christmas day, and the national fasts.

THE CITY OF DUBLIN.

Very early attention was paid by the Trustees to the establishment of the cambric manufactures in Ireland, and before the building of the Linen Hall, an order was dispatched to Holland to search out a person capable of teaching the art, to be sent to this country; in the year 1730, a cambric press was shipped at Amsterdam and erected in the Hall, which was recently finished. A bleach-green also on the model of that at Haarlem was established at Drumcondra, but on trial, it did not answer expectation, and was discontinued. The encouragement of printed linen became an object of the care of Trustees so early as the year 1719. The weavers and others concerned in the silk and woollen manufactures in England, complained to Parliament, that the stains and stamps of linen were injurious to their trade, and they hoped and expected that they would be prohibited. The Irish linens at this time, were almost entirely consumed in England, where they were sent in a raw state, and there stained and printed; a prohibition of their use would therefore deprive one half the manufactures of employment. The Trustees petitioned the legislature forthwith, and prayed that the Irish printed linens might at least be allowed to be exported to the plantations; at the same time an English printer was invited over to assist in establishing the printing of linens in Ireland. In consequence, in the year 1727, Ball's Bridge near Dublin was fixed on as a proper site to establish the manufacture. The Trustees took a lease of the ground, which they granted to Mr. Chappel for the purpose of erecting buildings and the necessary machinery. This was for some years supported and encouraged by the Board; it has however since failed, the business of printed linen has become extinct in Ireland, and the prints and process transferred to the fabrics of cotton, to which the factory at Ball's Bridge is now appropriated.

In 1785 an inspector was appointed to examine the linens for exportation, and, ascertain if they are of a quality entitled to the bounty; a suit of apartments in the Hall is assigned for this purpose.

A Cotton Hall has also been opened, in which the cotton factors are accommodated with chambers for the deposit of their goods.

There is no linen manufacture carried on in Dublin, or bleach-green in the vicinity.

By an order of the House of Commons, 9th July 1807, an Account of the establishment of the Trustees of the linen and hempen manufacture in Ireland was called for, when the following return was made.

THE HISTORY OF

Number of Persons.	Departments.	Salaries, Allowances, and Fees.			Net Receipts after Deductions.		
72	Trustees,	£0	0	0	£0	0	0
7	Linen Office,	850	0	0	767	14	4
4	Linen Hall,	456	0	6	456	16	6
4	Yarn Hall,	171	8	4	161	8	4
1	Inspector General,	700	0	0	500	0	0
3	Provincial Inspectors,	1100	0	0	700	0	0
35	County Inspectors of Linen and Yarn,	2114	0	8	1595	19	7
5	Port Inspectors of Linen,	256	13	0	246	13	6
16	Flax Inspectors,	1655	10	10	1602	14	0
8	Other Offices,	710	9	9	658	7	4
3	Contractors,	386	3	5	237	18	5
158 Persons,		£8401	3	0	£6927	12	9

PARLIAMENTARY GRANTS.

1713. When the Trustees were appointed, £ 2153 7 4
1728. When the Linen Hall was opened, 3989 4 10
1816. The present year, 21,600 0 0.

In the year 1816, the following appropriation was made of the rooms in the Hall.

- Linen, including 4 vacant, 441
- Yarn, - - - 56.
- Cotton, - - 30
- Damask and Diaper, - 4
- Establishment, - 4
- Blank or dark rooms, 22

Total number of rooms, 557

These are occupied by 36 factors, and 130 country drapers.

LINENS
entered at the Linen Hall for five years, from January 1812 to 1816.

Years.	Inwards.		General Value.			Outwards.				Excess.
						Exports.		Home Consumption.		
		Total					Total.		Total.	
1812.	Packs 3360 / Boxes 3731	7091	£1,040,503	0	0	Packs 6000 / Boxes 5553	11,553	Packs .... / Boxes	....	4462
1813.	Packs 3979 / Boxes 3811	7784	1,085,610	0	0	Packs 3800 / Boxes 3402	7202	Packs .... / Boxes	....	583
1814.	Packs 3408 / Boxes 3394	6802	954,915	0	0	Packs 3694 / Boxes 3219	6913	Packs 405 / Boxes 1209	1614	1724
1815.	Packs 3302 / Boxes 3891	7193	1,026,335	0	0	Packs 3320 / Boxes 3893	7213	Packs .... / Boxes	....	20
1816.	Packs 3606 / Boxes 4812	8418	1,157,625	0	0	Packs 2930 / Boxes 4542	7472	Packs 319 / Boxes 620	939	7

COTTON MANUFACTURE.*

In the year 1718, a petition was presented from Arthur and George Sherston to the Trustees of the Linen Board, praying for some encouragement for carrying on a cotton manufacture in Dublin. They were desired to

* It is a singular fact that the commencement of this important branch of manufacture in the North of Ireland, was in a poor-house. In the year 1777 the manufactures of Ireland were in the lowest state of depression; to give some stimulus to desponding artizans by opening a new source of manufacture, Mr. Joy conceived the idea of introducing the cotton machinery from Scotland. In conjuction with Mr. M'Cabe, he employed the children of the Belfast poor-house in spinning cotton yarn as a preparatory step; but the common wheel with which they commenced rendered their progress so slow and unprofitable, that it was necessary to construct a spinning machine similar to those used in Scotland. This was done in Belfast at his expence, and a spinner brought over to instruct the children. Having thus originated the measure, he now proposed to transfer all his machinery to the poor-house at prime cost, but the governors, unwilling to embark in a new undertaking, declined the offer. A firm therefore was formed of Joy, M'Cabe, and M'Craken to complete the project; they contracted with the governors of the poor-house for the employment of their children, and the use of their vacant rooms; they dispatched to England a skilful mechanic, who, like Sir H. Lombe, contrived at considerable personal hazard and expense to make himself master of the most improved machinery which was mysteriously concealed, and on his return they erected a carding machine, and a spinning jenny of 72 spindles on the improved plan, then deemed an extraordinary piece of machinery. So far from wishing to conceal their improvements or deriving profit from their exclusive knowledge, they exposed their machinery to public view, and invited numbers, without any charge, to be taught the use of it, and disseminate the practice in other places. From these liberal and enlightened men, the project was soon adopted by others; a mill for spinning twist by water was first erected in Ireland in 1784, and since that period the manufacture may be said to be permanently established. So rapid was its improvement that in the year 1800, in a circuit of 10 miles, comprehending Belfast and Lisburn, it gave employments in various ways to 27,000 individuals.

In several parts of Ulster, the linen looms are exchanging for those of cotton; several causes conspire to induce a preference to cotton. The material can be sooner bleached, the capital employed is sooner returned to the employer, and the wages are much higher to the workmen. It has therefore spread considerably round Belfast and the vicinity.

In other parts of Ireland the progress was equally rapid. Sir John Parnel built a large factory near Maryborough in the Queen's County with machinery worked by water; Lord De Vesci erected extensive buildings at Abbey-Leix, and placed a colony of weavers in Tullamore and Philipstown. It was established on the Boyne near Sack Allen, and at Stratford in the county of Wicklow, where they are so respectable as to have a library attached to their factory; and the muslin manufactory was set up by the Quakers at Mount Mellick. In effect, notwithstanding the pressure of a foreign war, and the interruptions of domestic disturbances; notwithstanding the discouragements it received by reducing the bounty on manufactured goods from 5 to $2\frac{1}{2}$ per cent. and the limited issue of machinery, it con-send in their proposal at the next Board, but it does not appear that they ever did so, or that the manufacture was then established. About the year 1760 two men, Sherrard and Edkin, were engaged in it to some extent. They employed 600 looms in the fabrication of jeans and common cottons, which were the only kind of goods then made; the machinery was rude tinued, by its own energies, rapidly to encrease; so that it appears by the returns of the inspectors of yarn, made to the Linen Board in 1802, that 10,000 looms were employed in the province of Ulster. In the counties of Dublin and Kildare 3500, Wicklow and Carlow 1500, Meath, West-Meath, King and Queen's Counties 2400, to which it was supposed might be added in Cork, Waterford, and Limerick 3000, making in the whole 20,500 looms engaged solely in the manufacture of cotton, producing 200,000 yards of cloth every week, and employing and supporting 600,000 individuals.

Since that period the business in Ireland has rapidly declined. The want of a resident legislature to protect it at home, and the state of other countries hastened its fall. The vigilance of the enemy to exclude our manufactures from the continent of Europe, and the embargo laid on the ports of America, inundated our markets with English cotton goods, which could nowhere find a mart, and against which a small duty of 10 per cent. on heavy goods, and 2d. per lb. on spun cotton, afforded a feeble protection. Some of the most respectable manufacturers withdrew their capital from the business, and others failed altogether; Lord De Vesci's company declined; Sir John Parnel's mills closed; and the factories at Cork ran to decay. Nor is there a hope that in this country it can ever revive. On the restoration of peace it was expected that some arrangements might be made with the French government. While this was under consideration, men of approved knowledge and integrity were deputed by some leading manufacturing towns in England, to proceed to France, and examine the grounds of its propriety. It appeared from their report, that such was the state of the cotton manufacture in France, from the low price of provisions and other local causes, that they could undersel us in the London market from 25 to 50 per cent. On the petitions of Nottingham, therefore, and other towns, the project of commercial regulations was abandoned. The secret progress of this manufacture in France is very striking. It appears by the Exposé, published immediately after the treaty of Paris, that the cotton manufacture in 1781 was very low; an Englishman of the name of Hawkins had worked 20 looms at Lyons on narrow goods, and a Lancashire weaver of the name of Miles had set up two small carding engines at Passy; there were besides 4 spinning machines of 56 spindles each; and this was all the machinery in France. In pursuance of the plan of hostility to the arts in these countries, their embryo of manufacture was silently but carefully cherished by the Revolutionary Government. In the suspension of intercourse we could not note its progress, and in the trouble and tumults of the war, we disregarded it. The infant, it appears, is now become a giant. It employs, says the Exposé, 449,000 persons in the Provinces of Normandy and Bretagne, and 690,000 souls in all France are supported by it. We cannot enter into competition with it abroad, and if we suffer it to enter into competition with us at home, it will completely undersel us in our own markets. In America the cotton manufactory has made but small progress, but the greater part of the cotton consumed in those countries is the produce of their soil, and it is not probable that an enterprising commercial people will long suffer the raw material to be exported, and returned enhanced in value in a manufactured form for their own consumption.

and imperfect, and the spinning performed on a common worsted wheel, which spun one thread only at a time. The cotton yarn used in the cheques and stripes was of an inferior quality obtained from Manchester, or Turkey spun cotton imported by the way of England About the year 1779 corduroys were first introduced, and on the following year commenced the æra of enterprise in Dublin, which distinguished the cotton manufacture in a remarkable manner.

Mr. Robert Brook had returned to Ireland and brought with him a large fortune acquired in the East. When the freedom of commerce was declared, he was among the first that availed himself of its advantages, and determined to employ his great wealth, and setting a spirited and patriotic example to his native country. With this view he embarked largely in the cotton business, and suddenly raised an obscure and scanty trade into a great national manufacture. He commenced by drawing to Dublin English artists, and importing the most improved machinery. These he established and set to work in the Liberties, and to complete the process, he erected a dry-house and finishing factory in Cork-street. But his great and important work was established out of Dublin. In order to remove the manufactures from the confinement, insalubrity, and expensive living of the metropolis, he commenced building a new-town at 19 miles distant from it in the County of Kildare, and in the short period of three years it was completely finished for all the different branches of the manufacture, including the printing cotton and linen goods on a very extensive scale; and that nothing might be wanting to give it permanency, he established there, with Mr. Kirchoffer, the business of making machinery on the most perfect and improved models. In these spirited pursuits he expended the sum of £18,000., and from the fair and flattering prospects with which he commenced, he called his rising colony by the appropriate name of *Prosperous*. This spirited example was followed by several gentlemen and manufacturers in Dublin and in its neighbourhood. Mr. Jackson established it in Cork-street, Mr. Talbot at Malahide, and Baron Hamilton at Balbriggan, who all imported machinery, nd erected extensive edifices for the purpose; while the great improvements of the fly-shuttle introduced from Chorlay at this time into Dublin, quickened in a wonderful degree the prolix operations of the weaver, and added a new impulse to his exertions. Meantime the public Societies were no less anxious to cherish and bring to maturity those young establishments. The Trustees of the Linen Board and the Dublin Society granted machinery to manufacturers, and bounties on goods, and the Legislature with correspondent liberality freely enabled them. But the Parliament of Ireland did more. Mr. Brooke, in cutting aqueducts and in making other extensive and expensive improvements in his works, had expended sums considerably exceeding his own private fortune; and Messrs. Talbot and Hamilton had found their properties insufficient for their spirited projects. £25,000. were therefore granted to the former, and £5000. to each of the latter; and other individuals who had embarked in and were extending the manufacture in Dublin, shared also their bounty. With these aids machinery was erected on the Liffey near Celbridge, and at Balbriggan, for spinning cotton by water; and farther sums were raised by these spirited adventurers to complete the improvements. But in a novel work undertaken by people of different pursuits, and established in a country where such things had never been before, it is not to be wondered at that men of liberal views and ardent minds should speculate beyond their means of accomplishment. In 1786, Mr. Brooke was compelled again to apply to Parliament for aid, but unfortunately he was not again successful. He was no longer able to answer the immediate demands of his widely extended establishment, and his creditors were pressing. He became insolvent, and, without notice or the slightest expectation of the event, the whole machine of industry suddenly stopped, and in the course of 24 hours 1400 looms, with all their apparatus and dependences, were struck idle, the artizans dismissed from their unfinished work, and the colonies, which a few hours before displayed such a picture of regular and thriving industry, exhibited a scene of confusion, and distress, and dismay, unparalleled perhaps in any other country. Mr. Brooke never again attempted to revive the manufacture. Mr. Talbot and Mr. Hamilton were equally unsuccessful; and thus a few short years had seen the rise and fall of a very extraordinary commercial enterprise of three private gentlemen*.

* The situation of Prosperous seems not to have been judiciously chosen. It is a low marshy country surrounded by turf bogs, which supply abundant fuel but give no command of water. The manufactures continued there under the directions of different individuals on a small scale till the year 1798, when it became an object of attack to the rebels; since that time it has run to decay, though a few scattered weavers still linger among its ruins. The village erected at Malahide, on the contrary, was beautiful and healthy. It also laboured under a want of water, but the enterprising proprietor supplied the

But their example was of signal service to the metropolis; those who had engaged in it with more experience and circumspection succeeded better, and availed themselves of their imported improvements. Mr. Jackson established himself in Cork-street, Mr. Grey in Francis-street, and Mr. Greenham at Roper's Rest, where he extended very much his business by erecting spinning machinery to work by water. He built a new factory at Harold's Cross, and filled it with machinery; he purchased the cotton-mills at Celbridge, and continued so to expand his concerns that in some years it is supposed he manufactured every week 27 tons of cotton in his different factories, and the number of cotton weavers in Dublin amounted to 1600 men, principally undertakers for the people called manufacturers.

The number of manufactures crowded together in the Liberties of Dublin had often been the subject of serious objection, not only on their own account but that of the community; among the objections of the latter kind was the spirit of combination and riot, readily excited among a number of people connected by regulations peculiar to themselves, constantly associating in great numbers, and roused to sudden irritation by every temporary fluctuation of their employment. To separate such a mass of irritable materials into different habitations in remote parts of the country, and induce every man to live in a cabin of his own, like those of the North, seemed to be the most likely means to benefit themselves and remedy the evil. With this view Parliament granted the sum of £96,000. to establish manufactures in different parts of the country. In this way many of the best artists and at the same time of the principal leaders and promoters of discontent, were drawn at different times from Dublin and established in the country. There are at present (1816), not more than 300 looms in the cotton manufacture in the metropolis, and of these 100 only are in the employ of masters; the rest have lately established a new system of commerce and excluded the agency of the manufacturers altogether. Since the formation of the Meath loan, a number of poor weavers have set up

---

deficiency. It stands on the sea coast at the bottom of a bay; the water of the tide was received into a canal, from whence it was raised by forcing engines to a height sufficient to command the work and set the machinery in motion. As the houses were well built and regularly laid out into streets and courts, they are still kept in repair, and generally occupied in summer by families from Dublin, and it forms one of the neatest and most rural bathing villages in the vicinity. The factory at Balbriggan was afterwards converted into flour and corn stores.

for themselves. Enabled by its aid to command a small sum of money, they laid in a stock of materials on their own account, and having wrought them into fabrics, dispose of them without the intervention of the manufacturers; by these means the profit of an intermediate person is saved, and they are enabled to sell the goods at a cheaper rate to the purchaser, and at the same time at an advanced price to themselves. It is said that they have established a depot for their goods, and a regular market in the Liberties for the sale of them, to which country shopkeepers repair, and above 200 working manufacturers are concerned in it.

The factories at present in existence in Dublin and the vicinity, are as follow:

Spinning.	- Roper's Rest, Green Mount,	Greenham.
Do.	- Palmerstown,	O'Briens.
Do.	- Mardyke,	Clark's.
Do.	- White Church, Rathfarnham,	Jackson.
Do.	- Tolka Bridge,	Dickinson.
Do.	- Celbridge,	Greenham.
Printing.	- Ball's Bridge,	Duffy.
Do.	- Love-Lane,	Anderson.
Do.	- Island Bridge,	Burton.
Do.	- Lucan,	Ryan.
Do.	- Palmerston,	Clark.
Do.	- Clondalkin,	} not now at work.
Do.	- Beggar's Bush,	

SILK MANUFACTURE.

This is peculiarly confined to the metropolis, and never extended to any other part of Ireland. It is generally supposed to have been introduced by the French refugees, and established in the Liberties of Dublin shortly after their residence in this city. In the year 1764 an Act passed to place it under the direction of the Dublin Society as far as it extended within $2\frac{1}{4}$ miles round the Castle, and they were empowered to make such laws and regulations for its management as they should deem necessary. To encourage the manufactory, the Society immediately established an Irish silk warehouse in Parliament-street, and the management of it was placed under the superintendance of 12 Noblemen, who were appointed directors, and a Commitee of 12 persons, annually returned by the Corporation of weavers, to examine the quality of the goods sent in by the manufacturers, to whom the Dublin Society paid a premium or discount of 5 per cent. on all sales made in the house. While the trade was thus managed the sales were on an average £70,000. per annum, and the silk manufacture in Dublin arrived at the highest state of prosperity. But this source of encouragement was, for some motive not well explained, done away by an Act of Parliament passed in the the 26th year of his present Majesty, by which the Dublin Society was prohibited from disposing of any part of its funds for the support of any house in which Irish silk goods were sold by wholesale or retail.* From that time the Irish silk warehouse declined, and was soon totally ruined; and hundreds of people supported by it were thrown out of employment.

According to a return made in 1809, there were 3760 persons employed in manufactures of unmixed silk. Lord Sheffield computed the number of silk weavers in Dublin at 1500. Of the sorts manufactured, the silk handkerchiefs were deemed superior, and other articles equal to those of England. The general distress, and failure of markets which have arrived at the lowest depression this year (1816), have completed the ruin of the silk manufacture in Dublin, and thrown out of employment and left destitute almost all those who were maintained and subsisted by it. The fate indeed of the silk manufacturers in London has been no less disastrous, as it appears that not fewer than 48,000 persons in Spitalfields were returned as wanting charitable aid.

The tabinet and poplin fabrics, for which Dublin has been long famous, have not however experienced so heavy a declension. The exportations to Great Britain in 1815 amounted to 64,000 yards, whilst 80,000 yards were exported to the United States of America. The latter indeed became a losing concern, as the exporters were undersold at the market by the light silks from France and Italy, so that no price could be got for them but at a great loss†.

* See 25th Geo. III. Chap. 62, and 26th, Chap. 48. It is said in the Act that it did not answer the ends proposed!

† It seems impossible that any more exports can be attempted unless a bounty or draw-back be

The capital employed in the silk trade amounts to about £250,000.

The silks imported are not brought direct from Italy, but purchased in London of the agents of the Italian houses, and the raw silks are bought at the sales at the East India House. The silk trade of Ireland is protected, as yet, by paying a less duty on organized silk than the London merchant; but as that was one of the commercial regulations made at the Union, it will cease in 1821, when the duties will be equalized; and as, notwithstanding this protection, there is about as much English silk goods at present imported, as are manufactured at home, the Irish manufacturer will then no longer be able to stand a competition, and the trade, in all probability, will be totally annihilated.

But it should seem extraordinary that while the Irish manufacturer is thus protected, he should not be able to supply at least his own market; for this two causes are assigned,—the want of a resident nobility and gentry to encourage the manufactures at home, and a perverted preference for that which is foreign. It appears by the items in the civil list laid before Parliament in the year 1815, there was a sum of £143,000. to silk mercers for silks made for Carlton House, while the Irish silk trade for the same time did not receive £20.; and it further appears from a report of the manufacturers at the Weavers' Hall in December 1816, that the quantity of silk goods imported and consumed would employ 1600 looms, while 500 were idle in the Liberties. The equal quality and equal price of our silk goods have not been disputed. " We ask not for charity for " our starving manufacturers," says the Report, " but to give them employ-" ment by using the work of their hands."

allowed, fully equivalent to the duty paid on the quantity of silk contained in them. At present the import duty on the silk contained in a piece of tabinet is L2. 18s. 6d. British, and the draw-back when it is exported is only 9s. 7d. equal to 3 farthings per yard. Now the manufacturing exporter of this beautiful fabric from this country never can meet the French, Italian, Dutch or Chinese in a foreign market, unless the bounty he receives on exportation be made equal to the import duty he is obliged to pay, that is, 5s. per lb., or 6d. per yard, which would be exactly equal to L.2. 18s. 6d. paid on the import of the raw material. The want of machinery seems also an impediment to the completion of the silk manufacture in this country. Silk throwsting in Dublin is confined to the preparation of shutes or wefts. They cannot organize the superfine silks imported from Italy and used in the warps.

THE CITY OF DUBLIN.

An Account of the Manufactured Silks imported into Ireland for three years, ending 1798, and for three years, ending 1815, with their value, and the duties paid.

		Stockings		Lace	
Years.	Quantity.	Value.	Duty.	Quantity.	Value.	Duty.
	Pairs.	£ s. d.	£ s. d.	lbs.	£ s. d.	£ s. d.
1796	134	67 0 0	28 9 6	230	2,300 0 0	181 2 6
1797	367	183 10 0	77 19 9	233	2,231 5 0	175 14 2
1798	49	24 10 0	12 3 0	213	2,126 0 0	183 18 3
Totals.	550	275 0 0	118 12 3	676	6,657 5 0	540 14 11
1813	13,777	7,564 2 6	821 12 6	1362	14,244 19 2	1,528 2 4
1814	12,230	6,115 0 0	959 12 2	957	9,570 0 0	1,089 1 9
1815	12,108	5,907 0 0	1,137 11 5	977	10,417 16 8	1,127 16 5
Totals.	38,115	19,586 2 6	2,918 16 1	3296	34,232 15 10	3,745 0 6

		Ribbands.		Other Manufactures.	
Years.	Quantity	Value.	Duty.	Quantity.	Value.	Duty.
		£ s. d.	£ s. d.	lbs.	£ s. d.	£ s. d.
1796	1739	5,653 3 5	913 4 9	5641	16,843 10 0	2,952 8 6
1797	1088	3,536 0 0	571 4 0	6621	19,864 10 0	5,476 5 5
1798	755	2,356 5 0	425 8 8	4453	13,358 8 9	1,400 3 9
Totals.	3572	11,545 8 5	1,909 17 5	16715	50,068 8 9	7,828 17 8
1813	3356	17,329 9 2	2,159 6 0	9532	53,898 14 2	6,596 13 4
1814	6190	35,283 0 0	3,684 6 2	13542	81,252 0 0	9,497 6 9
1815	5269	24,603 13 4	3,268 1 10	12510	73,651 0 0	9,478 5 9
Totals.	14815	77,216 2 6	9,111 14 0	35584	208,801 14 2	25,572 5 9

An Account of the Quantities of Orgazine, Thrown, and Raw-silks imported into Ireland for three years, ending 1798, and for three years, ending 1815.

Years.	1796	1797	1798	1813	1814	1815
	lbs.	lbs.	lbs.	lbs.	lbs.	lbs.
Orgazine.	50,870	40,284	49,208	78,280	69,833	61,035
Thrown-dyed.	9,587	787	743	4,841	7,766	7,678
———undyed.	1,613	539	38			172
Raw India.	30,200	29,988	17,918	15,837	11,415	9,855
Net India.	15,538	3,740	4,702	10,110	6,195	7,811
Totals - -	107,808	75,338	72,609	109,068	95,381	86,379

WOOLLEN MANUFACTURE.

So early as the Reign of Henry III., about 50 years after the landing of the English, the woollen manufactures of Ireland were imported into England and used as an article of dress.* In the time of Edward III. in 1327, Irish frizes were freely imported into England, and what is still more extraordinary, were allowed to be imported duty free. But the most remarkable fact attesting the early celebrity of our woollen manufacture was, that the serges of Ireland were exported to Italy in the year 1357,[†] at a time when the woollens of that country had attained an high degree of perfection at home, and dress was carried to so extravagant an excess that sumptuary laws were necessary to restrain it.[‡] In the year 1482 not only serges but other kinds of woollens, and the very fashion of the country were held in such estimation on the continent, that the Pope's agent obtained from Richard II. a license to export, duty free, mantels made of Irish cloth. From the slow progress of manufactures in any country, and the small comparative intercourse of those early times, it is inferred that it must have been long established and highly wrought, to make it at that period an object known and sought after by distant countries. In 1542§ woollen yarn is enumerated among the most considerable branches of trade pos-

* Maddox's History of the Exchequer, vol. 1. p. 550.
† Anderson's Commerce, vol. 1. p. 204.
‡ The passage from which this circumstance is inferred, is found in an Italian author, Fazio delli Uberti, the date of whose work is ascertained to have been in 1357. The passage is as follows:
    Similamente passamo en Irlanda,
    La qual fra noi è degna di fama,
    Par le nobile saie che ci manda.
        Cap. 24, lib. 4.

See an Essay on the Antiquity of the Woollen Manufactory in Ireland, published in the first volume of the Transactions of the Royal Irish Academy, by their President, the accomplished Lord Charlemont. It is remarked by him that the superiority of the fabric and the extent of the manufacture, must have been invariably acknowledged and extensively known to have entitled the country to the character of *degna di fama*, and the manufacture to the epithet of *nobile*. Without recurring to the æra of Milesius, it is not improbable that the early intercourse with the Spaniards, whose descendants are still so distinct a race in the county of Galway, might have introduced Spanish wool very early into this country, and given that excellence to the fabric which it is a favourite project to establish at the present day by the same means.
§ 33 Henry VIII.

THE CITY OF DUBLIN. 981

sessed by the natives of Ireland; and in an act of Elizabeth* it is recited that the merchants of Ireland had been exporters of woollen yarn for 100 years before; from hence it is asserted that the article was a native commodity, produced in such abundance as to supply the spinner and manufacturer at home, and leave a considerable quantity for export at a very early period. Whatever be the credit due to these facts and inferences, it is certain that the woollen manufactory attained in this country some time after an high degree of prosperity,† and excited the jealousy and apprehension of the rival trade in England. In the year 1673, sir W. Temple, at the request of Lord Essex, then Viceroy of Ireland, published in Dublin a formal overture for relinquishing the woollen trade, except in the lower branches, that it might not interfere with that of England, and urges the superior fitness of this country for the linen trade.‡

Immediately after the cessation of the disturbances in Ireland, in 1688, the woollen manufacture was established to a considerable extent in the Liberties of Dublin. The security of property ensured after the capitulation of Limerick, induced a number of English manufacturers to avail themselves of its local advantages, the cheapness of labour, the excellence of wool, and the abundance of the necessaries of life: and to emigrate with their properties and families, to settle here.§ The Combe, Pimlico, Spitalfields, and the Weaver's square were then built, and it soon became the residence of all that was opulent and respectable in the city ||

* 13 Elizab.

† By an act 13th Elizabeth, severe penalties were laid on the exportation of linen, flax, and linen yarns, and the Irish making only linens 14 inches wide, and not in demand out of Ireland, they turned all their industry to the woollen, which soon attained such perfection and celebrity, as to alarm rivals in the same trade.

‡ Collect. Polit. p. 87. Reports to Parliament.

§ See petition to William III. presented by the Lords of England.

|| The greater number of the leases were granted at that time by the Meath family, and the lessees are generally denominated aldermen and esquires. Yet the Liberties had been in existence before, and the woollen manufacture probably established there. In the reign of Charles I. Lord Meath's sheep of the English breed were in high estimation, and at an auction brought a price that would be extravagant at the present day. A gentleman in the vicinity of Dublin, mortgaged his estate to purchase some of them. In the reign of Charles II. a patent was granted to hold a market there. It was held in the large street now called New-market, which was so denominated from that circumstance. A patent was granted by Lord Meath, in the same reign, to act plays in the theatre built in Ransford street. The residence of the Meath family was in Thomas-street, and the mansion house was so fine that sir William Petty

But this prosperity was scarcely established when it was subverted. A petition was presented to William III., by the lords of England, stating that the further growth of the manufacture would greatly prejudice that of England; they therefore prayed that his majesty would declare in the most effectual manner, that the growth and encrease of the woollen manufacture had long and will ever be looked upon with jealousy, and if not timely remedied, might occasion very strict laws totally to prohibit and suppress the same. On the 30th of June, the commons presented a similar petition, praying that his majesty would enjoin all those whom he employed in Ireland to make it their care, and use their utmost diligence to hinder the exportation of wool, and discourage the woollen manufactures. Accordingly his majesty addressed two letters on the 29th of June and 7th of July, in the same year, to his Lord Justices in Dublin, reciting these addresses and requiring them to take the most effectual care to avoid all occasions of giving jealousy to his subjects, by carrying on this manufacture. In consequence of these proceedings, the Irish parliament passed a law 25th March, 1699, laying 4 shillings additional duty on every 20 shillings value of broad cloth, exported out of Ireland, and 2 shillings on every 20 shillings of serges and baise, and in the same sessions a law passed in England, restraining the exportation of woollen manufacture, including frise, to any other part except England and Wales.* The distress which Ireland suffered by this sudden suppression of her woollen trade is notorious. The whole number of inhabitants was not above one million, and this manufacture was almost their only trade; many wealthy employers immediately left the country, and brought their capitals and assistants with them, while the natives, who had neither agriculture nor other means of industry,

mentions it as the principal house in Dublin, second only to the Castle. Indeed, this end of the city seems to be that naturally pointed out for the residence of the opulent. Its airy and elevated site renders it in many respects more eligible than the low swampy soil at the east end of the town, which, like that of London, should be appropriated to that class of the community connected with ships and commerce. It is well known that the site first fixed on for Leinster-house was James-street, and its noble proprietor with reluctance erected it in the marshes of Merion-square.

* To compensate for this loss of the woollen trade, it was proposed to give every encouragement to the linen, for which it was said the country was better adapted, and where no rivalry or competition could exist between the sister kingdoms. In consequence of this commutation, those beneficial laws were enacted, and liberal bounties given which has raised our linen manufacture to such a height of prosperity.

remained in the greatest distress, without employment or the means of support.* From that time the decline of the Liberties was almost as rapid as their rise. For a short period their local advantages struggled with discouragement, but by degrees they became deserted by those opulent tradesmen who had established their consequence. The linen manufacture, for which the woollen had been commuted, was never tried in this district, and one source of industry failed without the substitution of another.

The manufacture of wool, however, did not at any time become totally extinct in the Liberties; it continued to languish there till about the year 1760, when the use of Spanish wool was introduced, and a brisk trade was carried on for some years for goods manufactured with that article; but the greater capital of the clothiers of Yorkshire, enabling them to extend their credit to a longer date, induced the Dublin shopkeepers to stock their warehouses with goods, which they were not so soon called on to pay for, and after a short effort, the trade again sunk to the manufacture of coarse articles.

The year 1773 however was a memorable æra for the manufacturers of this district. The trade was taken under the patronage of the Dublin Society, and a woollen warehouse was opened in Castle-street, in which were deposited superfine cloths made of Spanish wool, refines of a mixture of Spanish and Irish, with cassimeres and livery cloths of all descriptions. The steady encouragement given in this way to the home consumption of the produce of our looms, established a very regular trade in the Liberties, which continued for a long period; in the year 1792 there were 60 master clothiers and upwards of 400, broad looms, which employed 5000 persons, besides 100 narrow looms on cassimeres, cassenets, and beaver druggets, and machinery was then first introduced. Further to encourage the trade, an order was issued by the Privy Council that the Irish army should be clothed with Irish cloth. Many contracts were given for this purpose to the manufacturers of the Liberties, and great benefits derived from them; but the order was not long attended to, the contracts were left to the discretion of the colonels, and thrown open to all competitors.

The present state of the woollen manufacture in Dublin is very low; it

* Collect. Polit. p. 88. Report to Parliament.

appears from a survey lately made with a view to the relief of the unemployed poor, that 170 looms only were employed out of 700, which once were kept in motion in this district; of these, many are the property of masters who themselves work,—a new species of manufacturers which the Meath loan has contributed to set up both in the woollen and cotton business.

All the goods manufactured are for home consumption, with the exception of a small quantity which has been exported at different times to North America.*

TENTER HOUSE.

THE distresses to which the poor manufacturers of the Liberties are occasionally exposed, had long rendered them objects of sympathy and interest to the rest of the metropolis, and to remove the causes or alleviate the effects was a prime object of charity. The causes of this distress are of two kinds, extraneous and local; the first being such as could neither be directed or controlled, are beyond the means of charitable relief; the want of raw materials from a foreign port could not always be supplied, nor the demand for manufactured goods in a foreign market could not always be created. Among the evils which were local, and which might be removed,

* From the early notices of the woollen manufacture in Ireland it is pretty evident that we were never indebted to any other nation in these times for a supply, but were always capable of manufacturing our own fleece, and every village was a woollen factory. At a very early period manufactures of woollen were carried on to a considerable extent in Limerick, Galway, Cork, Birr, and Wexford. In more modern times Carrick on Suir was famous for ratteens and frizes, and Kilkenny for blankets. One of the objects of the Dublin Society was to remove the woollen workers from the metropolis and disperse them over the country like the linen: with this view Moore, an army clothier, emigrated to Carrick on Suir, and Long to Kilkenny; but the project did not succeed. A factory for superfine cloth has been for some years established in Kilkenny by a Mr. Nowlan, a gentleman of much enterprise and ingenuity. At this factory is worked up most of the Merino and South Down wool produced in this country. The factory is directed on an excellent system of internal regulations, stimulating industry, and promoting good conduct by an ingenious code of rewards and penalties, which renders it, independent of its commercial advantages, of importance to the moral improvement of the vicinity. A warehouse for the sale of the goods of this factory has been recently opened in Westmoreland-street in Dublin, and the cheapness and excellence of the superfine articles render them deserving of public encouragement. The manufacturers of the Liberties are invited to send their goods for sale to this warehouse without any profit to the institution.

there was one which long called for a remedy. In the process of the woollen manufacture there are certain stages when the materials must be sized and dried before the manufacture can proceed. The usual mode to effect this, was by suspending them on tenters in the open air; but in a climate so humid and uncertain as that of Ireland, this was often attended with great difficulty and delay, and days, weeks, and even months elapsed before it could be fully accomplished. In the mean time, the labours of the loom, and all the appendages of its industry were suspended. It was calculated that in ordinary years, and in a season where nothing impedes their employment, 550 woollen looms are at work in this district; each affording employment to 8 persons in the different gradations of trade. These amount to 4490, and supposing that 5 persons in a family depend upon each, it will follow that 22,000 individuals are deprived of the means of support, as long as the weather continues unfavourable.

To remedy this enormous evil, applications by petition were made at different times by the poor manufacturers to the Dublin and Farming Societies, praying them to erect some edifice in which the materials of their trade might be dried at any season of the year, by artificial heat, and by these means every person kept in constant employment, without the periodical recurrence of these calamities, which often sent, as their petition truly states, " one portion of them to the streets,[*] another to the jails, and a third to the hospitals." These petitions were treated with due attention, and taken into consideration by the public bodies to whom they were addressed; but they were not complied with. In the mean time it became a matter of such local importance, that some individuals determined to undertake it not only as a plan of high public expediency, but as a speculation of great private emolument; and it was proposed to erect such a

[*] It is on these occasions that the streets of Dublin exhibit to a stranger such an extraordinary spectacle. When industry is thus suspended, and the people of this district unemployed, the whole population emigrates from their desolate homes, and pours down upon the more opulent parts of the city. The passenger is every moment surrounded by groups of strange figures, remarkably different from those to which his eye has been accustomed. Their greasy and squalid dress, and pallid faces strikingly distinguish them, and a certain cast of countenance on which sickness and famine stamp a ghastly expression, often excites surprise and alarm. It is much to the credit of the poor people that the alarm is unfounded. Their distresses often render them importunate, but they never behave with incivility, much less with outrage.

building by debentures, the holders of which would be entitled to the profits which must accrue from so indispensable an establishment. But while the hopes of these poor people were thus suspended between the discussions of public expediency and the speculations of private emolument, an *individual** at his own expense, and without hope of remuneration, effected what neither petitions or debentures could accomplish. Having obtained the most approved models for such an erection, he commenced it on an improved plan, and in 1815 a noble and extensive building suddenly rose among the ruins of the Liberties, almost before the public were aware that the foundation was laid. It is situated in an open space, in Brown-street, at the rere of the Weavers'-square; in the centre of the manufacturing part of the Liberties. It consists of a long edifice of 3 stories in height, ornamented at each end, with the weavers' arms emblazoned in the front, and the centre surmounted with a cupola and spire. In the front is an extensive area neatly laid out with grass plats, gravel walks, and shrubs, and the whole exterior has a cheering air of prosperity in a desolated district. The interior consists of three stories and a ground floor. In this latter, are four furnaces, from which issue large metal tubes, which run horizontally to each extremity of the building; by means of these, the whole edifice is heated, as the flooring of each story is formed by iron bars through which the heat permeates. Along these floors run the tenters constructed on machinery, by which the cloth is stretched to any breadth or degree of tension. The upper story is appropriated to drying chains of woollen warps before they are wove, which requiring less heat, are more remote from the stoves. The whole cost £12,964. 12s. 10d. The only charge to which the poor manufacturer is liable, is such as barely pays for coals and other current expenses; it amounts to 2s. 6d. for every piece of cloth, and

---

* The individual alluded to is Mr. Pleasants, well known for his public munificence. He has lately had a noble accession to his fortune, of which he makes a noble use. In 1814 he made a donation of £6000. to the Meath hospital, for erecting an operation room and other useful purposes. His acts of private beneficence are not less useful because they are sometimes tinctured with an amiable eccentricity. Happening one Sunday to hear a sermon of which he approved, he conveyed a request to the preacher that he would suffer him to read the manuscript, which was readily complied with. The next day he returned the sermon with a letter of thanks, intimating at the same time that he had taken the liberty of adding *a note* to a passage which particularly struck him. On referring to the place, the astonished preacher found a *bank note* for a considerable amount folded in the leaf.

5d. for every chain of warp. In winter it is always filled. The establishment is vested in the hands of trustees, for the benefit of the public—the beneficent proprietor himself seeking no other remuneration than that which his own heart and the heart of others can bestow.

COMMERCIAL BUILDINGS.

It may appear superfluous, after the erection of the Royal Exchange, for the transaction of mercantile concerns, to raise another edifice for the same purpose; but the object of the exchange is very confined; it is intended for the purchase of bills on London; on three days of the week, Monday, Wednesday, and Friday, it is open from three to four o'clock for that purpose, and is applied to no other commercial object. Long after its erection, the merchants were obliged to transact their wholesale business in Crampton-Court, where samples were exhibited, and commodities purchased. Here the crowd was sometimes so great, and the space so confined and unwholesome, that it was deemed expedient to adopt some other mode and place. Accordingly, some of the most respectable merchants opened a subscription to erect a building as near the centre of the city as possible. Shares of £50. each were issued, and in a short time were filled up to the number of 400. The ground on which the Old Post-Office Yard and Crown Alley stood was taken in College Green, and in 1796 the building was commenced by Mr. Parks, the architect. In three years it was completed, and opened for the transaction of business in 1799.

The exterior of the edifice is plain, but chaste and elegant. It is built of mountain granite, and stands simple and grand in the spacious area, on one side of which it is placed. It consists of three stories, surmounted by a cornice; the bottom is in rustic; in the centre of which is the doorcase, supported by Ionic pillars; the middle story consists of seven windows, surmounted with alternate angular and circular pediments.

The apartments within are approached by a hall and grand stair-case; on the right hand, is the Marine Insurance Company, established by subscription, and on the left is the coffee-room, extending from front to rere of the building. This large apartment is 60 feet in length, 28 in breadth, and 20 feet high, and has a finer effect because its dimensions are unbroken by pillars, or any other projection; it is lighted in the day by three large circular windows at each end, and at night by two gilt branches, suspended from the ceiling. It is supplied with English and Irish newspapers.* Beside the coffee-room, eight apartments in the building are allotted for an hotel. There are also, the merchants' private subscription room, a room appropriated to occasional purposes, and the Stock Exchange, immediately over the coffee-room. In the rere is a spacious court, round which are the Royal Exchange and Commercial Insurance Offices, and the several brokers offices, where samples are exhibited.

The expense of the building was defrayed by

Subscriptions, amounting to	£20,000 0 0
Loan, guaranteed by Government,	13,000 0 0
Sale of ground,	4,000 0 0
	£37,000 0 0

For the first years the subscribers received no interest for their money, but the loan is now paid off, and they receive 5, and latterly 6 per cent. This interest arises from the rents of the building, after deducting the repairs and expense of the establishment.

A Chamber of Commerce was some years ago established among the merchants of Dublin, who held their meetings in an appropriate apartment in the Commercial Buildings. Their object was to regulate the commercial concerns of the city, and communicate with Government on any subject which affected trade in any important particular. On their representation, the fees formerly paid by the merchants to the different officers at the Custom-house were discontinued, and a commutation was made by an additional percentage paid by the merchants on all their goods entered,

* There is one practice in this coffee-room which deserves reprobation. In the Tontine at Glasgow, and in every other public coffee-house, the papers are left indiscriminately for every person who enters to take up, and a stranger is never embarrassed; but here the waiters seize on the newspaper the moment it is out of the hands of the person who uses it, and sometimes before he has done; it is then secreted carefully, and dealt out only to those to whom they please to give it. If this practice arises from a scarcity of newspapers, a sufficient number ought to be provided to supply every person who may want them; if it be adopted to compel people to drink coffee, and pay in some way for the indulgence of reading, it is a mean expedient, and unworthy of such a public establishment.

THE CITY OF DUBLIN. 989

which afforded a compensation to the officers deprived of their fees, and who have now augmented salaries.* This reformation was, at first, highly approved of, as substituting a certain duty for an indefinite exaction; but in practice it has been found much to interfere with the convenience of the merchant; the business is slowly and methodically executed, and there is no attention paid to the occasional emergencies of trade; the merchant, in his greatest haste, is obliged to wait for the regular routine, and he often repents that he is withheld from offering, as the officer from receiving, a small gratuity, which would expedite his business. The Chamber of Commerce has for some time discontinued its meetings.

The business of brokers at the Commercial Buildings, was formerly much more extensive than at present. The brokers office was a mart where samples of all kinds of commodities were exhibited, and the buyer and seller relied on the broker's integrity, as a confidential agent, to transact business between them. At present there are but three brokers offices open, and their samples are exclusively confined to sugars, while other persons go about with samples of other goods in their pockets, searching for a purchaser, and obtruding them upon his notice in a manner much less reputable to the dignity of commerce.

The trade of Dublin may be classed under the following general heads:

EAST INDIES. In the year 1793, an act passed to allow Ireland to participate in this trade, but restricted the amount to 800 tons of a few specified articles to be carried from Cork, and the returns made through Britain:—of this privilege Dublin never availed itself. All East India produce is imported from London or Liverpool.

WEST INDIES. This trade was formerly carried on through Liverpool, but the direct communication has lately much increased. There are at present, belonging to the port of Dublin, two vessels which trade to Jamaica, ten which trade to Barbadoes, Antigua, and Trinidad, and occasionally to St. Lucia, St. Vincent's, and Demarara; besides these, about eighteen more, not appertaining to Dublin, trade directly from the islands, and are chartered by Dublin merchants. They bring sugar, rum, cotton, and coffee, and take from hence, glass, foreign wines, provisions, soap, candles, linens, and coarse manufactured cotton for slaves.†

---

* See Appendix, No. 5.

† The trade to Jamaica was, some years ago, much greater than at present. The balance of trade with Dublin depends much on the price of bills, which are sometimes 20 per cent. above, and at other,

990   THE HISTORY OF

UNITED STATES. The trade with the States, is principally confined to New York, and generally carried on in American bottoms. There is not a single American trader to the States at present, belonging to the port of Dublin. The principal imports are, tobacco, flax seed, corn, (when the ports are open), cotton, pearl ashes, tar, rosin, and turpentine. American timber is generally imported from the British settlements in Canada. The exports are, glass, coals, hay, lime, bricks, manufactured iron goods, and linens.

BALTIC. There are about twenty mercantile houses engaged in this trade; no vessel is regularly employed, but Russian and other produce is brought direct from the Baltic in British and foreign bottoms. The imports are, hemp* and flax, iron, timber, and tallow, bristles, isinglass, rein deer tongues, and cavear from the Caspian sea occasionally. The exports are very trifling since the cessation of hostilities, before that time, French and Portugal wines were sent from Dublin.

MEDITERRANEAN. In this trade, there are about six mercantile houses engaged in Dublin, which import direct from Italy, the Levant, and the Islands. The trade is carried on by chartered vessels. They import silk, marble, liquorice and drugs, currants and fruits, with a small quantity of wines. The exports are too trifling to deserve notice.

HOLLAND sends geneva, madder, toys, and flax-seed. The trade is very inconsiderable.

FRANCE sends corn, wine, oil, vinegar, brandy, cork wood, fruits, and kid skins, which are in high esteem for gloves. The principal trade is from Bordeaux. The quantity of claret formerly consumed in Dublin was immense. In the year 1753, the imports amounted to 8000 tons, and the bottles alone were estimated at the value of £67,000.†

10 per cent. below par. When the former is the case, returns are made for exported goods in West India produce; when the latter takes place, the value is returned in bills. The exports from Dublin to Jamaica generally exceed the imports, and they are all the produce and manufacture of Ireland, the merchants not having yet adopted the practice of exporting foreign produce, with the exception only of wines.

* Within a few years, a duty of ten pounds per ton was laid upon hemp imported into this country. Before that period, considerable quantities were purchased in Dublin by the rope makers, and much advantage held out to foreign vessels to purchase their cordage here, where the article was not liable to the same duty as in England. This duty is now felt severely by fishing vessels particularly, and in fact, it operates as a discouragement to the fisheries of Ireland, as well as to the manufacture of salt fish, both of which were formerly objects of particular care and encouragement by the resident legislature.

† This extraordinary circumstance is detailed by Rutty, but it is not very clear, whether he intended

Claret is now little used in Dublin. The import of French wines of every kind, from France, in the year 1816, was only 211 tons, 2 hds. 49 gal. The principal cause assigned for this decrease of consumption is, the increase of duty. In the year 1793, the duty on claret was £32. per ton; in 1816, it was £143. an increase more than four times as much. The duty on vinegar was then £6. 10s.; it is now £48. 13s. 4d. per ton, nearly eight times as much. French vinegar is therefore as little used as French wine. It is much the practice at present, to use home made-wines and vinegar, which almost every family in Dublin manufacture for themselves. The first is made from currants subject to the vinous, and the latter from brown sugar subject to the acetous fermentation. Before the French revolution, from ten to twelve vessels of 100 or 150 tons each, belonged to Dublin merchants, resident in Dublin or Bourdeaux; and were in constant employment, carrying wine, brandy, vinegar, turpentine, rosin, cork-wood, fruit, and a variety of articles under the denomination of perfumery, and they brought back beef in barrels, butter in casks, a little linen, wheat, and flour. There is now but one small vessel, under 100 tons, engaged in the trade from Dublin. The exports to France are reduced to nothing. The French now victual their ships with pork of their own feeding, and take butter from Holland.

ENGLAND. The principal trade is with Liverpool, from which, latterly, East India produce is imported to Dublin. The imports are, seeds, steel, coal, woollen drapery, with all colonial and other foreign produce. The exports are, provisions, corn, oatmeal, flour, linen, live cattle, with bones, raw hides, and horns, which three latter are returned in a manufactured form.

The quantity of coal imported into Dublin from Great Britain, averages annually, about 220,000 tons, and is brought over in 700 sail of vessels, which arrive generally in four fleets at different times of the year. These ships are navigated by about 5600 men and boys. The coal is brought principally from Whitehaven, Workington, Liverpool, Irwin, Glasgow, and Swansea.

---

it as the importation and consumption of the city of Dublin, or of all Ireland. He, at the same time, recommended port in preference to claret, as more balsamic, but is liable, he says, to one objection, " that it would not admit of so long a sitting,—a great advantage to wise men in saving a great deal of their precious time." Rutty Nat. Hist. Co. Dub. vol. i. p. 12. The advice of this honest Quaker has been adopted both in the disuse of claret, and the use of port, and, in comparison to the potations of his day, the saving of much precious time in drinking.

The duty on coals coming into Dublin harbour is 2s. 9d. per ton, namely, one shilling and ninepence old, and one shilling new duty. If coals be imported for the glass, sugar, and salt manufactories, the latter additional duty is not charged.

SCOTLAND. The principal trade is from Glasgow, whence the imports are fish, including ling, cod, and herrings, some coal, wrought metals, and ale. The principal exports, corn, oatmeal, and flour.

AFRICA. With this quarter of the world Dublin has had no commerce, and either the poverty or the principle of our merchants, have exempted them from the abomination of the slave trade.

The COASTING TRADE is very considerable. About ten years ago, a marine list was published in Dublin every day, containing an account of all the vessels which arrived in port, with their cargo, and to whom consigned. This useful list has been discontinued these few months; but the *day notes* are regularly printed and sent about to subscribers, comprising all the imports and exports, the places from and to which they arrive or sailed, and the amount of duties paid every day. These day notes exhibit a singular instance of the fluctuation of trade in the port of Dublin: by one it appeared, that a single merchant paid duties, in one day, to the amount of £20,000. by another, that the whole receipts of the day from all the merchants of the metropolis, was £8. The first was attributable to the expectation of new duties, and the last to the prevalence of westerly winds. The average daily receipts of duties in the last five years, amounted to £4000.

The bonding system has been much extended in Dublin, and its accommodation well adapted to the merchants of the metropolis. It was principally confined to tobacco, but is now occasionally extended to sugars, wines, and foreign spirits, and in fact, to every description of goods. The whole duty on any quantity imported, is entered in the day note, as having been paid at one time; but the merchant only passes his bond for the amount, and pays it as the goods are disposed of; meantime, they are deposited in the king's stores, and withdrawn at such times, and in such quantities, as may suit his convenience. For this purpose, in addition to the confined stores at the Custom-house, others were taken in different parts of the town, as the increasing trade of Dublin made them necessary. The ground under George's church, contains extensive receptacles for spirits—that under the Lying-inn-hospital for other goods, and several places besides, are thus appropriated to the service of the revenue.* But the great inconvenience arising from the distance of these stores, and at the same time, the necessity of them for the accommodation of the merchants of Dublin, induced Government to determine on erecting others in a more convenient site. For this purpose, a large space of ground lying on the east side of the Custom-house, was taken, and marked out for new docks and stores, and the excavation commenced in 1816. They will consist of two large docks, one 250 feet by 320; the other 650 feet by 300. These will communicate with the Liffy, by means of a flood-gate, forming a semi-circular projection into the river, and with each other, by means of a canal. The interior dock will extend towards Buckingham-street, and will form a communication with the basin of the Royal Canal, if the increase of trade require it, and continue it even to the harbour of Howth, by means of a canal through the strand of Clontarf, and across the isthmus. Round these extensive docks it is intended to erect equally extensive stores, consisting of six ranges, three stories in height, and forming a front of from 5 to 600 feet each.—That for tobacco, will be 500 feet long, and 160 feet wide. We trust, the trade of Dublin will be progressive with these extensive precautionary accommodations.

It has been an opinion generally entertained, that the trade of Dublin has progressively declined since the Union, and indeed, the general distress that has been felt and complained of in the mercantile part of the community, would seem to justify such an opinion; but the fact is otherwise. In the year 1784, when the commerce of Ireland received its most powerful impulse from the removal of those fetters with which it had been before shackled, and which has been deemed the period of its greatest prosperity, the number of ships invoiced in the port of Dublin, was 2803, and the tonnage, 228,956. In the year 1800, the number of shipping was 2779, and the tonnage 280,539; and in the year 1816, the number of ships was 3164, and the tonnage 318,142. Thus then it appears, that for sixteen years before the Union, the commerce of Dublin was stationary, or rather declining, and for the same period since the Union, it has increased more than one-eighth,

---

* The number of private stores in the possession of Government, amount to forty-seven;—of these, six are rented for the sum of 1300*l.* 16*s.* per annum; six more have been purchased—fifteen are timber yards on the quays, and twenty are merchants' stores in different parts of the city, let at a rent equal to the storage of goods bonded in them.

notwithstanding that the last was a year of unexampled embarrassments to the commercial interest of the United Kingdoms. The following Table exhibits the comparative increase both of customs and excise duties, the different periods, and the progressive increase for the last ten years, of the customs, and the last five years of the excise. The vessels are those trading with British and foreign ports, coasters are not included.

PORT OF DUBLIN—*Customs and Duties.*					CITY OF DUBLIN—*Excise.*
Table of the gross produce of Customs and Duties.					Gross amount of Excise Duties for each of the last five years, viz.
Periods.	Amount.		Ships invoiced.	Tonnage.	Years ending 5th Jan. 1813..*L.*1,951,697
Year ended					1814.. 2,029,745
25th March, 1784	*L.* 485,039	14 9	2803	228,956	1815.. 2,726,275
1800	826,848	18 6	2779	280,539	1816.. 2,712,976
5th Jan. 1806	1,042,695	0 0	2584	281,077	1817.. 2,143,009
1807	999,006	0 0	2893	314,659	Particular amount of each article for the year 1816.
1808	1,230,678	0 0	2605	290,175	Spirits - - *L.*1,123,617
1809	1,346,506	0 0	2892	329,583	Malt - - - 389,793
1810	1,518,391	0 0	2437	257,836	Tobacco - - 556,732
1811	1,095,810	0 0	3346	358,955	Glass bottles - 375
1812	1,223,406	0 0	3036	339,510	Paper hangings - 1228
1813	1,405,367	11 3	3562	381,567	Paper - - 21,420
1814	1,304,487	17 0¼	2913	302,232	Auctions - - 5645
1815	1,228,567	2 3¼	3046	304,813	Mead - - 63
1816	1,309,908	0 2	3483	349,000	Vinegar - - 216
1817	1,046,318	6 7¾	3164	318,142	Leather - - 41,230
					Plate - - 2690

For the accommodation of the commercial world, there are at present, in the metropolis, six banking houses, besides the national; viz. Newcomen, La Touche, Finlay, Ball, Shaw, and Alexander; besides two country banks, B fast and Lurgan whose notes are payable in Dublin.

There are also nineteen life, fire, and marine insurance offices, viz. Dublin, Hibernian, Commercial, Marine, British and Irish, Albion, Hope, Globe, Phœnix, Norwich, Westminster, Eagle, London, Atlas, Pelican, Union.

CORN EXCHANGE AND CORN TRADE.

THE metropolis has largely participated in the agricultural improvements of Ireland, and corn has become an export from Dublin, which has gradually and greatly increased within a very short period. So little had this branch of commerce been understood or followed, that in the year 1765, there were in Dublin but three corn merchants, whose speculations were very limited, and principally confined to importation for the consumption of the city. In the year 1783, an important alteration took place: the Grand Canal was opened for the passage of boats, and the produce of the southern and midland counties found a ready conveyance to the metropolis. To encourage further this communication, an act was passed by the Irish Parliament, granting liberal bounties on all corn conveyed to Dublin by land or water carriage, either by canal or coastways. These judicious premiums were eagerly claimed, and their good effects speedily felt. In the year 1788, 65,936 tons[*] of corn were conveyed to Dublin, and bounties paid to the amount of £77,702.

In a very short time this commerce was so well established, that the encouragement held out to create, was deemed no longer necessary to support it. In the year 1797, the bounties were withdrawn, but not diverted from their object. The average amount was granted by Parliament to complete the canals, and promote the inland navigation, on which the corn trade so much depends, while the current of commerce continued to flow to the metropolis with an increasing stream, though the cause which first gave it impulse and direction, had ceased to operate: so rapid has been its increase, that in the year 1814, no less than fifty-three mercantile houses were engaged in it, by whom, in that year, 321,232 barrels of corn, and 104,965 of flour and meal, were exported from Dublin to different parts of the world.[†]

The corn brought to Dublin is principally from the southern counties, which have more advanced in agriculture: the value of ground for bleacheries, the divided avocation of the peasant engaged in the linen manufacture and the cultivation of flax having much retarded the correspondent improvement of the north, where the tillage is little more than sufficient to supply oats for local consumption: two thirds of the corn bounties granted by Parliament, were received by counties connected with the Grand Canal, and the river Barrow. Corn is now conveyed to Dublin almost exclusively by land and inland water carriage. Flour is brought by coasters sometimes from Cork.

Of the corn brought to Dublin, much is consumed in breweries and

---

[*] By land carriage, 24594 tons—coastwise, 23055 tons—canal, 18287 tons.
[†] See Appendix, No. VI.

distilleries.* The consumption of flower is estimated at 5000 bags, each containing 2 cwt., per week, but this varies not only with the price of bread, but also with that of meal and potatoes, the usual substitutes with the people of Dublin in cases of high assize. This great variation will appear by the following comparisons of receipts and sales, for four weeks in January, in three respective years.

	lb.	oz.	dr.	s.	d.		cwt.
1815, Loaf,	4	5	8,	at 1	5,	receipts,	61,215
						sales,	53,064
1816, Ditto,				at 0	8,	receipts,	46,225
						sales,	42,568
1817, Ditto,				at 1	9,	receipts,	37,542
						sales,	27,034

Previous to the year 1806, the interchange of corn between England and Ireland was subject to various regulations, founded on the state of the markets in each country, and permitted at the discretion and by the proclamation of the Viceroy; but in the above year, a bill was brought into the imperial parliament, by Sir J. Newport, by which all restrictions are taken off, and the corn intercourse between the two countries is perfectly free. But the import of corn from foreign countries is still subject to regulations and restraints. By an act passed in 1815, it is directed, that an average shall be taken of the prices of twelve maritime ports in England previous to the 15th of February, May, August, and November, and that no foreign corn shall be imported for home consumption while wheat is under 80 shillings per quarter; but corn may at any time be stored in warehouses.

As the corn mart of Dublin is one for export as well as import and home consumption, the want of a Corn Exchange, conveniently situated for both purposes, was long felt. The merchants were under the control of the corporation, who claim a toll on all corn coming into Dublin; and the regulations directing the manner of sale were annually varying with every Lord Mayor. It was determined, therefore, to erect an edifice where merchants might meet and dispose of corn by samples, as in Liverpool and London, and by these means supersede the necessity of sending large quantities, and evade the control which the corporation exercised over

* See Breweries and Distilleries.

them.* In the year 1816 a charter was obtained for this purpose, and a building was immediately commenced under its sanction. It is judiciously situated on the south bank of the Liffey, nearly opposite the Custom-house, and not far from the debouches of the Grand and Royal Canals into the river. It thus unites the local advantages of the internal navigation by the canals, the import and export by sea, with the convenience of a central situation, being near the Custom-house and Commercial Buildings, and the general residence and resort of merchants concerned in the trade. It is built of mountain granite. Its façade to the river consists of two stories— that of the basement rusticated, having three circular topped windows, and two doors. In the second are five windows, surmounted alternately with angular and circular pediments, above is a cornice, terminated by a ballustrade.† The interior consists of a large hall, 130 feet by 70, from wall to wall. The central ceiling is supported by six metal pillars, of the Tuscan order, on each side, and two at each end, with massive pilasters at the angles. These metallic columns are $19\frac{1}{4}$ feet in height, and $2\frac{1}{2}$ in diameter at the base. They were cast in one piece, including the plinth and capital, at the works in Colbrookdale, and conveyed entire to their present situation. They are hollow cylinders, having a surface of $\frac{1}{4}$ of an inch in thickness, each weighing $5\frac{1}{4}$ tons. This metallic colonnade supports a cornice, over which is a range of windows reaching to the roof, and lighting the hall below—behind the colonnade are four ailes, two of which are lighted by lanthorns in their ceiling; and at each end are two spacious apartments extending the breadth of the building, intended for coffee and committee rooms. The estimate of the expense is £22,000. and is defrayed by a duty of 2s. 6d per ton, granted by Government to the merchants of Dublin on the entries of merchandize. It produced no more at the time of passing the act than £400. per annum: and was assigned to build the Royal Exchange and Commercial Buildings. It now produces, on an average,

* Much controversy has lately ensued between the corporation of Dublin and the citizens on the subject of tolls, particularly of corn; and legal decisions have been made, but the right yet remains undetermined. The toll for corn claimed by the corporation is one farthing, per barrel, from which it is generally considered that corn coming by water carriage, or sold by sample, is exempt.

† The exterior of this new and conspicuous edifice resembles the front of the Commercial Buildings, from which it seems to have been copied, but its style and proportions are by no means so chaste. The building is too high for one of only two stories, and the eye is offended by the blank space and disproportioned interval between the upper windows and the cornice.

£2000. per annum, on which the directors, under the charter were authorised to raise £15,000. When this shall have been defrayed by the produce of the duties, the fund will again revert to Government, to be again probably employed in erecting other useful public edifices. The remainder of the estimate is defrayed by subscription shares, each subscriber limited to four of £50. each. The interest of this, it is expected, will be amply repaid by the rents of coffee-room, vaults, &c. but particularly by the rents of tables let in the hall to market-house factors. On these tables the samples of corn to be sold are exhibited, and afterwards carefully lodged with the secretary, to be produced should any difference arise or reference be made to the correctness of the sample. This building has proceeded with such dispatch, that it will be completely finished before the expiration of the year 1817.

There are besides this corn market, two others for the sale of grain in Dublin—one in Thomas-street, and the other at the Grand Canal harbour, in James-street; the first was erected by the corporation, who are obliged, by their charter, to provide a mart for the sale of corn—the other was erected on the speculation of an individual.* In the year 1798, and subsequently, the market house in Thomas-street was occupied by the military, and converted into a fortress, commanding the great pass into the city from the west; and, in the mean time, that on the canal was rented from the proprietor, by the corporation, at £200. per annum. The edifice in Thomas-street, standing a rude and deformed obstruction in the midst of a great public avenue, is now about to be taken down by the commissioners of wide streets; and the market-house on the canal will perhaps again be employed for the city purposes.

PROVISION TRADE.

PREVIOUS to the French revolution, a considerable quantity of provisions were sent from Dublin to France, for her own consumption and for her colonies, but since the year 1793, the demand for colonial supply from France necessarily ceased with the loss of the colonies, though they are still supplied from Dublin, through the medium of England. The principal export of provisions now is to London and the West India islands.—Live cattle are

* Sir James Blond.

driven to Dublin principally from the counties of Meath and Roscommon, and occasionally from other counties in Connaught—they are slaughtered in the metropolis, salted, and barrelled. Pork is principally sent from Meath and Westmeath. The bacon sent to Dublin is entirely consumed here, as none is ever exported. Butter for exportation is brought by the canals—that which is sent from the county of Wicklow is merely for home consumption. The merchants of Dublin are not much in the habit of curing pork for exportation, which is principally confined to the northern ports and Waterford: but during the war the curing of beef gradually increased, so as that Dublin became a port for the exportation of that article more extensive than any other in the kingdom. The following exhibits the state of the exports of provisions from Dublin to England and the West Indies, for two years during the war, from the 5th of January to the 5th January in each year.

	Beef.	Pork.	Butter.
1811,	27,383	4318	30,905 Casks.
1812,	21,072	362	23,798 Ditto.

Since the restoration of peace, this commerce has much declined in Dublin, but not in the same degree as in other victualling ports in Ireland. There are eight mercantile houses engaged in it. No duty is paid either on the import or export of provision. A bounty of two shillings drawback is allowed upon the salt used in curing, to make it equivalent to the duty paid on it.

BREWERIES AND DISTILLERIES.

BEFORE the introduction of porter, the malt drink brewed and used in Dublin was a description of brown ale. About forty years ago the first porter brewery was established in Dublin. At the time, considerable quantities had been sent from London; but the home brewing has now so increased both in quantity and quality, that for some years no English porter has been imported into Dublin. It had been a vulgar prejudice for some time entertained, that river water, and that of the Thames, in particular, from its softness, had some quality which rendered it exclusively adapted for porter; the water used in Dublin is not drawn from the river Liffy, but conveyed from the city water-courses, and is that used for ordinary purposes. The number of breweries now at work in Dublin amounts to 35, and the quantity of corn malted for brewing, is estimated at 10,000 barrels per month. The following gives the average quantities brewed for the last 5 years, and the places of its consumption:

	Barrels.
Porter, &c. brewed in Dublin annually	300,000
Consumed in the city.	269,000.
Sent to other parts of Ireland,	30,000.
Exported,	1000.

Some of the porter used in Dublin is sent from Cork.

The ardent spirits used in Dublin before the introduction of whiskey were rum and brandy, particularly the latter.* About the year 1750, whiskey was first introduced, but it was not in general consumption for many years after. There are now in Dublin 9 distilleries. The quantity of malt used, in the spring and winter months, when only they are at work, averages at 18,000 barrels per month. The following statement shews the quantity of spirits distilled and consumed in Dublin, and exported, in the year 1816.

	Gallons.
Spirits distilled,	1,969,726
consumed in Dublin,	1,553,741.
exported to Barbadoes,	134.
Lisbon,†	59,373.
St. John's,	959.
Newfoundland,	237.
Quebec,	42,214.
Nova Scotia,	484.
New York,	3,682.
London,	6111.
Liverpool,	6085.
Whitehaven,	7316.
	129,995.

* The houses vending malt and spirituous liquors are still called in Dublin " Ale-houses," and " Brandy shops," though little of either liquor is sold in them. The word whiskey is a corruption of the Gaelic *uisgé*, which literally signifies water. That modification of it called Usquebagh, is a common whiskey with some aromatic ingredients; the term is corrupted from uisgé-biodh, which signifies literally " the water of life," and is synonymous with aqua vitæ, and eau de vie.

† It is said that the greater part of the Irish whiskey sent to Portugal is consumed in the manufacture of port wine. They distil for private use, in Oporto, an ardent spirit from the lees of wine; but from the empyreumatic flavour with which it is tainted, it cannot be used in the preparation of their strong wines, for which the tasteless purity of Irish whiskey is so well adapted. The quantity sent from Dublin to Lisbon nearly equals the whole exportation to every other country.

THE CITY OF DUBLIN.

Besides the ardent spirits used in the city, the produce of its own distilleries, much is consumed from other places, particularly from Roscrea in the county of Tipperary.

It had long been a subject of enquiry both in and out of Parliament how the consumption of ardent spirits in Dublin could be restrained, and that of porter encouraged, but while much discussion took place and many statutes were enacted, little was effectually done; at present there is no exclusive encouragement given to brewers, except the exemption from excise be considered as such. It is however a pleasing circumstance, that the consumption of ardent spirits in the metropolis, among the lower classes, has decreased within these few years; the number of licenses issued for vending spirits and ale usually averaged at 1000 annually; for the year 1816 there were issued but 879.

POST AND POST-OFFICE.

The Post-Office system, in its present improved state, is the most perfect system of finance, and the most important department that can exist under any government. It is the most perfect system of finance, because it yields an immense revenue, by the only mode of taxation where the tax is immediately collected, and cheerfully paid; and it is the most important department, because it is the great bond of connection which unites distant and numerous bodies of men, and it is the great medium through which their interests, feelings, and properties, rapidly, secretly, and safely circulate; and whether considered with a view to public convenience or private feeling, it is the most interesting establishment that can be found in any country. Hence, it has been the care of the governments of all civilized nations, from the remotest antiquity, to establish communications, by post, throughout their dominions.* The ancient Persians are historically noticed

* The most ancient writings extant abound with intimations of, or allusions to, *posting*.

In the book of Job, perhaps the oldest in existence, there occurs this allusion—" My days are swifter than a post—Job, 9 c. 25 v.;—and in Jeremiah—" One post shall run to meet another—Jer. 51 c. 31 v. And in the following passages the Persian custom is clearly intimated. The Jews were evidently connected with the Persians by the closest ties.

" She (Jezebel) wrote letters in Ahab's name, and sealed them with his seal, and sent the letters to

as the first people who established a regular system of postage. Prior to the reign of Cyrus, intelligence was conveyed by a sort of oral telegraph— centinels were placed at certain intervals, who delivered it from mouth to mouth, and thus diffused it in a very short period over the whole empire. But as secrets of state could not be properly committed in this way, that great monarch invented a mode for sending letters and dispatches very like the present one. He appointed postmen, mounted on horseback, who rode day and night, and who were the bearers of sealed letters, both those of a public and private nature.* Notwithstanding the obvious utility of public and regular posts, the Greeks, who have described, and who were consequently acquainted with, the Persian method, do not appear themselves to have adopted it. Nor had the Romans, who were indebted to the Greeks for every art and science, any regular system of postage before the reign of Augustus Cæsar.

" the elders"—1 Kings, 21 c. 8 v. What follows happened in Persia itself. " And he (Mordecai) " wrote in King Ahasuerus' name, and sealed it with the King's ring, and sent it *by post on horseback.*" —Esther, 8 c. 10 v.

* Cyrus himself seems to have been instructed by Harpagus, before he ascended the throne, in the art of secret corresponding. Epistola, quia neque palam ferri nequibat, exenterato lepori inseritur, lepusque in Persas Cyro ferendus fido servo creditur.—Justin. lib. 1, cap 5. Carrying pigeons were also employed by the ancients, and recently by the moderns; for an instance of which see the account of the siege of Haerlem, in Watson's Philip 2d, vol. I. page 378. But the most remarkable example of secret letter writing is to be found in Herodotus, an author whose extraordinary stories were once discredited, but which are now found to be generally true.

ὁ δὲ τῶν δηλων τον πιςοτατον αποξυρησασ την κεφαλην εςιξε και αναμεινε αναφυναι τας τριχας· ὡς δὲ ανεφυσαν ταχιςα, απεπεμπε ες Μιλητον, εντειλαμενος αυτῷ αλλο μεν ᾀδεν, επεαν δε απικηται ες Μιλητον κελευιν Αριςαγορην ξυρησαντα μιν τας τριχας, κατιδεσθαι την κεφαλην. ΤΕΡΨΙΧΟΡΗ. ε. λε.

Histéus wishing to escape from his exile at the Persian court, urged Aristagoras to excite the Ionians to revolt. In order to convey this dangerous message from Susa to Miletus, he shaved the head of a slave, and wrote with indelible marks on the naked scalp, and detaining the slave till his hair grew again, he dispatched him to Miletus. When the head was again shaved by Aristagoras, the characters became legible, and thus a correspondence was formed by a scheme preconcerted by the parties. Herod. book 5, chap. 35.

The operation of this curious manuscript is expressed by the Greek word εςιξε, which signifies to puncture. It is therefore probable that a method of tatooing was practised by the ancients, which appears to be exactly similar to that frequently made on their naked arms by our soldiers and sailors. It is remarkable that such a custom should prevail among savage and civilized nations, ancient as well as modern.

THE CITY OF DUBLIN.

During the dark ages which succeeded the fall of the Roman empire, there were neither roads nor posts. Travellers were obliged to explore their way, sword in hand, under the protection of some feudal baron or chief, from one place to another. When governments at length assumed a settled form, the University of Paris appointed messengers to go to certain towns and places, in and out of the kingdom, which were the residence of the students, to bring letters backwards and forwards for their convenience. This was the origin of the posts in France and modern Europe,—for Louis XI. made it a public measure; and about 1475 he established posts throughout all his dominions, but only for the conveyance of state information.

In England, letters and news were transmitted, before the Reformation, by private hands and special messengers. Edward VI. settled the rate of post horses at a penny a mile. Elizabeth attempted to improve the mode of conveyance, by appointing a post master; but the merchants elected one of their own, and at length the department fell into individual hands, who conducted it for their own profit. Thus the Post-office appears to have continued until about the year 1643, when Charles I. by proclamation, ordered his post-master for foreign parts, to settle a running post, to run day and night, between London and Edinburgh, which journey was to be performed in six days, delivering letters at all places lying in the route. Similar regulations were made for Ireland, by Chester and Holyhead, and a regular post became finally established between the three kingdoms.

The Post-office was considerably improved under the protectorate of Oliver Cromwell. An ordinance was published, touching the office and postage of letters in Ireland, of the date September 2d, 1654, which set forth, " that the office of post-master, inland and foreign, was in the sole " power of parliament, by whose authority it was farmed under certain " conditions, to John Manley of London, Esq. for the consideration of ten " thousand pounds a-year, to be paid into the Treasury in quarterly pay-" ments." All letters and expresses were to be forwarded to Government free; and packet boats to be established, to ply weekly between Dublin and Chester, and Milford and Waterford, exclusive of packets on foreign stations. The posts were to ride seven miles an hour in the summer, and five in the winter months, including all stoppages. The rates of postage that Manley was authorised to receive, were—for every single letter within

80 miles of London, two-pence—for more than 80 miles, three-pence—to and from Scotland, four-pence, and to and from Ireland, sixpence. Double letters paid double postage. Cromwell's regulations, as well as his rates of postage, were confirmed at the Restoration. In 1711 the Post-office was new modelled, under the inspection of a post-master-general, appointed for the three kingdoms and the British colonies.

The independence of Ireland on the English Parliament, having been ascertained and established in 1782, the Irish Post Office became separate and independent. New Government packets were appointed to sail, in 1787, between Milford and Waterford;* but so early as 1662, a packet was established between Donaghadee and Port Patrick.

The Union having consolidated the separate interests of both countries, the Post Office department, and the post-master-general for Ireland, remained, notwithstanding, as before.

The last and most important improvement in the system was, the establishment of mail coaches, which took place in 1784, on the excellent plan of Mr. John Palmer, which was generally adopted, notwithstanding the considerable opposition it encountered.†

A desire to extend to Ireland, the important benefits derivable from mail coaches, induced the late Marquis of Buckingham, during his viceroyalty, to advertise for proposals for contracts. At that time, the state of the roads was so bad, between Dublin and Cork, that there was no intercourse by coaches, except by hiring them for the entire journey, which was performed in five or six days, and commonly with the same set of horses. This great inconvenience at length induced three respectable merchants of Cork, Messrs. Anderson, Fortescue, and O'Donoghue, to become the contractors. Upon which, the Lord-lieutenant purchased two coaches in London, one of which he gave to Mr. Anderson, and the other to Mr. Griers,

* Packets on this station were first appointed, as hath been already noticed, by Cromwell, in 1652, but they appear to have been soon discontinued, and were not re-established until 130 years afterwards.

† To Mr. Palmer, father of the present member for Bath, the United Kingdom is indebted for his great and patriotic exertions in ultimately establishing the mail coach system. Had he attended only to his own individual interest, he might have obtained a contract from Government, wh·ch would have rendered him 20,000*l.* per annum. Superior, however, to any emolument of which the public did not partake, he declined any other reward for his service, than 2¼ per cent. on the net revenues which he should create by his plan. At that time, the Post Office revenue for Great Britain, amounted only to 178,000*l.*; it now exceeds 1,500,000*l.*

merchant of Newry, who at the same time, contracted to run a mail coach to Belfast. These first mail coaches in Ireland, commenced running 5th July, 1790.

Since that period, the general establishment of mail coaches, throughout the island, has engaged the attention of some of the most respectable characters in the country, who have become contractors for the purpose.

Amongst the important advantages resulting from the mail coach system, is the improvement of the roads. The act of Parliament which vested the tolls of the road between Naas and Limerick, in Messrs. Anderson and Bourne, stipulated, that they should expend £27,000. on its immediate improvement and future repair; by such means, the change was rapid, and the roads, from being in many places nearly impassable, are now allowed to be among the best in Europe.

In the year 1804, the Act passed for making new roads; since that time the Post-office has expended in surveys £60,000., and grand juries have presented about £35,000 towards completing them. All the intended lines are now surveyed, and the roads are in progress. Through this extensive circulation of the mails, it will not appear extraodinary that the tolls of the coaches amount at present to £10,000. per annum.

Bad roads, however, were not the only impediments to be removed. There were so few drivers competent to the management of four horses, and most of these were so addicted to intemperance, that Mr. Bourne found it necessary to bring over, and to retain, ten English coachmen, to train and to render docile, a sufficient number of the natives. This experiment was very successful. Their skill is now as distinguished as their sobriety and general conduct is meritorious. But the introduction of this mode of travelling —whilst it has improved the roads, has deteriorated the inns, few good ones being now to be found, where the practice is to travel so much during the night. On some of the roads, however, houses are fitted up by the contractors, and let to proper persons, during good behaviour, for the exclusive accommodation of the coach passengers, and under heavy penalties, to entertain no other persons, thus confining the attention of the proprietors of those houses to the coaches—and there is no instance on these roads, of a coachman stopping at any other than the appointed places. But while the mail coaches have thus increased, the number of the stage coaches has diminished. This has been attributed to many causes—the difficulties of the times impeding the usual intercourse of business—the disembodying of the Irish militia, and several reductions of the army, particularly the English military, who constantly adopted that mode of conveyance; but probably the most efficient cause was, the introduction of a cheaper mode of travelling by stage jaunting cars, of which eight now leave Dublin daily, for the following places; viz. Slane and Ardee, Athboy, Navan, and Kells, Newry, Monastereven, Kilkenny and Carlow, Athy, Naas, and Kilcullen.

Travelling or posting in Ireland, has been the theme of severe animadversion and much ridicule, but from such, the mail coaches ought to be wholly exempt. The coaches themselves, are at least as well built, as strong, light, and more roomy, than those of Great Britain.* Some of them are constructed of sheet copper or iron: for in the various insurrections which have, unhappily, lately prevailed, it was the plan of the insurgents to attack the mail, which passed through the disturbed districts—and these metallic pannels were found to be effective in turning off a musket ball. They are further protected by a double guard, and now and then by an escort of cavalry.

The roads in Ireland are more hilly than those of England, over which the mail coach travels with equal rapidity, at the average rate of five Irish miles per hour, including stoppages. The number of coaches employed in conveying the mail through Ireland are ten, from Dublin.† They all set out from the General Post Office every evening, at eight

---

* In England, the contractors with the Post Office being provided with coaches by the same person, the vast expense of altering so many, restricts improvements, but in Ireland there is no second interest, and the principal contractors having their own factories, not only adopt all the improvements made by others, but have invented several of their own.

† Besides the mail coaches which leave Dublin, the following traverse the cross roads in the interior, from the following cities and towns:

   One from Waterford to Cork, by Youghal.
   One from Waterford to Clonmell.
   Two from Cork to Limerick, by Fermoy.
   One from Cork to Skibbereen.
   One from Cork to Tralee, by Kilearny.
   One from Limerick to Ennis.
   One from Mullingar to Sligo.
   One from Belfast to Derry, by Colerain.

o'clock, and their departure forms a novel feature in modern Dublin. The bags are not sent in carts, as in London, to the different inns, but are delivered to the coaches, as they are drawn up in order, before the Post Office, in College Green. The coachmen and guards in scarlet uniforms—the crowd of spectators attracted by curiosity, or to take the last greeting of their friends—the sound of the horns—the prancing of the horses, as they depart in quick and regular succession, form altogether an animated picture, and make a strong impression as to the utility and importance of this department.

The mail for England is dispatched every day, except Sunday, when the tide serves, of which notice is posted up at the Office. A long coach, holding forty inside and outside passengers, conveys them to the Pigeon House Dock, where the packet lies ready to sail the moment the mail, which is dispatched in a gig, is put on board. Seven packets, and two wherries, which last are used in contrary winds and stormy weather, are employed in this service. The average passage to Holyhead, is estimated at twelve hours, but when the new harbour at Howth shall be completed, the packets can sail at any time of the tide, and the passage will be shortened to eight hours *

Offices to receive letters, and bell-men to collect them, are on the same plan in Dublin as London, for which purpose there are 65 letter-carriers for the Irish, and 20 for the English; but the letters from the South and those from the North of Ireland are sent by the Waterford and Donaghadee packet. The average passage from these stations is estimated, the first at fifteen, and the latter at five hours.

The great increase of the intercourse and trade of the interior with the metropolis may be estimated from the number of post-towns which has so rapidly increased within the last thirty years, that in the present year (1816), there are three hundred and sixty-eight post-towns in Ireland, to which

> One from Belfast to Donaghadee.
> One from Newry to Dungannon, by Armagh.
> One from Monaghan to Armagh.
> One from Ballinsloe to Westport

Nineteen mail coaches leave London at eight o'clock every evening. The number of persons immediately contracting with the Post Office, exceeds eighty. The aggregate of miles travelled by the several coaches, in England, including those on the cross roads, amount to about 13,000 miles per day.

* See Howth Pier.

twenty more are about to be added. Before the post-roads had penetrated the country, in every direction, some of these places were in very remote, wild, and unfrequented situations. The town of Cahircavan, in the county of Kerry, 160 Irish, or 203¼ English miles from Dublin, was 30 miles from the nearest post-town, and so completly cut off from all communication with the metropolis, that having some intercourse with America, the Dublin newspapers and letters used sometimes to arrive there *via* New York, having twice crossed the Atlantic.

The penny-post is the medium of conveyance from the several parts of the city with each other, and is of the greatest utility to the citizens. Many years ago the convenience of this office was so little appreciated, that letters were delivered but twice in the day, and the revenue amounted to no more than £400. per annum, which for 30 years remained stationary. It is now so much improved by increasing the facilities of communication, that every one avails himself of it, and its revenues have encreased within the last five years to £3500 per annum. Sixty receiving houses are established in different parts of the town, which are paid by a salary of £5. and one-tenth of the produce of the letters. From these, letters are delivered four times a day by 60 letter-carriers, and with such regularity and dispatch, that two persons, dwelling in the most distant parts of the city, may write four letters and receive three answers every day for the trifling expence of three-pence. There is no surcharge for enclosures, provided the packet be under the weight of four ounces. This conveyance extends four miles round the metropolis.

The total revenues of the Post-office for the year 1800 were £85,000. The gross receipts for the year 1816 were £250,000., from which deducting £150,000. for expenses, left a net profit of £100,000. in favour of the establishment. The great encrease of business requiring a great encrease of room, the Post-office has been removed at different times to more convenient situations. It was originally established on the north side of Dame-street, near Anglesea-street, which, after its removal, was still called the "Post-office yard." From thence it was transferred to the south side of College-green, where sundry efforts were made to enlarge the too narrow limits of the increasing office, without removing it from the convenience of a central situation. At length finding it impracticable to transact the business there much longer, a more spacious site, and one no less con-

New Post Office.

THE CITY OF DUBLIN.

venient was chosen whereupon to erect a new post-office. It was an open space of ground on the west side of Sackville-street. A long litigation had prevented it from being built on before, and an arrear of 20 years rent had accumulated. This was purchased by the Post-masters-General, and the first stone of the new edifice laid by his Excellency Lord Whitworth on the 12th August 1815. This extensive and magnificent building has proceeded with a degree of rapidity unexampled in this country. It is 223 feet in front, 150 feet in depth, and its height is 50 feet to the top of the cornice, consisting of 3 stories from the surface. In the centre is a very grand portico 80 feet in length, consisting of a pediment supported by six pillars of the Ionic order 4 feet 4 inches in diameter, which is considerably larger than that of any other in the metropolis. The pediment is surmounted by three beautiful statues executed by the younger Smith. That in the centre represents Hibernia, resting on her spear and harped shield; on the right is Mercury, a nude figure with his caduceus and purse; that on the left is emblematic of Fidelity, with her finger on her lips and a key in the other hand. The tympanum of the pediment is ornamented with the Royal arms in high relief; an handsome balustrade surmounts the cornice all round the top, and gives an elegant finish to the whole. The bold and superb portico projects from the body of the building so as to range with the street, and to admit the flagged foot-way under it. The portico itself is of Portland stone, but the main structure is of mountain granite. The expense of this grand and useful edifice will not, it is said, amount to more than £50,000., to be defrayed from the net revenue of the post-office.

It is worthy of remark, that similar inconveniences have been so much felt respecting want of room in the post-office departments of the three capitals of the united kingdom, that more commodious situations have been chosen, and they are now actually building three new post-offices in London, Edinburgh, and Dublin.

STAMP OFFICE.

THIS department of the revenue was first introduced into Ireland in 1774, during the administration of Lord Harcourt. Its first business was transacted in a confined and inconvenient house in Eustace-street, but on the

3rd of May 1811, it was removed to William-street, and it now occupies one of the most striking public edifices in the metropolis. It is situated on the east side of the street, and presents a noble front, which would highly ornament a better situation. It was erected by Lord Visc. Powerscourt, in 1771, as his town residence, when Dublin had attractions for our nobility. He raised the stone from the mountains on his estate, and engaged Mr. Mack, a stone-cutter, to display all his skill on its erection. It is approached by a flight of steps which formerly led to a portico supported on four Doric pillars which is now removed. The first story is enriched with rustic arched windows, and an entablature of the Doric order which is continued throughout the front to two gateways, surmounted by pediments which stand as wings to the building. In the centre of the second story is a Venetian window of the Ionic order; the other windows are ornamented with their proper architraves and pediments. Above is a cornice with a central pediment, in the tympanum of which is a coronet. But what peculiarly marks the edifice, is a quadrangular building elevated above the whole, erected for the purpose of an observatory, and commanding an extensive view of the bay of Dublin and the surrounding country.*

This fine edifice was purchased from Lord Powerscourt, for £15,000., and an extensive wing has been added in the rere, extending down Coppinger's row, on which, and the alterations of the house, to render it suitable for a stamp office, the additional sum of £15,000 has been expended.

The receipts of this office since its first establishment, have greatly increased. The average for the first five years, was £21,365. per annum.

The receipts for the last five years ending Jan. 5th 1815, were

    For Dublin - - £237,653. per annum :
    For all Ireland - £741,400. per annum :

The annual disbursements for discounts, distributions, postage, management, and salaries, £65,000.

Since the 5th April 1815, the excise licenses have been taken out of this department, which has reduced its receipts nearly one third.

* This building exhibits a specimen of the only defect perhaps with which our mountain granite can be charged as a building stone. The granulated texture presents a rough surface, in the asperites of which, the floating films of soot with which the atmosphere of the narrow street is charged from sea coal fires, are entangled, and the hue of this fair stone is so entirely discoloured, as to leave no trace of what it was: Powerscourt house is now so black, that the quality of the stone can only be recognized by breaking off the surface.

RECORD OFFICE.

THE manner in which the public records of Ireland had been formerly kept, is a singular proof of the negligence and inattention which marked so many of the habits and practices of this country. There was no safe and general repository in which they could be securely placed, and conveniently consulted; but these muniments of national property were entrusted generally to the keeping of the several officers appointed to take care of them, who exercised a discretionary power of bestowing them where they pleased.* Their private houses were the record offices, which were scattered over different parts of the town, and were continually moved from place to place, on every new appointment, whenever the officer died, or as often as he changed his residence. The first effectual remedy applied to this evil, was the erection of the several offices attached to the Four Courts, to the repositories of which the records more immediately connected with the different courts, were removed. Still, however, much remained to be done, as many of the most valuable documents were unprovided with a repository in these offices. To remedy this defect also,

* Besides the national loss occasioned by the general conflagrations of the repositories in Ireland. (see Annals, page 166), the records also suffered great diminution from the connivance, negligence, or wilful abduction of the documents, by the several officers to whom they were entrusted from time to time, as appears by the subjoined curious document, which also proves that there had been an Irish *doom's-day book*. The extract is from one of the returns from the remembrancer of the English Exchequer on the state of the public records. Among other matters respecting Ireland, is the following item of one Henry de Ponte a justice's clerk, in the reign of Edward I. who carried away doom's-day book and placed it under the head of his bed, where it was consumed by fire, and also several other records were taken by him at his discretion and were likewise burned.

" Memorandum quod illud quod erat de bono ad evidentiam feodorum et jurium Regis ac quorundam privilegiorum et memorandorum in Scaccario fuerat in quodam magno libro qui vocabatur Domesday. Et ille liber asportabatur in castro per Henricum de Ponte, clericum justic. posito dicto libro extra Thes. ad caput lecti sui per ignem et malam custodiam cum aliis q. debuerunt remansisse in Thes. succendebatur, et sic ut dixit Dominus justic. quod multa brevia sua de libertate ibidem portata per dictum H. combusta fuerint."

That there had been many surveys and a doom's-day book, like that under the conqueror in England, had been long since asserted by the learned Doctor Ledwich. In his statistical account of Aghaboe, he says, " We knew such were common in the 16th century, for Spencer, who published his " View of Ireland" in 1596, makes Eudosus ask, " Where will you quarter the army ?" and Ireneus answers, " Perhaps I am ignorant, but I will take the *maps* of Ireland, and lay them before me."

the commons of the Imperial Parliament on Tuesday the 25th of May, 1810, addressed his Majesty on " the necessity of providing for the better arrangement, and preservation, and more convenient use" of the public records in Ireland, which, though preserved with order and regularity in some repositories, were in others wholly " unarranged, undescribed, and unascertained ;"* to this, his Majesty replied, that " he will give directions as desired by said address." On the 20th of August following, letters patent issued for forming a commission to execute the matters so recommended. The commissioners† are to appoint a secretary, and such other persons of diligence and ability to be sub-commissioners under their direction, to methodize, regulate, and digest the records, rolls, instruments, books, and papers in any of the public repositories and offices appertaining to government, to cause such as are decayed and in danger of being destroyed, to be bound and secured, and to make exact calendars and indices, and to superintend the printing of them, and of such original records and papers as the commissioners shall cause to be printed. Further, the commissioners are empowered to remove the secretary and sub-commissioners, and they are enjoined to certify under their hands and seal to the commissioners of the treasury from time to time, what shall be a suitable recompense for their labour, and to report annually to the king in his privy council, their own and the sub-commissioners proceedings.

In virtue of these powers, the commissioners immediately proceeded to execute the important task assigned them. They first resolved on concentrating the principal record offices, for which no provision had been made in building the Four Courts. In order to accomplish this, Mr. Johnson the architect, immediately after finishing the Castle chapel, commenced fitting up the wardrobe tower‡ in the Castle yard as a repository. The combustible materials formerly used in the floors and stair cases of that ancient building were removed, and stone every where substituted to guard against the accident of fire. The whole wall of the upper story was built anew,

* See report made to the commissioners on public records of England, in 1806.

† The commisioners appointed by the patent, are, the Lord Chancellor, Archbishop of Dublin; Chancellor of the Exchequer, and chief Justice of the King's Bench, Common Pleas, and Exchequer, Master of the Rolls, and Lord Lieut. Chief Secretary, all for the time being, together with the Bishop of Kildare and the Earls of Meath, Charlemont, and Ross.

‡ For some account of this tower, see p. 52.

and the exterior summit terminated with a circular range of strong projecting battlements.* In 1813, the whole was completed, and the interior appropriated to the following allocations.

No. 1. Ground floor, are the first fruits and record commission clerks offices, in a building which forms a vestibule to the tower.

No. 2. Commissioners committee room and secretary's office, immediately over the former.

No. 3. Appropriated to the books and papers of the deputy-keeper of the parliamentary records.

No. 4. Second story of the tower, books and papers of the civil department and council office.

No. 5. Third story, is another of the deputy-keeper's offices for the statute rolls and parliamentary records.

No. 6. Parliamentary records and printed statutes.

No. 7. The surveyor-general's offices, containing the various maps and books now remaining of the several surveys, estimates, and distributions, at different periods in Ireland. Among these documents the *Down Survey* is the most interesting.

No. 8. Contains books and manuscripts of the sub-commissioners.

No. 9. Appropriated to the records and plea rolls formerly kept in Birmingham tower.

No. 10 The office of Ulster King at Arms.

The labours of the sub-commissioners have been constant, and the object of their appointment has been already considerably advanced. They have formed an analysis or alphabetical index of all the records in the 3

---

* The foundation of this structure is 16 feet below the level of the street, and laid on a substratum of calcaerous earth or lime-stone, which dips so deep and suddenly within 20 yards of the base of the tower, that, in building the chapel wall, on the same line, though they sunk 23 feet, nothing appeared but turf and other soft alluvial remains; they were therefore obliged to lay the foundation of the east part of the wall on wooden piles. Those on which the foundation of the old chapel was laid, in the same place, were found to be of hazel wood, the timber which covered the ridge of the hill extending westward from Castle-street to the Foundling Hospital. This circumstance seems to establish the propriety of the designation of this early city in Irish, Drom-coll coill, the Ridge of the Hazel Wood. Some years ago, Mr. Williams, a silversmith, residing in Castle-street, sunk a foundation for a new building in his yard. The labourers met with a stratum, in which were interspersed the branches of trees, one of which was found to be that of an oak, and had a perfect acorn yet remaining on it. Hazel is the constant companion of oak in the woods of Ireland.

offices of the Birmingham tower, record office, and registry office of deeds and wills, 5 state offices, 15 chancery offices, 5 king's bench offices, 10 common pleas offices, 36 exchequer offices, with those of the ecclesiastical courts, cathedrals, colleges, public libraries, and public boards, including all the repositories and registry offices in different parts of Ireland. This analytical index points out the several records in Ireland in the ecclesiastical, civil, and military departments, and where they are to be found, a laborious compilation, particularly useful to the antiquary, law agent, and ecclesiastic, who may wish to consult them. They have besides published, a splendid folio volume, containing, among other things, *fac-similes* of the palæography of Ireland, and the different hands used in record deeds from Hen. II. to the present day, and they have ready for publication, several volumes of transcripts of the more ancient patent and close rolls, in questions and decrees in chancery, containing in a methodical and abridged form, the most important information on the various grants and transfer of property in this country.*

The remuneration awarded by the board to the sub-commissioners and others employed in the various departments, is made out on the principle of *quantum meruit*, and is proportioned to the difficulty of the work performed, and the time employed in its execution. The salary of the secretary is £200. per annum; and, with the remuneration as a sub-commissioner, is limited to £500. The annual expenditure of the commission is estimated at something under £5000. The number of sub-commissioners and clerks engaged in this important investigation, amounts to forty individuals, who are all well qualified by education for the task, and among whom are barristers, and clergymen of the established church.

* The more valuable records investigated by the sub-commissioners are those formerly deposited in the Birmingham Tower—those in the rolls and the remembrancer's offices, and various others in the four courts. The *Repertorium Viride*, so called from its green cover, contains ecclesiastical and other records, formerly deposited in St. Patrick's, but now in Christ Church. The *Liber Albus* and *Liber Niger* —the *Liber Ruber*, or red book of the exchequer, contains a copy or inspeximus of the *Magna Charta*, by which the commissioners of the records in England have made valuable corrections of their copy— besides the records of about 400 other offices in Ireland. It is remarkable, that in those vast repositories, not one M.S has been found in the Irish character or language, though constant allusions to such occur in the others. In the inquisitions, &c. such words as the following are frequently met with— " At constat, per indenturam in *Hibernica lingua* in hæc verba."

THE CITY OF DUBLIN.

INNS OF COURT.

AFTER the subversion of the Roman empire, all Europe became subject to a military code, called the feudal system. People and property were subject to military chieftains, in whose persons were united the legislative and executive power. In Ireland landed property was vested in the chiefs of the clans or septs, and the people were only tenants at will. These chiefs however, delegated the judicial power to one of their dependants, who was instructed in the forms and usages of legal decisions. They were called brehons or judges, and they presided with a true patriarchal simplicity, on a tribune in the open air, composed of green sods.

By the brehon laws, all sorts of crimes, from a simple misdemeanor, to wilful murder, were punished or comprised by a fine, called Erick, and so prompt, just, mild, and impartial did these primitive laws appear to the English colonists, that they universally adopted them in preference of their own. So that from the first coming over of the English, in the reign of Henry II. to that of James I. a period of more than 400 years, there were none other in use in Ireland, except only in a few of the principal towns and their vicinage within the Pale. These brehon laws were viewed by the English government with the greatest jealousy and alarm, and their use was declared, by the statute of Kilkenny, high treason.*

The brehons committed their code of laws to writing, called by them the Phanian dialect, but in a language and character difficult to be decyphered by the best Irish scholars of the present day. The key for expounding both was possessed by the clan of the M'Egans, who were the hereditary recorders so late as the reign of Charles I.†

Whether the Ostmen of Dublin had laws peculiar to their state of society, or adopted the brehon code, there are no documents to ascertain, but the latter is probable, after their conversion to christianity. However, when the Ostmen power in Ireland became utterly extirpated, by the conquest of their maritime towns, in all those towns—as Dublin, Waterford, Wexford, and Drogheda—the English laws were promptly introduced, and even applied and appropriated, by the father of English legislation, the celebrated

* 40th Edw. III. Vide Sir John Davis's Reports, passim.
† Vide Collectanea de Rebus Hibernicis for 1774 and 1782.

Randolph Glanville; for in England itself the laws before that period were neither precise, firmly established, or well arranged.

Henry II. kept his Court in Dublin in November 1172, where it is said he held a Parliament for the enacting statutes for the establishment of the English laws, and the erecting of Courts of Justice. These statutes have been lost, and there are no records of the proceedings of the law courts of Dublin before the establishment of the first inns of court in the reign of Edward I. These were erected outside the walls near Dame's Gate, on the site of south Great George's-street, and Exchequer-street, where also the superior courts of justice were held; but by an incursion of the Irish from the Wicklow mountains,* the Exchequer was plundered and the records burnt. From this circumstance the hours of court were held within the walls, and the courts of justice sometimes in the Castle and sometimes at Carlow, which town, on the frontiers of the Pale, appears to have been the strongest fortified place in Ireland possessed by the English.

In the 7th of Edward III., Sir Robert Preston, Chief Baron of the Exchequer, fitted up his large mansion, which occupied the site of the present Royal Exchange, and with its offices, extended almost down to the river, for the inns of court. Here the benchers and barristers lodged for two centuries.†

After some time it became inconvenient to hold the courts of law in the Castle, as the military occupied all the spare room, and the Preston family claiming the grounds on which the family mansion had been built, the courts were removed in 1542 to the monastery of the Dominicans,‡ situated on the north side of the Liffey, where the present magnificent pile of the four courts now stands, which monastery was dissolved by Henry VIII., and in compliment to the granter who first assumed the title of King of Ireland, the building was called "THE KING'S INN."

A statute now declared, that every person entitled to practise at the Irish bar, should previously be a resident a certain number of years at an English inn of court, on the principle that no man should profess the law in Ireland who has pursued an inferior or different course of study from an English barrister.

In the 33d Henry VIII. was granted for 21 years as an aid for the support of the establishment, the monastery of Friars Preachers, with 15 messuages,

* Vide Annals.   † See page 80.   ‡ See page 358

in St. Michan's parish, one messuage in Patrick-street, one in New-street, and a meadow in Gibbet's-mead.' A new term was granted by Elizabeth for the same time, and the statute of education rendered permanent.

In 1607, Lord Deputy Sir Arthur Chichester was enrolled a member of the inns of court, and the Society renewed; and this seems to be the first in which judges, barristers, and attornies were enrolled, and the Society assumed a regular form. The price of commons for a judge was settled at 7s. per week; and barristers at 5s. A brew-house was attached to the establishment, and chambers appointed. It was also ordered that every gentleman of the house shall be on commons one whole and two half weeks in each term.

In 1609, the Society was so respectable that Jones, Archbishop of Dublin, and Loftus, Lord Chancellor, became members, and Usher, afterwards Archbishop of Armagh, was appointed Chaplain.

In 1672, Patrick Usher claimed the ground granted to the King's Inns, and stated its value at £1500. per annum. He however failed in his proof; but the disputed ground was called after him " Usher's Quay."

For more than a century little satisfactory occurs respecting the King's Inns; the troubles and unsettled state of Society during that period having interrupted the progress of this institution as well as of others, the effects of which continued after the cause had ceased. So late as the year 1742, neither commons nor servants existed. The buildings were mouldering in decay, and no charges were allowed for keeping them in repair. In 1762 a committee was appointed to review the proceedings relative to building public offices ; and a report was made in 1771, that such a repository was much wanting for the public records, and they offer the grounds of the King's Inn as an appropriate situation for the same. The annual rents of the Society about this time amounted to £420. 9s. 6d. This is a great defalcation from its former income, as in the reign of the Stewarts it amounted to £1500.

By the appropriation of the ground of the King's Inns for the erection of the new courts of justice, the inns of court in Dublin were no more a local habitation, but a "name" only.* Other grounds and a situation by no

---

* When Lord Chancellor Bowes was first sent over from England as Chief Justice of the Common Pleas, having dined with his brethren on his first admission to chambers, and finding his reception very agreeable, he told them, that being a batchelor, he should dispose of his house and live among them

means convenient, were selected for a new building where the Members of the law might be accommodated with lodgings not merely nominal.

After the adoptions and rejections of various plans and situations, in which much money and time were expended, the Society finally chose a piece of ground of about three acres, at the top of Henrietta-street, called the Primate's garden, upon which site the foundation stone of the Inns of Court was laid in 1802.

It is not a little remarkable that the whole body of Irish lawyers should make erroneous calculations with respect to a public building appropriated solely for their use and accommodation; that they should choose one piece of building ground at an exorbitant rent, which excluded their law-courts from all approaches on three sides; and that they should take another piece of ground without a valid title, and that to rectify such mistakes, they should be compelled to consult an English attorney and solicitor-general. The ground on which the buildings are erected, was the property of a dean and chapter, who could only make a lease for 41 years; loud complaints were therefore made that so much money had been expended on a terminable lease, and it was necessary to get an Act of Parliament vesting the fee in the Society, subject however to the rents payable to the dean and chapter.* The plan of the buildings comprises a hall, library, and square of chambers;† but only a part of it is yet executed.

The edifice already erected, stands on the summit of the hill, and is composed of two wings, with a very narrow space between, and a front which connects the wings at the west extremities. Had this building fronted Henrietta-street, or ranged with one of its sides, it might be deemed an ornamental termination or continuation of that spacious avenue, but its front looks towards Constitution-hill, to which there is yet no passage open, and its rere forms an obtuse angle with the upper end of the street, which it serves to blockade in such an awkward position, as perhaps no building was ever placed, where the architect could command the foundation. It was

in chambers. But he was no less surprised than disappointed when he was informed, that such accommodation existed only by King's Inn intendment and Irish fiction of law.

* 38 Geo. III.

† Every barrister admitted since 1791 was compelled to pay 20 guineas to be allowed in the purchase of chambers there. Upon the memorial from about 100 of them, 12 or 13 years ago, soliciting some value for this money, the benchers answered, that they meant to build chambers.

originally intended, that the north wing should be appropriated to a dining hall, and the south to a library; but the former only is yet completed, in which is included both apartments, and the latter, by an Act passed in 1814, has been appropriated to a record office,* and is now completing for that purpose, at the expense of Government. The hall is a noble apartment, 81 feet long and 42 broad. It is ornamented at each end by four three-quarter columns, of the Ionic order, fluted, and supporting a massive frize and cornice, on which repose statues of the four cardinal virtues, under an arched ceiling. It is lighted on one side by five large circular headed windows, between which are niches: the uniformity of the opposite wall is broken by corresponding compartments. It is intended to fill the niches with statues, and the blind windows with portraits; at present there are but two of the latter—Lord Manners and Lord Avonmore. The floor of the farther end of the hall is elevated one step. Here three tables are placed for the benchers; below are those for the barristers and students on the left hand, and those for the attorneys on the right. The library is a smaller apartment, originally intended for another object, but now appropriated to this use, since the intention of completing the other wing for a different purpose; it is 42 feet long and 27 broad. It contains many volumes on miscellaneous subjects, but none very rare or valuable. It is accessible to members at all hours,† but it is always open during term time from two to four o'clock before commons, when it is more frequented than at any other time. The façade of the external front of this wing is chaste and classical. It is built with mountain granite, and ornamented with a pediment and windows, surmounted with architraves, with their proper pediments. Beneath are ornaments in relief, one of which represents an ancient sacrifice. The door case is very striking; it is surmounted by a cornice, supported on each side by gigantic caryatides, representing Plenty with

* The society complain, that for this alienation of part of their building, they received no compensation. The Act says, to "beautify and improve." It is certainly beautifying an edifice to complete an unfinished and ruinous part of it, but it can be no improvement to deprive the society to which it belongs, of one half of its accommodation.

† It contains a tolerable collection of law and history, and will soon be overloaded with books of all sorts; Mr. Duhig, the late librarian, having procured for it the benefit of the copy-right act. But if publishers must give away so many copies, it should suffice to send books of the above description to this library, and books on other subjects to libraries which suit them better, such as Marsh's library and that of the Dublin Society, which have no benefit from the act. Mr. Duhig has published a History of the King's Inns in Ireland.

her cornu-copiæ, and a Bacchante with a cup of grapes and wine—emblems very appropriate to the entrance of a banquetting hall, and the more striking, as they are the only caryatides to be met with in any public building of the metropolis.

The exterior of the unfinished wing will be completed in a correspondent manner; and the two fronts will form one continued façade, pierced in the centre by a lofty arched passage, over which will be an ornamented screen-front, with columns correspondent to those at the extremity of the dining-hall, and the whole surmounted by an octangular cupola, with a clock in the pedestal. The ornaments in relief are peculiarly appropriated to the allocation of the wing of the building. One represents Truth and Wisdom holding hands over a blazing altar, while Justice lowers her sword and suspends her scales over them. On the right is a group representing History between Time and Fame. On the left, Fidelity or Vigilance with a cock and keys, standing beside History, while she transcribes the records. The other entablature over the centre connecting the wings, represents Queen Elizabeth sitting in the middle; on one side, the bishops present her with a translation of the Bible; on the other, the barons present her with a copy of Magna Charta; her head seems rather inclined to the other side. The original design was by Messrs. Gandon and Baker, architects, and the figures and ornaments executed by Smith.

With a view to the more effectual completion of the plan of the new buildings, the Society have made rules for that purpose, which are included in their books of regulations; these set forth: that all buildings within their precincts, shall be built according to elevations settled and approved by the Society. That qualified persons may build their own chambers on the ground annexed to the premises. That the tenant shall pay to the Society a fine of admission equal to one-fourth of the yearly rent. That all expences relative to keeping the buildings in good repair and order, shall be paid by the Society.

The admission fines are,	£.	s.	d.
For a student	-	5	6	8
For a barrister	-	5	6	8
For a bencher	-	11	7	6
For an attorney	-	2	13	4
———when sworn	1	6	8
	4	0	0

The admission fee to the library is five guineas to each member.

The deposit for chambers are,   £. s. d.
For barristers and benchers   22 15 0
For Stamps - 10 0 0
          —— 32 15 0
For attorneys - 11 7 6
The benchers pay for pensions each term - - 1 2 9

The other principal regulations of the Society are:

That computations of time shall be by terms, commencing from the 1st day of Hillary term, 1794.

That no person to become an attorney, shall be admitted a member, who has not served 20 terms as an apprentice to a member.

That no person shall take an apprentice before he attain the age of 16 years.

That before his admission, he shall be publicly examined in the hall of the Society.

That he shall produce his master's certificate of his good conduct during his apprenticeship.

That persons desirous of becoming students, shall memorial the Society to be admitted members, setting forth their connections and professions, &c. which memorial must be certified by a barrister of at least 40 terms standing.

That a person being candidate for the degree of barrister, shall certify that he has kept 8 whole terms at least, at an inn of court in England, and if a student of the Society, that he has kept commons, &c. in the halls for 9 whole term*

---

* The following clause occurs in the Act of Henry VIII.: " But such person or persons hath or " shall be, for the same at one time, or severall times, by the space of   yeres complete at the least " demmurrant and resiant in one of the Innes of Court." 33 Hen. VIII. chap. 3. It appears that in the draught of the act, a blank had been left for the number of years, which by some accident was never afterwards filled up; it was subsequently understood however, to be intended for five years, and that was the term of service appointed, till the time of Chancellor Hewit; he finding a blank before—years, exercised a discretionary power to fill it up with two years, which he thought sufficient, and for a short time this period of service was all that was required for admission to the Irish bar. The present term was adopted after year 1792. It was hoped that graduates in the University would be allowed some exemption, and a degree in Trinity College, Dublin, be considered equivalent to two years attendance at the Inns; with this view Yelverton's act made 8 terms with a degree of A. M. or LL. B. sufficient; but it was repealed in 1792, whereby the act of H. VIII. was revived. The blank in that act, it should appear, could not be expounded to mean more than two years, because it was a penal statute, which must be construed

That commons shall be provided in the dining hall during the law term, and in vacation during the sitting of the court of exchequer. The 2nd Thursday in each term to be kept as a grand day. The exceedings to be at the expense of the Society. Dinner to be on the table at 5 o'clock in Hillary and Michaelmas, and at ¼ past 4 in Easter and Trinity terms, and the hall to be cleared in two hours after. That absentees shall be fined the amount of two days commons, and shall be admonished or suspended on continuing absent; and that each mess consist of ten persons. The number of benchers shall not exceed forty-five.

There was formerly a chaplain appointed to the Society, and many men eminent for learning and piety, and who afterwards held the highest ranks in the church, filled that office; among these are to be found the name of Dean Swift. The Society at the present day have divested themselves of this appendage. A barrister who became a clergyman, lately applied in vain for this office. Connected with the courts, and who make their constant or occasional residence in Dublin, are 45 benchers, 950 barristers, of whom 25 are advocates in the ecclesiastical courts, 2000 attornies, 12 proctors in the ecclesiastical, and 8 in the admiralty courts, and 50 public notaries.

The character of the Irish bar has long been held in estimation, and there is no body of men among whom are to be found a greater number of individuals of genius and learning. As they mix much with the social parties of the metropolis, where they are always bidden and welcome guests, they are generally distinguished by their convivial talents; varied knowledge unconnected with profession, playful fancy exercised on present incidents, and promptness of repartee, which habitual practice confers, gives them a superiority in this respect over the other learned professions of this country, and over their own in England. The daily practice of a profession which calls forth unstudied wit, and demands the constant exercise of prompt ingenuity and ready reply, will account why a lawyer is generally found to engross more attention in private mixed societies than a physician or a clergyman, whose habits are generally more reserved; but the dissimilarity between an English and Irish barrister must proceed from another cause;

---

strictly. The penalty mentioned in it was 100 shillings, which was actually offered by some students, who had kept eight terms under the former act, but wanted a week of two years. The period of study for the English bar is only eight terms.

this has been well assigned by an English writer in a recent publication.*
"There is a Society," says Wakefield, "with an establishment called King's Inns, where students of the law are admitted to the bar; but there are no chambers for transacting business, as in London. Barristers therefore live in all parts of the city, and during every stage of their profession, mix with society at large, and participate in the general feelings of the great mass of the people. They do not confine themselves to one court, as is the case in London, but plead occasionally in all. Those who have had an opportunity of witnessing the severe duties of an eminent barrister in London, know, that from the multiplicity of his business that he is closely confined to his chambers, and secluded from general society, of course little leisure is afforded him of acquiring a knowledge of mankind or manners; but in this respect the Irish barrister has the advantage—he is in consequence a more agreeable companion in private life."

Yet this convivial talent does not prevent the exercise of the severer duties of the profession; men of the gayest humour and most playful fancy are to be found in the highest ranks, and who have attained their eminence by the knowledge acquired by intense application: the bench has been frequently distinguished by such men.

The eloquence and wit of the Irish bar have been celebrated; these qualities are admitted to be the natural growth of our soil. The upper gallery abounds with humour, and every peasant is an orator.† When these faculties are cultivated, the natural gifts refined by education, and the business of every day gives them habitual practice, they are displayed with a promptness and applied with an effect that is seldom equalled in other countries. There are not indeed many examples of closeness of argument and logical precision, in which English lawyers so much excel. Few works on legal subjects have been published by Irish barristers, and those few have been generally reports. But speeches in the courts have been edited in profusion; and it is no unmerited eulogy to say that some of them display fancy, wit, a fund of classic lore and pathetic appeal that have not been exceeded; at the same time that they abound with a luxuriance of thought that is redundant, and a copiousness of language that degenerates into

---

* Wakefield's Account of Ireland, vol. II. p. 341.
† See genuine specimens in Edgeworth's Essay on Irish Bulls.

verbiage.* But the quality which most remarkably distinguishes the forensic pleading of this country is a propensity for *punning*. This amusing but inferior species of wit is so inveterate a habit in the courts, as to be called the distemper of the Irish bar; it equally prevades the hall, the courts, and the bench, and there is no rank in the profession exempt from the contagion. The good things in this way that have been collected and reported form but a small part of the multitude which every day produces. It is this habit of punning, and the mirth it causes, which contribute to give that air of levity to the solemnity of our courts which foreigners see with surprize, and mark with reprobation "a pun is the Cleopatra for which our " greatest orators have lost the world, and, like Shakspeare, are content to " lose it."

The moral character of the bar stands high; there are a few instances in which it has been disgraced by the improper conduct of its members, and many in which it has been exalted by principle and integrity. Gentlemen usually by birth, and always by education and profession, they support the characters well in the several social relations, and the public are willing to confer that consideration to which they are justly entitled. A nobleman of high rank had said something injurious to the character of an Irish bar-

* " On every subject," says the Edinburgh Review, in a critique on the eloquence of the Irish bar, " it aspires to what is pathetic and magnificent; and while it adorns what is grand or kindles what is interesting with the rays of its genius, is apt to involve in the redundant veil of its imagery what is either too low or too simple to become such drapery."

THE HISTORICAL SOCIETY in Trinity College was the cradle in which the infant eloquence of the bar was nursed, and where all the great men who have in these later days adorned it, made their first essays. While we deplore its extinction in common with all those to whom early academic associations have endeared its recollection, we are happy to pay another tribute to the memory of a venerable friend, by the following account of its origin, and assign to its founder that merit which he was himself too diffident to assume when he noticed it under the head of Trinity College.

HISTORICAL SOCIETY.

This society commenced in 1769, under the immediate superintendance of the *Rev. James Whitelaw*. It was confined to under graduates, and was rather a religious than a literary society. They met at each others rooms on Friday evenings during term, and were examined in a portion of the Old and New Testament, and also of profane history. Mr. Whitelaw was president, and appointed the portions of history for each week. The original members were Mat. Young, Digby Marsh, Rev. —— Read, Brinsley Nixon, Henry Duquerry, —— Johnson, Wm. Reily, Dr. Mercer, Somerset Bradfield, York Sterling, Henry Wilkinson (now Sir Henry), and Rev. —— Goldsbury. As their number increased, application was made to Provost Andrews for leave to meet in the Regent Loft, which was granted.

rister, who was held in little estimation by his own associates, or by the public: he however brought his action for defamation, and the jury awarded ample damages for a slight injury. The judge who presided asked the jury with some surprise, if such was their verdict on that occasion, "at " what price could they possibly estimate the character of the gentlemen " around him." On a more recent occasion, it was attempted by some of themselves to disbar one of their members* for incorrect conduct. When the question came to be tried, it was found that no such power existed in the society. Their members are amenable to the common law only, and subject to no control from the body to which they belong.†

In the relations of private life they display, with a few exceptions, very amiable examples. They eagerly retire from the bustle of public business to the bosom of their families, and in the sacred charities of the domestic circle, seem to feel their greatest happiness.‡

* The gentleman here alluded to was charged with no other offence than resisting with some warmth the intemperance of a judge on circuit.

† Attornies convicted of improper conduct can be prevented from practising in the courts, and this is technically called "*stripping them of their gown.*" It was supposed that a lawyer could in a similar manner be "*disbarred.*"

In England, a candidate, who was refused admission to the bar by the benchers of one of the inns of court, brought a mandamus to compel them; but the King's Bench decided, that the inns of court were mere voluntary societies, which, like other clubs, may exclude ad libitum. But this club law has never been extended to expelling without a crime, any barrister who has paid a large price for his profession, though an Irish barrister was struck off the roll by Lord Clare, for signing an appeal in a case where he was not concerned. This arbitrary sentence was submitted to because Lord Clare was dreaded and his victim despised.

‡ The highest character at the Irish bar is a remarkable instance of this. He is known to relax his great mind in sharing in the simple amusements of his children, with an interest apparently as great as their own. When Demosthenes appeared in public in a gay robe on the day his daughter died, he was justly reproached by his antagonist,—" A bad father," said Æschines, " can never be a good patriot."‖ —The deep affliction of this gentleman upon a similar occasion is yet recent. The rival of the Grecian in manly eloquence and zealous patriotism, he has shewn himself far his superior in an admirable union of the softer feelings of an affectionate heart in private life, with the severer virtues of intrepidity and integrity in the discharge of his public duties.

‖ Εἑδομην δ'ημεραν της θυγατρος αυτω τελευληκυιας, πριν πενθησαι και τα νομιζομενα ποιησαι ςεφανωσαμενος και λευκην εσθητα λαβων εβαθυτει, και παρηνομει· την μονην ὁ δειλαιος, και πρωτην αυτον πατερα προσειπεσαν, απολεσας, και ᴂ το δυςυχημα ονειδιζω, αλλα τον τροπον εξεταζω. Ὁ γαρ μισοτεκνος και πατηρ πονηρος ᴂκ αν ποτε γενοιτο δημαγωγος χρηςος, ᴂδε ὁ τα φιλτατα και οικειτοατα σωματα μη ςεργων, ᴂδεποτε ὑμας περι πλειονος ποιησεται τᴂς αλλοτριᴂς· κ. τ. λ. ΑΙΣΧΙΝ. κατ' ΚΤΗΣ. xϑ.

6 P

The Irish bar has been charged with want of patriotism. It is certain, that on the great struggle for political existence in this country, they shewed collectively but little energy. Of all the orders in the state they had apparently most to lose by a legislative union with England A seat in the Irish parliament was the great object of their ambition—it was the high road to reputation, profit, and honour, and it was readily accessible to the first display of abilities as a public speaker.* The Irish bar was the earliest to meet as a public body on this momentous question. The eyes of the nation were turned upon the result of their deliberations, and the energy of their resolutions was to give a tone to that of all the rest. They magnanimously resolved that the annihilation of the parliament of Ireland would be an innovation! A contemporary pamphlet remarked, that innovation meant the introduction of something new, and that they intended to imply by the resolution, that the union would introduce Sir B. R. into the House of Commons of England, which would certainly be, to the English members, the introduction of a very extraordinary novelty. Among the supporters of public charities, many lawyers are conspicuous. The excellent institution for establishing a general system of education among the poor is greatly indebted to them, insomuch so, that it is popularly called the Lawyers' Society.

ECCLESIASTICAL COURTS.

OF this description there are four held in Dublin, two casual and two permanent, viz. the Convocation, the Court of Delegates, the Consistory Court, and the Prerogative Court; to these may be added, as deciding by the same code of laws, the High Court of Admiralty.

* To compensate for the loss of parliamentary avenues to promotion, 32 places of assistant barristers, six of divisional magistrates, &c. have been distributed among the profession since the Union; and it is computed, that there are about 200 lucrative offices usually held by barristers, although the whole number of attendant barristers does not exceed 300.

THE CONVOCATION.

This is the highest, and that in which the ecclesiastical government of Ireland is properly lodged. In its structure and constitution it resembles the parliament, and was called together in the same manner, and, by ancient usage, now discontinued at the same time. The King directs his writ to the archbishop of each province, requiring him to summon all bishops, deans, archdeacons, &c. according to their best discretion and judgment, and assigns to them the time when, and appoints the place where, they shall meet, in the same writ. On the day of meeting, they assemble in two distinct chambers, and form an upper and a lower house. In the first the archbishop presides, and in the second they choose a prolocutor or speaker, who is presented for approbation to the upper house, and, after two speeches delivered in Latin by the person elected, and the Archbishop in reply, he is approved of with the consent of the bishops.

Though the matter to be debated on be purely ecclesiastical, and referring only to religion and the state of the church, yet the convocation seems to have a jurisdiction which extends further. It can, with the royal assent, make canons, which bind not only themselves, but the laity, in matters of religion, and this without the consent, it is asserted, of the Lords and Commons assembled in parliament. In debating any question, it is usual to propound it first in the upper house; it is then communicated to the lower, and when discussed, decided in both by a majority of voices.

Before the 12th century, various synods or convocations of the clergy were holden in different parts of Ireland, to discuss any important question which occurred. In the year 1172, a memorable synod was held at Cashel, where every archbishop and bishop gave sealed charters to Henry II. conferring on him and his heirs for ever, the kingdom of Ireland. They also enacted several canons, amongst others, one for an uniformity of divine offices with those of England.*

A convocation was called in Dublin by James I. in 1614. It established in Ireland the 39 articles.†

In 1641, a convocation met at Kilkenny, while the rebel parliament sat there. At this meeting, it appears that the provincial of the Augustineans

---

* Ware's Bishops, p. 468.   † See Annals, 486.

was treated with little ceremony; he was hissed from the assembly for claiming the possessions of his order from the lay impropriators.*

A synod was holden in Dublin by Charles I., in the 10th year of his reign. It was begun on 24th May 1534, and sat at St. Patrick's cathedral. It drew up the 100 canons and constitutions ecclesiastical which are in force at the present day.

In the 10th of Anne, anno 1711, another convocation was holden in Dublin, at which 5 canons were added to those already in force.

It had been usual to call a convocation with every parliament, but since the reign of Anne the practice has been discontinued, and no convocation has been called in either England or Ireland.

HIGH COURT OF DELEGATES.

This court is next in dignity and authority to the Convocation. It consists of the bishops, judges, and masters in chancery, who are mentioned by name in the commission which appoints them; and the duty is usually imposed in rotation, as they receive no compensations for their attendance. They act by special commission under the great seal, and an appeal lies to them from the highest metropolitan court. Their decision is final, though they sometimes reconsider the cause with the addition of other delegates, which is called a commission of adjuncts; they usually sit in the King's bench chamber courts.

PREROGATIVE COURT

Was originally established for the trial of all testamentary causes where the deceased has left *bona notabilia* within two different dioceses; in this case the probate of wills belongs to the archbishop of the province by way of special prerogative. The person who presides is appointed by the archbishop, and is called the judge of the prerogative court; he takes cognizance of wills, administrations, and legacies. From this court an appeal lay to the pope, but by a statute of Henry VIII. it now lies to the King in chancery.†

The office is held in Henrietta-street.

* Ledwich, p. 486. † 25 Henry VIII. cap. 19.

CONSISTORIAL COURT.

This is the tribunal or place of justice in the spiritual court appertaining to archbishops and bishops, and has been held from time immemorial in every diocese for the trial of all ecclesiastical causes which occurred within them. The court anciently sat in the nave of the cathedral, or some convenient aisle, where the bishop, assisted by his clergy, presided. The judge who now presides is appointed by the bishop. He is usually called in England a chancellor, but in Ireland universally a vicar-general. An appeal lies from the court of the suffragan bishop to that of the archbishop of the province, which however, as far as respects his province, is his consistorial court, from whence there is a final appeal to the high court of delegates. The consistorial office is held on the west side of Stephen's-Green.

In these courts all causes are cognizable which do not belong to the common law of England, such as blasphemy, apostacy, heresy, schism, ordinations, institution of clerks to benefices, celebration of divine service, rights of matrimony, divorces, general bastardy, tithes, oblations, obventions, mortuaries, dilapidations, reparation of churches, probates of wills, administrations, simony, incest, fornication, adulteries, procurations, with others of a similar nature.

HIGH COURT OF ADMIRALTY.

This court takes cognizance of all contracts on the high seas, seamen's wages, bottomry bonds, cases of salvage and collisions, &c. It is the only high court of Admiralty in the British dominions, with the exception of that of London. The courts of all other dependencies on the British empire are vice-courts, from which an appeal lies to that of England, but appeals from this lie to the high court of delegates in Ireland; and this independancy has been particularly reserved by the act of union.* No prize commissions, however, are annexed to this court. It is held in the Four Courts. Its officers are a judge, a register, and a king's advocate.

The proceedings of this court, like those of the ecclesiastical, are administered by the civil law. The mode of process is by citation. Proofs are

* See Brown's Civil Law.

adduced—witnesses are examined—presumptions admitted, and matters of argument drawn from the canon and civil law; and finally, the judge, without the intervention of a jury, passes the definitive sentence.*

The study and practice of the civil law was early introduced into Ireland, and was well understood when the common or statute law of England was very imperfectly known.† The early connection of Ireland with the see of Rome, caused the introduction of the Roman civil law from Italy, immediately after its discovery; and as the property and rights of the clergy were of prime importance, the study of the canon and civil law became a necessary part of education. Hence they obtained the reputation of being the best canonists,‡ and professors from Ireland were found in the English colleges, where they acquired great celebrity. The cultivation of the learned languages had always been particularly attended to, insomuch so, that at a period when war and dissension had for several centuries continued to obliterate the pursuits of learning and peace, the Irish had their schools of physic and law, in which they learned to speak Latin, and practise it as their vernacular language.

BOARD OF FIRST FRUITS.

The annats or primitial profits of ecclesiastical benefices, was a tax paid previous to the Reformation, to the Pope, by every person put into possession of a spiritual living. By a statute of Henry VIII. this tax, in the realms of England and Ireland, became vested in the crown, and every archbishop, bishop, dean, dignatory, rector, and vicar, paid one year's value of their respective income, and also one twentieth part of the same every year, except only for the first year, when it was supposed to have been paid by the first fruits.

* Ledwich, page 320.

† Quod plerique scriptores tradunt Hibernicorum ingenia valde propensa esse ad jus civile et canonicum. Roselius apud suos percrebuisse dicit, Hibernos olim studio juris pontificii delectari solitos et fuisse optimos canonistas.—Duck. p. 416, ap. Led. He also mentions a celebrated Irish professor at Oxford, in the reign of Edward III. who was called, from the place probably of his birth, William of Drogheda. Polydore Virgil, in the reign of Henry VIII. bears the same testimony; and Campion, in 1570, says they spoke Latin like a vulgar language.

This tax continued to be paid to the crown till the reign of Anne, when this excellent sovereign, taking into consideration the poverty of the Irish church, the want of glebes and glebe houses, with the ruinous state of the churches, which the parishioners were not able to rebuild or repair, was pleased, by letters patent, in the 10th year of her reign, to grant to certain trustees, all manner of first fruits arising from ecclesiastical benefices, amounting at that time to about £400. per annum, to be applied to the building and repairing of churches, and to the purchasing of glebes, and also releasing the clergy altogether from the payment of the 20th part, amounting to £561.* This was confirmed by an act passed in the 2d Geo. I. and by a further act passed in the 10th of the same king, the trustees were constituted a corporate body.

The trustees, aided by the talents and integrity of Archbishop King, and Marm. Coghil, seem to have been very assiduous and successful in the discharge of their important duty. In the year 1728, they had applied the following sums to the following purposes.—

  £3368. 2s. 7d. for purchasing 16 glebes.
  5856 3 1 for purchasing 14 tythes.
  4080 0 0 for building 45 glebe houses.†

The value of livings from which the rates of first fruits are proportioned, is deduced from taxations made at different times in the reigns of Henry VIII. Elizabeth, James I. and Charles I. since which there has been no valuation. Of 2400 benefices in Ireland, 1500 only had been valued, and 900 were passed over, and are not liable to any charge, besides all vicarages rated at or under £6. 13s. 4d. and parsonages at or under £5. are released altogether from the tax. These circumstances, with the surrender of 20th part of the annual value, had so reduced the produce of the benefices, that it was found altogether inadequate for the benevolent purposes to which it was appropriated, for while it remained stationary, the value of every thing else was advancing. The Irish parliament, therefore, made annual grants of certain sums to the trustees, in aid of the revenue, derived from the first fruits. These grants have been uniform since the accession of his present

* " Valor Beneficiorum in Hibernia"—a curious work printed in Dublin in 1741. It contains an account of the formation of the Board of First Fruits; and also the " taxatio" of all the benefices in Ireland, and when made. A transcript of the official copy is in the remembrancer's office.

† Valor Beneficiorum Hib.

Majesty, amounting to £5000. per annum till the Union, and since that period increased to £10,000. In the 46th Geo. III. besides this sum, £50,000. were granted to the trustees, to be lent interest free, for the erection of glebe houses, and purchasing glebe lands; and in the 48 Geo. III. it was extended to building churches also.*

By an act passed 29th George II. a further power had been conferred on the Board of First Fruits. The effects of primate Boulter were vested in them for the purpose of augmenting small livings under £60. per annum. The powers therefore possessed by the trustees are as important as their means are extensive; every thing connected with the external improve-

---

* Before a clerk receives institution, he must apply at the First Fruits office. If it appear that his benefice is under the sum liable to the tax, or that it be not charged at all in the king's books, he receives a negative *constat* from the office, stating either that the benefice is not charged, or, if charged, not liable. If it be charged or liable, he is allowed the option either to pay the total at the time, or enter into bonds, conditioned to pay one fourth each year till the whole be discharged. The sums at present arising from the first fruits average at 350l. annually, and are still paid into the Court of Exchequer in the first instance, as was done in the reign of James I. before their appropriation to their present use.

When any aid is requested from the board, a memorial is presented by the parties. If for a glebe house, it must be approved of by the bishop of the diocese; if for a church, it must be signed by seven protestant parishioners. The aid granted is either a gift or a loan, or both. The proportion of the gift is regulated by the inverse value of the living, and increases in a scale as the value of the living decreases, to a certain amount. The greatest gift is 450l. and the least 100l.; this is never repaid. The proportion of the loan is regulated by the direct value of the living. The greatest is 1500l. and the least is equal to two years income of the benefice. It is lent interest free, and is repaid by instalments of 6 per cent. on the principal, so as to be liquidated at the end of 17 years. On the removal of an incumbent by death or otherwise, what remains unpaid is a lien on the benefice, to be discharged by a successor. Gifts and loans for churches are regulated by the same law. A gift, however, is not granted for a church unless there has been no service in it for 20 years before; it amounts to 100l. and 200l. if a steeple be built. A loan may be had to any amount which the parish may choose to borrow.

In the 11th and 12th of Geo. III. by the exertion of Primate Robinson, an act was passed, by which any sums expended by the incumbent on his own account, are repaid in the following proportion. The immediate successor to repay the whole amount, his successor to reimburse to him three fourths, the next, two-thirds, and the next one-fourth. Thus the greatest encouragement is held out to building comfortable glebe-houses. The incumbent receives a certain sum of money, which he never repays; and a further sum as a loan, for which he is charged no interest, and if he expend any more for the improvement or comfort of his dwelling, he is reimbursed in such an equitable way, that the charge is moderately divided among four successors, who participate in the benefits of his improvements.

ment of the Irish church is at their disposal. The erection of churches, the building of glebe houses, the purchase of glebe lands, and the encrease of small livings.

In the year 1806 a return was made by the archbishops and bishops of Ireland, to several queries addressed to them by order of his Majesty, on the state of the Irish church. It appears by this return that grants had been made from the year 1786, to the year 1806, by the trustees of First Fruits, for the following purposes:

Churches	210
Glebe houses	209
Glebes	73

But though much had thus been done, much remained undone; there were still in the several provinces the following deficiences in the year 1807.

	Armagh.	Dublin.	Cashel.	Tuam.	Total.
Benefices without churches,	34	57	140	7	238
Without glebe houses,	198	185	273	68	724
Without glebes,	70	104	137	47	358*

These deficiences the present board are employed in supplying with such effect, that the change is conspicuous even to a cursory traveller. He every where meets with neat parish churches, and comfortable glebe-houses rising beside the road, and the opprobrium that "many extensive parishes in "Ireland had neither residence for the clergy nor church for the laity," will be speedily removed.

The board consists of the archbishops, bishops, dean of St. Patrick's, Lord Chancellor, chief judges and law officers. They meet twice in each year, in February and October, for transacting business. The office of the First Fruits was formerly held in Stephen-street, it is now removed to the Castle-yard, where an apartment is allotted to it in the Record Office.

SESSIONS HOUSE.

In the year 1792 the foundation of this building was laid, and in the year 1797 it was opened for the dispatch of business. It is erected between the

* This statement is taken from the return in 1806, and Carlisle's Topography, 1807.

prison of Newgate and the sheriff's prison, and its confined and unwholsome site adds much, during the sessions particularly, to the insalubrity of that crowded spot. Its front consists of a pediment supported by six three-quarter circular pilasters, and its interior is approached by two narrow passages extremely inconvenient for the throngs that press in and out whenever the court is sitting. The hall of justice itself is sufficiently spacious. The roof is supported by four Ionic columns, between which are deep galleries for the accommodation of witnesses and others who may have business in court.

In this edifice are held four courts, viz.

The quarter sessions for the city.
The commission of oyer and terminer.
The lord mayor and sheriff's court.
The court of record.

The quarter sessions are holden four times in every year, and are opened by the lord mayor. Before the erection of the present edifice they were held at the Tholsel. The recorder and two aldermen at least, as assessors, preside, and the court is held by adjournment generally once a fortnight. It may take cognizance of all offences, but is generally confined to those of minor importance.

The commission of oyer and terminer sat originally at the four courts. It is held by special commission for a general goal delivery, and usually sits six times in each year for a week at each sessions. Two judges of the land preside in the court, and take cognizance of those offences of a more atrocious kind passed over by the jurisdiction of the quarter sessions.

The lord mayor and sheriffs hold their court every Thursday to hear and determine complaints of apprentices, journeymen's wages, and other cases coming within their cognizance.

The recorder holds his court four times in each year, in January, April, July, and October, to decide on actions for debt by civil bill process.

Here is also held the town clerk's office.

A list of the offences and convictions of all the culprits tried at the commissions and quarter sessions, at the sessions house in Green-street in the year 1816 is here annexed.

Offences.	Commissions. tried.	Commissions. convicted.	Quarter sessions. tried.	Quarter sessions. convicted.
345 Assault.	10	1	335	62
51 Forgery, having and uttering forged notes,	23	7	28	18
805 Felony, including larceny,	50	22	755	442
47 Misdemeanour,	0	0	47	6
7 Perjury,	4	1	3	0
30 Receiving and having in possession stolen goods,	18	8	12	4
10 Vagrancy,	7	3	3	3
2 Murder,	2	0	0	0
1297 Total.	114	42	1183	535

Of the 577 convicts 2 were executed, the judgment of 87 was respited, and the rest were punished by fine, imprisonment, and transportation.

A list of the committals and executions in Dublin for 5 years.

Year.	Committed.	Executed.
1812	947	2
1813.	947	2
1814.	999	4
1815.	1354	3
1816.	1439	2
Total in 5 years,	5686	13

It appears by the above lists that the quantity of crimes has encreased in the metropolis within the period of five years almost one-third. This rapid indication of growing immorality among the lower orders would be alarming, was it not to be accounted for by local and temporary causes. The usual causes which encrease the number of committals to prison are the encreasing population, the encreasing vigilance of the police, the encreasing depravity, or the encreasing distress of the people. The first cause could not possibly operate in so short a space of time in Dublin, where the population is known for a much longer period to be nearly stationary. The police has been always active, but they have not latterly exercised any unusual degree of strictness and severity. The vicious propensities of the common people have not encreased, it appears, by the concurrent testimonies of all those who are conversant with them. In no city perhaps can this be so well ascertained; it is the important business of many individuals, who are members of different charitable societies, to visit personally and inspect minutely the state of the poor, and all their reports detail their encreasing distress, but not their encreasing inimorality. Indeed, the very nature of the offences in the above list concur with their reports; two trials, and not one conviction for murder; but one for perjury; 392 for assaults and misdemeanours, offences rather of intemperance than depravity, and more frequently in Ireland the effect of an irritable mind than of a bad propensity. It is probable, then, that the great distress of the poor of the metropolis for the last two years, may be the principal cause that has crowded our courts and prisons with culprits. The prejudices of the common people of Dublin against the House of Industry, or as they call it, "Channel-row," were some years ago insuperable, and it was necessary to use compulsion to fill its apartments. The well known black cart was constantly seen in the streets, surrounded by the officers of the Institution, dragging the reluctant vagrant along, and compelling him to accept of shelter and protection. The pressure of calamity was so great for the last years that the cart was no longer seen. The poor people themselves came voluntarily to beg admission till 3100 persons were crowded into the house, and its extensive accommodation could contain no more. Still they pressed for admission; and the governors were reduced to the afflicting, and to them extraordinary necessity of rejecting those who begged to be let in; and in this way 450 persons in a few months were thrown back into the streets, where many of them were known to have perished. Provisions[*] were a common

---

[*] Potatoes were a particular object of theft among the poor; it is the custom to bury them in pits in the fields where they grew, and these were constantly plundered in the vicinity of Dublin. A gentleman had been stopped and attempted to be robbed in one of the suburbs. He gave notice of the circumstance to the police, and he was called on the next day to identify some prisoners brought into the police house: he found five men who had been taken up the night before in their way to Dublin, with potatoes which they had purloined from these pits. Nothing could exceed the apparent wretchedness of these unhappy men; their whole covering was a ragged coat tied round their otherwise naked bodies with a hayband. Their misery had obliterated all distinction of the moral turpitude of the action, and without sense of shame or feeling of apprehension, they seemed to exult in being conveyed to a place where they would get something to eat and cover them. This is one of many similar instances. The large sums raised for the relief of the poor afforded another proof of indiscriminate distress; they were properly expended in public works which will long remain as useful memorials of judicious charity. All the poor who were out of employment were invited to work, and the public roads were every where crowded with labourers arrayed in all garbs and of all trades, whom common calamity had reduced to a common lot.

THE CITY OF DUBLIN.

object of theft, and to protect them was the constant employment of the police. If then the pressure of distress arising from want of employment and scarcity of food was extreme in Dublin at the time that public offences were multiplied, may we not charitably hope that the encrease of culprits does not indicate an encrease of profligacy; that 805 might be arraigned and 460 convicted of petty larceny in one year, and distress be the principal cause, more particularly so as it happened where there were but 13 public executions in five years, among a population of nearly 200,000 individuals?

POLICE.

The first act for establishing a watch in Dublin passed in the reign of Elizabeth,* and a constable was appointed to preside over the establishment, from Michaelmas to Easter, under a penalty of 3d. per night for every omission. This continued till the riegn of George I. when sessions or leets were directed to be held, to appoint parish watch houses, raise district contributions, and ascertain the quantity of halberts to be distributed. The watchmen were appointed by the magistrates, and any person refusing to watch or find a substitute, was subject to a penalty of 12 shillings. The chief governor might require protestants only, and every papist was to find a substitute, or pay 12 pence per night.† A few years after, it was directed, that notice should be given in every parish church on the 3d of February, to appoint nine substantial parishioners as supervisors, to regulate the number of watchmen, with their stands and wages, and appoint protestant constables for one year, to set the watch from ten till six from Michaelmas, and from five till four from Lady-day. No publican was allowed to be a constable, and if any watchman was found drunk on his stand he was liable to the punishment of whipping.‡ The watch thus constituted continued to guard the city till the year 1785, when Mr. Orde, among his other propositions, produced a plan for instituting a more efficient watch in the metropolis; and in the following year an act passed, repealing the former, and establishing the memorable police.§ As this establishment had the appearance of an armed force, and created much patronage to Government,

* 5th of Elizabeth.   † 2d and 6th Geo. I.   ‡ 10th Geo. I.   § 26th Geo. III.

it was ill suited to the irritable temper of these times, and met with violent opposition both in and out of parliament.* It was repealed in 1795, and the old watch restored, which was found so inefficient for the growing population of the metropolis, that after some years it was finally abolished, and the present substituted in its place.†

The present police establishment of Dublin was instituted by an act of parliament passed in 1808, during the time the present Duke of Wellington (then Sir Arthur Wellesley), was chief secretary to the Lord-lieutenant. Its jurisdiction extends to all places within eight miles of the Castle of Dublin. This district consists of six divisions : there is to each division a public office, and three justices, of whom one is a barrister of not less than six years standing, one an alderman of the city, and the other a sheriff's peer, or a member of the common council, who have each a salary of £500. a-year. The appointment of the six barristers to be justices is made by the Lord-lieutenant, and also of three of the aldermen, and three of the sheriff's peers. The remaining six are elected by the common council

* No political event perhaps which occurred in Dublin, exclusive of the rebellion and the union, excited more agitation among the citizens for several years than this local establishment. It gave rise to the memorable controversy before the privy council, between the aldermen and commons, on their respective right to elect a chief magistrate. The former returned a police magistrate to serve the office of lord mayor, and the latter rejected him, and elected one who was not so. The privy council could not decide on the right, and for some time there were two lord mayors in the metropolis. In 1790, a motion was made by Tr. Hartly, the respectable member for the city, that the police was expensive and inadequate ; and retired from parliament after making his last effort for his constituents. At length, after 10 years violent discussion, the offensive act was repealed, but not till it had excited much discontent and angry feeling, and was perhaps among the causes that led to the melancholy events that followed.

† During the disturbances of 1803, a singular species of police was established in Dublin, called, " Conservators of the Public Peace." This was founded on a plan of King Alfred's, who restored and preserved the peace of England by similar regulations. A letter issued from the Lord-lieutenant 21st August 1803, recommending the plan. The city of Dublin was divided into 50 districts—24 on the north, and 26 on the south side of the Liffey. Ten or more inhabitants, of unquestioned loyalty, in each district, were to form a committee, who were specially charged with the peace of it. They were to keep registers of every house in the district, the number and quality of the occupiers, with their means of livelihood, and their removals ; and to give notice of any unusual number of strangers coming to the city. They had a regular office in each district, elected a president, and met once a day ; and each citizen was sworn a constable, that no one might question their authority. This institution continued one year, during which they took a census of the inhabitants, which is noticed in the Appendix, No. I. They insensibly dissolved when there was happily no longer any occasion for them.

THE CITY OF DUBLIN

of the city, subject to the approbation of the Lord-lieutenant and the privy council. One of the divisional justices being an alderman, is appointed by the Lord-lieutenant chief magistrate of police; he is also one of the justices of the division in which the Castle is situated. He is allowed a house to reside in, and £600. a year salary.

At each of the public offices, one or more of the divisional justices attends every day, from eleven o'clock in the morning until eight o'clock in the evening, and at such other times and places as may be found necessary: two of the justices attend together at each of the public offices, from eleven o'clock in the forenoon until three o'clock in the afternoon. The barrister attends at all hours, although not his turn for duty, whenever any matter of weight or difficulty occurs to require his presence.

The public office belonging to the Castle division, in which the chief magistrate presides, is called the head police office; the other offices make returns every week into this office, and all public carriages are under the exclusive control of the justices of this division, with whom complaints of misconduct against the owners or drivers are to be lodged, within 14 days after the offence has been committed.

This police is extremely active and effective. The men who compose it are in general stout, young, and able-bodied. They have been principally discharged militia men, whose spirit and good conduct have been certified. Patroles are selected from the watchmen, to be continually in motion during the night, to see that the posts of the watchmen are properly filled, and are on the alert to take care that no depredation or outrage be committed in the intervening spaces between the watchmen's posts. Over these are the peace officers, who are in attendance day and night, to await the commands of the magistrates, to see that the several duties are performed properly, and to report accordingly.

The establishment consists of the following persons.—

Aldermen	6	Peace officers	63
Sheriff's peers	6	Constables of the watch	30
Barristers	6	Horse patrole	30
Secretary	1	Foot patrole, city and country	170
Clerks	12	Watchmen	484
Officers	31	Effective men	777

THE HISTORY OF

The horse patrole are quartered in Kevin's-street barrack, and the watchmen distributed through the city, having 13 watch-houses, over each of which preside two chief constables, and in the more turbulent parts of the town, three.

Beside the stations in the city, police houses are established in nine villages in the vicinity, through which 70 police men are distributed.* From these, patroles perambulate all night, through the avenues leading to the town; and as far as they extend, have rendered the approaches to the city remarkably secure and peaceable at all hours. The expence of the establishment for the city is defrayed by a tax on all houses within the circular road; that for the county, by grants from the Treasury.

MANORS.

BESIDES the police and the courts of justice, there are four manors which exercise a jurisdiction in Dublin, in those streets which are within their precincts, viz. Glasnevin, Thomas-court and Donore, St. Sepulchres, and the Deanery of St. Patrick's; to these might be added Kilmainham, but as it includes none of the streets of Dublin, it does not come strictly within the enumeration.

MANOR of GLASNEVIN. This manor is more usually known by the appellation of Grange Gorman, but the latter is not mentioned in any charter of the deanery, and it was so designated only because the courts were held in a place of that name nearer to the city than the village of Glasnevin. Hence, the whole took its common designation from a very small parcel of its very extensive jurisdiction. It includes a district stretching from Balscadden near Drogheda, to Killiney near Bray.† In

* These are Rathfarnham, Tirrhouse, Chapelizod, Castleknock, Crumlin, Finglas, Coolock, Williamstown, and Dundrum.

† The extent of this manorial jurisdiction may be seen from the following extract from the plan of a charter and reformation of the prior and convent of the Holy Trinity, in and near to the cathedral and metropolitical church of Dublin, commonly called Christchurch, by the act of three royal commissioners in the year 1539.

This extract relates to the manors only. " Necnon omnia et omnimodo fructus, redditus, proventus, proficia et emolumenta quæcunque parcellas possessiorum dictæ ecclesiæ cathedralis Sanctæ Trinitatis, Dub. quæ aliqui vel aliquis Decanus vel Decani dictæ ecclesiæ unquam vel ad aliquod antehac habuerunt

THE CITY OF DUBLIN.

this is comprehended all the streets of Dublin which are beyond the precincts of the city on the north side of the Liffy, as appertaining to the baronies included in the district. These streets are marked by a line commencing at Ballybough-bridge, and drawn over Summer-hill down Great Britain-street, through the centre of N. Frederick-street, across Dorset-street to White's-lane, thence through Nelson-street, across Blessington-street, and through the orchards in the rere of Paradise-row, across Upper Dominick-street down to Constitution-hill to Manor-street, and so to Stoney Batter. This line includes 33 streets, together with Mountjoy-square, which are subject to the jurisdiction of this manor.*

seperunt vel gavisi fuerunt, de in vel infra separalia 'maneria sive Dominia de Glasnevin et Clonemell, Clonem, Clonkein, Dalkeya, Killiney, Ballylogan, et Ballhunter, Ballebrenan, Balletper, Balliogan, Bloghon, Firnescort, Kilmahyocke cum suis pertinentiis tam in spiritualibus quam in temporalibus, Ballifinch et Ballechere in spiritualibus necnon Balscoddan et Smothsio quoad Temporali.

In 1542 a charter was passed, among other things, enabling the dean and chapter to make such a division of the common property of the late priory as they might think fit, and they confirmed the assignation of the above manors to the deanery.

The immunities of this manor were formerly as great as its jurisdiction was extensive, as appears by the following curious document :

Wheare yt appeared unto us by sufficient proofs shewed by the Deane and Chapter of Christ church within Dublin, that the town and lands of Glasseneviue in the County of Dublin, parcel of the auncient inheritance of the said Dean and Chapiter, had and hathe an auncient fredome graunted by Acte of Parliamente, and yt the inhabitants and tenants of the same have quietlie enjoyed the said fredome accordinglie, untill of late some sessors have gone aboute to wex and trouble wrongfullie the inhabitantes of the said towne, as amongest the newe fredomes, supposing that such matter, as was shewed under th'ands of the Lord Lieutenante and counsaile forbiddinge the cessors, to change the same, had byn but a concordatum of a fredome then newlie graunted, whereas in deed the same was a declaration of the auncient fredome, so as the same by statute beinge est sones moved and declared before us. Wee think it good to declare by the tenor hereof, that the saide towne and landes of Glassenevan ought to be free and from hence for the discharged of all cesse of subsedie cariag and all other charges whatsoever accordinge to the tennor and purporte of the said Acte of Parliamente, willinge and commanding all cessors, &ca. to suffer the inhabitants and tenants of the said towne and lands of Glassnevine from time to time to have and to enjoy the full effect and benefit of the saide fredome without their lett &ca. Dublin 18th June in the 20th year of her highnes reign.

Wm. Geurard canc. Thomas Armachanen. Adam Dublin. M. Bagenall. Wm. Drury (et aliis).

Patent Roll. 22 Elizabeth, 7th Art.

* These streets are, Summer-hill, Upper Rutland-street, Great Charles-street, Fitzgibbon-street, Belvidere-place, Russel-place, Russel-street, Margaret-place, Richmond-place, Mountjoy-square, Middle and Upper Gardiner's-street, Mountjoy-place, Temple-street, Great George's-street, Cavendish-row, N. Frederick-street E. side, Hardwicke-street, Hardwicke-place, Gardiner's-row, Denmark-street,

It holds a *court leet*,* *court baron*, and *court of record*. In the first, it examines weights and measures, and swears grand juries at Easter and Michaelmas; in the second, it holds pleas under 40 shillings, which are regularly held every Friday; in the last, it exercises an unlimited jurisdiction in all personal actions which are tried by a jury.

The prison appertaining to this manor existed in the precincts of Christchurch within 30 years; it was called *Borendo*. It was pulled down by an order of the dean and chapter then in being; but it is presumed that committals of prisoners had been made to the superior court of Kilmainham, which being a king's court of record, takes this liberty into its cognizance. At present it has no prison or court-house, but it holds a kind of ambulatory sessions occasionally in Constitution-hill, Dorset-street, or other places, at the discretion of the seneschal.

Its officers are a seneschal, register, and marshal, who are appointed by the bishop of Kildare, as dean of Christ-church.

The Liberty of Thomas Court and Donore, generally called the earl of Meath's Liberty, is partly within the city and partly within the county of Dublin. It includes the entire parish of St. Luke's, and three fourths at least of the parish of Saint Catharine. It is divided into four wards; the Upper Coomb-ward, the Lower Coomb-ward, Thomas Court-ward, and Pimlico-ward. That part of the liberty called Donore, was erected into barony

---

Gardiner's-place, Upper Dorset-street, Sinnot-place, Eccles-street, White's-lane, Nelson-street, Blessington-street West-end, Upper Dominick-street North-end, Constitution-hill, House of Industry, Grange Gorman-lane North-end, Manor-street, Aughrim-street, and Prussia-street.

* The Court Leet seems to have grown from the Saxon word Lebe, which, as appears from the laws of Edward, was a court of jurisdiction above the Wappentake or Hundred. According to others, it is derived from *Lete*, parvus quasi, a little court, or from the German *Laet*, a country judge.

Smith, de Rep. Angl. b. 2. c. 18, Lamb. No. 34.

The Court Leet enquires of such transgressions as are subject to its correction, and is accounted the king's court, because its authority originally belonged to the crown. These are all offences under high treason committed against the crown and dignity of the king, though it cannot punish many, but must certify them to the justices of assize. In the county of Dublin there are no assizes held, therefore the seneschal must certify great offences enquired of before him to the court of King's Bench.

The Leet is also a Court of *Record*.

In the Court *Baron*, the proceeding is by summons and attachment against the person or goods to enforce bail. In case of appearance the plaintiff declares; if there be no pleas, judgement goes by default; and the practice is nearly the same as in the court of Common Pleas. Habeas corpus cum causa, removes, certiorari, and writ of error lie to the proceedings in this court.

THE CITY OF DUBLIN.

by act of parliament, in the year 1756. The boundaries of the Liberty, commencing at its most eastern extremity, run in an ideal line between New-row on the Poddle and New-street, in a southerly direction across the Circular-road, forming the eastern limit of the ground on which the New Penitentiary is now building, dips by a tunnel under the Canal, embraces the western side of Harold's-cross, passes by Cupbage's paper-mill on the Rathfarnham-road to the south of the skin mills on the same road; then takes a north-westerly direction until they meet the Dark-lane; are coincident with that lane until they nearly reach Dolphin's-barn, then turn almost due north, and across Cork-street near the Dipping-bridge, pass at the back of that street at an equal distance between the City and Liberty watercourses; again cross the Grand Canal south of the harbour, and continuing in the same direction parallel with the city bason, turn round the rere of the canal buildings and stores, run along the east of Echlin-street, between Ransford-street and Thomas-street to Thomas-court; then under Thomas-street near the church, include that part on the south of the last mentioned street between the church and Meath-row, pass between Meath-street and Ash-street until they reach the Coomb; continue along the Coomb, enclosing within the Liberty that side on which the Meath hospital is situated until they arrive at the Poddle within two houses of Lower Kevin-street. It thus includes 40 streets and lanes of Dublin within its jurisdiction.[*] The population of it is calculated at about 40,000 souls. The court of the earl of Meath's liberty is of very ancient foundation; it was erected under a charter granted by King John. Its authority both as to the nature of the action in civil cases, and the amount of the sums sought to be recovered, is unlimited, but it proposes no criminal jurisdiction whatsoever, being constituted to hold all pleas except pleas of the crown.

In this court the seneschal, with the assistance of a jury, decides upon pleadings, all cases where the cause of action exceeds 40s.; when the debt is under that sum, the seneschal decides alone, as in a court of conscience; and as the circumstances of the debtor are carefully inquired into, and the amount of the sum allowed made payable by instalments proportional to his means of payment, imprisonment for small sums is not frequent.

---

[*] The streets included, in this circuit are, New-row, Ward's-hill, New-market, Mill-street, Ardee-street, Chambers-street, Weaver's-square, Ormond-street, Cork-street, John-street, Summer-street, Brathwaite-street, Pimilico, Cole-alley, Earl-street, Meath-street, &c.

The senenchal, at his Easter and Michaelmas courts, swears in grand and market juries, who remain in office for six months; he also swears in 12 constables, three for each ward; the better to secure the order and decorum of the court, and the execution of all such warrants and precepts as issue from it. His municipal authority within the liberty, is nearly equal to that of the lord mayor within the city, and has been enlarged and regulated by various statutes; under the 17th. Geo. II. cap. 5, he regulates the markets; the 10th Geo. I. cap. 3. gives him authority over beggars and vagrants; by the 25th. Geo. II. cap. 15. he enforces the law as to weights and measures, and is authorised to fine offenders against it upon a view; 27th. Geo. III. cap. 46. authorises him to fine and imprison persons countervening the provisions of that act when brought before him by the market jury; under 14th. Geo. I. cap. 7. no soldier can be quartered on the inhabitants of the Liberty except by his warrant. The manor had also power of paving and lighting its own streets and of levying taxes for that purpose; but this power has been transferred to the Paving-board, and grand juries are now unfrequent in the manor.

The Court-house is a very ancient edifice, and is situated in Great Thomascourt. The Liberty Marshalsea is at a small distance from it in Marrowbone-lane. One of the three export butter-cranes of the port of Dublin belongs to the Liberty, and is regulated by the seneschal, to whom the weighmaster, taster, and other officers are made answerable in case of measurement by the 56th. of Geo. III.

The officers are a seneschal, register, and marshal, who are appointed by Lord Meath, to whose ancestor, William Brabazon, the monastery of Thomascourt, with a carrucate of land called Donower, were granted in 1545, by Henry VIII.

THE LIBERTY AND MANOR OF SAINT SEPULCHRES lies partly within the city and partly in the county of Dublin; and the several other manors belonging to the archbishop of Dublin lie in the counties of Dublin, Kildare, and Wicklow; part of the parishes of Saint Peters, and that of Saint Kevin, in the county of Dublin, and Saint Nicholas without, which lies in the county and the city of Dublin with their streets,* compose the immediate Liberty of Saint Sepulchres. The other manors are Finglas, Swords, Luske, Ballymore, Seneghkile, Castlekevin, Clondalkin, and Rathcoole, over each of

* These streets are New-street, Kevin's-street, Kevin's-port, Cambden-street, Charlotte-street, Portobello, Charlemont-street, Harcourt-street, &c.

which is a magistrate called a portrieve, who is annually appointed by, and sworn before the head seneschal of Saint Sepulchres, at his Easter court-leet and court of oyer and terminer and goal delivery, and for all which manors and liberties there is a common goal in the Liberty.

The grants from the crown to the lord of the manor of Saint Sepulchres, &c. who is the Archbishop of Dublin for the time being, are from a very early period (commencing in the reign of King John), and have been confirmed and extended by several subsequent monarchs, and particularly by a charter granted by King Charles the First, and are of a most extensive nature.

By those charters are granted court-leets, courts-baron, and a court of record, wherein all pleas arising within the jurisdiction are tried without any limitation as to amount. A court of *oyer* and *terminer* and gaol delivery was formerly held twice in every year, at Easter and Michaelmas, wherein all pleas of the crown, with a very few exceptions, were tried, but the criminal jurisdiction has not been exercised for some years past.

By the charters of this liberty it has its own coroners, clerks of the market, assay master, &c.; and no sheriff, coroner, justice of peace, or other officer of the crown, or magistrate of the city of Dublin, or counties of Dublin, Kildare, or Wicklow, are privileged to enter into said Liberties to execute any thing which to their offices belongs, unless in case of default of the seneschal or other officers of said Liberties.

The lord of those manors is entitled, by charter, to have a boat on the river Liffy, to take salmon and other fish. He is also entitled to all the fines imposed on jurors for non attendance at the King's Bench, Common Pleas and Exchequer, commission of oyer and terminer and sessions of the peace of the city and county of Dublin, as well as all forfeited recognizances, amercements, or fines in the places aforesaid.

Some of the principal markets for the supply of Dublin are held within the Liberty of Saint Sepulchres, viz. the great corn, butter, bacon, and fowl market, &c. in Kevin-street, where is also held a straw and hay market, twice a week, on Tuesdays and Saturdays, equal, if not more extensive than Smithfield. The same, with the exception of hay and straw, at Spittalfields. The great meat and vegetable market in Patrick-street, Blackhall-market, and Camden-market, to and from whence, through the city of Dublin, all matters are toll and custom free.

At the Easter and Michaelmas leets, the seneschal swears in a grand and market jury, who remain in office for six months. He also swears in constables for the different wards. His municipal authority is similar to that of the lord mayor within the city, and is regulated by several acts of parliament, and the Liberty is free from the quartering of soldiers, except by the seneschal's authority.

The court of this Liberty was formerly held in the Palace of Saint Sepulchres, which is a very ancient edifice. It is situated in Kevin-street, and was purchased in the year 1803, by Government, for a barrack, from which period to the present there was no fixed court-house or marshalsea. There is now a very handsome court-house erected, with suitable offices for the register, and a marshalsea contiguous thereto, for the Liberty of Saint Sepulchres, and all the other manors of the archbishop in the archdiocese of Dublin, in a new street, which is a continuation of Bride-street, to the new basin at the Grand Canal, and is situated nearly in the centre of the Liberty of Saint Sepulchres.

The officers of the court are a seneschal, register, and marshal, who are appointed by the Archbishop of Dublin, to whom the manor appertains.

DEANERY OF ST. PATRICK'S.—The jurisdiction of these liberties is included in a line drawn along Bride-street, to No. 44, opposite Peter-street, from thence, at the back of the houses, till it issues at the building adjoining the barracks in Kevin-street, which it crosses, embracing the western side of Cathedral-lane to the Cabbage-garden, and from thence to the Dean's-vineyard, on the south side of Long-lane; returning to Kevin-street near New-street, it passes west to Mitre-alley to the Church, round which it enters Patrick-street, and thence to Walker's-alley, from the north part of which it proceeds to Bull-alley again. It is thus an insulated spot, circumscribed by the contiguous manors of Thomas-court and Saint Sepulchres, including a few poor streets.

The seneschal is appointed by the Dean and Chapter of St. Patrick's, but he holds no court. Hence it has become a kind of sanctuary for debtors of small sums. The parties are not amenable to the jurisdiction of the contiguous manors, and cannot be summoned to the city court of conscience. The only court which can take cognizance is that of the Civil Bill-court of the county, which is never resorted to. It is therefore a *refugium peccatorum* for the poor of that neighbourhood.

PRISONS OF DUBLIN.

NEWGATE.

THE old gaol in Corn-market, called Newgate, from its having formerly been one of the city gates, being small, inconvenient, and from its ruinous state, insecure, it was determined to erect a new prison, in which should be united permanence and security, with such an arrangement as would at once prevent the communication of contagious diseases, and contribute to the convenience and comfort of its unhappy inmates, as far as their circumstances will allow. In pursuance of this determination, on the 28th of October 1773, the foundation-stone of the present building, to which has been absurdly given the old appellation of *Newgate*, was laid in the Little Green, a piece of ground in the north part of the city, which was chosen, but we are sorry to add, very injudiciously, for its site, as it was not only insufficient in extent to admit of sufficient yards and other necessary accommodations for the different descriptions of prisoners usually confined in gaols, but environed by dirty streets, and in so low a situation as to render the construction of proper sewers to carry off its filth impracticable.

The expense of this prison, amounting to about £16,000. was defrayed by a tax on the inhabitants of the city of Dublin, aided by a parliamentary grant of £2000.; and though built on a plan drawn by a reputed able architect, the late Mr. Cooley,[*] and under his immediate direction, yet, from its insufficient extent, bad arrangement, and wretched execution, the materials and workmanship being of the worst description, it is a disgrace to the metropolis. In consequence of its being circumscribed on three sides by streets, and on the fourth by the Sessions-house, which absurdly joins it, and prevents all ventilation on that quarter, its limits cannot be enlarged, and from the walls being composed generally of small stones and bad mortar without bond, it is deficient in the essential points of perma-

[*] THOMAS COOLEY was an Englishman, and served his time to Reynolds, a carpenter. He was originally brought to Dublin in 1769, by the committee of merchants, who offered premiums for designs for the Royal Exchange, when his was selected from 61 sent in on that occasion. He received a premium of 100*l*. and was appointed the architect to erect the building. He afterwards made Dublin his constant residence, and built Newgate, the Record-offices on the Inns Quay, the Marine School, and the little Chapel in the Park. He imitated the manner of Inigo Jones, but did not always succeed as well as his great model. He died in Anglesea-street, Dublin, of a bilious fever, in 1784, at the age of 44.

nence and security, which, it is to be lamented, can be attained only by rebuilding it from the foundation.

It is a quadrangular pile of three stories, 170 feet in front and 127 in depth. The principal front, which is to the east, forming one side of Green-street, consists of a centre break of mountain granite rusticated and crowned with a pediment: on each side is a plain façade of black limestone, and at the external angles are four round towers, through which the filth of the gaol was intended to be conveyed, and which were of course to contain the necessaries: these, however, are not at present appropriated to this purpose. When the commissioners for inspecting the gaols of Ireland visited this prison in 1808, one had been roofed in, and converted into a room, and of the other three, which were open at the top, one formed the gaoler's back yard, and the other two were useless, though from their situation and dimensions, being 17 feet in their interior diameter, they might be converted into common halls, in which this goal is shamefully deficient. It is the prison for criminals of all descriptions for the county of the city of Dublin, and for persons confined under coroners' writs, and is also occasionally the receptacle for transports from many of the inland gaols of Ireland, who are sent hither previous to their being sent on shipboard; on which occasions it is often extremely crowded.

In the front are the guard-room, gaoler's apartments, hospital, common hall, long room, chapel, &c. and in the other sides of the quadrangle are the cells, which are universally 12 feet by 8, injudiciously disposed, badly ventilated, those in the upper stories accessible by narrow staircases, and all opening off corridores only three feet four inches wide. The interior area, totally insufficient to admit of proper and separate courts for the sundry classes of prisoners, is divided into two nearly equal parts by a passage for persons who visit the prisoners, with whom they can converse through grated apertures in the walls on either side. The part on the south, 61 feet by 56, and of which the centre was in 1808 occupied by an offensive necessary without a sewer, formed a court-yard for all the male prisoners under criminal charges of every description, who were crowded together from the number of 8 to 13 persons in the same cell: off this opened their only common hall, 20 feet by 17, and here consequently the tried and the untried, those charged with felonies, and with petty offences, and even persons under sentence of death, were all indiscriminately mingled, without any attempt at classification. The northern part of the area is divided into two yards, one 54 feet by 43, off which are the cells for prisoners of a better description; the other only 54 feet by 17, for females, where there was, in 1808, the same mixture of prisoners as in the male side; the untried and the convicted promiscuously herded together, and in general from 10 to 14 women of all descriptions in a cell 12 feet by 8. The hospital, 20 feet by 17, was injudiciously situated, ill contrived, ill ventilated, and destitute of hot and cold baths. The chapel, situated in an upper story, was accessible with difficulty by narrow winding stairs; and there was no room set apart for the chaplain, in which he could hold private communication with a prisoner under any circumstances.

The commissioners found that the excessively crowded state of the cells on the ground floor, was occasioned by a great proportion of those on the upper floors being no longer used, under a pretence of their comparative insecurity, but in reality, to save the keeper and his deputies the inconvenience of an encrease of trouble in attending to them: they found the hospital totally destitute of proper bedsteads, bedding, linen, and other articles essentially necessary for the sick: the surgical department badly attended; the cells also throughout the prison without bedsteads, beds, and bedding, and the persons of the prisoners, with the cells themselves, extremely filthy. At the same time it appeared from the testimony of the chaplain, that from a total want of proper discipline and supervision, not only insubordination and anarchy had universally prevailed in former years, but that frequent instances of robbery had occurred, which was not only permitted but encouraged, and the plunder shared with the turnkeys and watchmen; and that even rape and murder had been perpetrated within the prison:* that a salutary change, however, had latterly taken place, in

* Among the acts of misconduct charged on this prison, was one of a nature so atrocious as to be hardly credible. During the unhappy period of the rebellion, many persons were confined here in a situation of life above the ordinary class of criminals. As attainting the blood and exposing the bodies of traitors, were considered usages more consonant to the principles and practices of feudal and barbarous than of modern and more enlightened times, there were few recent instances in Ireland of either, and the remains of these unfortunate men were generally ordered to be restored to their friends after their persons had undergone the sentence of the law. But of this melancholy indulgence their friends were often deprived, by the brutal avarice of the gaoler and his assistants. An exorbitant price was demanded for their bodies, often greater than the means of their relatives, exhausted in their trial and defence, could provide; and as their remains became putrid, the demand was encreased with an

consequence of the laudable conduct of the keepers, particularly of the deputy gaoler, under whose more immediate supervision the care of the prison necessarily falls; but though many improvements had taken place, and that the conduct of the prisoners was at present, with a very few exceptions, decent and inoffensive, yet numerous evils still existed, which were the necessary result of the injudicious and confined structure of the gaol; that of these, the principal were a want of any kind of industrious employment, a general admixture of persons of all descriptions, and a want of personal cleanliness, evils which, in his opinion, might be mitigated, though not totally removed by enforcing the occupation of the vacant cells. It appeared also to the commissioners that the allowance of provisions, which were good in their kind, was regularly and fairly distributed, and that the practice of putting on irons (except in cases of gross misbehaviour, or of persons under sentence of death) has been almost entirely discontinued.

Such are the principal features of the state of this gaol in 1808, as represented by the commissioners, who so ably and faithfully discharged the trust reposed in them by Government. Their report was followed by an act of the imperial parliament in 1810, for correcting abuses and redressing grievances in the gaols of Ireland, at once distressing to humanity, and degrading to the national character. Under this act a happy reform has taken place in the prisons of this metropolis, a reform for which we are in a great measure indebted to the indefatigable exertions and unwearied humanity of the late Right Hon. Secretary, Mr. Pole, whose repeated visits and personal inspection has brought about a change in those regions of filth, disorder, and misery, that no delegated authority could probably have produced.

We visited this gaol in December 1812, and found that a great reformation indeed had taken place. In consequence of the cells on the two upper floors having been taken into use, it was no longer crowded, and sufficient room had also been obtained for establishing distinct infirmaries and convalescent rooms for both males and females, small indeed, and from necessity

arbitrary exaction proportioned to the anxious affection of the survivors. In this way the head of an unfortunate young gentleman, as much distinguished by his genius and talents as by his unhappy misapplication of them, was detained, and at length sold to his friends for the sum of £50.! We relate the circumstance as it is reported, without pledging ourselves for its authenticity. The report of the commissioners on the former practices of this prison renders it not improbable, though we 'trust' the improvements effected, will make such a recurrence impossible.

imperfectly ventilated. Three of the round towers, before useless, had been roofed, divided into two stories, supplied with fire-places, and converted into six comfortable common halls and kitchens, an accommodation in which this prison was miserably defective. To remedy as far as possible the defect of sewers, the privies are frequently cleansed. The beds and bedding were good. A part of the male felons' yard also has been walled off, and appropriated to convicts under rule of transportation; but no farther attempt at classification has been made, or from the imperfections of the prisons, is indeed possible.

To the zeal and humanity of the Rev. Mr. Jones, the late local inspector, this prison is much indebted, and his last report is very favourable to its improvement. It states, that no lingering or infectious disease had occurred within the last twelve months, and every practicable care was taken to prevent it by cleanliness; fresh straw was plentifully supplied once a month, and an allowance of soap once a week, which with the daily sweeping and cleansing every cell and corridor, gave an appearance of cleanliness and comfort to the prison at large, and of health and decency to the prisoners. The entire prison undergoes a general white-washing at least three times in the year, no accumulation of filth or other nuisance is suffered to exist within it, and there is a commodious bath also, with an abundant supply of water at all times. The provisions are of a wholsome and nutritious quality, and the bread always good and well baked, of which a loaf of three pounds weight is supplied to each prisoner, whose indigent circumstances require it, on Sundays, Mondays, and Wednesdays, with an adequate allowance of potatoes on Fridays, together with herrings during the winter months, and milk during the summer. No refractory or disorderly spirit had appeared in this gaol during his inspection, with one or two exceptions of a trivial nature, in which cases, recourse was had to a few hours close confinement, which produced the desired effect; nor has it been found necessary to resort to such coercion a second time. The peaceable and orderly conduct of the numerous offenders was rather surprising, the use of irons being totally dispensed with, expect in cases of capital convictions. It might be truly stated, that every attention was paid to supply their reasonable wants, and to promote their necessary comforts, which seemed to produce a more salutary effect on their habits and morals, than rigorous or coercive severity. The conduct of the gaoler and his deputy, seemed to blend the strictest vigilance with humane indulgence, and great mildness with a faithful discharge of their arduous and important duties.

Notwithstanding all that has been done (and much indeed has been done), to promote the comfort of the unhappy inmates of this prison, yet when we consider its insufficient extent, its want of effective sewers, its imperfect ventilation, its low, damp, and confined situation, its insecurity, occasioned by the bad materials and wretched execution of the building, and above all, the impossibility of classification, solitary confinement and industry, every friend of humanity must wish to see it rebuilt in a more elevated, airy, and unconfined situation, on a larger scale, and on a better plan.

The following are the sums which have been presented for the support of this prison, at the Michaelmas and Easter terms, for three years.

Michaelmas 1809, 2799*l*. 0*s*. 10*d*.   1810, 2149*l*. 8*s*. 3*d*.   1811, 1800*l*. 3*s*. 4*d*.
Easter   1810, 2146 14 3   1811, 2482 12 2   1812, 1218 19 6

This statement we give with pleasure, as it shews that, while the gaol has been improved, and the condition of its inmates greatly ameliorated, the spirit of economy has been progressive, and the reduction of expense in the last year great indeed.

The following are the officers and servants of Newgate, with their respective salaries.

Gaoler, £400. per annum; deputy-gaoler, £113. 15*s*.; five watchmen, £260. or £52. each; city architect, £56. 17*s*. 6*d*.; local inspector, £200.; chaplain of the established church, £100.; dissenting chaplain, £100.; Roman catholic chaplain, £100.; physician, £300.; surgeon, £227. 10*s*. Total amount of salaries, £1858 2*s*. 6*d*.

SHERIFF'S PRISON.

This prison, situated in the little Green, to the northward of the Sessions-house, was built in 1794, by grand jury presentment, with the good intention of preventing the abuses of sponging houses, and it appears to have answered, in some degree, this laudable purpose, the fees demanded in sponging houses having been much more exorbitant than those in the sheriff's prison, and many cruelties having been practiced in the former which are not exercised in the latter. But it has by no means afforded an adequate remedy, the building being totally insufficient in extent for the number of prisoners, who, although none are confined here whose debts are under £10. often amount to 130.

This prison consists of a centre building and two parallel wings, three stories above ground in each, and a range of cells, three under each wing below. In the centre building there is a large stone staircase, and lobbies looking into the yard behind. When the commissioners visited this prison in 1808, five of the cells were appropriated for the reception of the poorer class of prisoners; the other, under the north wing, being near the privy, was so extremely filthy as to be unfit for the occupation of any human creature: they were all deplorable habitations—dark, damp, noxious, and badly ventilated. The last inconvenience was in some degree mitigated, in consequence of the windows being wholly unglazed; but the excessive cold occasioned by this circumstance induced the prisoners to stuff the apertures with straw and other materials. For these cells no rent was payable to the keeper, but some of the occupiers exacted sums under the denomination of rent, from others. Two of the cells under the centre building were occupied as a tap; the other as a common receptacle for all the dirt of the prison, the offensive effluvia from which diffused itself through the entire building. In the cells occupied as lodging rooms, there were neither beds, bedsteads, bedding, blankets, straw, or any allowance of fuel or provisions supplied at the public expense; the necessities of the prisoners were relieved only by casual donations, the subscriptions of some wealthier prisoners, and sometimes by a distribution of bread and meat at Christmas, under the superintendance of the Lord Mayor and Sheriffs of the preceding year, arising out of a charitable fund created by the will of a person named Powell, who had been himself a prisoner.*

· The windows of the lobbies, and those of the staircase and centre building were all unglazed. The rooms above ground in the centre building, nine in number, were let unfurnished, at 7s. 7d. and furnished, at £1. 2s. 9d. per week: the rooms in the wings, 18 in number, were let unfurnished at 3s. 9½d. per week; but greater rents than these were exacted by the original occupiers of all these apartments, from persons whom they accommodated with share of their rooms.

In this prison, at that period, there was no common hall, no chapel, or provision for a chaplain, no infirmary, no wards for solitary confinement of

* See page 902.

the refractory, and no separate accommodation for male and female prisoners: to which we may add, that there were no rules or regulations for its internal government or means of enforcing them, no regular fund for repairing it, and no legal provision for the maintenance of the poorest class of debtors. The keeper, who is appointed from year to year, by successive sheriffs, and who enters into security to the amount of £10,000. conditioned for the performance of his duty, the safe keeping of the prisoners, and the indemnification of the sheriffs, rented his office, to which no salary was then annexed, from the sub-sheriff, at £100 *per annum*, in direct violation of an existing law; and was, of course, dependent for remuneration on the fees of his office, with the rent of rooms, among which we must include those let to the tapster, at £108. 8s. 10d. *per annum*: and hence arose a strong temptation to encourage the consumption of spirituous liquors, and a direct emolument was derived from the riot and dissoluteness of the prison.

When we visited this prison in December 1812, we found that a considerable degree of reform had taken place. The keeper no longer rented his office; he received a salary; and appeared from the general testimony of the prisoners, as well as of the local visitor, to be a man of humanity, and strictly attentive to the duties of his office. The windows were, with one exception, framed and glazed; printed rules were hung up in the corridores, which served as places for the prisoners to walk in when the weather was severe or wet; an infirmary had been provided, with necessary medicines, and proper medical and surgical attendance; the lobbies, rooms, and corridores were clean, and chaplains of the established, dissenting, and Roman catholic religions, performed divine service in the lobby every Sabbath day. The inconveniences and abuses, however, arising from the insufficient extent and bad plan of the building, unfortunately remain. There is no common hall; no separation of sexes; the privies in the wings are still offensive; and the wretched cells of the poor prisoners, though kept clean, are cold, damp, and ill ventilated; and their inmates without any allowance of food, beds, bedding, straw, or fuel; the necessities of these prisoners are relieved only by casual donations, the subscriptions of some of the wealthier prisoners, and sometimes by a distribution of Powell's bread and meat at Christmas; to which we may add, that notwithstanding the prohibition of the sale of spirituous liquors in the tap-room, they are constantly introduced through the front windows: an attempt was indeed made to prevent this abuse, by securing those windows by a strong and close iron wire work, but this has been torn down, and the evil continues.

FOUR COURTS MARSHALSEA.

This prison is in an elevated and healthy situation, adjoining Thomas-street, built of good materials, but on a scale much too small. This being a national prison, used for the debtors of all Ireland, who are occasionally removed hither from every county in this part of the united kingdom, in the hope of their obtaining the benefit of the maintenance and insolvent acts, it is imperative on the marshal, to receive them into the court yard in any numbers, though the prison be ever so inadequate to accommodate them.

Exclusive of the marshal's house and offices, which are his private property, it occupies an area of nearly 180 feet by 120, divided into an upper and lower court-yard; but the exterior wall having no perforations (though such might be made without danger or insecurity to the establishment) the ventilation of the apartments is extremely bad; in consequence of this total exclusion of thorough air. The marshal's house is on the south side of the upper court-yard, round the other sides of which are the principal buildings; the deputy's apartments, the tap, and three rooms let with it, with the entrance or hatchways, being on the east, and the guard-rooms and common halls on the west and north, over which are the prisoners' rooms. In the lower court-yard is a detached building intended for an infirmary, one room of which, nearly 20 feet by 17, is the chapel: here also are the privies, a ball court, and a common bath.

When the commissioners visited this prison in 1808, two rooms only of the infirmary were appropriated to the use of the sick; that which was designed for the hospital kitchen, nearly 20 feet by 17, was let by the marshal to a hatchman or turnkey, who underlet it to prisoners, of whom there were eleven, besides children, then sleeping in it: another apartment of the infirmary, of similar dimensions, was occupied by female prisoners of all descriptions, six of whom were then confined in it, being the only place within the precincts of the Marshalsea allotted to their separate accommodation. On the ground floor, a third room under the kitchen, originally designed for a charnel house, and in its construction manifestly adapted for this purpose, was let by the marshal to another hatchman, who underlet it to the poorest description of prisoners, who paid 5d. a night for the wretched accommodation of straw and a scanty portion of blanket. The privy, in the same yard, was in a most filthy state; and what was formerly a bath was then entirely choaked up, and wholly useless.

Exclusive of three rooms let to the tapster, and which, not excepting the very tap room itself, were occupied at night by prisoners, who rented them from the tapster, there are in this prison 25 apartments set by the marshal at a weekly rent, and seven common halls for the men; these latter, only 16 feet wide by from 18 to 20 long, on the ground floor, and flagged, they found greatly crowded, some of them having from 13 to 19 men lodging in them. All these halls were filthy and loathsome beyond description; into them all debtors on their first committal were obliged to go, until they could obtain a room to rent, or share of a room from some other prisoner: in these miserable halls all the windows were broken; and here, crowded together, all such prisoners as could not afford to pay for a room, or the share of one, were obliged to lodge.

Such was the state of this prison in 1808. We are happy, however, to state, that on visiting it on the 30th of November 1812, we found that a complete reform had taken place, and that "in the short space of 18 months (to use the words of the inspector-general), from being a scene of filth and disorder, it had been converted into a place of comparative comfort and tranquillity, which proves the wisdom and efficacy of the act of 30th Geo. III. and of the rules and regulations formed by the Lord Chief Justice, and the other judges of the Court of King's Bench, for its government and discipline." The too confined area of this prison had been enlarged by an additional yard on the west, 126 feet by 42, in the centre of which an insulated building of one story contained an excellent cold bath, and convenient privies, with well constructed sewers: this yard is kept perfectly neat and clean, forms a commodious place for walking, and is open during certain hours only.

The upper yard, which is also perfectly neat and clean, has two pumps, with an ample supply of good water, and in the lower yard a separate building has been erected, containing six comfortable apartments, supplied with beds and bedding, and capable of accommodating 48 pauper prisoners, who are not only perfectly rent free, but when their indigence appears to require it, supplied by government with bread. The chapel, though small, is neat and convenient; the infirmary and convalescent room, supplied with good beds and bedding, are well ventilated, and in the same yard two cells have been constructed for the solitary confinement of turbulent and refractory prisoners. Over these, a scaffolding has been erected, with convenient seats, where the prisoners are permitted in their turns to view the amusements of the ball yard, which they overlook, and where, from their elevated situation, they breathe, notwithstanding the height of the exterior wall, a pure and uninterrupted air: the ball court, which is neatly flagged, is closed on the Sabbath, and during the hours of prayer on other days. The hall for walking in is floored with brick, as is also the working hall of similar dimensions, and in both, as they are liberally supplied with coals, constant fires are kept during the winter months.* The tap has been put under strict regulations, the sale or introduction of spirits except for medical purposes is positively forbidden, and malt drink and cyder are the only liquors permitted to be sold. In effect, perfect order and cleanliness are at present visible in every department of the Four Courts Marshalsea, and the general conduct of the prisoners such, as shews that they are sensible how much they owe to the interference of the legislature.

It is perhaps to be lamented, that the observation of an intelligent architect, Mr. Francis Johnston, " that perforations in the exterior wall, and also in the central wall of the interior buildings might be made without producing danger or insecurity to the establishment," has not been attended to: hence every apartment in this prison is destitute of thorough air, the infirmary convalescent room, with three of the six pauper rooms excepted, which are partially ventilated, having windows in two contiguous sides: this want of thorough air is very perceptible. The approach to the Four Courts Marshalsea by a narrow lane, is an inconvenience which Mr. Pole, who has done so much for the Dublin prisons, was anxious to have removed.

This building, surrounded by distilleries, breweries, and stores, cannot

* In consequence of the coal-vaults of this establishment not being sufficient to contain a large supply of coals sent in by Government, they were stowed in the working hall, which was thus perverted from its proper destination. It had not latterly, however, been made use of, as there had not, for a considerable time, been any working tradesmen confined here, who were inclined to be industrious.

1058   THE HISTORY OF

easily be extended farther. It is certainly too small to answer as a general depot for the confined debtors of Ireland. The number of prisoners confined here sometimes have amounted to 270.*

CITY MARSHALSEA.

This prison, adjoining the Sessions-house, in Green-street, was built by the corporation of the city of Dublin, by contract with Mr. William Pemberton, who finished it in 1804, at an expense of £2174. 14s. 6d. The contract was badly executed, as it was already out of repair when visited by the commissioners in 1808. In this prison are confined persons under process of the Lord Mayor's court, and the Court of Conscience.

There are two common halls, where prisoners pay one penny per night for lodging; a chapel, hospital, nurse-tender's room, doctor's room; four rooms in the occupation of the keeper, and seven for prisoners who can afford to pay a higher rent. There is no stated public allowance for beds,

* A plan has been proposed by the Rev. Mr. Archer, inspector-general of prisons, to remedy this inconvenience. " The two following measures would tend to prevent this prison from being crowded, and consequently render it capable of conveniently lodging all that may be committed to it. 1st, A clause empowering the marshal to grant a license to prisoners to go out at certain hours in the day time during term, within certain limits, as is the practice in the King's Bench and Fleet prisons in London. The marshal being properly secured for the safe return of the prisoners, who should pay a small fine for this indulgence. As the Four Courts are not remote from this prison, the limits should comprehend them: this would facilitate the adjustment of many particulars which occur to those in embarrassed circumstances, and be found perhaps eventually as advantageous to the creditor as it would be beneficial to the confined debtor, who would be thus enabled to compromise his own affairs, without being compelled, as is now the case, to employ a gaol solicitor, who too often proves to be equally the adversary of plaintiff and defendant.—2dly, A clause which might be annexed to the maintenance act, 50th Geo. III. and which would extend relief to a very poor description of prisoners, who have in that act been somehow overlooked—that is, those persons who are committed on decrees and orders from the inferior courts: it would be therefore desirable to empower and require recorders of cities and towns, barristers of counties, and other more subordinate officers of manor courts, to extend the benefit of that act to imprisoned debtors in the county gaols, on their own application or that of others, each prisoner to be examined in that court only from whence the process is issued. A clause for that purpose would be attended with advantage to debtor and creditor: the parties would in that case, without inconvenience or expense, be present; the assessors or magistrates, being acquainted with the persons, could not easily be deceived; frauds and expense would be prevented: justice administered, and the real object of the bill, the unfortunate imprisoned pauper, would be quickly released, whilst the fraudulent swindler or solvent debtor, would be compelled to fulfil his engagements. If these two measures were adopted, applications for insolvent bills would be rendered less frequent."

THE CITY OF DUBLIN. 1059

bedding, blankets, fuel, or provisions of any sort, for the poorer prisoners, who depend for their supply of these necessaries upon casual charity: they are generally of the poorest order of society, confined for small debts, of from 15 to 40 shillings, on Tholsel warrants, and many of them objects of compassion. A benefaction of the interest of £1000, for releasing poor prisoners has been lately deposited in the hands of the lord. mayor for that purpose, by order of the Rt. Hon. Secretary of State.

There is a pipe to supply the prisoners with water, but no pump or bath; there is a privy, but without a sewer; and in 1808 it appears that the windows of the corridores were unglazed, that the common halls were destitute of bedsteads, forms, and tables, and that there was not any separate accommodation for males and females. The keeper exclusive of his legal fees, and the rent of the common halls and other rooms, receives from the corporation a salary of £20. *per annum.*

KILMAINHAM GAOL.

This prison, which is the gaol of the county of Dublin for debtors as well as felons, is in an elevated and commanding situation, near the stream that runs by the village of Kilmainham, which affords a great facility for an abundant supply of that essential article, wholesome water. It is large, well built, and on a good plan. The main building 178 by 102 feet, consist of two quadrangles, enclosing two court-yards, 55 feet by 40 each, one for persons confined for capital offences, the other for the condemned; and round it are judiciously disposed eight other spacious yards, three of which are supplied with pumps, the whole secured by a substantial lofty wall, which encloses a rectangular space of 283 feet by 190. The central pile separating the interior court-yards, with the eastern and western ends, rise three stories; of these, the former contains the keeper's apartments, hall, chapel, and principal staircases; and in the two latter are the common halls and work-rooms, with the infirmaries, which are placed judiciously in the upper story, and are well ventilated. These are connected by intermediate buildings of two stories only, which contain the cells, 52 in number, 10 feet by 6 each; and opening off corridores 5 feet wide, which are well ventilated by grated openings in the exterior walls; and exclusive of these, a detached building, containing 4 cells, for those under sentence of death, occupies the centre of the condemned yard. In the centre of the front which faces the north is a detached building, containing the hall of entrance, door-keeper's office, and the guard-room; as this building is connected to the prison by a well secured passage only, the guard has no communication with the prisoners, a circumstance which should be provided for in every gaol.

The walls of this prison are of limestone, in consequence of which the cells are often damp in wet weather, particularly in the lower story: though it is well supplied with privies situated in the angles of the building, yet from a shameful neglect in keeping the forcing pump and pipes in order, they have been frequently offensive, notwithstanding every effort that could be used: the circumstance also of the condemned yard being overlooked by two ranges of cells, is objectionable. With these exceptions, this prison is, in its construction, provided with all the requisites for carrying into effect a complete classification of prisoners, according to their several offences; a perfect separation of persons confined for debt and petty offences, from felons, and of male from female prisoners; and affords sufficient room for the introduction of a system of industry into the prison.

This gaol has also in some measure experienced the salutary effects of the humane interference of Mr. Pole; as to him it is indebted for the introduction of a system of industry within its walls; the continually crowded state of Newgate has occasioned the removal of several convicts guilty of minor offences to the Penitentiary established here under his directions, several of whom are employed in weaving and other handicraft occupations. The experiment seems to promise success, as some whose exemplary conduct has given expectations of amendment have been liberated on bail, and others have been admitted into the army and navy. The convicts also from the northern parts of Ireland have been latterly transmitted to this prison, previous to transportation:* this has been an advantageous change,

* " If a depot," says the Rev. Mr. Archer, " were established at Cork, whither all convicts should be moved four times in the year from the city and county of Dublin, and twice, immediately after the assizes, in each year, from the other counties, it would be attended with great public advantage, and at the same time save government the expence of removal, which might be paid by the respective counties from whence they were transferred. An infinity of anguish and indisposition to the wretched convicts would be thus prevented, as it is a fact, that they often sustain more misery in the tedious, difficult, and dangerous coasting voyage from Dublin to Cork, than in the greatly longer voyage from thence to New

THE CITY OF DUBLIN.

as formerly they were deposited in Newgate, which was not sufficiently capacious for their reception, until a ship could be provided to convey them to Cork for transportation to New South Wales.

The county allowance of bread and milk is extended to the debtors, as well as the felons of this prison, and the distribution is regularly superintended by the chaplain, who is also local inspector.

DUBLIN PENITENTIARY.

The first stone of this large edifice was laid by the Duke of Richmond, in 1812, and it is proceeding rapidly to its completion. It is situated contiguous to the House of Industry, and presents its front to Grand Gorman-lane, which extends 700 feet. It is plain and substantial, formed of hewn blocks of limestone. In the centre of the front is a very bold pediment of 80 feet in length. The cornice of this is formed of mountain granite, which contrast well with and enlivens the dark blue of the limestone, and gives to the whole a grand and not inelegant appearance, perhaps more cheerful than comports with the purpose of the institution. The depth of the building is 400 feet, and the whole stands on an area of three acres. It is intended as a substitute for Botany Bay, and those criminals who cannot be reclaimed by the discipline of the house, will ultimately be transported thither. It is formed on Howard's plan of solitary confinement, with a gradual progress to society, as the convict becomes reclaimed; with this view the interior of this immense building is arranged: the convict passes from a solitary cell to an apartment containing 10 or more persons of his own rank of moral improvement, with whom he associates, entirely separate from the rest of the buildings; from which he is advanced to large workshops, and less restraint, as his conduct merits. The cells are in the rear,

South Wales. Moreover, the immediate removal after conviction would be attended with other beneficial consequences: these unhappy people would be at once cut off from their vicious associates, and be freed from the evil councils of their ill-advising friends, who continue to visit them while they remain in the country prisons. The certainty also of this partial transportation to the extremity of Ireland, would terrify other offenders: the gaols would not be broken, and young culprits would not be so expeditiously corrupted as they are by these convicts, who are permitted to remain, often for years, in the county goals, before sentence is carried into execution."

and the shops in the more cheerful part of the edifice. The estimate of the building is £40,000.*

HOUSE OF CORRECTION.

This edifice is intended as a substitute for the very poor and inadequate House of Correction in James-street. It stands on the Circular road, near New-street, with its front to the road, and its rear to the canal. The aspect of this building has more of that appropriate gloom which corresponds with the purposes for which it is intended, than the former. It is ponderous and massive, and has a marked air of precautionary contrivance to prevent a crime or to punish it. Before the main body of the building is the keeper's lodge, which stands in advance like the outworks of a fortress; at the angles are projecting turrets, which command the main walls on the outside, as bastions flank the curtains; in them centinels are to be placed, who will effectually prevent any attempts at escape, either openly or secretly under these turrets. Outside the main building, but within the enclosing wall, are rope makers walks, under the eye of the centinels. On the front of the main building is this inscription " Cease to do evil, and learn to do well ;" and over the gateway of the keeper's lodge, are emblazoned on a shield, the city arms, three blazing castles, with this appropriate motto,
Obedienta Civium Urbis felicitas.

In this edifice it is intended to confine all young vagrants of both sexes, and the interior is arranged so that each sex may be kept distinct, and both be separated into different classes, and employed in various departments of industry. The whole stands upon an acre and a half of ground, besides three for a garden, and will contain 400 persons. The estimate of the expence is £28,000., and is raised by presentment, amounting to £1000. laid on the city of Dublin, at the presenting term of Easter and Michaelmas by the grand jury. The first stone was laid by the Duke of Richmond, in 1813.

* See House of Industry, p. 629.

CORPORATION.

The first charter of the city of Dublin, conferred by Henry II. gave the city of Dublin to the citizens of Bristol. A variety of subsequent charters modified this original grant, and the constitution of the corporation was altered by rules and regulations made at sundry times.* In the year 1760, however, an act passed repealing some of the former rules, and establishing those by which it is at present regulated. It consists of a lord mayor and 24 aldermen, sitting by themselves, who form an upper house, and the sheriffs, with the sheriffs' peers, not exceeding 48, with the representatives of 25 corporations, not exceeding 96, form the lower house. The lord mayor was originally denominated Provost in 1308, and was first called by his present appellation in 1665. He is elected annually from the board of aldermen, on the first quarter assembly in April, and continues lord mayor elect till the 30th of September following, when he is sworn into office,† and continues chief magistrate of the city till the ensuing year. The board of aldermen are chosen for life from among the sheriffs' peers, by the Lord Mayor, Aldermen, and Common Council. They are all magistrates for the city, and, with the Lord Mayor and Recorder, are judges of oyer and terminer for capital offences or misdemeanors committed in the city. The common council are elected in November every third year, and the members continue only for the three years following, except the sheriffs' peers, who are perpetual members. In the commons the sheriffs for the time being preside. They are two in number, annually elected from the commons, though any quali-

* For a synopsis of those charters, see page 377, et seq., for a full detail of the old and new rules of the corporation, see page 214, and for various anecdotes, see Annals, passim. We present a fac-simile of the original charter, recently brought forward by the record commission, and obligingly communicated by the secretary; it is a curious document.

† On this occasion, the Lord Mayor and Aldermen, accompanied by the Recorder, proceed in state from the Mansion-house to the Exhibition-house in William-street, where they are joined by the Commons, with all the corporation officers in full costume—hence they march in procession to the Castle, accompanied by music, and the battle-axe guards, where they are entertained with cake and wine, and the Lord Mayor is sworn into office before the Lord-lieutenant, and hears a charge on his duty from one of the judges of the land. From hence they proceed to the Sessions-house, where they open the courts, and swear the high sheriffs. The evening is concluded by an entertainment at the Mansion-house, at which the Viceroy is generally present.

fied freeman is eligible. They swear before their election that they are worth £2000. above their just debts. Persons who have served the office of sheriff, or who have paid a fine for exemption, become sheriffs' peers. The portions of the civic parliament, thus composed, always sit apart, except at the interval of three years, when they form one body, to examine the qualifications and returns of the members of the common council. The commons are elected by the several guilds. The following exhibits the number each guild returns, the name of its patron, its order of precedence, and the hall in which it assembles. There were originally but 20 guilds, the five last were subsequently added; that of the apothecaries was not incorporated till the year 1745.

No. of Representatives.	Guild.	Patron.	Halls.
31	Merchants	Holy Trinity	Exhibition House, William-street
4	Tailors	St. John Baptist	Back-lane
4	Smiths	St. Loy	Ditto
2	Barbers	St. Mary Magdalene	Ditto
4	Bakers	St. Anne	Audeon's Arch
3	Butchers	The Virgin Mary	Ditto
3	Carpenters	Fraternity of the Blessed Virgin	Ditto
4	Shoemakers	Guild of the Blessed V. Mary	Ditto
3	Saddlers	Ditto	Back-lane
2	Cooks	St. James the Apostle	Morrison's, Dawson-street
2	Tanners	St. Nicholas	Greenhide Crane
2	Tallow-chandlers	St. George	Audeon's Arch
2	Glovers and Skinners	Blessed Virgin Mary	Back-lane
3	Weavers	Ditto	Combe
2	Sheermen and Dyers	St. Nicholas	Ditto
4	Goldsmiths	All Saints	Golden-lane
2	Coopers	St. Patrick	Stafford-street
2	Feldt-makers		Audeon's Arch
3	Cutlers, Painters, Stationers, &c.	St. Luke	Capel-street
2	Bricklayers	St. Bartholomnew	Audeon's Arch
2	Hosiers	St. George	Weavers'-hall, Combe
2	Curriers	St. Nicholas	Back-lane
4	Brewers	St. Andrew	Morrison's, Dawson-street
2	Joiners		
2	Apothecaries	St. Luke	Mary's-street

Of these, the tailors, carpenters, weavers, goldsmiths, cutlers, and apothecaries, only, have halls built by and appertaining to their respective guilds. The rest meet at places, not halls, or use those of the guilds to which they belong. The Tailors'-hall is one of the oldest in Dublin; it is situated in Back-lane, and used for a variety of other purposes. It is ornamented with some paintings, among which are portraits of Charles I.

THE CITY OF DUBLIN.

William III. and Dean Swift.*—The tailors claim to be the oldest guild, and originally took precedence of all others, but resigned it to the merchants by compact between them. They had also a considerable estate in the county of Wicklow, but improvidently let it for ever at a small rent.

The Weavers'-hall is on the Combe. It is an ancient edifice, but rebuilt. The interior of the hall is spacious, and contains also many portraits, particularly one of the earliest of the Latouche family, who settled in Dublin, and was a member of this corporation.†

The original charter of the weavers was granted by Edward I. in 25th year of his reign, but James II. when he seized upon the franchises of the city, dissolved all the former charters, by judgment obtained in the Court of Exchequer. He granted to the weavers a new one, in the 4th year of his reign, and united them with the clothiers, who were before attached to the sheermen and dyers. In a similar manner he dissolved the charter of Edward I. granted to the tanners, and united them by a new one with the curriers, who before were a separate guild. Formerly, every person following a trade or craft in Dublin, and not free of that corporation, paid a certain sum, called quarterage, for so doing, whence they were called quarter brothers, but in the year 1782, this tax was repealed, and since that period every person exercises his trade at his own discretion. The quarterage was applied to defray the expences of riding the franchises and other incidents of the guilds.

The franchises were a perambulation performed every three years to ascertain the boundaries of the city jurisdiction.‡ They were formerly rode with much pomp, the guilds vying with each other in the richness of their decoration, and people assembling from different parts of the kindom to be spectators; but they have for some years been entirely discontinued,

---

* There is also an old painting on wood, representing a man clothing some naked figures; an inscription indicates that it is St. Hommebon of Cremona, a tailor, who gave " all his gaine and labour to the poor," and was canonised for his holy life and miracles by Innocent the III.

† There is besides, a curious portrait of Geo. II. executed in tapestry, when that manufactory was attempted to be introduced into Dublin about 60 years ago; an inscription imports that it was executed

By John Vanbeaver,

Liberty weaver.

‡ For a full account of the perambulation of these limits, both ancient and modern, see page 90, et seq.

6 U

though the Lord Mayor performs the perambulation every three years through the accustomed boundaries. The day selected is in the first week in August, when the tide is lowest. He proceeds into the sea between the Black Rock and the Light-house, as far as his horse can wade, and hurling a lance, his jurisdiction is supposed to extend as far as his cast reaches. In performing this perambulation, a singular custom is still observed. In the year 1660, a valuable gold collar had been presented to the city by Charles II. Eight years after, Sir Michael Creagh was Lord Mayor of Dublin, and during his mayoralty he absconded, carrying with him this valuable collar, which, from the shape of its links, was called the collar of SS.

It is a part of ancient usage to open by proclamation certain courts at the city gates, and here the delinquent is regularly called on to appear. * Sir Michael, however, never having since appeared, or returned the collar, in the year 1697, Bartholomew Vanhomrigh, † then lord mayor, obtained from William III. a new collar of SS for the city, valued at that time at a £1000. This has been preserved with care, and is that worn by the chief magistrate of Dublin at this day; it has the miniature portrait of the royal donor attached to it.

The Mansion-house is a low edifice, unworthy of its appropriation, and ill according with the other public buildings in the metropolis.‡ It is situated

---

* By the following citation.—" Sir Michael Creagh, Sir Michael Creagh, Sir Michael Creagh, come " and appear at this court of our Lord the King, holden before the right honourable Lord Mayor of " the city of Dublin, or you will be outlawed." At Essex Gate this is repeated nine times.

† It is not generally known, or at least not noticed, we believe, in any edition of Swift's works or life, that this worthy alderman was father to the celebrated Vanessa. Lord Orrery says, in his Life of Swift, that " Vanessa's father was Bartholomew Vanhomrigh, a Dutch merchant, who went to Ireland on the Revolution, and was made a commissioner of the revenue by William III." p. 34. At the time he obtained the chain from his Majesty, he was, as appears by the annals, a commissioner of the revenue, as well as an alderman. He purchased an estate at Celbridge, near Dublin, which descended to his family. Miss Vanhomrigh lived with her mother in London when Swift first met her. On the death of her mother and brothers she came to Dublin, and in 1717 retired to this paternal property, where she lived and died in seclusion.

‡ Various plans have been devised in the Corporation for erecting a mayoralty-house worthy of the residence of a chief magistrate. Among others, it was suggested to build one in Stephen's-green, which is the property of the City. The plan proposed, that the edifice should be erected in the centre of this fine area, with suitable architectural ornaments, and four grand avenues of approach lead to it from the opposite sides of the green. Whatever objection it is liable to, it would be at least preferable to the

in a recess in Dawson-street, presenting a mean brick front, and distinguished principally by being the most unsightly edifice in the street in which it stands. It has, however, some large apartments, well adapted to the convivial purposes to which they are appropriated. They are ornamented with whole length portraits of Charles II., William III. and some of the Viceroys of Ireland.*

The City Assembly-house in William-street is equally mean. It was originally built by a society of artists, as a house of exhibition; and purchased by the Corporation, when the Tholsel was no longer habitable. The Corporation here meet quarterly for the dispatch of civil business, and hold post assemblies for any extraordinary occasion. In this representative assembly all political questions are freely discussed; and since the removal of the Legislative Body from Dublin, it gives some faint image of a resident parliament. Here much warm and acrimonious discussion has taken place, and much talent has been at different times displayed by political opponents. Latterly, however, little has occurred to agitate discussion; and questions are generally carried, with little opposition, by large majorities.

The rental† of the City is ample; it amounts to £13,917. 9s. 7d. This, with the tolls and customs, amounting to £4867. and other sources of revenue amounting to nearly as much more, and producing altogether an income of nearly £23,000. per annum, should fully answer every corporate purpose: but the affairs of the Corporation have been so much deranged by bad management,‡ that notwithstanding the several plans of retrench-

disproportioned ornaments of an enormous pyramid, or a diminutive statue. Leinster-house was also mentioned. It is much to be wished that the Corporation had anticipated the Dublin Society.

* In Dublin they elevate and pull down pictures, as in ancient Rome they treated statues. Mr. Foster's picture was once among the number of those in the mayoraltry-house; but he brought forward an oppressive tax, and his picture was pulled down. Mr. Grattan's portrait experienced similar treatment in the Fellowship-hall of the University.

† For the rental and income of the Corporation, its tolls and customs, salaries and other expenditure, with a list of the mayors and sheriffs, see Appendix, No. VIII. and IX.

‡ The City formerly possessed a considerable estate on the sea-shore, extending from Ringsend and Irishtown, to the Black Rock and Stilorgan. This had been let on a lease of lives renewable for ever, and though the rent was not augmented, the renewal fines amounted annually to a considerable sum. By some mismanagement, of which curious stories are told, the City afterwards granted it in fee-farm. About six years ago this extraordinary alteration of the original tenure was contested by the Corporation; but the deed, duly executed by themselves, was produced, and the City was non-suited. The present income to the lessee is said to be about 16,000l. per annum.

ment carried into effect, it appears by the last Report of the Committee of Accounts for the year 1816, that the expenditure still exceeded the income by £3000. per annum. The Corporation have in their gift some benefices, Taghadoe, in the diocese of Dublin, of which they enjoy the tythes, amounting to £120, and pay the rector a salary of £25.; Rathmenie, in the diocese of Ferns, and Rathdrum; this last is the most valuable: it had always been usual to confer each of those on some candidate who had merit or interest to obtain it; but this practice is now abandoned; and the right of presentation of the last living has been disposed of for £2861. 4s.*

ALDERMEN OF SKINNER'S-ALLEY.

When James II. arrived in Dublin in 1688, the Protestant corporate establishment retired, and took refuge in Skinner's-alley, an obscure avenue in the Liberties, leading from the Weavers'-square to the Combe. Here they brought with them whatever regalia and emblems of office they could provide, and continued the semblance of their former state, with all its officers, while a Roman Catholic Lord Mayor and Corporation occupied the Chair of the City. To this little remnant all the independent gentry of the same party resorted; and they kept up their institution and the spirit of their party, till the arrival of William, and the battle of the Boyne restored to them their former situations. The memory, however, of this transaction was still cherished; and the institution was preserved with great zeal, as the nucleus of independence and civil liberty: in the year 1784, it was one of the most celebrated institutions in Ireland, and comprehending among its members all the nobility and gentry then most remarkable for their spirit and patriotism. About the year 1790, however, dissensions began to arise, and a spirit of party to interrupt the harmony of their

* Among the other retrenchments of the Corporation, the City chaplain was deprived of his entire salary; he looked forward, however, to future remuneration by the presention to one of these benefices, and the present injury was not felt or complained of. It is with deep concern that every friend of the corporation heard of this disposal. If the right of presentation to livings in the Established Church be thus publicly sold by great public Bodies, who profess to be its most zealous supporters, we know not that a greater injury could be inflicted, or calumny uttered by its worst enemies. We wished to refute this imputation, but the fact makes an item in the public accounts!
Pudet hæc oppiobria nobis
Et dici potuisse et non potuisse refelli.

THE CITY OF DUBLIN. 1069

members. A bust of King William had been presented to the Society, which always stood on the table—an appropriate memorial of the cause of their institution. Constant allusions to this excited controversy, and it was proposed to exclude altogether the offending bust. On this occasion two aldermen* of the City took opposite parts, and a schism and separation immediately ensued. One party bore off the bust and plate, and another took the records: they formed afterwards separate societies, and continued for some years to hold their meetings at the same time in different places; one of these, however, has ceased to assemble, and the other continues its meetings regularly: they first retired to the Weavers'-hall on the Combe, but now meet in Dawson-street. The great anniversary-day is the 4th of November, the birth-day of King William: but they meet besides on the 4th day of every month. The qualification to be a member is, that the person must be an undoubted supporter of the Protestant ascendancy, and a freeholder of the county, or freeman of the City of Dublin. From the numbers of this Society and their decided opinions, their support makes a material feature in all the elections of the county and city.

The officers of the Society are still designated by such titles as represent the different offices of government. A Governor, who is styled "Most Noble;" a Deputy Governor, Lord High Treasurer, Primate, Chancellor, Almoner, Sword and Mace-bearer. The present Governor is Sir Richard Musgrave, Bart.

PIPE-WATER COMMITTEE AND CITY BASINS.

Before the great extension of the city towards the east, the western part of it was much more respectable than at present, when it is almost exclusively consigned to the lower class, to poor working manufacturers or their employers; who, as they acquire wealth by their exertions, desert their former habitations, and follow the tide of fashion and elegance to the eastward: hence the City Basin, notwithstanding its decided superiority over

* The hostile aldermen on this occasion were Alderman Hugh Crothers, and Alderman Jacob Pool: the latter gentleman was a brewer in Black-pits; had been Lord Mayor in 1803; was afterwards distinguished by much pretorian celebrity, and noticed in the Familiar Epistles. He was a man of strong wit and coarse drollery, who said and did a number of good things worthy of notice, but not fit to be recorded here.

every other public walk in this metropolis, is now in a great measure deserted, except by the lower classes, and begins to exhibit evident symptoms of neglect and decay. This fine piece of water, above half an English mile in circumference, has suffered a small diminution at its southern extremity, where a portion of it has been filled up, to facilitate the extension of the Grand Canal to its present harbour near James's-street: including its surrounding walk, it still occupies an area of nearly five and a quarter English acres, and commands an uninterrupted view of a richly ornamented country, terminating in that range of mountains which occupy the confines of the counties of Dublin and Wicklow.

Its destination as a reservoir to supply an extensive city with water rendered it necessary to give its surface as great an elevation as was consistent with moderate expense: for this purpose it is supported by a firm embankment of earth several feet higher than the adjacent fields, on the summit of which is a walk, bounded on both sides by quick-set hedges, judiciously kept low not to interrupt the view, while the outer fence is planted with elms, still in a good state of preservation, with their branches expanded so as to entwine with each other and form graceful arches: and as these, from the moisture of the soil, are clothed in spring and summer with luxuriant verdure, they add much to the beauty of this charming scene. The form of the basin is an oblong parallelogram, 1210 feet in length, and varying in breadth from 225 to 250 feet. The entrance is by a neat iron gate from Basin-lane and Pig-town, the latter appropriately so called, from being perpetually infested with those animals, and forming by its filth a strong contrast to the salubrious air and cheerful tranquillity of the scene within.

The reservoir, which covers an area of nearly three and a half English acres, is supplied by a cut from the River Dodder, the waters of which, near Temple-Oge, are kept at the proper elevation for the purpose, by a dam or rampart of stone, so firmly constructed as to resist the floods of that furious torrent. As this cut is the joint property of the city of Dublin and the Earls of Meath, as proprietors of the Liberties of Thomas-court and Donore, it is at a place called the Tongue, at some distance from the city, accurately divided into two streams by a stone pier, terminating in a very acute angle, and dispensing to each their respective proportions; to the corporation for the supply of the city basin one third, and to the Earls of Meath two thirds for the accommodation of their tenantry. These pass.

under the circular road branch of the Grand Canal, and while the one circulates through the Liberties, the other, called the City Water, is, in consequence of the elevation of the basin, carried along the summit of an equally elevated rampart of earth and stone, during the latter part of its course; in consequence of which circumstance it frequently inundates the vicinity to a considerable extent, an inconvenience which might be easily prevented, by judicious overfalls to carry off the superfluous water in times of extraordinary floods. Passing in tunnels under the James-street branch of the canal, it reaches the City Basin, where it deposits its earthy particles, becomes pure and limpid, and by means of a curious system of metal and wooden pipes, formerly supplied almost the entire, and still a considerable part of the city with water.

The ancient city occupied the eastern part of a hill, which commencing at the Castle, terminates at Mount Browne, near which it attains its greatest elevation. On this summit the basin has been judiciously placed, and hence a gradual descent has been secured for the main pipes that run along the summit of this eminence through James-street, Thomas-street, High-street, Skinner-row, and Castle-street, and which may be considered as the grand artery of this system, from which the lesser pipes diverge, carrying the salubrious fluid, so essential to health and comfort, to every part of the city south of the river; while another great branch issuing from this, and descending down Watling-street, crosses the Liffy on Barrack-bridge, which forms an aqueduct to support it, and thus communicates similar advantages to the northern parts of the metropolis.

From these issue lateral pipes of lead, which convey water to each house as the main pipe passes. This is received in a cistern, which serves as a reservoir, as the water is suffered to run but a certain time each day. To prevent a waste of water as well as the damage and inconvenience arising from the overflow of the cistern, the cock of the pipe is turned by a rod to which is affixed a hollow ball; this is suffered to float freely on the surface, and when the ball rises to a certain height, it closes the cock before it can overflow; every person is obliged under a penalty to keep this apparatus in order. About the year 1802 an important improvement was made in the structure of the pipes.[*] It was found that those of wood rapidly decayed,

---

[*] By 42d Geo. III. cap. 92, the corporation are empowered to lay down new pipes, and to make new reservoirs, not exceeding two acres in each.

and the pavement of the city was constantly broken up to repair them; thereby incurring considerable expense, and interrupting in a disagreeable and dangerous manner the communication of the streets; to obviate this, iron tubes were laid whenever the wooden ones decayed, and a new tax called *the metal main* imposed upon the citizens to defray the expenses.

The supply of water from the single reservoir in James-street, however copious, having become inadequate to the wants of the continually encreasing population of the metropolis, application was made to the Grand and Royal Canal Companies, and two additional reservoirs were excavated on the banks of the canals, one at the extremity of Blessington-street, near the Royal Canal, for the north-eastern, and the other at Portobello, near the Grand Canal for the south-eastern parts of the city. The first of them is six feet higher than the basin in James street; and the latter on a level with it; they cost £30,000., paid from the fund of the metal main. These reservoirs are intended, like that of James-street, to be promenades for the citizens in the vicinity, and are laid down with gravel walks and shrubberies. The water thus procured is not only abundant in quantity, but excelcellent in quality, the Grand Canal deriving an unfailing supply from the Morrel-river, and the Royal Canal having attained to its grand reservoir the spacious and limpid Lough Owil in Westmeath. Thus the western parts of the city only are dependant on the basin in James-street, to the wants of which it is fully adequate.* By the system now perfected, the pipes ramify

* Notwithstanding the abundance of water with which Dublin is supplied, it has been visited sometimes with a scarcity of this necessary article. One of these occasions is so well described in a satyrical little work which appeared in 1804, that we shall quote the passage. The account professes to be " an intercepted Letter from China." Quang-tcheu is Dublin.

" China may be truly called the country of canals, those watery ways being here almost as numerous as the high roads of Great Britain. Quang-tcheu is absolutely surrounded by them, and yet from a circumstance which its folly would render ridiculous, did not its injustice make it serious, this town has been during the three hottest months of summer deprived of water, the first and commonest necessary of life, for which, during those very months, the inhabitants were paying an heavy impost.

" I shall relate you the transaction, because it will most strongly shew how tamely this ingenious people will sometimes submit to the most barefaced imposition.

" The inhabitants of Quang-tcheu have for many years paid to a committee of the Ta-whangs an heavy tax, in consideration of which this committee is bound to supply them with water. Of this tax the Ta-whangs have hitherto given a share to the proprietors of the Drang-la-nac, (or Great Canal) for permission to apply the waste water of their water-works (which surround the city) to the public accommodation.

for near 70 miles, and water is conveyed to every house in the metropolis at the moderate rate of one halfpenny per day.

" You will say that it is sufficiently ridiculous to buy waste water from any body, but what will you think when I inform you that the society of the Drang-la-nac who sold their waste water to the public, have received from that very public 523,621 tahels towards the formation and support of these very water works! what follows is more surprising still.

" By some unfortunate accident it was lately discovered that water had become more plenty than it used to be, and the consequence was, that it became scarcer than ever.

" The La-nac society asserted " as there was a probability that the waste water of some other works might be had at a cheaper rate than theirs, that therefore it was reasonable that they should have a double price." This style of argument (which you perceive is not that of Adam Smyth) did not persuade the Ta-whangs, who were told by some Chinese logicians that the contrary conclusion should have been drawn, viz. that the more water there was the cheaper it should be. The Ta-whangs, who generally hold their own when they can, being thus backed by the logicians, and not remembering the sentence of Con-fu-tze, which advises one not to throw out dirty water till they get clean; the Ta-whangs, I say, stoutly refused to give the Drang-la-nac society a greater share of their profits, and the Drang-la-nac society as stoutly resolved that neither the Ta-whangs or the citizens should have any more of their waste water, which they very spiritedly turned into the common sewer, in the first instance, instead of letting it pass thither through the bodies of four hundred thousand people; this, though very bad for the people, and not very profitable for the La-nac society, was very good for the Ta-whangs, who saved their money, and for the common sewer, which, instead of its being a filthy kennel as it was, is now become a very pretty trout stream.

" You will ask, were all the parties mad? I cannot answer that; but I am sure the people were not wise to continue for three hot months paying for liberty to die of thirst, because two societies quarrelled about the division of what they paid. Ah! my friend, the Chinese are not yet as enlightened as we are; in Dublin if such circumstances had occurred, you would have thrown both the societies into the common sewer, and have given the people the waste water to drink.

" In Quang-tcheu, however, the affair ended exactly where it should have begun, viz. in the Viceroy's ordering the water to be distributed to the city, and leaving the two angry societies to squabble at their leisure about their profits."

Public fountains have been among the ornaments of many cities. The beauty of those in Paris and the singularity of those in Brussels strike every traveller. With all the expense incurred in Dublin, the city is not ornamented by one public fountain. Some years ago, during the residence of the Duke of Rutland, an attempt was made to erect them in different parts of the town. Some were of cast metal, and some of less durable materials. They are now, we believe, all removed except one, which remains in Merrion-square, a mouldering memorial of a mutilated Naiad drooping over a broken conch. This had been first erected in Mary's-street, and in one night was disfigured in a most disgusting manner. A placard appeared the next morning on her breast, with the following inscription:

> A warning for the public weal
> My hapless figure shows;
> My virgin charms I scarce unveil,
> When lo! I lost my nose.

6 X

Notwithstanding the great convenience and excellence of the pipe-water system, the citizens justly complain of the enormous expense, which is raised by a tax on every house. In the year 1760, it amounted to £2500. in the year 1800 to £7000.; and in the year 1816 it has encreased to a sum exceeding £21,000. per annum! The new department of the system called the Metal Main,* amounts to half this sum; but it was expected that a correspondent reduction would ensue in other expenses. The quick and constant decay of wooden pipes induced an expense of £1800. for timber, and £600. for paving over the pipes, when laid down, which was proposed to be saved by the substitution of metal. The following Table exhibits the state of the funds for the last year.

Account of the Receipts and Disbursements of the Pipe-water for the Year ending September, 1816.

Dr.

	£.	s.	d.
Cash received from different collectors	10915	15	8
From paving commissioners for supplying fountains with water	150	0	0
From Ditto for supplying watering fountains	100	0	0
Balance due by treasurer, September, 1815	631	12	6
Interest per interest account	84	5	10
Cash paid on account of salary by last treasurer	17	19	1¼
	11899	18	1

Contra.

	£.	s.	d.
Cash paid Grand Canal Company 12¼ per cent. on gross receipts of the pipe-water revenue to June, 1815	1469	11	10¼
Ditto Royal Canal ditto 15 per cent. north side	734	10	7¼
Salaries	2133	11	6
Rent and taxes	2813	17	4½
Tradesmen's bills	332	6	1¼
Annuities	45	0	0
Store-keeper's weekly bills	960	3	11
Contractor's ditto	376	0	3¼
Commissioners of paving for paving over mains	436	10	2
Balance due by treasurer	2598	6	2¼
	11899	18	1

* The Pipe-water establishment had incurred a debt of one hundred thousand pounds. By the Metal Main Act of 1809, two thousand per annum is to be paid to a sinking fund, so as to liquidate the debt in about seventeen years, during which time the Metal Main tax is to continue.

Dr. Metal Main.	£.	s.	d.		£.	s.	d.
Cash received by different collectors	10409	6	9	Brought forward	1650	0	0
Balance due by treasurer, Sept. 1815	792	16	9	Storekeeper	100	0	0
				Overseer	120	0	0
	11202	3	6	Measurer	100	0	0
Contra.				Inspector	90	0	0
Interest on debentures to March, 1815	5806	0	0	Messrs. Quintin and J. Despard	73	11	6
Paid off 29 debentures by sinking fund	2900	0	0		2133	11	6
Interest on ditto	99	0	0	Rents and Taxes.			
Salaries	560	0	0	To City one year's rent of basin	2500	0	0
Tradesmen's bills	450	16	4	Rent of Assembly-room	100	0	0
Storekeeper's weekly bills	223	18	11½	Sundries	213	17	4
Contractor's ditto	339	0	0				
Paving commissioners for paving over mains	147	9	3		2818	17	4
Balance due by treasurer	675	18	3¼	Salaries Metal Main.			
				Supervisor	150	0	0
	11202	3	6	Engineer	150	0	0
				Storekeeper	100	0	0
Salaries paid by Pipe-water.				Overseer	60	0	0
Lord Mayor and treasurer in lieu of				Measurer	50	0	0
poundage	1000	0	0	Inspector	50	0	0
Secretary	200	0	0				
Supervisors	200	0	0		560	0	0
Engineer	250	0	0				

The management of this expensive and important establishment is entrusted to a Committee of the Corporation, called the "Pipe-water Committee." It is composed of the Lord Mayor, Sheriffs, Treasurer, 12 Aldermen, and 24 Common Council-men, who meet every Monday at the City Assembly-house in William-street.

COMMISSIONERS FOR PAVING AND LIGHTING.

AFTER several Acts of Parliament, by which this Board was variously modified, a most important one was passed in the year 1807,* by which the former were repealed, and the present Board constituted, with enlarged powers and more extensive means. It consists of three commissioners, who, with a secretary, treasurer, and supervisor, are appointed, removed, or encreased by his Excellency the Lord Lieutenant. This Board is authorised to levy rates of taxation on the City of Dublin, in whatever proportion they shall think fit, to a certain amount,† and recover the same by dis-

* See 47 Geo. III.
† Once in every year, or oftener, if the Commissioners shall see occasion, rates of assessment shall be made on every house, &c. in such sums as they, or any two of them, shall order, not exceeding, however, 4s. 6d. in the pound on the rates of houses valued for ministers' money. 47 and 54 Geo. III.

tress;* no more, however, than two years taxes can be recoverable, and unoccupied tenements to pay but half rates.† They are also empowered to make sewers and water streets, at the expense of the inhabitants of those streets. Their powers originally extended only to the Circular Road; but in 1814 they were enlarged to the north-west side of the Grand Canal.‡

The salaries, as appointed by the act, are as follow.—

Chief Commissioner	£600.
2 other Commissioners, each	500.
2 Supervisors, each	400.
Treasurer	500.
Secretary	300.

The conduct of this establishment has excited much animadversion, and commissioners have been heretofore appointed to inquire into it.§ The most remarkable circumstance, however, connected with it, is the enormous expense incurred, which the citizens of Dublin, loaded with such a weight of other taxes, loudly complain of. It is but just, however, to say, that, notwithstanding the unpopularity of this board, the objects of its establishment are well attended to.|| Great and important improvements have taken place in paving, lighting, and constructing sewers, and, we believe, no city can exceed Dublin in these particulars.¶

The establishment was originally conducted in Dawson-street; it has, within these few years, been removed to a large mansion in Mary's-street.

* See 47 and 54 Geo. III. sec. 8. † See 47 Geo. III. sec. 45.
‡ 54 Geo. III. By this Act, also, the street dirt belongs to the Board, and goes to encrease their funds.

§ A debt of 97,000l. had been incurred by former boards, of which 44,000l. were discharged out of the consolidated fund, and debentures issued for 53,000l. the interest to be paid also out of the consolidated fund, in order that the present funds for paving and lighting should be free from all debts. This was in lieu of 10,000l. per annum, formerly granted for paving and lighting, but now discontinued. 47 Geo. III. sec. 34.

|| See page 448. A bill was brought into Parliament last session to light the city of Dublin with gas, but in consequence of the petitions of the citizens, who thought it would induce an additional tax, the bill was abandoned, and this important improvement for the present postponed. The taxes paid at present by the citizens amount to 350,000l. annually.

¶ The city is at present lighted by 6000 lamps. These were formerly crowded together in some places, and thinly scattered in others, where they were more necessary. They are now judiciously distributed over every part of the city. The want of sewers was much felt in Dublin. The waste water was usually received in *cess-pools*, which were large excavations made in the front of each house, and covered in. It was supposed that the water would filter through the soil, and continually disperse; but the clay and limestone strata of Dublin are so very tenacious, that the contents of the pools were

The following gives a view of the expenditure of the board for the year
1815.— £. s. d.
Paving - 13,448 17 2¼
Scavenging 5,903 19 7¼
Lighting 14,348 18 3
Flaging - 2,137 10 9¼
Paid expense of fountains, 231 15 7½
Annuities, under act 47, Geo. III. - 1,650 0 0
Poundage to collectors - - 986 2 5
Rent, taxes, and other incidental expense of corporation house 572 19 4½
For information of nuisance - - 308 18 1
Advertisements and newspapers 53 6 4
Stationery and printing 689 14 8
Horses, forage, and stables 1,124 8 9

retained till they were filled up, and it became necessary to remove them, by opening the pool, which constantly exposed in the public streets an highly putrid and offensive mass. By the 47th Geo. III. the commissioners are empowered to make such sewers as they shall think fit, to which the inhabitants of the street are to contribute rateably. Under these powers, the commissioners formed several main sewers, and commenced a large and important one in Capel-street, which, notwithstanding, was covered in at the desire of the inhabitants, and left incomplete. In Sackville-street and elsewhere, these *cess-pools* still continue.

The great water-course which cleanses the Liberties and the old parts of the city, is called the *Poddle*. This is a stream of considerable magnitude, which rises near the Dublin mountains, and is augmented by several land drains from the ground near Tallagh Hill. After communicating with the Dodder, it enters the Liberties at Pimlico, where it divides, one branch passing through the Upper and Lower Comb, and the other through Black Pits, near the end of Fumballie's-lane, and so through Three Stone-alley, and meeting the first under the Cross-poddle, the united stream runs under Patrick-street, Ross-lane, Bride-street, and one side of Ship-street, through the Lower Castle-yard, where it once formed the moat of the fortress, and passing under Dame-street, and between Crampton-court and Sycamore-alley it empties itself into the Liffey, under the Old Custom-house-yard—now Wellington-quay. This water, in some parts of the Liberties, is not covered in, but runs through the streets, from which it is only divided by a parapet wall, and is used for the purposes of manufactures; from thence, however, it is arched over, and forms an immense sewer, carrying off the filth in its current, and purifying the streets under which it passes. It occasionally however bursts from its caverns, and inundates the vicinity to a considerable extent, particularly Patrick-street, Ship-street, the Castle-yard, and Dame-street, where it has been sometimes necessary to use boats till the flood subsided. This subterraneous river has thus been the occasion of much mischief, and many acts and regulations have been made to restrain it.—(See page 485). In the year 1814 a boy fell into the current, from an arch which they were erecting over it in the Castle-yard. He was carried by the stream under Dame-street to the Liffy, and was taken up just as he had emerged from the subterraneous passage into the river. Two mills were recently turned by this subterranean current in Little Ship-street and Ross-lane, but they were removed in 1796 by Act of Parliament.

	£.	s.	d.
Brought forward	41,456	11	1¾
Smith and carpenters' work, iron, ropes, &c.	1,673	13	2
Incidents	30	6	8¼
Sundry small expenses on collection of taxes	69	4	2
Expenses passing act of parliament	757	11	4
Salaries	5,095	8	8
Expenses of granite pavement	514	12	2¼
Sewers	1,342	18	4¼
Expenses of Corporation-house, Mary-street	408	18	2
Law expenses	142	18	8
Total paid up to January 1815	£51,492	0	6

The accounts of this Board are annually audited by the proper officers, from whose report to Parliament the above is extracted.

WIDE STREETS COMMISSIONERS.

AFTER Essex bridge was built, the only avenues to it from the frequented parts of the town in the vicinity of the seat of Government, were through the Blind quay on one side, and Crane-lane on the other. The inconvenience felt by the Castle from these indirect and narrow passages, occasioned an act of parliament, in the year 1757, " to open an avenue from his Majesty's royal palace to Essex bridge ;" and certain persons were appointed by name, under the appellation of " Commissioners for making a wide " and convenient street from Essex bridge to the Castle of Dublin," to meet at such times and places as they should think fit; and they were empowered to make a passage through such ground, and to have the houses built on each side the new street in whatever manner they should deem most eligible; and they were further empowered to agree for the purchase of such ground with all the parties concerned, and in case any refused to sell or shew their title, then to summon a jury, to inquire into the value and assess the purchase money for which the commissioners were to give judgment conclusive, and on paying the sum awarded, the premises were to be conveyed to them to build the street, and sell and demise the overplus.[*]

[*] 31 Geo. II. When the Commissioners proceeded to exercise those powers, they found, it seems, some opposition on the part of the inhabitants. Gorges Edm. Howard, who says he was a principal

THE CITY OF DUBLIN.

By subsequent acts, the commissioners were enjoined and directed to proceed to other great plans of public utility, and their powers were enlarged. Their improvements were to extend to the Circular Road, and half a mile beyond it, and if persons whose houses were valued, did not surrender them, they were to issue a precept to the sheriff to deliver possession.* The revenues of the commissioners to carry these projected improvements into effect, were derived partly from King's letters, and partly from parliamentary grants, and the produce of appropriate duties. A duty of 1s. per ton was laid on all coal brought into Dublin not from any part of Ireland,† and every house-keeper was to take out a card license, 5s. 5d. for houses value from 20 to £30. 11s. 4d. from 30 to £40. and £1. 2s. 9d. for 40 and upwards;‡ and all members of clubs were to pay the same, under a penalty of £20.§

With these ample powers and aids the Commissioners commenced their improvements; and after opening and building Parliament-street, in 1762, they proceeded in 1768 to enlarge the passages to the Castle from the Exchange, through Palace-street and Cork-hill.‖ Having opened a grand avenue of communication between the south and north sides of the Liffy, and rendered more convenient the passages leading immediately into the Castle, their next object was to open a suitable avenue between the seat of the executive and the legislative bodies. For this purpose an act passed in 1781, for widening the approach from the Castle to the Parliament House, between the Castle-gate and George's-lane, and the sums of £5000. and £21,000., in addition to the duty on coal were granted for that purpose,¶ and they were empowered to borrow £100,000., restricted to an interest

---

agent on the occasion, relates the following odd incident. " When the bargains for the houses were concluded, the inhabitants refused to quit possession, alleging they had six months to remain, and prepared bills of injunction against the Commissioners. A host of slaters and labourers with ladders, were secretly prepared in the night before the day in which the injunctions were to be filed, who proceeded at the first light in the morning to strip the roofs, and in a short time left the houses open to the sky. The terrified inhabitants bolted from their beds into the streets, under an impression that the city was attacked, of which there was some rumour, as it was a time of war. On learning the cause, they changed their bills of injunction into bills of indictment; but the Commissioners proceeded without further impediment."

* 21 Geo. III. † 21 Geo. III. ‡ 39 Geo. III. § Sec. V.
‖ It is to be regretted that the Commissioners, among their extensive plans, omitted to remove or throw back the short range of houses between Palace-street and Exchange-alley; these houses ought surely to be made to range with Dame-street, which would not only complete the uniformity of that side of the street, but would open the façade of the Royal Exchange to Trinity College, and give a consequence and dignity to that superb edifice to which it is so justly entitled.
¶ 21 Geo. III.

of four per cent, which they accordingly did in the year 1790. With this sum they paid of a debt of £47,500. incurred in opening Dame-street, and applied £21,000. to continue the improvement. Meanwhile, Parliament made sundry grants* for promoting similar plans in other parts of the city to the east, and the Commissioners then turned their attention to the narrow avenues *west* of the Castle. The great passage leading from the southern road, to the east end of the town, was obstructed by the narrow passes of James-gate, Cut-purse-row, and Skinner-row. Of those, Cut-purse-row was particularly inconvenient and dangerous; the passage itself was not more than 15 feet wide, in the most crowded thoroughfare of the city, and its entrance was obstructed by the Market-house in Thomas-street. In 1790, James-gate was opened, and the ground of Cut-purse-row was valued at £11,221., but for several years it remained a nuisance and a deformity, without the commissioners being able to pay the award. It was proposed by them to open a treaty with the Dean and Chapter for certain premises in Thomas-street, on which to erect a market-house, so as that one side should front Thomas-street, and the other Francis-street; but the plan was abandoned.† In the year 1810, Cut-purse-row was opened, and the act for widening Skinner-row is now before Parliament.‡ Meanwhile the commissioners were proceeding with other improvements no less useful than ornamental. They opened Fleet-lane, Drogheda-street, and the Barley-fields, forming Westmoreland-street, Sackville-street, and North Frederick-street, by which, one of the finest avenues perhaps in Europe is completed from Dorset-street to College-green. They have removed the obstructions which deformed our quays at the bottom of Wine-tavern-street, in rere of Temple bar, and between Burgh and George's quays. They further propose to open the quay on the north side from Barrack-bridge to the Park-gate, which will form a spacious and uninterrupted passage on one side from the

* £25,000. for continuing Sackville-street, (30 George III.) £5600. for opening Dorset-street to Rutland square, then called the Barley-fields, now North Frederick-street, (Sec. X.) and for opening a passage from Sackville-street to Carlisle bridge, and laying out streets to the eastward (36 George III.) £11,000. to purchase houses to open the Custom-house.

† The Corn Exchange Corporation are now erecting a Corn Exchange on Burgh quay, where the corn business is to be transacted as in Mark-lane, London. When this is completed the Market-house in Thomas-street is to be removed, for which purpose an act is now before Parliament.

‡ It was the object of the Chapter of Christ-church to have a Deanery-house with residences for the Chapter contiguous to the cathedral; and we understand the opening of Skinner-row has been suspended hitherto in consequence of some arrangements for that purpose not having been agreed upon.

Park to the Custom-house, and on the other, from Watling-street to Rings-end, equal in extent and almost in beauty, to the celebrated Quays of Paris. They are completing Abbey-street to Beresford-place, and have opened the passages to the Custom-house, from Carlisle bridge; presenting to the stranger at one view from that bridge, such a cluster of architectural beauties grouped together, or scattered in every direction which he turns, as are not to be seen from any other spot in any other city. On the south are to be seen, at the termination of Westmoreland-street, the perspective façades on each side of the College and House of Lords; on the east, the front of the Custom-house, which an accidental flexure of the river presents obliquely in a most striking point of view. On the north, the noble perspective of Sackville-street terminated by the Rotunda, and ornamented with the new Post-office and Nelson's Pillar; and on the east the Quays to a long extent, connected by seven handsome bridges, among which the light and elegant arch of the Iron-bridge in the foreground is very conspicuous. Strangers who visit Dublin are particularly struck with the beauty of this assemblage of objects. Next to the view from Carlisle-bridge, College-green displays the finest architectural scenery. The extensive front of Trinity College, the National Bank, Daly's Club-house, the Commercial buildings, and the equestrian statue of king William III. on a lofty pedestal, are all fortunately grouped, and produce a grand *tout ensemble.*

If, therefore, the Commissioners did no more, they deserve well of the public for the active discharge of their trust reposed in them; but their projected improvements will equal in utility, though not perhaps in beauty, those already effected. By the intended line of New Brunswick-street, and D'Olier-street, they will open and render healthy the whole vicinity of Townsend-street, which, though in immediate contact with the finest parts of the town, was proverbial for its filth and insalubrity. They further propose to open the passages on the north and south side of Richmond bridge, and pierce the dark and narrow obstruction through the very heart of the city; for this purpose they have commenced on one side at Inns-quay, and are opening from Church-street to the Four Courts; and on the other, they propose to take down the west side of Wine-tavern-street, throw open the obstructions that obscure and block up our cathedrals, by removing Skinner-row from Christ-church, and the alleys from round St. Patrick's, and having pushed this open avenue through Patrick-street and Three-stone alley, form a grand passage through the centre of the town from Richmond bridge to the extremity of New-street, in which our venerable cathedrals, brought into view, will form striking public objects.*

The Commissioners of wide streets are not a corporation. The act provides that, upon death or resignation, the Board is to elect a new member, subject to the approbation of the Lord Lieutenant. They receive no salaries.

EXPENSE OF IMPROVEMENTS.

EXPENDITURE.

	£.	s.	d.
ne of Dame-street	206.646	3	0
South Great George-street	11.029	6	3
Sackville-street	84.767	0	0
Lower Abbey-street from Sackville-street, to the Custom-house including Beresford-place	192.010	10	3
Sundry other streets	11.124	10	0
Barley Fields, now North Frederick-street	11.596	1	6
Westmoreland-street, D'Olier-street, Burgh Quay and Hawkin's-streets	132.256	4	0
Fleet-street, and College-street	19.742	5	5
Great Brunswick-street	14.880	1	6
Wellington Quay, (site of the old Custom-house)	10.186	1	6
King's Inns Quay	9.380	17	6
North Cope-street	2.154	13	3

ote. The foregoing expenditure has been provided for by a duty of one shilling per ton on coals imported into the city, a tax on houses and clubs, and grants from Parliament. And

he following improvements are provided for by Local Grand Jury Presentments, pursuant to the Act of the 47th of the King.

	£.	s.	d.
ine of Merchants Quay	9.935	6	7
Cutpurse-row	9.936	11	0
Werburgh-street	5.757	15	0
Nicholas-street	100	0	0
Patrick-street	5.044	12	6
High-street, and Corn-market	36.071	19	7
Wine-tavern-street	15.652	13	6

RECEIPTS.

	£.	s.
Ground sold in line of Dame-street	83.116	18
Ditto line of South Great George-street	6.831	1
Ditto line of Sackville-street	20.313	
Ditto Rents, old materials, &c. in line of Lower Abbey-street, and Beresford-place	25.304	1
Ditto Rents, materials, &c. line of Barley-fields	2.261	1
Ditto ditto, line of Westmoreland-street, D'Olier Burgle Quay and Hawkin's-street	30.231	1
Ditto in line of Fleet-street and College-street	3.327	1
Ditto ,and , materials sold, line of Great Brunswick-street	1.382	1
For materials sold in line of Wellington Quay	270	1
Ditto line of King's Inns Quay	690	
Ditto line of North Cope-street	141	1
For materials sold on line of Merchant Quay	419	1
For ground sold and materials in line of Cutpurse-row	1.986	1
For materials sold in line of Werburgh-street	109	1
Ditto, line of Patrick-street	343	1
Ditto, line of High-street, and Corn-market	1.369	

* When this is effected we hope it will be found practicable to continue the line on the north side of the Liffy, through Greek-street and Beresford-street by the Linen-hall; by which means a spacious street may be continued almost in a right line over Richmond-bridge, from the Grand to the Royal canal, from New-street to Constitution-hill.

EXPENSE OF IMPROVEMENTS.

ANNUAL EXPENSE.	£. s. d.	£. s. d.	£. s. d.	ANNUAL INCOME. £.
nded Debt, viz.				Coal duty - - 12.000
bentures £4. per cent. - - -	76.400 0 0			Club and House Card Tax 1.688
tto, at £6. per cent. - - -	22.600 0 0			Rents receiveable - - 1.312
·rtificates at £6. per cent. - -, -	107.636 19 3¼			Annual Income 15.001
	206.636 19 3¼			Annual deficit - 4.111
which the annual interest is - -	- - -	10.870 4 5		
an from Treasury - - -	38.985 19 7			
which the annual interest is - - -	- - -	1.949 6 0		
	245.622 18 10¼		12.819 10 5	
an from Corporation for preserving and improving the Port of Dublin - }	12.500 0 0			
a which the annual interest at £5. per cent. is	- - -	625 0 0		
an from the Corn Exchange Corporation -	4,500 0 0			
a which the annual interest at £6. per cent. is	- - -	270 0 0		
	17.000 0 0		895 0 0	
nnual expense of establishment - -	- - -	680 0 0		
ιw costs and other contingent expenses - -	- - -	3.200 0 0		
			3.880 0 0	
:nts payable - - - - -	- - -	- - -	1.525 19 0	
Annual expenditure	- - -	- - -	£19.120 9 5	£19.12

BALLAST OFFICE, OR CORPORATION FOR PRESERVING AND IMPROVING THE PORT OF DUBLIN.

It appears, that the first incorporation for the improvement of the harbour of Dublin, was by an act 6th Anne, 1707, for cleaning the port, harbour, and river of Dublin, and erecting a ballast office, which vested powers for the purpose in the Lord Mayor, Commons, and Citizens of Dublin, and laid a small tonnage on shipping for that purpose; their operations began in the following year; before this period, the lower part, of the river and the harbour were in the state the currents of the river Liffy and the other streams that communicated with it, and the natural effect of the winds and tides, had placed it.* The first step for improvement appears to have been by employing lighters to cut a new and more direct channel, of about 100

* See page 436.

yards wide, and to stop up the old one. About the same time, the inclosing the ground at the south side of the river, now Sir John Rogerson's Quay, was undertaken. About the year 1714, surveys were ordered relative to the propriety of piling below Ringsend, and in consequence thereof the preparatory work was soon after begun, by sinking wicker-work kishes, filled with stones; and in the year 1717, the piling commenced.

In the same year, the attention of the public was turned to the enclosing of the strand on the north side of the river, which was then an open waste, from below where the present Custom-house stands to the bay, the property of the near part whereof appears to have been in the city of Dublin. To effect this important purpose, and defray the expense, an act of assembly of the city was passed for letting the ground in perpetuity, rent free, to a set of subscribers, who were to undertake the inclosure of it; and a map of the whole ground was made out, which divided it into lots, denominated foot and acre lots, leaving room for proper quays and roads.*

Shortly after the commencement of the piles, they were found to be inadequate to the intended purpose, as they did not keep the sand out of the harbour, and it was therefore determined on to form a wooden framing, carefully filled with stones, and which was accordingly completed.

In the year 1735, a light ship, being a small sloop, with a lantern at her mast head, was placed at the end of these piles or frames, near to the situation where the present light-house stands; and in the year 1748, the building of the wall from what is now called the Pigeon-house to Ringsend began. The light ship having been found very difficult to be kept at her mooring, and being a very important light, the building a permanent light-

* The foot lots were those that fronted the river, or were near it, and they varied as to their dimensions according to their vicinity to town, so as to be considered of equal value; those distant having in extent what might be supposed to compensate for their being more remotely removed. The entire number of lots were 132 of each class; and the subscribers were obliged to pay a certain sum into the general fund, for the enclosure of and dividing the grounds, making roads, &c. The whole of these lots being numbered, each subscriber was entitled to a foot and an acre lot. The numbers were drawn as a lottery, and leases made out to the several subscribers. In conformity to the drawing, what is now denominated the *north lots* were taken in, inclosed, and laid out from the fund; but an almost equal part of the original scheme, which was to have extended the inclosure to the Clontarf Strand road, leaving a channel for the Ballybough river, remains unexecuted, either from a dispute with the family of *Vernon* (Clontarf), as to the property of that part of the Strand, or to the expense of the enclosure already made having been so great, or probably from the combination of both these circumstances.

house* was determined on and completed, partly out of the funds belonging to the Ballast-office, and partly by small parliamentary grants. After the completion of the light-house, the present great south wall, composed of solid masonry, and cut granite stone was commenced and proceeded on, but from the uncertainty of funds, and various untoward circumstances, the progress was slow; and the frame piles had become so much decayed, that the stones with which they were filled were displaced, and the land which had accumulated on the South Bull, was washing into the river continually, and filling up the channel. The merchants and others concerned in the trade and navigation of the port, applied, by petition, to the legislature, to have a new modification of the laws relative to the conservation of the port; and expressed their willingness to contribute more liberally to its improvement, if the superintendance and expenditure were placed in a less changeable body, and who were more closely connected with and interested in the maritime commerce of the city. After considerable opposition, an act of the legislature passed 1786, which transferred all powers relative

* For an account of this light-house, &c. see page 456.

The time when it is proper to erect a signal, there noticed, for passing the bar, is intimated by a simple but ingenious piece of machinery. In a wooden frame, which stands on the wall, near the building, is suspended a bell. When the tide rises to a certain height, it communicates motion to the bell, which tolls for a short period, and gives a distinct signal, particularly useful at night, when to notify the circumstance to the shipping. This was the invention of Dr. Bernd. M'Mahon, a Roman catholic clergyman, to whose ingenuity the public is much indebted.

Previously to Dr. M'Mahon's time, many vessels were cast away in and about the bay of Dublin. Many valuable lives were consequently lost, for want of an accurate knowledge of the phenomena of the tide on the bar and the adjacent coasts. To ascertain this, Dr. M'Mahon's genius was peculiarly adapted. An admirer of Newton, well skilled in the science of mathematics, endued with an inventive and mechanical genius, and of an active mind, he represented to government the necessity of fathoming the bay, and of deducing from actual observations and experiments, *a posteriori*, a set of tables like those formed for Brest, Plymouth, and other ports, for ascertaining the tide. For this he was favoured with the use of a yacht equipt and ready at all hours. On this business the Doctor employed above three years of his life, to the no small detriment of his health, till he was ultimately enabled to form that system of tide-tables adopted by the Commissioners of the Custom-house and of the Coast-office, to the great advantage of the public at large.

This gentleman, after devoting a long life to the service of the public, and the duties of his own profession, died last year (1816) at his chapel in Hadwick-street, at the advanced age of 80, leaving a high character behind him for learning and piety. He was of a cheerful, pleasant temper, abounding with anecdotes—his disposition was amiable, and his views of religion liberal and enlarged.

to the river Liffy, the bay and harbour of Dublin, together with the regulation of the pilotage of the port in a new corporation, to be composed of the *Lord Mayor* and *Sheriffs* for the time being, of three aldermen, elected by, and from that board, and of seventeen other persons named in the act, of which a portion were of highly respectable *public characters*, and the remainder merchants, at the time considered much interested in promoting the commerce of the metropolis. They were denominated—*The Corporation for Preserving and Improving the Port of Dublin*, and had perpetual powers given to them for filling up all vacancies occasioned by death or otherwise.

At that period, there was built of the great south wall, from the lighthouse upwards toward the Pigeon-house, 1522 feet, and the particular attention of the corporation was necessarily applied to the completion of this great work, as also to removing the different banks and shoals in the river. The former was completed in the year 1796, by joining this wall to that formerly built to the Pigeon-house, and forming a basin there for the convenience of passage and other vessels. The dredging and deepening the channel has been progressively carried on, and still continues; all the great obstructions have been removed, so that loaded vessels, drawing from 13 to 14 feet water, now come up to the Custom-house quay, and further improvements are in progress. To enable them to proceed with their works, they were empowered to receive the following rates from all vessels coming to the port of Dublin.—

    Foreigners   - -   1*s*. 6*d*. per ton.
    Natives   - -   0 9 ditto.
    Colliers and coasters   -   0 6 ditto.

Besides this, every vessel is obliged to take all its ballast* from the corporation, for which

    Foreigners pay   -   2*s*. 6*d*. per ton.
    Natives   1 8 ditto.

* The ballast is raised from the bed of the river, and is the means of rendering it deep. Eighteen large lighters, of 60 tons each, and containing nine men, are employed in this work, and perhaps display an instance of as much strength and laborious exertion as can any where be found. The lighters, having proceeded at the ebb tide down the river, take their station over the appointed place. A spoon formed of a strong ring of iron, to which is attached a net, is fixed to the end of a long pole. This is let down to the bottom, perpendicular at the bow of the boat, and by means of a rope, fastened to the

The amount of this revenue and the improvement of the port of Dublin, inviting commerce, may be estimated by the following average of shipping invoiced at the period of the incorporation of the board, and since.

Average of ten years previous to 1786.

Foreign shipping	- -	15,983 tons.
British ditto	- -	232,600 ditto.
Total	-	232,600

Average for three years ending January 1816.

Foreign shipping	.	21,284 tons.
Merchant ditto	- -	84,776 ditto.
Colliers ditto	- -	210,517 ditto.
Coasters ditto	- -	37,907 ditto.
Total		354,484

The quay walls of the river, the building and keeping in repair of which had heretofore been made good by the proprietors of the opposite ground, had been so much neglected, that on a remarkable high tide in 1792, the waters of the Liffy broke over the wall at Sir John Rogerson's quay, and complelely inundated the south lots, at which time a very singular circumstance occurred: a deep laden collier of 200 tons was coming up the river under full sail, and when opposite that part of the wall which had given way, the rapidity of the current through the breach carried her into the middle of a field, from whence she was re-conducted at the ebb of tide into the Liffy; in consequence of this accident, and after a parliamentary enquiry into the circumstances that led to it, an act was passed, vesting the care of all the quays eastward of Carlisle bridge, in the ballast office corporation,

spoon, and passing over a windlas, is dragged along and raised at the stern, filled with sand, which it had scooped up in its passage. By this simple machine, the boat is filled in four hours, and returns with the flood tide, each loaded with 60 tons of sand, which is transferred immediately to the vessels wanting ballast, who, besides the price of the sand, pay 5d. per ton for loading. The quantity of sand removed from the bed of the river in this way amounts to from 1500 to 2000 tons per week. The utility of this process in improving the river is every day becoming apparent. Since the incorporation of the board, the depth of the bed has been increased from three to four feet. It was formerly the practice for lighters to attend all merchant vessels at Poolbeg, and lighten them of part of their cargo, before they could venture up the river. Vessels of larger burden and deeper draught now proceed up to the Custom-house and Carlisle bridge without discharging any part of their cargo.

Besides the important and primary object of deepening the harbour, the corporation derive a revenue of £2000. per annum for the sale of their ballast.

and directing a small tax on the proprietors of ground in front of the river, as also a quayage duty on shipping, towards defraying the expense thereof. The great advantage that has arisen from building regular quays, which then began, appeared so obvious, that in the year 1803, at the desire of the grand juries of the city and county of the city of Dublin signified to the Lord Lieutenant, application was made to the ballast office corporation, conveying to them a wish that they should undertake the care of the quay walls and bridges, from Carlisle bridge to Barrack bridge, on the north side, and from the west end of Aston or Crampton quay, to Barrack bridge on the south side: and on their acquiescence, an act was passed,[*] which placed those important works under their management, the plan and expense of such works being first laid before the Court of King's Bench, and the respective grand jurors of the city and county of Dublin, who were to present money for their execution. Since the passing of this act, the building of quay walls has been nearly finished. One beautiful bridge has been completed, another commenced, and ballustrades opposite the Courts executed, by which that elegant building can, from the opposite side of the river, be viewed with advantage from its base, so that within a very short period, probably not exceeding two years, there will be completed, the most extensive mole and wall in Europe, stretching from the light-house to the Pigeon-house, a length of 9816 feet, from thence to Ringsend, 7938, and from thence to Barrack bridge, 11,800, nearly six English miles.

The walls are completed by a tax of two shillings per foot on every house, and the bridges by presentment of the grand jury.

The care and superintendance of the *light-houses* round the coast of Ireland has passed through various hands. Charles II. first laid a tonnage duty upon all vessels inwards and outwards, to maintain six light-houses in Ireland, and a patent was granted to the earl of Arran for that purpose. In the year 1703 the Irish House of Commons finding only two of the six light-houses maintained, passed resolutions on the subject, which were presented to the Lord Lieutenant. The patent was revoked, and the care of the light-houses placed under the commissioners of the revenue. By an Act passed in George I. it was vested in the commissioners for barracks; but the Chancellor of the Irish Exchequer, Mr. Foster, with the approbation of

---

[*] See 43 Geo. III. cap. 127.

THE CITY OF DUBLIN. 1089

Government, and of the commissioners of customs, intimated to the corporation for preserving and improving the port of Dublin, that he considered it would be a measure of public utility, if the management of the lights around the coast of Ireland, were assimilated to that in Great Britain; and for the purpose of carrying this measure into effect, proposed that the corporation should be formed into a body, somewhat like the Elder Brethren of the *Trinity-house, London:* the corporation acquiesced in the measure, as being one of vital importance to navigation, and the principle of assimilation has been carried into effect under an Act of the Legislature, passed in 1810, which vested and committed to their management, the superintendance of all the light houses in Ireland, building new ones, towers, and beacons, or other sea marks, with a stipulation that all new works should, prior to their execution, be communicated to the Elder Brethren of the Trinity-house; and after their opinion obtained, to the Lord Lieutenant of this kingdom, and the Lords of the Treasury. The measure of the communication with the Trinity-house arose from a consideration that the arrangement of lights on each coast should be such as would not clash with each other, and to prevent the possibility of mistaking one for another.

All the lights in Ireland were formerly from coal fires, which it must be evident were highly objectionable, as in bad weather, when they were *most* required, they were *most* liable to be obscured, or totally extinguished by rain. The first alteration that took place in this kingdom, was at the time when the light house at the extremity of the great south wall, Dublin, which was, on being completed, illuminated with candles.* Howth was the next that underwent a change, a new light-house having been built near the very high ground where coal light had formerly stood. It appears to have been the universal principle when fixing on a situation for a light-house, to choose the highest ground the neighbourhood admitted of; this was the case with respect to Howth, but experience has since proved the mistake, such elevated situations being liable to, and very frequently obscured by fogs. This light the corporation determined on altering to a situation on a point of land considerably lower, called the Little Bailey of Howth, and

---

* This is now lighted with oil, as are all others, with the exception of the light-houses on Wicklow Head, which are still lighted by candles; but will be re-built the ensuing season, and then altered on the new principle.

near to the verge of the sea, where has been constructed a very commodious building, and which is found most excellently adapted to the intended purpose, not being liable to be obscured by vapour, and can be seen at a much greater distance, than if from a higher situation.

The establishment of a floating-light ship, on a bank called the *Kish Bank*, south-east of Dublin Bay, about nine miles, engaged the attention of the corporation at a very early period after receiving their powers; for this purpose, a properly constructed vessel, *Dutch built*, was provided, and fitted out for the purpose, bearing three lanthorns, one at each mast, the centre one about four feet higher than the two others, and manned with fourteen seamen, and placed at her moorings on the 16th November, 1811, where she has since safely rode out all weathers, and proved a most extensively useful light to the trade of the Irish channel * This bank was, and is still marked by a very large buoy at either end; but in the night, vessels running for Dublin, could not with safety venture to stand in, and, not unfrequently, lost a passage thereby; all which is now obviated, seamen relying so confidently on the light, consider themselves in safety (particularly the packets) the moment it is visible, which is not unfrequent in two or three hours

---

* The light-ship is a strong flat built vessel, about 140 tons burthen, with three masts, to each of which is attached a large lanthorn, in which there is six properly constructed lights, with small reflectors: these lanthorns slide in a groove on the masts, are hoisted by the crew without much difficulty; although heavy, the centre one is elevated from four to six feet higher than the other two; thus completely distinguishing her from all other lights, particularly Wicklow, where there are two near to each other. She is moored off the north-end of the Kish Bank (distant from Dublin harbour about nine miles), being the tail or extremity of this dangerous shoal—composed of quick sand, which begins off the coast of Wexford, and extend with different intervals from thence along the coast of Arklow and Wicklow, and may be said to die away at the Kish Bank.

The light-ship is moored by what is called a mushroom anchor, from its exact resemblance to a mushroom; the chain to which the cable is attached, is fastened to what may be called the stalk of the mushroom. The advantage derived from this form of anchor is, that the vessel can freely swing; preserving the vessel at her station, and making her, as the sea term is, *ride easy*, by accommodating the length of the cable to the height and strength of the waves and the swell of the sea. The greater they are, the more cable is given out, to prevent the possibility of any sudden jerk raising the anchor or straining the cable. The quantity of chain cable attached to the anchor is about 30 fathoms, and being immediately adjoining, lies on the ground; to this is properly fastened 240 fathoms of the best patent cable, being double the length of an ordinary cable for such a vessel, when the whole is let out, which however is seldom.

THE CITY OF DUBLIN.

after losing sight of the light-house on the South Stack, Holyhead. A light-house on the Tuscar rock* next seemed most desirable, and has been erected: and was lighted on the 4th of June, 1815. The rock is situated near the coast of Wexford. The base extends a considerable way under.

* The Tuscar rock stands about seven miles from the south-east extremity of the coast of Wexford; it is about 300 feet in length, 150 in breadth, and its most elevated part 30 feet above the level of the sea at high water mark. It stands projected from the coast to meet the unbroken and tremendous surge of the Atlantic bearing up the channel; its base runs a considerable way, shelving towards the sea, on which the surge ascends as on an inclined plane; and though the summit is so considerably raised above the level of the tide, it is constantly submerged by the wintry storms. The importance and exposure of its situation, the arduous difficulty of erecting an edifice on it, and the dreadful accidents to which it has been liable, all combine to render this rock the Edystone of Ireland. When the Corporation determined to build a light-house, they commenced by laying horizontal beams across the rock, and connected to it firmly by iron cramps; on this was laid a platform, and huts erected capable of containing and sheltering 41 workmen. They were scarcely lodged here, when a West Indiaman from Barbadoes, bound to Liverpool with a valuable cargo, and having soldiers and other passengers, to the amount of 107 on board, was wrecked on the base of the rock, and went to pieces. The night was dark, and the greater part of the crew must have perished, but for the aid afforded by the workmen stationed in these huts, who by ropes raised them to the summit, and, with the exception of four, saved and sheltered the whole crew. About six weeks after this accident, on the night of the 18th of October, a sudden storm arose, and the sea was agitated with unusual violence. Some of the men in the huts ran naked from their beds to the highest point of the rock, but before the rest could escape, a surge striking the foundation of the huts, swept the whole completely away, while the men in their beds; the others were miraculously preserved by clinging to the rock all night, while the waves beat over them: several vessels attempted to assist them here, but they were compelled to remain from Sunday morning at four o'clock, till the Wednesday following, when the surge subsided, and they were rescued from their perilous situation. This awful catastrophe made a deep impression on the minds of the people of that neighbourhood; præternatural visions and warnings were reported to have been seen and heard, and no offers could induce the workmen again to approach the rock: materials to the value of several hundred pounds lay the whole winter in perfect security without a guard, for no one would venture near to take them. At length the Corporation undertook the work themselves. Smeaton's plans of the Edystone light-house were taken as a model; the stones were raised from the granite rocks near Dublin, and the materials of the light-house were fitted, and the whole of the building completed on the spot. From hence they were conveyed by Dublin workmen to Tuscar. Over each course runs a chain of cramps, counter-sunk, and leaded; on this the next course was laid, and the lead sunk in that above. In this way the whole is cramped; and as the iron is protected from the action of the air or sea, it will not be eroded: in about 18 months it was completed, at an expense of 30,000*l.* The Corporation have humanely granted pensions to the widows and children of the unfortunate workmen who were drowned, which amount to 150*l.* per annum. On the night the accident happened, the "Smalls" light-house near the Land's-end was almost entirely destroyed, and other similar disasters occurred on many parts of the coasts of England and France.

the water which encreased the danger of being entangled with it. The light-house is a circular building 82 feet high. The apparatus for illuminating it is on a revolving principle, with a red light at intervals to distinguish it. To a vessel at a distance it presents a strong light once in two minutes, being the period of revolution, and every third appearance is of a deep red colour, caused by coloured glass: to the building there is also attached two very large bells, those placed under the outer gallery of the light-house, are tolled by machinery, in thick weather, snow, &c. to warn vessels of the danger when the light might not be discernible.

By the activity of this corporation there are now 8 new beacons added to the 14 which existed on the coast of Ireland in 1810,* many of which

---

* It may not be uninteresting to detail the light-houses that existed on the coast of Ireland in 1810, when committed to the care of the Corporation, and those since added; in which they are noted in the order they are situated, proceeding from Dublin northward.

+. Howth, and S. Wall, Dublin Bay.
Balbriggan Pier.
Cranfield. Entrance to Carlingford Bay.
D South Rock. A revolving light on a half tide rock, three miles off the coast of the county of Down, near Strangford.
+ Copeland Island. Three miles off Donaghadee.
Arran More. Island of Arran, coast of Donegall.
Clare Island. In Clew Bay Coast, county of Mayo.
+ Loophead. Entrance to the river Shannon, county of Clare side.
D Old Head, Kinsale. Entrance to Kinsale.
Charles Fort. In the Harbour of Kinsale, direction up the river.
+ Hook Town. Entrance to Waterford. This is a tall circular tower of great antiquity, and was found standing by Strongbow when he landed near this spot in 1070. (Smith's Hist. of Waterford, p. 249.)
Duncannon Fort. Harbour light, direction up the river, same as at Kinsale.
Wicklow Head. Two light-houses, so situated that the mariner keeping them both in one line is thereby guided to avoid the Arklow banks.
Thus the coast was lighted in 1810.
Since that, there has been erected by the Corporation, namely, one called
Inishtrahul Light-house. On the Island of that name nine miles off the most northern point of Ireland coast, county of Donnegal, a revolving light distinguishable to the mariner once in two minutes; revolving, to distinguish it from the light at Copeland, and that at Arranmore.
Tuscar Rock. Seven miles off Grenore Point, county of Wexford.
Floating Light-ship, at the Kish Bank, nine miles S. E. of Dublin Bay.
Fannel Point. At the entrance of Loughswilly. Seeking this place, the Saldanagh frigate was lost some short time since, when all on board perished.

THE CITY OF DUBLIN.   1093

latter were also repaired and relighted. The expenses are defrayed by the following duties :*

For every British or Irish ship or vessel which shall pass any such lighthouse or floating-light, for, and in respect of every time of passing the same, whether outward or homeward bound, the sum of one farthing British currency, for every ton burden of such ship or vessel.

For foreign vessels, duty one halfpenny.

Vessels in ballast coastways in Ireland, half the rates above on British vessels.

His Majesty's vessels and fishing smacks are exempt.

OF THE RIVER LIFFEY, THE QUAYS AND THE BRIDGES.

ALTHOUGH the Liffey, as it passes through the centre of Dublin, cannot be denominated a great river, its current at low water being inferior to the Seine at Paris; yet being confined between walls of granite, when the tide-water flows into its channel it assumes an aspect of considerable importance, as vessels, some of even 500 tons, are floated up to the last bridge that crosses its stream to the east.

The old Quay walls becoming ruinous, a tax was granted by Parliament

---

Roches Point. Entrance to the Harbour of Cork, which harbour, although the resort of the trade of the United Kingdom, and what is termed a Blind Harbour not discernible at night for the high lands, have hitherto escaped being considered a situation for a light.

Arran Island. Galway Bay (in progress of building.)

Mutton Island. Near to the Town of Galway as a direction after entering the Bay.

A Beacon. On the Beerces Rock on the river Shannon.

And the ensuing season's work will consist partly in the erection of a light-house on *Cape Clear*, the most southern point of Ireland; a beacon on the Black Rock in Sligo Bay; and the rebuilding the two light-houses of Wicklow Head, (continued to be lighted with candles), and probably removing the site of the new ones to a lower situation for the same reason as at Howth.

Of the old light houses this mark + signifies that they have been replaced by permanent new buildings, and ☽ signifies that a new apparatus was added.

* By Act 52 Geo. III. cap. 115.

for rebuilding them. This work, under the direction of the Ballast-office, has proceeded with so much diligence and expedition, as to be now (1817) nearly complete, and it is executed in a style that does the greatest credit to that Board. The walls, 12 feet thick at the foundation, are faced with large blocks of hewn mountain granite. To the eastward of the bridges they are constructed without parapets to facilitate the landing of goods. Huge blocks of that material connect them with the quays on the same level, and give stability to the whole. Above Carlisle-bridge the walls are finished with parapets, interrupted at convenient distances by iron gates, stone stairs and slips, to accommodate the interior navigation.

Before the execution of this meritorious work, the line of quays on either bank of the river was, in various places, interrupted by unsightly buildings, wharfs, and warehouses, which projected into its channel. All these obstructions are now removed, and few cities can exhibit a grander architectural effect than is displayed by the combination of those fine quays with superb public buildings and elegant bridges. The quays at the south side of the river extend from the grand Canal Dock to Barrack-bridge, being a line of two English miles and a quaater; and those on the north side, from the Royal Canal Docks to the vicinity of the Barracks, being an extent of one English mile and three quarters.

From the western to the eastern extremity of the bridged-river, the stream is crossed by seven bridges, and an eighth bridge is just begun. The most westerly is 256 feet long and 38 broad, and is composed of a single elliptic arch, which spans the stream with a segment of 104 feet, and an altitude, from the key stone to the surface of the current at low water of 30 feet; this Dublin Rialto, being in fact, 7 feet wider in the span than the famous Venetian-bridge makes a fine feature in the general view. The foundation was laid June 22, 1791, by Sarah countess of Westmorland, and was named after the vice-queen SARAH-BRIDGE.

The next bridge was first constructed of wood in 1671, and in consequence of an affray on it, in which four persons lost their lives, was called Bloody-bridge. Being afterwards built of stone, and situated not far from the barracks, it has been since named BARRACK-BRIDGE. It is a plain structure of four semicircular arches, but at the south end, there has been lately erected a grand Gothic gateway leading to the Royal Hospital of Kilmainham, having four towers at the angles, one of them being much higher than the others, which, with the accompaniment of rural scenery in the back ground, gives to the whole a striking and romantic appearance.

The bridge next in succession was first built in 1683, and called after the then Lord-lieutenant, Arran-bridge, but, being swept away in a flood, it was rebuilt in 1768, and named QUEEN'S-BRIDGE, in honour of her present Majesty. It is of three arches, of hewn stone, and is admired, though small, for its neatness, and the justness of its proportions.

The next bridge, which connects two of the oldest streets in Dublin, and which was the most ancient of all the bridges, has been known by the several names of Old-bridge, Dublin-bridge, and Ormond-bridge, and was for a long time the only passage across the river. It is uncertain when it was first erected, but in 1385 it fell down, and was not rebuilt till 43 years after, in 1428.* It remained a long time mouldering in decay; a blemish amidst so many fine pontal edifices, when, at length, it was overturned by the great flood of 1802.† Its ruins still encumber the bed of the river, but it has been lately replaced by the magnificent erection of Richmond-bridge; and on the other side westward, there is a new one begun, whose foundation was laid 16th October, 1816, by his Excellency Lord Whitworth, from whom it derives its name of WHITWORTH-BRIDGE.

RICHMOND-BRIDGE—so named from the late Lord-lieutenant, the Duke of Richmond, the foundation stone being laid by her excellency the Lady-lieutenant, August 9th, 1813, was finished and opened for the public on St. Patrick's day, 1816. It exceeds in breadth any of the London bridges, being 52 feet broad, and 220 long. It is built of Portland stone, and consists of three arches, whose key-stones are ornamented with six colossal heads, executed by Smith, which represent Peace, Hibernia, Commerce, on one side, and Plenty, the Liffey, and Industry on the other. It is further embellished with lamp pillars, and a ballustrade of cast iron, which is prolonged the whole front of the courts of law, and which will connect Richmond bridge with the new one just commenced.‡ The cost was

* Vide Annals, page 180, for some curious particulars.

† Among the peculiarities of Dr. Rutty, (a sketch of whose life is given, page 835) were certain preventions which no experience could correct. He was impressed with a belief that the Old bridge would fall whilst he was crossing it, and for thirty years he made a detour to avoid passing over it, which nothing could induce him to attempt.

‡ In sinking for the foundation of the south abutment of Richmond-bridge, opposite Wine-Tavern-street, there were found in the excavations made four feet below the bed of the river at low water,

£25,800. raised by presentments on the county and city of Dublin. James Savage of London, was the architect, and it was executed by G. Knowles of Dublin, engineer.

Essex Bridge, first built in 1676, was named in honour of the then Lord-lieutenant, Arthur Earl of Essex. It began to be rebuilt in 1753, and was finished in 1755. This structure was raised of hewn stone on the exact model of Westminster-bridge; it consists of five noble arches, which are proportioned to the five central arches of the other, as three to five. It is 51 feet broad, that of Westminster being only 44 feet, and 250 long. It is the largest and grandest of the Dublin bridges. Ordinary tides rise ten feet at Essex bridge, and eleven feet at Westminster. The nett cost was £20,661. An equestrian statue of George I. was erected on this bridge

several pieces of German, Spanish, and British coins; the latter, of Phillip and Mary and Elizabeth, together with cannon balls, (about 12 pounders), pike heads, and other implements of war. These were all lying upon a stratum of sand, about seven feet thick, under which was a bed of clay, eight feet thick, which rested on the solid rock, where the foundation was laid.

In sinking for a foundation for the north abutment two very ancient, in appearance, and rudely formed boats, were discovered. These were 18 feet long from stem to stern. They were caulked with *moss*, and in one of them was found a large human skeleton. They were imbedded in a stratum of sand about seven feet thick, which appeared to have been deposited, at once, by some great flood, as it was not in layers, and was perfectly free from sediment. It is further remarkable, that the foundation of the old Liffey wall was laid about four feet above these boats and sand-bank, and rested upon them.

In sinking for a foundation for the south abutment of Whitworth-bridge, it was found that the foundation of the old bridge, which occupied the site, stood upon the ruins of another still more ancient. The stones of which it was formed rather resembled Portland stone than any of the sorts found in Ireland. These were regularly laid, connected by iron cramps, on a platform of oak-timber, supported by small piles, shod with iron, which was completely oxidated, and being incrusted with sandy matter, the lower ends of the piles were as hard as stone, as if entirely petrified. It is supposed the old bridge was first constructed as early as the reign of King John, but these ruins indicate that a bridge of a better and more artificial construction had, at a more remote period, preoccupied the situation.

THE CITY OF DUBLIN.

in 1720; it was removed in 1753, whilst the bridge was rebuilding, and is now placed near the Mansion-house in Dawson-street.

There is a long space from Essex-bridge to the last one eastward. Between them, an IRON BRIDGE, for foot passengers only, who pay a toll of one halfpenny, has this present year (1816) been opened. It is 140 feet long, exclusive of the end piers, and 12 feet wide. It was constructed by Alderman John Claudius Beresford and William Walsh, Esq. who derive their right to the tolls, as a remuneration, from the corporation of Dublin, whose tenants they are, and in whom the ferries and fisheries of the river are vested. On a previous notice, however, from the corporation for improving the port of Dublin, of twelve months, this bridge must be removed. It consists of one arch, forming the segment of an ellipse, has a light and picturesque appearance, and adds much to the convenience and embellishment of the river.* It cost about £3000.

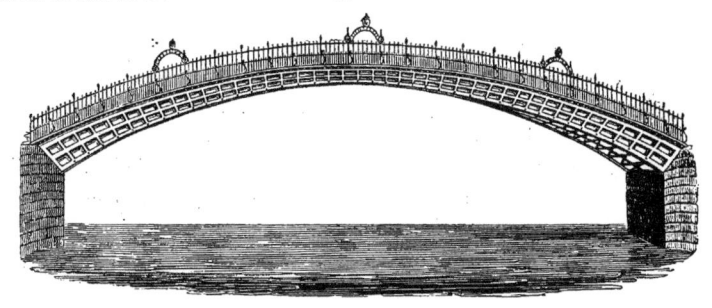

The old Custom-house was originally situated close to Essex-bridge, but the river, before the construction of docks, became most inconveniently crowded with shipping. When, therefore, the new Custom-house was built nearer the harbour, it necessarily occasioned the building a new bridge, which was begun in 1791, and opened in 1794; and, according to custom, was named after the then viceroy—CARLISLE BRIDGE. It is exceedingly well finished with cut stone, 48 feet in breadth, and 210 feet long, consisting of three arches, of light and elegant proportions.

* This elegant bridge was originally deformed by toll-houses at each end, which blocked up the entrance, and ill accorded with the structure of the bridge. These mean and unsightly edifices have been lately removed.

7 A

From the middle of Carlisle-bridge, there is a very fine panoramic view of the interior of Dublin.

Besides those bridges, the river is crossed by three ferries, one of which is immediately above, and another below the Custom-house.

PUBLIC MONUMENTS.

EQUESTRIAN STATUE OF KING WILLIAM III. COLLEGE GREEN.

THIS statue is of bronze, on an elevated marble pedestal, of good proportions. But by an effusion of more loyalty than taste, both statue and pedestal get a new coat of paint every year.*

From the first erection of this statue, it seems to have been a source of discord: In the government of the Duke of Wharton, an attack was made upon it by the party who thought its elevation an insult on their feelings, which called forth the notice and interference of Government.† In more modern times it has been a source of discord and exasperation among the lower orders, and serious disturbances have taken place at the annual commemoration of its erection. It is the practice on these occasions to decorate the statue with orange ribbons, and other party emblems, which,

---

* For inscription, see Annals, page 225.

† On Sunday, 25th June, 1700, the Jacobites or Tories, very much defaced this statue—twisted the sword it had in one hand, and wrested the truncheon from the other, daubed the face with dirt, and offered it many other indignities. The House of Lords immediately addressed the Duke of Wharton, to issue a proclamation to discover the authors, which was done the next day, offering one hundred pounds sterling for apprehending any of the persons guilty. The House of Commons was then adjourned, but when they met, the 1st of August following, they also sent an address to his Excellency, expressing their pleasure for the early care he took to bring to punishment " the insolent miscreants who, with equal malice and baseness, insulted the statue of his late Majesty King William III. of glorious memory." It does not appear that the authors of the outrage were ever discovered, but the city caused the statue to be repaired, and a new truncheon put into its hands, the 24 companies of the city attending the solemnity, on which occasion the thanks of the House of Commons was given to the Lord Mayor and citizens, nem. con. for their zeal and care in repairing that noble monument of their gratitude.—Wharton's Life, p. 83.

THE CITY OF DUBLIN.

though harmless in themselves, have unfortunately become badges of distinction. These practices every well-wisher to peace and good order would be pleased to have discontinued, and accordingly they have been latterly much discountenanced.

EQUESTRIAN STATUE OF GEORGE I.

This statue was first erected on Essex-bridge in 1720, but on rebuilding the bridge, it was taken down, and in 1798, re-erected near the Mansion-house in Dawson-street.

The following inscription is on the pedestal.
Be it REMEMBERED that
at the time when REBELLION and DISLOYALTY
were the CHARACTERISTICS of the day,
The loyal CORPORATION of
the City of Dublin re-
elevated this STATUE of the
FIRST MONARCH of the
ILLUSTRIOUS HOUSE of HANOVER.
THOMAS FLEMMING, Lord Mayor,
JONAS PAISLEY and WILLIAM HENRY ARCHER, Sheriffs.
Anno Domini 1798.

EQUESTRIAN STATUE OF GEORGE II.

This statue was first erected in 1758, in the middle of St. Stephen's Green. On the late alteration and improvement of that grand square, the low pedestal on which it stood was removed, and another, much more elevated, substituted. The statue, notwithstanding, from the largeness of the area, is almost lost and overlooked. It was proposed to remove it to a more suitable site, of which the removal of the statue of George I. was a precedent. This was, however, over-ruled, and it remains insignificant in itself, and no ways ornamental to the place. For inscription, and further account, see page 460.

PEDESTRIAN STATUE OF GEORGE III.

This stands in the Royal Exchange, and has the following inscription.*

* For further notice of this statue, as also for that of Doctor Lucas, see page 552.

Front.
GEORGIO III
M. B. F. ET H. REGI.
OPTIMO PRINCIPI

HUGO PERCY
NORTHUMBRIÆ COMES
HIBERNIÆ PROREX
PRO SUA IN CIV. DUBL.
BENEVOLENTIA
AD. MDCCLIV
P H C..

On the back of the plinth.

HUGNI PERCY
NORTHUMBRIÆ COMITI
HIB. PROREGI
HOC QUALECUNQUE TESTIMONIUM
CIV. DUBL.
A. D. MDCCLXXXVII
DESCRIBI VOLUIT

But one of the finest statues in Europe has been lately erected in the Court of Proprietors of the Bank (late House of Lords). It represents his present Majesty George III. in his parliamentary robes, with the ensigns of the Orders of the Bath and of St. Patrick, and is allowed to be a correct likeness. It stands on a beautiful pedestal, decorated with the figures of Religion and Justice, and having the following inscription—

GEORGIUS III
REX

This very excellent statue was formed out of a single block of white marble, and was executed by the younger Bacon; it cost two thousand pounds.

NELSON'S PILLAR.

The testimonials of national gratitude and admiration to the memory of this favourite naval hero are already numerous in the British dominions. That erected by public subscription in Dublin is perhaps the greatest of any of them. It is situated in the centre of Sackville-street, opposite Mary-street and Earl-street, and is composed of a pedestal, column, and capital of the Tuscan order, on the summit of which a colossal statue of

THE CITY OF DUBLIN.

Lord Nelson stands. On the four pannels of the pedestal are inscribed the names and dates of his principal victories, together with the name NELSON. On the south side is inscribed, TRAFALGAR XXI OCTOBER MDCCCV.—On the north, THE NILE I AUGUST MDCCXCVIII.—On the west, ST. VINCENT, XIV FEBRUARY MDCCXCVII.; and on the east, COPENHAGEN, II APRIL MDCCCI.

Within the pedestal and column there are 168 stone steps, to ascend to the top, which has a parapet of iron railing, from whence there is a superb panoramic view of the city, the country, and the fine bay.

The foundation stone of this monument was laid with much ceremony, attended by the civil and military authorities, with the Lord-lieutenant at their head.

A brass plate, covering a recess in the stone, filled with various coins, has the following inscription.

By the
Blessing of Almighty God
to commemorate
The transcendant heroic atchievements of
The Rt. Honble. Lord Vicount NELSON
Duke of Bronte in Sicily
Vice Amiral of the White Squadron of His Majesty's Fleet
who fell gloriously in the Battle off
CAPE TRAFALGAR
on the 21st October 1805.
When he obtained for his country
A VICTORY
over the combined fleets of France and Spain
unparalleled in naval history.

The first stone of a triumphant Pillar
was laid
by his Grace
Charles Duke of Richmond and Lennox
Lord Lieutenant General and General Governor of Ireland,
on the 15th day of Feby.
in the year of our Lord 1808,
And in the 48th year of the reign of our most
Gracious Sovereign
GEORGE THE THIRD.

The design of this triumphal column was given by William Wilkins, Esq. architect, fellow of Caius College, Cambridge. It is of most ponderous proportions,* which is not relieved by the least decoration. Its vast unsightly pedestal is nothing better than a quarry of cut stone, and the clumsy shaft is divested of either base, or what can properly be called a capital. Yet with all this baldness and deformity, it might have had a good effect when viewed at a distance, or placed any where else; but it not

* The Dimensions of the Pillar are as follows.

	Feet.	Inches.
The pedestal, whose diameter is 20 feet, is	30	1
Shaft of column, diameter 20 feet at bottom,	71	8
Capital of do.	7	0
	78	8
Epistilion and plinth at top, for the statue,	12	6
Statue,	13	0
Total height of column and statue,	134	3

only obtrudes its blemishes on every passenger, but actually spoils and blocks up our finest street, and literally darkens the two other streets opposite to it, which, though spacious enough, look like lanes. These were objections to its site at first, but they are now become still stronger, since the building of the new Post-office close to it, for, by contrast, it in a great measure destroys the effect of one of the largest and finest porticos in Europe.*

THE WELLINGTON TROPHY,
OR,
"TESTIMONIAL."

It having been resolved by a number of the most respectable inhabitants of Dublin, and of other parts of Ireland, to erect a monument commemorative of the great achievements of their illustrious countryman, the Duke of Wellington; the expense of which, estimated at twenty thousand pounds, was to be defrayed by voluntary subscription; when, therefore, sixteen thousand pounds had been subscribed, a select committee was chosen from among the subscribers, to conduct the work.

The first act of the committee was to issue proposals and assign premiums for models and plans, in consequence of which a considerable number were sent in by artists from various parts of the united kingdom. Out of these, six models, judged of superior merit, were selected, and submitted to public inspection at the Dublin Society's exhibition rooms, in Hawkins'-street. Finally, one of the six was pitched upon, which had been transmitted by Mr. Smirke, the English architect; as, in the opinion of the committee and majority of the subscribers, uniting in itself all the requisites for the intended

* Materials, expenditure, and receipts.

22,090 cubic feet of black stone, and 7310 ditto of cut mountain granite, with stone cutter's bill, per contract, - L.4876 11 3	Amount of Subscriptions,	L.6608	16 6
	Concert at Rotunda, -	137	9 10
	Interest on money lent, -	499	7 3
Flagging, railing, painting, and carpenter's bill, - 710 15 8	Entrance money to ascend the column for one year, at 10d. each person, deducting cost of attendance, - -	92	13 7
Cost of pillar, L.5587 15 8			
William Kirk, sculptor, 300 0 0			
Portland stone, model, scaffolding, 329 2 3	Total receipts,	L.7138	7 2
Cost of statue (L. 629), with lamps and flag staffs, - 83 0 9	Total expenditure,	6856	8 3
	Balance Cr.	L. 281	18 11
Total cost of pillar and statue, L.6299 18 8	Laid out in stock, which, with the entrance money, is to keep the monument in repair.		
Contingent expenses, - 556 9 7			
Total expenditure, L.6856 8 3			

monument. But despotism in the fine arts can least of any be submitted to, and the maxim, *Nullius adictus jurare in verba magistri*, is peculiarly applicable to the arts and literature.

Before offering a remark, let the reader judge from a just and exact description of the chosen model, (of which the annexed vignette is a correct figure), how far it is likely to produce the effect and promote the design intended.

On the summit platform of a flight of steps, of an ascent so steep and a construction so uncouth, that they seem made to prohibit instead of to invite the spectator to ascend them, a pedestal is erected of the simplest square form, in the die of which, on the four sides, are as many pannels, having figures in basso-relievo emblematic of the principal victories won by the Duke. Before the centre of what is intended for the principal front is a narrow pedestal insulated, and resting partly on the steps and partly on the platform. This pedestal supports an equestrian statue of the hero. From the platform, a massive obelisk rises, truncated and of thick and heavy proportions. On the four façades of the obelisk are inscribed the names of all the victories gained by the Duke of Wellington, from his first career in India to the battle of Waterloo. The whole structure is to be of plain mountain granite, without any other decoration whatever.

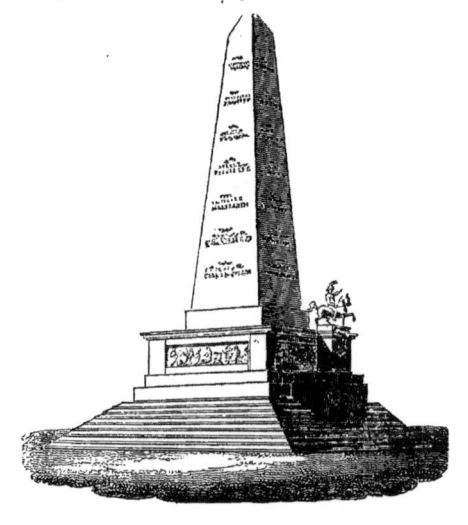

THE CITY OF DUBLIN.

The dimensions are as follow—

Base, formed by the lowest step, 120 feet on each side, or in circuit 480 feet.

Perpendicular section of steps, 20 feet.

Subplinth of pedestal on the top of steps, 60 feet square by 10 feet high.

Pedestal, 56 feet square by 24 feet high.

Obelisk, 28 feet square at the base, and 150 feet high, diminishing in the proportion of one inch in every foot.

Total heigth of the monument 205 feet.

A public monument at once magnificent and beautiful, rich and appropriate in its decorations, yet striking and impressive in its general effect, is, it must be confessed, not easy to invent or construct. If the ancients are our supreme masters in any art or science, it is in architecture. The more we deviate from the specimens left by them, the more we run into absurdity and deformity. Now, the obelisk is not classical for a triumphal trophy. If it be admissible, it must belong to the funereal order, ranking with the pyramid and such mausolea. It originated in Egypt, where it was also used as a gnomon to mark the meridian. Obelisks are already numerous enough in Ireland. The figure, simple as it is, betrays a great poverty of invention. The model seems to have been borrowed from those little obelisks made of spar, the common ornaments of chimney pieces, which the monument in question resembles in every thing but size and polish. But the obelisk form is not the only objection to the Wellington Testimonial. Its base, composed of an inclined plane of inconvenient steps, is abrupt and unsightly. The pedestal, with the basso-relievos, though the least exceptionable part, resembles a huge tomb-stone, to which a minor pedestal is attached, like an excrescence, on which is placed the Equestrian Statue, that contrives to conceal the figures sculptured on the front entablature, whilst the shaft of the obelisk is remarkably clumsy. Judging therefore from the model, the *tout ensemble* produces an effect singularly heavy, bald, and frigid.

This monument was proposed to be erected in the middle of Stephen's Green, or of Merion-square, but the inhabitants seeing that its inelegant form, and lumpish shape, making its huge unadorned base equal in magnitude to the highest house, refused to give it admission. Upon this rejection, the site of the Salute Battery in the Phenix Park has been given for its erection, and this change of place is fortunate for the design. Situated in a large romantic park, on elevated ground, surrounded with plantations, and accompanied with rich and extensive scenery, its vast size and towering height will doubtless produce an imposing and grand effect, whilst its defects may perhaps be overlooked or disregarded.

Nevertheless, a national monument of such importance ought surely to be erected within the city; it should every where meet the public eye, and not be sought for to be visited. Besides, above all other cities, Dublin is most in want of elevated and aspiring public structures, to relieve the immense flat mass of buildings of which it is composed. It is therefore to be regretted, that a design less exceptionable was not selected from among the six. It would then have readily gained admission in the centre of one or other of the squares. Such was that sent in by Mr. Hamilton, which, although of the obelisk order, had much more elegant proportions, whilst its base was conspicuous for grandeur, beauty, and variety. Such was also the design given in by Mr. Baker, master of the Dublin Society's School for Architecture. This was a triumphal arch, with a double tier of arches, which gave it a rich and noble elevation. The emblematic decorations were beautiful and appropriate, and under the superior centre arch was placed the equestrian statue of the hero.

BARRACKS.

The city of Dublin has to boast of the most noble erections of this kind perhaps in Europe, whether considered in reference to salubrity of situation, extent of building, or excellence of architecture. These barracks were erected in 1706, at the expence of the crown; they stand at the western extremity of the city, on an airy and elevated eminence which overhangs the Liffy, and commands an extensive view of the town and the country contiguous to the river. They consist of several squares, three of which are built only on three sides, leaving the fourth open to the fine view and wholesome breeze. In the rere of these is the Palatine square, which forms a very noble quadrangle; it is built of hewn granite, and ornamented with a cornice and pediments at the opposite sides; at the western extremity is the horse barrack. The whole is capable of containing four battalions of foot and one of horse, or about 5000 men. It is entered by two gates from

Barrack-street, and several posterns from Arbour-hill, to which it extends. Notwithstanding the extent and accommodation afforded by these barracks, it was unfortunately found necessary to augment the military protection of the metropolis, and temporary barracks were formed during the last 25 years, in ten different parts of the city, viz.—Stephen's Green and Baggot-street, for cavalry; Marlbrough-street, James-street, Cork-street, Essex-street, George's-street, Henry-street, Kevin-street,* and the Combe, for infantry. When the necessity for this distribution of the military force had ceased, it was deemed expedient to remove the inconvenience which they, caused. They have all been discontinued, with the exception of that in George's-street, which accommodates one regiment of infantry, and is to be permanent; and to supply the place of others, two large edifices were erected in the vicinity of Dublin, to accommodate the troops which had been quartered in the city, one at Golden Bridge, near Kilmainham, and the other near Portobello. The first of these is called Richmond Barracks, from his excellency the Duke of Richmond. It is erected on an elevated and healthy situation, not far from the prison of Kilmainham, between Golden Bridge and the banks of the Canal. It consists of two fronts, with extensive courts, open to the north and south; these are connected in a right line by a row of light and elegant houses, 300 yards in length; on the east and west fronts are two spacious areas, and in the centre a communication through a large portal, surmounted with a cupola and spire. The second is also on the bank of the same Canal, where it passes Portobello, and is called for that reason Portobello Barracks. It is very extensive, covering 27 acres of ground, and has two very spacious open courts on each side of

* This barrack had formerly been the residence of the Archbishop of Dublin, and disposed of in times of peril and disturbance to government, as a fit situation for quartering soldiers. It is a melancholy appropriation of a prelate's residence, who has now no palace in Dublin. Oliver Cromwell had formerly converted Westminster Abbey into a barrack for his horse, and James II. had assigned Trinity College, Dublin, for lodging for his foot soldiers; but they were again restored to their original use when the melancholy periods of their respective alienations were passed away.

It must be confessed, however, that this Archiepiscopal residence in Dublin was unfit for the accommodation of a prelate, and its present appropriation has materially improved both the appearance and security of the part of the town in which it is situated. Part of it is now assigned to the accommodation of the police patrole. When the Palace was suffered to run to decay, it was purchased by Government for the sum of 7000l. which was deposited in the Bank of Ireland, and placed there to an account entitled, " The Fund for providing a See-house for the Archbishop of Dublin," with suitable offices, in some convenient place, and also to erect a court-house for the manor of St. Sepulchre's within the manor. See 44th Geo. III.

a range of buildings which communicates by a central gate. Richmond barrack is for infantry, and Portobello for cavalry. Besides these, there is a barrack for artillery at Chapel Izod, about two miles from Dublin.

THEATRES.

BEFORE the erection of a regular Theatre in Dublin, plays were exhibited, as in London, at the private houses of noblemen and gentlemen. In the reign of Elizabeth, the ball room of the Castle was converted into a theatre, in which the nobility were the principal performers. The play at that time in highest esteem was Gorboduck, which was performed at the Castle on her Majesty's birth day. It was one she was fond of, and had been represented before her at Whitehall, in London, by the students of the Middle Temple, some years before; but it was not till the reign of Charles I. that any regular theatre was established in Dublin. In the year 1635, during the government of Lord Strafford, John Ogilby, the early translator of Homer, was master of the revels, and he erected, at his own expense, a theatre in Werburgh-street, which cost him £2000. To this he invited all the itinerant players of merit, who strolled from booth to booth; and to give his stage celebrity, Shirley, who was the popular writer of the day, and an intimate friend of Ogilby, wrote for him the "Royal Master," which was first performed here. It seems also to have called forth native talent, and roused the dormant genius of Dublin. Henry Burnet, an Irishman, wrote "Langartha," which was also performed here, and was the last play ever acted at this theatre. The rebellion now broke out, and for some time threw its dark shade on every intellectual amusement. This theatre was closed by an order from the Lords Justice, and it never was reopened.

After a lapse of twenty years, Ogilby's friends procured for him the renewal of his patent, and the nobility and gentry entered into a subscription to erect a new theatre. The site chosen was near the Castle, and the centre of the city; it was then called Orange-street, but since Smock-alley. The edifice proceeded with great dispatch, and it was finished in 1662, the same year it was commenced. It was opened with the play of "Pompey," translated from the French of Corneille, by Mrs. C. Philips, the celebrated Orinda, and it was followed by another called "Horace." These plays were not performed in England till the death of the translator, which happened two years after, and thus they received their first currency on the infant Dublin stage. But the haste with which the theatre was erected, proved fatal to its existence; about nine years after it was built, it fell upon the audience during the representation of a play, and killed and wounded several persons. Theatrical amusements were again suspended in Dublin, and the company was so dispersed during the commotions which followed at this period, that, on the restoration of peace, after the battle of the Boyne, no players could be found in Dublin to express the joy of the citizens, and commemorate the event by a theatrical representation. The citizens themselves, therefore, formed a company for this purpose, and performed Othello in the repaired theatre of Smock-alley, to which the public were gratuitously invited. Amongst these gentlemen was Mr. Wilkes, who played the part of Othello, and was then first introduced to the notice of the public as a dramatic performer.[*]

On the death of Mr. Ogilby, the situation of master of the revels, and the patent for acting plays, were conferred upon Mr. Ashbury. He had been an officer in the Irish army, and had distinguished himself by his zeal and activity in the royal cause; the Duke of Ormond, therefore, remunerated his services by appointing him to succeed Ogilby. He invited several actors of eminence to Dublin, and the theatre prospered under his management in a degree unknown to his unfortunate predecessor. Among the performers who appeared at Smock-alley during his administration, was the celebrated George Farquhar.[†]

[*] WILKES was born at Rathfarnham, near Dublin, in the year 1670. His grandfather, Judge Wilkes, had raised a troop of horse at his own expense for the service of Charles I. and was obliged to take refuge in Ireland when the royal party were discomfited. Wilkes received a liberal education, and was placed as principal clerk under Secretary Southwell. Here he contracted an acquaintance with Richards, an actor of some merit; and from hearing him rehearse his parts, acquired a strong propensity for the stage, and was so well known for his private theatrical talents, that he was unanimously chosen to play Othello on the public occasion above noticed: his success induced him to leave his lucrative employment and devote himself to the stage. In 1698 he went to London, and was engaged at Covent Garden, at a salary of £4. per week. He soon became the rival of Betterton, and attained the head of his profession. In 1711 he paid his last visit to his native country, and played Sir H. Wildair nineteen nights successively at Smock-alley Theatre.

[*] GEORGE FARQUHAR was born in Derry, in the north of Ireland, in the year 1678, and entered

In the year 1701, a circumstance arose characteristic of the manners of the times. On the first night of performing Shadwel's " Libertine," a very profligate play, the galleries of the theatre were uncommonly crowded, and suddenly gave way. This was considered by the people as a visitation of Providence for encouraging such a representation. The play was immediately discontinued, and the superstition of the time happily contributed to banish for a season vice and immorality from the stage.*

On the death of Mr. Ashbury, in 1720, the management of the theatre devolved on Thomas Ellrington, his son-in-law. Under his direction, Smock-alley arrived to a considerable degree of respectability, as he was a

the University of Dublin in 1694. His father dying soon after, he was left to follow the bent of his own inclinations, which led him to the stage. He appeared at Smock-alley Theatre in the year after his entrance into college, and commenced at a salary of 20 shillings a week. His first character was Othello, in which he gained some applause, though he had personal defects which precluded the possibility of his ever rising to eminence as an actor, a weak voice which nobody could distinctly hear, and a timidity which nothing could assure. He was, however, driven from the stage by a very different cause. He was performing the part of Guyomer, in the " Indian Emperor;" by some negligence he forgot to change his sword for a foil, and when he encountered Vasquez, he severely wounded a Mr. Price, who played that character. He now determined to leave a profession which rendered him liable to an accident which he deeply felt and deplored, and he applied himself solely to write for the stage. He soon composed " Love and a Bottle," and set out from Dublin, with the manuscript in his pocket, to try his fortunes in another country. His play was well received in London, and he soon after produced " The Constant Couple," which had an astonishing run both in England and Ireland. He had now obtained a commission in the army, but he felt an irresistible propensity to return once more to his native country, and play a part in one of his own celebrated comedies. For this purpose it was necessary to obtain the permission of the Duke of Ormond, the then Viceroy of Ireland, which was granted. By this second attempt on the Dublin stage he gained more profit than fame, and soon after returned to England, where he was persuaded to sell his commission, on the faithless promise of a nobleman, who proferred to procure him another. The frustration of his hopes broke his heart. He prematurely died in 1707, leaving behind him a character as a dramatic writer which shed a lustre on his native country. It was said, that he has taken so much liberty with his country and his profession in some of his comedies, that had he not been an Irishman and a soldier, he would have been called to a severe account for it. His plays are—

Love and a Bottle	1699	Twin Rivals	1703
Constant Couple	1700	Stage Coach	1705
Sir Harry Wildair	1701	Recruiting Officer	1705
Inconstant	1702	Beaux Stratagem,	1707

* It is this play which has been altered and exhibited since in London and Dublin under the less exceptionable form of " Don Juan, or the Libertine Destroyed," with considerable success.

THE CITY OF DUBLIN.

man of no less talent as an actor, than skill as a manager. Performers of the best reputation were invited to Dublin, and every play of merit on the London stage was carefully got up and strikingly exhibited. His premature death, however, was a blow to the rising character of the Irish theatre, which it did not for a long time recover. The exhibition of infant performers on the public stage, though considered a modern extravagance, is of very early date,* and was at this time a favourite project in Dublin. In the year 1731, Madam Violante had attempted to establish a booth for the performance of rope dancers, but the public were soon tired of the exhibition, and she converted her booth into a theatre. To make her performance more attractive by its novelty and singularity, she exhibited all theatrical pieces with a company of children under the age of 10 years. It is remarkable, that the Beggars' Opera was first introduced to the notice of a Dublin audience by these infants, and that Mrs. Margaret Woffington made her first theatrical effort among them in the character of Polly.†

* In the year 1578, the children of St. Pauls performed dramatic entertainments in London. In the beginning of the reign of Elizabeth, the children of the Royal Chapel were formed into a company, and a few years afterwards another company was formed, called the "Children of the Revels." These two juvenile companies became very famous; all Lily's plays and many of Jonson's were first performed by them. So great was the estimation in which they were held, that the adult companies in Shakespeare's time grew jealous of them. It is said in Hamlet,—" There is, Sir, an aiery of young " children, little Eyases, that cry out on the top of the question, and are most tyrannically clapped for " it. These are now the fashion."—Act II. sc. II. In these latter years, the fashion was revived. In 1803, Master H. W. Betty, aged 13, and in 1805, Miss Mudie, aged eight years, astonished the London and Dublin Theatres with their precocious powers. They were both natives of Ireland. Miss Mudie, and it is said Master Betty also, was born at Belfast.

† The house in which this infant company exhibited stood on the spot where Fownes-street is now built. It belonged to Chief-justice Whitehal, and had behind it a spacious garden, which extended to the ground on which Crow-street Theatre now stands. It was entered by an avenue called Fownes-court. At the entrance of this court, the mother of Mrs. Woffington kept, for many years, a stall or shop, and sold fruit to those who frequented the theatre. Here it should appear her daughter was first seen and noticed by Madam Violante, and introduced to the public among her infant company. She afterwards removed with her to George's-lane. Her first appearance at Aungier-street was as a dancer, and the first speaking character she performed was Ophelia. When arrived at some eminence on the Dublin stage, she was called on by several persons of quality to attempt the character of Sir H. Wildair. In this she succeeded so admirably, that she was immediately invited to London, where the novelty of the attempt and its astonishing success attracted immense crowds for 20 nights in succession. The public had never before witnessed such a display of talent; they now for the first time comprehended how the conceptions of an author could be embodied on the stage, and the finished portrait of

The growing propensity of the people of Dublin for theatrical amusements and public spectacles was now very strongly evinced. It was determined to erect another theatre, and a large piece of ground was taken in Aungier-street, at the corner of Longford-street, for the purpose. This site was selected as being near Stephen's Green, and the centre of the then polite world, and all persons of rank and fashion became subscribers to it. The first stone was laid with great pomp on the 8th of May 1733. Medals were struck for the occasion, some of which were placed under the foundation stones, and an immense concourse of people attended, who were liberally supplied with refreshments. The theatre was raised with such great expedition, that it was completely finished in ten months, and opened with Farquhar's " Recruiting Officer," on Saturday the 19th of March following.

To accommodate the trading part of the town also, a new theatre was opened in Rainsfoad-street, in the Liberties. This part of the city now so desolate, was at that time the residence of all that was wealthy in the trading and manufacturing world. This theatre opened the same year to a crowded audience, with a new tragedy called the " Fate of Ambition," which had not merit however to rescue it from oblivion. Between these theatres of the court and citizens a rivalry commenced, which continued some years with various success.

There had been, it appears, in Dublin, three theatres in which dramatic

fashionable life be justly represented by the careless gaiety and elegant vivacity of an accomplished performer, whose innate genius surmounted the supposed insuperable difficulties of birth, sex, and education. She now returned to her native city, where her singular eminence procured her as singular a distinction. A convivial society connected with the theatre had been formed, called the Beef-Steak Club; it consisted of 30 or 40 members, who were generally peers or members of parliament. They met at the manager's house, and by their rules all females were excluded; an exception, however, was made specially in favour of Margaret Woffington. She was not only admitted a member, but, by unanimous consent, elected president, and continued for many years to fill the chair with an ease and gaiety peculiar to herself. Though raised to an unexpected height of favour, admired, courted, and caressed by all ranks, it made no alteration in her manners. She continued to shew the same affability and kindness to all around her that marked her conduct in obscure life. It is told, to her singular honour, that she never refused to exert her astonishing powers for the lowest retainer of the theatre; and of 26 benefits in one season, she acted for 24. The characters she principally excelled in were, Charlotte in the Nonjuror, Lady Townly, Hermione, and Sir H. Wildair, displaying a talent varied with surprising versatility. She died in 1760, having reigned for 20 years the unrivalled favourite of the London and Dublin theatres.

THE CITY OF DUBLIN.

pieces, properly so called, were exhibited—Madam Violante's, Fownes-court, Ward's Theatre in Dame-street, and Smock-alley. Two more were thus added. A new music hall had been also erected in Crow-street, at which ridottos were performed; and an entertainment, called "Ashton's Medly," was exhibited in Patrick's-close, a neighbourhood now more desolate than even Rainsford-street. Thus, it appears then, that Dublin, nearly a century ago, supported in one season seven places of public amusement, in five of which dramatic pieces were represented. To these the price of admission was nominally the same, but comparatively much greater than at present. Boxes 5s. 5d.; lattices 4s. 4d.; pit 3s. 3d.; gallery 2s. 2d. All ranks and orders of the community flocked to these spectacles in every part of the town—rivalry of interest in the managers produced a competition of talent. New plays by native authors received their first currency here,[*] and every

---

[*] As a native author, HENRY BROOKE was at that time a deserved favourite with the Dublin audience. This gentleman was the son of the Rev. Mr. Brooke of Rantavan, county of Cavan, rector of Killincar, &c. He was educated at Dr. Sheridan's school, and sent early to Trinity College, Dublin, from whence, at the age of 17, he removed to the Temple. In due time he was called to the bar, and practised in Dublin as chamber council. After some time, however, he returned to England, took up his residence at Twickenham, and became the friend and companion of Pope, Swift, Lord Littelton, and Lord Chatham, by whom he was introduced to Frederick Prince of Wales, who shewed him many marks of good will. Under this patronage he wrote "Gustavus Vasa, or The *Deliverer* of his Country." This noble drama was first prepared for exhibition at Drury-lane, but when every thing was ready for the representation, the Lord Chamberlain interfered and prohibited it. Mr. Brooke now returned to Dublin, and as the authority of the Chamberlain did not extend to the Irish stage, the play was prepared with great care for a Dublin audience, and was represented for the first time at Aungier-street, in February, 1741, where it was received with the highest applause, and kept possession of the stage for many years. His next play was the "Earl of Westmoreland, or The *Betrayer* of his Country," as a companion to the former, acted also in Dublin for the first time in the year 1741. The independent spirit of Mr. Brooke's dramatic Muse seemed ill to accord with the then government of either England or Ireland. In 1748 his piece called "Jack the Giant Queller" was brought out by Mr. Sheridan at Smock-alley. It was as usual highly relished by the audience, but the next day an order was issued by the Lords Justices prohibiting the further representation of it, and the play was accordingly withdrawn. The piece contained general reflections on bad governors, which the then administration applied to themselves. Mr. Brooke, after enjoying the tributes of applause and good will from a public who admired his talents and respected his worth for a long period, received a violent shock by the death of his wife, which impaired his faculties and clouded the evening rays of that genius whose meridian was so brilliant. He became an enthusiast on religious subjects, and died in Dublin, the 10th of October, 1788. His talents will be justly appreciated, perhaps, by the estimation in which he was held by his contemporaries. He is mentioned with

performer of eminence on the London stage was to be seen in Dublin. Quin and Cibber were found at Aungier-street at the same time that Woffington and Garrick exhibited at Smock-alley; and so great were the crowds which frequented the theatres in the hottest months of summer, that an epidemic disorder appeared in the city, which carried off numbers, and, from the circumstance of its supposed origin, it was called the Garrick fever.

A few years after, another theatre was added to the number. On the occasion of some dispute at Smock-alley, several of the performers seceded, adopted the appellation of the City Company of Comedians, and under the sanction of the Lord Mayor, erected the little theatre in Capel-street, which opened with the Merchant of Venice. This continues to be occasionally used at the present day, and is the only one of those already mentioned that either yet exists or has not been appropriated to some other purpose. But it was not till the year 1745, that the Dublin Theatre assumed the form of a well regulated dramatic establishment. Dublin was at this time infested with a number of idle and profligate young men who seem to have taken a license from their rank to violate the laws of the land, as well as those of decency and decorum. They frequented all public assemblies, where trampling on the orders and regulations of the place, and terrifying the more peaceable seemed to be the end and object of their coming. The theatre was their particular haunt, where both the performers and the audience were entirely under their control, and subject to their caprice. The actors also were in a state of great insubordination; the irregular payment of their salaries was a frequent source of discontent, and constant pretext for disregarding the directions of the manager, and neglecting the regulations of the theatre. The drama in Dublin, thus assailed from without, and

distinguished praise by many. B. Whitehead thus characterizes him in reference to Shakespeare.—

Lured by his laurels never fading bloom,
You boldly snatched the trophy from his tomb,
Taught the declining Muse again to soar,
And to Britannia gave one poet more.

Mr. Brooke's works were published in Dublin in 4 vols. in 1778, and again in 1792. He was the author of 14 plays, including those mentioned above. He wrote beside, many miscellaneous works, among which the most noted are, "The Farmer's Letters," written in the style of Swift's Drapier's Letters, and two novels, "The Fool of Quality," and "Juliet Grenville."

in a state of mutiny within, was feeble and fluctuating, without system, order, or regularity. At this time Mr. Sheridan happily succeeded to the management, and set himself to remedy those evils. A union had taken place between the theatres of Aungier-street and Smock-alley, and Mr. Sheridan was now called upon to direct both. For this situation he was eminently qualified. His temper was remarkably mild and gentle, yet unremittingly persevering; though he had rather convince than command, yet he was resolute in enforcing compliance with whatever he was assured was right. Passionately devoted to the theatre, he beheld with regret the humiliating condition to which it was reduced at this time, despised and deserted by the grave, the rational, and every lover of order and decorum. His first care was to give respectability to the character of his actors. He raised their salaries liberally in proportion to their merits, and he scrupulously discharged whatever he engaged to pay. The pretexts for irregularity were thus prevented, and the reproach annexed to debts and poverty was removed. Nor did his public conduct yield in firmness to the punctuality and honour of his private engagements. He resisted, though at the hazard of his life and property, the intrusion of the dissolute and profligate young men behind the scenes, and by his spirited exertions a principal offender was brought before a legal tribunal, which inflicted an exemplary punishment.* Since that period the insolence and impunity of

* These young men were generally distinguished by the name of " Bucks," which was frequently prefixed to their surname, as an agnomen to distinguish the most eminent. In this way the names of several " Bucks" in Ireland have descended to posterity. It was their practice to walk up and down through Lucas's Coffee-house, with a train to their morning gown, sweeping the floor, and challenge any man to fight who by accident trod upon it. They also assumed the appellation of " Mohawks" and " Cherokees," and their actions would not disgrace their savage archetypes. The incident which occurred in the theatre would be hardly credited in a civilized country. On the 19th of January, 1746, a young man of the name of Kelly, went to the pit much intoxicated, and climbing over the spikes, got upon the stage, and proceeded to the green-room, where he insulted some of the females in the most gross and indecent manner. As the play could not proceed, he was taken away and civilly conducted back to the pit; here he seized a basket of oranges, and amused himself by pelting the performers, particularly Mr. Sheridan, whom he publicly abused in the grossest manner. A few nights after he returned with 50 of his associates, who, climbing over the spikes of the stage, proceeded to the dressing rooms, in search of Mr. Sheridan, with drawn swords, which they thrust into the chests and presses of clothes to *feel*, as they facetiously observed, if he was there, and not finding him, they proceeded to his house in Dorset-street, with the same murderous intention. After much riot for several nights in the theatre of a similar kind, in which the celebrated Dr. Lucas took a decided part in favour of decorum

these men has ceased, and the Dnblin public are indebted to him for that propriety, order, and regularity which now exits in our theatres, equally serviceable to the audience and to the actor, by ascertaining and vindicating the privileges of both.

The Irish stage continued to prosper under Mr. Sheridan's management till the year 1754. But at that period party spirit ran very high, and a speech* in the tragedy of "Mahomet," which was appropriated by a particular party, was the signal for the complete destruction of the theatre. He now retired from public life, but afterwards resumed the management, till an important event in the theatrical annals again compelled him to quit it for ever.

An idea had been for some time entertained of erecting a new and rival theatre in Dublin. For this purpose the walls of the late music hall in Crow-street, and several contiguous buildings were thrown down, and a new theatre erected on the foundation, which opened on 23d of October, 1758, with the play of "She Would and She Would Not." To this Barry and Woodward brought a new company, and established an opposition to Sheridan. The contest was carried on with various success for a short period, till at length a ship, bringing over a reinforcement from England to the company in Smock-alley, was lost on the coast of Scotland, and all

and the manager, the cause was brought to a legal decision, under a general impression in Dublin that a jury could never find a gentleman guilty of an assault on a player. It was on this occasion that a barrister remarked, "he had never seen a gentleman player," when Mr. Sheridan replied, "I hope you see one now, sir." Kelly was found guilty of the assault, and sentenced to a fine of 500*l.* and three months imprisonment. This critical and salutary chastisement had an excellent effect in restraining the insolence of those licentious men, and the *ebrius ac petulans* was afterwards rarely met with at the theatre.

* The passage which excited the uproar was in the speech of Alcanor, in the first act. It was as follows.

      If, ye powers divine,
  Ye mark the movements of this nether world,
  And bring them to account—crush, crush those vipers
  Who, singled out by the community
  To guard your rights, shall, for a grasp of ore,
  Or paltry office, sell them to the foe.

This was loudly applauded and encored by a party in the pit. The first night their commands were complied with, but on the next occasion the speech would not be again repeated, and they immediately destroyed the house.

on board perished, including Mr. T. Cibber and Mrs. Maddox. This was decisive of Mr. Sheridan's fate, and he left the management of the Dublin Theatre never to resume it.

On the retirement of Mr. Sheridan, the sole management of the Dublin Theatres devolved on Barry and Woodward, till a new opposition arose in Mr. Mossop,* who assumed the management of Smock-alley Theatre; between him and Barry the rivalry continued till the year 1767, when the latter resigned, and Mossop became sole proprietor of both theatres. On the death of Mr. Mossop, in 1761, Mr. Ryder† succeeded as manager, and continued

* For a further account of Sheridan and Barry, see "Biographical Sketches," annexed. HENRY MOSSOP was the son of a clergyman who possessed a living in the diocese of Tuam, where he was born in 1729. As his father resided entirely at his rectory, he sent his son to his uncle, who kept a bookseller's shop in Dublin; by him he was placed under the care of Mr. Butler, a clergyman, who kept a classical school in Digges-sreet, where, in five years, he completed his preparatory studies, and entered Trinity College, Dublin. Having graduated, he proceeded to London, to another uncle, who had promised to promote his views, but not meeting the reception he expected, he turned his attention to the stage, to which he was long and early attached in Ireland. He first offered himself to Garrick and Rich, but after displaying the best specimens of his ability, these judges pronounced him "utterly unfit for the stage." Rejected in England, he applied to the theatre in Ireland, and was introduced to Mr. Sheridan by his friend Francis Gentleman. Sheridan at once detected his latent genius, and allowed him his choice of characters to make his debut. He chose Zanga, and astonished the audience with a fervid but untutored energy which at once established his character and the manager's penetration. After a chequered life of celebrity and misfortunes, he retired from Dublin to London, where he died in 1761, in great distress, having swayed a stormy sceptre for 10 years.

† It is not very certain where THOMAS RYDER was born. The "Biographia Dramatica" asserts only, " it is said he was born in Lincolnshire." It is by some asserted he was an Irishman, born at Carlow, and others, that he was born in Dublin. This much is certain, that he was known to the Dublin public as a printer and bookseller in Castle-street, and that he made his first appearance at Smock-alley Theatre, in Captain Plume, on December 7, 1757. His first acquaintance with opulence arose from an unexpected incident. Mrs. Ryder met accidentally with a lottery ticket on her toilet, where it had lain for a long time neglected; on examining the drawing books it was found to be a prize of a considerable amount. This fortunate incident was the cause of much future distress. He not only established a splendid equipage, with a house in the country, but he built a splendid house in the city, which is yet standing in Eccles-street, and to this day known by the name of " Ryder's Folly." On this he expended 4000*l*. and sold it before it was finished for 600*l*. He exercised at the same time the professions of manager, player, and printer, in which latter capacity he established a " Theatrical Journal," which he published three times a week. His profits, however, bore no proportion to his extravagance. His company were left unpaid; and on one occasion, when the Lord-lieutenant of Ireland was in the house, they mutinied, and refused to play for his Excellency, who, with his suite, immediately left the house. Encreasing embarrassment obliged him to resign the management which he held

1118   THE HISTORY OF

a fortunate and unopposed career, till an unexpected opposition appeared from a quarter little expected. A number of performers, lead by Vandermere and Waddy, established themselves in a theatre formed on the site of the music-hall in Fishamble-street. This new company he silenced by a singular manœuvre. They had brought forward, at considerable expense, Mr. Sheridan's favourite opera of the Duenna immediately after its representation in London. A short-hand writer was deputed by Ryder to take down the dialogue, and being thus master of the words, he immediately brought forward an opera advertised as the "Governess," including the songs of the Duenna which had been published; to the dramatis personæ he gave new names, having called Isaac the Jew, Enoch, which he himself represented. A prosecution was commenced by the injured party, but it was the opinion of the Irish bench, that any person may make memoranda of what is publicly exhibited and which he pays for hearing, and Ryder silenced his opponents. In order to prevent any further opposition he rented both theatres, in Smock-alley and Crow-street, the latter only of which he kept open, but his improvident extravagance involved him in bankruptcy. The vacant theatre was occupied by Mr. Daly, who soon became too powerful for his embarrassed rival. Ryder finally resigned to him both theatres in 1782, and consented to become a performer under his management. During the administration of Mr. Daly, the theatre in Smock-alley was converted into merchants' stores, and the drama was solely and exclusively confined to Crow-street.

In the year 1794 a new competitor for the management appeared, who seemed to have more pretensions than most of his predecessors. Mr Jones had been for some time manager of a private theatre in Fishamble-street,* to

for 10 years, and consent to play in the same house under the management of another. He died at Sandymount, near Dublin, November 26, 1791, and was buried at Drumcondra. He wrote two plays—

Like Master Like Man - - 1770
Such Things Have Been - - 1789

* A number of the nobility and gentry not finding the Theatre Royal at this time conducted in a manner to meet their approbation, and to afford that rational amusement which a theatre ought, resolved to enter into a subscription to establish a theatre in Dublin under their own direction. For this purpose they took the old music-hall in Fishamble-street; and under the management and direction of the late Earl of Westmeath, and Frederick Jones, Esq. they fitted it up with a degree of elegance hitherto unknown in the metropolis. The interior of the house formed an ellipse, and was divided into three compartments—pit, boxes, and lattices, which were without division. The seats were covered with

which all persons of rank and fashion in Ireland had become subscribers. In the conduct of this fashionable concern he had given so much satisfaction, and displayed such taste and judgment in dramatic management, that his friends, it is said, procured for him a promise of the patent of the Theatre-Royal, or liberty to open another in Dublin. The latter purpose was prevented by Mr. Daly compromising the affair with Mr. Jones, who, with the general

rich scarlet, and fringe to match, while a stuffed hand rail carried round gave them the form of couches, and rendered them particularly agreeable for any attitude of repose or attention. The pilastres which supported the front of the boxes were cased with mirror, and displayed various figures on a white ground, relieved with gold. The festoons were fringed with gold, and drawn up with golden cords and tassels. The ceiling was exquisitely painted. In the front was a drop curtain, on which was depicted an azure sky with fleeting clouds, from the centre of which was Apollo's lyre emerging in vivid glory; on each side were the figures of Tragedy and Comedy, appearing between the pillars in perspective, to support a rich freeze and cornice; in the centre was the appropriate motto, " For our Friends." The stage and scenery were equally brilliant; and that nothing might be wanting to complete the costume, servants in rich and costly liveries attended on the stage and in the box rooms, to accommodate the company. The orchestra was filled with amateurs and professors. The male characters were performed by gentlemen subscribers, but the female by public actresses engaged for the purpose. In effect, every thing that could contribute to the splendor and elegance of the ornament, the excellence of the performance, and the decorum of the company, was scrupulously attended to. The house opened for the first time on the 6th of March, 1793, with the Beggars' Opera and the Irish Widow. The following were the dramatis personæ.

Beggars' Opera.

Macheath,	- Capt. Aske	Polly,	-	Mrs. Mahon
Peachum,	——— Brown	Lucy,	-	Mrs. Garvey
Locket,	——— Stewart	Mrs. Peachum,		Mrs. Dawson
Mat of the Mint,	Sir H. Butler	Jenny Diver,		Miss Kingston
Filch,	Mr. Howard	Mrs. Coaxer,		Miss Atkins
Drawer,	Sir Vere Hunt	Mol. Brazen,		Mrs. O'Reily
		Sucky Taudry,		Mrs. Wells

Irish Widow.

Whittle, -	Mr. Howard
Kecksy, -	Mr. Stewart
	Mr. Holms
Nephew,	Capt. Withrington
Sir P. O'Neil,	Mr. Nugent
Servant, -	Capt. Brown
Widow, -	Mrs. Garvey.

Among the performers, Captain Aske and Lord Westmeath were particularly distinguished. His lordship's performance of Father Luke in the Poor Soldier was considered a masterpiece, and gained for the noble representative the celebrity of having his portrait in that character exhibited in all the print shops and magazines of the day. The audience were always distinguished by rank and fashion, but by the rules of the theatre, were almost entirely females, no gentleman who was not a subscriber being on any account admitted. The theatre closed on the appointment of Mr. Jones to the management of the Theatre-Royal. This, however, is still occasionally used by private parties, though its splendor is entirely faded. The talents of the fashionable world in this way are now transferred to Kilkenny, where private theatricals have long been celebrated. Besides Fishamble-street, there is a small private theatre in Drury-lane, for more humble aspirants.

approbation of the citizens of Dublin, little satisfied with the attention, or capacity of the former manager, obtained the exclusive direction, not only of the Theatre-Royal Dublin, but of Cork and Limerick also; and in order to give greater efficacy to this monopoly, an act was passed in 1796, by which any other person than the patentee is prohibited, under a penalty, from exhibiting any kind of dramatic representation even in booths or tents,* which has extinguished all shadow of rivalry, and established the present patentee absolute monarch of the Irish drama.

The ill effect of a monopoly in any department of society, by extinguishing emulation, and conferring a careless security, has been so well established as to be recognised as an axiom by all who have thought on the subject. Its effects on the Dublin theatre may be further adduced, if necessary, to confirm the fact. While there existed a rivalry between two managers, and each hoped for success only by his exertions to obtain the approbation of the public, the public enjoyed a display of varied and excellent dramatic talents, in which they are now not destined to participate. Garrick, Sheridan, Macklin, Digges, Mossop, Barry, Woodward, Quin, King, Ryder, Brown, and Sparks, appeared successively, and sometimes collectively before them; while Mrs. Woffington, Mrs. Crawford, Mrs. Bellamy, and Mrs. Fitzhenry, exerted their various powers to excite their tears, or animate their gaiety. It would be invidious to compare this constellation of dramatic genius with the single stars which now and then rise above our horizon only to make the surrounding obscurity more remarkable. It was opposition that elicited those talents—it is monopoly that has extinguished them. The proprietors of the theatres may sometimes have suffered by the rivalry, but the public, for whose amusement and instruction they were established, were highly benefited by the consequence.

The only theatre now in the metropolis stands in Crow-street; it occupies the space between Fownes-street and Crow-street, and is approached from Dame-street and Temple-bar, by four narrow inconvenient avenues.

* The act states, that it is intended to establish a well regulated theatre, productive of public advantage, tending to improve the morals of the people. It grants a patent for 21 years for keeping one or more well regulated theatres in the City and Liberties of Dublin, and inflicts a penalty of 300*l.* on any one else who shall act plays—tragedy, comedy, prelude, opera, burletta, farce, pantomime, or any part of them, on any stage, theatre, booth, tent, or public house, except feats of horsemanship, puppet shows, and the like.—26th Geo. III. cap. 57.

THE CITY OF DUBLIN.

The exterior of the edifice is singularly rude and unsightly, an irregular mass of brick defying all symmetry, and divested of any architectural ornament that should distinguish it as a public building. The interior of the theatre, which is semi-circular, is less exceptionable : it consists of a stage, orchestra, pit, boxes, lattices, middle and upper gallery, besides the usual apartments annexed to the stage and box lobby. The house is capable of containing about 2000 persons, and is so well constructed, it is said, that those in the remotest part can distinctly hear and see the performance. The ceiling is well painted with allegoric figures, representing Hibernia supported by the manufactures of Ireland, protected by Jupiter, and crowned by Mars. The pannels of the boxes are tastefully executed in compartments, representing different incidents in the classic writers. The house opens in November, and closes in August; the summer period is called the after season, during which only the metropolis is visited by any performer of eminence. The nightly expense of the house is estimated at £60. The custom of admission to half play at half price is not known in Dublin, but several families possess free tickets, which admit them at all times to the theatre.*

The general decorum that reigns in this theatre is certainly very praiseworthy; the house is never disturbed by those riots which formerly disgraced it;† nor is female delicacy wounded by the shameless admixture of

* This privilege originated with the building of Crow-street Theatre. Barry and Woodward borrowed 3000l. to complete the house. To raise this sum they issued 30 debentures for 100l. each, entitling the holder, besides the usual interest, to a free ticket on the house till the sum was paid off. These debentures have been increased by their successors. They are often disposed of by the possessors; they usually sell for 50l. or 60l. as the only benefit derived to the holder is the privilege of admission.

† From this remark, however, must be excepted a recent riot which originated in a singular cause. Some years ago, the melo-drame of the " Forest of Bondy, or Dog of Montargis," was exhibited at Crow-street, the principal incident of which turns upon a dog discovering a murder. There was found in Dublin an extraordinary animal belonging to a rope-maker in Francis-street, who volunteered his services for the occasion, and delighted the audience several nights by his untutored sagacity. On Friday the 16th of December, 1814, the Duenna and the Dog of Montargis were announced, by command of his Excellency the Lord-lieutenant, but during the night the entertainment was altered, and the Dog did not appear. It was rumoured that the Dog had received no compensation for his services, or return for the extraordinary profits of the managers. The audience took his part; the manager was called for, and when he would not appear, they became outrageous, and proceeded to demolish the lustres; when they were all broken, except one, a young collegian called out that he was going to strike the *ultimus Romanorum ;* the light was extinguished, and the rioters groped their way out of the house. For several successive nights these riots were renewed. The manager still refused to appear,

7 D

those degraded females who are suffered to obtrude themselves into Drury-lane and Covent-garden, and exclusively occupy the lobbies and saloons. The only occasion on which this ever happens is one peculiar to the Dublin Theatre. So early as the first rise of the stage in Ireland the manager received a certain annual sum for performing plays on particular nights—such as those of the King and Queen's birth-day, and others of public commemoration On these occasions the ladies were complimented with the freedom of the boxes. For a long period these nights were marked by a brilliant audience, and ladies of the first distinction and character only attended. It is now, however, a " custom more honoured in the breach than the observance." When the boxes are announced " free for the ladies," it is an invitation for every female to avail herself of the privilege. The boxes are therefore crowded with improper characters of both sexes, who banish every respectable person from the house, and for one night vice and profligacy exclusively occupy the seats of decency and decorum.

Theatrical strictures occupy a considerable part of every newspaper and magazine published in Dublin, and some of them are not remarkable for the justice or impartiality of their criticisms; but the only work dedicated exclusively to the stage was The Theatrical Journal, published by Ryder during his management,*

and at length, on December 26, he published an advertisement, stating, that as " it was proposed to him to appear personally and apologize, or quit the management, he preferred the latter." A new patent and a second theatre were now talked of; but the affair passed away without any alteration in the established order of things. This was the only serious riot which happened in a Dublin Theatre since the days of Sheridan.

* In the year 1788, " A View of the Irish Stage," from the earliest periods, was published in Dublin, by Robert Hitchcock, prompter to the Theatre-Royal. It proposed to carry down the view to the period in which it was published, but it terminated with the year 1775; and there is an hiatus in the theatrical annals of Dublin since that period. It is an useful and impartial work as far as it goes, and of sufficient authority to be quoted by the Biographia Dramatica, and other works since published, on the general subject of the stage. Much of the foregoing account has been extracted from it, where it has been generally confirmed by Victor, Chetwood, Cibber, Davies, &c. But the work which has recently excited most attention on a local subject was " Familiar Epistles," in verse, published in 1804. The author has never avowed his name, and like Junius, is to this day a subject of various conjecture. They contain strictures on the then state of the Dublin stage; and in humour, point, and critical acumen, they are supposed to have exceeded any thing published on the subject since the days of Churchill. The wit, however, was censured for its severity, and the satire for its personality. The effects of these are

THE CITY OF DUBLIN.

MARKETS.

The great wholesale market in Dublin for cattle and hay is Smithfield, situated at the extremity of King's-street. It is an oblong square, extending to the rere of Ormond Quay, and forming a fine, airy, spacious place, of not an unpleasing aspect. On one side, Lord Bective has erected an handsome edifice,* which he once intended as his town residence, and on

recorded by a public memorial in Dublin, the most extraordinary perhaps that ever was displayed since the days of Archilocus, and the *agentia verba Lycambem*. The following epitaph is to be seen on an upright marble slab in the middle of St. Werburgh's church-yard, erected over one of the performers of Crow-street Theatre, who was censured in the " Familiar Epistles," and died immediately after.

Here lie the remains of
MR. JOHN EDWIN
of the Theatre Royal, who died
February 22 1805 aged 33 years.
His death was occasioned by the
ACUTENESS of his SENSIBILITY.
Before he was sufficiently known to the public
Of this City to have his talents properly appreciated,
He experienced an ILLIBERAL and
CRUEL ATTACK on his professional Reputation
from an ANONYMOUS ASSASIN. This
circumstance preyed on his mind to the extinction
of Life while he apparently enjoyed bodily vigour; he
predicted his approaching DISSOLUTION.
Consciousness of a Brain rending with agony
Accounts for that prescience, & incontrovertibly
establishes the cause of his death.
This stone is
Inscribed to the MEMORY of an AFFECTIONATE
HUSBAND as a tribute of DUTY & ATTACHMENT
by her, who best acquainted with the qualities of his
HEART, can best record their AMABILITY.

* All the avenues leading to it from the south are very narrow and inconvenient, and the space on the whole is found to be much too small for a market where the commodities for sale occupy so much room. The sheep are penned in the middle, and the black cattle are generally kept at random close to the houses, so as to render the passages choked up and very difficult through the horns of the animals. These poor creatures are kept together only by the sticks of a set of urchins called penny boys, who sometimes exercise their authority with the most wanton cruelty. Hay carts are often excluded altogether from the market for want of room, and obliged to stand in the adjacent streets, where they suffer great

the other is the front of the Penitentiary; but it is ill calculated, notwithstanding, for the purposes for which it is appropriated.

The great cattle market is held here twice in the week throughout the year, on Monday and Thursday, for kine, sheep, and pigs. The butchers here supply themselves with fatlings of every kind for the markets, and dairymen and others with milch cows. The purchases are generally made, not with the owners, but with certain intermediate persons called salesmasters, who act as confidential agents between the buyers and sellers. As the functions of these persons are very important to the agricultural interests of the country, and the convenience of the city, several acts of parliament have been made to regulate and define their duty, and, as it is now conducted, the business of a salesmaster is found to be of great importance and utility. They are bound to sell fairly and truly for the best price, and to pay and account with the owner on demand.* In the seasons of the year when there is no meat made up for export, and the cattle exposed for sale is solely for the consumption of the metropolis, Smithfield exhibits, on market days, an appearance which strongly impresses a stranger with the quantity of animal food used in Dublin and the vicinity. The quantity of

depredation from a gang of pilferers, who are known to attend for the very purpose, and the passages are so very dirty, that gentlemen who come to purchase hay and straw in wet weather are obliged to ride through it. It has been proposed to open this market up to Brunswick-street and down to the Liffey. This, it is said, might be done at a small expense, as the houses are old and of little value. It would afford ample space for this important market, and render it perhaps one of the finest in Europe, in the centre of a city.

* The regulations of this market, and the duties of salesmasters, have been settled by acts of Parliament since the reign of Geo. I. They are not graziers themselves, under a penalty of 5*l*. per week, (31 Geo. II.); they are not to sell in Smithfield till security is given to the Lord-Mayor in a bond for 1000*l*. with two sureties, the bond to be lodged in the Tholsel for the use of any person aggrieved, who may peruse it gratis, and have a copy for 1*s*. (10 Geo. I.) All calf and lamb to be retailed in the markets of Dublin must be first purchased in Smithfield, and not contracted for in the country or on the road, (31 Geo. II.) and notice must be given of the opening of the cattle market by the toll of a bell, (10 Geo. I.) Besides this market, there are annually 14 cattle fairs held in the county of Dublin, and some in the immediate vicinity of the town, the principal of which is Donnybrook.—Tallagh 4, Balruddery 2, Newcastle 2, Taggard 3, Rathfarnham 1, St. Margaret's 1, Rathmichael 1. The prices of cattle vary with the time of the year, local causes, and the fatness and quality. When soup shops were open, a cow sold from 10 to 20 guineas; the general price, however, has been within these latter years, in April, for an ox of 700 st. prime beef, 28*l*.; sheep 24 lb. per quarter, 4*l*. In August, an ox of the same size and quality brings 20 guineas, and a sheep 3 guineas. Besides the beasts sold for

cattle bought and sold here, and annually slaughtered in Dublin, amounts, on an average, to 30,000 head; and it is not an unusual circumstance to sell 5000 sheep and lambs in one day. These are driven to the different markets, which are generally situated, for convenience, in the most crowded parts of the town, and are there slaughtered.

the consumption of the markets and slaughtered for exportation, a large quantity of the cattle sold is driven from the fairs and markets to the quays, and embarked alive. The following table gives the numbers for the last year.

Live cattle exported from Dublin from November, 1816, to November, 1817.

	November.	December.	January.	February.	March.	April.	May.	June.	July.	August.	September.	October.	Totals.
Oxen and Cows	1010	398	47	50	55	70	126	837	720	2714	1849	1351	9229
Sheep	540	230	600	200	100	0	0	730	1370	4827	2609	1140	12,346
Swine	200	250	1114	1460	1730	2700	1720	2590	1330	568	555	255	14,472

Live cattle was formerly one of the prohibited exports of Ireland—a circumstance which Sir W. Petty complains of as one of the causes which obstructed the prosperity of the country. " Why should they breed more cattle," said he, " when it is penal to import them into England." (Polit. Anal. p. 99.) By some it is doubted if it would not be better if the penal statute still continued. The hides, horns, tallow, &c. are so much raw material sent from the country, to which it is afterwards returned in a manufactured state—thus depriving a people of so many sources of employment, among whom the want of employment is the greatest evil. Without adverting to the number of hands required in slaughtering, salting, and coopering an ox prepared at home for exportation, or those engaged in the ordinary process of tanning the hide, the following are some of the less obvious uses to which the several parts of our animal are applied in other countries, when exported alive. The *hide* prepared with oil produces buff, a name derived originally from buffalos skins; from this soldiers belts, &c. are formed. The *hair* extracted from the interior of the ear makes pencils for painting earthenware. The *cartilage* and *sinews* produce glue; the best and most tenacious is said to be extracted from the ears and tendons of bulls. The *horn*, having undergone a process of fire, is formed into combs, lanthorns, knife-handles, drinking vessels, hunters tubes, curtain rings, buttons, &c. The *hoofs* are worked into snuff-boxes, and are held in more esteem in England and France than those produced from their own beasts. The *tibial* and *carpal bones* yield an oil most essential to coach-makers and other trades, for dressing and preparing harness, and all the leather used in the appointment of coaches and other vehicles. The *shank* bones are worked into buttons, knife and razor handles, &c. The *metatarsal bones*, when burnt, produce an ash of which copels are formed, for purifying and ascertaining the quantity of silver in lead mines. The *bones* in general, well burnt and ground, form the noir d'os, much used in painting, and the substance of which copper plate ink is composed. Many of these applications of the parts of this most useful animal the Dublin Society laudably encouraged at home. Cow-hides milled with oil were formed into buff under their auspices; kilns were erected in Dublin for burning ashes to form copels, and glue was one of our exports. Little attention, however, seems now to be paid to these objects.

THE HISTORY OF

For the sale of this meat, there are nine established markets, in different parishes, containing 360 stalls, besides 39 others, dispersed through different places within the circular road.

Meath market, in St. Catherine's parish, was originally established by patent in the reign of Charles II. and intended to supply a neighbourhood much more opulent and populous than it is at present. It is distinguished by an advantage in which some others are deficient. The animals for sale are not killed in the market, but in adjoining slaughter-houses. The number of butchers' stalls occupied is 32.

Ormond market was erected in 1682, and has been long esteemed among the first in Europe. It extends from Ormond quay to Pill-lane, and from Charles-street to Arran-street, from all of which there are approaches to it. The passages of the market are flagged, and kept tolerably clean, but they are all inconveniently narrow for the crowds that frequent it. Besides the stalls occupied by butchers, which are of great extent, and all well filled every day, there are others for poultry, bacon, butter, cheese, fruit, vegetables, and every sort of fresh or cured fish. Nor is there, perhaps, any article of food according with the climate or season of the year, or any sauce which luxury could require, which may not be had at this market. The number of meat stalls is 73.

Castle market originally stood in the vicinity of the Castle, in the rere of the south side of Dame-street, and was remarkable for its dark and narrow passages. When Dame-street was widened by the Commissioners of Wide Streets, this nuisance was necessarily removed, and a new market built as a substitute, extending from George's-street to William-street, and opened in the year 1782. Its passages are flagged and kept clean, and the approaches to it, from two wide streets, very convenient. It is much inferior to Ormond market in size and variety, but superior in cleanliness; it is too narrow, however, for proper ventilation. The number of butchers' stalls is 37.

St. Patrick's market was very early established near the centre of the city, in a low narrow and dirty street, periodically subject to inundation, from the bursting of the poddle in the vicinity of St. Patrick's Church. The butchers stalls or rather shops are ranged on one side of the street, and the other is occupied by poulterers, stands of fishmongers, &c. Notwithstanding its situation, it is said to be an excellent market, where good meat is exposed in the midst of revolting and offensive objects and in large quantities. The number of stalls is 43.

Blackhall market, called also the City market, was erected in the year 1783, by Sir Thomas Blackhall, an alderman of the city; his object was to draw the butchers from the former market to one much more eligibly situated. It is erected on an eminence, between Patrick-street, Francis-street, and Back-lane, and is of considerable extent, and entirely flagged. Not able to effect his original purpose,* this market was occupied chiefly by those who sold inferior meat, and was soon frequented exclusively by the poor of that part of the city. Mutton and lamb are the only meats exposed here for sale, except a small quantity of pork in the spring months. It is a market much frequented, and the sales by retail have amounted usually to 1000 sheep and lambs per week.† Notwithstanding its favourable situation, it is very filthy. The animals are killed in the stalls in which they are sold, where the offal is suffered to accumulate, and there is no fountain to cleanse or purify them. The number of stalls is 63.

Clarendon market was erected in a convenient site, where King-street, William-street, Stephen-street, Mercer-street, Clarendon-street, and Henry-street, terminate. It was also flagged, and neatly finished; notwithstanding it has not succeeded, and the greater number of the stalls remain unoccupied. Besides a few held by poulterers, &c. there are but 18 opened for the sale of meat.

* The butchers of Patrick-street were opulent, and they obstinately refused to give up situations where they were thriving, and houses in which they had interests. To compel them to remove, they were no longer allowed to expose their meat for sale in a public street; they, therefore, sold it in their houses. The prohibition, however, ceased to be inforced—the stalls were again thrust into the public passage, and the nuisance has increased with the market, and become greater than ever. It is hoped that when the projected improvements of the Commissioners of Wide Streets take place in that direction, this unsightly and offensive market place will be removed.

† Some of the butchers here are wholesale dealers, and send the meat to be disposed of in other markets after it has been killed here, but by far the greater quantity is sold in the stalls. From this circumstance it may be inferred, that the use of animal food by the lower classes in Dublin is much more general than it is supposed, or than is usual in other parts of Ireland. One butcher in this market is said to kill on an average 350 sheep per week, principally for their consumption. Lamb is much used by the working people, and continues longer in season in Dublin than perhaps in any other place. It is to be bought through almost the whole year, and for five months it is by far the most cheap and plentiful animal food. Pork is also very cheap, and plenty in the Dublin markets. A pig is the constant inmate of a poor man's cabin, and is the stock on which he always relies to help to pay his rent.

Leinster market has been erected within these few years in the vicinity of Carlisle-bridge, and leads from Dolier-street to Hawkins-street, through' the new buildings. It is entered by handsome iron gates, the passages are flagged, and the whole kept perfectly clean and neat. As yet but five of its stalls are occupied for the sale of meat.

Fleet market.—There are two markets in this vicinity, the new and old, which are entered from Townsend-street. From the proximity to the river, they are those to which seafaring people resort, and the ships in the harbour are generally supplied from them. The number of stalls occupied is about 16.

Rotunda market, or as it is now more generally called Norfolk market, from a bust of the Duke of Norfolk erected at one entrance, was originally a few mean and dirty stalls in Cole's-lane. As it was situated, however, in the extensive and opulent parishes of Mary's, Thomas, and George, and was the only market to supply the whole north-east side of the Liffey, it soon increased in size and consequence. It now has extended from Cole's-lane to Denmark-street on one side, and to Moore-street and Great Britain-street, through which it is approached on the other, and become the rival of Ormond market, to which, however, it is yet much inferior. It is not flagged, the passages are confined and dirty, and though equal in extent, is by no means so in variety. The number of stalls occupied is 79.

It is much to be regretted that these markets, so convenient in every other respect, and so well supplied with cheap and excellent meat, should not be better laid out, or kept in neater order. They are generally placed in low and confined situations, either blocking up the passages of streets or lanes, or surrounded by high houses, where the free circulation of air is prevented; the approaches are narrow and inconvenient, and the avenues confined and dirty. To increase those objections, there are no public slaughter-houses,[*] and the animals for sale are killed either behind the

---

[*] So early as the year 1388, one of the clauses in the oath taken by the Lord Mayor of Dublin was that he should see the markets kept decent and in order, and not suffer any cattle to be slaughtered within the walls (12th Richard II.); and by an act passed in the year 1777, butchers are prohibited from killing or dressing meat for sale in the markets or stalls (17th Geo. III.) Notwithstanding the practice is permitted, to the manifest tendency of tainting the food, and corrupting the atmosphere of the metropolis. In consequence of some dispute between the graziers, salesmasters, and butchers, in Smithfield, it has been recently proposed to erect public slaughter-houses in or near the city, in

THE CITY OF DUBLIN.

stalls, or in the very place where the meat is sold; and the accumulation of ordure and offals in the market is sometimes highly offensive. An attention, however, to the goodness and quality of the meat is strictly paid. Forty-eight citizens are periodically returned by the sheriffs to the sessions, on the justices precept. Of these 24 are sworn as market jurors, who continue in office three months; they inspect the provisions for sale in markets and shops. If any be of a quality not sufficiently good, they are empowered to carry it before the Lord Mayor, who may condemn or dispose of it, and punish the owner by a fine. The Lord Mayor himself, who is sworn escheator and clerk of the markets, is exceedingly active in the performance of this duty. Large quantities of meat and other provisions have been seized in this way, and applied to charitable purposes.

Besides these markets, there are about 60 poulterers shops dispersed through different parts of the town, who each keep three or four journeymen constantly employed in drawing and skewering fowl, which are generally plucked before they are sent to market. These shops are profusely furnished, according to the season, with chickens, barn door and crammed fowl, geese, turkeys, hares, rabbits, and all kinds of game. These shops are generally supplied from the wholesale markets, which are held every day early in the morning, at the little green, near Newgate, where convenient markets have been recently built for the sale of fruit, poultry, and eggs. Eggs are in exceeding great abundance in Dublin, and are to be had in vast numbers in every obscure street, either in shops or exposed in baskets. In the market which supplies these shops 200,000 eggs is not an uncommon sale in one day, besides numbers which are sold by country people, who supply private families, where they invariably form part of the breakfast.* The general use of eggs and poultry is a circumstance which

convenient situations. We trust they will be excluded altogether from the town. The vicinity of Fisher's-lane and Cole's-lane, where the cattle is slaughtered for Ormond and Rotunda markets, is sometimes so intolerably offensive, that many of the inhabitants are obliged to remove from it. The custom also of using baskets to convey the meat home to the purchaser is exceptionable. They are seldom washed, and the fragments and fibres of the flesh, divided into small portions, readily entangle in the twigs, and remaining in the interstices till they become putrid, must also have a tendency to taint such fresh meat as comes in contact with it. The substitution of trays would be a great improvement.

* " As to the customs peculiar to the Irish gentry I know of only three. The first is that of having " boiled eggs for breakfast with their tea."—Twiss's Tour, p. 40. This remark was made while resi-

distinguishes Dublin. In other places they are generally confined to the opulent—here they are universally used by all classes. About a fortnight before Christmas it is supposed that 1000 geese and turkeys are daily sold in Thomas-street, principally to labouring people, besides large quantities purchased in the different avenues leading to the city. The barn door and crammed fowl are excellent, and turkeys proverbially the finest that are exposed for sale in any city.* Game is not in any plenty or variety where the laws for its preservation are so, negligently enforced.†

The bacon consumed in the city is purchased at the great wholesale markets, held every morning in Kevin-street, for bacon and butter, and in Spittalfields for bacon and potatoes. The whole quantity of bacon sent in from the country and disposed of here, is consumed in the city, as none has yet been exported by the merchants. From the quantities exhibited for sale in retailers' shops, it would seem almost exclusively the diet of the lower classes, of which it certainly constitutes a considerable part. Cheese, however, is not in such general use. It is not an article of rural economy

---

dent in Dublin, and before he had visited the rest of Ireland. Notwithstanding this notice of the learned fellow of the Royal Society, the peculiarity still continues in 1817 as prevalent as in his time, 1775. Poultry are the constant companions of pigs in the poor man's cabin, even in the immediate neighbourhood of the metropolis, and every peasant's wife has eggs to sell, with the produce of which she supplies herself and children with sundry conveniences. From Michaelmas to Shrovetide they sell from 1s. to 1s. 6d. per dozen; from Shrovetide till Michaelmas from 8d. to 10d. per dozen.

* Fowl is always best and cheapest in Dublin in autumn. At this time they are turned into the stubble after the harvest is gathered in. Geese and turkeys are frequently driven in flocks through the streets, and purchased at the doors of houses as the droves pass by. The price of fowl, as of every thing else, is enhanced with the demand. The practice of serving up green geese with gooseberries in the Common-hall of the University on Trinity Sunday, and the general use of full grown geese by the citizens of Dublin on Michaelmas day, raises the price of the markets in those articles at these times.

† The BARNACLE, found in the bay of Dublin, is held in little esteem. It feeds on fish spawn and sea wreck, which has a sensible effect on the flavour of its flesh; but that which is sent from Wexford and Belfast is much prized. The flooded sands on which they feed at the entrance of these harbours abound with a species of marine grass, the roots of which contain a saccharine juice, which not only fattens but gives a high flavour to the flesh of these birds. They are seldom exposed for sale, but frequently sent as presents to people in Dublin.

A species of Pigeon is sold in the markets of Dublin which is almost peculiar to the county. It is found to frequent a wide stream called the Lough of the Bay, near St. Margaret's, about seven miles to the north of Dublin, and is distinguished by the name of the *Easterling*. It is a delicious bird, and has now become very scarce.

THE CITY OF DUBLIN.

in Ireland, except for domestic use. That sold in Dublin is generally English, from Cheshire and Gloucestershire, with the exception of a small thin cheese of an excellent flavour, made at Kinnegad, in the county of Westmeath, and frequently cried about the streets.

Roots and vegetables are plenty, and of a good quality. Those usually found in the markets are parsnips, carrots, turnips, cabbages, &c. the whole year; cauliflowers, brocoli, pease, beans, particularly Windsor beans, asparagus, artichokes, sea kale, &c. in their seasons. Salsafy sorsonera, &c. less common.* But the root most abundant is potatoes; where this vegetable is still used almost universally as a substitute for bread with animal food, the consumption must be proportionably great. The average quantity sold is 56,000 stone per week.†

Fruit in Dublin is not so good or so abundant as in other places. The science of practical gardening is not so well understood, nor carried on with such zeal and emulation as elsewhere, and there were no societies formed

* The carrots of Dublin were once remarkable for their excellence. They were cultivated in the sandy soil near Rush, without any manure, where they grew to an immense size, some of the roots measuring, according to Rutty, seventeen inches in circumference. They were red at the heart, and sweeter than those raised in manure It is proposed, in the survey of the county of Dublin, to appropriate all the sandy soil between Howth and Balbriggan to the purpose of raising carrots and parsnips, for which it seems peculiarly adapted.

The use of sea kale as an esculent vegetable is supposed to be of very recent date, and was first introduced, it has been said, by the present Bishop of Carlisle, who cultivated it in his garden for asparagus; but so long ago as the year 1764 this plant was cultivated in the gardens of Dublin, and the seeds sold in the shops. When the seeds were sown they were covered over with stones. The shoots were used in spring as they are now, and preferred to any other species of kale. It was the practice, however, to boil them in two different waters, to extract the salt with which the plant was supposed to be impregnated from its marine origin. The valuable property also which distinguishes it from all other kale, that the root is perennial, and will last cutting 40 years, was well known. See Rutty, vol. I. p. 4. It grows at present in abundance on every part of the sandy shore round the bay, and is cultivated in every garden in and near the metropolis.

† The use of potatoes by the Irish excited the animadversion of Mr. Twiss, as well as that of eggs. "The second practice is the universal use of potatoes, which form a standing dish at every meal; they "are eaten by way of bread—even the ladies *indelicately* placing them on the table-cloth on the side "of their plate after peeling them."—(Page 40.) The judicious practice of serving up this fine root simply in its skin, without peeling or any other previous preparation, is still adhered to; but if in Twiss's time it was served up at *every meal*, its use is by no means so constant in the metropolis as it was; even the working people eat it but once a day, and have generally substituted tea for breakfast and supper, particularly in the Liberties.

or premiums proposed for excellence till so late as the year 1816.* Apples, pears, plums, cherries, and the common small fruits, are sufficiently plenty in their season, but peaches, apricots, nectarines, melons, and pines, are scarce and dear. Those sold are generally the superfluities of gentlemen's gardens, and therefore not the choicest; they are seldom raised in the grounds of professed gardeners. Strawberries, however, is an exception; they are very plenty, and of an excellent kind.†

* The science of gardening does not seem ever to have made a great progress in Ireland. The little that was known was confined to the different religious houses, to each of which was attached a garden which the monks cultivated. On the dissolution of those edifices their gardens ran to decay, and the turbulent periods that succeeded afforded the natives but little opportunity to attend to this pursuit. It appears, however, that grapes were very early and successfully cultivated in Ireland; every monastery had its Finavain or vineyard attached to it; and an Irish almanack, in the possession of the late General Valancey, printed in the fifteenth century, notices the time for gathering grapes and drinking mus'd or new wine. Cherries were first introduced by Sir Walter Raleigh, and propagated at Affane, in the county of Waterford. Cauliflowers, artichokes, and melons, seem to have been introduced about the reign of Charles I. Father Lombard, who wrote a Latin treatise, De Regno Hiberniæ, in 1632, says, they throve well at that time, though transplanted from other countries. Pine apples were first brought to Dublin by a man of the name of Bullen, who, in the reign of Queen Anne, settled in the vicinity of Dublin, and held an extensive nursery in New-street, where traces of it remain to this day. In the reign of George I. the Hugonots established a Florist's Club, for the purpose of promoting the cultivation of flowers, and held their meetings at the Rose tavern in Drumcondra. They were continued till the reign of George II. But the science of gardening was from that time entirely neglected, till a number of the principal gardeners in the vicinity of Dublin, assembled at the Rose tavern, in Drumcondra, on the 30th of September, 1816, and formed themselves into an "Horticultural Society." The cause assigned for their formation was " the deep regret they felt that the art of gardening was falling away and rapidly declining in all its various branches, particularly in the growth of fruit and flowers." This Society is patronised by Lords Charlemont, Leitrim, Manners, Judges Downes, Fletcher, George, and several gentlemen who have devoted their attention to the cultivation of fruit and flowers in the vicinity of Dublin. They held their first shew of flowers in Donneybrook, on Easter Monday, 1817; and of fruit and flowers on August 18 of the same year, at the Rotunda in Dublin, where the emulation excited was displayed pleasingly by the fine specimens exhibited, proving that any deficiency in the production of the gardens of Dublin, did not arise from ungenial soil or unskilful cultivation, but from want of due encouragement. Premiums were given for the best pines, grapes, melons, cucumbers, peaches, nectarines, gooseberries, and currants; and for auriculas, polyanthuses, hyacinths, and carnations, specimens of each of which were produced not inferior to those of any country in flavour, size, beauty, and early maturity.

† Some situations in the vicinity of Dublin are peculiarly adapted to the cultivation of strawberries, and the proprietors have availed themselves of the circumstance. Between Chapel Izod and Lucan, about three miles from Dublin, the ground rises very abruptly on the north bank of the Liffey, and

THE CITY OF DUBLIN.

The fish markets in Dublin contain-an abundant supply, and in great variety. The practice of using fish not only in Lent, but on every Friday in the year, is very general, even by those who do not feel it imposed by any religious obligation; hence the quantity consumed is proportionably greater than in London. The markets are supplied in their different seasons with cod, haddock, whiting, ray, gurnard red and grey, turbot, plaice, soal, salmon, mackarel, and herrings, in great abundance, and at a very reasonable price. Besides these, mullet, bream, dory, polluck white and black, hake, bret, bass, eels, and trout, are frequently sold, though not in such abundant and regular supply as the former. Carp, tench, pike, sturgeon, and holybut, are scarce, and rarely appear.* Of testaceous fish,

presents a sloping aspect, exposed to the strongest heat of the sun. These banks for a considerable distance are cultivated to the summit, and display a surface of several acres, covered exclusively with the finest strawberries. They are beautifully situated in the romantic and highly wooded valley of the Liffey, and it is one of the most delightful recreations of the citizens to resort in the season to this spot and eat strawberries and cream, of a quality, and in the midst of a scenery, not to be surpassed in any country. The Dublin markets are plentifully supplied from these exhaustless hills.

* HERRINGS appear in the Dublin markets from July till Christmas. Those which first come in are sent from the Isle of Man, and different parts of the Irish coast, and continue till Michaelmas, when a new variety of the herring appears, which is peculiar to Dublin, and found for three following months in great abundance in the bay. They are smaller, more firm, and less oily than the common kind, and are distinguished as Dublin-bay herrings, by the more deep and vivid green of their backs. These are much prized, and usually sell at an advanced price; these are frequently found in the bay long after the shoals disappear from the coast. Notwithstanding the abundance of herrings, it is remarkable, that the sardine or sprat is never seen in the markets, though, in the time of Rutty, it was taken in the Liffey, between the City and Island bridge. It is now found only on the southern coast of Ireland, particularly in the harbour of Waterford, where it is smoked and sent in small casks to Dublin.

STURGEON is sometimes but rarely exposed for sale. It is occasionally found in the bay or adjacent coast; one was taken between Howth and the Isle of Man in September 1746, which measured six feet in length and three in breadth, and is mentioned by Rutty rather as a curiosity. It is now more plenty, and is brought to market once or twice in the year, and sells for 1s. per lb. It is the roe of this fish which makes the celebrated cavear, and the membrane of the stomach, isinglass. A transverse section of this fish is unlike that of any other. The flesh is as white and firm as veal, and the bones, particularly of the spine, a bright orange. It has therefore a strange appearance when cut into junks, and exposed for sale in the markets.

COD and LING, salted and cured, are imported in considerable quantities from Newfoundland, but that which is taken on the Dublin coast is of a superior quality. At the fishing villages of Rush and Skerries, in the district of Fingal, they pursue a mode of curing which preserves the fish in great perfection. They are first seasoned with the best salt; then dried in the sun, care being taken to remove

THE HISTORY OF

Crabs are very plenty, but seldom arrive at a great size. Lobsters and cray fish are scarce and dear. Shrimps and prawns are rarely met

them to shelter every night, or in wet weather. They are daily pressed with a weight to give them a shape, and finally packed in straw. These are more prized than foreign fish, as preserving a better flavour, having a firmer consistence, and swelling more when boiled. It is a great article of food in Lent, and at such seasons as other fish is scarce in Dublin, and sells on an average for 5d. per lb.

SKATE or RAY is taken in abundance at Howth, Baldoyle, and Skerns, where it is dried by suspending it outside the walls and roofs of the fishermen's huts, and eaten with parsnips. It is held in little estimation in Dublin, where a prejudice exists against it, and it is rarely sold in the markets.

HADDOCK is in great abundance. It is always to be met with in the markets of Dublin, to which it seems almost peculiar. Mundius, an old writer, asserts, that " it is not agreeable food by reason of " the hardness of its flesh, though it serves the necessities of the poor;" and Rutty, " that among the " East Frieslanders it is thought to be 'so unwholesome as to excite fevers!" Notwithstanding, it is highly and justly esteemed in Dublin, both as an agreeable and wholesome food. The size and price vary perhaps more than that of any other fish; and they sell on the same day from five pence to 27 shillings a piece; they are thus the food of all ranks of people. The fish is distinguished by two black marks on each side of its neck, which the common people assert were impressed by the fingers of our Saviour, who took from its mouth the tribute money. These marks at present are of use to the inexperienced, who by their means distinguish this fish from codling, which those who sell it sometimes attempt to impose on the buyer. It sometimes happens that the haddock is brought up with the entrails torn out. It is supposed to be thus mutilated by cod or other voracious fish, which attempt to prey on it while on the hook. The fish thus lacerated is more highly esteemed than others. It is supposed that by thus bleeding it becomes more firm and curdy.

The SALMON most esteemed in Dublin is taken at Island-bridge, in the Liffey, close to the town, because it is always the freshest. The fishery rents for 200l. per annum; and in the last year produced 1762 salmon, weighing from five to 30 lb. and bringing sometimes into the market 3s. per lb. The next in esteem is that which comes from the Boyne, because next in freshness. But neither the Liffey or Boyne fish is equal in quality to that which is brought from the Barrow, Suir, and Shannon, by the mail coaches of Ross, Waterford, Limerick, and Cork. On the roof of the coaches are large boxes called imperials, lined with lead, that the fish may be kept cool, and the sides formed of wire, that the air may freely permeate. In these the salmon are laid when the coaches are setting out, and conveyed to Dublin in 20 or 30 hours after they are out of the water; each box contains about 2 cwt. of fish. The southern coaches brought this year, 1817, during the season from December to August, 2700 fish, producing to the proprietors for the liberty of conveyance about 350l. and to those who sold it about 1500l. The abundance of salmon with which the rivers in Ireland teem has made it at all times so cheap and common an article of food, that it was supposed to be the cause of distemper among the Irish. Boate, in his Natural History, assigns it as the cause of the leprosy once so prevalent in Ireland. The disorder arose, he says, from the " foul gluttony" of the inhabitants in devouring unwholesome salmons after they had spawned, " and were covered over with filthy spots, like a scald man's head." The English made laws against eating it in that state, " whereby hindering those barbarians against their

THE CITY OF DUBLIN.

with.* Of other shell fish, oysters, cockles, and scollops are very plenty. Limpins, perriwinkles, razor fish, muscles, and a species of bivalve called dog cockle, are also sent to the markets, and used by the citizens, but in smaller quantities.† When fish arrives in Dublin, it is sent to Pill-lane, to be disposed

will from eating poisonous meat," which quite abolished the leprosy, " which great benefit that hateful people rewarded by seeking to destroy their benefactors."—(Nat. Hist. ch. 29, p. 101.)

Dr. Gerarde Boate derived all his information on the subject of Ireland from his brother Arnold, who resided in Dublin for eight years. He himself had been in the country but a few months, and died here in the year 1649. He had been appointed physician to the Commonwealth under Cromwell, which accounts for the fanatic virulence with which he speaks of the people of this country, and the complexion of absurdity which his prejudice gave to his physiology. The laws were then made, and continue still in force, to protect the fish during the season of spawning, and are not confined to Ireland; and the leprosy had at that time become an extinct disease in countries where it formerly prevailed, and where no such cause could be assigned.

EELS are not plenty, or in much esteem; those brought to Dublin are principally from Athlone, on the Shannon, and from the Lakes of Westmeath.

† The scarcity of LOBSTERS and SHRIMPS is a circumstance which distinguishes Dublin from London. The lobsters found on the south side of the Bay are so bad, that those sold from that neighbourhood are brought from Wexford and Waterford—fed there, and sent from thence to the Dublin markets. They are taken also at Lambay, where they are good, but the great supply is brought from the Isle of Man. Shrimps were formerly abundant on our coast, but the hard frost in 1739 destroyed such numbers that the species here has become almost extinct. SEA CRAY FISH is brought from the county of Cork, where it abounds, and the fresh water CRAY FISH is found in small quantities in the river Tolka.

* The OYSTERS of Dublin are not remarkable for their quality, though pains are taken to improve the breed. In the vicinity of Dublin are two artificial and three natural beds of oysters. One of the artificial beds lies near Sutton, on the west side of Howth; the other near Clontarf, usually called Crab-lake, from the quantity of crabs found there before planting the oysters. The oysters are taken in the month of May, immediately after they are spat or spawned, from the neighbourhood of Arklow and Wexford, and brought to these beds nearly in a gelatinous state; here they are suffered to remain till they have acquired a sufficient size, and are well fed when they are taken up for use. Of the natural beds but one only is in the bay; it is situated at Pool-beg, near the light-house wall; it produces oysters with large brown shells, which frequently contain pearls. The two other natural beds lie outside the bay—one at Ireland's Eye, and the other at Malahide. The first of these beds lies 20 fathom under water, and produces oysters of a remarkably large size; they are dredged up with a strong net, and distinguished by the appellation of dredge oysters. They are of a quality coarse in proportion to their size, &c. They sell so high as half a guinea per hundred. Malahide bed produces fish with green fins, which is much esteemed. It has also the singular property of yielding oysters in season in every month in the year; and fine fish have been taken from the beds and sold in June and July. Besides these, the metropolis is supplied from Skerries, Arklow, and other places on the Dublin and Wicklow coast, but the bay oyster is readily distinguished from the rest, by its less

of by auction ; here at the gate of Ormond market it is set up in lots, and sold to the highest bidder : the auctioneer is generally a woman, who holds in her saltish taste, the admixture of fresh water diluting in a perceptible degree the juice contained in the shell. It sometimes happens that all the beds in the bay are confounded together. On occasions of great storms the foundations have been rent, and the fish scattered in all directions, and cast on the shores all round : at these times they are found dry after the reflux tide, and carried away in sacks by any casual passenger. All these oysters are sold in the crude state in which they are taken, without any of that management which in London gives them firmness and delicacy. In London, besides other precautions of feeding and preserving, particular attention is paid even to the outside of the shell, which is carefully washed and brushed, and every excrescence removed, which, like the conferva, growing to the surface of the pots of green-house plants, is supposed to imbibe the nutrition, and materially to impede the artificial growth of the fish. In Dublin, the oyster is never fed or cleaned, but it is sold with a crop of fuci and other marine plants growing on the surface, or covered over with an extraneous incrustation of the lepas, anomia, or other parasitical shell fish ; the consequence is, that they are watery in consistence, and coarse in flavour. But besides the oysters found near Dublin, there are other kinds more esteemed, which are sent from a distance. One of these is found at Burrin, a district of the county of Clare, on the south west extremity of the bay of Galway. From hence the oysters are brought in baskets on small horses backs, each carrying about 1200, a distance exceeding 130 Irish miles. They are cried about the streets in a peculiar tone and accent. They have a small thin shell, which is filled with a delicious fish. The people who bring them take back lemons and oranges in their emptied baskets, and in this way establish a reciprocal commerce between the metropolis and this remote district. Another kind is brought from Carlingford, in the county of Louth, a distance of 50 miles. They are conveyed in boats to a tavern on Aston's-quay, particularly established for the sale of them. They are very highly esteemed, and considered superior to those of Colchester.

The COCKLES of Dublin-bay are remarkably fine ; that called the *black cockle* is in most esteem; it is found on the north side of the bay, about Clontarf, and is supposed to derive its colour from the black mud brought down by the Tolkay and Liffey, in which the cockle is usually found embedded ; for the same reason they are larger and fatter, as this mud and the slime with which it is impregnated afford a richer food. The cockles here are good even in the winter months : there is a variety found at Malahide, which are said to have green fins like the oysters. When the season for oysters is past, and they begin to cast their spat, that is when the months without an R commence, the season of cockles commences, and the approach of winter and summer is alternately indicated to the people of Dublin by the cries of the persons vending these fish, and the first cry of oysters conveys with it a melancholy association. They are carried about in sieves, and always cried by women whose harsh and dissonant screams from evening till near morning, "startling the dull ear of night," distinguish Dublin, perhaps from any other city in the world. They are sold in vast quantities, and constitute alternately the great article of supper, as well in private houses as in taverns, through the whole year, particularly cockles during the summer months. Some houses where they are vended are called cockle warehouses.

Next to oysters and cockles the PECTEN or SCOLLOP is more generally used than any other shell fish. They contain a quantity of offal, which is exceedingly sickening, and is carefully cleaned away,

THE CITY OF DUBLIN.

hand a plaice or other flat fish by the tail, instead of a hammer. It is sometimes purchased in this way for private use, but more generally by those who retail it. In the metropolis there is but one fishmonger, who vends fish in a shop exclusively fitted up for the purpose; he resides in William-street, and his shop is superior perhaps to any in London. There are besides sundry stalls in the different markets, where it is exposed for sale; but by far the greatest quantity is purchased and sold by fish women, who carry it through the city in open sieves on their heads, and cry it as they proceed. If the fish be not soon sold it is lost to these poor people; exposed to the sun and bruised by the carriage, it soon taints and is unfit for use. The losses sustained in this way are severely felt by them, and, in

leaving a small portion of coraline adhering to a cartilaginous substance, which is alone fit to eat. It is in season in March, April, and May. Many of these fish were destroyed by the great frost in 1739. The shell is regularly striated and beautifully marked. It has been used for several domestic purposes, and latterly for forming the sides of purses and ridicules.

The SOLEN or RAZOR FISH is sometimes, though rarely, sold in the markets. It is found on the Bull and other flat sands in the vicinity of Dublin-bay. This fish seems to be endued with a power of loco-motion which no other bivalve possesses in the same degree. It lies buried in the sand, and the fishermen at Skerries search for its retreat by striking the surface above, when a small jet of water from an aperture in the sand discovers it; a grained fork is immediately thrust under the spot in an horizontal direction, and the fish is raised up. Should the fish escape the first effort, it retires so fast through the sand that it cannot be overtaken. Another method is said to be sometimes practised on the Bull. The fisher proceeds with a little bag of salt, and having ascertained where the fish lies, a few grains are dropped into the aperture in the sand; as they dissolve, the fish rises, and is seized as it protrudes itself above the surface; if it be not taken at the first attempt it retires so fast as to elude all further search. It is supposed to be attracted to the surface by the salt impregnating the water, from an instinctive feeling of the approach of the flood tide, which it rises to enjoy.

MUSCLES are not much used in Dublin. They are found to occasion great sickness when incautiously eaten. It has been doubted whether the offensive part resides in the beard, or in some poisonous insect eaten by the muscle. It was not supposed by Rutty to reside in the substance of the fish, for sometimes a large quantity was eaten with impunity, and sometimes one or two caused the most violent symptoms. The symptoms he describes are shortness of breath, anxiety, loss of memory, delirium, convulsions, and other violent effects, which frequently terminated in death. The fish most in esteem were formerly found adhering to the piles leading to the light-house, and at Clontarf, and at Sutton, on the south side of Howth. The muscle, like the razor fish, is endued with a power of spontaneous loco-motion. Smith, in his History of the County of Cork, describes minutely the manner of their progress, which was traced by long furrows in the sand.

For a catalogue of all the shell fish found in the bay of Dublin and the vicinity, see Conchology of Howth, Appendix.

7 F

consequence, they appear to be the most ragged, squalid, and forlorn class of the community.

Dublin is the great and only market for selling grain in the country. The market is held on two days in every week, in the market-house of Thomas-street, where the act appoints that all corn brought by land shall be sold.* It is under the control of the Lord Mayor, and from its prices that of bread is regulated. The clerks are required to make returns of the middle price of wheat and flour each week. They allow 29¼ stone as equivalent to one quarter of wheat, and settle the price of bread accordingly; the baker is allowed not more than 15 or less than nine shillings per quarter, and it is required that the weight shall be full for three days after baking; formerly the price of the loaf was stationary, and its weight fluctuated with the price of wheat; it has latterly been found more convenient to fix the quartern loaf to a certain weight, and let the price vary with the markets. It now must always contain 4 lb. 5 oz. 8 dr. The monthly sales of grain are as follow.

Market note for one year, exhibiting the quantity of grain, meal, and flour, sold in the Dublin market from November, 1814, to November, 1817.

	November.	December.	January.	February.	March.	April.	May.	June.	July.	August.	September.	October.	Totals.
Wheat, per bar.	7375	4363	4775	5233	5290	1969	3833	4369	3501	2706	3630	5549	52593
Barley, bar.	2360	4979	4818	4398	5541	2435	609	348	65	52	165	1129	26899
Bere, bar.	433	56	253	358	589	113	123	0	0	32	110	196	2263
Oats, bar.	23508	17322	17671	19382	15406	6734	6336	7024	2246	2714	13694	9685	141722
Oatmeal, cwt.	6983	5638	7519	13323	12345	8045	15181	19275	8655	5258	3192	5142	110556
Flour, cwt.	38365	28123	28307	37036	44299	28422	64079	41726	41245	43488	31312	144732	571154

As wheat is the standard by which the comparative value of other grain may be estimated, the following prices of that article for different periods for a century, may serve to ascertain the fluctuation of the value of corn in the Dublin markets. They are taken in the months of the respective years when the variation was greatest.

* Under a penalty of forfeiture of the corn and 20s. per barrel, 23d, 24th Geo. III. Corn brought by the canal may be sold at the canal harbour; 26th Geo. III. Wednesdays and Fridays are the appointed market days for the former; Tuesdays and Thursdays for the latter; ibid.

THE CITY OF DUBLIN.

Highest and lowest price of wheat per barrel in five years, from 1716 to 1816.

1716.	1730.	1742.	1765.	1816.
L. s. d.	*L. s. d.*	*L. s. d.*	*L. s. d.*	*L. s. d.*
May 1 4 9	May 0 17 0	January 0 12 0	April 2 7 0	May - 1 7 7
October 0 12 3	June - 0 13 3	May - 0 8 6	October 1 12 6	December 3 5 7

Bread is in general of a good quality, and though not always so white or well raised, is generally more free from adulteration than that of other places. Particular attention is paid by the Lord Mayor, market jurors, and seneschals of the several manors to this important object. They proceed, accompanied by beadles, with a weight and scales, at all hours, through the bakers and retailers shops both in Dublin and the vicinity, and inexorably confiscate all the bread found at all deficient either in weight or quality. This is invariably given to some charity, to which it often affords a seasonable supply. All weights and measures are under the control of the Lord Mayor, and standards for each are kept in his possession, and to prevent abuses, none are permitted to be used without being previously examined and stamped by the clerk of the market.*

* The following are the measures and weights as regulated for the Dublin markets.

In grain of every denomination weight is assigned for measure. The nominal barrel is thus divided.
1 barrel = 4 bushels, 1 bushel = 4 gallons.

WHEAT, pease, beans, and potatoes, 1 barrel = 20 stone.
BARLEY, 1 barrel = 16 stone.
OATS, 1 barrel = 14 stone.
MALT, 1 barrel = 12 stone.
BUTTER—Meat and all kinds of provisions, grocers and shop goods, are sold by avoirdupois weight, 16 oz. = 1 lb.—14 lb. = 1 st.—8 st. = 1 cwt.
TALLOW, 15 lb. = 1 stone.
WOOL, 16 lb. = 1 stone—7 stone = 1 cwt.
HAY sold by the load—1 load = 4 cwt.
COAL.—By an act passed in 1727 (1st Geo. II.) all coal brought to Ireland is measured in vessels of the following dimensions and contents.

	Bottom.	Top.	Winchester measure.
Half barrel,	24 inches.	25½ inches.	20 gallons.
Bushel,	20 ditto.	21 ditto.	10 ditto.
Half bushel,	15 ditto.	16 ditto.	5 ditto.
Peck,	11 ditto.	12 ditto.	2½ ditto.
Half peck,	10¼ ditto.	11¼ ditto.	1¼ ditto.

Coal is usually sold by the ton—1 ton = 8 barrels.

Milk and butter bear a high price in Dublin. Milk is a nutritious and necessary article of food to the poor, and cannot be carried from a distance; its scarcity in any place cannot be supplied from another. The number of dairies in the year 1800 had considerably declined, which was attributed to two caues. The suspension of distilleries, from which the Dublin dairies were principally supplied with fodder; and the number of soup-shops established in Dublin, so enhanced the value of meat, that the dairy-man was induced to sell where he got a price, considerably beyond what he himself paid.* It seems a strange paradox in political economy, that the supply of the most mild and nutritious food to the poor, must in Dublin depend upon the increase of the most pernicious poison, and an embarrassing impediment to the efforts of charity, if providing them with soup be a means of depriving them of milk. Previous to the year 1801, it was calculated that there were in Dublin and the vicinity for four miles round it, 7000 milch cows, which supplied the markets with milk and butter. In that year, and subsequently, there were not more than 1600.† The breed of Irish kine is now nearly extinct, and their places supplied in Dublin by the Dutch and English breed, and some few Kerry cows. It is asserted by the dairyman, that the former gave more milk, though the latter were more profitable to the butcher. The average quantity of milk produced in a Dublin dairy every day is eight quarts in summer, and five in winter, which, compared with a London or a country dairy, producing 12 or 14, is a melancholy deficiency.‡

But not only the quantity is thus scanty, but the quality is very bad; the best butter sent to the Dublin market is derived from the mountainous district on the south side, where the cattle feed on a sweet and natural herbage; the butter supplied from hence is excellent, and yields perhaps to none in any country.§ But that made in Dublin is very different, and is

LIME.—Roach lime, 1 barrel = 40 gallons, 1 gallon = $217\frac{6}{15}$ cubic inches.

It is to be regretted that the wishes of the Board of Agriculture in England have not been complied with, and the weights and measures equalized in every part of the united kingdom. In Ireland scarcely two counties use the same or measure different commodities by the same standard. In Dublin eight barrels of coal are contained in a ton; in Waterford six; and the contents of a barrel of potatoes vary from 20 to 120 stone in different places. In our own markets, why should 1 stone of rough tallow contain 15 lb. or 1 cwt. of wool 7 stone, to the manifest inconvenience and confusion of the dealers?

* Archer's Survey, p. 59.   † Ibid.   ‡ Dutton, p. 79.

§ Besides the butter made in Dublin, which is generally used fresh, considerable quantities are sent adulterated and deteriorated in a variety of ways. The milk from whence it is procured, is the scanty and morbid produce of sickly cows, confined in unwholesome yards, littered in putrid filth, and fed on decaying vegetables; the offals of gardens and green grocers stalls, and what is still worse, the intoxicating refuse of breweries and distilleries.

In the process of making it, a quantity of hot water is added, both to quicken the process and to render it white, and in moulding it into prints and other forms for sale, old butter is frequently beat up with new, and more water is added to increase the weight;[*] it is thus served up to table a porous, watery mass, sometimes tasteless, and sometimes rank, occasionally palid and colourless, and occasionally streaked with a variety of different tints. The milk has scarcely the consistency of whey, and the cream will not keep, but becomes tainted in 24 hours, while that from the country will preserve its sweetness in the same season for several days.[†] The consequence of this is, that several families, who have no other accommodation than a yard or a stable, keep a cow instead of a horse, to preserve to their children this indispensible diet in a wholesome and nutritious form.[‡] The salted from the neighbouring counties—Meath, Wicklow, Wexford, Carlow, Louth, and some from Roscommon. It is brought to the City Cranes in Thomas-street, Queen-street, and Spitalfields, appointed by act of parliament, where its quality is ascertained by certain tasters, appointed also by the act, who extract a portion from the centre with a long iron scoop, and the price is fixed accordingly. It is sold also at the market in Kevin-street, the Little Green, &c. That which is sent for home consumption is packed in bowls, containing from three to 30 lb. or in cools, which are large flat tubs, open at the top, and containing from 40 to 60 lb. each; that which is intended for exportation is packed in small barrels, closed at both ends, called casks or firkins, containing from five to six stone each; they are weighed at the crane, and the contents branded on the outside. The following exhibits the Quantity of butter sold at the City Cranes, and exported from Dublin for one year from Nov. 1816, to Nov. 1817.

	November.	December.	January.	February.	March.	April.	May.	June.	July.	August.	September.	October.	Totals.
Casks	12,010	3652	1808	444	30	100	40	0	0	800	3187	2900	24,962
Firkins	12,752	4394	158	380	66	403	20	0	0	2550	4700	3700	29,123

* Archer, Dutton. † Rutty's Co. Dub. vol. 1, p. 267.

‡ A gentleman lately paid a visit to a medical friend resident in the centre of the city. He was surprised to see a large bin just erected in his hall, and found on enquiry that this reservoir was intended to keep meat for his cow, for which he had exchanged his horse, in order that he might have the necessary articles of milk and butter in a wholesome state for his children.

This important consideration has occupied the attention of the faculty, and various expedients have been proposed for detecting adulterated milk, and ascertaining its purity. Some years ago, Mr. Kirwan directed the attention of his powerful mind to this subject, and printed for the benefit of the public

cow is fed on hay and oatmeal, and occasionally the fresh tops of turnips and other vegetables, which they procure from the market in a fresh state, and at a very trifling expense. To remedy this public evil, several gentlemen have recently established dairies on speculation, in the vicinity of the city, at Ballymuir, Glasnevin, Rathfarnham, and other places. The produce of these is vended through Dublin in hand-carts, in which are several churns suspended on springs. These churns are secured with locks, of which the proprietor keeps the key, and the person who sells it cannot increase the quantity at any time by adulteration. They stop at every door, and the milk is distributed through a brass cock. Whether from the novelty or real comparative excellence of these establishments, they are increasing in public estimation, and likely to supersede, or at least improve, the old dairies.*

In the article of fuel, Dublin is much more deficient than, from the abundant store of that important article in Ireland, and the vicinity of the great collieries in England, it is reasonable to expect. The only substances used for fuel are coal and turf. The coal is always imported from England or Scotland;† but more frequently from the former, particularly

an easy method of estimating the richness of milk, by which citizens may know how much the milk commonly sold is adulterated with water. He directs three saucers to be balanced in scales, which will turn with a half grain weight, and in one of them to pour half an ounce of water, and in the other two the same quantity of milk, but not warmer than the water. In a short time all will lose part of their weight by evaporation, and at first all the same quantity in the same time; but as the cream forms, the milks will lose less, and that which loses least of the two is least adulterated. The specific gravity of good milk at the temperature of 62° is 1.0324; if heavier, it is adulterated in proportion to the increased weight.—See Transactions Dub. Soc. 2d vol.

* Among those new dairies, that established near Glasnevin, by the Lord Bishop of Kildare, is the most remarkable. With a view to ascertain how the most wholesome milk and butter, and at the cheapest rate, could be supplied to the public, he has erected an extensive range of buildings on a new construction, capable of feeding about 30 cows. His principle is to render the confined and consequently unnatural state of the animals as near a state of nature as possible. With this view they are merely, protected from the inclemency of the weather by a tiled roof, but immediately under it are open spaces through which the air permeates and freely circulates round the building. Below is a platform on a gently inclined plane, the floor of which is formed perfectly smooth, and free from projections. On this the cows repose without litter, and from its construction must remain clean and dry. Minute attention is paid to the quantity and quality of the food, and the times and manner of feeding; and some of the produce of the dairy is served up morning and evening at his Lordship's table as a kind of barometer to ascertain the variations of the quality. In this not inexpensive experiment his lordship has no personal concern further than the public spirited motive, and the general management. The cows are the property of another, and in the profits he has no interest.

† The only native coal used in Dublin is that brought from the collieries of Castle Comer, and called Kilkenny coal. The mine was discovered a few years before Boate wrote his Natural History of

THE CITY OF DUBLIN.

Whitehaven. The great supply is brought in two annual fleets, at September and January. When it is usual for the citizens to lay in a store for the whole year, an order is given to a coal factor, and the quantity required is sent in with punctuality and integrity, with great convenience, and little additional expense to the consumer. It sometimes happens, however, that the usual supply of fuel fails, when the periodical fleets are detained by contrary winds or other causes, and the citizens of Dublin suffer extreme distress from the absolute want of this important article. To obviate this, public coal yards have been established, in which a large supply is deposited; they are opened only in times of scarcity, and afford to the poor on these occasions a most seasonable relief, who are then supplied at reduced prices.

The annual consumption of coal averages at 200,000 ton.

Besides coal, Dublin ought to be abundantly supplied with turf. The great bog of Allen, situated within 20 miles of the metropolis, presents an inexhaustible source of fuel; and intersected in every direction by the Grand Canal, should furnish a regular supply of fuel at a very moderate price to the citizens; but from the high price at which it is sold, enhanced by the tolls exacted on the canal, it is in little use except by the poorer classes. Turf is used for lighting fires; also wood dug out of the bogs, called bog-wood; any other kind of wood has long ceased to be an article of fuel.

The following tables present the prices of different articles used in domestic economy in the several markets of Dublin for the last year.

Ireland in 1649, who thus describes it. " This mine is in the province of Leinster, county of Carlow, " seven miles from Idof, in the same hill where the iron mine was of Mr. Christ. Wandesworth. In " that iron mine, after that for a great while they had drawn iron oar out of it, and that by degrees " they were gone deeper, at last, in lieu of oar, they met sea coal. There be coals enough in this mine " to furnish a whole country, nevertheless there be no use made of them further than among the " neighbouring inhabitants, because the mine being situated far from rivers, the transportation is too " chargeable by land. These coals are very heavy, and burn with little flame, but lie like charcoal, " and continue so the space of seven or eight hours, casting a very great and violent heat. In the place " where the mine standeth, do lie little smith-coals above the ground, from whence the smiths dwelling " in the parts round about did use to come and fetch them, even before the mine was discovered."— (Boate's Nat. Hist. ch. 19, p. 84.) It is a substance peculiar to Ireland, and to the Castle Comer collieries; it contains no bitumen, but an extraordinary proportion of sulphur. It produces no smoke, and therefore " fire without smoke" is one of the local boasts of Kilkenny, where it is much used; but the extrication of sulphureous acid gas is sometimes highly dangerous, and causes suffocation when the coal is incautiously used in a confined place. The coal produces a more intense degree of heat than any other known, and is used in Dublin principally by smiths and nailors. It is conveyed by the Nore to the Suir and the Barrow, and is principally brought by the Grand Canal to Dublin, and deposited near Ring's-end, where a coal yard, under the direction of the company, is opened to vend it.

Market Table, exhibiting the Prices of Butter, Bacon, Meat, Grain, and Fuel, for each Month in the Year from November, 1816, *to November*, 1817.

	January.			February.			March.			April.			May.			June.		
											lb.			lb.			lb.	
	L.	*s.*	*d.*	*L.*	*s.*	*d.*	*L.*	*s.*	*d.*	*L.*	*s.*	*d.*	*L.*	*s.*	*d.*	*L.*	*s.*	*d*
Butter, in casks,	3	15	0	3	17	0	4	18	0	0	0	9	0	0	11	0	0	9
Do. in cools,	0	0	10	0	0	9½	0	0	11½	0	0	9½	0	1	0	0	0	10½
Green Pork	1	10	0	1	16	0	1	16	6	1	19	0	1	16	0	1	16	6
Bacon -	2	13	6	2	11	6	3	0	6	2	19	6	2	18	6	2	19	0
Hams -	2	1	0	2	1	0	2	7	0	2	6	2	2	5	0	2	6	8
Beef -	0	0	5	0	0	6	0	0	6¼	0	0	6½	0	0	6	0	0	6½
Mutton -	0	0	6½	0	0	7½	0	0	7	0	0	7½	0	0	7	0	0	7½
Pork -	0	0	4½	0	0	5½	0	0	5	0	0	5¾	0	0	4¼	0	0	5¾
Veal -	0	0	8	0	0	9½	0	0	9¾	0	0	9½	0	0	8½	0	0	7½
Raw fat -	0	6	0	0	6	0	0	6	0	0	6	0	0	6	0	0	6	0
Tallow -	3	4	0	3	6	0	3	5	6	3	6	0	3	6	0	3	3	0
Candles, dipt,	0	0	9	0	0	9	0	0	9	0	0	9	0	0	9	0	0	9
Do. mould,	0	0	10	0	0	10	0	0	10	0	0	10	0	0	10	0	0	10
Soap -	0	0	8	0	0	7	0	0	7	0	0	7	0	0	7	0	0	8
Bread -	0	1	9	0	1	9	0	1	9	0	1	8¼	0	1	6	0	1	6¼
Wheat -	2	0	8	1	18	8½	2	3	2¾	1	14	8½	1	7	7¼	2	13	4½
Flour -	1	18	0	1	14	0	1	19	0	1	10	0	1	4	4	2	4	0
Bere -	1	3	10	1	2	6	1	5	5¾	1	5	8	1	0	3½	0	0	0
Barley -	1	8	8½	1	4	2½	1	6	4½	1	11	1½	0	18	6½	1	10	11½
Oats -	1	0	6½	0	19	8½	1	3	6½	1	3	7½	1	2	3½	1	14	5¾
Oatmel -	1	5	1¾	1	4	4½	1	10	6	1	9	6	1	5	5	1	13	5¾
White Potatoes	0	0	0	0	7	0	0	7	7	0	0	0	0	0	0	0	0	0
Black ditto	0	4	9	0	3	9	0	5	6½	0	4	4	0	4	4	0	7	6
Apple ditto	0	5	8	0	5	9	0	6	10	0	6	9	0	6	4	0	8	8
Hay -	0	3	3	0	2	11	0	3	4	0	3	8	0	3	1½	0	3	7
Wheaten straw	0	2	7	0	1	7½	0	1	11	0	2	5	0	1	6	0	2	0
Oaten ditto	0	2	7	0	1	7½	0	1	11	0	2	5	0	1	6	0	2	0
Whitehaven coal	1	9	0	1	9	0	2	0	0	1	5	0	1	5	0	1	3	0
Scotch ditto	1	8	0	1	8	6	2	2	0	1	4	0	1	4	0	0	0	0
Harrington ditto	1	8	9	1	8	0	0	0	0	1	4	0	1	5	0	1	2	6
Workington do.	1	9	5	1	9	0	0	0	0	1	5	0	1	5	0	1	2	6

	July.			August.			September			October.			November			December.			
		lb.			cwt.			cwt											
	L	*s*	*d.*	*L.*	*s.*	*d.*	*L.*	*s.*	*d*	*L.*	*s.*	*d.*	*L.*	*s.*	*d.*	*L.*	*s.*	*a.*	
Butter, in casks,	0	0	8	4	4	0	4	4	0	4	14	0	4	3	0	3	12	6	per cwt.
Do. in cools,	0	0	9¼	0	0	10	0	0	9¾	0	0	10	0	0	10	0	0	9	per lb.
Green Pork	0	0	0	0	0	0	0	0	0	0	0	0	1	12	6	1	12	6	per cwt.
Bacon -	2	19	0	3	1	3	2	18	6	2	17	6	2	10	0	2	8	6	ditto
Hams -	2	12	6	2	15	4	2	10	0	2	13	0	2	9	0	1	19	6	ditto
Beef -	0	0	6½	0	0	5	0	0	5	0	0	5¾	0	0	4	0	0	4	per lb.
Mutton -	0	0	6½	0	0	5¾	0	0	5½	0	0	6	0	0	6	0	0	6	ditto
Pork -	0	0	0	0	0	0	0	0	0	0	0	0	0	0	4½	0	0	3½	ditto
Veal -	0	0	7¾	0	0	7	0	0	6½	0	0	6¾	0	0	6	0	0	6½	ditto
Raw fat -	0	6	0	0	6	0	0	6	0	0	5	6	0	6	0	0	6	0	per stone
Tallow -	3	3	0	3	3	0	3	3	0	3	2	0	3	4	0	3	4	0	per cwt.
Candles, dipt,	0	0	9	0	0	9	0	0	9	0	0	9	0	0	9	0	0	9	per lb.
Do. mould,	0	0	10	0	0	10	0	0	10	0	0	10	0	0	10	0	0	10	ditto
Soap -	0	0	8	0	0	8	0	0	8	0	0	8	0	0	8	0	0	8	per lb.
Bread -	0	1	4¾	0	1	2	0	1	2	0	1	1¾	0	1	7	0	1	9	{ per quartern loaf 4 lb. 5 dr. 8 oz.
Wheat -	2	4	0	1	15	2	1	15	9	2	2	9	2	8	6	3	5	7½	per barrel
Flour -	2	0	0	1	10	0	1	9	8	2	9	6	2	18	8	3	18	3	per cwt.
Bere -	0	0	0	0	14	8	0	13	1¼	0	14	2½	1	1	4½	1	2	0	per barrel
Barley -	0	14	0	0	14	0	0	17	11½	1	0	2½	1	3	6	1	8	7½	ditto
Oats -	1	3	3½	0	18	6½	1	0	4¾	0	15	5	0	18	10¼	1	0	7	ditto
Oatmel -	1	5	5¾	1	0	5½	0	19	11¼	0	13	6	1	3	11	1	1	7½	per cwt.
White Potatoes	0	0	0	0	6	0	0	3	4	0	2	9	0	4	10	0	0	0	ditto
Black ditto	0	6	8	0	0	0	0	0	0	0	2	8	0	4	5	0	4	8	ditto
Apple ditto	0	9	0	0	0	0	0	3	0	0	0	0	0	5	11	0	5	9	ditto
Hay -	0	4	1	0	3	2	0	3	5	0	2	11	0	2	10½	0	3	10	ditto
Wheaten straw	0	1	11	0	1	9	0	2	3	0	1	9	0	2	3	0	2	7	ditto
Oaten ditto	0	1	11	0	1	9	0	2	3	0	1	9	0	2	7	0	2	7	ditto
Whitehaven coal	1	2	9	1	2	0	1	3	0	1	3	0	1	8	0	1	8	0	per ton
Scotch ditto	1	3	0	1	3	0	1	3	0	1	3	0	1	5	0	1	6	0	ditto
Harrington ditto	1	1	0	1	1	0	1	2	0	1	2	0	1	6	0	1	6	0	ditto
Workington do.	1	1	0	1	1	0	1	2	0	1	2	0	1	6	0	1	7	0	ditto

THE CITY OF DUBLIN.

verage Price of Fish, Poultry, Game, Fruit, and Vegetables, in the Dublin Markets, for the Year 1817, the variation of the price depending on the size and season.

	From s. d.	To L. s. d.	Usual Price L. s. d.
ılmon, per lb.	0 6½	0 2 8½	0 1 1
ɔd, per piece,	2 2	0 6 6	0 3 3
addock ditto	0 5	1 7 6	0 0 10
urbot ditto	0 10	2 5 6	0 16 3
laice ditto	0 2	0 3 0	0 0 10
ɔal, per pair,	0 10	0 7 0	0 2 2
ullet, per piece,	0 10	0 2 0	0 1 7½
hiting ditto	0 1	0 0 5	0 0 3
errings, per dozen,	0 10	0 2 2	0 1 1
ackarel ditto	0 10	0 2 8	0 1 0
rabs, per piece,	0 2	0 1 0	0 0 5
ɔbsters ditto	1 1	0 8 8	0 2 2
ysters, per hundred,	0 10	0 13 0	0 4 4
itto Carlingford	6 6	0 7 7	0 6 6
itto Buroin	5 5	0 6 6	0 5 5
ockles, per pottle,	0 4	0 0 4	0 0 4
callops, per doz.	0 3	0 5 5	0 2 2

FRUIT.

	From s. d.	To L. s. d.	Usual Price. L. s. d.
Apples, eating, per hundred	10 0	0 16 0	0 12 0
Ditto, baking ditto	10 0	0 16 0	0 12 0
Pears, ditto	12 0	0 20 0	0 10 0
Plums, Mogul, per dozen,	2 6	0 4 0	0 3 3
Ditto, green gage, ditto,	1 6	0 2 6	0 2 0
Ditto, Orleans, ditto,	0 10	0 1 8	0 1 0
Damascenes, per quart,	0 8	0 1 1	0 0 10
Peaches, per dozen,	16 3	1 3 0	1 0 0
Apricots, ditto,	5 0	0 8 0	0 6 0
Nectarines, ditto,	6 0	0 10 0	0 8 0
Grapes, per lb.	4 0	0 17 4	0 6 6
Melons, per piece,	8 0	0 16 3	0 12 0
Pines, ditto,	16 3	2 0 0	1 0 0
Cherries, May Duke, per lb.	1 4	0 2 6	0 2 0
Ditto, black hearts, ditto,	1 4	0 2 6	0 2 0
Strawberries, per leaf,	0 5	0 1 8	0 0 10
Raspberries, per noggin,	0 6	0 0 10	0 0 8
Currants, per leaf,	0 4	0 0 6	0 0 5
Gooseberries, per quart,	0 6	0 0 8	0 0 7
Filberts, ditto,	0 10	0 1 3	0 1 1
Walnuts, per hundred,	1 8	0 2 6	0 2 0

POULTRY AND GAME.

	From s. d.	To L. s. d.	Usual Price. L. s. d.
Geese, per piece,	3 4	0 5 0	4 4
Turkeys ditto	3 4	0 7 0	0 5 0
Fowls ditto	2 2	0 5 0	0 3 3
Chickens, per pair,	2 6	0 3 9½	0 3 3
Ducks ditto	3 4	0 5 0	0 4 4
Wild Ducks ditto	5 5	0 8 8	0 6 0
Pidgeons ditto	1 8	0 3 3	0 2 2
Partridges, per brace,	5 5	0 7 0	0 6 6
Woodcocks			
Snipe			
Quail			
Widgeon			
Tail			
Barnacle			
Hares, per piece,			
Rabbits, per pair,	1 8	0 2 8½	0 2 0
Venison, per lb.			

VEGETABLES.

	From s. d.	To L. s. d.	Usual Price. L. s. d.
Parsnips, per bunch,	0 8	0 1 4	0 1 0
Carrots, ditto,	0 6	0 0 10	0 0 8
Turnips, ditto,	0 2½	0 0 8	0 0 5
Cabbages, York, per dozen,	0 5	0 1 4	0 0 8
Ditto flat Dutch, ditto,	0 10	0 1 8	0 1 4
Ditto red, per head,	0 3	0 0 6	0 0 4
Brocoli, ditto,	0 5	0 0 6	0 0 6
Cauliflowers, ditto,	0 1½	0 0 5	0 0 4
Windsor Beans, per quart,	0 2½	0 0 6	0 0 4
Marrowfat Pease, ditto,	0 3	0 0 6	0 0 5
Kidney Beans, per lb. or leaf	0 8	0 1 4	0 0 10
Sea Kale			
Celery, per bunch,	0 4	0 1 7½	0 0 8
Artichokes, per dozen,	0 10	0 2 0	0 1 3
Onions, per stone,	1 0	0 4 0	0 2 2
Picklers ditto, per quart,	0 4	0 0 8	0 0 5
Cucumbers, per piece,	0 3	0 1 4	0 0 0
Asparagus, per hundred,	3 3	0 8 8	0 5 0
Spinach			

7 G

THE HISTORY OF

NEW BUILDINGS, &c.

RICHMOND LUNATIC ASYLUM.—The hospital attached to the House of Industry in Dublin was the only receptacle originally for the poor who laboured under mental derangement, and the cells attached to the infirmaries or poor houses in some counties were by no means calculated for the restoration to sanity, or even the safe custody and care, of the unhappy persons who suffered under this malady. In the year 1810, therefore, application was made to Parliament on this purpose, who granted the necessary aids, and a new hospital, called from the then viceroy of Ireland, " The Richmond Lunatic Asylum," was commenced, and in the year 1815 it was completed, at an expense of £50,000. This noble charity is arranged on the plan of the London Bethlem Hospital. It contains eight convalescent apartments, and 210 cells, arranged in 12 corridors; at the extremity of each corridor is a keeper's room, which looks into and commands the whole. This not only gives the keeper a ready facility of interfering when necessary, but acts as a salutary restraint on the patients who know and feel they are thus watched. As soon as the arrangements were complete, 170 patients were removed to this asylum from the House of Industry, and the whole number was soon filled up by others transmitted from the country. The only recommendation for admission from any part of Ireland is an affidavit, sworn before a magistrate, of the poverty of the patient, and a certificate of his insanity from a physician. The patients are attended by two physicians and one surgeon, and guarded by 33 nurses and keepers. The whole is under the superintendance of a moral governor, who watches the conduct of the patients, and applies the treatment of the malady rather to the mind than the body. In conformity with this, regulations are suspended in each corridor, to be strictly observed by the domestics of the institution.*

---

* *Directions to be strictly observed by the domestics of the Institution.*

To allow every patient all the latitude of personal liberty, consistent with safety.

To proportion the degree of coercion to the obvious necessity of the case.

To use mildness of manner or firmness, as occasion may require.

Every cause of irritation, real or imaginary, is to be carefully avoided.

The requests of the patients, however extravagant, are to be taken graciously into consideration, and withheld, under some plausible pretext, or postponed to a more convenient opportunity.

They breathe a mild and benevolent spirit, and do no small credit to the author. But the effects prove that the mode of treatment is not less judicious than the principle of it is humane. The patients are tractable, and remarkably cheerful; and the proportion of cases in which restoration has followed the treatment, has been so great, and the general knowledge of it had induced the transmission of such numbers to Dublin, that it was necessary to give public notice that no more could be received from the country parts of Ireland.*

The institution is under the direction of five governors of the House of Industry, with ten more nominated in the Act of Parliament passed in 1815, constituting them a corporate body. It is supported by annual Parliamentary grants.

STEPHEN'S GREEN.—The improvement of this noble square had long been an object with the inhabitants, but it was not till it was seriously determined to appropriate it to another object that the improvement was determined on. About ten years since, the corporation of Dublin, to whom it belongs, exhibited a plan for dividing it into streets for building, which alarmed the inhabitants, who were naturally anxious that the finest square in Europe should not be destroyed. Nothing, however, conclusive was determined on till the successes of the Duke of Wellington induced the citizens of Dublin to erect a trophy to commemorate his victories. As it was then in agitation to erect the trophy in Stephen's Green, the inhabitants determined to effect their long meditated plan of improvement in conformity to the design. They accordingly applied to Parliament, and an act was passed in 1815,† appointing by name certain commissioners for carrying

All violence or ill treatment of the patients is strictly prohibited, under any provocation, and shall be punished in the most exemplary manner.

The mild acts of conciliation are to be the constant practice in this hospital.

These laws are of fundamental importance, and essential to the prudent and successful management of this Institution.

* See an highly interesting Report of the Select Committee for the Lunatic Poor of Ireland, made to the House of Commons in 1817. They propose that four or five distinct asylums, similar to the Richmond, should be erected in different parts of Ireland, and earnestly recommend an entire conformity to the system laid down and acted on here with signal success, having no doubt that the restoration of patients in this malady depends more on the adoption of a regular system of moral treatment than casual medical prescription.

† 54th George III. cap. 97.

the provisions of the act into execution. In pursuance of the powers vested in them, they entered into a negociation with the corporation for the disposal of their interest in the interior of the Green,* who finally came to an agreement to grant it in fee farm to the inhabitants, at the rent of £300. per annum, but with a clause that the rent should be reduced to £200. if the Wellington trophy should be erected in it—the corporation expressing their willingness to contribute so much as their subscription to this national monument. The managers, however, for erecting the trophy, could not agree with the commissioners in the design; it was determined, therefore, not to admit it within the interior of the Green; they therefore pay the original rent agreed, and are content to give up the exemption of £100. per annum for the exclusion of the obelisk. Meantime they proceeded with expedition in their plan. Empowered by the act, they laid a tax of 5s. per foot on all the houses in the Green, which amounted to £991. they beside issued 60 debentures for £100. each, at 5 per cent. and with this fund they soon completed their improvements. The offensive ditch was filled up, the old trees removed, and the walls and hedges levelled. The obstructions thus cut down, the whole area presented the view of a noble plain of seventeen acres, surrounded by houses. From this was marked off 60 feet of pavement for the common street in the front of the houses. This space was bounded by granite pillars, connected by chains, and surmounted by lamp posts. Within this was formed the public gravel walk, 20 feet wide, the innerside of which was bounded by iron palisades, standing on a dwarf wall, which separated it from the interior area. This was laid down with plantations and walks; 1800 trees, shrubs, and evergreens, were grouped and scattered through it, of which nearly 1000 are forest trees, so that when the timber acquires some growth it will present a fine wooded spectacle in the midst of the metropolis. The exterior area laid down for the public passages occupies 3 A. 2 R. 22 P. and the interior

* On investigating the right of the corporation on this occasion, they were found to be levied in fee, but no chartered grant appeared on record from the Crown, When the Blue Coat Hospital was established, in the time of Charles II. the outskirts of St. Stephen's Green, then a common, were set out in lots for building, forming a square in the centre, and the chief rent of the lots were appropriated, with other funds, to the support of the school. Since that time, the corporation have exercised rights of ownership over the interior of the square, having assigned it as an appurtenant to the mansion-house of the Lord Mayor. This right of prescription was not now however disputed.

occupied by planting 13 A. 1 R. 20 P. Irish measure. After much debate on the propriety of removing the statue of George II. and substituting some ornament more proportioned to the magnitute of the square, it was at length finally determined that it should remain in its present site; and a special clause is inserted in the lease, that it shall not be removed from the interior area except the express consent of the Prince Regent be previously obtained. It is intended, when the debenture debt of £6000. is paid off, to erect a grand Gothic Lodge for the gate-keeper, and though the immediate object be accomplished, the present tax on the inhabitants is to continue, for the liquidation of debts, and the effecting further improvements.

Items of the expense of the improvement of Stephen's Green.

Iron railing	- -	£4915 4 4
Walks	-	2220 1 5
Planting, &c.		194 4 9
Act of Parliament	-	237 10 0
Keeper's salary	- -	119 5 8
Other incidents		1832 18 8¼
		£9519 4 10¾

NEW FRONT OF TRINITY COLLEGE.—To accommodate the increasing number of students in our University, it was found necessary to erect a new and extensive range of apartments.* The site chosen is the north side of the new square, which had not been before completed. This wing forms a new front to the College, and occupies a considerable space of New Brunswick-street, formerly a part of Lazar's-hill. The front extends 270 feet in length. It is 48 feet in height from the street, and 30 in depth. It consists of four stories, containing 32 windows in each. The basement is rusticated, and the windows plain; those of the principal story are enriched with architraves, freeze, and cornice, supported by small consoles, which give a neat effect. The windows in the attic are decorated only on three

* The increase of students in our University has recently been very rapid. At the commencement of the present reign they did not exceed 300. In 1775 they amounted to 400. In 1812 Mr. Whitelaw states them only at 500. In February, 1816, there were on the college books, under the degree of A. M. 1090; and at the monthly entrance in November, 1817, 114 candidates presented themselves, of whom 111 were admitted, making the present number of students 1230, of whom 293 are fellow commoners, and 927 pensioners and sizars. Of these only 200 were accommodated within the walls before the erection of the new wing.

sides by a plain architrave, resting on the window stone. The whole is terminated by a very unornamented cornice and a blocking course. The entire front is enclosed from the street by a circular range of iron palisades, similar to that in College Green, but of less projection. It is built of mountain granite. It cost £26,000.* of which the College borrowed £20,000. from Government. It will accommodate 64 under graduates, and four fellows. The architect was Mr. Ward, who contracted for it.

It is to be regretted that the appearance of this extensive front is so very plain as to add little to the beauty of the new projected street. Had it been ornamented with a pediment and portico, it would form an highly interesting structure, as it stands in a very prominent situation, and presents an object from Carlisle-bridge and other points of view. In its present form it fatigues the eye with its long and unbroken uniformity, ill according with its kindred front in College Green, or the portico of the former House of Lords, with which it stands in immediate contrast.

CASTLE CHAPEL.—The old edifice attached to the Castle for public worship had become so ruinous as to be altogether unworthy of the seat of Government. It was therefore resolved, in the administration of the Duke of Bedford, to remove it, and erect a more suitable fabric. Accordingly, in 180$\frac{7}{7}$, it was taken down, and a new one commenced on its site. In laying the foundation, some difficulty occurred. The old chapel had been erected partly on the excavation of an old quarry and partly on the solid rock. As the new chapel was intended to be a much more ponderous edifice, it was necessary to make the foundation of the whole equally firm, and to pile the eastern end, which rested on the soft alluvial soil formed in the excavation. The building is raised with calpe or common Irish black stone. It is 73 feet long and 35 broad. It was finished in seven years, and

* Of this sum 6500*l*. was expended in laying the foundation! In sinking for this purpose, a deep excavation was discovered, extending towards Westmoreland-street and the Liffey. It was filled up with soft mud and sludge immediately below the surface, and the flowing of the tide was indicated by the oozing and bubbling up of the water in several places when the workmen sunk below the level of the river. There had formerly been an extensive quarry in this place, of calpe or common black Irish stone. In laying the foundation for the portico of the House of Lords, the workmen came to the western margin of this quarry, on the edge of which the pillars rest, except one, which is within the excavation. The new front of the College stands within the eastern extremity, and to secure the foundation it was necessary to drive piles 20 feet long.

opened for divine service on Christmas Day, 1814, and cost, including the organ, £42,000. It consists of a choir, without nave or transept, finished in the richest style of Gothic architecture. Each side is supported by seven buttresses, which terminate above in pinnacles. These spring from four grotesque heads in each buttress, ornamented at the angles with rich foliage, and terminate in a Gothic final. Between the pinnacles runs a monastic battlement, ornamented with moulding. On each side are six pointed windows, between the buttresses, surmounted by labels, which spring from two heads, some of which are fanciful and some historical. In the centre of the east end is a pointed door, surmounted by a rectangular label, which springs at one side from the head of St. Patrick, and at the other from that of Brian Boromhe, the Irish monarch. Over this is a tablet, with the following inscription.

X
HANC ÆDEM
DEO OPTIMO MAXIMO OLIM DICATAM
VETVSTATE PENITVS DIRVTAM
DENVO EXTRVI IVSSIT
JOHANNES BEDFORDIÆ DVX HIBERNIÆ PROREX
IPSEQVE FVNDAMENTA POSVIT
ANNO A CHRISTO NATO. M.D.CCCVII.

A monastic battlement surmounts the door-way. Immediately over this is the great east window, richly ornamented with Gothic foliage, and surmounted by a label, which springs from the heads of Hope and Charity, and is terminated at its point by a demi-figure of Faith holding a chalice. The gavel terminates above in a rich antique cross, the arms of which are enclosed in a circle. At each angle of the east end are square towers, rising to the height of the roof, These contain the robing apartments and stairs which communicate to the galleries of the chapel, and are entered by the eastern door.

The great entrance is on the north side of the west end, where the chapel is united to the Record Tower. This gate is surmounted by a fine bust of St. Peter, holding a key, and above it, over a window, the bust of Dean Swift. The gate opens into an arcade, through which is the passage from the Castle on one side, and into the body of the chapel on the other, under the organ. The interior is singularly beautiful. The east window in the

THE HISTORY OF

front is adorned with stained glass. The subject is Christ before Pilate, and the execution is very fine. The glass was purchased by Lord Whitworth on the Continent, and presented to ornament the chapel. The compartments beneath this piece are filled with the four Evangelists executed in Dublin. Beside the window are the whole length statues of Faith, Hope, and Charity in modelled stucco, and the busts of the four Evangelists. The roof is supported by six clustered pillars on each side opposite the buttresses. They are formed of pitch pine, which is preferred to oak for durability, and terminated with capitals covered with foliage. Ranging with these pillars are the pews, below which they go hence to the side walls and the gallery above. The ceiling is formed of groined arches springing from grotesque heads of modelled stucco above the capitals of the columns; it is richly ornamented with tracery and painted in imitation of stone.

On the front of the organ gallery are armorial bearings carved in oak and highly finished. The king's arms are in the centre pannel with supporters, and at each side are those of the Duke of Bedford, who commenced and of the Duke of Richmond who completed the chapel. From these are placed alternately the arms of the respective viceroys to the earliest periods, with inscriptions containing the dates; the whole presenting a history of the arrival and departure of each in a chronological series.

The pulpit is supported on a shaft issuing from an open bible, which lies cushioned on a base of clustered Gothic foliage raised two feet from the floor. The capital of this shaft is formed of the heads of the four Evangelists, from which springs the cone of the pulpit. The pannels are enriched with the arms of the archbishops and bishops of Ireland, including those of Kirwan and three other deans eminent for talent and piety; between their arms are those of the monarchs, Henry, Edward, Elizabeth, and William, the four great supporters of the Reformation. The organ was made in England expressly for the chapel, with appropriate carving to correspond with that of the chapel.

With the exception of the organ and the stained glass, the whole of this beautiful chapel was planned and executed by native artists. The design by Johnson, the sculpture by the two Smyths, and the carved work and modelling by Stewart, and perhaps more beautiful specimens of each are not in existence. The heads on the outside are formed of dark blue marble from the quarries of Tullamore, which is found to possess the closest grain,

Metropolitan Roman Catholic Chapel.

and best adapted for sculpture. It has a susceptibility of expression not inferior to the finest statuary marble, and a durability of texture which the action of the atmosphere will not erode in any given time. Of these heads no less than 90 ornament the exterior, displaying an infinite fund of invention and variety of expression, and while other Gothic edifices are mouldering away, and the hand of time is obliterating the features of their ornaments, we trust that these will long remain durable and unimpaired memorials of what Irish talents can effect when duly fostered.

METROPOLITAN CHAPEL. This fine edifice is intended to accomodate the Roman Catholic congregation who frequented Liffey-street chapel. The income of the titular sees in Ireland being very moderate, the bishops are incumbents of some living in their respective diocese. The titular archbishop of Dublin is incumbent of the parochial district annexed to Liffey-street chapel, and hence the new chapel is called metropolitan, as appertaining to the archbishop. It was commenced in the year 1816 in Malbro-street, the site of Lord Anneley's mansion-house, the fee of which was purchased for £5100. The principal front extends 118 feet, and is taken from the celebrated temple of Theseus at Athens. It consists of a noble portico of six fluted columns of the Doric order, of Portland stone, four feet nine inches each in diameter. Over the entablature is a pediment ornamented with the figures of Faith, Hope, and Charity. The portico projects 10 feet on an extended flight of steps, and beneath it are three grand entrances for the congregation. The flanks extend 160 feet in depth, and in the centre of each are two large recesses enclosed by a colonnade on a lesser scale than the portico, but like it, surmounted by emblematic figures appropriate to the edifice. This colonnade is intended as the entrance of the more humble part of the congregation; the rere of the building being entirely concealed from public view, is unornamented.

The interior of the building is supposed to be taken from St. Mary Major at Rome, but it is more on the model of St. Philip du Role at Paris.* It is divided into three parts, a body and side aisles, by a splendid colonnade which runs parallel to each side, and forms at the west end a circular ter-

* It has this great advantage over the church of St. Philip du Role, that the side aisles behind the colonnade are carried entirely round the western end, and pass behind the great altar In the church of St. Philip the passage is obstructed by walls at each side, and the aisles extend only as far as the chancel.

7 H

mination, under which the principal altar is placed. There are also two side altars near the grand entrance; the ceiling is circular, the arch springing from the summit of the entablature over the colonnade, and is beautifully laid out in compartments of ornamented pannels and fret work. The expense is estimated at L 50,000. which is raised entirely by private subscription. It is intended to accommodate a congregation of 1000 persons.

It is to be regretted that this grand and classic edifice is not displayed in a more open site. Its principal front ornaments an unfrequented street, and its sides are obscured by the close contiguity of private houses. Had it been raised in a commanding situation, it would have formed one of our most striking public structures. Two architects are concerned in its erection, Mr. Morrison and Mr. Taylor. Several models were presented by others who gratuitously contributed their advice and assistance.

COUNTY INFIRMARY. In the year 1814, T. Pleasants, Esq. made a liberal donation of £6000. to the Meath Hospital; £2000. of which were to be funded according to the donor's wish to purchase with the interest, cordials and medicines for the patients, and £4000. to be laid out in erecting a new dissecting room. To this latter sum £800. were added by the subscription of other individuals, and ground was purchased in the Long lane between Cambden and New-streets, for the erection of a new hospital, which has been commenced. As this is intended for a county infirmary, and the reception of patients from the county as well as the city, its magnitude is proportioned to its application. The estimate of its expense is £8475. exclusive of £6000. paid for the purchase of the ground. When finished, it will be an important substitute for the Meath hospital, not only on account of its more extensive accommodation, but because the patients will be removed from a confined and unhealthy street, to an open airy situation in the immediate vicinity of the country, to which the hospital will on two sides be entirely open.

NEW FEVER HOSPITAL. To accommodate the inhabitants of the north side of the city, and those in that vicinity. It is proposed to erect a new fever hospital on the same scale as that of Cork-street, which shall receive patients not only from the parishes of St. Michan's, St. Mary's, St. Thomas and St. George, and St. Paul, but also from Drumcondra, Santry, Glasnevin, Clontarf, Finglas, and all the country contiguous to the north suburbs of the city. Several meetings of the promoters of this excellent and useful

THE CITY OF DUBLIN. 1155

charity have been held, but the building has not yet commenced, nor its site been determined on.

CARLISLE BUILDINGS. This edifice was intended originally for a city tavern. It stands near Carlisle bridge in D'Olier-street. Its appropriation has been lately changed, and it is now a public exhibition house, where pictures and other objects worthy of public notice are occasionally displayed.

CHARITABLE INSTITUTION HOUSE. The subscribers and conductors of several charities in Dublin have been in the habit of paying an annual or occasional rents for the use of rooms to conduct their affairs, in which their books, &c. have been kept, thus constantly subject to the inconvenience of confinement, disturbance, expense, and change of situation. To remedy this it has been proposed to erect a building appropriated to this purpose, and vested in the hands of six trustees for providing accommodation for various charitable Institutions. This edifice has not yet been commenced.

FREE MASONS' HALL. To accommodate this respectable and numerous body, it is also proposed to erect a suitable edifice in Dublin, and proposals have been published for that purpose, but the building is not yet commenced. A large edifice however has been erected in Nassau-street, by a private individual, containing a very extensive apartments suitable for, and with a view to accommodate, those public bodies.

OF THE STATE OF LITERATURE AND THE FINE ARTS IN DUBLIN.

There is no clear evidence existing, that letters, (with the exception of some theological writings) were cultivated in the city of Dublin prior to the reign of Elizabeth. The reformation was indeed preceded by the dawning of science in some countries of Europe,* it was however that great

* In other countries the art of printing was the precursor of the reformation. In Ireland the reformation was the precursor of the art of printing. In the year 1550 pursuant to an order from government, the new liturgy was first read in Christ church on Easter Sunday, and in order to provide books for the service, Humphry Powell established the first printing press in Dublin, and printed Edward 6th prayer book in the following year. "This book, which is with reason supposed to be the first ever printed in Ireland, is still preserved in the Library of Trinity College. It was among the books of Usher,

event which produced its glorious morning, not only in the countries which embraced its doctrines, but in those which still adhered to the ancient faith. Prior to that æra, an University was attempted, more than once, to be founded in the capital; but from the ignorance, the poverty, and the troubles of the times, the attempt always failed. The literature of Dublin then may be deemed coeval with the foundation of Trinity College, and from that time to the present no place in the world has advanced more rapidly in science and the Belles Lettres than the Irish metropolis. Of this, there cannot be a more convincing evidence than the many illustrious names (an enumeration and brief account of which are given in a subsequent

and is to be found in the Bibliotheca Usseriana. It is printed in black letter, and has the following title page.

THE BOKE
of common prayer and admi-
nistration of the Sacramen-
tes and other Rites and
Ceremonies of the
Churche; af-
ter the
use
of the Churche of
England
DUBLINIÆ IN OFFI
CINA HUMFREDI
POWELI
Cum Privilegio ad impri
Mendum solum
ANNO DOMINI
M.D.LI.

N. B. The first line is red, and in Roman characters, the next is black, and in black letter, and every alternate line is red and black.

The following extracts from the Rubric and Baptismal service are curious:

"As touchyng, kneeling, crossyng, holding up of handes, knocking upon the breast, and other gestures, they maie be used or left out, as every man's devotion serveth without blame."

"If there be a sermon or for other great cause, the curate by his discretion, maie leave out the Latenie, &c."

The form of exorcisme also at baptism was still retained.

"Then let the priest lookyng upon the children saie, I command thee uncleane spirite in the name of the Father, and of the Son, and of the Holy Ghost, that thou come out and depart from these infantes, &c."

THE CITY OF DUBLIN. 1157

Chapter) which reflect so much honour on their native city, and which, perhaps, no city of the same extent can surpass. Elegant literature and the fine arts require the fostering protection of the sovereign or the government, and the patronage of the nobility and the opulent to cause them to flourish, without such support they are found rarely to attain any degree of perfection in a provincial capital, and truth compels us to state, that not only have they declined most perceptibly in Dublin since the union, but the very taste and inclination for them are deteriorated.

When Dublin possessed a parliament, it had also a press of its own. Its acts and debates awakened the literature of the law and the University, and party views, and political interests, excited the attention of, and imparted a literary impulse to the public. Eloquence was not confined within the walls of the parliament-house, it embellished the courts of law, and enlivened the University, whilst the weapons of wit and satire were wielded with effect and dexterity by all parties. Now, the lively tumult is at rest, and all is secret or silent, as in a Turkish Divan.

As the copy-right of books was confined to Great Britain; the reprinting of smaller and cheaper editions, became a considerable branch of trade in Dublin, and many works respectable for their execution and correctness, thus republished, were exported to America, and to other countries. Whilst the act of union was still pending, application was made by petition to the Irish parliament to secure to the Irish printers a continuance of that right so advantageous to the Irish press; but by the neglect or mismanagement of those who were to conduct the petition—it was lost, and nothing here was effected.* Meanwhile the English printers availed themselves imme-

* While the act of union was in progress, the booksellers of Dublin prepared a petition to parliament to secure their rights, and prayed to be heard by counsel upon the subject. To conduct the petition and defray the expense, a subscription was entered into by the booksellers, and some gentlemen eminent at the bar were feed for the purpose. It happened by some accident that the petition was not heard on the night appointed, and it stood over for another. When it was to come on the lawyers were called on, but they refused to attend without a retaining fee. The subscriptions were exhausted, and they actually sat in the parlour of a house in College Green, opposite the Parliament house, while the proprietor went out to collect fresh subscriptions; before this could be effected, parliament was up, and no subsequent opportunity occurred till its final dissolution. But the English booksellers were determined to compensate for this neglect and watch over those rights which had been neglected in this country. With great apparent zeal for the interests of the trade in Dublin, six months after the act of union, a bill was passed in the United Parliament to extend the *benefits* of the copy-right to

diately and effectually of the act of union. Under the plausible pretence of securing to the Irish publisher the benefit of the copy-right, the English act was extended to Ireland, which secured indeed a nominal right, that they well knew would be wholly unavailable in competition with the trade at London, Glasgow, and Edinburgh. Thus have the Dublin booksellers ceased to be publishers by act of parliament, and must be content to be the agents of those of London.*

Besides the injury the trade has sustained, great numbers who formerly were in the habits of reading are by this act interdicted from doing so, as the books which once, by their comparative cheapness, were within their means of purchasing, cannot be procured. The printing business is therefore confined to devotional and moral tracts, which are paid for by charitable societies for gratuitous distribution—to printing hand-bills and playbills—to some half dozen newspapers, which are by no means remarkable, and to one or two very middling magazines, which can scarcely maintain an ephemeral existence.† The Royal Irish Academy publish their Transactions at their own cost, as do the editors of the statistical work now in progress under the patronage of the Dublin Society. The University press,

Ireland, and the original draught went so far as to extend to all books already published; but it was after confined only to those which should be published for the first time after the passing of the act. The benefits of the act were nearly to extinguish printing and literature in Dublin. It conferred a nugatory advantage, of which no author has yet, or perhaps ever will avail himself, by printing his works in Dublin; and it took away a most important privilege, the source of great profit to the bookseller, of extensive employment to the printer, and adapted to the state of the country, by putting within the reach of ordinary readers, those works of merit which are now removed altogether beyond their attainment.

* Among the former Dublin editions of authors of repute, may be enumerated Swift's works, edited by George Falkener, under the inspection of the Dean himself; a quarto edition of Johnson's Dictionary, by Ewing, which Dr. J. said was more correct than the folio edition completed under his own inspection; Kennicot's Bible, with plates, printed by Jackson, and the Doway Bible, by Cross. A duodecimo edition of Shakspeare, by Ewing, is in great request. Paine's Geography, 2 vols. 4to. Moore's Encyclopædia, Ledwich's Antiquities, 4to. Chambers's Dictionary, 4 vol. folio; and Don Quixote, by Chambers, Leland's History of Ireland, 3 vols. 4to. Collectanea de Rebus Hibernicis, and the Anthologia Hibernica, are works creditable to the Dublin press. A republication of old Chronicles and Tracts, illustrative of Irish history, by an Hibernian Press Company, was published in a good style since the Union, but the publishers became bankrupts by the undertaking.

† The following is a list of newspapers, magazines, and almanacks, which have appeared in Dublin since the year 1700. Those marked with an asterisk are become extinct. Of the monthly and weekly

in the College Park, was formerly distinguished for its correct editions of several of the classics; it has, however, long since ceased to work.

periodical pamphlets (except a monthly religious publication,) not one exists in Dublin, or any other part of Ireland. They " come like shadows—so depart."

Newspapers.

Dublin Gazette, twice a week	* Universal Journal
* Pue's Occurrences, daily	* Volunteer Evening Post
Falkener's Journal, ditto	* Volunteer Journal
Saunder's News Letter, ditto	* Hoey's Mercury,
Freeman's Journal, ditto	* Bell's Weekly Pacquet
Hibernian Journal, ditto	* The Meridian
Dublin Evening Post, three times a week	* Magee's Weekly Pacquet
* Morning Post	* Weekly Messenger
* Phœnix	* Irish Pacquet
* Evening Star	* Pimlico Journal
* Antiunionist	* Telegraph
* Press	* Sunday Oracle
* Herald, Evening	* Lanthorn
* True Born Irishman	* Monitor
* M'Donald's Weekly Journal	* Express
* Patriot	* Review
Carrick's Morning Post, daily	* Chronicle, weekly
Correspondent, Evening, ditto	* Western Star
Dublin Chronicle, twice a week	* News
Farmer's Journal, weekly	* National Reform
Weekly Gazette	* Impartial Enquirer.

Magazines and Periodical Works.

* Weekly Advice of Dublin Society	* Dublin Satirist
* Exshaw's Gentleman's Magazine	* Flapper
* Walker's Hibernian Magazine	* Antiunion
* Baratariana	* Medical Journal
* Batchelor	* Examiner
* Pranceriana	* Sentimental Magazine
* Cyclopedian Magazine	Evangelical Magazine
* Anthologia Hibernica	* Gleaner
* Masonic	* Union Star
* New Hibernian Magazine	* Panorama
* Cox's Irish Magazine	* Milesian Magazine
* Ireland's Mirror	* Minerva Magazine

Pue's Occurrences was the first newspaper ever established in Dublin; it commenced in the year 1700, and was called from the proprietor, who conducted it. It maintained itself for more than half a century.

THE HISTORY OF

Another reason of the depression of the Irish press, and paucity of original literary publications in Dublin, is the facility with which the best

Falkener's Journal was established by the celebrated George Falkener in 1728, and displayed in its composition that honest blundering simplicity so conspicuous in the character of the man. The sheet was remarkable for the paleness of the ink, and the darkness of the paper; and the peculiarities of the style have been happily imitated on several occasions, of which the following is a specimen: "House of Industry first contrived by Mr. Ben. Houghton, weaver, and several other worthy clergymen, for taking up cripples that lie in the street, folks without legs that stand in corners, and such like vagrants. We have the pleasure to hear, that all ballad singers, blind harpers, hackhall, and many other nefarious old women, are in there already." It was afterwards conducted with ability and party spirit. It has recently been re-established, on new principles.

Freeman's Journal came out in 1763. It was established by a committee for conducting a free press, and assumed as its emblem and motto, "The Wreath or the Rod." In this first appeared several of the essays afterwards collected and published in "Barrataria," and evinced a spirit and energy not inferior to Junius. It afterwards was edited by a person called the "Sham Squire," and degenerated. It has within some years, however, revived, and regained some of its original spirit.

Hibernian Journal was established in 1771, and, like the former, conducted by a committee for a free press. The fate of Mills, its first printer, is characteristic of the summary mode of proceeding at that time in Dublin. Some of the numbers of "Pranceriana" first appeared in that paper, and it became the organ of attack by one party of the College on another. On a dark evening in February, a coach drove up to the printer's door in Dame-street, to which he was called out, and while he was talking to those in the inside, he was pushed in by some one behind, and immediately carried to the College pump, which then stood in the middle of the front court, and almost suffocated. A reward was offered by the common council, and a scholar of the house, who was concerned, was admonished by the board. The printer is thus noticed in the admonition, which was the production of the celebrated Dr. Leland : " Cum " constet scholarium ignotorum cœtum injuriam admovisse in typographum quendam famosum nomine " Mills, qui nefariis flagitiis nobiliora quæque Collegii membra in chartis suis lacessiverat," &c.

Morning Post was also called the Dalkey Gazette. A convivial society some years ago existed in Dublin, who periodically assembled at the island of Dalkey, and elected a king and other officers of state. A column of this paper was always devoted to their proceedings, which were then interesting, as the society comprised a number of respectable citizens. The last monarch was a bookseller of the name of Armitage, who was always called "King Stephen."

Volunteer Evening Post was established about the year 1780, and its fate displays a lively trait of the temper of those times. The spirit of opposition to the then Government was so strong that no Irish printer could be found to compose a paragraph in its favour against the popular cause. Government was therefore obliged to send a press and printers from England for this purpose; but it required some management to establish it. It first assumed a popular name, and professed to take a warm part on that side. To increase the deception, the portrait of a volunteer in full uniform was exhibited every night in an illuminated transparency, and a prize medal was proposed and given by the editors for the best poetical composition on the Volunteer Institution, and every thing was practised, and with great success to complete the deception. At length the secret transpired, and the mob proceeded to take

THE CITY OF DUBLIN.

English works may be procured. All the London and Edinburgh periodical works are taken in at the two library societies, "The Dublin," and "The

summary vengeance. The editor escaped, but the printer was dragged to the Tenter-fields, and tarred and feathered. But the most extraordinary proceeding was that of the counties of Ireland, some of which actually came forward with resolutions, that the paper was established on fallacious principles, and for the wicked purpose of putting down the Volunteer Institution; they therefore conjured their countrymen not to read it. The effect of this prohibition to a literary work was as singular as the cause. It was fatal to the newspaper; no one was found to purchase it, and the editors returned to England after three years fruitless effort.

The Press was established in the year 1797, and was conducted with an energy and ability too successful at that perilous period. The first conductor had been convicted of a libel on Lord Camden, and the celebrated Arthur O'Connor became the avowed editor. The paper was suppressed by the military a short time previous to the rebellion. The essays and other pieces contained in it were published in one volume, with the imprint of London, under the name of " The Beauties of the Press," and afterwards circulated in Dublin.

Baratariana appeared in 1770. It was a keen and vigorous attack on the administration of Lord Townshend in this country, and conducted with great ability.

Anthologia Hibernica commenced in the year 1793, and was strictly a national work, devoted to the antiquities and literature of Ireland. All the literary men resident in Ireland contributed to the undertaking, and it was a valuable repository of ingenious essays and learned communications. Political discussion, however, soon superseded every other, and this excellent periodical work expired in two years, as several others had before, in the distractions of the country.

Union Star. This atrocious composition appeared in the year 1797. It was published at irregular intervals, printed only on one side, and was secretly posted during the night in the most conspicuous parts of the city. It commenced with the motto, " Perhaps some arm more lucky than the rest may " reach his heart, and free the world from bondage," and denounced by name and description such men as were inimical to the cause it advocated. A reward of 700*l.* was offered by government for the author and publisher, but though well known he was never avowed.

Antiunionist. This appeared in 1799, with a view to oppose the legislative union then in agitation. It displayed some wit, but it seemed to want the energy and spirit which alone give efficacy to opinions in great political discussions. Like the last efforts of the French under Napoleon, the Antiunionist displayed the imbecility of an exhausted subject and worn out people.

Irish Magazine. This was first published in 1807. It was edited by an extraordinary man of the name of Cox, a gunsmith, whose father, as he says himself, was a bricklayer in the county of Meath. The magazine was almost exclusively matter compiled by himself. It contained biographical notices of the dead, and severe attacks upon the living. The work was a series of scurrility, calumny, and vulgarity; but there was withal a fund of information, a strong sense, and a humour and drollery so captivating, that its circulation extended to all parts of Ireland, and continued for some time the only periodical publication, and became even a school book in some of the hedge schools. The usual number printed and circulated annually amounted to 60,000, or about 5000 monthly. The author was convicted of a libel in 1811, continued his magazine while in Newgate, with an increased circulation,

1162 THE HISTORY OF

Institute," to one or other of which almost every respectable inhabitant of the capital is a subscriber. The circulating libraries are also early supplied with popular works.

It must not, however, be inferred, that Irish genius or talent has declined. It is true, there is no encouragement for literary exertion in the Irish metropolis, because the cautious Dublin bookseller will run no risk in was convicted of a second, and finally agreed to transport himself to America, and put an end to his magazine in 1815. He is since dead.

Medical Journal was first published in 1807. It was the first ever attempted in Dublin, and intended as a receptacle for all medical essays and communications which might be made on the subject; but notwithstanding the extensive hospitals of Dublin, the rising reputation of the schools of surgery and physic, and the talent supposed to exist in the respective professions, this work could only be supported for eighteen months. Its place is now, in some measure, supplied by " Hospital Reports," two volumes of which appeared in the summer of 1817; one anonymous, and the other under the sanction of the College of Physicians.

Dublin Examiner was the last attempt to establish a respectable periodical work in Dublin. It commenced in May 1816, and was continued monthly. It contained a critical review of recent works, with essays, and other original matter; and proposed in some measure to establish a Review in the metropolis of Ireland similar to those of Edinburgh and London. It continued only to the end of the year, exhibiting a melancholy instance of the low state of literature in a country which, while its talents contribute largely to enrich literature abroad, cannot support at home one single periodical publication.

Almanacks.

An Irish Almanack, so early as the 15th century, is stated to have been in the possession of General Valancey.

In 1696, an Almanack was published in Dublin by Andrew Cumsty, Philomath, who kept a school at the sign of the Royal Exchange, Wood Quay. It should appear by the preface, that it was only established the year before. It contained a calendar, fairs, tide-tables, and astrological observations.

In the same year another, pirated from this, was published by Wilde.

Watson's Almanack, first published in 1729; still continues.

Ryder's, published a few years after, failed in a short time.

Merlin, published by Alexander Stewart.

Kelly's, printed in the year 1793. This was a very copious and useful work, and contained, in addition to the usual information, brief biographical notices of the existing members of both Houses of Parliament, present state of schools, public and private, &c. This expired in a few years.

Grant's, now *Lady's*. This, besides the calendar, contains a great number of charades and enigmas, proposed each year, to be answered in the next.

Smith's, lately established.

The *Directory* was first published about forty years ago.

The *Registry* is a republication of an English work.

The Almanack, Directory, and Registry, bound together, form perhaps the completest body of information on local subjects to be found in any city in Europe.

THE CITY OF DUBLIN. 1163

publishing an original work, however great its merit. It must first appear in London, or not at all. Nevertheless, Dublin can even now boast of many existing characters in the various walks of literature and the arts, as well as in the senate, the church, the bar, the army, and the theatre, which uphold its pretensions to the high rank that it has obtained in these respects.

With respect to the progress of the fine arts, and especially of painting, very little has been known of their early state in Ireland. Bindon, a gentleman of fortune, and an amateur artist, made laudable attempts to encourage them. He painted portraits of Swift, Dean Delany, and Dr. Sheridan. Shortly after this period, James Latham, (an Irish artist, born in Tipperary in 1696), having studied at Antwerp, cultivated his art with singular success. He painted portraits of the beautiful Mrs. Woffington, Geminiani the composer, and a few others, with so much truth, clearness, and purity of style, that he obtained the distinguished title of the Irish Vandyke. Although polite literature about the same time had attained its highest degree of excellence in England, yet painting was there still in its infancy, so far as regarded a school of native artists, for the principal painters were foreigners, and even Jervas, a native of Dublin, arrived at distinction, although he is now better known by his translation of Don Quixote, than for any pictorial celebrity. It was not, indeed, till Reynolds founded the English school that painting began to be distinguished in England. He became first president of the Royal Academy, which was founded so late as the year 1768. The same remark is applicable to sculpture, which, until lately, was wholly in the hands of foreigners If therefore the fine arts were thus backward in arriving at maturity in the metropolis of the British empire, it is not surprising that their establishment should be of a recent date in Dublin.

But the Irish Government were not wanting to encourage the arts; for prior to the founding of the Royal Academy in London, the Dublin artists formed themselves into a society, in the year 1764, consisting of twelve members, who elected from their number a president, secretary, and treasurer. The society soon after proceeded to build an exhibition-house, and were assisted by Government with £500. and by subscriptions, which amounted to £300. This money, however, being insufficient to finish the building, three of the members gave bonds in behalf of the society, to satisfy the demands incurred by the undertaking.

The first exhibition was opened in 1765, and for a few years the rooms were well attended, but the admission money being small, the receipts were insufficient to pay the interest of the bonds and debt. The house-rent, which was £33. per annum, was defrayed by the rent of the ground floor, which was set for a school. Under these circumstances, Richard Cranfield, treasurer of the society, took up the bonds on his own account, and forthwith had the whole management of the concern.

About the year 1773, a schism took place in the society. The seceders opened an exhibition in Great George's-street, which met so much encouragement that the exhibition in William-street was obliged to be discontinued. At length a coalition was effected, and the society, now become respectable—were distinguished on festive days and public exhibitions by a gold medal, which each member wore on the breast, suspended by a garter blue ribbon round the neck. The medal was struck with emblematic figures of painting, sculpture, and architecture on one side, and on the reverse, with the name of the wearer.

From the year 1776 to 1782, the yearly exhibitions, although the admittance money was raised to one shilling, did not pay the interest on the bonds, and the treasurer, Cranfield, brought in the society his debtor to the amount of £800. William Ashford, therefore, the then president, called a meeting, which resolved to dispose of the concerns; but there being no offers at all adequate to the claims of Cranfield, the society was compelled to assign over to him all its interest in the premises, with a clause of redemption, when it was rich enough to pay his demand. It was also stipulated to pay him £30. annually for the use of the rooms, whenever they were used for exhibition. The exhibitions, however, were discontinued until the year 1800, when the society's house in William-street was disposed of for other purposes. There was now a general meeting of all the artists in Dublin, who determined on an exhibition, and hired suitable rooms in Dame-street for that purpose. Soon after, by the liberality of Earl Hardwick, the Parliament-house, at that time fitting up for the national bank, was assigned them, and here they exhibited with much effect for two years. A permanent institution was at length established, under the patronage of the late Lord-lieutenant—the Duke of Richmond, with the title of THE SOCIETY OF THE ARTISTS OF DUBLIN. Meanwhile, the Dublin Society had erected, in their buildings in Hawkins's-street, a most noble exhibition room. In this grand room the first exhibition was displayed in the summer of 1810, and another the following year; both were numerously attended and much applauded.

But symptoms of dissension had already appeared among the members, some of whom wished to form a society more select and independent. They therefore seceded from the rest, took commodious rooms at Del Vecchio's in Westmoreland-street, and opened an exhibition under the title of the IRISH SOCIETY. But the public did not approve of these disputes, and the separate exhibitions met with no encouragement. This at length produced a re-union. The united members then adopted another title, that of the HIBERNIAN SOCIETY; and the public applauded this conciliation by giving the most distinguished support to the exhibition of 1814. But the embers of discord, though smothered, were not extinguished; another separation took place, and similar consequences were the result. The exhibitions were neglected and became a losing concern, whilst the public directed their attention to a new institution, formed on the plan of that of London, for exhibiting the works of the old masters.

This exhibition was founded June 4th, 1813, under the title of the "ROYAL IRISH INSTITUTION FOR PROMOTING THE FINE ARTS IN IRELAND." It is supported by names of the highest rank; H. R. H. the Prince Regent being the Patron; his Excellency Earl Whitworth, Lord-lieutenant, the Guardian; his Grace the Duke of Richmond the Vice-Patron; and his Grace the Duke of Leinster the President. The subscriptions already amount to upwards of £3000. The exhibitions take place at the great rooms in Hawkins-street, and paintings of the old masters of the Flemish and Italian schools are supplied by the nobility and gentry of Ireland who possess collections. The Earls of Charlemont, Farnham, and Milltown, are the principal contributors.

With all those liberal measures and plans for the encouragement of the arts, it must be confessed that the door is too widely opened for the admission of young candidates, whose friends or patrons, unfortunately for them, fancy they discover a genius for painting. Many a good mechanic is spoiled by becoming an indifferent artist; and after furnishing half a dozen drawing masters and some artizans whose trades are intimately connected with drawing, as cotton printers, paper stainers, &c. there yet remain numbers who cannot earn a moderate subsistence by any exertion of moderate talents. Nay, even distinguished talents if they aim at fame or fortune, must not expect to find them in Ireland. The country is too poor, and if it were not so poor, there are too few real connoisseurs in it to appreciate and reward the merit of a living artist.

On the other hand, it would be unjust to conclude that the Dublin Society's school for drawing, sculpture and architecture had failed to produce the results expected from it. The two masters,[*] the Wests, father and son, who so long presided over the Academy, though eminent themselves, were yet more conspicuous for the number of celebrated artists which they had the honour of initiating in the art ; among whom were James Barry, George Barret, Hugh Hamilton, Henry Tresham, Thomas Roberts, Henry Brooks, Edward Smith the statuary, Thomas Ivory the architect, together with several others still living, but not less known to fame.[†]

[*] For an account of the native and other artists, and those practised in Dublin, see Addenda.]

[†] Among the living and native artists of Dublin is one who has particularly distinguished himself, and rendered essential service to the community, by a discovery arising from his profession, but altogether unconnected with it. This gentleman, Mr. Oldham, served his time to an engraver, and was afterwards engaged in the calico printing manufactory of Duffy and Hamel at Ball's-bridge, where he first imbibed a taste for mechanics and optics, and from his study of the camera obscura became a painter, and practised in miniature for several years in Dublin. He had long turned his mind to discover a means of preventing the forgery of bank notes, and invented an engraving machine on the principles of a diagonal motion, something after the manner of Maillardet's writing automaton, which has been since adopted in the bank of Ireland. The important improvement of this machine is—that it produces a species of ornamental engraving at once comprehensible to all capacities, and yet beyond the possibility of being imitated by any manual operations, and by a rotatory motion is capable of engraving twenty copper plates at the same time. His next discovery was the application of steam to the department of copper plate printing. Heat and power are necessary to this art, and for this purpose a small engine of eight horse power has been erected under his direction for the purpose of turning the printing presses of his original construction ; in these presses are a feeding machine in place of the accustomed prolix mode of charging the plates with colour, and also a precaution for registering the notes, by which the superintendant, though not present, may ascertain the number struck off, and thus prevent the possibility of frauds. The same steam which sets the instrument in motion is also used instead of charcoal braziers to heat the plates. It also sets in motion an air pump, which heats and ventilates the entire of the printing establishment. It turns a paper mill, and a colour machine of his own invention, which consists of a table and a cylinder ; three motions are communicated to both. The table turns slowly upon its axis, while the cylinder revolves quietly on its surface, and has a lateral motion from side to side of the table in a horizontal direction ; by these means a complete levigating effect is produced, as no part of the colour can escape unground ; the advantage of this to the preservation of the plates is very important, as the friction on their surface is reduced to nothing by the tenacity of the materials

THE CITY OF DUBLIN.

It is however more especially in architecture that the inhabitants of the Irish capital have evinced a decided predilection. Every city may be said to prefer a particular style in their public buildings. That of London is grave and massive, being mostly of the Doric and Tuscan orders. That of Dublin is much lighter, affecting the bold portico and airy colonnade of the Ionic and Corinthian orders.

In ecclesiastical structures, the captial of the empire admits of no competition; but, excepting two churches in Dublin, St. George's and the Castle chapel, and two or three half finished façades of others, so left for the erection of future steeples; the rest seem to set at defiance every principle of architecture. Moreover, with the exception of the cathedral of St. Patrick, and the new church of St. George, there is not a steeple with a spire among them all. To this rude unsightly stile, the new R. C. Metropolitan chapel will, when finished, afford one more striking exception. The interiors of most of the churches are, however, handsome, and a few even grand. But in edifices allotted to civil purposes, Dublin is not excelled by any city in Europe.

PRESENT STATE OF SOCIETY AND MANNERS IN DUBLIN.

It is an established maxim in politics, that in every clime and country political events and changes of government have had at all times, a most decided influence in forming the character and manners of the people. Dublin, besides experiencing this influence in common with the progress of civilization of the British empire, has been affected by causes which were peculiar and

---

composing the ink. In addition to those services of this engine, it turns forcing pumps to supply water for the whole establishment, and can be applied as an engine to extinguish fire in any part of the edifice. The numbering presses are also his invention. The numbers and dates formerly written with a pen, are now printed by a machine, after the note has been thrown off from the copper plate. This machine is a piece of clockwork which produces the numbers in successive order from 1 to 100,000 by its own internal operation, and without any attention requisite to such changes on the part of the operator, who has only to change the type according to the accustomed mode of printing. The whole series of numbers occupied eight weeks in throwing off. By these means one boy performs the operation of eight clerks.

appropriate to the metropolis of Ireland alone. It partook in far more than a proportional degree of the rapid advances which Ireland made in population, commerce, civilization, and literature, in the latter half of the eighteenth century, and yet more particularly, at the period when the kingdom enjoyed a flourishing but too transitory legislative independence. Within that half century, all the public institutions of utility or elegance, all those embellishments and improvements which still exist, were completed or commenced; whilst the inhabitants boasted, and not without just pretensions, of their superior urbanity, state, gaiety, hospitality, and active charitable disposition; but it is now very apparent, that in all these qualities there has been a visible declension, except only in the last. The reason of the decline is sufficiently obvious. Prior to the legislative union, a splendid vice-regal court, with frequent and crowded levees, a stationary parliament, and the occasional residence of all the nobility and gentry of the kingdom diffused wealth and animation over a metropolis of a size sufficiently moderate to feel the effects, and imparted to the inhabitants in general a tincture and tone of that civility and good-breeding which are supposed exclusively to belong to the higher classes of society. Since the period alluded to, these acquisitions and advantages have, in a great degree, been lost to Dublin; between four and five hundred families of rank and opulence which once were residents, are no longer to be found in it, and those few who might still be inclined to make it their occasional abode are prevented by their attendance in London on their parliamentary avocations.* Thus that overgrown and bloated

The bank of Ireland so highly appreciates these important discoveries that they have approriated an entire wing of their new erected building for the operation, and have appointed the ingenious inventor, Mr. Oldham, to superintend the whole.

* Before the Union, the society of the Irish metropolis was very numerous, as well as highly respectable. Dublin was then the constant or occasional residence of 249 temporal peers, 22 spiritual peers, and 300 members of the House of Commons. Politics and party imparted a spirit and animation to all ranks; and social intercourse was rendered brilliant and interesting, when the most eminent characters, still more remarkable for their talents than their rank or fortune,—in the Castle, the Parliament, the Courts of Law, the Church, and the University contributed to make it so. Amongst these might be distinguished: Lords Charlemont, Clare, Clonmel, Montjoy, Mornington, and Moira; Anthony Malone, Henry Flood, Hussey Burgh, Bushe, Jephson, Courtney, O'Hara, Grattan, Curran, Foster, Yelverton, Hely Hutchinson, the two Kirwans, George Ogle, Charles Sheridan, Forbes, Toler &c.

Since that period, the Irish members of both houses, visit Dublin only for a short time in their transit to England. At present its society is composed of the following classes, the individuals of which have a dwelling in the city, namely: 29 peers and peeresses temporal, 6 peers spiritual, 13 baronets or

capital absorbs all the wealth, and engrosses all the talents of the sister metropolis, and, indeed of the whole sister kingdom. Although the commerce of Dublin has not, on the whole, experienced this general depression, yet the diminished importation and very limited consumption of wines is a striking proof of it. During its flourishing period, claret was universally drank after dinner, in the upper ranks, nor were the tables of the middle classes, on days of entertainment without it; and it was particularly esteemed for its purity and excellence. Claret, except at the very first tables, is becoming almost as rarely to be met with as tokay. Port wine, which formerly was only admitted on the table, during dinner, almost every where supplies its place, together with the native beverage whiskey. With the pleasures of the convivial board, the relish for public amusements seems also to have greatly abated. Formerly, two theatres, royal and a circus were supported in Dublin, with a proportional exhibition of other spectacles. Now one solitary playhouse scarcely finds encouragement, though duly supplied with first rate performers from London; and Astley's Circus in Peter-street is converted into an asylum and meeting-house. With the too frequent circulation of the bottle, which formerly was the custom, the spirit of gambling has also almost wholly declined. The once-fashionable Club-houses are no longer attended. Gaming of all kinds indeed is so much discountenanced, that scarcely a card table is to be met with in private parties.

The character of the people of Dublin seems to have undergone a complete change. It was once gay, convivial, and in some degree dissipated; it is now more serious, prudent, and religious; but it still maintains its reputation for unfeigned benevolence and genuine charity. It may be truly asserted that in no city in Europe of the same extent are public morals purer. The crimes of the populace proceed rather from the pressure of distress than from vicious habits. The unfortunate females who walk the streets are fewer in number than are usually found in second rate sea-port towns in England, and even these are the inevitable appendages of a large garrison.

ladies, 5 members of the House of Commons, 93 Protestant clergymen, 170 Roman Catholic clergymen, 25 Dissenting clergymen, 1851 lawyers and attorneys, 204 physicians and surgeons, 1484 gentry and private families, and 4911 persons engaged in commerce, bankers, merchants, head-manufactuers, and dealers. To these may be added the officers of the garrison about 200,

The are, however, many signs of prosperity still to be observed in Dublin; its public and private buildings are increasing, though not in the same degree as formerly; according to the port returns, to which we refer, the commerce of Dublin is augmenting, particularly in its exports; the Castle, though with diminished bustle and brilliancy, still keeps up a little court; the University is increasing in buildings and students; the law courts attract the accustomed crowds during terms; and the officers of a large garrison consisting of about 7000 men, embellish and keep up the spirit of public amusements and private parties; for the latter, indeed, the people of Dublin seem to have a decided predilection, and to prefer that unreserved and good humoured intercourse which constitutes the sweetest charm of society, to every other amusement. Public balls and concerts are frequently given at the Rotunda, either for some charity or to support the Lying in Hospital: these are always well attended. The distinction of ranks and conditions is not particularly observable in public, but in private meetings it is more strictly preserved. When by the act of union, so many of the superior classes became absentees,* and were necessarily estranged from their attendance at the Castle, a door was opened for the admission of the

* The absentees of Ireland have been from the earliest times a constant theme of complaint, as the prime cause of the unprosperous state of the country. So early as the year 1368, an ordinance of the 42d of Edward III. respecting Ireland, states :—Les ditz mals (the conduct of the absentees) aveneez en perdition de la dite terre. In 1601, a writer of "Remarks on the Affairs of England and Ireland," states, that the amount of drainage of wealth by absentees in different ways, was L136,018. per annum. In 1729 a work, ascribed to Thomas Prior, contains a list of absentees, and the money they drew from the kingdom in various ways, which amounted annually to L627,799. Arthur Young, in 1779, states, it at L732,200; but an alphabetical list of names and particulars published in 1782 makes it amount to the enormous sum of L2,223,222!. What then must it amount to since the union?

Among other indications of the effect of absentees on the prosperity of Dublin, may be mentioned the increased number of hotels. Heretofore every nobleman and gentleman of distinction either rented or built a house in the metropolis, in which he resided half the year. Some of these, such as Leinster, Powerscourt, and Tyrone house, &c. were among the first architectural ornaments of the city; the greater number of these are now converted into public buildings and hotels, where the former proprietors occupy a room for the few days he remains in the metropolis in his transit to England. The number of principal hotels now amount to 43, in a city where formerly such an accommodation was scarcely known. Such houses as are not applied to public use are sometimes deserted by the proprietors to avoid the taxes. These amount to so serious a sum, and have borne so heavily on the citizens of Dublin, that it has been found necessary to make certain exemptions in favour of those whose houses lay on their hands unoccupied for a certain length of time. The multitude of houses in almost every street advertised for sale by bills on the windows, is a melancholy proof of the cause and effect of this

THE CITY OF DUBLIN. 1171

upper ranks in the commercial world, in consequence of which the Castle assemblies soon became so inconveniently thronged, that the future entré of these *novi homines* was restricted. Nevertheless, that honour is by no means difficult to be obtained. Strangers and visitors complain that they do not always find that hospitality so generous and inviting as they were taught to believe; as if it were incumbent on the inhabitants to convert their houses into hotels and taverns for the exercise of this virtue. Dublin, like other great cities, is never averse from receiving strangers, when properly introduced; but in later times, the pressing claims of its own distressed citizens have diminished the ardour, as well as the means of being extensively hospitable.

Among the amusements of a populous town, public gardens, opened in the evening, for the entertainment and refreshment of those who have devoted the day to business, seem to be in other cities almost a necessary appendage to the habits of a citizen. In Dublin the custom is scarcely known. About 50 years ago, the garden of Ranelagh, in the southern

exemption. The following are the taxes to which houses in Dublin are liable, with their probable amount. The rate of taxation is regulated generally by the minister's money paid by each respectively.

General.

Hearth money and window light,	L180,000	Minister's money, - -	L8000
Paving and lighting, usual average,	40,000	Parish cess, - - -	12,000
Pipe water, - -	10,000	Clerk's dues, - -	600
Metal main, - - -	10,000	Foundling Hospital, -	10,000
Wide-street, - -	8,000	Anna Liffey, - - -	12,000
Grand Jury, - - -	25,000	Watch tax, - -	- 12,000

Local or partial,
Card tax,   Square,   Private still fine,
Club house,   Poddle,   Mob tax,
Quay,   Occasional, Watering streets,

The *card tax* is only paid by houses rated at 20s. minister's money. The *quay tax* by houses on the Quays for keeping the walls, &c. in repair. It is an additional tax of 2s. per foot on each house. The *square tax* by houses in the public squares rated by the breadth of the front of the house. In Stephen's Green it amounts at present to 5s. per foot, in addition to the other taxes. *Poddle tax* is paid by the houses built over the course of that stream, to keep the arches, &c. in repair. Those local and occasional taxes may be estimated at 10,000l. per annum. The aggregate of all these taxes sometimes exceed the rent, and often bears no proportion to the value of the house. The amount of the whole paid by the citizens is estimated at 340,000l. and in some years at 350,000l. per annum. To these grievances the tax levied by street beggars must be added. This is a nuisance that has long existed in Dublin, and notwithstanding the asylums prepared and the precautions taken, it seems daily to be increasing. It is supposed that there are 5000 persons in the city who support themselves by begging in different forms, and that they levy a tax in this way of £100,000. per annum; but it is endured, in consequence of being exempt from a still greater evil—the Poor Laws.

suburbs, was for some time opened, and frequented by the citizens. The amusement, however, did not seem congenial to the temper of the people, and after some time the garden, with all its gay appendages, was converted into a nunnery, which it continues to be at the present day. About 30 years ago, a number of tea houses were opened at Drumcondra, on the northern suburbs; the city, however, extending in that direction, obliterated the gardens attached to these houses, and they never revived in any other place. In the year 1817, an attempt was made to remedy this deficiency, and the grounds of Lord Clonmel, in Harcourt-street, were deemed a proper situation. This extensive lawn, comprising twelve acres, was laid down with walks, benches, and alcoves, for promenade and recreation—a theatre was erected for public exhibitions,—grand illuminations by lamps and fire works, were prepared, and they opened in May, 1817, under the appellation of the " Coburg Gardens." The public habit, however, was not in unison with these preparations, and from the ill success of the proprietors, it is probable that this attempt also will fail, like all the former. In effect, the social habits of the people of Dublin are only exercised in their own or in their friends' houses. Their amusements are domestic, and they seldom look abroad for that recreation which they enjoy best at home. Hence it is, that a citizen will not appoint a stranger to meet him at a tavern, but at his own house; and writers of other countries have remarked with surprise, that he invites not only the individual, but all the party he is with, to accompany him.* For this convivial gratification, he neglects the theatre, the tavern, and the tea garden. The only public evening amusement which has been well and uniformly attended, is a public charity. The promenades in the gardens of the Rotunda, for the benefit of the Lying-in-Hospital, were constantly crowded, on Sunday evening, with all ranks of persons, till the " Association" interfered, and they were discontinued. They have, however, been revived on the evenings of week days, when they are illuminated, and attended by a band of music. There is no refreshment distributed, and the price of admission is only 5d. During the summer months the citizens of Dublin are frequently deprived of all public amusement, with this solitary exception

But while they are thus indifferent to those amusements which others so much enjoy, the citizens of Dublin carry one to an excess peculiar to them-

* See " Philosophical Survey," in 1775, &c.

THE CITY OF DUBLIN.

selves. The vicinity of the city to the sea, and the lovely and inviting coast which surrounds it, are attractions which have universal influence. The whole population of Dublin seem to crowd to the water in the summer months, and all ranks and ages think bathing a specific for the preservation of health or the cure of distemper. On these occasions the roads to the sea, at particular times of the tide, present extraordinary spectacles. Every vehicle,* both public and private, is seen filled with people crowding the

* Besides hackney coaches, which are common to all classes and other places, there have been other vehicles used by the middle and lower classes, which were of a description peculiar to Dublin. The earliest and rudest of these machines were called " Ringsend Cars," from their plying principally to that village and Irish Town, then much frequented for bathing. They consisted of a seat suspended on a strap of leather, between two shafts, and without springs. The noise made by the creeking of this strap, which supported the whole weight of the company, peculiarly distinguished this mode of conveyance. These were succeeded by an improved machine, called a " Noddy." This was a low small vehicle capable of holding two persons, and drawn by one horse; it was covered in with a calash, and open before, but the aperture was nearly closed by the back of the " Noddy Boy," who was generally a large sized man, and occupied a seat which projected into the laps of the company. This race also became extinct about 25 years ago, and its place was supplied by " Jaunting Cars." This machine originally consisted of a platform laid upon shafts, without springs, from which foot-boards hung at each side. On this platform the company, four in number, sat, with their feet very near the ground, and were dragged along sideways, and sitting back to back; from which latter circumstance the vehicle was sometimes called an Irish " Vis à Vis." The last improvement, and which still holds its place, are " Jingles," so called from the ringing sound of the lose iron work. These consist of a circular open body, placed high upon springs, and rolling on four wheels. In these the company, six in number, sit face to face, sometimes sideways, and sometimes front to rere. They ply between Dublin and the villages in the vicinity, particularly Black Rock and Clontarf. They are drawn by one small starved horse, which is drove with little intermission, at the top of his speed, for twelve hours every day. The performance of some of these apparently wretched animals is incredible. They have been known to perform 20 journeys to and from the Black Rock in one day, a distance on the whole, of 60 miles, and to carry at each time seven people. They seldom, however, outlive a season, and frequently die in the harness. The fare of each person is only sixpence. The great convenience and cheapness of these jaunting cars had induced almost every respectable citizen to keep one for the private use of his family, and occasionally to hire a horse to draw it to the sea water; but the tax having within these few years been extended to these also, they were universally discontinued, and the citizens of Dublin, deprived of a convenience which contributed essentially not merely to the comfort, but health of their families, parted with them not as luxuries, but as articles of prime necessity.

Besides the use of the open sea, several cold and hot baths have been established in Dublin and the vicinity, for those who prefer them. They are also much frequented, and are at the following places.

| Irish Town, | Black Rock, | North-hall, | Temple-street, | Dublin. |
| Merrion, | Sea Point, | Annesley-bridge, | Crane-lane, | |

avenues that lead to the salt water on both sides of the bay, particularly on the south. As the shore is flat, and the period of bathing is but short at each tide, they hasten to avail themselves of it, and rush altogether into the water. The swarm of naked figures thus seen on the shore from Ringsend to Sandymount is as singular as it is surprising, while the noise and sportive merriment seem to indicate that it is not practised so much for health as festive recreation. It is supposed that 20,000 people bathe every tide in Dublin-bay during the summer months, and many continue the practice through the winter.

In the present state of Europe, the upper classes every where assimilate; it is from the lower that the true character of a city or state should be deduced. That of the Dublin populace was much more strongly marked some years ago than at present, when industry and plenty took up their abode in the now miserable streets of the Liberty. The high spirits of the people were frequently exhibited in pitched battles, fought with the national weapon, an oak stick. Bull baiting was also a constant amusement; and every Sunday evening there were large assemblies in the fields, who exercised themselves in hurling, cudgel playing, and wrestling, in which they were allowed to have excelled the London populace, though inferior to them in the pugilistic art. Memorable days and festivals have been always particularly observed by the Irish. The feast day of the Patron Saint is especially honoured by all ranks and classes in Dublin, when the national emblem, the shamrock, is drowned in libations of the native beverage. Riding the franchises was once an occasion of high festivity with all the artizans and mechanics. It took place every fourth year. The individuals of every trade or guild walked in procession in their best dresses, the master and wardens being mounted, and pageants, illustrative of the trade, moved at the head of each. This custom has been discontinued more than 30 years, but still, at the same periods, the Lord Mayor and City Officers perambulate the city, to shew the extent of his jurisdiction. This is a usage interesting to the populace, who avail themselves of it to assert an ancient privilege. At the street of the Cross Poddle, part of which is beyond the boundaries of his jurisdiction, the Lord Mayor is stopped by a Liberty party, and not suffered to pass until he surrenders his sword, which is not returned without a present from his Lordship, and a promise to liberate a prisoner.

After St. Patrick's day, the eve of St. John the Baptist, or Midsummer's day, was observed as a high festival throughout the whole island. In many places, bonfires still continue to be lighted, and kept up with various ceremonies all night. This the Irish antiquarians maintain was a relict of the Pagan fire worship, or Baal-tinné. These bonfires were interdicted by the magistrates in Dublin, on account of the danger which might arise from fire, but in lieu thereof the inhabitants formerly used to light candles, which were fastened to a bush, and planted in the middle of the street. The only public notice at present of this feast is the assembling of great numbers of people at St. John's well, to drink its waters, which are supposed to have peculiar efficacy to cure diseases on this day. This well is situated near Island-bridge, where tents are pitched, and the people observe the festivities which commemorate a day dedicated to a tutelar saint, and called for that reason in Ireland a " patron." On St. James's day, the populace repair in great numbers to St. James's church-yard, which is the general cemetry of the lower classes, when they garnish and decorate the graves, being persuaded that prayers are offered up on that day by his Holiness the Pope, for the souls of all those who were there buried. Some of these decorations are strong indications of the affectionate attachment of the Irish to the memory of the dead. They form effigies or images of all the persons who have been buried in the same grave, or represent them by shirts or shifts made of paper, of a size proportioned to the age of the persons. These are laid on or hung round the place where they are buried; and a mother is frequently seen sitting on a grave surrounded by the rude figures of her deceased children, with whom she is holding a communication, to which strong affection and an ardent imagination give a reality unknown perhaps elsewhere Holy. Eve, or the Eve of All Saints, is also still generally observed in Ireland, and in the capital, with all those superstitious rites so admirably described in Burns's poem of " Hallow E'en." On the other hand, the protestant inhabitants do not fail to commemorate the 1st July, the anniversary of the battle of the Boyne, on which day, the Lord Mayor and Corporation, attended by the military in garrison, used to parade round the statue of King William, which, on this occasion, was fresh painted and decorated with orange ribbons. The practice, however, has been of late years discountenanced, and but partially continued.

It is however at the fair of Donnybrook, that the natural humour and

THE HISTORY OF

peculiar character of the lower classes of the metropolis are best seen. Donnybrook is a pleasant village contiguous to the south suburbs of the city. It has a green or common, on which the fair is held, in the month of August. It is regularly proclaimed, and is attended by police officers, whose interposition is indispensible to preserve the peace. The fair, which is held for the sale of horses and black cattle, lasts a week, during which time every mode of amusement and gymnastic exercise peculiar to the Irish is practised, each day concluding with a pitched battle, in which much blood is spilled, and many heads broken, but rarely any life lost. The Green is covered with tents, and filled with pipers, fiddlers, and dancers; and of late years they have introduced mimes, mountebanks, shows of wild beasts, and all those spectacles, but on a much more limited scale, which are to be found at Bartholomew fair. During the continuance of this fair, Harcourt-street, and the other avenues leading to it, present extraordinary spectacles, particularly in the evenings. Almost all the carriages which plied at other parts of the town now assemble here, and while they go to and from the fair they are crowded at all hours with company. The din and tumult of the roads on these occasions is inconceivable, particularly during the stillness of the night; from the vociferation, laughter, and fighting of these turbulent cargoes, a noise ascends which is heard for several miles in all directions. The attachment of the populace to this amusement is so great, that the Lord Mayor finds it necessary to proceed there in person at the expiration of the limited time, and, striking the tents, compel the people to go home. These annual scenes of turbulence and riot ought not to detract from the general good principles and quiet demeanour of the Dublin populace. They are even now by no means so prevalent as formerly, not so much on account of any improvement of morals in the people, as from that depression of spirits which is the consequence of the decline of the manufactures in the Liberty, and the state of abject misery which the lower classes at present suffer from the pressure of the times, but which we trust will not be of very long continuance. The common people of Dublin have been always celebrated for the richness of their humour and the liveliness of their repartees. The discrimination of the upper gallery, by which theatrical talent is estimated, can no where else be surpassed. The greatest clamour and riot instantly subsides into the deepest silence and attention when superior acting or singing require them, and the judgment of the house on a piece or an actor is often directed, and justly directed, by the mob of the gallery.

The people of Dublin assert that the English language is spoken better in that city than in any other in the British dominions. There is indeed some truth in this assertion, for although that intonation of voice in speaking, called the Brogue, be sufficiently perceptible to strangers, yet there are few colloquial barbarisms and grammatical blunders, and no provincial *patois* to be met with in the ordinary conversation of the inhabitants;* and the many illustrious examples of the natives of Dublin having distinguished themselves on the stage and in the imperial Parliament are further corroborations of it.

* There was in Dublin a phraseology used by the lower classes, and peculiar to them. Specimens of this language has been preserved in Edgeworth's " Essay on Irish Bulls," and happily contrasted with the slang of a similar class in England. It abounded with shrewdness, metaphor, and whimsical allusion. It was particularly used by "shoe-blacks," a class of the community once very numerous, and celebrated by all strangers who visited Dublin for their wit, wickedness, dirt, and dialect. This last has been well imitated in several songs which excited much curiosity at the time, and were attributed to men eminent for genius and talents. The most celebrated of these are " Lord Altam's Bull," " De nite afore Larry was stretched," and " Luke Cassidy's Kilmainham minuet." One of these is inimitably descriptive of the incidents of a bull-baiting, and another of the custom of waking a malefactor the night before his execution, and playing cards on his coffin. The former practice was prohibited by act of parliament, and happily ceased in Dublin 30 or 40 years ago, when several persons were killed by the military who were called out by the sheriffs to prevent it; the latter was put an end to by the excellent system of regulations adopted in our prisons, substituting order, decorum and solemnity, for outrage, indecency, and levity. The race of shoe-blacks and their associates have become entirely extinct, and with them all memory of their customs and language, except only such as are preserved in the above and similar songs. Indeed there seems to have been a total subversion of all those peculiarities which once distinguished them. So late as the year 1775, a traveller of some celebrity asserts, that " the common people of Dublin seldom shave."—" It is deemed almost a reproach for a gentlewoman to be seen walking the streets."—" Hotels are novel in Dublin, and only set up a few years."—" I was advised by my banker to lodge in Capel-street, near Essex Bridge, being in less danger of being robbed, two chairmen, it seems, not being a sufficient protection." &c. (Philosoph. Survey, p. 46 et seq.) At present the common people shave as well as others. Ladies walk the streets universally without a sense of impropriety. Hotels are more numerous than in London, if the respective population be compared; and the streets are so secure that a robbery does not occur in them once in several years, and

THE HISTORY OF

To complete the account of the rise, progress, and present state of the arts and literature in Dublin, it is thought adviseable to subjoin a brief notice of the Artists themselves, as well as of " Eminent Natives."

people return to their lodgings in the remotest parts of the town in perfect safety, without the protection of chairmen who are now almost unknown in the metropolis.

ADDENDA.

A Brief Account of ARTISTS, *Strangers as well as Natives, who made* DUBLIN *their Residence, and adorned it by their Works.*

☞ For other Native Artists see " Biograpical Sketches."

PAINTERS.

——— BINDON, portrait painter in oils. This gentleman was among the earliest of the Irish artists; he lived in habits of intimacy with Dean Swift, Delany, and ,Dr. Sheridan, and painted their portraits.

JAMES LATHAM was a native of Tipperary; he studied at Antwerp, and practised in Ireland in 1725: he died in Trinity-street, Dublin. This gentleman may be probably considered as the father of the polite arts in Ireland, as there is no celebrated production extant by any native of this kindom previous to those executed by this artist. His portraits of Mrs. Woffington the actress, and Geminiani the composer, were painted in so pure a style as to procure him the title of the Irish Vandyke. Some of his pictures would do honour to a modern painter for colour, breadth, facility of execution and good drawing. A curious anecdote is told of this artist; while in the zenith of his prosperity in Dublin, a lady with coarse features sat for her picture, which he faithfully delineated; she was however so displeased at the likeness as to abuse the painter, who forthwith tore the portrait from the frame, and nailed it on the floor of his hall as a piece of oil-cloth. Every one who entered knew the likeness, the anecdote circulated, and the lady offered any money for her portrait; but the artist was inflexible; it remained nailed to the floor till the features were trodden out by the feet of his domestics.

——— LEE, portrait painter in oils. He flourished in 1724, and is ranked as one of the earliest painters that ever practised in Ireland.

RICHARD MANNING was invited to Dublin to fill the department of Ornamental Master to the Dublin Society. He principally excelled in flower painting, and was distinguished as the master of Williams, Roberts, Barret, Baralet, Waldron and Mackenzie. He died in 1779.

——— WEST, the first master of the historical department in the National Academy for Design in Dublin, was the son of Alderman West, of Waterford, where he was born, in 1720, and studied in Paris under Vanloo and Boucher. He principally excelled in his drawings of the human figure in chalk and crayons. He established the first academy for design in Ireland, in Shaw's-court, Dame-street, Dublin, under the patronage of the Dublin Society. This gentleman was superseded for several years, in consequence of a mental infirmity, by Mr. Ennis, one of his pupils, but he was reinstated afterwards, and died possessing the situation. He is considered as the parent of the arts in Dublin. The late Mr. Moser mentions his figures in high terms of approbation.

FRANCIS ROBERT WEST, his eldest son, succeeded his father as master of the Academy. This gentleman executed several historical subjects in chalk and crayons, but had a very imperfect idea of the harmony of colours in oil. He died in Dublin.

―――ENNIS, historical painter, learned the rudiments of his art under the elder West. He was sent to Italy by Mr. Neville Jones about the year 1754. He painted in the Academy, and studied in the Vatican at the same period with Sir Joshua Reynolds; on his return to Dublin he painted history and portrait. One of his best efforts was the decoration of the ceilings of his patron's house near the Rotunda. He was master of the Figure Academy in Dublin, and was killed by a fall from his horse in the county of Wicklow in 1771.

JOHN BUTTS was a native of Cork; he painted figures and landscapes. This artist is considered as one among the best that Ireland has produced. He was accustomed to paint the grotesque assemblage usually seen in alehouses on pannel, which he executed in a manner little inferior to Teniers. He worked for several seasons as scene painter to Crow-street Theatre, Dublin, when under the management of Mr. Barry. The distresses of this ingenious man were so great, that he was occasionally compelled to paint signs and coach pannels for the present wants of a numerous family.

GEORGE MULLINS, a landscape painter, was pupil to Mr. James Manning. He married a respectable young woman who kept an alehouse in Temple-bar, called the Horse-shoe and Magpie, which was the accustomed resort of the theatrical performers. He worked at Mr. Wise's manufactory at Waterford, and painted snuff-boxes and waiters, in imitation of the Birmingham ware. After residing in London several years he returned, and died in Dublin about the year 1798.

JAMES BARRY, R. A. was the son of a bricklayer, and was born in Cork in 1740, and first attracted public notice by painting the sign of Neptune for an ale-house in that city. This was a production so uncommon for a lad so cirumstanced, that Dr. Longfield immediately took notice of him, and rescued him from oblivion. He was first sent to Dublin, where he became a pupil of the Academy, and at the age of 19 obtained a premium for an historic painting, which introduced him to the notice of Edmund Burke. From Dublin he went to London, and immediately after to Italy, being pationized and supported there by Burke. On his return he attained the pinnacle of his art in historic, or rather epic composition ; but no influence, entreaty, or money, could ever induce him to condescend to paint portraits. The works of this extraordinary man, as well as his eccentricities, are already so well known, that they need not here be repeated. Barry died in 1806.

ROBERT HAYLEY was a pupil of the elder West; he drew cattle and the human figure in black and white chalk in a manner entirely his own. He died in Dublin about the year 1770. His principal drawings are now in possession of the Marquis of Hastings, Lady Louisa Connolly, and the Marquis of Wellesley's family, and are admirable for their free spirit, correctness, execution, and exquisite softness; they look like fine proof prints of the most capital mezzotinto engravings.

—— KILVERLY, painter and picture dealer, lived in Ranelagh-road near Dublin. This extraordinary man made a pedestrian journey to Rome about the year 1738, where he purchased a collection of pictures by the Italian masters, for the Earl of Ely and other gentlemen. It is presumed that an exhibition which he made of these pictures at William-street, was a principal excitement to the gentry of Ireland to become more generally the lovers of virtù. He died at his house near Ranelagh, in 1789.

THOMAS ROBERTS was a landscape painter of merit. He was the son of an architect, and born in Waterford; he studied under Mr. George Mullins, but was improved by Butts. He was patronised by the Duke of Leinster and Lord Powerscourt, and is considered one of the best landscape painters Ireland ever produced. He died in Lisbon of a pulmonary complaint.

PHILIP HUSSEY, portrait painter of whole lengths in oil, was a native of Cork, but resided in Dublin. He began his career as a mariner, and was shipwrecked five times. He evinced his disposition for the polite arts by drawing the figures from the sterns of vessels. He was particularly noticed and protected by Lord Chancellor Bowes. He entertained his friends in the evening sometimes in his kitchen, where he informed them by his discourse, and improved them by his manners. He evinced to the end of his life great simplicity of heart and suavity of disposition. He died at an advanced age at his house in Eustace-street, Dublin, in 1782, lamented by all who had the pleasure to know him.

JOHN BLOOMFIELD, a miniature painter; he was born in Ship-street, Dublin, and was a pupil of Mr. West.

WALTER ROBERTSON, miniature painter, was the son of a jeweller in Dublin. He was considered as the first professor of the arts in Ireland for several years. He went from Dublin to America, and from thence to the East Indies, where he died.

—— SADLER, historical painter, son of a professor of music; he studied under the first Mr. West, at the Dublin society's school. He was patronised by the family of La Touche. He painted portraits in oil and miniature, and also engraved some mezzotinto plates, the principal of which latter is a likeness of Kemble in the Count de Narbonne. He died in Dublin about 1788.

ROBERT HUNTER, portrait painter in oils, studied principally under Mr. Pope, senior. He was esteemed the first limner in his nation until the arrival of Mr. Hone from England.

MICHAEL KANE, a native of Dublin, studied at the Academy under Mr. West, and practised miniature painting in Dublin and London. He was originally a pupil to Mr. Smith, the Irish statuary. He settled in Derby, and became a china manufacturer.

M. T. QUADAL was a native of Moravia. In the year 1779 he came to Dublin and practised as a painter of animals. The Dublin Society have purchased many of his designs for the use of their students; he also painted portraits. It was remarked of him, that he had been employed by more sovereigns and travelled through more countries than any man living. It was said that Mr. Quadal went to Russia some years ago, and was appointed master of the Academy at St. Petersburgh, in which situation he died.

JONATHAN TROTTER studied in Rome, and practised portrait painting in oil in Dublin. He married the daughter of Mr. Hunter, portrait painter, a lady who possessed great merit in the same pursuit: he died some years ago.

—— REILY was a miniature painter in water-colours of considerable talents; he lived in Grafton-street, Dublin, and died in 1780.

ROWLAND OMER made several views of buildings in Dublin and Ireland, which have been engraved by Mazell and others.

THOMAS CHAMBERS studied the art of drawing and engraving first in Dublin, and afterwards at Paris. His principal work is the death of Marshal Turenne. His own death occurred in London in the year 1792. He had been importuned by his landlord for rent, and went out, leaving the following note on the table: " If I do not return by to-morrow night, I desire you will sell my effects and pay yourself." He did not return, and his body was found floating at Battersea.

THOMAS WOGAN, miniature painter, studied at the Dublin Academy under Mr. F. R. West. He practised both in Dublin and London, and acquired much reputation. He died in Dublin, in 1780.

SOLOMON WILLIAMS, historical and portrait painter, was born in Dublin. He studied at the Dublin Academy, and in Rome and Bologna; he was afterwards in London engaged in the composition of a large historical picture, the subject of which is the trial of Algernon Sidney.

FRANCIS WHEATLEY, R. A., came to Dublin from England some time previous to the memorable year 1782. He was chiefly employed in painting likenesses in small whole lengths, and was greatly encouraged; but the work which rendered him famous in the metropolis, was an interior view of the House of Commons of Ireland, with portraits of all the celebrated members. The point of time he selected was that important moment when Mr. Grattan was making his motion for the repeal of Poinings' laws. This picture was afterwards disposed of by raffle in Dublin.

THOMAS MALTON formerly kept an upholder's shop in the Strand, London, and published an elaborate treatise on perspective; from hence he went to Dublin, where he lived as professor of perspective for many years.

THOMAS MALTON, junior, also resided in Dublin, where he made several architectural drawings, which he executed with more accuracy than any of his competitors. He also painted scenes for the theatre.

VANDER HASEN, a native of Holland, practised in Dublin as a painter of landscape and shipping: he was an eccentric man, and worked only when pinched by necessity, on which occasion he would retire to a public house, and paint a picture to pay the reckoning. He died in Dublin in 1760.

―― ROSABELLA, an Italian lady of high eminence in the arts, practised crayon painting in Dublin; many of her works are in the possession of Mr. Stewart and Mr. Hamilton.

CAPTAIN FRANCIS GROSE. This gentleman came to Ireland to investigate the antiquities of the country, and sketch its ruins; while preparing his work in Dublin, he was invited to pass the evening with Mr. H. Hone, in Dorset-street. Here, in the act of relating a humourous story, he was struck with a fit of apoplexy, and suddenly expired. He had written but seven pages of his work, which was afterwards published by the learned Dr. Ledwich. He was interred in Drumcondra, where a stone near the entrance of the church has the following inscription:

To the Memory
of
CAPTAIN FRANCIS GROSE
F. R. S.
who, whilst in cheerful conversation
with his friends
expired in their arms
without a sigh
18th of May 1791
Aged 60.

BARTHOLOMEW STOKER studied in the Dublin Academy under Mr. F. R. West. He was the son of an upholder, and worked at that business for some time. He afterwards practised crayon painting in Dublin, with great success, but died in 1788, of a decline brought on by intense study.

GEORGE PLACE, miniature painter, studied under Mr. F. R. West. He was the son of an eminent linen draper on Essex-bridge, Dublin. He practised in London for several years, where he acquired a considerable portion of reputation; from thence he went to the East Indies, and met with great success. He died there about the year 1809.

JEFFREY WILSON, historical and landscape painter, was a native of the north of Ireland. He was remarkable for painting large pictures, which he copied from prints.

―― ROACH, a native miniature painter, practised in Dublin. This artist was self taught, and deaf and dumb.

JOHN ELLIS, a native of Dublin, was originally apprenticed to a cabinet maker; he practiced scene painting in Dublin and London, and received the premium of the silver palette from the Dublin Society for a drawing in body colours, which involved the most intricate and difficult specimen of a thorough knowledge of perspective.

―― HICKEY, portrait painter, was brother to the sculptor of that name: he was born in Batchelor's-walk, Dublin. He studied at the National Academy, and afterwards at Rome. This artist was apppointed to accompany Lord Macartney in his extraordinary mission to China, to make drawings of that country and the dresses of the people.

GEORGE MADDEN, miniature painter, studied at the Dublin Academy. He went to Italy with the Bishop of Derry, and at his return he painted miniature in Dublin.

J. J. BARRALET, painter of history, flowers and landscape, studied in the Dublin Academy. This gentleman drew landscapes with Italian chalk, in which he affected to imitate Vernet. During the illness of Mr. Manning he superintended the ornament department in the Dublin School, and at his demise became candidate for the situation, in opposition to Mr. Waldron, but lost it, as his rival had the protection of the Duke of Leinster. When he lost his election, he had the honour of having a sum of money voted to him by the Dublin Society as a compliment to his ability and a reward for his attention. Since that period he was engaged in staining glass in concert with Messrs. Hand.

THOMAS WALMSLEY, landscape painter, was born in Dublin. He studied under Mr. Columba, principal to the Opera house in London. He executed many of the scenes for Crow-street Theatre, during the management of Mr. Daly. This gentleman has published various picturesque views in Wales, and of the lake of Killarney. He was remarkable for his rich illuminations of the skies He lately resided at Bath, where he died in 1806.

HENRY HODGINS, landscape painter, was a native of Dublin, and the pupil of Robert Carver. He was a respectable artist, had been for several years one of the principal scene painters to Covent-garden Theatre, and died about the year 1807.

WILLIAM HINKS, historical and portrait painter, was born in Waterford, and was the son of a blacksmith. This ingenious and indefatigable artist was self-taught. While practising in the north of Ireland, he drew and engraved a series of designs, exhibiting the progress of the linen manufactory; he also executed several interesting works from Tristram Shandy, and the historical representation of the last interview of Louis Seize with his family. He painted principally in crayons. He died some years ago.

JONATHAN BUCK, LL. D. was born in Dublin and educated at Trinity College. This gentleman painted small landscapes in oil with a delicate pencil.

—– DE GREE. This amiable man was born at Antwerp, and was the son of a taylor. While exercising his art in his native city, he was engaged to paint some pictures for Mr. La Touche, who invited him to Dublin for the purpose of painting more. He arrived in Dublin in the year 1781, where he continued to exercise his pencil till his death; he excelled in painting groups of boys in imitation of alto-relievo on marble, and some of them are such masterly deceptions as to resemble exactly real perspectives. He made some attempt at portraits, but did not succeed. He died in Dublin in 1788; his death was accelerated by privation: he continued to work at the low prices he demanded in Flanders, and the greatest part of his earnings he remitted to his aged parents.

JONATHAN FISHER, landscape painter, was born in Dublin; he was originally a woollen draper in the Liberty. This gentleman was self educated. He has been particularly indebted to the patronage of Lord Portarlington. About the year 1782 he published a set of views of the Lake of Killarney, which were engraved in London from his paintings. He held a lucrative situation in the Stamp-office till his death, which happened in the year 1812.

ANGELICA KAUFFMAN visited Dublin in the year 1775, and was hospitably received by

THE CITY OF DUBLIN.

Mr. Tisdal, then Attorney general, at whose house she exercised her talents and etched her first plate. She executed, while she remained in Dublin, among many other pictures, whole length portraits of the Earl of Ely's family; but her most admired portrait was that of the celebrated *Dolly Munro*, who at that time was the reigning beauty of the metropolis, and had captivated, it is said, the heart of the Viceroy. She is thus described by a cotemporary writer: " Her stature was majestic, but her air and demeanour was nature itself. " The peculiar splendour of her carriage was softened and subdued by the most affable con- " descension ; and as sensibility gave a lustre to her eye, so discretion gave a security to her " heart; and while her charms inspired universal rapture, the authority of her innocence " regulated and restrained it. The softest roses that ever youth and modesty poured out on " beauty, glowed on the lips of Dorothea; her cheeks were the bloom of Hebe, and the " purity of Diana was in her breast. Never did beauty appear so amiable, or virtue so " adorned, as in this incomparable virgin." To execute faithfully the portrait of such a lady was an arduous task, and a lady as singular and as accomplished as herself was selected for the purpose. This picture is now at Rathfarnham Castle near Dublin, and is more distinguished by the subject, and the artist, than by any intrinsic excellence.

JAMES PEARSON, a painter on glass, was born in Dublin, but learned the principles of his art at a glass-house in Bristol. He executed the painted window of the altar in Aldersgate church, London, and many others, after the designs of Barry.

ENGRAVERS AND SCULPTORS.

JAMES MACARDEL, engraver in mezzotinto, learned the rudiments of his art from John Brooks. This ingenious artist went from Dublin, where he was born, to London, at an early period of his life, where he acquired the highest honour in his profession. He used the scraping-tool with more boldness, decision, and freedom, perhaps, than any other person that ever existed. His portrait of Captain Thomas Coram is an astonishing instance of his proficiency in the art, and will be admired as long as taste has any influence in the human mind. He died in London, June 2d, 1765.

CHARLES SPOONER was an engraver in mezzotinto. He was born in the County of Wexford but practised principally in London, where he died, 1767. Two portraits engraved by him in Dublin in 1752 were much prized; one is Dr. Samuel Madden, the other Thomas Prior: the latter is well executed, and dedicated to the Dublin Society.

RICHARD HOUSTON served his time to John Brooks, engraver on Cork Hill, Dublin, and practised in mezzotinto; he left Ireland young and settled in London, where he lived a dissipated life, and died in 1775, at the age of 54. His chief performances were portraits and running horses.

LUKE SULLIVAN, engraver and painter in miniature, was born in the county of Louth; he flourished in 1750, and possessed the friendship of Sir Joshua Reynolds, and Mr. Hogarth. He is said to be the son of one of the grooms of the Duke of Beaufort. His first employment was in the stables; but shewing strong marks of a genius for drawing, he was placed an apprentice with Major. He engraved the " March to Finchley-Common" from Hogarth, for which he received only one hundred pounds. Hogarth drew his portrait in the character of the Angel in *Paul before Felix*, in the Dutch taste. Sullivan afterwards applied himself to miniature painting, but soon fell a victim to intemperance.

WILLIAM SHERLOCK, engraver, was born at Dublin. He studied at Paris under Le Bas ; he was the son of Sherlock the celebrated prize-fighter, who opposed Faddi, the stout Hungarian, at Broughton's Amphitheatre in Tottenham Court Road, before the Duke of Cumberland and many of the nobility. His principal work was some of the heads illustrative of Smollet's history of England. He flourished in 1762.

J. DIXON, mezzotinto engraver, was originally a silver engraver in Dublin. He studied at the Dublin Academy; but disdaining this inferior department of his art, he suddenly surprised the world with his admirable engraving of Garrick in Richard III.; but soon after marrying a lady of rank, the arts lost the benefit of his talents.

GILES KING, an engraver, resided many years in Dublin, where he engraved views of the Waterfall at Powerscourt, and Salmon Leap at Leixlip.

THOMAS MILTON practised in Dublin as an engraver of small views, principally of noblemen and gentlemen's seats in Ireland. They were executed with exquisite neatness and delicacy, published in numbers, and highly esteemed.

CHARLES HENECY was born in Dublin about the year 1785. He engraved some of the plates for the Anthologia Hibernica, and Paine's Geography, published by Jackson. He died about the year 1808.

SAMUEL CLOSE was a native of Dublin, born deaf and dumb. He was much addicted to intemperance, and was employed at low prices by others, who affixed their names to his engravings. He died in 1817.

VANNOST was brought to Dublin about the year 1750, where he was distinguished as an artist. He executed the Equestrian Statue of George II. in Stephen's Green, and many statues and ornaments which adorn the Castle of Dublin. He also made some statuary half lengths of private individuals, particularly of Thomas Prior and Samuel Madden, from which Spooner executed mezzotinto engravings. He died in Mecklenburg-street, Dublin, in the year 1787.

SIMON VERPOYLE, a statuary, and a native of Italy. He was a pupil of Sheemaker, and was invited to Dublin by Lord Charlemont, to make models to ornament his demesne at Marino. He was concerned in most of the public works then carried on in Dublin, particularly the front of St. Thomas's church, which he executed from a design of Palladio at Venice. He lived for many years on the Batchelor's-walk in Dublin, where he died. He is now principally distinguished as the master of Edward Smyth.

EDWARD SMYTH was born in the county of Meath in the year 1746. His father was a captain in the army, and designed him for his own profession, but his son's taste for modelling was so decided at an early age, that he thought it better to cultivate it, and indented him to Verpoyle. In his service he contributed to ornament several public works, but it was not till he commenced on his own account that he attracted any notice. His first public work of this kind was the statue of Dr. Lucas, in statuary marble, in the Royal Exchange, which was a spirited and admirable likeness, and at once established his reputation. His other works are the colossal heads on the key stones of the arcades of the Custom-house, the figures on the Bank of Ireland, the Four Courts, and the King's Inns: his last work is the beautifully sculptured heads in black stone on the Castle chapel; these he did not live to complete, but they are ably finished by his son after his models. He died in 1812, leaving behind him exquisite specimens of sculpture, not to be exceeded perhaps in any city in Europe. He was a man of singular modesty and retired habits; his genius qualified, and his respectable family entitled him to mix with the best society; but he was embarrassed in such company; and he unfortunately sought for other less reputable, but where he felt himself more at ease.

—— FAGAN, a statuary, educated by Verpoyle, and employed in Dublin about the year 1794.

CHARLES MOUNTSTEPHEN was born in the county of Meath, and resided some time in Dublin, from whence he went to London in 1787. Here he commenced modeller in wax, and executed a fine head for the Duke of Orleans. He died on the Continent. He was supposed to have brought this inferior department of the statuary art to a higher degree of perfection than ever it attained before.

—— PERCY was a native of Dublin, and practised as a modeller of likenesses both in Dublin and London.

ARCHITECTS.

THOMAS IVORY, architect, was self educated; the only monument of his ability is the Blue Coat Hospital on Oxmantown Green, Dublin. It is a fine proof, though still unfinished. He died in Dublin in 1786. He was also master of the Architectural School of the Dublin Society.

THOMAS COOLEY. See page 1047.

RICHARD CASSELS was born in Germany, and invited to this country by Sir Gustavus Hume, of Castle Hume, in the county of Fermanagh, in 1773. There was scarcely one private residence in Ireland at that time which displayed any taste; but he introduced the models of Palladio, and a rapid improvement immediately succeeded. He commenced with Castle Hume; he next erected the mansion of Hazlewood, county of Sligo, Powerscourt-house, county of Wicklow, Carton-house, county of Kildare, and Bessborough, county of Kilkenny. In the city of Dublin he erected the Marquis of Waterford's house in Marlborough-street, Leinster-house in Kildare-street, now the Dublin Society house, Lord Bective's house in Smithfield, and sundry private houses in Sackville-street, Stephen's Green, and other parts of the city. His public works were not so numerous: he built the cupola of the old chapel in the College, now removed; the beautiful Printing-office in the College park, which happily yet stands as a memorial of his skill; and the Lying-in-hospital. Moreover he was the first architect that ever built a stone lock in Ireland, which he constructed on the Newry canal. He was a man of integrity, but much addicted to intemperance. He had besides many peculiarities; he was prepossessed with an opinion that some barber would cut his throat, and he never would suffer one to shave him; but as he could not perform the operation himself, he prevailed on a Mr. Simpson, a stucco worker, to act as his barber for several years. When he disliked any part of his work, he collected his men together, marched them to it in procession, and immediately pulled it down. He died in the act of writing a letter to a carpenter engaged at Leinster-house. He was sixty years of age, and was buried at Maynooth.

SCULPTORS OF GEMS AND MEDALS.

—— Stanly was the first seal engraver of whom there is any record in Dublin: it does not appear when he died.

Edward Lyons was born 1726, died 1801. He was on the committee who established the first exibition of the arts in Ireland.

—— Madden was an artist of great genius, but so addicted to the use of spirits, that he died at last in extreme poverty, about the year 1789.

John Logan was born 11th of August, 1750, in Duncannon fort, county Wexford: he studied his art with such assiduity that he materially injured his health, and died in the year 1805, in a state of mental derangement.

William Mossop, medallist, was born in St. Mary's parish, in the city of Dublin, in 1754, and was nearly related to the actor. He commenced his professional pursuits under the direction of Mr. Johnstone, in the linen seal cutting, and by progressive steps in 1784 he appeared a medallist. His first work was a medal of Thomas Ryder, comedian, which was so much admired as a production of art, that it drew the attention of every person of taste in Dublin, and established his character as an artist. His subsequent works were numerous; his last was the medal of the Dublin Society, which for delicacy of finishing, boldness and spirit of execution, has not been surpassed by the work of any modern artist. He died in 1806 of a fit of apoplexy. As a son, husband, and father, he was exemplary, and as an artist he was unrivalled, and had the honour to be, if not the creator, at least the reviver of the art in his native country.

Hugh Caddell studied at the Dublin Academy, and was a pupil of Logans. He fell into a decline, and died young.

Benjamin Clare was born in Dublin, in 1771. He was a man of extraordinary talent; but neglected to improve it by due application. However he was held in great estimation, and most justly deserved the name of a fine artist. He was a man of a benevolent disposition. He died greatly lamented in 1810.

Although the grand mart for the arts and polite literature be London, yet the sister metropolis can still boast of a number of *living* resident artists who do not suffer a taste for them to expire, and who maintain an honourable emulation with their brethren in London, if not in numbers, in talent and genius.

THE CITY OF DUBLIN.

BIOGRAPHICAL SKETCHES.
OF
EMINENT PERSONS BORN IN DUBLIN,

Chronologically arranged, according to the dates of their Birth.

ST. LAURENCE O'TOOL was born in Dublin about the year 1100. He was first consecrated Bishop of Glendeloch, and was thence translated to the Archiepiscopal see of Dublin. O'Tool signed the capitulation of the city with Earl Strongbow; but while the treaty was completing the Anglo-Normans forced an entrance, led on by Miles and Raymond de Cogan, and sacked and plundered the place. (Vide Annals.) However, such was the esteem and veneration that the archbishop was held in, both by the Ostmen and Anglo-Normans, that his property alone was spared. The next year he went to attend the Lateran Council at Rome, at the head of a deputation of Irish Bishops. On his return he was detained in Normandy, where he died November 1180. His bones were afterwards sent to Ireland, and interred in the cathedral of Christ's Church. He was canonized by Pope Honorius the Third in 1225. Vide Ware's Antiquities.

CHRISTOPHER PEMBRIDGE was born in Dublin, A.D. 1347. He wrote the Annals of Ireland, published by Camden.

JAMES YOUNG, or Junius, was born in Dublin in 1407. He was the author of " Monita Polita."

JAMES STANIHURST, a lawyer and recorder of Dublin, was born there in 1496. He wrote " Pias Orationes plures." " Epist. ad Corcagiens. Decanum ;" he died in 1573 His daughter Magaret was the mother of Archbishop Usher.

JAMES KING, born in Dublin 1498, was the author of Latin poems, " Carmina in laudem Hen. Sidnei, et Epigrammatica. He died in 1569.

JOHN USHER, born in Dublin about 1529, was Mayor of the city in 1574. He wrote " De Reformatione Hiberniæ."

WILLIAM BATHE was born in Dublin about 1532. He travelled on the Continent, and became a learned Jesuit. He was professor of languages at the University of Salamanca, and published there "Janua Linguarum." He also published in London, where he died in 1614, " an Introduction to the Art of Music," and some pious tracts.

RICHARD STANIHURST, son of James, and uncle to Archbishop Usher, was born in Dublin A.D. 1535. He went abroad, took priest's orders, and became chaplain to Duke Albert, Governor of the Netherlands. He died at Brussels in 1618. He published, 1. ". De Rebus in Hibernia gestis." 2. " Vita S. Patricii." 3. " Harmonia seu Catena dialectica in Porphyrium." 4. " Translation of the first four books of Virgil's Æneas." This is a scarce and very curious version, being written in uncouth English hexameter lines.

THE HISTORY OF

WALTER QUIN was born in Dublin about 1540. He published a volume of poems, Latin and English, in Edinburgh, 1600. Neither the place nor time of his death is known.

CHRISTOPHER HOLLYWOOD, vel, A Sacro Bosco, born in Dublin A.D. 1552, was a learned Jesuit, and was appointed professor of divinity at the University of Padua. He published abroad several Polemic works, and presided over the Jesuits of Dublin 23 years, until his death in 1626.

JAMES USHER, descended from an ancient family, was the son of Arnold Usher, one of the six clerks in Chancery, and was born in Dublin 1580. Trinity College had been recently founded by order of Queen Elizabeth, by his paternal uncle Henry Usher, Archbishop of Armagh, and James became the first scholar on the foundation. After filling with infinite applause various arduous situations in church and state, he was elevated to the Primacy in 1626. His profound erudition, his learned writings, and the energy of his character, have rendered his name justly celebrated throughout Europe. Archbishop Usher died in London 20th March, 1656, and was buried in Westminster Abbey. Vide his life by Dr. Parr.

ROBERT STRAFFORD was born in Dublin in 1584, and educated at Oxford. He published in 1634. " a Geographical Description of all the Empires of the World." The time of his death is not known.

WILLIAM MALONE was born in Dublin in 1586, and became a Jesuit at Rome in 1606, being only 20 years of age. He returned to Ireland by order of the Pope, and from thence after a sojourn of 14 years, he was sent for by His Holiness and made Regent of St. Isidore's College at Rome. Six years after, he went again to Ireland, and was three years Superior of the mission there, when he was thrown into prison, from which he contrived to escape, and retired to Spain, where he died in 1659. He wrote a reply to Dr. Usher's answer concerning the "Judgment of Antiquity of the Romish Religion."

HENRY FITZSIMONS, a merchant's son, was born in Dublin about 1590. He was educated at Oxford a protestant, but on going to the Continent he embraced the Roman Catholic faith, and became a zealous Jesuit. He returned to Ireland, and publicly disputed with the protestant clergy, Usher being at their head. He was imprisoned in the Castle, and on his enlargement went to Rome, from whence he was again sent to Ireland, where he was accused of fomenting the rebellion of 1641. He however absconded in 1643, nor is it known when or where he died. He published several polemic works in Latin as well as English.

JOHN PERROT, a Quaker, was born in Dublin about 1593. He made a pilgrimage to Rome to convert the Pope, and was thrown into the Inquisition; but being deemed insane, he was enlarged and sent back to Ireland, where he published a book, entitled " The Battering Ram against Rome." The time of his death is not noted.

SIR JAMES WARE, eldest son of Sir James Ware, was born in Castle-street, Dublin, 26th November, 1594. He was educated at Trinity College, and in 1632 succeeded his father in his office of Auditor General. During the rebellion he retired to England; but was sent to the Tower by order of the Parliament. At the restoration, however, he was reinstated in his place, and died in Dublin in 1666. Sir James married the daughter of Jacob Newman of Dublin, Esq. by whom he had ten children, of which two sons and two daughters survived him. These were connected by intermarriage with some of the first families in the kingdom. Sir James Ware wrote several works, chiefly in Latin; but his Antiquities of Ireland have justly gained him the appellation of the Irish Camden.

JAMES BARRY, Lord of Santry, was born in Dublin in 1598, which city his father represented in Parliament. Having made the law his profession, he rose through all its gradations until he became Lord Chief Justice of the King's Bench. He was a firm friend of the great but ill fated Earl of Strafford, and died in 1673. He published The Case of Tenures, &c. in folio, 1637, republished in 12mo. 1725.

ARTHUR ANNESLEY, Earl of Anglesea, was born in Dublin in 1614; he was educated at Oxford, and became a zealous royalist. He was sent a commissioner into Ulster, and contributed greatly to effect the restoration in Ireland. In 1667 he was made Treasurer of the Navy, and created Earl of Anglesea, and soon after Lord Privy Seal. In 1680 he was accused at the bar of the House of Commons, as being accessary to the Popish plot, but by his spirited remonstrance to Charles II. he shewed himself favourable to the cause of the exclusioners, for which he was dismissed from all his employments, and retired to his seat in Ireland, where he died in 1686. Several of his children survived him. Lord Anglesea wrote the History of the Civil Wars, which is lost; but his " Memoirs of his own time" is very curious and interesting.

SIR JOHN DENHAM was born in Dublin, in 1615. He was the son of Sir John Denham, Chief Baron of the Exchequer, by Lady Eliza, daughter of Lord Millefont. In his early youth he was profligate, and gave no indications of future celebrity. He followed the fortunes and was the companion of Charles II. on the continent. He died at Whitehall, 1688, and was buried in Westminster Abbey. By his celebrated poem of Cooper's Hill, he is reckoned among the improvers of English poetry. Vide his life by Dr. Johnson.

DUDLEY LOFTUS was born in 1630 at Rathfarnham in the Liberties of Dublin. He was a great Oriental scholar. He translated the New Testament from the Ethiopic, and the Psalms of David from the Armenian into Latin. They were published in Dublin in 1661. He also wrote against the increase of Popery in Ireland, and died in 1695.

THOMAS BLOOD was a disbanded officer of Cromwell's army, and born in Dublin about 1630. In 1663, he was engaged in a conspiracy with several desperate adventurers to seize the Castle of Dublin. Being defeated in the attempt by the vigilance of the Duke of Ormond, then Lord Lieutenant, who had his accomplices tried and executed, he meditated a signal vengeance against that nobleman, whom he followed to London, where he was waylaid and seized in his coach, and would have been murdered on the spot, if Blood, by a refinement of revenge, had not deferred the murder until he should have hanged his victim at Tyburn. The delay gave the Duke an opportunity to escape. Blood and his associates were imprisoned, but afterwards pardoned by Charles II. at the intercession of the Duke of Ormond. After which, the daring act of this petty Catiline in carrying off the crown and regalia from the Tower, is well known. For this exploit he became a favourite at court, and received an estate in Ireland of the value of £500. a year. At length having libelled the Duke of Buckingham, he was committed to gaol, where he died June 24th, 1680.

Vide Annals, p. 211.

HENRY DODWELL was born in Dublin, October 15th, 1641. He received his education both at Oxford and Trinity College, Dublin, of which last he was a Fellow. He resigned the Fellowship in order to return to Oxford, where, in 1668 he was elected Camden Professor. He inherited from his father a good estate in Ireland, but being a nonjuror, he refused to take the oaths to King William, and thereupon resigned his professorship He died at Shottesbrook in Berkshire, in 1711. Dodwell was one of the most learned men in Europe. He published about seventy different works in both Latin and English.

RICHARD FLECKNOE was born in Dublin in 1643 He was a dramatic writer, and dedicated his play of " Love's Dominion" to lady Eliza Claypole, daughter of Oliver Cromwell. He was the Mac Flecknoe of Dryden's Satire. The time of Flecknoe's death is not noted.

NAHUM TATE was born in Dublin in 1646, and was educated at Trinity College In 1692 he was appointed Poet Laureat and died in the Fleet prison, where he was confined for debt, in 1715. Tate had merit as a poet and dramatic writer. He altered and adapted for the stage with much success some of Shakespeare's plays ; but the work by which he is best known, is the poetic version now in use of the Psalms of David, which he composed in conjunction with his countryman Doctor Brady, who was a prebend in the cathedral of Cork.

ROBERT LORD MOLESWORTH was the son of a Dublin merchant, and was born in that city, in 1656. He performed essential services in Ireland for King William, by whom he was made a member of the Privy Council, and sent Embassador to Denmark. He was ennobled by George I. in 1716, and died in 1725. Lord Molesworth published a History of Denmark, which was esteemed in his time.

WILLIAM MOLYNEAUX was born in Dublin in 1656, and received his education at Trinity College, where he founded, and was the first secretary of the Physico-historical Society. He was appointed Chief Engineer and Surveyor of the Works, and in 1685 was elected a member of the Royal Society. After settling with his family in Chester, he ultimately returned to Dublin, for which city he was chosen representative in Parliament, and the next year was elected to represent the University. He died in 1698, aged 42 years ; and was buried in St. Audeon's church, where there is a monument erected to his memory. Molyneaux contributed some papers to the Philosophical Transactions ; he was the inventor of the telescopic dial, and his other mathematical and political writings are held in estimation. In his celebrated tract, " The Case of Ireland considered," he ably vindicates the independance of his country. He was, moreover, the intimate friend and correspondent of John Locke. His son Samuel became Secretary to George II. when Prince of Wales, and distinguished himself by his improvements of the telescope.

THOMAS DOGGET was born in Dublin in 1658. He was early attached to the stage, and was distinguished as a comic actor at Drury-lane, of which house he at last became

THE CITY OF DUBLIN.

joint manager. He died in 1721. Dogget was the author of a farce which was once popular called " Flora, or Hob in the Well." But that for which he is chiefly remembered, is his Legacy of a coat and badge to be rowed for annually, on the 1st of August, by six waterman, from London Bridge to Chelsea.

SIR THOMAS MOLYNEAUX, Bart. M.D. younger brother to William, was born in Dublin in 1660, and educated at Trinity College. He was made state physician and created a Baronet. He died in 1733. Sir Thomas published various tracts on medical subjects, botany, and the natural history of Ireland.

THOMAS SOUTHERNE was born in Dublin in 1660, and educated at Trinity College. He went to London to study the Law, but quitted that pursuit for a Captain's commission in the Duke of Brunswick's regiment. After the Revolution of 1688, he became a poet and dramatic writer. Of his ten dramatic pieces " Isabella," and " Oronooka," still keep possession of the stage, but these two plays rank after those of Shakespeare and Otway in tragic effect. Southerne was the first that raised the value of acting plays, getting for the author three free benefits for a successful piece, instead of one. He may be reckoned among the very few *prudent* poets, as he died in affluent circumstances in 1746, aged 83.

JONATHAN SWIFT, Dean of St. Patrick, was born in Hoey's-court, Werburgh-street, November 30th, 1667, was educated at Trinity College, and died at the Deanery, October 19th, 1745. He was buried in St. Patrick's Cathedral, where a monument is erected to his memory. Swift's works have been repeatedly edited and his life written by the most celebrated biographers. The best is by T. Sheridan and Walter Scott.

CHARLES JERVAS was born in Dublin about the year 1670. He received a good education, and having evinced a decided taste for painting, he studied under Sir Godfrey Kneller, and became an eminent portrait painter in London, where he was much employed by the higher orders. He had the honour of teaching drawing to Pope, with whom he was intimate, who paid him in kind by an elegant poetical epistle, well calculated to flatter his vanity, of which he had no small share. He was amiable and pleasing in private life, and was more esteemed as a man than a painter. He published the best translation of Don Quixote, by which he is now better known than by any production of his palette. Jervas died in London in 1733.

SIR RICHARD STEEL was born in Dublin in 1671. His father, who was secretary to the Duke of Ormond, sent him to be educated at the Charter House school, London. He was afterwards a commissioner of stamps, and some time Member of Parliament, and died from the effects of a paralytic stroke, near Caermarthen, South Wales, September 1729. Steel was the editor and principal writer of the Tatler, being the first of that series of Essays of which he may be deemed the inventor, and to which he largely contributed, that became so famous under the titles of " Tatlers," " Spectators," and " Guardians." Steel's Dramatic Writings were once in much repute, though now seldom or ever acted ; " The Conscious Lovers," however, is the prototype of the English sentimental comedy, or of that species which the French more properly call " *La Comedie Larmoyante.*" For this play George I.

presented him with five hundred pounds. He was also the author of a moral work, once much esteemed, called " The Christian Hero," and of many political pamphlets, in support of his party, the Whigs.

MARMADUKE COGHIL was born in Dublin, Dec. 28, 1673, and was admitted a Fellow Commoner of Trinity College, in 1687. Here he took his degree as doctor of civil law, and was chosen one of its representatives in parliament, which mark of respect and esteem his constituents conferred on him till his death. After filling several important offices, he was appointed Chancellor of the Irish Exchequer in 1735, which situation he held during the rest of his life. He died of the gout in his stomach, in 1738, and was buried in St. Andrew's church-yard. In public life he was a man of unwearied diligence and clear judgment, an equally upright counsellor of the crown and independant representative of the people. As one of the first commissioners of the Board of First Fruits, he may be said to have organized that body, and to have been the prime cause of all the benefits which arise to the established church in Ireland, from his exertions. In private life he was universally beloved for his benevolence, affability, and mildness of temper. His sister, Mary Coghil, erected the church of Drumcondra near Dublin as a monument of respect and affection to his memory, and ornamented it with a tomb sculptured by Scheemaker.

THOMAS PARNELL was born in Dublin, A. D. 1679, and educated at Trinity College. On taking orders, he obtained the living of Finglass near Dublin, and was afterwards Archdeacon of Clogher. He was one of the constellation of wits which made the reign of Queen Anne so illustrious. Besides his poems, he wrote " the Life of Homer," prefixed to Pope's translation of the Iliad, and assisted him in that great work. He wrote also " The Life of Zoilus," " the Origin of the Sciences," and some elegant essays in the Spectator and Guardian. He died at Chester in 1717, aged only 38. Parnell is deemed to have given to English versification its highest degree of polish, in which his poetry supasses that of Pope himself. Vide his Life by Dr. Johnson.

CHARLES MACKLIN, or Macloughlin, was born, according to the most authentic accounts, in Dublin, in the year 1690. His native place has however been a subject of dispute, though it is certain his parents resided there during his infancy. His father, William Macloughlin, was a gentlemen of the County of Down, and commanded a troop of horse on the part of King James, at the battle of the Boyne. His mother was Alice O'Flanigan, daughter of I. O'Flanigan, of Black castle, county of Westmeath, Esq. Charles was born two months previous to that decisive battle, and in consequence of the loyalty of his parents for the cause of King James, their estates were confiscated, and the family at once brought from affluence to indigence. In 1704 his father, being reduced to poverty, died broken hearted in Dublin, and his mother married a second husband. Young Macklin, having become acquainted with some under graduates of Trinity College, was fain to accept the place of Badgeman in the University, where however he had an opportunity of pursuing his studies with success, until he attained his 21st year. In 1716, Macklin went over to England and commenced strolling player. In 1729 he made his first appearance on the London stage, at the theatre royal Lincoln's-inn-fields, and after some time got an engage-

THE CITY OF DUBLIN 1195

ment at Drury-lane. In this theatre he had the misfortune to kill Mr. Hallam, by giving him a thrust in the eye with the end of his cane, which wounded the brain. For this he was tried, and acquitted of the murder, but found guilty of manslaughter. After this unfortunate affair, Macklin engaged himself at various times with all the principal managers of the three kingdoms. He had frequent and violent altercations, and was often involved in lawsuits, from which he extricated himself with honour and success. At length he took leave of the stage in his favourite part of Shylock, which he performed for his own benefit, January 10th, 1790, being then on the verge of one hundred years. His memory however failing him during the performance, he gave up the attempt in a short and pathetic appeal to the audience, and retired amidst commiserating plaudits. This centenary of the stage died July 11th, 1797, in the one hundred and seventh year of his age, and was buried in the Chancel of Covent-garden church. Macklin was twice married, and had a son and daughter, who died before their father. Notwithstanding his public life was so stormy and turbulent, he was in private, a tender husband, an affectionate father, a steady and generous friend, and a frank and decided character. As an actor, in three or four prominent parts he had no competitor, and his last two dramatic pieces still continue great favourites, being composed with much judgment, vigour, and discrimination.

Macklin's dramatic works are Henry;VII. a Tragedy, 1746; The Married Libertine, a comedy, acted at Covent Garden, January 1761; The True born Irishman, a comedy, acted with great applause at Smock-alley theatre, Dublin, October 1763; Love à la Mode, a comedy, 1770; The Man of the World, a comedy, 1781. Macklin also altered and adapted for the stage some of the older dramas. He wrote besides several pieces, some of which were acted but never published. See Kirkman's Life of Macklin, 2 vol. 8vo. 1799.

ROBERT CLAYTON, son of the Dean of Kildare, was born in Dublin in 1695. He was Fellow of Trinity College, and became the intimate friend of Dr. Samuel Clark, and though an Arian, he was successively preferred, and translated to the sees of Killala, Cork, and Clogher. In 1756 he made a motion in the Irish House of Lords, for expunging the Athanasian and Nicene creeds from the Liturgy, but not being seconded, a prosecution was soon after instituted against him in consequence of a royal mandate, by which he was so deeply affected that he was attacked with a nervous fever, which carried him off February 26th, 1758. Bishop Clayton published many theological works, the chief of which is his " Essay on Spirit."

SAMUEL BOYSE, the son of a dissenting clergyman, was born in Dublin, 1708. He was educated at Glasgow, where he improvidently married, and speedily became involved in all the distresses of poor authorship. He died miserably in Shoe-lane London, in 1749, and was buried at the expense of the parish. Boyse wrote a great deal in prose and verse, and was also a proficient in music and painting; but his works are forgotten, except his poem entitled " The Deity," which has gained some celebrity, and is still read.

DOCTOR THOMAS BURKE, titular Bishop of Ossory, was born in Dublin in 1710, and died in 1776. For a further account of this active Roman Catholic prelate see notes, page 807.

WILLIAM HAVARD, the son of a vintner, was born in Dublin about the year 1710. He was educated a surgeon, which he quitted for the stage. He continued to perform at Drury-lane with much reputation until 1769, when he retired, and died in London in 1778. The talents of Havard, both as an actor and author, were respectable, although he did not rise above mediocrity; but his character in private life was held in high estimation by his contemporaries. The following epitaph by Garrick is inscribed on his tombstone, Covent-garden church-yard:

"Havard from sorrow rests beneath this stone,
An honest man, beloved as soon as known,
Howe'er defective in the mimic art,
In real life he justly play'd his part,
The noblest character he acted well,
And heav'n applauded when the curtain fell.

Havard was the author of the following plays, which, though now scarcely noticed, were once acted with applause: Scanderbeg, a tragedy, 1733; King Charles I., a tragedy, 1737; Regulus, a tragedy, 1744. See Biographia Dramatica.

LETITIA PILKINGTON, the daughter of Doctor Vanlewin, a physician of Dublin, was born in that city in 1712. Her husband was a clergyman, and a needy author, from whom a separation took place by mutual consent. Mrs. Pilkington was one of Dean Swift's female coterie, and perhaps surpassed all the party in wit and genius not less than in levity. She died in Dublin in 1750. Her "Memoirs," written by herself, and her Letters, are still entertaining.

MARY BARBER, another of Swift's *bas bleu* society, was born in Dublin about 1712. She married a person in business, and appears to have been an estimable character. She published a small volume of poems under the patronage of Dean Swift and Lord Orrery, which are moral and not inelegant. Mrs. Barber died in 1757.

DR. CHARLES LUCAS, according to the most probable account, was born in Dublin about the year 1713; others, however, state that he was born at Ballymagaddy, in the county of Clare. Indeed, since the age of Homer, the birth-place of those who raise themselves from obscurity to distinction is often uncertain and disputed, and sometimes cannot be ascertained by the parties themselves. The ancestors of Lucas were substantial farmers of the above place, but his father lost the family property by mismanagement, and settled in Dublin; and the first certain notice that we can obtain of the son is, that he kept an apothecary's shop at the corner of Charles-street. Afterwards, he took out a degree in medicine. Dr. Lucas soon began to be distinguished as a political writer, and in consequence of the bold freedom of his opinions, he found it advisable to withdraw to the Continent. Whilst at Aix-la-Chapelle, he published an Essay on its waters and hot-baths, which was translated into French. On his return to Dublin, he was patronised by the Earl of Charlemont, and became a member of the Common Council, in which situation he exerted

THE CITY OF DUBLIN. 1197

himself with so much zeal and effect in the popular cause that he was elected Member of Parliament for the city. Upon this occasion he addressed his constituents in a spirited pamphlet, beginning with these words, "Yesterday I was your equal, to-day I am your servant." He himself enjoyed that moderate independance for which he so powerfully pleaded, being alike unincumbered with debts or riches at the time of his death, which took place in 1771. Dr. Lucas was thrice married, and had children by all his wives. It is related of him, that on the wedding night of his last wife, who was a remarkably fine woman, he was so crippled by the gout, that he was obliged to be lifted into bed. His funeral was attended by the Lord Mayor and Corporation in full costume, together with all the most distinguished characters then in the metropolis, and a statue of white marble was erected to his memory in a niche on the grand stair-case of the Royal Exchange. (See page 222.) In talents and in energy of character, Lucas resembled Wilkes, but the morals and principles of the former were much purer and more consistent; indeed his admirers consider him among the very few upright, unshaken, and incorruptible patriots who have rescued the name of Patriot from reproach and scorn. Dr. Lucas has written several political, and some medical tracts, which have been collected and published in four volumes 8vo., among which, his Treatise on Waters is much and justly esteemed.

JOHN GAST, Archdeacon of Glandeloch, son of Daniel Gast, a French Protestant refugee, who settled in Ireland in 1684, was born in Dublin July 29th, 1715, and received his education at Trinity College. Having taken orders, he officiated as pastor to the French congregation at Portarlington, and on his return to Dublin, he received a Doctor's degree from the Provost and Fellows of Trinity College, and was presented in 1761 with the living of Arklow and Archdeaconry of Glendeloch. He died in 1788. Dr. Gast published a History of Greece, which was held in much estimation; he was also remarkable for his active charities and benevolent plans for the relief of the distressed.

THOMAS FRY. This excellent artist was a native, it is generally believed, of Dublin, where several families of his name at present reside. He was born in 1710, and his first essay was a picture of Frederick Prince of Wales at the age of 28. While resident in England, he devoted his time and attention to the porcelain manufactory, which he is said first to have brought to perfection there. He was in high repute in London in the year 1744, where he executed those mezzotinto engravings which are the admiration of the present day. They chiefly consist of heads as large as life. The principal of these are His present Majesty, the celebrated Miss Pond, and his own portrait. This last is an admirable effort of genius, representing the character of the man with a truth and spirit which other mezzotintos are scarcely susceptible of. He died a martyr to intense application to his beloved art in 1762. Messrs. Boydells are in possession of 20 plates of his execution, consisting of portraits and fancy heads.

CHARLES MULLOY was born in Dublin in 1716, and educated at Trinity College. He studied the law in London, and was the editor of a periodical paper called " Common

Sense." He died in 1767. He wrote some Dramatic Pieces which are now scarcely remembered.

MARGARET WOFFINGTON was born in Dublin in 1718, and died in 1760. This celebrated actress made her first appearance in England at Covent Garden in 1738. She was the " Lovely Peggy" of Garrick. In face and form, in fascinating manners, and in the representation of sprightly characters she had no rival on the stage in her day. See note, page 111.

THOMAS SHERIDAN, M. A. Long before the arrival of the Anglo-Norman settlers in Ireland, the Sept of the Sheridans or O'Sheridans was seated (together with the O'Reillys) in a midland district called Hy-Breffny, comprising the present county of Cavan and parts of the adjacent counties, where the name and the descendants are still met with. Part of the Clan embraced the principles of the reformation, but the greater part adhered to the old religion and to the Stuarts; of the former was the family of Thomas Sheridan, some of whom held respectable situations; Doctor William Sheridan was Bishop of Kilmore at the Revolution, but resigned his see rather than conform.

Thomas Sheridan, father of Doctor Thomas Sheridan, possessed a small estate in the county, which became so incumbered by the generosity of his disposition, that his only son was indebted for his education to the exertions of his relation, the deprived bishop. Doctor T. Sheridan entered into orders, took out his degree, and obtained a Fellowship in Trinity College, which however he soon lost by his early marrying, before he had succeeded to a College living. His wife was Elizabeth, daughter of Mr. McFadden, a gentleman of Ulster. His acquaintance with Dean Swift commenced soon after, and continued in the closest habits of intimacy during his whole life. It is confidently stated, that the Dean was indebted to Dr. Sheridan for all his classical acquirements, as it is well known he was so inept or negligent at College as to have obtained his degree *Speciali Gratiâ*. Dr. Sheridan opened a grammar-school in a large house in Capel-street, which had been the mint where the base coin of King James was struck. In this house his third son, Thomas, was born in 1719, and was baptised in St. Mary's Church, Dean Swift being his godfather; after which, he removed to Quilca, in his native county. T. Sheridan received the elements of education at his father's seminary at Quilca, which soon became very famous. From thence he was placed in Westminster school, and after a residence of two years he returned to Dublin and entered the University. In the year 1738 he lost his father, and having nothing but his own exertions to depend on, he gave lectures on elocution in the College, which were well attended. Encouraged by success he took a decided taste for the stage, and made his debut at Smock Alley theatre in the part of Richard III., January 29th, 1743. His reception equalled his hopes, and from that time he played at the theatres royal in London and elsewhere with encreasing fame, so that he divided the theatric bays with his great cotemporaries Garrick and Barry. In the year 1747, he underwent a violent persecution in Dublin in consequence of his attempt to reform the abuses of the stage. This materially injured his finances, and obliged him to recur to his Lectures on elocution, which became so celebrated that he obtained degrees of Master of Arts

THE CITY OF DUBLIN.

from the Universities of Dublin and Cambridge, and ultimately a pension of £200. a year from the king.

Whilst embroiled in the law dispute when manager of Smock-alley, he became acquainted with Miss Frances Chamberlaine, in consequence of a spirited pamphlet which she published in his vindication. This led to a matrimonial alliance, which took place in 1748. He now resided with his wife's maternal uncle, Captain Solomon White, until a house was built for the new married couple near his own, in Dorset-street. In this house all his children were born.

After surmounting many difficulties and vicissitudes, Mr Sheridan, in 1776, succeeded Garrick in the management of Drury Lane, which he resigned in 1779, in consequence of his increasing infirmities; after which he went to Margate with a view of improving his health, which however was so much impaired that he died there, August 14th, 1788, in the 69th year of his age.

Many trying situations in his life have proved Thomas Sheridan to have been a man of the strictest honour and probity, whilst his useful writings evince his great learning, sound judgment, and extensive information.

His productions are as follows: 1. A Course of Lectures on Elocution, 4to.; 2. A Dissertation on the Causes and Difficulties which occur in Learning the English Tongue; 3. British Education, or the Source of the Disorders of Great Britain, 8vo.; 4. Elements of English, 12mo.; Lectures on the Art of Reading, 2 vol. 8vo.; 6. A Dictionary of the English Language, one Main Object of which is to Establish a Plan and permanent Standard of Pronunciation, 1 vol. 4to. and 2 vol. 8vo.; this has become a standard book. 7. Life of Swift prefixed to his works of which Sheridan was the editor, 1 vol. 8vo.

SPRANGER BARRY was born in Dublin in 1719. He was brought up a silver-smith, and had a shop in Skinner-row, which he quitted for the stage. Barry only played in tragedy, and in that line was for some time at Covent Garden a successful rival to Garrick; he lost his fortune in mismanagement of the Irish theatres, and died a martyr to the gout in 1774. Barry married Mrs. Dancer, who became no less celebrated in the tragic walk than her husband. She survived him many years, and continued long an ornament to her profession after her marriage with councillor Crawford of Dublin.

JAMES USHER was born in the vicinity of Dublin in 1720. He was of the same family as the Primate. He and his family, however, were Roman Catholics. He received a good education, but he failed in his attempt at farming, which was his father's occupation; upon which he settled, as a linen draper, in Dublin; married, and found himself in a few years a widower with four children. He now changed his mode of life, took priest's orders in the church of Rome, went to London, and set up a school at Kensington Gravel Pits; in which, at length, he was very successful. He died in 1772. His writings, which are elegant, ingenious, and moral, are: 1, A Treatise on a New System of Philosophy; 2, Letters by a Freethinker; 3, Clio, or a Discourse on Taste, in much estimation; 4, An Introduction to the Theory of the Human Mind.

THE HISTORY OF

THOMAS LELAND, D. D. a citizen's son, was born in Dublin in 1722. He was first educated at Doctor Sheridan's school at Quilca, and entered Trinity college in 1737, where he rose to a senior Fellowship. He was chaplain to Lord Townsend, and held the prebendary of Rathmichael, in St. Patrick's cathedral, being compatible (as under-rated in the King's Books,) with retaining his Fellowship. He died in 1785.

Doctor Leland was an excellent divine and a most eloquent preacher. He was highly esteemed by his contemporaries, especially by Doctor Johnson and Dr. Parr, by whom he was eulogized. His works, which hold a respectable rank in the republic of letters, are: 1, Translation of the Orations of Demosthenes, 2 vol. 4to. 1754; 2, The Life of Phillip of Macedon, 2 vol. 1758; 3, Longsword Earl of Salisbury, a Romance; 4, The Principles of Human Eloquence, which was attacked by Warburton; 5, Reply to Doctor Warburton, 1769. In this controversy Doctor Leland was deemed to have had the superiority; 6, History of Ireland, 3 vol. 4to 1773: 7, Sermons, 3 vol. posthumous.

MERVYN ARCHDALE was born in Dublin 22d April 1723, and graduated at the University there with reputation. He soon evinced such a decided taste for antiquarian pursuits as recommended him to the notice of several learned antiquarians and particularly to Doctor Pococke, Archdeacon of Dublin, who, as soon as he became Bishop of Ossory, presented him with a living. He died in 1791, leaving a character no less amiable than learned. After spending forty years in collecting materials for his " Monasticon Hibernicum," which was to be published in two vol. fol. he was compelled, for want of encouragement, to abridge it into one vol. 4to. It appeared in 1786. Archdale also published an enlarged edition of Lodge's Peerage, in 7 vol. 8vo. Mr. Lodge had left additions to his work written in a cypher which no one could comprehend; at last, Mrs. Archdale, like the wife of Leonidas, decyphered the tablets, by discovering the key to them.

MRS. FRANCES SHERIDAN was the daughter of ———— Chamberlaine, Esq. whose father, Sir Oliver Chamberlaine, was descended from a respectable English family, that had been settled in Dublin since the reformation.

Mrs. Sheridan was born in that city May 1724. A disposition naturally happy was improved by a refined education, and she appears to have been a very accomplished female, when she married Mr. Thomas Sheridan in her 23d year. The issue of this marriage were Thomas, who died an infant; Charles Francis; Richard Brinsley; Alicia, and Maria, all of whom appear to have been chiefly indebted to their excellent mother for the celebrity they attained in life. In the many vicissitudes and trying situations to which Mr. Sheridan was exposed, his wife bore her share with exemplary cheerfulness and fortitude; but her exertions and feelings were too powerful for her delicate constitution, which began to give way, until she sunk under a rapid decline at Blois in France, Sept. 26, 1766, in the 42nd year of her age. Such was the spirit of intolerance which then reigned in this part of France, that this amiable woman was denied the rites of Christian burial, and her body had been excluded from the church yard as a heretic but for the kind exertions of Major Maurias, the friend of her husband.

Mrs. Sheridan has attained a high rank among the literary females of the British empire.

THE CITY OF DUBLIN.

Her writings have received the sanction and approbation of the most eminent of her contemporaries: of Richardson, Dr. Young, Dr. Johnson, Garrick, and Murphy; and though one of her two comedies failed in the representation, owing to violent party opposition, yet they both had great success in the closet. There is said to be another comedy of hers, of still superior merit, as yet unpublished. Mrs. Sheridan's published works are: Memoirs of Miss Sidney Biddulph, 3 vol 8vo. 1761; Nourjahad, 1 vol. 12mo. 1762; The Discovery, a comedy, performed with great applause at Drury-lane, Feb. 1763; The Dupe, a comedy, withdrawn from the stage, and published Jan. 1764. She also wrote some occasional poems; and " A Trip to Bath, a comedy," is also ascribed to her pen.

FRANCIS GENTLEMAN was born in York-street, Dublin, 23d October, 1728. His father was a major in the army. He himself entered young into the service, and obtained a company in a new raised corps, which was reduced in 1748, at the conclusion of the war, and Gentleman, like many other officers, was left destitute without half pay, or any means of subsistence. He therefore betook himself to the stage for support; but though respectable in the middle walk of the drama, and still more as an author, he never rose to distinction, and died in great indigence in Dublin, December 1804. Gentleman had the advantage of a liberal education: he was a worthy and amiable character, which unhappily was latterly clouded by an intemperate use of spirits—the last desperate resource and only solace of the miserable! His writings are: The Stratford Jubilee, a comedy, 1769; The Sultan, a tragedy, 1770; The Modish Wife, a comedy, 1774; besides some dramatic pieces that never were published. He also altered and adapted for the stage some of the plays of our old dramatists; and he published the Dramatic Censor, 2 vol. 8vo. 1770.

NATHANIEL HONE, R. A. was born in Dublin about the year 1728. He painted History and Portraits with considerable success, in a manner peculiarly his own; but in consequence of some satirical attempts reflecting on the President, he became unpopular in the Royal Academy. He died in London, in 1784.

JAMES CAULFIELD, Earl of Charlemont, son of James the third Viscount Charlemont, and of Elizabeth, daughter of Francis Bernard, of Castle Bernard, County Cork, Esquire, was born in Dublin, 18th August, 1728. His education was domestic, by private tutors. Lord Charlemont spent his early years in travelling, and sojourned a long time in Italy, where he patronized Sir William Chambers, who, on his lordship's return to Ireland in 1754, erected for him the beautiful Temple at Marino, from designs drawn by Lord Charlemont. His elegant house in Palace-row was also planned by himself. In 1763 he was advanced to the dignity of Earl. In 1783 Lord Charlemont was elected President of the Volunteer Convention, held at the Royal Exchange by delegates from all the volunteer corps in Ireland. In 1786 he was elected President of the Royal Irish Academy, and was also Fellow of the Royal Antiquarian Society in London. In 1768 Lord Charlemont married the very amiable and accomplished Miss Hickman, daughter of Richard Hickman, of County Clare, Esq. by whom he had the present Earl, and other children. He died at Charlemont House, Dublin, 4th of August 1799. He composed the following simple and modest epitaph for himself:

THE HISTORY OF

" Here lies the Body of
James Earl of Charlemont,
a sincere zealous and active friend
to his Country.
Let his posterity imitate him in that alone
and forget
His manifold Errors"

Lord Charlemont contributed some valuable papers to the Transactions of the Royal Irish Academy, particularly " An Essay on the Antiquity of the Woollen Manufacture of Ireland." He also wrote the " History of Italian Poetry," and some light poems, as songs, sonnets, epigrams, inscriptions, &c. Being intimate with all the celebrated men of his time, his seat at Marino was long the temple of taste, science, and hospitality.

Vide Hardy's Life of Lord Charlemont, 1 vol. 4to. 1810.

HUGH HAMILTON, D. D. Bishop of Ossory, was born in the environs of Dublin, March 26, 1729. He received his education at the University, where he obtained a fellowship in 1751, and was also elected Erasmus Smith's Professor of Natural Philosophy. In 1767 he resigned his fellowship for the living of St. Anne in the city of Dublin. In 1777 he married an Irish lady of good family, and was preferred to the Deanery of Armagh. In 1796 he was consecrated Bishop of Clonfert, and in 1799 was removed to the See of Ossory, where he remained until his death, which happened Dec. 1, 1805. Doctor Hamilton was not less excellent as a philosopher than exemplary as a divine and prelate. His works have been published by his son, 2 vol. 8vo. 1809. Their contents are as follows: 1. " De Sectionibus Conicis;" 2. " An Essay on the Existence and Attributes of the Supreme Being;" 3. " An Essay on the Permission of Evil;" 4. " Three Philosophical Essays,—on the Ascent of Vapours; on the Aurora Borealis; on the Principles of Mechanics;" 5. " Remarks and Hints on the Improvement of Barometers; 6. " on the Power of fixed alkaline Salts to preserve Meat from Putrefaction; and 7. Introductory Lectures on Natural Philosophy.

Right Hon. EDMUND BURKE was born in Dublin, January 1st, 1730. His father was a respectable Protestant attorney, who had removed from Bruff, County Limerick, his native town, and settled in Dublin. Burke received the groundwork of his education at the Quaker Academy of Ballytore, near Carlow, under Abraham Shackleton, which distinguished school has been continued ever since by Shackleton's immediate descendants. He himself never after crossed over to Ireland without visiting the family of his old preceptor. From Ballitore Burke entered Trinity College, where he was made a scholar of the house in 1746. After leaving College he entered of the Middle Temple in 1753; but he never studied at St. Omer, or professed the Roman Catholic religion. He married a daughter of Dr. Nugent, at whose house he was domesticated. By this lady he had an only son, Richard Burke, whose premature death hastened that of his father. He had for some time retired from all public affairs to his seat at Beaconsfield, in Buckinghamshire, where he died July 8th, 1797, and was buried in the parish church, near the body of his much loved son.

THE CITY OF DUBLIN.

In this limited sketch it is not possible even to enumerate the active duties or numerous writings of this great statesman, orator, and author. His works have been collected and published in 5 vol. 4to; the last edition in twelve 8vo. volumes; and for the particulars of his life we must refer to " General Biography," and to Doctor Bissett's work. But a well written life of Edmund Burke is still a desideratum in British biography. All the family of Burke were men of talents, and distinguished themselves, though at an awful distance from the head. His brother, William Burke, was Recorder of Bristol, and published some pamphlets, esteemed in his day. His son Richard was just beginning a promising career in parliament when he died, and his cousin, —— Burke, was a political writer of some eminence.

JOHN CUNNINGHAM was born in Dublin about the year 1731. He was bred to business, but left it for the stage, on which he was not successful. A gentleman of Newcastle-upon-Tyne, struck with his amiable deportment, received him in his family, at whose house he died in 1773. Soon after, a volume of his poems was published, with a sketch of his life prefixed. Cunningham's pastorals and songs are among the best in the English language, and they have obtained for their author a place among the English classics.

DOCTOR GABRIEL STOKES was born in Dublin in 1732. His father was an eminent optician in Capel-street, who had made some inventions in mechanics, and composed a treatise on calculation. He was subsequently appointed Deputy Surveyor General. Doctor Stokes was educated in Trinity College, under his brother Joseph, the senior fellow. He obtained a fellowship in his twenty-third year, and soon after accepted the Rectory of Artree, county Tyrone, which he served in person fourteen years. From thence he removed to Waterford, where he presided over the Corporation Grammar School with great reputation. He was presented by Bishop Newcome to the Chancellorship of the Cathedral of that city. From Waterford he went to reside at Desart Martin, in the diocese of Derry. Here, at the age of 74 he exercised all the duties of his profession with diligence. In the year 1806, returning home from preaching a very energetic sermon, he found a fire had broken out in his glebe-house, which he exerted himself to extinguish ; retiring to rest after the fatigues of the day, he was found dead by some of his family.

Doctor Stokes edited " Hippolitus" and " Iphigenia in Aulis." He published an Essay on Primate Newcome's Harmony of the Gospels, and a volume of his sermons was published after his death, 12mo. 1812. He had commenced an useful work on " the Errors and Dangers of the vulgar Misapprehension of several Texts in Scripture taken in an insulated sense," which he expounded by their connexion with the contexts, &c. but it has been left in a state too imperfect to publish.

ISAAC BICKERSTAFF was born in Dublin about the year 1732. His father held the situation of Groom Porter in the Castle, which place was abolished during the Lord Lieutenancy of the Earl of Chesterfield, in 1745. But the services of the father were recompensed by a pension, and his son Isaac was made a page. After the departure of Lord Chesterfield, Bickerstaff got a commission in the marine corps, which it is said he left in disgrace, in consequence of being suspected of a most disgraceful crime. It appears, notwithstanding, that he continued to write for the stage for several years, when perhaps the charge was renewed by his enemies, which drove him at last into banishment. The law is justly severe against detractors of this nature, but it was not in the power of the law to restore a repu-, tation so deeply wounded as his by the imputation of such a crime. If the robust nerves of Samuel Foote were unable to sustain a similar charge, made at the instigation of an infamous woman, although he was exculpated in a court of justice,—how much less could one of Bickerstaff's refined sensibilities (if one might judge by his writings) support it? It is now generally believed, at least in Ireland, that the accusation was alike malicious and unfounded. Be that as it may, the sweet and prolific muse of Bickerstaff was silenced for many years. He was known to be living in London in 1811, but there are later reports of his death, which it is supposed took place two years ago.

The earliest and best of Bickerstaff's operatic pieces, aided by the delightful music of Doctor Arne, still keep possession of the stage, and, if we except the Beggar's Opera and the Duenna, without a rival. In his retreat he wrote some popular after-pieces, which have been adopted by others. The celebrated sea songs published by the late Mr. Dibdin, who it is said furnished the music only, are asserted also (but probably not truly) to have been written by Bickerstaff, whose published works are: 1. Leucothoe, a dramatic poem, 1756; 2. Thomas and Sally, a comic opera, 1760; 3. Love in a Village, a comic opera, 1763; 4. Judith, an oratorio, 1764; 5. Maid of the Mill, a comic opera, 1765; 6. Daphne and Amintor, a comic opera, 1765; 7. Love in a City, a comic opera (altered into the farce of the Romp) 1767; 8. Lionel and Clarissa, a comic opera, 1768; 9. The Absent Man, a farce, 1768; 10. The Padlock, a comic opera, 1768; 11. The Ephesian Matron, a musical farce, 1769; 12. The Captive, a comic opera, 1769; 13. The Recruiting Sergeant, a musical farce, 1770; 14. The Sultan, a musical farce, 1775. The Deserter; The Waterman; The Spoiled Child, and other pieces are said to have been written by him, though published under other names.

HUGH KELLY, according to the most probable accounts was born in Dublin in 1732, though there are others which state that he was born in the county of Kerry, where his family was respectably connected; but being in reduced circumstances they removed to Dublin, where young Kelly was bound apprentice to a stay-maker; this business not exactly suiting his lofty *Milesian* spirit, he soon changed the needle for the quill, and became assistant to an attorney in London, and after struggling with great difficulties, he was at last enabled to take chambers in the Temple. He then married respectably, and enjoyed an estimable private character. He died in 1777.

Kelly was a voluminous writer, and lived to see all his writings successful, though at present, notwithstanding their merit, they are not much known. His works are: 1. False Delicacy, a comedy, which had a great run; 2. A Word to the Wise, a comedy; 3. The School for Wives, a comedy; 4. The Romance of an Hour, a comedy of two acts; 5. The Man of Reason, a comedy: 6. Clementina, a tragedy; 7. Thespis, a poem, being the best dramatic satire after Churchill's Rosciad; 8. Louisa Mildmay, or The Memoirs of a Magdalen, an original and pathetic novel; and 9. The Babler, a series of essays; together with many political pamphlets. See his life prefixed to his works.

GEORGE BARRETT, R.A. an eminent landscape painter, was born in the Liberties of Dublin in 1732; he was self-taught, having been apprenticed to a stay-maker, and while yet a youth gained the principal prize in Dublin, and afterwards that in London. He had the honour to be among those who planned the Royal Academy, and was one of its first members. He died in 1784. His pictures are in great estimation, and are in the collections of the dukes of Buccleugh and Portland, &c. Pilkington's Dictionary of Painters.

KANE O'HARA, descended from an ancient and respectable Irish family, was born in Dublin about the year 1733, and was educated at Trinity College. O'Hara had an exquisite taste for music and was well skilled in musical composition, which, with his social and lively humour, introduced him to all the wits and literati of his day. He had the misfortune, in his latter years, to lose his sight, and died at his house near Dublin, June 17th, 1782. O'Hara was the author of a new species of comic opera called the English Burletta. His dramatic works are: Midas, a burletta, 1764; The Golden Pippin, a burletta, 1773; The Two Misers, a musical drama, 1775; April Day, a burletta, 1777; Tom Thumb, a burletta, 1780.

HUGH HAMILTON, an eminent painter, was born in Dublin about the year 1734. He studied the elements of his art at the Academy House in Grafton-street, and was the inventor of a species of portrait painting, being a mixture of crayons and chalks, in which he so much excelled that his likenesses were held in high estimation. He followed his art with encreased success in England, where he had the honour of having the King, Queen, and several of the royal family sit to him. From England he went to Italy, where he resided twelve years, and whilst studying the models of excellence in that country, he exchanged his crayons for the palette and pencil. His portraits in oil were not less distinguished for characteristic likeness, knowledge of half-tint, and good drawing, than his former works in crayons; and his efforts in historic painting prove how much he would have excelled had his genius taken an earlier direction in that line. A Cupid and Psyche, in the possession of Lord Charleville, and a fine sketch of Prometheus snatching Fire from the Car of Apollo, are strong evidences of his talents in the higher walks of the art. Hugh Hamilton died in Dublin in 1806.

ROBERT JEPHSON was born in Dublin about the year 1734. He received the rudiments of his education at Ryder's grammar school, from whence he was removed to Trinity College in 1750, and studied under Doctor Ratcliffe. On leaving the university he entered the army and obtained a company in a new raised regiment, on the reduction of which he held the appointment of Master of the Horse at the Castle given to him by Lord Townsend, whom he captivated by his wit and convivial qualities. He was also happy in the friendship and constant attachment of Mr. Secretary Hamilton, better known by the name of Single-speech Hamilton, who introduced him into the Irish Parliament, where he gained the attention of the House by an unpremeditated flow of facil witty eloquence. Captain Jephson died of a paralytic stroke at his seat at the Black Rock, May 31st, 1803.

The first production of Jephson, which at once introduced him to notice, was that exquisite piece of humour, "The Heroic Epistle to Georges Edmund Howard by Alderman George

Faulkner," 8vo. 1772; it ran through eight editions. His tragedy of Braganza was acted at Drury-lane in 1775, with distinguished applause, upon which occasion he received a very flattering epistle from Horace Walpole; The Law of Lombardy was performed in 1779; The Count of Narbonne, which had great success at Covent Garden, in 1781; and Julia, his last tragedy, in 1786. All these plays met a very favourable reception. His other dramatic pieces are The Campaign, a comic opera; Love and War, a farce, 1787; The Hotel, or Servant with Two Masters, a farce, 1791; which still continues a favourite in Dublin; and The Conspiracy, a tragedy, 1791.

Jephson published, in conjunction with Mr. Courtney and the Rev. Mr. Burrows, a series of satiric essays, replete with wit and humour, called The Bachelor. He also wrote a satire on the French Revolution, called The Confession of J. Baptist Couteau. His last publication was Roman Portraits, a poem, 4to. 1800.

The tragedies of Jephson, although at present seldom acted, are written in a fine dramatic style, at once elegant and forcible; the plots are well conducted and interesting, and they may be justly placed, " if not first, in the very first line" of *modern* tragedies.

HENRY BROOKE, an historical painter of some eminence, of the same family as the excellent author of Gustavus Vasa, was born in Dublin in 1738. Mr. Brooke went to London in 1761, where an exhibition of his paintings obtained him both fame and money. In 1767 he married and settled in Dublin, where he lost a considerable property in unlucky speculations. He however followed his profession with much credit, and died in Dublin in 1806. Brooke was employed in painting altar pieces for some Roman Catholic chapels, which are much admired. The death of Seneca, in chiaro scuro, has also met with great applause.

DOCTOR STOCK was the son of a hosier in Dame-street, Dublin, where he was born, 22d December, 1741. He was educated at Trinity College, of which he became, in due course, senior fellow. He was promoted to the see of Killala, and was taken prisoner in his palace by Humbert, who made his descent at that place with a French force in 1799. By his address and conciliating conduct he succeeded in restraining the excesses of both the French and the rebels. From Killala he was translated to the see of Waterford, where he died, August, 1813.

Doctor Stock edited " Demosthenes," and the edition is now read in the university course. He published " An account of the Landing of the French at Killala, by an Eye Witness;" an interesting narrative. And lastly, A Paraphrase on the Book of Job, which has been severely, and in many respects justly, criticized.

JOHN JARVIS, an eminent painter of glass, was born in Dublin about 1749. He first practised his art in his native city, in the prosecution of which he was much assisted by the chemical instructions of the late Doctor Cunningham. He then removed to London, where he was soon distinguished, and was employed to execute those beautiful works in painted glass at Oxford and Windsor, from the designs and under the inspection of Sir Joshua Reynolds and Mr. President West. Jarvis died in London in 1804.

HENRY TRESHAM, R. A. historical painter, was born in Dublin in 1749, and studied under the elder West. He was sent to Italy under the patronage of Sir Clinton Wetherington, where he remained, completing his studies, for several years. On his return he finished several pictures in a grand style. That of Milton's Adam and Eve, as large as life, is known by a fine print of it ; the original is in the possession of Lord Powerscourt. He also painted several subjects for the Shakespeare Gallery, and was employed, at the time of his death, in making selections from the ancient masters for a series of engravings ; that event took place, June 17th, 1814. Tresham was also a poet of no mean talent. He published an odd, but well written poem, called the Sea-sick Minstrel, 4to. 1796; also Rome at the Close of the 18th Century, 4to. 1799; and A Heroick Epistle from Britannicus to Bonaparte, 4to. 1813.

CHARLES FRANCIS SHERIDAN, the second son of Mr. Thomas Sheridan, and elder brother of Richard Biinsley, was born in Dublin, July, 1750. He received the elements of science, together with his brother, at the seminary of Samuel White, in Grafton-street, and completed his education under his father, whom he assisted for some years in his public lectures. He was afterwards oppointed Envoy to the Court of Stockholm, and on his return became Under Secretary at War for Ireland, and a member of the Irish Parliament, where he distinguished himself by his wit and eloquence. He died in 1795.

Charles Sheridan published The History of the Revolution of Sweden, 1 vol. 8vo. a work of repute.

Right Hon. RICHARD BRINSLEY SHERIDAN.—This' celebrated dramatic writer completes the list of authors, natives of Dublin, who have successfully cultivated the drama, and in extending the enumeration to the whole kingdom, which would include Congreve, Farquhar, Goldsmith, Murphy, &c. it may serve to confirm and illustrate the general opinion of the natural talent of the Irish for wit, humour, and eloquence. In the graver and more scientific walks of literature the pretensions of Ireland are not so high ; but in works of humour, in dramatic composition, and especially in comedy, she must be allowed to excel. Congreve (who was born in the Castle of Lismore, where his father was steward to Lord Orrery) brought English comedy to perfection ; and but for his licentiousness, (the vice of his age,) would remain unrivalled. Sheridan inherited the regularity, wit, polish, and variety of character of Congreve's drama, with greater purity of style. In the present degenerate state of the stage, it is quite hopeless to expect any thing approaching the excellence of The Way of the World or The School for Scandal.

R. B. Sheridan, the third son of Thomas and Frances Sheridan, was born in Dorset-street, Dublin, Oct. 26, 1751. The name of Brinsley was given to him in compliment to Brinsley Butler, Lord Lanesborough, a friend of the family. His mother took much pains with his early education, in which she was assisted by her cousin, Samuel White, of the Academy in Grafton-street. From this school he was removed to Harrow, where he finished his studies under Doctor Sumner and Doctor Samuel Parr ; after which, in 1769, he went to reside with his father at Bath, and though he entered of the Middle Temple, he never studied there, or followed the law as a profession. It is said that Sheridan gave no indications at school of that intellectual pre-eminence for which he became afterwards so distinguished, and that his capacity did not appear above the level of ordinary boys. This may possibly be true; the developement of the mental powers has been late in some of the greatest geniuses. It was love, however, that expanded the first blossoms of genius in Sheridan. His passion for Miss Linley, a celebrated vocal performer at Bath, bordered on the romantic. He fought two duels with sword and pistol on her account, in the latter of which he was dangerously wounded, but was rewarded on his recovery by the fair hand of the lady.

Sheridan having interdicted his wife from singing in public, and having no patrimony or resources for maintaining his family, became an author from necessity. His first comedy, The Rivals, was acted at Covent Garden in January 1775, and his last piece, The Critic, appeared at Drury-lane in October 1779, (of which theatre in 1776 he became a joint patentee,) so that all his original dramatic works came out in less than four consecutive years. It is ascertained that the four first acts of the School for Scandal were in rehearsal whilst he was writing the fifth; a proof at once of his negligence and the exuberance of his wit. The drama, unfortunately for its admirers, was too soon superseded by politics; and what a fertile source of taste, elegance, wit, and genius was absorbed and swallowed up in the whirlpool of politics!

At the general election in 1780, Sheridan was chosen member of Parliament for the borough of Stafford, which he continued to represent for 26 years. His political career was in the highest degree brilliant. As a parliamentary orator he holds an equal rank with Burke, Pitt, and Fox; indeed all three voluntarily conceded to him the palm of eloquence at the trial of Warren Hastings. With such great talents, his political conduct was ever consistent with his principles, which, though on the popular side, determined him to support the just prerogatives of the crown, no less than the rights of the people. When therefore there was cause for real alarm, when actual danger threatened the country, then, waving his attachments to his friends and his party, without however deserting them, he devoted all the energies of his mind exclusively to its support. Of this generous devotion, his successful exertions during the awful mutiny of the fleet, and afterwards, when Napoleon was preparing to invade England, are proofs which should never be forgotten. Latterly, Sheridan held the appointment of Receiver of the Revenues of the Duchy of Cornwall; but this belonged to the establishment of the Prince Regent, as Duke of Cornwall, and is by no means to be considered as a place under government. It was bestowed on him, on the demise of General Lake, as a particular mark of the friendly consideration of his Royal Highness.

It is, but too true that Sheridan was totally deficient in prudence; had he possessed that "one thing needful," the want of which no genius or talent can redeem, he might have attained the summit of fortune, as of fame. It is not intended to apologize for his failings, (for which he has been most severely judged,) by the trite observation, that genius and prudence are seldom united; but it may be remarked, that his great contemporaries, Fox and Pitt, were never celebrated for either prudence or temperance. Nevertheless, it is astonishing between the blandishments of his two favourite mistresses, Indolence and Dissipation, where or how he acquired those rich and copious stores of knowledge, and that versatility of intellect, which he could instantly command on every occasion. He never would submit to the drudgery of consulting documents, or searching among papers; like the French Abbé, " his siege was made" without them.

Having lost his first wife, by whom he had one son, Thomas, he married in 1792 Miss Esther Ogle, youngest daughter of the Dean of Winchester. In the last general election, Sheridan was an unsuccessful candidate for Westminster, and also failed in being returned for Stafford, upon which he gave up all political and literary pursuits, and lived in privacy with his family. He had previously lost his chief revenue by the accidental burning of Drurylane Theatre; an event which he bore with the utmost philosophy; but the " res angusti domi," together with a painful chronic complaint, embittered his latter days; however, he was supported by the consolations of a most amiable and affectionate wife and son. He died in London at his house in Saville-row, July 7th, 1816. His funeral was attended by persons of the highest distinction, and he was interred in Westminster Abbey near the tomb of Addison. A plain blue slab was placed over his grave by his friend Peter Moore, marked simply with the usual inscription of name and age.

Of the detailed events of Sheridan's public and private life, of his unrivalled wit and eloquence, of his dramatic and other poetry, a good history remains yet to be published; for the accounts which have already appeared are surely not worthy of the subject. Indeed it is hopeless to expect a fair and impartial biography of any public character, so long as party spirit guides the pen, and despotically sways the press. His published writings are: 1. The Rivals, a comedy, 1775; 2. St. Patrick's Day, or the Scheming Lieutenant, a farce, 1775; 3. The Duenna, a comic opera, 1775; 4. The Camp, a dramatic entertainment, 1777; 5. The School for Scandal, a comedy, 1777; 6. The Critic, a dramatic satire, 1779. Sheridan altered, retouched, and adapted to the present taste, Vanburg's comedy of A Trip to Scarborough, and the plays of Pizarro, and the Stranger from Kotzebu. He also wrote a monody on Garrick, and occasional poems, a collection of which it is hoped will be published. His parliamentary speeches have lately been given to the public, in 4 vol. 4to. but his political pamphlets should also be ascertained and collected for publication.

Rev. WILLIAM PETERS, LL. B., R. A. was born in Dublin about the year 1752. His father held a respectable situation in the Custom-house, from whom he received an excellent education; but having evinced a decided taste for drawing, he was sent to the Dublin Academy, and acquired the elements of the art under West. He then went to Italy, where he studied and remained for some years, during which he was elected member of the Academy of Florence. On his return he was patronised by the Lord Lieutenant, the Duke of Rutland, who sent him to Paris to take a copy of Le Brun's celebrated picture of Madame de la Valiere. At the same time, the late Duke of Manchester, then our Embassdor at the French court, requested the Queen of France to permit Mr. Peters to make a portrait of the young Dauphin. A council being summoned on the occasion, it was decided that the smell of paint might prove injurious to the child's health, and the proposal was declined. The subsequent fate of this unfortunate boy and his parents is strongly contrasted with these early precautions.

Mr. Peters was elected a Royal Academician, and soon after took orders in the Church, in which he became Prebendary of Lincoln, and obtained other valuable benefices. He married a niece of Dr. Turton; by which alliance a large fortune ultimately came into the family. He died at Basted-place in Kent, April 20th, 1814.

The early productions of his palette were subjects of rather a warm tendency, which he painted in a rich florid style, but with great taste. After he had taken orders, his style became more chastened and severe, and he dedicated his pencil to designs calculated to inspire religious and pious sentiments: The Resurrection of a Pious Family; The Spirit of a Child; and other such subjects he treated in an original manner, so as to give them an air of spirituality which perfectly conveys the idea.

Some years ago Mr. Peters resigned his academicial honour, and with it his palette and pencils, except that occasionally he reassumed these to gratify his particular friends.

WILLIAM PRESTON was born in the year 1753, in St. Michan's parish, Dublin; at the age of two years he was deprived of his father, who went to the East Indies, and was never after heard of. Young Preston discovered early energies of mind. He selected for his master Doctor Campbell, then esteemed the most severe in the metropolis, and on the decline of his school pursued his studies by himself. In three years he finished the whole College course prescribed for entrance, and in the year 1766 was admitted a pensioner of Trinity College at the age of 15, having selected Doctor Law for his tutor. Here he highly distinguished himself by obtaining a premium or certificate at every quarterly examination, and when at a proper standing became a candidate for a fellowship. The College was at this time much agitated by political disputes, and every man of talents exerted the to aid his friends or annoy his opponents. Preston took an active part, and was a principal contributor to a work called "Pranceriana," of which he wrote the 16th, 24th, 25th, 29th, 31st, and 33d numbers. In due time he sat for a fellowship, but was twice unsuccessful; and if the author of Lachrymæ Academicæ is to be relied on, it was his political opinions, and not his want of merit, that excluded him. He now became a student of the Middle Temple, and was called to the Irish bar in 1777. His attention to his profession did not detach him from his favourite studies: he became a member of a literary society in the University, called *Neosophers*, and with them was instrumental in founding the Royal Irish Academy. To this society he was chosen a secretary shortly after its commencement, which he continued till his death. He contributed the following essays to its Transactions: 1.Thoughts on Lyric Poetry, with an Ode to the Moon; 2. Essay on Wit and Humour; 3. On the Choice of a Subject for Greek Tragedy; 4. On Credulity; 5. On the Ancient Amatory Poets Ovid, Propertius, and Tibullus; 6. On the German Writers; 7. On the Natural Advantages of Ireland, which gained the prize of £50. During the political discussions which took place at this memorable period, Preston was intimately connected with Lord

THE CITY OF DUBLIN.

Charlemont and his associates, and he contributed his share to the publications of the time. In the year 1780 he first published his poem of The Contrast, which though too violent for the present day, was then highly applauded and admired, not less for the patriotic than for the poetic spirit which it breathed. In the year 1781 his poems were collected and published in one volume, on which occasion a remarkable literary incident occurred :—The author gave them to the printer without receiving any compensation for them, and after the publication he obtained a few copies to distribute among his friends; the printer became a bankrupt, and on inspecting his books, Mr. Preston was found to be entered a debtor for so many books as he had received, and was actually furnished with a bill for 12 copies of his own work, which was the only compensation he had ever received for 500, which were published in the edition. Another circumstance occurred—Doctor Stock had deposited some time before, in the hands of the printer, paper for an edition of Tacitus; the needy printer applied it to the use of Preston's poems, as the more popular subject: Doctor Stock never received any compensation for 50*l.* worth of paper, his book was not published, and Preston silenced Tacitus. He some years after turned his attention to the drama. His first effort in this way was Offa and Ethelbert, founded on an event in Saxon history; it was published in 1791, but never acted. In 1792 he produced Messenè freed, written on an incident recorded in Le Voyage du jeune Anacharse; it was performed for several nights with much interest at the Theatre Royal Crow-street. His next dramatic piece was Romanda, taken from the murder of Albinus, King of the Lombards, by his wife, as recorded by Gibbon. But his last drama was by far the most celebrated, it was called Democratic Rage, and founded on the events of the French Revolution, then recent: this play was first printed, and received with such unparalleled popularity, that three editions were called for in three weeks; the manager of the theatre considering it public property, put it into rehearsal without ever consulting the author, and its success on the stage was not less than in the closet. On this occasion the Guillotine was exhibited on the stage. It was sanctioned by the more horrible Wheel in Venice Preserved. In 1793 he collected all his pieces together, and gave an edition of them to the public in two volumes large octavo: it contains all his poetic and dramatic works, with the exception of Democratic Rage: it was printed in Dublin, ornamented with a portrait and elegant vignettes by Dublin artists; and from the care with which the publication was super intended, and the manner in which it was executed, affords perhaps the best specimen of an elegant edition that ever issued from an Irish press. The patriot mind of Preston was anxious for the literary reputation of Ireland, even in its subordinate departments; he therefore encouraged the arts by publishing his works in his native city, and set an example, which if followed, would rescue us from the too frequently merited censure passed on Irish editions. He now published a translation of The Argonautics of Apollonius Rhodius; and about this time was principally instrumental in establishing the Dublin Library Society, the selection of whose books was left to his judgment. As some remuneration for his public services, the situation of Commissioner of Appeals had been conferred on Mr. Preston by his political friends at an early period; but when they had again an opportunity of serving him they treated him

THE HISTORY OF

with great neglect. This circumstance preyed upon his mind till the hour of his death, which it probably accelerated by predisposing him to a mortal disease. He had sat a whole day in December, in wet clothes, in his Court, presiding at a trial of some consequence: on his return home he was seized with an illness which terminated in a miliary fever, and proved mortal in a few days, in January 1807. As a testimony of respect to his memory, the Dublin Library Society evinced their regard by an Address and Resolution, in which they denominate him " an honour to their institution," and gave a ticket of perpetual admission to his son. The University took the whole edition of his Apollonius Rhodius, to distribute as premiums at quarterly examinations; and one of its former fellows testified his regret, and that of the world, by an impressive epitaph.

Preston was a man of great literary attainments; his mind was highly cultivated, and richly stored with Roman and Grecian literature. It is probable, there was not a more elegant or accurate classical scholar in the United Kingdom. To this was added an extensive knowledge of modern languages, and an intimate acquaintance with the poets and writers of his own and other countries. On the occasion of any new publication either at home or abroad, he generally had the earliest intelligence; his oral criticisms supplied to his friends the functions of a Literary Review, and his early judgment was generally sanctioned by the subsequent testimony of public opinion. Besides the works of greater consequence to which he affixed his name, he was the author of a variety of anonymous pieces both in prose and verse. His active mind and ready fancy catched at every flying topic; the town was amused, and the fugitive effusions appropriated, but Preston used to say to his friends—
" Hos ego versiculos tulit alter honores."

He left behind him unpublished plays, poems, and letters, comprising a correspondence with some of the most eminent characters of his day both in England and Ireland.

Two years after his death proposals were printed to publish the poems, to which were to be prefixed a copious account of his life, and a critique on his writings; the life and critique were omitted, and we believe the present Sketch is the only biographical notice of this excellent scholar published since his death in his native city.

ALICIA LE FANU was born in Dorset-street, Dublin, in the year 1754. She was the daughter of Thomas and Frances Sheridan, and sister to Richard Brinsley. At an early age she accompanied her excellent mother to Blois in France, where she received her education in a convent, and acquired that correct knowledge and fluent use of the French language which afterwards distinguished her. On her return to her native city, after her mother's death, she married Joseph Le Fanu, Esq. the respectable descendant of a French refugee family, who held a lucrative situation in the Custom-house of Dublin. Here, her house became the resort of all that was excellent in the literary society of the capital. On one night in the week it was open for the reception of unbidden guests, who, after the first introduction, came uninvited: reading select passages, in which Mrs. Le Fanu excelled, poetic compositions, and other literary pursuits, excluded cards; and the rooms were generally filled with those who preferred such delightful and rational sources of amusement to the fashionable frivolities of other assemblies. After having long reigned chief of the gifted few who compose the lettered society of Dublin, the arbitress of taste, and the patroness to whom the rising genius of Ireland dedicated their first works, she was affected with a painful and lingering distemper, which she bore with the cheerful fortitude characteristic of her family, and died at her son's residence in the Phœnix Park, on the 5th of September, 1817; leaving behind her two sons, Thomas and Joseph, and one daughter, Eliza.

This talented lady did not exercise those powers which she eminently possessed, in the composition of many pieces. She published but two—Suzette's Marriage Portion, an elegant translation of La Dot de Suzette; and the Sons of Erin, a dramatic composition, in which she has rendered justice to the calumniated character of her country in her hero, by conquering the feelings of inveterate prejudice against him. This excellent comedy was first acted in London, and afterwards in Dublin, with distinguished success.

JOHN HICKEY, statuary, was born in Dublin in 1756. He was pupil to Cranfield, an eminent carver. He worked in Dublin with success, and came to London under the patronage of Mr. Burke and Sir Joshua Reynolds. His Basso Relievo of the Massacre of the Innocents obtained for him the gold medal of the Royal Academy. He died in London from the effects of intemperance in 1787.

J. COOPER WALKER was the son of an eminent cabinet-maker in Capel-street, Dublin, where he was born in 1761. He received a liberal education, but a delicate frame and weak constitution induced him to seek a warmer climate. He resided some years in Italy, of whose manners, language, and literature he became master, and was enrolled a member of some of its learned societies. He returned to his native country, rich in elegant acquirements, but still poor in health. He died at his romantic little villa at St. Valori, near Bray, April 10th, 1810. He wrote, 1. Memoirs of Alessandro Tassoni; 2. Essays on the Customs and Institutions of Ancient Ireland; 3. Historical Memoirs of the Irish Bards, 4to. 1786; 4. On the Dress, Weapons, and Armour of the Antient Irish, 4to. 1799; 5. An Historical Memoir of Italian Tragedy, 4to. 1799; 6. On the Revival of the Drama in Italy, 8vo. 1805; 7. Brookiana, 2 vols. 12mo. 1807. He also contributed to the Royal Irish Academy, of which he was an early member.

WILLIAM GARDINER was born in Dublin, June 11th, 1766. Although his parents were of the lower class of society, he received a good education, and evinced a strong natural talent for literature, painting, and music. He was accordingly sent to the Dublin academy, where he studied for three years, and obtained a prize medal. Afterwards he migrated to London, and supported himself there for some time by making profile shades. He then tried the stage, but without success. At last, having accidentally met with Captain Grose the antiquarian, who was pleased with the versatility of his genius, he was placed by him with Mr. Godfrey the engraver. He also worked for Bartolozzi, and imitated his style so correctly that his engravings were often passed for those of that great artist. He was now much employed by print and booksellers, and was engaged in the illustrations of Harding's

THE HISTORY OF

Shakespeare, Memoirs of the Count de Grammont, and particularly in Lady D. Beauclerk's fine edition of Dryden's Fables, all the prints of which are marked by the name of Bartolozzi, although several were executed by Gardiner. He now might have attained independence and fame, but he was too volatile and unsteady for any sedentary occupation. He was induced to leave his business in London and go to Dublin, where he expended all his money, and irreparably injured his health. Afterwards, on his return to England, he was admitted, (by the favour of Doctor Farmer), of Emanuel, and then of Corpus Christi College, Cambridge. He remained there five years, with a view of qualifying himself for holy orders, and was a candidate for a fellowship. Failing in his attempt, he left the University, and turned painter. Even in that line he had great merit as a copyist; but he grew tired of his employment, and finally became a bookseller. He had made a collection of scarce and curious books, in which he dealt for the last thirteen years of his life. At length, grown dissatisfied with mankind, and brooding over his disappointments, he put a period to his wordly existence at his house in Pall-mall, June 21st, 1814. Immediately prior to his committing this desperate act, he wrote the following impressive letter, to a friend; which, from its calm rational tenor, seems to prove that he was one of those few unfortunate suicides whose crime cannot be well referred to mental derangement.

"Sir,—I cannot descend to the grave, without expressing a due sense of the marked kindness with which you have favoured me for some years. My sun has set for ever;—a nearly total decline of business, the failure of my catalogue, a body covered with disease, though unfortunately of such a nature as to make life uncomfortable without the consoling prospect of its termination, has determined me to seek that asylum " where the weary are at rest." My life has been a continual struggle, not indeed against adversity, but against something more galling; and poverty, having now added herself to the list, has made life a burthen. Adieu, Sir, and believe me your sincere and respectful humble servant, WILLIAM GARDINER."

MARY TIGHE. The father of this lovely and interesting woman was the Rev. William Blashford, Librarian of St. Patrick's Library, Dublin, and her mother Theodosia Tighe, of Rosanna, county of Wicklow. She was born in Dublin, in 1774, and had the misfortune to lose her father while yet an infant; but by the care of an excellent mother, her fine intellectual powers were developed and cultivated. She married her cousin Henry Tighe, some time member of the Irish parliament. The pleasant and romantic seat of Rosanna now became the temple of Taste, of the Muses, and of all the social virtues. It was there the poem of Psyche was first printed at a private press, and a few copies only distributed to friends, together with her other shorter occasional poems, some of which are of distinguished merit. In the midst of such refined enjoyments she was attacked with a fatal complaint, which for a long time she bore with the mild fortitude of a christian, and at length, in the full bloom of life and fame, calmly resigned all her prospects of earthly happiness. She died at Woodstock, county Kilkenny, the seat of her brother-in-law, William Tighe, Esq. on the 24th of March, 1810, in the 37th year of her age: and to use the words of the Editor of the 4th edition of her poems : " After six years of protracted malady, her fears of death were perfectly removed, before she quitted this scene of trial and suffering; and her spirit departed to a better state of existence, confiding with heavenly joy in the acceptance and love of her Redeemer."*

With the profits accruing from Mrs. Tighe's poems, an hospital ward has been endowed and attached to the House of Refuge, a charitable institution founded by her mother in the county of Wicklow,—it is called the "Psyche Ward."

The beauty, goodness, and accomplishments of this highly gifted woman, have consecrated her memory even more than her elegant poetry. A mausoleum has been dedicated to her virtues in the demesne of Woodstock. It is of Italian statuary marble, executed by Flaxman, in his best manner, and represents her fine form, reclined on a couch in the tranquil sleep of death, whilst attending angels are waiting her resurrection.

W. P. LE FANU was born in Dublin in the year 1774. His ancestors were French refugees. They settled in Dublin on the revocation of the edict of Nantz, and were among those who contributed to the moral and intellectual improvement of the metropolis. His father had four brothers; one was the Rev. Philip Le Fanu, D. D. known as the author of an abridged "History of the Proceedings of the Council of Constance," published in Dublin in 1787; and also as the translator of that excellent work, "Les Lettres de certains Juivs à M. Voltaire." Another is the Rev. Peter Le Fanu, a prebendary of St. Patrick's cathedral, and curate of St. Bride's parish, Dublin. He has been long noticed as one of the most popular preachers of the metropolis, and was the cotemporary and rival, but not the imitator, of Kirwan; without the energy and fire of his great competitor, he possessed more ease and fluency, and is peculiarly persuasive by the colloquial familiarity of his address; he may be said to have founded a school of pulpit oratory, on principles directly opposite to Kirwan, but, like him, he adopted the extemporaneous form of address from the pulpit, and is one of the very few who still retain it in the established church. His other uncles were in the army, and are commemorated in "Drinkwater's Siege of Gibraltar," for their extraordinary escape through the Spanish fleet at the time of the great siege. One of these married a sister of Richard Brinsley Sheridan, who has published "The Sister," a novel, and other works. His father was married to a young lady of Dublin, on whose death he married another sister of Sheridan, eminently distinguished for her literary acquirements. W. P. Le Fanu was the offspring of the first marriage, and was therefore unconnected with the Sheridans by blood, but under his father's roof he imbibed their genius, and seemed to inherit the talents and benevolence of two excellent families, as it were by descent and adoption. Having graduated in Trinity College, he was called to the Irish bar in 1797, where his abilities could aspire to the highest rank, but preferring a pursuit more congenial to his disposition, he early left his profes-

* The editor of Psyche has himself lately paid the debt of nature; and thus Ireland has to lament the loss of another of her few resident patriots. Mr. Tighe represented the County of Wicklow, in the Imperial parliament, at the time of his death. He was the author of "The Statistical History of the County of Kilkenny," thick 8vo. 1799; by far the best of those county histories published under the auspices of the Dublin Society.

sion, and gave up the prospect of fame and emolument to himself to promote the welfare of others; possessed of a small patrimony, and happily of very moderate desires, he devoted all his time and half his fortune in forwarding different plans of public and private charity. He first turned his attention to medicine, and qualified himself by attending a course of lectures in Trinity College, to practise among the poor, which he did to a great extent and with considerable success. In the same spirit he founded schools, established dispensaries, and enlarged his sphere of charitable exertions to a degree that seldom falls to the lot of a private individual, and never perhaps before to one of such a limited income.

As a literary man his character stood very high; his talents were of the first order, and always exerted in the cause of virtue, religion, and humanity. In the year 1798 a pamphlet was published in Dublin, entitled " The Situation to which Ireland is reduced by the Government of Lord Camden." This pamphlet charged Lord Camden with weakness, because he did not go far enough in blood; and Lord Cornwallis with folly, because he rather attempted to reconcile than to destroy; it reprobated the protections granted to repentant rebels as lures held out to deceive, and the invitations to abjure unlawful oaths as incentives to perjury. The design of the pamphlet was to defeat the merciful intentions of Government by rendering abortive the Act of Amnesty, and to extend the system of blood, by cutting off all hope of reconciliation; and notwithstanding the atrocity of its object, such was the temper of the times, that it had gone through six editions without an answer. In this hour of peril and dismay Mr. Le Fanu, then a very young man, was the only person found to reply. His first literary essay was " A Letter addressed to Lord Cornwallis," in which he vindicated the mercy of Government, and exposed the pernicious sophistry of the pamphlet. In a spirited and eloquent sketch he detailed the real causes of the disturbances in Ireland, and conjured Lord Cornwallis, in a pathetic appeal, to exert the unlimited power with which he was vested, " in behalf of those whom oppression had embruted, whom interest had vilified, and who had none to help them." The measures suggested were happily adopted, and tranquillity restored without further effusion of blood. Though capable of the highest works of fancy, he had rather instruct than amuse, and all his writings had for their object something useful: with this view he devoted much of his time to the composition of tracts on popular and familiar subjects, and assisted in the composition of all those which had the same intentions. Among these were " Ledbeatter's Cottage Dialogues." He positively declined having this popular work dedicated to him, though he could not prevent the author from acknowledging her obligations in the preface. But the most useful work of this kind was the " Farmer's Journal," established by him in 1812, and no less novel than necessary in this country. This work is published in Dublin every Saturday, and in order to render it as valuable as possible, he invariably devoted some of its columns to the service of the following day; these Sunday Readings, like the Saturday Papers in the Spectator, were equally admired for the matter, as the manner in which it was conveyed; divested of sectarian enthusiasm, they are plain and rational, but eloquent and pathetic appeals on the best interest of the human soul, periodically circulated, familiarly applied, and judiciously submitted, at the very time when those to whom they are addressed would have leisure and inclination to attend to them. He so highly appreciated the importance of this department, that he specially provided in his will, that it should be conducted after his death by his brother and another competent friend, who should appropriate a certain proportion of the profits to the support of particular charities. It is to be regretted, that some informality has frustrated this request; but it is the intention of these Gentlemen to collect and publish those Sunday Readings in a separate work, as a valuable volume of moral and religious instruction. But while he thus devoted an useful life to the service of his fellows, and delighted and instructed the public, his literary and charitable works were equally unobtrusive; he never suffered his name to appear in either—possessed of singular modesty of nature, he shrunk from any thing like a public display, and studiously declined all occasions of notoriety; but while he fancied that the hand which dispensed the bounty was unseen, and the ability which penned the precept was unknown, his reputation grew with his exertions. There was no man more highly esteemed and admired by the public, and he himself was the only person who did not know it.

In private life his character was no less estimable, his goodness extended to all, but his intimacy was confined to a very few, who highly prized it, possessed of a rare talent for conversation; the originality of his remarks and the playful fancy with which they were accompanied were equally delightful. He saw with a penetrating eye the vices and follies of society, and touched them with a happy raillery. But his satire was of the benevolent kind, and his wit, poignant without causticity, gave only pleasure to the objects of it. In this spirit he published the "Gallery of Portraits," a work founded on Erle's Characters, with much original matter of his own; and from his known talent in this way, many anonymous satirical publications were attributed to him; among these were " the Intercepted Letter from China," " The Metropolis," and " The Familiar Epistles." The first is generally believed by his friends to have issued from his pen, the general satire and playful humour exactly according with his genius and disposition; but the personality of the two latter were abhorrent from the feelings of a man who was never known to wound a present or depreciate an absent individual, by malevolent aspersion.

He had in early life formed a tender attachment, but some circumstance broke off the connection, when it was on the eve of taking place. This deeply affected him, and for some time preyed so upon his mind and body as almost to derange one and destroy the other. After a long seclusion, he returned again to society, and sought for relief by resuming those benevolent pursuits, which this incident had suspended; but his constitution had received a violent shock, and a train of morbid symptoms embittered the few enjoyments he allowed himself. In the month of June 1817, he was seized with an excruciating pain in his head, which terminated fatally in a few days. On examining the cause after his death, a considerable quantity of water was found not only in the ventricles of the brain, but extending down the spine. It was supposed that intensity of thought, and anxiety of mind might have induced a predisposition to generate it. He was buried in St. Peter's church, and in conformity to his last wishes, the few friends who shared his intimacy, attended him to his last home, accompanied by the children of the schools he founded and patronized. But the church was crowded with others, whom good will had attracted to pay the last tribute of respect to his memory. The scene was awfully affecting. The solemn service of the dead was at first interrupted by those bursts of grief which could not be suppressed, while the stifled sob and silent tears of a numerous and mixed congregation were the unbought and genuine expressions of affection for an estimable man, whose public and private loss will not soon be repaired by an equal.

He would never gratify the wishes of his friends, by suffering his likeness to be taken while alive, they were therefore anxious after his death to rescue from oblivion those features which genius and benevolence had impressed with a marked and striking character. A cast of his face was taken a few hours after his decease; but it displayed a melancholy proof how inefficient is any modification of matter to represent immortal qualities. The impression was perfect, and the features accurate, but it did not retain the most distant trace of the man it represented. The mind which had lighted up the countenance and constituted its whole essence had passed to another place, and the clay which remained behind did not seem to belong to him.

GEORGE M'ALISTER was the son of Mr. M'Alister, head porter to Trinity College, Dublin. He was born in 1786, and early bound apprentice to Mr. Ergue, jeweller; but an irresistible desire to discover the art of painting on glass, long extinct in this country, induced him to give up his profession, and apply himself wholly to chemistry. In his pursuit, he succeeded to the utmost extent of his wishes. By unwearied industry and untutored ingenuity, he may be said to have actually rediscovered, by reviving an art, which its professors had carefully concealed, and selfishly carried to the grave with them. On the 21st of December 1807, in the 21st year of his age, he made a public display of the result of his application before an astonished and delighted public; and the Dublin Society, after minute examination, bestowed on him the most flattering testimonial of their approbation. His fame now expanded, and he was engaged in the execution of several works. He finished the great east window for the cathedral of Lismore, and was proceeding with that of Tuam, when intense application to his chemical pursuits brought on an inflammation of the brain, and he died a martyr to his art on June 14th, 1812, at the early age of 26. His last, is his most admired work, and gave a promise of what perfection this ingenuous young man would have brought his art to, had he not been arrested by premature death. He, however, communicated his principles, and instructed his three sisters, who completed the windows of Tuam cathedral on his model, and still preserve and practice their brother's art in his native city.

CITY OF DUBLIN.

Index to Artists and Eminent Natives of Dublin.

Name	page	Name	page	Name	page
Annesley, Lord Anglesea,	1191	Hickey, John,	1213	Peters, Rev. William, R. A.	1209
Archdale, Mervyn,	1200	Hincks, William,	1184	Pilkington, Letitia,	1196
Barber, Mary,	1196	Hodgins, Henry,	1184	Place, George,	1183
Barralet, I. I.	1184	Hollywood, Christopher,	1190	Preston, William,	1210
Barret, Geo. R. A.	1204	Hone, Nat. R. A.	1201	Quadel, M. T.	1181
Barry, James, R. A.	1180	Houston, Richard,	1185	Quin, Walter,	1190
Barry, Lord Santry,	1191	Hunter, Robert,	1181	Reilly,	1182
Barry, Spranger,	1199	Hussey, Phillip,	1181	Roach,	1183
Bathe, William,	1139	Ivory, Thomas,	1187	Roberts, Thomas,	1181
Bickerstaff, Isaac,	1203	Jarvis, John,	1206	Robertson, Walter,	ibid.
Bindon,	1170	Jephson, Robert,	1205	Rosabella,	1183
Bloomfield, I.	1181	Jervas, Charles,	1193	Sadler,	1181
Blood, Thomas,	1191	Kane, Michael,	1181	Sherlock, William,	1186
Boyse, Samuel,	1194	Kauffman, Angelica,	1184	Sheridan, Thomas, A. M.	1198
Brooke, Henry,	1206	King, Giles,	1186	Sheridan, Frances,	1200
Buck, Jonathan,	1184	King, James,	1189	Sheridan, Charles, F.	1207
Burke, Doctor T.	1195	Kelly, Hugh,	1204	Sheridan, Rt. Hon. R. B.	ibid.
Burke, Right Hon. Edmund,	1202	Kelverly,	1181	Smythe, Edward,	1186
Butts, John,	1180	Latham, James,	1179	Southerne, Thomas,	1193
Cadell, Hugh,	1188	Lee,	ibid.	Spooner, Charles,	1185
Cassels, Richard,	1187	Lefanu, Alicia,	1212	Stanihurst, James,	1189
Chambers, Thomas,	1182	Lefanu, William,	1215	Stanihurst, Richard,	ibid.
Charlemont, Earl,	1201	Leland, Thomas, D. D.	1200	Stanley,	1188
Clare, Benjamin,	1188	Loftus, Dudley,	1191	Steel, Sir Richard,	1193
Clayton, Dr. B. of Clogher,	1205	Logan, John,	1188	Stock, Dr. B. of Waterford,	1206
Close, Samuel,	1186	Lucas, Doctor Charles,	1196	Stoker, Bartholomew,	1183
Coghill, Marmaduke,	1194	Lyons, Edward,	1188	Stokes, Gabriel, D. D.	1203
Cooly, Thomas,	1187	M'Alister, George,	1218	Strafford, Robert,	1190
Cunningham, John,	1203	Macardel, James,	1185	Sullivan, Luke,	1185
Degree,	1184	Macklin, Charles,	1194	Swift, Doctor Jonathan,	1193
Denham, Sir John,	1191	Madden, George,	1183	Tate, Nahum,	1192
Dixon, John,	1186	Madden,	1188	Tighe, Mary,	1214
Dodwell, Henry,	1192	Malone, William,	1190	Tresham, Henry, R. A.	1207
Dogget, Thomas,	ibid.	Malton, Thomas, senior,	1182	Trotter, Jonathan,	1182
Ellis, John,	1183	Malton, Thomas, jun.	ibid.	Usher, John,	1189
Ennis,	1180	Manning, Richard,	1179	Usher, James, Archbishop,	1190
Fagan,	1187	Milton, Thomas,	1186	Usher, James,	1199
Fisher, Jonathan,	1184	Molesworth, Robert, Lord,	1192	Vanderheusen,	1182
Fitzsimmons, Henry,	1197	Molloy, Charles,	1197	Vannost,	1156
Flecknoe, Richard,	1192	Molyneaux, William,	1192	Verpoyle, Simon,	1186
Fry, Thomas,	1197	Molyneaux, Sir Thomas,	1193	Walker, Cooper I.	1213
Gast, Archdeacon,	1197	Mossop, William,	1188	Walmsley, Thomas,	1184
Gardiner, William,	1213	Mountstephen, Charles,	1187	Ware, Sir James,	1190
Gentleman, Francis,	1201	Mullins, George,	1180	West, senior,	1179
Grose, Francis,	1183	O'Hara, Kane,	1205	West, R. T. junior,	1180
Hamilton, Hugh, D.D. Bishop of Ossory,	1202	Omar, Rowland,	1182	Wheatley, Francis,	1182
		O'Tool, St. Lawrence,	1189	Williams, Solomon,	1182
Hamilton, Hugh,	1205	Parnel, Thomas,	1194	Wilson, Jeffery,	1183
Havard, William,	1196	Pearson, James,	1185	Woffington, Margaret,	1198
Hayley, Robert,	1180	Pembridge, Christopher,	1189	Wogan, Thomas,	1182
Hencey, Charles,	1186	Peicy,	1187	Young, James,	1189
Hickey,	1183	Perrot, John,	1190		

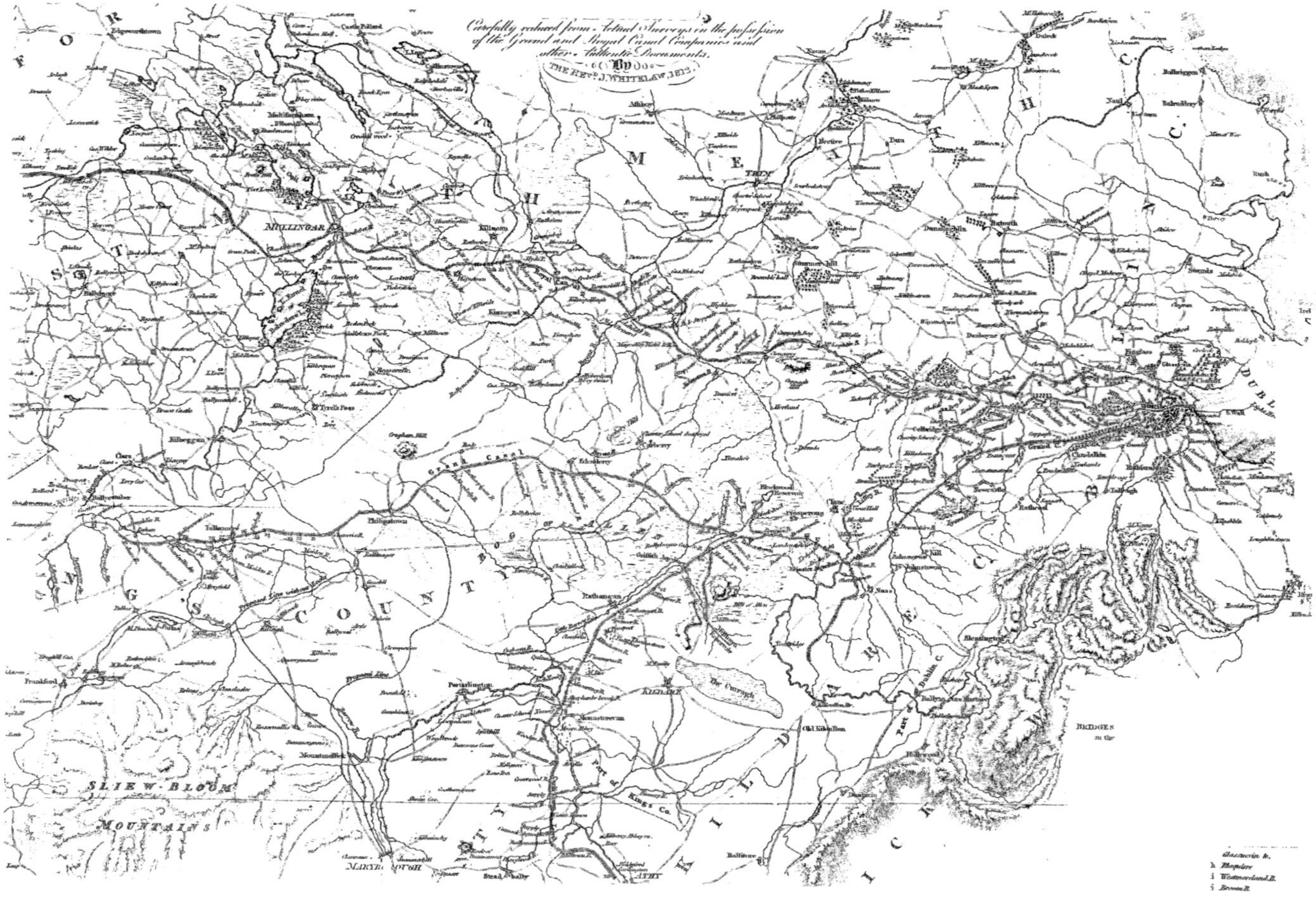

ENVIRONS.

THE ENVIRONS OF DUBLIN are exceedingly curious and interesting. The country, in a circuit of twelve miles from the Circular Road, abounds in those objects which compose the grand and beautiful features of landscape; but it is not intended here to 'enter into a description of this diversified scenery, other important objects demand more particular attention—public works and establishments of great magnitude, which, though comprised within the Environs, centre in the City itself, are intimately connected with its present state of improvements and commerce, and are constructed with a view to its future grandeur and prosperity. Of these, the foremost are—

THE GRAND AND ROYAL CANALS.

As these canals both terminate in the metropolis, from whence they diverge, so as to connect it with a very considerable and fertile tract of the interior of the kingdom, they promise to be, in a very considerable degree, the common medium of prosperity to both; to the latter they offer an easy and inexpensive access to an unfailing market, and thus invigorate the hand of industry; to the former they promise, not only an abundant supply of the necessaries of life for its consumption, but, under proper regulations, the materials of an extensive export; and thus promote both its comfort and opulence: a general view therefore of these two great conduits of plenty and wealth seems naturally to form a part of our plan.

In every continent and island the soil, by the wise arrangement of Providence, ascends towards the centre, thus facilitating the descent of its waters, which would otherwise stagnate and form great lakes or pestilential marshes: where the ascent is sudden, its rivers must be too rapid for the purposes of navigation, and if the central elevations form, as it often happen, continued chains, they render the union of distant tracts by navigable canals difficult or impracticable: in this point of view Ireland has been highly favoured; the descent from the interior to the surrounding sea is almost every where gradual, and hence its rivers are generally so gentle, as to invite the industry of man to remove their few obstructions, and thus improve what nature seems to offer with a liberal hand; and it is singular that in this island there is no elevation that merits the appellation of a chain; its mountains are so disposed in groups, that while they diversify its scenery and amply supply the sources of its rivers, they offer no obstruction to navigation by projecting ridges, and future canals may circle round them to enrich the plains which they shelter and adorn.

When the line of greatest elevation runs nearly through the centre of an island or continent, intersecting it longitudinally, the course of its largest river seldom exceeds half its breadth; of this an obvious instance occurs in Great Britain, in which the courses of the Thames, Severn, and Trent, are not computed to exceed 150 miles each, though they water that highly favoured island where its breadth is greatest and not short of 300 miles. In Ireland, where its great elevations, as already observed, are dispersed in groups, some have been placed by the hand of Providence on or near its coast line, and emitting rivers which pursue an opposite direction, these, before they reach the sea, have room to acquire a magnitude, which, relatively to the extent of the island, is truly surprising: such is precisely the case with the Shannon, which, issuing from a lake embosomed in a group of mountains distant not more than ten miles from the bay of Sligo, flows to the southward, and before it is lost in the Atlantic, runs a course of 180 miles in an island whose greatest breadth does not exceed 150. This noble river, issuing from an extensive lake, with an abundant stream, seems as if exempted from the imbecility of youth, and is at its very source considerable; flowing to the southward through a spacious and fertile plain, and with a calm and steady course, that justifies its name, which implies the gentle river, it expands in its progress into lakes, irregular in their forms and beautifully wooded; of these, two are very considerable; Lough Ree, or the Royal Lake, occupying nearly the centre of the kingdom, and interspersed with above seventy islands; and Lough Derg, or the Red Lake, farther south, invironed by the most beautiful scenery: this fine river, which waters ten counties, and which, by the removal of a few inconsiderable obstructions, would be navigable to its parent lake, receives at Limerick, sixty miles from its mouth, ships of 500 tons, and in the last thirty miles of its course resembles a fine arm of the sea, or rather one

THE CITY OF DUBLIN.

continued harbour, varying in breadth from one to nine miles, of easy access, well sheltered, free from any hidden danger, and capable of receiving any number of the largest ships of the line.

The uniting this fine river to the capital by a navigable canal, was an object of great importance, and the nature of the intervening ground seemed to encourage the idea, by holding out the fairest prospect of success to those who should undertake a work of such national advantage. The spine or line of highest elevation of this part of Ireland passes between Dublin and the Shannon, and is in reality only the summit of an extensive plain, from which rivers diverge in almost all directions to the surrounding ocean. To the eastward run the tributary waters of the Boyne, which reaches the Irish sea: the Barrow takes a southern direction, with a gentle navigable stream, encreased by its sister rivers the Nore and Suire: while the Inny and Brusna, issuing from considerable lakes on or near the summit level, flow to the westward and mingle with the Shannon. From the capital to the summit level of this plain is an ascent of from 200 to 300 feet, and from thence there is a less considerable descent to the navigable parts of the Barrow and Shannon. A finer field of exertion could scarce present itself; but though the idea of affecting this union seems to have occured as early as the administration of Lord Strafford, yet every effort to have it executed was, until a few years since, feeble and ineffectual. " From the first settlement of the English in this country, (says the ingenious Mr. Griffith,) the Government appears to have been disposed to take advantage of the facility with which inland navigation might be extended in this island, and our Statute Books are crowded with laws intended to encourage this wise and important improvement; but the general ignorance that prevailed, the unsettled state of the country, the want of public credit, the spirit of jobbing, together with the shackled state of our commerce and legislature, repressed the ardour of every advance towards national improvement; and these laws, like may other specious regulations for public benefit, served but to mock our wretchedness."

Parliament finding that there was neither capital nor spirit of adventure sufficient among the people to accomplish the great works they had projected, at length appointed Commissioners for promoting and carrying on inland navigation in Ireland, and provided them with a fund sufficient, if well directed; these gentlemen, incompetent to the discharge of a trust that required great knowledge of the business, with unremitting and minute superintendance, instead of confining their attention to one great object at a time, divided it among not less than twenty-three different works, not one of which, after an expenditure of nearly £600,000. in fifty-five years, was completely finished.

At length, the only mode likely to procure that unremitting attention which alone can insure success, was sought for in that most powerful stimulus—self-interest. Our various inland navigations have been accordingly vested as properties in the hands of associated companies, upon certain conditions, and under certain restrictions, and to these have been granted one-third of their expenditure, as a bounty from the public. "In England," says the ingenious author already quoted, "this bounty is not demanded or even thought of, because canals there are the effect of internal wealth and population, of an improved state of agriculture, manufactures, and commerce; in Ireland we must look to inland navigation as an efficient *cause* of producing, or at least as the best means of facilitating, those happy effects: in England it is almost impossible to extend a canal ten miles in any direction, without intersecting two, three, or more populous manufacturing towns; in *Ireland it may be expected*, that in the process of a few years, manufacturing towns *may* be raised on the banks of our navigable waters."

This plan promises the most beneficial effects both to the undertakers and the public, and with respect to the Grand Canal, has been attended with complete success. This line was originally commenced in the year 1755, by the Corporation for promoting and carrying on an Inland navigation in Ireland. In 1772 a subscription was opened, and the subscribers were incorporated by the name of "*The Company of Undertakers of the Grand Canal;*" and the indefatigable and well directed perseverance with which these gentlemen have conducted the works, has enabled them, after combating a variety of difficulties, to conduct this great work to an happy termination, by uniting the capital both to the Shannon and Barrow by still-water navigations; the former extending sixty-one miles and three quarters, and the latter forty-miles and a half, Irish measure.

The harbour, where this work commences is situated near James's-street, in the western extremity of the capital, from whence it ascends seventeen miles, by four double and fourteen single locks, to the summit level, which is 202 feet four inches above the level of the harbour in James's-street, and

THE CITY OF DUBLIN.

261 feet ten inches above the tide water in the Liffey. From this level, and at the distance of twenty and a half Irish miles from Dublin, the canal divides into two branches; by one we descend 103 feet half an inch in twenty-two and a quarter miles, to the Barrow at Athy, and through two double and nine single locks, with one ascending single lock of eight feet six inches, at Monasterevan; by the other we descend 163 feet eleven inches in forty-one miles, to the Shannon, at Shannon Harbour, about two miles northward of Banagher, and through one double and seventeen single locks; the double locks varying in elevation from thirteen feet four inches to nineteen feet seven inches, and the single locks from four feet three inches to thirteen feet four inches.

The Barrow is navigable from Athy, the termination of the Grand Canal, to its mouth in the fine harbour of Waterford, and from thence navigation extends up the Suire to Waterford and Carrick. The navigation of the Shannon from Athlone to Portumna belongs to the Grand Canal Company, and the communication along that river is at present open from Shannon Harbour to Limerick and the Atlantic ocean, in one direction; and to Carrick, a few miles from its source, in another.

The dimensions of this noble canal are on a large scale: its width at the top is forty-five feet, at the bottom twenty-five feet; the depth of water six feet in the body of the canal and five feet on the sills of the lock gates, and the locks are generally seventy feet long, fourteen wide, and calculated to pass boats of sixty tons in from five to two and a half minutes.

A spacious artificial harbour has been finished, adjoining to the mouth of the Liffey, with which it communicates by three sea locks. This harbour, which is one of the noblest works of its kind in Europe, covers an area of twenty-five English acres, has sixteen feet of water, and is capable of containing 600 ships: it consists of two arms at right angles with each other; the western, about 1600 feet long and 300 wide, is passed by a handsome draw-bridge; and adjoining to the northern branch, which is 1700 feet long by 360 wide, are three excellent graving docks for vessels of different dimensions; the whole is surrounded by spacious wharfs and stores, and is executed in the best manner and of the best materials. From this harbour a canal of communication leads, in a semicircular form, round the south side of the city to the Grand Canal, which it enters, after a course of three miles, immediately below the first lock; this is crossed by twelve bridges, consisting of single beautiful elliptic arches, over which are the approaches to the city, and these having been secured by palisades during the late unfortunate rebellion, the whole formed a line of circumvallation round the capital on the south, and sufficiently secured it from any sudden attack on that side. From the harbour you ascend fifty-nine feet six inches, in a distance of about one mile and a half, and through seven single locks to Portobello, from whence to the Grand Canal and the harbour in James's-street, is one level without a lock. The remoteness of this last from the central parts of the city, with which it communicates by streets, in some parts narrow and embarrassed, rendering it an ineligible station for the Company's passage boats, they were, in July 1807, judiciously removed to Portobello, where a harbour, and graving docks for building and repairing boats, have been constructed on the best plan, and an elegant hotel erected for the accommodation of passengers. This edifice, which does great credit to the taste and judgment of the company's architect and assistant engineer, Mr. Colbourne, is spacious and convenient; it is three stories high, with a handsome portico in front, supporting a platform enclosed with an elegant iron balustrade, which opens from the coffee-room, and commands a fine view of a charming country, richly decorated with numerous villas, and finely terminated by the Wicklow mountains at the distance of about five miles. The portico is of the Doric order, and its columns, with the other ornamental stone work, were brought along the line, a distance of nearly forty-five miles, from the Company's quarries at Tullamore, in the King's county; the stone is of a bluish tinge, of a good grain, and seems excellent.

The summit level of the Grand Canal is amply supplied from the Milltown and Blackwood rivers, which are branches of the Barrow, and cuts have been made to take in their waters; one, of nearly five miles, of which three and a half are navigable, terminating at Milltown, near the Curragh of Kildare; the other, of nearly two miles, terminating at the Blackwood reservoir. Of these supplies the Milltown river is by far the most considerable, as it issues from abundant and perennial springs, which probably have their sources in the bowels of that extensive group of mountains, which occupies part of the counties of Dublin and Wicklow; so abundant indeed is this river, that at Milltown, not more than a mile from its remotest, spring a considerable bolting-mill heretofore received from it an ample and unfailing supply during the whole of the year.

THE CITY OF DUBLIN.

Before the Grand Canal divides, it may be called the main trunk, and passes through Sallins and Robertstown, leaving Lucan, Leixlip, Cellbridge, and Clane, all on the Liffey, at a small distance to the northward; and to the southward, Newcastle, Johnstown, and Naas, with which last it communicates by a navigable lateral branch, executed by the Kildare Canal Company, and reaching at present within one mile of Kilcullen bridge on the Liffey, from whence it will probably be extended into the county of Wicklow; it crosses the Kilmainham, Esker, and little Morell rivers, over aqueducts of a single arch; about twelve miles and a half from Dublin takes in the Morell, which affords such an abundance of wholesome water, as enables the Directors to give an ample supply of that indispensable necessary of life to the capital, and at the distance of fifteen miles passes over the Liffey, on an aqueduct bridge of five arches, with two others, and a circular tunnel to carry off superfluous waters, in extraordinary floods. This admirable work, which is seventy-eight feet longer than the Pont de Cesse, the largest aqueduct on the Royal Canal of Languedoc, is built in five feet water, in a river subject to violent floods, that often rise to fifteen feet, and of course required great care in the construction: the foundation was accordingly sunk seven feet through sand, gravel and large stones, to a firm substrate of strong blue clay, and notwithstanding the difficulties necessarily attending such a work, was passable by boats in eighteen months, from the day of laying the foundation; it is constructed on the most ingenious and permanent principles, cost £7500., and does great credit to the architect.

The branch to the Barrow visits Rathangan, Monasterevan, Vicarstown, and Athy, leaving Kildare to the east, and Portarlington, Mountmellick, and Maryborough, at some distance to the west; while the branch to the Shannon passes by Phillipstown and Tullamore, leaving Edinderry, with which it communicates by a lateral navigable cut of one mile, to the north, and approximating on the south to Frankford, Birr, and Banagher, two miles to the northward of which it terminates in the Shannon.

Two miles from the Leinster aqueduct, seventeen nearly from Dublin, and at the commencement of the present summit level, is the hill of Downings, consisting of loamy gravel, through which the canal has been carried almost two English miles, at a depth of forty feet below its summit, and of course at a very great expense. At the termination of this hill the canal enters the Bog of Allen, the largest in this island: this, like every other bog, consists of decayed vegetable substances, and as the principal agent in the formation of bogs is stagnant water, it occupies that situation precisely most likely to produce it; a level space with scarce any descent to carry off its waters, and where every stream of course creeps on with a lazy current: it was originally covered with wood, and at present, wherever it has been opened or bored, timber has been found at various depths. Of this timber the lowest stratum is generally oak, the others fir, and on both the marks of the hatchet or fire were frequently visible; this, when felled, whether by design or accident, not being removed, naturally promoted a stagnation of the springs and rivers that watered this tract, and thus became the chief efficient cause of the bog itself; and it is an extraordinary fact, that the original soil has completely disappeared, being no longer distinguishable from the bog, which every where rests on a bed of gravel, without any intermediate stratum of clay or mould.

Here the Company encountered difficulties almost insuperable, from the redundant moisture and want of firmness in the soil; and in consequence of the drainage occasioned by opening the canal, the surface sunk so considerably, that objects beyond the bog, which were formerly concealed by its interposition from the gentlemen's seats in its vicinity, became suddenly visible. The bog of Ballyteague, particularly, between the twentieth and twenty-first locks, sunk above thirty feet below its original level: thus tracts formerly deemed inaccessible, afford at present coarse pasture or fine meadow ground; the hand of industry is encouraged to new exertions, and at no very distant period tillage will, probably, cover what may now be considered only as a vast turbary to the city of Dublin.

The turf of this bog is various in quality; near the surface it is light, porous, and of swift combustion; that taken from a sufficient depth is heavier, and good. A boat containing about 200 kishes pays a toll to the Company of about £6., and is brought to market by a single horse and two men, but in consequence of combination and other circumstances, it is sold at a price which renders it, even when of the best quality, much more expensive than foreign coal; which circumstance, with the room required for stowing such bulky fuel, must exclude every idea of its becoming a sufficient substitute for that essential article: it is however a matter of great convenience and comfort to the poor of this capital, who, too indigent or too improvident to lay up coal, can purchase turf in the smallest

THE CITY OF DUBLIN.

quantities, even so low as a halfpenny worth. The Company have shewn a laudable desire to prevent combination, and at the same time to diminish the expense of carriage of that article from the boat. In former years, fleets of turf boats, if the expression may be used, lay in the canal, above the harbour in James's-street, waiting for berths, or quay room at that harbour; then, the only market for turf on or adjoining to the canal; in which station, their unemployed crews became a dangerous banditti; but such fleets are now seldom, if ever, to be seen; the company having, partly by bounties, induced, and partly by judicious regulations compelled, a distribution of that trade along the before mentioned circular line compassing the south side of the city, where, at convenient stations, and generally where the principal avenues to the city cross the canal, markets for the sale of turf have been established; by this division of the market, combination has been rendered more difficult, and the expense of carriage to a very considerable part of the purchasers, has been materially reduced; and it may be thought worthy of observation, that the bounties and regulations, without which this arrangement of the trade, at first much resisted, could not have been accomplished, are now considered as being no longer necessary; such division of the market having not only greatly increased the general consumption of the article, but much accelerated the sale of each boat load.

The eye of the passenger, however familiar with the wretched hovels of the poor of this country, must be immediately struck with the singular construction of those which he will meet with in the Bog of Allen. To a moderate distance on each side of the canal the bog is let in small lots to turf cutters, who, for convenience and the facility of guarding their property from theft, take up their residence on the spot, however dreary and uncomfortable. The first care of one of these, is to seek a dry bank above the influence of floods; and here he excavates his future habitation, to such a depth that little more is visible than the roof; this is sometimes covered with scanty thatch, but oftener with turf pared from the bog, which, as the herbage is upwards, so perfectly assimilates with the surrounding scenery, that the eye would pass over it unnoticed, were it not undeceived by a number of children sallying from a hole on one side, accompanied frequently by the cat, the pig, and the goat; the joint inmates of the hovel, and sometimes a cloud of smoke, which finding no other vent, issues through the roof, which from its slight texture, is every where pervious to it, betrays the habitation.

The wretched manner in which the lower class of the inhabitants of this country is lodged, has been long a subject of reproach to us, as a civilized people, and it must be acknowledged, that rack rents and unfeeling landlords are among the efficient causes of this evil : that it may however be sometimes traced to other sources, is evident from a contemplation of the present scene ; the proprietors of these hovels earn an easy subsistence; nay, some are comparatively opulent, and one was pointed out to me by a person of credibility, who had saved above one hundred pounds, and yet his habitation, the only one he possessed, was perfectly similar to that of his neighbours. To what must we impute this seeming inconsistency? Not surely to any peculiar attachment of an Irish peasant to inconvenience and dirt, but to the neglected state of his mind ; to the want of an education, that raising him above that semi-barbarism which now marks his character, would give him a taste for the conveniences and comforts of life.

This vast level supplies but few objects on which the eye, fatigued by its sameness, can repose : on the south, the high grounds of the isle of Allen present some pleasing scenes of intermingled plantations, pasture, and corn fields : to the east the Wicklow mountains appear melting into the horizon; while to the north and west the distant hills of Carbery and Croghan start, like elevated islands, from the dreary waste, and are visible at a great distance : the intelligent traveller, however, will find amusement of a superior kind in reflecting, while he passes along the line, on the wonders which human ingenuity, thus well directed, can perform, and in anticipating, in idea, the seats that may arise, the plantations that may flourish, and the harvests that may wave, at no very distant period, over tracts now consigned to heath and sterility.*

Near the bog of Ballyteague, the canal crosses the Milltown river over the Griffith aqueduct of three arches, with perforated cylinders, built on piles and counter arches, in soft bog and marl ; and at Monastrevan it falls into the channel of the Barrow, from whence ascending to a second summit of nearly ten miles, called the Cardington level, by one lock of eight feet

---

* The banks of the Grand Canal, for about six miles from its termination in the harbour, are planted with rows of fine elms. There are also parts of the lins, here and there, very partially planted.

THE CITY OF DUBLIN. 1231

six inches, it receives an ample supply from the Anianagh and Stradbally rivers, and again joins the Barrow at Athy. Here a boat regularly attends the arrival of the Company's packet, to receive such of the passengers as are bound to Carlow, ten* miles lower down the river: the voyage along the Barrow to this neat and thriving town is delightful in favourable weather, as it is through a beautifully diversified country, rising boldly from the banks of the river, and richly ornamented with intermingled seats, tillage, and pasture.

Five hundred and eighty-seven boats, mostly capable of conveying sixty tons, have been already built for the trade on the Grand Canal, and the number of passage boats now plying on it is ten. The Company, whose capital stock has been lately increased to £400,000., have expended above one million and a half of their private property on this extensive work, since their incorporation in 1772. For many years they made no dividend; they did, at one time, receive six per cent. per annum, and their income was supposed to be in a progressive state of prosperity.

The ROYAL CANAL Company of Subscribers was incorporated by a charter from his Majesty in 1789, and had additional powers granted afterwards by the legislature. The object of this Company, like that of the undertakers of the Grand Canal, was a still-water navigation from the capital to the same noble river the Shannon, which has been emphatically called the grand artery of the kingdom; but as the latter pointed their line towards the middle and lower parts of it, so the former have directed theirs towards its source, where the rich treasures of coal and iron, which encircle Lough Allen, seem to offer an ample recompense to their spirited exertions. This canal is on a large scale, being forty-two feet wide at the surface, twenty-four at the bottom, and with locks and a depth of water calculated for boats of from eighty to one hundred tons burden. Like the Grand Canal it has two terminations in the capital by a short branch of about half a mile; it communicates with a spacious harbour adjoining Brunswick-street and Broad-stone, the station of the Company's boats both for the trade and passengers, into which it enters by a noble aqueduct built over the great north-western road, and consisting of one arch of thirty feet span, and fifteen high, with two smaller side arches for foot passengers.

* The miles and distances on the canal line are Irish measurement, (except otherwise stated,) which are to English as eleven to fourteen.

This, which is executed in a masterly manner, with the best materials, does great credit to the architects, Messrs. Millar and Roddery, is plain and neat without any superfluous ornament, and possesses a solidity that seems to bid defiance to the hand of time.*

The other branch of one mile and a half terminates, after a descent of sixty-two feet, through four locks, in the spacious docks in the North Lots, which communicates with the Liffey to the eastward of the Custom-house, by sea locks capable of admitting ships of one hundred and fifty tons.

From the union of these two branches the canal passes near Lucan and Leixlip, crosses the Rye water, a tributary stream of the Liffey, on an aqueduct of one arch, supporting a vast bank of earth, on the summit of which the canal and track-ways pass, at an elevation of near 100 feet above the river; visits Carton, Maynooth, and Killcock, crosses the Boyne on a plain but elegant aqueduct of three arches, of forty feet span each, passes near Kinnegad, with which it will communicate by a lateral branch of two and a half English miles, and circling round Mullingar, which is on its summit level, terminates at Coolnahay, about forty-six miles to the westward of that town, and fifty-three and a half Irish, or above sixty-eight English miles from its commencement at the docks, contiguous to the Liffey. From the spring tide high water mark in these docks, the ascent to the summit level is 307 feet, through twenty-five locks, of which eleven are double and fourteen single. The ascent is at first rapid, requiring eleven locks in five miles and a half, afterwards they are less frequent, the thirteenth level being six miles, the eighteenth sixteen miles, and the summit level above twelve miles.

Before this canal reached the summit level the supply of water was so scanty that boats could not ply in the summer months; at present, however, all apprehensions on that head have vanished, as Lough Ouil, adjacent to the summit level, affords such an abundance as to enable the Company, after attending to their own wants, to *contract* with the corporation of Dublin to supply the pipes in the north eastern part of the city with excellent water.

* On the front is the following inscription:
FOSTER AQUEDUCT.
Serus in cœlum redeas diuque per ora, &c.
This was intended as a compliment to the Right Hon. John Foster, but by an unlucky position of the name and the Inscription, the words " serus in cœlum redeas" are addressed to the aqueduct.

This singular lake, situated in the county of Westmeath, on the highest part of the great plain extending, as before observed, from the Irish sea to the Shannon, is about eighteen inches higher than the summit level of the Royal Canal; it is of considerable extent, being six miles long and one broad, and spreading over on area of 1785 Irish, or 2856 English acres. It is environed by a fine fertile country, interspersed with country villas, and appears to be fed by copious springs, as it receives only one inconsiderable rivulet, and yet emits two rivers that run from it in opposite directions: one of these, known to the natives by the name of the Silver Hand,* issues from its north-western extremity, and falls, after a short but rapid course of one mile, into an expansion of the Inny, called Lough Iron; the other, denominated the Golden Hand, flows with a gentle stream from its south-eastern point, visits Mullingar, and is soon lost in Lough Innel, or Belvidere Lake, from which issues the Brustna: hence it happens that Lough Ouil, with the rivers Inny, Brustna, and Shannon, completely insulate a considerable portion of Westmeath, Longford, and King's counties, a geographical singularity, which though frequently represented in maps, seldom occurs in nature. The property of these two rivers, the Golden and Silver Hands, has been purchased by the Company; who, to secure as ample a supply of water as possible, have cut off the latter, and dammed up the former, which feeds their summit level so as to keep the lake always full to its winter level; and with these precautions it is supposed that no canal in Europe can boast a more abundant reservoir.

From Coolnahay, its present termination, this canal is to be carried across the Inny and through the county of Longford to the Shannon, at or near Farmonbury, a distance of about twenty-two miles, and with a descent requiring probably about fifteen locks; two lines, one direct by Ballinalack, Edgeworthstown, and Newtown-Forbes to Rookey-bridge; and another more southerly, more circuitous, and through a much worse country, have been already surveyed; but the Directors have, with a very justifiable degree of caution, suspended their final determination until further surveys are made, which it is anxiously hoped may obviate such difficulties as have occurred, and be the means of bringing this important work to a happy termination.

* See Description of the County of Westmeath, by Sir Henry Piers, written in 1682. The Silver and Golden Hands are appellations not at present known to the inhabitants of the vicinity.

THE HISTORY OF

Some persons have expressed an opinion, that the line of this canal was not judiciously laid out in all its parts, and that by a direction more northerly at its commencement many difficulties and much expense might have been avoided, and particularly, that incurred by the aqueduct over the Rye, amounting to above £30,000. On the justice of this opinion, which can be ascertained by an actual survey alone, it is not possible to decide, but it is certain that the Company have encountered, and by persevering energy surmounted vast difficulties in the execution of their plan. Near Dublin the canal is cut through a solid rock,* about thirty feet below the surface, for a space of a mile and a half; a similar obstacle opposed its progress near Mullingar, and in the vicinity of the Boyne, and in many other parts the canal and trackways are supported for miles together on the summit of an embankment raised twenty feet above the adjacent country, in order to preserve its level. The preservation of such an embankment necessarily requires great care and attention, the Company are therefore constantly employed in adding to its breadth and solidity, and as the accidental bursting of the bank must, especially in very long levels, be productive of serious consequences, stop gates have been constructed in the most convenient situations, to limit the extension of the evil as much as possible.

The Royal Canal, in its proposed extension, must, as already observed, cross the Inny, the upper part of which flowing generally with a deep and placid stream, may, on the removal of a very few obstructions, be considered as a lateral extension of the navigation through the lake of Donore and some other less considerable expansions, to its source in Lough Sheelin; this last, fed by some considerable streams, is a fine large expanse of water, environed by the three counties of Cavan, Meath, and Westmeath; it is interspersed with some islands decorated with ruined castles; its shores are adorned by intermingled pastures, cultivated fields, and gentlemen's seats; and future surveys will ascertain, it is hoped, the facility of uniting it by a navigable cut to Lough Gawna, the source of the Earne, and only a few miles distant. Donore Lake also is a

---

* The quality of the rock is limestone, not regularly stratified but curling together, so as to form a texture of most stubborn tenacity, which renders it necessary to proceed with excavation, by blasting so constantly as to consume a most extraordinary quantity of gunpowder.

THE CITY OF DUBLIN.

beautiful expansion of water, but gradually narrowing to the southeastward, where it terminates near the foot of Knock Eyné, whose lofty summit commands an interesting view, not only of its cultivated and embellished shores, but of the surrounding country to a vast extent.

A cut of a few miles only, commencing at Mullingar, would unite the Royal Canal to Lough Innel, or Belvidere Lake, one of the most beautiful of our Irish lakes, and of considerable extent: it emits the river Brustna, and is situated in a fertile country, well cultivated, and decorated with numerous villas and plantations; to this lake the Grand Canal Company are meditating a lateral branch, and we may entertain a hope, that a desirable communication will be thus opened between our two great inland navigations.

The Royal Canal Company have also in contemplation a lateral branch to the Shannon at Athlone, to issue from the main trunk.

The Company's works are every where executed in the best manner; but their plan being as yet incomplete, they have not hitherto made any dividend.

From the completion of these canals, not only the tract in their immediate vicinity, but the neighbouring country to a considerable extent, has already derived many essential advantages, which are in a continued state of progression; large tracts of bog have been reclaimed and improved, and lands already in an improved state, have almost every where, along the line of the Grand Canal, risen to more than double their former value: by both lines flour, corn, potatoes, and other provisions, with native timber, turf, stone, bricks, lime, sand, gravel, &c. are conveyed with safety, cheapness, and expedition to the metropolis, which sends in return coal, culm for burning lime, bricks, manure, foreign timber, iron, ale, spirits, groceries, and such other necessaries as render the intercourse between the city and country of reciprocal benefit: to these advantages we must add, the many comforts and conveniencies which the traveller finds, by the establishment of clean and commodious passage-boats, constantly moving along the various lines, passing at stated hours from stage to stage, uninterrupted by any change of weather, and with a rapidity and security, that, added to the reasonable terms of accommodation, afford one of the most pleasant, comfortable, and expeditious modes of travelling to be found in any part of the world; of these there are at present ten plying on the Shannon and Barrow lines of the Grand Canal, and with such expedition, that the passage from Dublin to Shannon Harbour, sixty-three Irish, or above eighty English miles, is performed in one day, between the hours of four in the morning and ten in the evening, and at an expense, exclusive of entertainment, of one guinea for the first cabin, and 14s. 1d. for the second; the passage to Athy, of above fifty-four English miles, requires twelve hours and thirty-five minutes, and the intermediate stages are performed in periods nearly in the same proportion to their distances. The Royal Canal as yet employs only four passage-boats, and the passage to Mullingar, of forty-two Irish, or fifty-three and a half English miles, is performed in thirteen hours and a half, at an expense, exclusive of entertainment, of 12s. 6d. for the first, and 7s. 7d. for the second cabin. In the passage-boats on both canals, the entertainment is excellent, and the prices of every article are, to prevent imposition, stated in tables hung up in the cabins;* there is no charge for attendance, and to preserve sobriety and decency of manners, the use of spirits is prohibited, and no individual allowed more than one pint of wine.

The present unparalleled state of Europe forces on us a system of defence in some degree new: exclusive of a powerful navy, a considerable military force must be kept on foot in both islands, and so stationed, as to be able to move with rapidity to any point of the surrounding coast that may be assailed. Athlone on the Shannon, and nearly the centre of this island, seems to have been judiciously selected, as an important military station for this purpose; and the facility and expedition with which, not only military stores, but an army itself, can be carried along the line of the Grand Canal between this central point and the capital, must place it in a new and important point of view, particularly when we consider that the troops so conveyed, will arrive at their destination not encumbered with

---

* In justification of the offensive practice of mulcting passengers with gratuities to servants, or, in other words, compelling them to pay the servants' wages, it has been alleged, that it is a tie on their conduct, and being voluntary, may be given or withheld as their assiduity merits; but besides that custom has now so sanctioned the usage, as not to leave it optional, the practice of the canal boats is a proof that it is not necessary. The attendants are no where more civil and obliging, without expecting or receiving the smallest remuneration from the passengers. It was intended to introduce a similar regulation into the hotels connected with the canals, but by some inattention, the attendants are here suffered to violate it, and the traveller is teazed with the exaction of this undefined charge, as much as at an ordinary inn.

baggage, or fatigued by forced marches, but fresh and fit for immediate action. This central station communicates also with Limerick by the Shannon, and with Waterford by the Barrow; the projected line from the Suck at Ballynasloe to Galway, will connect it with that town; and by the upper part of the Shannon, troops may, on removing the few remaining obstructions in that fine river, be landed within twelve miles of Sligo: actual surveys have ascertained the facility of uniting the Shannon to the Earne and its beautiful lakes; thus opening a communication between Athlone and Ballyshannon, and navigable lines from Lough Earne to the Foyle and Blackwater, would extend the same, with many other signal benefits, to the remote and important cities of Londonderry and Belfast. These capabilities of defence are worthy of consideration, and that this statement is not a mere ideal project, is evinced by experience: before the rebellion in 1798, vast quantities of military stores were conveyed to different parts of the kingdom, by the Grand Canal; and when the French landed at Killala, the Marquis Cornwallis embarked a considerable number of troops at Dublin and Salins, and proceeded with them fifty-six English miles to Tullamore, where they arrived in a few hours, fresh and fit to-proceed on their march to Athlone.*

The advantages thus mutually resulting to the country and metropolis, from this system of inland navigation, are obviously both great and numerous; there are, however, two considerations of such superior interest, as to merit peculiar attention, viz. the certainty of our being thus able to afford Great Britain a supply of corn and other provisions, at all times, equal to her greatest demand, and the high probability that the capital may be supplied, through the same channel, with fuel from our own collieries.

Every man, who wishes the prosperity of the British empire, must feel an anxious solicitude to see the bands of amity between the sister islands drawn as close as possible, and the more external dangers threaten, the more foreign connections become precarious and delusive, the dearer should this principle of union be to the heart, and the more ready should we be to

---

* The sudden return of peace, since the above was written, has affected, in some measure, the concerns of the Canals, as well as those of almost every establishment. The effects, however, can only be temporary; their utility, as contributing not a little to promote the prosperity of the British empire, is unquestionable.

seek for national independence and prosperity in our own internal resources. One of the principal, one of the most indispensable of these resources under the existing circumstances of Europe, is the promoting the agriculture of Ireland. Great Britain, in consequence of her increased population, and of the number of hands employed in her manufactures, which within the last half century have been improved to such a degree, as to excite the astonishment and envy of Europe, is no longer able to grow corn for her own consumption, and is, of course, under the necessity of importing what may supply her wants, by long and tedious voyages from the countries round the Baltic and the Mediterranean, or from North America: countries that may be hostile or unfriendly, and from which such supply may be precarious; the annual average value of grain imported into Great Britain in the three years preceding 1799, was £2,714,406.

This immense sum may be considered as an annual bounty given by Great Britain,* to improve the agriculture, and encrease the population and resources of countries, in whose welfare the British empire can have no interest, and is, in reality, only contributing to raise future navies for nations, whose object it is to rival her commerce and subvert her power: how erroneous must be the policy of continuing dependant on those nations for so large a supply of the essential necessaries of life, which may be raised at home? Ireland possesses vast tracts of land inviting cultivation by its extraordinary fertility, and requiring nothing but the hand of industry, to enable her to yield ample stores, not only for her own internal consumption, but for every want of her sister island. The wisdom, and it may be added, the necessity, of withdrawing these tracts from pasturage, and appropriating them to tillage, is obvious to every enlightened mind, and accordingly the Imperial Parliament, by the act lately passed, to permit the free interchange of every species of grain between Great Britain and Ireland, holds out the greatest encouragement for promoting this salutary plan; all therefore that seems to remain to be done towards its completion, is to procure an easy and cheap conveyance of the produce of the fertile tracts alluded to, to the capital, from whence it may be exported to the sister kingdom: this can be done effectually by canals alone, and

* See an excellent pamphlet written on the great utility of an extensive plan of inland navigation, published in 1800 by Mr. Archer.

THE CITY OF DUBLIN.

recent surveys, made by order of the Directors of the Grand Canal, have ascertained a very singular fact, which promises an extraordinary and almost unparalleled facility of inland navigation—one great level, extending its various branches nearly 100 miles, without a lock, through the King's, Queen's, Westmeath, and Tipperary counties, contains an extensive tract of the most fertile part of Ireland, and peculiarly adapted to the production of grain.

From these surveys, which were taken with great care in 1808, by the Company's very intelligent and experienced engineer, Mr. John Killaly, it appears that the present summit level of the Grand Canal may be lowered to that of Philipstown, by sinking about sixteen feet through the hill of Downings, removing the seventeenth and eighteenth locks on the main trunk, the nineteenth and twentieth on the Shannon branch, and also the nineteenth and twentieth on the Barrow branch, these locks being no longer necessary. The new summit level thus formed, by a very slight deflection of the line from its present course, will commence at Digby-bridge, and the sixteenth lock on the main trunk, and terminate at the present twenty-first lock on the Shannon branch, which will thus become the seventeenth. The summit level will receive a small prolongation on the Barrow branch also, of nearly one mile, terminating at the present twenty-first lock on that line, which will thus become the seventeeth from Dublin.

At Ballycommon, two and a half miles west of Philipstown, and nearly the western termination of this proposed summit level, the great southern line, as it may justly be denominated, will issue from it: this, which is properly a continuation of the summit level, will visit the vicinity of Frankford, Birr, Roscrea, Nenagh, and Silvermines; will approach within a mile and a half of the Shannon below Killaloe, and will finally terminate about two miles and a half from the town of Tipperary, after a course, uninterrupted by a single lock, of ninety-five Irish, or 121 English miles, from Ballycommon, and Digby-bridge, which is properly the commencement of this surprising level, and only sixteen miles from the capital.

But the Philipstown, or proposed summit level, may, as appears from actual surveys in possession of the Company, be extended from the same point of Ballycommon, by the town of Kilbeggan, on the river Brustna, to a point only five miles from Athlone; and thus it has been ascertained, that an inland navigation of nearly 200 English miles, on one great level, and constituting at the same time a summit abundantly supplied with water to feed the several branches that may descend from it, is practicable, and at an expense which, if we consider the importance and magnitude of the object, will not appear extraordinary.

Where this level, unrivalled in extent by any ascertained line in any country, approaches the Shannon, it presents a point most favourable for descending by locks into that river, directly opposite to the Doonass Canal, which is already navigable to the city of Limerick: this descent will require one double and seventeen single locks; but if executed, the navigation from Dublin to Limerick would be much safer than that at present used, in which, boats calculated for canals only, must encounter much delay, difficulty, and danger, in passing that expansion of the Shannon, called Lough Derg.

The fine valley, along the side of which it is proposed to carry this great level to the southward, is bounded, on the east and south-east, by that line of eminences that extending from Sliew Bloom mountains, forms part of what may be called the spine of Ireland, and which here separates the waters flowing to the Shannon, from the sources of those streams that pay their tribute to the three sister rivers, the Barrow, Nore, and Suire. This seemed to oppose a barrier to any further extension of this important navigation, but a careful survey of the same able engineer has ascertained the practicability of passing it by seven ascending locks in a space of one mile, to a summit level of one mile and three quarters between the towns of Tipperary and Cahier, and from thence by thirty-two descending locks in a distance of thirty-nine miles and a quarter, passing through Clonmel, and terminating at Carrick on the Suire, which river is naturally navigable from thence to Waterford and the sea. This line, which may with propriety be called the Suire canal, would form the southern termination of this very singular inland navigation, and its principal level of nearly twenty miles, might by an off branch of only three miles and a half, and without a lock, communicate nearly with the city of Cashel. Thus, the completion of this splendid plan would open an easy communication through the finest part of Ireland, not only between the three great sea-ports of Dublin, Waterford, and Limerick, reciprocally, but between the numerous towns on the various navigable branches of the Shannon and the three sister rivers, the Suire, the Barrow, and the Nore; and it is a circumstance of too much national

THE CITY OF DUBLIN. 1241

importance to be overlooked, that thus also a complete navigation across the island from east to west will be produced, commencing at the entrance of the fine harbour of Waterford, visiting Waterford, Carrick, Clonmel, and Limerick, and terminating, after a course of nearly 160 miles, at the mouth of the Shannon in the Atlantic ocean.

It may be observed, that the course of the great southern line is necessarily circuitous; this very circumstance, however, by extending its benefits to a larger tract of country adapted to cultivation, will greatly promote a spirit of agriculture, one of the essential ends of inland navigation.

The Naas or Kildare Canal, issuing, as already mentioned, from the main trunk near the Leinster aqueduct, and of which about six miles have been finished, has been deserted for some years, but will, it is hoped, be shortly resumed in consequence of its obvious utility. From an actual survey of Mr. John Killaly in 1808, this line, intended to pass through the counties of Kildare, Carlow, and Wicklow, will cross the Liffey on an aqueduct at Kilcullen bridge, and after a course of sixteen miles and a half, and through twenty ascending locks, will reach its summit level at Bumbo Hall: this level, after crossing the river Slaney, and visiting Baltinglass, and also Hacketstown by a winding course, will terminate at Killabeg, about two miles and a half from the town of Shilelagh, thirty-seven from its commencement, and fifty-one and a half Irish miles from Dublin.

Although the tract of country that environs Wicklow on the north and west abound in the finest lime-stone, it is singular, that this county, in other respects so highly favoured, should be totally destitute of an article, essential as a manure, peculiarly appropriate to the nature of its soil. The demand for it is of course great, and the tract situated on, or contiguous to the sea, is supplied with excellent lime from the quarries at Sutton, on the peninsula of Howth, and partly with an inferior kind produced by calcining the pebbles on the sea shore; but the inhabitants of the western part of this county are under the necessity of bringing it by land carriage from the county of Carlow, at a vast expense, amounting on an average to at least 6s. per barrel when laid down; yet under this disadvantage, such is its effects as a manure, that the consumption is incredible, and upwards of 25,000 tons are now annually sent from Carlow, Clogrennan, Tullow, and Clonnegal to this tract. The Company, therefore, sensible of the advantages that must result from facilitating the transport of an article so indispensable, have, by an actual survey taken by the same able engineer, Mr. J. Killaly, in 1809, ascertained the practicability of extending the present summit level from the Miltown reservoir, so as to pass to the southward near the towns of Kildare, Castle-Dermott, Ravilly, Tullow, and Clonnegal, through a country abounding in limestone, from whence assuming an easterly direction, by Shilelagh, Tinahaly, and Aghrim, in the county of Wicklow, it will terminate within four miles of the copper mines of Ballymontagh and Cronebane. Such an extension of their canal would, it is computed, double, or perhaps treble, the consumption of lime, and of course proportionably that of culm. This would be far preferable to the upper line, as it would pass through a more fertile country, bring in an abundant supply of water to the summit level, and save an aqueduct over the Liffey. A descent by a few locks from this canal near Clonnegal, would connect it to Newtown-Barry and Enniscorthy, whence the Slaney is naturally navigable to Wexford and the sea.

Although Kilkenny is the most considerable inland city in Ireland, possessing a population of above 20,000 souls, in a very fertile country, abounding, among other objects of commerce, in excellent stone-coal and beautifully variegated black marble, articles for the export of which, on account of their weight, water carriage is indispensable; yet it is totally destitute of the advantages resulting from inland navigation, the Nore, on which it is situated, not being navigable higher than twelve miles below the city. To connect it, therefore, by a navigable line to the Barrow branch, and thus with the capital, has naturally become an object, not only interesting to the Company, but of serious importance to the gentlemen of landed property in the county of Kilkenny. At the instance therefore of several of these gentlemen, and with the permission of the Company, the same indefatigable engineer, Mr. J. Killaly, has carefully surveyed the intermediate country, and has ascertained an interesting fact, viz. that the Cardington level of the Barrow branch may be extended from its present southern termination, without a lock, to the city of Kilkenny, thus producing an uninterrupted still-water navigation of forty Irish, or nearly fifty-one English miles, on one level, from that city to Monastereven.

This line, which will commence immediately above the twenty-eighth lock, will run to the southward, in a direction nearly parallel to the Barrow, along the valley between that river and Sliew Margy till it reaches Gouran; when winding round the southern termination of that groupe of mountains, to the west and north-west, it reaches Kilkenny, after a course of twenty-nine and a half Irish miles. The only serious difficulty in opening this important canal, will occur in its passage round the south-western extremity of Sliew Margy, where it must be excavated to the medium depth of twenty-three feet, through clay and gravel, for a space of three miles and a quarter : a similar excavation, but of three furlongs only in length, will take place to the southward of Clogrennan: but when the importance of the object to be attained is considered, these difficulties will not, it is hoped, be deemed as serious objections.

An extension of the Grand Canal from the Shannon to Galway, so as to open a navigable communication between the capital and that sea-port, and nearly across the centre of the kingdom, must necessarily be an object of importance with the Grand Canal Company, though confessedly subordinate to the great southern level. Accordingly Mr. Thomas Colbourne, in 1808, by their directions surveyed this line, and found the proposed extension practicable. According to this gentleman's plan, the river Suck is to form the commencement of this navigation, and at a point about six miles and a half from its conflux with the Shannon, where it ceases to be naturally navigable, the proposed canal begins, visits the great fair town of Ballynasloe, and by nine ascending locks in a distance of eighteen miles, reaches its summit level of eight miles and a half, from whence it passes through nineteen descending locks, of which one is double, in a space of nineteen miles and a half to Galway, with an off branch to the river of Clare-Galway, which falls with a navigable stream into Lough Corrib; this large lake, inferior in magnitude only to the great lakes of Neagh and Erne, would thus extend the benefits of navigation to its farthest shore above twenty miles from Galway. The summit level of this canal is 203 feet 6 inches above the harbour of Galway : its course is circuitous, and future surveys may, perhaps, discover a shorter practicable line.

Mr. Thomas Colbourne has also surveyed a proposed line, from the northern end of Lough Derg to the lake on which the town of Loughrea is situated : but this line of about twelve miles, with sixteen ascending locks, would require a supply of water to which that lake, notwithstanding its considerable extent, appears unequal, has been relinquished.

Every friend of Ireland, every friend to the empire, must anxiously wish that the Imperial Parliament may see the wisdom and the necessity of promoting by their judicious aid, the execution of these most desirable extensions of the Grand and Royal Canals; these various lines, passing through the most fertile parts of this fine island, and terminating like converging radii in Dublin, as their common centre, would render it a vast storehouse, ever ready to supply the wants of our sister island, by a short navigation through an inland sea nearly environed by the great mass of the empire, and undisturbed by hostile cruisers. Thus would our capital be, in some degree compensated, for the injury it has sustained, by the non-residence of such of our nobility and gentry, as the union of the two kingdoms has necessarily drawn to the seat of empire.

It is a circumstance well worthy of remark, that as one system of converging canals thus serves to convey the essential necessaries of life to the port of Dublin, so, from the opposite port of Liverpool, another system of canals diverges, and traversing England in all directions, happily facilitates the conveyance of these necessaries to her numerous, great, and populous manufacturing towns, and even to London.

The great probability of being able to supply the capital and other places on or adjacent to our navigable waters, with fuel from our own collieries, is a consideration of such real importance, that it should stimulate the exertions of both the Grand and Royal Canal Companies, to extend their respective navigations to the collieries of Boulavoneen, Dunane, and Castlecomer on one hand, and to those at the sources of the Shannon on the other.

The quantity of coals imported from Great Britain in 1794, is stated by Mr. Griffith at 392,952 tons, and from the continually increasing state of our population, that quantity is probably at present much more considerable; if we estimate it at 400,000 tons, and its present average price at 30s. per ton it will appear, that little or no recompense is made to Ireland for the immense sum of £600,000. annually sent to Great Britian for fuel, as it is a well known fact, that the colliers who carry it hither, generally return in ballast, taking nothing of the produce of Ireland, except a small quantity of provisions for the immediate consumption of their respective crews.

In the south-eastern part of the Queen's county, and in the vicinity of the famous collieries of Doonane and Castlecomer, the Company of Undertakers of the Grand Canal are possessed of the royalties of a considerable tract, which are found to contain stone-coal of the same superior quality; and in the year 1805, by boring in various parts, it was ascertained in the most satisfactory manner, and indeed to a degree of physical certainty, that at Boulavoneen, a space of at least 300 acres, contained a bed of this coal, from three feet to three feet four inches thick, from twenty-four to forty-three yards below the surface, with a comparatively small quantity of water to encounter, and in such an elevated situation, as to be easily drained by a subterranean tunnel: the Company are also possessed of four other collieries in this vicinity, which have been ascertained to contain different seams of coal and culm, from two to three feet in thickness: the superior heat and durability of Kilkenny coal, is to that of the best Whitehaven coal, as four to three, and this circumstance has given it such a preference to all others in manufacturing and for culinary purposes, that in Dublin it is in such request, as to sell from 45s. to 50s.; and on the banks of the Shannon from four pounds to four guineas per ton: and yet, notwithstanding these high rates, (arising from the extravagant price of land carriage,) the demand for it is considerably beyond the present supply: the Company, therefore, were amply justified in meditating their plan of uniting these collieries, which are probably inexhaustible, to their grand line of navigation, and thus affording a cheap and easy communication, not only with the towns on its different branches, but with Dublin, and by the Shannon and Barrow with Limerick and Waterford, The plan proposed for effecting this purpose was—an extension of the Grand Canal near Athy, in one level of nine miles, to the foot of the hills within four miles of the collieries, and a rail-way from thence up an ascent to a navigable tunnel of two and a half miles, terminating in the collieries, and serving not only to unwater them, but by the rail-way to convey the coal to the canal: the dimensions of the tunnel were proposed to be ten feet four inches wide, and eight feet six inches high, including three feet seven inches depth of water, similar to those of the Duke of Bridgewater near Worsley in Lancashire; the expense of the whole was estimated at about £130,000. On a moderate computation, it appeared highly probable, that 100,000 tons would thus annually be disposed of, at the cheap rate of £1. 5s. per ton in Dublin and the interior of the country, and that after allowing a sufficient profit to all the persons concerned in raising and vending it, the Company, by a moderate toll, not exceeding 10s. per ton, on any distance it might be carried on the canal, would, after all expenses, have a clear annual profit of near £40,000.

This plan, however, has unfortunately been considered as interfering with the rights of the Barrow navigation Company, as the proposed extension of the canal would run parallel to that river, and at a small distance from it; it has of course been for the present suspended; but it is to be hoped that the good sense and patriotism of the Companies may induce them to adopt such an amicable adjustment of their respective claims as may facilitate the execution of a plan so evidently conducive to the welfare of their common country.

It is however to the collieries on the banks of Lough Allen that we must look for the chief supply of this essential article. The mountains surrounding this lake for twenty miles on the west and east, abound not only with coal of the finest quality, but with iron ore, producing iron equal if not superior to that which Great Britain imports at a heavy expense from Sweden and Russia. The coal has, on repeated trials, been found not only excellent for all the ends of fuel, but after the process of coaking peculiarly adapted to the purpose of smelting the iron ore. The strata, as far as trials have been made, incline with a gentle dip, are near the surface, may be drained without steam engines, and are so easily wrought that they sell at the pits for 8s. 8d. per ton, notwithstanding the very unreasonable and injudicious royalty of 2s. 2d. per ton, which is about four times the usual charge in the English collieries. The seams which have been hitherto wrought, are on the west side of the lake, and do not exceed three feet in thickness; however, there cannot be any reasonable doubt, but that on sinking to greater depths, thicker strata will be found here, as in the collieries of England, where the most valuable seams of coal are found at depths varying from 200 to 800 feet.[*] At the head or north side of the lake are the Dobally mountains, where a seam appears of ten feet thick, but as no attempts have been made here, this coal is as yet seen only at its outburst on the side of the mountain, when from its exposure to the atmosphere it is of course tender and culmy, but on going deeper into it, it will, no doubt, be found of the usual hardness.

* At the colliery of St. Anthon near Newcastle the first workable stratum is the ninth, of six feet thick, and 456 feet below the surface, and another stratum of six feet six inches lies at the depth of not less than 812 feet.

Were the Royal Canal finished to the Shannon, the navigation of that river opened to Lough Allen, and both freed from tolls by a proper compensation from Government to the Company, these coals, it is computed, might be conveyed to Dublin and sold there at 14s. per ton; and as inland navigation is not subject to the interruptions to which sea voyages are liable, this price would be invariable, or at least not subject to those great and distressing fluctuations which, whether from a real scarcity of the article, or from combinations among the venders, we have often experienced; from these causes we have seen English coals rise suddenly, in the depth of winter, from 17s. 4d. to £2. and even to £3. per ton; a circumstance of real distress to the poor of this city, who are generally lodged in damp cellars or wretched garrets.

At a period when the woods in the vicinity of Lough Allen supplied charcoal in abundance, the iron mines on the eastern side of that lake were wrought, and the ruins of the iron-works then erected are still visible at Dumshambo, a village near its southern extremity; these woods, however, have long since disappeared; but it having been discovered that the pit-coal on the spot, when coaked, answered every purpose of charcoal, the business was again resumed, and an iron-foundery was established some years since by Messrs. O'Reiley of Dublin, about one mile from the western shore of Lough Allen, on the west side of the river Arigna, at the southern foot of the mountain of Brahlieve, and in the county of Roscommon. Messrs. John Grieve of Edinburgh, and Thomas Guest of Dowlais iron-works, Glamorganshire, gentlemen possessing much practical knowledge, took an accurate survey of these works, the former in May, 1800, the latter in October, 1804; and their reports coincide in representing the situation being highly favourable; as iron-stone, coal, lime-stone, free-stone, fire-clay, common clay, with every other material that can be wanted, are on the spot or in its immediate vicinity, and are all excellent of their kind and in abundance; to which we may add, that the Arigna will afford a sufficiency of water, not only to work machinery, but to supply a level canal of two miles, to facilitate the carriage of iron ore and coal from the pits to the furnace, which are at present brought on horses backs.

A quarry of iron-ore has been discovered at Drummond, on the banks of the Shannon, about twelve miles below where that river issues from

Lough Allen, and it is thought by good judges, that a mixture of this ore with that of Arigna, would correct the softness of the iron produced there, and thus prevent the great waste at present suffered in converting pig into malleable iron.

On the Arigna works, which are complete and well executed, Messrs. O'Reiley expended above £25,000.; but these gentlemen not being possessed of sufficient capital, (a misfortune that too often occurs in the plans that have been hitherto adopted for promoting the manufactures of Ireland,) the foundery, after having been for some time generously protected and supported by Peter La Touche, Esq. has at length become his property: but however great the patriotic zeal and resources of that worthy individual may be, the business, we fear, can only languish until the completion of the Royal Canal, and the removal of all obstructions in the Shannon, shall afford an easy and cheap conveyance of such weighty manufactures to their proper markets, whether in the capital, or in the towns along that noble river, or the various navigable lines that communicate with it.

Mr. Griffith, in the excellent pamphlet already quoted, affirms on the authority of Lord Sheffield—" that from 15 to 20,000 tons of Swedish iron are annually imported into Great Britain, the quality thereof being superior in toughness to the English iron. This iron in bars was valued at from £10. to £10. 10s. per ton, and when manufactured produced an average profit of about £28. per ton, and this produced a balance in favour of Great Britain amounting to upwards of £484,500. The iron of Lough Allen has been frequently assayed by persons of skill in this branch, who have all pronounced it equal to the best Swedish iron. Here, then, is a new source of mutual wealth and advantage to Great Britain and Ireland," in an article of essential consumption, which, it thus appears incontestably, we can have from the interior of our own empire, not only free from the risk of long and expensive voyages, and a precarious dependance on the connection of a foreign state, but enhanced by this delightful reflection, that we are thus providing employment and comfortable subsistence to thousands of our, at present, idle and consequently discontented poor.

These facts added to the consideration that the country adjacent to this lake every where abounds with flint, pipe-clay, and every material necessary for the manufacture of earthen and stone ware, which employs so many industrious hands in the sister kingdom, should be powerful stimulants to the company of undertakers of the Royal Canal, to persevere with that energy which they have lately evinced in attaining to their summit level, and acquiring such an inexhaustible supply as that noble reservoir Lough Ouil. They have conquered the great difficulty, and we trust that their patriotic efforts will be soon brought to a termination, equally advantageous and honourable to themselves and beneficial to their country. Indeed the exertions both of the Grand and Royal Canal Companies seem, in some degree, to have freed Ireland from the melancholy but just reflection of a celebrated nobleman, who emphatically called it—"The island for which nature had done so much and man so little." It is deeply to be regretted, that the unexampled state of the country has involved these noble works in that embarrassment which has been felt more or less by every public establishment. In the year 1812 the Royal, and in the year 1816 the Grand Canal Companies were obliged to suspend the payment of the interest on their respective loans, and the further prosecution of their projected improvements. We have annexed in the Appendix statements of their affairs.

HARBOURS OF HOWTH AND DUNLEARY, WITH THEIR ENVIRONS.

THE north and south shores of the Bay of Dublin, leading to the harbours of Howth and Dunleary, present many objects worthy of remark. Having passed over Annesly-bridge, on the north side, the road leads along the sea coast. The first object that presents itself is the small sandy island of Clontarf, formerly of greater magnitude, and having still to be seen the ruins of a house, to which the citizens resorted to recreate themselves. It seems to have been formed by the sand brought from the South Bull, sweeping round the east wall of the Lots. Since this sand has been intercepted by the South Wall, the island has gradually decreased, and is now nearly washed away by the torrents of the river Tolkay, confined in this direction by Annesly-bridge, and which here discharge themselves.

From hence there is an embankment, raised upon the sand above the level of the tides, and protected by a strong stone abutment, against the incursion of the water; it leads under the lawn of Marino, from which it is divided only by a sunk fence. This beautiful demesne was once the resort of the citizens of Dublin, to whom its liberal proprietor freely threw it open. It had then a number of attractions; it was the favourite of Lord Charlemont, who exhausted his large fund of classic taste in embellishing it. The Cassino stands naked and simple in the middle of an open lawn, forming the most striking and beautiful model of the chastest style of Doric architecture to be found in Ireland. Contrasted with this is Rosamond's Bower, erected at the upper extremity of a lake, in a dark sequestered retreat embosomed in trees. Its stained glass, fretted mouldings, and pointed ornaments, giving as pure a model of a Gothic, as the other of a Grecian temple.[*] These things have now lost their attraction, the demesne has long been seldom neglected, and a stranger visits it. Contiguous to the demesne is the Crescent, a semicircular range of buildings, looking to the sea, and divided from the shore by a parterre and shrubbery; on this also the marks of neglect and decay are already visible, though it is of recent erection, and forms a fine front to the bay in a distant view. The dome of the Charter School now strikes the eye, and a little further on the shore the shaft of the lead mine appears. This mine has been opened at different times, and the remains of old works are found in the field inside the road. Within these few years they attempted to work it, like the celebrated wherry mine at Penzance, by sinking a shaft in the sea; the project failed, and it remains filled with water, and sometimes covered with the tide. This mine,

---

[*] The motive for erecting this edifice was as amiable as the building is beautiful. When Lord Charlemont came to Ireland in 1773, he built Marino, not merely from a love of architecture, but from a sense of duty as a citizen, who was bound to cultivate the interests of the country that gave him birth. "I was sensible," said this excellent man, "that it was my indispensible duty to live in Ireland, and I determined by some means or other to attach myself to my native land, and principally with this view I began those improvements at Marino, as without some attractive employment I doubted whether I should have resolution to become a resident."—Hardy's Life, vol. i. p. 325. For this purpose he invited to Ireland Simon Verpoyle, to make models and ornaments for his new building, and in this way contributed to encourage that taste for architecture which distinguishes Dublin. Verpoyle was the master of Smith. He was also assisted by Sir William Chambers.

Royal Chester Iron Church Antwerp.

however, ramifies in various directions, and was found also at Crab Lough, where it had been worked by Mr. Vernon, on whose estate it lies. The vein recently explored was first opened in the year 1768, and fourteen ton of good ore taken from it. The shafts were sunk about eighty yards from the shore, and not more than thirty feet deep. They were, even at that distance, filled with the sea water oozing through the soil at every tide. The ore raised yielded twelve hundred weight in every ton, and some silver was found in assaying it, but not worth refining. The ore recently extracted from this mine was sufficiently abundant in quantity and of a good quality. It produced some good specimens of compact galæna, though the greater part of the vein was of the cubic kind: it was said to contain a certain proportion of antimony, and to be calculated for casting printers' types, without any other alloy than this primary combination. The antimonial sulphuret of lead is a rare ore, and the proportions of antimony found in combination with galæna, very different from that necessary to form printers' type. This ore, however, was analyzed in 1813, by Mr. Higgins, at the request of the Dublin Society, and no antimony was detected, as appears by the following statement:—

100 parts of galæna yielded - - - pure lead - - - 75
            sulphur - - - 25
                   100

From hence the town, and further on, the sheds of Clontarf* stretch into the bay, forming, with its white-washed houses, a picturesque promontory very conspicuous, floating as it were on the dark green water. This village is now the great resort of bathers from the north side of the city. Its rere is intersected by rural alleys, called green lanes, which are laid out with neat villas for the accommodation of company in the summer months. From the shore a wooden wharf ran to a considerable distance into the sea, at the extremity of which was a platform with seats, for the accommodation of company; it was an attractive spot, and where, on a summer's evening, the sea breeze was enjoyed with peculiar pleasure.† Some time since,

---

* This name is a corruption of *Cluain-Taribh*, the " Recess," or " Bay of the Bull," so called from its situation behind the sand bank called the North Bull.

† This was called Weekes's Wharf from the benevolent individual who erected it. It was intended to afford to ships a facility of procuring water, for which purpose pipes conveyed it under the platform.

Clontarf was a celebrated fishing town, and this part was called the sheds, from the number of wooden edifices erected there for the purpose of drying fish. But it was much more celebrated for the scene of the memorable battle of Clontarf,* fought between the Danes and Irish on Good Friday, in the year 1014, in which the Danes were defeated, and the Irish monarch, like Epaminondas, fell in the arms of victory. The memory of Bryan Boromhe is still cherished; his victories and his virtues were the favourite theme of Irish historians; † like the Grecian general, he was a philosopher, a statesman, and a soldier; and with him too, the rising prosperity and independence of his country sunk to rise no more! An elegant modern writer (Walker, in his Irish Bards, page 60) says—" This great prince repaired the ravages of the Danes, and restored tranquillity to the kingdom. He re-edified the theological and Tilean colleges, opened new academies, erected public libraries for the use of indigent students, animated timid merit by well gounded hopes, and patronised with steady zeal all professors of the liberal arts." Among these liberal arts he was particularly attached to music, and excelled in the practice of that delightful science. His favourite harp, on which he is said to have played on the eve of the battle, is still preserved in the museum of Trinity College, Dublin, and is a fine memorial of the scientific and mechanical skill of the Irish artists in his reign. It is an universally received tradition in the county of Clare, where he was born, that the beautiful Irish air—*Thugamuir fein an samhra lin*, "We brought summer with us," was his favourite composition, and that he played it on this occasion, both in allusion to the time of the year in which the battle was fought, and the prospect of prosperity to Ireland from the expected expulsion of the Danes. This air is preserved in Bunting's first collection of Irish Melodies, where another anecdote is

Mr. Weekes built it at his sole private expense, and sought not praise nor expected reward. When he left the neighbourhood his useful work was suffered to decay.

* The battle of Clontarf seems to have had a much wider range than is generally attributed to it. Bones and human remains have been found in excavating streets on the north side of Dublin; and in Knock-brush Hill, near Finglas, besides human bones, those of horses, and remains of military weapons are still constantly dug out. Part of the hill is evidently artificial, and tradition says, it was raised over those who fell on the spot at the battle of Clontarf. The hill is about five miles inland from the sea; its present name, Knock-brush, is a corruption of *knock an bhrisé*, the hill of the breach or overthrow.

† See Keating, M'Curtin, O'Halloran, Warner, &c.

THE CITY OF DUBLIN. 1253

told of it.—It was this battle of Clontarf, and the death of Bryan, that gave a subject to Gray's ode of the " Fatal Sisters," which he translated from Torfæus and Bartholinus :—

> Fate demands a nobler head,
> Now a king shall bite the ground.   Ode viii.

alludes to the death of the Irish monarch. This ode is given in the original Norse, with a Latin literal translation, in Barn. Hist. of Orkney Islands, 1808.

> Et Hibernis
> Dolor accidet,
> Qui nunquam
> Apud viros delebitur.

Gray thus paraphrases :—

> Long his loss shall Erin weep,
> Ne'er again his likeness see,
> Long her strains in sorow sleep,
> Strains of immortality!

With such recollections, it is impossible to pass this village without feelings of interest and respect.

Hence the road takes a semicircular sweep along the north side of the bay, and presents a view of the southern shore no less singular than beautiful. From the water's edge rises a rich and wooded country, thickly strewed with villas, which seem to ascend to the summit of the mountains. These mountains, commencing to the eastward, form a chain of conical hills, which skirt the horizon with the most picturesque and singular outline. Among them, the tetonated promontory, formed like the Paps of Jura, which overhangs the harbour of Bray, the greater and lesser Sugarloaf, and Shank-hill are the most remarkable. It sometimes happens, that the artillery stationed at the Pigeon-House exercise their guns and mortars at objects placed on the Bull; should the traveller pass at this time, the effect will be much heightened: the explosion caught by the echoes of the southern hills, and reverberated from summit to summit, is rolled in distinct and measured intervals along the chain, till it seems to travel round the bay, and lose itself in the ocean.* Before him lies the Great

---

* A faint imitation of this effect is produced near Bownass, on Winandermere Lake, in Cumberland, where a small cannon is kept on the shore, and the traveller's curiosity gratified at six shillings a shot.

Bull, called so from the bellowing of the waves, which at particular times of the tide, roll over it on the calmest days with a loud and continued roaring.* Beyond this, on the north, the majestic ridge of Howth rises, and seems an island separated from the main by a considerable interval, the low and sandy isthmus by which it is connected, not appearing above the level of the water. This isthmus, which is about half a mile across, is bounded on the north by the bays of Balldoyle and Malahide,† and on the south by

* The North and South Bulls presenting themselves to a stranger at his entrance into the bay among the first objects he sees and the first names he hears, have been the occasion and subject of silly sarcasm. In justification of the name we shall only observe, that Homer adopts the terms βοάᾳ, βοόωσιν, from βῦς, a bull, for the same reason :

Ουτε θαλλασσης κυμα τοσον βοαα προτι ροον.   Ιλ. ρ. 265.
Ἠϊόνες βόοωσιν ερευγομενης αλος εξω.   Ιλ. ξ. 394.

and that Cowper, his most judicious translator, despairing of attaining to the beauty of the orignal word in the last line, endeavours only to imitate it by a juxta position of others :—

As when within some deep-mouth'd river's bed
The stream and ocean clash—on either *shore*
Loud sounds the *roar* of waves ejected wide.

Those who have passed between the Bulls and witnessed the conflict of the stream and ocean at certain times of the flood tide, will acknowledge the accuracy of Homer's onomatœpoeïa.and Cowper's paraphrase Miss Edgeworth, we trust, will add these " Irish Bulls" to the next edition of her ingenious and classical defence of the metaphorical language of the Irish. It may be added, that the Irish name for Clontarf, *Cluain-Taribh*, " the Recess of the Bull," is a proof of the antiquity of the name of the great sand bank behind which it lies.

† Malahide, or as it is more properly called in the Records, *Mullagh-hidé*, " the head-land of the extremity of the tide," lies at the bottom of a deep bay, having at its entrance the islands of Lambay and Ireland's Eye, and divided from the bay of Dublin by the promontory and isthmus of Howth. It was formerly a place of much consideration, and had several singular immunities and privileges annexed to it. It was granted to the Talbot family, in the reign of Henry II. who immediately assigned Mullaghide-beg to St. Mary's Abbey, Dublin. In the year 1372, Thomas Talbot was summoned to Parliament by the title of Lord Talbot; and by a grant of Edward IV. bearing date March 8th, 1475, besides the usual manorial privileges of receiving customs, holding courts leet and baron, &c." Thomas Talbot is appointed high admiral of the seas, and no other admiral to intrude to exercise any thing to the office of admiral belonging, within the town of Mullaghide ; but that he shall have full power and authority to hear and determine all trespasses, covenants, contracts, or any other offences done on the high seas or elsewhere by the tenants, or vassals, or other residents in the town of Mullaghide, in 'a court of admiralty ; and have all fines, amercements, ransoms, issues, and forfeitures, without any account or return to any crown officer, and to be keeper of ferries, water-bailiff, guager, and searcher of the town and arm of the sea, with all advantages and profits of such offices, him and his heirs, &c." In 1641, Thomas Talbot was outlawed for acting in the Irish rebellion, and the castle of Malabide, with 500 acres of

that of Dublin; the road divides here into two parts, one leading round Sutton on the south, and the other rising over the north shore, and conducting the traveller along the cliffs, presents a view extremely beautiful. On the left the horizon is skirted by the mountains of Mourne, distant forty Irish miles, and stretching far into the eastern sea; more near is the island of Lambay,* and still nearer the picturesque and rugged isle

land, was held for seven years by Miles Corbet, the regicide, who lived in the castle. In later times the town was noted for the cotton factories established there by Mr. Talbot, which was one of the spirited, but unsuccessful attempts of some private gentlemen to establish the manufactory in Dublin. The castle is a grand structure, much improved by modern additions. It was originally moated, with battlements and embrasures for wall pieces; the moat is now turned into an ornamental slope, the battlements still remain, presenting a fine front, terminated at the angles by circular towers. The house is entered by a low stone Gothic door, and the rooms above are approached by stone spiral stairs, which open into a striking Gothic apartment, lighted by a corresponding window, with stained glass. This room is wainscotted with Irish oak, pannelled and divided into compartments, ornamented with sculptured figures, representing different events of the Old and New Testament; over the chimney is the Assumption, of which a curious tradition is preserved :—When Miles Corbet occupied the castle, the Virgin immediately withdrew from his unhallowed presence, and disappeared from the compartment in which she stood; the morning of his departure, however, she again came forward, and has continued visible ever since. In the adjoining apartments are some valuable pictures : Charles I. by Vandyke; the Duchess of Portsmouth and the first Duke of Richmond, by Sir Peter Lely, presented to Mr. Talbot's grandmother by the Duchess herself; James II. and his viceroy Tyrconnel. But the most valuable is a small picture, divided into compartments, representing the Nativity, Adoration, and Circumcision, by Albert Durer; this had been the altar-piece of Mary Queen of Scots.

Beside the castle is a dilapidated chapel, unroofed, it is said, by Corbet, who used the materials to cover a barn; there is also a curious well, dedicated to the Virgin Mary, enclosed in a stone building. Malahide is one of the parishes which forms the union of Swords, from which it is distant two miles and a half.

* LAMBAY lies about two miles from the coast, in the barony of Balruddery. It is about three miles in circumference, and rises into a considerable ridge, contrasted with the flat sandy shore of the main. There is yet on it a castle, which was built by John Chaloner, in the reign of Edward VI. as appears by the licence of alienation made anno fifth Edward VI. 1551, of which the following is a translation :

" In consideration that John Challener, Gent. had brought over into the island of Lambay for the profit thereof, a proper and oportune colony of the King's subjects, to inhabit that island, and render it safe and defensible from the sudden incursions and spoils of pirates, from which they might the more easily and advantageously be driven, the king hereby granted a license to George, Archbishop of Dublin; with the consent of the Chapter of Christ Church, to alien and grant to said I. Challener and his heirs in feefarm, the entire island of Lambay with the Courts Leet and all other hereditaments thereto, and to the whole coast of Ireland belonging, at the rent of £6. 13s. 4d. Irish. Provided that he or his

of Ireland's Eye,* whose eastern extremity rent by some convulsion from the main cliff forms a detached mass of great height and magnitude and

heirs should within six years, build on the said island a town or village, (villam sive pagum) for the habitation of fishermen, with one place of refuge defended with a ditch and wall, or mound (aggere) to retire to in case of need from any sudden insults of enemies; and make within the said term on such part of the shore of said island as he shall think fit, a harbour for the boats and small ships of said fishermen."

Lambay is a fee simple, paying a quit rent of £1. 10s. per annum to the See of Dublin. In the reign of Elizabeth, it was granted to Archbishop Usher, who resided for some time on it, and wrote there, it is said, a considerable part of his works. A clause in the leases especially provides " that the Castle shall be kept in repair to enable the Usher family to retire there whenever the plague shall appear in Dublin." It was purchased from the representatives of Usher by the Talbots of Malahide, in whose family it continues. It has been recently surveyed, and contains six hundred and fifty-two acres, three poles, nineteen perches, Irish, the greater part of which is highly susceptible of cultivation, and is well watered by a number of streams. The castle is in good and habitable repair. The population of the island consists of eight families. It abounds with rabbits; the sea pie or parrot; and the alca arctica or puffin, with which it is sometimes confounded, are also found here in great numbers : from the taste of their flesh, so exactly resembling fish, on which they constantly feed, they are sometimes used in Lent as such. The corvus graculus, or Cornish chough, with red bill and shanks, also frequents this island. Among the fossil productions, indications of copper have been found on the south side, and fine specimens of porphyry capable of very high polish have been dug up in different places. This stone is so abundant that the whole substratum of the island is said to be composed of it.

* Ptolomy describes the islands which lie contiguous to the coast of Ireland in the following passage :
ὑπαρεχεινται δε νησοι της Ιυερνιας ἁι τε καλυμεναι Εϐουδαι ϛ τον αριθμον, ὡν ἡ μεν δυτικωτερα καλειται Εϐουδα· Ἡ δ' εξης προς ανατολας ομοιως Εϐουδα, ειτα Ρικινα, ειτα Μαλεος, ειτα Επιδιον. Και απ' ανατολων της Ιυερνιας εισι ἁι δε νησοι Μοναοιδα, Μονα νησος, Εδρου ερημος, Λιμνου ερημος.

In the Palatine manuscript Εδρυ is written Αδρυ and Λιμνυ Λινυ. Of these islands, which are also mentioned by Pliny and other writers, Λιμνος is supposed by commentators to be Lambay, and Εδρος to be Ireland's Eye ; though the learned Cambden asserts that Εδρος is the island of Ramsey off the coast of Pembrokeshire in Wales :—Air Anglus hodie novum nomen Ramsey. Hæc Sancti Davidis Episcopali sedi adjacet ad quam spectat; hanc autem esse quæ Ptolomæo Edri et Plinio Ardrus et Adros, audacius ex vi verbi conjectare possum. Brit, p. 794. Ware, however, is of a different opinion.

IRELAND'S EYE stands about one mile from the north side of the hill of Howth, and is about one mile in circumference. There are still to be seen on it the ruins of a church, appertaining to an abbey founded here by St. Nessan, in the year 570, in which the Saint passed his life in fasting and prayer. The book of the four gospels called " the Garland of Howth," was preserved here. Archbishop Allen, in his Liber Niger, thus speaks of it : " That book is held in so much esteem and veneration that good men scarcely dare take an oath upon it for fear of the judgements of God being immediately shewn on those who should forswear themselves." Archd. Monast. Ware states that the book

CITY OF DUBLIN. 1257

resembles the curious fragments of the Giants Causeway, called the Chimney. On the right is the Castle of Howth,* whose white battlements

was in possession of Lord Stafford and quotes from it a curious circumstance. The stone called *lias fail*, on which kings had been formerly crowned, always *spoke* when a worthy candidate sat on it. This stone was brought from hence to Scotland, and afterwards to England by Edward I. and is that on which the English monarchs are crowned at this day. Ireland's Eye is in the barony of Cooluck, and appertains to the estate of Lord Howth. It affords pasturage to cattle, which tradition says were formerly driven across on a causeway which extended over the sound. Among the objects of natural history is a fine breed of goshawks. They are noticed by Rutty, and continue still to build among the rocks, where they are sought after with avidity.

* This castle has been the residence of the Howth family since the arrival of the first adventurers from England. The name of the first knight was Sir Armorey Tristram, and the adventures recorded of his life received as authentic, are more extraordinary than those of any hero in romance. Happening to meet with Sir John De Courcy, who was married to his sister, in the church of St. Mary at Rouen, he there made a compact with him, that whatever they should win in any realm, either by conquest or otherwise should be divided between them. On the faith of this agreement, they sought adventures together through Normandy, France, and England, and finally proceeded to Ireland, where the first land they made was Howth. De Courcy was confined by illness to his ship, and the command devolved on Sir Armoricus. Having pushed to shore, he was opposed by the Irish at the bridge of Evora, and a fierce encounter ensued, in which seven sons, nephews, and uncles of Sir Armoricus were slain. The Irish were finally defeated, and the land and title of Howth were allotted to him as his share of the conquest. The bridge of Evora, where this battle is said to have been fought, crosses a mountain stream, which falls into the sea, on the north side of Howth, nearly opposite the west end of Ireland's Eye. In clearing out the foundation for the new parish church, erected a few years ago near this spot, a quantity of bones were discovered scattered over an extensive space; and in the neighbourhood, an antique anvil, with bridle bits and other parts of horse harness. It is conjectured, with some probability, that the armourers' forge was erected in this spot, where the knights were accoutred preparatory to the battle. Sir Armoricus, after a variety of perilous and wild adventures in Ireland, was surrounded by a superior force in Connaught. His knights were inclined to avail themselves of their horses, and save themselves by flight; but their leader dismounting, drew his sword and kissing the cross of it, thrust it into his horse's side, his example was followed by all the knights except two, who were sent to a neighbouring hill, to be spectators of the approaching combat. The Normans were cut off, not a man escaping, but the two who afterwards testified the circumstances of the heroic transaction. Some time after, the original family name of Tristram was changed to St. Laurence, for the following reason:—One of them commanded an army near Clontarf, against the common invaders, the Danes. The battle was fought on St. Laurence's day, and he made a vow to the Saint, common in these days, that if he was victorious he would assume his name, and entail it upon his posterity. The Danes were defeated, and his vow was religiously observed. Clogher's MS. quoted by Lodge, v. iii. p. 180.

This incident may be contrasted with another, to shew the difference of times and opinions. The battle of St. Quentin was gained also on St. Laurence's day; but, to commemorate it, Phillip II. built the palace of the Escurial, in the form of the gridiron, on which the Saint suffered martyrdom.

7 X

rise from the dark wood in which it is embosomed; in the front is a park well stocked with deer. In the rear, this wood proceeds up the hill to the base of a steep mountain, by whose abrupt side it seems suddenly stopped. In the front lies the town of Howth, consisting of one street running along the ridge of the cliff. It is entirely inhabited by fishermen who, by prescription, hold their cabins rent free; they do service however for the tenure, by giving to the lord of the soil the prime fish of every boat, of which there are ten engaged in the fishery. It was formerly remarkable for its filth, and the foul smell generated by the offals of putrid fish, and

---

Another romantic circumstance is related of this family. The celebrated Grana Uille, or Grace O'Malley, was noted for her piratical depredations in the reign of Elizabeth. Returning on a certain time from England, where she had paid a visit to the Queen, she landed at Howth, and proceeded to the castle. It was the hour of dinner, and the gates were shut. Shocked at an exclusion so repugnant to her notions of Irish hospitality, she immediately proceeded to the shore, where the young lord was at nurse, and seizing the child, she embarked with him, and sailed to Connaught, where her own castle stood. After some time, however, she restored the child, with the express stipulation that the gates should be always thrown open when the family went to dinner, a practice which is observed at this day.

The castle stands in a situation which commands no view. It is a long battlemented structure, flanked by square towers at each extremity. In advance of the left wing is a castellated edifice, forming a large archway. This is entirely detached from the main building, and seems to have formed an entrance to some works which are now no more. The castle is approached by a large flight of steps, which are modern. These lead to a spacious hall, extending the whole front of the building; round this hall are hung weapons and armour of ancient days, and among the rest, the actual two-handed sword with which Sir Tristram defeated the Danes. In a chamber, to which a flight of steps leads from the hall, is a painting, said to represent the abreption of the young Lord Howth. A female is mounted on a white horse, receiving a child from a peasant; above, the sky seems to open, and a figure is represented looking down on the group below. It is probable the picture alludes to some other subject, though the tradition of the castle refers it to this. In the saloon are some portraits; among others, a full length figure of Dean Swift in his robes, with the Draper's Letter in his hand; the figure of Wood is crouching beside him, and his halfpence are scattered about. Over a door way to a range of offices, connected with the west end of the castle, is an incription, the fac-simile of which is below. Christopher, the twentieth Lord of Howth, usually called the *blind Lord*, married Elenor Plunket; their initials are at the extremities of the tranverse line, and their arms are impaled on the shield; the date indicates the time, and the motto is that of the Howth family.

```
   ┌─────────────QVE PENCES─────────────┐
   │       1564        ▓▓▓▓     DEVS AI     │
   │  CSL ─────       ▓▓▓▓    ─────────  E P │
   │       IDNS                SERIT? ИRI    │
   └────────────────────────────────────────┘
```

THE CITY OF DUBLIN. 1259

it was seldom free from contagious fever. The present Lord Howth, by a strict edict, enjoins cleanliness and white-washing, and the houses, both inside and out, exhibit a cleanly appearance, and emit a less offensive smell. Notwithstanding, the natives are a singularly hardy, healthy race of men, and generally above the common stature. Their life is a scene of privation and fatigue; after days of incessant labour, they snatch a few,hours rest in the wet clothes in which they are drenched, recruit their spirits with fish, potatoes, and whiskey, their only diet, and proceed again to the repetition of their danger and toil. Till very lately, they were noted smugglers, and added the perils of this illicit calling to the hardships of their ordinary life;* yet they live to a great age, and instances of longevity beyond the age of 100, are not uncommon.

About the middle of the town, and impending over the sea, is the venerable abbey of Howth.† From below the basis of this edifice, and on the beach, was

* These fishermen are frank and intelligent, some are particularly so; they freely acknowledge that their fathers and grandfathers had been concerned in smuggling, and that some had died in consequence of wounds they had received in this service. In one encounter with the revenue officers, a Howth man was killed; on examination it was found that a sleeve-button was lodged in his heart; a revenue officer had expended his ammunition and loaded his pistol with this extraordinary bullet.

† It is very remarkable, that notwithstanding the complete records which exist of the Howth family from the earliest periods in this country, the history of this venerable abbey should be buried in obscurity. It is conjectured to have been erected by Sitric the Dane, who, in 1038, bestowed part of that tract of land on ecclesiastical foundations. It is dedicated to St. Mary. The present ruins derive much interest from the striking aspect they present, and the romantic site on which they are placed. They are enclosed in an area of 189 feet by 168 feet. This is defended by a battlemented rampart, which on one side impends over the sea, and on the other over a deep fosse, the usual appendage of ancient religious edifices. Within this enclosure, which is now a church-yard, stand the abbey and the college: the former is entered through a large arch in the steeple, which is a singular structure, ascended by stairs on the outside from the roof, and displaying a front curiously pierced with arched windows. The church within is thirty-one yards by fourteen, divided into two aisles by a partition wall of six pointed arches: this may be of a later erection, as the porches and doors are of the form of the semi-circular Saxon arch. It is remarkable in this church, that the aisles do not correspond, though they are of equal length, and apparently built at the same time; the gabels of each mutually projecting several feet beyond the other. In the south aisle is an ancient monument of Christopher, the thirteenth baron of Howth, erected in 1430; his effigies are represented in relief, in armour, with his wife beside him; his feet resting on a dog: the traces of an old inscription are still visible on the edge of the tomb. It is thus modernized in Lodge—" Christopher, Baron Howth, alias De St. Lawrence, and a Lord of Parliament, and Anne Plunket, daughter of ——— Plunket, of Rathmore, in the County of Meath." There are other tombs and vaults in the aisle, which have

constructed the old quay, at which the fishing boats of the town unladed themselves.

been made receptacles for smuggled goods, from whence they are sometimes disinterred by revenue officers. In the wall of the north aisle is a slab of black marble containing the following inscription :—
To the Memory of
ANNE FLIN,
A friend that lov'd thy earthly form when here,
Erects this stone to dust he held most dear;
Thy happy genius oft his soul reviv'd,
Nor sorrow felt he till of thee depriv'd:
Peace to thy gentle shade, and endless rest
To thy fair soul, now numbered with the blest !
Yet take these tears—mortality's relief,
And, 'till I share thy joy, forgive my grief:
These little rites—a stone, a verse—receive,
'Tis all a father, all a friend can give!
Deceased, September 18, 1766,
Aged near 21 years.

The Mr. Flin who composed the above affecting epitaph on his daughter, was a bookseller in Limerick, and a native of Howth. His family are supposed to have come over among the first English adventurers, and established themselves on this spot; they are possessed at present of two houses in the town of Howth, which are insulated spots in the centre of Lord Howth's property, supposed to be reservations made to the ancestors of this family, and held as a tenure coeval with that of the family of Tristram.

On the south side of the enclosure is the college; it is entered from the south. It consists of a hall, kitchen, and the remains of seven cells. The ruins are sufficiently tenantable to afford shelter to a number of poor families, who have thatched some of the cells, and seem to live in a kind of monastic community, shut up in the college walls.

The bells which once hung in this abbey were recently discovered by an accident. When the new church was built, it was necessary to provide for it a bell. A tradition existed, that the bells of the abbey were somewhere in the castle, and they were searched for with a view to recast them for the service of the new church. Three were found in a remote apartment, but they were deemed objects of such curiosity, that they are properly preserved by Lord Howth, and a new bell provided for the church. These bells are about two feet and a half in height and one foot and a half in diameter at the base. Near the summit of each runs an inscription, which forms a belt round the surface. On two of the inscriptions are sufficiently legible in the following words, in old Roman characters.
Sancta Maria ora pro nobis.
Jesu Christe ora pro nobis.
But on the third, which is the largest, and apparently the most ancient, the legend is not so intelligible :

Nicholas: own: car: ofmaeuguer.

The New Harbour of Howth.

THE CITY OF DUBLIN. 1261

This has been chosen for the site of the new harbour, which, with the front of the abbey above, Ireland's Eye opposite, and Lambay in the distance, forms the annexed view.

The importance of an harbour of shelter for the port of Dublin, is strongly enforced by the consideration, that there is not, from Carlingford bay to the harbour of Waterford, a single port in which a vessel can take shelter at low-water. The insecurity of Dublin bay is notorious: from the year 1797 to 1803, 124 vessels were damaged in the bay, with the destruction of property to the amount of £262,312.* independent of vessels not insured and total wrecks. In one winter alone fifty lives, and £100,000. were lost; † in this calculation is not included the tremendous loss of the Rochdale transport, and the Parkgate packet in the year 1807, and other calamities which annually occur. Among a variety of stations pointed out, a harbour at Howth seems to possess superior advantages, and nature marked the sound of Ireland's Eye as a site already formed. This small island extends almost half a mile in length, at the distance of one mile from Howth. From Howth pier at one side, and from the south-east point of the island on the other, run two ledges of rocks to meet each other, leaving a space between of half a mile, called the south entrance, having five fathom depth at low water. At the north-west end of the island runs a similar ledge, leaving between it and the sand-bank under Howth a similar passage, having one fathom and a half at low water. These two passages lead into the sound or anchorage, the bottom of which is a soft bed of fine sand with a mixture of black mud, but towards the shore it is partly rocky and partly sand, having twenty-four feet depth of water at the lowest tides in the centre, but shoaling toward the coast at each side. Through the sound the velocity of the tide is only one mile and a half per

To one of these inscriptions is annexed the following characters:

A.D.RIL IU S2

It is conjectured that these characters are a contraction of the words *ad domum religiosam*, and imply that the bells were a donation to the abbey; and further, that they contain a chronogram, ascertaining the date, the letters MLII. standing for the numerals 1052. The tradition is, that the bells were cast in Italy, and presented to the abbey immediately after its foundation, and before the arrival of the Anglo-Normans.

* Testimonial entries made with one notary-public, Mr. E. Hammerton.
† Parliamentary Report.

hour.* From the Hill of Howth there runs a perennial stream of pure fresh water, copious at all seasons, and so situated that it might, at a trifling expense, be conveyed into boats and the holds of small vessels. In effect, the contiguity of this sound to the open sea, its uninterrupted approach, its great depth at low water, its pure bottom, its natural enclosures, and its abundance of fresh water, seem to point it out as a place intended by nature for a harbour, which, if judiciously improved by art, might not only be an asylum of safety for all vessels bound to the port of Dublin, but also a receptacle for ships of war for the protection of the channel, and a general rendezvous for the vessels from the north ports bound southward, as its space is sufficiently capacious to contain a large fleet, from whence they could put to sea at all times of the tide, with the wind in almost any direction, and in a few minutes be clear of rocks or shoals. The next consideration was, how to take advantage of these important and natural circumstances. Among the many plans presented, one seemed to be peculiarly adapted for the purpose. It proposed merely to raise a superstructure on the foundation which nature had already laid; to run two piers on the ledges of rocks, from the points of Ireland's Eye to meet correspondent ones from Howth, and so to form a capacious bason, by enclosing for a harbour *the whole sound* between the island and the peninsula: at the extremities of these piers, it was intended to leave two passages where they are already formed by nature, to be marked by beacons on the piers, which would afford vessels a ready entrance on either side, at any hour of the tide, or in any weather.† Unfortunately this bold and noble plan was rejected, and one more limited and ineffectual, but not more unexpensive, has been adopted. A pier has been constructed on the eastern

* A singular circumstance is observed in the tides through the sound. From the commencement of the flood to half tide, the stream runs north; it then changes to the south, and continues its course in that direction till low water. Thus, instead of the current coinciding with the ebb and flow of the tide, it runs in one direction for three hours and in another for nine.

† The gentleman who proposed this plan, and published a very intelligent pamphlet to recommend it, was Mr. Thomas Rogers, inspector of light-houses to the Commissioners of his Majesty's revenue; Captain Bligh concurred with him in opinion, "that from the nature of the place, it might be circumscribed by a wall to shelter every way;" and Sir Thomas Page agreed with him in essential points—see pamphlet, p. 51. Another plan was proposed by the Hon. and Rev. W. Dawson, for constructing an harbour immediately to the east of the sound, by running a pier from the eastern point of Pul Scadden bay, which would form a capacious and deep harbour at low water.

THE CITY OF DUBLIN.

ridge, as far as the Carline rocks, it is 200 feet wide at the base, and eighty-five feet at high water mark; it is thirty-eight feet high, and runs 1503 feet from the shore; here it forms an obtuse angle * with its first direction, and proceeds north-west for 990 feet. The space inside these two was the original harbour, but it was apprehended that the drift sand, sweeping round the shore of Balldoyle, would be stopped by this obstruction, and continually deposited within the piers. It was therefore necessary to construct another to the east, to intercept the sand, and £40,000. more were granted by Parliament for this purpose. This western pier is 170 feet wide at the base, and eighty at high water mark; it is thirty-six feet high, and runs 2020 feet north-east, to meet the return, and between them a space of 300 feet is left for an entrance. The area inclosed within these vast masses of masonry is fifty-two English acres. To erect these piers, every engine that could facilitate or give stability to the work, was employed; railways conducted immense fragments of rock down steep roads from quarries above, so well constructed, that while a line of loaded carts descended, a similar number of empty ones ascended, and this rotation was constant, with the aid of only two men to unite and disunite them. These rude fragments formed the bases of the interior of the wall. The fronts are faced with hewn granite brought from the other side of the bay, where this excellent stone abounds. But their foundation is laid with blocks of red grit stone, brought from the quarries of Runcon in Cheshire.† To place

* When the wall was completed and the angle was about to be turned, a surge of the sea, on a stormy winter's night, turned several yards of its extremity into the harbour, without dispersing the stones. On this foundation, thus singularly formed, they continued the wall, so that in fact, the east and north piers do not join at an angle, but are connected by a short caut. The sea which bursts into the sound of Ireland's Eye, from the east, is tremendous in stormy weather. In order to protect the extremity of the work in winter, one of the Danish prizes taken at the attack of Copenhagen, was filled with large stones and sunk near it as a break-water: in a short time it was dashed to pieces, and not a fragment of the wreck, or the rocks it contained, were left.

† When exposed to the action of the air, this stone rapidly decays, and the docks at Liverpool and the pier at Douglas in the Isle of Man are melancholy memorials of its perishable nature; but in submarine architecture it is particularly useful. The soft texture of the stone renders it easy to hew the largest blocks from the quarry, to adapt them readily to any form, and when submersed in water they acquire the hardest texture. Each of those brought to Howth weighed four ton, and were managed with surprising facility; a small rectangular excavation was made on one surface, near the centre of gravity; in this was sunk three small bars of iron, kept together by a yoke. The centre bar was cuneiform, with the base downwards, and sliding between the other two; through the apex of the wedge was passed a

them below water two diving-bells were used, in which the workmen descended, and by a supply of air forced in from above, remained under water for several hours.

The surface of the piers form a spacious road, and along the outside edge of them are high parapet walls; towards the sea the extremities are marked by beacons, the eastern a red light in a turret, the western a lanthorn, to point out the entrance. The sums already granted by Parliament amount to £333,000. and it is supposed they will require £346,606. 15s. 3d. for their completion; the first stone was laid in the year 1807, and they are now ten years in constructing.* The number of men daily employed amounts to from 500 to 700, and a little town has been built to accommodate them; while the crowds of people who flocked from Dublin to view these novel works gave great animation to a place which a few years ago was solitary and deserted.

It is much to be regretted that this noble and expensive work should be liable to so many objections. The deepest and best anchorage the sound affords, is left *outside* the pier; one third of the space within is dry at half ebb, and two thirds at low water; at which time the deepest part near the entrance is only twelve feet, consequently it denies access to any vessel which draws more water, and most of the foreign shipping trading to Dublin draw from thirteen to sixteen. Add to this that the bottom is rocky, and that part only which is dry and useless can be cleaned with certainty, and the access is difficult at times of peril, when it is most wanting. In effect, it is said that as an harbour of safety in bad

---

ling, which was linked to the hook of a chain suspended from a crane. As the force was applied, the inverted wedge was drawn up, and pressed the bars laterally against the sides of the excavation. By this simple apparatus these ponderous blocks were in a few minutes attached to a crane and swung into their berth beneath the low water mark, where workmen in the diving bells received them; bags of small shingles were let down, on which they were bedded, and when the chain was relaxed the wedge descended, and the bars immediately slipped from the cavity and released the stone.

* The act for building the pier, passed in the 45th George III. and since that period to the end of the sessions in 1816, 333,000l. have been granted by Parliament, 41,217l. 4s. 5d. of which had been expended previous to passing, the act of 50th George III. constituting the present commissioners. Mr. Rennie's estimate for the completion of the work, is 305,389l. 10s. 10d. exclusive of the sum expended before the appointment of the present board. Mr. Rennie is the engineer, and his calculations have been found accurate.

weather it is ineffectual: but as a packet dock it is useful, by allowing the packet to sail at all times, and abridging the passage ten miles of the most difficult and tedious part of the navigation.*

From the town, the road leads over the hill, ascending which the prospect enlarges, and presents in succession a view of the islands, town, harbour, ruins, and Martello tower, in a new interesting group below; and at length, the isthmus, by which the peninsula is connected with the main land; the sweeping coast of Baldoyle on the one side, and the bay of Dublin at the other, start into view.

* Much controversy has arisen on the subject of this harbour, even as a packet dock; and a select committee of the House of Commons appointed to consider the state of the roads, and conveyance of the mails between London and Dublin, in the year 1817, published five reports on the subject, one of which exclusively relates to Howth harbour. It states, that all the objections urged against it had been foreseen and fully attended to before the construction of it was undertaken; that evidence satisfactorily shows that a sufficient space within the harbour will be prepared in the course of next spring, in which the packets may be perfectly safe, and that the apprehensions of the difficulty of navigating the channels by which the harbour is approached are not well founded.

Is is calculated that the time of communication between London and Dublin may be abridged one half, by the packet sailing from Howth, and corresponding regulation at the other side. At present the packet lying in the Pigeon-house dock, sails at different hours, from six to twelve in the evening, as the tide serves, but when it serves between twelve and six, it waits for it, so that taking the average, there are three hours lost for one half of the year. If the wind blow fresh from east or north-east, the packet cannot sail at all; and thus an entire tide, and sometimes two or more are lost. If it blow fresh from the north at neap tides, she is neaped in the dock. Even when she gets under way, unless the wind be west, she has considerable difficulty and great loss of time in working out of the bay, and when at length she arrives at Holyhead after an average passage of eighteen hours, the mail takes forty eight hours, though allowed but forty six, to arrive in London through the sands and mountains. The same delays occur in returning, so that an answer to a letter sent from Dublin to London cannot be expected in less than seven or eight days. But if the packet lie and take in the mail at Ireland's Eye, it could be dispatched at a certain hour every night, with any wind, and in weather when she could not work out from the Pigeon-house dock, and in fifteen minutes she would be completely at sea, lying her course. The mail in this way might arrive at Holyhead in thirteen hours on an average, after leaving the post office in Dublin, and by some improvements in the road to Shrewsbury, might arrive in London in thirty-two hours after. Thus, if the letter was dispatched from Dublin at eight o'clock on Saturday evening, it would arrive in London at five on Monday evening; and suppposing an answer were sent by that night's mail, leaving London at eight o'clock, it would arrive in Dublin at six on Wednesday evening, in four days, instead of eight. The advantage of this to the commercial world is unnecessary to dwell on. See Parliamentary Reports.

Two steam packets made several trips across from Howth harbour with passengers, but they received so much damage in a storm, that they were obliged to be laid up.

THE HISTORY OF

At some distance below, on the left hand of the road, is the singular precipice called *Puck's rock*.* At the end of this road and at the eastern extremity of the peninsula, on a steep cliff, stands the old light-house, which is now discontinued. It was lighted by large refractors, about two feet in diameter; the light of the lamp was received in a concave reflector behind, which threw it on the lens before, in the focus of which it was placed; and the light passing through, was dilated to a vast blaze by its immense refractive powers.† From hence, a new road is lately made to the southern point of the promontory, on which a second light-house was erected a few years ago. The site of this is rendered interesting by a traditionary anecdote; it is a small promontory nearly detached from the main by a steep cavity. The little peninsula thus formed, from its constant and bright verdure, was called the *Green Baillé*, which in Irish signified a town or enclosed habitation. Here, it is said, a remnant of the Danish army retired after the battle of Clontarf, insulated the promontory, and defended themselves till they were carried off in their vessels. It is certain that the excavation had all the appearance of an artificial fosse, before

* This wild rock seems to have been detached from the main by some convulsion, which also cleft it nearly in two, by a deep perpendicular fissure. On one side, and near the summit, is the rude representation of a colossal human figure on the face of the rock, of which tradition preserves a story. St. Nessan, whose sanctity is still venerated by the people of Howth, was assailed in his retreat on Ireland's Eye by an evil spirit, who to terrify him the more, assumed a frightful gigantic form. The Saint, by good luck, was reading the holy book called " the Garland of Howth," which rendered him invincible by any thing unearthly and unholy. As his enemy approached, he struck him on the forehead with the book, and drove him with such force against the opposite coast, that he split the rock and impaled the evil spirit in the fissure, where he remains to this hour, struggling to extricate himself. In the course of centuries he has nearly disengaged his body and arms, but one leg still remains firmly wedged in the rock. This imaginary figure is frequently viewed from boats, but few have courage to venture into the chasm of the rock, within. It was however a noted haunt of smugglers.

† These lenses are plano-convex, and serve another purpose; when not in use, they are covered behind by a copper plate, and form convex mirrors, in which the miniature landscapes all around are beautifully reflected. They have been used in this way for the purpose of sketching the scenery, like a camera obscura. A gallery on the outside leads round the building, and affords convenience for this end. The sun's rays passing through these immense burning glasses are very dangerous, of which the keeper warns a stranger. He tells, that the clothes of a lady were set in a blaze by accidentally crossing near the focus, when the sun was shining, and the cap incautiously lifted up. An alarming conflagration recently occurred in the vicinity of Dublin, in which several cabins were consumed; it was said to have been occasioned by a thatcher accidentally leaving his spectacles on the straw of the roof of one of them.

the ancient marks were obliterated by the road, and the works of the present light-house constructed upon it.* Behind the light-house is a large room, which opens by folding doors on a platform, at the utmost extremity of Howth: here an excellent telescope is kept, and the shoals which obstruct the entrance of the bay distinctly viewed; these are the Great Kish,[†] and the Bennet and Burford banks, which are links of the chain extending along the Wicklow and Wexford coasts, and called the Irish grounds; these, though not visible, are distinctly marked in stormy weather by the surf, which breaks over them with uncommon violence, and form a very dangerous approach to the bay. From the light-house, the road leads along the south side of the hill, presenting every where new objects, and romantic scenery, and after passing under the base of Shell Martin,[‡] a conical mountain rising near the centre of the peninsula, it returns by the hamlet of Sutton into the isthmus.

Howth is called in the Irish MS. by the bold appellation of *Bin Eider*, or the Cliff of the Eagle. Its circuit includes an area of 1500 square acres, Irish measure. It is noted as an extraordinary circumstance, that it has continued for 600 years in the family of Lord Howth, without increase or diminution, we might also add, without improvement or alteration. The

* In this beacon the convex lens is disused, and it is lighted by lamps and reflectors; refractors are now generally excluded from all the light-houses on the Irish coast.

† The Kish extends about six miles, running north and south, across the entrance of the bay, distant in the nearest parts about five miles; at low water in some places it has only one fathom depth. Its place was marked by a ton buoy with a flag moored about the middle, and a white buoy at the north extremity; these were only seen by day; and within these two years a vessel carrying a floating light, marks its place both by day and night. To the north of this lies Bennet's bank. In the year 1798 a large vessel was lost on this bank, and the disaster was only discovered by her main mast, which some fishermen of Howth saw above the water, and brought away with them. The Burford is a small bank nearer Howth, so called from the Burford man of war striking on it, in the year 1780, and receiving some damage. Besides these, the Rosebeg bank runs off the south promontory of Howth, from under the new light-house into the bay about two miles and a half, in a south-west direction. Through these banks are two passages into the harbour; one between the south end of the Kish and Tolkey, frequented only by small craft; the other between the north end and Howth, called the east passage; it is five miles wide, and safely passed by the largest vessels.

‡ The summit of Shell, or more properly Slieu Martin, is crested with a large cairn, and near its base are the ruins of a very ancient chuich, dedicated to St. Fonton. Just below it, on the north side, stands a lesser hill, called Carric-mor, on which is erected a signal post to communicate with the Pigeon-house on the other side of the bay. The face of this rock is very steep, and formed of vast fragments which seem to have been rolled by some convulsion from the summit, like one side of the Scalp.

greater part of the hill seems to be in the state in which it emerged from the flood. The fine lime stone* with which it abounds is exported to fertilize distant fields; and travellers view with surprise this bold and beautiful promontory, within a few miles of the metropolis, with scarcely a single habitation to mark its surface, while the opposite coast, at a greater distance, is covered with villas to the summit of the mountains. It stands in the

At some distance from the face of Carric-mor, in a meadow below, stands a large *Druid's Altar*, of which the annexed is a correct view.

These erections are called in Ireland *crom-laac*, which literally means a crooked stone, from the inclined position in which the upper stone is laid. They are generally attributed to the Druids; and Sir J. Ware assigns them an origin of even higher antiquity. He deduces them from Abraham and the patriarchs, who were directed not to strike a tool on the stones of their altars (p. 140). It is certain these rude structures have no impression of any implement. It is called by the people of Howth, Fin's quoit, and supposed to have been chucked into its present position by Fin M'Comhl, (or Fingal) when engaged in that spot with a Dane. It consists of a ponderous mass of rude rock probably rolled down from the mountain beside it; it is of an oblong shape, fourteen feet long and twelve broad, and in one face six feet thick. It was originally supported in a more horizontal position, on seven perpendicular stones, rising seven feet above the ground, and apparently placed without any order; the superincumbent stone has now slided from its supporters to the north side, and rests with one edge on the ground; one of the supporters is broken in two by the oblique pressure of the weight above. This monument rests in a hollow, and from its position, seems to favour the opinion that the perpendicular stones were sunk in pits under it as it lay on the ground, and that the earth was afterwards digged away, and it was left supported on these pillars, to which it was impossible that any number of men, in these rude times, could raise it. Rowland, in his " Mona Antiqua," conjectures, that the ponderous imposts at Stonehenge and other Druidical remains were placed by a similar contrivance.

* This *lime stone* is much prised. It is sent to Wicklow, Arklow, &c. where there is none, and even to Holland heretofore by the Dutch, who set a high value on it. It bears a high polish, equal to marble, and some specimens exhibit curious vermiform impressions. In erecting the new light-house

THE CITY OF DUBLIN. 1269

barony of Coolock, county of Dublin. The living is a prebend of St. Patrick's cathedral valued at £24. 6s. 10d. in the King's books, and has now a new church, for which the sum of £500. was lately granted. A neat Roman Catholic chapel has also been recently erected in the town of Howth.

Proceeding from the Liffey * along the south side of the bay, the first object which occurs is the village of Ringsend,† once a celebrated bathing resort of the citizens, and affording, for their accommodation, the only public vehicles used in Dublin, called from the place where they were

on the Green Baily, fine specimens of carbonate of lime were found, crystallized generally in six-sided prisms terminated by pyramids and tinged with ochre.

Porphyry, both white and red, has been found in large rocks, bearing a high polish, and much harder than marble. It is of so fixed a nature, that Rutty kept it ten hours in a pipe-maker's furnace without effecting any change.

Potter's clay of a remarkably good quality is found in great abundance in a cleft a little to the north of the old building on the sea shore.

Indications of coal were discovered in a cliff near the bathing-house, preceded by a stratum of black clay which burnt white.

Galæna was found in scattered specimens in excavating the rock to form the pier; it was of the cubic kind, and mixed with spots of *copper*, but no regular vein of either was discovered on the shore. In blasting the rocks, however, which obstructed the anchorage in the new harbour, a vein of lead was discovered under water, and considerable specimens were raised of a quality supposed to be so rich as to make it an object to work it.

A vein of compact gray ore of *manganese* was discovered on the south side of the hill, towards Sutton. It consists of manganese mixed with compact brown iron stone and hæmatites; specimens of which are found among the rocks of the coast near the mine. About fifteen years ago it was worked, and some cargoes sent to England. In consequence, however, of some dispute about the proprietorship, it has been discontinued; and notwithstanding the recent application of an English company who have proposed to re-establish the works, no agreement has been effected, and this valuable ore remains unexplored, while several tons are annually imported into Dublin, from Devonshire, through the agency of a Cornish miner who resides not far from the mine at Howth.

* Between Annesley-bridge and Ringsend lies a flat shore, forming the bottom of the bay of Dublin. It is an alluvial tract, formerly inundated by the torrents of the Tolka, Dodder, and Liffey, between which it lies. It is now drained, and the inroads of the sea and rivers kept off by embankments called the North and South Walls. That on the north side of the Liffey is called the Lots, (see page 1084.)

† The name of *Ringsend* has been noted among the blunders of Irish appellations, and has been facetiously enumerated as the third bull which a stranger meets on his entrance into Dublin, after passing between the North and South Bulls. It is probable, that the name, like that of Phœnix, has been a corruption of some Irish word, for which a more familiar English one which resembled it in sound, was substituted. It is supposed by O'Halloran to have been originally *Rin-ānn*, the point of the tide, from the confluence of the waters of the Dodder and the Liffey which takes place here.

1270   THE HISTORY OF

used, Ringsend cars. The town is now only remarkable for its ruined and neglected aspect, striking a stranger on his first landing from the packet, with unfavourable impressions of the first town he meets: the place has been ruined by extensive salt works established there, the fumes of which are intolerable. At Ringsend the river Dodder empties itself into the Liffey. This stream rising from the Dublin mountains, is subject to very sudden and extensive inundations, laying the low grounds in the vicinity under water, and carrying away the bridges. Various plans have been devised for diverting the water by another channel through the low grounds between Irishtown and Sandymount; but none of them were effected, and by the embankments formed to confine the river, and the massive bridge now erected at Ringsend, the stream continues in its old channel, without further apprehension of its violence.*

* This river has been, from very early times, a dangerous and turbulent stream, in which many lives have been lost, and much property destroyed About the year 1649, Sir William Usher was drowned in crossing the current, though many of his friends, both on foot and on horse back, were beside him. Immediately after, a stone bridge was erected over it, to which an odd circumstance occurred: the bridge was scarcely built, and a safe passage effected across the current, when it suddenly altered its channel, leaving the bridge on dry ground and useless, " in which perverse course it continued," says Boate, " until perforce it was constrained to return to its old channel," (ch. viii. p. 36.) In the year 1796, powers were vested in the Corporation for improving the port of Dublin, to change the course of the Dodder, from the north of Ball's-bridge, and lead it by a canal of sixty feet wide, to the south of the SouthWalls, so as not to fall either into the Liffey or harbour, with a view by this means of removing the obstruction called the bar of the Dodder, caused by the deposit of its sand in the bed of the river Liffey, 26 Geo. III. This act was not carried into effect; and in 1802, another great inundation destroyed the old bridge; since which a new one has been erected of mountain granite, very strong and massive, capable, it is supposed, of resisting any force of the water. This bridge joins Ringsend to the south-east suburbs of the city.

About half a mile west of the Dodder and south of Ringsend, stood Baggot-rath Castle, formerly of much strength and importance.

So early as the year 1234, in the reign of Edward III. there was an order for removing W. Fitzwilliam from the castle and manor of Baggot-rath, and giving them to the Bishop of Meath. In 1649 the castle was rendered famous by the defeat of the King's troops by the Parliamentarians. The Marquis of Ormond had encamped at Rathmines, and determined to seize on this castle, in order to prevent Jones's cavalry from grazing on the fine pastures on the banks of the Dodder, and streighten Dublin on that side. General Purcel was sent for this purpose in the night with 1500 men, and to favour his operations, the Marquis remained under arms all night. The next day, when the Marquis had retired to take some repose, the garrison of Dublin made a sortie, retook the castle, and brought on the fatal battle of Rathmines, in which 4000 men were killed, 2500 taken prisoners, and the Royal

Contiguous to Ringsend, on the shore, stands Irishtown, another bathing village, but not so ruinous. In this is the church of Ringsend, a building ornamented with an ancient steeple, and dedicated to St. Matthew. It is a chaplaincy attached to the living of Donneybrook. Along this shore the sea is kept out by strong dykes, which would otherwise inundate the grounds which lie below its level. Farther on are Cranfield baths, much frequented for the purity of the water, which is not diluted with any fresh stream; and beyond them is the village of Sandymount, which is comparatively large and populous, and much resorted to in summer for the benefit of bathing. From hence the shore is solitary, naked, and deserted to Booterstown, where the road from Dublin opens upon it. Here the features of the coast assume the most beautiful appearance. On one side are seen the bay extending to Clontarf, and the bold promontory of Howth with its low sandy isthmus, over which the islands of Ireland's Eye and Lambay rise in the most picturesque manner; on the other the land swells into the romantic hill of Roebuck, presenting a view of a sloping country, richly clothed with wood to its summit, and thickly scattered with villas and demesnes. In the front projects the promontory of the Black Rock, and the bold shore beyond it. It is peculiar to this place, that vegetation flourishes within the immediate reach of the spray, and trees root themselves almost in the sand and water; the beauty of the view of the Black Rock is much heightened by those plantations, which clothe the slope of the ground down to the waters' edge, and bathe their branches in the tide. The villages of Booterstown, Williamstown, and the Black Rock, form an extensive town, exceedingly crowded by the citizens of Dublin during the summer months, who generally prefer this to the north side of the bay, as having more pure and undiluted salt water for bathing.*
The road is therefore filled to an uncommon degree with all kinds of

---

party in Ireland totally ruined. Part of this castle, with the entrenchments, were standing beside the road, leading from Baggot-street to Ball's-bridge in 1794, when Grose wrote his Antiquities, in which there is a view of the ruins; but not a vestige of them now remains; and thus it has fared with the remains of many other ancient buildings in Ireland.

* Another cause perhaps why the south side of the bay is much more frequented than the north, is the open roads, which are not impeded by turnpikes, while all the avenues on the north are blocked up with gates in the immediate vicinity of the city. Several attempts have been made to erect them on this road, but they have been uniformly opposed with success.

vehicles, and presents a scene of bustle and population more striking perhaps than the most crowded outlets of London.

One mile from the Black Rock stands the church of Monkstown. This was built in 1797, with a steeple, and is perhaps one of the largest and finest edifices erected for a country congregation in Ireland. The parish was united by Act of Council, in 1780, to the curacies of Bullock, Carrick-Brennan, Dalkey, Kill, and Killeiny, and the church accommodates all the nobility and gentry of a very rich and populous vicinity: it is, therefore, always much crowded.*

Half a mile beyond Monkstown, and five miles and a quarter from Dublin, is the village of Dunleary, now become an object of considerable interest from the new harbour just commenced in its vicinity.

* The want of churches is much felt and complained of in this neighbourhood, where there is a more numerous population of the established religion than in any other part of Ireland. Yet, with the exception of Stillorgan, this is the only church from Ringsend to Bray, the extremity of the county, an extent including eleven populous villages, and a very thickly inhabited country.

NEW PIER OF DUNLEARY.

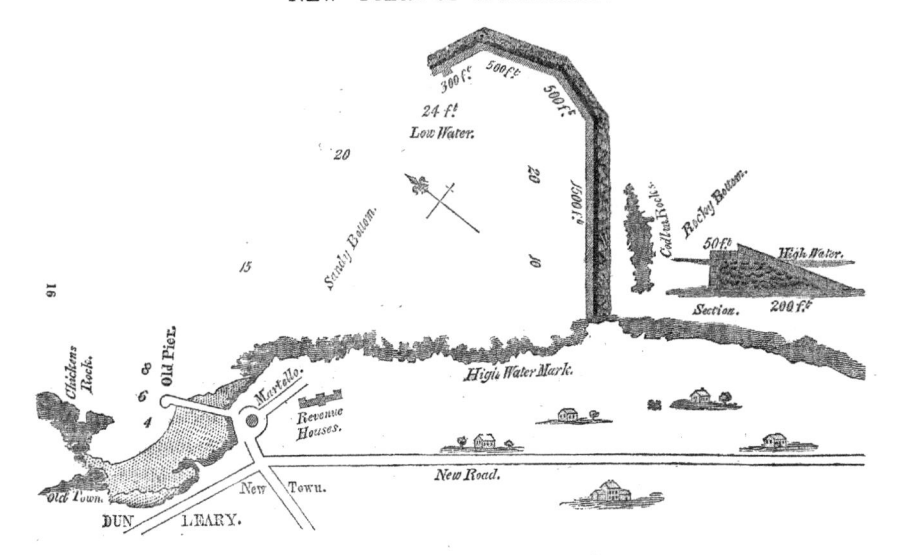

DUNLEARY, as an harbour affording shelter to the shipping on the inside of the bay, was early acknowledged to be an object of prime importance. Within the bay of Dublin there was no other situation which could be eligibly chosen, when a vessel was once embayed by a storm from sea. The northern shore had been searched, and not one situation could be discovered to form an artificial harbour. The western passage is interdicted for the greater part of twenty-four hours, during which time the bar is impassible. Any harbour formed outside would be unattainable, and consequently hopeless. To the southern shore, therefore, vessels could only look for shelter, by forming an artificial harbour in such a situation, as would be sufficient to the east or windward, to secure the depth of water at all times necessary to shelter large trading vessels and ships of war, and so far to west or leeward, as to offer security to fleets of smaller vessels attempting, in vain perhaps, at that time to cross the bar, and incapable of reaching the finest harbour, if too far to windward. Such a situation Dunleary afforded; by an indentation of the coast, a small bay was formed, with a fine soft sandy bottom. This

7 Z

was protected on the west by a natural bank, and on the east a small pier of rude structure was run out. Within this pier many vessels had taken shelter, and lives and property to a considerable amount had been saved by it, when vessels availed themselves of it at a particular time of the tide; but at other times, wanting depth of water, and a light, it only afforded a softer bottom for a vessel to strand herself upon, to prevent her striking on a worse place. Several petitions had been presented on this subject, and in 1809 one was addressed to the Duke of Richmond, signed by all the magistrates and gentlemen on the south side of the bay. This was taken into consideration, and on the 11th of July, 1815, an Act passed the Imperial Parliament, for the erection of an Asylum Harbour and Place of Refuge at Dunleary, and five Commissioners were appointed to cause surveys and estimates to be made. By the direction of the Commissioners, accurate surveys were made of the coast, from the present pier to Dalkey island. It was found that midway nearly between these points, the Codling Rocks formed a distinct division of the shore; all to the eastward was a rocky bottom, all to the westward a fine sand. It was therefore determined to form the pier as far to the east as the Codling Rock would permit, by these means excluding all the rocky bottom, including the sand, and affording the greatest possible depth of water; and an estimate of the expense was sent to Parliament, amounting to £505,000. On the following year another Act passed, appropriating certain duties, to be vested in the Commissioners, to defray this expense;* and on the 31st of May, 1817, the

* Duties for building Dunleary Harbour, under the Act of 56 George III.

	£.	s.	d.
Foreign vessels entering the port of Dublin, per ton	0	0	6
Native ditto, except colliers - ditto	0	0	4
Colliers - - ditto	0	0	2
Entry of goods - - ditto	0	1	0
Every invoice, cocket, &c.	0	2	0
Every coast and cross-channel permit	0	2	0
Every bond, except masters' and mates'	0	2	0
Every bond of masters and mates	0	7	6
Every certificate of registry	0	7	6
Anchorage, slippage, and city dues, each vessel	0	7	6
Every bill of view, &c.	0	2	6
Every license to navigate	0	10	0
Every transire certificate	0	10	0

THE CITY OF DUBLIN.

first stone was laid by his Excellency Lord Whitworth, with the usual ceremonies. The pier commences about half a mile east of the old one, immediately to the west of the Codling Rock. It will extend 2800 feet, and consist of four parts; the first running directly from the shore to the distance of 1500 feet in a direction north-east; the next returning in a direction north 500 feet; the third running north-west 500 feet; and the fourth west 300 feet. The base of the pier will be somewhat more than 200 feet in breadth, terminating in a perpendicular face on the side of the harbour, and an inclined plane towards the sea. A quay fifty feet wide will run along the summit, protected by a parapet eight feet high on the outside. At the extremity will be a beacon to mark the harbour. Close to the pier-head, there will be a depth of water of twenty-four feet, at the lowest springs, which will admit a frigate of thirty-six guns, or an Indiaman of 800 tons, and at two hours flood, a seventy-four may take refuge with safety. This depth varies withinside, and gradually lessens to fifteen or sixteen feet nearest the shore.

The materials which compose the pier, are mountain granite of a remarkably sound texture.* This stone is brought from Dalkey hill, a distance of two

    It was supposed by Parliament that these duties would yield annually about £17,000. but the Commissioners have found that, since the peace, they average only at £12,000. Notwithstanding the value and importance of this pier, the citizens of Dublin complain that it was not erected like Howth and others, by Parliamentary grants, defrayed in the general expenditure of the country, but that it imposes an indirect local tax on them of £12,000. a year for fifty years. It is supposed, however, from savings already made in various contracts, that the work will be completed for a sum considerably less than the estimate. A canal communicating with the South Docks at Ringsend, forms no part of the present plan, though the great advantage of such a communication renders it probable that it may be undertaken at a future day. A western pier also would be an important addition to complete the harbour, and prevent the accumulation of sand, though it is said that none is brought along this shore by the western currents, but that it is found always to accumulate at the east side on any obstruction, and is brought by east currents from the Arklow banks.

    * Granite, in the theory of Werner, is deemed a rock of primary formation, and supposed to have been formed when the earth was covered to a vast height by the waters of the general ocean, and that the particles of which it is composed were suspended in a state of chemical solution, and were deposited slowly in a crystalline form. It is supposed to occupy the lowest place, and that it rises from the nucleus at the centre to the surface of the earth, in an uninterrupted stratum. It is called granite from its granular texture, and consists of quarts, felspar, and mica. It is the stone of all others perhaps best calculated for marine architecture. In England it is scarce; it is found principally in Cornwall, where it is called *moor-stone*, and highly prized. It was the stone of which Smeaton wished to construct the Eddystone light-house; but from the difficulty of procuring it, he was compelled to use

miles, by means of railed ways. These ascend the mountains by parallel and inclined planes, and discharge the hill so fast into the sea, that the vast work proceeds at the rate of 100 feet per month since its commencement, and it is conjectured that in three years the rough breakwater will be constructed, and in three years more the whole pier faced and and completed. The number of men daily employed, averages at 600.

From the speculation of this pier, and the benefit it is likely to confer on the vicinity, the value of every thing is highly encreased, and the village from being the inconsiderable and dirty abode of a few fishermen, in the bottom of a valley, has now extended itself along the cliffs in every direction. Dunleary was heretofore the last residence in this direction, the country lying between it and Bullock presented a sterile solitary tract covered with furze and heath, without road or inclosure, and passable only

Portland stone in the interior. It is faced, however, with granite, and that edifice, which was twice destroyed by the elements, is raised with blocks of this stone, simply dovetailed into each other, and has now acquired a durability equal to the rock on which it is erected. This valuable stone abounds on our coast. The whole extent of the southern shore of Dublin Bay is one vast stratum of granite, and affords an inexhaustible mine of the finest materials for building, which modern architects avail themselves of, though their predecessors ignorantly neglected it. The spire of Patrick's church was probably among the first erections in which granite was used as a building stone in Dublin. In London Waterloo-bridge is built of granite which was brought from Cornwall and Scotland.

The granitic tract is bounded on the east by schist rocks, which join it on on the sea side beneath Killiney-hill, and on the west by lime-stone, which appear on the sea coast on the strand of Booterstown and pass over towards Merrion. The interval is a vast mass of granite, its northern edge washed by the sea, and its southern penetrating to an indefinite and unexplored distance through the Dublin mountains. On this substratum vast hills repose, of different materials; Bray Head, the greater and lesser Sugarloaf, and Shank-hill, whose conical summits give so remarkable a feature to the southern horizon, consist of quartz, which seems disposed to assume the form of a cone in terminating similar mountains in different parts of the globe. The granite, on the shores of Dublin bay, is in general of a gray colour, consisting of yellowish, white, and gray felspar, grayish quartz, and a variable proportion of mica of different shades, gray and brown; in some places the proportion of mica greatly predominates, and gives to the surface of the worked stone, when the sun shines, a very glittering and brilliant appearance; schorl, garnet, and beryl are sometimes accidental ingredients. The felspar of the granite is found in some places in a state of decomposition, forming *porcelain earth*, of a purity equal to the Cornish china clay. As this decomposition is very extensive, it suggests a most important object of further enquiry. This interesting tract of country has hitherto been but little explored. The Rev. Walter Stephens commenced an attempt, and as far as he proceeded, made valuable discoveries; his premature death in 1808 prevented the completion of his design. His notes were printed in 1812, by Mr. W. Fitton, with additional remarks, and the whole forms a brief but elegant sketch of the geology of this country.

by a few foot paths. Within ten years, the aspect of the country has been, changed; it is pierced by good roads in all directions, fields are enclosed and reclaimed, and the whole space is covered over with neat and even elegant villas, built of hewn mountain granite. From the pure air, dry soil, and bold coast of this tract, it is now preferred as a summer residence to the sandy shore of the interior of the bay.

The next part of the coast which attracted public attention is SANDY COVE point, where Sir Thomas H. Page proposed that a pier of an extraordinary construction and at an enormous expense should be formed;* and farther on is BLOYKE or BULLOCK, seven miles from Dublin. This village stands close on the sea; has a small key, and is defended by a castle and ramparts. It is not known when these defences were built. The castle was erected to protect commerce, as well from the pirates by sea, as from the Tories from the Wicklow mountains. It is now in good repair, and an habitable residence.

The last village within the bay of Dublin is that of DALKEY; it stands at the base of a high mountain, and was one of the ancient manors of the see of Dublin. The town of Dalkey is seven miles from the city. Our ancestors seemed to have an higher notion of the value of a harbour at this place than we entertain. It was formerly so considerable that fairs and markets were established so early as 1480, to favour foreigners, who resorted here for trade, and seven strong castles were built to store their goods and protect them.† It could raise twenty men at arms, and the tolls of the markets were appointed to pave the town. The castles are now dismantled, and some of them destroyed, and the town is reduced to a poor decayed village; but what remains of both, indicate much former importance, and appear venerable even in ruins. An extensive common, on which the inhabitants claim

---

* See page 439. It was to consist of an immense break water, detached from and lying obliquely to the shore, and having a narrow entrance at the south-east, and a wider one at the north-west extremity. The estimate of the expense exceeded one million! It has since been found by the report of those employed to sound the coast by the commissioners of Dunleary pier, that this part of the coast has a rocky bottom unfit for anchorage.

† Three of these castles yet remain in good preservation. One was repaired, and forms part of a private house. Another is a house and store, having on the top a summer-house erected, which affords an extensive view of the bay and country. A third is used as a forge. One was pulled down in 1769, for the materials, and what remains of the other three form parts of cabins.

a right of pasturage, is annexed to the town, at the extremity of which, on the sea coast are lead mines,* formerly worked to some extent, but now discontined. Opposite the lead mines is the island of Dalkey ;† it forms the south-eastern extremity of the bay of Dublin, which from hence to the south-eastern point of Howth is six miles broad. The north side of the bay lies in the barony of Cooluck, and the south side in the half barony of Rathdown.

* In the time of Rutty this mine was extensively worked, and several hundred tons of ore extracted from it. He fluxed it with equal parts of salt of-tartar, and obtained forty-two grains of lead from ninety grains of ore.

† The ISLAND OF DALKEY contains about eighteen acres of good marsh land for cattle. The island was formerly dedicated to St. Benedict, and there are still to be seen on it the ruins of a church, and Kistvaens or receptacles of human bones are found near the shore. Tradition says that the citizens of Dublin retired here when the city was visited by the great plague in 1575. In modern times the citizens resorted to it for convivial purposes. It was the custom to elect here a mock-king and officers of state, whose proceedings were recorded in a newspaper called the Dalkey gazette. A society called the Druids, established about 1790, also held their anniversary meetings on this island. To the east are a number of small rocks called the Muglins, in whose cavities are found abundance of fish. Dalkey island is separated from the main by a channel called the Sound, 3650 feet long, 1000 feet wide, at its south-east, and 700 feet wide at its north-west extremity, with a sunken rock near its centre, and a rocky shore on each side. This place had been surveyed among others, as affording a proper site for an asylum harbour, and a plan was proposed by the Committee of Inland Navigation, but from the objections to which it was liable, it was abandoned. It was considered, however, in former times a very safe and convenient harbour, where vessels lay secure in ten fathoms water, protected from the north-east wind and ready to sail at any hour. Hence the port of Dalkey was that used on state occasions. In 1538 Sir Edward Bellingham landed here, and proceeded to Dublin. In 1553, Sir Anthony St. Leger also landed here, and in 1558 the Earl of Sussex shipped his army from this port, and proceeded to oppose the Scotch invaders at the island of Raghery on the coast of Antrim.

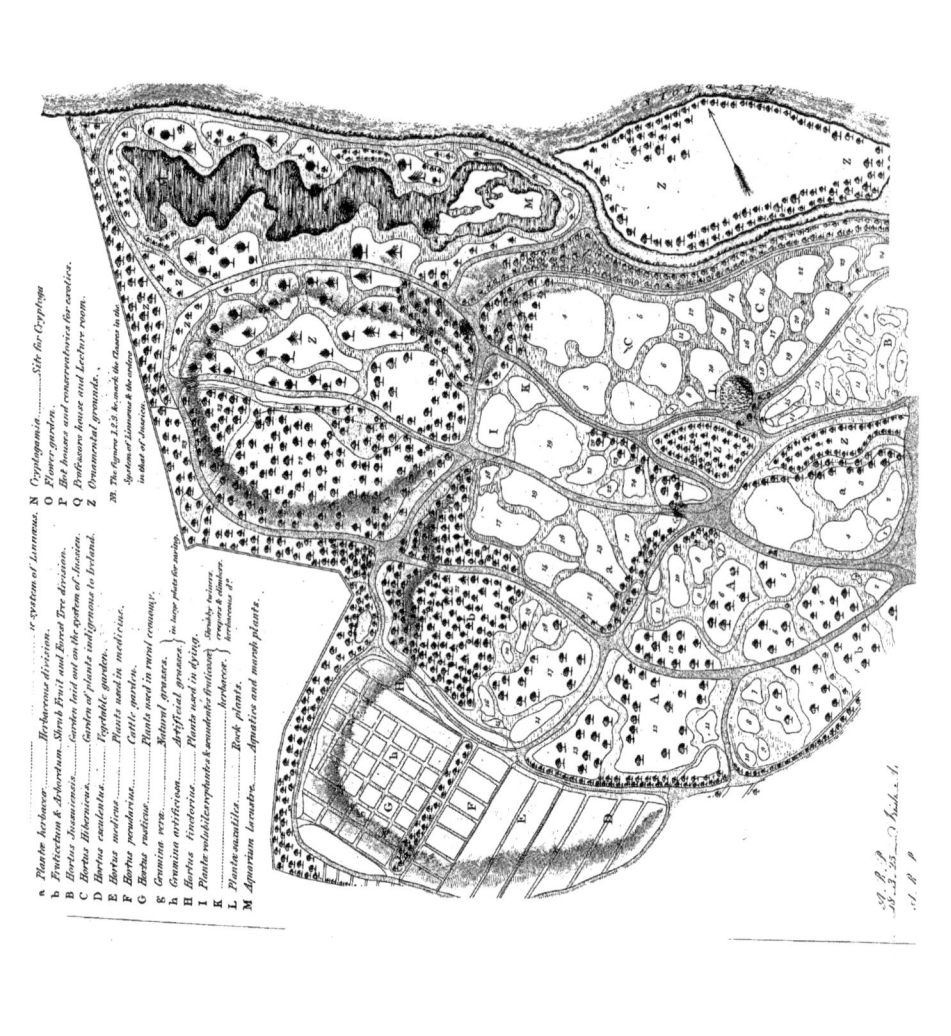

a Plantae herbaceae............or system of Linnæus. N Cryptogamia............Site for Cryptoga
b Fruticetum & Arboretum. Shrub Fruit and Forest Tree division. O Flower garden.
B Hortus Jussiæsianus........Garden laid out on the system of Jussieu. P Hot houses and conservatoria for exotics.
C Hortus Hibernicus............Garden of plants indigenous to Ireland. Q Professors house and Lecture room.
D Hortus caulolenthus........Vegetable garden. Z Ornamental grounds.
E Hortus medicus..............Plants used in medicine.
F Hortus pecuaricus..........Cattle garden. 39. The figures 1.2.3 &c. mark the Classes in the
G Hortus rusticus..............Plants used in rural economy. System of Linnæus & the orderes
g Gramina vera................Natural grasses. in that of Jussieu.
h Gramina artificica..........Artificial grasses. } in large plots for sowing.
H Hortus tinctorius............Plants used in dyeing.
I Plantæ volubiles ryphvites & scandentes frutices } Shrubby twiners
                                                     creepers & climbers.
K   herbaceous d°.
L Plantæ saxatiles..............Rock plants.
M Aquarium lacustre..........Aquatics and marsh plants.

THE CITY OF DUBLIN.

BOTANIC GARDENS.

The earliest pursuit of man, and that science to which he first applied himself, immediately after his creation, was botany. Emerging himself from the earth, he was every where surrounded by the production of a common parent; and the Being who called them both into existence, seemed to have united them together by primæval and inseparable association. The cultivation of the vegetable kingdom became man's first care, the contemplation of its beauties his first pleasure, the collection of its fruits his first support, and the distinctions of its kinds his first knowledge. The science of botany, therefore, must have been coeval with the creation, and Adam its first professor : " For him God planted a garden eastward, in Eden, that he might dress it, and keep it."*

The pursuit of botany in this way, and the culture of gardens for ornament and utility, seemed to have occupied the greatest characters in the earliest ages. Homer celebrates those of Alcinous at Phaeacia :†

> Without the courts, and to the gates adjoin'd,
> A spacious garden lay, fenced all around :
> There grew luxuriant many a lofty tree:——
> And on the garden's verge extreme,
> Flowers of all hues smile all the year, arrang'd
> With neatest art judicious.

Diodorus and Josephus celebrate the hanging gardens of Semiramis, at Babylon,‡ and Xenophon commemorates those of the younger Cyrus, at Sardis, who so highly prized them, that his reply is recorded as a memorable

---

* Genesis, chap. ii.

† Εκτοσθεν δ' αυλης μεγας ορχατος αἶχι θυραων
Τετραγυος· περι δ' ερκος εληλαται αμφοτερωθεν——
Ενθα δε κοσμηται πρασιαι παρα νειατον ορχον
Παντοια πεφυασιν επηετανον γανοωσαι. Odysseis, lib. 7.

From whence it appears that a part of the garden at least was laid out with botanic regularity, as the words κοσμηται πρασιαι import.

‡ Diodorus, lib. 2. Το δε εδαφος εξωμαλισμενον πληρες ην παντοδαπων δενδρων των δυναμειων κατα τε το μεγεθος και την αλλην χαριν τοις θεομενοις ψυχαγαγωγησαι.

Joseph. contr. Ap. lib. 1. Εν δε τοις βασιλειοις τετοις αναλημματα λιθινα υψηλα ανωκοδομησας—κατασκυασας τον καλεμενον κρεμαςον παραδεισον.

trait of the character of that celebrated man:—" What," said he to Lysander, who was admiring their beauties, " do you think has created the varied vegetable productions of these gardens?—the labour of mine own hands."* Amongst the Romans, Plutarch extols the splendid gardens of Lucullus;† Cicero the more modest one of his Tusculan villa; ‡ and Pliny is most copious and minute in the detail of all the regular and formal beauties of his Laurentine villa.§

In the varied pursuits of the wisest man, we find botany formed a prominent feature. Solomon's view of the subject seemed to have embraced the whole science, from the largest to the minutest vegetable, for " he discoursed of trees from the cedar of Lebanon to the hysop that groweth out of the wall." ‖ And the smallest plant had in his estimation more value than the riches of Egypt; conscious, that in all his glory he was not arrayed like one of those.

This interesting study engaged the attention of the wisest men of prophane as well as sacred history. Theophrastus, the disciple of Aristotle, thought that the manners and habits of plants were as worthy objects of his pursuit as those of men,** as bearing to them a striking analogy. He has, therefore, been as minute in investigating the characters of the one as of the other. To facilitate the pursuit he thought it necessary to adopt some system. He has accordingly divided the whole vegetable world into classes, and arranged them conformable to their qualities and uses—into †† esculent, succulent, and condiment. Dioscorides adopted his plan, but altered his arrangement, ‡‡ into aromatic, alimentary, medicinal, and viscous; and

* Xenophon. Memorab. Œconom. lib. 5. De Administ. domestic. Επει δε εθαυμασεν αυτον ο Λυσανδρος ως καλα μεν—πολυ τε μαλλον αγαμαι τε καλαμέιρησαντος και διαπραξαντος εκαςα τητων Κυρον ειπεν—εγω παντα διεμετρησα και διεταξα, εστι δ' αυτων ο και εφευτευσα αυτος—και ο Λυσανδρος ειπειν—συ γαρ ταις σαις χερσι τητων εφευτευσας ; .
† Plutarch. Vita Lucul. ‡ Cicer. Epist. § Plin. Epist. lib. ii. Ep. xvii.
‖ 1 Kings, chap. iv. v. 33.
** Των φυτων τας διαφορας και την αλλην φυσιν εκ της προς τα ζωα αναλογιας ληπτεον κατα τε μερη και τα παθη και τας γενεσεις και τους βιης. Theophrast. a Bodæo, κεφ. ά. Amstædol. 1644.
This proposition, identifying the animal and vegetable kingdoms in their parts, passions, generations, and modes of living, is a singular proof the sagacity of this primitive botanist. A similar identification is the *ne plus ultra* of modern botany, and gives to the science so much of the interest it at present possesses.
†† Milne's Botanical Dictionary. Article—Method.
‡‡ J. Bambini et Fab. Column. Comment.

these seem to be the first attempt of systematic distribution ever adopted in the science.* But while these philosophers endeavoured to promote the science, the very method they employed contributed to retard it. Such divisions must be vague and indefinite, or even if certain, the knowledge of the properties of a vegetable cannot promote an acquaintance with a particular plant, for it can only be of use to him who already knows what the plant is. It supposed every thing and taught nothing; it separated things which ought to be united, and confounded things which ought to be separated: of this the inutility of the works of these great men is a melancholy proof. The properties of the plants they describe, remain to the present day a memorial of their discernment and industry; but most of the plants to which these properties belong are no more known, notwithstanding the labours of their commentators,† than if they never had been described. Divisions, therefore, founded on signs more determinate in their natures, and more sensible to the eye of the observer, were necessary to extend our knowledge of individual plants, and to give that knowledge permanency. The earliest method of this kind was founded on the comparative size and duration of plants; but this also was found to be of too fluctuating a nature for accurate information, depending on climate, temperature, and other adventitious causes; the same vegetable was found to assume such a variety of appearances, that the method, though adopted by eminent writers, was finally abandoned for one more constant in its character.

For a long period, botanists were much embarrassed to find what particular character to adopt as affording a similitude and distinction always permanent; many were proposed, and some remarkable for their singularity. In the year 1588, J. Bapt. Porta published at Naples a work entitled "Phytognomia," or the "Astrology of Plants." In this strange collection, he has classed them from their resemblance to men and other animals, and from their supposed relation to the stars; asserting that a strong connection exists between them, founded on this similitude. Thus, that a plant which resembles the liver has properties which renders it serviceable in diseases of that organ, and so of others. Many names of this fantastic writer are found in the nomenclature of botany at the present day. Pulmo-

* J. Bambini et Fab. Column. Comment.
† Bodæus, Scaliger, Bauhine, Columna, &c.

naria was so called by him from a fancied resemblance of the surface of the leaves to the substance of the lungs; it still retains the name he gave it, is called Lungwort, and is frequently exhibited, with supposed good effect, when the lungs are distempered.

But it is to Gæsner that the world is indebted for a classification founded upon the characters pointed out by nature herself. This great man had observed the invariable regularity which always exists in the parts of fructification under every change of place or temperature, and he first suggested the propriety of adopting these parts as external marks of discrimination. Cæsalpinus, a physician of Pisa, immediately availed himself of this suggestion. In the year 1583 he published his arrangement, formed upon this plan, and gave to the science a new character, by founding the æra of systematic botany. The permanence and minute regularity of nature, in every part connected with the important function of fructification, is as wonderful as the knowledge of the fact is useful in extending the science. The acquisitions of botany were no longer fugitive, for they were founded on immutable marks, and the progress of the science was as rapid as the knowledge it conveyed was certain. The comparative value of this great discovery may be appreciated by the following fact:—The ancients have professed to describe the vegetable kingdom; they have only distinguished about 200 plants, and even those so imperfectly that, perhaps, not fifty of them are recognized at the present day; while the moderns, in their systematic arrangement, have described upwards of 80,000, and these with such precision, and in characters so perfect, that they can be recognised in any age or country, as long as their descriptions shall endure. But, besides the accuracy and wonderful conciseness which the moderns, and the illustrious Linnæus in particular, have introduced into the language of botany, their assigning to the parts of fructification a sexual system, and breaking down the fancied partition which separated the contiguous kingdoms, and restoring to the vegetable those habits, sympathies, and preferences which it has in common with the animal, has given a new interest to the science by the singular discoveries it has made, converting the ordinary and scarcely noticed appearances of plants into subjects of wonder and admiration.* To ascer-

* The common nettle (Urtica,) has ever been the most despised and abundant weed of our vegetable tribes. In one species, the Urtica dioicia, the parts of fructification are found on separate plants, and

tain by experiments and inspection the reality of these singular facts; to bring the whole vegetable world under our eye; to place in order before us the several nations, tribes, families, and individuals which compose it, and view at once their various habitudes, attachments, and relations in a given time and in a limited space, was the object of Botanic Gardens. Here the botanist first observed what character was permanent and what accidental; whether it constituted a distinct species, or only a variety of the individual; whether a singular appearance was casual or the regular and constant effect of some cause; in fine, here his knowledge acquired a certainty which no other means could give to so minute, yet so vast a subject.

BOTANIC GARDENS.

The family of the Medici, to which literature and science are so much indebted in a dark age, were the original founders of these establishments, and the first garden, dedicated exclusively to the science of botany, was opened in Padua in 1540, under their auspices.* In imitation of this example, several were established in different countries of Europe; at Upsal in Sweden in 1657; at Paris in 1626; at Edinburgh in 1675; and at Oxford in 1683. Since this last period, sundry others have been opened, not only as national establishments, but at the expense of private individuals; but the two which most claim the attention of the present day, both for extent and arrangement, are those of Jamaica,† and of Glasnevin, near Dublin. The first consists of seventy acres: one of the objects of its establishment was to preserve, without artificial means, the productions of various climates. Such a project could only be executed in a tropical latitude, where the various elevations of the ground would regulate the required temperature. The site chosen for this purpose is about seven miles from Kingston, on the side of the Liguanea mountains, the summit of which is 3600 feet

according to the Linnæan system, are of different sexes. At a particular period, the elastic stamina of the male plant expand, and shedding their farina round them like a vapour, it is borne on the breeze to its neighbouring plant, which, without such a communication, would not be productive. It is thus then, that the sexual system opens to us new and unthought of views of ordinary phenomena, points out to us how the sympathies of plants are communicated, and gives to the fixed and motionless vegetable, the animal faculties of loco-motion and sensibility. For further examples of this interesting fact, see Valisneria, Parietaria, &c. &c.

* Milne's Bot. Diction.
† There are in fact two botanic gardens in Jamaica, but we only notice the most remarkable.

above the level of the sea. Here, ascending from the base, are found the productions of the various countries of the earth : every change of elevation represents a change of latitude, and the whole surface of the mountain may be clothed with the appropriate vegetation of every climate from the pole to the equator. By means of this noble and useful establishment, the vegetable productions of various climes have been naturalized to the soil, and the plantations of Jamaica have been enriched with many valuable trees, shrubs, and plants which were heretofore unknown in the island.[*] Next to this in size and situation, and not perhaps inferior in beauty, is the botanic garden of Glasnevin. Till a very late period, the science of botany had made but a small progress in Ireland. Nor was it till the year 1790, that the public attention was directed to this interesting subject; in that year a petition was drawn up by Doctor Walter Wade,[†] on the subject, and presented to the Irish Parliament by Mr. Toler, now Lord Norbury. This was ably supported in the house, and the sum of £5000. was granted the same year to the Dublin Society, £300. of which was to be appropriated to the establishment of a garden. In the following year, the grant was continued, and in 1793, a plan of a garden was drawn up by Doctor Wade, by the direction of the Society, and distributed among the members of both houses of parliament. In the subsequent year, similar applications were made, and similar grants followed; and in the year 1800, the last act of the Irish Parliament was a patriotic grant of £10,000. in addition to £5000. granted before, making altogether the sum of £15,000. to the Dublin Society for that year: out of which, £1500. was to be appropriated to the

[*] In the year 1782 a French ship was taken by Rodney; she was bound from the isle of Bourbon to Cape François, and had on board sundry oriental plants; they were placed in the Botanic Garden, where they soon adapted themselves to a congenial soil, and multiplied through the island; they were cinnamon, mangosteen, mangoes, bread-fruit, sago, star apple, camphor, gum arabic, olives, sassafras, &c. &c. Part of this garden had been a coffee plantation, Edwards's Jamaica, vol. 1. p. 188.
In the year 1812, the whole was sold by the House of Assembly for the small sum of £4000. to an apothecary in Kingston.

[†] This gentleman, an enthusiast in the pursuit of botany and most zealous to promote it, exerted himself with the most indefatigable industry, to excite the attention of the public. He published a catalogue of the plants indigenous to the county of Dublin, which was highly approved of by the Dublin Society, who ordered five hundred copies to be printed and distributed at their expense. It is no unmerited eulogium to say, that the country is principally indebted to him for the establishment of a botanic garden, and for that zeal and activity in the pursuit of the science which his lectures have promoted.

completion of the garden. This sum has since been continued by the Imperial Parliament, the expense some years amounting to £2000. Meantime, the garden was established and in progress.* The site chosen for the purpose was near the village Glasnevin,† not quite two miles from the Castle of Dublin, a situation equally convenient and beautiful. The air of this romantic village had long been celebrated for its salubrity, and its mild temperature, and was no less calculated to promote the health and vigour of the vegetable than of the animal kingdom. Here then, the various

* The original plan proposed that it should be established in the Phoenix Park, on a royal grant.

† Glasnevin is a manor annexed to the deanery of Christ church, and its name frequently occurs in the records in its true orthography. It was called *Glaseen-even,* " the pleasant little field," from the amenity of its situation on the sloping banks of the Tolka. It had early been the most favoured and frequented residence in the vicinity of Dublin, and several mansions yet standing attest its former celebrity.

Tickel the poet came to Ireland with Addison, who was secretary to Lord Sunderland in 1714. In 1726 he married in Dublin, and vacated his fellowship in Oxford. He occupied the house and laid out the demesne on which the botanic garden is now arranged. One of the walks was planted under the direction of his friend Addison, and is to this day called Addison's walk. It is a straight avenue of yew trees crossing the walk which leads to the well. Tradition says it was here Tickel composed his ballad of Colin and Lucy, commencing with " In Leinster famed for maidens fair."

On the other side of the Tolka stood Delville, laid out by Dr. Delany, the friend of Swift. Delany was an Irishman, the son of a farmer, born in 1686. He was entered a sizar, and afterwards became a fellow, of Trinity College, Dublin. He obtained preferment from Lord Carteret, was made Dean of Down, and married, as his second wife, the widow of a Cornish gentleman, and daughter of Lord Lansdown. She was a lady highly accomplished; she excelled in painting, and was so expert a botanist that she completed a British Flora containing 980 plants. In concert with his friend Dr. Helsham, a physician, and also fellow of Trinity College, he erected the house and laid out the grounds of Delville. It was called Hel-Del-ville, formed from the initial syllables of the names of the proprietors, to intimate their joint property in the place, but the first was soon dropped, as having a strange association. The demesne consists of eleven acres, and was laid out in a style then new in Ireland. It is said by Cowper Walker to have been the first demesne in which " the obdurate and straight line of the Dutch was softened into a curve, the terrace melted into a swelling bank, and the walks opened to catch the vicinal country." Notwithstanding this eulogy, it still retains the stiffness of the old garden; walks in right lines terminating in little porticoes, and valleys crossed by level artificial mounds. On the most eminent point stands a temple decorated with specimens of Mrs. Delany's skill in painting. On the rere wall is a full length portrait of St. Paul, in fresco, and excellent preservation, and above is a medallion of the bust of Stella, said to be taken from the life, and an excellent likeness. It represents a female face with sharp and disagreeable features, and gives a very unfavourable impression of the celebrated original. On the frieze in the front is the inscription *fastigia despicit urbis*. This is attributed to Dean Swift, and supposed to be a punning allusion to this rural retreat on an eminence which literally looks

productions of different climates would naturally thrive, and many, perhaps, of the tender exotics acquire in the open air the luxuriance of indigenous plants. The garden was originally the demesne of Tickel the poet, and was purchased from the tenant in possession, and Tickel's representatives, for £2000. subject to a reduced rent. To this; other ground has been since added, so that the whole garden and its appendages now occupy the space of thirty English acres. Nothing can exceed the command of aspect which the irregular beauty of the surface presents, and of which the planners of the garden have been careful to avail themselves. Having ample room for every botanical purpose, they have not sacrificed taste to convenience, or disturbed such objects as contributed to the beauty of the old demesne. The summit, having considerable elevation, gradually or abruptly slopes to the river Tolka, which forms a sweeping boundary to one side of the garden. Here large clumps of venerable elms, or other forest trees, shade the sloping steeps, or, running along the ridges, separate the ground into irregular divisions. Through these, the ivy-crowned ruin of some venerable arch presents a passage, so that many of the compartments are approached by some picturesque or striking entrance. Nor is the systematic arrangement

down on the city. The house displays also many specimens of Mrs. Delany's taste. The rooms are decorated with admirable imitations of Chinese paintings on crape, which cannot be distinguished from the originals; and the ceiling of the domestic chapel is ornamented with entablatures of real shells disposed in the manner of modelled stucco with singular taste and beauty. A discovery was some time ago made in one of the old out offices of this house, which gives colour to a current tradition. Swift's intimacy with Delany, and his frequent visits to Delville, are well known. He passed there the summer of 1735, and in 1736 his Legion Club appeared. It is generally understood, that this bitter satire was not printed in Dublin, where no one would undertake so dangerous a libel, and it was supposed to have been composed and struck off at some private press. In removing the lumber of an out office at Delville, preparatory to its being pulled down, a printing press was found concealed among it, and it is a tradition current in the house at this day, that it was here the first copy of the Legion Club was printed. Delville is now in the occupation of J. K. Irwin, Esq. The Committee of Agriculture proposed to take this demesne for the Botanic Garden, but on investigating the title, they found they were to be restrained from breaking up the ground, and the negociation of course terminated.

Higher up in the village is the once celebrated demesne of Mitchel, extending along the banks of the Tolka opposite Tickel's. It is now in the occupation of the Bishop of Kildare. Farther on is Hampstead, formerly noted as the residence of Sir Richard Steele, and in the contiguous parish Parnel resided, who was vicar of Finglas. Thus, then, this vicinity was no less celebrated for its beauty than for its classic society. Those men whose names ennobled the age in which they lived, and whose writings for near a century have delighted and instructed the world, here took up their abode, and Tickel, Addison, Swift, Delany, Sheridan, Steele, and Parnel, made it their constant or occasional residence.

CITY OF DUBLIN. 1287

less judiciously managed. Nothing can be conceived more ungraceful than the formal regularity necessary in such an arrangement; every plant following in its order, and labelled with its name, presents to the eye an irksome sameness. To avoid this appearance, each class is subdivided into smaller compartments, insulated in green swards, and communicating by pathways, and the intervals filled up with scattered shrubs; so that while the most exact regularity is observed in the classification, and ,the series of plants follow each in such succession that the most minute can be immediately found,—the whole presents the aspect of unstudied confusion. The whole garden is arranged under the following divisions.

*A. *Hortus Linnæensis,*
Divided into two Parts.
a. *Plantæ herbaceæ.* Herbaceous division.
b. *Fruticetum et arboretum.* Shrub, fruit, and forest-tree division.

Each plant is here arranged by its parts of fructification, according to its class, order, genus, and species, beginning with Monandria, and proceeding to Cryptogamia; for which last class, however, a separate and congenial site is allotted. As this great collection is intended to include the whole series of nature; such plants as are exotics, and too tender to stand in the open air in their proper places in the class and order to which they belong, will be found in the conservatory by a reference to the printed catalogue. This extensive compartment occupies, at irregular intervals, the whole centre division of the garden, having no less than six acres assigned to it. Prefixed to each plant is a metal label incribed with its number in the Glasnevin Catalogue, and its class and order, generic, specific, and English names; by which any vegetable production, known only by description may be immediately found, and any known only by its aspect, may be immediately classed; in fact, the student in botany at once combining his knowledge, is furnished with plants for his names and names for his plants. The Arboretum and Fruticetum, containing trees and shrubs arranged in the same manner, occupy the west and south sides, forming a screen five or six perches wide, with a broad gravel way winding through the centre. The trees are planted from twenty to thirty feet asunder. To protect those which were tender, partitions of elms and other hedge rows originally sur-

* The letters refer to the plan.

rounded each compartment; these, however, are now cut away as useless, and the formal regularity removed; leaving this division to expand in all directions its rich and luxuriant foliage, forming groves and shrubberies not to be surpassed for variety and picturesque beauty. In the arrangement of Linnæus and of others, no notice is taken of varieties, as being merely incidental to the plant, and presenting no permanent or scientific character; but here, every variation, even those merely seminal, is to be found in its proper place; giving the whole a completeness of collection, and exhibiting the vegetable world, not only as it is constantly found, but also in all the varieties incidentally assumed by the individuals which compose it. Here the scientific botanist resorts, sees the whole vegetable kingdom arranged under his eye, and the very irregularities of nature coerced within the limits of an artificial system, so admirably contrived, that among so many thousand vegetable beings, he is instantly enabled to discover the individual he is in search of, sees its relations with those that surround it, and assigns to it at once its rank in the scale, and its link in the chain of vegetation.

B. *Hortus Jussieuensis.* Garden laid out on the system of Jussieu.

In order that the botanical student may have a view of the different systems which are noted for their excellence, and compare their utility by actual inspection, this compartment has lately been arranged on the method of Jussieu. It is comparatively limited, yet sufficiently extensive to comprise all the orders, and to convey a perfect knowledge of the method of that celebrated botanist.

C. *Hortus Hibernicus.* Garden of plants indigenous to Ireland.

In this department is collected every plant which is indigenous to the soil of Ireland, arranged on the Linnæan system. This extensive division is perhaps one of the most useful and interesting in the garden. Ireland, abounding with a copious variety of plants, which the exuberance of the soil spontaneously furnished, had hitherto been but little explored.[*] The first

---

[*] Among the Irish manuscripts in the Seabright collection, and in the possession of the Gaëlic Society, there are many on the subject of botany; a translation of these would throw curious light on the early state of the science in this country. A passion for botany is very prevalent among the Irish peasantry at this day. There is in every village some person who makes plants his study, and some of them attain a considerable share of knowledge, which they are not always willing to communicate. That the old Irish were well acquainted with the plants of their native country, is evident from this, that

THE CITY OF DUBLIN.

attempt ever made in modern times to investigate its vegetable productions was by Doctor Threlkeld. In 1726, he published a short treatise on native plants, especially such as grow in the vicinity of Dublin.* He was followed, by Keough, and sometime after, by, Dr. Rutty, who, in his Natural History of the County of Dublin, has devoted some portion to the consideration of its plants. These, with a few incidental notes in Smith's History of Waterford: and Kerry, were all that had been attempted in Ireland, till Dr. Wade, in 1794, published his Catalogue, adopting in his arrangement the artificial system of Linnæus. From that period, the public attention seems to have been excited in no small degree. The Garden was established, a professor was appointed, and the public crowded to hear a course of lectures on a novel and interesting subject, to which they were liberally invited by the professor, who was content to forego the emolument, he was allowed to derive from pupils, and was anxious only to promote and diffuse an interest and zeal in pursuit of the science. It was now that groups of botanical students were seen in all directions, exploring the treasures of their native soil, and adding new discoveries to its scanty collection; not only the County of Dublin, but the remote parts of Ireland were explored. In 1804, Dr. Wade published the result of his own researches,† and added

---

Keough and Threlkald were able to obtain Irish names for almost all they collected. It also appears, that considerable advances were made towards a systematic classification. Thus, they called by the genuine name of *Meacan*, such plants as had tap roots; *Brumsean*, such grasses as had creeping roots; *Trathnin*, such as had naked wing stems; *Raithleadh*, such as had imbricated heads, &c. &c. These genera, though including many heterogeneous plants, were yet no greater deviation from the present systems than Linnæus's fragments of natural orders are from his artificial arrangement. See his order Sarmentaceæ, &c.

* Synopsis Stipium herbarum alphabetice dispositarum, sive Commentatio de Plantis indigenis præsertim Dubliniensibus instituta. Being a short treatise of native plants, especially such as grow spontaneously in the vicinity of Dublin, with their English, Latin, and Irish names; and an abridgement of their virtues, with several new discoveries. The first essay of the kind in the kingdom of Ireland. Auctore Caleb. Threlkeld, M.D. Dublin. 1726.

Botanologia Universalis Hiberniæ. Containing a description of 500 plants, with their names in Latin, English, and Irish. By Doctor Keough, Chaplain to Lord Kingston. Cork, 1735.

Dr. Rutty has devoted 230 pages of his Natural History of the County of Dublin to a description of its indigenous plants, of which he describes 377. These he divides into three classes; such as are esculent 219, such as are œconomical seventy-six, and such as are used in dying fifty-seven; to which he subjoins a list of those which are poisonous, twenty-five. Published for the Author, Dublin, 1772.

Dr. Patrick Brown wrote a fasciculus of Irish botany, and printed the first sheet, which, with the manuscript of the whole work, is in the possession of Dr. Wade. It is noticed in the Linnæan Transactions, and intended as a complete Flora Hibernica. Brown was born in the county of Mayo, in 1720. He took a degree at Leyden, and fixed his residence for five years at Jamaica, of which he published the natural and civil history in 1750. He died in Ireland in 1790. † Plantæ rariores.

494 rare and curious plants to his former Catalogue. Several excellent botanists* have explored different parts of the country, and successfully contributed to increase the knowledge of indigenous botany. Recent specimens of the newly discovered plants were always sent to the Garden, where they were set down in their proper place, and in this way the indigenous plants were progressively increasing by new accessions. When the Garden was first arranged, it contained little more than those noticed in the Flora Dubliniensis, about 500 specimens; nothing having been added to the imperfect collections of Threlkeld and Keough, made more than half a century before. In the first prospectus, therefore, there was no separate compartment for Irish plants, but it proposed, that a Hortus Hibernicus should be established when Ireland should be explored. This has now been done with some success, and the proposed compartment has been for some years established, though it is still far from being complete. However, even already, the collection amounts to 1345 species, including Cryptogamics, an increase that strongly marks the spirit of inquiry which this noble establishment has excited, and the zeal and assiduity with which it has been pursued.†

* Mackay, Templeton, Miss Hutchins, &c.

† This total increase will be more striking by considering the increase of particular genera. There were known at that time, and planted in the garden, but one native species, of the genus Ulex; there are now three: there were then but thirty-nine grasses; there are now eighty-four, &c. &c.

The following Table presents a comparative view of the indigenous plants in their respective classes. The first column shews, as nearly as can now be ascertained, the number of Irish plants scattered through the garden in its first arrangement. The second is an accurate statement of the collection now in the Hortus Hibernicus. The third gives the increase in each class.

	First Collection.	Present Collection.	Increase.		First Collection.	Present Collection.	Increase.
Monandria	4	4	0	Polyandria	18	43	35
Diandria	15	31	16	Didynamia	31	79	48
Triandria	48	124	76	Tetradynamia	21	46	25
Tetrandria	22	52	30	Monadelphia	9	22	13
Pentandria	77	146	69	Diadelphia	24	49	25
Hexandria	22	54	32	Polyadelphia	7	9	2
Heptandria	0	0	0	Syngenesia	56	95	39
Octandria	14	33	19	Gynandria	10	22	12
Enneandria	0	1	1	Monoecia	14	71	57
Decandria	21	67	46	Dioecia	16	39	23
Dodecandria	9	13	4	Polygamia	9	17	8
Icosandria	15	38	23	Cryptogamia, Filices, about	50	76	26
					512	1092	585

THE CITY OF DUBLIN. 1291

),(/ (l)).... D. ' *Hortus Esculentus.* ' Kitchen Garden.

This compartment is devoted to the cultivation of such plants as are fit for culinary purposes.* Here experiments are made on the best mode of cultivation; the different kinds of manure, and the earliest and most productive kinds of culinary vegetables.† To promote and extend its utility,

To these may be added the three other orders of Cryptogamia not yet arranged in the Hortus Hibernicus, amounting to 250, making the number of indigenous plants already known, 1345 species, exclusive of varieties. Of these, the following may be noticed as a few of those which are peculiar to Ireland.

A new species of *Ulex*, which has not yet received a trivial name, was some time ago found in the county of Down, and even there it is very rare, It is distinguished by spines softer than those of the common species, and by its very seldom flowering even on its native mountains. The specimen in the garden flowered but once in several years.

ERICA DABŒCIA. This was formerly Andromeda, and now Menziezia polyfolia, but the latter name is not universally adopted. It is a beautiful heath, and peculiar to Ireland, where it is confined to a particular district. It was first called St. Daboe's Heath, by Ray, who asserted that it was carried about by the female peasantry of Ireland, as an infallible preservative of chastity. It was supposed to have been called St. Daboe's Heath from its abounding in the solitary island in Lough Dearg, dedicated to that saint; but it was ascertained that no trace of it had ever been found in the island, nor is there any tradition extant why or when the saint took it under his patronage. It is, however, with strict propriety called Irish Heath, to which name it has exclusive pretensions.

ROSA HIBERNICA. This is an intirely new species of rose, recently discovered in Ireland by Mr. Templeton. It is distinguished from the Rosa canina and other natives, by the sphæricity of its pericarpium, and other marks, which give it a decided claim to be a new species which has never before been described. It was at first supposed to be exclusively confined to Ireland, but it has been also found in Iceland.

ARENARIA CILIATA and TURRITIS ALPINA are foreign plants, and were not supposed to be natives of any part of Great Britain. The first, however, has been lately found in Sligo, and the last in Conemara, by Mr. Mackay of the College Botanic Garden.

SAXIFRAGA GEUM and SAXIFRAGA HIRSUTA, with other species of the same genus not yet described or published, have also been lately found by Mr. Mackay.

* All that are found to be fit for the food of man are occasionally introduced into it, so that the department contains not only the usual culinary vegetables, but all others in which wholesome and nutritious qualities, reside, so as that they may be converted into human aliment.

† Among other experiments on culinary vegetables made under this compartment of the garden, those on potatoes have been particularly attended to. On the 23d of January, 1810, an order was made by the Dublin Society, and transmitted to the professor, to make a series of experiments on potatoes, in various soils and manures, and by every mode of setting and planting, by shoots, cuttings, scoopings, and seed of the apple, for the purpose of giving certain information to the public on the subject. In the ensuing spring, therefore, a portion of the garden was allotted for the purpose, and a number of experiments, exceeding 100, were tried with different manures and modes of planting, and a diary of the weather was kept during the whole process. The result was returned on oath to the

six apprentices are received into the Garden, who, having passed the usual period under private gardeners, are received here to complete their knowledge

Society, but it was never given to the public. Among other curious facts it was found that an American white potatoe, weighing seven ounces, cut into seven parts, produced two stone, or an increase of sixty-four fold.

The long use of this vegetable by the natives of Ireland, has given them a kind of prescriptive claim to it, as if it was indigenous to the soil; and every thing relating to its history and origin is highly interesting. The potatoe was supposed to have been known to the ancients, and to have been the same which Theophrastus calls δραχιδνα, and Dioscorides πυκνοκωμον. It was used in India under the name of Chunno, and Bauhine found it in a wild state by the way side in Peru, in 1590. It was first introduced to Ireland by Sir Walter Raleigh, from whence its use became general in Europe. It is asserted, however, by Campbel, that this happened in the year 1610, (Polit. Survey, vol. i. p. 95.) but it appears that the potatoe was known and used in England before that period. It is mentioned by Shakspeare, and all the cotemporary writers—" Luxury with her potatoe finger." (Troilus and Cressida, act i. scene 4.) " Surphaling waters and *potatoe* roots," (He and She Coney Catchers, 1592.) " Larks, sparrows, and *potatoe* pies," (Every Man out of his Humour, act ii, scene 3.) " Some artichokes and *potatoe* roots, (Menechmi of Plautus translated, 1595.) From these and sundry other passages it appears, that the potatoe was in general use so early as the year 1592, both in pies and other culinary preparations, and was highly esteemed as an aphrodisiac. Either then, the potatoe there mentioned was a plant different from that now in use, or it must have been well known in England some time before the æra assigned for its introduction into Ireland.

It appears from Gerarde, who wrote his Herbal in 1597, that there were two kinds of potatoes known in his time. One, the *Sisarum Peruvianum*, or Spanish Batate, called in English potatoe, potatus, and potades; which he planted in his garden, but could never cause to flower; it had a trailing stem, triangular leaves, and knobbed roots like pionies: it was much used by the Spaniards, Italians, and Indians; and in England it was boiled with prunes, or roasted with oil, vinegar, and salt, " strengthning the bodie, and procuring bodilie lust, and that with gredinesse." The other kind he calls the Virginian potatoe; he had some plants from Virginia, which grew and prospered as in their native soil. The leaves, blossoms, fruit, and tuberous root he describes with great accuracy, and illustrates the whole with an excellent cut, so as to leave no doubt of its kind. It was at the time a rare plant, had temperament and virtues like the *common potatoe*, and was eaten either roasted in the embers, or boiled " or dressed in any other way by the hand of some cunning in cookerie." The first of these potatoes was that of Shakspeare, and the cotemporary writers, it is at present classed under the genus Convolvulus, and called *Convolvulus batata*. The second is our plant, classed by Bauhine under the genus Solanum, and called *Solanum tuberosum*, a name adopted by Linnæus, and retained at the present day.

The period of its introduction into Ireland assigned by Campbel must be erroneous. Sir Walter Raleigh first visited this country in 1569, an adventurer and a very young man, and again in 1580, under Lord Grey, the Lord Deputy, a captain, and of some repute; in 1584 he was sent on a voyage to America by Queen Elizabeth, and discovered Virginia, which he called from her supposed state of maidenhood; and in 1586 he obtained a grant of three seignories and a half of land, containing 42,000 acres, in the counties of Cork and Waterford, the warrant bearing date the last day of February, 1586.

THE CITY OF DUBLIN. 1293

and experience; and while in the Linnæan garden they acquire a knowledge of systematic botany, and are admitted into the higher walks of their profession, they learn in this compartment the more useful knowledge of correcting the errors of ignorance and prejudice, and improving on common practice by the light of scientific experience. After passing two years here they are received as gardeners into private houses, and are naturally much sought after, from the opportunities they have had of such important advantages.*

E. *Hortus medicus.* Plants used in medicine.

It is a melancholy fact that as our knowledge of botany encreases, its application to the most important purpose of life becomes more limited. We have, with good reason, rejected hundreds of plants from the use of

In 1603 he was tried for high treason, and on conviction, was confined for fourteen years in the Tower, from whence he was only liberated to discover a gold mine in Guiana; returning unsuccesfsul, he was sacrificed to the jealousy of Gondamir, the Spanish Ambassador, and executed 29th October, 1618. (See his Life prefixed to the History of the World, folio; also Smith's History of Waterford, p. 68.) It was impossible therefore that he could have visited Ireland in 1610, or at any period subsequent to 1603. The time truly assigned for the introduction of potatoes into Ireland is 1586. In this year Sir Walter Raleigh returning from his expedition to Virginia, landed on an estate he had near Youghal, which he afterwards sold to the Earl of Cork, and left behind him a specimen of the strange root he had brought with him from the new world. When they grew up, his steward mistook the apples for the edible part of the plant, and finding them very unpalatable, the vegetable was entirely neglected." He discovered, however, some time after, the tuberous roots in turning up the ground, when they were also tried, and found to be nutritious and palatable. Tradition also says, that they were likewise planted on some land in the diocese of Tuam, which Sir Walter afterwards left to endow a school. From Ireland they were accidentally brought to England by a vessel wrecked on North Moels in Lancashire, a place and soil still famous for their production. In the year 1662, a letter was read in the Royal Society, recommending the culture of them; the recommendation was adopted by the Society, and their members requested to plant them; while the celebrated Mr. Evelyn inculcated the project in his Sylva. From this time their use became more general, though prejudice long existed against the plant in some parts of Europe. In Burgundy it was prohibited from a supposition that it caused the leprosy; and the culture of potatoes was little known in France till after the revolution. Before the cultivation of potatoes became general in Ireland, the peasantry made use of parsnips as an article of food.

Its use on the Continent is now so general, that it has become an article of export within these some years from the port of Dublin. It is packed in baskets made for the purpose, each holding about six stone. These make part of the cargoes of ships freighted for different parts of France and Spain, where they are disposed of to considerable advantage in the way of barter, each basket bringing goods in exchange to the value of seven or eight dollars.

* A premium of five guineas is given by the Society to those who are recommended by the Superintendant for assiduity and good conduct during that period. The Superintendant receives five pounds as a gratuity for his trouble in instructing them.

medicine which were once supposed to be highly efficacious, but out of the many thousands which swell the botanical catalogue, recently discovered, how few have been substituted to supply their place. The study of botany and medicine were once almost synonymous terms; there is now but little connection between them, and it is every day growing less.* This great alteration in the practice of medicine, and the experienced inefficacy of that multitude of simples which filled our dispensatories, gardens, and apothecaries shops have much reduced the extent and interest of this compartment. It is however arranged on the plan of Woodville's Medical Botany, and here will be found every plant in which any medical virtue is known really to reside. Such as are exotics and natives of a climate too warm to bear the open air of this country will be found in the hot-houses and conservatory.

F. *Hortus pecudarius.* Cattle garden.

Here are arranged on the Linnæan system all plants which the animal, to whom the plant is appropriated, is fond of eating, and which are wholesome food for it; also such as he is not fond of eating, though not unwhole-

* In the Pharmacopœia Londinensis published by Salmon in the year 1707. A particular account is given of the virtues of 737 herbs, the knowledge of which was an indispensible requisite to every practitioner in medicine. In Lewis's Dispensatory, published in 1789, the number is reduced to 347, exclusive of gums and resins, and the virtues even of many of these much doubted. In the London Pharmacopœia of the Royal College of Physicians for 1809, all the vegetable substances, including, root, leaf, flower, bark, wood, oil, and gum, were 147! On the continent, however, the Galenical practice is still in high repute, and the Materia Medica consists principally of vegetables.

Among the native Irish the application of indigenous plants to the purposes of medicine was very general. In every village at this day, there resides a cow or fairy doctor, who is continually employed in collecting herbs, and examining their properties. The medical virtues attributed to some of these were very extraordinary, and excited the attention of the learned; of which the EUPHORBIA HIBERNICA, is a memorable example. This was formerly called *Tithemallus Hibernicus* from the milky juice which oozes from the broken stem, as from a nipple. It is known in Ireland by the name of *Meacan buidhe,* corruptly *Mackinboy,* and from the earliest times extraordinary virtues have been attributed to it. It was deemed so efficacious a purgative that it was sometimes placed under a saddle, and operated, it was said, on both horse and rider. Its high character induced some members of the Royal Society of London to enquire into its qualities, and the following report was made by Dr. Ache, Bishop of Cloyne, in 1698 : " Dr. Mullen lately tried an experiment on the famous Irish herb called Mackinboy, or Tithemallus Hibernicus, which is by the natives reported to be so strong a purge, that even carrying it about their cloaths is sufficient to produce the effect. This fabulous story, which has long prevailed, he proved false, by carrying its roots for three days in his pocket without any alteration of that sort." It possesses in a high degree all the acrid qualities of the spurge. The medical properties of the digitalis, or fox glove, have also been long known to the peasant practitioners of Ireland.

some. On the opposite side are arranged such plants as the same animal will eat, but which are injurious to it, and likewise such as it refuses to eat, whether injurious or not. Each of these particulars is noted on the label pointing out the plant, as also whether the plant be indigenous or foreign. The great utility of this division is obvious, the farmer sees at once before him the result of long experience, and without the tedious and expensive test of his own practice, he may at once adapt his stock to his field, promote the growth of such vegetables as are useful, extirpate such as are injurious, and convert the hitherto despised weed into an useful and wholesome pasturage.

G. *Hortus Rusticus.* Plants used in rural economy.
  g. *Gramina vera.* Natural grasses.
  h. *Gramina artificiosa.* Artificial grasses.

This contains all the plants of which hay can be made, and dry fodder saved for cattle, whether from grasses properly so called, or from those which are called artificial. In one division, single specimens of the Gramina vera are arranged in alphabetical order, in the other, they are arranged according to the time when each is fit for cutting, and those which are most valuable are carefully distinguished from those which are less so.* The central plats here are quite distinct, and each sufficiently large to allow their produce to be mowed and saved into hay, so that such grasses as require the same length of time to ripen, may be assorted together, and such specimens of seed collected as will propagate each species distinct, and afford the means of extending the culture of the most valuable. To promote, as much as possible, the utility of this department, premiums are proposed by the Dublin Society to those persons who collect abroad certain quantities of the seeds of such natural grasses as are pointed out,† specimens of which are distributed from this compartment. This department of botany had been, till lately, very imperfectly known. The distinctions between the genera and species of the gramina vera or natural Grasses are so minute as to elude the notice of a common observer, and the farmer saw under his eye a copious variety of kinds which he supposed possessed

* An important alteration is about to take place in the arrangement of this department. The natural and artificial grasses are to be placed according to their respective importance on the Bedford plan.

† These are Poa trivialis, Poa pratensis, Poa annua, Dactylis glomeratus, Festuca ovina, Festuca, pratensis, Avena elatior, Alopecurus pratensis, Anthoxanthum odoratum.

one common character. Even the scientific botanist formerly made but few distinctions. But under the auspices of this institution, White* has found indigenous in Ireland twenty-six genera, and eighty-four species; to these, new accessions are likely to be made, as a taste for the study becomes diffused, and a knowledge of it promoted by this department. Each of these grasses has its peculiar *habitat;* and flourishes in proportion to the aridity, moisture, elevation, and composition of the soil, to which it is congenial; each has also its peculiar property, and is in degree better calculated for meadow, pasturage, and different kinds of cattle. What infinite advantage then may not be derived from the pursuit of such an inquiry. The different kinds of corn used as food for man were originally no more distinguished than the grasses which our fields present, till his industry and sagacity separated them, and now keeps them distinct for the most important purposes. To keep the grasses separate for cultivation will be a matter of equal facility, or to combine them in such proportions as the nature of the soil may dictate. In the vast fecundity of nature nothing has been done in vain, each soil has its peculiar grass, as each animal its appropriate food. It may not be in the power of man to alter the site and soil, but it is within the scope of his industry to improve its produce by selecting for it congenial subjects.† Some grasses will clothe an arid and gravelly soil, where all other vegetation becomes extinct,‡ others love a humid situation and afford a luxuriant and succulent herbage, where promiscuous vegetation rots and decays.§ Some that are less valuable afford a necessary support to those that are more so, and the coarse form an important

* This self-taught botanist is one of the Society's gardeners. Without any advantage of education, he has acquired a scientific knowledge of botany and an accuracy in its nomenclature, rarely met with in one unacquainted with the learned languages. Under the auspices of the Society he has been very successful in exploring different parts of Ireland, and seems to have an almost intuitive knowledge of native plants, which he is able to distinguish in any state of vegetation. He has published a work on indigenous grasses, valuable for its information and curious for the Irish names, which his knowledge of the language enabled him to apply with precision.

† Bromus steriles, Hordeum murale, Poa annua.

‡ Alopecurus geniculatus, Agrostis canina, Festuca fluitans, Poa aquatica, Aira aquatica.

§ Dactylus glomeratus, Festuca elatior, Avena elatior, Phleum pratense, } when sowed with { Agrostis stolonifera, Agrostis mantina, Holcus lanatus, } support their debile stems and suffer the air to permeate their matted fibres.

addition when judiciously mixed with these of a finer texture. In effect, our pastures abound with a copious variety of grasses, as yet little distinguished because little explored; and the mildness and humidity of the atmosphere clothes our soil with a luxuriant and ever verdant herbage, amongst which have been recently discovered kinds hitherto unnoticed or despised, which are found to surpass the most valuable in succulent nutrition and fecundity.* That nothing might be wanting to complete the utility of this compartment, a separate course of lectures are delivered on the subject by the professor, at a season of the year when the grasses are in blossom, and their parts of fructification in the greatest perfection. To this, every one is gratuitously invited, specimens of the different kinds are distributed, their distinctions marked, their properties noted, their application to the different soils and situations in Ireland pointed out, and every thing that can give interest to the science and utility to the knowledge is explained to the numerous auditory, who never fail to assemble on this attractive occasion.

H. *Hortus Tinctorius.* Plants for dyers' use.

Here are to be found all the plants used in dying, particularly those which are indigenous to Ireland.†

* Of this the *fiorin* grass, Agrostis stolonifera, is an abundant proof. The circumstance of the discovery and numerous valuable qualities of this extraordinary vegetable are too well known to be recited here. In addition to the properties already well known, it is found to possess others not less important; an antiseptic power that resists the ordinary progress of putrefaction and decay, and a superabundance of saccharine matter, from which a large proportion of ardent spirits may be distilled. The first is highly valuable in our humid climate; but it is devoutly to be wished, that the latter may never add to that poison which is already productive of so many moral and physical evils.

† The colours most in repute with the ancient Irish, were yellow, purple, scarlet, and black. The first was extracted, not from saffron, as the act of Henry VIII. erroneously states, but from the *Reseda luteola*, called by the ancient Irish *Buidhe mor*, or the great yellow, from its constant application to this purpose. It grows in great abundance in arid situations in every part of Ireland, and is collected and used at this day in factories. Purple was procured from the *Lichen calicaris*, called by the Irish *corcair*. Scarlet was obtained from the *Buccinum capillus*, a shell which abounds on all the shores. The curious process of extracting the dye is minutely described by Pennant in his Zoology. Black was extracted from the matter of bogs, consisting of decayed vegetables of a highly astringent nature, set with urine.

Rutty enumerates the indigenous plants which yields different dyes. The greater number of them are in use at the present day. Red, purple, black, and blue are produced from one or more species of the following genera: Anchusa, Betula, Centaurea, Erica, Galium, Spartium, Iris, Lichen, Lycopus, Nymphæa, Origanum, Populus, Prunus, Quercus, Rosa, Rubia, Rubus, Salix, Rhamnus, Tormentilla, Vac-

8 C

I.—K. *Plantæ volubiles repentes et scandentes, frutuosæ et herbaceæ.*
Twiners, creepers, and climbers; shrubby and herbaceous.

These, though found in their proper places in the respective Class and Order to which they belong, are here collected into two compartments, that the various modes adopted by nature to support a plant or extend it, may be at once seen, and her various precautions examined and compared.

L. *Plantæ saxatiles.* Rock plants.

To afford a congenial site for plants of this description, which the garden did not naturally give, an artificial mound was constructed on the most elevated part. The fragments of rock for this purpose were transported from the hill of Howth, and such were selected as were already cloathed with various species of mosses and lichens. These were piled together without any apparent order, so as to give the appearance of a natural rocky mound. But it is so constructed, that spiral walks winding round the sides, but not visible to the eye, conducts the visitor to the summit. Here, as he ascends, he sees every gray stone cloathed with its appropriate vegetation. In every fissure of the rocks some Alpine plant has struck its roots, from which it issues forth, shading the mimic cliffs with its waving foliage.[*]

When arrived at the summit of this mount, the eye is gratified with a view of the whole garden, which the irregularity of the surface prevented when viewed from a less elevated point. It lies beneath, displayed as in a map, and presents at one view the variety and extent of its arrangements. This fantastic hill is a favourite walk, and on public days its sides and summits are usually filled with crowds of visitors.

M. *Aquarium, lacustre et palustre.* Aquatic and marsh plants.

This important addition has within these few years been made to the garden. Originally the marsh and aquatic plants stood in the class to

cineum. Yellow, green, and brown, are extracted from Betula, Anthyllis, Arundo, Berberris, Caltha, Chrysanthemum, Corylus, Crocus, Erica, Euonymus, Galium, Ligustrum, Malus, Pinguicula, Primula, Prunus, Pyrus, Ranunculus, Reseda, Rubus, Rhamnus, Rumex, Sambucus, Scabiosa, Trifolium, Verbascum. The mordants used are sulphate of iron and alum.

[*] At intervals, under the projecting shade, a variety of ferns wave their palmate fronds, among which the rare and beautiful OSMUNDA REGALIS, or flowering fern, retires from the obtrusive eye :—

There hid in caves, clandestine rites she proves,
Till her green progeny betrays her loves.

THE CITY OF DUBLIN. 1299

which they belonged, and languished for a short time in scanty reservoirs, giving for examination but a brief and imperfect specimen. But the happy site of the garden provided a remedy for this defect. On the banks of the Tolka lies an extensive flat lower than the bed of the river, which presented a ready site for inundation ; through this an extensive excavation was made, which is constantly kept full by the command of water from the stream above it. On the humid shores of this lake, and on an island formed for the purpose at one extremity, marsh plants thrive, and among other natives the beautiful *Butomus umbellatus,* or flowering rush, decorate the green margin.* The surface of the water is covered with aquatics, and among the most conspicuous is the *Nymphæa alba,* or great Water Lily ;† giving to the limpid lake an uncommon glow and richness. At convenient intervals, green promontories project into the water ; which, while they give a picturesque variety to the banks, afford an opportunity of approaching such plants as the botanist may wish to examine. This sheet of water is 200 yards in length, but of irregular breadth. It winds through a valley embosomed in high grounds which rise about it. These grounds are entirely devoted to ornamental decoration. Contiguous to the lake, American pines and other transatlantic woods that love a swampy soil are beginning to flourish, and above, the hanging woods are cloathing the side of the steep ; already they present from some points very interesting views, and when the plantations arrive at sufficient maturity, this lake will form another fair feature in the garden, where the hand of taste embellishes the formal face of science.

N. *Cryptogamia.* Site for Cryptogamics.

The incomprehensible and anomalous nature of this class of plants placing them beyond the scope of ordinary cultivation, it became necessary to select a peculiar and congenial site for them. This is a steep bank sloping to the river, and shaded with lofty trees ; through this, the Cryptogamics

* This rare and highly ornamental native inhabits the banks of the Shannon. It was not found in the first arrangement of the garden, but as the country became explored, it was transported with sundry others equally rare, from the remotest parts of Ireland, and added to the increasing collection.

† This beautiful native is not noticed because it is very rare, but because it is very abundant ; there is not a solitary pool from Donegal to Bantry where it is not found in the wildest profusion. Yet in the texture of its petals, the richness of its colour, and the magnitude of its flower, it does not yield to the most beautiful exotics. Its beauty in the lakes of Scotland did not escape the notice of Walter Scott.

are dispersed, and in a dark and gloomy retreat are solicited to indulge those habits of vegetation in which they are supposed best to thrive. Yet there is something in this class which seems to elude all inquiry and management; and it is not more difficult to develope their concealed manner of fructification, than it is to direct their solitary and sequestered propensities. This spot, which is dank and gloomy, seems as little adapted to their stubborn natures as the other compartments of the garden, and they seem to vegetate as imperfectly in one situation as the other: this division, therefore, is very incomplete.*

O. Flower Garden.

Here are planted in parterres, without order or arangement, these vegetable exuberances from which art has excluded the characters of nature. However beautiful, therefore, in the eye of the florist, they possess little interest in the eye of the botanist, who regards them as monsters in his creation. Perhaps it is for this reason that this garden, is not of corresponding interest. The flowers in it are neither remarkable for beauty or variety.

P. Hot-houses and Conservatories for Exotics.

Five houses were erected for this purpose, standing ranged together

* Cryptogamics, particularly mosses, abound in Ireland; the humidity of the soil is supposed to be the cause, as peculiarly promoting their vegetation. Several botanists have been very successful in discovering new species, which have been called after their names. Miss Hutchins was chiefly distinguished for her successful researches in this way. She was a native of the south of Ireland, who prosecuted the study of the plants of her native country with zeal and assiduity; and indigenous botany has suffered by her death a considerable injury. She discovered—

JUNGERMANIA HUTCHINSIA, peculiar to Ireland, and justly distinguished by her name.

JUNGERMANIA CALYPTRIFOLIA. This grows on furze near Bantry bay, and is marked by the singular structure of its leaf like the calyptic of a moss or the extinguisher of a taper.

ORTHOTRICHUM HUTCHINSIA.

TRICOMANES BREVISETUM was found by Dr. Stokes, but first found in fructification by Mr. Mackey, Curator of the College Botanic Garden, near Killarney. It has since been found in fructification at Madeira; and as the south of Ireland and Madeira are the only parts of the world where this vegetable has yet been found in that perfect state of vegetation, it might indicate something peculiarly analogous in the air or soil of these places.

JUNGERMANIA MACKEI was first discovered at the Lover's Leap at the Dargle, County of Wicklow, by Mr. Mackey, and called after his name.

JUNGERMANIA TAYLORI was discovered at Lough Bray by Mr. Taylor, and called after his name.

BAXBAUMIA APHYLLA was not supposed to be a native of the British islands till Dr. Wade discovered it on the Purple Mountains, Killarney.

THE CITY OF DUBLIN.

parallel to each other, and communicating by a common passage at the north end. Behind the passage and below it, were the furnaces which communicated by flues each to its respective conservatory. These magnificent houses of glass were each sixty feet long, sixteen broad, and twenty high, except the centre one, which is twenty-three feet broad and twenty-three feet high; they stood ten feet asunder, their gavels projecting into the flower gardens, of which they formed one side; they were covered with many thousand square feet of glass, and illuminated on three sides to within a few inches of the ground. They consisted of a dry-stove for such succulent exotics as required heat without moisture, as *Crassulas, Mesembrianthemus, Aloes, Cotyledons*, &c.; a hot-house for such as require an extraordinary degree of heat; a green-house for such as are sufficiently small to be contained in pots, and are arranged on stands; and a conservatory for such as are too large for pots, and are bedded in mould. The large house in the centre is of this last description, and reared trees twenty feet high. They contained 8000 plants, some of the most rare and valuable kinds, in the purchase of which no expense had been spared. One green-house was appropriated almost exclusively to heaths, of which there were displayed no less than 136 species. The site of these houses had been censured as not affording a proper aspect; that their vicinity to each other impeded a free circulation of air; and their unmanagable size prevented the due distribution of any uniform heat, so that the plants were continually exposed in winter, particularly to considerable and sudden variations of temperature.* In consequence of these objections they have been removed,

* The general healthy state of all the plants, and the uncommon vigour and luxuriance of some, would seem to be a refutation of this opinion.

The KOBEA SCANDENS, though not deserving notice as a rare plant, is yet remarkable for the rapid and prolific vegetation it displayed here. The first produced in this country was from a single seed, scarcely larger than that of a parsnip. When it began to vegetate, its progress could be distinctly marked by the naked eye; its diurnal growth was four inches, and in sixteen months it extended 130 feet, creeping round the whole extent of the conservatory, and completely cloathing its sides.

The CACTUS GRANDIFLORA is another example of this exuberant vegetation. This singular exotic it is well known only blows in the night, beginning to expand when the sun declines below the horizon, and to fade when he rises above it. It is therefore addressed by Darwin in the beautiful apostrophe—

Nymph, not for thee the radiant day returns;

Nymph, not for thee the glowing solstice burns.

The approach of this expansion is generally notified, and the curious assemble to witness it. On one

and two others erected on improved plans and in better situations. One stands on the elevated ground nearly in the centre of the garden. The range is 153 feet in length; the centre is a conservatory, seventy-five feet by eighteen; and the wings are green-houses, forty feet by fifteen each. The wings are nine feet high, the centre somewhat more elevated. Close to the entrance of the garden is another on the same plan, but of smaller dimensions. These conservatories are built without any attention to architectural ornament. They are obtruded into the most conspicuous parts of the garden, where they are coarse and formal objects, destroying that picturesque effect which was so particularly attended to in every other arrangement.

Q. Professors' House and Lecture Room.

This house was once the residence of Tickel, and consecrated to Poetry before it was dedicated to Science. The large apartments at present appropriated to a lecture room, has corresponding decorations. The frieze is ornamented with pipes, lyres, and other Doric emblems of the Muse, probably the device of the poet himself. It communicates by folding doors with the garden on one side and the conservatories on another. Through the former the public enter to the lectures; through the latter such exotics are introduced as it may be necessary to exhibit. Lectures commence in May and continue till September. The introductory lectures are given at the Society's house in Dublin, but the course really commences at the garden at eight o'clock in the morning, and is continued on three

occasion a few years ago, this nocturnal beauty attained a most extraordinary magnitude; when measured at midnight, the flower was found to be *two feet and a half* in circumference, exceeding any that has been yet recorded.

But the plant which challenges most admiration, and is likely to render these conservatories objects of uncommon interest, is the DOMBIA, or *Pine of Norfolk Island*. This magnificent tree in its native soil attains to the height of 300 feet, and is unrivalled for the majesty of its air and the beauty of its foliage. Several plants have been brought to Europe; some languish in too close confinement, and some have perished by exposure to the open air, while that at Glasnevin seems to have found a soil and temperature exactly adapted to its nature. It has already far outstripped all its competitors, and grown too large for the conservatory in which it is placed. It is proposed, therefore, to raise over it a dome, and to lay a foundation sufficient to bear the weight of a superstructure which may be elevated, if necessary, to the height which the tree would obtain in its native soil. When this magnificent idea is carried into effect, it will be a grand spectacle of human ingenuity, and present the largest vegetable production that ever was raised and supported by artificial means.

CITY OF DUBLIN. 1303

days in each week. It is very copious, detailing not only the science of botany, the method of discriminating plants as they are learned in the natural and artificial systems of writers, and every thing that is curious or interesting in the structure, nature, or habit of the plants ; but it also embraces the application of botany to all the useful purposes of life, and details the various properties of the vegetable kingdom as far as they concern the farmer, the artist, or the physician, to know them. In this full developement, nothing is wanting to complete the information conveyed by the Professor. Abundant specimens are sent round in their most perfect state, that every auditor may examine the plant while it is described, and may carry away with him materials for forming an Hortus Siccus. Different soils are exhibited and submitted to the test of chymical analysis ; and the result of experiments in the different departments to which a knowledge of the properties of plants may be usefully applied. The interest naturally excited by such a course of lectures, the most liberal invitation of the Society and the Professor to every one to attend them gratuitously; and the attention paid to the accommodation and instruction of those who frequent them, always attract such crowds, that the lecture room in its original state was found altogether insufficient to contain them. It has been recently fitted up with seats rising behind each other, so as to accommodate the greatest number in the smallest space, but though the room in this way contains more than 150 persons, it is still very insufficient for the growing interest of the public.* The gardens are thrown open on two days in the week for every one to visit, and it is only required, that those who avail themselves of the permission shall enter their names in a book lying open on a desk in

* In consequence of a donation of £700. from Mr. Pleasants, the old Doric cottage at the entrance has been removed, and another entrance similar to that in the plan, is now erected. The lodges on each side the gate are for the superintendant, and one of his assistants. There are many who think the Garden not improved by those gates, and regret the removal of the Doric structure which formerly stood at the entrance, which was more appropriate to the place. It was proposed to erect the new gates on the farther side of the bridge of Glasnevin, and have the entrance to the Garden through the island formed by the Tolka, in the valley between the high wooded grounds on each side; here grand gates would be correspondent ornaments to an extensive view of an highly ornamented landscape. Where they are now placed, the stranger at once meets with the systematic part of the Garden, which the removal even of the buildings cannot remedy. It is said, however, that in consequence of this new gate, the flower garden, professor's house, &c. which now obstruct the view, are to be removed, and new ones erected on improved plans and better situations.

the gate-lodge: on days that are not public, it is necessary to have an order from certain members of the Dublin Society. To the studious in botany an order is readily granted for admission at all times and seasons. The establishment and expenditure of the garden is as follow:—

Permanent.	£.	s.	d.
A professor	300	0	0
A superintendant	100	0	0
Two assistants, £60. each	120	0	0
Twelve gardeners at 12s. per week	374	0	0
Six apprentices at 9s. ditto	140	0	0
Rent	73	0	0
	£1107	0	0
The casual expenditure for alterations, repairs, and the purchase of plants, coals, and tools, is very fluctuating; it may be averaged at	393	0	0
	£1500	0	0

COLLEGE BOTANIC GARDEN.

THE ground for this garden was taken in 1807. It is situated in the low grounds near Ball's-bridge, about two miles from the Castle. It contains three Irish acres and a half, and has been inclosed by a very fine wall, twelve feet high. The garden is of an irregular figure: its longest side, which faces to the south-east, is 600 feet; it is lined with brick, and is well adapted for delicate creepers, Madeira, and Cape plants, with many from New South Wales.

There are separate arrangements for trees, shrubs, and herbaceous plants, according to the Linnæan system, and a very full collection of medicinal plants, arranged according to Jussieu's natural method, having the botanic and English names, together with the Number, Class, and Order both of Jussieu and Linnæus marked on each label.

The annuals and biennials are for the most part arranged separately from the perennial herbaceous plants. The grasses also form a separate division.

The hardy collection is now very extensive, little inferior to any in the United Kingdoms: an addition of nearly 400 herbaceous plants has been made to it lately, and a catalogue of the whole is now preparing.

Only one wing of the intended range of glass has yet been built, which comprises a stove, thirty-five feet by sixteen, and a green-house, forty feet by sixteen. These contain an extensive collection of stove and green-house plants, although more room is wanting to enlarge it, and to display fine specimens to advantage.

In the front of the conservatory is a small aquarium, which might be encreased to any size. A fine stream of water runs on the outside of the garden wall; if it were turned through it, it would be a considerable addition to its beauty.

THE PHŒNIX PARK.

This pleasant, diversified, and extensive demesne derives its name and origin from a manor-house, on whose site the present Powder Magazine was erected in 1738. The manor was called in the Irish vernacular tongue *Fionn-uisge*, pronounced *finniskè*, which signifies clear or fair water, and which articulated in the brief English manner, exactly resembled the word *Phœnix*;* at length the Park became known, even at an early period, by no other appellative. The spring or well so called, still exists.†

* The origin of this name for the Park has puzzled many scholars unacquainted with the Irish language, " Whence it got the name of Phœnix, I cannot learn," (Phil. Survey of Ireland, p. 5,) &c. The appellation occurs in many places in Ireland with the same import. · A river called the *Phinisk*, falls, at the presnt day, into the Black-water. (See Smith's Hist. County of Waterford, p. 239.) It was so called because its *fair* stream is contrasted with the deep hue of the Black-water, with which it mingles.

† It is situated in a glen, beside the lower lake, near the grand entrance into the Viceregal Lodge, and has been frequented from time immemorial, for the supposed salubrity of its waters. It is a strong chalybeate. It remained, however, in a rude and exposed state till the year 1800,when, in consequence of some supposed cures it had effected, it immediately acquired celebrity, and was much frequented.

THE CITY OF DUBLIN.

The Phœnix manor made part of the lands of Kilmainham, which belonged to the Knights Templars, and which, on the suppression of the priory of St. John of Jerusalem, was surrendered to the Crown by Sir John Rawson, knight, the prior, 32d Henry VIII. The priory was re-established by Queen Mary and King Philip, who re-granted it to Sir Oswald Massingherde, knight, on his becoming the prior. The estate remained in his possession until 1559, 2d Elizabeth; but Sir Oswald having fled the kingdom, it reverted to the Crown, upon which the Queen resolved to form it into a deer-park.

This resolution, however, does not appear to have been put in execution before the year 1662, when James Duke of Ormond, then Lord Lieutenant, purchased on behalf of his Majesty, King Charles II. for the sum of £3000. of Christopher Fagan, of Feltras, county of Dublin, Esq. and Daniel Hutchinson, of the city of Dublin, Alderman, their interest in a lease of sixty years, of the lands of Phœnix and Newtownland, in the parish of Kilmainham, containg 467 acres, 10 perches. This first formation of the Park had its limits greatly extended by various additions from the surrounding lands, To make these purchases, the sum of £10,000. was first issued by the Treasury; and that being found insufficient, a further sum of £10,000. was granted in 1665. These several estates were conveyed by deed to Sir John Temple, knight, Solicitor-General, and to Sir Paul Davies, the then Secretary of State, in trust for his Majesty.

In consequence of such large additions of land, the Park became very extensive, stretching on both sides the river Liffey, from Chapel-Izod to

About five years after, it was enclosed, and is now among the romantic objects of the Park. It is approached by a gradual descent through a planted avenue. The spa is covered by a small structure of Portland stone, on which sits a colossal eagle, as the emblem of longevity. This appropriate ornament was erected by Lord Whitworth. Behind the spring, under the brow of the hill, is a rustic dome, with seats round it for the accommodation of those who frequent the spa; in the back of which is an entablature with the following inscription:—

This seat,
Given by her Grace,
CHARLOTTE, DUTCHESS OF RICHMOND,
For the Health and Comfort
Of the Inhabitants
Of Dublin.—August 19, 1813.

The Duke of Richmond and Lord Whitworth used this spa with much benefit, and their example has been followed by the citizens of Dublin. In the summer nearly 1000 persons frequent it every week. The price for the season is 5s., and for a single tumbler 1d.

THE HISTORY OF

Dublin, and including the site and demesne of the present Royal Hospital of Kilmainham.* But much inconvenience arose from this disposition of the grounds; the high road ran through the Park, and the deer trespassed on the neighbouring fields, and were destroyed in great numbers. It was therefore resolved to give the highway another direction, and to enclose all that part of the Park with a stone wall, which was situated on the north side of the river. The wall, 527 perches in length, was accordingly built by Sir John Temple, at the cost of about one thousand pounds; whilst on the opposite side of the Liffey, the Royal, or Old Man's Hospital, was erected.

The completion of the Phœnix Park was effected by that accomplished nobleman and friend of Ireland, Philip Dormer Stanhope, Earl of Chesterfield, who, during his Lieutenancy, erected the column with the Phœnix surmounting the capital;* and laid out and embellished the grounds with walks and plantations.

* The following are the denominations and extent of the estates in possession of, or purchased by the Crown for the formation and subsequent enlargement of the Phœnix Park:—

	A.	R.	P.
1. The manor of the Phœnix and Newtownlands, Crown lands	467	10	0
2. Part of the lands of Chapel-Izod, purchased of Sir Maurice Eustace, Knt. Lord Chancellor of Ireland	441	0	0
3. The whole of the remaining lands of Chapel-Izod, with the mills, manor, and town, purchased of the said Sir Maurice; but its dimensions, or the additions to the Park, are not stated	0	0	0
4. Part of the lands of Grange-Gorman, purchased of Colonel John Daniel, for £126.1s. Extent not stated	0	0	0
5. Certain lands from Thomas Pooley, of Dublin, Gent. for £600.	0	0	0
6. Certain lands from Sir John Temple, Knt. for £200.	0	0	0
7. Part of the lands of Upper Castleknock, purchased of John and William Warren, of Corduff, for £240.	16	0	0
8. Part of the lands of Ashtown, in the parish of Castleknock, purchased of John Connell, of Pellett's Town, Gent. for the sum of £2270.	152	1	2
9. Part of the lands of Castleknock, from Philip Hore, Gent. in consideration of his other lands being confirmed to him	28	0	6
10. Fields near Kilmainham, from T. Musgrave, for £35.	16	0	0
11. The interest in certain lands and a house in Chapel-Izod, part of the estate of Sir Maurice Eustace, Knt. purchased from David Edwards for £150.	30	0	0
12. Certain lands from Thomas Boyd? Extent not stated	0	0	0
13. A meadow near Oxmantown, purchased from Robert Bowyer, for £44.	01	0	10

† The pillar was erected in 1745. It stands in the centre of an area where four great avenues meet, and from which there are entrances to the Viceregal Lodge, and that of the Chief Secretary. The

Although the Park may be said to have been finished by Lord Chesterfield, yet various improvements and public buildings have been erected at different periods, of which the following is a brief account and enumeration:

1. The Powder Magazine, erected in 1738. This is a regular square fort, with demi-bastions at the angles, a dry ditch, and drawbridge; in the centre are the magazines for ammunition, well secured against accidental fire, and bomb proof, in evidence of which no casualty has happened since their construction. The fort occupies two acres and thirty-three perches of ground, and is fortified by ten twenty-four pounders; as a further security, and to contain barracks for troops, which before were drawn from Chapel-Izod, an additional triangular work was constructed in 1801.

2. The Salute Battery, situated on the highest ground in the Park. It mounts twelve pieces of cannon, twelve pounders, which are fired on rejoicing days; but as such are not likely to occur as often as formerly, its site has been given by the Board of Ordnance to the Wellington Committee, for the erection of the Grand Trophy.*

trees which shade the avenues form vistas through which the perspective view of the column forms a picturesque object.

*The pillar is formed of Portland stone, and is of the Corinthian order, fluted, and highly ornamented. The base and pedestal five feet in height, the shaft and capital twenty, and the Phœnix which surmounts the column five feet, so that the whole presents on object thirty feet high. On the east and west sides of the pedestal are the following inscriptions:—

    CIVIVM OBLECTAMENTO
   CAMPVM RVDEM ET INCVLTVM
     ORNARI IVSSIT
    PHILIPPUS STANHOPE,
   COMES DE CHESTERFIELD,
      PROREX.

    IMPENSIS SVIS POSVIT
   PHILIPPUS STANHOPE, COMES
   DE CHESTERFIELD, PROREX.

On the north and south sides are the crest and arms of Stanhope in relief. It is to be regretted that from the perishable nature of the stone, this ornament to the Park even already exhibits symptoms of decay; to protect it from accidental violence it has been enclosed by a circular iron railing; but this defence, while it keeps off the hand of man, cannot keep off the hand of time, which is fast obliterating its ornaments.

* In the rere of the Salute Battery, on the ground between the great avenue leading through the Park and the road to Island-bridge, stand the remains of another fortress, called the *Star Fort*, and

3. The Vice-Regal Lodge was originally built by Mr. Clements, from whom it was purchased. It was a plain structure of brick. In 1802 Lord Hardwicke made the first important improvement, by adding the wings, in one of which is the great dining-hall. In 1808, the Duke of Richmond added the north portico, a structure of the Doric order and the lodges by which the demesne is entered on the side of Dublin. But the most striking addition to the building is the north front, added by Lord Whitworth. This is ornamented with a pediment supported by four Ionic pillars of Portland stone, from a design of Johnson's. The whole façade has been new faced to correspond with this portico, and it now stands a fair architectural ornament in the Park—a residence befitting a viceroy.

4. The Hibernian School; and
5. The Royal Infirmary, both of which have been already described under their respective heads.

The Park also contains the houses of the Ranger and the Principal Secretary; these are not worthy of further notice, nor are they ornamental to the place. A grand gate has been lately erected at the entrance from the city.

A law suit was instituted some years ago, respecting certain rights and claims in the Phœnix Park;—the Citizens of Dublin *versus* the Crown. This suit was first promoted by Napper Tandy, who resisted an attempt made by Lord De Blaquiere to add some ground to the demesne of his lodge, which he occupied in the Park as Secretary of State. In this trial the citizens were defeated.

In 1776, the Phœnix Park was surveyed by Bernard Scale, when its extent

also the Citadel. It is a regular polygon of considerable diameter. It was the work of the Duke of Wharton, when Viceroy of Ireland, and is sometimes called Wharton's Folly. It is said, that this excentric nobleman intended it as a fortress to which he might retire, in the event of any disturbances in Dublin, some symptoms of which appeared in the attack on the statue of King William, in College-green, shortly after his arrival. His apprehensions, however, were happily not verified, and the Citadel never was completed. It is further added, that he employed in its construction the Palatines who had come over to England, in 1709. Lord Wharton procured an address from the Privy Council of Ireland to her Majesty, that as many as should think fit, should be kindly received and advantageously settled here. The petition was referred to the Commissioners for disposing of the money for their settlement and maintenance, and it was resolved that 500 should be sent to Ireland, where such a colony of Protestants would add to the security and advantage of the English interest.

Wharton's Life, p. 66.

THE CITY OF DUBLIN.

and dimensions were found to be as follow:—From the Dublin gate by the Magazine and Hibernian school to Knockmaroon gate, two miles and sixty-six perches. From the Dublin gate by the Phœnix Column to Castleknock gate, two miles and thirty perches. From the Dublin gate by the rere of the Viceregal Lodge to Castleknock gate, two miles one quarter and twenty-seven perches; and from Castleknock gate to Knockmaroon gate, half a mile and fifty-four perches. Its contents were found to be 1086 acres, Irish plantation measure; or 1759 acres and twenty-two perches, English statute measure; contained in a circumference of five and a half Irish, or seven English miles.

The following seats and demesnes are comprized within the limits of the Park:—

	A.	R.	P.
The Viceregal Lodge and demesne	100	0	15
The Principal Secretary of State's	34	3	16
The Under Secretary's, at War	11	0	0
The Under Secretaray's, Civil Department	31	2	12
The Barrack demesne, formerly Lord Mountjoy's	31	2	5

The officers attached to the Park are—A Chief Ranger, with a salary of £50. a year, besides fees, lodge, and ground; he has moreover an allowance of fuel, and maintenance for twenty cows, one bull, and twenty horses. Two Park-keepers, who may appoint deputies; they have salaries, fees, lodges, fuel, and grazing. A Bailiff, with a salary of £9. a year and fees, together with a lodge and grounds, and grazing for eighteen cows, six horses, and twenty sheep, with a power of appointing deputies. A Gate-keeper and two under gate-keepers are appointed by the Ranger, with a salary of £17. 18s. and £13. 2s. 6d. in lieu of fuel, to be divided amongst them.

It may readily be conceived, that so extensive a demesne must comprise a variety of situations and scenery. In fact, the ground is very unequal, producing an undulating surface of hill and dale, agreeably diversified with wood and water. The exterior views from the Park are grand and beautiful. In the fore ground the river Liffey meanders through rich meadows, until it flows beneath the magnificent arch of Sarah's bridge. The city itself terminates the horizon on the east In front is a rich landscape highly embellished with country seats, through which the Grand Canal passes, marked in its course by fine rows of elms; and beyond all, the soft contour of the Wicklow mountains forms a suitable frame to the picture. Within the Park are several picturesque and romantic spots, forming very delightful and retired walks; some of these are skirted with groves of hawthorn of a large and venerable growth; these trees clothe the sides. of glens, which are intersected by paths that lead to " alleys green, dingle, and bushy dell in the wild wood," strongly contrasted with the regularity of the other plantations. In spring, the beauty of these spots is much heightened by the rich blow of hawthorn blossoms which cover the trees, and load the air with their fragrance. Among these woods, there is but one open level space that can be properly termed a plain; this is called the *Fifteen Acres*, and here the troops in garrison are exercised: it has also been noted, though formerly much more so than at present, as the spot where private disputes were decided by single combat.

The Park is not destitute of water, though the magnitude of the space it occupies bears no proportion to the extent of the place. There were formerly three lakes, one of which has been some years ago drained, and its place occupied by an extensive plantation; the others still remain, forming fine objects in the approach to the Viceregal Lodge.

Viewing all the particulars which should distinguish a place set apart for public recreation; the Phœnix Park, on the whole, would not suffer on comparison with any other in Europe. It is, like Hyde Park, most conveniently situated at one extremity of the town; and, if the latter be laid out in a neater manner and more trimly dressed, with nicely gravelled walks better suited to pedestrians; if it even boast a finer piece of water, in what is miscalled the Serpentine River:—yet, in extent, in variety of grounds, and in grandeur of prospects—the other indisputably possesses a decided superiority; whilst the concourse, bustle, and splendour of the gay and fashionable world, give an animation and eclat to the avenues of Hyde Park, which, it must be confessed, are never seen in the more rural solitudes of its rival.

OBSERVATORY.

The Observatory of Trinity College Dublin, was founded by the will of Dr. Francis Andrews, Provost of the College, who died in 1774. He left a rent charge of £250. per annum, for supporting, and the sum of £3000. for erecting and furnishing the Observatory with instruments. Some years

THE CITY OF DUBLIN.

elapsed before this bequest took effect, but the Provost and Fellows, in the mean time, began the erection of the edifice, and expended considerably more than the original sum bequeathed, in building it, and furnishing it with instruments.

The site chosen is an elevated ground about four English miles north-west of the City of Dublin, and one from the village of Finglas. It is founded on a solid rock of limestone of some miles in extent. Near the observatory this rock rises within six inches of the surface, and is so hard as to require to be blasted with gunpowder, for the ordinary uses of the farmer. The soil around is composed of loam and limestone gravel, which is very absorbent. The horizon is remarkably extensive, without interruption on any side, except on the south, where it is bounded by the Wicklow mountains, at the distance of fifteen miles, rising about one degree and a half. When clouds come from the south they are arrested by those mountains, leaving the space from thence to the zenith serene, while on the east and west, where no such obstacles intervene, the sky has been obscured with flying vapours.

The principal front of the building is to the east. It presents a façade of two wings, and a projecting centre, which is surmounted by a dome.

The principal apartments of the interior, devoted to the purposes of astronomy, are the Equatorial and Meridian Rooms.

The Equatorial Room is that surmounted by the dome; it overlooks every other part of the building, so as to command the entire range of the horizon. For this purpose the dome is moveable, containing an aperture of two feet six inches wide, which opens six inches beyond the zenith, by means of a lever fixed in the wall, and applied to cogs projecting from the base of the dome, it is readily moved round, and the aperture directed to any part of the horizon. The Equatorial instrument with which the observations here are taken, rests upon a solid pillar of masonry sixteen feet square at at the base, which rises from the rock below, and issues through the floor in the centre of the dome. It is so constructed, that it stands insulated and unconnected with the floor or walls, and the instrument which rests on it remains undisturbed by any motion of any part of the building: round this dome is a platform which commands a most extensive and varied prospect.

The Meridian Room stands on the west side of the building. It is intended for observations on the heavenly bodies passing the meridian, and on their meridian altitudes. It requires, therefore, an uninterrupted view from north to south, which it commands, and an attention to a variety of particulars which has been carefully paid.

A mass of solid masonry, forming a broad cross, rises from the rock, and is totally unconnected with the walls. On one end is laid down a solid block of Portland stone, nine feet two inches in length, three feet in breadth, and one foot four inches thick. This block supports the pillars of the transit instrument; these pillars are seven feet six inches in height, three feet in breadth at the base from north to south, and two feet six inches from east to west. They are formed each of a solid piece, and all effects arising from lime, mortar, and iron cramps are avoided. Such minute attention has been paid to these particulars, that the blocks were selected as they lay beside each other in the quarry, and though they are heterogeneous in their parts, yet the relative portions at given altitudes are perfectly similar; thus the effects of unequal expansion or contraction, from variations of heat cold or moisture, are guarded against. The temperature of the pillars, at different heights, is shewn by thermometers; the tubes of which are bent at right angles, and their bulbs inserted into the stone surrounded with its dust. At the other extremity of this cross of masonry rise four pillars, for the support of the frame of the great vertical meridian circle; the vertical axis of which is placed on another block of Portland stone, and so placed as not to touch the pillars or floor. Besides these precautions to ensure the stability of the instrument, similar ones, no less judicious and necessary, are adopted to provide for the equability of temperature, by admitting as free a passage of external air as is consistent with the safety of the instruments and the observer.

It was at first intended to furnish the Observatory, thus carefully planned, with the best instruments that could be procured; with this laudable view, the Provost and senior Fellow employed the celebrated Mr. Ramsden to make a transit instrument of six feet in length, and an astronomical circle ten feet in diameter. The transit instrument was early furnished to the Observatory; but the circle, without which the transit instrument was comparatively of little use, was not finished for many years after it had been ordered. This delay was partly caused by the procrastination, and partly by the indecision of Mr. Ramsden, who first began a

THE CITY OF DUBLIN.

circle of ten feet in diameter, which he rejected for one of nine feet. This he also rejected, after it was actually divided, for one of eight feet, which last was finally completed, by Mr. Ramsden's successor, after twenty years had been occupied in its construction, and placed in the Observatory in the year 1808.

This noble instrument is the largest of the kind that ever was made. It consists of a circle supported in a frame, which frame turns on a vertical axis. The axis of the circle is a double cone four feet in length, and the pressure of the weight of the circle on it is relieved by an ingenious application of friction wheels and the lever. The circle of brass is divided into intervals of five minutes, which are subdivided by micrometic microscopes into seconds and parts of a second. There are three microscopes, one opposite the lower part of the circle, a second opposite the right, and a third opposite the left extremity of the horizontal diameter. By these microscopes the minute subdivisions of the circle, which are indistinct to the naked eye, are marked with the greatest accuracy. From the vast size of the instrument, and the great interval between the upper and lower parts, the temperatures above and below must occasionally differ; and hence, the relative positions of the points of suspension of the plumb line, ten feet long, which adjusts the vertical axis and the point below over which it passes, must be changed; to obviate this, which would be fatal to the accuracy of the observations, the point of suspension and the point below are on similar compound bars of brass and steel; and hence the distance of the plumb line from the vertical axis remains always the same, as has been proved in a most satisfactory manner. The circle and the frame are also found to turn on their respective axes with equal steadiness.

The first Professor appointed to this Observatory was Doctor Henry Usher, senior Fellow of Trinity College, Dublin, under whose superintendance the Observatory was built, and the instruments ordered. He died in 1790, and was succeeded by Doctor Brinkley, the present Professor.

It is much to be regretted, that the delay in completing the necessary instruments should have retarded the advancement of astronomical knowledge in this country. Had they been furnished twenty years earlier, they would have supplied observations which would have assisted, as well as those taken at Greenwich,[*] in bringing to their present degree of perfection

[*] The present perfection of the astronomical tables is almost entirely owing to the observations made during the last sixty years at the Royal Observatory, Greenwich.

those astronomical tables which are of such importance to navigators and practical astronomers. Since the erection of the great instrument, however, two important objects of astronomical research have engaged the attention of Doctor Brinkley. These are the parallaxes of the fixed stars, and astronomical refractions. His observations seem to point out, that several of the fixed stars have a visible parallax, and that AQUILA particularly, is nearer to us than others which appear to be much brighter than that star. The particulars of this important discovery Dr. Brinkley has published in the Transactions of the Royal Irish Academy.*

Since the year 1799, the students of Trinity College have been much aided by a treatise on astronomy published by Dr. Brinkley for their use, and by a course of lectures delivered on the subject in Michaelmas term, in the philosophy school of the College.

* The notice of this discovery was given in a paper read before the R. I. Academy on the 6th of May, 1814. It was published in a quarto pamphlet in 1815, and finally inserted in the Twelfth volume of the Transactions of the Academy.

Maynooth College.

ROYAL COLLEGE OF ST. PATRICK, MAYNOOTH.

WHATEVER controversy the original colonization of Ireland, and other facts of her early history may have caused, however the advocates of her early civilization may differ from the assertors of her more recent barbarism, there is yet one claim that is openly or tacitly admitted by all,—a passion for literature in every period of her history. When hordes of northern barbarians had burst into southern Europe, and centuries of war and rapine had extinguished almost every ray of knowledge, Ireland,[*] remote and insulated, enjoyed a happy tranquillity; devoted to learning, she not only produced men of genius,[†] who were successively eminent in different parts of Europe, but also, at home, displayed an attachment to the sciences and a generous ardour to promote them, unparalleled perhaps in the annals of literature. She not only liberally endowed seminaries for the instruction of native pupils, but she invited every foreigner to participate in the same pursuit, and with a disinterested liberality, unknown in the similar establishments of any people in their highest state of refinement, she defrayed every expense, and gratuitously supplied her literary guests with every accommodation.[‡]

It was thus, that not only the natives were highly improved, but Ireland

[*] Carens bellis externis. Bede.

[†] Did the subject call for extensive illustration, it were easy to prove from undoubted testimony, that Ireland, at a very early period, produced men eminent in the different departments of literature. Let the notice of one or two suffice.

Johannes Erigena, in theology, the friend and preceptor of Alfred King of the Saxons, was very eminent in the age in which he lived. He opposed the Real Presence and other doctrines then first promulgated, with great acuteness; and the letter of Pope Nicholas, bearing testimony to his excellent learning, but charging him with heterodox opinions, is still extant. He must not be confounded with Johannes Duns Scotus, who was called the irrefragable Doctor, and lived some time after.

Virgilius, surnamed Solivagus, afterwards Bishop of Saltzburgh, was a man of astonishing knowledge for the age in which he lived. He taught the sphæricity of the earth, and held the doctrine of the Antipodes. He drew his opinions, it is said, from the early Grecian writers, who adopted the theory of Pythagoras, having travelled into Greece to consult them. These illustrious men were the precursors of Wickliffe and Luther, Galileo and Copernicus. One was therefore the harbinger of reformation in religion, as the other was of astronomy in Europe. See Ware, Usher, Mosheim, Spotswood, Dupin, &c.

[‡] Bede has these remarkable words: " Quos omnes Scoti libentissime suscipientes victum quotidianum " sine pretio, libros quoque ad legendum et magisterium gratuito præberi curabant." (lib. 3, cap. xxvii.) Bede was born in the year 678.

was crowded with learned strangers,* who having no means of prosecuting their studies at home, flocked to this Athens† of the middle ages from every part of Europe; and while native genius received liberal encouragement and was highly cherished in its native land, foreign talents were invited to participate, and received into a secure and hospitable asylum.

But how different was the scene of more modern centuries! even the barrier of the ocean was no longer a protection against the restless barbarians of the north.‡ War and rapine burst into our hitherto tranquil island, and overturned every peaceable establishment; from that inauspicious period, the vestiges of our former state of refinement were gradually destroyed, external force and civil dissention successively overthrew the monuments of our improvement, and revolving centuries so deformed the face of our fair island, that the highly cultivated soil and no less cultivated mind were converted apparently into mental and physical deserts.

But the energies of the unsubdued mind were not entirely destroyed; under every vicissitude a passion for poetry and letters continued among the people, which is to this day remarkable among the poorest and remotest

---

* It was here that Alfred retired to study: " In Hibernia omni philosophia animum composuit." (Gul. Malms. lib. 1) Alfred was the politest and most learned person in Europe. On his return from his studies he invited Johannes Erigena to his court, and about that time founded the University of Oxford. Possibly on the model of Lismore, or some university in Ireland where he had studied.

† " Amandatus est ad disciplinam in Hibernia" was the necessary character to constitute the polite and learned gentleman of the middle ages, no less sought after than the " Doctus Athenis vivere" among the Romans.

"Certatim hi properant diverso tramite ad urbem
" Lismoriam, juvenis primos ubi transigit annos,"

says Morinus in his life of the founder of the university of Lismore, county Waterford.

Ivit ad Hibernos Sophia mirabili claros. Vita Sullegeni in Cambden.

Du temps du Charlemagne 200 ans après *omnes* vera *docti* étoient d'Irelande. Scaliger the younger.

‡ The bright æra of Irish literature commenced at a period of which there are no authentic records, and terminated in 815, in which year the country was over-run and subdued by the Danes, under Turgesius; the pacific and studious habits of the natives giving no effectual opposition to these ferocious barbarians, who were, at that time, fierce Pagans that regarded Christianity with hatred and contempt. They were afterwards converted, which greatly softened their manners. The persevering ravages of these enemies to every art of peace for two centuries, will account for the state to which Ireland was reduced in the reign of Henry II.

This dark interval was, however, illuminated by a transient gleam of national prosperity during the reign of Brian Boromhe, under whose protection literature and the arts experienced a temporary revival. He fell gloriously at the battle of Clontarf, together with his valiant son Murtoch. By this decisive

peasantry.* While the bolder and more enlightened, quitting at different times their native soil, now so uncongenial in their exertions, pursued abroad the cultivation of those talents which adverse circumstances denied them at home,†

victory the Danish power in Ireland was indeed effectually broken, and it is worthy of remark, the same year (1014) in which Canute the Dane was crowned King of Norway, Denmark, and England. But the death of Brian threw the country into inextricable confusion, in consequence of the unceasing contests for superiority among the provincial *Reguli*. The radical vice of the Pentarchical frame of government could only be remedied by revolution or ,conquest. It opened an obvious road to the first invader; and Ireland was destined at last to submit to those redoubtable Goths, who settled in France by the name of Normans, and who took possession of this country under Henry II. Henry himself was Norman by birth, as were the chieftains who attended him in Ireland. They were the origin of most of the principal families of the nobility existing at present. Had Henry II. followed the policy of William upon his conquest of England, and portioned out the country among his followers, gradually incorporating the natives with the conquerors, in place of making a partial and detached settlement, similar effects would as certainly have followed; but the nerve was punctured instead of being divided, which brought on a state of constant irritation, and produced those horrible wars, insurrections, and massacres, that for 500 years devastated the island, and checked the progress of science and of civilization.

Those who wish to enter minutely into these subjects will consult Bede, Cambden, Usher, Lhuid, Rowland, &c. Those who have not leisure for such a research will find a most interesting and eloquent sketch, and the authorities from which it is quoted, in " Hamilton's Letters on the Coast of Antrim.

* The proficiency of the peasantry of the coury of Kerry in classical knowledge is well known. Greek and Latin form part of the course of education in almost every hedge school in the country. It is not uncommon for women to acquire a knowledge of the former, and the latter is the language always used in common conversation in every school where it is taught.

† The numbers who emigrated for this purpose will be best estimated by considering the provision made in foreign countries for their reception. The following was the state of the establishment on the continent for the education of Irish Catholics, previous to the French Revolution:

	Masters.	Scholars.
Paris, College des Lombards,	4	100
—— Community Rue Chavel vert,	3	80
Nantz,	3	80
Bourdeaux,	3	40
Douay,	2	30
Toulouse,	1	10
Lisle,	1	8
Total in France,	17	348
Louvain,	2	40
Antwerp,	2	30
Salamanca,	2	32
Rome,		16
Lisbon,	2	12
Total on the Continent,	27	478

and sought for that literary asylum in foreign lands which their ancestors had so liberally afforded to all the world.*

In these our days, a happier æra has opened upon us, liberal reflections on the sorrows of the past, and mutual intercourse are wearing down the asperities of mutual intolerance, and enlightened systems are dispelling the darkness of past prejudices. Native talents are no longer compelled to search elsewhere for fostering protection. Schools are every where established for the young, without infringing on that sacred conscience which is the dearest feeling of every principled mind; the honourable pursuit of every liberal profession is thrown open, without the restriction of any particular mode of faith; and finally, the establishment at home of a seminary for the Catholic priesthood, and giving a liberal education in their own country to those who are supposed to control the principles and sway the opinions of the greater mass of the community, is no less an act of strict justice than of sound and enlightened policy.

The period at which this great concession was made was most important; all intercourse with the continent of Europe was suspended, and it was rendered almost impossible for a subject of Great Britain to avail himself of any advantages offered to him in a country where his presence was interdicted. That the Irish Catholic therefore should be denied the means of education at home, and no longer suffered to obtain it abroad, was a proscription of the human faculties which no people were ever subject to; accordingly, in the year 1795, an Act was passed in the Irish Parliament, for the purpose of removing the difficulties of procuring a suitable education, to which students intended for the Catholic ministry were subject, in consequence of the suspension of intercourse between that country and the continent.

The site chosen for this College was the town of Maynooth, in the county of Kildare, at the distance of ten miles from the metropolis. It is situated at the south-western termination of the principal street, which is

---

to have compelled so many enlightened men to leave their home for conscience sake, to receive the only mental improvement they were permitted in a foreign country, to imbibe at a period when the human mind is most susceptible of them, the interests, passions, and prejudices of nations directly hostile to the government under which they were to live, and to return home with feelings naturally attached and grateful to the people that had afforded them an asylum, and averse from those that had denied it, seems to have been, independant of its injustice, very unwise policy.

* " Give these the means of education at home who formerly gave it to all the world."

(Debates on the Establishment of Maynooth College.)

THE CITY OF DUBLIN.

very wide, and forms a spacious vista to the front of the College, from which it extends to the noble avenue leading to Cartown, the princely country residence of his Grace the Duke of Leinster. The edifice, of which the centre is formed, was originally a handsome private house, built by the steward of the late Duke of Leinster, from whom it was purchased by the Trustees of the institution. To this, extensive wings have been added of the same elevation, so that the whole front now presents a grand and ornamental façade of 400 feet in length. It consists of three stories; the centre pile, which was the original building, standing forward fifty feet, the extremities of the wings being of corresponding form and projection. In this front, besides the spacious lecture rooms, &c. are the chapel and refectory, neat and commodious; the latter is of considerable dimensions, and judiciously divided into different compartments by handsome Ionic columns and arcades which support the ceiling. It was originally intended that this front range should form one side of a square, and that the supplementary buildings to be added, should form, behind it, a spacious quadrangle of corresponding elevation; but for want of sufficient funds, the front and north-west wing only have been as yet completed. This wing is principally laid out in dormitories, opening off galleries about 300 feet in length, which serve as ambulatories to the students in wet weather, and on a plan not only judicious in the arrangement, but in the execution neat, simple, and inexpensive. The Kitchen is lofty and spacious, and over the principal fire-place is the following admonition to the cook, in large characters:—

<blockquote>
Be always cleanly, show your taste,
Do not want, but do not waste.
</blockquote>

The library, which is so important a part of any seminary, is yet in its infancy; it consists of books ranged on plain shelves round not a very large room. The books are principally on theology, and are in number about 5000, among which are to be found commentaries on the Scriptures, written by men of all religious persuasions. The collection on other subjects is so limited, that the professor of philosophy is obliged, from paucity of books, to compile his treatise and dictate it to his pupils. In this library all students of a certain age are permitted to read.

Attached to the College are about fifty acres of land. In the front is a lawn of nearly two acres, laid out in gravel walks and separated from the street by a handsome semicircular iron railing on a dwarf wall, erected by the original proprietor of the central building. In the centre is the principal gate of entrance, the piers are ornamented with sphynxes, while other piers gracefully break the iron railing into parts, and are decorated with lions couchant and sculptured urns. The piers, dwarf walls, and decorations are of the best Portland stone, and executed in a fine style.* The lawn is termimated on the right hand by the tower of the parochial church of Maynooth, beautifully mantled with ivy from top to bottom, and on the left it extends to the stately ruins of the castle of Maynooth, the ancient residence of the Fitzgeralds ancestors of the Duke of Leinster; connecting these objects is this classic and highly ornamented railing, and behind is the lawn and the façade of the College. These circumstances present a fine perspective, and render the approach very interesting.

In the rere of the building is an extensive tract of level ground, part of which is appropriated to a garden, and part laid out in spacious retired gravel walks for the convenience of the students; this is decorated with plantations, and particularly with a fine avenue of stately elms.

The number of students is about 250. The proportion to be sent from each district is prescribed by the satutes:—Armagh and Cashel to furnish sixty each, Dublin and Tuam forty each; in consequence of an additional grant from Government, fifty more have been added, sent in the same proportion. They are provided with lodging, commons, and instruction from the funds of the establishment; but each student pays £9. 2s. entrance money, and his personal expenses through the year are calculated at £20.† There is a recess during the months of July and August, and a recess for a few days at the festivals of Christmas, Easter, and Pentecost. As it is requisite, even during the time of vacation, for students, who wish to be absent from College, to obtain the permission of their respective prelates, they, for the most part, remain during the whole year, and are employed in study, composition and preparation for the ensuing course. During term, the obligation of residence imposed by the statutes is religiously enforced. For the

* Either because it was supposed to be an insufficient barrier on the side of the town, and a greater degree of seclusion was considered as favourable to study and the maintenance of internal discipline, or from some other motive, of which every spectator must lament the necessity, a wall of coarse masonry and mean appearance has been built in front of this fine railing, and completely conceals it from public view. It is much to be wished that the Trustees may devise some means to remove this deformity.

† He provides himself with cloaths, books, bedding, and chamber furniture, and pays for washing, mending, and candle-light for his room.

admission of a student, besides other conditions, the recommendation of his prelate is required.* He is to be examined in the classics, and admitted by the majority of examiners. The following is an outline of the course of studies prescribed to all the students, who are divided into seven classes: first, Humanity; second, Logic; third, Mathematics; fourth, Divinity; fifth, sixth, and seventh, Modern Languages.—*Humanity:* under class; Latin and Greek, Sallust, Virgil, and Horace explained; select passages of Goldsmith's Roman History occasionally translated into Latin; portions of the Greek Testament, Lucian, and Xenophon construed and explained.—*Belles Lettres:* or first class of Greek and Latin: Greek; Gospel of St. Luke, Acts of the Apostles, Epistles of St. Paul, Homer, Epictetus, Xenophon, explained, &c.— Latin: Cicero's Orations, Offices, Livy, part of Seneca, Pliny's Letters, Horace, explained, &c.; rules of Latin versification.—*Philosophy:* Logic, Metaphysics, and Ethics; Seguy's Philosophy and Locke.—*Natural and Experimental Philosophy:* different branches of Elementary Mathematics, Algebra, Geometry, Conic Sections, Astronomy, Mechanics, Optics, Hydraulics, &c.; Chemistry.— *Divinity:* Dogmatical, first course, de Religione; second course, de Incarnatione et Ecclesia; third course, de Sacramentis in genere, de Eucharistia. The Professor is obliged to compile these treatises, which are chiefly taken from the following books; Hooke, Bailly, Duvoisin, Le Grand, Tournely, N. Alexander, P. Collet, C. Tour.—*Moral:* first course, de Actibus Humanis, de Conscientia, de Peccatis, de Matrimonio; second course, de Legibus, de Virtutibus theol. et moral.; de Sacramento pænitentiæ; third course, de Jura, de Justitia, de Contractibus, de Obligatione Statuum, de Censura, &c. P. Collet, Continuator Tournellii. There is at present no regular Professor of Sacred Scriptures, but a portion of the New Testament is committed to memory every week, the Gospels and the Acts of the Apostles are explained, the Epistles from Dom. Calmet, Maldonatus, Esthius, Synopsis criticornm, and other biblical expounders. The modern languages which are taught are English, native Irish,† and French; these

* The usual mode is to select a certain number from the candidates in each diocese, on the recommendation of the respective parish priests; but in the diocese of Cashel a strict examination is previously held, and the best answerers are sent forward; the consequence is, that students from this district hold a decided superiority in the course.

† It is an extraordinary fact, that there was originally no provision made for a Professor of Irish in this College, and that the deficiency was supplied by the bequest of an individual in humble circumstances. See Gaelic Society.

are merely incidental, and not a necessary part of the course. There are on an average sixty students annually in the Irish class, to promote whose progress the professor has published a copious Irish Grammar in its native character.

The following is the general order of each day :—The students are summoned by a bell; at half-past five they meet for public prayer; from six they study in the public halls; at half-past seven, mass is performed; at eight they breakfast; at nine, study in public halls; at ten, attend class; at half-past eleven, recreation : at twelve, study in public halls; at half-past one, attend class; at three, dinner; at five, class for modern languages; at six, study in public halls; at eight, supper; at nine, common prayer; and at half-past nine all retire in silence to their chambers.

There are two public examinations held in each year, at Christmas and Midsummer, and premiums are given, whose value is proportioned to the merit of the answerer. The period of study is usually five years; two devoted to Humanity, Logic, and Mathematics, and three to Divinity. Sometimes this period is abridged by the omission of Mathematics.

The bye-laws chiefly relate to internal regulations, enforcing much of discipline and formality, tending to train up the students to the habitual observance of exterior decorum; yet there are three anniversary days in the year observed with unusual festivity—Foundation Day, Christmas Day, and St. Patrick's Day. On these occasions wine is allowed, and three bottles are given with each mess. During meals, the Scriptures, and other profitable books, selected by the President, are to be read. The students are to be obedient to the President, and to use only such books as shall be recommended by the President and Professors.

The statutes are employed in describing the duties and qualifications of the Members of the institution. The President must be a native subject of the British empire, not under thirty years of age, in priest's orders, and must have passed through a complete course of academical learning. It is his duty to superintend the general discipline of the College. In the performance of his office he is assisted by a Vice-President. The Dean, who is likewise styled Magister Officii, inspects manners and morals, and is to be of the same order, age, and country, &c. as the President. The fifth and sixth chapter of the statutes relate to the professors and lecturers, the seventh to the choice of professors, the eighth to the students. The ninth chapter respects public examinations; the tenth and eleventh describe the parts of the Librarian and Bursar.

The allegiance of the Members of the institution to the Government from which they derive their support, is testified in various ways. Each student on his admission, takes an oath, that he is, and will remain unconnected with any conspiracy The duty of fidelity to the civil government is strongly inculcated by the theological professors. Prayers are offered on Sundays and holidays for the King in a prescribed form.

This Institution is obviously highly deserving the liberal support of Government, not merely on the moral and religious consideration of justice and conscience, but as a measure of high political expediency, as forming perhaps the strongest bond of attachment between the great majority of a country and the Government under which they live. It is supported by annual Parliamentary grants,* aided in some degree by private donations

---

* The annual grant from Parliament heretofore amounted to £8000. In 1807 application was made for an augmentation, and the sum of £2500. was granted in addition. Since that period the annual grant has amounted to £9250. by which fifty students were added to the original number of 200. The following was the establishment of the officers and professors at that period. See Report of the House of Commons, 1808:—

	£. s. d.	Allowances.
A President General, Governor of College	227 10 0	commons, groceries, and servant.
A Vice-President General, Governor in the absence of the preceding	85 0 0	commons, lodging, fire, and candles.
A Dean	85 0 0	ditto, ditto.
A Procurator or Bursar	106 0 0	ditto, ditto.
A Professor of Dogmatic Theology	106 0 0	ditto, ditto.
A Professor of Moral Theology	106 0 0	ditto, ditto.
A Professor of Natural and Experimental Philosophy	85 0 0	ditto, ditto.
A Professor of Logic	85 0 0	ditto, ditto.
A Professor of Belles Lettres	85 0 0	ditto, ditto.
A Professor of Greek and Latin	75 0 0	ditto, ditto.
A Lecturer on Dogmatic Theology	75 8 0	ditto, ditto.
A Lecturer on Moral Theology	75 0 0	ditto, ditto.
A Lecturer on Logic	55 0 0	ditto, ditto.
Carry over	£1250 18 0	

THE HISTORY OF

and legacies, which have amounted since the commencement of the institution to more than £8000. The buildings have cost £32,000, and are yet far from complete, and on the whole it is said, that the present state of the establishment is not fully adequate to the wants of the Irish Church; if this be so, it is earnestly to be wished that the same liberal and enlightened policy which dictated the establishment, may complete its boon, so as to render it fully effectual to all the purposes intended.[*]

The following are its present Officers:

President	Rev. B. Crotty, D.D.
Vice-President	Rev. M. Montague.
Dean	Rev. John Cantwel.
Bursar	Rev. John Cummins.
Sub-Dean	Rev. Ph. Dooley.

	£. s. d.	
Brought forward	1250 18 0	Allowances.
A Professor of the Irish Language	75 0 0	commons, lodging, fire, and candles.
A Profesor of English Elocution	100 0 0	
A Treasurer and Secretary to the Trustees	79 12 6	no allowances.
A Physician	56 17 6	
An Agent	300 0 0	
	£1862 8 0	

[*] This College having been exclusively founded for those who are intended for holy orders, its benefits, therefore, could not be imparted to those who were intended for any lay profession: in consequence of which, in 1802, a subscription was entered into, and a LAY COLLEGE was opened in the vicinity, for those who were not intended for the priesthood. The plan of education adopted here, comprises the Latin, Greek, French, and English Languages; with History, ancient and modern, sacred and profane. To these are added Geography and Arithmetic, Book-keeping and Mathematics. The building is on an handsome plan, and sufficiently spacious to accommodate ninety students.

Another seminary of a similar kind, called the JESUITS' COLLEGE, has been established within these few years at Castle-Brown, about fourteen miles from Dublin, near the village of Clare, in the County of Kildare. The College was the family residence of Wogan Brown, who sold it to the Jesuits. It consists of a Gothic building, flanked with four round towers, and a demesne of fifty acres. It is superintended by three Principals, who are Jesuits; and receives 150 pupils, who are clothed in uniforms, and besides the usual classical course and modern languages, they are instructed in music and every other polite accomplishment Each boy is clothed, dieted, and educated for £50. per annum.

Professors:

Of Dogmatic Theology - Rev. L. Delahogue, D.D.
Moral Theology   Rev. Fr. Anglade, L.D.
Sacred Scriptures - - Rev. James Browne.
Dunboyne Establishment Rev. P. Magennis, D.D.
Natural Philosophy - Rev. Corn. Denvir.
Logic   -   Rev. Ch. M'Nalty.
Greek and Latin   -   Rev. R. Gibbons.
Hebrew   -   -   Rev. Christ. Boylan.

Professors of Modern Languages:

Of Irish   -   -   Rev. P. O'Brien.
French   -   Rev. Fr. Power.
English Elocution   - Rev. Chr. Boylan.

Lecturers:

Of Dogmatic Theology - Rev. J. M'Keale.
Moral Theology   - Rev. D. Malone.

SITUATION, CLIMATE, SOIL, AND DISEASES.

THE situation of Dublin is, in general, pleasant and healthy. The lower or south-eastern parts lie in a flat plain, much of which has been rescued from the sea, and the inundations of the rivers which fall into it. The soil of this part is alluvial, soft, and muddy, and the situation is sometimes liable to the inconvenience and insalubrity of a humid air and damp exhalations. But from hence the City, rising into considerable elevations, forms many airy and spacious streets and squares running along the brow, or sloping down the sides of these hills, whose substratum is a dry gravel or rocky soil. These, constituting the greater portion of the town, enjoy an elastic air and pure atmosphere, ventilated by the wholesome breezes either of the sea or the mountains in the vicinity. It is computed that the greatest height of Dublin above the level of the sea is sixty feet, and it is not uncommon when a fog prevails, to stand in any street at this elevation, breathing a pure air and enjoying a clear sky, and to see the streets below buried in mist, and every object obliterated in the vapour that floated over them.* These mists, which do not often occur, would perhaps be more frequent but for the winds to which the City is exposed. It lies contiguous to a long range of mountains, which, at the distance of five or six miles, runs for a considerable way parallel to the direction of the bay and river. Along this acclivity is a constant draught of air in the direction of the bed of the river, more frequently from west to east, but sometimes from east to west. This alternate current disperses any stagnant vapours, and contributes to give salubrity to the air by continued circulation.

* This appearance particularly presents itself from the top of Frederic-street, North, down Sackville-street, and from Mountjoy-square, down Gardiner-street; the top of Nelson's Pillar in one, and the dome of the Custom-house in the other, appearing the only objects, as if they floated on the surface of the mist. Dublin has been sometimes, but very rarely, visited by dense and dangerous fogs, when ordinary business has been suspended and the streets rendered impassible from the obscurity which attended them. On these occasions the vapour appears bursting from the ground, like steam from the surface of a cauldron. In Townsend-street and College-green, some years ago, a curious phænomenon was observed—A dense white vapour was seen to issue in flakes and curling wreaths from the pavement; it rose but a few feet above the surface, and then formed small circumscribed lakes of dense opaque vapour in different parts of the street; in the vicinity of these the air was perceptibly colder than in other places, from the absorption of the caloric of the atmosphere.

THE CITY OF DUBLIN. 1329

The winds in Dublin are not so variable as is generally supposed, but, contrary to the description of the poets, zephyrs are not the vernal breezes, at least they are not the breezes which prevail in the spring.

East, north-east, and north winds prevail most in spring.

West winds predominate generally in summer and autumn.

South and south-west winds blow most during the winter months.

The west and south-west winds are found to be the most healthy and agreeable. The first is attempered by the land over which it blows, and the violence of the latter is broken by the Dublin mountains which intercept its progress; they are the warmest winds in winter. The north and north-east, on the contrary, are the most insalubrious, and attended with the most disagreeable effects; they come directly from the sea, bearing with them the cold of the northern parts of Europe, and their violence is unbroken by any higher land in the vicinity. These winds are particularly dreaded in Dublin, as they are in Edinburgh, by valetudinarians; and many who survive the winter, fall victims to the severity of the spring. The vegetable no less than the animal kingdom feel their influence. In the gardens about Dublin the buds and first shoots are constantly burnt, the blossoms destroyed, and the fair prospect of fruit blasted by one day's north-east wind; and it frequently happens, that the tender plants which outlive the winter, perish in the spring from the prevalence of these harsh winds.

But it also happens, by the bounty of Providence, that the wind most healthy should be the most frequent. The westerly winds blow, on an average, for eight months in the year.* The indefatigable Rutty, who kept a diary of the weather in Dublin for forty-one years, particularly noted the winds which prevailed during that period, and the summary of his observations gives the following result, which is fully confirmed by subsequent experience.†

* Boate notices this circumstance in a manner indicative of the state of navigation as well as of the winds in his day. "It is worth observation, that not only stormy winds, but others, do much seldomer blow out of the east than out of the west; so that commonly there is no need of a wind to be wafted over to England, where, on the contrary, those who out of England will come over into Ireland, very ordinarily are constrained to waste two or three weeks, and sometimes five or six weeks; yea, it hath fallen out so more than once, that in two whole months there hath not been so much east wind as to carry ships out of England into Ireland." Nat. Hist. p. 96.

† Since the time of Rutty no regular diary of the weather has been kept in Dublin, but several

8 G

Winds—west, south-west, and north-west, 9061. Winds—east, south-east, and north-east, 5141.

In the year 1800, winds from some point of the west prevailed for nine months. The south-west wind is the most prolific in storms; of eighty-six noted by Rutty, fifty-seven were from the south-west, and but two from the east or north-east.

The south-east is most productive of rain. The proximity perhaps of the sea in that direction might be the cause of this; but next to the south-east, the south-west is the most humid, which blows across the island, and would not probably bear so far the vapours of the Atlantic, if a range of mountains interposed.

It appears, by a mean of observations, that the fair days of Dublin are to the rainy as 110 to 255, being a proportion of nearly one-third in the year; it is further remarked, that the nights are finer than the days, and frequently when it rains for three or four days in succession, the intervening nights are clear. The mornings commencing fine, and the rain setting in at twelve o'clock at noon; this is particularly the case with the early frosts in autumn. The year 1792 was remarkably wet; 30,700 inches of rain fell in the year: of which fell in the month of August, 5,8588 inches; the humidity of autumn, Kirwan remarks, was perfectly extraordinary. It was, however, exceeded by 1816, which was a year of unparalled wetness.

The floods occasioned by the rains are very sudden and dangerous. In 1687, the water rose in Patrick's-street as high as Patrick's-gate. In 1744, the poor were entirely dislodged from their cellars, and the bridges

individuals have noted it for interrupted periods, and published their remarks. Among others, Mr. Kirwan, who read his observations before the Royal Irish Academy, which are published in their Transactions; he bears testimony to the accuracy of Rutty's remarks, and makes them the foundation of his own. He observes, that in forty-one years there were—

Of springs - 6 wet, 22 dry, 13 variable.
Of summers - 20 wet, 16 dry, 5 variable.
Of autumns - 11 wet, 11 dry, 19 variable.

Hence, in the commencement of the year, a calculation might be made of the probability of the weather in Dublin:—

Of a dry spring - $\frac{22}{41}$, of a wet $\frac{6}{41}$, of a variable $\frac{13}{41}$.
Of a dry summmer - $\frac{16}{41}$, of a wet $\frac{20}{41}$, of a variable $\frac{5}{41}$.
Of a dry autumn - $\frac{11}{41}$, of a wet $\frac{11}{41}$, of a variable $\frac{19}{41}$.

Transactions of the Royal Irish Academy, Vol. V.

on all the rivers and streams running into the bay of Dublin, were carried away; and in December, 1801, the rain continued without intermission from Wednesday night to Friday morning, swelling the Liffey to a most extraordinary height, inundating the city, and destroying several bridges.

The greatest falls of snow have been in the latter end of January, or the beginning of February. The year 1814 was memorable for a remarkable fall. It commenced on the 18th of January, and continued undissolved in some places till the beginning of April. The avenues leading to Dublin were impassable, and the poor were employed, in every direction, in cutting passages. Snow, however, seldom lies long; the fall usually sets in with a western wind, which veers to the south-west, and the snow gradually passes to sleet and rain. The tops of the Dublin mountains are seen from the city covered with snow, sometimes in the latter end of May and the beginning of June, while the air below is very temperate. It is remarked, however, that a change takes place, and the air becomes perceptibly warmer, when this snow disappears. Snow, however, for a continuance, rarely occurs. Frosts are seldom severe or of long duration.* They frequently return at intervals, twice or three times in the same winters, and last for a few days each time. Those of a more intense degree are rare, and occur at distant periods. The following years were remarkable. In 1683, frost continued from the end of December till the 25th of March, wind east-north-east; in 1708, it held for nine weeks, wind north-east; in 1715, ten weeks, wind east and north-east; in 1739-40, seven weeks; it commenced with a south-east, and ended with a north-east wind, and produced ice eighteen inches in thickness. The hard frost in 1783 commenced on Christmas-day, and continued till the 21st of February, the wind north-east.

Thunder and lightning are rare and almost always innocuous; sometimes the latter is unaccompanied by any audible sound, and the former by any visible flash. They have, however, visited Dublin in an awful form. On the 17th of July, 1719, a storm of thunder and lightning burst over the city

* The amusement of skating is seldom enjoyed by the citizens of Dublin, as the ice usually dissolves before it acquires sufficient strength to support the weight of a man. It frequently happens that the newspapers announce this diversion in London many days before it has commenced and many days after it has ceased in Dublin, in years when it is practicable; and often, that the Serpentine river in Hyde Park is thronged with skaters, when there has been little or no appearance of ice on the canals, or the lakes of the Phœnix Park in Dublin.

from the south, which lasted without intermission, from six in the evening till three in the morning. It did much damage, burning hayricks and blasting corn, and was followed by a deluge of rain, which inundated the low parts of the city. Another occurred in September 1808. It commenced from the east, at eleven o'clock at night, and lasted without intermission till two in the morning. The electric cloud seemed to burst directly over the city, where it remained stationary. The profound darkness, the vivid flashes, the near and incessant peals of thunder, excited in the inhabitants, unused to such a solemn scene, the most anxious alarm. They left their beds, and continued all night in indescribable terror. Happily, no other injury was sustained by them.* Intervals, however, of eight or ten years occur without any indications of thunder which deserve notice in a meteoric table, and when they do appear they are, not unfrequently, in the winter, accompanied with showers of hail and snow.

Halos, parhelia, or mock suns, Aurora borealis, and balls of electric fire have been seen and noted among the meteoric phænomena of the atmosphere of Dublin.

The summer in Dublin is remarkably temperate, the heat is never sultry or oppressive; the west wind, which generally prevails, is bracing and elastic,

* The only accident that happened on this occasion occurred in a street leading into Smithfield. The lightning struck the chimney of a house which seemed to act as a conductor. It penetrated the roof where it joined it, and entered a garret room in which a man and his wife were in bed. The man was forcibly raised and again dashed to the ground; while the woman attempted to escape in her first alarm, but was thrown back by some obstruction, which afterwards appeared to be the partition wall and door case, which were torn away and thrown into the middle of the room. From hence the lightning passed into the room below, having pierced the floor and ceiling with a small circular perforation, burnt at the edges, similar to that made by a red-hot poker. In this room seven people slept. The windows of the room were shattered, and some of the glass reduced to fragments like sand, as if it had been pounded in a mortar. A girl who slept on the floor was awakened, and having felt an uneasy sensation in her face, she instinctively put up her hand to guard it; she felt immediately an acute pain in her little finger, and it appeared, in the morning, that she had lost nearly the whole of the top joint. From hence, the lightning made its way through the pannel of the door into the stairs, and following the course of the wall, burst out the window on the landing place, and returning down the last flight by the opposite wall; it rent a large iron bolt and lock from the hall door, which it twisted into a variety of contortions, and having forced open the door, it passed off through a common entry. The progress of this electric fluid was distinctly marked on the walls and floor from the chimney to the hall door, and though it passed with such violence through twelve people lying close together in a small house, the only personal injury experienced, was by the girl whose finger it seared.

THE CITY OF DUBLIN.

and the aridity of the season obviated with seasonable showers. Fahrenheit's thermometer seldom exceeds seventy-eight. The longest day is sixteen hours forty-six minutes; and from the third of May to the thirteenth of July, night is never dark, for the northern horizon is lighted by a crepuscular illumination.

The winter is equally mild and open; cattle remain night and day unhoused, and certain herbaceous vegetables, which in England and the Netherlands perish to the roots, are seen in the neighbourhood of Dublin green and above ground all the year.* Fruit trees frequently blossom, like the Glastonbury thorn, at Christmas; and in December 1817, laburnums and other flowering shrubs were in full and luxuriant blossom at Glasnevin and other villages in the vicinity of Dublin. The thermometer is very seldom below twenty, in the severest winter, and the shortest day is seven hours fourteen minutes.

The testimony of Giraldus Cambrensis, on the mildness of the climate, is very striking :—" Terra terrarum hæc omnium temperatissima. Non Cancri calor exestuans compellit ad umbras, non ad focos Capricorne rigor urgenter invitat." He particularly notices its effects on the vegetable kingdom:—" Sicut æstivo sic et hïemali tempore herbosa virescunt pascua, unde nec ad pabula fœna seçari nec armentis unquam stabula parari solent, aëris amœnitate temperieque tempora fere cuncta tepescunt."—Cap. 9. The herbage was so green and succulent all the year, they had no occasion to save hay.

The following Table is drawn up from observations taken at the Botanic Garden, Glasnevin, under the direction of the Dublin Society.

* This is particularly the case with the primrose and violet; it is not uncommon to meet with primroses, cowslips, and violets in blossom in the hedges all the winter months. Different species of the Senicio, &c. throw up radical leaves, which form verdant tufts in every field. In the gardens, artichokes and other esculents are verdant and vigorous without that covering which garden books direct, and which is used in England.

Monthly Registry of the Weather for the two last Years.

N.B. The Observations were taken at 12 at Noon and 4 in the Afternoon. The Thermometer stands in shade in a North aspect.

1816.

Months	Thermom. highest	Thermom. lowest	Barom. highest	Barom. lowest	Wind points	Weather days wet	Weather cloudy	Weather sun s.	Rain G. inch.	Rain G. lines
January	49	24	30.30	23	N.E. & W.	10	8	13	2	0.00
February	50	27	30.30	29	N.E. & W.	7	10	12	0	5.59
March	53	26	30.20	28.80	N.E. & E.	13	7	11	1	1.20
April	63	29	30	29.40	E. & N.E.	7	8	15	2	0.00
May	64	39	30	29	N.W. & E.	16	7	8	3	5.70
June	73	45	30.60	29.50	W. & N.E.	8	7	15	3	0.00
July	70	53	30	29.10	N.E. & W.	18	7	6	4	2.80
August	69	47	30.29	29.20	W. & N.E.	11	14	6	6	6.00
September	67	45	30	29	E. & S.	11	12	7	3	2.20
October	64	30	30.20	29.10	W. & S.W.	16	7	8	5	0.00
November	56	24	30.50	29	N.E. & W.	17	18	5	1	2.00
December	46	25	30.50	28	W. & N.W.	8	10	13	3	4.50

1817.

Months	Thermom. highest	Thermom. lowest	Barom. highest	Barom. lowest	Wind points	Weather days wet	Weather cloudy	Weather sun s.	Rain G. inch.	Rain G. lines
January	56	23	30.50	28.70	W. & S.E.	10	11	10	1	7.10
February	55	37	30.50	29.80	W.	8	11	9	2	0.00
March	55	31	30.10	28	E. & N.E.	10	12	9	1	0.45
April	57	37	30.40	29.10	E. & N.E.	1	0	29	1	0.43
May	66	37	30.30	29.20	E.	12	8	11	1	0.80
June	78	53	30.50	29.50	W. & S.W.	10	10	11	2	4.70
July	74	54	30.60	29.10	S. & W.	14	12	5	5	1.60
August	71	57	29.70	29	S. & W.	14	8	9	3	3.00
September	75	30	30.20	28.60	S. & E.	4	10	16	0	3.30
October	56	29	38.30	29.30	W. & S.W.	7	7	17	1	0.00
November	61	30	30	29.10	W. & S.	8	10	12	3	5.00
December	50	22	29.70	28	E. & N.	7	6	18	2	1.50

Annual Registry of the Quantity of Rain which fell in Dublin for the last sixteen Years.

N.B. The Rain guage is graduated into inches, 10ths of an inch, and 100ths of 10ths of an inch.

The aperture is 1 square foot and 8¾ oz. of water = $\frac{1}{10}$ of an inch.

Years	Inches	Lines
1802	26	9.93
1803	18	9.70
1804	29	7.20
1805	22	4.70

Years	Inches	Lines
1806	24	4.90
1807	26	5.00
1808	23	1.82
1809	28	8.99

Years	Inches	Lines
1810	22	6.63
1811	18	1.12
1812	25	7.48
1813	23	2.70

Years	Inches	Lines
1814	24	6.16
1815	19	6.72
1816	30	9.97
1817	23	7.88

THE CITY OF DUBLIN. 1335

The two last years are given, not as confirmations of former observations, but rather as remarkable exceptions. They exhibit no extraordinary prevalence of the winds which has been so constantly observed in Dublin. The year 1816 was a year of unparalled rain, the distressing effects of which were severely felt; the quantity that fell, measuring in the guage nearly thirty-one inches, was a circumstance which, perhaps, never before occurred. On the first nine days in October in that year, it rained three inches. In the year 1817, the month of April was singularly dry, it rained but a small portion of one day, and the quantity that fell was but the forty-third part of the hundredth of the fourteenth part of an inch. On the twenty-first of June the thermometer stood at seventy-eight, and the weather was oppressively hot and sultry, which continued till the twenty-third. The evening of that day was marked by such lightning as is seldom seen in this country. It commenced at nine o'clock, from the east, and continued to blaze in the eastern horizon till three in morning with continued flashes. It was not attended in Dublin with any audible thunder. The month of September was also distinguished by much peculiarity. The variation of the thermometer in that month was greater than it usually is during the period of a whole year; during the greater part, it stood at 75°, two degrees higher than it had been in the preceding year; but on the thirtieth it suddenly fell two degrees below the freezing point, and was accompanied by a cold that was unknown at that season of the year. The unusual dryness of the spring had so retarded vegetation, that much of the oats and potatoe crops in the neighbourhood of Dublin were still green and vegetating; they were suddenly prostrated by this premature severity of the weather, and the greater part, particularly of the apple potatoes, were destroyed. These irregularities are remarkable deviations from the usual gradual and general progress of Dublin seasons.

The substratum of Dublin is composed of different modifications of lime-stone, particularly that sort called black-stone or calp. This substance is in some measure peculiar to the county of Dublin, and was first noticed by Kirwan in his Elements of Mineralogy, and deemed of sufficient importance to deserve a name and place as a distinct species. It is arranged by him under the genus Argyl, as possessing the distinctive character of that earth, more than that of any other. Subsequent analysis, however, has found, that the proportion of that substance is so comparatively small, that it can hardly be distinguished by that generic character.. The following analysis was made by the Hon. G. Knox, and published in the eighth volume of the Transactions of the Royal Irish Academy.

100 parts of calp contained
- Carbonate of lime - 68 grains.
- Oxid of iron - 2 ditto.
- Argyl - - 7¼ ditto.
- Silex - - 18 ditto.
- Carbon and bitumen - 3 ditto.
- Water - - 1¼ ditto.

100

The properties of this modification of lime-stone are singular. Though it effervesces with acids and scratches glass, it neither burns into lime nor strikes fire with steel; and when breathed upon, it gives the smell peculiar to argillaceous earth. It is usually found under a bed of vegetable mould and layer of lime-stone gravel, and commences with black lime-stone; in some places separated by layers of argillaceous schist, which gradually passes, as it descends, into calp, by an imperceptible transition. It particularly abounds in the neighbourhood of Lucan, and in the quarries of Tolka-bridge and Glasnevin. From these two extremities it ramifies in all directions through the City, of which it probably forms every where the sub-soil, except perhaps of the alluvial tracts at the east extremity. In laying the foundation of Essex-bridge, it was not met with at the bottom of the river, and extensive quarries of it had been formerly worked near Stephen's-green, in the Lower Castle-yard, and in Townsend-street. The fact is noticed by Rutty, as enriching its proprietor, and the two last were met with in laying the foundation of the Castle Chapel, the House of Lords, and the new front of Trinity College.

Connected with calp, is *magnesian lime-stone*, which is also found in considerable quantities, particularly at Miltown and other places in the immediate vicinity of Dublin, and probably accompanies calp in forming part of the lime-stone substratum of the city.

100 parts of the stone contains - Carbonate of lime - 21 parts.
Carbonate of magnesia 18 ditto.

It effervesces slowly with muriatic acid, and is rendered friable with the blow-pipe, and acquires a dark brown colour. It is remarkable, that the pro-

THE CITY OF DUBLIN.

portions of the ingredients of this stone are the same wherever it is found, and the chemical properties differ materially from those of a mixture of its components, of which the injurious properties of its lime in vegetation is a remarkable example.

The soil of Dublin abounds with mineral springs. In some places a mixture of saline and other mineral substances strongly impregnates the water, and forms a great nnmber and variety of spa wells, for which Dublin has been from the earliest times remarkable, and to which recent discoveries are every day adding new ones. About the year 1750, the Physico-Historical Society directed that they should be analysed, and their properties ascertained. This was done by Doctor Rutty, who examined ten mineral springs issuing from different parts of the soil on which the city is built; viz.: five in Francis-street, at the signs of the Burnes Arms, the Plough, the Pump, the Vernon's head, and the Wheat sheaf; one on the Combe, one on the Liberties of Donore and Thomas Court, and one in Engine alley; besides two others discovered ten years after in Francis-street and Hanover-lane. These were all saline purgative springs; and some of them so strongly impregnated as to yield on evaporation from three to four hundred grains of solid contents in each gallon; in which the salts bore a proportion, varying from sixteen to one, and four to one. The purgative qualities of some of these salts were so strong, that two drachms operated as a brisk cathartic. They had been in extensive use in the latter end of the preceding century, and after a lapse of fifty years, had been again brought into notice by the Physico-Historical Society, and many important cases of their efficacy recorded. They stood upon the highest part of the city, and issued from a surface generally sixty feet above the level of the sea; the salts, therefore, with which they were impregnated, were unconnected with any marine filtration. They have again fallen into disuse and oblivion, and from sewers, and other excavations made near their sources, it is probable they have drained away never to reappear.

It is remarkable, that the Lucan waters known and analysed at that time, were considered as a weak chalybeate, and entirely neglected. They have since wonderfully changed both their quality and reputation. In the year 1758, a sulphureous spring was discovered to the north-west of the chalybeate; but so near the river, and in a situation so low, that it was constantly overflowed by the river floods, till Agmondisham Vesey, Esq. on whose

THE HISTORY OF

estate it was discovered, protected it by a wall. The well is very superficial, and not more than fifteen inches in depth. It contains about eighty gallons of water, and when emptied fills again in an hour. The soil from which it issues is a lime-stone gravel, supposed to contain coal. The water is limpid, but throws up a blueish scum to the surface, and turns whey coloured in rain, and after standing for some time. The odour it emits is peculiarly offensive, and in smell and taste resembles the washing of a foul gun barrel, or the flavour of a semi-putrid egg; it is caused by the sulphuretted hydrogen gas with which it is strongly impregnated. This gas is extricated in considerable quantities from the surface, and diffuses itself for several yards round the well, strongly tainting the air, particularly in frosty or rainy weather. Of all the analyses made of this water, it is probable, that that of the Hon. G. Knox is most correct; it was read before the Royal Irish Academy, and published in the eighth volume of the Transactions, and it is as follows:.

Two gallons contain - Carbon of magnesia - $1\frac{1}{4}$ grain.
————— of lime - 23 grains.
————— of soda - 39 ditto.
Muriate of soda - 4 ditto.
Sulphur - - 16 ditto.
Bitumen 0

$83\frac{1}{4}$

The carbonate of lime is held in solution by an excess of carbonic acid gas, amounting to thirty-two inches in two gallons of the water. The sulphur is in a state of sulphuretted hydrogen. The experienced efficacy of these waters in all cutaneous and some other diseases, induced great numbers to use it. For their accommodation a spacious hotel and a range of lodging houses have been erected, which for several years have been the resort of the gay and fashionable of the metropolis.

In laying the foundation of Essex-bridge, Semple, the architect, found a spring issuing from the bed of the river, the substratum of which was a lime-stone rock, and by fixing into it iron pipes, he raised it many feet. It does not appear what the nature of this water was, but the circumstance appeared so curious to Darwin, that he has quoted it in his Phytologia.*

* Sec. IX. 1—10.

THE CITY OF DUBLIN.

A chalybeate spring in the Phœnix Park had long been known. In the year 1800, it was recommended to public notice by some efficacious cures recently performed. It has since attained much celebrity, and is now greatly frequented by the citizens of Dublin.*

A tepid well of many reputed virtues, was early known at St. Margaret's, near Finglas, about four miles north of Dublin. It was dedicated to St. Bridget, and was enclosed by Plunket, of Dunsoghly-castle, with a battlemented wall; forming a pleasant bath, six yards long and three broad, which is still in good preservation. The temperature of the water is very low, being colder than the air in summer, but perceptibly warmer in winter, when it raises the thermometer to fifty-one. It is said to contain lime, muriate of soda, nitrate of kali, and a sulphur, but not in any notable proportion. The water is extremely pure, soft, and limpid; and frequently bottled and sent to Dublin; but the bath is seldom used.

In the year 1793, another tepid spring was discovered about a quarter of a mile north-west of the village of Leixlip, about eight miles from Dublin. The workmen employed in excavating the Royal Canal, cut into its spring, and it immediately issued in a narrow perpendicular stream from the bottom of the bed, and astonished and alarmed a labourer with whose naked leg it came in contact. The engineer communicated the discovery to Mr. Conolly, on whose estate it was, and the waters were sent to Professor Higgins to be analysed.

A wine gallon yielded the following contents:

Gaseous, at the heat of 212, Carb. acid gas and atm. air 4 cubic inches.
Solid   -   -   Muriate of soda   -   30 grains.
                         Lime   -   23 ditto,

with a small quantity of sulphur of kali, magnesia, argillaceous and siliceous earths, and bituminous matter.

Heat of the water   -   75¼ degrees Fahr.

This water was recommended to the notice of the Canal Company, who secured the current of the spring by directing its course to the neighbouring bank, under which it was conveyed into a cistern, and the redundant water was received into a basin, formed for the purposes of a bath. This was much frequented, particularly by the poor, and the spa at Leixlip was for some time the rival of Lucan. A rumour, however, was spread, that the

* See Phœnix Park.

original spring was lost; and in the year 1803, it was highly recommended to the public, in a pamphlet, published in Dublin by Ch. Fletcher, M.D. who denied the fact. It has however lost its reputation, and it is now little frequented.

A few years since, an important addition was made to the mineral waters of Dublin, by the accidental discovery of the springs at Golden-bridge. These are situated near the new barrack, on the south side of the Liffey, and are on the ridge which overhangs the river, and extends with little intermission from Francis-street to Lucan, the soil of which seems impregnated with saline ingredients. On the first discovery of these springs miraculous qualities were attributed to them, and immense crowds resorted there. They are still much frequented, and another of a similar quality has been discovered in the vicinity. The waters were analysed under the direction of the Dublin Society in 1813, by Professor Higgins, and gave the following results:

		Grs.	Parts.
One gallon yielded	Sulpht. potash	7	0
	Chrystal. carb. pot.	8	12
	———— C. soda	25	38
	Carb. lime	13	50
		54	0

with a portion of sulphuretted hydrogen usually condensed in sulphuretted mineral water, and a quantity of carbon of iron too minute to be collected.

About two years ago, another spring was discovered of a very different quality and in an opposite direction. It issues from the low grounds near Sir Patrick Dunn's Hospital, and was analysed by Mr. Wharmsby, in the laboratory of the Dublin Society in 1817. A wine gallon contains—

Gaseous, Carbon. acid gas, 25 0 cubic in. Sulph. of soda, - 10 50 grs.
Solid, Oxyde of iron, 4 0 grains. ——— of lime, 30 50
   Mur. of magnes. 18 0 Carbon. of magnes. 8 50
   ——— of soda, 12 0 ———— of lime, 18 50
   Sulph. of magnes. 23 0
                                         125 0 grs.

The ingredients of this newly discovered spring are similar to those of Cheltenham, but the quantities and proportions very different.

In sinking for a pump in the lawn before the Stone Tenter-house, in the

Liberties, in the year 1817, another mineral spring was discovered. It was analysed by Dr. Barker, chemical professor to the University, and produced the following results. One wine gallon of the water contained—

Carbonic acid gas,	8 16 cubic inches.	Muriate of soda,	2 95 grs.
Oxide of iron, -	1 15 grains.	Sulphate of lime,	4 77 do.
Muriate of magnesia,	4 17 do.	Carbonate of lime,	15 90 do.
Sulphate of ditto,	7 50 do.	—— of magnes.	10 9 do.
—— of soda,	2 60 do.	Silex, a trace,	

Total - 49 13 grs.

This water issues from the same ridge which furnished the mineral springs known in Rutty's time, and is probably derived from the same impregnation. It has been tried and found useful in some cases, and from the alkaline muriates which it contains, hopes are entertained that it may be found useful in scrophulous disorders.

The general character of the water, which is raised in pumps or wells, as it issues from the calp and lime-stone rocks, is remarkably hard, and impregnated with a considerable portion of sulphate or nitrate of lime. This is readily decomposed, by pouring a solution of soda, or other alkali, into the water, which becomes immediately cloudy, and deposits a copious calcarious sediment. In some manufactories and distilleries where it is used, the pans are sometimes covered with an encrustation of gypsum nearly an inch thick.* This is not the water, however, which is used for domestic purposes; that which is distributed by pipes to every house, is the product of a remote soil. It descends from the summit levels of the canals, or from the Dodder. It is brought, therefore, from the lakes of Westmeath, the county of Kildare, or the Dublin mountains; and is thus sometimes conveyed forty miles to supply the city. It is here received in large reservoirs, where it rests and deposits its impurities, and is then distributed to the cisterns, abundant, sweet, soft, and limpid.

The food of the inhabitants is wholesome and nutritious; it consists in a most abundant and constant supply of flesh, fish, and vegetables, of the best quality, of which an account has been given in the "Markets." It is probable, that no city in Europe exceeds Dublin in this respect.

* From the boiler of a distillery in Bow-street, near Smithfield, flakes of selenite, half an inch thick, are frequently taken.

From all these circumstances then of free air, dry soil, mild climate, pure water, and wholesome and abundant provisions, Dublin should be a very healthy residence, and the usual distempers arising from the contrary causes be absent. But though nature has done much for its salubrity, art has done more to counteract it. Nineteen church-yards attached to as many parish churches, and nine slaughter-houses * behind or within their respective shambles, in the heart of the city, expand the noxius effluvias of animal putrefaction in every direction, and so taint the air as to render it highly offensive to all the neighbourhood, and frequently to compel the inhabitants to seek another residence.† Where these are wanting, offals of every kind are suffered to accumulate in the front and rere of every narrow lane, till they become impassible and intolerable, and engender and perpetuate the germs of contagion among a population which is here more crowded than elsewhere, and sometimes averages at twenty-eight to a house. To this is to be added, the extreme distress of some of these poor people, arising from frequent suspension of industry and want of employment. The privations they suffer of every comfort, the bad quality and scanty quantity of the food they are able to procure, their exposure to wet and cold, with scanty and insufficient covering both night and day; habits of intoxication, which are promoted by 900 houses licensed to vend spirits, and 300 more, perhaps, unlicensed, together with those moral effects which arise from anxiety and depression of mind ‡ and irregular passions, all these

* Among the Romans the Laws of the Twelve Tables prohibited the burial of the dead in the city. Hominem mortuum in urbe ne sepelito. Tab. x. Lib. 12. The Jews usually buried their dead outside their cities; and it is remarkable, that they are the only sect who adhere to the practice in Dublin. In the year 1765, all slaughter-houses were removed from Paris to the Isle de Cignes, below the town.

† In the intelligent Reports of the Fever Hospital, Cork-street, it is stated as probable, that the infectious miasma arising from animal substances in a state of putrescency, is capable of producing deleterious effects in a much wider sphere than that which arises from the patient himself; and that families were often attacked with the same symptoms of fever for several months, of which some neighbouring collection of filth was found to be the common origin.

‡ This depression of mind, which sometimes leads to an absolute indifference of life, and a neglect of all the means of preserving it, has been remarked by all medical men who have practised among the poor of Dublin. It is thus noticed in the Report of the Fever Hospital for 1816, by Doctor Stoker, one of the attending physicians:—" Many years continuance of misery have nearly extinguished all that hope and buoyancy of spirit for which the poor people of this city were remarkable in their better days. These have been succeeded by indifference to their situation, or the encroachment of disease, or even

latter circumstances predispose them to receive diseases which the preceding causes had engendered. Hence it is, that sickness is prevalent in Dublin, and that twelve hospitals and five dispensaries cannot afford adequate accommodation and relief. The following Table exhibits the diseases among the poor of Dublin, and the comparative number afflicted with each, as they appear on an average of several years from the reports of the different dispensary institutions.

Annual Average of Diseases among the Poor of Dublin.

Apoplexy	21	Herpetic Eruptions	153	Paralytic affections	90
Amaurosis	18	Hooping Cough	15	Palpitations	135
Amenorrhœa and Chlorosis	285	Hysteria	48	Piles	69
Asthenia	75	Hydrophobia	3	Petechiæ et Purpura	
Afterpains	24	Hypochondriasis	15	Hæmorrhagia	12
Catarrh	123	Inflammation of the eye	507	Prurigo	30
Cholera	354	—— of the ear	6	Psorophthalmia	45
Colic	216	—— of the intestines	21	Porrigo Capitis et Barbæ	66
—— of Poitu	15	—— of the kidneys	3	Pulmonary Consumption	399
Cough and Dyspnœa	3765	—— of the lungs	243	Rheumatism, Acute	533
Constipation	387	—— of the liver	90	—— chronic	549
Dysentery	345	—— of the mamma	15	Retroversio uteri	3
Deafness	66	—— of the peritonæum	42	Rickets	6
Diarrhœa	381	—— of the parotid gland	21	Scarlatina	1024
Dropsy, Anasarca	337	—— of the tonsils	642	Small pox	114
—— Ascites	240	—— of the trachea	3	St. Vitus's dance	3
—— of the chest	84	Indigestion	792	Scrofula	42
—— of the ovarium	9	Idrosis	12	Spasms	15
Erysipelas	105	Insanity	30	Typhus	807
Ear-ache	36	Itch	93	Tabes Mesenterica	15
Epilepsy	12	Jaundice	39	Tape Worm	12
Fever not contagious	105	Leucorrhæa	162	Tenesmus	135
—— intermittent	102	Lumbago and Sciatica	297	Tooth-ache	57
Hæmorrhage from the lungs	156	Measles	108	Trismus dolorificus	6
—— from the nose	30	Menorrhagia	165	Venereal complaints	78
—— from the stomach	15	Nettle-rash	24	Vomiting	147
—— from the uterus and abortion	93	Opacity of the cornea	36	Worms	216
		Peripneumonia Notha	162	Wry-neck	18
Heart-burn	36	Pleuritic stitches	1020	Water on the brain	42
Head-ache and Vertigo	305	Pain of the stomach and bowels	75		
Hemicrania	18				

death itself; surprising and unaccountable to a casual observer, and which is more to be deplored, as it leads many of them to neglect the means of preservation when afforded." (p. 47.) Yet it should be noticed, to the credit of these people, that with all that feeling of preference for death, they never accelerate its approach with their own hand; nor, careless as they are of their own life, are they equally so with respect to that of another: the great law seems to be deeply impressed on their minds, and suicide and murder are crimes unknown in Dublin.

To these may be added the patients received into the different hospitals, and those prescribed for as externs,* so that the whole number of the poor afflicted with some complaint every year in Dublin, may average at 45,000. The average number of deaths is about one in forty-one.

Among these complaints dyspepsia or indigestion always bears a considerable proportion. This arises from the constant use of tea, which has become the universal diet of all the poor in Dublin, and is prepared frequently as dinner. This alternates with ardent spirits, and both communicate that artificial and temporary exhilaration to which the poor resort with a fond but melancholy attachment. The prevalence of dropsy of different kinds, is another consequence of this diet, and very generally a fatal one. Pectoral complaints bear also a large proportion in the list ; the insufficient covering

* The hospitals which prescribe for extern patients, are the Meath, Jervis-street, Peter-street, St. Mark's, Mercer's, and Richmond. All these prescribe for surgical as well as medical cases, and for patients from the country as well as the city. The aggregate returns of their externs for one year amounted to 135,000! These, added to the dispensary reports, amounting to about 20,000, would give a sum of 155,000 patients annually exceeding the whole pauper population. To account for this apparent inconsistency, it is to be remarked, that there is no registry of names kept in the hospitals for externs ; they merely return the numbers prescribed for, without respect to persons, and the same patient is enumerated every time he returns to the hospital. It is here assumed, that the hospitals prescribe for about as many externs as the dispensaries, and that the intern patients amounting to 3500, with those labouring under typhus and syphilis received into their respective hospitals, and not noticed in the Dispensary Reports, amounting to about 5000 more, make an aggregate sum of 45,000.

To the hospitals already noticed are to be added—

St. Peter's. This was established in the year 1810, in Peter's-street, at the sole expense of Surgeon Kirby. It contains thirty beds, and receives patients from all parts, though nominally confined to St. Peter's and St. Bride's parishes. Attached to it, is an anatomical theatre, where the founder lectures, and devotes the fees of the pupils to the support of the hospital. Its patients are principally surgical.

St. Mark's. This was originally opened in Francis-street in the year 1753, and called St. Nicholas's Hospital. In 1808, it was removed to Mark-street, for the parishes of St. Mark and St. Anne. It contains ten beds. Its patients are both medical and surgical.

An important addition has also been recently made to the dispensaries, by attaching to them " Nourishment Departments," whence food is distributed to the poor convalescents. It is supposed that this has increased the number of patients, particularly in the Meath-street dispensary, where many poor creatures take physic to entitle them to food. After all, no just conclusions can be drawn from these vague and loose data ; for there are no weekly reports of christenings and burials extracted from the parish registers, ever published in Dublin ; nor any annual tables of deaths and diseases, graduated from infancy to old age, with the comparative increase or decrease of mortality, as are regularly published in London, and in most of the large towns of Great Britain.

of the poor may account for this. It is remarked, however, that they bear venesection better than those of a similar class in London. Small-pox is still very prevalent and often fatal among the poor of Dublin, and it is supposed that one out of every three perish who take it naturally.* The efficacy of vaccination was early recognised here, and no medical man in Dublin ever opposed it; but it was not so easy to persuade the poor to submit to it, from a prejudice on their minds, that if the cow-pock be introduced where the contagion of small-pox exists, both disorders will be fatal; they are, therefore, most decided against the practice of vaccination when the small-pox appears as an epidemic, and protection against it is most necessary. Within the last years, an eruptive complaint attended with violent symptoms was very common in Dublin, and as it nearly resembled smallpox, and vaccination was no safeguard, a very general alarm was excited. The disease, however, was found to be varicella, or chicken-pock; though there is no doubt that small-pox had, in a few unequivocal cases, succeeded vaccination, but not in sufficient numbers to justify any apprehension of its antivariolous security.

It is an opinion generally entertained by medical men in Dublin, that contagious fever had not prevailed in Ireland till within these last twenty-five years. Hence, that its causes are not of a permanent nature, and that it may be extinguished, or at least its type changed, and its malignity mitigated. Although the number of patients admitted to the Fever Hospital in Cork-street, has been gradually and progressively increasing since its commencement, yet the mortality of the disease has greatly lessened, as appears from the following comparison:—

Year.	Patients.	
Admitted in - 1805	- 1024,	- died 1 in $10\frac{1}{37}$.
Admitted in - 1815	- 3787,	- died 1 in $19\frac{140}{117}$.

Thus, while the number of patients affected with fever has increased in the ratio of three to one, the deaths are lessened in the ratio of two to one.

It is a fact worthy of notice, that the year 1816, so remarkable for the quantity of rain that fell, and the constant humidity of the atmosphere, was singularly healthy, not only in the United Kingdom, but on the Continent; but the evil was reserved for the following year, when all the morbid effects followed. Much of these are to be attributed to the

* Report of Meath-street Dispensary.

unwholesome quality and scanty quantity of food produced by an immature vegetation. The sickness most fatal and most universal was typhus fever. It first appeared in the spring of 1817, in Cork, and next in Derry, the southern and northern extremities of the kingdom, leaving Dublin and the centre long free from the infection; nor was it till the end of the year, and after the greater part of Ireland had been infected, that the contagion visited the metropolis.* In the month of November, the number of patients received into the hospitals amounted to forty per day. It was hoped that the frost, producing a salutary change in the state of the atmosphere, would have checked it; but cold, acting as a debilitating cause on the half-naked bodies of the poor of Dublin, was found to increase the fever to a most alarming degree. In December the number increased to fifty per day on an average, and in some days 100 patients were admitted. The alarm now became very general: besides the usual fever hospitals, wards in several others were fitted up for the purpose, and 800 beds were thus provided for their reception.† It happened, providentialy, that the malignity of the

* Among the causes which might account for this postponement of the contagion, may be assigned the precautions taken in the metropolis. In the spring of the year, the sum of £18,000. was subscribed by the opulent, to provide the means of employment for the poor. With this sum they were kept for several months engaged in public works about Dublin; they received as much as supplied their families with food, and were themselves kept in wholesome exercise; their anxiety was removed, their minds kept up, and they had neither the means nor the motives for intoxication. In addition to this, very early precautions were taken to remove such causes as might engender and propagate infection: by the active and judicious exertions of Mark Bloxham, Lord Mayor, offals and putrid filth of every kind were removed from those places where they had been suffered to accumulate, and a general ventilation and purification of the houses by cleansing and white-washing took place as far as it could be practised. The predisposing and the proximate causes of fever being thus removed, the city was for a long time preserved from its visitation, long after other parts of Ireland were suffering from its attack; and when it did appear, it did not assume a malignant character. The fever entered the city by the great avenues leading from the north and south, particularly by the former; through Swords, Santry, and Drumcondra; where every house was visited by it in its progress; and it is sufficiently remarkable, that it extended but a short way out of the high road, at either side. Through Dublin it was supposed to be propagated by 5000 beggars who conveyed the contagion in their clothes from street to street and from house to house. In a pamphlet written by Whitley Stokes, M.D. a plan was proposed for removing those 5000 beggars from the city, as a means of stopping the progress of the infection.

† The hospitals which received fever patients were Cork-street, St. George's, Hardwicke, House of Industry, Sir Patrick Dunn's, and Stephens'. In the House of Industry, the extensive Penitentiary was appropriated to this object, and supplied with temporary beds.

THE CITY OF DUBLIN. 1347

disease did not increase in the same proportion. The symptoms were rather mitigated, and the mortality was in a ratio rather less than usual among the number affected.

The diseases among the upper classes have nothing to mark them. Exempt from the causes which generate distemper among the poor, they are not liable to their effects.

Of the natural salubrity of Ireland, and of its once remarkable exemption from disease, there are abundant testimonies. Giraldus Cambrensis thus writes, temp. Hen. II. " Aëris clementia tanta est, ut nec nebula inficiens, nec spiritus hic pestilens, nec aura corrumpens. Medicorum opera parum indiget insula: morbidos enim homines, præter moribundus, paucos invenias, inter sanitatem continuam mortemque supremam, nihil fere medium." Cap. 9. And Boate observed about a century ago, that this immunity from disease was remarkable:—" There be few sickly persons," says he, " and Ireland's healthfulness doth further appear by this particular, that several diseases very common in other countries are here very rare, and partly altogether unknown." Chap. 23, sec. 102.

It becomes then a matter of great importance to inquire, what can have been the cause or causes of this deterioration of the health of the inhabitants, and of the great increase of diseases in the country? The soil and climate have not changed; nor is it evident, that the naturally robust stamen of the natives have suffered an alteration for the worse. Bodily vigour, when not reduced by debilitating causes, and instances of great longevity, are still as remarkable, and as numerous as they ever were; and Ireland exceeds, in these respects, most countries. To one cause alone, therefore, must be ascribed the present deplorable condition of the lower classes, and that is—the rapid and immense increase of population, which has nearly trebled itself during the last century, whilst the resources for its support have, by no means, kept pace with this increase. Nothing could check the early and improvident marriages of the peasantry, or the fruitfulness of the women; however, the pressure of increasing numbers was lessened by continual drains for the army and navy, and by occasional migrations to England, where, during the war, hands were required. Some considerable manufactures too, particularly those of cotton, were once in activity, though at present extinct. All these resources have now failed; even the demand for day labourers is partial and limited; and, with the exception of a few manufactures of woollen still struggling to maintain themselves in the city, and the linen manufacture, which alone employs great numbers—there is absolutely no permanent employment for this exuberant and importunate population. Hence arise extreme poverty, and the deficiencies of the necessaries of life, in the prime articles of food, cloathing, fuel, and habitations. This state of miserable destitution, with the mental anxiety and despondency attending it, is quite sufficient to account for the rise and propagation of various maladies. It is indeed a subject for serious and sad reflection—to witness such multitudes of the poorer classes thus suffering the extremities of want and disease, in perhaps, the most fertile and salubrious country in Europe!

APPENDIX.

APPENDIX.

No. I.

POPULATION OF DUBLIN.

THE strangely contradictory calculations with respect to the population of the principal cities of even civilized Europe has been already mentioned: with respect to that of Dublin, the same diversity of opinion prevailed until a few yeare since, when the Rev. J. Whitelaw, anxious to ascertain the truth, and influenced by an ambition, perhaps laudable, of being the first to offer to the public, what it has often wished for in vain, an accurate well arranged census of a considerable capital, availed himself of the favourable opportunity offered by the unhappy situation of that city at the commencement of the late rebellion; and, with the sanction of Government, but at his own private expence and toil, began a census of the inhabitants of the city of Dublin, early in the month of May, 1798.

When he first entered on the business, he conceived that he should have little more to do than to transcribe carefully the list of inhabitants affixed to the door of each house by order of the Lord Mayor. As the families of the middle and upper classes always contained some individual who was competent to the task, and as few had any motive to conceal or misrepresent, he found their lists, in general, extremely correct: but among the lower class, which forms the great mass of the population of this city, the case was very different. The lists on the doors of their wretched habitations, presented generally to view a confused chaos of names, frequently illegible, and generally short of the actual number, by a third, or even one-half. This he at first imputed to design, but was afterwards convinced that it proceeded from ignorance and incapacity. In order effectually to obviate this difficulty, he and his assistants, undeterred by the dread of infectious diseases, undismayed by degrees of filth, stench, and darkness, inconceivable by those who have not experienced them, explored, in the burning months of the summer of 1798, every room of these wretched habitations, from the cellar to the garret, and on the spot ascertained their population. In this business he expected opposition, but experienced none. So universal, at this period, was the dread of being suspected of disaffection, and so powerful was the Secretary's seal and signature, that

APPENDIX. No. I.

every person seemed anxious to assist; and, when this terror gradually subsided, a rumour circulated that he was employed by Government to take an account of the poor inhabitants, preparatory to the adoption of some system for the relief of their necessities; which produced a similar effect, from a far more pleasing motive. In the course of the survey, one only of his assistants received a serious insult. In attempting to remonstrate with a butcher of Ormond-market, on the incorrectness of his list, the human brute flung at him a quantity of blood and offals.

Mr. Whitelaw was at first much embarrassed by the inexperience of his assistants. He employed them, therefore, in taking surveys of streets which he had already surveyed himself, until he discovered that they had attained a sufficient degree of accuracy. He never, however, relied on their returns with implicit confidence, but made them frequently act as checks on each other. Two or more of them frequently surveyed the same street in succession, without any communication with each other, and, if any material variation occurred, he investigated it himself on the spot. He was, besides, constantly engaged, during the continuance of the survey, in taking the population of the poorest and most thickly inhabited houses of the poorest streets, as these were most likely to produce confusion and error, in order to serve as checks on their returns. Hence it happens that, in the poorer parts of the city, there are few streets that have not been twice, and some even three times surveyed.

In a country, where difference of religious opinions has been the source of so much misery, to ascertain the number belonging to each religious sect would be gratifying to many, and particularly at a period when animosities, that were supposed to be nearly extinguished, have been unfortunately revived. The calculations, or, to speak more properly, the conjectures on this subject, were so various and discordant, that he was anxious to determine the point, as far as it concerned the capital. On a nearer view, however, it was found to be a subject of extreme delicacy: the temper of the times seemed to discourage enquiry, and he was obliged, though with reluctance, to relinquish the idea. On this subject, however, we shall take the liberty to intimate, that truth may be sufficiently approximated by a little exertion on the part of the Protestant clergy. In their domiciliary visits, they may easily ascertain the number of their respective flocks, with sufficient accuracy, while engaged in the performance of an essential and pleasing part of their duty, and without giving alarm to any by the parade of a census. There may, at first view, seem to be some difficulty in discovering the habitations of poor Protestant room-keepers; but the parish registers of births and marriages, which, in consequence of the repeated injunctions of the late and present archbishops of Dublin, are now, it is presumed, kept with accuracy, will generally serve as guides where to enquire them; and, as each poor room-keeper has generally some knowledge of those of his own communion in his neighbourhood, the clergyman, who is willing to exert himself, will seldom want the necessary information: this mode would not have been suggested with so much confidence, had not experience convinced the author that it is practicable: he has, by the means proposed, obtained a complete list of the Protestant inhabitants of the parish of St. Catharine, at once the largest, and nearly the poorest in this city;

APPENDIX. No. I.

which specifies the age, sex, and occupation of every individual; together with their state of education, if children; and such other circumstances as may be singularly useful to a parish minister, in the execution of an indispensable, but too much neglected duty. The number of Protestants, deducted from the gross population of each parish, as ascertained by the present survey, will shew the number of those of the Church of Rome, without any material error, except, perhaps, in St. Catharine's parish, where allowance must be made for a considerable number of Quakers.

The materials, thus collected, with the incessant toil of at least ten hours each day, during five successive months, were next to be arranged. The plan adopted, he trusts, is such, that the work may be considered as a correct and faithful picture of the actual state of Dublin in the year 1798, and may, at any future period, be compared as such with its then existing state, in order to discover, at a single glance, the changes, whether for better or worse, which have taken place in the lapse of time. For this purpose, not only the position of every house is given, with the population, and the proprietor's name and occupation; but its elevation, or number of stories; whether it is modern built, or old; and whether, with respect to its state of repair, it is good, midling, bad, or ruinous, are all expressed by appropriate marks. The width of each street at either end is also given, with its commencement and termination, and the intersections of other streets, lanes, &c. with their breadth where they enter it. If the contiguity of the houses be interrupted by a dead wall, waste ground, or any other object, its position and extent in yards are carefully marked. Public buildings are placed in their proper situations. The position of the different sides of each street, with respect to the points of the compass, with the parish in which it is situate, are expressed; and if the boundary line between two parishes cross it, the houses between which it passes are accurately noted. This seeming multiplicity of objects, with a variety of others unnecessary to detail, are, it is presumed, minutely delineated, without the slightest confusion. For the truth of this statement the reader is referred to the work itself, where it may be observed, that each page is divided into six columns by strong lines. The first of these columns is subdivided into four by finer lines; of which the first contains the number of houses in regular order; the second the number actually on the door; the third its state of repair, in which the letters n, g, m, b, r, express *new, good, midling, bad, ruinous*; and the fourth column gives the elevation expressed in stories above the ground floor. The second column, titled *Upper and middle Classes*, subdivided into three, gives the males, females, and total of that description in each house; while the third column gives the servants of ditto, similarly divided. The fourth column, titled *Lower Class*, exhibits the great mass of the labouring poor, working manufacturers, &c. who are not in the service of others, similarly divided. The fifth column gives the grand total, divided into males and females; and the last column contains the name and occupation of the proprietor, if resident; if not, the letters P. T. intimate that he has it set in poor tenements. On the left-hand margin of the page, the extent of each side of the street is marked, with its direction with respect to the cardinal points; and, on the right-hand margin, the parish or parishes, in which the whole or different parts of it are situate.

vi APPENDIX. No. I.

The examination of a few pages of the work will, it is presumed, shew that its claim to perspicuity is not unfounded. But, as it is accessible to few, and its bulk (two folio volumes) renders its publication inexpedient, for the satisfaction of the reader, the table, containing York-street is annexed, as a sample of the method which has been adopted. Immediately after the name, its breadth at either end is given, in feet and inches. In the first horizontal space, Aungier-street is written, intimating that it commences at, and is numbered from thence; then follow the houses, in regular succession, from No. 1 to No. 13, where their contiguity is interrupted by the intersection of French-street, which is here twenty-nine feet wide. The series of houses is again resumed, until again interrupted by Proud's-lane, only eighteen feet wide, which is succeeded by a dead wall of forty-three yards to Lord Roden's house, where the south side of York-street, as appears by the left-hand margin, terminates in Stephen's-green. From the Green we return along the north side, in which we first meet a dead wall of eighty yards bounding the Quakers' burial ground, and from thence a continuity of houses to Aungier-street, interrupted only by the intersection of Mercer-street, thirty-one feet wide; and, by directing the eye to the right-hand margin, we find that the entire street is in St. Peter's parish.

Giving the breadth of the streets, and noting their waste or unbuilt-on spaces, may, perhaps, seem to some superfluous: but such persons will please to recollect, that these are points which plans seldom ascertain. In some of our latest productions, the narrowest alleys are widened into respectable streets; while streets that have but a few straggling houses, or that exist only in idea, are represented as completely occupied by buildings. Mr. W. was anxious, besides, to give posterity a work, which may enable them to compare the same street with itself at very distant periods, in order to discover its improvement or decline; and, in such a point of view, these are most essential features. Had such a delineation of ancient Rome or Athens, or even of London in an early period of its existence, reached our time, how would it be prized?

The corner or angle houses are, it is obvious, situate in two streets; and hence it is necessary to specify in which of them they are numbered.

The limits of several of the parishes are so very irregular, that streets of a very moderate extent frequently pay ministers money to three different incumbents. This is the case with the Poddle, (see the table). The north side of this street commences we find from Francis-street, in which the corner house is numbered; and by the left-hand margin we see, that the ten first houses between Francis street and Patrick-street belong to the parish of St. Nicholas Without: the 11th and 12th, between Patrick-street and Upper Kevin's-street, belong to the Deanery of St. Patrick; the 13th, 14th and 15th, on the south side, to St. Nicholas Without; and the remainder of the south side to St. Luke's. This is so clearly expressed, that any person of common understanding, with the table in his hand, might instantly find the limits on the spot, not only by the numbers of the houses, but where these may happen to be erased or altered, which frequently happens, by their relative situation with respect to the intersecting streets.

From the survey of the squares, streets, lanes, alleys, courts, &c. of the city of Dublin

Number of Houses	Number on Door	State of Repair	Stories High	UPPER AND MIDDLE CLASS Males	Females	Total	SERVANTS OF DITTO Males	Females	Total	LOWER CLASS Males	Females	Total	Total Males	Total Females	Grand Total	NAMES AND OCCUPATIONS OF PROPRIETORS, &c.

† NORTH SIDE. †

ST. FRANCIS-STREET.—38.3 Feet wide.

CORNER HOUSE IN DITTO.

1	1	n	3	0	0	0	0	0	0	0	0	0	0	0	0	T. O'Brien, Publican, P.T.
2	2	n	3	0	0	0	0	0	0	7	10	17	7	10	17	J. Leigh, Toy-shop / Samuel Spencer, Pawnbroker.
3	3	n	3	0	0	0	0	0	0	2	3	5	2	3	5	Lydia Barry, Linen Draper.
4	4	n	3	0	0	0	0	0	0	4	2	6	4	2	6	Michael Jones, Chandler, P.T.
5	5	n	3	0	0	0	0	0	0	3	3	6	3	3	6	J. Wilmot, China-shop.
6	6	n	4	0	0	0	0	0	0	7	16	23	7	16	23	John Murray, Tin-man.
7	7	n	3	0	0	0	0	0	0	3	3	6	3	3	6	John Tench, Grocer, and Dram-shop.

ST. PATRICK-STREET.—26.7 Feet wide.

CORNER HOUSE IN DITTO.

| 8 | 8 | n | 3 | 0 | 0 | 0 | 0 | 0 | 0 | 2 | 3 | 5 | 2 | 3 | 5 | Mc. Donald, Huxter. Holt, Publican. |

UPPER ST. KEVIN'S STREET, in Continuation.

| 9 | 9 | n | 3 | 0 | 0 | 0 | 0 | 0 | 0 | 3 | 6 | 9 | 3 | 6 | 9 | Dunn, Publican. |

THREE-STONE-ALLEY.—10.4 Feet wide.

10	10	n	3	0	0	0	0	0	0	8	9	17	8	9	17
11	11	n	3	0	0	0	0	0	0	3	2	5				Tate, Old Iron shop. William Erskine, Publican. James Butler, Starch Manufacturer. Costello, Publican, P.T.
12	12	B	3	0	0	0	1	0	1	1	4+	26	11	26	37	
13	13	m	2	0	0	0	0	0	0	11	21	21	9	21		Dureen, Baker, P.T.
14	14	b	3	0	0	0	1	1	3	0	10	19	9	10	19	Molloy, Huxter, P.T. Peter Ryan. Daniel Kennedy, Distiller.
15	15	B.H.		3	2	5	0	0	0	0	0	0	5	6	11	
16	16	B.H.		3			0	0	0							
17	17	B.H.														
18	18	B.H.														
19	19	b	3													
20	20	B.H.														
21	21	B.H.														
22	22	B.H.														
23	23	b	3													

† SOUTH SIDE. †

NEW-Row.—23.9 Feet wide.

TOTAL .. || 11 || 5 || 16 || 0 || 5 || 5 || 76 || 116 || 192 || 87 || 126 || 213 ||

+ ST. LUKE. +   ST. NICHOLAS WITHOUT.   DEANERY OF ST. PATRICK.   ST. NICHOLAS WITHOUT.

NOTE.—The letters B.H. in the second column express Back Houses; of these there are three; and the passage to the yard, in which they are situate, appears, from the table, to lie between the houses No. 14 and 15. The letters P.T. annexed to the name of a Proprietor in the last column, imply, that he has set in tenements to the poor, the shop, and perhaps one room excepted, which he occupies himself.

Number of Houses.	Number on Door.	State of Repair.	Stories High.	UPPER AND MIDDLE CLASS. Males.	Females.	Total.	SERVANTS OF DITTO. Males.	Females.	Total.	LOWER CLASS. Males.	Females.	Total.	Total Males.	Total Females.	Grand Total.	NAMES AND OCCUPATION OF PROPRIETORS, &c.

AUNGIER-STREET.

1	1	m	4	0	0	0	0	0	0	8	10	18	8	10	18	Elizabeth Nowlan, Haberdasher.
2	1	m	4	0	0	0	0	0	0	5	6	11	5	6	11	Lau. Birmingham, Porter-house.
3	2	n	4	1						0	0	0	1	5	6	George Shee.
4	3	m	2	0						4	7		3	4	7	I. Woffington, Hair-dresser.
5	4	m	2	0	0	0	0	0	0	5	7	12	5	7	12	{ John Maxwell, Law Scrivener. Thomas Irwin, Taylor, shop o
6	5	n	4	1	0	1	1	1	2	0	0	0	2	1	3	P. Marsh
7	5	n	4	0	0	3	0		1	0	0	0	3	1	4	Samuel Montgomery.
8	6	u	4	2	4		1		2	0	0	0	3	3	6	Mr. Cary.
9	7	n	4	3	7		1		3	0	0	0	5	5	10	George Lyndon.
10	8	n	3	0	1	0			2	0			1	2	3	Charles Fleetwood, Attorney.
11	9	n	4	2	3		1		2	0	0	0	2	3	5	Mrs. Robnet.
12	10	n	4	3	6	3			5	0	0	0	6	5	11	William Glascock, Attorney.
13	11	n	4	1	2	3			6	0	0	0	4	4	8	James Glascock, Attorney.
14	12	n	4	3	6	1			3	0	0	0	4	5	9	W. Bourne, Attorney.
15	13	n	4	3	5		3		9	0	0	0	5	9	14	Thomas Walker, L. L. D.

FRENCH-STREET.—29 Feet wide.

16	14	g	4	0	0	0	0	0	0	2	10	12	2	10	12	Thomas Byrne, Publican.
17	15	n	4	2	5		0		2	0	0	0	3	4	7	——— Mc. Nemara, Attorney.
18	16	g	4	1	6		1		2	0	0	0	6	3	9	John Sweeny, Merchant.
19	17	n	4	3	5	2			3	0	0	0	4	6	10	Matthew Franks, Attorney.
20	18	n	4	1	3	2			2	0	0	0	4	3	7	Molesworth Green, Attorney.
1	19	n	4	5	10	1			2	0	0	0	6	7	13	Rev. E. Ledwich, L. L. D.
2	20	n	4	3	7	1			2	0	0	0	5	5	10	Andrew Moller, Merchant.
3	1	n	4	2	3	2			1	0	0	0	3	3	6	Joseph Hone, Merchant.
4	2	n	4	5	7	1			2	0	0	0	3	7	10	Nicholas Fitton, Esq. Attorney.
5	3	n	4	1	5	3			2	0	0	0	1	7	8	Counsellor O'Farrell.
6	4	u	4	4	5	0			3	0	0	0	4	3	7	Francis William Green, Counsell
7	5	n	4	2	3	2			2	0	0	0	3	4	7	Mr. Mc. Donnel.
8	6	n	4	2	4	3			4	0	0	0	5	6	11	Edward Westby, Master in Chan
9	7	n	4	3	6	2			3	0	0	0	5	6	11	Joseph Hone, Jun. Merchant.
30	8	n	4	1	2	1			1	0	0	0	2	2	4	William Johnson, Counsellor.

PROUD'S-LANE.—18 Feet wide.
DEAD-WALL, FORTY-THREE YARDS.

| 31 | 0 | g | 3 | 1 | 3 | 4 | 4 | 8 | 12 | 0 | 0 | 0 | 5 | 11 | 16 | Earl of Roden. |

STEPHEN'S-GREEN, WEST.
QUAKER'S BURIAL GROUND, EIGHTY YARDS.

32	9	n	4	5	6	11	2	3	5	0	0	0	7	9	16	Mr. Handy.
3	30	n	4	1	2	3	3	3	6	0	0	0	4	4	8	Robert Eustace, Attorney.
4	1	n	4	1	2	1	1	1	2	0	0	0	2	2	4	Arthur Thomas, Attorney.
5	2	n	4	3	6	3	3	3	6	0	0	0	6	6	12	David Sherlock, Brewer.
6	3	n	4	1	2	3	2	5		0	0	0	4	3	7	Nicholas Morrison, Counsellor.
7	4	n	4	5	9	2	3	5		0	0	0	6	8	14	Thomas Bell, M. D.
8	5	n	4	1	3	2	2	4		0	0	0	4	3	7	Thomas Lyster, D. D.
9	6	n	4	2	4	2	2	4		0	0	0	4	4	8	Joseph Jameson, Counsellor.
40	7	n	4	2	3	1	2			0	0	0	3	2	5	Mrs. Reily, L. H.
1	8	n	4	3	6	2	3	5		0	0	0	5	6	11	Counsellor Burston.
2	9	n	4	4	8	3	2	5		0	0	0	6	7	13	Baron George.
3	40	n	4	2	2	0	3	3		0	0	0	0	5	5	Mrs. Knott.
4	1	n	4	3	4	2	4	6		0	0	0	3	7	10	Thomas Garde, Attorney.

MERCER'S-STREET.—31 Feet wide.

45	42	n	4	2	6	1	2	3		0	0	0	5	4	9	Gerard Macklin, Surgeon.
6	3	n	4	0	2	1	3	4		0	0	0	3	2	5	Rich. and Edw. Pennefather, M.
7	4	n	4	2	4	1	3	4		0	0	0	3	5	8	William C. Hogan, Attorney.
8	5	n	4	0	2	1	3			0	0	0	4	1	5	William Knott, Counsellor.
9	6	n	4	2	5	2	3	5		0	0	0	5	5	10	William Keon, Attorney.
50	7	n	4	3	5	0	3	3		0	0	0	2	6	8	Mrs. Jane Carey.
1	8	n	4	1	5	1	5			0	0	0	6	4	10	Surgeon Richards.
2	9	n	4	4	6	2	3	5		0	0	0	4	7	11	Counsellor Grady.
3	50	n	4	4	7	3	2	5		0	0	0	6	6	12	Charles Farren, Attorney.
4	1	n	4	3	4	1	2	3		0	0	0	2	5	7	Robert Stoney.
5	2	n	4	2	3	1	1			0	0	0	2	3	5	Mrs. Bentley, L. H.
6	3	g	2	3	3	0	1	1		0	0	0	0	4	4	Jane Robinson, Haberdasher.
57	54	g	3	5	12	1	2	3		0	0	0	8	7	15	Thomas O'Neil, Grocer and Dram

AUNGIER-STREET.

[To face Appendix page vii.

General Table of the Population of Dublin in 1798, as divided into its nineteen Parishes and two Deaneries.

INDEX to Tables	NAMES OF PARISHES, &c.	UPPER AND MIDDLE CLASSES. Males.	Females.	Total.	SERVANTS OF DITTO. Males.	Females.	Total.	LOWER CLASS. Males.	Females.	Total.	TOTAL Males.	TOTAL Females.	GRAND TOTAL.	No. OF HOUSES. Inhabited.	Waste.	Average to a House.
I.	Parish of St. James,	342	367	799	97	201	298	2432	2665	5097	2871	3233	6104	538	32	11.34
II.	St. Catherine,	991	846	1837	378	660	1038	7608	9693	17301	8977	11199	20176	1481	140	13.62
III.	St. Luke,	150	148	298	32	75	107	2846	3990	6836	3028	4213	7241	454	41	15.95
IV.	St. Nicholas without the Walls,	347	347	694	50	169	219	4861	6532	11393	5258	7048	12306	950	55	12.95
V.	St. Nicholas within the Walls	163	153	316	45	92	137	306	362	668	514	607	1121	107	10	10.48
VI.	St. Audoen,	585	513	1098	156	302	458	1612	2023	3635	2353	2838	5191	415	53	12.5
VII.	St. Michael,	124	108	232	10	50	60	1064	1243	2307	1198	1401	2599	163	20	14.68
VIII.	St. John,	316	333	649	46	118	164	1577	1752	3329	1939	2203	4142	295	31	15.94
IX.	St. Werburgh,	609	551	1160	98	253	351	941	1177	2118	1648	1981	3629	305	33	11.9
X.	Deanery of Christ-church,	25	10	35	3	4	7	80	111	191	108	125	233	23	2	10.1
XI.	St. Patrick,	76	64	140	14	30	44	832	1065	1897	922	1159	2081	162	11	13.84
XII.	Parish of St. Bridget or St. Bride,	1287	1445	2732	195	580	775	2054	2448	4502	3536	4473	8009	744	27	10.76
XIII.	St. Peter,	2283	3017	5300	1117	2048	3165	3390	4108	7498	6890	9173	16063	1512	116	10.61
XIV.	St. Anne,	1486	1737	3223	715	1286	2001	870	1134	2004	3071	4157	7228	711	36	10.17
XV.	St. Andrew,	1489	1373	2862	289	661	950	1738	2132	3870	3516	4166	7682	709	63	10.83
XVI.	St. Mark,	599	684	1283	121	354	475	3127	3797	6924	3847	4845	8692	646	61	13.45
	Total Population on the South side of the River Liffey,	10872	11695	22567	3466	3417	6883	35338	44232	79570	49676	62821	114497	9215	731	12.2
XVII.	Parish of St. Paul,	781	1002	1783	186	444	630	3321	4170	7491	4288	5616	9904	1050	116	9.43
XVIII.	St. Michan,	1312	1409	2721	374	772	1146	6375	7850	14225	8061	10031	18092	1520	141	12.56
XIX.	St. Mary,	2452	3014	5466	979	1771	2750	3859	4579	8435	7290	9364	16654	1590	43	10.47
XX.	St. Thomas,	1316	1624	2940	650	1087	1737	1787	2098	3885	3753	4809	8562	892	82	9.6
XXI.	St. George,	817	1011	1828	706	997	1703	688	877	1565	2211	2885	5096	587	89	8.68
	Total Population on the North side of the River Liffey,	6678	8060	14738	2895	5071	7966	16030	19574	35604	25603	32705	58308	5639	471	
	Spring-garden, a suburb beyond the circular-road, omitted in the return of the Conservators, in 1804.												1286	345	0	
	Total Population North of the Liffey, taken from the Parishes of St. Thomas and St. George;												59594	5984	471	
	Total Population of Dublin in 1798,												172091	5199	1202	

APPENDIX. No. I. vii

thus arranged with persevering patience, the tables of the population of its parishes were formed. In these, the first column expresses the streets or parts of streets that compose it; the second, third, fourth, and fifth, give their population properly arranged ; the sixth exhibits the number of houses in each street, distinguished into inhabited and waste; the seventh shews the average population to an inhabited house, both for the entire parish, and its principal streets; and, finally, the left-hand margin serves as an index to the page, where the particular survey of each street, &c. may be found.

We have annexed these parochial tables, but in an abridged form; the population being divided into males and females only, and not ranged according to their classes, as in the original work.

From the addition of the totals of these parochial tables, was formed the general table of the population of Dublin, in which the classification of the inhabitants is retained, with the hope that it may be satisfactory to the reader.

To the total of this table, viz. - -	172,091
We must add for the Garrison, about - -	7,000
Royal Hospital - -	400
Foundling Hospital, in July 1798	558
St. Patrick's Hospital, ditto - - - -	55
House of Industry, ditto - -	1,637
Trinity College, at present 597, in 1798 -	529
Castle - - - -	000
Total population of Dublin, in 1798, may be estimated at - -	182,370

As a salutary precaution against the revival of that disaffection, which in 1798 pervaded the poorer parts of Dublin, Government, in 1803, ordered that the city and its immediate vicinity should be divided into 53 wards or districts, which, from motives of œconomy, were afterwards reduced to the number 21. These were entrusted to the inspection of Conservators, who were directed to make accurate lists of the population of their respective districts. As there is reason to belive that this work was generally executed with care, and in some instances with minute precision, its general result is here laid before the public. It is arranged, in the annexed table, in such a manner, as to shew the population, both of the former, and lately existing districts. As no return was made by the Conservators for the districts of Grange-Gorman, Broadstone, and Grand Canal, distinguished in the table by an asterism[*], the deficiency has been supplied from the survey of Mr. W. To the district of St. Kevin's, No. 37, 13 houses, and 95 souls, the population of Old Portobello, omitted by the Conservators of that district have been added; and a comparative view of the general result of the two surveys in 1798 and 1804, is annexed.

The district of Harold's-cross, with that of Sandy-mount and Black-rock, cannot with any propriety be considered as parts of Dublin. If, therefore, we deduct their population, the comparative statement of the surveys, in 1798 and 1804, will stand thus :

APPENDIX. No. I.

	Houses.	Inhabitants.
Population according to Mr. W's. survey in 1798,	16,023	170,361
Ormond market not returned by him, taken from the Conservators survey,	33	444
Spring-garden not returned by him, as lying beyond the circular road; but properly a part of Dublin, taken from ditto	345	1,286
Total population in 1798	16,401	172,091
Population, according to the Conservators, in 1804, supplying deficiencies as above,	16,234	172,042
Population of the district of Harold's-cross, with that of Sandy-mount and Black-rock deducted, as not being parts of Dublin	589	4,143
Total population in 1804	15,645	167,899
The return of 1798, therefore, exceeds that of 1804, by	756	4,192

Of the 16,023 houses, returned by Mr. W. in 1798, 14,821 were inhabited, and 1,202 waste: the exact position of every one of which is distinctly marked in the survey.

If to the 16,401 houses, which are stated as existing in 1798, we add 401 houses, which appear, from the returns in 1804, to have been built, in the intermediate period, in the parishes of St. Thomas and St. George only, the Conservators must have omitted 1157 houses at least, which were probably waste. In consequence of this increase of new houses, it was reasonable, that the return of the Conservators, for the districts on the north side of the Liffey, should exceed Mr. W's. by 1455 souls. A greater encrease of population might indeed have been expected; but many of these 401 houses were probably untenanted in 1804, as they appear to have added only 2474 souls to the parishes of St. Thomas and St. George, which gives an average of only 6.1 to an house.

Of the above excess, of 4182 inhabitants in 1798, 3960 were found in that portion of the city westward of Fishamble-street, Werburgh-street, and Bride-street; and, of these, the far greater part in the districts which were the center of rebellion. But whether this excess is only apparent, and owing to inaccuracy in the returns of the Conservators of these districts, or was occasioned by an influx of rebels from the country at that period, we do not presume to determine: nor, indeed, are we possessed of *data* sufficient to enable us to form any decided opinion on the subject. It may be necessary to observe, that a considerable number of Protestants of condition, took shelter in Dublin just at this period: their names, however, appeared in the lists under the head of *visitors;* and, as they properly formed no part of its population, they were not included in the survey.

That the population of a great city may become, from local causes, so crouded as to become a nuisance, is obvious; and that this is peculiarly the situation of many parts of Dublin is a melancholy truth: with the hope therefore, that a wise Legislature may be induced, by an

FORMER DISTRICTS.

Nos.	NAMES.	Houses.	Population.
1 2 3	Barrack, Mountpelier, Aughrim,	228 410	3157 2516
4 7 8	Grange-Gorman,* House of Industry, Broadstone,*	154 146 158	883 1482 739
5 6	Smithfield, St. Michan's,	310 396	3143 6289
12 13	New Gaol, King's Inn's,	357 609	4025 5939
9 10 11	Royal Circus, Dorset-street, Linen-hall,	186 126 183	1263 931 1831
14 21	St. Mary's, Henry-street	401 475	4417 5362
15 16 17 18	Simpson's Hospital, Rutland-square, St. George's, Mountjoy-square	161 159 449 264	1793 1805 4095 1970
20 22	St. Thomas's, Marlborough-green,	314 125	2861 1919
19 23 24 51	Gloster-place, Custom-house, North Lotts, Spring-garden	272 66 186 345	2002 494 841 1286
	This population gives an average of 9.42 to a house,	6480	61049
25 26 33	Grand Canal,* St. Mark's, Trinity College,	1 294 406	7 3773 5555
27 32	Merion-square, St. Anne's,	290 435	2264 4362
28 29 30	Fitzwilliam-square, St. Stephen's-green Harcourt-street,	174 77 487	1686 679 4145
31 34	Powerscourt, King William's,	694 549	7700 6512
35 36	Castle, St. Peter's,	746 376	7406 4277
37 38 53	St. Kevin's New-street, Harold's-cross,	316 291 190	3968 3170 1200
42 43	St. Patrick's, Christ-church,	822 532	11146 7549
44 45	Usher's-island, James's-gate,	551 234	3281 4205
40 41	St. Luke's, St. Catherine's,	594 646	7390 7845
39 46	Weaver's-square, Marybonne-lane,	229 241	2506 3596
47 48	City Bason, St. James's,	187 127	1820 1582
49 50	Royal Hospital, Kilmainham,	179	2049
52	Sandymount and Black-rock,	599	2943
	This population gives an average 11.38 to a house,	9754	110993
	Average, 10.51 to a house,	16234	172042

APPENDIX. No. I.

accurate statement of facts, to adopt some mode of obviating so serious an evil, much pains have been taken to ascertain the density of population in various parts of this city. For this purpose, Roque's plan of Dublin, on a scale of twenty perches Irish to an inch, was taken as the ground work, as it was found, on examination, a few errors in the limits of the parishes excepted, sufficiently accurate. These errors having been corrected, and the streets that have been built since the period of its publication having been added, a number of right lines were traced round its contour, which separated the surrounding waste ground from the space actually occupied by buildings, and thus the entire city was reduced into one great irregular polygon. This polygon was subdivided into several smaller ones, by tracing with care the boundary lines of the parishes, and also lines inclosing the area occupied by the Liffey, our great squares, the College Park, the Castle and its dependencies, and other considerable spaces not built on. The plan thus prepared, the area both of the entire polygon and its parts were measured, and its appropriate population being applied to each, the following table was formed.

APPENDIX, No. I.

	Number of Inhabitants.	Area in English Acres.			Number of Inhabitants on an Acre.	HOUSES. Inhabited.	Waste.	Average to an Inhabited HOUSE.
		A.	R.	P.				
Paul's,	9904	88	0	37	112.2	1050	116	9.43
Michan's, (including Ormond-market,)	18092	99	0	13	182.6	1520	141	12.56
Mary's,	16654	115	0	33	144.5	1590	43	10.47
Thomas's.	8562	98	0	37	87.1	892	82	9.6
George's,	5096	53	3	21	96.4	587	89	8.68
occupied by buildings, North of the Liffey,	58308	454	2	21	128.5	5639	471	10.35
WASTE GROUND.								
green, in St. Paul's parish,		12	0	20	The Blue-coat-hospital is on this ground.			
re, in St. Mary's parish,		6	3	28	The Lying-in-hospital is on this ground.			
are, in St. George's parish,		4	1	34	The area of Mountjoy and Rutland-			
		23	2	2	squares are taken within the railing. The suburb of Spring-garden is not			
		478	0	23	included, as I am ignorant of its area.			
James's,	6104	59	1	36	102.5	538	32	11.34
Catherine's,	20176	112	1	28	179.4	1481	140	13.62
Luke's,	7241	31	0	21	232.6	454	41	15.95
Nicholas, without the walls,	12306	47	0	25	261.0	950	55	12.95
Nicholas, within the walls,	1121	5	0	32	215.0	107	10	10.48
Audeon's,	5191	24	2	29	210.0	415	53	12.5
Michael's,	2599	5	3	27	439.0	163	20	15.94
John's,	4142	11	2	32	355.0	295	31	14.08
Werburgh's,	3629	10	3	35	331.0	305	33	11.9
Bridget's, or St. Bride's,	8009	36	3	8	217.6	744	27	10.76
Peter's, (St. Kevin's included),	16063	141	0	21	114.0	1512	116	10.61
Anne's,	7228	63	0	27	114.0	711	36	10.17
Andrew's,	7682	42	2	30	179.8	709	63	10.83
Mark's,	8692	59	0	31	146.6	646	61	13.45
nery of Christ church,	233	1	1	2	184.4	23	2	10.1
nery of St. Patrick,	2081	9	3	35	208.7	162	11	12.84
	112497	662	3	19	169.7	9215	731	12.2

	A.	R.	P.
te ground in Saint Audeon's parish,	3	0	19
In Saint Catherine's parish.			
al-harbour, stores, &c.	23	2	4
ter fields,	12	2	39
In Saint Werburgh's parish.			
le-garden, Castle and its dependencies,	9	0	4
In Saint Peter's parish.			
t Stephen's-green, within the wall, 17 0 2 Irish acres, including gravel walk,	27	0	24
Do. within the ditch, pasturable, 13 1 20.			
ion-square, within the railing,	12	2	21
In Saint Mark's parish.			
ege-park, bowling-green, &c.	25	1	33
In Saint Anne's parish.			
ster-house, offices and lawn,	7	3	36
In St. John's parish.			
Custom-house and quay,	0	3	25
otal waste ground, South of the river Liffey,	122	2	5
otal area of Dublin, South of the river Liffey,	785	2	24
otal area of Dublin, occupied by buildings,	1117	2	0
otal waste ground in Dublin,	146	0	7
rea of the Liffey, included in Dublin,	36	0	26
otal area of Dublin, including its waste grounds and the Liffey,	1299	2	33

APPENDIX. No. II.

POPULATION TABLES *of the* NINETEEN PARISHES *and* TWO DEANERIES *of the* CITY *of* DUBLIN, *A. D.* 1798. *Shewing what Streets, and Parts of Streets, &c. are comprehended in each Parish; with the Number of Inhabitants, whether Male or Female; and of Houses, whether Inhabited or Waste.*

☞ *Where a Street, Lane, Alley, Square, &c. extends into more than one Parish, the Alphabetical List, annexed to this Work, refers to the Number of the Parochial Tables, in which its several Parts will be found.*

No. I.
Parish of Saint James's.

NAMES OF STREETS, &c.	POPULATION.			HOUSES.	
	Males.	Females.	Total.	Inhabited.	Waste.
Watling-street, E. side from No. 1 to 30; W. side entire, -	193	201	394	46	6
Lord Galway's walk,	13	26	39	3	1
Cook's-lane, -	27	32	59	5	0
St. James's-street, -	1139	1197	2336	181	12
Conoly's-lane,	17	17	34	5	0
Glannan's-lane, -	4	5	9	1	0
Sherlock's-yard, -	3	5	8	2	0
Bason-lane, -	17	23	40	3	0
Pig-town -	50	39	89	12	1
Bason-place, from No. 1 to 7, -	30	31	61	7	0
Echlin's-lane, -	47	58	105	11	1
Cherrytree-lane, -	48	55	103	5	0
Stevens's-lane, -	18	19	37	3	0
Bow-lane, -	407	528	935	63	4
Irwin-street, - -	179	199	378	21	0
Rope-walk, -	22	21	43	10	0
Bow-bridge, -	137	209	346	26	1
Kilmainham-road & town,	237	255	492	68	5
Commons-lane, -	5	12	17	4	1
Dolphin's-barn-lane, -	269	281	550	57	0
Rehoboth-lane, -	9	20	29	5	0
TOTAL -	2871	3233	6104	538	32

Parish of Saint Catharine.

NAMES OF STREETS, &c.	Males	Females	Total	Inhabited	Waste	NAMES OF STREETS, &c.	Males	Females	Total	Inhabited	Waste
Coomb, N. side, from No. 40 to 69, to Pimlico,	232	374	606	33	4	Flag-alley, Pimlico,	11 231	23 281	34 512	5 45	0 3
Ardee-street, or Crooked Staff, W. side only,	75	86	161	11	0	Delany's-court, off Pimlico,	5	6	11	1	0
Francis-street, part of W. side, from No. 150 to 159, to Thomas street,	40	56	96	10	1	Jackson's-alley, do.	34	94	128	8	1
						Tripilo,	138	213	351	22	0
						Thomas-court,	370	539	909	54	4
						Miller's-alley, off Thomas-court,	53	85	138	7	0
Cut-purse-row, N. side,	1	2	3	2	6	Gilbert's alley, do.	8	19	27	3	1
Sweeny's-gate and Tenter-lane,	15	29	44	6	0	Meath-row,	77	71	148	9	3
						Cole's-lane,	7	5	12	2	1
Stirling-street,	13	32	45	2	1	Swan-alley,	21	30	51	5	0
Corn-market, N. side, Nos. 17 and 18,	3	7	10	2	0	Little Thomas-court,	68	119	187	11	0
						Hanbury-lane,	126	130	256	20	4
Thomas-street,	1154	1300	2454	181	9	Scanlon's-court, off Hanbury-lane,	25	45	70	3	0
Molyneux's-yard, off Thomas-str.	11	23	34	5	0	Meath-market,	58	63	121	31	8
Black-horse yard, do.	24	22	46	3	0	Earl-street,	223	262	485	36	5
Talbot-inn-yard, do.	14	11	25	1	0	Cole's-alley,	283	408	691	40	5
Reily's-court, do.	3	3	6	1	0	Gill's-square, off Cole's-alley,	56	86	142	8	0
New-sun-inn yard, do.	17	11	28	3	0	Cambden-court, do.	4	7	11	2	0
Churn-inn-yard, do.	8	9	17	2	0	Elbow-lane,	264	370	634	36	0
Cherry-tree-inn-yard, do.	4	3	7	1	0	Gibraltar, off Elbow-lane,	35	58	93	6	2
Yellow-lion-inn-yard, do.	5	5	10	1	0	Little Elbow-lane,	42	45	87	6	1
White-horse-lane, do.	38	58	96	5	0	Cork-street,	752	868	1620	126	15
Brown's-alley, do.	14	27	41	6	0	Love-lane,	21	20	41	5	0
White-bull-inn-yard, do.	6	6	12	1	0	Chamber-street,	167	176	343	34	9
						Weaver's-square,	112	149	261	19	1
Lime-kiln-yard, do.	34	58	92	3	0	Ormond-street,	122	143	265	14	4
New-row, Thomas-street,	167	188	355	40	2	Brown-street,	135	173	308	20	3
Wormwood-gate,	22	25	47	6	0	Marybonne-lane,	607	797	1404	90	5
M'Cracken's-alley,	49	80	129	13	0	John-street,	91	101	192	13	0
Croager's-alley, or Meeting-house-lane,	65	106	171	8	0	Braithwaite-street,	161	206	367	30	1
						Pool-street,	160	220	380	26	1
John-street,	78	72	150	9	3	Summer-street,	48	59	107	9	0
John's lane,	24	48	72	5	0	Robert-street,	79	78	157	15	0
Mullinahack,	87	70	157	9	0	White-hall,	18	26	44	6	0
Dirty-lane, or Bridgefoot-street, from No. 1 to 14, E. side; from No. 52½ to 69, W. side,	200	225	425	32	3	Water-row or Russel's-lane	34	52	86	6	0
						Bowes's-lane,	15	17	32	4	3
						Taylor's-lane.—No population.					
						Belle-view,	36	41	77	6	0
M'Cormick's-court off Dirty-lane,	18	28	46	3	0	Crawley's-yard, now School-street,	27	47	74	7	6
						Ransford-street,	395	500	895	46	2
Collison's Fields, or Black-ditch, do.	11	18	29	4	0	Bardon's-yard, off Ransford-street,	20	25	45	2	0
						Davis's Coal-yard, do.	15	16	31	3	0
Bonham-street,	59	49	108	11	3	Sugar-house-lane,	37	25	62	7	0
Marshalsea-lane,	13	16	29	4	0	Clane-street,	80	86	166	14	6
Mass-lane, no population.						Rope-walk,	39	36	75	8	2
						Portland street,	27	23	50	6	0
Meath-street,	525	619	1144	81	3	Canal-place,	40	55	95	6	1
Vicar-street,	217	222	439	33	2	Canal Stores,	22	21	43	5	0
Engine alley,	200	206	406	27	0	Washerwoman's-lane,	33	57	90	10	0
Catharine-street,	42	46	88	6	0	Bason-place, No. 8, 9, & 10,	9	13	22	3	0
Crosstick-alley, entire, except No. 4.	48	70	118	10	3						
						TOTAL	8977	11199	20176	1481	140

No. III.

Parish of Saint Luke.

NAMES OF STREETS, &c.	POPULATION.			HOUSES.	
	Males.	Females.	Total.	Inhabited.	Waste.
Coomb, S. side entire,	525	614	1139	73	8
Cain's-alley, -	56	72	128	6	0
Green's-alley, -	8	16	24	4	0
Daniel's-alley, -	56	120	176	11	0
Three-nun-alley, -	23	32	55	5	0
Stillas's-court, -	58	74	132	7	0
Poddle, S. side, from No. 13 to No. 17,	40	58	98	8	0
New-market, - -	432	614	1046	62	6
Ardee-street, or Crooked-staff, - -	151	177	328	12	2
Ardee-row, or Mutton-lane, - -	95	167	262	16	1
Atkinson's-alley, -	18	29	47	4	0
Brabazon's - street, or Truck-street, -	122	160	282	18	3
Brabazon's - row, or Cuckold's-row, -	75	94	169	13	5
Hunt's-alley, -	31	58	89	5	0
Fordam's-alley, -	328	570	898	53	1
Skinner's-alley, .	322	491	813	52	1
New-row on the Poddle,	359	453	812	52	7
Ward's-hill, - -	28	24	52	6	2
Mill-street, - -	139	206	345	25	4
Warren's-mount, -	25	15	40	3	0
Mill-lane, - -	19	42	61	4	1
Sweeney's-lane, -	54	64	118	6	0
Black-pitts, W. side, -	64	63	127	9	0
TOTAL -	3028	4213	7241	454	41

No. IV.

Parish of Saint Nicholas Without.

NAMES OF STREETS, &c.	Males	Females	TOTAL	Inhabited	Waste	NAMES OF STREETS, &c.	Males	Females	TOTAL	Inhabited	Waste
St. Francis-street, E. side entire; W. side, from the Coomb to No. 149 inclusive	853	1078	1931	154	13	Poddle, North side, from No. 1 to 10; S. side, No. 1, 11 and 12.	38	62	100	12	1
Handkerchief-alley, off Francis-street,	16	15	31	4	0	Upper St. Kevin's-street, S. side, from New-st. to the Poddle,	48	49	97	6	0
Binns's court, do.	56	69	125	8	3	Coomb, North side, from No. 1. to 39,	277	372	649	45	0
O'Brian's-alley, do.	10	14	24	3	3	Crosstick-al. one house, viz. No. 4,	6	9	15	1	0
Francis's-court, do.	19	1	20	2	0						
Chapel-alley, do.	18	26	44	4	0						
Sun-inn-yard, do.	7	11	18	1	0	New-street, E. side, from No. 14 to 31; W. side entire,	694	929	1623	114	10
Red-cow-gate yard, do.	5	6	11	2	0						
Calender-yard, do.	19	28	47	3	0	Three-stone-alley	36	44	80	8	0
Churn - inn - yard, do.	4	5	9	1	0	Fumbally's-lane,	73	71	144	13	0
						Malpas-street,	31	50	81	9	2
Infirmary-yard, do.	69	92	161	6	0	Bonny's-lane,	35	43	78	10	0
Plunket-street,	701	1103	1804	92	0	Ducker's-lane,	2	14	16	3	0
Hanover-lane,	192	246	438	35	1	Fatal-alley,	20	23	43	7	0
Hanover-square,	28	19	47	9	0	Donovan's-lane,	11	9	20	4	0
Limerick-alley,	2	5	7	2	0	Black-pits, E. side,	121	166	287	26	0
Ash-street,	140	186	326	30	0	Bride's-al. S. side, from No. 1 to 9; N. side, from No. 28 to 34,	43	63	106	26	0
Swift's-alley,	41	107	148	9	1						
Garden-lane,	272	380	652	39	1						
Carman's-hall,	81	101	182	16	1	Mill-yd. off Bride's-alley,	18	30	48	0	0
Pye-alley,	1	13	14	1	0						
Park-street,	84	123	207	13	3	Draper's-court, do.	62	82	144	8	0
Hanover-street,	27	47	74	9	1	Bull-alley, S. side, from No. 1 to 9; N. side, from No. 31 to 38,	72	85	157	15	2
Mark's-alley,	82	115	197	23	3						
Spittle-field,	173	173	346	25	1						
Wall's-lane,	57	66	123	12	1	Walker's-alley, N. side,	36	79	115	6	0
St. Patrick's-street, W. side, from No. 1 to 32, and from 36 to 49; E. side, from 50 to 56, and from Walker's-alley to Nicholas-street,	510	722	1232	92	4	City-market, from No. 1. to 43,	147	185	332	41	2
						Cut-purse-row, S. side,	11	17	28	5	2
						Lamb-alley,	10	15	25	3	0
						TOTAL	5258	7048	12306	950	55

APPENDIX. No. II.

No. V.
Parish of Saint Nicholas Within.

NAMES OF STREETS, &c.	Males.	Females.	TOTAL.	Inhabited.	Waste.
High-street, No. 70 only, the corner house of Nicholas-street,	0	0	0	0	1
Skinner's-row, from the Tholsel to No. 5, S. side,	23	29	52	7	0
Prince of Wales-court	27	23	50	5	0
Nicholas-street, entire, No. 19½ and 25 excepted,	173	228	401	35	3
Kennedy's-lane,	52	65	117	15	1
Back-lane { N.side, from Nich.-street, to No. 18, S.side, from No.49, to Nicholas-street	202	242	444	34	5
City-row, part of City-market, from No. 44, to 52, as correct,	31	19	50	9	0
Angel-alley, No. 3 and 4, as correctly numbered,	6	1	7	2	0
M'Cullough's - alley, in part, no inhabited houses Ram-alley, no inhabited houses.					
TOTAL	514	607	1121	107	10

No. VI.
Parish of Saint Audeon.

NAMES OF STREETS, &c.	Males.	Females.	TOTAL.	Inhabited.	Waste.
Watling-street, E. side, from No. 31 to 42, and Usher's island,	39	50	89	8	2
Usher's island,	80	114	194	23	3
Usher's-quay,	184	173	357	41	3
Usher's street,	33	57	90	11	1
Usher's-lane,	30	38	68	10	1
Island-street,	111	109	220	11	1
Dog-and-duck-yard,	32	39	71	7	0
Usher's-court, or Meeting-house-yard,	69	86	155	16	1
Bridge-street,	216	224	440	48	2
Chapel-alley,	22	15	37	5	0
Wolfe's-alley,	7	19	26	3	0
Brazen - head - inn-yard,	9	15	24	2	0
Minor's alley,	4	7	11	1	0
Upper Bridge-street,	19	25	44	9	17
Merchant's - quay, from No. 10 to 34,	121	81	202	22	5
Cook-street, from No. 16 to 85,	427	480	907	56	5
Swan-alley,	4	3	7	1	0
Archibold's-court,	9	11	20	3	0
Keizar's lane,	31	53	84	3	0
St. Audeon's arch,	37	67	104	9	1
Hope's-yard	36	49	85	7	0
Schoolhouse-lane W. side,	55	77	132	3	3
Bethel's-court, off Schoolhouse-lane,	8	27	35	2	0
Corn-market entire, No. 17 and 18 excepted,	137	215	352	33	2
Purcell's-court,	73	134	207	10	4
Bear's-court,	11	12	23	2	0
High street, from No. 17 to 43, and Gorely's alley,	208	247	455	27	3
Back-lane, from No. 19 to 48,	301	367	668	33	2
Byrne's court	40	44	84	5	0
Skipper's-alley, W. side, no inhabited house.					
TOTAL	2353	2838	5191	415	53

APPENDIX. No. II.

No. VII.
Parish of Saint Michael.

NAMES OF STREETS, &c.	Males.	Females.	TOTAL.	Inhabited.	Waste.
Cook-street { Merchant's-quay, from Rosemary - lane to Skipper's-alley,	40	48	88	7	1
N. side, from Rose-mary-lane to Skipper's-alley S.side, from School-house-lane to Michael's-lane,	96	137	233	21	2
Rosemary-lane, W. side,	24	21	45	5	0
Chapel-yard,	6	2	8	1	1
Skipper's - alley, E. side, no inhabited houses.					
Schoolhouse-lane, E. side,	102	122	224	9	1
Michael's-lane,	321	323	644	24	1
Crosby's-court,	27	30	57	2	0
Cox's-court,	43	43	86	6	0
Boor's-court,	55	77	132	6	1
Cock-hill, from No. 5 to 12,	51	60	111	9	1
High-street { Christ-church-lane, W. side,	53	57	110	8	1
Chapter-court,	6	9	15	2	1
N. side, from Christ-church - lane to Schoolhouse-lane S. side, from Gorely's-alley to No. 69,	302	398	700	45	6
Jones's-court,	23	27	50	5	0
Gorely's - alley, part of E. side, no inhabited houses.					
M'Cullough's - alley, in part,	13	12	25	2	0
Angel-court,	18	10	28	3	2
Angel-alley, in part, viz. No. 1, 2, 5, 6, 7, correct,	7	16	23	5	0
Skinner's-row, N. side, from No. 32 to 37,	11	9	20	3	2
TOTAL	1198	1401	2599	163	20

No. VIII.
Parish of Saint John.

NAMES OF STREETS, &c.	Males.	Females.	TOTAL.	Inhabited.	Waste.
Essex-bridge street,	32	35	67	9	0
Essex-quay,	110	154	264	23	1
Wood-quay,	244	300	544	27	1
Fisher's-alley,	11	9	20	4	0
Johnston's-court,	46	74	120	8	0
Redmond's-alley,	18	26	44	3	0
Rose-alley,	41	41	82	4	0
Merchant's-quay, No. 1 on the S. side, and 35, 36, 37, on the N. side,	9	7	16	4	0
Lower Exchange-street,	142	157	299	24	10
Upp. Exchange st. from No. 12 to 17, W. side,	32	36	68	6	0
Smock-alley,	88	97	185	16	6
Copper-alley { No. 1, 2, 3, 4, 5, on the S. side, No. 35, 36, on the N. side,	10	14	24	4	3
Fishamble-str. from No. 2, to 55, properly 57,	423	468	891	55	3
John's-court.	31	19	50	3	0
Sall's-court,	5	7	12	1	1
Virginè-court,	11	21	32	2	0
Molesworth-court,	9	19	28	4	2
Fleece-alley,	40	25	65	7	0
Deanery-court,	5	2	7	1	0
Medcalf's-court,	14	15	29	3	0
Wine-tavern-street,	449	457	906	51	2
Brazil-court,	10	15	25	2	0
John's-lane,	44	63	107	13	0
Ball-court-yard,	9	7	16	3	0
Plowman's-court,	9	7	16	2	0
Cotk-hill, No. 1, 2, 3, 4, and a back-house,	49	57	106	5	0
Rosemary-lane, E. side,	11	29	40	3	1
Howard's-lane,	2	3	5	1	0
Cook-street { N. side, from Wine-tavern - street to Rosemary-lane, S. side, from Michael's - lane to Winetavern-str.	35	39	74	7	1
TOTAL	1939	2203	4142	295	31

APPENDIX. No. II.

No. IX.
Parish of Saint Werburgh.

NAMES OF STREETS, &c.	POPULATION. Males.	Females.	TOTAL.	HOUSES. Inhabited.	Waste.
Werburgh-street,	191	207	398	23	3
Hoey's-court,	103	118	221	18	0
Darby's-square, No. 1, 5, 6, 7, 8, as correctly numbered,	27	36	63	4	1
Skinner's-row, from No. 6 to 31,	103	134	237	27	1
Bolton-court,	19	16	35	2	1
Wilme's-court,	12	12	24	3	0
Castle-street,	237	299	536	59	1
Garter court,	10	9	19	3	1
Cole's-alley,	87	110	197	22	3
Silver-court,	3	5	8	2	1
Pembroke-court,	67	75	142	11	0
Temple-court,	26	20	46	3	0
Fishamble-street. { No. 1, E. side; No. 58, 59, 60, W. side,	32	36	68	4	0
Copper-alley, from No. 6 to 34,	207	254	461	20	9
Orpin's-court,	15	30	45	4	0
Cork-hill,	70	70	140	14	2
Upper Exchange-street. { E. side, entire; W. side, No. 18, 19, 20,	70	104	174	9	2
Parliament-street,	119	105	224	27	2
Essex-gate, S. side,	7	6	13	2	0
Essex-street. { N. side, from No. 2 to 10. S. side, from No. 42, to 53,	114	142	256	18	3
Crane-lane,	74	123	197	13	1
Crampton-court, No. 1, 2, 3, 18, 19,	2	12	14	4	1
Dame-street. { S. side, No. 1, 2, and half No. 3, a double house, N. side, No. 90, 91, 92, 93,	31	35	66	6	1
Exchange-court,	22	23	45	7	0
TOTAL	**1648**	**1981**	**3629**	**305**	**33**

No. X.
Deanery of Christ Church.

NAMES OF STREETS, &c.	POPULATION. Males.	Females.	TOTAL.	HOUSES. Inhabited.	Waste.
Christ-church-lane, E. side,	17	12	29	4	0
Hell,	16	26	42	3	1
Christ-church-yard,	58	78	136	14	1
Fishamble-street. { Two Houses on each side of the entrance into Christ-church-yard, both numbered 57,	17	9	26	2	0
TOTAL	**108**	**125**	**233**	**23**	**2**

No. XI.
Deanery of Saint Patrick.

NAMES OF STREETS, &c.	POPULATION. Males.	Females.	TOTAL.	HOUSES. Inhabited.	Waste.
Bride-st. W. side, from No. 29 to 44,	85	80	165	16	1
Canon-street,	130	150	280	15	0
Patrick's close,	131	176	307	24	2
Miler's-alley,	78	91	169	15	3
Goodman's-alley,	30	33	63	5	1
Walker's-alley, S. side,	14	20	34	5	0
Bull-alley, one house, viz. that next Bride-street on the S. side,	3	2	5	1	0
Patrick-str. W. side, from No. 33 to 35; E. side, from the Cathedral to Walker's-alley,	35	44	79	11	2
Patrick's back-close,	30	57	87	8	2
Mitre-alley,	54	74	128	11	2
Upper Kevin's-street, N. side, from No. 1 to 12; S. side, from New-st. to Edge's-court,	193	229	422	28	0
New-st. No. 1, 2, and a B. H. on the E. side,	13	18	31	3	0
Edge's-court,	55	100	155	8	0
Cathedral-lane, W. side,	37	41	78	5	0
Corbaly's-row,	25	38	63	5	0
Poddle, two houses between Patrick-st. and Upper Kevin's-street,	9	6	15	2	0
TOTAL	**922**	**1159**	**2081**	**162**	**11**

APPENDIX. No. II.

XII.
Parish of St. Bridget.

NAMES OF STREETS, &c.	Males.	Females.	TOTAL.	Inhabited.	Waste.
St. Bride-street, E. side entire; W. side, from No. 1 to 28,	448	504	952	83	3
Cummin's-court,	1	1	2	1	1
Sherry's-court,	10	13	23	2	1
Derby's square, off Werburgh-street, Nos. 2, 3, 4, as correct,	25	21	46	3	0
Ross-lane,	75	71	146	12	4
Bride's-alley, S. side, from No. 10 to 15; N. side, from No. 16 to 27,	48	53	101	17	0
Bull-alley, S. side from No. 10 to 17; N. side, from 22 to 30,	113	119	232	16	3
Bishop-street, N. side,	81	176	257	27	1
Peter's-street,	101	147	248	32	2
Wood-street,	198	276	474	41	2
Golden-lane,	342	423	765	61	1
Dobbin's-court,	3	3	6	1	0
Maiden-lane,	70	87	157	14	0
Oliver's-alley,	8	2	10	1	0
Peter's-row, W. side,	28	54	82	12	0
Whitefriar's-st. W. side,	86	112	198	15	0
Chancery-lane,	194	254	448	40	1
Great-ship-street,	199	247	446	48	3
Clarke's-court,	14	19	33	4	0
Michael-a-Pole,	24	24	48	1	0
White's-court,	19	30	49	7	0
Buckridge's-court,	20	29	49	5	0
Little-ship-street,	178	237	415	31	0
St. Stephen's-st. N. side,	161	226	387	40	0
Great-George's-st. S. W. side, from No 47 to 61: E. side, from No. 22 to 46,	271	304	575	59	1
Tinkler's-court,	4	5	9	1	1
Rothery's-yard,	8	22	30	2	0
George's-court,	15	19	34	4	2
Fade-street,	95	135	230	18	0
Joseph's-lane,	62	79	141	14	1
Drury-lane	231	299	530	43	0
Castle-market and its dependencies,	54	48	102	18	0
Exchequer-street, { South side from Great George's-street, to William-street,	193	204	397	29	1
Clarke's-court,	13	16	29	2	0
William-street, W. side,	144	214	358	40	0
TOTAL	3536	4473	8009	744	27

No. XIII.
Parish of Saint Peter.

NAMES OF STREETS, &c.	Males	Females	TOTAL	Inhabited	Waste	NAMES OF STREETS, &c.	Males	Females	TOTAL	Inhabited	Waste
Grand-canal-street, S. side, no inhabited houses.						Cuffe-lane, -	31	33	64	5	0
						Montague-court,	24	30	54	9	0
Wentworth-place S. side,	35	37	72	6	1	Harcourt-street,	155	190	345	36	7
Denzille-street, S. side,	68	57	143	19	1	Harcourt-road, -	9	12	21	3	0
Hamilton's-row, S. side, no inhabited houses.						Montague-street, -	34	59	93	14	1
						Kevin's-port, -	225	324	549	38	1
Harcourt - place, one house, viz. S. side,	3	7	10	1	0	Protestant-row, -	3	2	5	1	0
						Cambden Market,	13	20	33	5	0
Lower Merion-st. E. side,	15	16	31	3	0	Long-lane, -	12	19	31	4	0
Upper Merion-st. E. side,	64	83	147	12	0	Cambden street, -	239	351	590	74	1
Merion-square, entire, -	400	459	859	69	2	Gunpowder - office-yard, -	23	27	50	3	0
Holles-street, -	135	171	306	32	1						
Lower Mount-street, -	40	54	94	13	9	Charlotte-street.	85	93	178	23	2
Grant's-row, -	36	55	91	9	1	Charlemont-street, -	220	369	589	65	5
Holles-row, -	42	34	76	4	0	Charlemont-row,	5	6	11	2	0
Wilson's-place	19	29	48	3	0	Gordon's lane, -	20	43	63	9	1
Kelly's place, -	21	32	53	3	0	Clarke's-lane, -	10	21	31	6	0
M'Clean's-lane, -	30	27	57	6	0	Fennell's-lane, -	13	17	30	5	0
Upper Mount-street, -	5	15	20	4	2	Canal-quay, W. of Charlemont bridge	8	7	15	2	1
Fitzwilliam-street, -	10	26	36	6	4						
Fitzwilliam-lane,	35	42	77	4	0	Charlemont-place,	27	31	58	7	0
Fitzwilliam square, -	19	22	41	4	0	Peter-place, -	26	32	58	8	2
Baggot-street, -	153	195	348	38	9	Porto-Bello, -	105	156	261	30	1
Baggot-court,	13	10	23	4	0	Old Porto-Bello, -	37	58	95	13	0
Chancellor's lane,	6	9	15	1	0	Redmond's-hill, -	45	76	121	12	5
Merion-row, S. side, -	8	22	30	5	0	Bishop's-street, S. side,	94	110	204	24	2
Hume-street, -	53	73	126	15	2	Lower Kevin's-street,	552	700	1252	83	3
Ely-Place, -	99	103	202	20	1	Liberty-lane, -	132	144	276	24	0
Ely-lane, -	13	9	22	1	0	Church-lane, -	33	41	74	6	0
Leeson-street, (not including the Magdalen Asylum), -	157	234	391	43	6	Tool's-lane, -	11	16	27	3	0
						Ferns's-court, -	34	40	74	4	0
Leeson-place, and Quinn's-lane,	135	184	319	23	7	Bride-street, from Upper Kevin's-street, to No. 45,	72	94	166	13	
St. Stephen's green, E. S. and W. side, -	373	545	918	88	6	Grogan's court, -	15	21	36	4	0
						Faucett's court, -	10	8	18	3	1
Proud's-lane, -	7	13	20	2	0	N. side, from No. 16 correct, to Bride - street ; S. side, from Lower Kevin's-street to Edge's-court,	287	335	622	40	0
Glover's-alley, -	47	39	86	5	0						
King's-st. South, S. side,	261	305	566	35	0						
King's-court, -	65	70	135	10	0						
St. Stephen's-st S. side,	149	224	373	31	2						
Whitefriar's-st. E. side,	32	74	106	12	1						
Peter's-row, E side, -	6	6	12	2	0	Cathedral - lane, E. side,	61	84	145	11	1
York-street, -	225	282	507	57	0						
Aungier-street,	344	489	833	80	3	Leinster-row, -	28	21	49	4	2
Whitefriar's-lane,	43	62	105	5	0	E. side, from No. 3 to 13, and from No 32 to the Circular road,	134	176	310	35	4
Longford-street, -	74	104	178	18	0						
Longford-lane, -	32	51	83	3	0						
Little Longford-street,	41	53	94	12	2						
Mercer-street, -	70	85	155	19	0	Williams's-lane, -	8	12	20	5	5
Bow-lane, -	56	52	108	9	2	Circular - road, E. of New-street,	11	18	29	5	0
Digges's-lane, -	157	180	337	18	1						
Digges's-court	42	42	84	5	0	St. Patrick's Library,	7	4	11	1	0
French street,	127	195	322	37	1	Magdalen Asylum, Leeson-street, -	0	32	32	1	0
Little Digges's-street,	9	11	20	3	0						
Cheater's-alley	14	11	25	4	0						
Digges's-street, -	49	127	176	19	2	TOTAL -	6890	9173	16063	1512	116
Cuffe-street,	196	297	493	46	5						

No. XIV.

Parish of Saint Anne.

NAMES OF STREETS, &c.	Males	Females	TOTAL	Inhabited	Waste	NAMES OF STREETS, &c.	Males	Females	TOTAL	Inhabited	Waste
Lower Merion-st. W. side,	12	16	28	7	0	Adam-court,	37	43	80	8	0
Upper Merion-st. W. side,	108	145	253	21	2	Grafton or Spann's-lane	97	126	223	10	0
Lacy's-lane,	27	41	68	4	0						
Merion-row, N. side,	28	31	59	7	3	Tangier-lane,	18	20	38	3	0
St. Stephen's-green, N.	139	213	352	31	2	Chatham-street,	67	91	158	18	3
King's-st. South, N. side,	110	191	301	28	0	Pitt-street,	41	48	89	13	0
Lime-kiln-yard,	7	5	12	3	0	Harry-street,	23	30	53	7	0
Johnston's place,	13	27	40	6	0	Johnston's-court,	51	49	100	8	4
William-street, E. side,	127	153	280	29	2	Dawson-street,	269	373	642	60	3
Exchequer-street, S. side from William-street to Grafton-street,	72	104	176	19	1	Duke-street,	119	150	269	23	0
						Anne-street,	113	168	281	30	0
						Molesworth-street,	160	233	393	37	0
Wilson's-yard,	8	7	15	3	0	Frederick-street,	110	169	279	35	3
Clarendon-street,	211	306	517	55	3	Kildare-street,	170	232	402	46	0
Clarendon-market, in stalls,	6	11	17	5	0	Schoolhouse-lane,	36	63	99	4	0
						Nassau-street, S. side,	119	168	287	34	1
Clarendow-row,	63	76	139	4	0	Nassau-lane,	8	6	14	1	0
Chatham-row,	25	27	52	3	1	Leinster-street, S. side,	65	85	150	13	0
Coppinger's-row,	11	18	29	3	1	Clare-street,	82	141	223	26	1
Grafton-street, E. side entire; W. side, from King-street to Exchequer-street,	438	497	935	92	4	Clare-lane,	34	29	63	4	0
						Park-st. E. side & S. side,	47	65	112	11	2
						TOTAL	3071	4157	7228	711	36

No. XV.

Parish of Saint Andrew.

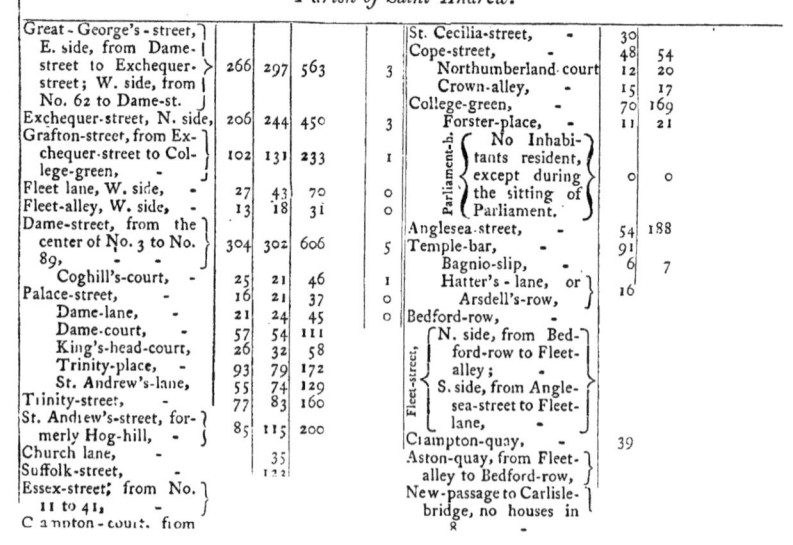

Great-George's-street, E. side, from Dame-street to Exchequer-street; W. side, from No. 62 to Dame-st.	266	297	563	3	St. Cecilia-street,	30		
					Cope-street,	48	54	
					Northumberland-court	12	20	
					Crown-alley,	15	17	
					College-green,	70	169	
Exchequer-street, N. side,	206	244	450	3	Forster-place,	11	21	
Grafton-street, from Exchequer-street to College-green,	102	131	233	1	No Inhabitants resident, except during the sitting of Parliament.	0	0	
Fleet lane, W. side,	27	43	70	0				
Fleet-alley, W. side,	13	18	31	0				
Dame-street, from the center of No. 3 to No. 89,	304	302	606	5	Anglesea-street,	54	188	
					Temple-bar,	91		
					Bagnio-slip,	6	7	
Coghill's-court,	25	21	46	0	Hatter's-lane, or Arsdell's-row,	16		
Palace-street,	16	21	37	0				
Dame-lane,	21	24	45	0	Bedford-row,			
Dame-court,	57	54	111		N. side, from Bedford-row to Fleet-alley; S. side, from Angle-sea-street to Fleet-lane,			
King's-head-court,	26	32	58					
Trinity-place,	93	79	172					
St. Andrew's-lane,	55	74	129					
Trinity-street,	77	83	160					
St. Andrew's-street, formerly Hog-hill,	85	115	200		Crampton-quay, Aston-quay, from Fleet-alley to Bedford-row, New-passage to Carlisle-bridge, no houses in	39		
Church lane,		35						
Suffolk-street,		132						
Essex-street, from No. 11 to 41,								
Crampton-court, from								

No. XVI.
Parish of Saint Mark.

NAMES OF STREETS, &c.	Males	Females	TOTAL	Inhabited	Waste
College-st. entire, No. 12 excepted,	90	106	196	15	2
Fleet-lane, E. side,	33	54	87	5	0
Fleet-alley, E. side, no inhabited houses.	0	0	0	0	0
Fleet-street, E. of Fleet-lane and Fleet-alley,	218	310	528	40	3
Townsend-street,	764	1012	1776	136	20
Fleet-market,	43	66	109	11	0
Tucker's-yard,	35	31	66	6	2
Spring-garden-lane,	23	18	41	3	1
Tennis-court,	72	57	129	6	0
Park-place, or Carter's-alley,	127	218	345	13	0
Sandwith-street,	11	8	19	2	1
Hawkins-street,	148	181	329	29	3
Sugar-house-lane,	2	1	3	1	0
Aston's quay, E. of Fleet-al	157	177	334	17	1
Stewart's-court,	7	10	17	3	0
George's-quay,	303	375	678	30	0
City-quay,	269	315	584	41	0
Banfield's-lane,	6	9	15	3	0
Sir John Rogerson's-quay,	284	233	517	28	0
Hanover-street,	2	8	10	1	0
Nowland's lane,	8	6	14	2	0
Lime-street,	2	2	4	1	0
Poolbeg-street,	224	293	517	42	4
Stocking-lane,	129	189	318	20	0
Luke-street,	69	76	145	14	3
White's lane,	52	53	105	11	2
George's street, E.	44	57	101	12	0
Moss-street,	205	263	468	34	4
Prince's-street,	13	15	28	3	1
Gloster street, S.	79	80	159	11	0
Mark-street,	30	65	95	13	2
Nassau-street, N. side,	10	17	27	5	1
Leinster-street, N. side,	30	20	50	2	0
Park-street, W. side,	20	29	49	4	0
Harcourt-place, N. side,	17	17	34	5	0
Hamilton's row. N. side,	16	39	55	8	0
Denzille-street, N. side,	13	36	49	7	2
Wentworth-place, N. side,	29	46	75	9	0
Grand-canal-street, N. side, no houses as yet.	0	0	0	0	0
Westland-row,	18	49	67	4	0
Cumberland-street, S.	55	71	126	21	5
Boyne-street, rere of do. and Boyne-lane,	190	231	421	27	0
Erne-street,	0	2	2	1	0
Great Clarence-street, no inhabited houses,	0	0	0	0	1
TOTAL	3847	4845	8692	646	62

No. XVII.
Parish of Saint Paul.

NAMES OF STREETS, &c.	Males	Females	TOTAL	Inhabited	Waste
Park-gate-street,	120	190	310	36	3
Barrack-street,	587	858	1445	99	3
Granby-court,	18	17	35	6	0
Featherbed-lane,	6	17	23	2	0
Boot-yard,	25	53	78	6	0
Dawson's-yard,	44	98	142	7	0
Silver-street,	62	81	143	11	1
Liffey-street,	42	51	93	8	2
Flood-street,	83	122	205	15	4
Kane's-court,	18	20	38	3	0
Pembroke, or Sand-quay,	21	38	59	5	2
Tighe-st. or Gravel-walk,	329	466	795	51	4
Browne's-alley,	11	12	23	2	0
Ellis's-quay,	34	51	85	9	0
John-street,	18	22	40	3	1
Queen-street,	339	438	777	79	4
Queen's-court,	5	3	8	2	5
Burges's-lane,	16	16	32	1	1
Bridewell-lane,	11	14	25	2	0
Hendrick-street,	58	90	148	19	1
Hendrick-lane,	16	28	44	4	0
Blackhall-street,	59	66	125	15	6
Blue-coat-hospital,	134	24	158	1	0
Parade at St. Paul's church	4	5	9	2	1
Temple-street,	41	59	100	13	1
Mountpelier,	56	77	133	19	0
Arbour-hill,	119	158	277	42	9
Stony-batter,	219	188	407	52	3
Chicken-lane,	17	28	45	10	5
Manor-street,	429	534	963	127	7
Daly's-court,	13	12	25	7	2
Swan's-lane,	15	12	27	6	0
Garden-lane,	51	62	113	22	2
Prussia-street,	183	227	410	64	5
Aughrim-street,	116	163	279	46	5
Brunswick-st. N. side, from No. 17 to Stony-batter; S. side, from Stony-batter to No. 49.	103	178	281	31	3
George's lane,	20	29	49	3	1
Red-cow-lane,	45	46	91	8	2
Smith's-court, off Red-cow lane,	22	34	56	6	0
Grange-Gorman-lane,	191	240	431	76	18
Fitzwilliam-place,	8	16	24	3	0
Love-lane,	6	10	16	5	0
Stanhope-street,	13	23	36	5	0
King-street, North, N. side, from Red-cow-lane to Stony-batter; S. side, from Stony-batter to Smithfield,	156	240	396	40	7
Smithfield, W. side only,	185	225	410	26	0
Hay-market,	84	90	180	15	0
Arran-quay, from No. 19 to Queen-street,	88	110	198	26	0
West-Arran-street, E. side, from Arran-quay to Phœnix street; W. side entire,	48	69	117	11	3
TOTAL	4288	5616	9904	1050	115

No. XVIII.
Parish of Saint Michan.

NAMES OF STREETS, &c.	Males	Females	TOTAL	Inhabited	Waste	NAMES OF STREETS, &c.	Males	Females	TOTAL	Inhabited	Waste
West - Arran - street, from Phœnix - street to Smithfield,	25	38	63	4	0	Ormond-market, Mountrath-street,	0 102	0 124	0 226	0 19	0 3
Smithfield, E. side only,	205	253	458	30	2	Toshe's-court, Mass-lane,	9 10	15 21	24 31	2 4	0 0
Duck-lane	3	4	7	2	0	Morgan-place,	0	3	3	1	3
Carter's-alley,	35	58	93	6	0	Mary's-lane,	451	517	968	67	4
Factory-lane,	28	34	62	5	0	Boot-lane entire, except No. 1, belonging to Bank of Ireland, and in Mary's parish,	207	231	438	34	0
N. side, from Bolton-street to Redcow-lane; S. side, from Smithfield to Capel-street,	647	836	1483	122	8	Fisher's lane, Bradogue-alley,	179 15	195 27	372 42	50 3	1 0
Whitehall-court,	19	28	47	5	1	Bull-lane,	129	164	293	19	0
N. side, from Upper Church-street to No. 16; S. side, from No. 50 to Upper Church-street,	131	168	299	34	3	Greek-street, Lattin's-court, Anderson's-court, Beresford-street, Stirrup-lane, Kelche's-yard,	97 36 24 202 53 2	138 59 32 279 68 9	235 95 56 481 121 11	30 7 5 42 8 3	3 9 2 6 1 0
Snugborough,	13	11	24	3	0	Simpson's-court,	8	15	23	4	2
Arran-q. from Church-street to No. 18,	54	78	132	18	0	Anne-street, North, George's-hill,	85 49	129 42	214 91	27 12	3 0
Phœnix-street,	206	287	493	27	2	Halston-street,	77	108	185	14	2
Lincoln-lane,	37	50	87	13	0	Ball's lane,	9	17	26	3	1
Ball-yard,	16	16	32	6	4	Cuckow-lane,	17	17	34	4	0
Bow-lane,	111	108	219	14	2	Petticoat-lane,	24	32	56	4	1
Hammond-lane,	182	206	388	29	5	N. side, from No. 5 to Green-street; S. side, from Petticoat-lane to Stable-lane,	53	66	119	12	1
Church-street,	1293	1517	2810	189	24						
Field's-court,	9	10	19	3	4						
Townley-court,	18	18	36	5	1						
Cole's-conrt,	38	48	86	4	0						
Russell's-court,	10	12	22	2	0	Green-street,	94	122	216	16	0
George-inn-yard,	11	14	25	2	3	Coleraine-street,	58	87	145	15	1
Byrne's court,	23	31	54	3	0	Linen-hall-street,	52	56	108	14	0
Catherine's-lane,	18	26	44	4	1	Lurgan-street,	27	30	57	9	0
New Church-street,	142	169	311	17	0	Lisburn-street,	10	21	31	4	0
Bow-street,	339	429	768	46	9	Linen-hall,	12	22	34	1	0
Bedford-street,	26	36	62	6	0	Constitution - hill, or Glasmanoge,	236	287	523	45	4
Browne-street, between King-st. and Bow-st.	36	61	97	8	0	Townsend-st. off do.	27	30	57	4	0
Kavanagh's court, off do.	13	16	29	4	1	Broad-stone,	230	322	552	112	11
May lane,	119	139	258	18	0	Monk's-place,	30	39	69	11	1
King's inns-quay,	51	55	106	13	1	Phibbsborough-lane,	45	73	118	22	1
Upper Ormond-quay,	147	158	305	35	1	Yarn-hall. — No Population.					
Pill lane,	507	626	1133	97	12						
Blue-hand-court, off Pill-lane,	30	24	54	5	1	N.E.side,except the house next Bolton-street; S. W. side, except the house next Bolton-street,	100	106	206	13	0
Arran-street,	128	159	287	26	1						
S. side, from Arran-street to No. 6; N. side, from No. 17 to Arran-street,	116	140	256	18	0	Henrietta-place, Stable-lane, off Henrietta-street.—No Population.	16	29	45	4	0
Johnston's-alley.— No population.											
Charles-street,	304	390	694	40	0	TOTAL	7865	9783	17648	1487	141

APPENDIX. No. II. xxiii

No. XIX.

Parish of Saint Mary.

NAMES OF STREETS, &c.	Males	Females	TOTAL	Inhabited	Waste	NAMES OF STREETS, &c.	Males	Females	TOTAL	Inhabited	Waste
Capel-street,	612	767	1379	162	4	Cross-lane, off Cole's-lane,	16	20	36	3	0
Little Strand-st. S. side, from No. 7 to Capel-street; N. side. from Capel-st. to No. 16,	76	81	157	10	0	Sampson's-lane,	77	85	162	16	0
						Bennetting's-lane, now Cole's-lane market,	99	125	224	28	0
						Stable-lane, off middle Liffey-street,	10	11	21	2	0
Mary's-abbey,	146	136	282	36	2						
Meeting-house-lane,	26	4	30	4	0	Moore-lane,	27	30	57	5	0
Little Mary-street,	233	230	463	30	0	Sackville-lane,	66	73	139	12	0
Stable-lane,	16	22	38	2	0	Off-lane,	81	88	169	8	0
Little Britain-street, N. side, from Capel-st. to No. 45 S. side, from Stable-lane to Capel-st.	21	25	46	6	0	Back-yard, off Moore-st.	22	21	43	4	1
						Bolton-street,	295	426	721	64	0
						M'Manus-court,	15	17	30	5	0
						Bryner's-alley,	6	6	12	1	0
Lower Ormond-quay,	160	185	345	34	4	Ryder's-row, (N B. This	31	49	80	7	0
Batchelor's-walk, from Lower Liffey-street, to Sackville-street,	121	147	268	32	0	Britain-lane,	62	86	148	10	0
						Loftus-lane,	111	149	260	20	0
						Cross-lane,	117	176	293	23	0
Abbey-st. S. side, from Capel-st. to No. 53; N. side, from Williams's-lane to Capel-st.	492	632	1124	109	11	Cherry-lane,	47	94	141	10	0
						Turn-again-lane,	36	48	84	11	0
						Dominick-street,	243	344	587	59	0
						Granby-row,	174	245	419	44	0
Great Strand-street,	192	191	383	39	2	Granby-place,	26	30	56	4	0
The Lots, N. side, West of the rere of No. 54 Abbey-street; S. side entire,	14	15	29	4	1	Palace-row, (N B. This is extra-parochial, as also Mrs. Dean's house in Granby-row.)	91	110	201	12	0
Murry-court, off Strand-street,	12	29	41	4	0	Frederick-street, North, the S. W. side only,	23	26	49	6	1
Prince's-street, West of Williams's-lane,	21	22	43	4	0	Yarn hall-street,	6	6	12	1	0
Mary-street,	210	318	528	52	2	Henrietta-st. 2 houses next Bolton-street,	6	5	11	2	0
Henry st. S. side, from Middle Liffey-street to No. 22; N. side, from Off-lane to Denmark street,	248	323	571	50	2	Stable-lane off Henrietta-street,	14	24	38	3	0
						Dorset-street, S.E. side, from Dominick-st. to Frederick-st,; N. W. side, from White's-lane to Bolton-street,	484	611	1095	99	0
Great Britain-st. S. side, from Capel-street to Moore-lane; N. side, from Cavendish-row to Capel-street,	512	655	1167	127	0						
						Gilshenan's-lane,	18	25	43	7	0
						Gooding's-yard,	44	58	102	8	0
						King's-lane,	51	69	120	21	2
Stafford-street,	156	224	380	41	4	Kelly's-lane,	20	38	58	7	0
Jervis-street,	185	371	556	62	3	Bishop's-yard,	10	14	24	5	0
Swift's-row,	83	95	178	11	1	Blessington-stieet, no population in 1798.					
Lower-Liffey-street,	131	144	275	31	0						
Middle Liffey-street,	287	318	605	34	1	Paradise-row,	117	178	295	43	0
Denmark-street,	273	404	677	39	0	Graham's row,	24	29	53	10	0
Cole's-lane,	243	254	497	33	2	Lane from Paradise-row to the Royal Circus,	11	16	27	6	0
Moore-street,	274	349	623	56	0						
Chapel-lane,	34	52	86	6	0						
Wheeler's-alley,	15	18	33	3	0						
M'Cann's-lane,	19	21	40	3	0	TOTAL	7290	9364	16654	1590	43

No. XX.

Parish of Saint Thomas.

NAMES OF STREETS, &c.	Males	Females	TOTAL	Inhabited	Waste	NAMES OF STREETS, &c.	Males	Females	TOTAL	Inhabited	Waste
Lower Sackville-street,	104	141	245	25	6	Summer-hill, S. side only	152	251	403	51	3
Upper Sackville-street,	275	341	616	59	1	Rutland-street, -	19	13	32	6	2
The Lotts, Abbey-street, { N. side, E. of the rere of No. 54, Abbey-street,	9	7	16	3	0	Morgan's-lane, - -	12	14	26	5	3
						Portland-row, - -	13	13	26	3	3
						Buckingham street, -	36	45	81	10	0
Abbey-street, { S. side, from No. 54 to Lower Sackville-st; N. side, from Lower Sackville-street to Williams's lane, -	76	92	168	25	5	Meredith-place, -	3	4	7	1	0
						Washington-row, - -	3	3	6	2	4
						Caroline - row, without the Circular-road,	0	0	0	0	0
						Stratford row, -	12	19	31	5	0
						Gloucester-street, -	139	197	336	41	0
Prince's-str. E. of Williams's-lane, -	20	25	45	4	0	Lower Gloucester-street,	41	39	80	10	1*
						Cumberland-street,North,	144	200	344	41	1
Henry-street, { S. side, from No. 23 to Lower Sackville-st.; N. side, from Upper Sackville-street to Off-lane, - -	40	57	97	8	2	Cumberland-lane,	37	51	88	6	0
						Stable - lane, off Cumberland - st., between No. 4 and 5, -	2	3	5	1	0
						Stable - lane, off Cumberland - st. between No. 38 and 39, -	7	8	15	2	0
Batchelor's - walk, from Sackville - street to Union-street, -	72	73	145	7	0						
Lower Abbey-street, -	352	482	834	54	3	Lower Gardiner-street,	47	64	111	15	10
Custom-house, -	20	38	58	1	0	Gloucester-place, - -	18	20	38	6	1
Berresford-place, -	3	4	7	1	4	Upper Gloucester-place,	0	0	0	0	0
Union-street, - - -	57	57	114	6	0	Mecklenburgh-street,	272	397	669	78	7
Marlborough-street, -	426	520	946	99	5	Mecklenburgh-lane, No. 1,	18	21	39	5	0
Tucker's-row, - -	98	92	190	13	0	Mecklenburgh-lane, No. 2, - -	23	37	60	3	0
Stable-lane, between Tucker's-row and Earl-street, -	53	59	112	8	0	Mabbot-street, -	137	150	287	31	5
Back yard, off do.	11	18	29	2	0	Back yard,off Mabbot-street, -	8	0	17	3	0
Roach's - lane, off Marlborough-st.	7	12	19	2	0	Mabbot-lane, No. 1,	15	11	26	4	0
Earl-street, North, -	95	149	244	25	2	Do. No. 2, -	34	39	73	11	0
Elephant-lane, -	24	32	56	4	0	Montgomery-street, -	296	320	616	72	3
Gregg's-lane, -	34	42	76	6	0	Barlow's-square, -	17	20	37	7	0
Potter's alley, -	33	39	72	6	1	Martin's-lane, -	7	5	12	3	0
Entrance to Marlborough-green, -	19	18	37	3	0	North Strand, -	134	179	313	39	3
Cope-street, North, -	25	33	58	8	0	Mayor-street, - -	34	28	62	5	2
Great Britain-st. S. side, from Moore-lane to Summer-hill, -	186	275	461	46	4	North Wall, - -	34	43	77	11	1
						TOTAL - -	3753	4809	8562	892	82

No. XXI.

Parish of Saint George.

NAMES OF STREETS, &c	POPULATION.			HOUSES.	
	Males.	Females.	Total.	Inhabited.	Waste.
Great Britain-st. North side from Cavendish-row to Summer-hill,	243	353	596	59	0
Johnston's-court,	31	58	89	7	4
Summer-hill, N. W. side,	135	196	331	48	2
Lane's-lane,	29	39	68	14	1
Cavendish-row,	126	142	268	24	0
Frederick-street North, North-East side only,	9	10	19	3	0
Dorset-str. { S. E. side, from Frederick-street to Lower Dorset-st. N. W. side, one house only,	17	27	44	5	0
White's lane,	12	34	46	8	0
Lower Dorset-street,	257	335	592	78	5
Kelly's-row,	35	43	78	14	0
Synnot's-place,	16	28	44	6	2
Great George's-street, N.	237	273	510	48	2
George's-court,	10	14	24	2	0
Upper Temple-street,	90	121	211	23	2
Lower Temple-street,	56	89	145	14	6
Stable-lane, off Upper Temple-st.	16	23	39	6	0
Temple - court, off Lower Temple-st.	43	53	96	9	0
Gardiner's-row,	44	48	92	8	0
Great Denmark-street,	62	55	117	11	1
Gardiner's-place,	94	153	247	28	3
Stable-lane,	12	22	34	4	0
Grenville-street,	49	48	97	11	7
Stable-lane,	5	9	14	3	3
Mountjoy-square, N. side,	50	50	100	10	3
Mountjoy-square, W. side,	37	30	67	9	6
Mountjoy-square, S. side,	91	99	190	16	2
Mountjoy - square, East side, no population in 1798,	0	0	0	0	0
Middle Gardiner-street,	72	87	159	21	7
Russel's-lane,	24	19	43	4	0
Belmont place,	10	10	20	2	1
Mountjoy-place,	11	18	29	5	7
Great Charles-street,	15	14	29	4	7
Stable-lane,	15	10	25	3	0
Mountjoy-court, off ditto,	8	14	22	4	4
Fitzgibbon-street,	4	3	7	1	1
Belvidere-place,	40	54	94	10	5
Upper Gardiner-street,	36	54	90	12	8
Eccles-street,	163	246	409	51	0
Eccles-lane,	7	4	11	2	0
TOTAL	2211	2885	5096	587	89

[xxvi]

APPENDIX, No. III.

DOWN SURVEY.

In the Surveyor General's Office, (No. 7, of the Record Tower) are deposited the various Maps and Books now remaining of the several surveys, estimates, and distributions of the territory of Ireland, made at different periods.

Amongst the important documents in this repository those of the Down Survey are the most interesting (see p. 474, &c.). Mr. Whitelaw had commenced an investigation of the Survey, and had proposed to present a table of it, but it was left at the period of his death imperfect and unfinished. We have been enabled, by the kindness of the Record Office, to subjoin a new and complete analysis of an article which will be found important and necessary to be consulted by the agent, the clerical incumbent, and the landed proprietor or farmer.

Conformably to an order of the Record Commissioners in July 1814, these maps were repaired by a skilful bookbinder. Such of them as had been damaged by fire, injured by use, or worn by attrition, were carefully inlaid and pasted down on the best and strongest drawing-paper, and all of them were then uniformly bound in thirty-five broad atlas-sized folio volumes, lettered with the names of the counties on the backs, and of the baronies on the sides of the several books. General Vallancey's copies of the barony-maps are also similarly bound and lettered, in four atlas-sized folios, to match the original maps of the Down Survey.

APPENDIX, No. III.

Catalogue of the Maps of the Down Survey.

Counties and Baronies.   Parishes and other Sub-denominations.

Co. Antrim, perfect maps; not damaged by the fire.

Toome.   V.* Dunean, Drumall and Magherivchill, part of. A plot of church lands in Drumall and Magherivchill.

Antrim.   V. Skirre, Rocavan, Kells, Connor.

Kilconway.   V. Dunaghy and Grange of Dundermount, Oghill, Balimonie part of, Killagha part; Maghirisharkan, Magherioghill, Finvoy.

Glenarne.   V. Larne, Killoghter, Carnecastle, Glenarne, Ardclunis, appendix to Glenarne, Layde.

Carie.   V. Calfaghtrim, Rathmoan, Billy, Rathlin Island, Ardmoy, Derrichechen.

Co. Antrim, imperfect maps; damaged by the fire.

Belfast, including Carrickfergus. V.

County Palatine of ditto. V.

Dunluce.   V. Loghgreely, Derickehane, Ballyroshan, Billy, Killagan and Kilraghtis, Portcommonals, Dunluce, Balliwillin.

Massareene.   V. N. P.

Co. Armagh, perfect maps; not damaged by the fire.

Orier.   V. Kilsleeve, Loughilly forfeited lands, Tawnaghlee forfeited church lands.

Fews.   V. Cregan, Armagh and Mulloghbrack part.

Co. Armagh, imperfect maps; damaged by the fire, &c.

Armagh.   V. Armagh.

O'Nealand.   V.

Fowrany.   V. Fynan in two parts, Armagh.

Co. Carlow, perfect maps; not damaged by the fire, &c.

Ravilly.   V. Rahill, Ravilly, Kingath, Rathmore two parts, Tullogh, (Adriston, Ahad, and Fernagh parts).

Forth and part of St. Mullin. V. Myshall, Templepeters and Aghad, Fenno, Adriston and Ballymolden, Ballin, Barrow Pobbledrum.

Catherlogh.   V. Clodagh and Painstown with part of Killerig, Catherlogh, Ballinacarrigge, Tulmaghgimagh, Killestowne and Lordship of Grange, Forth, (Barnycary and Killerig parts of,) Urlagh.

Idroney.   V. Cloghguenan Manor, Kilcrene and Loughland, Kilmcene and Wells part, Dunlearny and (Wells part of) Clonvgosh and Balliellin, Sleagoe and part of Lorum, Acha, Arnie, Senagh part, Kilishynal, St. Mullins part.

St. Mullins part.   V. Ballolin and Ullard parts Mullin.

Co. Cavan,† imperfect maps; damaged by the fire, &c.

Castlerahan.   V. Killinkeirin, Crosserlogh.

Clonehy.   V. Monebolge, Killane, Knockbride and Dromgoone.

---

* By V. here is meant that there is a copy of the barony-map, made from the Paris maps by General Vallancey.
† In this county General Vallancey's copy has the half-barony of Tullaghanoho, not mentioned in the Down Survey.

xxviii APPENDIX, No. III.

Counties and Baronies.		Parishes and other Sub-denominations.
Clonmoghan.	V.	Ballitample, Kilmore, Ballimohugh, part of Denne, Kildrumsartan, als. Crosserlogh Drumloman.
Loghtee.	V.	Kilmore, Crosserlogh and Denn, Orny, Annaghgelene, Annagh, Lowry or Lawry, Casterra and Larragh, Killinkerin and Killinkeare, Drumlane and Tomregan.
Tullaghah.	V.	Kildallan, Killasandra and Kildallan, Templeporte, Killinagh.
Tullaghgary.	V.	Larragh, Drong, Killiserdimny, Dromgoone Annagh.
Clonchy.	V.	Inniskeene.

In the county of Clare General Vallancey has the following baronies, Corcumrve, Bunratty, and Moyferta, not mentioned in the Down Survey.

Co. Cork, perfect maps; not damaged by fire, &c.

Imokilly.	V.	Killeagh, part of Dunganedunavane and Itermurrogh, Inchy, Corkebeg, Aghaddy, Garran Cloyne, Ballintemple, Kilmaghene, Titeskin, Rostellane, Garivoe and Boghland, part of Itermurrogh and Mogeally, Kilmaedonogh and Clonpriest, Ballyoughtragh, Mogeally and parts Inchenebacky and Ballynecore.
Barrimore.	V.	Gortroe, Kilguane, Killvillan and Killafvane, Templerobin, Killshanahane, Carrigtuoghill, Moyessey and Ballycrany, Ardnegihy, Templenecarrigg and Ballyspellane, Downebullogh and Templeusky, Templebodan and Lisgoolde, Clonmell, Caherlagh and Little Island, Rathcormuck, Castle Lyons and Brittway, Dungorney and Clonnalt, Ballynacorra Gatranekinefeaky, Abadda and Titeskin.
Liberties of Cork.	V.	Finbarris, Carrigoline and Killinally, Inchkiny, Carrigaline, Ballinaboy, Kilgroghan and part of Kilnaglory, Rathcoany, Kilcully, Currykippane and Shandon.
Liberties of Kinsale and Barony of Coursey.	V.	Ringrone part, Ringrone, Kilbroan and Templetrine, Rincoran, Clanteade, Tesaxon, Dundorrow and parts, Rincoran and Barrymartle.
Barriroe and Ibawne.	V.	Rothbarry, Killkeranmore and Ardfield.
Ibawne Barony.	V.	Temple Omalice and Temple M'Quanlane, Abbeymahoone and Lislee.
Muskerry and Barretts.	V.	Oven, Ballynaboy and Finbarris, Knockavilly and Desertmore, Kilbonan, Moviddy, Aglish Maclonehey and Kanaboy, Kilmorris, Kilmichael, Inchigeelagh, Ballyworney, Clondrohid, Drishane and Killcorney, Killmartery, Macrompe, Aghabollog and Aghinagh, Kilcoleman, Mattehy and Inniscarragh, Donoghmore, parts of Dunbollog, Whitechurch, and Grenagh, Templemighell part.
Barrett.	V.	Currycrohanbeg and Inniscarragh, Aglish, Mattehy and Kilcolman, Donoghmore, Ovens Desert and Granagh, St. Finbarris, Killnaglory and Currycroghanmore parts of.
Beare and Bantry.	V.	Kilmacomoge, Kilcaskane, Killaghaninagh, Killcatierin and Killmallagh, Durrous,
Kerricurrihy and Kinalea.	V.	Killmurhy, part Lisnacleary and Carrigoline, Monkstown impropriation and land between Lisnacleary and Carrigoline, Killinelly and part of Carrigoline, Vyrnekelly and part of Carrigoline and Lisnacleary, Ballinaboy, Templebride and part of Kilpatrick, part of Kilpatrick and Carrigoline, Lisnacleary.
Kinalea.	V.	Templemichael, part Taxaxon, part Inishonan and Dundurrow, Leoffoly, Brinie and Knockavilla and part Inishonan, Ballymartle and part Ballynevoy, and Dundurrow, and Knocknemannagh, Cullen Bealefoile and part Nogaval, Kilmahonogue, Kilpatrick and Carrigoline, Kinnure and part of Nogaval, Bealaseard.

APPENDIX, No. III. xxix

Counties and Baronies.		Parishes and other Sub-denominations.
Carbury.	V.	Ballinedeghy, part of Inishanon, Templetown and Rinerone, Kilbrittane, part of Ballymodon, Rathclarin, Kilmolody and part of Timoleage, Desert, Kenneth, Funlobbish, and part of Kilmihil, Drinagh, Ballymoney, Killmine, Garriff, and part of Innishdonny, Castroventry, part of Temple-M'Guinlane and Templeomalus, Killnegrosse, Kilmaclkabea, Roscarbry, Kilfanaghbeg, Miros, Castlehaven, Creagh, Tulloghal, Baltimore and Island of Capeclear, Affodowne, Abbyshrowry, Caheragh, Drummaleige, Durrous, Kilcroghan, Kilcoe, Skul, Kilmoe.

Co. Cork, imperfect maps; damaged by the fire.

Armoyal, Fermoy.	V.	Monenemi, Killathy and Ballyhooly, Downerayle, and part of Ballyhay part of Whitechurch, Kilcrumper, part of Clondelon and Templetheogan, Cabirdugan, part of Clenor and Carrigtemleary, Castletown, Raghan, Whitechurch and Moyallow, Wallstown and Carrigdownan, Clenor, Pharihy and Templervan, Killgollane, Ballyloghy and Glannor.
Condons and Clongibhon.	V.	Castlelions, Knockmore, and Muckollap, Macrony, Kilgollane and Glannor, part of Marshalstown and Brigoon, Preb. of Phelan and Nelan, Kilworth, Kilcrumper, Templetheogan and Glennor, Clondollan and Letrim.
Duhallow.	V.	Kilmeene, part of Ballyclough, Killishannock, Drumterrif, Knockatemple, Tullelish and Clonfert, Clonemeene, Kilbrin, Noghavall, Cullin, and Drishane.*
Orrery and Kilmore.		Ballyclough, part of, and Castlemagnor, parts of Liscarrol and Templebrady, Cotoyne and Aglishbradew, Kilbolane, Rathgogan and Ballyhay, Shandrum.

Co. Donegal, perfect maps; not damaged by the fire, &c.

Tyrehugh.	V.	Carne alias Farmon M'Grah, part of, parts of Kilbarran and Ennish M'Saint, Drumhone, part of, another part of ditto.
Boylagh and Bannah.	V.	Inver and Killomard, parts of, Killbeg, Killrean, Capella, Letter M'Ward, Kilcarrha, Glancollankill, Templecron, and Killaghty, Inishkeel.
Raphoe.	V.	Raphoe, Lifford, Taybone, Ray and Lecke, Donaghmore and Stranorlan.
Kilm M'Crenan.	V.	Garton, Conwel, Athnengin, part Tully, Aghnish, Killgarvan, Clondevadoge, Mevagh, Ciandehura, Revagh, Tulloghobegly.
Ennishowen.	V.	Movill, Clanmany, Clancae, Coolduffe, and Donagh church lands, Deserteene and Templemore escheated lands, Fanthen.

Co. Down, perfect maps; and damaged by the fire, &c.

| Kinealearty. | V. | Loughmiland and Kilmoremorean forfeited lands, Magheredril, Magherehowlett. |
| Evagh, Lower. | V. | Forfeited part of Segoe and Corumbie, with Anakett quarter, Dromore, Drumara, forfeited part Magherelin, Donoghglonnie, Tullelish, and Aghaerig, and forfeited part of Seapatrick, Magherally Glebe. |

Co. Down, imperfect maps; damaged by the fire, &c.

Ards.	V.	Ardquin, Ballyphilip, Slane, Utter, Ballygagott Grange, Grayabbey.
Lecale.	V.	Kilmegan, Down, Kilclief, Balliculter, Ballee, Bright, Terella, Dunsford.
Evagh, Upper.	V.	Kilmegan, Kilbrony, Drumgagh, Garvaghy, Dromgolane, Aghaderrigh, Anaghecloane, Maghera, Cloneallen, Cloneduff.

Co. Dublin, perfect maps; not damaged by the fire.

| Rathdown, half barony. | V. | Donnabrooke, Tannee, Kill, Monkstowne, Killeny, Tully, and part of Whitechurch, Kilternon, Conough, and Rathmichell. |

* General Vallancy has Killnatalloon and Kilcalmaky, not mentioned here.

APPENDIX, No. III.

Counties and Baronies.		Parishes and other Sub-denominations.
Newcastle and Upper Cross.	V.	Talaugh, part of, Lucan, Adery, part of, Sagard, Rafarnam, part of Creevagh, Whitechurch, Racoole, Killmatalway, Callestowne, Newcastle, Palmerstown, Kilmainham, Clondalkin, and Ballyfermot, parts of.
Coolock.	V.	Santry, St. Margarett's, Killeegh and Killostry, Malahide, Coolock, Raheny, Cloghran, part of Swords and Finglass, Portmarnock, Howth.
Castleknock.	V.	Malahedert, Ward, Kilsoghan Castleknock.
Nethercross.	V.	Swords, Portrane, and bigger part of Luske, Clonmedon, and part of Finglass and Luske.
Ballruddery.	V.	Balruddery, Garestown, Balmadon, Naule, Holywood, Wespelstowne, Ballibroghell, Donabate, Palmerstown, and Bulscaddan, Old Patrick, Baldongan, and part of Luske.
Upper Cross.	V.	Ballymore, Eustace, the part of Ballibought and Tipperkevan.

Fermanagh, imperfect maps ; damaged by the fire, &c.

Clanawly.	V.	Killnally, Clinish, Boha, Killagher.
Magheraboy.	V.	Beagh, Innish M'Saint, Devenish, Rossury.
Magherestephana.	V.	East and West parts of Aghalurcher, Aghaveigh.

In the County of Kerry, not mentioned here at all, General Vallancey has Iraghticonnor, Clanmorris, Corkaguinny, Trughanackny, Magunnihy, Dunkerrone and Iveragh.

Co. Kildare, imperfect maps ; damaged by the fire.

Naas.	V.	Naas, Whitechurch, Sherlockstown, and Bowdinstown, Killisha, Rathmore, Carnalway.
Carbery.	V.	Dunfert, Ballinadrumnie, Cadamstown, Moylerstown, Archill, Nurney-Carrick.
Claine.	V.	Downing, Clane, and Killibegs, Timiocho, Ballinasso, Brideschurch.
Great Connell.*	V.	Old Connell and Morristownbiller, Kilmeag, and Ratherning, Ladytown, Fecullen, Great Connel.
Ikeathy, and Oughterany.	V.	Mayneham, Kilcock, Dunmurchill, Donada and Skulogstown, Cloncurry, Clonshanboe, Balraine.
Kilcullen half barrony.	V.	
Ophaly.	V.	Kilrush, Ballisanarr, Carne, and Ballisax, Tully, Killdingan, Duneny, and the Nurney.
Salt.	V.	Kildrought, Donoghcomper, largest part of Oughterard, Teightooe, Kilteel, part of Castledillon, and Donoghcromper, Leixlip.

King's Co. perfect maps ; not damaged by the fire.

Coolestown.	V.	Monesteron, and Ballineklil, part o lRathangan, called Moyligh in Coolstown Barony, Clonsart.
Warrenstown.	V.	
Philipstown.	V.	Harristown and Belaghbreckan, Killadurhy, Kilclonfert and Croghan, Ballykeene, two parts of Cloonehorke, Ballicoman.
Ballycowen.	V.	Durrough and Killeride parishes united, Linury and Rahan united.

* General Vallancey has in this county the baronies of Norragh and Rebane, and Kilcah and Moone, not mentioned here.

APPENDIX, No. III.   xxxi

Counties and Baronies.		Parishes and other Sub-denominations.
Kilcoursoy.	V.	Kilbride, part of Ardmurcher, part of Kilcumririagh, Kilmanaghan.
Balliboy.	V.	Killagby, Balliboy.
Clonlisk.	V.	Etagh, Sinrone and Kilmory, Cullenane, Dunkerrin, Killcomin, part of Castletown, Aghenemedall, Finglis, and the other part of Castletown, parts of Roscrea, Dunkerrin, and Corbally, Killcolman.

King's Co. imperfect maps ; damaged by the fire, &c.

Ballibrit.	V.	Birr, Kinnity, Skirkheran and Roscomroe, Aghacon, part of Kilcolman and Etagh, Roscrea and Corbally.
Eglishals Fercale Teritory.	V.	Eglish Drumcullen.
Garricastle.	V.	Lismanaghan, Clonemacnoisse, Killegally, Reinagh, Lushina.
Geshill.	V.	Geshill.

Co. Kilkenny, perfect maps ; not damaged by the fire, &c.

Fassahdining.	V.	Donaghmore and part of Killmenan, Conohy, Coolcrahin, Mayne, Kill-midimoge, and part of Dronomore, Mothill, Killmodum, and part of Castlecomber, Muculley, and part of Desert.
Galmoy.	V.	Dorrow, Agharny, Bayllin, Coolcashin, Fertagh, Eirke, Urlingford.
Granagh.	V.	Ballycallan and part of Tullaghan, and part of Killaloe, lying together, Kilmanagh, Tullervan, and part of Killaghy, Ballilurkan, and a small part of Tubbrid, Clonetubrid and Glashcrow, Freshford, and part of Coolerahin, Belanemara, Bannoghals, Bannonough, Tubride and part of Kilcooly and Boelicke, Cloghmantaghs, part of Farlagh, and part of Jerypoint Abbey.
Libertie, City Kilkenny.	V.	Canice, St. Patrick, and part of Canice, St. Johns.
Gowran.	V.	Graige, Ullard, Powerstown, Jerpoint, Inisteage, the Liberties of Thomastown, Collumkill, Kilfane, Dungarvan, Tullehelim, Killerney, Dunbell, Blanchfield and Smithstown, Blackrath, and part of St. Martin's, Teighscoffin, Churchclaragh, Kilderry, Rathcoole, Kilmodum, Upper Grange, Shankhill, Killmacahill.
The Liberties of Callan.	V.	

Co. Kilkenny, imperfect maps ; damaged by the fire, &c.

Ida, Igrin, and Ibercon.	V.	Gauleskill and Dunkitt, Balligurin and Shanbogh, Killcolomb, Rowre, Desertmoane and Listertin, Kilmackenoge, Killiridie, Cloane, Rathpatrick, Rosbercon, Killeleheene.
Iverk.	V.	Clonemore and Fiddown, Kilmacroe, Ullud and Rathkerane, Templegawle, Aglish, Ballitursny and Portnescully, Owney and Teighbraghny, Tubbrud, and part of Muckully.
Kells.	V.	Kells, Kilree, and Dunamagon, Killowry, Clolaghamore, and Whitechurch, Earlstown, and Ballaghtovin, Killmagany.
Knocktopher.	V.	Derinehensy and Killkeneady, Kilbeacon and Listerling, parts of Knocktopher and Jerpoint, Kilkerhill and Aghaverviller, parts of Fiddown and Muckully, Killahy and Kilkeasy.
Sheelogher.	V.	Callen, Maysetowne, Earlstown, and Burnchurch, Dunfert, Enishnagh and Stamcartie, Inshewlachan, Grange and Tullaghane, Killalow, Kilree, Kilfera and Oughtragh.

xxxii   APPENDIX, No. III.

Counties and Baronies.   Parishes and other Sub-denominations.

Leitrim, perfect maps ; not damaged by the fire.

Carrigallin.   V. Carrigallin, Dromrealy, Oughteragh, Cloone.
Moyhill.   V. Moyhill, Cloone, Anaghduffe, Finagh.
Leitrim.   V. Killahorke, Finagh, Kiltibret, Anaghduffe, Moyhill.
Dromahcre.   V. Dromleas, Killinumerie, Killarga, Inishmacra, Clonlogher and
                        Cloonclare.
Rosclogher.   V. Kilasnett, Rosehver.

Co. Limerick, perfect maps ; not damaged from the fire, &c.

Liberties of Limerick. V. Stradbally, Killicknegarruffe, Kilmurry, Derrigalvan, Carrig-I-Parson,
                         Carnarry, Cahiravally, Donaghmore, St. Michael and St. Nicholas,
                         Knocknegaule, Mongret, St. Patrick, with part of St. John's and
                         St. Lawrence.
Clanwilliam.   V. Stradbally, Killicknegarruffe, Clounkeene, Cahirkinlisk, Drumkeene
                        and Greane, Ballyleroode and Agliscormuck, Rathjourdan, Caherelly,
                        Insenlawrence, Rochestown and Feadmore, Cahire-Ivrahally, Lud-
                        denbegg, Abbyony.
Owntheneybeg.   V. Abbyownthenebeg, Tough and part of Downe.
Small County.   V. Killteely and Ballinloghy, Kilfrush and Any, Urgare and Athenesy,
                        Monisterneany, Glynogry and Tulloghbracky, Feadmore and Kilpea-
                        can, Cahirconly, Kilkilane, Ballinemonymore, Ballinegard, part of
                        Brury.
Coshma.   V. Tankardstown and Kilbreedy, Drommin, Athlackcogh, Effin, Tullo-
                        bracky, Uregare, Ballingaddy.
Liberties of Kilmallock. V. Galbally, Ballingarry, Ballinlondry and Ballinascaddane, Downe and
                         Longe, Athenesy and Kilbreedy, Ballingaddin, Elphin and Kilcoone,
                         Kilfinane and Particles.

Co. Limerick, imperfect maps ; damaged by the fire, &c.

Castlea.   V.
Connelloe.   V. Kilidy and Monigaine, each in two parts, Corkamohide and Clonecreave,
                        Doonemoy and Kilcolman, Rathronan, in two parts, Cloneagh, Kil-
                        bradran and Killscannell, Ballingarry, Kilfiny and Athdare, Ardagh
                        and Grangy, Brury, Croagh and Cloneshire, Abbyfeale, in two parts,
                        part of Askeaton and part of Nantenan, Kilmoylan, Robertstown and
                        Shanagolden, Rathkeale, Clonecagh and Clonisty, Loughill.
Coonagh.   V.
Kenry.   V. Kildimoe, Kilcornane, part of Athdare, Ardcany, Askeaton.
Pobblebrian.   V. Ballycahen, Killinaghten, Crecory and part of Killpeacon, and part of
                        Knocknegaule, Monesterneany and Crome, Kileonahama, in two
                        parts, Kilkeedy and Mongret, Cluonona.

Co. Londonderry, perfect maps ; not damaged by the fire.

Tyrekerin.   V. Faughanvall, Clondermount and Cumber, Churchland of Faughanvall,
                        the Churchland in Cumber, part of Clondermount and Templemore.
Kenought.   V. Part of Fynnlaghan, or Templefinlaggan, part of Drumcross and Bal-
                        tiagh, part of Drumcross, Ardmagilligan, also Tamloghara, part of
                        Banagharr, Bouevy, Dungevan, Aghalow and Banagher, forfeited
                        parts.

APPENDIX; No. III. xxxiii

Counties and Baronies.		Parishes and other Sub-denominations.
Colerain.	V.	Church land of Dunbo, parts of Camus and Killowen, Aghadowny part, Desertoghinn and Arragell.
Liberties of Colerain.	V.	Ballyrasheran and part of Ballemony, Ballewillin, Ballyagharen.
Loghinshollin.	V.	Part of Towlagochrill and Ballyskulen, part of Killelagh, Maghera, Farmonery and Kilranaghan, the church land of Lissan and Desertmartin, Ballinskein, part of Arboe, Artrea. Tawlaghtkilligh and Ballinderry.

Co. Longford, perfect maps ; not destroyed by fire, &c.

Moydow.	V.	Ballimackormack and Killish, Kilglasse, Fashinode and Moydow, and part of Ardagh, Kildacomoge.
Ardagh.	V.	Templemichael, Rathrea, Kilglasse and Ardagh, Ballimacarmoth, Streete, half part, Mastrim.
Granard.	V.	Bigger part of Abbylarra, Granard, Clonbrone, Colomkill.
Longford.	V.	Killishea, part of, Clongish, Moghill, Killoe.

Co. Longford, imperfect maps ; damaged by the fire, &c.

Abbyshrewl.	V.	Aghara, Abbyshrewl and part of Kilglass, Forghnie and part of Knockavole, Faghshinnie and part of Kildocomoge.
Rathline.	V.	Rathlin, part of Rathlin, of Kildocomoge, Coshall, Shrewre.

Co. Louth. imperfect maps ; damaged by the fire, &c.

Atherdee.	V.	Tallonstown, Mapperstown and Charlestown, Shanlish, Killdemock and Smermer, Clonkine, Atherdee, Kilsaran and Dromcar.
Dundalk.	V	Carlingford, Dundalk.
Ferrard.	V.	
Louth.	V.	Louth.

Co Meath, perfect maps; not damaged by the fire, &c.

Dunboyne.	V.	Dunboyne.
Ratooth.	V.	Rathbeggan, Rathregan, Killeglan and part of Trivett, Ballymaglassan, Dunsaghlin, Cookstown and Creekstown, Kilbrew, Dunamore and Greenogg, Ratooth.
Duleek.	V.	Duleek and Abbey. Ardcath, Piercetown and Clonalvy, Stamullen, Moorchurch, Ballyart, Ballingarry, Killmoon, Kentstown, Fennor, Painstown and Brownstown, Killcarvan, Colpe and Julianstown.
Moyfenragh.	V.	Trim, Laracorr, Rathcore, Rathmullain, Castlerickard, Killian, Clonard, Ballyboggan, Castle Jordan.
Kells.	V.	Kells, Rathboyne, Burry, Girly, Kilskyre, Moynatty, Donagh Patrick, Telltown, Emlogh, Loghan, Duleene, Newtown, Kilbeg, Stahalmok, Crucetown, Kilmainham, the poles of Ballyattyknaffe, Ballybreachy, and Castle Kearan, Ardmagh and Bregagh.
Foore, half Barony.	V.	Killallon, Diamore and Clonebreny, Loghcrew, Moylagh, Oldcastle, Killeigh.
Deece.	V.	Ballsoone and Assey, Drumlargin and Killmore, Rodanstown, Ballfeehan, Gallow, Agherpallis and part of Rathcor, Culmullen and Knockmark, Moyglare and Killone, Trubley, Balsoone and Killmessan, Scurlogstown, Galtrim, Kittall and Dirpatricke.
Lune.	V.	Moyagher and Rathmore, Killaconican, Kildasky, Athboy.

APPENDIX, No. III.

Counties and Baronies.		Parishes and other Sub-denominations.
Morgallion.	V.	Nobber, Cloonegill, Kilberry, Killpatrick and Knock, Kilsaney and Drakestown.
Navan.	V.	Donoghmore, Churchtown and Ratone, Trimilstown and Trim, Tullahanoge and Moymett, Clonmacduffe, Killcooley and Newtown, Ardsallagh, Navan, Rathkenny, Rathboyne and Martery; Donoghpatrick, Liscarten and Ardbracken.
Screene.	V.	Tymoole, Rathseigh and Cullingstown, Templekeran, Monkstown and Lismullen Skreen, Maccetown, Dainestown, Killeen and Dunsany, Trevett, Athlumny and Killcarne, Ardmulchan and Foliestown, Dowestown and Taragh.
Slane.	V.	Part of Uniskeene, or Iniskeene and Nobber, Drumcondrath, Manor and parish of Dowth, Slane Ardagh, Gernonstown and Stackallen, Loghbracken and Mitchelstown, Killary, Innismott and Siddan.

Co. Mayo, imperfect maps; damaged by the fire.

| Tyrawly. | V. | Ardagh, Kilfinan, Magawny, Addergowle, Kilbealfadda, Kilalow, Rathreagh, Crosmolina, Kilcommin, two parts, Templemurrie, Leckan, Ballinaglasse, Ballyshikilly and Kilmoremoy, Kilbridy, Doonefinny, and Kilfyan and Commons to Tyrawly barony. |

Co. Monaghan, imperfect maps; damaged by the fire.

Cremorne.	V.	Aghnemullan, Tehallan, part, Tullycorbet, Clowntebret.
Dartry.	V.	Aghabog, Edergale, Kilevan, Clownish, Currin.
Monaghan.	V.	Tehallen, Teelownet, Monaghan, Tollecorbet, Kilmore, Drumsnatt, Clonish.
Trough.	V.	Douough.

Co. Queen's, perfect maps; not damaged by the fire.

| Upper Ossory. | V. | Clonkin and Roxonnel, part, Durrow, Killeny, Agharney, part, Coolkerry and Aghmocart, Bordwell and Killermgh, Aghavoe, Eirke, part, Rathsaran, Rathdowny, Skeirke, Downamore, Kildilligie, Offerillan and Kilballiduffe. |
| Balliadams. | V. | Kilmackedy, Fonstown, and St. John's part, Rathnespug, Tankardstown, Killibane. Monksgrange. |

Co. Queen's, imperfect maps; damaged by the fire, &c.

Cullinagh.	V.	Cloneheene, Ballyroan, Fossi.
Moryborough.	V.	Kilcolmanbane and Timochoe, part, Burres, Clonenagh, Cloneheene.
Portnahinch.	V.	Coblebanchor, Lea.
Slewmargigh.	V.	Killebran and Rahaspuge, Killeshin, Steaty, Shrowle.
Stradbally.	V.	Corcloane, Ballyallan, part.
Tenehinch.	V.	Rossandlis, Rerymore, Kilmannan, Castlebracke.

Co. Sligo, imperfect maps; damaged by the fire. &c.

Carbury.	V.	Dromcliffe, Kilmac Owen, Killasbegbrown, Aghamlisk, St. John, Calrie.
Corran.	V.	Tumover, Killturroe, Cloneghill, Killmurrogh, Killoshally and Drumratt, Emlaghfadda.
Leyncy.	V.	Achonry, Kilm^c.teige and Kilorin, Kilm^c.teige, Balishandra.
Tireragh.	V.	Castleconnor, Kilglasse, Skrein, Templeboy, alias Corkagh, Estenagh, Dromard, Kilm^c.shalgan, Kilmoremoy.

APPENDIX, No. III.

Counties and Baronies.	Parishes and other Sub-denominations.
Tirrarill.	V. Townagh, Kilrasse, Ballysandragh, Kilm^c.allan and Dromcollom, Killery and Ballisomaghan, Sankuagh, Athchanagh. Ballinakill, Killodowin, Kilmactrany.

Co. Tipperary, perfect maps; not damaged by the fire, &c.

Slevardagh and Compsey.	V. Fennor two pas. Kilcowly in three pcls. Buolick, Graystown, Ballinure, part, Killinaile, Croaghan, Mowny, Ballingarry, Lismalin, Modeshell, Cloneen, part, Isartkeiran, Kilmanenan, Grangemockleer, Newtownlenane, part.
Kilnemanagh.	V. Castletown, Down, part, Trome, Donnaghill, Agherow, Ballintample, Kilpatrick. Oghterleagh, Clonoltie, Clogher, Holicrosse, part, Meallife, Templeoughteragh, part.
Kilnelongusty.	V. Moulliffe, part, Ballaghcahill, part, Templeoughtragh, Templebeg.
Owny and Arra.	V. Youghill, Musea, part, Burges, Castletown, Templeically, Kilmacstully, Killoscully, and Killcommonty, Stradbally, part, Kilmilamand, Kilneragh and Abbeyowny.
Upper Ormond.	V. Aghnamaydull, part, Ditto and Latherath, Ballimackie, Balligibbon, Templederry, most of Templedonie and part of Kilkiery, Ballymaccloghie, Kilroan, part, Lisbunny, Killeniffe, Dullow, Kilmore, Nenagh, part.
Lower Ormond.	V. Lorhoe, Durrow and Bonocum, Loghkeene, Ballingarry Eglish, Piraglass, Uskean, Bores, Fenogh, Kilbaran, Moderenhy, Arderony and part of Kilruan, Cloghprior, Killodiernan, Knigh, Musea and Dromeneire, united parts, Nenagh, part.

Co. Tipperary,* imperfect maps; damaged by the fire, &c.

Clanwilliam.	V. Curroge, Templenoe and Doonegore, Tampulanery, Templebridane, Emly and Kilcorman, Kilshane, Cordangan, Religmury, Sollohoodbeg Sronill, Lattin, Donaghill and Killmilkane, Tipperary, Sollowhood, Bruis and Clonpett, Clonbulloge and Killardiff, Rathleyny.
Eliogurty, half Barony.	V. Loghmore, Thurles, Burrishleagh, Moyne, Drumspernan, Holycross and Bellacahill, Inchifogurty, Kilfishmone, Cullabeg, Balliomurrin, Rahetty and Shian, Templemore, Mokearry.
Ikerrin half Barony.	V. Castletown, Killovinoge, Templetoshow, Templemore, Templeree, Corbally, Roscrea, Burrine, Rathmoveage.
Middlethird.	V. Crumpsland, Coolmundri and St. Aug^{ts}. Abbey, Ballycleirahan, part, Red City, Rathcoole, Boytonrath and Dangandergan, Cooleagh and St. John'stown, Clony, Pepperstown, Mogerbane, Kilconnell, Knockgrafford, Oughtera, Donoghmore and St. John Baptist, Grange, St. Patrick's, Magowny and Drangan, Moortown-Kirk, Killynane, Ardmayle, Holycross and Gale, Ballyshiane and Erry, Ballymere, part, Tullaghmayne.
Dungannon.	V. Lissan, Derriloran, Killdresse, Ballidoge, Artrea Ballinderry, Arbo, Desertcreagh, Donaghhenry, Cunio, Tulliskan, Donaghmore, Drumglas, Clonfickle and Killaman, Glebe lands and Carnate e, forfeited part, Carntele church lands, with Aghavowe and Killishell, Ditto and Killishel and Aghavow, forfeited parts, Clonfickle, forfeited part of, and Aghalow or Aghavoe.
Strabane.	V. Ardstragh, Cappy, Bodony, Camos, Urnie and Leckepatrick, church lands of, church land, in forfeited lands of Donaghkiddy.

* General Vallancey's copy has, in this county, the baronies of Illeagh, and Iffa and Offa, not mentioned in the Down Survey.

APPENDIX No. III.

Counties and Baronies.		Parishes and other Sub-denominations.
Omy.	V.	Tarmonmagurke and Dronaragh, Maghericross and Urnie, Tarmonomongan and Longfield, church lands in Drummoore and Kilskerry, escheated lands in.
Clogher.	V.	

Co. Waterford,* perfect maps; not damaged by the fire, &c.

Galtier.	V.	Kill St. Laurence, Bishop's Court and Ballimakill, Balligunnertemple and Fathbeg, Kill St. Nicholas and Crookes, Killea and Killmacombe, Rathmelan and Ballimacleag.
Middlethird.	V.	Drumcanon, Ilandicane, Reiske, Killbride, Kilronan, Killoteran, Kilburan, Ballycashin, Loughdahy, Lisnekilly Kilmeaden, Newcastle, Donhill.
Upperthird.	V.	Kilbarrimeaden, Munecksland, Rosmeere, part, Ballylankeene, Mothill, Rathgormucke, Desert and Glasspatricke, alias Coolesheelane, Fenogh and Clonegaure, division of Coolefine and Gilcah.
Glaneyhery.	V.	Abbyslunagh, Clonmell, Commons, Kilronan.

Co. Westmeath, perfect maps; not damaged from the fire.

Farhill.	V.	
Delvin.	V.	Killuah. Castletown, greater and lesser part of, Kilvollogh, Killagh Kilcumly, Clonarly, part of.
Moycashell and Magheredernon.	V.	Newtown. Rathue, Killcrumriagh, Ardnorcher, Castletown.
Clonlonan.	V.	Killmonaghan and Killorumraghragh, Ballylaughlow, Killcleagh.
Brawny territory.	V.	Brawny territory and Moydrum lands.
Corkeree.	V.	Taghmon, Leney and Tyfarnan, Portneshagan, Portloman, Lacken Multifarnan, Stonehall.
Moygoish.	V.	Kilbixy, Templeorane, Kilmackinnan, Russagh, Streete, Rathaspick.
Kilkennywest.	V.	Noghevale, Drumrany, Kilkenny, Bunowen.
Rathconrath.	V.	Rathconrath, Churchtown, Conry, Ballimore, Templepatrick, Killare, Ballimorin, Piercetown.
Moyashell and Magheredernon.	V.	Mullingar, Raconnell, Dysert.
Turtullagh.	V.	Lyn, Mullingar, part, Enniscoffy, Castlelost, Pace-Kilbride, Newtown and Clonfadda, Carricke, Moylasker and Kilbride.
Foore, alias Demifoore.	V.	Foyran, St. Teighan, St. Mary's, Kilpatricke, Fashalstown, Maine, Rathgarve, Luckblea.

Co. Wexford,† maps; not damaged by the fire.

Shelborne.	V.	
Bantry.	V.	Clonmore, Killcowan, Ballikeoge, Whitechurch, Corleckan and Downony, Old Rosse and Adamstown; Whitechurch, Ballilane and Carnagh, parts of, Templedican, Killany and part of St. Molings, Kellegny, Chappell and Rosdrehid, New Ross, alias Rosse liberties.
Shelmalier.	V.	St. Margaret's, Ardcollum and part of Skreene, Ardcavan, Ardcroman, Killpatrick, Ballinslaney, Takillen, Carrigge, Kilbride in two parcels, Ardcanrush, Custuffe, Tirghmon, Ballimitic and Ballingley, Ballilo-

* General Vallancey has the baronies of Deecies, with Coshmore and Coshbride, not mentioned here.
† General Vallancey has Bargy barony, not mentioned here.

APPENDIX, No. III.

Counties and Baronies.	Parishes and other Sub-denominations.
	Ian, Inch and Clongeene, in two parcels, Adamstown, part, Kilgarran, Horetown, Chappelcarran and Kelluringe, St. John's and Clonmore, parts of.
Forth.	V. St. Peter's, Rahaspicke, Killeane and Drinagh, Kilmackree and Rathmacknee, Kildevan, Maglass, Ballimore, Shartmond, part, and Killinick; part, St. Michael's, Ballybrenan and Killinicke, Kilscorane, Tecumshine, St. Iberious iland and St. Margaret's, Carne, St. Ellens and Kilrane, Roslahir.
Scarwelsh.	V. Cloyne and Fernes, Kilrush and part of Camowe, Macoyne, Templeshanuogh.
Ballagheen.	V. Kilmocrish and part of Killancomy, part of Killancomy and part of Killenemanagh, Ballivalden, Ballevalloe and part of St. Margaret's, Arddemaine, Killenagh, Donoghmore, Monnemoling, Kilnemananagh, part, Milienagh, Killilly, Castle-Ellish, Kilcormock, Skreene and Nicholas, Killiske. Kilmallocke, Balleslane, Edermine, Ballihaskart, Templeshannon,
Gory.	V. Monemolin half part, Kiltricke half part, Ballyconnowe, Liskin, Killmaclogue and part of Toome, Killcormuck, Killkeavan and Killkorman, Killenor, forfeited part of, Arklow, half part of, Inch parish, Rosmenoge and part of Toome, Killenhue.

Co. Wicklow,* maps not damaged by the fire, &c.

Rathdowne, half Barony.

Newcastle.	V. Delling, Kilcoole, Newcastle, Newragh and Killiskee, Wicklow, Clonelly and Dellalosery, parts of.
Arklow.	V. Kilcomin, Kilmachooe and Radrum, Clanily, Wicklow and Killpoole, Ennishboyne, Balledonnell, Castle n.ʳ. Adams, Templemichell, Newrille, and Arklow abbey land.
Ballinecur.	V. Killdalogh, Rathdrum, Kilpipe and Hackelstown, part of.
Talbotstown.	V. Castlesallogh, Talbotstown and Baltinglass, lordships of, Bishop's lordship, Ditto of Boyestown, and Holywood and Burgage, and part of Ballibough, Kilbride and the lordship of the Three Castles.

* General Vallancey has the barony of Arklow, not mentioned in the Down Survey.

[xxxviii]

APPENDIX No. IV.

ANALYSIS OF THE FOURTEEN REPORTS OF THE BOARD OF EDUCATION.

1st. *Schools of Royal Foundation.*

The following schools are the schools of royal foundation in Ireland; they were founded by Charles the First, and liberally endowed with large estates by Charles the Second.

				Boys educated.	
			£. s. d.	Boarded.	Day Scholars.
Armagh	1530	English acres producing	1043 4 6	87	29
Dungannon	1600	Ditto.	1481 4 9	27	12
Enniskillen	3360	Ditto.	1461 0 0	65	16
Raphoe	5946	Ditto.	750 0 0	8	30
Cavan	570	Ditto.	900 0 0	0	0
Banagher and Carreysfort	3 336 }	Ditto.	} 165 0 0	0	30
			5800 9 3	187	117

2nd. *Schools of Private Foundation.*

In the year 1686, Alderman Joshua Preston of the City of Dublin was possessed of the lands of Cappalaughlin, in the Queen's county, containing 790 acres, then estimated at 80*l*. per annum. These he conveyed to trustees to pay three school-masters; one in the town of Navan, one in Ballyroon, and one in King Charles's Hospital, Oxmantown; a litigation took place, in which 2800*l*. were consumed at law: the lands, however, were re-let in 1806, and yield an annual rent of 1465*l*. 15*s*. With this fund two inefficient schools are kept at Navan and Ballyroan, the master of which was the same person; he received two salaries for 13 years, and never himself instructed a boy.

3rd. *Charter Schools,* (see page 635.)

4th. *Diocesan Schools* were established in the reign of Elizabeth.* It was enacted by an Act of Parliament, that there should be a free school in each diocese, the master to be appointed by the Lord Deputy, or other chief Governor, except in Armagh, Dublin, Meath and Kildare, whose respective archbishops and bishops should appoint the school-house to be erected in the principal shire town of the diocese, at the cost of the whole diocese. The salaries of the master to be apportioned by the Lord Deputy and Privy Council, and paid one-third by the ordinary, and two-thirds by the parsons, vicars, and prebendaries.

Under this Act schools were established in all the dioceses of Ireland, but they are very inefficient, and no account of them appears before the Restoration; after which a commission was appointed to carry into effect the Act of Elizabeth; and in the reign of George the First,† an Act passed, empowering archbishops and bishops to set apart an acre of ground out of

* 12 Elizab. ch. 1.   † 12 Geo. I.

APPENDIX, No. IV.

any lands belonging to them, for the site of a free school, and grand juries to present sums for building and repairing them. Notwithstanding these powers and provisions, the whole number of effective schools is only 13 out of 34, which might have been established; and the whole number of scholars 380. The inadequacy of the stipend seems the principal cause of this deficiency; in no instance does it exceed 40*l.* and in some it is only 25*l.* per annum. The Board propose, that 12 schools should be established in places most convenient; that the contributions of each of the dioceses, which averages at present at 36*l.* per annum, should be raised to 40*l.* and the endowments of each school should be 102*l.* per annum; and the sons of the poorer clergy and curates, should be admitted as free scholars. No diocesan school in Dublin.

5th Report. *Wilson's School, County Westmeath*;
income from rents and tythes 4000*l.* per annum; supports 18 old men, and educates and supports 107 boys.

6th. Report. *Blue Coat Hospital*, (see page 564.)
7th. ——— *Hibernian School, Phœnix Park*, (see page 602.)
8th. ——— *Foundling Hospital*, (see page 578.)
9th. ——— *Erasmus Smith's Schools*, (see page 655.)
10th. ——— *Hibernian Marine School*, (see page 613.)
11th. ——— *Parochial Schools.*

By an Act* passed in the reign of Henry the Eighth, every clergyman on induction shall swear that he will teach, or cause to be taught, an English school within his vicarage or rectory. Children who are educated in these schools in different parts of Ireland amount to 23,000. There are in Ireland 1122 benefices: returns have been made from 736, in which were 549 schools.

12th Report. *Classical Schools of Private Foundation.*

	Years.	By whom endowed.	Land.	Money.	Boys educated. Boarded.	Day Scholars.
Clonmell	1685	R. Moore	370 acres	£. 0	0	21
Carrickmacross	1611	Lord Weymouth	0	70	12	19
Kilkenny	1684	Duke of Ormond	2	140	46	39

In 1773, the patronage of this school devolved upon the Provost and Board of Fellows of Trinity College, Dublin; and Parliament granted 5046*l.* with which a noble school-house has been erected; it is called the College of Kilkenny, and is governed by statutes.

| Middleton | 1796 | Countess of Orkney | 2000, set for | 200 | 14 | 0 |

These lands are set on a lease of lives renewable for ever, at 200*l.* per annum; the salary of the master is fixed at 100*l.* a year, with one acre of ground.

| Waterford | — | Corporation | 0 | 100 | 6 | 20 |

The school-house was erected by the Corporation at an expense of 1300*l.* Dr. Downes of the cathedral of Waterford endowed it with an exhibition of 15*l.* for the use of a student sent to Trinity College, Dublin, till he attains the standing of A. M.

| Dundalk | — | Corporation | 0 | 100 | 14 | 22 |

The salary of the master is paid by Lord Rodden, as representative of Lord Clnabrasil.

Lismore	1610	Earl of Cork	half acre	36	0	0
Bandon	1610	Earl of Cork	0	20	20	25
Kinsale	1767	Lord de Clifford	0	50	3	30

* 28th Hen. VIII.

APPENDIX, No. IV.

	Years.	By whom endowed.	Land.	Money.	Boys educated. Boarded.	Day Scholars.
Castlebar Charleville	1798	Lord Lucan—now discontinued Lord Cork	0	L. 40	8	10

The Deeds of this school, with the school-house, were destroyed by fire.

| Lifford | Reign of Jas. I. | Sir R. Hansard | 50 | 0 | 0 | 0 |

There is no school kept on this foundation.

| Clonakilty | 1808 | Earl of Shannon | half acre | 60 | 65 | 12 |

This is the most respectable endowed seminary in the south of Ireland.

| Rathfarnham | . 1752 | Richard Wetherell | | | | |

This charity has never been carried into effect, though a suit was instituted, 1788, for the proper application of the bequest.

13th Report. *English Schools of Private Foundation.*

Diocese.	Schools.	By whom Endowed.	Revenue.			Number of Children.	
			L.	s.	d.		
Armagh	Forkhill	Rob. Jackson, 1787.	375	0	0	380	Receive 5l. and a loom
	Drelincourt	Widw. of Drelincourt, 1732	267	0	0	17	Female orphans
	Maherafield	Hugh Rainey, 1707	175	0	0	9	
Dublin	Female Orphan	(See page 849)					
	Calverstown	Sir R. L., 1747	91	16	0	7	
	Blessington	Marquis Downshire	15	0	0	20	
	Castleknock	R. Crosthwaite, 1720.	10	0	0	12	
	Morgans	R. Morgan, 1773	1562	3	1	0	N. B. 8000l. have been expended in erecting two noble school-houses near the banks of the Royal Canal, 4 miles from Dublin, where they form very striking objects: they are not yet entirely completed.
	Holywoodrath	D. Jackson, 1706— 3 acres	6	0	0	0	
	Sandry	D. Jackson 20	20	0	0	0	
	Swords		0	0	0	0	The Compensation

Fund paid L. 15,000. for each borough at the time of the Union, which, at Swords, was applied to building and endowing a school, in which 261 children are educated. In 1703, a sum of money was bequeathed by Dean Scardeville, for a school here, but no trace of it can be found.

	Finglas	Sundries	20	0	0	25	N. B. Now 65 children.
	Dublin City	James Knight, 1725	60	0	0	20	No school kept
	Celbridge	Wil. Connely, Geo. I.	450	0	0	106	Now a charter school
	Rathcoal	Mrs. Mercer, 1734	635	0	0	50	
Cashell	Fethard	Morgan Hicky	10	0	0	34	
	Ballintemple	Ditto	5	0	0	0	No school
	Toer	J. Doherty	4	0	0	10	
	Templeneiry	Ditto	4	0	0	20	
	Doon	Ditto	4	0	0	0	

APPENDIX, No. IV.

Diocese.	Schools.	By whom Endowed.	Revenue.			Number of Childrn.	
			L.	*s.*	*d.*		
Cashell	Tubbrit	G. Vaughan, 1735, 3 acres	816	13	0	40	
Cork	Blue Coat	Ed. Burk, Bp. Killala, 1699	457	0	0	24	
	City Green Coat	Sundries	134	0	0	40	
	Do. Dean's	Moses Dean, 1726	113	15	0	100	
	Do. Sharman's	Mrs. Sharman	33	0	0	75	
Clogher	Leslie's	Bishop Leslie, 1762	25	0	0		Interest of *L.* 500—money was never applied
	Garnett's	Doctor Garnett	100	0	0		No further account.
	Tihallow	Captain Richardson	3	0	0		Ditto
	Monaghan	William Cairnes,	20	0	0	53	
Cloyne	Cloyne	Doctor Crow, 1719	165	0	0	41	9 taught the Classics
	Youghal	Earl of Cork, 1610	30	0	0		No school kept
	Buttevant	Lady Lanesborough, 1698	20	0	0		No salary. Ceased
	Castle Hamson	H. Hamson	20	0	0		No school
Clonfert	Eyrecourt	Rev. R. Banks	42	0	0	14	Master does not attend
	Belfast	Lord Donegal, 1777	20	0	0	100	
	Bangor		5	0	0		
	Batteritay	Mrs. Jane, 1760	15	0	0	25	
	Drumbo	One of Ld. Donegal's family, 1722	10	0	0	50	
	Donoghadee	Lady Mt. Alexander, 1764	60	0	0	25	*L* 30. is allotted to clothe the boys and pay apprentice fees.
	Lisburn	John Handcock, 1764	76	11	4	42	This is a provincial Quakers' school, and is further supported by subscription.
Derry	Cloncagh	Lord Donegal	10	0	0		
	Camies	J. Hamilton, 1666	32	0	0	24	Salary not paid, and the school supported by subscription.
	Primrose Grange	Rev. Ed. Nicholson, 1721	118	0	0	9	
Kildare	Betaghstown	Doctor P. Hewitson, 1770	304	6	7	16	
	Cardiffstown	Lord Mayo	20	0	0		Not carried into effect
	Portarlington	Lord Galway—William III.	32	0	0		For French and English master; the salary is not paid, and there is no school; suit pending.
Laughlin & Ferns.	Aghola	Marq. Rockingham, 1717, 10 acres	0	0	0	50	
	Kilcommon	Rev. Mr. Barton, 1798	50	0	0		Income ceased, and school discontinued
Killala	Frankfort	Dr. Valentine	75	0	0	34	
Killaloe	Ballymakee	Lady A. Cole, 1724	6	0	0		No return of scholars
	Drumolan d	Lady O'Brien	60	0	0		Ditto
	Killaloe	Bishop of Killaloe	40	0	0	50	
Kilmore	Tullavin	William Moore, 1803	240	0	0	60	Suit pending.
Limerick	City Blue School	Mr. Ald. Craven, 1724	90	2	6	15	*L* 4. apprentice fee.
	Ditto Halls	Doctor Jer. Hall, 16 7	30	0	0	40	No account of funds
Meath	Athlone	Arth. St. George	5	0	0		Heir refuses to comp'y with his will, as not duly witnessed.
	Ditto	William Handcock, 1705	24	0	0	29	
	Oldcastle	Laurence Gibson, 1809	500	0	0		This was the bequest of

an Irishman who died in London, for establishing a school in his native place—school to

f

Diocese.	Schools.	By whom Endowed.	Revenue.	Number of Children.
	\multicolumn{4}{l}{be on Lancaster's plan—master to be either Protestant or Catholic—scholars, an equal number of each. Half the endowment to be drawn by the priest, the other by the minister of the parish. Legal opinions were had, that this does not come within the act of Mortmain, but it is not yet carried into effect.}		
			L. s. d	
Raphoe	Robertson's schools,	Colonel Robertson, 1790	445 0 0	775	The sum of *L* 15. was left to each of the 31 parishes of the diocese of Raphoe, which, by a decree of Chancery, was estimated at a principal sum of *L*. 9300: it is now augmented to *L*. 15,500, and there are 25 children in each of the schools.
Tuam	St. Johnstown	Sir Walter Raleigh	120 0 0		This school was founded by the celebrated Sir Walter Raleigh, who endowed it with 60 acres of land. The land was left, about the year 1780, by the schoolmaster to his son, who sold it to an attorney, and no school is since kept. It is valued at about *L* 120. per annum, and a suit is pending to recover it.*
	Jamestown	Earl of Montrath	34 0 0	80
Waterford City	Blue Girls	Mrs. Mason	143 7 6	34
	Blue Boys	Bishop Foy, 1707	466 11 0	67	It is expected when the present leases expire, that the whole income of this charity will amount to *L* 2547. 3s. 3d. The trustees have besides, a fund of *L* 4900. in hand, and another in accumulation, with which new school houses are building near Waterford, the expenses of which are estimated at *L*. 9000: here it is intended to keep 75 boys, and raise the expenditure of the establishment to *L* 2047. 10s. per annum.

14th *Report*—Contains general remarks on the foregoing, and further states, that exclusive of the Charitable Institutions, there are, in seventeen out of twenty-two dioceses, 3786 schools, in which are taught 162,476 children, of which 45,490 are Protestants—116,977 Roman Catholics; that the whole number of schools, including parochial, is 4600, and the scholars 200,000, being an average of forty-three to each school. That the instruction extends no further than reading, writing, and the common rules of arithmetic; that the average price paid per annum is, 10s. for reading, 17s. 4d. for writing, and *L* 1. 6s. for arithmetic; but that the masters are deficient in knowledge, unacquainted with regular system, and unaccustomed to uniform discipline; and the books read, are calculated to excite lawless adventure, cherish superstition, and lead to dissension;—that the lower classes are extremely anxious to instruct their children, even at an expense which the small means of many of them can ill afford. It recommends that some uniform plan should be substituted for those ill taught and ill regulated schools, which would at once gratify the thirst for information, and form habits of regularity and discipline;—but proposes that *supplementary schools* should be added on a new plan, that a spirit of improvement might gradually correct the old, rather than that the superintendance of the old should be transferred to commissioners to new model them;—that evening schools should be encouraged, and that the books used, should be selections extracted from the most important parts of the scriptures, which would be as effectual as the bible itself, and not liable to the objections made against its use.

* It is asserted, and not without probability, that the first experiment of planting potatoes in Europe, was made by Sir Walter on this land.

[xliii]

APPENDIX, No. V.

Salaries of the Officers of the Customs in the Port of Dublin.

First commissioner, { £1,200	
House and allowances, { 600	
Second commissioner,	1,200
Five others, each	1,000
Secretary, { 800	
House and allowances, { 400	
Assistant secretary,	300
First clerk,	600
Second clerk,	400
Third clerk,	300
Fourth clerk,	240
Fifth clerk,	220
Sixth clerk,	200
Seventh clerk,	160
Eighth clerk,	140
Ninth and tenth clerk, each	130
Eleventh and twelfth clerk, each	120
Thirteenth and Fourteenth clerk, each	110
Fifteenth and Sixteenth clerk, each	100
Seventeenth and eighteenth clerk, each	90
Nineteenth, twentieth, and twenty-first clerks, each	80
First messenger,	80
Second, third, fourth, and fifth messengers, each	60
Clerk of the portage,	100
Clerk of the petitions,	150
Messenger,	60
First commissioner's clerk,	100
Wool accountant,	50
Clerk of the stationary store,	300
His first clerk,	150
His second clerk,	100
His third clerk,	80
Messenger,	60
Housekeeper,	60
Six servants, each	13
Surveyor of revenue buildings,	7 300
First clerk,	100
Second clerk,	80
Messenger,	60
Counsel,	100
Solicitor,	200
Clerk of securities,	100
Clerk of information,	350
Assistant,	120
Clerk,	80
Server of notices,	80
Register of seizures,	20
English agent,	200
Agent in London	400
Accountant general	600
First clerk,	350
Second clerk,	250
Third clerk,	150
Fourth clerk,	120
Fifth clerk,	80
Examinator of customs,	848
Assistant,	600
First clerk,	350
Second clerk,	250
Third clerk,	160
Fourth clerk,	140
Fifth clerk,	130
Sixth and seventh clerks, each	120
Eighth and ninth clerks, each	110
Tenth and eleventh clerks, each	100
Twelfth, thirteenth, and fourteenth clerks, each	90
Fifteenth, sixteenth, and seventeenth clerks, each	80
Examiner of incidents and charity fund,	150
Assistant,	90
Clerk,	80

APPENDIX, No. V.

Examiner of fees	£ 60	Assistant	£ 80
Examiner of navy payments,	200	Three surveyors of the quay, each	500
Examiner of army payments,	100	Gauger ditto,	400
Examiner of information books,	200	Assistant,	400
Examiner of incident bills,	220	Assayer of spirits,	150
Examiner of surveyor's and landwaiter's books,	500	Eight landwaiters, each	400
Two clerks,	90 & 80	Two ditto, each	250
Examiner of spirit books	200	Five debenture officers, each	120
Assistant	80	Nine quay tide waiters, each	80
Inspector of revenue boats,	670	Seven quay scale-porters, each	80
Three clerks and messenger,	360	Ten quay porters, each	100
Register of corn return,	200	First gatekeeper,	120
Register general of shipping,	300	Six others, each	80
Registry officer ditto,	250	Clerk for counting lambskins,	20
Clerk,	80	Dock master,	80
Inspector general of imports and exports,	500	Aston's Quay, a surveyor and four landwaiters,	1,600
First clerk,	200	Inspector of the tide,	200
Nine others together	1,000	Coxswain,	60
Equalizer of duties and inspector of hereditary revenues,	200	Six boatmen, each	50
Four surveyor generals and their clerks, with an allowance per day, when out on duty,	2,400	Jervis's Quay, surveyor or scale-porter,	280
Collector and six clerks,	1,810	Northwall surveyor, two officers, seven boatmen,	710
Clerk of the commissioners cheque-book,	350	Rogerson's Quay, surveyor and four officers, two tidewaiters, one coxswain, six boatmen, and a watchhouse-keeper,	1,040
Two clerks and messenger to ditto,	240		
Clerk of ship entries,	110	Ringsend, four surveyors, each	200
Ditto and of the coast,	350	Forty-four tidewaiters, each	80
Three clerks and a messenger,	320	Fifty-five super. ditto, each	60
Officer to swear coasters to their permits,	20	Two coxswains, one carpenter, and eleven boatmen, each	50
Jerquer and two clerks,	530	Curate of Ringsend,	200
Debenture and cocket clerk,	350	Surgeon for sick and wounded officers,	100
Three clerks,	260	Clerk of the king's yard, Ringsend,	120
Cheque on permits,	80	House and allowance.	
Three permit officers,	406	Dunleary, surveyor, mate, six tidewaiters, one coxswain, eight boat-men,	1,090
Surveyor of the stores,	500		
Two scale-porters, 160l. marker, 80l. doorkeepers, 60l.	300	Clontarf surveyor, coxswain, five boatmen,	400
Storekeeper,	40		
Nine clerks of delivery in ditto, each	80	Baldoyle and Howth surveyor, coxswain, five boatmen,	400
Cooper,	60	Princess Charlotte revenue cruiser. Commander, 300l. five officers, 360l. two boys and forty men, 1,084l.—total 1,644	
Book-keeper and cheque in the stores,	400		
Four clerks,	480		
Cheque on the store of seizures,	200		

STRACT *View of the Corn, Flour, and Oatmeal exported from Dublin from the Year ending 5th Ja 5, to the Year ending 5th January 1816, both inclusive; with the Places to where exported. The fi te the number of barrels of Barley, Oats, and Wheat, and the Cwt. of Flour and Oatmeal.*

	England.	Scotland.	Isle of Man.	Guernsey.	Jersey.	France.	Spain.	Portugal.	Italy and Straights.	Denmark.	Canada and Nova Scotia.	Newfoundland.	Antigua.	Demerara.	St. Croix.	Trinidad.	St. Vincent.	Barbadoes.	Jamaica.	St. Kitts.	Surinam.	Total.	Total Grain.
rley	—	—	—	—	—	—	—	—	—	—	—	—	—	—	—	—	—	—	—	—	—	—	
its	575	—	—	—	—	—	—	—	—	—	—	—	40	—	—	—	—	—	—	—	—	615	
heat	2243	—	—	—	—	—	—	—	—	—	—	—	—	—	—	—	—	—	—	—	—	2243	2858
our	394	—	—	—	—	—	—	—	—	—	—	—	—	—	—	—	—	—	—	—	—	394	
atmeal	2400	1408	—	—	—	—	—	—	—	—	—	—	—	—	—	—	—	—	—	—	—	3808	—
rley	500	620	—	—	—	—	—	—	—	—	—	—	—	—	—	—	—	—	—	—	—	1120	
its	3483	1000	—	—	—	—	—	—	—	—	—	—	—	—	—	—	—	—	—	—	—	4483	
heat	14642	40	—	—	—	—	—	—	—	—	—	—	—	—	—	—	—	—	—	—	—	14682	20285
our	4854	400	—	—	—	—	—	—	—	—	—	—	—	—	—	—	—	—	—	—	—	5254	
atmeal	6290	—	—	—	—	—	—	—	—	—	—	—	—	—	—	—	—	—	—	—	—	6290	
rley	20	858	—	—	—	—	—	—	—	—	—	—	—	—	—	—	—	—	—	—	—	878	
its	14126	7634	—	—	—	—	—	—	—	—	—	—	160	—	—	—	267	—	—	—	—	22187	
heat	1518	—	—	—	—	—	—	—	—	—	—	—	—	—	—	—	—	—	—	—	—	1518	24683
our	24	—	—	—	—	—	—	—	—	—	—	—	—	—	—	—	—	—	—	—	—	24	
atmeal	3820	1160	—	—	—	—	—	—	—	—	—	—	—	—	—	—	—	—	—	—	—	4980	—
rley	1858	214	—	—	—	—	—	—	—	—	—	—	—	—	—	—	—	—	—	—	—	2072	
its	38326	5030	—	—	—	—	—	—	—	—	—	—	340	200	146	—	75	40	—	—	—	44157	
heat	7385	—	—	—	—	—	—	—	—	—	—	—	—	—	—	—	—	—	—	—	—	7385	53614
our	153	—	—	—	—	—	—	—	—	—	—	—	—	—	—	—	—	—	—	—	—	153	
atmeal	2083	600	—	—	—	—	—	—	—	—	—	—	—	—	—	—	—	—	—	—	—	2683	—
rley	6882	700	—	100	—	—	—	—	—	—	—	—	—	—	—	—	—	—	—	—	—	7682	
its	89274	22695	6	316	—	—	—	—	—	—	—	—	106	—	—	—	—	—	—	—	—	112397	
heat	17698	694	—	—	—	100	—	—	—	—	—	—	—	—	—	—	—	—	—	—	—	18492	38571
our	4091	—	—	133	—	—	—	—	—	—	—	—	—	—	—	—	—	—	—	—	—	4224	
atmeal	2853	3802	100	—	—	—	—	—	—	—	—	—	—	—	—	—	—	—	—	—	—	6735	—
rley	1023	654	—	—	1550	19466	—	—	—	—	—	—	—	—	—	—	—	—	—	—	—	22693	
its	12312	—	140	—	—	1350	—	—	—	—	—	—	—	—	—	354	85	—	—	—	—	24441	
heat	22661	—	—	—	260	6299	—	—	—	—	—	—	—	—	—	—	—	—	—	—	—	29220	76154
our	17298	—	20	—	600	5750	—	—	—	—	—	—	—	—	—	—	—	—	—	—	—	23668	
atmeal	1384	545	—	—	—	—	—	—	—	—	—	—	—	—	—	—	—	—	—	—	—	1929	—
rley	690	—	—	—	2154	23396	—	—	—	—	—	—	—	—	—	—	—	—	—	—	—	26240	
its	6865	3328	—	20	—	13297	—	—	—	—	—	—	—	—	—	—	—	100	—	274	—	23884	
heat	45795	1036	—	—	6124	7375	—	—	—	—	—	—	—	—	—	—	—	—	—	—	—	60330	110454
our	21928	—	—	—	2700	17282	—	200	—	—	—	—	—	—	—	—	—	—	64	—	—	42174	
atmeal	1864	100	—	—	—	260	—	200	—	—	—	—	—	—	—	—	—	—	—	—	—	2424	—
rley	21766	111	—	548	2640	2232	—	—	—	—	—	—	—	—	—	—	—	—	—	—	—	28197	
its	101558	9758	—	100	1080	1460	1520	—	—	—	—	—	248	240	—	80	—	—	—	—	—	116046	
heat	41795	—	—	100	4441	3732	—	—	—	—	—	—	—	—	—	—	—	—	—	—	—	50068	194311
our	24128	120	470	—	2720	3153	3822	—	—	—	—	—	—	—	—	822	—	—	—	—	—	35235	
atmeal	4166	3010	—	180	—	—	—	—	—	—	—	—	—	—	—	—	—	—	—	—	—	7356	—
rley	14431	1751	—	592	383	12485	24665	—	—	—	—	—	—	—	—	—	—	—	—	—	—	54307	
its	157050	33719	—	58	684	8488	3653	—	—	230	285	—	391	—	—	—	—	—	931	—	—	205489	
heat	57952	960	—	239	40	845	1400	—	—	—	—	—	—	—	—	—	—	—	—	—	—	61436	321232
our	64561	1078	184	—	350	4919	—	—	200	54	—	705	1050	—	—	—	—	3231	—	262	—	76594	
atmeal	17695	8244	80	200	92	—	1030	—	—	—	—	—	—	—	—	1030	—	—	—	—	—	28371	—
rley	—	—	500	—	—	24999	—	—	—	100	—	—	—	—	—	—	—	—	—	—	—	25419	
its	118320	4280	104	—	—	11546	—	—	—	—	300	100	—	—	—	—	—	—	—	—	—	124650	
heat	73623	989	—	—	—	1776	—	—	—	—	—	—	—	—	—	—	—	—	—	—	—	76388	226848
our	55783	3170	400	—	60	620	—	40	864	544	—	—	400	400	—	—	—	—	—	—	—	62281	
atmeal	8198	1066	—	140	—	—	—	—	—	100	—	—	—	—	—	—	—	—	—	—	—	9504	—
rley	335	34	—	—	330	11732	2790	—	—	—	—	—	—	—	—	—	—	—	—	—	—	15222	
its	66331	9241	—	—	—	—	—	—	—	—	315	—	—	—	—	—	200	—	—	—	—	76287	
heat	23999	506	—	—	—	3347	4976	1540	—	—	—	—	—	—	—	—	—	—	—	—	—	34368	125877
our	—	921	320	—	—	—	—	—	—	—	—	—	—	—	200	—	—	—	—	—	—	1440	
atmeal	—	80	—	—	—	—	—	—	—	—	—	—	—	—	—	—	—	—	—	—	—	80	—

An Estimate and Taxation of the Revenues ... drals, in the year 13... Black ... ublin.

Prebends, &c. &c.	Annual Value.	Tithes.	Prebends, &c. &c.	Annua
Prebend of the Archbishopric of Dublin	700 marcs	£.46 13s. 4d	Preb. of Tassagard	10 p
Preb. of Cullen (Archbps.)	40 pounds	4 0 0	Preb. of Maynooth	20 p
Deanry	100 marcs	10 marcs	Vic. of Porcio	10 m
Precentorship	40 marcs	4 marcs	Preb. of Yago Town	10 m
Treasurership	40 pounds	40 shillings	Preb. of Dunlonan	20 p
Chancellorship	40 pounds	4 pounds	Preb. of Moninehenoke	10 m
Archdiocese of Dublin	40 pounds	4 pounds	Preb. of Tymothan	10 p
Preb. of Sweides	60 pounds	6 pounds	Preb. of Typper	10 p
Vicarage of Swerdes	100 shillings	10 shillings	Preb. of Typerkevny	10 p
Preb. Jac. de Spaniæ in Luske church	£.33 6s. 8d.	5 marcs	Vic. of Tavolagh	5 m
Preb. of Mast Ric. de Wyndon in Luske church	33 6 8	5 marcs	Vic. of St. Kevin's Preb. of Stagonyllde, not ascertained on account of the war	5 m
Two Vicarages of Luske	26 13 8	4 marcs		
Preb. of Clynmethan	20 marcs	2 marcs	Archdeanry of Glandelagh	10 m
Preb. of Houeth	£.23 8s. 8d.	45s. 7d.	Preb. of Aderk	114 sh
Preb. of Ja. Palke in Castleknock Church	13 6 8	2 marcs	Amount of the whole Taxation of all the Prendaries of the Archbishoprick	
Preb. of J. de Dene in do.	13 6 8	2 marcs		
Vic. of Castleknock Church	10 marcs	1 marc		
Preb. of Rathmyell	20 marcs	2 marcs	I XX	
Preb. of Newcastle	20 pounds	40 shillings	£.M IIII XIIIs. Tithes L	

Taxation of the Revenues of St. Patrick's aforesaid.

Churches and Places.	Annual Value.	Tithes.	Places.	
Keyvin's (St. Patrick's)	10 pounds	20 shillings	Ashtown (Villa Fraxini) Donaghmor in Omayl not ascertained on account of the war	
Crumelyn Church	10 pounds	20 shillings		
Castlecnock Ch.	20 marcs	2 marcs		
Kymesentan Ch., not ascertained on account of the war			Terenemok Land	20 sh
Tamelog Ch.	40 shillings	4 shillings	Dublin City revenue or rents, not levied on account of the war	40 sh
Kylbryde Ch.	40 shillings	4 shillings	Pelyok Land	10 sh
Breynok Town	60 shillings	6 shillings	S. Nich. Alterage in St. Patrick's	100 sh
Mon. Derton and Arscoll	20 pounds	40 shillings		
Rathsallagh	100 shillings	10 shillings	Amount of the Taxation of the Community	75l.
			Total of the two preceding accounts	1156

Calculation and Tithe Tax of the Goods, Income, and Rents of the Church of the Holy Trinity D Tithes, adopted at Vienne.*

	Annual Value.	Tithes.	
In the Deanry of Dublin.			In the Deanry e
St. Michael's Church	6 pounds	12 shillings	Balyscadan Church
St. John's Church	100 shillings	10 shillings	Yearly rent thereof
St. Michan's Church	4 pounds	8 shillings	
Dublin City revenue	£.16 5s. 0d.	32 sh. 6¼d.	Total Amount
Total of Trinity Church	31 5 2	62 sh. 6¼d.	In the Deanry of . . . (illegible)
In the Deanry of Franche.			Killcolyn Church, held by the Prior and Convent of Holy Trinity aforesaid, with the chapels and appurtenances thereof
In Grange-Gorman four carucates	24 pounds	48 shillings	
Tithes of same carucates	8 pounds	16 shillings	
In Glasnveyvyn Manor 3 carucates	24 pounds	48 shillings	
Total amount	56 pounds†	112 shillings	Total of the above sums - £.226
In the Deanry of Bree. (Bray.)			A true translation from the Latin
Clonken-Manor 7 caruc. of which 2 with a mill as a farm, set at	£.14 13s. 4d.	24sh. 4d.	
Also 1 carucate, set as a farm for	4 10 0	9 shillings	
Also 1 carucate at Tylagh, set for	6 0 0	12 shillings	
Also 3 caruc. remaining in the manor	18 0 4	36 shillings	
Cionken Church and adjoining Chapel	18 3 4	36sh. 4d.	
Total Amount	£.61 6s. 8d.	£.6 2s. 8d.	

* This is entitled Taxatio bonorum proventuum et Reddituum Ecclesiæ Sanctæ Trinitatis Dublin Secundum exact This ordonance for levying tithes, seems to have been issued by the General Council, held at Vienne, in Dauphiné, for unfortunate Knights Templars, in 1311 and 1312, or during the Pope's residence at Avignon, in France. It must ha years subsequent to the first evaluation above stated of 1306.

† In some of the totals, the sums do not seem to agree with the amount of the particulars.

[xlvii]

APPENDIX, No. VIII.

A Rental of the Estate of the City of Dublin, for one year, ending the 29th of September, 1816.

Ancient Revenue.

No. of Receipt	Tenants' Names.	Denominations.	Yearly Rent £. s. d.
1	Richard Ginn,	The Tower over St. Audeon's Arch	1 5
2	John Esmonde,	A Tenement near Newgate	40
3	Joshua and Joseph Wills,	A House in Thomas-street	6
4	William Ellis,	Ground near Oxmantown and the Strand	38 10
5	James Lord Santry,	Ground called the Pill, in Oxmantown	8
6	Sir William Usher,	The Island behind his House	1
7	Sir William Davis,	Two Lots of Ground on Hogan-green	9
8	Sir John Rogerson,	Part of the Strand behind Lazor's-hill	200
9	Richard Norton,	A piece of Ground west of the Bridge	5
10	Sir William Usher,	A piece of Ground near his House	2
11	Arthur Dawson,	The Fish Market in Ormond-market	50
12	Viscountess Mazarene,	Loughboy	6
13	Richard Ginn,	A Tenement in Hamond-lane	7
14	Patrick Grogan,	Part of the Town Ditch, Wormwood-gate	81
15	Saint Andrew's Parish,	The Church and Church-yard	0 3 4
16	Jonathan Armory,	The Strand north side of the Liffey	2 10
17	John Murphy,	A House in High-street	30
18	Richard Jackson,	Ditto Ditto	27
19	Ditto	Ditto Ditto	33
20	Joseph Hearne	Ditto corner of Corn-market and Back-lane	35
21	John Barlow,	A Lot of Ground, Schoolhouse-lane	6 6
22	His Majesty,	Out of the Receipts of the Irish Exchequer	500
23	James King,	Part of the City wall in Bridge-street	1
24	Mary Byrne and J. Gilmore,	The Commons' Bakehouse in Winetavern-street	8
25	Doctor Nicholas Forster,	The Tower over Dame's Gate, Buttevant's Tower, &c.	1 17 8
26	Matthew Pierson, Alderman,	Part of the Town wall and ditch, near Werburg's-gate	5
27	Earl of Limerick,	Part of the City Water, Jame's-gate	6
28	John Smith,	Izod's Tower, Ground end of Kenedy's-lane	1
29	James King,	Part of the Town Wall, near Newgate	0 5 0
30	Isaac Ambrose,	Ground on the left side of Fyan's Castle	13
31	John Temple and Wife,	Part of Hogan-green	40
32	Thomas Pleasants,	Ground at the upper end of Capel-street	18
33	Richard Geering,	A piece of Ground opposite Steven's Church-yard	6 13
34	Lord Palmerston,	A lot of Ground in Oxmantown	5
35	L. Gardener and Mrs. Mercier,	Part of the Ground behind Lazor's-hill	3
36	Robert Dixon,	Part of Souter's-lane behind Skinner-row	4
37	William Quaile,	A House in High-street	20
38	His Majesty,	Out of the Irish Exchequer	300

APPENDIX, No. VIII.

No. of Receipt	Tenants' Names	Denominations	Yearly Rent
			£. s. d.
39	Benjamin Everard,	Ground in Glasminogue	3
40	Daniel Cooke,	Ground on the Blind Quay	15 4
41	Anthony Barkey,	Ditto Ditto	15
42	Edward Forde,	Ditto Ditto	9 6 4
43	Hosea Coates,	Ditto Ditto	12
44	James Mullen,	Ditto Ditto	7 10
45	Darby Eagan,	Ditto on the South Strand	29 11 8
46	Thomas Ellis,	Ditto Ditto	0 5 0
47	Thomas Wilkinson,	Ditto Ditto	16 11 8
48	Nathaniel Dyer,	Ditto Ditto	18 13 4
49	John Vareilles,	Ditto Ditto	5
50	John Taylor,	Ditto Ditto	5
51	William Wilde,	Ditto Ditto	5
52	Anthony Barkey,	Ditto Ditto	5
53	Arthur Lamprey,	Ditto Ditto	4 14
54	Barnaby Middleton,	Ditto Ditto	0 5 0
55	Jane Jacob,	Seven feet of the Blind Quay	3
56	David Latouche,	Part of the City-wall south side of Castle-street	6
57	James King,	A Shed south side of Newgate	2
58	Richard Faulkener,	Ground north side of the Coombe	10
59	Benedict Arthur,	Part of Booker's-lane	2
60	Corporation of Carpenters,	Ground in Oxmantown	0 3 4
61	Lewis Jones and Wife,	Part of Lazor's-hill	5
62	Sterne Tighe,	The Old Bridewell near Oxmantown	24
63	Elizabeth Walker,	Part of Souter's-lane	2 10 0
64	Agustine Thwaites,	Part of the back of the Blind Quay	20
65	John Crowe,	Part of Essex-street and the Blind Quay	20
66	David Reed,	Part of the Blind Quay	10 3 4
67	John Daniel,	Ground near the City Stables	3
68	William O'Neal,	Ground in Little Booter's-lane	10
69	Samuel Sandwith,	The Lots, Nos. 26 and 27, South Strand	5 5
70	Ballast Office,	Ground on the South Strand	5
71	William Mc. Gowan,	Part of Cow-lane behind Castle-street	7
72	John M. Allen,	Ground on the Blind Quay	11
73	Henry Aston,	Ground and Houses in Temple-bar	41 5
74	Walter Donegan,	A Messuage in College-green	26
75	Bridget Fitzpatrick,	Ditto Ditto	86
76	Elizabeth Stoyle,	Ditto Ditto	16
77	Francis Smith,	Ditto Ditto	26
78	John Murragh,	Ditto Ditto	25
79	Arthur Thompson,	Ditto Ditto	25
80	Thomas Dames,	Two Houses in Trinity-street	12
81	Samuel Fenton,	A Messuage, corner of Trinity-lane	13 10
82	Alderman Edward Hunt,	A House in Kenedy's-lane	6
83	George Lamprey,	A part of the City wall in Castle-street	3
84	William French,	Part of Souter's-lane	2 10
85	Thomas Allen and Wife,	Ground on the South Strand	11 4
86	Philip Crampton,	Ditto in Temple-bar	66
87	John Biindly,	Ditto Ditto	40
88	Francis Perry,	Ditto Ditto	83
89	William Dunne,	Ditto Ditto	30
90	James Ware	A House north side of Castle-street	20
91	Ephraim Cuthbert,	Part of Croker's Lane	6
92	Parish of St. Bridget,	Ground in Little Ship-street	0 5 0
93	Arthnr Shepherd,	Ditto Ditto	7

APPENDIX, No. VIII.

No. of Receipt	Tenants' Names.	Denominations.	Yearly Rent.
			£. s. d.
94	Henry Aston,	Ground on Aston's Quay	90
95	Thomas Blair,	Ditto Ditto	32 16
96	Ditto	Ditto Ditto	42 6
97	Michael Eagle,	Ditto on Aston's Quay	37 10
98	Thomas Carmichael,	Ditto, Ditto	37 8 7½
99	Thomas Blair,	Ditto in Fleet-street	50 5
100	William Adair,	Ditto Ditto	36 6
101	Stephen Reed,	Ditto Ditto	36 6
102	John Magrath,	Ditto Ditto	22 9
103	Morris Humphreys,	Ditto Ditto	22 2
104	James Edwards,	Ditto Ditto	23 11 3
105	John Baptiste Cuville,	Ditto Ditto	40 10
106	Edwin Thomas,	Ditto Ditto	37 16
107	Ditto Ditto	Ditto Ditto	39 12
108	Samuel Laban,	Ditto Ditto	39 12 0
109	Nicholas Kempston,	Ditto on South Strand	19 19
110	Benjamin Pemberton,	Ditto Ditto	23 2
111	Pricious Clarke,	Ditto Ditto	25
112	Thomas Bell,	Ground north side of Fleet-street	37 1
113	Thomas Gorman	Ditto on Aston's Quay	52 14 1¼
114	Peter Wilson,	Ditto in Grafton-street	75 10
115	James Dexter,	Ditto in Church-street and King-street	17 10
116	Samuel Johnson,	Ditto in Temple-bar, formerly Ferry-slip	11 7 6
117	Michael Nowlan,	Ditto in Trinity-street	40
118	Revd. Deane Doyne,	Ditto in Steven-street	43 10
119	Sir William Mayne,	Houses in New-row	200
120	Benjamin Lett,	Ground in College Green	28 1 2
121	Edward Beatty,	Ground in St. Andrew's-street	20 14
122	Thomas Mayler,	Ditto Ditto	12 1 6
123	Ditto,	Ditto Ditto	18 2 6
124	Thomas Truelock,	Ditto Ditto	17 6 6
125	Ditto,	Ditto Ditto	15 18
126	Edward Beatty,	Ditto Ditto	12 1 6
127	John Kerr,	Ditto Ditto	13 13
128	Ditto	Ditto Ditto	18 7 6
129	Edward Beatty,	Ditto in Exchequer-street	10
130	Thomas Meyler,	Ditto Ditto	12 10
131	Ditto,	Ditto Ditto	14
132	Edward Beatty,	Ditto Ditto	14
133	Thomas Truelock,	Ditto Ditto	11
134	Ditto,	Ditto Ditto	9
135	Edward Beatty,	Ditto Ditto	9
136	Joseph Sirr,	Ditto west side of Trinity-street	19
137	Thomas Blakeney,	Ditto in St. Andrew's-street	19
138	William Ferguson,	Ground in St. Andrew's-street	18 1
139	Ditto,	Ditto Ditto	17 2
140	John Morgan.	Ditto Ditto	13 15 6
141	Ditto,	Ditto Ditto	11 17 6
142	Ditto,	Ditto Ditto	11 8
143	Ditto,	Ditto Ditto	7 12
144	Ditto,	Ditto Ditto	9 10
145	Ditto,	Ditto Ditto	12
146	Revd. Benedict Arthur,	Ditto in Werburgh's-street	20
147	Sir Thomas Blackall,	Part of Arundel-court	19 17
148	Jane Curtis,	Ditto Ditto	73

g

APPENDIX, No. VIII.

No. of Receipt	Tenants' Names.	Denominations.	Yearly Rent. £. s. d.
149	Richard Ginn, - -	A House in Cooke-street - -	9
150	William Adair, - -	A Lot of Ground in Suffolk-street -	12 13
151	William Smith, - -	Ditto Ditto - -	13 15
152	Thomas W. Mahon, -	Ditto Ditto - -	15 8
153	Thomas Todderick, -	Ditto Ditto - -	14 17
154	Ditto, - -	Ditto Ditto - -	13 4
155	Nugent Booker, - -	Ditto in Grafton-street - -	33 15
156	Ditto, - -	Ditto Ditto - -	18
157	Thomas Todderick, -	Ditto Ditto - -	20 14
158	Graham Myers, - -	Ditto Ditto - -	23 2
159	Elms Hailey, - -	Ditto in Suffolk-street -	18 19 6
160	Thomas Truelock, -	Ditto Ditto - -	21 7 5
161	Nugent Booker, -	Ditto Ditto - -	31
162	Ditto, - -	Ditto Ditto - -	22 12 3
163	Ditto, - -	Ditto Ditto - -	18 14 11
164	John Giffard, - -	Ditto Ditto - -	23
165	Ditto, - -	Ditto in Grafton-street -	52 18 0
166	William Ralph, - -	Ditto Ditto - -	34 10
167	John Exshaw, Alderman,	Ditto Ditto - -	35 1 6
168	Michael Boylan, -	Ditto Ditto - -	31 12 6
169	Edward Byrne, - -	Ditto Ditto - -	31 12 6
170	George Grant, - -	Ditto Ditto - -	22 11
171	Ditto, - -	Ditto Ditto - -	20 18
172	John Darragh, - -	Ditto Ditto - -	18 3
173	Ditto, - -	Ditto Ditto - -	25 11 6
174	Edward Tracey, - -	Ditto in Exchequer-street -	11
175	Ditto, - -	Ditto Ditto - -	12 2
176	Patrick Matthews, -	Ditto Ditto - -	15 19
177	Ditto, - -	Ditto Ditto - -	10 3
178	James Dawling, - -	Ditto Ditto - -	13 15
179	William Adair, - -	Ditto in Exchequer-street -	8 16
180	John Locker, - -	Ditto Ditto - -	11 10
181	Ditto, - -	Ditto Ditto - -	11 10
182	Ditto, - -	Ditto Ditto - -	10 7
183	Thomas Meyler, - -	Ditto Ditto - -	11 10 10
184	Ditto, - -	Ditto Ditto - -	12 13 2
185	Andrew Culloden, - -	Ditto Ditto - -	13 15
186	Edward Beatty, - -	A piece of Ground taken off 37 in Ditto -	1
187	Richard Campsie, - -	Ground west side of Back-lane - -	1 5
188	James Horan, Alderman,	The Mills at Island Bridge - -	200
189	Richard Manders, - -	Ground at Ditto - -	20
190	Richard Williams, - -	City Lot North Strand - -	60
191	Edward Stephens, - -	Ground Part of the Pipes -	8
192	Charles Williams, - -	Part of the Pest Houses Thomas-street No. 1	15 10 0
193	Ditto, - -	Ditto Ditto No. 2	18 19 6
194	Ditto, - -	Ditto Ditto No. 4	17 12
195	Richard Manders, - -	Ditto Ditto No. 5	15 10
196	Matthew Gibbon, - -	Ditto Ditto No. 3	15 8
197	Sir Thomas Blackall, - -	Part of Arundel Court - -	20
198	Alexander Sparrow, - -	Part of the Tower Ditch near Arundel Court	15
199	Henry Hutton, - -	A Shed in Rosemary-lane - -	1 6
200	Michael Dwyer, - -	A House in College-green -	113 15
201	Robert Whitestone, - -	A House in St. Andrew's-street -	40
202	Rev. James Nevin, - -	Ditto Ditto - -	35
203	Thomas M'Donald, -	Rere Ground in Lurgan-street - -	5 10

APPENDIX, No. VIII.   lix

No. of Receipt	Tenants' Names.	Denominations.	Yearly Rent.
			£. s. d.
204	Hugh Crother, Alderman,	Rere Ground in Lurgan-street	5
206	John Beatty	3 Lots of Ground in Exchequer-street	48 3
205	St Paul's Parish,	A Lot of Ground in Oxmantown	5 5
207	Sir William Worthington,	Ditto Ditto	37 9 2
208	Michael Dwyer,	A House in Trinity-street	50
209	John Willis,	Ditto Ditto	34 2 6
210	Thomas Barker,	Ditto Ditto	35
211	John Shea,	Ditto in College Green	70
212	David Courtney,	Ground in Oxmantown	15 4 6
213	Frederick Darley, Alderman,	Ditto in Little Ship-street	13 10
214	Ditto,-	Ditto Ditto	15
215	Bartholomew Herbert,	Ditto Ditto	20 9 6
216	Ditto,	Ditto Ditto	6 6
217	Ditto,	Ditto Ditto	14 8
218	Robert Boylan,	Ditto in North King-street	25 16
219	Robert Mallet,	Ditto in Exchequer-street	21 12
220	William Grumley,	The Green-hide Crane, Bonham-street	40
221	John Still,	A Lot of Ground in Cuffe-street	2 15
222	James Fegan,	Ground in Bonham-street	12
223	Bryan Murphy,	A House next the late Tholsel, Skinner-row,	25
224	Ditto,	Ground in Skinner-row	40 15 6
225	Thomas E. Thorpe,	Ditto Ditto	41 14 11
226	William Craig,	Ditto Ditto	34 19
227	Timothy Cahill,	Ditto in Grafton-street	47 6
228	John Adam,	Ditto Ditto	42 14
229	Drury Jones,	Ditto Ditto	104 10
230	William Fry,	Ditto Ditto	51 14
231	Thomas M'Cready,	Ditto Ditto	52 16
232	Michael Dunne,	Ditto in Thomas-street	74 8
233	James Porter,	A House in St. Andrew's-street	35
234	James Sanders,	Ditto Ditto	32
235	Richard Manders, Alderman,	Ground west end of James-street	37 10
236	William Roe,	A House in William-street	7 6 3
237	George Wildridge,	Ditto Ditto	5 11 10¼
238	Ditto,	Ditto Ditto	7 0 3
239	James Troy,	Ditto Ditto	11 6 3
240	Drury Jones,	A Lot of Ground in William-street	25 4
241	Ditto,	Ditto Ditto	17 6 6
242	Ditto,	Ditto Ditto	21 6 7
243	Ditto,	Ditto in Exchequer-street	11 5
244	Ditto,	Ditto Ditto	13 10
245	Ditto,	Ditto Ditto	15 15
246	Ditto,	Ditto Ditto	9 15
247	Ditto,	Ditto Ditto	15
248	Ditto,	Ditto Ditto	15
249	Ditto,	Ditto Ditto	15
250	John Stamper,	Ditto in St. Andrews-street	35
251	Ditto,	Ditto in Church-lane	35
252	William Humphreys,	Ditto on Merchants Quay	5
253	Hugh Crothers, Alderman,	Ditto in North King-street	51 3 9
254	Prudence Payne,	A House in College Green	113 15
255	William Bond,	Ground east side of Kevin's port	21
256	Ditto,	Ditto Ditto	18 15
257	Ditto,	Ditto Ditto	27 15
258	Richard Skelleron,	East Side of Montague-place	6 15

APPENDIX, No. VIII.

No. of Receipt	Tenants' Names.	Denominations.	Yearly Rent.
			£. s. d.
259	Richard Skelleron,	East side of Montague-place	11 5
260	George Cummins,	Ditto rear of Cuffe-street	18 15
261	Sarah Gartside,	Ditto Ditto	6 15
262	Peter Burnett,	Ditto Ditto	6
263	Mary Read,	Ditto Ditto	3 10
264	Commissioners St. Stephen's Green,	St. Stephen's Green	500
			7220 6 2¼

Saint George's Rents.

1	Joseph Barret,	A House in Castle-street	50
2	John Lloyd,	Ditto Ditto	35
3	Joseph Ridley,	Ditto Ditto	45
4	William Andrews,	Ditto Ditto	30
5	John Donnelly,	Ground north side of Thomas-street	57 16
6	Christopher Usher,	A House in Castle-street	5
7	William Usher,	A Lot of Ground in Cooke-street	9
			231 16

All Hallows, or All Saints Rents.

1	Sir John Coghill,	The Lands of Clonturke	40
2	Earl of Charlemont,	The Lands of Donaghcarney	709 15
3	William Usher,	Lands near Donnybrook	100
4	William Slicer,	Ground in Golden-lane	30
5	John Furnace,	Part of Baldoyle, with the Warren	172 10
6	William Montgomery,	Ditto Ditto	41 18
7	John Wyue,	Ditto Ditto	12 15 6
8	Charles Boyde,	Ditto Ditto	22 14 6¼
9	John Adamson,	Ditto Ditto	17 11
10	Ditto,	Ditto Ditto	26 0
11	Ditto,	Ditto Ditto	29 5 5
12	John Templeton,	Ditto Ditto	22 14 9
13	Thomas Adderly,	The House and Demesne of Baldoyle	85 6
14	Jeremiah Byrne,	A House in High-street	24 5
15	Charles Napper,	Ground in George's-lane	16 10
16	Ditto,	Ditto Ditto	12
17	Thomas Barber,	Ditto Ditto	15
18	Peter Le Maistre,	Ditto Ditto	14 5
19	Henrietta Le Maistre,	Ditto Ditto	14 5
20	John Reynell,	A Tenement in Castle-street	10
21	St. Werburg's Parish,	Ditto Ditto	8
22	Peter Butterton,	Ground in George's-lane	15
23	Peter Le Maistre,	Ditto Ditto	23 8 2
24	Jeffrey Foote,	Ditto Ditto	18 19 10
25	Thomas Barber,	Ditto Ditto	22 10 6
26	Ditto,	Ditto Ditto	22 10 6
27	William Dawson,	Ditto Ditto	15
28	John Rosiveau,	Ditto Ditto	11 5
29	James Bamber,	Ditto Ditto	8 8
30	Neptune Vero,	Ditto Ditto	7 5 3
31	John Franklin,	Ditto Ditto	4 15 0

APPENDIX, No. VIII.

No of Receipt	Tenants' Names.	Denominations.	Yearly Rent.
32	Thomas Keatinge,	Ground in George's-lane	6
33	John Fawcet,	Ditto Ditto	10 14 6
34	John Rossiveau,	Ditto Ditto	8 11
35	William Adair,	Ditto Ditto	8 10
36	Thomas M'Mahon,	Ditto in Grafton-street	14 17
37	Ditto,	Ditto Ditto	17 12
38	Alderman Darragh,	Ditto Ditto	19 16
39	Alderman Crampton,	Ditto Ditto	16 5
40	John M'Grath,	Ditto Ditto	16 16
41	Ditto,	Ditto Ditto	18
42	Ditto,	Ditto Ditto	18
43	Ditto,	Ditto Ditto	19 11
44	Jacob Jolly,	Ditto Ditto	21 17
45	William Gibson,	Ditto Ditto	18 19 6
46	Ditto,	Ditto Ditto	17 16 6
47	William Carter,	Ditto Ditto	14 7 6
48	William Evans,	Ditto Ditto	5 3 6
49	Thomas M'Mahon,	Ditto in Chatham-street	7 7 3
50	James Horan, Alderman,	Ditto Ditto	5 14
51	Ditto,	Ditto Ditto	5 14
52	Pricious Clarke,	Ditto in Pitt-street	5
53	Fergus Fowler,	Ditto in Chatham-street	6 15
54	Ditto,	Ditto Ditto	7 5
55	John Haydon,	Ditto Ditto	8 0 0
56	Ditto,	Ditto Ditto	9 5
57	William Millikin,	Ditto Ditto	5 5
58	Alderman Darragh,	Ditto Ditto	5 15 6
59	William Millikin,	Ditto Ditto	9
60	Ditto,	Ditto in Pitt-street	6
61	Thomas Truelock,	Ditto Ditto	3 5
62	George Bradshaw,	Ditto in Chatham-street	5 10
63	Pricious Clarke,	Ditto in Pitt-street	4 10
64	John Darragh, Alderman,	Ditto Ditto	3 12
65	Captain Evans,	Ditto Ditto	2 6
66	William Fernsley,	Ditto in Chatham-street	3 16
67	Ditto,	Ditto Ditto	5
68	Joseph Higginson,	Ditto Ditto	5 10
69	Thomas Truelock,	Ditto in Pitt-street	3 10
70	Ditto,	Ditto Ditto	3
71	James Horan, Alderman,	Ditto Ditto	1 17
72	William Millikin,	Ditto Ditto	3 10
73	Thomas Truelock,	Ditto Ditto	3 10
74	Ditto,	Ditto Ditto	3 10
75	Ditto,	Ditto Ditto	3 10
76	John Darragh, Alderman,	Ditto Ditto	3
77	Ditto,	Ditto Ditto	2 15
78	Ambrose Leet,	Lot of Ground in Dawson-street	80
79	Joseph Kelly,	Part of the Lands of Ballycullen	103 1.10
80	James Hamilton,	Ditto Ditto	175 4 6
81	Bernard Foy,	Ditto Ditto	45 14 10
82	George Garnett,	Ditto Ditto	72 16 9
83	Timothy Mahon,	Ground near Bow Bridge	18 11 6
84	James Manders and J. Glennan,	Sundry Lots of Ground near Ditto	77 10 9½
		Total	2542 19 8

APPENDIX, No. VIII.

St. Mary's Abbey and Thomas Court Rents.

No. of Receipt	Tenants' Names.	Denominations.	Yearly Rent.
			£. s. d.
1	Patrick Aylmer,	A House and Garden in Oxmantown	9
2	Francis Humphreys,	A Ditto in Church-street with Shop and Garden	59 18 5
3	Nathaniel Cavanagh,	Ditto Ditto	8
4	Ralph Gregory,	Ground on the Merchants' Quay	4 10
5	William Jones,	A House in Thomas-street	32 11 2
6	Ditto,	Ditto Ditto	30 19 11
7	William Parry,	3 Tenements in Cooke-street.	0 0 0
8	Keane O'Hara,	Dames Mills	20
9	Joseph Andrews,	A House &c. in Church-street	26 5
10	John Oldham,	A Lot of Ground in Lincoln-lane	17 1 3
11	Richard Workman,	A House in Castle-street	18
12	Edward Torton,	A Concern in Nicholas-street	16
13	John Cooke,	A Messuage in Oxmantown	14
14	Mary Dalton,	A Tenement in Fishamble-street	30
15	Benjamin Archer,	2 Lots of Ground in Church-street	12
16	John Phibbs,	2 Houses in Nicholas-street	15 2
17	Rev. Thomas M'Donnell,	A Tenement in Cooke-street	5
18	William Brown,	A House North side of Castle-street	24
19	John Cooke, Alderman,	Ground James's-street	6 7 6
20	Nathaniel James,	A House in Castle-street	20
21	George Sutton, Alderman,	Ditto in Nicholas-street	21 15 8
22	Richard Grady,	Ditto Ditto	18 14
23	Benjamin Ward,	Ditto Ditto	20 13 3
24	James Dexter,	Ground in Church-lane	25
25	George Maquay,	Ditto in Thomas-street	12
26	Rev. Henry Ware,	A Tenement in Castle-street	18
27	Richard Power,	A House North side of Ditto	30
28	John Donnely,	A Lot of Ground in Thomas-street	49 17 6
29	Arthur Guinness,	A Holding called the Pipes	10
30	John Hart,	A Lot of Ground in Bason-lane	1
31	Arthur Guinness,	A Piece of Ground near James-street	1
32	Robert Mercer,	Ditto near the City Bason	0 0 0
33	Francis Dunne,	A House in Castle-street, formerly N. James	20
34	Joseph Rose,	2 Lots of Ground in Blackall-street No. 1 and 2	9 18
35	Robert Walker,	5 Ditto Ditto No. 3, 4, 5, 6 and 7	27 10
36	Ditto,	2 Ditto Ditto No. 8 and 9	9 13 6
37	Ditto,	15 Ditto in Walker-street	23 9 6
38	Joseph Ashley,	3 Ditto in Blackall-street No. 10, 11 and 12	15 15
39	Representatives of William Arnold	3 Ditto in Upper Bridge-street No. 1, 2 and 4	68 5
40	Thomas Potter,	1 Ditto Ditto No. 3,	27 9
41	William Arnold,	Ditto Ditto No. 5,	19 10
42	John Langan,	Ditto Ditto No. 6,	19 10
43	Gerald Dillon,	Ditto Ditto No. 7,	18
44	Patrick Tommins,	Ditto Ditto No. 8,	18
45	Gerald Dillon,	Ditto Ditto No. 9,	17 1 3
46	Ditto,	Ditto Ditto No. 10,	17 1 3
47	Charles Ryan,	Ditto Ditto No. 11,	17 1 3
48	Ditto,	Ditto Ditto No. 12,	17 1 3
49	Ditto,	Ditto Ditto No. 13,	17 1 3
50	William Arnold,	Ditto Ditto No. 14,	23 5

APPENDIX, No. VIII.

No. of Receipt	Tenants' Names.	Denominations.	Yearly Rent.
			£. s. d.
51	William Arnold,	1 Lot of Ground in Upper Bridge-street, No. 15,	20 18 6
52	Ditto,	Ditto Ditto No. 16,	36 11 6
53	Ditto,	Ditto Ditto No. 17,	15 18 9
54	Allen Forster,	Ditto Ditto No. 18,	31 10
55	Thomas Potter,	Ditto Ditto No. 19,	12 15
56	Gerald Dillon,	Ditto Ditto No. 20,	17 1 3
57	Ditto,	Ditto Ditto No. 21,	17 0 3
58	Ditto,	Ditto Ditto No. 22,	17 5
59	Sir William Worthington,	Ditto Ditto No. 23,	15
60	Ditto,	Ditto Ditto No. 24,	19 10
61	Ditto,	Ditto Ditto No. 25,	18 15
62	Ditto,	Ditto Ditto No. 26,	24
63	Thomas Potter,	Ditto Ditto No. 27,	18 15
64	Sir William Worthington,	Ditto Ditto No. 28,	20 14
65	Philip Cassidy,	Ditto Ditto No. 29,	17 3
66	Samuel Read, Alderman,	Ditto Ditto No. 30,	17 17
67	Daniel Sulivan,	Ground north side of Cooke-street in Winetavern-street	20 8 6
68	Ditto,	1 Ditto in Winetavern-street	16 2 6
		Total	1319 13 2

A List of New Settings of City Lands.

Ancient Revenue.

1	Thomas Kennan,	Houses and Premises in Fishamble-st. and Copper-alley	26
2	Lawrence Byrne,	Part of the Timber-yard Essex-street	45 10
3	Samuel Linfoot,	A House in Essex-street	100
4	Edward Bambrick,	Ditto Ditto	87 10
5	Jacob Jackson,	Ditto Ditto	120
6	Ditto,	Ditto Ditto	25
7	Charles Alder,	Ditto Ditto	36
8	John Forster Burnett,	Ditto on Essex Quay	25
9	Thomas Mason,	Ditto on Essex Bridge	80
10	Francis Castro,	Ditto in Saint Andrew's-street	13 10
11	William Walsh,	The City Ferries	335
12	Stewart King,	Part of the Land of Baldoyle	113 15
			1000 7 5
		Colganstown	425 14
		Tythes of Taghadoe	120

APPENDIX, No. VIII.

A List of Tenants to part of Humphry Butler's Holding; being Ground formerly set to Neville Pooley.

No. of Receipt	Tenants' Names.		Denominations.		Yearly Rent.
1	Representatives of Tuite	-	A Tenament in Essex-street	- - -	£. s. d. 10
2	Ditto	-	Ditto Ditto	- - -	0 0 0
3	Ditto	Scriven -	Ditto Ditto	- - -	15
4	Ditto	Trueman -	Ditto Ditto	- - -	40
5	Ditto	- -	Ditto Ditto	- - -	11 7 6
6	Ditto	Beauviere	Ditto Ditto	- - -	30
7	Ditto	Sheridan -	Ditto Ditto	- - -	38
8	Ditto	Fleming -	Ditto in Eustace-street	- -	44 10
9	Ditto	Moore -	Ditto in Essex-street	- -	18
10	Ditto	Fenton -	Ditto Ditto	- - -	32
11	Ditto	Farris -	Ditto Ditto	- - -	20
12	Barrack Board	- -	The Old Custom House in Ditto	- -	60
13	Richard Gregg	- -	A Tenement in Ditto	- - -	26
14	M. J. Kimberley	- -	Ditto Ditto	- - -	30
15	Ditto Ditto	- -	Ditto Ditto	- - -	22 15
16	Samuel Alker	- -	Ditto Ditto	- - -	35
17	John M'Robin	- -	Ditto Ditto	- - -	20
18	John Robinson	- -	Ditto Ditto	- - -	30
19	Margaret Quinn	- -	Ditto Ditto	- - -	55
20	Jacob Jackson	- -	Ditto Ditto	- - -	30
					567 12 6

Settings of Part of the Lands of Clonturke.

John Carlton, Alderman		Part of the Lands of Clonturke	- -	148	
J. C. Beresford, Alderman		Ditto Ditto	- - -	270 10	
Charles Connolly	- -	Ditto Ditto	- - -	17	
Charles Kavannagh	- -	Ditto Ditto	- - -	54	
Ditto Ditto	- -	Ditto Ditto	- - -	15	
Bryan Clifford	- -	Ditto Ditto	- - -	17	
Hugh Hamill	- -	Ditto Ditto	- - -	83	
Edward Hughes	- -	Ditto Ditto	- - -	14	
John Duvall	- -	Ditto Ditto	- - -	30	
Ditto	- -	Ditto Ditto	- - -	24	
William Williams	- -	Ditto Ditto	- - -	61 10	
Audrew Coffey	- -	Ditto Ditto	- - -	7 10	
Ditto	- -	Ditto Ditto	- - -	34	
John Woodhouse	- -	Ditto Ditto	- - -	130	
John Duvall	- -	Ditto Ditto	- - -	32 10	
George Collens	- -	Ditto Ditto	- - -	7 10	
John Curtis	- -	Ditto Ditto	- - -	11 10	
Thomas Kirwan	- -	Ditto Ditto	- - -	46	
Elizabeth Meehun	- -	Ditto Ditto	- - -	57	
William Benson	- -	Ditto Ditto	- - -	4	
Rev. J. Fitzpatrick	- -	Ditto Ditto	- - -	15	
J. C. Beresford, Alderman		Ditto Ditto	- - -	39 16	
Mary Connor	- -	Ditto Ditto	- - -	22 10	
				1141 6	

APPENDIX, No. VIII.

Amount of the Annual Rents of the City of Dublin.

		£.	s.	d.
1	Ancient Revenue	7220	6	2¼
2	Saint George's Rents	231	16	0
3	All Hallows' or All Saints' Rents	2542	19	8
4	St. Mary's Abbey and Thomas Court Rents	1319	13	2
5	New Settings Ancient Revenue	1007	5	0
6	Humphry Butler's Holding	567	12	6
7	Clonturke	1141	6	0
		13917	3	6½

Received of the above from the 29th Sept. 1815 to the 29th Sept., 1816 — 12732 9 7¼

By Cash paid Interest, &c.

1815. Dec.

	£	s.	d.
To Interest on advance	537	8	6¼
To the Lord Mayor and Sheriffs one year's Interest on the late Mr. Powell's Legacy	40	0	0
To Interest on City Bonds to 25th March, 1816	11590	16	0
To Ditto on English Tontine remitted William Coningham	2669	9	11¼
To Ditto on Irish Ditto payable in Dublin	75	10	0
	14913	4	6

By Cash paid Casual Expenses.

1815.
Oct.

		£	s.	d.
To T. Burn, for removing Rubbish from Market House		13	4	6
To Stamps and Postage		17	13	11
To Margaret Smith for lighting Fires in Market House		4	11	0
To Pells and Poundage at Treasury at receipt of 800l.		26	1	0
To Alderman Beresford, late lord mayor, usual Grant		1000	0	0
To Ditto for Weigh Houses for Smithfield-market		96	19	4
To Benjamin Eaton for Work done at City Marshalsea		11	4	2
To Arthur R. Neville for Maps		58	8	10
To Work done at the Market House		11	4	11
To Watchmen at Colganstown and Market House		39	1	11
To Fisher and Greene on account of Costs		374	8	9
To Carriage of Articles to Market House, Thomas-street		0	10	0
To painting the statue of King William III.		3	8	3
To Robert Norris for Hats for City Beadles		5	13	9
To Recorder for attending contested Elections		34	2	6
To Richard Quinton for providing Candles for Commons' Room		5	0	0
To County Cess Colganstown		14	17	11
To J. C. Beresford per Act of Assembly		50	0	0
To Jonas Paisley on account of Rent paid J. C.		18	4	0

	£	s.	d.
To William Leet for Great Coats for City Beadles	8	0	0
To Margaret Smith for attending Assemblies	5	13	9
To Fisher and Greene per order of Finance Committee	100	0	0
To George Waller for Receipts for City Rents	1	1	8
To D. Latouche on account of Rent overpaid by J. C.	7	10	0
To R. Spear for a Set of Liquid Measures	28	8	9
To Gordon and Fletcher for winding-up Mansion House Clock	0	8	1¼
To J. C. Beresford deposit on Tolls and Customs	2433	15	0
To Fisher and Greene on account of Costs	200	0	0
To Coals for the Market House	1	4	0
To Arthur R. Neville for Surveys	49	12	1
To Ditto Ditto	70	0	0
	4691	8	1¼

By Cash paid Gifts and Alms.

	£	s.	d.
To sundry poor Persons	91	0	0
To Mary Gregg ordered per Christmas reduced	20	0	0
To Elizabeth French Ditto	10	0	0
To Catharine Darquire, Michaelmas	16	0	0
To George Dickenson	2	0	0
To Rose Emmerson	34	2	6
To Mary A. Kelly	5	13	9
To Sarah Walker	40	0	0
	218	16	3

APPENDIX, No. VIII.

By Cash paid Annuities.

	£.	s.	d.
To Robert Hart, one year, due Sept. 1815, reduced	200	0	0
To Mrs. Lucas, ditto, due July, 1816	40	0	0
To Miss Lucas, ditto, due April, 1816	18	4	0
To Miss Hart, ditto, due June, 1816	36	8	0
To Mrs. Vance, ditto, due ditto	40	0	0
To Mrs. Andrews, ditto, due April, 1816	16	0	0
To St. Nicholas within, ditto, due March, 1816	5	0	0
	355	12	0

By Cash paid Rents and Taxes.

	£.	s.	d.
To the Commissioners of Paving, &c. one year's composition money, for Paving, Lighting and Cleansing the Streets, ending 25th March, 1816	2320	0	0
To sundry Quit Rents	108	15	2¼
To one year's Rent of the City part of the Assembly House, due 25th of March, 1816	50	0	0
To one year's ditto of the Tholsel, due ditto	60	0	0
To one year's ditto of Ground, Skinner-row, due ditto	25	0	0
To one year's ditto' of Ground, Essex-bridge, due ditto	23	0	0
To one year's ditto of Tolls and Customs, due ditto	15	0	0
To one and a half year's ditto of Ground, Molesworth-street, due ditto	30	0	0
To one year's ditto of the Green Hide Crane, due ditto	13	13	0
To one year's ditto of Ground, Patrick-street, due ditto	6	6	0
To one year's ditto of Hearing-room, due ditto	19	0	0
To one year's ditto Ground in Cooke-street, due ditto	14	0	0
To one year's ditto part of the Tholsel, due ditto	32	5	0
To Richard Smith and J. S. Fleming, one year's Rent; out of the Lands of Merrion, due 29th Sept. 1815 (as High Sheriffs)	65	0	0
To one year's Rent of Essex-street, due 25th March, 1816	840	0	0
To one year and eleven months of Toll Houses, due August, 1816	118	16	8
To sundry Taxes on Mansion House and Colganstown and Insurance	508	7	6
	4249	3	4

By Cash paid Salaries.

	£.	s.	d.
To Alderman Shaw, one year's Salary as Lord Mayor	1320	0	0
To Recorder one year due 30th May, 1816, reduced	400	0	0
To Town Clerks, half year, due, 1st January, 1816	135	0	0
To ditto, one year's ancient Salary due ditto	3	0	0
To Law Agents, one and a half year's ditto, due March, 1816, reduced	136	10	0
To Sword Bearer, one year, due 7th August, 1816, ditto	80	0	0
To ditto as Clerk of the Corn Market, due 10th August, 1816	60	0	0
To ditto for striking the Assize, due ditto reduced	18	4	0
To Timothy Allen, one year, due March, 1816, ditto	91	0	0
To John Lambert, one year ditto due ditto ditto	16	0	0
To Officer of Commons, one year due ditto ditto	80	0	0
To the High Constable, one year, due 24th June, 1816, reduced	80	0	0
To Keeper of City Marshalsea, one year, due 16th April, 1816, reduced	32	0	0
To Harbour Masters, one year, due 24th June, 1816	10	0	0
To Ticketmen, Market House, one year, due 24th Sept. 1816	45	0	0
To Crier, Sessions Court, one year, due 24th June, 1816	5	0	0
To Alexander Faulkner, Beadle, one year, due ditto, reduced	12	0	0
To Matthew Leigh, ditto, one year, due ditto	10	0	0
To Keeper of Freemen's Gallery, one year, due 24th April, 1816	4	0	0
To Beadle of Smithfield, one year, due Easter, 1816	3	8	3
To Beadle of Christ's Church, one year, due Sept. 1815	5	0	0
To Mary Stone, Keeper of Court of King's Bench, due ditto	1	0	0
To Curate of Taghadoe, Rev. H. Savage, one year, due April, 1816	25	0	0
To Curate of Baldoyle, Rev. J. Lewis, one year, due ditto	10	0	0
To Treasurer, one year, due Sept. 1816	500	0	0
To A. Crane, late Greenkeeper, one year and quarter, due Sept. 1815	18	15	0
	3101	7	3

By Cash, paid Tradesmen's Bills.

To Amount of sundry Accounts furnished   791 14 11

The Account of Alderman William Henry Archer, Treasurer to the Corporation of the City of Dublin; commencing Michaelmas, 1815, *and ending Michaelmas,* 1816.

Dr. *Alderman William Henry Archer.*	£.	s.	d.
To Cash from Alderman Beresford for the Court of Conscience - -	50	0	0
To Cash from Tenants at will, Colganstown - - -	12	9	1
To ditto from J. Flood, Deposit of one year's Rent of Ground, Essex-street	18	7	
To ditto from William Dixon, ditto of ditto of ditto - - -	15	15	6
To ditto one year's Rent Basin, Water-course, &c. - - -	2500	0	0
To ditto from Allen and Greene on account of Disallowances -	138	0	0
To nett amount of Rents from 29th Sept. 1815 to 29th Sept. 1816 -	12732	9	7¼
To twelve months' Tolls and Customs	4867	10	0
To twelve ditto Slippage and Anchorage, per Edward Hamerton -	704	17	7
To Freemen's and Sessions Fines per Allen and Greene - -	20	0	4
To Stalls at the Market House -	57	15	5½
Alderman Manders, six months deposit of Tolls and Customs - -	1875	0	0
To Receiver's Fees from 29th Sept. 1815 to 29th Sept. 1816 -	33	6	9½
To Balance due to Treasurer -	8228	14	3
	31254	5	7¼
To Cash received from Commissioners of Wide Streets; being purchase of premises, east side of Essex bridge	1326	0	0
To Cash received from ditto, being balance of purchase of Leather-crane	35	0	0
To Cash for the right of presentation to the living of Rathdrum -	2861	4	0
To twelve months Interest on 1361*l.*	81	13	2
To 124 days Interest on 2861*l.* 4*s.*	58	6	4½
	4362	3	6½

Contra	£.	s.	d.
By Balance due Treasurer, 29th Sept. 1815 - - - -	2632	19	2¼
By Cash paid Interest - -	14913	4	6
By Cash paid Rents and Taxes	4249	3	4½
By Cash paid Salaries - -	3101	7	3
By Cash paid Tradesmen's Bills -	791	14	11
By Cash paid Casual Expences -	4691	8	1½
By Cash paid Gifts and Alms -	218	16	3
By Cash paid Annuities - -	355	12	0
By Cash paid Alderman Beresford, one year's Rent of Stephens Green -	300	0	0
	31254	5	7¼
By Balance due by Treasurer on this account - - - - -	4362	3	6½
	4362	3	6½

A Docket of the Customs of the Gates belonging to the City of Dublin.

At a Post-Assembly held at the Tholsel of the City of Dublin, on Monday the 13th of June, 1763, the following Order was conceived, relative to the undermentioned Docket, to wit—

" That from and after the 24th day of June, 1763, all Goods and Merchandises, that are really the property of any Freeman of this City, do pass Custom Free, into and out of the City, provided such Freeman do certify to the Collectors of the Customs, the quantity and quality of such goods, and that they are his property; that if any Freeman of this City shall presume, after the said 24th of June, to certify that any Goods are his property which are actually the property of any other person not Free of this City in order to defraud this City or their Farmers, of the Customs of such Goods, such Freeman

APPENDIX, No. VIII.

to be proceeded against by the City Agent, as Mr. Recorder shall advise, in order to his being disfranchised for such fraud and breach of oath."

" And it is further ordered—That from and after the said 24th day of June, all Raw Hides going out of this City, to any of the adjacent Liberties to be Tanned, shall be free from Custom going out; that Bark going out of any of the adjacent Liberties, to be made use of for Tanning, shall likewise be free; that all Iron going out to the several Mills near the City to be manufactured, and returning to this City manufactured, shall be likewise free from Custom; that all Salt, manufactured in Ireland, shall be free from any Custom; that all Goods going to be manufactured, and the materials made use of therein, shall be free from Custom, if they are returned to this City manufactured; and that the Committee be empowered to regulate the Docket accordingly."

A

Of every Sack of Ashes, one halfpenny.
———— Car load of Apples, or other Fruit, two pence.
———— Horse load ditto, one penny.
———— Flasket ditto, on one Car, one halfpenny, not exceeding the price of a Car load.
———— Barrel of Ale coming in, brewed without the City or Liberties adjoining, two pence.

B

———— Tub of Butter, one penny.
———— Crock or Basket of ditto, containing ten pounds or upwards, one halfpenny.
———— load of Deal Boards, exceeding six, one penny.
———— load ditto, under six, one halfpenny.
———— Car load of Brushes, two pence.
———— Horse load ditto, one penny.
———— Back load ditto, one halfpenny.
———— Horse load or Car load of Bed-Mats, two pence.
———— Back load ditto, one penny.
———— Barrel of Bark, one halfpenny.
———— Sack of Green Beans or Peas, one halfpenny.
———— Bull, Bullock or Cow, one penny.
———— Sack of Button Moulds, two pence.
———— Flitch of Bacon, one penny.
———— Car load of Brooms, two pence.
———— Horse load of Brooms, one halfpenny.
———— Car load of Brandy or other Spirits, three pence.
———— Runlet ditto, on one Car, one penny, not exceeding the price of a Car load.
———— dozen ditto, one penny, not exceeding the price of a Car load.
———— pedlar's box, carried on his back, one halfpenny.
———— Car load of Brass, three pence.
———— Horse load ditto, two pence.
———— single Brewing Pan, two pence.
———— Car load of Baskets, two pence.
———— Car load of Boymore, two pence.
———— Car load of Bent, one halfpenny.
———— Sack of Brogues, one penny.
———— Car load of Bays, Serges, Frizes, Stockings, &c. three pence.
———— pack of Flannel, two pence.

———— Bundle ditto, one penny.
Of every Horse load of Frizes, Serges, &c. two pence.
———— Car load of Heel Blocks or Patten Boards, two pence.
———— Car load of Bulrushes, two pence.
———— Back load of ditto, one penny.
———— Car load of Brussels, three pence.
———— Piece of Buckram, one penny.
———— Horse load of Earthen Ware, one penny.
———— Car load ditto, three pence.
———— Bedstead, one halfpenny.
———— Dozen of Barrows, one penny.

C

———— Car load of Cheese, three pence.
———— Hundred weight ditto, one penny, not exceeding the price of a Car load.
———— Horse load ditto, two pence.
———— Calf, one halfpenny.
———— Car, to be sold, one halfpenny.
———— Kish of Charcoal, three halfpence.
———— Horse load of Charcoal, one halfpenny.
———— Car load of Candles or Soap, three pence.
———— Horse load ditto, two pence.
———— large Hair Cloth, one penny.
———— Car load of Cradles, two pence.
———— Car load of Chairs, two pence.
———— Dozen of Chairs, one penny.
———— Bag of Corker, one penny.
———— Sack of Cutlins, one halfpenny.
———— Car load of Cyder, three pence.
———— single Dozen ditto, on one Car, not exceeding the price of a Car load, one penny.
———— Kish of Kilkenny Coal, one penny.
———— Dozen of Woollen Cards, one penny.
———— Hundred of Conyfell, one penny.
———— Barrel of Corn, as Wheat, Oats, &c. one farthing.

E

———— Horse load of Eggs, one penny.
———— Clieve load ditto, on Backs, one halfpenny.

F

———— Horse load of dead Fowl, two pence.
———— Clieve of Chickens, carried on Backs or Arms, one halfpenny.

APPENDIX, No. VIII.

Of every Dozen of dead Fowl, on one Car, one penny, not exceeding the price of a Car load.
────── Car load ditto, three pence.
────── Horse load of Fish, one penny.
────── Car load ditto, two pence.
────── Salmon, one farthing.
────── small Basket of Fish on one Car, one halfpenny, not exceeding the price of a Car load.
────── Trail of Figs or Raisins, one halfpenny.
────── Horse load of Feathers, two pence.
────── Car load ditto, three pence.

G

────── Crib of Glass, two pence.
────── Back load ditto, one halfpenny.
────── load of Grass, one farthing.
────── Goat or Kid, one farthing.
────── Gage of all sorts, two pence.
Of all manner of Grain, per Barrel, one farthing.

H

Of every Bag of Hops, three pence.
────── Pocket of Hops, two pence.
────── small parcel ditto, on one Car, one penny, not exceeding the price of a Car load.
────── Horse load of Hats, three pence.
────── Back load ditto, two pence.
────── dozen of Hats, on one Car, one penny, not exceeding the price of a Car load.
────── Cow or Bullock Hide, tanned or untanned, one halfpenny, not exceeding sixpence in the whole, on one Car.
────── Car load of Herrings, four pence.
────── Barrel ditto, two pence.
────── Mease ditto, on one Car, one penny, not exceeding the price of a Car load.
────── Hog or Pig, one halfpenny.
────── sucking Pig, one farthing.
────── load of Broad Hoops, two pence.
────── load of Small Hoops, one penny.
────── load of Hay, one farthing.
────── Firkin or Runlet of Honey, one penny.
────── Crock of ditto, one halfpenny.
────── Car load of Horns, three pence.
────── Bag of Hairsell, one penny.
────── Cart of Hay, one penny.

I

────── Car load of Iron, three pence.
────── Horse Back load ditto, two pence.
────── Bar ditto, on one Car, one halfpenny, not exceeding the price of a Car load.
────── Bundle of Nail Rod Iron, one halfpenny.
Rod Iron per Hundred weight, on one Car, one penny, not exceeding the price of a Car load.
Of every New Iron Pot, one halfpenny.
────── Bar of old Iron, one halfpenny.
────── Car load of Iron Mine, one penny.
────── Hundred of Horse-shoes, and Cart Clouts, three farthings.

Of every Hundred of Iron Shovels or Spades, three halfpence.
────── Car load of Iron pots, three pence.
────── Horse load ditto, two pence.
────── Hundred Trips and Brand Irons, one halfpenny.
────── Dozen of Griddles, one penny.
────── Car load of Nails, three pence.
────── Horse load of Nails, two pence.
────── Hundred weight ditto, on one Car, one penny, not exceeding the price of a Car load.
────── Hundred weight of wrought Iron, on one Car, one penny, not exceeding the price of a Car load.

K

────── Keeve, one penny.

L

────── Car load of Lead, three pence.
────── Lamb, one farthing.
────── Car load of dressed Leather, six pence.
────── Horse load ditto, three pence.
────── Leaden vessel, one penny.

M

────── Car load of Merchant's Goods not herein particularly specified, being the property of one person, three pence.
────── Hore load ditto, two pence.
────── Bundle ditto, or what a man carries under him, one penny.
────── Barrel of Malt, one farthing.
────── Mill Wheel, two pence.
────── Mill-stone, three pence.
────── Barrel of Meal, one halfpenny.

N

────── Car load of Nuts, three pence.
────── Horse load ditto, two pence.
────── Bag ditto, one halfpenny.

O

────── Hogshead of Oil, three pence.
────── Runlet ditto, on one Car, one penny, not exceeding the price of a Car load.
────── Barrel of Oil, two pence.
────── Car load of Oysters, two pence.
────── Horse load ditto, one penny.
────── Car load of Onions, three pence.
────── Horse load ditto, two pence.
────── Flasket ditto, on one Car, one halfpenny, not exceeding the price of a Car load.

P

────── Sack of Potatoes, one halfpenny.
────── Car load of Pewter, three pence.*
────── Horse load ditto, two pence.
────── Car load of Paper, three pence.
────── Horse lead ditto, two pence.
────── Car load of Plants, one halfpenny.
────── Barrel of White Peas, one farthing.
────── Barrel of Pitch or Tar, two pence.

APPENDIX, No. VIII.

R
Of every Car load of White Rods, two pence.
—— ditto Green, one penny.
—— Barrel of Rape-seed, three halfpence.
—— Horse load of Rabbits, two pence.
—— Dozen ditto, on one Car, one penny, not exceeding the price of a Car load.
—— Car load of Rushes, two pence.

S
—— Barrel of Salt, two pence.
—— Hundred weight ditto, three farthings.
—— Car load of Sheep Skins, three pence.
—— Horse load ditto, two pence.
—— Dozen ditto, on one Car, one penny, not exceeding the price of a Car load.
—— Horse Skin, one farthing.
—— Car load of Lamb Skins, three pence.
—— Horse load ditto, two pence.
—— Dozen ditto, on one Car, one farthing, not exceeding the price of a Car load.
—— Car load of Slink Lamb Skins, or Kid, two pence.
—— Horse load ditto, one penny.
—— Back load ditto, one halfpenny.
—— Dozen ditto, on one Car, one farthing, not exceeding the price of a Car load.
—— Car load of Calf Skins, three pence.
—— Horse load ditto, two pence.
—— Dozen ditto, on one Car, one penny, not exceeding the price of a Car load.
—— load of Barrel Staves, one penny.
—— load of Straw, one farthing.
—— Car load of Rabbit Skins, three pence.
—— Horse load ditto, two pence.
—— Man's Back load ditto, one penny.
—— Dozen ditto, on one Car, one halfpenny, not exceeding the price of a Car load.
—— Sheep, one farthing.
—— Dozen of Stockings, on one Car, one penny, not exceeding the price of a Car load.
—— load of Silver Mine, three pence.
—— load of Flag Stones, one penny.
—— load of Slates, one penny.
—— load of Marble Stones, two pence.
—— load of Grinding Stones, one penny.
—— Car load of Bazils or Pelts, three pence.
—— Horse load ditto, two pence.
—— Dozen ditto, on one Car, one farthing, not exceeding the price of a Car load.

T
—— Hogshead of Tobacco, three pence.
—— Horse load or Back ditto, two pence.
—— single Roll ditto, on one Car, one farthing, not exceeding the price of a Car load.
—— Hogshead of Tallow, three pence.
—— Barrel ditto, two pence,
—— Cake ditto, on one Car, one halfpenny, not exceeding the price of a Car load.

Of every load of made Timber Ware, two pence.
—— load of Timber, one penny.
—— load of Tazels, two pence.
—— Back load ditto, one penny.
—— Cart load of Turnips, Parsnips, and Carrots, one halfpenny.
—— Car load of Trees, two pence.
—— Horse load ditto, one penny.
—— Back load ditto, one halfpenny.
—— Timber Stutch or Chest, one penny.
—— load of Tin, one penny.

W
—— Hogshead of Wine, three pence.
—— Horse load ditto, two pence.
—— single Hamper ditto, two pence.
—— Dozen ditto, on one Car, one penny, not exceeding the price of a Car load.
—— Runlet of Wine, one penny.
—— Pack of Wool, three pence.
—— Horse load ditto, two pence.
—— Pocket ditto, on one Car, one penny, not exceeding the price of a Car load.
—— Car load of Wadd, three pence.
—— Hundred of Bees' Wax, three pence.
—— Car load of Worsted, three pence.
—— Horse load ditto, two pence.
—— Hundred of Yarn, one penny.

N. B. All Goods coming in for private Use, to be exempted from Custom.
Examined by
ALLEN and GREENE, Town-Clerks.

The Docket of Toll of every single Barrel of Grain, at the Gates belonging to the City of Dublin.

Wheat,	Oats,	Bere,	Malt,	Meal,
lb. oz.	lb. oz.	lb. oz.	lb. oz.	lb. oz.
3 10	2 4	2 1½	2 1	2 9

Barley,	Flour,	Rye, or Meslin,	Crush,
lb. oz.	lb. oz.	lb. oz.	lb. oz.
2 12	2 7	3 9	3 12

A Docket of the Petty Customs of the Markets.
Of every Car load of Fruit two pence.
—— High load of ditto, one penny.
—— Flasket of ditto, one halfpenny.
—— Butter standing per Week, two pence.
—— Root Standing, per Week, two pence.
—— Standing for Fowl, per Week, two pence.
—— Standing in Corn-Market, per Day, one penny.
—— Car load of Hay and Straw, at Smithfield, one halfpenny.

APPENDIX No. IX.

the Names of the Chief Magistrates of the City of Dublin under the different appellations of Provosts, Bailiffs, M and Sheriffs, from the second year of King Edward the Second, 1308, to 1816.

Mayors.	Bailiffs or Sheriffs.		Provosts or Mayors.	Bailiffs or Sheriffs.
ecer	Richard de St. Olave, John Stakebold	1363	Richard Highgreen	Maurice Young, Walter Cromp
ecer	Richard Lawless, Nicholas Clerk	1364	John Beake	Thomas Brown, John Passavant
ttingham	Richard de St. Olave. Hugh Silvester	1365	David Tyrell	William Herdman, John Grandsett
iwless	Nicholas Golding, T. Hunt	1366	David Tyrell	John Grandsett, Richard Chamberlain
iwless	Richard de St. Olave, Robert de St. Moenes	1367	Peter Woder	Thomas Brown, Richard Chamberlain
iwless	John de Castlenock, A. Phelipot	1368	John Wydon	Roger Beakford, John Beake
ttingham	Robert Woder, Robert Burnell	1369	John Passavant	Roger Beakford, John Hoyle
iwless	Robert Woder, Robert de Moenes	1370	John Passavant	William Herdman, Edward Berle
ttingham	Luke Brown, William le Marechal	1371	John Passavant	William Herdman, Edward Berle
ttingham	Robert Woder, Stephen de Mora	1372	John Wydon	John Field, Richard Chamberlain
ttingham	Robert Woder, Robert de Moenes	1373	John Wydon	John Field, Richard Chamberlain
Moenes	Luke Brown, William le Marechal	1374	Nicholas Serjeant	Robert Stackbold, Robert Piers
ttingham	Robert Woder, Stephen de Mora	1375	Edward Berle	Stephen Fleming, John Ellis
ttingham	Robert Woder, Robert de Cyton	1376	Robert Stakebold	Walter Passavant, William Bank
ant	John Crekes, Walter de Castlenock	1377	Nicholas Serjeant	Roger Folliagh, Robert Piers
once	Stephen de Mora, John de Moenes	1378	Nicholas Serjeant	Roger Folliagh, Robert Piers
ecer	William le Marechal, Robert Tanner	1379	John Wydon	William Bladon, Roger Kilmore
ant	William Walsh, Philip Dodd	1380	John Hull	William Tyrell, Roger Folhagh
nner	John de Moenes, Richard Woodfold	1381	Edmund Berle	Robert Burnell, Richard Bertrain
arechal	Richard Swerd, John Crekes	1382	Robert Burnell	John Bermingham, John Drake
nner	John de Moenes, Philip Cradock	1383	Robert Wakepont	Thomas Mereward, Roger Serjeant
ock-	Richard Swerd, Robert de Walton	1384	Edmund Berle	Thomas Cusack, Jeffry Callan
nce	John Crekes, John Serjeant	1385	Robert Stackbold	Nicholas Finglass, Richard Kerklus
es	William Walsh, John de Callon	1386	John Bermingham	Robert Piers, Richard Cravis
p.	John Crekes, Giles de Walderson	1387	John Passavant	Walfran Bran, Simon Long
yden	William de Winerton, Roger Grancourt	1388	Thomas Mereward	Thomas Cusack, William Wade
iyden	Kenelbrock Sherman, John de Callon	1389	Thomas Cusack	Richard Kercluis, Jeffry Gallan
es	Robert Honey, Roger Grancourt	1390	Richard Chambers	Jeffry Gallan, Jeffry Douwick
lock	Giles de Walderson, John Crekes	1391	Thomas Mereward	Thomas Dovewick, Ralph Ebb
es	John Crekes, Robert de Haughton	1392	Thomas Cusack	Ralph Ebb, Thomas Duncreet
nner	John Callon, Adam Lovestock	1393	Thomas Cusack	William Wade, Hugh White
Sherman	John Crekes, William Dancie	1394	Thomas Cusack	Richard Giffard, Jeffry Parker
k Sherman	William de Winerton, Roger Grancourt	1395	Thomas Cusack	Richard Giffard, Jeffry Parker
c Sherman	John Crekes, Walter de Castlenock	1396	Jeffry Gallan	Thomas Duncreef, John Philpot
ant	William Walsh, John Taylor	1397	Thomas Cusack	Jeffry Parker, Richard Clark
ant	William Walsh, John Taylor	1398	Nicholas Finglas	Richard Bacon, Richard Bove
ant	William Walsh, John Taylor	1399	Ralph Ebb	Richard Bove, Richard Taylor
ant	William Walsh, John Taylor	1400	Thomas Cusack	Richard Taylor, Walter Tyrell
ant	William Walsh, John Taylor	1401	John Drake	John Philpot, Walter Tyrell
up	William Walsh, Walter Lusk	1402	John Drake	Walter Tyrell, Simon Long
k Sherman	John Callon, John Deart	1403	John Drake	Walter Tyrell, Robert Gallery
ant	John Deart, John Beake	1404	John Drake	John Philpot, Walter Tyrell
	Robert Burnell, Richard Highgreen	1405	William Wade	Robert Gallery, Nicholas Woder
enes	John Deart, Peter Moynul	1406	Thomas Cusack	Richard Bove, Thomas Shortall
ovestock	John Callon, Peter Woder	1407	Thomas Cusack	Richard Bove, Thomas Shortall
erjeaut	Maurice Dundrean, David Tyrell	1408	Thomas Cusack	Richard Bove, Thomas Shortall
ant	Maurice Dundrean, T. Woodlock		Mayors.	
ant	Peter Barfet, William Wells	1409	Thomas Cusack	Richard Bove, Thomas Shortall
irnell	Thomas Woodlock, Thomas Brown	1410	Robert Galleon	John Walsh, William Heyford
et	Robert Walsh, John Wydon	1411	Robert Galleon	Richard Bove, John White
or	Thomas Woodlock, Roger Delwick	1412	Thomas Cusack	Stephen Taylor, Nicholas Fitz Eustace
et	Peter Moynul, John Passavant	1413	Luke Dowdall	Stephen Taylor, Nicholas Fitz Eustace
et	Roger Delwick, Thomas Brown	1414	Luke Dowdall	Stephen Taylor, Nicholas Fitz Eustace
ighgreen	David Tyrell, Thomas Woodlock	1415	Thomas Cusack	John White, Thomas Shortall
rnell	William Herdman, John Grandsett	1416	Thomas Cusack	John White, Thomas Shortall

APPENDIX, No. IX.

	Bailiffs or Sheriffs.		Mayors.	Bailiffs or Sheri
rs.	John Barrett, Thomas Shortall	1483	John West	Reynold Talbot, John Gayd
rell	Nicholas Fitz Eustace, Ralph Pembroke	1484	John West	Henry Talbot, Henry Mole
usack	John Barrett, Robert de Ireland	1485	John Serjeant	John Bourk, John Gaydon
usack	John Kilberry, Thomas Shortall	1486	Jenico Marks	John Bennett, Robert Blanc
rell	John Kilberry, Thomas Shortall	1487	Thomas Meilier	William English, Robert Boy
ıell	Stephen Taylor, Thomas Shortall	1488	William Tew	Thomas Birmingham, Patric
ıell	Ralph Pembroke, Robert de Ireland	1489	Richard Stanihurst	Robert Foster, Thomas Wes
usack	Ralph Pembroke, Robert de Ireland	1490	John Serjeant	Robert Lawless, William Br
te	John Kilberry, Thomas Shortall	1491	Thomas Bennett	Richard Tyrell, Thomas Ne
usack	John Kilberry, Thomas Shortall	1492	John Serjeant	John Blake, William Browne
ır Tyrell }		1493	John Savage	Nicholas Herbert, Henry La
lsh }	John Kilberry, Thomas Shortall	1494	Patrick Fitz-Leones	Thomas Philips, John Archb
ıh	John Barrett, Robert de Ireland	1495	Thomas Bermingham	William Cantrell, John Heyn
ıortall	Thomas Bennett, Thomas Ashe	1496	John Gaydon	John Beckett, Edward Long
hortall	Thomas Bennett, Thomas Ashe	1497	Thomas Collier	Thomas Dugan, Bartholome
usack	Thomas Bennett, Robert Chambers	1498	Regnold Talbot	Richard Humphrys, Robert
te	John Hadsor, John Bryan	1499	James Barby	William Fleming, John Oulo
te	John Hadsor, John Bryan	1500	Robert Forster	Patrick Boys, John Stanton
ior	Nicholas Woder, Robert de Ireland	1501	Hugh Talbot	William Hodgson, Richard
oder	Philip Bryan, Thomas Newberry	1502	Richard Tyrell	Richard Moyer, Richard Da
ıbroke	James Dowdall, Richard Willett	1503	John Blake	John Loughtan, John Good
rry	Richard Willet, Robert Stafford	1504	Thomas Newman	Walter Peppard, Maurice Co
ımbers	John Bryan, Nicholas Clark	1505	Nicholas Herbert	John Blanchfield, Patrick H
wberry	Nicholas Clark, John Bennett	1506	William English	William Talbot, Nicholas Ro
ıder	Robert de Ireland, John Bryan	1507	William Cantrel	John Rochford, Patrick Fie
Robert	John Fitz-Robert, David Row	1508	Thomas Philips	Walter Eustace, Henry Gore
oder	John Bryan, John de Veer	1509	William Talbot	Nicholas Quaytrot, James H
broke	Thomas Walsh, Robert Stafford	1510	Nicholas Roach	John Fitz-Simons, Robert Fr
oder	John Walsh, William Curragh	1511	Thomas Birmingham	Christopher Usher, Thomas
oder	Philip Bellews, John Tankard	1512	Walter Eustace	John Sheriff, Stephen Ware
oder	John Walsh, William Curragh	1513	Walter Peppard	Nicholas Hancock, James Re
ıwberry	Robert Wade, Thomas Savage	1514	William Hodgison	Richard Talbot, James Halte
oder, Jun.	Thomas Savage, John Bateman	1515	John Rochford	William Newman, Robert Co
ett	Walter Donagh, William Cramp	1516	Christopher Usher	John Sarsfield, Giles River
: Burnell	John Bateman, John Tankard	1517	Patrick Field	Walter Kelly, Hugh Nugent
ewberry	Walter Donagh, William Cramp	1518	John Loughan	Henry Gaydon, William Kell
ewberry	Richard Fitz-Eustace, John Tankard	1519	Patrick Boys	Nicholas Gaydon, Patrick Fi
ıs Woder	Richard Fitz-Eustace, John Tankard	1520	Thomas Tue	Robert Shillingford, Michael
: Burnell	James Blakney, William Chamberlain	1521	Nicholas Herbert	Arlanton Usher, Thomas Bar
ew	John White, William Bryan	1522	John Fitz-Simons	John Bayley, James Browne
alsh	John Tankard, Thomas Savage	1523	Nicholas Quaytrot	Bartholomew Blanch, John
ett	John Tankard, Thomas Savage	1524	Nicholas Hancock	Walter Fitz-Simons, William
:wberry	Thomas Savage, Thomas Walton	1525	Richard Talbot	John Shelton, Simon Gaydon
Burnell	Thomas Savage, John Heigham	1526	Walter Eustace	Alexander Beswick, Richard
alsh	Thomas Boys, Simon Fitz-Rery	1527	William Newman	James Fitz-Simons, Nicholas
Burnell	Arnold Usher, William Purcell	1528	Arlantor Usher	Francis Herbert, John Squire
:wberry	John Tankard, Thomas Barby	1529	Walter Kelly	Thomas Stephens, Nicholas
ewberry	John Shanagh, Nicholas Burk	1530	Thomas Barby	Nicholas Stanihurst, Nicholas
s Newberry	Nicholas Cook, John Bowland	1531	John Sarsfield	William Tyrell, William Qua
-Rery	Nicholas Cook, John Bowland,	1532	Nicholas Gaydon	Simon Lutterell, Brandom Fc
amp	Nicholas Cook, John Bowland	1533	Walter Fitz Simons	Walter Forster, John Peppar
er	John Bowland, John Walsh	1534	Robert Shillingford	Henry Plunkett, William Wh
alton	John Bowland, John Walsh	1535	Thomas Stephens	John Money, Christopher Co
er	Thomas Fitz-Simons, John Bellew	1536	John Shelton	Thady Duffe, Patrick Burges
alton	Richard Fitz Simons, John Bellew	1537	John Squire	Michael Pentany, Robert Cus
-Rery	Richard Parker, John Dancie	1538	Sir James Fitz-Simons	Richard Berford, Mathew Go
	Thomas Molygan, John West	1539	Nicholas Bennett	James Hancock, Robert Tayl
w	William Donaugh, Patrick Fitz-Leones	1540	Walter Tyrrell	Thomas Fyan, Thomas Spenfi
urk	John Rowland, Walter Pierse	1541	Nicholas Humphrys	Richard Fyan, Bartholomew
tz-Simons	Richard Stanihurst, William Tue	1542	Nicholas Stanihurst	Richard Fitz-Simons, Barnab
tz-Simons	John Savage, Mathew Fowler	1543	David Sutton	Richard Quaytrott, Thomas
tz-Leones	Thomas Collier, Thomas Herbert	1544	William Forster	James Segrave, John Ellis
	Jenico Marks, Richard Arland	1545	Sir Francis Herbert	John Callener, John Worral
	William Cramp, Thomas Meilier	1546	Henry Plunkett	Oliver Stephens, Nicholas Pen
ɔvewick	John Serjeant, William Whitaker			Sheriffs.
olygan	John Russell, James Barby	1547	Thady Duffy	John Ryan, Thomas Comin *
tz-Leones	Thomas Meilier, Richard Barby	1548	James Hancock	Edmond Brown, Robert Goldi

* Mr. Harris says, Thomas Fining, and Sir James Ware's list calls him Thomas Fleming.

APPENDIX, No. IX.

ors.	Sheriffs.		Mayors.	Sheriffs.
Fyan	Charles Sedgrave, John Nangle	1614	Richard Browne / John Goodwyn	Patrick Fox, Robert Bennett
ıey	Patrick Fitz-Simons, Thomas Fitz-Simons			
entony	Richard Barnwell, William Hancock	1615	Richard Browne / John Dows	Simon Barnwall, George Springh
ısack	Walter England, Richard Drake			
ew Ball	Walter Rochford, Robert Usher	1616	John Benes / George Dew	Nicholas Kelly, Daniel Birne
rsfield	William Sarsfield, Robert Jones			
ogers	Patrick Buckley, Patrick Giggen	1617	Sir James Carroll	William Bishop, Robert Linaker
oner	John Usher, Edward Peppard	1618	John Long	Thomas Russel, Henry Cheshire
ıfield	John Dempsey, Walter Cusack	1619	Richard Forster	John Lock, Robert Teyzar
olding	Michael Fitz-Simons, Nicholas Fitz-Simons	1620	Richard Brown	Edward Jones, William Allen
er Sedgrave	Richard Gattrim, Edward Barren	1621	Edward Ball	Christopher Forster, Christopher
itz-Simons	Patrick Gough, James Bellew	1622	Richard Wigget	Thomas White, Thomas Evans
iher	Henry Brown, Michael Tyrrell	1623	Sir Thady Duffe	Christopher Wolverston, George
leming	Edmond Barron, Walter Clinton	1624	Sir William Bishop	Sir Walter Dungan, William Wes
ısack	John Fitz-Simons, John Lutterell	1625	Sir James Carroll	Adam Goodman, Nicholas Sedgr
yan	James Dortas, Patrick Dowdall	1626	Thomas Evans	Robert Arthur, Francis Dowde
itz-Simons	Christopher Fegan, John White	1627	Edward Jones	Michael Brown, Thomas Sheltor
n Sarsfield	John Gaydon, John Gough	1628	Robert Bennett	James Bellew, William Baggott
Simons	Giles Allen, John Lutterell	1629	Sir Christopher Forster	Sanky Silliard, John Fleming
ıe	Nicholas Duffy, Richard Rowncell	1630	Thomas Evans	William Tyrrell, John Stanley
sack	William Fitz-Simons, John Lenan	1631	George Jones	David Begg, Walter Kenedy
wn	Nicholas Ball, John Grow	1632	Robert Bennett	Thomas Wakefield, Charles Bric
owdall	Andrew Lutterell, Thomas Doyne	1633	Robert Dixon	Thomas Wakefield, Christopher
lew	Walter Ball, Thomas Cosgrave	1634	Sir James Carroll	Edward Brangham, John Gibsor
er Fegan	John Coyne, Patrick Brown	1635	Christopher Forster	John Carberry, Thomas Ormsby
r	Henry Cusack, Thomas Cane	1636	Sir Christopher Forster	Thomas Arthur, William Smith
ıugh	Richard Fegan, William Barnwall	1637	James Watson	Philip Watson, William Bladon
ҫh	Edward White, Edmond Devinish	1638	Sir Christopher Forster	Sir Robert Forth, Andrew Clark
	Walter Sedgrave, James Barry	1639	Charles Forster	Edward Lock, Richard Barnewel
owncell	John Forster, William Pigot	1640	Thomas Wakefield	John Bamber, Abraham Riccasis
uffe	Henry Shelton, Thomas Smith	1641	Thomas Wakefield	Laurence Allen, John Woodcock
l	John Durning, James Malone	1642	William Smith	John Pugh, Thomas Pemberton
on	John Malone, Philip Couran	1643	William Smith	John Miller, Peter Flacker
all	Robert Stephens. Edward Thomas	1644	William Smith	John Brice, Morice Pugh
l	John Barren, William Brown	1645	William Smith	Edward Hughes, John Collins
sgrave	John Dungan, Laurence White	1646	William Smith	Robert Caddell, Robert Deey
got	John Gerald, James Ryan	1647	William Bladden	Walter Springham, Thomas Hill
ownsell	Francis Taylor, Edmond Conran	1648	John Pugh	Peter van Hoven, Robert Miles
uffe	Nicholas Weston, Michael Chamberlain	1649	Thomas Pemberton / Sankey Silliard	Thomas Waterhouse, Richard T
wn	John Tyrell, James Bellew			
on	Mathew Hancock, Thomas Brown	1650	Rapheal Hunt	George Gilbert, Richard Cook
evinish	Walter Galtrim, Nicholas Burren	1651	Richard Tigh for D. Wybrant	Ridgly Hatfield, John Brown
ııth	George Kenedy, John Miles			
ıan	John Usher, Thomas Fleming	1652	Daniel Hutchinson / Richard Tigh	John Cranwell, William Cliff
s	Richard Ash, John Murfey			
rald	William Gough, Ralph Sankey	1653	John Preston	Thomas Clarke, Tobias Cremens
lor	John Elliott, John Marchal	1654	Thomas Cook	William Cox, John Desmynieres
amberlain	John Shelton, Alexander Palles	1655	Richard Tigh	Daniel Bellingham, Richard Palf
eston	Robert Panting, John Goodwin	1656	Ridgely Hatfield	Rice Philips, Henry Bollardt
w	John Brice, Edward Purcell	1657	Thomas Waterhouse	John Forrest, John Totty
ıng	John Brice, Edward Purcell	1658	Peter Wybrants	Robert Arundell, John Eastwood
rren	John Cusack, John Arthur	1659	John Deey	John Price, Hugh Price
ndcock	Robert Kenedy, William Turner	1660	Sir Hu. Adrianverner	Peter Ward, Thomas Jones
ırrell	Nicholas Stephens, Peter Dermot	1661	Sir George Gilbert	William Whitsed, George Hewlet
ough		1662	John Crauwell	Christopher Bennett, Elias Best
t	James Tyrrell, Thomas Carroll	1663	William Smith	Thomas Kirkham, William Brook
on		1664	William Smith	Joshua Allen, Francis Brewster
ll	Edmond Malone, Richard Berry		Lord Mayors.	
	John Benes, Richard Brown	1665	Sir Daniel Bellingham	Charles Lovett, John Quelsh
r	John Laney, Nicholas Purcell	1666	John Desmynieres	Philip Castleton, Joseph Dobson
urren	Thomas Bromgold, James Bee	1667	Mark Quin	Mathew French, Giles Mee
lunket		1668	John Forrest	William Cressingham, John Sinig
k	Thomas Allen, Robert Eustace	1969	Lewis Desmynieres	William Story, Richard Ward
	Thomas Long, William Preston	1670	Enoch Reader	Richard Honway, Isaac John
ry	Edward Hall, Richard Eustace	1671	Sir John Totty	Henry Reynolds, Nathaniel Philp
hop	William Chalkret, Richard Wigget	1672	Robert Deey	Thomas Clinton, John Castleton
arroll	Edmond Cullen, John Francton	1673	Sir Joshua Allen	Abel Ram, George Blackhall
orster for / ſalone	Thady Duffy, William Taylor	1674	Sir Francis Brewster	Humphry Jervis, William Sands
		1675	William Smith	John Knox, Walter Motley

APPENDIX, No. IX.

	Sheriffs.		Lord Mayors.	Sheriffs.
ayors.				
er Lovett	William Watt, Benjamin Leadbeater		⎧ Sir Richard Grattan, ⎫	
:h	James Collingham, William Billington	1735	⎨ 9 months. ⎬	Robert King, John Twigg
rd	William Cooke, Thomas Tennant		⎩ George Forbes, 3 ⎭	
wood	Thomas Taylor, Robert Bridges		ditto.	
ther	John Coyne, Samuel Walton	1736	James Somervell	Richard White, Edward Hun
hry Jervis	John Fletcher, Edward Hains	1737	William Walker	Charles Rossell, Robert Ross
hry Jervis	William Watt, Edward Hains	1738	John Macarrell	Thomas Baker, George Ript
3est	George Kenedy, Michael Mitchell	1739	Daniel Falkiner	J. Bern. Hoffshleger, John A
lam	Charles Thompson, Thomas Quin	1740	Sir Samuel Cook	James Dunn, Benjamin Hunt
Knox	Richard French, Edward Rose	1741	William Aldrich	W. Grattan, Q. Somervell, T
Castleton	James Howiston, Isaac Holroyd	1742	Gilbert King	George Fraser, John Bradsh
as Hacket	Thomas Keiron, Edmond Kelly	1743	⎧ David Tew ⎫	George Swettenham, Thom
el Creagh	Christopher Pales, John Coyne		⎩ William Aldrich ⎭	
Dermot, 9 ⎫		1744	John Walker	Daniel Walker, Patrick Ewir
s. ⎬	Ignatius Brown, John Moore	1745	Daniel Cooke	John Espinase, Andrew Mur
Motley, 3 ⎭	Anthony Piercy, Mark Rainsford	1746	⎧ Richard White ⎫	William Cooke, Thomas Tay
			⎩ William Walker ⎭	
ington	Mark Rainsford, Edward Loyd	1747	Sir George Ripton	John Hornby, John Cooke
el Mitchell	Thomas Bell, Henry Stephens	1748	Robert Ross	Matthew Weld, Hans Baihe
el Mitchell	Francis Stoyte, William Gibbons	1749	⎧ John Adamson ⎫	Thomas Mead, Robert Dono
Logerson	John Page, Robert Twigg		⎩ Sir Samuel Cooke ⎭	
lackhall	Benjamin Burton, Thomas Denham	1750	Thomas Taylor	George Reynolds, Thomas
Vatts	Andrew Brice, William Stowell	1751	John Cooke	James Taylor, John Tew
m Billington	Robert Constantine, Nathaniel Whitwell	1752	Sir Charles Burton	John Forbes, Patrick Hamil
mew Van ⎫	William Fownes, John Pearson	1753	Andrew Murray	Edmond Huband, H. Wray,
gh ⎭		1754	Hans Bailie	Philip Crampton, Timothy
uin	Robert Mason, Samuel Cook	1755	Percival Hunt	Arthur Lamprey, Charles R
' Piercy	Charles Forrest, James Barlow	1756	John Forbes	Peter Barré, Charles Nobiles
Ransford	John Eccles, Ralph Gore	1757	Thomas Mead	Michael Sweeney, William F
alton	John Stoyte, Thomas Bolton	1758	Philip Crampton	Benjamin Geale, James Tay
ell	Thomas Pleasants, David Cossart	1759	John Tew	Benjamin Barton, Edward S
e	John Hendrick, William French	1760	Sir Patrick Hamilton	Francis Fetherston, George
s Stoyte	Thomas Wilkinson, Robert Cheatham	1761	Sir Timothy Allen	Mathew Bailie, Thomas Blac
ibbons	Anthony Barkey, Michael Leeds	1762	Charles Rossell	John Read, Joseph Hall
Burton	John Godly, William Quail	1763	William Forbes	William Brien, Francis Book
rson	M. Pearson, R. Hendrick, W. Dixon	1764	Benjamin Geale	Henry Hart, Robert Montgo
n Fownes	Thomas Kirkwood, Thomas Curtis	1765	James Taylor	William Rutledge, Richard
Forrest, 6 ⎫		1766	Edward Sankey	William Lightburne, Thoma
s. ⎬	Joshua Kane, Nathaniel Shaw	1767	Francis Featherstone	P. Boyde, H. Bevan
ge, 6 ditto. ⎭		1768	Benjamin Barton	William Dunn, Henry Willia
Eccles ⎫	Michael Sampson, William Dobson	1769	Sir T. Blackhall	Kilner Sweetman, An. King
re ⎬	Humphry French, Richard Blair	1770	George Reynolds	Blen. Grove, Ant. Porrier
l Cooke ⎭	Thomas Bradshaw, Edward Surdeville	1771	⎧ F. Booker ⎫	James Hamilton, James Hor
			⎩ W. Forbes ⎭	
Barlow	Peter Verdoen, William Aldrich	1772	Richard French	James Shiels, James Jones
te	John Porter, John Tisdall	1773	Willoughby Lightburne	Nat. Warren, John Tucker
olton	William Empsom, David King	1774	Henry Hart	John Wilson, Thomas Truel
Barkey	John Reyson, Vincent Kidder	1775	T. Emerson	Fielding Ould, Geo. Alcock,
uail	Percival Hunt, Charles Hendrick	1776	Henry Bevan	John Rose, William Alexanc
Vilkinson	William Milton, Daniel Falkiner	1777	William Dunn	Henry Howison, Henry Gor
orbes	James Somerville, Nathaniel Kane	1778	S. A. King	William Worthington, Rich
urtis	Nathaniel Pearson, Joseph Nuttall	1779	James Hamilton	William James, John Exsha
ickson	John Macarrell, Robert Nesbitt	1780	Kil. Sweetenham	P. Bride, Thomas Andrews
er	Gilbert King, Henry Borrowes	1781	John Darragh	James Campbell, David Dick
sin	Ralph Blundell, George Curtis	1782	Nathaniel Warren	John Carlton, Samuel Read
ine	William Walker, Casp. White	1783	Thomas Green	Alexander Kirkpatrick, Ben
mpron	Philip Pearson, Thomas How	1784	James Horan	Caleb Jenkin, Ambrose Leet
a Whitewell	Henry Daniell, Richard Grattan	1785	James Shiel	John Sankey, Hugh Trevor
urrowes, 9 ⎫		1786	George Alcock	William Thompson, Thomas
s. ⎬	John Holliday, Benjamin Archer	1787	William Alexander	William Humfrey, Brent. Ne
ge, 3 ditto. ⎭		1788	John Rose	Thomas Tweedy, Jeremiah
Verdoen	David Tew, John Sterne	1789	John Exshaw	Charles Thorpe, James Vanc
l Pearson	Samuel Cooke, Eliphal Dobson	1790	Henry Howison	Joseph Dickinson, James W
uttall	George Tucker, Edward Dudgeon	1791	Henry Gore Sankey	Benjamin Gault, John Nortc
French	Daniel Cooke, Henry Hart	1792	John Carlton	Henry Hutton, Jacob Poole
How	William Woodworth, Charles Burton	1793	William James	Meredith Jenkin, John Giffa
l Kane	John Walker, Thomas Cooke	1794	Richard Moncrieffe	Robert Powell, Richard Ma

APPENDIX, No. IX.

d Mayors.	Sheriffs.	Lord Mayors.	Sheriffs.
ım Worthington	William Stamer, Humphry Minchin	1808 Frederick Darley	George Sutton, John George
el Reed	William Lindsay, Joseph Pemberton	1809 Sir Wm. Stamer, Bart.	Sir Edward Stanley, Kt. Sir J
as Fleming	Jonas Pasley, William Henry Archer	1810 Nathaniel Hone	Matthew West, Brent Neville
as Andrews	Frederick Darley, Nathaniel Hone	1811 William Henry Archer	Robert Harty, John Kingsto
ı Sutton	} Thomas Kinsley, John Cash	1812 Abraham Bradley King	George Studdart, Lewis Mor
ı Exshaw		1813 John Cash	George Warner, John West
es Thorp	Francis Fox, John Ferns	⎧ John Claudius Be- ⎫	
.rd Manders	Bradley King, Nathaniel Craven	⎪ resford resigned, ⎪	
Poole	Drury Jones, George Walsh	1814⎨ and John Smith ⎬	Richard Smith, John Plunke
ɼ Hutton	Joshua Pounder, Mount. John Hay	⎪ Fleming elected ⎪	
lith Jenkin	Mark Bloxham, George Thorp	⎩ in his stead ⎭	
s Vance	James Blacker, John Tudor	1815 Robert Shaw	Samuel Tyndall, Charles P. A
h Pemberton	Isaac Manders, Edmund Nugent	1816 Mark Bloxham	William Dixon, John Read
Trevor	Alexander Montgomery, John Alley	1817 John Alley	George Wheeler, William Le

APPENDIX, No. X.

CANAL COMPANIES.

These afford another strong proof that Ireland is not qualified to carry on great national works by private companies. In England, it has succeeded: In France, these works are executed by the Government. Now as the circumstances of Ireland, are nearer to those of France, than of England, the mode of executing national works, should assimilate to the peculiar circumstances of the country, and especially of the national character. In the infancy of the introduction of canals into use in England, it is probable, they met with those difficulties inseparable from a new attempt; but after the accumulation of wealth by trade, and manufactures, established for centuries, canals became secure servants to national wealth, and not precursors of trade and manufactures, as in Ireland. The experience of ages has qualified English financiers in private life, to manage the concerns of a company in a national work; and the English character of prudence, thrift, and regularity, so opposite to the Irish, sanguine, venturous, and extravagant in pecuniary affairs, would alone draw a distinction between these two countries in the mode of conducting public works.

These remarks are illustrated by the immense impost of county cess in Ireland, from the plausible system which vests this great power of taxation in the grand juries, who, at their pleasure, can make roads, bridges, &c. more ornamental to their respective demesnes, than useful to the public.

It is not for want of public Boards, that the national works are confided to private committees; no city has more of them; there is a Board of Works and a Board of Inland Navigation; but the public works require, along with a rich treasury, talents of the most experienced excellence. Ireland presents to canal undertakers, all the encouragement a fertile soil can give; but it is peculiar to Ireland, that a premium of no less than exemption from tythe, is given to the grazier; and thus vast tracts, which should be covered with waving harvests, and inhabited by a busy population of industrious peasantry, are to be seen without a human creature. The gates are shut on the herds of lean cattle in May, and are opened to take them out fat for the market in November: thus one proprietor, with his herds, easily occupies thousands of acres; and if a few famished labourers established a hamlet, they must make up for their want of work by theft, or

lxviii   APPENDIX, No. X.

see their families perishing with cold and hunger. If the grazier undertook tillage, although the rector instead of a tenth, may only demand the twentieth of the value, this proportion being made off the gross produce, is really at least a sixth part of the net produce; and sometimes, where rent is high, it amounts to more than a third part; the land in tillage is therefore laid down in grass, except when the exorbitant price of corn over balances the tythe; and as yet it has not obtained to employ cattle-boats on the canal, although two or three attempts were made; cattle being found in better health making easy journeys, than shut up with unusual fodder in a canal boat.

The difficulty of paying interest on the stock and loan, drives the directors to levy tolls as high as possible; and this operates to make the canals but little frequented: hence potatoes by the canal, are undersold by potatoes brought in coasting vessels, or on cars from the neighbourhood of the city. Hay is carried on those barbarous cars which are so small as to contain only a load of 4 cwt. and yet this conveyance successfully withstands the conveyance of hay by canal boats; there is a want of system, of safety-stores and markets, and of punctuality, which time and experience may produce in the canal conveyance, to give it the preference of land carriage. The canal seems eminently calculated for the conveyance of turf; yet the price of carriage is so high, that a quantity which costs one shilling in the bog, is, after the carriage of twenty or thirty miles in a canal boat to the metropolis, sold for six shillings; and there is no central turf market, to save the carriage of turf on cars, a mile or two from the canal harbour in the outlets of the City, to the house of the consumer, which adds 25 per cent. to the cost. The late survey of the bogs of Ireland may lead to produce cheaper turf; the chief expence is in draining the turf bank, preparatory to cutting it; and this drain, formed in the fluctuating spongeous substance of the bog, fills up with the dissolved matter of turf in winter, so that the cost of temporary draining for a series of years would have compleated a permanent drain in the substratum, had the levels been known. The levels are now ascertained, and printed by order of the House of Commons, and a scale is adapted of so many feet above or below the base of Nelson's Pillar, Sackville-street, Dublin, which points out the height of the surface of the bog above the level of the sea, the depth to the substratum, and its variations; but as these surveys could not originate at individual expense, neither can individuals apply them to use; the Government alone can follow it up, by making small canals in the substratum of bogs to drain off the water; and however practicable the production of grass and corn, from such reclaimed grounds in length of time; an invaluable advantage will be derived much sooner, by the retiring waters leaving the turf banks dry.—This fuel will then become so cheap as to add much to the tolls of the inland navigation.—The collieries and iron-works on the Royal Canal have not fulfilled expectation; their produce is undersold by Cumberland coal and foreign iron.

Since the failure of the Company, the canal is under the direction of the Government Board of Inland Navigation; the tolls have been reduced, and the income is at present about 15,000*l*. per year. The particulars of the dissolution of the Company and the state of the funds are as follow:—It was stipulated in the charter of 1789, that the grant of 66,000*l*. from Parliament was to be added to 134,000*l*. subscription of the Company of undertakers, and a power given them, to encrease that capital stock of 200,000*l*. by any further sum not exceeding 300,000*l*. with several other regulations for the obtaining and disposing of the said grant and stock.

In 1796 the whole of the capital stock and sums then borrowed were expended on a line of 15 miles from Dublin to Kilcock! In 1797 the Company received 25,000*l*. from Government, on condition of completing their line to Thomas-town, which is 33 miles; and in 1801 the Company

APPENDIX, No. X. lxix

contracted to reduce their tolls, and received 95,866*l*. part of a sum granted by Parliament to the disposal of the Board of Inland Navigation.

By an act of Parliament passed in 1813,* commissioners were appointed to investigate all improper practices in the execution of the powers given to the Royal Canal Company, and to ascertain how far the stok-holders were individually implicated in the said alleged irregularities. These commissioners have published two reports, in which it appears that the conditions of the charter made in 1789 have been broken; and that some of the directors who were most concerned, had notwithstanding, appeared to have acted with pure motives for the eventual good of the undertaking, but which unfortunately ended in its failure. The commissioners suggest for the formation of a new company that the old *stock-holders*, who are innocent sufferers, should be allowed shares in proportion to their claims, without giving priority to the *loan-holders*. Before the dissolution of the Company the loan-holders had the priority, and if on its failure, they had taken upon them to complete the canal, and succeeded, their priority would have been established; but as the canal must now be completed at the public expense, all those who have contributed to the undertaking, whether for stock or loan, are upon an equality for an equitable arrangement; provided they did not actively or passively partake in the mismanagement: every stock holder of £300. share had a right to vote: if he did not exercise this right, knowing the extent of the chartered powers of the Company, by opposing the violation of them, he has failed in duty to the *loan-holder*, who had no such privilege; and if the stockholder chose to neglect the care of his own stock, it does not excuse him for neglecting the care of the loan, confided to him in trust for others. The lender is, therefore, on a par only with those stock holders who were excluded from the management, or from electing the managers; for the act of the directors becomes the act of those who elected them; and those who neglected to attend the election, are equally guilty for not opposing the appointment. At the same time it must be allowed, that the appointed meetings of the Company could not conveniently be attended by all the Company, and that the minority who disapproved, are blameless of those acts which they could not prevent.

The stock debentures issued were 200,000*l*. in 1795, 30,000*l*. in 1797, and 70,000*l*. in 1799; of this 300,000*l*. total stock issued, the amount proved to have been purchased or subscribed is 265,535*l*., and the total price paid for same by the present holders (about 500 persons) is 130,975*l*., on which the present proprietors received interest, dividend, or annuity, 16,994*l*. The loanholders, about 1200 persons, have proved a debt in 4 per cents., 27,900*l*. for which they paid 19,725*l*., and in 6 per cents, 783,850*l*. for which they paid 749,002*l*. Those who purchased under par, it was supposed, would only be allowed shares on what they paid.

Abstract of the TOTAL EXPENDITURE *on the Royal Canal.*

	£.
The grants of Parliament to the Royal Canal,	186,866
The amount of Stock really cost the present proprietors,	130,975
The Loan debt really cost the present creditors,	768,727
	1,086,568

This sum total is exclusive of the sum lost by individuals who sold their shares under first cost. But there is an unascertained deduction to be made from this sum where the first cost was lower than the payments made by the present creditors. Great sums were gained at different

* 53 Geo. III. p. 101.

APPENDIX, No. X.

periods of public delusion, by those who sold out when the funds were artificially raised to a price far above the first cost; in this class of purchasers, are many of the present creditors, the amount of whose debts, as claimed, was not altogether expended on the canal, but was partly realized by successful speculators in the funds.

At the time the Royal Canal Company stopped payment the canal had been completed to Coolnahay, about 6 miles from Mullingar, on the summit level. Since that period Government have finished, at their own expence, the canal from Coolnahay to Tarmonbury on the Shannon, about 24 miles, in the middle of the summer of 1817. The revenue of the canal from Dublin to Coolnahay has been suffered to accumulate in addition to a sum of 16,000l. which was in hands, and given over to the commissioners of Government in 1813 by the then directors.

	£.	s.	d.
The Royal Canal Company's Account, from 1790 to 1810 inclusive, states the amount expended on Works, including purchase of Land and Mills,	763,617	11	3
Ditto on Sundries, Interest, &c. Incidents, Coaches, Boats,	444,415	5	5
And the *exceeding* of the Permanent Expenditure Establishment, Interest, and Annuity, over the Permanent Revenue in these ten years,	355,198	17	7
The total of the Dividend, Interest, Annuity, Expenditure, and Establishment, for ten years,	1,373,635	12	10
Total of the annual debts to 1810,	842,550	0	0
Loss on the 300,000l. stock,	66,795	1	5
Loss on 128,366l. 7s. 10d. parliamentary grants,	7,377	4	9
Loss on 842,551l. loan both 4 and 6 per cents,	97,086	3	1
Capital to be raised, Grants, Loans, Debentures issued, and Income,	137,351	15	8
Money actually raised,	1,208,032	16	8

The failure of the Grand Canal Company in fulfilling their engagements to their creditors, has not extended so far as that of the Royal Canal; and the Legislature has not interfered to take the management of their affairs out of their own hands. The loan-holders assembled in September, 1817, and resolved to accept a reduced interest, and the Company proceed with the management of their affairs, in the hope of paying off the loan-debt, and then making dividends of their revenue among the stock-holders. When the payment of their interest was suspended in 1816, they published an account of the state of their affairs, of which the following Abstract is subjoined from the official document.

An Abstract of all Sums received and paid by the Grand Canal Company for six years and half, commenced 28th February, 1810, *and ended* 31*st August,* 1816.

	£.	s.	d.
Permanent Revenues arising from Rents, per centage, on Pipe-water Tax, Tolls, Passage Boats, and Docks, for six years and half ended 31st August, 1816, - -	465800	7	10
Interest on 30,000*l.* vested in Government Stock for same period, at 5 per cent. - -	9750	0	0
Cash, Balance in the hands of the Treasurer, 28th February, 1810,	1211	3	3½
37,807*l.* 14*s.* 9*d* Government Stock, 3½ per cent. on hands 28th February, 1810, which stood the Company in - - -	24862	17	10½
8,800*l.* Grand Canal Loan Debentures, 6 per cents, which were sold in half year ended 31st August, 1810, for - -	8848	15	0
Dividends on Grand Canal Stock purchased for the Company, - -	636	0	0
Deposits on Grand Canal Stock, -	65	0	0
Interest on Government Stock, in which part of the Company's Funds have been from time to time invested, - - -	10630	13	6½
Balance received from the Directors General for completing the River Shannon Navigation, -	11916	10	7½
Profit on Sales of Government Stock,	2009	14	3
Subscription towards Grand Canal Stock in 1810, -	141598	11	7
Subscription towards Grand Canal Stock in 1814, - -	19159	9	7
Profits produced within these six and half years by the Collieries, exclusive of the Stock of Coal on hand, 31st August, 1816, -	27864	3	2
Old Boats, Stores, Furniture of Hotels, Oak, and Stones sold, -	835	6	5
Received from sundry Persons, on account of old Debts and Advances, &c. prior to 28th February, 1810,	2630	10	7½
Received from Government, on account of the grants from Parliament for liquidating the Company's debt,	121000	0	0
Balance due to the Bank of Ireland, 31st August, 1816, - -	15715	10	0
	864534	13	10

	£.	s.	d.
Permanent Expenditure and Establishment for six years and half, ended 31st August, 1816, -	167455	7	11
Interest on the Company's Debt for same period, - -	410906	8	7
Arrear of Interest due prior to 28th February, 1810, and paid subsequent thereto, - -	5470	14	11
Dividend paid on the Company's Stock, subsequent to the 28th February, 1810, - -	72897	15	0
New and casual Works within the six years and a half, - -	18456	15	4½
Grand Canal Note paid, - -	5	13	9
12,700*l.* Grand Canal Stock purchased for the Company, pursuant to their Resolution of the 22d January, 1810, - -	10475	1	3
Advances to sundry persons, -	1690	0	4½
*155,500*l.* Grand Canal 6 per cent. Debentures paid off and purchased, and Interest thereon to the period of payment, - -	156064	0	11
† 34,474*l.* 4*s.* 10*d.* Government Stock, 3½ per cent. on hands 31st August, 1816, which being purchased at low rates, and several other Sums in Government Stock having been sold at a profit, makes this stand the Company in only,	19373	10	3
Cash, Balance in the hands of the Treasurer, 31st August, 1816, -	1738	5	6
	864534	13	10

N. B.

* 155,000*l.* of the Grand Canal 6 per cent. Debentures have been paid off, but 500*l.* thereof was not called for by the Treasurer, until after the 31st August, 1816.

† This 34,474*l.* 4*s.* 10*d.* would now sell for 78*l.* per cent. and therefore in the half-yearly Account is stated as worth 26,889*l.* 18*s.* 3*d.*

GRAND CANAL.—*Account of* EXPENDITURE *and* REVENUES, *for six months, ending August* 31, 1816; *together with the amount of Interest on Loan, which became due and payable within said half year.*

Dr.	£.	s.	d.
To Interest on 249,000*l.* six months, due March 25, 1816, at 2 per cent.	4980	0	0
Ditto 17,100*l.* ditto, at 2½ per cent.	427	10	0
Ditto 745,650*l.* ditto, at 3 per cent.	22369	10	0
To Tolls, - drawbacks, -	339	3	2
To Passage Boats, - -	3855	2	2½
Repairs of Passage Boats, -	221	7	1
Permanent Expenditure and Establishment: General Harbour Returns, -	732	15	9
Charges General, - -	1229	17	8
Charges on Docks and Circular Road Line, - -	217	18	0½
Salaries, - - -	1975	4	8
Stationary, - - -	174	4	9
Rents payable, - -	272	7	11½
Repairs of Locks, - -	203	17	10½
Repairs of Old Line, - -	393	3	11
Repairs of Shannon Line, -	442	5	10½
Turnpikes, - -	31	16	9½
Hotel at Robertstown, (now let) -	0	12	7
Hotel at Tullamore, (now let) -	7	16	7
Hotel at Shannon Harbour, ditto	31	4	0
Kildare Canal, - -	50	1	8
River Shannon Navigation, -	31	4	0
Fines reimbursed to Contractors,	62	16	0
Incidents, - - -	781	17	1½
	38831	17	8½

Cr.		£.	s.	d.
By Interest on Government Stock,		262	4	1
Permanent Revenue: By Tolls, - - -		17886	8	3
— Passage Boats,	7957 10 1	8064	19	3½
— Parcels & Luggage,	107 9 2½			
— Dockage, - -		59	17	2
— Floating and Graving Docks, -		477	19	11½
— Wharfage, - -		91	15	2½
— Turnpikes, - -		95	14	5½
— Traders for Repairs of Boats,		7	17	0
— Hotel at Portobello, Revenue Account, - -		193	18	8½
— Rents receiveable, -		1598	17	2
— Pipe Water per Centage receivable, about, - -		730	0	0
Balance deficient of Revenues to pay Interest, permanent Expenditure, Establishment, - -		9362	6	4½
		38831	17	8½

Newtown Colliery, for half year ending August 31, 1816.

Dr.	£.	s.	d.
To amount of Coal on hands, 23d February, 1816, valued at 12*s.* per Ton—7347 Tons, 8½ cwt. -	4408	9	0
To amount of Culm on hands, 23d February, 1816, valued at -	2000	0	0
To amount of Charges paid on Coal and Culm for working and raising, and which were sold in the half year ending August 23d, 1816, together with Watchmen, Clerks, and Artificers' Wages, particulars in returns furnished each fortnight to the Directors, - - - -	6912	1	8
To six months Rent of Royalties payable by the Company, -	500	0	0
To Manager and Cashier's Salaries,	288	14	6
To amount of Stores sent from Dublin, furnished by the Company's Storekeeper, - - -	161	13	10
To amount of Cash advanced the Colliers within this half-year on account of Stock on hands, -	1736	15	6
To Balance, being profit on the Coal and Culm sold within this half year,	3254	14	0
	19262	8	6

Cr.	£.	s.	d.
By amount of Coal sold for half year ending August 23, 1816, at 20*s.*—9134 tons, 1¼ cwt. - -	9134	1	3
By amount of Culm sold for half year ending August 23, 1816, - -	1718	10	6
By amount of Cash stopped for Tools furnished to Contractors, -	264	12	3
By amount of Coal on Bank, 23d August, 1816, valued at 12*s.* per ton, 10,075 tons, 7½ cwt. -	6045	4	6
By amount of Culm on Bank, 23d August, 1816, per valuation at 3*s.* per Ton, 14,000 tons, -	2100	0	0
	19262	8	6

N. B. The price of 12*s.* per Ton affixed to the Coal and 3*s.* per Ton to the Culm on hands, is but nominal, as the Charge for raising fluctuates according to the

Signed by the Manager.

APPENDIX, No. X.

Farm attached to Colliery.

r.	£.	s.	d.	Cr.	£.	s.	d.
o·six months Rent payable by the Company,	267	4	0	By six months Rents receivable,	505	8	7¼
eturns, for Expenses on Farm,	22	5	6¼				
gents' Fees paid on Rents received,	80	2	6				
o Balance, being the profit this half year,	135	16	7				
	505	8	7½		505	8	7½

Signed by the Steward.

The Canal, Collieries, and Farm, collectively.

r.							Cr.						
anal, including Interest, as above stated,			38831	17	8¼		Canal, including Interest, as above stated,			29469	11	4
Collieries,	ditto		16007	14	6		Collieries,	ditto,		19262	8	6
arm,	ditto		369	12	0¼		Farm,	ditto,		505	8	7½
							Balance deficient of Revenues, Collieries, and Farm to pay Interest, permanent Expenditure, and Establishment,			5971	15	9¼
			55209	4	3					55209	4	3

Casual Expenditure and Receipts.

aw Expences,			321	5	7	Received for Coal sold at Coal-yard,	253	0	0
oal-yard at Docks Ringsend,			163	12	11¾	Value of Coal, &c. on hand there,	160	7	0½
oals stored therein,			413	7	7½	Received on account of Sums advanced last half year,	25	0	0
epair of Breaches, on Shannon Line, (Balance)			277	18	3				
arret Moore, damages, ditto,			120	0	0				
			1296	4	5		438	7	7

Sworn by the Accountant.

State of the Funds, 31st August, 1816.

Cash, Balance in the hands of the Treasurer,		1738	5	6
Government Stock, 3½ per Cent. 34474l. 4s. 10d. at 78 per Cent.		26889	18	3
Due to the Bank of Ireland,		15715	10	0
		12912	13	9
Coal on hand, as returned by Manager, 10,075 Tons, 7¼ Cwt. will sell at 20s. per Ton,		10075	7	6
Culm ditto, ditto 14,000 Tons, per Valuation,		2100	0	0
		12175	7	6

Sworn the 11th day of October, 1816.   EDWARD GEOGHEGAN.

[lxxiv]

APPENDIX, No. XI.*

rative Table of Population Returns for the City and Suburbs of Dublin, from 1798 to 1813 inclusiv

	No. 1. Mr. Whitelaw's Return of 1798, corrected by that of the Conservators in 1804		No. 2. Official Return of 1813, as given in Whitelaw's Life.		No. 3. Return revised by William Gregory, 1816.		Vacant Houses according to Gregory, 1816.		*₊* Mr. Gregory was o those employed by Govern to take the census in 1813. published his return 1816.
s, &c.	Inhabit- ed Houses	Total Inhabitants	Inhabited Houses.	Total Inhabitants.	Inhabited Houses.	Total Inhabitants	Building.	Un- tenanted.	
-	709	7682	703	7070	703	7074	0	27	It is evident, that Mr. Whi
-	711	7228	764	8324	764	8324	1	25	enumerated the county parts
-	415	5191	412	4667	412	4667	7	51	Catherine's, (his own parish,
-	745	8009	745	9639	745	9639	6	47	which county part has been w
ie's -	1481	20167	1350	17104	1350 } 1692	17104 } 21012	11	414	omited in No. 2.
nty part	- -	- -	- -	- -	342 }	3908 }	8	41	St. George's parish has
h Deanry	23	233	23	250	16	254	0	2	also omitted by No. 2, but
-	587	5096	590	5100	1794	13012	49	89	plied from No. 1, not incl
-	538	6104	455	5649	455	5649	12	19	the outlets, Drumcondra,
-	295	4142	277	4346	277	4346	0	21	bough, &c.
-	454	7241	460	7300	461	7002	5	33	St. Luke's parish having
- -	646	8592	720	11066	720	11063	30	48	omitted by No. 2, is also su
-	1590	16654	1670	19268	1778	19268	21	108	from Mr. Whitelaw's Tables
-	163	2599	130	2011	130	2011	1	8	a small variation.
-	1520	18092	1488	20563	1604	20593	17	101	The remark that was ma
within	107	1121	102	1447	102	1447	3	9	St. Catherine's is applicable
s without	960	12306	722	9409	722 } 250	9409 } 2899	12308	0	42	county part of St. Nicholas
nty part	- -	- -	- -	- -			0	12	out, which was included b
Deanry	162	2081	149	2246	149	2246	0	3	Whitelaw, but omitted i
-	1050	9914	746	9560	746	9560	0	28	Official Return, No. 2.
-	1512	16063	1264	13478	1264 } 605	13478 } 7012	20490	69	104	The above remark applie
nty part	- -	- -	- -	- -			28	32	to the county part of St. Pete
-	892	8562	1680	13766	1680	13766	50	133	was included in Mr. Whit
's -	305	3629	246	3052	246	3052	0	22	Return, not omitted in No.
n -	345	1286							The Return of Spring Gar
									omitted by all except Mr. W
TALS -	15199	172091	14696	175319	17315	196783			law, who notices that of the
			Additions, No. 3.						servators.
, No. 1.			St. Mary's Donnybrook	684 } 290	974	4910 } 1974	6884	11	10	Kilmainham (which is ir
- -	- -	7000	Ditto, county part -					1	0	the county town) is as much
tal	- -	400	St. Kevin's -		547		6102	1	28	of Dublin as Dorset-street
Hospital	- -	55	Kilmainham		794		4718	13	54	same may be said of Doll
lustry -	- -	1637	Manor of St. Sepulchre		797		9001	11	40	Barn, Harold's Cross, Rathr
-	- -	529	Ditto, Donore -		803		10910	13	74	&c.; also Grange Gorman,
			Ditto, Grange Gorman		809		7735	9	104	manogue, Phibsboro', &c. o
Total Inha	bitants	182370								north side; they are all on
Houses -	1202				22039	242133	393	1710	interrupted continuation o
			Untenanted Houses -		2103					suburbs, except where inters
otal Houses	16401		Total Houses		24142					by the Circular Road.

* In the Preface to the first volume, this is referred to as Appendix No. I.

APPENDIX, No. XI.

The discrepancies of these Returns are to be ascribed to the assigning parts of the city (the newest and best parts) to the county, because not in the jurisdiction of the Lord Mayor. On the other hand, Gregory's estimate goes too far out of town, and takes in too much of the scattered out-lets.* If the city and suburbs of Dublin be taken out of the county, the latter will then be the smallest county in Ireland. There is not what may be termed a market town in the whole county. It contains eighty villages, but ten of the principal of these are absorbed in, and make part of the city. Now suppose seventy villages average each forty houses and 200 inhabitants, which make 14,000, and that the remainder of the county contains 46,000, on the whole - - - - - - (souls) 60,000
But according to the last Official Census, the city and county together contain 270,784
From this total deduct the number in the county - - 60,000

The population of the city and suburbs will therefore be - - 210,784
Add from the other side the garrison and inmates of public buildings - 15,030

Total inhabitants - 225,714
Although this is more than 30,000 short of Gregory's statement, (for he does not include the garrison, &c.) yet it perhaps comes nearer the truth.
But to strike a medium between the Census of Mr. Whitelaw and that of Gregory, we shall say that the inhabitants of Dublin were in 1816, in round numbers 220,000

Which divided by ten,† not too high an average, gives the number of houses - 22,000
Houses building and untenanted - - - - 2,000

Total of Houses - 24,000

Inmates of Public B
Men, Women, and Cl

Six Barracks -
House of Industry, old
 and new -
Foundling Hospital
Royal Hospital, Kilmain
Steven's Hospital -
Blue Coat Hospital
Lying-in Hospital
Swift's Hospital -
Mercer's Hospital
Twenty other Hospitals,
 Asylums, and Peni-
 tentiaries, at 50 each
Newgate -
Kilmainham Gaol
Marshalsea
Six other Prisons, at 50
Seven Friaries, at 20
Seven Nunneries, at 20
Trinity College (residen
Castle -

* Registers of christenings and burials, which are of such assistance in computing the population, are very partially kept, and never published in Dublin.
† Others make the average eleven, and even eleven and a half to a house; but Mr. Whitelaw inclines to ten, which is greater than the average of London.

[lxxvi]

APPENDIX, No. XII.

IRISH Manuscripts in the Irish Character, still existing in the archives of Trinity College, Dublin, and in the private libraries of Members of the Gaëlic, or Hiberno-Celtic Society of Ireland.

Tracts illustrative of the ANTIQUITIES and early state of Ireland.

No.
1. Psalter Theamhra.
2. Psalter Chaisil.
3. Analaidh Thighearnaigh.
4. Analaidh Ulladh.
5. Analaidh Multigh fhearnain.
6. Analaidh Innisfaidhliné.
7. Analaidh Chonacht.
8. Analaidh Thuamhumhain.
9. Analaidh Chabhain.
10. Analaidh Dun-na-ngall.
11. Leabhar Binín, or na Ccart.
12. Leabhar Gabhala.
13. Leabhar Baile-an-mhota.
14. Leabhar Breac mhic Eoghain.
15. Leabhar Leacain.
16. Leabhar Gleandalocha.
17. Leabhar Mhidhe.
18. Leabhar Oirghial.
19. Leabhar Na-naomh.
20. Leabhar Chluain mic-naois.
21. Leabhar Fhearmuidhe.

No.
22. Leabhar Chluain-an-mhuilinn.
23. Leabhar na Gcuigidhe.
24. An Reim Rioghraighe.
25. Leabhar Cheannanus.
26. Leabhar Dhruim sneachta.
27. Leabhar Choimh-aimsireacht.
28. Leabhar Mhaolchonairé.
29. Leabhar mic Phartholain.
30. Leabhar na CCeart.
31. Chroinic na-Scuit.
32. Iomarbha-na-m-bárd.
33. Din-seneachais Eiriond.
34. Eocha O Floinn. Historic verses.
35. Duan ghiolla Chaomhain.
36. Duan Thorna Eigios.
37. Duanairé ui Ghadhra.
38. Tuirhead Seain ui Chonnel.
39. Feiliré Aonguis.
40. Duan Firf laha ui Ghniomh.
41. Amhra choluim-chillé.

Particulars BATTLES, in Irish called *Cathaith*, with the supposed year in which they were fought.

42. Cath Odbha, County Westmeath   B. C.   78.
43. Cath Chiliach, County Carlow   -   9.
44. Cath Aichle, County Meath   A. D. 70.
45. Cath Muigh-agha   -   -   122.
46. Cath Chnuca   -   154.
47. Cath Magh lena, King's County   -   181.
48. Cath Muicriove, County Galway   - -   195.
49. Cath Chrionda, near Tara   -   230.
50. Cath Fionn traighe, Ventry Harbour   240.
51. Cath Druim da vairé, Knock-long   -   268.
52. Cath Ghaabhra, near Tara   -   296.
53. Cath Dubhchomairé   322.
54. Cath Acha   -   '   -   478.
55. Cath Rath beg, King's County   -   558.

APPENDIX, No. XII.

lxxvii

No.		A.D.	No.		A.D.
56. Cath Bealgduin m-bolt	-	594.	64. Cath Bealach muichna, County Carlow		909.
57. Cath Sliabh-thua, County Galway	-	610.	65. Cath Greallach kille, County Meath		910.
58. Cath Moigh-ratha, Moyra	-	639.	66. Cath Cuan Fuah, against the Danes		918.
59. Cath Aire-cealtrach	-	673.	67. Cath Roscré, against the Danes		942.
60. Cath Locha gabhuir	-	675.	68. Cath San aingel, County Limerick	-	942.
61. Cath Almhuin, Allenhill, County Kildare		721.	69. Cath Aitha-cliath, Dublin	-	946.
62. Cath Drom-foinacht	-	724.	70. Cath Altha-cliath, Dublin	-	948.
63. Cath Focharta, County Lowth	-	730.	71. Cath cluain tairbh, Clontarf	-	1014.

JURISPRUDENCE.

72. Dlighé Breitheamhain, or Brehon Laws, fragments.
73. Seanchais mōr, or great ancient Code, with other miscellanies.
74. Brehuin Laws, fragments.
75. Another Collection.

76. Treatise on the Brehuin Laws.
77. Two volumes, quarto, on the Brehuin Laws.
78. Dān Seanachid.
79. Ancient Laws, fragments; with interlineary glosses.

MEDICAL and BOTANICAL TRACTS.

80. Causes of diseases and mode of treatment.
81. Tracts, Surgical and Physiolgical.
82. Cord.Valer.Dispensatory,with a Medical Tract, transcribed 1592.
83. Diseases and their treatment.
84. Silan. de Nigr. on Almanzor, a Botan. and Med. Tract.
85. Treatment and Cure of Palsies, Apostems, and Dropsies, with an account of Plants, and their uses.
86. Medical and Botan. Miscellany; large folio.
87. Medical Miscellany; large folio.
88. Treatise on Medicine; quarto.
89. Donoch ōg O Hickey's Transcript of Medicine and Botany.
90. Melaghlin O Maolchonairé, from Peter D'Argillata, of Bal-loch-reach.

SCIENTIFIC TRACTS.

91. De Philosophia.   Trin. Col.
92. De Logica.

93. Tract on Geometry.   Trin. Col.
94. De Astronomia.

MORAL and RELIGIOUS TRACTS, illustrative of Church History.

95. Fiech's Hymn of St. Patrick, with interlineary comments; folio.
96. Columkille's praise of St. Bridget.
97. St. Patrick's consolations against death.
98. Comments on Columkille's Vision.
99. Account of Lands and other Abbey Donations.

100. Hagiography, Irish & Psalter Latin,writ.1484
101. Fiech's Hymn; second copy.
102. Sermons.
103. New Testament.
104. Old Testament.
105. Lives of St. Bridget, &c. with glosse.

lxxviii

APPENDIX, No. XII.

PHILOLOGICAL TRACTS, on Vellum and Paper.

No.	No.
106. Uraiceapt na m-bārd.	111. Plunket's Glossary of Irish, Latin, and Biscayen.
107. Naghten's Irish-English Dictionary.	
108. Etymologies of Persons and Places.	112. Vocabulary of difficult words.
109. M'Naghten's Latin-Irish Dictionary.	113. Clerigh's Vocabulary.
110. Cormac's Glossary.	114. Glossary of difficult words.
	115. Ureacepts, Glossaries.

ROMANCES and DRAMATIC TRACTS, including Eachtraidh, or Adventures, and Agallaidh, or Dialogues.

116. Eachtra chonail Charnaigh.	123. Eachtra Ridiré an Leoin.
117. Eachtra cheallachain Chaisil.	124. Eachtra Chonail Ghulbain.
118. Eachtra mic na Miochomhairlé.	125. Agalladh Phadruig agus Oisiñ.
119. Eachtra an ghiolla dhecair.	126. Agalladh Phadruig agus Oisiñ.
120. Eachtra Toreili mic Stearn.	127. Agalladh na Seannoiridh.
121. Eachtra Lomnochtan Sliabhriffé.	128. Agalladh na n-Oirimhidighi.
122. Eachtra an Mhadra Mael.	129. Dearg ruathar chonail golban.

NOTES.

1. Of the Manuscripts, Psalters, Annals, and Poems of Ireland, some are anonymous, and some bear the name of their real or supposed authors; a detailed account of the origin and contents of the greater number will be found in Nicholson's Irish Historical Library, printed in Dublin in 1723. The most remarkable mentioned by him are noted in the following Catalogue, with such further information as occurred since his time, and which he had not detailed.

As all the compositions of the bards were in verse, they were thence called *Psalters*, or sonnets; there were three of great eminence in Ireland, quoted and referred to by more modern writers, with great respect. First, the *Psalter of Teambar*, or Tarah, was a collection of Chronicles authenticated in a solemn convention of the States of Ireland, in the reign of King Laoghairé. This venerable document has disappeared for many centuries, with the exception of some fragments.

2. Second, *The Psalter of Cashel* was written by Cormac, son of Culinan, King and Bishop of Cashel or Munster, A. D. 900; it was extant when Nicholson wrote his Irish Historical Library in 1724; but there is now no perfect copy in Ireland; it is said there are two in England, one of which the Rev. Dr. O'Connor has met with in his researches there. Third, *Psalter na Rann* was written by Oengus O'Colidé, one of the Culdees; it contains a catalogue of kings, from Heremon, A. M. 2935, to Brian, killed at Clontarf, A. D. 1014; it is mentioned by Nicholson, but it does not appear that there are any remains of it now in Ireland, except extracts in other works. Printed translations of these Psalters and Annals have long been a desideratum in the learned world, " Histories of the middle ages, found in other countries, have been published," says E. Burke, "and I do not see why the Psalter of Cashel should not be printed as well as Robert of Gloster."

3. These Annals were commenced by Tighernach, an Eranach of Clanmacnoise, and carried down to the time of his death, which occurred in 1088. They were then continued at irregular intervals by

APPENDIX, No. XII.

other hands to 1395. Messrs. Macnamara and O'Reily, members of the Gaëlic or Hiberno-Celtic Society, have transcripts of these, and the greater number of the works that follow, both on vellum and paper.

4. These Annals are written in Irish and Latin, and principally of the affairs of Ulladh, or Ulster; they commence in 444, and end in 1541. They are called *Annales Senatenses* by Colgan, who says they were written by Cathal M'Guire, of Senat-mac-magnus, county Fermanagh.

5. The monastery of Multifernam or Montfernand, from whence these are called, lay in Westmeath; the annals commence in the year 45, and end in 1272.

6. Innisfathlean, so called from a monastery on an island, in Loch Lean, county Kerry, where they were written. The annals commence with universal history to 250, and continue the affairs of Ireland down to 1215, when the compiler died and they were continued by another hand down to 1320. They are now translated by Mr. O'Reily, and ready for the press.

7. These are very brief, extending only from 1232 to 1282; they were written in the abbey of Boyle, and were called by way of eminence Leabhar na manaistreach, or the Book of the Abbey.

8. Thomond is the country of the O'Briens, or Clare; the annals contain the succession of reigns, the fiscal property, and the territorial possessions of the princes of that district.

9. Contains an account of the O'Reily dynasty in the county of Cavan, and are continued to the revolution in 1692.

10. The Annals of the Four Masters, were so called from Michael and Cuchoigcriché O'Clerigh, Cuchoicriché O'Duigenan, and Fearfeasa Conry, the principal persons who compiled them from all the annals then to be found in Ireland. They are also designated the " Annals of Donegal," from their being transcribed in the convent of Strict Observantines in that town, 1636. These are generally considered the most valuable, accurate, and consistent compilations towards a general history of Ireland, in the Irish language. There are some few copies in the hands of members of the Gaëlic Society, and others in this country, and two in the library of Trinity College, Dublin, one of which is in four volumes. There is also one in the Marquis of Buckingham's library at Stow, where Doctor O'Connor deposited all his grandfather's Irish manuscripts. From these he is now publishing some extracts illustrative of Irish history, under the patronage of the present Marquis. One quarto volume of the Prolegomena has already appeared. In this he gives an account, from Muratori, of an Irish manuscript, called the " Bangor Antiphonary," written about 1100 years ago, and now in the Ambrosian library at Milan. In this St. Patrick is mentioned, and if the manuscript be of the era assigned to it, it must tend, with the proofs adduced by Usher, to remove the doubts entertained of the Saint's existence, which are founded on the silence of Bede, who lived posterior to this era.

11. Binín, or St. Benignus, who wrote this book, was Bishop of Armagh; it is also called " Leabhar na Ccart," or " Book of Rights" or revenues of the crown of Munster.

12. This was written by Mich. O'Clerigh, one of the Four Masters, and finished in the reign of Charles I. at the Observantine Monastery, Donegal.

13. This venerable repository, called improperly by Lluid, the Book of Ballymore, contains various genealogies of the ancient families in Ireland, a treatise on education, the art of writing in the various characters of the Ogham, historical matter of the Argonautic expedition and war of Troy; valuable only for the purity of the language. Mr. Charles O'Connor says, it was carried on under the patronage of Timothy M'Donagh, chief of a district, now comprehending the counties of Sligo, Roscommon,

and Leitrim, at Ballymote, his ancient residence. In 1390 it was transcribed, and in 1522 it was purchased by Hugh Duff O'Donnel, Prince of Tyrconnel (Donegàl), for 140 milch cows; and after many revolutions of times, places, and persons, it became the property of the Chevalier O'Gorman, of Cathair Murchaghé, in the county of Clare. This gentleman early left his native country, he entered the Irish Brigades and married a sister of the Chevalier d'Eon, and remained ignorant of the sex of his sister in law till it was publicly discovered. He was singularly well skilled in the language and history of Ireland, and collected a very valuable library of scarce manuscripts on these subjects. He presented the book of Ballymote to the Royal Irish Academy, on his return to Ireland, about the year 1785, and left the remainder at his death, which happened in 1810, to a gentleman who reserves them as an important addition to the course of Education he proposes for his son.

14. This is called the " Speckled Book," and sometimes " Leabhar ruadh,' or " Red Book," like several others, from the red spotted colours of its cover. It was written about 400 years ago, and contains the annals of Ireland, stated by Nicholson to be of undisputed authority. The present copy was found near Nenagh, in the county of Tipperary, by one Michael Longan, a schoolmaster, and brought to Dr. J. O'Brian, Roman Catholic Bishop of Cloyne, who used it to complete his Irish Dictionary, published in France in 1767, whither he had retired from the disturbances in this country. The Leabhar Breac was left by Doctor O'Brien, at his departure, in the house of a relation, who brought it to Dublin, and disposed of it to the Royal Irish Academy for the trifling sum of three guineas.

15. The Book of Leacan was so called from Leàcan, a well known residence of hereditary antiquarians in the county of Sligo. It contains a large collection of Irish treatises, generally historical, and was held in high authority by Usher, O'Flaherty, and other Irish writers. It had been in the library of Trinity College Dublin, but some time before Nicholson wrote, it had been lost, or, as he says, purloined from the library. The time and manner of its disappearance are variously reported. It is stated by the Abbé M'Geohegan, that James II. caused a great manuscript folio volume, called the Book of Leacan, to be taken from Trinity College, Dublin, and deposited in the Irish College at Paris, of which a formal acknowledgement was there executed before public notaries. (Hist. d'Ireland, page 39.) The book, however, appears to have been in the library of Trinity College Dublin many years after that prince's abdication. In Lluid's Archæologia, printed in 1707, this manuscript is particularly described, and its contents enumerated. In the preface to O'Connor's translation of Keating's History of Ireland, printed in Dublin in 1723, he states that he obtained the perusal of this book for six months, on giving security for £1000. sterling. General Valancey mentions in his Green Book, that about thirty years ago Doctor Raymond, lent a manuscript volume out of the library of Trinity College Dublin, to a person of the name of Thady Naghten; a man of the name of Egan stole it from Naghton, and gave it to Judge Marlay, his master, in whose library it was at his death, from whence it was by some means conveyed to the Lombard College in Paris. The superior of the Irish College presented it the Royal Irish Academy in 1788.

Doctor Aherne, professor of Theology in Maynooth College in the year 1797, was many years previous to the French Revolution, professor to the Irish College. When he first became a member of that community, about the year 1740, he was informed by some of the elders of that seminary, that the Book of Leacan was originally brought there by an Irish priest, who being well known to be deeply read in the ancient language of Ireland, prevailed on the Librarian of Trinity College, Dublin, to lend him

APPENDIX, No. XII.   lxxxi

the vellum manuscript, on the deposit of a sum of money, as he could find no other security. Implicated in the troubles of the times, he was obliged to fly suddenly from his native country, and brought with him the book he had borrowed, which he deposited in the library of the Irish College in Paris. In 1773 the Dublin Society addressed the members of the Irish College of Paris on the subject of Irish manuscripts. In consequence of this, the Irish community returned a polite and patriotic answer, formed a committee to explore the libraries of the Continent, and collect books and manuscripts illustrative of the antiquities of Ireland, and ordered a transcript of the Book of Leacan to be made out for the Dublin Society, but it does not appear that the transcript was ever completed.

From these varying accounts, however, it is certain, that this celebrated book has been at all times an object of great importance and interest; that it was early deposited in the library of Trinity College, Dublin; that it disappeared from thence about the year 1723; that it was deposited by some means in the library of the Lombard College in Paris, where it continued till 1788, when it was presented to the Royal Irish Academy, in whose library it now remains.

16. Nicholson calls this an ancient and valuable record; it contains an account of the Assembly at Dromceat, at which St. Columnkill was present, which sat for one year and one month, and established excellent laws for protecting the liberty and restraining the licentiousness of the bards.

17. This is an enumeration of the names of the monarchs of Meath.

19. This was compiled by Augustine M'Graidon canon, regular of the Isle of Saints in the river Shannon, near the county of Longford. He continued these historical records to the year 1405, when he died.

20. The annals of Clanmacnois consisted of miscellaneous matters, with the births and obits of great men. It was included in the great work of the Four Masters.

21. Contains in prose and verse an account of the possessions of the Roaches of Fermoy, with historical and other micellaneous tracts; among others, a curious tract on the metampsychosis.

22. This Book of St. Moling, is a transcript of " great antiquity," according to Nicholson.

23. Contains a statistical account of the provinces of Ireland.

24. " The Reigns of the Kings." This book was taken by Lynch as his great authority.

25. This is the " Book of Kells."

26. This old " White Book," contains an account of the fabulous æra of Ireland.

27. The Book of Synchronisms contains an account of the cotemporary events and reigns of Ireland and other countries.

28. This is a geneological tract, written by Conaing O'Maolchonairé, called " The Scribe." It commences in 428, and ends in 1014.

30. A book of fiscal rights. This is probably another copy of the Leabhar Benín.

31. Chronicon Scotorum.

32. In the fifteenth century, an emulation was excited among the bards of Ulster and Munster to celebrate their respective kings. The contest was carried on in verse, and included a considerable portion of the history of Ireland.

33. Contains a topographical description of Ireland.

34. Eochaid O'Flinn was a poet and antiquary of great note, who sung the adventures of the most early times of the Milesians and sons of Partholanus.

APPENDIX, No. XII.

35. Giolla Chaomhain was a celebrated poet, who composed an account of the arrival of the Milesians in Egypt, and their expulsion from it.

36. Thorna Eigios was a learned poet, who lived towards the latter end of the fourth century; he described the interment of the ancient kings in the royal cemetery of Roilic na Riogh, near Ciuaghan, in Connaught; and left numerous rythmical compositions on the history of Ireland.

37. This book contains 214 folio pages, 168 of which are historic, moral, genealogic, and comic poems. They were collected among the extra-national Irish convents in French Flanders, by Mich. Feargal dubh O'Gadhra, a native of Galway and an Augustine Friar, who was obliged to leave Ireland in 1688. It was among the books of Daly of Dunsandle, and Lady Moyra, supposing it might contain matter illustrative of the history and antiquities of Ireland, commissioned her chaplain to purchase it at Mr. Daly's sale; it was put by Lady Moyra into the hands of the late T. O'Flanagan, in the hope that he would translate it and publish the contents; from him it devolved to Mr. Macnamara, in whose possession it now is.

38. This poem is elegiac and historic on the subject of Ireland.

39. This contains an account of the festivals celebrated in Ireland down to the ninth century.

40. Fear Flatha O'Gnimhe was hereditary bard of O'Neil, of Claneboy, in the reign of Elizabeth. He was the Tyrtæus of Ulster, and was often too successful in rousing his countrymen against the English. He is mentioned with great applause in Campbel's Philosophical Survey of Ireland.

41. These poems are supposed to be of great antiquity, and said to be written in the sixth century, by Dallan Forgaill, or as he is sometimes called Eochaid Eigias. He was chief poet in the reign of Hugh Mōr. It was his province to examine the abilities of the several candidates, and on admission to send them to the several provinces. He established a poet of learning in the family of every great lord in the kingdom.

42. These are detached accounts of battles fought at different times in different parts of Ireland. Some of them are facts, and others, though founded on fact, are highly embellished with poetic imagery. They are all descriptive of ancient customs, and are so far valuable as they convey a picture of the manners of the supposed ages assigned to them.

52. In this battle the Finian Knights destroyed each other, and terminated the chivalrous or heroic history of Ireland.

64. It is by some asserted that the celebrated Cormac O'Cullenan, King of Munster, and compiler of the Psalter of Cashel, was killed in this battle.

71. This describes the memorable battle of Clontarf, in which the integral and independant state of Ireland, may be said to have terminated with the death of the last monarch, Brian Boromhe.

72. The system of laws by which the ancient Irish were governed, was not left to the uncertainty and fluctuation of oral tradition, but has been very early reduced to order, and preserved in the permanent characters of a written code. These were administered by Judges, called Brehons, and hence the maxims by which they were guided were called Brehon Laws. A compilation called "Breithé-neimhé," or Heavenly Judgments, was said to be formed A.D. 90, and another in 254, which is still supposed to be extant. After continuing 1200 years to be the guides of Irish jurisprudence, these laws were at length abolished by Act of Parliament, in 1366, and the manuscripts which contained them were so dispersed, that little more than fragments escaped the ravages of time and proscription. In 1723, there

APPENDIX, No. XII.   lxxxiii

were several specimens in public and private libraries, the most perfect of which was in the Duke of Chandois' collection, it contained twenty-two sheets and a half, close written in two columns. This Chandois Repository of Irish manuscripts had been formed both before and after the rebellion of 1641, by Sir James Ware, who collected together all that could then be procured. In the reign of James II. when Lord Clarendon was Viceroy of Ireland, he obtained this collection from the representatives of Sir J. Ware, about the year 1686, and brought them to England. After his death they were sold to the Duke of Chandois. In 1697, a Catalogue of Contents was printed, and Dean Swift having met with it, he became very desirous that these national records should be restored to the country to which they appertained. Accordingly he wrote to the Duke a letter, dated August 31, 1734, stating—That several worthy persons of this City and University, had importuned him to solicit his Grace to make a present of those ancient records on paper or parchment, which are of no use in England, and naturally belong to this poor kingdom. This request, however, was not complied with.

But the most valuable and extensive repository of these laws is now in the library of Trinity College, Dublin. In consequence of a correspondence with General Valancey, on the subject of Irish literature, Edmund Burke prevailed on Sir John Seabright to give his valuable collection of Irish manuscripts to our University. They were accordingly sent to Dublin by Doctor Leland, and deposited in the library, in order that the learned in Ireland might have access to them, and their contents might be investigated and given to the public. The Brehon Laws form a considerable portion of this collection.

The obscurity of a character abounding in contractions, and the technical language of a remote age, long disused, had been considered as insurmountable obstacles to this investigation, and had baffled many of those who had attempted it. It was even said by the learned Charles O'Connor, that a key for expounding the laws had been kept by the M'Egans, and had been lost since the time of Charles I. This seemed to render hopeless any attempt at exposition. An effort, however, had been made by General Valancey in the Col. de rebus Hib. in 1774 and 1782, and a translation of part of the laws given to the public, so curious as to excite much interest for the remainder. Nothing further, however, was done till the formation of the Gaëlic Society in 1806. Since that time the pursuit has been followed up. The Society have now fourteen volumes of fragments of these laws, copied on paper from the original vellum; which Mr. O'Reily is arranging for the press.

77. This copy was the property of Mr. Forbes, of Lecan, in 1666, who was the preceptor of the learned O'Flaherty, and had been instructed by the M'Egans, hereditary expounders of the Brehon laws. He was considered by Mr. O'Connor to be the ablest scholar instructed by the M'Egans, and to have been concerned in compiling a Law Lexicon, for the purpose of elucidating the obscurity of the Brehon code. All the copies of the Brehon Laws noticed above, are on vellum.

89. It should appear from the numerous tracts of the subjects that the study of medicine and botany has been pursued with much assiduity very early in Ireland, and with success. It appears from some passages that have been translated, that the circulation of the blood was known and described in these books, particularly in O'Hickey's transcript made from an older work, in 1432, two centuries before the discovery of Harvey. The manuscripts, Nos. 88, 89, 90, are on vellum, and belong to members of the Gaëlic Society. They are at present in the possession of one Michael O'Casey, an old Milesian, noticed in page 761 of this work, who practices medicine among the people of his neighbourhood from the prescriptions directed in them.

95. Fiech was the disciple of St. Patrick, and Bishop of Sletty, near Carlow, and the poem is supposed to be the composition of the fifth century.

lxxxiv APPENDIX, No. XII.

‾ Besides the tracts mentioned here, the Feilerés in prose and verse, with the lives, genealogies, and praises of saints, on vellum and paper, are very numerous. The records kept in particular churches are also sources whence much may be deduced towards the ecclesiastical state of ancient Ireland. Of these, as well as of the genealogies and histories of particular families, there are numerous and multiplied copies in the archives of Trinity College and in the collections of private individuals.

99. This account is in a Roman Breviary, once the property of the Culdee Church of Armagh.

102. These were composed and transcribed on vellum, in 1041, for the brethren of Foure Abbey, in county Westmeath.

103. Nicholson mentions a very beautiful vellum transcript of the Gospels, in the library of Trinity College, Dublin, written in Irish, and called the Book of St. Columbkill. It had on the cover a silver cross, inscribed, it was said, by St. Columba's own hand.

106. This work contains a model for bardic compositions; it also includes a grammar of the Ogham and Foras Focall or Etymon of words. It is a vellum folio.

111. This dictionary was originally written in 1662. There are copies of it in Marshe's library, and in that of Trinity College.

110. This venerable glossary of difficult words, is said to have been compiled by Cormac, King of Cashel, in the tenth century.

125. There are many Irish poems extant attributed to Oisín, and either addressed to St. Patrick, or in the form of a dialogue. One of these has been beautifully translated by Miss C. Brooke, in her Reliques of Irish Poetry.

Besides these compositions here noticed, there are various others on similar subjects yet extant, which it would be superfluous and beyond our limits to enumerate. Among others, Dr. John Murphy, Roman Catholic Bishop of Cork, has already 10,000 quarto pages transcribed from Irish manuscripts, the more modern compositions of the two last centuries. From what has been stated in the above brief and imperfect sketch, it will be seen that there is yet in this country, and accessible to the lovers of the Irish language, many compositions in history, jurisprudence, medicine, botany, geometry, logic, ethics, philology, poetry, and polite literature, not less interesting for their subjects than venerable for their antiquity; and whatever difference of opinion may arise on the relative value of the information contained in them, it must be admitted by all, that the investigation of these manuscripts must be highly important, as affording the only certain information of the early state of science and literature in this country, and the pretensions of the Irish to the character of a polite and lettered people. Nor is this investigation an object of interest to the people only who are resident in this country and of the present day; men the most distinguished for their talents and attainments elsewhere, have long since recommended it. Dr. Johnson in his letter to Charles O'Connor says—" I have long wished that Irish literature were cultivated in Ireland; and surely it would be acceptable to all those who are curious either in the original of nations, or affinities of languages, to be further informed of the revolutions of a people so ancient and once so illustrious." Edmund Burke constantly recommended in his correspondence with General Valancey, that the originals of these manuscripts, with literal translations in English and Latin, should be printed. " Until something of this kind be done," said he, " the ancient period of Irish history which precedes official records, cannot be said to stand on any proper authority: a work of this kind, pursued by the University and a society of antiquaries, would be an honour to the nation."

The Gaelic Society, in order to carry into effect the wishes of Johnson, Burke, and others on this

Fac similes of the Types used in Irish Books.

	at Lovain & Rome. *Molloy*	Paris. *Donlevy*	Dublin. *Vallancy*	Dublin. *Halliday*	Proposed Alphabet.	No
A	a a	x a	a a	a a	a a	1
B	b b	b b	b b	B b	B b	2
C	c c	c c	c c	C c	C c	3
D	d d	d d	d d	D d	D d	4
E	e e	e e	e e	e e	e e	5
F	f f	f f	f f	F f	F f	6
G	g g	g g	g g	g g	g g	7
H	h h	h h	h h	h h	h h	8
I	i i	i i	i i	i i	i i	9
L	l l	l l	l l	l l	l l	10
M	m m	m m	m m	m m	m m	11
N	n n	n n	n n	N n	N n	12
O	o o	o o	o o	O o	O o	13
P	p p	p p	p p	P p	P p	14
R	r r	R r	r r	R r	R r	15
S	s s	s s	s s	s s	s s	16
T	t t	t t	t t	t t	t t	17
U	u u	u u	u u	u u	u u	18

Fac simile from Ancient Vellum M.S.S.

[facsimile alphabet specimens 1–18]

Ogam.

Clar na n-dott

APPENDIX, No. XII.

subject, have now ready for publication copies of the Brehon Laws and other manuscripts in the above catalogue, and they only wait for that patronage which can alone enable them to complete their undertaking.

The form of the characters used in Irish books has varied like that of other nations, with the age in which they were written. The annexed plate exhibits that which has been used at different periods. The first compartment shews that which has been already used in printed books, with an alphabet proposed to the Gaelic Society, by their Secretary, as a model for their future publications. The second is the varied forms used in the vellum manuscripts, of which we have given an account. The third displays the characters of the Ogham, with those which they represented placed above or below the lines.

The fourth is that peculiar mark called in Irish "Con fá acté," or the turn of the plough. It was placed at the termination of a paragraph, and intimated that the line next following should return to that point.

The last contains specimens of the different contractions, with the words for which they stood.

APPENDIX, No. XIII.

Botany of Dublin Bay and its Vicinity.

This List includes such plants as have been found on the coast, or within one mile of it, from Killiney to Mallahide. The more common plants are arranged systematically, the grasses and rarer plants alphabetically.

MONANDRIA.
Salicornia herbacea
Hippuris vulgaris
Callitriche verna
——— autumnalis.
DIANDRIA.
Veronica officinalis
——— v. fl. carneo
——— serpyllifolia
——— anagallis
——— becabunga
——— scutellata
——— chamædrys
——— arvensis
——— hederifolia
——— agrestis
Pinguicula vulgaris
Lycopus Europæus
Salvia verbenaca.
TRIANDRIA.
Valeriana officinalis
Iris Pseudacorus
Schœnus nigricans
Scirpus palustris
——— cespitosus
——— lacustris
——— v. minor
——— maritimus
——— sylvaticus
Montia fontana
TETRANDRIA.
Dipsacus sylvestris
Scabiosa succisa
——— arvensis
Sherardia arvensis
Galium palustre

Galium Mollugo
——— verum
——— montanum
——— Aparine
Plantago major
——— lanceolata
——— v. prolifera
——— maritima
——— Coronopus
Alchemilla vulgaris
——— Alpina
Ilex aquifolium
Potamogeton natans
——— crispum
——— gramineum
——— pectinatum
Sagina procumbens.
PENTANDRIA.
Myosotis arvensis
——— palustris
Lithospermum officinale
——— arvense
Cynoglossum officinale
Borago officinalis
Lycopsis arvensis
Primula vulgaris
——— officinalis
——— v. flor. Coccineo
Menyanthes trifoliata
Lysimachia nemorum
Anagallis arvensis
——— tenella
Convolvulus arvensis
——— sepium
Campanula rotundifolia
Samolus Valerandi

Lonicera periclimenum
Verbascum Thapsus
Hyoscyamus niger
Solanum Dulcamara
Hedera Helix
Glaux maritima
Chenopodium Bonus Henricus
——— murale
——— viride
——— olidum
——— album
——— rubrum
——— maritimum
Beta maritima
Salsola Kali
Gentiana } Centaureum
Chironia }
——— pulchella
Gentiana campestris
——— Amarella
Eryngium maritimum
Hydrocotyle vulgaris
Caucalis Anthriscus
——— nodosa
Daucus carota
Bunium flexuosum
Conium maculatum
Crithmum maritimum
Heracleum Sphondylium
Angelica sylvestris
Sium nodiflorum
——— repens
——— angustifolium
Sison inundatum
Oenanthe fistulosa
——— pimpinelloides

APPENDIX, No. XIII.

Oenanthe crocata
Æthusa cynapium
Scandix Pecten Veneris
─────── Anthriscus
Chœrophyllum sylvestre
─────────── temulum
Smyrnium olusatrum
Anethum fœniculum
Pimpinella saxifraga
─────────── dissecta
Apium graveolens
Sambucus Ebulus
─────── nigra
Alsine media
Statice Armeria
─────── Limonium
Linum catharticum
Euonymus europæus
HEXANDRIA.
Anthericum } ossifragum
Narthecium }
Juncus effusus
─────── bufonius
─────── campestris
─────── pilosus
─────── glaucus
─────── conglomeratus
─────── compressus
─────── articulatus
Peplis Portula
Rumex crispus
─────── pulcher
─────── acutus
─────── obtusifolius
─────── Acetosa
─────── Acetosella
Triglochin palustris
─────── maritimum
Alisma Plantago
─────── ranunculoides.
OCTANDRIA.
Epilobium hirsutum
─────── montanum
─────── tetragonum
─────── palustre

─────── parviflorum
Chlora perfoliata
Vaccinium Myrtillus
Erica vulgaris
─── v. hirsuta
─── v. squarrosa
─── cinerea
─── v. fl. albo
Polygonum Persicaria
─────── v. fl. alb.
─────── aviculare
─────── Convolvulus.
DECANDRIA.
Saxifraga granulata
Silene maritima
Stellaria graminea
─────── holostea
─────── glauca
Arenaria peploides
─────── serpyllifolia
─────── marina
Cotyledon Umbilicus Veneris
Sedum acre
─────── anglicum
Oxalis Acetosella
Agrostemma Githago
Lychnis Flos Cuculi
─────── dioica
Cerastium vulgatum
─────── semidicandrum
─────── viscosum
─────── arvense
Spergula arvensis
─────── nodosa
DODECANDRIA.
Lythrum Salicaria
Agrimonia Eupatoria
Reseda Luteola
Euphorbia Peplis
─────── exigua
─────── paralia
─────── helioscopia
Sempervivum tectorum.
ICOSANDRIA.
Spiræa Ulmaria
Prunus insitia

Prunus nigra
Rosa arvensis
─────── spinosissima
─────── v. a.
─────── v. b.
─────── canina
Rubus fruticosus
─────── corylifolius
Cratægus mespylus
Oxycantha vesca
Fragaria visca
─────── sterilis
Potentilla anserina
─────── reptans
Tormentilla erecta
Geum urbanum
Comarum palustre.
POLYANDRIA.
Glaucium luteum
Papaver hybridum
─────── Argemone
─────── Rhæas
─────── dubium
─────── somniferum
Ranunculus Flammula
─────── Ficaria
─────── sceleratus
─────── bulbosus
─────── repens
─────── acris
─────── aquatilis
─────── hederaceus
Caltha palustris.
DIDYNAMIA.
Ajuga reptans
Teucrium Scorodonia
─────── v. fl. aur.
Mentha aquatica
Glecoma hederacea
Lamium album
─────── purpureum
─────── amplexicaule
─────── dissectum
Galeopsis Ladanum
─────── Tetrahit

APPENDIX, No. XIII.

Galeobdlon luteum
Stachys sylvatica
——— palustris
Ballota nigra
Thymus Serpyllum
Scutellaria minor
Prunella vulgaris
Rhinanthus crista galli
Euphrasia officinalis
Bartsia odontites
Melampyrum pratense
Pedicularis palustris
————— sylvatica
Antirrhinum Linaria
Scrophularia majus
————— aquatica.
TETRADYNAMIA.
Draba verna
Thlepsi arvense
——— campestre
——— Bursa Pastoris
Cochlearia officinalis
————— anglica
Coronopus Ruelli
Cardamine hirsuta
————— pratensis
Sisymbrium Nasturtium
————— Irio
————— Sophia
————— palustre
Erysimum officinale
————— Barbarea
————— Alliaria
Brassica campestris
Sinapis arvensis
——— nigra
——— alba
Raphanus Raphanestrum
————— maritimus
Bunias Cakile.
MONADELPHIA.
Geranium pyrenaicum
——— molle
——— v. fl. alb.
——— dissectum

Geranium Robertianum
Erodium cicutarium
——— v. fl. alb.
Malva rotundifolia
——— sylvestris
——— v. fl. cyaneo.
DIADELPHIA.
Fumaria officinalis
——— capreolata
Polygala vulgaris
——— v. fl. alb.
——— v. fl. incarn.
Spartium scoparium
Ulex Europeus
——— nanus
Ononis arvensis
——— v. fl. alb.
Anthyllis vulneraria
Lathyrus pratensis
Vicia Cracca
——— sativa
——— lathyroides
——— angustifolia
——— sepium
Ervum hirsutum
Ornithopus perpusillus
Trifolium officinale
——— repens
——— pratense
——— fragiferum
——— agrarium
——— procumbens
Lotus corniculatus
——— v. pilosus
Medicago lupulina.
POLYADELPHIA.
Hypericum Androsæmum
——— quadrangulum
——— perforatum
——— humifusum
——— pulchrum.
SYNGENESIA.
Leontodon hirtum
——— hispidum
——— autumnale
——— taraxacum

Sonchus oleraceus
——— asper
——— arvensis
Tragopogon pratense
Hieracium paludosum
——— pilosella
Crepis tectorum
——— biennis
Hypochæris radicata
Lapsana communis
Arctium lappa
Serratula arvensis
Carduus arvensis
——— lanceolatus
——— palustris
——— v. fl. alb.
——— tenuiflorus
Carlina vulgaris
Eupatorium cannabinum
Tanacetum vulgare
Artemisia vulgaris
Gnaphalium sylvaticum
——— uliginosum
——— germanicum
Erigeron acre
Tussilago Farfara
——— Petasites
Senecio vulgaris
——— viscosus
——— sylvaticus
——— tenuiflorus
——— jacobæa
——— aquaticus
Aster Tripolium
Solidago Virgaurea
Inula dysenterica
——— crithmoides
Bellis perennis
Chrysanthemum Leucanthemum
——— segetum
Anthemis maritima
——— arvensis
——— Cotula
Achillea millefolium
Centaurea nigra

APPENDIX, No. XIII.

Centaurea Scabiosa	Carex paniculata	Scolopendrum vulgare
——— Cyanus	——- flava	Asplenium marinum
Viola hirta	——- pilulifera	——— tricomanes
——— canina	——- pallescens	——— Ruta muraria
——— tricolor	——- distans	——— Adiantum nigrum
——— arvensis	——- recurva	Polypodium vulgare
——— lutea.	——— præcox	Aspidium Filix mas
GYNANDRIA.	Littorella lacustris	——— Filix fœmina
Orchis pyramidalis	Urtica urens	——— aculeatum
——— mascula	——- dioica	Fucus sanguineus
——— masculata	Myriophyllum spicatum	——- vesiculosus
Ophrys ovata	——————- verticillatum.	——- alatus
Arum maculatum.	DIOECIA.	——- laciniatus
MONOECIA.	Mercurialis annua.	——- crispus
Chara vulgaris	POLYGAMIA.	——- mammillosus
Lemna minor	Parietaria officinalis	——- canaliculatus
——— trisulca	Atriplex laciniata	——- urcus
Typha latifolia	——— erecta	——- aculeatus
——— minor	——— patula.	——- coccineus
Sparganium ramosum	CRYPTOGAMIA.	——- plumosus
Carex leporina	Equisetum sylvaticum	——- Filum
——- muricata	——— arvense	Ulva compressa.
——- remota		

GRASSES alphabetically arranged.

Agrostis alba	Avena elatior	Festuca decumbens	Melica uniflora
——— canina	——- flavescens	——— dumetorum	Nardus stricta
——— vulgaris	——- pratensis	——— duriusculus	Phalaris arenaria
——— maritima	——- pubescens	——— elatior	Phleum nodosum
——— pumila	Briza media	——— fluitans	——— pratense
——— stolonifera	Bromus arvensis	——— loliacea	Poa angustifolia
Aira aquatica	——— asper	——— ovina	——— annua
——— cæspitosa	——— erectus	——— pratensis	——— aquatica
——— caryophylla	——— mollis	——— rubra	——— distans
——— cristata	——— secalinus	——— vivipera	——— maritima
——— flexuosa	——— sterilis	Holcus lanatus	——— pratensis
——— præcox	——— sylvaticus	——— mollis	——— rigida
Alopecurus geniculatus	Cynosurus cristatus	Hordeum murinum	——— trivialis
——————- pratensis	Dactylus glomeratus	——— pratense	Rotbelia incurvata
Anthoxanthum odoratum	Elymus caninus	Lolium perenne	Triticum junceum
Arundo arenaria	Eriophorum angustifolium	——— temulentum	——— loliaceum
——— colorata	——————- polystachion	Melica cærulea	——— repens.
——— Phragmites	Festuca bromoides		

APPENDIX, No. XIII.

PLANTS more rare or remarkable, arranged alphabetically.

Allium.   The odour of these plants, particularly of the last, is so penetrating,
carinatum,   mountain garlic.   that it renders the butter of such cows as feed on it in the vicinity of
vineale,   crow.   Dublin, sometimes unfit for use.
ursinum,   ramson.

Artimisia.   This genus of plants is remarkable for producing a finer alkaline salt
Absinthium,   common mugwort.   than any other vegetable, and hence the vegetable alkali was long
maritima,   sea mugwort.   known by the peculiar appellation of Sal'Absinthii. It is here noted for this reason rather than for its rarity. Rutty mentions that geese were stuffed with it, both for its grateful taste and to help digestion.

Artiplex.   Rutty says it was used by the poor in broths.
littoralis,   grass leaved orache.
purtulacoides, sea purslane.

Blechnum.   This small fern is sufficiently common in Ireland; it is called in the
boreale,   rough spleenwort.   north She-Bracken, to distinguish it from the larger fern called Lady-Bracken; it is popularly supposed to be an infallible cure for the farcy in horses. It is so rare in France, that Jussieu in his herborization through the woods in Montmorency, offers a premium to any person who can find it.

Carex.   All these species of sedge are noted among the plantæ rariores,
arenaria,   sea sedge.   though some are sufficiently common. They are all found on Howth.
binervis,   double nerved.
cæspitosa,   turfy.
dioicia,   diœcious.
hirta,   hairy.
ovalis,   naked.
panicea,   pinked.
pulicaris,   flea.
vulpina,   great.

Carum.   This aromatic was found growing in a field near Ringsend.
Carrui,   common caraway.

Convolvulus.   This elegant species of Convolvulus grows in sufficient abundance on
Soldanella,   sea bindweed.   the sandy banks behind the beach at Killiney strand, which it clothes and adorns with its variegated flowers, adding one of the lesser features of beauty to that picturesque coast. It is said to possess in a considerable degree the purgative properties of the C. jalappa.

Crambe.   So early as the time of Rutty this plant was cultivated in the gardens
maritima,   sea kale colewort.   round Dublin. It is found in the sands on every part of the coast.

Corrigiola.   This plant is among the rarissimæ, and not found in Hudson. It
littoralis,   sand strapwort.   grows on the south side of Howth, at Sutton.

Coriandrum.   Notwithstanding the doubts entertained of this plant, its seeds are
sativum,   com. coriander.   generally used with impunity. Coriander comfits are constantly found in the confectioners' shops in Dublin.

APPENDIX, No. XIII.

Drosera.		The leaves of this plant are armed with bristles which contract and pierce flies like the Dionæa muscipula. But it is more remarkable for the globules of a transparent fluid which are entangled on the points of these bristles, and crown the leaves with little diadems. Darwin calls it for this reason " Imperial Drosera." This small plant is often detected by its glittering crown.
rotundifolia,	round leaved sun-dew.	
Equisetum.		This rare plant was found on Portmarnock sands by Doctor Taylor.
variegatum,	varied horse tail.	
Erodium.		These two species, particularly the latter, emit when bruised, a strong odour of musk, so as not to be distinguished from that animal substance.
maritimum,	sea heron's-bill.	
moschatum,	musk.	
Fucus.		The first of these is a rare fucus, and was found on the strand of Malahide. The second is that which is cut from the rocks to make kelp. The two next species are sometimes thrown on the shores in vast quantities, particularly on the south isles of Arran, and when mixed with the Fucus nodosus make the richest kelp, and bring a higher price than that which is made on the main land. The Fucus palmatus is dried and sold in the fruit stalls in Dublin, made up in paper bags, under the name of dulisk. It is gathered from the rocks about Dalkey, and has an odour of violets. In Norway sheep and goats flock to the sea side in great numbers to eat it, when the tide is retiring. The Fucus serratus is preferred to any other for packing lobsters. The fishermen in Norfolk suppose it has some charm in preventing these hostile animals from fighting together.
ceranoides,	sea wrack.	
digitatus,	sea girdle.	
palmatus,	dulisk.	
sacharinus,	sea belt.	
serratus,	serrated.	
Geranium.		This, though not a rare plant, is one of the most beautiful of the crane-bill tribe, whether foreign or indigenous. A plant found at Howth was nearly four feet in height, and was equally remarkable for its ample foliage and rich flowers of bright purple.
sanguineum,	bloody crane's-bill.	
Jasione.		
montana,	hairy sheep's scabious.	
Juncus.		
acutus,	great sheep rush.	
bulbosus,	round fruited.	
squamosus,	moss.	
uliginosus,	little moss.	
Leontodon.		This curious plant which seemed to be a variety of the L. taraxacum, was found by Mr. White on the sea shore near Dalkey. He transferred it to the Botanic Garden, Glasnevin, and found that it propagated a similar plant both from seeds and roots. It is distinguished from the L. taraxacum not only by its colour, but by the laciniæ of the leaves, which are more numerous, hooked, and pointed, and these
maculosum,	Dandelion spotted.	

APPENDIX, No. XIII.

characters continuing permanent, seem to mark it not as an accidental variety, but a new species not noticed by Smith, or any other botanical writer on indigenous plants.

Lichen.
calicaris, channelled lichen.
caperatus, sulphur.
omphaloides, purple rock.
Perellus, crabs eye orchal.

All these species are found to possess the property of dying, in different shades and degrees, but the L. perellus is the most valuable; when steeped in volatile alkali, it communicates any shade of purple or crimson, and from it litmus is prepared. Dr. Smith says it costs £1000. per ton in times of scarcity. The curious accident by which its valuable properties were first discovered, is well known. It is thus related in Sampson's Statistical Survey of Derry. A Florentine merchant, who traded to the Levant in the fourteenth century, happening to make water on a rock, observed that the green vegetable substance on which the urine fell, was changed to an azure tint; this hint he improved to an art of dying, by which he acquired a large fortune: his name was *Rucellai*, whence the dye was called *Archill*. It was afterward manufactured in Glasgow, and called *cudbear*. Considerable quantities are sold at Dingle, made up into balls, which when steeped in urine produce a beautiful purple dye.

Linum.
angustifolium, pale flax,
Orchis.
conopsea, sweet scented fool-stones.
latifolia. broad leaved.

All the Orchidæ produce the nutritious vegetable substance called salep. The farina is said to have the valuable property of rendering sea water fresh, and is therefore proposed as an important addition to sea store to provide against a scarcity of fresh water. There is no plant more abundant in our upland meadows than the different species of this genus.

Osmunda.
Lunaria, moon-wort.
Phalaris.
arundinacea, sea canary grass.
Pyrus.
Aria, white beam-tree pyrus.

This grows on a mountain on the north-east side of Howth.

Reseda.
lutea, base-rocket reseda.
Luteola, wild woad.

The first of these species is rare, and resembles mignionette, but is inodorous. The second is very common, but valuable for its properties. It was highly prized by the ancient Irish for the yellow dye which it yielded. It thrives well in sandy soils, and was formerly cultivated to a considerable extent at Portmarnock, by Will. Plunket, who supplied the dyers of Dublin with it. It grew to the height of three feet and a half, and stained as deep a yellow as that raised at Rouen in France, which was imported sometimes at £200. per hundred.

APPENDIX, No. XIII.

Rubia. peregrina,	wild madder.	The roots of this possess the property of dying red, and are sometimes used by the peasantry for that purpose.
Sagina. cerastoides,	mouse-ear pearl-wort.	This insignificant and useless plant is one of those which has excited much botanical controversy. It is hardly yet settled to what it should belong, or in what class it should be placed. It is very common on the shore leading to Howth.
Saponaria. officinalis,	officinal soap-wort.	This plant grows on the North Strand, near Ballybough-bridge. It is also found in great abundance on the banks of the Dodder, near Ball's-bridge, and is supposed, by Dr. Wade, to have been used in the factories established there instead of soap. When bruised it emits a saponaceous viscid fluid, which possesses an abstersive property, and raises a lather like soap.
Saxifraga. granulata,	root-grained saxifrage.	
Schœnus. rufus,	red bog-rush.	This grows on the salt marshes near Baldoyle.
Scirpus. acicularis, glaucus, fluitans, multicaulis, paucifloris, setaceous,	least club-rush. azure. floating. many-stemmed. scanty flowering. bristly.	All these species of the Scirpus are noted as rare, particularly the S. acicularis and pauciflorus; they were found by Mr. White in the brick fields near Clontarf. Mr. Mackay met with the S. acicularis but once in Ireland, on the banks of the Shannon, near Portumna. The S. fluitans is noted among the plantæ rariores of Doctor Wade, who found it on Howth.
Scrophularia. nodosa,	great fig-wort.	This is held in high respect by the common people, and considered a specific in fevers. Nine leaves are plucked, the ninth is thrown away, and the juice of the rest is given in a cup of salt and water. It has a refrigerant quality. The scrophularia, however, has acquired celebrity among the medical practitioners in Dublin. Doctor Stokes directed his attention to a fatal complaint among children, called white blisters, and purchased a receipt from a woman in the country, who was famous for curing it. The principal ingredient of her ointment was found to be S. nodosa.
Scutillarea. galericulata.	com. scull-cap.	
Serapias. palustris,	marsh heleborine.	
Serratula. mariana,	milk thistle.	This fine plant is not common. It grows in great luxuriance in Kilbarrick church-yard, near the isthmus of Howth, where it attains the height of five or six feet. The milky veins of its ample foliage, make it a curious and conspicuous object. The young stalks, Rutty says, pulled and soaked in water, are eaten raw, and the heads are used as artichokes.

APPENDIX, No. XIII.

Sium. latifolium,	broad-leaved water parsnip.	This plant is found but sparingly in marshy habitats on Howth; but too frequently in other situations in the county of Dublin; its roots are deadly poison, and fatal to both men and cattle.
Solanum. nigrum,	garden nightshade.	
Stellaria. uliginosa,	marsh stich-wort.	
Tormentilla. reptans,	creeping septfoil.	As early as the year 1739, a vote of the House of Commons passed, in favour of a Mr. Maple, who published an account of the properties of this plant in tanning leather instead of oak bark. Notwithstanding the great importance of the object, it has never been followed up since. The plant abounds at Howth and on other mountains, and has a very large root. If it really possess the properties ascribed to it, it would be a mine of wealth to a country deprived of its oak woods. It is said to have been used by the ancient Irish for tanning.
Trifolium. arvense, maritimum, scabrum,	hare's foot trefoil. teazle-headed. rough.	This first species is a singular and beautiful little plant; it is found in great abundance creeping over the sandy isthmus of Howth, with its silky foliage and furry head, no unapt resemblance to a hare's foot.
Tropæolum. majus,	great Indian cress.	This inhabitant of Peru was found growing in great luxuriance on the open shore on the Sutton side of Howth, and remote from any garden. It is highly probable, however, that it strayed from one. The electric property of its petals is noted by Darwin, and sufficiently known, as also his beautiful personification:

"Round her fair form the electric lustre plays,
And cold she moves amid the ambient blaze."

Botanic Garden.

Ulva. Lactuca, umbilicalis,	oyster green laver. navel laver.	These two are gathered principally from the rocks near Portrane, on the north shore of Malahide bay. When boiled in sea water they are packed in little earthen pots, and sold in Dublin under the name of *Sloke*. It is in highest season in winter.
Utricularia. vulgaris,	greater hooded milefoil.	This species of Utricularia is called vulgaris, though by no means common. It derives its generic name from a singular precaution of nature, which has furnished the plant with sundry vessels filled with air attached to the leaves, which like inflated bladders support them on the surface of the water.

APPENDIX, No. XIII.

IRELAND'S EYE.

Aira.
flexuosa.
Euphorbia.
portlandica, portland spurge.
Iris.
fœtidissima, gladwin flagger.

Lavatera.
arborea, tree mallow.
Scilla.
verna, vernal squil.
nutans, harebel.

Rosa.
villosa, garden rose.

Thalictrum.
minus, lesser meadow rue.
flavum, yellow.

When this plant is broken or bruised, it emits an odour said to be like that of roast beef, and hence it is vulgarly called the roast beef plant. The smell, however, is particularly sickening and offensive.

A fine specimen was found here, which attained the height of five feet.

This sweet and romantic flower abounds in the south of Ireland, but is considered a planta rarior in the county of Dublin. It is found on Ireland's Eye and Howth, with blue and white bells. It was formerly a hyacinthus.

It is not easy to determine how this inhabitant of the garden became wild in this island. It is found in a state which precludes all possibility of its having been planted there within any given time. It has been found, however, in an apparently wild state in other parts of Ireland.

APPENDIX, No. XIV.

Conchology of Dublin Bay and its Vicinity.

THE study of this interesting science in Ireland has been of very recent date. The first persons who published any thing on the Testacea of Ireland were Dr. Rutty, and Smith the historian of Cork, Kerry, and Waterford; and their notices are merely of the commonest shells. Whitley Stokes, Esq. M.D. F.T.C.D. presented a collection of Irish shells, about twenty years since, to the museum of Trinity College, which, considering the infancy of the science, does credit to his industry and scientific acquirements. The next person on record who cultivated this science was Thomas Taylor, Esq. M.D. who presented 120 species of shells to the museum of the Dublin Society, for which he received their thanks. From this time the science made rapid progress, several collections were formed, the shores about Dublin being remarkably abundant in shells. Nothing, however, was yet published, until Captain Brown, of the Forfar Regiment, sent a paper on the subject to Professor Jamieson, which was read before the Wernerian Society, on the 16th of December, 1815, and is dated 20th of August, 1815. Captain Brown in that paper says—" My residence having been in situations remote from the coast, has prevented me from making the list of the marine species more complete. The variety to be met with in one day on the beach of Dublin Bay and Portmarnock, exceeds any thing I ever before witnessed; and it appears to me, that the land and freshwater Testaceæ are more plentiful in Ireland than in England or Scotland, as almost every ditch abounds in shells; I have frequently seen old ditches cleared out, with a solid mass of decayed shells, from twenty inches to two feet thick at bottom." Captain Brown's catalogue contains 232 species; it was ordered to be printed by the Wernerian Society in their Transactions.

The first catalogue of Irish Conchology published in Ireland, was from the pen of Dr. Turton, the translator of Linnæus's Systema Naturæ. In the Doctor's catalogue, which was published in the Dublin Examiner, July 1816, he observes—" The following catalogue will exhibit a beautiful assemblage of native shells, some of them known to inhabit foreign shores, but hitherto not found in the sister kingdom; many of great variety, and many non-descript."

Besides those gentlemen, several others resident in Dublin, have devoted their attention to the study of Conchology, and have formed cabinets of Irish shells; amongst the principal of which are those of M. J. O'Kelly, Esq. of James's-street, John Nuttall, Esq., Miss Lawless, James Tardy, Esq. Camden-street, and Alfred Furlong, Esq. Aungier-street.

The following catalogue contains the shells that have been found in the bay of Dublin, or its immediate vicinity. The strand of Portmarnock, on the north-west side of the isthmus of Howth, is particularly abundant, so much so, that Miss Lawless collected in one excursion there upwards of 100 species, and it is supposed that all the shells found in Ireland, with few exceptions, are here to be met with.

The shells marked thus (*) in the following list, have not yet been found on the shores in the neighbourhood of Dublin. They are added, however, to the catalogue in their order, that the series of Irish shells may be given as complete as it is at present known; also, that the fecundity of Dublin Bay and its vicinity in shells, may be more obvious by displaying the very few that are not found there.

APPENDIX, No. XIV.

CATALOGUE OF IRISH SHELLS.

MULTIVALVES.

Chiton fascicularis. Found at Balbriggan and Lough Strangford abundantly.
—— *marginatus.*
—— *lævis.* Rarely at Portmarnock.
—— *cinereus.* Dublin Bay.
—— *punctatus.* In the collection of Mr. O'Kelly.
Lepas Balanus.

Lepas balanoides.
—— *Tintinnabulum.*
—— *rugosa.*
—— *intertexta.*
—— *costata.* Rare.
*—— *elongata.* Rocks below Bantry Bay. Rare.
—— *anatifera.* On drifted wood.†

---

† These shells are sometimes thrown in on different parts of the bay, and particularly at Howth; and when discovered, have been advertised for exhibition, as curiosities, in a tent erected on the shore. The curiosity excited originated in the story of this shell being the parent of the barnacle-goose, a circumstance still believed by the multitude, and gravely related by several historians. Giraldus Cambrensis first introduced the story into Ireland, and devotes to it a whole chapter: " Sunt et aves hic quæ *Barnacæ* vocantur quas mirum in modum contra naturam natura producit. Ex lignis namque abietinis per equora devolutis primo quasi gummi nascuntur, deinde tanquam ab alga ligno cohærente conchilibus testis ad liberiorem formationem inclusæ, per rostra dependent. Et sic quousque processu temporis firmam plumarum vestituram indutæ, vel in aquas decidunt vel in aëris libertatem volatu se transferunt." Cap. viii. His account was followed by the naturalist Gerarde, who presents his readers with a plate of a bird hanging by the bill to the shell of the fish, as described by Giraldus, and prefaces his own narration with the following words: " What our eyes have seen and our hands have touched, we will declare ;" he afterwards adds, " When it (the fowl) is perfectly formed, the shell gapeth open, and the first thing that appeareth is the aforesaid lace or string, next come the legs of the bird, hanging out, and as it groweth greater, it openeth the shell by degrees, till at length it is all come forth and hangeth only by the bill; in short space after it cometh to feel maturitie, and falleth into the sea, where it gathereth feathers, and groweth to a fowle bigger than a mallard and lesser than a goose." This supposed fishy origin gave rise to the practice very early adopted in Ireland, of eating them in Lent, which Giraldus condemns for the following extraordinary reason : " Si quis enim ex primo parentis carnei quidem licet de carne non nati, femore comedisset, eum a carnium esu non immunem arbitrarer." The practice, however, was defended by Stanihurst, 400 years after, in as extraordinary a syllogism :

" Quicquid est caro ex carne communi naturæ cursu gignitur,
" Ast talem ortum Bernaculæ non habent,
" Non sunt igitur Bernaculæ carnes."

R. Stanihurst, Dublinensis, de reb. in Hib. gestis, Ap. p. 232.

The fiction was first confuted by the Dutch, who, in a voyage to discover the north-east passage to China, found, in an island in eighty degrees north latitude, plenty of Barnacles eggs and geese sitting on them; they brought over one goose and sixty eggs, to convince an incredulous world.

Pontan. rer. Amsted. Hist. c. 2. l. 22.

Fabius Columna was the first conchologist who published the real nature of those shells. " Conchas vulgo *anatiferas* non esse fructus terrestres nec ex iis anates oriri, sed *Balani* marini species."

Phytobas. sub finem.

xcviii   APPENDIX, No. XIV.

*Lepas anserifera. ⎱ Found on the shores of the   Pholas candida.
*—— sulcata.   ⎰ Atlantic, by Mr. O'Kelly.   —— crispata.
Pholas Dactylus.†

BIVALVES.

Mya truncata.   Mya inæquivalvis.
—— arenaria. ‡   —— ferruginosa. Dr. Turton.
—— declivis.   —— nitens? Ditto.
—— convexa. Of Wood's conchology.   —— bidentata.
—— prætenuis.   *—— pictorum. Rivers about Cork. Rare.
*—— pellucida. §   Solen Siliqua. ††
*—— margaritifera. ‖   —— Vagina.

† The power which this soft animal possesses of penetrating limestone and timber, has excited the attention of philosophers, though hitherto they have been unable to divine the cause. The opinion of Reaümur, that they work their way into limestone and other hard substances, by the continual rotation of their valves acting as a rasp, is not, as Wood observes, satisfactory, some species being smooth, and all of them are softer than limestone.

The faculty which this and other species possess of penetrating limestone, a substance harder than themselves, and therefore not to be penetrated by mechanical means, may be accounted for by supposing the animals capable of secreting muriatic acid from their bodies, as it abounds in the element in which they live. The impression on the stone resembles the erosion effected by acid, and they have not been found in any rock but limestone. One valve of this shell was found at Howth.

‡ This fish is brought to the London market about February, and sold at two shillings a dozen, but is not much esteemed. It is used only as bait in Ireland.

§ Two opposite valves of different sizes, of this shell, were found by Miss Hutchins at Bantry Bay, and are now in the cabinet of Dr. Taylor of Dublin.

‖ It is upon record, in the second volume of the Philosophical Transactions Abridged, that several pearls of great size were procured from this shell, in the rivers of the county of Tyrone and Donegal, in Ireland. One that weighed thirty-six carats was valued at £40. but being foul, it lost much of its worth. One was sold a second time to Lady Glenlealy, who put it into a necklace, and refused £80. for it from the Duchess of Ormond. It was the fame of the pearls of this shell that caused Cæsar to invade Great Britain.

†† The hole which this shell makes is two or three feet in depth; the animal descends to the bottom, on the ebbing of the tide, and returns to the surface as it flows. They may be seen near low water mark, with their bodies protruding from their shells, in search of food; but on the approach of any one to disturb them, they immediately shrink back and sink into the sand. A slight pinch of salt, laid upon their holes, is sufficient to make them come to the surface; and this, though often repeated, will always succeed. It has been asserted, however, that if the animal be once handled, and afterwards suffered to retire, it can never be raised again by a similar application. These fish are eaten in Italy, in France, and sometimes in England. The English writers say the Irish eat them during Lent.

APPENDIX, No. XIV.

Solen ensis.
—— *Legumen.*
*—— *Novacula.* Of small size.
—— *pellucidus.*
*—— *fragilis.* South of Ireland. Rare.
—— *minutus.*
—— *antiquatus.*
—— *vespertinus.* South of Ireland.
**Tellina maculata.* †
*——*fragilis.* ‡
—— *Ferröensis.* §
—— *tenuis.*
—— *Fabula.*
—— *depressa.*
—— *flexuosa.*
—— *solidula.*
—— *Radula.*
—— *crassa.*
*—— *carnaria?* South of Ireland. Very rare.
*—— *bimaculata?*
*—— *inæquivalvis.* ‖
—— *Donacina.* Bantry Bay and Bray.
—— *cornea.*
—— *amnica.*
*—— *lacustris.* A rare and beautiful species in ponds.
—— *jugosa.* ††

**Cardium medium.* One valve, from Rathgarmont, Lough Strangford.
—— *exiguum.*
—— *aculeatum.*
—— *echinatum.*
—— *ciliare.*
—— *lævigatum.*
—— *edule.*
*—— *elongatum.* ⎫ From Dr. Turton's Cata-
*——*fasciatum.* ⎭ logue.
Chama Cor. ‡‡
Mactra Stultorum.
—— *solida.*
—— *truncata.*
—— *subtruncata.*
—— *Listeri.*
—— *Boysii.*
—— *lutraria.*
*—— *hians.* About Cove. Rare,
—— *minutissima.* In drifted sand at Portmarnock.
Donax Trunculus.
*—— *denticulatus.*
**Venus verrucosa.* In the south of Ireland, Wexford. Rare.
—— *Casina.* At Bray in abundance.
*—— *reflexa.* At Bantry Bay. Very rare.

---

† A perfect specimen of this long lost shell, which Dr. Turton was fortunate enough to find at Bantry Bay.

‡ This addition to the British conchology was found with the last.

§ This beautiful shell is very rare on the British coasts. It is very plenty at Portmarnock.

‖ Specimens of this rare shell are in the cabinet of Mrs. Travers, at Cove; they were found below Bantry. The Solen Pinna of Montague is probably the young of this shell.

†† This shell was lately found in the blue clay opposite Clontarf, by Mr. Furlong. It was found before by Miss Hutchins of Bantry Bay, and is now in the cabinet of Dr. Taylor.

‡‡ A fine specimen of this rare shell was dredged by fishermen in Dublin Bay, and is now in possession of Dr. Blake of Dublin; it was also found by Mr. Tardy, on the strand in Dublin Bay. "A magnificent specimen of this rare shell was found at Cork, by Samuel Wright, Esq. measuring $4\frac{1}{2}$ inches in length, and $3\frac{2}{4}$ in breadth." Captain Brown.

APPENDIX, No. XIV.

Venus fasciata.
———— sulcata. Dredged at Bray.
———— *antiqua.* New species found by Dr. Turton in Dublin Bay.
———— spinifera? Portmarnock. Very rare.
———— *Gallina.*
———— *triangularis.* Portmarnock. Very rare.
———— *Islandica.*
———— *ovata.*
———— *tigeriana.* Ringsend, Dublin Bay. Rare.
———— *undata.* This much sought for species was taken alive in Dublin Bay.
———— *exoleta.*
———— *decussata.*
———— *Pullastra.*
———— *perforans.*
———— *virginea.*
———— aurea.
———— *sinuosa.*
Arca pilosa.
———— *Nucleus.*
———— *Noæ.*
———— lactea. Calves' Island.
———— Glycymeris. Carrickfergus.
———— barbata. Lough Strangford. This very perfect and new shell on our coast was found alive adhering to an oyster.
Ostrea maxima.
———— *Jacobæa.*
———— *opercularis.*
———— *varia.*
———— *lineata.*

Ostrea sinuosa.
———— *lævis.*
———— *fragilis.*
———— *obsoleta.*
———— *edulis.*
———— pustulata. New species, on drifted wood. Dr. Turton.
Anomia Ephippium. †
———— *Squamula.*
———— *aculeata.*
———— *undulata.*
———— *cymbiformis.*
———— *pellucida.*
Mytilus Hirundo. ‡
———— *edulis.*
———— *bifidus.* New species, on rocks; west of Ireland. Dr. Turton.
———— *pellucidus.*
———— *incurvatus.*
———— *modiolus.*
———— *umbilicatus.* ⎫
———— barbatus. ⎬ Varieties of M. modiolus.
———— velutinus. New species, Dublin Bay. Dr. Turton.
———— *discors.*
———— *discrepans.*
———— *rugosus.*
———— stagnalis. In the bog of Allen. Rare.
———— Cygneus. In the Grand Canal, about twenty miles from Dublin. Plentiful.
———— anatinus. In the Shannon.

---

† This is found on oyster shells, adhering by a strong tendinous ligature, which perforates the contiguous valve. It probably derives its specific name Ephippium, from its lying on the oyster like a saddle on a horse. The exterior is coarse and rough, but it is lined with a pearly epidermis, beautifully varied with purple and silvery hues.

‡ This interesting addition to the British Testacea, Dr. Turton found on the sand bank between the Pigeon-house and the Light-house, Dublin Bay.

APPENDIX, No. XIV.

Mytilus fuscus. At Sligo; a new shell in the British seas. Captain Brown.

Mytilus lævis.
* *Pinna ingens.*†

Univalve Shells.

Nautilus crispus. ‡
——— *Becarii.*
——— *depressulus.*
——— *umbilicatus.*
——— *Beccarii perversus.*
——— *inflatus.*
——— *lobatulus.*
——— *Legumen.*
* ——— *spirula.* §
Cypræa Pediculus.
——— *bullata.*
Bulla lignaria.
——— *aperta.*
* ——— *Alkera.* Warren Point, among sea weed. Abundant. Captain Brown.
* ——— *halotoidea.*
* ——— *Hydatis.* Balbriggan. Rare.

Bulla cylindracea.
——— *umbilicata.*
——— *retusa.*
——— *obtusa.*
——— *fontinalis.*
* ——— *rivalis.* Near Naas. Very rare.
——— *Hypnorum.*
* ——— *fluviatilis.* ||
Voluta tornatilis.
——— *denticulata.*
——— *alba.*
——— *ringens.* New species; Portmarnock.
* ——— *plicata.* Seafield, on the Atlantic. Very rare.
Buccinum undatum.
——— *carinatum.*
——— *striatum.*
——— *Lapillus.*††

---

† A very fine specimen of this shell was found at Portrush, county of Antrim, by Mrs. Clewlow of Belfast. Another was found at Bantry Bay, by Samuel Wright of Belfast. Rutty mentions one found at Skerries, ten inches long and five broad. The natural history of the Pinna, as detailed by Linnæus and others, is very singular. It is thus noticed by his pupil Frederick Hasselquist, in his Letters from Smyrna: " The Pinna muricata (ingens?) or great silk muscle is here found in the bottom of the sea, in large quantities, being a foot long. The ὀκτωπόδια, or Cuttle fish, with eight rays, watches the opportunity when the muscle opens her shell, to creep in and devour her; but a little crab lodges constantly in this shell fish: she pays a good rent by saving the life of her landlady, for she keeps a constant look out through the aperture of the shell, and on seeing the enemy approach, she begins to stir, when the πίνα shuts up her house, and the rapacious animal is excluded." p. 407. The little crab is called Pinnophylax from this circumstance; and this connection between " the anchor'd pinna and her cancer friend," has afforded interesting matter to both poets and philosophers. The fibres of this muscle by which it is suspended to rocks, are sometimes twenty or thirty feet long, and yield the finest silk. It is supposed to have yielded the Byssus of the ancients.

‡ Dr. Turton has marked the eight small species of this genus as found at Howth and Portmarnock.

§ Mr. O'Kelly discovered this shell in Kerry on the shores of the Atlantic. It was never before found in Great Britain.

|| The Helix bulloides of Donovan, found by Captain Brown near Clonoony barracks.

†† The application of this shell to the purposes of dying purple, was a very important object before

APPENDIX, No. XIV.

Buccinum reticulatum.
—————— Macula.
—————— ambiguum.
—————— hepaticum.
Strombus Pes Pelecani.
*Murex pyramidalis. A new and magnificent species found by Dr. Turton, at Warren's Point, after a storm.
—————— erinaceus.
—————— Nebula.
—————— septangularis.
—————— costatus.
—————— Turricula.
—————— rufus.
—————— antiquus.
—————— carinatus. At Portmarnock. Very rare. M. J. O'Kelly, Esq.
—————— corneus.
—————— linearis.
—————— purpureus.
—————— muricatus.
—————— Bamffius.
—————— reticulatus. On the western coast and at Carrickfergus. Not common.
—————— gracilis.
—————— sinuosus.

Murex lævis. Portmarnock a new species. Dr. Turton.
Trochus Magus.
—————— umbilicatus.
—————— lineatus.
—————— tumidus.
—————— crassus.
—————— ziziphinus.
*Trochus conulus. Dredged up at Bray
*—————— papillosus. Ditto.
—————— exiguus.
—————— Erythroleucos.
—————— cinereus.
*—————— discrepans. Holleswood, Belfast Lough. Miss Templeton.
*—————— rugosus. At Portinarnock, in drifted sand; size, scarcely one-eighth of an inch. Dr. Turton.
Turbo littoreus.
—————— rudis.
—————— crassior.
—————— Ziczac.
—————— Cimex.
—————— Pullus.
—————— Ulvæ.
—————— sub-umbilicatus.

---

the introduction of the *coccus* insect superseded its use. It appears from Bede to have been early and extensively used in England for that purpose: " Sunt cochleæ satis superque abundantes, quibus tinctura coccinei coloris conficitur, cujus rubor pulcherrimus nullo unquam solis ardore, nulla valet pluviarum injuria pallescere, sed quo vetustior eo solet esse venustior."—Bede, Hist. Ecc. l. 1. c. 1. The curious mode of extracting the dye is minutely detailed in Pennant, from Cole's paper in the Philosophical Transactions, 1684. The shell is laid on the face and broken by a smart stroke of a hammer, so as not to bruise the fish. On removing the fragments of the shell, a white vein is found lying in a transverse furrow on the back of the fish. This is carefully picked out with a pointed pencil-brush of stiff horse hair. When cloth is tinged with the fluid of this vein, it assumes a light green, which gradually deepens on exposure to the sun's rays, and becomes watchet blue, and purple red; When washed, it at length assumes a bright crimson hue, which is permanent; while drying, it emits an odour of garlic. This shell abounds at low water mark on every part of the Irish coast. It was supposed to have been used by the ancient Irish, in common with other nations, in dying red.

APPENDIX, No. XIV.

Turbo Cingillus.
—— graphicus. † Dublin Bay, South Bull.
—— interruptus.
—— vinctus.
—— quadrifasciatus.
*—— elegans. At Portrush. Dr. M'Donnel, Belfast.
—— fontinalis.
*—— nautileus. At Naas, in a ditch. Capt. Brown.
*—— cristatus. Near Naas, and in ditches at Cloonony, King's County. Plentiful.
—— Clathrus. ‡
—— Turtonis.
—— pentangularis. New shell; one specimen found in Dublin Bay by Dr. Turton.
—— nitidissimus.
—— Terebra.
—— nigricans.
—— muscorum.
—— jugosus.
—— tenebrosus.
—— petræus.
—— semicostatus.
—— ruber.
—— unifasciatus.
—— ventrosus.
—— auricularis.
—— parvus.
—— reticulatus. Seafield. Very rare.
—— Bryereus.
—— striatus.
—— costatus.
—— unicus.
*—— subcancellatus. Seafield; either a new species, or the T. elegans of Mr. Adams.

*Turbo Ascaris. Seafield. A new and very elegant species. Very rare.
—— arenosus.
*Helix Lapicida. Near Belfast. Dr. M'Donnell. Also found by Mrs. Travers, Belgrove, Cove, in the stone step of her house.
—— subcarinata.
—— Planorbis.
—— planata.
—— Vortex.
*—— Spirorbis. At Salins, near Dublin.
*—— contorta. At Clonoony, Naas, and Ferbane; large size.
*—— alba. In ditches with the above, and on the Canal. Rare.
—— cornea.
*—— fontana. At Ferbane, in a ditch. Rare.
—— paludosa.
—— Ericetorum.
—— margarita.
—— serpuloides.
*—— cingenda. At Balbriggan strand.
—— virgata.
—— rufescens.
—— Cantiana.
—— hispida.
—— nitens.
—— radiata.
*—— umbilicata. At Clonoony Barracks, in a mossy stone; and at Cove. Plentiful.
*—— Pomatia. Enumerated by Dr. Rutty among the shells of the county of Dublin; but is not now to be found there.
—— arbustorum.
*—— elliptica. Found in moss on the stump of an old tree at the gate of Gillan, Ferbane,

† A variety is found more conic and paler, with yellowish marks on the body, which is larger in proportion than the rest, and more rounded and deeply defined.

‡ The Turbo clathrus, or clathratus, as it is called by Donovan, is one of the most singular species to be found on the British shores. It is called False Wentletrap, from its resemblance to the celebrated Scalaris, or Wentletrap, of the East Indies, which bears so high a price among conchologists.

APPENDIX, No. XIV.

King's County; and another specimen under a stone on a mud wall, Downpatrick.
*Helix janthina. †

*Helix vivipera. Newtown Ards, Co. Down. Rare.
—— nemoralis.
—— hortensis. ‡
—— elegans. §

---

† Many hundreds of this shell were found after a storm, at Portrush, county of Antrim, by Mrs. Clewlow of Belfast and Miss Kelly, with the animal alive in them. Some of them were found floating on the surface of the water, and they seemed to be buoyed up by a little reticulated membrane of a purple colour; there also exuded from the body of the animal a fine purple mucous substance. This shell is well known as a West India species, and we can only suppose that they have been carried on the surface of the water, during a long continuance of westerly winds, which prevailed at the time, as they have never since been met with.

Brown, in his Account of Jamaica, gives the following account of this shell. " *Purple Ocean Shell.* The creature which forms and inhabits this shell, is a native of the ocean, and lives frequently many hundred leagues from any land; but having met with many of the kind between Bermudas and the Western Islands, in my voyage from Jamaica, it enables me to communicate the following account of them:

" The creature probably passes the greatest part of life at the bottom of the sea, but rises sometimes to the surface, and to do so, it is obliged, *piscium more*, to distend an air-bladder, which, however, is formed only for the present occasion, and made of tough viscid slime, swelled into a vesicular transparent mass, that sticks to the head of the animal, at the opening of the shell. This raises and sustains it while it pleases to continue on the surface; but when it wants to return, it throws off its bladder, and sinks. I have taken up many of these insects alive, with the bladder yet affixed to the aperture of the shell, and still preserve some with it on, in spirits. I have also observed many of the vesicula themselves swimming upon the surface of the water about that place, which induced me to think they were thrown off as the creature retired. It is observable, that on touching the body of this insect, it diffuses a beautiful purple liquor, of which colour the shell generally appears when fresh."

Brown's Jamaica.

This shell was also found on the coast of Kerry by Mr. O'Kelly.

‡ Donovan, in his Conchology, relates a curious mode of courtship practised by this species. Within the cavity of the neck is contained a number of little darts. When they approach within a short distance, they continue to dismiss these at each other till the reservoir is exhausted, when a reconciliation takes place between them. The secretions of the animal are known to possess the property of uniting broken glass and and china; but this property resides in a remarkable degree in a small globule of white fluid contained in the apex of the shell. From hence there proceeds a spiral tube, which winds through the convolutions of the animal, and issues with it at the aperture. It is supposed to be a reservoir of calcarious matter to supply the developement of the shell.

§ One specimen of this very elegant shell was found in a field beyond Kilmainham Jail, near the turnpike of Golden-bridge, Dublin, by Mr. Edward Stephens, and is now in the cabinet of M. J. O'Kelly, Esq. Dr. Turton, in his Catalogue, calls this shell H. disjuncta, and says it is "a new and beautiful species." Mr. O'Kelly considers it only a variety of H. arenaria.

APPENDIX, No. XIV.

Helix Cochlea. In a pond, College Botanic Garden; in the cabinet of Mr. O'Kelly.	*Nerita Canrena.*
—— *elegantissima.*	—— *glaucina.*
—— polita. Bantry Bay. Rare.	*—— fluviatilis.* ‡
—— *bifasciata.*	—— *littoralis.*
—— *Lachamensis.*	—— *glaberrima.*
—— *obscura.* Neighbourhood of Dublin. Rare. One specimen found near Cloonony.	*—— Macula.*
	—— Mammilla.
—— *lubrica.*	*—— livida.*
—— *vitrea.*	*—— pallidula.* } Those seven from Dr. Turton.
—— *arenaria.*	*—— Traversiana.*
—— *stagnalis.*	*—— virginea.*
—— *palustris.*	*—— pellucida.*
—— *fossaria.*	*Haliotis tuberculata.* §
—— *succinea.*	*Patella vulgata.*
—— *putris.*	—— *ungariea.*
—— *limosa.*	—— *militaris.*
—— *tentaculata.*	—— *lacustris.*
—— *canalis.*	*Patella oblonga.*
—— *auricularia.*	—— *pellucida.*
—— *lævigata.*	—— *cærulea.*
—— *reversa.*†	—— *virginea.*
—— Naascensis. Near Naas; new species. Captain Brown.	—— *Fissura.*
	—— *græca.*
—— Punctura. Seafield. Rare.	—— *chinensis.*
—— fragilis. } From Doctor Turton's Catalogue.	—— *intorta.*
—— detrita.	—— *mitrula.*
—— lutea.	—— *Apertura.*
—— glutinosa.	*Dentalium entalis.*

† A new species, remarkable, as being the only known British reversed Helix. In the bark of trees, Wicklow; and Glasnevin gardens. Dr. Turton.

‡ In a stream at Clonoony; in the Shannon and Bresna; and in some places in the Canal, adhering to stones. Size of the shell one-eighth of an inch. Found by Dr. Turton in Dublin Bay.

§ One specimen was got by the dredge at Springfield, by Mr. Templeton of Belfast; and several specimens have been picked up on the shores of Down, particularly in the neighbourhood of Spring-field. One specimen was found at Bullock, and is in possession of James Tardy, Esq. It is frequently cast upon the south shores of England. When living, it adheres to rocks like limpets.

APPENDIX, No. XIV.

Serpula Spirillum.
―――― *Spirorbis.* ||
*―――― *granulata.* Balbriggan and Donaghadee. Plentiful.
*―――― *lucida.* Lough Strangford. Not uncommon.
―――― *vermicularis.*

Serpula triquetra.
*―――― *minuta.*
*―――― *vitrea.*
*―――― *tabularia.*
*―――― *Leminulum.*
*―――― *subrotunda.*
*―――― *oblonga.*

} From Doctor Turton's Catalogue.

|| This adheres to crabs and lobsters claws, but chiefly, Donovan says, to the Fucus serratus, the dark leaves of which it decorates with its pearly knobs; hence it is called *wrack-spangles.*

CORRECTIONS AND ADDITIONS.

Page line
4 32 Letters patents, *read* Letters patent.
42 last To the list of Chief Governors, *add*—
   1813, Aug. 26. Charles, Earl Whitworth, L.L. landed and sworn.
   1817, Oct. 9. Charles Chetwynd, Earl Talbot, L.L. landed and sworn.
45 8 litle, *read* little.
50 33 porteullis, *read* portcullis.
70 19 Chape-lizod, *read* Chapel-Izod.
72 29 wàs, *read* was.
78 last, note, *add*. This last specimen of the cage-houses of Dublin, was taken down by the Commissioners of Wide Streets, while in good repair. In 1812 the materials were sold for 40l. The frame work was of Irish oak, in a state of perfect preservation. It appeared from the date in the front, that it was erected in the reign of Edward VI. and from the arms, that it had belonged to the Fitzgerald family. Tradition says it was the residence of Oliver Cromwell while he was in Dublin.
85 19 Ballybrugh Bridge, *read* Ballybough Bridge.
132 20 at lengt, *read* at length.
138 5 note, wes erected, *read* was erected.
163 5 do. A.D. 1286, *read* A.D. 1266.
164 27 monumonuments, *read* monuments.
177 6 note, was began, *read* was begun.
184 1 do. the Ctiy, *read* the City.
194 21 Sunnday, *read* Sunday.
236 26 To the Annals *add*—
   1808, Feb. Foundation stone of Nelson's Pillar laid.
   1809, Oct. 25. A Jubilee of three days was observed in Dublin to commemorate the 50th anniversary of George the Third's accession to the throne.
   1811, Nov. 16. A floating light-ship was established at the Kish-Bank, south-east of the entrance into Dublin Bay.
   1812, Sept. 12. The Basin at Portobello, for supplying the south-eastern parts of Dublin with water, opened.
   Oct. 14. Mr. James Sadler, a native of England, ascended in a balloon, at half-past

Page line
two oclock, P.M. from the lawn in Belvidere-house, Drumcondra, with the intention of passing to England. After an intrepid but unsuccessful attempt to proceed to Liverpool, he fell into the sea near the south-east extremity of the Isle of Man, at six o'clock in the evening, and was rescued from the perilous situation by a Mank's boat, which conveyed him to Liverpool, from whence he returned to the Irish metropolis.
   1813, Feb. The Lord Mayor of Dublin proceeded to London with a petition of the Commons, in order to establish a privilege for the Chief Magistrate of the Irish metropolis, similar to that enjoyed in London, of presenting petitions at the Bar of the Imperial Parliament.
   Aug. 9. The foundation stone of Richmond bridge laid.
   1814, Jan. 18. The streets of the metropolis, and the avenues leading to it, are by a great fall of snow rendered almost impassable for three months; this occasioned much distress among the poor, and a subscription exceeding 10,000l. was raised for their relief.
   Aug. 12. The foundation stone of a new Post-office was laid in Sackville-street, on the celebration of the Centenary of the accession of the House of Hanover to the Throne.
   1816, March 16. Richmond bridge completed. Expence 25,000l.
   May 19. An iron bridge erected and finished for foot-passengers in one year.
   Sept. 13. Steam packets sailed for the first time from the Harbour of Dublin, and continued to ply across the channel till winter set in.
   Oct. 16. The foundation stone of Whitworth bridge laid.
   Dec. In consequence of the extreme wetness of the season and the scantiness of the crops, a subscription amounting to

CORRECTIONS AND ADDITIONS.

age line
18,855l. 11s. 9d. was raised for the poor, and expended in giving them employment, by repairing and improving the avenues leading into Dublin. The hill at the north entrance was cut down, and a fine level road formed through Drumcondra.

1817, May 31. The first stone of Dunleary Harbour laid by his Excellency Lord Whitworth.

June 18. The first stone of the Wellington testimonial laid in the Phœnix Park on the Anniversary of the Battle of Waterloo.

July 22. Mr. Windham Sadler, son to Mr. James Sadler, ascended in a balloon from Portobello Barracks, at half-past one o'clock, P.M., and by a bold and judicious management of his machine succeeded in reaching to opposite coast in six hours, and landed in the Isle of Anglesea two miles and a half south of Holyhead at half past seven o'clock, P. M., effecting at length what so many had attempted in vain to accomplish. This was the most perilous voyage, and performed with the most decided and uninterrupted success, that ever was attempted in an aerostatic machine.

Nov. 19. The public offices were closed and all business suspended in consequence of the lamented death of her Royal Highness the Princess Charlotte of Wales. The funeral service was performed in the different places of public worship on the day appointed for the interment.

Dec. Contagious fever appears in Dublin, and makes an alarming progress. The average number of sick suddenly amounted from thirty to fifty, giving an aggregate of 18,000 per annum. The number of beds provided for the reception of patients in hospitals, and the buildings connected with the House of Industry, amounted to 1000, which were always occupied.

240 4 Grandelough, *read* Glendalough.
13 as follows, *read* as follow.
243 11 54, Charles Agar, *add* created Baron Somerton, 1795, and Earl of Normanton, 1806. Translated from the see of Cashel to Dublin, 1801.

Page line
55, Euseby Cleaver, consecrated Bishop of Cork, March, 1789; and of Leighlin and Ferns, June, 1789; translated to Dublin, 1809.
279 1 note et seq. Wards Bps. *read* Ware's Bps.
297 17 prebend, *read* prebendary.
penult. prebendary, *read* prebend.
310 28 o fJanuary, *read* of January.
313 3 Chapel in Mary's-lane, *add*—Besides this statue part of the Abbey still remains in a state of very perfect preservation; it is at present occupied by Mr. Maziere, sugar-baker, Mary's Abbey, and forms part of his stores. It consists of buildings of four arches, forty-three feet by twenty-four wide. The arches are ten feet in height, groined and ribbed; the ribs formed of blocks seven or eight inches square, of stone resembling Portland or Bath stone, presents a front ornamented with two semicircular mouldings, separated by an angular fillet. Where the ribs intersect the crown of each arch, they are united at the angles by a knot of flowers, which appear to be an imitation of trefoil. The ribs spring in threes from the ground, where they are united, and probably rest on some corbeil or capital beneath the floor, which seems to have been raised; underneath are arched vaults, which evidently are of some modern erection, as they are formed of brick. The breadth of the building below is somewhat less than that above, and any shaft or capital on which the ribs above rested, is probably concealed by the new facing. The walls of this building are three feet nine inches thick, and are perforated in several places by Gothic windows, terminated in pointed arches. The edifice, which was probably the chapel, is still very perfect, and free from damps.
454 20 Dr. Rutley, *read* Dr. Rutty.
464 7 Rhus in urbe, *read* Rus in urbe.
465 2 innani, *read* inani.
471 27 was began, *read* was begun.
513 26 } Beresford-street, *read* Hardwick-street.
514 11 }
526 4 mancho capac, *read* mango capac.
Ollamh Todhla, *read* Ollamh Fodhla.

CORRECTIONS AND ADDITIONS.

Page line
527   5 has been, *read* have been.
     7 Consumption of last year; but the most expensive of any, *read* Consumption of last year, but the most expensive of any;
535   22 to the ite, *read* to the site.
536   9 Ollamh Fodlah, *read* Ollamh Fodhla.
547   28 note, Dr. Th. Ellrington, 1181, *read* Dr. Th. Ellrington, 1811.
548   8 the number of junior fellows is at present (1812), 15, *add*—They have since been increased to 18. The new fellowships were added from the funds of the College, and were filled up gradually, the last in 1817, when no natural vacancy occurred.
560   17 towvr, *read* tower.
582   1 note, Conduct; *read* conduct,
     10 who, *read* which.
     11 are, *read* is.
645   22 Charlemont-street, *add* now removed to Upper Kevin-street.
647   last, portion, *read* proportion.
648   9 table, 180 to 1804, *read* 1803 to 1804.
     31 do. Loregrea, *read* Loughrea.
663   32 Master Chaplain, *read* Master, Chaplain.
664   21 Superier, *read* Superior.
692   last, hey, *read* they.
697   29 prodvce, *read* produce.
699   8 76..302l. 4s. 7d. *read* 7630 2l. 4s. 7d.
808   17 in Arran-street, *read* Anne-street.
810   2 nine Chapels, *read* ten chapels.
     7 James-street, *add* Liffey-street or Marlbro'-street
     11 Mass-lane Augustinians, *read* John's-lane Augustinians.
812   18 150 girls, *add*, in Dublin and in different parts of the country.
     6000l. *read* 8000l.
820   24 Pool Baggot-street, *read* Poolbeg-street.
834   11 Downe and Thomas-court, *read* Donore and Thomas-court.
837   6 adherance, *read* adherence.
     13 of any, *read* of any other.
     17 applied he, *read* applied they.
842   3 Lucas-lane, *read* Lucy's-lane.
842   25 9 to 1, *read* 1 to 9.
866   9 table, parochial school, *read* parochial school.
892   10 Kildumo, *read* Kildeemo.

Page line
896   29 made by Dean Graves, *read* made to De Graves, as Secretary of the Association.
908   1 note. Miss Cheeses, *read* Misses Cheese.
911   35 its symphonies, *read* his symphonies.
919   24 continued till 1790, *read* till 1804.
918   5 Rutley's, *read* Rutty's.
920   26 between 9000l. and 12000l. a year, *read* abo 7000l. a year.
     last, Mr. Flood's Heirs, *add* The college has bee recently defeated in this suit on a constructic of the Mortmain Act, but there yet lies an a peal to House of Lords.
938   23 Ussiana, *read* Usseriana.
939   20 interuit, *read* intererit.
     Hallison, *read* Palliser.
958   6 note Cornucopiæ, *read* Cornucopia.
     8 do., Broad Room, *read* Board Room.
961   15 Committee, *read* Board of Directors.
     34 supplement, *read* implement.
962   28 forasmuch, *read* inasmuch.
964   12 panch, *read* punch.
968   10 fardeles, *read* fardles.
971   32 Sack allen, *read* Stackallen.
973   11 and setting, *read* in setting.
     32 nd erected, *read* and erected.
975   9 27 tons, *read* 7 tons.
992   11 coasting trade is considerable, *add*, employ ing annually 37,000 tons.
1001   last, Porsians, *read* Persians.
1005   14 60,000l., *read* 40,000l.
     15 95,000l., *read* 300,000l.
1009   24 50,000l., *read* 60,000l.
1011   19 note, Eudosus, *read* Eudoxus.
1014   last do., at constat, *read* ut constat.
1015   11 comprised, *read* compromised.
1016   12 hours of Court, *read* Inns of Court.
1029   penult. like those, *read* and those. citation, *read* libel.
1040   8 note, possessiorum, *read* possessionum.
1063   18 in the city, *read* within the district of th metropolis.
     11 note, swear the high Sheriffs, *read* swear th Lord Mayor into the office of Escheator o the markets, and the high Sheriffs into thei respective offices.
1065   5 note, his picture was pulled down, *read* i

CORRECTIONS AND ADDITIONS.

Page line
  was moved in the Commons that his picture should be pulled down.
1065 14 note, After the word, Corporation, *omit* the passage, but the deed duly executed by themselves was produced, and the City was nonsuited.
1068 .12 Weaver's-square, *read* New-market.
  2 note, presention, *read* presentation.
1077 16 do., the united stream runs through Patrick-street, to Ross-lane, *read* the stream runs on each side Patrick-street, unites at Ross-lane, and continues across Bridge-street.
  last, The north side of the city is cleansed by a similar stream, called the *Bradogue*; it rises about two miles from Dublin, on the lands of Upper Cabra, near a large pond, and passing through Lower Cabra, it enters a large quarry pit, in Quary-hole-lane; from thence it winds through a number of gardens which supply the city with vegetables, which it continues to fertilize in its passage, and crossing the circular road at the top of Grange Gorman-lane, it runs down one side of the lane, till it meets the wall of the New Penitentiary; under this it is conveyed by arches, and passing out through the gardens, in the rere, it runs under the bason of the Royal Canal, near the Aqueduct, and again becomes visible along the rere of Henrietta-street for some space. Hence, it is arched, and becomes the great water course of the north side of the city; it takes its way down Bolton-street, under Newgate and Halstone-street, crosses Mary's-lane, and Pill-lane; passes under Ormond-market, and enters the Liffey by a large arch opposite the Water-row. In this course it has been judiciously directed. It receives all the filth and offals of three great establishments, the Penitentiary, Newgate, and Ormond-market, and contributes much to the sweetness and salubrity of these places. This stream is represented in the old maps of considerable magnitude, and there is a tradition current among the common people, that it was formerly navigable for ships. Attempts have been made by the prisoners confined in Newgate to es-

Page line
  cape through this subterranean river; on one occasion some of them crept into the sewers which fall into it and appeared under the gratings, when they were supplied, it is said, with food by their friends, who thrust down slices of bread between the bars.
1100 13 HUGNI, *read* HUGONI.
1102 3 which is not, *read* which are not.
  1 note, follows, *read* follow.
1103 Europe*, dele *
1108 21 Burnet, *read* Burnell.
1111 4 note, Jonson, *read* Johnson.
  12 do., Whitehall, *read* Whitchal.
1117 9 1761, *read* 1771.
1119 17 note, Capt. Aske, *read* Capt. Ashe.
1123 26 do., AMABILITY, *read* AMIABILITY.
1124 8 do., not graziers, *read* not to be graziers.
  16 do., Taggard, *read* Saggard.
  19 do., 700 stone, *read* 700 lb.
1125 5 do., polit. anal., *read* polit. Anat.
  22 do., Ash, *read* Ashes.
1127 18 Harry-street, *read* Chatham-street.
1130 19 Pigeon, *read* Widgeon.
1131 8 Sorsonera, *read* Scorzonera.
1132 18 note, Rose Tavern, in Drumcondra, *read* Rose Tavern, in Donnybrook.
1141 13 do., meat, *read* meal.
1143 12 do., Sulphur, *read* Carbon.
  14 do., Sulphureous, *read* Carbonic.
1144 Table, oatmeal, *read* oatmeal.
1145 do., add,   from   to   usual price.
  Woodcock, per brace   5 5   8 8   6 0
  Snipe, do.   -   1 8   2 2   2 0
  Quail, do.   -   -   1 8   2 2   2 0
  Widgeons, do.   -   4 4   6 0   5 0
  Teal, do.   -   -   2 2   3 3   2 8
  Barnacle, per piece, 4 4   6 6   5 0
  Venison, per lb.   2 2   3 3   2 6
  Sea Kale per bundl.   1 8   3 4   2 2
1147 6 note, distinct Asylums, *read* district Asylums
1148 1 do., levied in fee, *read* seized in fee.
1150 20 180¾, *read* 1807.
1152 10 the pews, below which they go home to the side walls and, *read* the pews below, which go home to the side walls, and
1152 26 Deans, *read* Dignitaries.
1153 16 Lord Annley's, *read* Lord Annesley's.

CORRECTIONS AND ADDITIONS.

Page line
1155   2   *add*, in September 1817, it was commenced near the canal at Drumcondra.
       10 apartments, *read* apartment.
1160 12   note, Barritaria, *read* Barritariana.
1166   1   do., and those practised, *read* and those who practised.
       last do., tenacity of the materials, *read* tenuity of the materials.
1167   7   do. change the type, *read* charge the type.
1168   2   do., new erected, *read* newly erected,
1173 32   note, north hall, *read* north wall.
1175 27   elsewhere Holy. Eve, *read* elsewhere. Holy-Eve.
1192 19   Prebend, *read* Prebendary.
1196   Page 196, *read* 1196.
1203 19   Joseph, *read* John.
1209 11   res angusti, *read* res angustæ.
1218 17   Mr. Ergue, *read* Mr. Vigne.
1221 26   happen, *read* happens.
1226 penult. remotest, spring a, *read* remotest spring, a.
1230   Monastievan, *read* Monasterevan.
       last note, lins, *read* lines.
1264   3   Note on diving bells.

The first person who attempted to descend in a diving bell in the vicinity of Dublin, was Mr. Spalding, who had previously made several successful attempts in other places. He twice descended to the Kish bank at the entrance of Dublin Bay, in a bell of Halley's construction, to view the wreck of the Imperial Indiamen; he was accompanied by one of his young men, and returned in safety. In June 1783, they went down a third time, and remained one hour under water; two barrels of air were sent down to them, and no apprehensions were entertained for their security. After some time, however, the signals from below were not repeated as usual; the bell was drawn up, and the unfortunate philosopher and his assistant were found dead. The next attempt was made by Mr. Healy of Dublin. In 1799, a brig had foundered between Dunleary and Howth; in concert with Capt. Londsdale of the Experiment, Mr. Healy proposed to attempt raising her by means of a bell supplied with air on Smeaton's principles. On the deck of a ship moored above, was lashed a forcing or condensing syringe, capable of containing two quarts; to this was connected five fathoms of an iron, and an equal length of a leather tube which turned into the bell. When the piston was depressed, the air passed through the tubes, and thus a constant stream was propelled down. In the summer of 1802, he made the experiment, and descended on two different days. On the first, he remained down half an hour, and on the second, one hour and some minutes in seven fathoms water. The scheme, however, of raising the sunk brig was abandoned in consequence of the vessel above, breaking from her moorings.

The diving bells employed at Howth in constructing the pier, are formed of cast iron of the same shape and materials as those employed by Smeaton at Ramsgate, and are supplied with air from above, by forcing pumps on his principle. It is sent down in an uninterrupted current, attended with the most complete security and success; the workmen remain sometimes four hours under water, and many persons from motives of science or curiosity, occasionally accompany them.

Page line
1265   8   EAST, *read* WEST.
1266   8   note, impaled, *read* impacted.
1267 13   the Kish and Tolkey, *read* the Kish and Dalkey.
1267 14   note, object to work it, *add*, on further investigation, however, it appeared, that the mass brought up was not galæna but pure lead, and has probably dropped from some ship, as large fragments of wrought iron were found near it. About the same time, a rock weighing four or five ton, was taken up by the diving bell. This had obstructed the harbour in such a way, that the interstices of the upper surface were filled with fibres of wood, which it had abraded from the keels and bottoms of vessels as they passed over it.

CORRECTIONS AND ADDITIONS.

Page	line	
1270	11	note, St. Daboe's heath, *read* St. Daboec's heath.
1273		plan of Harbour, 10, *read* 16.
1294	17	do., Dr. Asche, *read* Dr. Ashe.
1296	8	do., steriles, *read* sterilis.
	11	do., mantina, *read* maritima.
1297	13	do., capillus, *read* lapillus.
1301	11	mesembrianthemus, *read* mesembrianthemums.
1302	5	note, Dombia, *read* Dombæia.
	6	do., 300 feet, *read* 200 feet.
1304	4	is, *read* are.
1307	12	Feltras, *read* Feltram.
1312	25	Zenith by means, *read* Zenith and by means.
1318	11	vera, *read* ferè.
1323	23	pænitentiæ, *read* poenitentiæ.
	24	de jura, *read* de jure.
1324		penult. Chapter, *read* Chapters.
1329	17	feil, *read* feels.
1333	16	Capricorne, *read* Caprecorni.
1335	10	fourteenth, *read* tenth.
	27	were, *read* was.
	28	general, *read* genial.
1336	21	it was not met with, *read* it was met with.
	23	the fact, *read* the first.
1338	16	Carbon of magnesia, *read* Carbonate of magnesia.
1340	20	Carbon of Iron, *read* Carbonate of Iron.
		last, Stone tenter-house, *read* Stove tenter-house.

Page	line	
1347	11	præter moribundus, *read* præter moribundos.
	23	occasconal, *read* occasional.
vi	11	Ap. dead wall, *add* now the Independant Chapel.
	14	Quakers burying-ground, *add* now the College of Surgeons.
lxiv		year 1508, Sheriff Henry Goreway, *read* Henry Gourway.
lxv		do. 1613, Sheriff Thady Duffy, *read* Thady Duffy.
lxvii		do. 1803, Sheriff Jothua Pownden, *read* Joshua Pounden.
lxxvii		No. 69, Aitha Cliath, *read* Atha Cliatha.
		105, glossa, *read* glosses.
lxxxv		line 10, Con fá acta, *read* Cion fa eité.
lxxxvi		32 fl. coiceineo, *read* fl. coccineo.
lxxxvii		9 oxycantha, *read* oxyacantha.
		10 visca, *read* vesca.
lxxxviii		1 galeobdlon, *read* galeobdolon.
1st, Col.		15 Scrophularia majus, *read* Antirrhinum majus.
		18 Thlespi, *read* Thlaspi.
2d. Col.		38 Raphanestrum, *read* Raphanistrum.
		20 Craeca, *read* Cracca.
lxxxix		
		Grasses 3d. col. 3 duriusculus, *read* duriuscula.
cxiii		20 Scutillaria, *read* Scutellaria.

London: Printed by W. Bulmer and Co.
Cleveland Row, St. James's.